Litigation and Trial Practice

Sixth Edition

DELMAR CENGAGE Learning

Options.
Over 300 products in every area of the law: textbooks, online courses, CD-ROMs, reference books, companion websites, and more – helping you succeed in the classroom and on the job.

Support.
We offer unparalleled, practical support: robust instructor and student supplements to ensure the best learning experience, custom publishing to meet your unique needs, and other benefits such as Delmar Cengage Learning's Student Achievement Award. And our sales representatives are always ready to provide you with dependable service.

Feedback.
As always, we want to hear from you! Your feedback is our best resource for improving the quality of our products. Contact your sales representative or write us at the address below if you have any comments about our materials or if you have a product proposal.

Accounting and Financials for the Law Office • Administrative Law • Alternative Dispute Resolution • Bankruptcy Business Organizations/Corporations • Careers and Employment • Civil Litigation and Procedure • CLA Exam Preparation • Computer Applications in the Law Office • Constitutional Law • Contract Law • Court Reporting Criminal Law and Procedure • Document Preparation • Elder Law • Employment Law • Environmental Law • Ethics Evidence Law • Family Law • Health Care Law • Immigration Law • Intellectual Property • Internships Interviewing and Investigation • Introduction to Law • Introduction to Paralegalism • Juvenile Law • Law Office Management • Law Office Procedures • Legal Nurse Consulting • Legal Research, Writing, and Analysis • Legal Terminology • Legal Transcription • Media and Entertainment Law • Medical Malpractice Law Product Liability • Real Estate Law • Reference Materials • Social Security • Sports Law • Torts and Personal Injury Law • Wills, Trusts, and Estate Administration • Workers' Compensation Law

DELMAR CENGAGE Learning
5 Maxwell Drive
Clifton Park, New York 12065-2919

For additional information, find us online at:
www.cengage.com/delmar

LITIGATION AND TRIAL PRACTICE

SIXTH EDITION

WILLIAM M. HART

RODERICK D. BLANCHARD

DELMAR
CENGAGE Learning

Australia • Brazil • Japan • Korea • Mexico • Singapore • Spain • United Kingdom • United States

8/9/10
Lan
$163.95

Litigation and Trial Practice, Sixth Edition
William M. Hart, Roderick D. Blanchard

Vice President, Career Education Strategic
 Business Unit: Dawn Gerrain

Acquisitions Editor: Shelley Esposito

Managing Editor: Robert Serenka, Jr.

Senior Product Manager: Melissa Riveglia

Director of Production: Wendy A. Troeger

Content Project Manager: Matthew J. Williams

Cover Design: Suzanne Nelson

Cover Images: Comstock Images/Alamy,
 Dennis MacDonald/Alamy Keith Levit/Alamy

Director of Marketing: Wendy E. Mapstone

Marketing Channel Manager: Gerard McAvey

Marketing Coordinator: Jonathan Sheehan

For product information and technology assistance, contact us at
Cengage Learning Customer & Sales Support, 1-800-354-9706

For permission to use material from this text or product,
submit all requests online at **www.cengage.com/permissions**
Further permissions questions can be emailed to
permissionrequest@cengage.com

Library of Congress Control Number: 2006014187

ISBN-13: 978-1-4180-1689-0

ISBN-10: 1-4180-1689-6

Delmar
Executive Woods
5 Maxwell Drive
Clifton Park, NY 12065
USA

Cengage Learning is a leading provider of customized learning solutions with office locations around the globe, including Singapore, the United Kingdom, Australia, Mexico, Brazil, and Japan. Locate your local office at **www.cengage.com/global**

Cengage Learning products are represented in Canada by Nelson Education, Ltd.

To learn more about Delmar, visit **www.cengage.com/delmar**

Purchase any of our products at your local bookstore or at our preferred online store **www.CengageBrain.com**

Printed in the United States of America
3 4 5 6 7 14 13 12 11 10

BRIEF CONTENTS

CONTENTS

CHAPTER 3   COURT ORGANIZATION 47

CHAPTER 4   CAUSES OF ACTION AND REMEDIES 78

CHAPTER 5   AFFIRMATIVE DEFENSES 126

CHAPTER 14   MEDICAL EXAMINATIONS AND RECORDS   387

CHAPTER 15   INSPECTION OF PROPERTY, DOCUMENTS, AND THINGS   425

CHAPTER 16   REQUESTS FOR ADMISSIONS   438

TABLE OF EXHIBITS

PREFACE

Introduction

Litigation and Trial Practice prepares paralegal students to work with lawyers as members of a litigation team. The book describes and explains the civil justice system. It explains how courts are organized, how they function, what lawyers do to make the system work, what paralegals may do, and how they should do it. The authors' premise is that, in addition to litigation rules and procedures, paralegals should understand why the system works the way it does. Otherwise, paralegals feel like outsiders—wondering what is happening and why. Outsiders are reluctant to take initiative and make suggestions. Paralegals who do not understand why the system functions as it does tend to make more mistakes and are less efficient. The book develops each subject by starting with the basics and building from there. It assumes the reader has little knowledge about courts, lawyers, and civil litigation. *Litigation and Trial Practice* is also an authoritative reference book. Although specifically written for paralegals, *Litigation and Trial Practice* can help anyone who works with lawyers and courts to be more effective, including persons in insurance claims work, court personnel, and legal secretaries who want to understand the reasons that underlie their work.

Development of *Litigation and Trial Practice*

The first edition of *Litigation and Trial Practice* was printed more than twenty-five years ago. It adopted a pragmatic approach to teaching civil litigation. The book's proven approach has been retained. Even so, this edition has been completely rewritten and reorganized to accommodate the dramatic changes in federal procedure that occurred about the time the fourth edition was published. This edition is even more comprehensive, providing more examples and more forms.

Organization

Litigation and Trial Practice begins by explaining that state and federal governments provide courts to resolve private disputes to keep people from using self-help, such as violence, as a remedy for perceived wrongs. Of course, people do not have to use courts to resolve their disputes, but courts are available when other civilized means are inadequate. The text explains the basic principles that guide courts, and that determine and limit their authority. Chapters 1 and 8 are important preview chapters. Chapter 1 provides an overview of litigation. Chapter 8 provides an overview on gathering evidence. These chapters prepare students for the detailed presentations that follow.

Lawyers are officers of the courts in which they practice. They must honor and protect the courts. At the same time, lawyers are advisers and represent their clients. Chapter 2 explains attorneys' dual roles. It discusses legal ethics problems that may confront paralegals and makes suggestions for avoiding problems. Chapter 3 explains how courts are organized, how they function, jurisdictional requirements, how courts obtain jurisdiction, and why courts can handle only certain kinds of disputes. The discussion is comprehensive, complemented with numerous examples and illustrative documents. Chapters 4 and 5 explain causes of action, remedies, and affirmative defenses. Building on the prior chapters, Chapter 6 describes the procedures for placing claims in suit and raising defenses. The role, preparation, and use of all pleadings are covered in detail so that students can understand them, prepare them, and use them.

Causes of action and affirmative defenses, as pled, determine what facts are material to a case. Therefore, the initial chapters prepare students to understand the importance of *material facts* and the need for *relevant evidence* to prove those facts. They prepare students to understand the role of evidence. Chapter 7 is a discussion about evidence and the exclusionary rules of evidence. It explains what evidence is, why certain kinds of evidence are subject to objection and exclusion, and the exceptions. The discussion is not a mere recitation of the rules of evidence. Chapter 8 is an overview of the processes for gathering evidence. It explains the importance of obtaining "the best evidence" and preserving evidence. Chapters 9–16 explain the various methods of obtaining evidence, including investigation, interrogatories, oral depositions, inspections, medical examinations, and requests for admissions. A separate chapter is devoted to each phase of discovery. Each chapter carefully describes the procedure and explains the paralegal's role. Each chapter contains helpful examples, illustrative documents, and appropriate responses to discovery requests. The text discusses the relative value and effectiveness of discovery procedures for various situations. It discusses the importance of coordinating discovery procedures with a party's investigation.

Chapter 17 covers motions of all kinds, including summary judgment motions. Again, the role of motions is explained, procedures are explained, examples and illustrative documents are provided. Many attorneys could benefit from the discussion and materials. The chapter prepares paralegals to understand and work with motions.

Chapter 18 is unique for a paralegal book. It explains and illustrates legal analysis, which is the foundation for a trial strategy. This is important because a trial strategy guides a lawyer's preparation for trial and her or his presentation of evidence. Of course, it is not enough merely to present the available evidence. The evidence must be presented in a manner that keeps it interesting, believable, persuasive, and memorable. *Litigation and Trial Practice* shows how a thorough legal analysis, starting with the pleadings, identifies the evidence a party needs. It examines the many choices lawyers must make for presenting evidence. It considers how a litigation team can anticipate and meet an opponent's evidence and plan alternative solutions. The teaching points in Chapter 18 may be applied to the hypothetical case or any case the instructor finds useful.

Chapter 19 explains the structure of a civil trial, from the preliminary conference with the judge through polling the jury and entering judgment. Each step is explained with an emphasis on the paralegal's role. Chapter 20 discusses judgments, entry of judgments, and enforcement of judgments, including executing on judgments and using supplementary proceedings. To round out the process, Chapter 21 covers appeals and what paralegals may do to assist with an appeal, such as organizing the record and reviewing the transcript to support the statement of facts. Chapter 22 provides a thorough discussion of settlements and releases along with illustrative documents.

Chapter 23 provides a comprehensive explanation about alternative dispute resolution procedures and what paralegals may do in the field. Paralegals who understand civil litigation can assume major roles in mediation and arbitration matters. Some casualty insurance companies are asking laypersons to handle intercompany arbitrations in an effort to adjust losses efficiently and economically. The construction industry is turning to arbitration to resolve disputes between owners and contractors, between contractors, and between contractors and suppliers. For many years, labor disputes have been resolved in arbitration and mediation by persons who are not lawyers. A person does not have to be a lawyer to be a mediator or arbitrator or to represent a person or company in arbitration, unless the case is already in litigation. Then the arbitrators and advocates must be lawyers, because the parties are entitled to have rules of law and legal standards applied.

Litigation and Trial Practice is comprehensive and detailed because it is a paralegal reference book as well as a textbook. It is very basic with "how-to" explanations about the law and procedures. At the same time, it attempts to relate court procedures to the substantive law. It discusses legal theory and explains why the law functions as it does. If an instructor finds some sections contain material offered in the school's other courses, she or he may skip or de-emphasize those portions. Instructors may focus on sections they deem most important in light of the time available. Down the road, some students will read the sections that time did not permit them to cover in class.

Features

The sixth edition has been updated, somewhat condensed, made more technology friendly, and more readable. Like the fifth edition, it includes an interesting hypothetical case at the beginning. The hypothetical case is based on an actual case that went to a state supreme court. The hypothetical case is carefully integrated into the text to expand the student's opportunities to apply and learn the material. Instructors will find that it contains an incredible number of procedural steps, which take students from basic principles to an appeal and settlement. The hypothetical case is fully developed and provides a basis for study assignments. Other features include the following:

- Each chapter begins with an outline providing an overview.
- Key terms and phrases are boldface, cited in the Marginal Glossary, listed at the end of the chapter, and defined in the end-of-book Glossary.

- Example documents and forms complement the text discussions.
- A chapter summary reviews important learning points.
- Chapter review questions help students to determine whether they have grasped the material.
- Case assignments at the end of each chapter give students an opportunity to apply the information from the chapter and preceding chapters to the hypothetical case. The case and assignments are an ongoing story with subplots. It may also be used as the basis for independent work and tests.
- *Litigation and Trial Practice* avoids esoteric discussions about legal issues and problems in the law.
- The Glossary is very comprehensive.

New to This Edition

Litigation and Trial Practice has been updated and edited to be more concise.

- Each chapter is more specific about a paralegal's role on the litigation team.
- Court organization has been moved to the beginning of Chapter 3 to provide a frame of reference for subsequent discussions.
- Juries had been covered in a separate chapter; that subject is now part of the court organization chapter, and the juror's role is discussed in the chapter on trials.
- The chapter on motions brings together all types of motions, including motions for summary judgment.
- The chapter on expert witnesses now follows the chapter on investigations to better explain all the ways in which litigants can use experts.
- The discussion on jurisdiction is expanded and illustrations have been added.
- A discussion about the preparation and use of trial notebooks has been added.
- The discussion on fact briefs is greatly modified and integrated into the materials on trial preparation.
- A valuable discussion about trial strategy has been added to trial preparation.
- The hypothetical case now appears at the beginning of the text and is augmented and integrated into the text.
- The hypothetical case provides the basis for specific Case Assignments at the end of each chapter.
- Most discussions about rules and procedures are now augmented with more examples, illustrative documents, and exhibits. The text is slightly longer because of the many additions.
- Major examples are clearly delineated in the text.
- The discussion concerning mediation and arbitration is expanded to provide clarification about what paralegals may do.
- Technology Notes have been added to many chapters to inform students about technologies relevant to civil litigation and the use of the Internet.

How to Use This Text

Litigation and Trial Practice is designed to give students the big picture while explaining in detail most aspects of civil litigation. It does this in an evolutionary manner. Each chapter builds on the prior chapters. Subjects build on one another. The text was written to be self-sufficient. Little, if any, outside reading should be necessary. Chapters 1 and 8 are overviews. Students should read them, but not necessarily study them. They prepare students to understand the material that follows. Students should read the hypothetical case at the beginning of the course. Hopefully, it will catch their interest and be a catalyst for questions and discussion. It provides a frame of reference for class discussion.

Supplemental Teaching Materials

- The **Instructor's Manual with Test Bank** is available on-line at *www.paralegal.delmar.cengage.com* in the Instructor's Lounge under Resource. Written by the author of the text the *Instructor's Manual* contains educational objectives, lecture notes, key terms, answers to review questions, "Using the Hypothetical Case", Web links, additional discussion questions, and a test bank.
- **Online Companion™**—The Online Companion™ Web site can be found at *www.paralegal.delmar.cengage.com* in the Resource section of the Web site. The Online Companion™ contains the following:
  - Study Notes
  - Chapter Outlines
  - Web Links
  - Key Terms
  - Supplemental Activities
- **Web Page**—Come visit our Web site at *www.paralegal.delmar.cengage.com*, where you will find valuable information specific to this book such as hot links and sample materials to download, as well as other Paralegal Studies products.
- **Westlaw®**—Delmar's on-line computerized legal research system offers students "hands-on" experience with a system commonly used in law offices. Qualified adopters can receive ten free hours of WESTLAW®. WESTLAW® can be accessed with Macintosh and IBM PC and compatibles. A modem is required.

Authors

Roderick Blanchard, senior author, has specialized in civil litigation since 1960. Over the years, Mr. Blanchard has tried hundreds of civil actions of all kinds, including automobile accidents, airplane accidents, construction site accidents, defective products, electric utility power line accidents, natural gas accidents, fire losses, medical malpractice, accounting malpractice, engineer malpractice, insurance agent malpractice, attorney malpractice, employment discrimination, sexual harassment, sexual transmission of disease, insurance coverage, business breach of contract, divorce, child custody, and even a few probate matters. One hundred thirty-four of those cases reached the appellate courts—both federal and state. He wrote numerous briefs and argued those cases in both the trial courts and appellate courts.

Mr. Blanchard's interest in paralegal programs began more than twenty-five years ago when the University of Minnesota asked him to teach a civil litigation course for a new paralegal program. He was impressed by the students' enthusiasm and talents. He began to appreciate how much paralegals could help lawyers to be better lawyers. Although his firm employed some investigators, it did not have any certified paralegals. Soon, the firm began to hire trained paralegals. Some of the paralegals came to the firm directly from colleges. Some had prior experience in other fields, such as nursing and accounting. Some came from other law firms. As his law firm grew, its paralegal staff grew even faster. Lawyers who worked with paralegals were more efficient. Mr. Blanchard became increasingly dependent on paralegals to keep on top of his case load. They quickly became part of the firm's litigation teams. The firm now has twenty-plus paralegals to assist seventy-plus lawyers.

Litigation and Trial Practice is a product of his years of experience with litigation and working with paralegals. The paralegals in Mr. Blanchard's law firm told him how much they appreciated the fact that lawyers in his office made the effort to explain *why* they did things the way they did. Because the paralegals understood the reasons why they were asked to handle matters in a certain way, they found it easy to adapt to office procedures and to work with the kinds of documents and forms the firm used. The firm's paralegals did not feel like outsiders who were looking in. They understood what to do, how to do it, and why. That has become the theme of *Litigation and Trial Practice*.

The new coauthor, Bill Hart, devotes his practice to appellate law, focusing on insurance coverage and general litigation matters. He has been voted a Minnesota Superlawyer and is currently listed in the top 100 of Minnesota Superlawyers and in the top 10 of Minnesota's appellate practitioners. He is also a frequent lecturer on appellate practice and procedure.

Acknowledgments

The authors would like to thank the reviewers who made suggestions for improving this sixth edition:

Sally Bisson
College of Saint Mary
Omaha, Nebraska

Melody Brown
Eastern Idaho Technical College
Idaho Falls, Idaho

Ramona DeSalvo
Southeastern Career College
Nashville, Tennessee

Robert Diotalevi
Florida Gulf Coast University
Fort Myers, Florida

Tim Hart
College of the Sequoias
Visalia, California

Sheila Merchant
Hillsborough Community College
Tampa, Florida

Jill Raines
Oklahoma University College of Law
Norman, Oklahoma

Rana Scarlett-Johnson
College of Saint Mary
Omaha, Nebraska

Ruth S. Stevens
Davenport University–Grand Rapids
Grand Rapids, Michigan

A Personal Note

A paraprofessional career in law should be interesting, fulfilling, and, on occasion, exciting. As you prepare to assume responsibilities that, historically, were reserved to lawyers, give some consideration to the attitude with which you will approach those responsibilities. I have a few suggestions that may help you to obtain the benefits a paralegal career has to offer.

You should be proud of your association with the legal profession and the judicial system. Conduct yourself as a professional person. Dress appropriately. Be courteous to all persons with whom you come in contact, especially when dealing with an adverse party or opposing lawyer. Strive to develop a reputation for reliability and candor. Keep appointments. Be on time. Avoid creating time conflicts. Use a calendar to schedule appointments and deadlines. By being timely, you will do the best job possible.

Recognize that each matter you handle is very important to someone, even when the work seems routine to you. Some matters you will handle will be very personal in nature. Avoid the temptation to make "innocent" disclosures about the cases you are handling. Guard against making accidental disclosures. When you handle an assignment for a client, demonstrate the same interest and concern that you would want for your own important matters.

Be thoughtful and innovative, but be careful not to exceed your authority. Look for ways to work effectively and efficiently. Keep copies of documents you prepare. When you work on other assignments, they will help you to do the job better and faster. One of the surest ways to gain satisfaction, if not enjoyment, from your work is to strive for excellence. There is always satisfaction in doing a job well—whether or not anyone else happens to notice. Even a tedious task can be made more interesting by approaching it with the intent of doing it as well as you can.

Lawyers and all others who serve the judicial system depend on effective communications, both oral and written. Strive to be precise in your statements and questions. Develop a concern for using words correctly. Be alert to the meaning of words you use in your correspondence and reports. Use the language of the profession. Legal terminology will help you to be precise in your thinking and effective in your communication. Organize your thoughts before you write your letters, reports, and memoranda. Prepare your reports while the information is fresh and clear in your mind. Learn to use short, specific questions when you make inquiries of witnesses and clients.

As you work on assignments, try to keep in mind the whole picture and the ultimate objective. Strive to be objective in analyzing facts. It is all too easy to become oversold on a client's claim or defense. Lawyers and paralegals must avoid deluding themselves about the client's cause while serving the client. A client is better served by objective advisers than by fervent "yes-persons."

Ask questions about assignments. Determine how your tasks relate to the overall project. Learn from your mistakes, and do not become defensive because of past mistakes. Accept responsibility for what you have done, and for what you should have done but failed to do. Accept advice, corrections, and suggestions graciously. Usually, there is more than one way to perform a task. Be agreeable if the lawyers you work with prefer a method that is different from that which you learned or prefer.

Do not violate court rules or court orders or professional ethics. On occasion, your litigation team might be able to gain some advantage by disregarding professional responsibilities. Do not do so. Do not let anyone mislead you into a violation. No case, no client, no employer is important enough to justify sacrificing your own integrity and professional standing for his or her convenience. More often than not, the perpetrator's unprofessionalism is exposed to his or her detriment. The adversary system works well because each party has the opportunity and responsibility to present her or his own case. The process would collapse if it were not conducted by professionals in accordance with rules and standards based on fair play. Do not do anything to upset that delicate balance. Continue your education by attending seminars and reading professional articles relative to your work.

Roderick D. Blanchard

HYPOTHETICAL CASE STUDY
RASKIN V. HARPER

Introduction

The hypothetical case is based on a real case that reached the Minnesota Supreme Court. The names, places, dates, and a few of the facts have been changed. The case arose out of a car accident on a rural roadway. A pickup truck attempted to pass a slow-moving car. But while the pickup was passing, the car driver tried to make a left turn. The pickup's right front corner struck the car's left rear. There are issues concerning both drivers' negligence and causation. The driver of the car sustained serious personal injuries that lead to his death. After he died, a trustee was appointed to bring a wrongful-death action against the pickup driver.

The driver of the pickup had purchased it from a lawyer. At the time of the sale, the lawyer (seller) could not find his certificate of title. Both parties thought the buyer could not register the pickup without the certificate. For that reason, the lawyer agreed in writing to retain insurance on the pickup until he could find the certificate and give it to the buyer. Unfortunately, the lawyer neglected to look for it. The buyer notified the seller about the accident. The seller reported it to his automobile liability insurance company. But the insurer had canceled the policy. The seller's adult son had told the insurance agent that the pickup had been sold and asked the agent to transfer the coverage to another family vehicle. The seller complained that the agent should not have terminated coverage without talking to him first. In the meantime, the trustee, seller, and pickup driver entered into a hybrid settlement agreement to authorize the trustee to pursue a malpractice claim against the insurance agent. Eventually, the agent prevailed on a summary judgment. The case was appealed to the Minnesota Court of Appeals, which affirmed. The trustee petitioned to the Minnesota Supreme Court for review. The petition was denied. See *Redmond, as trustee for the heirs and next of kin of Wayne Russell Nolta vs. Frank Brandt and State Farm Mutual Automobile Insurance Company*, 1995 WL 479609 (Minn. App.).

Carefully read the hypothetical case now, before you begin your study of the text. Do not be concerned if you do not understand some of the words or if the circumstances are confusing. Keep the case in mind and use it as a frame of reference for applying the text. Case Assignments at the end of each chapter ask you to assist parties with aspects of the litigation. Sometimes the assignments will require you to use information from a prior chapter as well.

Hypothetical Case
Raskin v. Harper
John Griffin

John Griffin is a lawyer. He is married and has two adult sons who live in his home. He owned several vehicles, which were used by family members. In 1998 he bought a used 1995 GMC pickup truck from a lien holder who had obtained it through a repossession. Mr. Griffin contacted his insurance agent, Frederick Burns. Burns is the owner and sole proprietor of the Burns Insurance Agency, which is not incorporated. Burns had provided the coverage on Griffin's other vehicles. Griffin asked Burns to provide $100,000 of liability insurance on the pickup. Agent Burns placed the coverage with the Security Insurance Company. Security sent the insurance policy to Griffin. It provided the coverage he had requested. Griffin's adult son, Carl Griffin, became the pickup's principal driver. Mr. Griffin and Carl treated the pickup as though it belonged to Carl. Carl bought the gasoline and paid for minor repairs, but Mr. Griffin paid for the insurance.

William Nordby

William Nordby was born in 1932. He was married and had an adult married daughter, Laura Raskin. He was a retired farmer. He owned a Chevette that from time to time lost engine power and died. Mr. Nordby had a mechanic look at it once, but the mechanic could not find the problem.

Sale of Pickup Truck

Carl decided he wanted a used Chevrolet Camaro instead of the pickup truck. He talked to his father about selling the pickup. Mr. Griffin agreed that Carl could sell the pickup and that he could use the proceeds to buy a used Camaro. A friend told Carl that Bradley Harper was looking for a pickup truck. Carl contacted Harper, and they were able to agree on a sale price of $2,100. Carl told Mr. Griffin about the buyer and the proposed terms for the sale. Mr. Griffin could not find his certificate of title for the pickup to give to Harper. He was concerned that he might be liable for Harper's operation of the truck until he could transfer title to Harper. He concluded that he would keep the Security insurance policy on the pickup to protect himself.

John Griffin prepared a handwritten buy-sell agreement, which provided for the following:

SALE OF MOTOR VEHICLE

Seller: 333 Bittersweet Lane
    Mitchell, Iowa

Buyer: Bradley Harper
    Goodthunder, Minnesota

I, Bradley Harper, hereby purchase from M. John Griffin a 1995 GMC pickup, Sierra Classic 1500 Series, today, April 6, 2000, for Two Thousand One Hundred Dollars ($2,100.00). The purchaser has inspected the vehicle and is purchasing the vehicle "as is," without warranty.

  The seller does not have the certificate of title as of today. The seller shall use his best efforts to obtain said title as soon as possible. Seller shall keep insurance on said vehicle until title is obtained.

Dated this 6th of April, 2000.

            /s/ Carl Griffin, Seller
           /s/ Bradley D. Harper, Purchaser

On April 6, 2000, Carl Griffin met with Bradley Harper at their friend's house. They went over the terms of the written proposal and agreed that it was correct. Both men signed the sale-of-motor-vehicle agreement on April 6, 2000. Harper paid the full purchase price in cash. Harper took possession of the pickup on April 10, Carl used the sale proceeds to buy a used Camaro.

Bradley Harper

Mr. Harper was born in 1973. He is single. He is self-employed with an annual income of $23,000. He had lost the use of both legs because of injuries sustained in a 1996 automobile accident. He is a paraplegic. He modified the pickup to include hand controls and a new stereo system. Harper operated the pickup as his own, but he did not buy insurance. As modified, the pickup had a fair market value of $3,500.

Insurance

On April 10, 2000, Carl Griffin informed the Burns Agency that his father had sold the pickup and that they had purchased a Chevrolet Camaro to replace it. Carl asked for insurance coverage for the Camaro. An insurance secretary at the Burns Agency completed the necessary documents to cancel the policy on the pickup and transfer the unearned premium to a new policy for the Camaro. The secretary sent the documents to the Security Insurance Company, which placed coverage on the Camaro and terminated coverage on the pickup. The Griffins received a credit for the unused premium on the pickup. The credit was applied to the insurance on the Camaro.

Harper called Mr. Griffin several times and asked him to provide the certificate of title. Although the buy-sell agreement provided that Mr. Griffin would use his best efforts to locate the certificate of title and deliver it to Harper, after six months passed he stopped looking for it. Unbeknownst to Mr. Griffin, the liability insurance terminated by operation of law at the time of sale to Harper, because Griffin no longer had an insurable interest in it. Harper had to buy his own coverage and pay whatever premium was appropriate for his status and risk. Nevertheless, Harper expected Mr. Griffin to "keep" insurance on the pickup for Harper's benefit. Although John Griffin was a practicing lawyer, he did not realize his coverage had terminated, and he made no effort to buy other insurance for Harper. Even if he could have paid for liability insurance for Harper, the policy would have to have been purchased in Harper's name.

The Accident

The accident occurred on October 17, 2000, on Hubbard County Road 13, two hundred yards west of County Road 118 in Minnesota. County Road 13 is a two-lane, asphalt, secondary highway. There are pastures and farmland on each side of the road and gentle rolling hills. County Road 118 forms a T intersection with County Road 13, going to the north. Harper was driving the pickup east on County Road 13. He had an adult passenger named James Patner. Patner lived in Iowa and was visiting Harper. The weather was overcast. A weather report for the nearest airport showed no precipitation that day. The highway was in good condition. Traffic was limited. Driving conditions were good in every respect.

Harper believes he was driving about fifty-five miles per hour, which is the posted speed limit. As Harper came over the crest of a hill, he noticed a Chevette in his lane. It seemed to be traveling slowly, slower than he wanted to travel. There were no oncoming vehicles. The County Road 118 intersection was about 200 yards ahead of the Chevette. Harper did not see any turn signal on the Chevette. He decided to pass. He moved left across the center line and into the westbound lane in preparation to pass. As he approached the rear of the Chevette, he says, the Chevette moved to the left but did not change speed. Harper applied his brakes and skidded forward. The front end of the pickup struck the left rear corner of the Chevette. The sheriff later measured seventy-eight feet of skid marks left by the pickup. The Chevette spun counterclockwise and came to rest north of the intersection on the east shoulder of 118. The pickup came to rest at the northeast corner of the intersection, facing southeasterly.

Mr. Nordby was driving to visit his daughter. He could have reached her house by going straight ahead on County Road (CR) 13 or turning left to go north on CR 118. The Hubbard County sheriff investigated. Harper told him Nordby's Chevette made a sudden lane change and/or left turn directly in front of him while he was attempting to pass. He had not sounded his horn. The Chevette did not signal for a left turn. He said he could not avoid the Chevette. Nordby was unconscious at the scene. An ambulance transported him to a regional hospital. He regained consciousness, but he never left the hospital. Nobody questioned him about the accident.

Injuries and Property Damage

Mr. Nordby's injuries led to his death on April 5, 2001. He was 69. His only income was from social security and from properties in joint tenancy with his wife. His wife

ACCIDENT REPORT

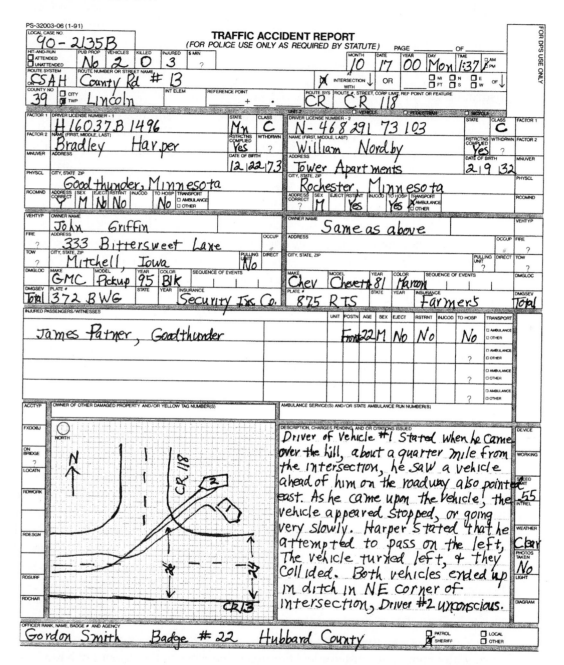

and adult daughter, Laura Raskin, survived him. They incurred $115,345 in medical expenses for Nordby's care and $4,772 for funeral and burial expenses. The Chevette was not repairable. It had a fair market value of $4,500.

Harper did not require hospitalization. He sustained some minor cuts on his face and scalp and suffered a neck and back sprain. He started having recurring headaches and was irritable for months following the accident. He saw his family doctor four times over the following six months. He had twelve chiropractic treatments for his neck and back during the second month following the accident. His condition improved, but his chiropractor believes Harper will have some permanent disability of his spine because of the accident. His medical expenses total $355. His chiropractic expenses total $375. All the expenses have been covered by Harper's medical insurance. The pickup truck could not be repaired and was considered to be a total loss.

Insurance Coverage Problems

Harper contacted John Griffin to get the name of the insurance company Griffin had used to insure the pickup, as provided in the April 6, 2000, buy-sell agreement. At that time, Griffin assumed he still had coverage, because he had not asked the agent to cancel it. He assumed that he had paid the premiums through an automatic payment plan. He was unaware that his son had told the agent that the pickup had been sold or that coverage had been transferred to the Camaro. John contacted agent Burns and told him about the accident. He explained the buy-sell agreement and related circumstances. Burns informed Mr. Griffin that the records showed coverage on the pickup had been terminated at the customer's request. Nevertheless, Burns contacted the Security Insurance Company about the accident and claim for coverage. Security responded that it did not provide coverage. Its records also showed that coverage had been terminated and the unused premium had been applied to the Camaro on April 10, 2000. Security had issued a notice of the change of the policy. It also sent monthly billings to Mr. Griffin showing coverage on a Camaro and no coverage for the pickup truck after April 2000. Mr. Griffin retained attorney Sandra Gillis to help him deal with the situation. In the meantime, he explained to Harper that he believed that Security Insurance should provide coverage, but the company was not cooperating.

Litigation

Laura Raskin hired attorney Donald Smith to seek money damages for her father's wrongful death. Attorney Smith filed documents to have Ms. Raskin appointed trustee to represent the heirs and next of kin. On July 29, 2001, the Hubbard County District Court appointed Laura Raskin to be trustee. She then commenced a civil action in the Hubbard County District Court against Bradley Harper. The suit is titled *Laura Raskin, as Trustee for the heirs and next of kin of William Nordby vs. Bradley Harper.* Because John Griffin did not own the pickup and was not vicariously liable for Harper's operation of it, no action was brought against him. The trustee alleged Harper was negligent for driving at an excessive rate of speed, failing to maintain control of his pickup, improperly passing, failing to signal his pass, and failing to keep a proper lookout. The trustee asked for money damages in the amount of $400,000.

Attorney Smith retained an accident reconstructionist to help investigate the accident. The accident reconstructionist was erroneously informed or assumed that the skid marks were 121 feet in length.

Harper retained attorney William Hoch to represent him. Attorney Hoch filed an answer to the trustee's complaint. He denied that Harper was negligent. He alleged that Nordby was negligent for failing to keep a proper lookout, failing to signal his intent to make a left turn, and failing to keep his vehicle under control. He filed a counterclaim for money damages for Harper's personal injuries and the loss of the pickup.

Harper brought a third-party action against John Griffin for indemnity based on John Griffin's breach of contract for failure to obtain or provide insurance on the pickup as provided in the buy-sell agreement.

Sandra Gillis filed an answer to the third-party complaint for John Griffin. Griffin did not deny the agreement with Harper, but he denied that the agreement was an enforceable contract. He alleged that Harper had not paid a consideration for Griffin's promise to provide insurance; therefore, there was no contract. The $2,100 Harper paid was the price of the pickup and not for insurance. Griffin also alleged there was no meeting of the minds concerning essential terms and conditions, such as the amount of coverage, the identity of the insurer, or the type of coverage. He claimed the alleged contract was contrary to public policy because he was not authorized by law to provide insurance for Harper. He contended that, at most, he would be liable for the minimum amount of coverage required by state law. He also alleged all the affirmative defenses that Harper had alleged as defenses to the trustee's action.

On behalf of John Griffin, Sandra Gillis commenced a fourth-party action against Agent Burns. Griffin alleged that Burns was negligent for "canceling" his Security Insurance policy on the pickup truck without his express authority. Further, he alleged that Agent Burns was negligent for not informing him that his son had canceled the coverage and/or transferred it to the Camaro. He alleged that if Burns had told him about changing coverage to the Camaro, he would have gone elsewhere to obtain the coverage he expected to provide to Harper.

Agent Burns has "errors-and-omissions" liability insurance. He notified his insurer about the claim and immediately sent a copy of the fourth-party complaint to the insurer. The insurer accepted coverage and provided an attorney, Catherine Dolan, to defend Burns. She interposed an answer to the fourth-party complaint. The fourth-party answer denied that he caused Griffin's coverage on the pickup to be canceled, because the coverage terminated by operation of law when Griffin sold the pickup to Harper. She alleged that Carl Griffin had actual or apparent authority to order cancellation of the coverage on the pickup and request coverage for the Camaro. She alleged that John Griffin could not have been damaged by Burns's "transfer" of the coverage to the Camaro, as Carl requested, because John Griffin could not insure the pickup after selling it. The answer also alleged all the defenses that Griffin had to Harper's third-party action and all the defenses that Harper had to the trustee's wrongful death action.

Each party needs legal representation, advice, and assistance. You are not expected to know what the law is. That is an attorney's responsibility. But once the attorney has decided how to proceed, the attorney will ask for your help with prosecution of the claims and defenses. You can expect to interview the client and witnesses. You may need to conduct an investigation, locate and interview experts, locate relevant documents, prepare pleadings, prepare motions, prepare deposition summaries, assist with discovery, and help bring the matter to a successful conclusion. If the case cannot be settled, you will help prepare for trial and assist at the trial.

Your assignments will come from the attorney. You will complete them in the form of intraoffice memoranda similar to the following:

Intraoffice Memorandum
(Privileged)

TO: File

FROM: Paralegal

SUBJECT: Accident Reconstructionist

The reconstructionist has formed the following opinions:

1. The Harper pickup laid down 121 feet of skid marks before entering the northeast ditch. The vehicle continued its skid in the ditch. The left-side skid marks start 46 feet west of the right-side skids.

2. The left-side skid marks start 10.6 feet north of the south edge of the traveled portion of, or totally within, the eastbound lane.

3. Harper's minimum speed prior to the initiation of braking was 51 miles per hour. After allowing for energy absorption by the collision itself and skidding or braking off the roadway, the likely speed at the time of initiation of braking activity was in excess of the speed limit of 55 miles per hour.

4. The roadway is generally flat and level to the west of the scene of the accident, with good visibility. Accordingly, there is no reason why Harper could not view the Nordby Chevette for approximately one-quarter mile and appropriately reduce his speed. It is apparent that he did not do so and was traveling at or above the speed limit at the point he initiated braking.

5. Harper gave a statement on 11/7/00 in which he stated that when he first saw the Nordby Chevette, both vehicles were in the eastbound lane. He stated that he did not feel at that point that he would be able to stop or avoid contact by remaining in his own lane and, accordingly, went into the left lane to pass or avoid a collision. This statement, together with the physical fact that Harper skidded 121 feet before going into the ditch, support the conclusion that Harper did not have his vehicle under control sufficiently so as to avoid collision with the Nordby Chevette. This was obviously a panic maneuver, due to a high rate of speed and lack of control.

EXPERT'S DIAGRAM

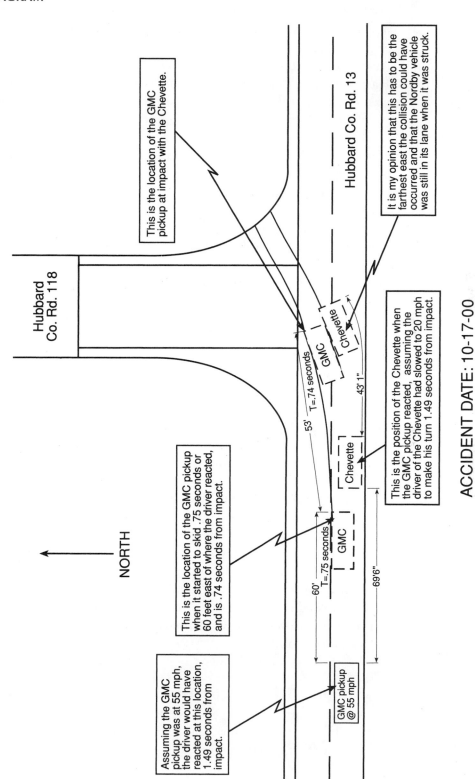

This is the location of the GMC pickup at impact with the Chevette.

It is my opinion that this has to be the farthest east the collision could have occurred and that the Nordby vehicle was still in its lane when it was struck.

Hubbard Co. Rd. 13

Hubbard Co. Rd. 118

NORTH

This is the location of the GMC pickup when it started to skid .75 seconds or 60 feet east of where the driver reacted, and is .74 seconds from impact.

Assuming the GMC pickup was at 55 mph, the driver would have reacted at this location, 1.49 seconds from impact.

This is the position of the Chevette when the GMC pickup reacted, assuming the driver of the Chevette had slowed to 20 mph to make his turn 1.49 seconds from impact.

53'   T=.74 seconds

GMC

Chevette

43' 1"

60'   T=.75 seconds

GMC

Chevette

69'6"

GMC pickup @ 55 mph

ACCIDENT DATE: 10-17-00

Considerations

The plaintiff trustee must allege and prove that Harper was negligent and that his negligence caused or contributed to the accident and Nordby's death. The plaintiff trustee also must prove the nature and extent of the heirs' and next of kin's damages. Harper can avoid liability if he was not negligent or if Nordby's causal negligence was greater than his. Harper can reduce the extent of his liability by showing Nordby's negligence contributed to the accident.

Harper has a claim against the trustee for Harper's injuries and loss of the truck. Harper has a claim for breach of contract against John Griffin for failing to provide some kind of insurance in some amount on the pickup truck. Harper must prove that he had a valid contract with John Griffin, that John breached the contract, and that Harper sustained damages.

Mr. Griffin claims negligence against Agent Burns on the grounds that Burns wrongfully canceled insurance coverage on the pickup. This is a type of professional malpractice action. John Griffin must first establish that Agent Burns owed him a legal duty that he negligently breached. John must then prove that Burns was negligent for terminating coverage or failing to inform him that the coverage was terminated; that Burns's negligence caused John not to have insurance coverage for Harper.

Agent Burns can avoid liability by showing that he was not negligent, and that he acted as a reasonable and prudent insurance agent by relying on information that Griffin had sold the pickup. But there is also a question whether Griffin *could* retain coverage on the pickup for the buyer after he sold it. If Griffin could not provide coverage for another owner, the agent's alleged negligence could not be the cause of Griffin's failure to have coverage for Harper. In other words, could Griffin legally contract to buy insurance for another owner?

The plaintiff trustee wants to obtain control over the insurance coverage issues, and Griffin and Harper want out of the case. Is there some way they can settle the matter among them so the trustee can pursue Griffin's claim against agent Burns?

In dealing with such a case, paralegals are not required to determine the parties' legal rights and obligations or to analyze legal issues. Instead, they help lawyers conduct the procedures that make the system work. Each party needs legal representation and assistance. Each party must be interviewed. The accident must be investigated. The suits must be commenced. An accident reconstructionist (expert witness) may be necessary. Discovery must be conducted. The claims must be prepared for trial.

Transcript of Telephone Interview

Q: Mr. Harper, this is Diane Kaplan. I am an investigator for the Security Insurance Company. Your accident has been reported to us. Mr. Griffin says that you are insured under his policy with this company. May I discuss the accident with you?

A: I guess so.

Q: Good. This should only take a few minutes. This telephone conversation is being recorded. I need to make a record of what we say. Is that all right with you?

A: Do I have any choice? . . . What are we going to talk about?

Q: Well, this is November 7, 2000. I want to get your version of the accident you had with William Nordby on October 15th—

A: October 17.

Q: I'm sorry. You're right. Yes. I need to talk with you about how the accident happened. The company needs to have your version.

A: I understand. Do I need an attorney.

Q: Do you have a lawyer?

A: Not yet. But I have talked to a couple.

Q: I can't tell you what you should do. I can tell you that I have to have a statement if Security is going to help you with this accident. You do understand that a recorder is running.

A: Yeah.

Q: What?

A: Yes.

Q: OK. What is your address?

A: Goodthunder.

Q: That's Minnesota.

A: Yes.

Q: What is your birth date?

A: December 22, 1973.

Q: Are you married?

A: No, I'm single.

Q: What's your occupation?

A: I am a computer programmer.

Q: What is your social security number?

A: 555-55-5555.

Q: Who is the title holder of the GMC pickup truck you were driving? Do you know?

A: John Griffin, I think.

Q: You were driving with his permission?

A: Yes. I bought it from him. He said he would keep the insurance on it until he could give me the title card.

Q: He did what?

A: He said he would keep the insurance on it.

Q: Why?

A: He put it in writing. I have the bill of sale.

Q: OK. What kind of condition was it in?

A: Good. Real good.

Q: Was there any physical damage on it before the accident?

A: Not that I know of.

Q: Well, where were you coming from?

A: We were coming from Goodthunder. We were on our way to Bob Johnson's place.

Q: Who is we? Did you have a passenger?

A: Yes. Jim Patner.

Q: Can you spell that for me?

A: P-a-t-n-e-r.

Q: And the other vehicle involved, do you know who owned it?

A: The guy who was driving, I suppose. Nordby. Bill Nordby.

Q: What kind of car was it?

A: A late-model Chevrolet, or Chevette.

Q: And how was the condition; any prior damage on it?

A: What prior damage?

Q: Hum?

A: You mean its condition?

Q: Yes.

A: It was totaled.

Q: No. I mean before the accident.

A: No idea.

Q: Were you wearing a seat belt?

A: No. Doesn't have any.

Q: I see. Are there any restrictions on your license.

A: Nope.

Q: Was your passenger wearing his seat belt?

A: Negative.

Q: Had you had any drugs or alcohol before the accident?

A: You mean that day?

Q: What time did the accident happen?

A: About one in the afternoon.

Q: Had you had anything that day?

A: No.

Q: The previous day.

A: I don't do drugs.

Q: Any alcohol?

A: Not that I remember.

Q: How were the weather conditions?

A: Sky was overcast. Maybe, slightly misting.

Q: And were—what road were you on, what street were you traveling on?

A: County Road 13, going east.

Q: What's the speed limit?

A: Fifty-five miles per hour.

Q: OK. I'm trying to picture this. I'm going to make a sketch here. You're going east on 13 at fifty-five miles per hour. Where was the other car? Could you place that for me?

A: Yeah, I'm going east. Nordby was also facing, going, east on 13. It's an old Chevette.

Q: OK. Was he ahead of you or behind you?

A: He is ahead, long way ahead when I first seen him.

Q: How many lanes for 13?

A: Two lanes, one each way. East, west.

Q: What about lane markers? Any dotted lines, anything like that?

A: To my recollect, I believe there are center line markings.

Q: Just the dotted or dash type?

A: Yeah. I believe so.

Q: Describe the surface?

A: I can't recollect for sure. The surface is blacktop.

Q: How long had it been misting?

A: I'd say about, probably less than an hour.

Q: And did—at the time of the accident, did you need, use, your windshield wipers?

A: No, that wasn't necessary.

Q: How about the lay of the road; is it straight or curved or what?

A: Thirteen is straight. A quarter mile from the [inaudible] of collision a rise in the road.

Q: OK.

A: Otherwise, it's flat and straight.

Q: In your own words, why don't you tell me what happened.

A: We—I viewed Mr. Nordby's car sitting—I believe I initially viewed him in the distance. I viewed the vehicle going real slow, maybe stopped, facing east in the right-hand lane; sitting there off center more toward the right without brake lights or blinker indicators. And viewed the vehicle as stationary and proceeded to pass him. It looked like he was sitting there and—watching him as I went into the left-hand lane to pass him or around him, seen him make a physical move to turn left, at which time I tried to move further to go around him, laying on my horn and going for the brakes and braking.

Q: How far back do you figure you noticed him making his left-hand turn?

A: Oh, I would say—I would say, I didn't view him actually making the physical move until point-blank range. When I was actually, had just made the lane change.

Q: OK.

A: I had seen him stationary. I was in a position where I couldn't brake the vehicle without—and avoid hitting him by staying in the same lane. I also didn't view the ability to go around him on the right, as I was making my commitment turn left at that time. I immediately, after I went into the left lane started to go there, I seen his head—turn—to the left, which, at that time I come to the realization possibly not to stay sitting there and was going to make some sort of action. I put on the horn. I would say . . . approximately twenty-five foot, thirty foot.

Q: What was he turning?

A: He turned left.

Q: Was it on a side road, or was he going to make a U-turn?

A: That's total subjectory [?] for me, 'cause we had impact before obviously he made a completion of what he was going to do.

Q: Was there an intersecting road?

A: There is a T-road there. There is a road to the left but no road to the right.

Q: OK.

A: It was a field driveway approach. There is a field driveway approach to your right.

Q: At this intersection, I mean, does it have a, you know . . . You were on County Road 13. Does that intersecting road have a county name or anything? An identifier?

A: One eighteen, I believe.

Q: And how fast were you going?

A: I was going the speed limit. Fifty-five miles per hour.

Q: Did you have your lights on or . . . ?

A: I can't recollect if I did or didn't. I believe I probably did not.

Q: And then what happened?

A: I went for the brake. I put the brakes on and tried to maneuver further to the left, around into the far ditch, and was unsuccessful at that. We had impact in a matter of short—or period of incident reactionary time of a second or two. He made contact with us in the front passenger fender at about the front wheel, right above the front wheel, and brought us together side to side, and we went into the left-hand ditch beyond the intersection.

Q: OK. Then what happened?

A: I got out of my pickup and viewed the individual in the vehicle, and the first vehicle arrived on the scene I flagged down, and immediately sent for an ambulance assistance, medical assistance, called at . . . And we waited by Nordby's car until they arrived.

Q: And how about injuries in your vehicle? Were there any injuries on your—

A: Injury to the party in my vehicle?

Q: Right.

A: No. Nothing of significance.

Q: Nothing of significance, but you didn't feel any—

A: Well, sure I was hurting, but . . . .

Q: And was your car—was the pickup truck you were driving drivable after the accident?

A: I guess that's within question. The vehicle—the engine ran. We did not drive it after the accident. It was towed from the accident scene and subsequently towed also. It hasn't been driven since. Whether it's movable by driving, it's questionable.

Q: And you say it was owned by John Griffin. Did you have permission to drive this car—or the pickup, I mean?

A: Yes, I did. We had a purchase agreement made on it.

Q: Could you tell me about the purchase agreement, like when it was made?

A: The first week of April, dated on, I would assume, was the 6th of April. I made an exchange of $2,100 with John's son, Carl, and signed an agreement that was written up by John and signed by John.

Q: But you said it was with John's son, Carl. Was Carl titled owner of the vehicle, or do you know if John was?

A: No, I believe John is.

Q: And when did you expect—when were they going to produce the title for you?

A: As quickly as possible. I was expecting it thereafter. Purchase agreement says that he would use his best efforts to obtain title as soon as possible.

Q: Was there another agreement?

A: No, this was an ongoing agreement with conversations following this.

Q: And did you report this to your insurance agent, or anything, that you would be driving this vehicle?

A: Yes, I did, actually. It was brought up that I would possibly, upon receiving transfer of the vehicle, that I would be insuring that pickup. Possibly in the winter of this coming year or whenever I obtained the title to said vehicle.

Q: And . . .

A: The last time I believe I had a conversation about renewal of my policy, that was brought up.

Q: Last time you had renewal. About April or so? Does that sound about—

A: No, this was discussed with my agent just briefly as a topic of my policy, which directions—I had insured a vehicle and had said possibly this standard policy hadn't held, that I would call and, depending on which vehicle, I would add or delete.

Q: Was it going to be—oh, you didn't know exactly if you were going to sell?

A: Recollect when this was?

Q: Well, you did know if it was going to be a replacement vehicle or an additional vehicle?

A: Right.

Q: On the—

A: Depending on, of course, what I would be driving and would be liable if I would continue to carry additional insurance on the minivan, or if it was decided that that vehicle . . . Then I would insure the other vehicle or one would be added.

Q: Did you do anything to the pickup after you got it?

A: Yeah, I put hand controls and a new stereo in it.

Q: Where can the truck be viewed?

A: I got it at home, now.

Q: Let's see, after the accident, did the police investigate?

A: Yes, there was the County sheriffs and, I think, state troopers.

Q: Did you talk with the police?

A: Yes, I did.

Q: And what did they say afterwards?

A: Not a whole lot.

Q: Did they issue any tickets?

A: No, no tickets were issued.

Q: The—Nordby, do you know where he was taken to?

A: I believe he was taken to Redeemers Hospital and then transferred.

Q: Were there any witnesses?

A: Not at the time. Some came later.

Q: Who do you think was at fault for the accident?

A: Well, I feel that I've done everything correct in my behalf, so I would say that William Nordby was at fault for not using blinkers or indicators. I didn't see any brake lights or anything of that sort, so . . .

Q: Is there anything else that you would like to add concerning the accident details?

A: I think I've described them just as comprehensive as I can.

Q: OK. Have you understood all of these questions?

A: Yes, I believe so.

Q: And to the best of your knowledge, the information given is true and correct?

A: Yes, it is.

Q: And you understand that this interview has been continuously recorded?

A: I understand that, yes.

Q: This is Diane Kaplan concluding the interview with Bradley Harper on November 7, 2000, at 2:30 P.M.

CHAPTER OUTLINE

Chapter Objectives

Chapter 1 introduces you to the civil justice system. The chapter identifies and discusses principles that guide courts in handling civil litigation and limit the power of the courts. These principles provide a frame of reference for the rules of law and procedure that are the subject of this text. Almost everything discussed in this chapter is covered in detail, with examples, in later chapters.

Introduction

Law is an interesting subject, but civil litigation is particularly interesting because of the human drama, types of problems, and need for creative problem solving. People resort to litigation because they need to resolve controversies they have with others. The law provides a means for peaceably resolving the disputes. Paralegals play an important role as members of litigation teams. They assist attorneys to actively develop and manage their cases. Paralegals have become invaluable to the judicial system, helping to resolve disputes in a timely, economical, and just manner.

The judicial system is constantly evolving with changes in society. It regulates itself through checks and balances and self-limitations to ensure that justice is administered according to law. It succeeds because it is founded on experience, reason, and fairness. It may not be perfect, but it works very, very well. The better a paralegal understands the law and legal procedures, the more effective she or he can be.

Overview of Civil Litigation

A person who has sustained an injury or loss need not resort to self-help or violence against the wrongdoer because our federal and state governments have given courts the power to resolve such controversies. The procedure for bringing a lawsuit has been kept *relatively* simple and inexpensive. If the civil justice system were too complicated, unpredictable, or expensive, people would avoid it. If any **party** were forced to bear the entire cost of their litigation—such as the cost of the courtroom or of court personnel salaries—the party might forgo valuable rights or concede rights to others. In fact, the parties to a civil lawsuit pay only a fraction of the actual costs of the litigation.

The United States Constitution provides for a federal judicial system that handles criminal and civil cases. The Constitution created the United States Supreme Court and delineated its powers. The Constitution gave Congress responsibility to create lower courts that function under the supervision of the Supreme Court. Congress created a **district court** for each state. For our purposes, we will think of federal district courts as courts in which trials are conducted. They are courts of **original jurisdiction**—a place where cases are first heard by a court. Most district courts have two or more divisions. The number of divisions is determined by the size of the district (state) and population. Each division has its own courthouse where most of the court's business is conducted.

Congress created eleven Circuit Courts of Appeals to handle appeals from district courts. Each Circuit Court of Appeals serves several districts. A party who appeals from a district court **judgment** must appeal to the Circuit Court that serves that party's district. Usually, a Circuit Court of Appeals' decision is final, but the United States Supreme Court may choose to review a Circuit Court's decision, especially when there is disagreement between Circuits about the law or when the case involves law that needs clarification. (See Exhibit 1.1.)

Each state also has its own state-run judicial system. Typically, a state has a number of trial courts. They often are described as district courts. It is common to have one district court for each county or parish. Most states have a two-tier appellate system similar to the federal system. For information about a particular state, see http://www.courts.net or http://www.findlaw.com. The state district courts handle

party A natural person, corporation, or other legal entity that is the plaintiff or defendant in a civil action.

district court Trial courts of the United States court system, and in some states, low-level state courts (or even appeals courts).

original jurisdiction The court in which an action may properly be commenced. A trial court has original jurisdiction. An appellate court does not have original jurisdiction.

judgment (1) A court's ultimate determination of the parties' rights and obligations concerning a particular matter.

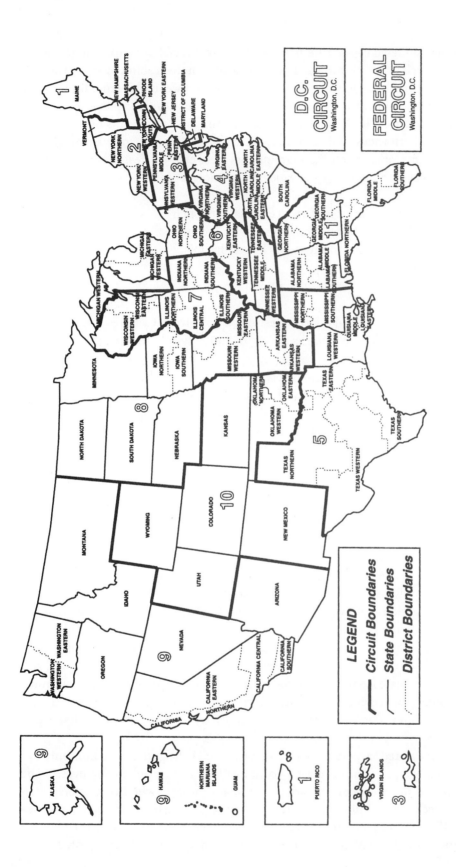

4   Chapter 1

both criminal and civil cases. The federal and state judicial systems function independently of each other. But in the few areas where there is some overlap, the federal system controls. Seldom is there any conflict between the federal and state judicial systems. Criminal and civil law are very different in their purposes and use different procedures. This book explains the manner and the means by which parties to a lawsuit, attorneys, and courts handle civil cases from beginning to end.

Civil lawsuits arise out of disagreements between parties. Civil courts are equipped to deal with the following types of questions.

- Did the transaction or occurrence actually happen?
- Was the defendant's conduct wrongful (unlawful)?
- Did the act or omission cause any loss or harm?
- What **remedy** is appropriate?
- How much money would be fair compensation?

The law to answer these (and other) questions comes from Congress, state legislatures, and the courts. When there is no controlling[1] statute to determine the parties' rights and obligations, the court has power to create legal rights and duties between litigants for the purpose of resolving their dispute. The law that a court creates is referred to as the **common law.** In an effort to find or create a rule of law that will resolve a pending dispute, a court looks first to its own precedent. Precedent is a rule of law that a court has expressly decided. The written decision in a previous case that sets forth a rule of law is often referred to as a precedent. Setting precedent for future cases is one critical function of an appellate court. In this regard, trial courts are required to follow the precedent of an appellate court. But when there is no apparent precedent, the trial court must find or create its own rule of law. Courts look to fundamental principles of fairness and society's needs in determining what a new rule of law should provide.

The civil law establishes our legal rights and obligations with regard to property, transactions, and conduct toward each other. Civil litigation is the process by which courts apply the civil law to resolve disputes between persons concerning property, transactions, and wrongful, injurious conduct. The term *person* includes any legal entity, such as an individual, corporation, trust, and other organizations created through law. The **substantive law** creates legal rights and imposes legal obligations. The substantive law includes contract law, property law, tort law, and all statutes that create legal rights. **Procedural law** determines how a lawsuit must be commenced, managed, and presented in court. This includes **rules of evidence,** which determine what **evidence** a party may use to prove facts that are in dispute.

As already noted, a person who engages in civil litigation is commonly referred to as a "party." And because a corporation is a "person" in the eyes of the law, a corporation also may be a party to a lawsuit. A party who brings a civil lawsuit is referred to as the **plaintiff,** and the opposing party is referred to as the **defendant.** This is true even if the defendant also makes a **claim** against the plaintiff in the same lawsuit. A civil lawsuit is often referred to as a civil **action** or, simply, an "action."

remedy   The means by which a right is enforced or satisfaction is gained for a harm done. The means by which a violation of rights is prevented, redressed, or compensated.

common law   A system of law that is based on precedent, rather than a civil code of laws. Most states rely on the common law to resolve disputes in civil litigation.

substantive law   Law that creates, defines, and regulates legal rights between persons.

procedural law   The rules of law that govern the conduct of a legal procedure or process, as distinguished from the law that determines the parties' substantive rights.

rules of evidence   Rules that govern the admissibility of evidence at trial.

evidence   Anything that tends to prove a fact, especially testimony and exhibits offered at a trial.

plaintiff   A person who brings (starts) a lawsuit against another person.

defendant   The person against whom a legal action is brought. This legal action may be criminal or civil.

claim   A demand for compensation or restitution for personal injury, property damage, or loss of profits.

action   A claim that has been placed in suit. A lawsuit.

A plaintiff commences a civil action by serving a **complaint** upon the defendant(s). The complaint must also be filed with a court that has **jurisdiction** over the defendant *and* over the subject of the lawsuit. Jurisdiction refers to the courts' authority to decide the case. When the plaintiff files the complaint, the court places the case in line for trial. In most cases, either party may ask the court to schedule the case for a jury trial in which a jury will resolve the disputed facts. If neither party asks for a jury trial, the case will be submitted to a judge to decide all fact issues.

The defendant is entitled to know, at the outset, what rights the plaintiff claims were violated. The plaintiff must clearly state each such violation. Therefore, the complaint must identify the time and place of the transaction or occurrence in which the plaintiff claims his or her rights were violated. The complaint also must describe the manner in which the plaintiff's legal rights were allegedly violated (i.e., by the defendant's wrongful act or by the defendant's wrongful omission). A defendant cannot simply ignore a lawsuit. The law requires the defendant to appear in the case by serving and filing an **answer** to the complaint. The defendant must admit the truthfulness of specific facts the plaintiff alleged in the complaint if the defendant knows them to be true. A defendant who falsely denies the plaintiff's specific factual allegations is subject to penalties. The defendant's denials raise issues between the parties. The issues may arise from differences on the facts or differences on the law or both.

Not every dispute between persons may be brought to court for resolution. Courts only resolve claims involving a violation of a person's *legal rights*. A defendant violates the plaintiff's legal rights if the defendant has a **legal duty** to act or refrain from acting for the plaintiff's benefit or protection and the defendant breaches that duty. For example, a homeowner might sue her neighbor for damage caused by a fallen tree that had died and become vulnerable to collapse. If the defendant owned the tree (i.e., it was on his property) it was his legal duty to act to prevent the weakened tree from falling on his neighbor's house. But if it turned out that the tree was owned by a different landowner, a court would dismiss the action for want of a legal duty. The law does not require people to protect others from things they have no right to control.

The above example also shows the difference between a question of fact (who owned the tree?) and a question of law (is there a legal duty to take action vis-à-vis a thing one does not own?). When there is a dispute about the facts—where is the property boundary?—it is the jury's function to resolve it. But when there is a dispute about the law, it is the court's function to resolve it. Consider this further example. The plaintiff may allege that the defendant defamed him by describing the plaintiff in a newspaper article as a "devious politician." It would be a *question of fact* for a jury to decide whether the defendant wrote the article, but it would be a *question of law* whether such a statement about the plaintiff qualifies as defamatory. For a statement to be defamatory, certain elements must be present, and that is for a judge to determine as a question of law. If the statement is not defamatory in the eyes of the law, it is not **actionable,** even though the defendant made the derogatory[2] statement. In order for a statement (or any other conduct) to be "actionable," it must state a claim for which the court can grant **relief.** In this case, as the judge would note, the defendant was not under a legal duty to refrain from saying that the plaintiff is a "devious politician."

complaint   A document used in civil litigation to state a claim against a defendant.

jurisdiction   The power and authority of a court.

answer   A defendant's pleading in which the defendant admits and/or denies the plaintiff's allegations.

legal duty   A duty that the law imposes on a person to act or refrain from acting.

actionable   An act or occurrence is actionable if it provides legal reasons for a lawsuit.

relief   A remedy, redress or assistance that a court awards to a party, other than money damages.

dismissal The termination of a lawsuit pursuant to Rule 41.

fact finder The fact finder must consider and weigh the evidence to resolve disputed facts and determine the ultimate questions of fact.

general verdict A verdict in which the jury simply finds in favor of the plaintiff by specifying an amount of money damages, or finds for the defendant.

special verdict A verdict form in which a jury answers specific questions about the facts of the case.

findings of fact A determination of facts made by the fact finder from the evidence produced in a trial.

conclusions of law Determinations judges make when applying the law to a given set of facts.

order for judgment A trial court's order directing the clerk or administrator to enter a judgment in the judgment book, including the terms of the judgment.

judgment debtor A person against whom a judgment has been entered declaring he or she is indebted to the judgment creditor for a stated sum of money.

The statement may be hurtful and bad manners, but it is not actionable. Therefore, the appropriate result would be **dismissal** of the plaintiff's case.

The plaintiff must prove his or her allegations against the defendant. A plaintiff must do this by convincing the jury that the greater weight of the evidence—sometimes described as "a fair preponderance of the evidence"—supports her case. As described, judges have the responsibility for deciding all questions of law, including whether the defendant owed a legal duty to the plaintiff. The **fact finder** looks to the evidence to determine whether there was a breach of that duty. It is the plaintiff's burden to produce the evidence and convince the jury that a breach of duty occurred in fact.

Given the jury's limited role as a fact finder, if there is no dispute concerning the material facts, there is no need for a trial. In that event, the parties may simply place the case before a judge who can apply the law to the agreed-on facts and determine the parties' legal rights and obligations. Otherwise, the parties are obligated to gather the evidence that is relevant to the disputed facts. They must adhere to rules of evidence when presenting their evidence. The rules are designed to keep the evidence relevant to the dispute, reasonably reliable and the presentation fair. Each party has a right to challenge the competency and credibility of the other party's evidence. Neither the government nor the court assists the parties to prove their claims and defenses.

A jury listens to evidence and decides what the facts are. The judge instructs the jury about the controlling rules of law and allows the jury to apply those rules to the facts as the jury determines those facts to be. When that procedure is followed, a jury returns a **general verdict.** Another way of handling trials is for a judge to ask the jury to answer specific questions posed by the judge. The jury's answers are called a **special verdict.** Then the judge prepares an order called "Findings of Fact, Conclusions of Law and Order for Judgment." The order contains the jury's **findings of fact.** The judge makes **conclusions of law** by applying the law to the finding of facts. The conclusions of law are the basis for the court's **order for judgment.** The clerk of court enters a judgment pursuant to the judge's order for judgment. The judgment declares the parties' legal rights and obligations. The defendant is then identified as a **judgment debtor.** A judgment is a public record. If a party refuses or fails to comply with a judgment, the prevailing party (judgment creditor) may invoke the court's help and the help of the state sheriff or federal marshal to enforce the judgment.

Considering the number of courts and the enormous amount of important litigation they handle, it is amazing that the courts work so well. Most lawyers who regularly appear in court have the utmost respect for the civil justice system. As a paralegal, you will have the opportunity to play an important role in the administration of justice and to serve clients who need your help. We will begin by examining the principles and concepts that guide the judicial process.

Everyone Is Presumed to Know the Law

Although it is a legal fiction, everyone is presumed to know the law, including all the state statutes, all the federal statutes, and all the common-law rules. The effect of the presumption is to obligate individuals to inquire about the law insofar as their conduct or situation might be affected by the law. For example, a motorist must make an effort to learn about the rules of the road before he or she can obtain a license to drive. Taxpayers must find out how the tax laws apply to them. Employers must find out what laws apply to them. One litigant cannot gain an advantage over another by claiming not to know the law. For example, a person cannot avoid liability for an accident by claiming she or he did not know that red means "stop." When a person has a concern about what the law is or how it applies, he or she must search the law or obtain a lawyer's advice. If the person obtains the wrong advice, that is not an excuse for failing to comply with the law.

A few examples might help clarify this important principle. Suppose state statutes provide that the maximum speed limit in municipalities is 30 miles per hour, unless a higher speed is posted. A motorist who travels more than the 30 mile per hour speed limit violates the law and cannot avoid the consequences by claiming he or she did not know the speed limit. But suppose vandals remove a stop sign at an intersection and the next day a motorist enters the intersection without stopping. Does the principle apply? No. The law is that a person must stop for a stop sign. Motorists must know that rule of law. If there is no stop sign, there is no legal duty to stop. May a defendant avoid liability for defaming another person by claiming he or she did not know defamation was against the law? No. Again, all citizens are required to learn what the law requires of them. Noncompliance on the basis of ignorance is not an excuse.

Legal Duty as a Basis for Claims

Courts are pragmatic about the types of claims they will handle. Courts cannot and should not use their powers and resources to resolve petty or trivial disputes. Some disputes cannot be resolved with the kinds of remedies courts can provide. Some disputes are not subject to a final resolution. There are at least three requirements that a claim must meet before a court will undertake to consider it:

1. The plaintiff must allege that the defendant breached a duty that the defendant owed to the plaintiff.
2. The plaintiff must allege that the defendant's breach of duty directly caused the injury or loss.
3. The plaintiff must allege that he or she sustained an injury or loss of a type for which a court can award compensation—usually a sum of money.

A claim on which courts may grant relief is often referred to as a **cause of action.** Again, such claims allege conduct that is actionable. Some of the more common causes of action are discussed in Chapter 4.

A legal duty may arise from a statute, a contract between the parties, or from the common law. The purpose of having statutes is to create legal rights that benefit or protect people and property. When a claim is brought under a statute, it must appear to the court that the legislature intended the statute to protect people in the plaintiff's position and to prohibit persons in the defendant's position from engaging in the alleged wrongful conduct. For example, each state has a highway code that provides in great detail what each driver and pedestrian must do and not do while

cause of action A claim that is recognized by law and enforceable through the courts; a claim in which a court may grant relief.

using the public roads. The highway code creates legal duties for the protection of those who are on or near the highways. The statutory duties are legal duties that, if violated, may give rise to a cause of action. But the highway code would not apply to a boating accident or a snowmobile accident on farmland. When courts create common-law legal duties, they have many factors to consider. For example, it is well understood that if a person drives a truck on another person's property and damages a tree, the driver is **liable** (i.e., responsible) for damages for trespassing. But suppose an airplane is inadvertently forced to land on the property and damages the tree; has the pilot breached a legal duty to the landowner? Should he or she be liable for making a forced landing to save his or her life and those of the passengers? Why should the landowner bear the loss? Those are the kinds of considerations that have shaped causes of actions and help courts decide the kinds of remedies to provide. The important point to understand is that particular types of transactions and occurrences give rise to particular legal duties.

When two or more people enter into a contract, they create a special relationship between themselves, and the law gives effect to the relationship. The phrase *special relationship* in law means a relationship in which the parties have legal rights and obligations between them, such as a landlord and tenant, employer and employee, or husband and wife. By contracting with each other, they voluntarily make commitments and acquire rights and duties. The breach of a contractual duty is the breach of a legal duty that is the basis for making claims on which courts grant relief.

A legal duty may require the defendant to do something or to refrain from doing something. The duties imposed by common law usually reflect the minimum standard of care that people must accord to each other and another's property to make it possible to be joined in a society. For example, long ago the common law determined that a person who owned land had a right to keep others from entering that land. Out of that principle, the common law developed a cause of action called trespass, which permits the owner or occupant of land to make a claim for harm to the land caused by an intruder. Similarly, courts recognized that people should be protected from harm caused by their justified reliance on another's false representations. From that principle came the cause of action called **fraud.** In yet another instance, courts concluded that every person should be protected from injury or loss caused by another person's culpable carelessness. From that principle came the cause of action called **negligence.** When a person negligently injures another person or another person's property, the actor may be held liable to pay compensation (damages) for the harm.

Sometimes a common-law rule does not work well and needs to be changed—perhaps because society has changed. Courts may **overrule** their own common-law rules and make new ones to accommodate society's needs. The legislature may also change the common law through legislation. When a statute is inconsistent with a common-law rule, the common-law rule is abrogated. If a statute is abolished for some reason, the common law rises to fill the void.

liable   To be legally responsible or obligated by law to another person.

fraud   An intentional misrepresentation of a material fact on which another person reasonably relies to his or her detriment.

negligence   A failure to exercise the degree of care that an ordinarily careful person would exercise considering the foreseeability of harm to persons or property.

overrule   A court order that denies a party's objection to another party's evidence or acts committed in prosecuting an action.

Courts' Authority

When the plaintiff commences a civil action to resolve a private dispute, in effect, the plaintiff asks the government to use its power to force a resolution. Courts have power to decide controversies between individuals, corporations, governmental agencies, states, the federal government, and other legal entities. The court is a forum that has procedures that the parties must follow. A court has power to directly order parties to appear, testify, and produce evidence as requested by an opposing party. By submitting to the government's power, the parties obtain access to the power. For example, both parties are able to use the court's **subpoena** power to compel another person to appear in court as a witness, testify, and produce any tangible evidence in his or her possession. A court may compel parties and witnesses who are under a subpoena to comply with court orders and rules by imposing penalties. The list of penalties includes monetary fines, forfeitures and even incarceration through **contempt of court** proceedings. The prevailing party obtains a judgment in his or her favor, which is enforceable against the losing party through the power of the executive branch of the government—a federal marshal or state sheriff.

subpoena (1) A process commanding a party, witness, or deponent to set aside all pretences and excuses, and appear before a designated court or magistrate at a specified time and place to testify.

contempt of court A person's act or omission that interferes with a court's functions and for which a court may impose a punishment.

Jurisdiction

Although courts have great power over people and even over other branches of the government, courts are not omnipotent. A court must have jurisdiction over a case to have the authority or power to issue a binding judgment. There are several aspects to jurisdiction. To have jurisdiction in a particular case, a court must have each of the following: **subject matter jurisdiction, territorial jurisdiction,** and **personal jurisdiction** (jurisdiction over the parties). A court's power comes from the government that created it. Therefore, it stands to reason that the court cannot function outside the government's territorial limits. So geography is a limiting factor on jurisdiction. By the same token, a court is no more powerful than the government that created it. The United States Supreme Court was created by the United States Constitution; therefore, the Constitution is the source of its power. The federal district courts and circuit courts of appeals were created by federal statutes; therefore, the statutes prescribe the scope and extent of the courts' jurisdiction. In other words, the statutes prescribe what types of cases those courts may handle, who may use the courts, in which geographical areas the courts may operate, and what kinds of awards the courts may make. Similarly, the highest court in each state is empowered and limited by the state's constitution. State legislatures prescribe the jurisdiction of the state's lower courts.

subject matter jurisdiction Jurisdiction over the type case and the subject of the litigation.

territorial jurisdiction The geographic area in which a court may function as determined by political boundaries.

personal jurisdiction A court's jurisdiction or authority over a person, obtained through due process.

A plaintiff has a pragmatic interest in making sure that the court has jurisdiction, because time and effort spent litigating in a court that does not have jurisdiction is wasted. Similarly, courts do not want to waste their time and effort, so they are very careful to consider jurisdictional issues before proceeding with a case. However, more often than not, the defendant is first to raise a jurisdictional issue, because lack of jurisdiction is a basis for having the entire case dismissed. Because a dismissal for lack of jurisdiction may or may not preclude the plaintiff from bringing the case in another court, court rules and procedures encourage the parties to resolve jurisdictional issues at the outset. As soon as a court becomes aware of any jurisdictional defect, the case must be dismissed.

Personal jurisdiction refers to a court's power to resolve the rights and liabilities of the persons who are parties to an action. Personal jurisdiction is largely a doctrine of fairness. For example, it would be unfair to require a Hawaii resident to defend himself in a New Jersey court in a dispute about an auto accident that happened in Honolulu. The New Jersey court is said to lack personal jurisdiction over the defendant.

Because it is based on fairness to the defendant, she or he may voluntarily submit to a court's jurisdiction by agreement or by failing to make a timely objection to the court's lack of jurisdiction. Once a party submits to the court's jurisdiction—even if inadvertently—the party cannot avoid the court's authority.

A court obtains jurisdiction over a person who is *not* a party when the court's subpoena is served on him or her. A subpoena requires the person to appear (actually come before the court) for purposes of the particular case at the time specified in the subpoena. The term *subpoena* means that the person is then under the penalty of law if he or she fails to appear as directed.

Subject matter jurisdiction refers to a court's power over the subject of an action. For example, certain types of actions may be commenced only in federal court. As to such an action, therefore, a state court would lack subject matter jurisdiction. Unlike personal jurisdiction—which is grounded in fairness—subject matter juridiction is grounded in a court's power and authority. Therefore, while a defect in personal jurisdiction may be waived, a defect in subject matter jurisdiction may not. Regardless of how far a case has progressed, a defect in subject matter jurisdiction requires dismissal.

Judges

waive To intentionally and voluntarily give up a legal right.

At the trial court level, a judge determines all questions of law and procedure. Some cases are conducted without juries, either because the law does not allow a jury in the particular type of case or because the parties **waive** the right to have a jury trial. In those cases, judges resolve disputed fact issues on the basis of the evidence the parties present. Judges are responsible to control all the people in the courtroom: lawyers, parties, witnesses, and spectators. If a person disrupts the proceedings in the judge's presence, the judge has the power to find that the person has acted "in contempt of court" and order punishment, including incarceration. Judges need this authority to ensure respect for the courts and for the justice system. Most of a trial judge's rulings are subject to review by appellate courts. But appellate courts want to give trial judges as much leeway as possible on procedural matters and still have a fair trial. Therefore, the appellate courts allow trial courts broad discretion when dealing with procedural issues and hold that a trial judge's rulings will not be corrected unless the trial judge abused his or her discretion. Appellate courts will not reverse a trial judge's rulings on the law unless the appellate court believes that the erroneous ruling may have affected the outcome of the case.

The physical features of the typical courtroom emphasize the dignity of the court and proceedings. The judge's robe sets the judge apart from everyone else. Robes are always black, emphasizing the solemnity of the proceedings. Professional ethics require lawyers to underscore the dignity of the court by always being respectful, even during moments of acute disagreement.

Juries

Juries act as fact finders. They do not make any decisions about what the law is or how the law applies. In this regard, they take their instructions from the trial judge, and only that judge. Jurors do not need any training in the law to handle their duties. Jurors are supposed to determine the facts only from the evidence that the parties present. Jurors are supposed to sort through the evidence and resolve conflicts to determine the truth. They are not supposed to guess (speculate) about facts that do not have any support in the evidence.

The right to a trial by jury is unique to English and American law. It is a right that stems from a distrust of judges when they were under the direct control of the king, who had absolute power. The right to trial by jury has been significantly abridged in England, but in America it is protected by the United States Constitution and by state constitutions.

With experience, a judge acquires knowledge and understanding that should be helpful in deciding cases. But a judge's experience may also cause him or her to acquire prejudices for or against certain lawyers, parties, and types of litigation. Even though a judge endeavors to keep personal feelings from affecting decisions, the potential for bias exists. Because jurors are exposed to only a few cases during their term of service, they are not likely to develop strong, fixed attitudes about a particular lawyer or a party or certain types of cases. Trial by jury provides the civil justice system with an important check that promotes the appearance of fairness and gives the parties confidence in the system.

Commencement of Lawsuit

A lawsuit is very easy to start. The first step is to prepare a document called a complaint, which sets forth the plaintiff's claim against the defendant. The complaint must state the basic facts that gave rise to the claim and alleges that the defendant breached one or more legal duties owed to the plaintiff. Finally, the complaint states the type of remedy or relief requested by the plaintiff, as well as the amount of damages. In federal court, the action is *commenced* when the complaint is filed with the clerk of court. The clerk then issues a **summons** directed to the defendant. The summons instructs the defendant that he or she must answer the complaint or be found liable to the plaintiff by default.

Once an action is filed, the summons and complaint must be served on each defendant within a specified period of time. Several methods may be used to serve the summons and complaint on a defendant. The traditional method is to have the United States marshal serve them by delivering a copy of each to the defendant personally or by delivering the copies to the defendant's residence and leaving the copies with a person who resides there. The person with whom the summons and complaint are left need not be related to the defendant but must be of suitable age to understand the importance of the papers. Many states now authorize service of the summons and complaint by mail. However, the service is not effective until the defendant decides to accept it by signing an acknowledgment, which the defendant then returns to the plaintiff's lawyer. Some types of cases, such as automobile accident cases, appoint a state official, such as the Secretary of State, to receive service on behalf of a defendant motorist or corporation. Under some circumstances, **service of process** (communication of the substance of the legal process initiated by the plaintiff) may be made by publication in a legal newspaper. These methods of service are discussed in greater detail in Chapter 6.

summons A court mandate that informs a person that a civil action has been commenced against him or her and requires that person to appear in the case and defend; otherwise, the plaintiff is entitled to judgment by default for the relief specified in the complaint.

service of process To deliver or communicate court papers to a person thereby giving the court jurisdiction over that person.

Remedies

The civil justice system strives to provide a suitable remedy to every person who has suffered an injury, damage, or loss as a consequence of another person's unlawful conduct. The task is monumental. Sometimes courts are able to restore to a party the very thing she or he lost through the wrongful conduct of another person. Included in such things may be real estate, personal property, documents, and, to a certain extent, intangibles such as a job or a reputation. In certain situations, a person may be able to **enjoin** (stop or prevent) an individual, corporation, or even a government from pursuing a course of conduct that is harmful to the person or the person's property. Courts can issue an **injunction** to prohibit wrongful conduct. In extreme cases, courts will issue a **restraining order** to prohibit the wrongful conduct while considering the merits of the plaintiff's claim for an injunction. Courts rarely, if ever, order a party to perform some service or act.

Where restoration or an injunction is not feasible, the law attempts to provide fair compensation for injury and other losses by awarding a sum of money. The award of money is commonly referred to as "money damages" or, simply, **"damages."** Money seems to be the best common denominator for compensating injuries and losses. Regardless of the specific remedy sought, the procedures for preparing and presenting claims and defenses are much the same. Civil litigation damage awards fall into three categories: (1) loss-of-the-bargain, (2) compensatory damages, and (3) punitive damages.

When parties enter into a contract, each expects to profit from the arrangement. If one party breaches the contract, the loss of the anticipated profit flows naturally from the breach. The law allows recovery of the lost profits. The loss of profit is often referred to as a loss of the bargain. Its purpose is to place the plaintiff in the same position the plaintiff would have been in had the contract been fully performed. Of course, the defendant is entitled to an offset against any expenses the plaintiff avoided by not having to perform her or his side of the contract.

Tort actions allow recovery for the plaintiff's actual loss. The objective of tort law is to compensate a party for her or his loss without providing profit. A potential profit is not an element of damages. For example, suppose that the defendant negligently damages the plaintiff's car. The defendant is liable for the cost of repairing it and for the loss of its use.

A judicial system must do more than merely decide who is right and who is wrong. The system must provide remedies that satisfy reasonable people. The remedies must be in proportion to the loss and comport with a generally accepted sense of fairness. The legal obligations must be consistent with what an obligor reasonably can do or can afford to pay, as well as what society can afford. In other words, awards must be appropriate in kind and reasonable in amount.

Civil Penalties

The matter of punitive damages and civil penalties must be distinguished from criminal penalties. The civil justice system operates alongside the criminal law system but is quite separate from it. The basic objectives of the two systems are different.

---

enjoin To order a person to stop or refrain from a particular activity or to abate a condition for which the person is responsible.

injunction A court order that prohibits a party from engaging in a specified activity.

restraining order An order a court issues to prevent a person from engaging in specified conduct until the court can hold a hearing to determine whether there is reason to believe the person is violating another person's legal rights.

damages (1) The injury, loss, or other harm to a person or property that is proximately caused by another person's breach of a legal duty.

The criminal justice system is designed to identify criminals, characterize their acts, and punish the guilty. Civil justice is concerned with resolving disputes and providing appropriate remedies for losses. Money damages reimburse a party for a loss caused by another party's breach of a legal duty. There is a trend in criminal law to require convicted criminals to provide restitution to victims as part of the criminals' punishment. Restitution is similar to compensation in that the purpose is to return to the victim that which was taken or lost. Of course, too often, the loss cannot be restored. Similarly, there seems to be a trend to allow plaintiffs to obtain punitive damages as a civil penalty.

Many states allow plaintiffs to recover **punitive damages**—a penalty assessed against the defendant—in addition to **compensatory damages** in cases where the defendant intentionally inflicts injury. For example, an intentional battery with a knife, gun, or even fist, may be the basis for imposing punitive damages. Punitive damages are recoverable regardless of the degree of injury or other harm—as long as some harm was sustained. The measure of punitive damages depends on the character of the wrongful conduct and the financial worth of the defendant. If the award is really going to penalize the defendant, its size must take into consideration the defendant's ability to pay—at least, that is the rationale. Consequently, in cases where punitive damages are allowable, the defendant's financial worth may become part of the evidence. The term *exemplary damages* is sometimes used instead of punitive damages, because the award is held out as an example to others to discourage wrongful conduct.

Opposition to allowing punitive damages in civil actions is considerable and growing. Members of this opposition argue that punitive damage awards subject the defendant to double jeopardy—in other words, the defendant pays twice (or more) for one mistake. Where more than one claim may result from a tortious act, the imposition of multiple penalties can have ruinous consequences for the defendant. Moreover, civil procedures lack the safeguards of criminal cases. For example, the burden of proof is lower in civil cases. Opponents argue that only the state should impose fines for criminal conduct. And a claim for punitive damages injects the defendant's financial worth into the case, which could adversely influence the jury on other issues and become a personal embarrassment to the defendant. Recently, the United States Supreme Court has examined the constitutional limits on punitive-damage awards. Punitive-damage awards that are out of all proportion to the compensatory-damage award violate constitutional due process.

Declaratory Judgments

Courts may resolve controversies requiring the interpretation of statutes and documents *even though a loss has not yet occurred.* A lawsuit brought for this purpose is called a **declaratory judgment action.** The court judgment determines the meaning and effect of the statute or documents in dispute. For example, if two parties have a disagreement over the meaning of a contract between them, either party may start a declaratory judgment action to have a court interpret the contract for them even though the contract has not been breached and no loss has been sustained. The

punitive damages Money damages awarded to a plaintiff in a civil action to punish the defendant for willfully committing a wrongful act that injured the plaintiff or damaged the plaintiff's property.

compensatory damages A sum of money that is awarded to a person to reimburse her or him for personal injury or property damage.

declaratory judgment action An action to obtain a declaratory judgment.

court declares the parties' rights and obligations. The controversy must be real, not hypothetical, or the action will be dismissed. Through declaratory judgments, parties also are able to establish legal status concerning employment, marriage, property ownership, and right to government benefits.

Litigation Expenses

Each party to a civil lawsuit must bear most of his or her own expenses, including investigation costs, most witness fees, and lawyers' fees. The few exceptions to this general rule usually involve special remedies provided by statute where the monetary loss may be relatively small, but the principle at issue is important. Such legislation makes the courts more readily available to those who have been the victim of some form of official harassment or discrimination. The prevailing parties in such lawsuits are usually allowed to recover all their expenses, including lawyers' fees. In most cases, however, **taxable costs** are limited to the filing fee, subpoena fees, United States marshal's fees, and some small portion of expert witness fees. Taxable costs are the costs of the litigation that may be added to the parties' recovery of money damages.

taxable costs Costs of litigation that a prevailing party is entitled to recover from the losing party.

Real Controversy

Courts will only hear controversies that are real, as opposed to hypothetical. They must arise from an actual transaction or occurrence. People could conjure up all kinds of interesting fact situations for which they would like a court's "advisory opinion." But courts were not created to resolve hypothetical questions. Until an allegedly *unlawful event and loss occurs*, there is nothing for a court to decide. To be the subject of litigation, a controversy must be subject to resolution by applying the law, not philosophical principles. The controversy must be of a type that permits a court to provide a remedy. Historically, courts have limited their remedies to those that a court can enforce through the executive branch of the government.

This principle has some very practical applications. For example, suppose that during the course of a trial the parties are able to reach a **settlement** so that their controversy is, in fact, resolved. It would be considered a fraud on the court for the parties to continue with the case just to see how it would have been decided. Their settlement ends the dispute, and they cannot impose on the courts. Similarly, if a person believes that another person is going to **trespass** on and damage the first person's property, it might be reassuring for the first person to obtain a court decree that declares the other person may not enter on the land. But a court will not act in the matter until there is evidence that a trespass has occurred.

settlement An agreement between parties that results in a resolution of their dispute.

trespass A cause of action in tort to recover money damages for damage to real estate resulting from a wrongful entry on the land. A trespass occurs whenever the entry is made without consent of the possessor and without legal authority.

Real Party in Interest

A lawsuit must be brought in the name of the **real party in interest,** as is expressly required by Rule 17 of the Federal Rules of Civil Procedure. The defendant has an absolute right to deal with the party who owns the cause of action. If it appears that

real party in interest A party who actually owns the cause of action and who is directly affected by the outcome of the litigation.

the plaintiff is not the real party in interest, the action must be dismissed by the court. A party may not send his "big brother" to do battle for him in court. The principle may be difficult to grasp because it is hard to conceive that someone other than the real party in interest would ever prosecute a lawsuit. But occasionally litigation strategy or matters of convenience suggest that someone else should prosecute the action.

As a general rule, personal-injury claims cannot be assigned or transferred. This principle tends to discourage intermeddlers from fomenting personal-injury litigation and from speculating in personal-injury litigation. However, there is a growing list of exceptions to the prohibition against **assignment** of personal-injury claims. For example, if a medical insurance policy has paid an accident victim's medical bills, the insurer may have a right of **subrogation** against the **tortfeasor** (someone who commits a tort). Subrogation allows a party who pays benefits to another—fire insurance and medical insurance are prime examples—to recoup the payments from a person who wrongly caused the loss.

assignment   A transfer of one's property or legal rights to another.

subrogation   The substitution of one person in the place of another to make a claim or prosecute a cause of action.

tortfeasor   A person who commits any kind of a tort.

Necessary Parties

To minimize the number of cases and trials, the plaintiff should join as parties to the case all persons whose presence is necessary to fully resolve the dispute. Those parties are termed **necessary parties.** If a person has not been joined who should be joined, the court may order that person joined through proper service of process. The person joined (added) in the action may be made an involuntary plaintiff or defendant. Of course, a court will not order a joinder of a party unless the court can obtain jurisdiction over the person to be joined [Rule 19(a)].

Suppose an "indispensable" party is outside the jurisdiction of the court and refuses to agree to join as a party. The court must consider the "equities" of the situation and decide whether it is more fair to let the action proceed without that party, or to dismiss. The concern is whether the court's action would be prejudicial to any of the parties. Rule 19(b) states

necessary party   A person whose legal interest will be affected by the litigation or a person who must be a party if the court is to grant a remedy or complete relief according to law.

> The factors to be considered by the court include: first, to what extent a judgment rendered in the person's absence might be prejudicial to the person or those already parties; second, the extent to which, by protective provisions in the judgment, by the shaping of relief, or other measures, the prejudice can be lessened or avoided; third, whether a judgment rendered in the person's absence will be adequate; fourth, whether the plaintiff will have an adequate remedy if the action is dismissed for nonjoinder.

In the following example 2, the defendant owner might be held liable and unable to obtain **contribution** from the other owner. However, if the plaintiff agrees to limit the damages to one-half of the total entitlement, the defendant owner would not be prejudiced. If the plaintiff could pursue the claim in another court and obtain full relief from all persons who should be joined, the first court would likely dismiss the plaintiff's claim. If the defendant will voluntarily agree to submit to the jurisdiction of another court where the action can be brought against all persons who should be defendants, the first court would probably dismiss the action.

contribution   A right or obligation between parties who are jointly liable to a third person, usually the plaintiff, for money damages recoverable in a civil action.

EXAMPLES

1. If the plaintiff is one of several owners of a building that was destroyed by a fire, and the plaintiff brought the action against the defendant to recover money damages for loss of the building, the rights of the other owners should be determined in the same action.
2. If the tenant in an apartment building claims an injury because of a premises defect and sues only one of the two persons who own the building, a judgment against the one owner would be unfair to the tenant. She or he is entitled to collect damages from the co-owner. Unless the co-owner is made a party, the court cannot provide complete relief.

Representatives

If a litigant is a minor or otherwise incompetent to make decisions concerning his or her litigation, the court must appoint a representative. This is true whether the incompetent person is the plaintiff or defendant. A representative acts to protect the incompetent party's legal interests and carries out the court's orders. If a guardian has already been appointed by a probate court, ordinarily that person is a proper representative to handle the incompetent party's litigation. Otherwise, the incompetent person, or a friend of the incompetent, or even an opposing party may ask the court to appoint a representative. Any interested person may nominate persons whom the court should consider.

guardian ad litem A guardian appointed by a court to help a minor to prosecute or defend a lawsuit in which the minor is a party. The minor may be the plaintiff or defendant.

A representative who is appointed to handle only the particular case is called a **guardian ad litem.** A guardian ad litem is discharged (released from official duties) by the court on conclusion of the litigation. A representative's status in the case is indicated in the title of the action (see the following example). The representative is a considered and treated as a party. A representative may be required to post a bond to guarantee due and proper performance. The pleadings usually contain a separate paragraph alleging that the representative was duly appointed to act in a representative capacity. Rule 9(a) specifically states, however, that such an allegation is not essential.

EXAMPLE

John Jones, as guardian ad litem of
Mary Jones, a minor,

                    plaintiff,

   vs.

Robert M. Smith and
Michael M. Smith,

               defendants.

Another kind of representative is needed when an action is brought to obtain money damages for a person's wrongful death. Because the recovery in such an action is for the benefit of the decedent's next of kin, a court must appoint a trustee to represent the next of kin. The trustee becomes the person or party who may then bring the lawsuit. A trustee is required to exercise judgment, to do what is best for the next of kin, and to comply with court rules and orders. But a trustee is not liable for any of the decedent's unlawful acts. Almost anyone can petition a court to be appointed trustee, but usually the petitioner has some special relationship to the decedent and beneficiaries.

Using this book's hypothetical case as an example, when Ms. Laura Raskin brings a wrongful death action for the benefit of William Nordby's next of kin, the action should be something like:

Laura Raskin, as Trustee for the
next of kin of William Nordby, deceased,

plaintiff,

vs.

Bradley Harper,

defendant.

The trustee is usually appointed by a state court even if the wrongful death action is to be brought in a federal district court.

A Claim Must Be Prosecuted as a Whole

Most claims have several bases or parts. For reasons of practicality, economy, and fairness, the law requires the plaintiff to prosecute (pursue) all parts in one lawsuit. There are several reasons why a plaintiff might like to pursue only a part of a claim and save the rest for later. But the law does not allow it. The plaintiff may pursue a portion of the claim to judgment, but any part omitted is lost, whether intentionally or inadvertently omitted. For example, suppose the defendant drives his car into the plaintiff's car and injures the plaintiff and damages the plaintiff's car. If the plaintiff starts a lawsuit to recover compensation for the car, the lawsuit must also include the personal-injury claim or the latter claim is lost. Another way of saying the same thing is that the personal-injury claim is "barred," or prevented from being heard by the court. Courts refuse to handle two or three lawsuits where one will do. This principle has been formulated into a rule of law. The rule prohibits parties from **splitting a cause of action.** The same rule precludes a party from prosecuting a **breach of contract** claim in a piecemeal fashion. Whatever losses were caused by one breach must be claimed in one lawsuit. The same principle prevents the plaintiff from pursuing a claim using one legal theory and subsequently making the claim by asserting a different legal theory. For example, if the plaintiff alleges that the defendant injured him or her in an **assault** and **battery,** the plaintiff cannot bring a subsequent lawsuit alleging that the injuries were caused by the defendant's negligent conduct.

splitting a cause of action Dividing one cause of action or claim into two or more lawsuits.

breach of contract A cause of action to recover money damages, flowing from a person's violation of the terms of a contract.

assault A cause of action in tort that allows the victim to obtain money damages for personal injury, usually mental suffering, caused by an intentional threat of serious bodily harm or death even though no physical contact occurs.

battery A battery gives rise to an action in tort for personal injury. An intentional, impermissible physical contact of an injurious nature, or a physical contact that is offensive to ordinary sensibilities.

EXAMPLE

The plaintiff bought a hunting rifle directly from a gun manufacturer, and the rifle exploded in his hands. The plaintiff may have a cause of action against the manufacturer for negligence, **breach of warranty,** and **strict liability** in tort. The three legal theories (causes of action) against the manufacturer arise from the same occurrence. The plaintiff is required to assert all three causes of action, if at all, in a single lawsuit. The plaintiff is not allowed to sue three times on three separate legal theories. The plaintiff is barred from seeking recovery on any cause of action not asserted in a first action.

---

breach of warranty A breach of an express or implied warranty relating to the title, quality, content, or condition of goods sold.

strict liability A cause of action in tort in which liability is imposed upon a person without regard to fault, such as negligence.

Combining Claims

A transaction or occurrence that causes a loss may give rise to claims against two or more persons. Although the law and court procedures encourage the plaintiff to include all appropriate defendants in the one lawsuit, consolidation is not mandated. There are practical reasons for the rule: Principally, the law does not want to encourage unnecessary litigation. Suppose that two cars collide in an intersection and the passenger in one car was injured. The passenger could bring an action against one driver. If that driver successfully defends against the claim, the passenger could later bring an action against the second driver. The determination in the first lawsuit, however, may encourage the remaining parties to resolve their dispute without litigation.

Counterclaims and Cross-claims

counterclaim A claim asserted by the defendant against the plaintiff to obtain compensation for a loss or damages suffered by the defendant, or the pleading in which such a claim is asserted.

A defendant is required to assert, by way of **counterclaim,** all claims that she or he has against the plaintiff arising from the same transaction or occurrence. If the defendant fails to counterclaim against the plaintiff, the claims are waived and the defendant is barred from bringing them in another lawsuit at another time. The entire controversy should be determined once, in one proceeding. It is more economical for the parties and the court to resolve the entire matter in one trial.

cross-claims Claims by one defendant against one or more codefendants, arising from the same facts that support the plaintiff's claim against the defendants.

When there are two or more defendants, they may assert **cross-claims** between them. The cross-claims will be litigated in the same action as the plaintiff's claim against the defendants. A cross-claim may seek compensation for the first defendant's own loss resulting from the transaction or occurrence on which the plaintiff's action is based, or a cross-claim may seek contribution toward the plaintiff's claim, or both. The presence of a cross-claim establishes adversity between defendants. When there is adversity between parties, they may treat each other as **adverse parties.** As such, they may cross-examine each other and each other's witnesses. The use of cross-claims is another example of courts trying to resolve as many issues as possible in one proceeding.

adverse parties Parties are adverse when their interests in the outcome of the litigation conflict.

Third-Party Claims

third-party action An action brought by a defendant against a person other than the plaintiff to recover money damages as contribution or indemnity to the obligation, if any, that the defendant has to the plaintiff.

If a defendant believes that someone who is not yet a party to the case should be liable for all or some of what the plaintiff seeks, the defendant may commence a **third-party action** to obtain indemnity or contribution. A claim for indemnity is a claim for complete reimbursement. For example, an employer who is **vicariously liable** to a plaintiff for an employee's negligence is entitled to indemnity from the employee. Contribution is a claim to have the plaintiff's damages shared proportionately by the defendants. This is done by having the jury assign percentages of fault to each defendant. If the plaintiff has only sued one of multiple at-fault persons, that defendant may commence a third-party action. For example, if two automobile drivers are negligent so as to cause injury to the plaintiff, but the plaintiff brings an action against only one of the drivers, the driver who was sued may bring a third-party action against the driver who was not sued to obtain contribution for any award the plaintiff may obtain.

A third-party claim is limited to the claims arising from the plaintiff's alleged loss. The defendant cannot use a third-party action as a basis for obtaining compensation for the defendant's own loss.

vicarious liability To impose legal liability on a person for the acts or omissions of another person.

Assignment of Claims

The owner of a claim (cause of action) for money damages has the right to prosecute the claim in court. The purpose of proving or establishing the claim in court is to have the claim adjudged to be an enforceable right. This right is established by a judgment. A cause of action that is subject to assignment, or transfer, to another person is sometimes referred to as a chose in action. It is a right that is not (yet) perfected; one that is not "completed" or enforceable against others. Though unperfected, the right is identifiable and has value. A chose in action can be bought and sold, or assigned. Whenever a cause of action is properly assigned, it must be prosecuted in the name of the assignee. The maximum amount of money damages that the assignee can recover is, ordinarily, the amount paid for the assignment. Proof that the assignment was duly consummated is part of the cause of action. The assignee must plead and prove the assignment as part of the case.

As a general rule, *personal-injury* claims cannot be bought and sold, or assigned. There is no commercial necessity for such assignments. This rule effectively prevents

EXAMPLES

1. If a dispute arises between a seller and a buyer of goods, and the buyer refuses to pay for the goods, the seller's alleged right to payment could be assigned or sold to another person or company, which could bring suit to recover on the claim. As part of the cause of action, the assignee would have to prove a valid assignment.

2. A trespass on real estate could damage the property. The owner of the damaged property may want to sell the property before he or she can bring suit against the trespasser. The buyer may be willing to take an assignment of the cause of action against the trespasser. The value of the assignment may be quite subjective and, therefore, negotiable between the seller and buyer. The buyer's recovery is often limited to the amount paid for the assignment, but not always. The law tends to discourage people from buying and selling causes of action for the purpose of making a profit.

lawyers and others from speculating in personal-injury claims. Suppose a plaintiff sustains injuries from the tortious (wrongful, as in the nature of a tort) conduct of the defendant. The plaintiff is the only person who is permitted to sue the defendant to recover money damages for those injuries. If the law were otherwise, the plaintiff might find it convenient to sell his cause of action to another person. It is not too difficult to imagine some well-to-do individual or company speculating in personal-injury lawsuits. Some injured parties would be willing to sell their claims for inadequate sums of money to obtain payment immediately. Such dealings would no doubt shortchange injury victims who are in need. The buyer might be able to turn a handsome profit on a subsequent settlement or jury verdict. But profit making is contrary to the objectives of civil litigation.

A common example of assignments occurs in the context of insurance. If an insurer pays the full amount of its insured's loss—a fire loss, for example—the insurer becomes the owner of the claim and is the real party in interest to bring an action against any person who wrongly caused the loss (a careless smoker, perhaps). When the insurer pays its own insured for the entire loss, the insurer is said to be subrogated to the claim against the defendant.

Res Judicata

res judicata   A matter adjudged; a thing judicially acted on or decided; a thing or matter settled by judgment.

A party may litigate a claim only once. The principle that precludes repeat litigation is referred to as **res judicata,** which means "the matter has been adjudged." Once a court of competent jurisdiction has decided a matter, the losing party may not pursue the case again—even by going to another court. If the loser attempts to relitigate the same issues in another case, the prevailing party merely needs to show to the second court the first court's judgment. The judgment is a complete defense. The second court will summarily dismiss the claim. The second court will not even litigate issues that should or could have been determined in the first trial, but were not. Also, neither party may go to another jurisdiction and contend that the first court reached the wrong result. However, if the first court lacked subject matter jurisdiction, its judgment or decree would be a nullity. Therefore, when a judgment creditor tries to enforce a judgment in a new (foreign) jurisdiction, the judgment debtor can try to avoid the judgment by contesting the first court's jurisdiction—power—to render the judgment.

Collateral Estoppel

estop   To bar or prevent by estoppel.

collateral estoppel   An affirmation defense that precludes the plaintiff from suing defendants not named in a prior case on the same cause of action, where the verdict against the plaintiff in the prior case held that the plaintiff either did not sustain a loss or was solely responsible for the loss.

A transaction or occurrence may give rise to a cause of action against two or more persons. For reasons of convenience or strategy, the plaintiff may elect to sue only one of the responsible persons. Sometimes the result is less favorable than the plaintiff wished. For example, the court may determine that the plaintiff did not sustain a loss, that the loss is less than the amount claimed, or that the loss was caused by the plaintiff's unlawful conduct. Such determinations may be used against the plaintiff in any new action the plaintiff brings against another person. The new party or parties in the next case may elect to **estop** (legally prevent or bar) the plaintiff from avoiding the results of issues litigated in the first case. This principle is called **collateral estoppel** or estoppel by verdict. The rationale is that the plaintiff pre-

EXAMPLE

A plaintiff was injured while riding as a passenger in an automobile that collided with another automobile. For convenience, or as a matter of strategy, the plaintiff elected to sue only one of the drivers. Suppose that the jury found the defendant liable for the plaintiff's injuries but awarded only a "small" amount of money damages to the plaintiff. The resulting judgment would *not* collaterally estop the plaintiff from suing the other driver in another lawsuit to obtain more compensation. However, the defendant in the second suit could, in effect, adopt the jury's verdict in the first suit and thereby *estop* the plaintiff from obtaining more damages. In other words, the plaintiff's damages would be limited to the amount set in the first trial. But if the first award were "large," the defendant in the second case could elect to require the plaintiff to prove the damages claim anew.

The plaintiff cannot encumber the defendant in the second case with any of the results of the first case. Again, the rationale is that the plaintiff had the opportunity and incentive to fully prove his or her damages in the first suit, and the courts should not be bothered with having to litigate that issue twice. But the second defendant has the right to a full trial, unencumbered by any mistakes made by the defendant in the first case. Consequently, when a plaintiff chooses to bring separate suits against two defendants, both of whom may be liable for the accident and injury, the plaintiff runs the risk of incurring a bad result in the first suit and being bound by that result in the second suit. The defendant in the second case has the option of asserting collateral estoppel against the plaintiff or trying to obtain a better result in the second suit.

sumably tried the original case as well as she or he could and presented all the material evidence and should not be allowed to avoid the result and obtain a "better" result by pursuing a second lawsuit against another person. This is one way in which the law encourages parties to join in one action all the persons who may be liable to the plaintiff. Courts do not want to be bothered by piecemeal litigation.

A party usually cannot use collateral estoppel against a person who was not a party to the first action. But if the jury in the first case finds that persons who were not parties caused the loss, collateral estoppel would not prevent the plaintiff from bringing a new action against those other persons. In that situation, the second action is not inconsistent with the determinations made in the first case. Collateral estoppel applies against a party only when that party obtains an unsatisfactory result in the first case.

Stare Decisis

The law must be fair, consistent, and predictable. If the law were not predictable, parties could only guess about their legal rights and obligations. If the law varied from case to case, the courts' decisions would be unfair to some litigants. Courts

EXAMPLE

A state court trial judge concludes that lie detector evidence should be allowed in civil actions for the purpose of determining whether a witness has testified truthfully. There is no controlling authority on the issue, so this is a new rule for that state. Other trial judges in the same jurisdiction need not follow that judge's decision. But if the issue is appealed and the appellate court affirms, the new rule of law becomes binding on all trial courts in the state. Then other trial judges *must* apply the same rule in similar cases.

stare decisis The doctrine of abiding by, or adhering to, decided cases.

must be consistent in how they interpret and apply the law. By being consistent, courts gain predictability and fairness. To be consistent, courts follow the principle of **stare decisis** in which once a court propounds a rule of law, that court and all lower courts in that jurisdiction must adhere to that rule in all similar cases. The decided rule controls all cases unless and until the legislature changes it or until a higher appellate court in that jurisdiction overrules the decision. In other words, courts will always follow their own decisions or the decisions of higher courts when deciding how the law applies in a new case.

But the law is not inflexible. A court may overrule its own decisions, and a higher appellate court may overrule a rule of law propounded by a lower court. In other words, a district court (trial court) may overrule its own court-made laws and decisions. A circuit court of appeals, which is an intermediate appellate court, may overrule a district court-made rule of law and decisions. The United States Supreme Court may overrule a rule of law propounded by any district court or any circuit court of appeals. The highest appellate court in a jurisdiction has authority to reverse itself and change the rule of law in a later case. When the court does overrule a prior decision, the prior case is unaffected. The parties to the prior case remain bound by the final decision in that case. The common law has a certain amount of fluidity; it is always changing to meet the changing needs of the community and society. The flexibility of court-made law is both a strength and a weakness. Courts cannot overrule or change the law propounded by the legislature in a statute. However, courts can and do find some statutes to be unconstitutional and, therefore, unenforceable. This is true in civil law as well as criminal law.

Appellate Courts

Appellate courts, such as the United States Supreme Court, decide questions of law that were first raised in a trial court. The issues of law may concern the substantive law, which determines the parties' legal rights, or procedural law, which determines how the case must be handled by the lower court. An appellate court will reverse the trial court only if it finds that the trial court erred and that the error could have affected the outcome of the case. As a rule, an appellate court will not consider whether a jury's verdict is correct or well reasoned. Indeed, appellate courts sometimes comment in their opinions that they feel that the evidence should have resulted in a different verdict, but the appellate court will not substitute its judgment about the facts for the jury's findings. However, if an appellate court determines that there is insufficient evidence to support the jury's determination, the appellate court will set aside the verdict. In that event, the appellate court has the option to order judgment for the other side or, more likely, remand the case for a new trial to give the parties the opportunity to obtain and present additional evidence.

Either the United Staes Supreme Court or a given state's highest appelate court has the power to change court-made rules of law. With limited exceptions, this power extends only to the laws in the system over which the particular appellate court presides, whether state or federal. An appellate court changes the laws by issuing a written opinion that expressly overrules all prior opinions that are inconsistent with the new holding. Often the new rule is made effective prospectively only. But if an appellate opinion does not expressly state that the new rule is to be given prospective effect only, its effect is retroactive as well. Then the new rule applies even to pending cases, but not to cases already adjudicated[3] or settled.

Settlements

Courts favor voluntary settlements. Parties settle their dispute by entering into a contract that provides that the claimant releases the defendant from any liability for the transaction or occurrence. To be valid, the settlement must have all the elements of a valid contract. Most settlements are the result of compromise. A valid settlement provides a complete defense to the settled claim.

People can be very creative to fashion a solution or remedy that meets the situation. Parties may take into consideration many issues that have no actual relevancy to their legal rights and obligations—such as the effect of the dispute on friends, business associates, or relatives. A defendant's lack of insurance or lack of financial responsibility may be an important element inducing the plaintiff to accept a compromise or a reduced settlement. A party might be constrained to settle because of the cost of litigation or the unavailability of witnesses. Parties are always free to settle their dispute on mutually satisfactory terms, even after one has obtained a judgment against the other.

Professional Ethics

Lawyers are subject to the **Model Rules of Professional Conduct.** The Rules dictate the obligations that lawyers owe to their clients, to the courts, to opposing lawyers, and even to persons with whom they do not have any direct contact or relationship. A lawyer who violates the Rules is subject to disciplinary action, including the loss of licence to practice law, *even if the violation does not cause any actual harm to anyone.*[4] The Rules also help lawyers deal with obligations and loyalties where there are apparent conflicts in their duties. Ethical considerations that govern lawyers' conduct are discussed throughout this book.

An unethical act committed by a paralegal is the ethical responsibility of the lawyer(s) who employ the paralegal. In other words, a lawyer could probably be censured for the mistakes or misconduct of a paralegal who has acted within the course

Model Rules of Professional Conduct American Bar Association rules stating and explaining what lawyers must do, must not do, should do, and should not do. They cover the field of legal ethics (a lawyer's obligations to clients, courts, other lawyers, and the public) and have been adopted in modified forms by most of the states.

of the paralegal's employment. It is doubtful that paralegals could be censured and punished in the same way that lawyers can be sanctioned by the courts and by the boards of professional responsibility. Nevertheless, paralegals must avoid involvement in any conduct that violates the Rules. Any violation of the Rules by a paralegal must be considered a matter of grave concern.

Courts control the unlawful practice of law. Anyone who tries to practice law without a license may be disciplined by a court. The practice of law consists of giving legal advice to another person or representing another person in a court proceeding. As is discussed in Chapter 23 a paralegal may fully participate in certain methods of **alternative dispute resolution** and not be guilty of the unauthorized practicing of law.

alternative dispute resolution (ADR) Any procedure or method for resolving disputes between persons that does not involve the courts. The primary methods of alternative dispute resolution are arbitration and mediation.

TECHNOLOGY NOTES

Litigation has become increasingly dependent upon technology. From finding the law, to managing large volumes of discovery documents, to serving and filing litigation documents, to scheduling meetings and recording your billable time, most of your duties as a litigation paralegal will have a technology application. This book will discuss some of the most important applications in the coming chapters.

In addition to specific legal applications, a valuable skill in this age of information is the ability to find information on the Internet. Here are some excellent sites for you to find legal and law-related technology information. The American Bar Association's Web site (http://www.abanet.org) has a vast store of information, but its Technology Resource Center might be of particular interest as you start your legal career. The related Information Centers have pages on law office technology, court technology, mobile computing technology, and more. Another excellent site, http://www.law.com, also has a wide array of information, including legal tech links, legal blog links, and an expert-witness locator. Finally, the Legal Information Institute (http://www.law.cornell.edu) provides free links to state and federal constitutions, state and federal statutes and court opinions, and up-to-date state and federal rules. Web searches can also provide valuable information to your litigation team about your party opponent (a corporation, for example), about an important witness, or about the subject of the litigation itself (a product, perhaps). Your ability to learn important information from the Internet is a valuable asset to any litigation team.

SUMMARY

Civil litigation is a highly structured means for resolving disputes between persons. A court that has jurisdiction over the subject matter and parties has the power to force the parties to participate in the process. A court provides the forum in which parties state their claims and present their evidence in an orderly manner. The purpose of a trial is to determine the truth about the facts that gave rise to the parties' dispute. The court applies the law to the facts to determine the parties' legal rights and obligations. The parties' legal rights and obligations are stated in the court's judgment. A court has the power to enforce its judgment against the parties. When the plaintiff is entitled to a remedy, the most common type of relief that courts provide is money damages. The award of money damages is intended to compensate the plaintiff for the loss he or she sustained.

A court's jurisdiction is its authority or power. To have the authority to decide a case, a court must have jurisdiction over the parties, the subject matter, and the territory. If a court decides a case without having complete jurisdiction, its judgment is a nullity and may be attacked in a subsequent action. Even though a court may not have jurisdiction over a party, that party may submit to the court's jurisdiction voluntarily or even inadvertently. Once the court obtains jurisdiction, it does not lose it.

A lawsuit must involve a real dispute, not a hypothetical problem. As a general rule, the plaintiff must show that the defendant has breached a legal duty owed to the plaintiff and has caused actual harm. This rule has one exception: A party may bring a declaratory judgment action to have the court interpret a contract or statute where the parties have an actual dispute concerning the application of the contract or statute but neither has yet breached a legal duty. A declaratory judgment action is authorized by statute but is prosecuted like any other civil action.

A plaintiff must be able to state her or his claim in the form of a cause of action, which is a type of claim for which the courts will provide a remedy. Each cause of action has certain elements and requisites. The plaintiff must present evidence to prove each element of the cause of action alleged. Regardless of the particular type of claim, a plaintiff must show that the defendant breached a legal duty that the defendant owed to the plaintiff and that the breach directly caused the plaintiff's loss or harm.

Courts are restricted in the kind of remedies or relief they can provide. The most common relief courts provide is money damages. Where the parties have a dispute over ownership of certain property, a court may determine who is the real owner. Where a party is engaged in a continuing course of wrongful, harmful conduct, a court may enjoin that conduct by issuing an injunction. In rare circumstances, a court may actually order a party to take some affirmative action, but courts are reluctant to do that because it is difficult to enforce the order.

The plaintiff commences a civil lawsuit by preparing a complaint. The complaint must state a claim on which a court may grant relief against the defendant. The plaintiff must file the complaint with the clerk of court. The clerk issues a summons with the title of the action and a court file number. The plaintiff must arrange to serve the summons and complaint on the defendant. The plaintiff may pay a United States marshal to serve the summons and complaint or arrange to have an adult who is not a party to the suit serve them. In federal court, and most state courts, the action is commenced at the time of the filing so long as service is accomplished within a specified time after the filing.

A lawsuit must be prosecuted by the real party in interest. The plaintiff cannot be a mere "front" for someone else. When a party assigns a claim to another person, the assignee becomes the real party in interest. The assignee must prove the validity of the assignment as part of his or her claim.

A plaintiff may not split a cause of action. All claims that arise from a single transaction or occurrence must be included in one lawsuit; otherwise, the omitted claim is barred. If the defendant fails to assert a defense to the plaintiff's claim or claims, the defense is lost.

The plaintiff must assert all claims against the defendant that arose from the transaction or occurrence, or give up the claims. In other words, if the plaintiff omits any claim for damages or omits any legal theory for recovery, the plaintiff is barred from trying to assert the claim in a subsequent action. Similarly, the defendant must assert all defenses to the claim and waives any defenses not duly asserted.

The plaintiff may not maintain a civil action in more than one court. If the plaintiff does commence the same suit in two courts, the defendant may move for a dismissal of one of the cases.

A defendant may assert a claim against the plaintiff by making a counterclaim. If the counterclaim arises from the same transaction or occurrence, it is mandatory; that is to say, if the claim is not brought in the same suit, the defendant loses it. Defendants may assert claims against each other in a cross-claim. A cross-claim may seek compensation for the defendant's own loss or it may seek contribution toward the plaintiff's claim or both.

A defendant may join another person in a lawsuit as a third-party defendant to obtain indemnity or contribution toward the claim made by the plaintiff. The defendant may not bring a third-party action to obtain compensation for the defendant's own loss.

When a person is under a legal disability, such as being too young to bring a lawsuit, the action may be brought by a representative. A natural guardian (e.g., a parent) may act on behalf of a child in a lawsuit. All other "representative" plaintiffs must be appointed by court order.

Where fact issues exist, the parties have a right to have a jury determine those facts. However, the interpretation of an unambiguous contract or statute is strictly the responsibility of the judge.

Stare decisis requires courts to follow established rules of law, at least until the rules are expressly overruled. A court may overrule its own decisions. A higher court may overrule a lower court's decisions. A legislature may also change a court-made rule of law.

Res judicata precludes a party from bringing the same claim against the same person a second time. The doctrine requires the plaintiff to include in one action all claims that arise from a single transaction or occurrence. Res judicata complements the rule against splitting a cause of action.

Collateral estoppel precludes a party from litigating the same issue more than once where the issue was decided adversely to that party. The doctrine differs from res judicata in that it applies to a subsequent action even though the later action involves a different party.

Courts allow the plaintiff to recover punitive damages from the defendant when the defendant has intentionally committed a wrongful act in willful disregard of the rights or safety of the plaintiff. Punitive damages are awarded (rarely) in addition to compensatory damages. The customary issues that the jury may consider in determining how much money to award include the degree of the defendant's culpability, the extent of the defendant's financial resources, and the nature of the harm to which the defendant exposed the plaintiff.

The prevailing party is entitled to recover some of the costs of the litigation as provided by statute. Usually, the recoverable costs include the filing fee, subpoena fees, witness fees, and some portion of the expert witness fees. As a general rule, each party must bear his or her own attorney's fees.

Courts favor voluntary settlements. Parties settle their dispute by entering into a contract that provides that the claimant releases the defendant from any liability for the transaction or occurrence. To be valid, the settlement must have all the elements of a valid contract. Most settlements are the result of compromise. A valid settlement provides a complete defense to the settled claim.

KEY TERMS

action
actionable
adverse parties
alternative dispute resolution
assault
assignment
answer
battery
breach of contract
breach of warranty
cause of action
claim
collateral estoppel
common law
compensatory damages
complaint
conclusions of law
contempt of court
contribution
counterclaim
cross-claims
damages
declaratory judgment action
defendant
dismissal
district court
enjoin
estop
evidence
fact finder
findings of fact
fraud
guardian ad litem
general verdict
injunction
judgment
judgment debtor
jurisdiction

legal duty
liable
Model Rules of Professional Conduct
necessary parties
negligence
order for judgment
original jurisdiction
overrule
party
plaintiff
personal jurisdiction
procedural law
punitive damages
real party in interest
relief
remedy
res judicata
restraining order
rules of evidence
service of process
settlement
special verdict
splitting a cause of action
stare decisis
strict liability
subject matter jurisdiction
subpoena
subrogation
substantive law
summons
taxable costs
territorial jurisdiction
third-party action
trespass
tortfeasor
vicarious liability
waive

REVIEW QUESTIONS

1. What are the sources of a court's authority?

2. How does a court obtain personal jurisdiction over the plaintiff and the defendant?

3. How does a cause of action differ from a claim?

4. How can an established rule of law be overruled?

5. What jurisdictional issues must a court consider in determining whether it has jurisdiction in a particular case?

6. Why do courts preclude plaintiffs from splitting causes of action?

7. What are the essential elements to every cause of action?

8. Who benefits from the application of the res judicata doctrine?

9. What is the purpose of an appellate court?

10. How do declaratory judgment actions differ from other civil actions?

CASE ASSIGNMENT

All case assignments are based on the hypothetical case that appears on pages xxvii–xli.

Laura Raskin is considering bringing a civil action against Bradley Harper to obtain money damages for William Nordby's next of kin. In two to four sentences describe how the following litigation principles would apply to her case: (1) cause of action, (2) real controversy, (3) res judicata, (4) representatives, (5) counterclaims, (6) litigation expenses. *Hint:* If "jurisdiction" were a topic, an appropriate response would be similar to the following:

> Raskin's lawyer would have to choose a court that has jurisdiction over the case. This means having subject matter jurisdiction and personal jurisdiction. Because Harper lives in Minnesota and the accident occurred in Minnesota, its courts should be used. Ms. Raskin will submit to the Minnesota court's jurisdiction by commencing the action. Raskin's lawyer will have to serve a summons and complaint on Harper to give the court jurisdiction over him.

Endnotes

1. "Controlling" refers to a source of law that is generally regarded as deciding an issue.
2. Many derogatory statements are not defamatory.
3. If something has been "adjudicated," it has been finally decided by judicial authority.
4. Contrast this with typical civil litigation, where (with very few exceptions), if the claim is actionable, the courts will also require *proof* of actual harm or injury.

 For additional resources, visit our Web site at www.paralegal.delmar.cengage.com

CHAPTER 2

LAWYER AND CLIENT RELATIONSHIP AND ETHICS

CHAPTER OUTLINE

Chapter Objectives

Chapter 2 describes lawyers and the role of lawyers in the civil justice system. They are representatives and advocates for clients. At the same time, they are officers of the courts. Lawyers' ability to faithfully perform both functions make the system work. You need to know about lawyers' responsibilities, what they may do, what they may not do, and why.

Introduction

As a paralegal, you will work closely with lawyers. Your responsibilities to the client parallel a lawyer's responsibilities. Although you are not licensed by a court, as are lawyers, you must adhere to court orders, rules, and standards. Therefore, you need to understand the role of lawyers in the judicial system, what they do, and the limits on what they may do. All the rules and ethical considerations that apply to lawyers indirectly apply to paralegals. A lawyer may not ask you to do anything that he or she cannot do in representing a client. To be able to function with a fair amount of independence, you must be able to make decisions about what you are authorized to do when serving a client, as well as how you may do it. If you correctly understand

29

the interrelationship among the client, lawyer, and court, and if you correctly understand the rules of conduct, standards, and ethical considerations, you can avoid being involved in any misconduct.

Qualifications to Practice Law

The principal qualification required to practice law is a license issued by a state. The highest court in each state establishes the criteria that individuals must meet to be able to obtain such a license and practice law in that state. Most states require applicants to be graduated from an accredited law school, and a college degree is a prerequisite to enter most accredited law schools. In addition, most states require each applicant to pass a bar examination. The examination tests applicants on their knowledge of substantive law, procedural law, and ethics. An applicant for a license to practice law is also screened to make sure the applicant has good moral character. A criminal conviction involving a minor crime usually requires a detailed explanation but will not preclude admission to the state's bar. Conviction of a crime involving moral turpitude[1] should preclude licensure. In states that have an **integrated bar,** a person cannot practice law without belonging to the bar association. The bar association is clothed with an official status and is given the initial responsibility for determining whether an applicant may be admitted to practice. A person who is not licensed to practice law may handle her or his own legal matters but cannot advise or represent others in legal matters.

After a lawyer has been admitted to practice in the courts of a state, the lawyer may petition to practice in the federal district court for that state. Federal district courts do not require petitioners to take any test; they presume that the state courts have adequately screened the petitioners for competency. The lawyer's petition must be supported by an **affidavit** of one other lawyer who is admitted to practice in the court. The sponsor must affirm that he or she knows the petitioner, that the petitioner is a competent lawyer, and that the petitioner has good moral character. Each federal district court periodically has a swearing-in ceremony. The petitioners must appear in person with their sponsors.

A lawyer's admission to practice in one federal district court does not give the lawyer a right to practice in other federal courts. If a lawyer wants to try a case in another district, the lawyer may obtain special leave from that court to appear in the one case. However, a local lawyer must move the applicant's admission. A lawyer obtains leave to practice in a federal circuit court of appeals by filing a petition with the court. The petitioner does not have to appear before the court for a swearing-in ceremony. Similarly, a lawyer may obtain leave to practice in the United States Supreme Court by filing a written petition.

A lawyer must not assume responsibilities beyond the lawyer's experience and competence. Merely having a law degree and a license to practice law does not guarantee competency. Every lawyer must determine for himself or herself whether he or she has the ability to handle any given case. This means a lawyer must have the education, experience, and skill to handle whatever case or other legal matter he or she undertakes. Of course, a lawyer must not only possess such abilities, but must also exercise the abilities with due diligence and due care. For this reason, new lawyers often choose to work with experienced lawyers, at least for a while, to obtain the necessary experience.

integrated bar A state bar association that controls the right to practice law. All lawyers in the state must belong to the bar association.

affidavit A written ex parte statement made under oath before an officer of the court or a notary public.

An integrated bar association also has responsibility for conducting disciplinary proceedings against lawyers who are found guilty of unethical conduct. In states that do not have integrated bars, the highest court in the state disciplines and disbars errant lawyers. The court ordinarily appoints personnel to conduct disbarment investigations and prosecute disbarment proceedings. Nevertheless, the authority and responsibility remain with the court, and it must make the final decision on any admission, disciplinary action, and disbarment.

A court disbars a lawyer by rescinding the lawyer's license to practice in that court. A court may disbar a lawyer for engaging in conduct that is unethical or for committing a serious crime. Conduct that involves moral turpitude is a basis for disbarment even if not committed in connection with the practice of law. Misconduct of a lesser nature, such as an ordinance violation or traffic offense is not grounds for disbarment. The privilege of practicing law is valuable and cannot be taken away at the "pleasure" of the court. A lawyer is entitled to have a hearing to contest any charges that may affect his or her privilege to practice law. Any individual who attempts to practice law without a license is subject to disciplinary proceedings by the court having jurisdiction of the matter, just as though the individual were a lawyer. Furthermore, an individual who unlawfully attempts to practice law is subject to criminal prosecution.

Paralegals do many of the things lawyers do in handling litigation. However, paralegals are not authorized to practice law, and some of the work must be performed under a lawyer's direction. You must not advise people about the law or how the law applies to any given situation. A lawyer must assume ultimate responsibility for whatever advice is given to a client and the consequences of any legal services provided. This is necessary so that courts can retain authority over the judicial process, which they do by licensing lawyers. Courts lack direct control over paralegals, because no license is required.

As the number of civil cases continues to skyrocket, state and federal courts would be overwhelmed in short order were it not for the increased popularity of **alternative dispute resolution (ADR).** The most common forms of this so-called ADR are **mediation** and **arbitration.** Mediation is an informal gathering of the parties and their counsel to negotiate about a possible settlement with the help of a professional intermediary—a mediator. Mediators are trained to help reluctant parties see the strengths of the opponent's case and the weaknesses of their own in a way that promotes settlement. Paralegals can provide valuable assistance in this process by helping to prepare a confidential mediation memorandum that shares critical legal, factual, and evidentiary strengths with the mediator, thus encouraging the mediator to put favorable pressure on the opponent to accept a settlement favorable to your client. Mediation is remarkably more effective than party-only settlement efforts.

Arbitration is best viewed as a privately run trial. The parties agree to submit their dispute to an out-of-court decision maker, usually a panel of three arbitrators. The parties' agreement provides the ground rules for choosing the panel and everything else about the proceedings. Parties can choose arbitration before they have a dispute—for example, by agreeing to it in a contract at the start of a commercial relationship—or after the dispute arises. Note, however, that parties cannot be compelled to give up their access to the court system; arbitration is a matter of agreement. But the advantage of arbitration is that it is quicker and less expensive than the court system, leading to an

alternative dispute resolution (ADR) Any procedure or method for resolving disputes between persons that does not involve the courts. The primary methods of alternative dispute resolution are arbitration and mediation.

mediation A dispute resolution procedure in which an intermediary facilitates communication between the parties, helps the parties overcome barriers in the negotiation process, and identifies the parties' real interests and needs so that they can make their own agreement.

arbitration A procedure by which parties submit their dispute to another person or tribunal for decision. The submission may be voluntary, pursuant to a contract to arbitrate, or pursuant to a dispute that requires arbitration.

efficient resolution of the dispute. The paralegal's role in preparation for an arbitration is much the same as it would be if the matter were in court. Because the arbitration itself is much less formal than a court proceeding, your role in an arbitration could be expanded to meet the needs of the particular case.

Court Officers

Lawyers are officers of the courts in which they practice. Each lawyer takes an oath to serve the courts honorably, to adhere to the courts' rules, to support the laws of the land, and to support the Constitution. Each state has a special set of rules that govern a lawyer's ethics. Many of those rules have roots in the ABA Model Rules of Professional Conduct. For uniformity, this book references these Model Rules as the source for discussion of a lawyer's professional ethics. They are discussed throughout this chapter. See http://www.law.cornell.edu.

Although lawyers have a special relationship with their clients and usually derive their income by advising and representing clients, a lawyer's highest duty is to serve and protect the courts. If a conflict arises between the court's integrity and a client's interests, a lawyer must choose to protect the court. This means a lawyer must not allow a client to disregard the law, present false evidence, or evade a court order. If a lawyer believes that his or her client is misleading the court, the lawyer must stop it and do what he or she can to persuade the client to be honest. If a lawyer cannot control the client, the lawyer must withdraw from representation. See generally Model Rules of Prof'l Conduct R.3.12(2004). (These rules will be abbreviated throughout as "Model Rules.")

Professional Responsibilities

Lawyers are trained and licensed to provide two distinct services to their clients:

1. Lawyers may give advice about the law and its application.
2. Lawyers may act as a client's **agent** in judicial proceedings by *representing* the client.

agent   A person or corporation that has authority to act for another person, usually called a principal, and to make legally binding commitments on behalf of the principal.

As advisers, lawyers may counsel others about what the law requires or permits them to do. As advisers, lawyers may prepare legal documents for clients, such as deeds, contracts, wills, and so on. Anyone may prepare legal documents for his or her own use, but only a lawyer is authorized by law to prepare legal documents for another person or legal entity. A layperson who engages in the **unauthorized practice of law** by preparing legal documents for another is guilty of a crime. Nevertheless, it is clear that real estate agents, banks, and accountants are successfully invading the lawyers' domain concerning legal advice and document preparation. Indeed, some states may have no proscription limiting laypersons in this regard.

unauthorized practice of law   Nonlawyers doing things that only lawyers are permitted to do. Who and what fits into this definition is constantly changing and the subject of dispute.

Lawyers commonly represent clients in courts, legislative hearings, regulatory agencies, arbitration hearings, mediation sessions, business negotiations, city council meetings, and county board meetings. Sometimes professional people such as physicians, ministers, teachers, and lawyers need lawyers to represent them in peer review hearings where the client has been charged with "unprofessional conduct." Obviously, no list of representations could be all inclusive.

When a lawyer undertakes to represent a client in litigation, the lawyer assumes the role of an agent as well as that of adviser, whether hired on a full-time basis for a salary or retained to handle only one legal matter for a fee. An agent is a person who is authorized by a **principal** to act on behalf of the principal. Here, the client is the principal. Lawyers speak for and perform acts on behalf of their clients. Their words and acts bind the client, just as if the client had performed them. Notices directed to a lawyer are binding on the client. However, an agent can bind the principal only to the extent that the agent acts within the scope of his or her authority. A lawyer's actual authority is limited to the particular case or matter for which he or she has been retained.

The client retains the ultimate authority concerning management of the client's litigation. A lawyer must abide by the client's decisions concerning time, expenses, and costs. A client has the right to reject his or her lawyer's recommendations. A lawyer must not start a lawsuit for the client without the client's authorization. The client may insist that the lawyer pursue a claim in some other manner, such as through negotiations, mediation, or arbitration, or abandon the matter. In settlement negotiations, the client ordinarily perceives the lawyer as the expert, who has the ability to decide when and how to proceed. Nevertheless, the lawyer is not allowed to accept or reject a proposed settlement without first obtaining the client's authority to do so—even if the settlement is clearly in the client's best interest. Similarly, a lawyer must not dismiss a lawsuit without the client's authority and direction to do so. If the lawyer believes or even knows that the client's claim lacks merit and will be subject to dismissal by a court and that the court may impose penalties on the client and lawyer for bringing the claim, the lawyer cannot dismiss the claim without the client's permission. The lawyer can extricate herself or himself by obtaining the court's leave to withdraw from the case. Under such circumstances, the sooner the lawyer withdraws, the better for the lawyer.

If a client wants to settle a claim on terms less favorable than those the lawyer honestly believes are fair and obtainable, the lawyer must accede to the client's preference even if the lawyer's fee is determined by the amount of the recovery. By the same token, if the client wishes to forgo a valid claim or dismiss a meritorious claim, regardless of the reason, the lawyer must comply, even if the lawyer risks losing the fee. In this regard, a lawyer's authority differs from agents who sell merchandise, commodities, and commercial services. Agents in commerce typically earn their fees when they have negotiated a sale whether or not the sale is consummated. A lawyer must accept the client's decision concerning the objectives of the litigation and the manner in which the litigation is prosecuted. A lawyer should not try to prosecute a claim, however, when the lawyer believes that the claim lacks merit. And, of course, a client cannot require a lawyer to commit an unlawful act.

A lawyer has implied authority to do whatever is reasonably necessary to prepare and manage a trial.[2] Lawyers and paralegals have implied authority to follow the customary practices and procedures for prosecuting and defending civil actions without consulting the client about each step. Lawyers are responsible to their clients for the manner in which they handle their clients' litigation, and they are always subject to the client's ultimate authority. When a lawyer strongly disagrees with the client about

principal In the law of agency, a principal is a person who directed or permitted another person to act for him or her and is subject to his or her control.

the client's choice and order, the lawyer should document his or her recommendation and the client's rejection.

Fiduciary Responsibility

A lawyer is considered a **fiduciary** of the client's properties and monies. A fiduciary voluntarily assumes a legal duty to act for another person, the beneficiary, for a particular undertaking in a position of trust and confidence. A fiduciary must put the beneficiary's interests ahead of the fiduciary's own interests. As a fiduciary, the lawyer must exercise the highest degree of care, not merely ordinary care, in handling the client's monies, properties, papers, and confidential communications. If a loss occurs, the lawyer has the burden of showing that it was for reasons beyond his or her control. The Model Rules specify a lawyer's duty for the safekeeping of a client's property, which is most often money. See Model Rules R.1.15. Generally, it is of utmost importance to keep all client money separate from all other money. The Rules specify that a lawyer must maintain a client trust account for this purpose. Intermingling lawyer funds with client funds is perhaps the most common basis for lawyer discipline and disbarment.

The fiduciary relationship lasts as long as the lawyer continues to possess or control the client's property. A lawyer's fiduciary duties are limited to protecting and maintaining the client's *property*. A lawyer is not a fiduciary when giving legal advice or representing a client in legal proceedings. In such matters, the lawyer owes a duty of reasonable care.

Professional Ethics

Violation of the Model Rules hurts the legal profession and contaminates the judicial system. The Model Rules provide guidelines for the resolution of various ethical problems. Seldom is there a direct conflict between a lawyer's duties to a client and the court. The Model Rules help lawyers to determine where their primary obligations lie and how to avoid or resolve conflicts. Many states have adopted the Model Rules as standards of conduct which, if violated, provide the basis for imposing sanctions—including disbarment.

Although the Model Rules are directed at lawyers, by implication they apply to any person who assists lawyers, whether as an investigator, a secretary, or a legal assistant. A lawyer must not direct or encourage a client to engage in conduct that is unethical for the lawyer. In other words, a lawyer may not do indirectly through a client that which the lawyer is forbidden to do. If a lawyer discovers that a client is guilty of some such impropriety, he or she must take affirmative action to correct the wrong. Model Rules R.3.3.

Lawyers are forbidden to engage in activities that stir up litigation. It is not difficult to imagine a lawyer, whose business is down, examining public records to find problems with ownership titles to real estate for the purpose of obtaining clients. Similarly, unscrupulous lawyers could research newspapers and magazines to find potential libel suits. By such conduct, lawyers would create problems solely for their own financial gain. Similarly, lawyers are in a good position to encourage accident victims to pursue litigation rather than settle or drop a claim. Such practices are degrading to the profession and could flood the courts with petty, unnecessary, and unwanted litigation. Society's interests should be served, not damaged, by lawyers and civil litigation. A lawyer who stirs up litigation is subject to disciplinary proceedings and possible disbarment. Paralegals, too, must avoid inciting litigation. That is not to say that a paralegal must avoid recommending a good lawyer when and where one is needed, but a paralegal should not create a controversy where none exists.

Lawyers must not insult or cast aspersions on the court in public. As court officers, lawyers must conduct themselves in a professional manner, showing due respect to the court—even when they seriously disagree with the judge. A lawyer's zeal and desire to serve a client must not lead to misuse or abuse of the court. If a lawyer believes that a judge has acted improperly in some respect, the lawyer has the right and duty to bring the problem to the attention of a judicial board. Of course, a judge's misconduct may also be the basis for appealing an adverse judgment.

If a lawyer discovers that a client has perpetrated a fraud on the court by suborning[3] perjury, or the like, the lawyer should urge the client to confess the wrongdoing to the other party with the hope that the matter can be resolved. If the client refuses, the lawyer's only recourse may be to inform the court about the wrongful act. Model Rules R.3.3(b).

If charged with a violation of professional ethics, a lawyer is entitled to a hearing that meets all the requirements of due process of law. A lawyer has a right to know the charges against her or him, to present evidence in defense, and to be heard by an impartial tribunal.

Conflicts of Interests

To avoid a **conflict of interest,** a lawyer must put the client's interests ahead of the lawyer's. The lawyer's failure to do so would be a breach of the duty owed the client of full and vigorous representation. For example, as noted previously, if a client wants to settle his case for less than the lawyer believes the case is worth, the lawyer must comply even though it means the lawyer's contingent fee will be less than the lawyer expected. Similarly, a lawyer must not put one client's interests ahead of another client's interests. When a lawyer has two clients who have a dispute between them, the lawyer should not represent either. Model Rules R.1.7(a)(1). Each client should go to another lawyer for legal advice or representation. Ethics even preclude a lawyer from representing a client against a former client. Model Rules R.1.9. There is a presumption that the former client disclosed important, confidential information and that the lawyer has special knowledge about the former client that would put the former client at a disadvantage. In a sense, the obligations from the relationship between a client and lawyer persist beyond the end of representation.

The rule concerning conflicts of interests has an important exception. Two or more clients may agree to allow one lawyer to represent them. Model Rules R.1.7(b). This often happens when the clients' objectives are similar. For example, a lawyer may represent two buyers in a real estate transaction. A lawyer may draw a deed for a buyer and seller who have made their own agreement and merely want the agreement formalized. A former client may also waive the right to object to a lawyer representing a new client against him or her. Model Rules R.1.9(a). The burden

conflict of interest A situation in which a lawyer's duty to a client to act or refrain from acting is or may be harmful to the interests of another client or a former client or to the lawyer's own interests. A lawyer must avoid conflicts of interests or obtain the client's express consent to act.

Example

A driver and passenger, both of whom were injured in an accident, may ask one lawyer to represent them against another driver involved in the accident. This often happens when a husband and wife are involved in the same accident. But there is a probable conflict of interests between the driver and the passenger, because the passenger may also have a claim against the driver. But suppose the passenger does not want to seek damages from the driver. The lawyer could undertake to represent both if the lawyer fully explains to the passenger that she or he is forgoing a valid claim and may, consequently, recover no damages. The lawyer's explanation and the clients' consent should be reduced to writing for the purpose of showing that the matter was clearly communicated and understood. The lawyer needs the clients' informed consent. As a further precaution against criticism, the lawyer could advise one or both of the potential clients to talk with another lawyer about the desirability of separate representation.

---

is always on the lawyer to inform both clients about the relationship and conflict. The lawyer must explain that either client has a right to object to the lawyer's handling the matter. Consent must be confirmed in writing.

A lawyer who represents several claimants may have a problem allocating the available settlement monies between them. If the defendant offers to settle all claims for an aggregate amount, the lawyer is in an awkward position to advise the clients how to allocate the proceeds. Suppose a husband and wife both have claims against a negligent driver and that the driver's liability insurer offers to pay the policy limits of $25,000 for a full and final settlement of both claims. The insurer may not care how the claimants divide the money, but no additional money is available. If the clients voluntarily agree on the allocation, there is no problem. But if they are unable to agree, their lawyer may counsel them but should not insist on a particular allocation. Each client may need to consult another lawyer about whether to accept the offer and what is an appropriate division. Ultimately, the attorney may not participate in an agreement settlement for multiple clients without both clients' written consent. Model Rules R.1.8(g).

Lawyer-Client Privileged Communications

A person who seeks legal advice must be free to tell the lawyer everything relevant to his or her legal problem. A lawyer must have all the facts and information, whether helpful or harmful, to be able to provide sound advice and effective representation. Therefore, when a person seeks legal representation, the person's communication with a lawyer is **privileged communication.** This means that a court cannot order the lawyer or person to disclose the contents of their communication—whether the communication was written or oral. If there were no such privilege, many clients would be unwilling to talk candidly to lawyers for fear that what they say would be obtainable by the government or an opponent and used against them. That would be counterproductive for the client and the judicial system. See Model Rules R.1.6.

privileged communication A communication that is protected by law from disclosure.

The privilege does not depend on the person paying a retainer or having a formal retainer agreement. The critical factor is that the person must be *seeking* legal advice or representation to make the communication privileged. See Model Rules R.1.18. But after a lawyer informs the person that the lawyer will not help the person, any further communications are not privileged. Similarly, once the potential client elects not to hire the lawyer, subsequent communications are not privileged. Of course, after a lawyer is hired by a client, any further communications are privileged.

A communication that is merely "confidential" is substantially different from one that is privileged. A matter that is kept secret between two or more persons would be considered confidential. For example, most businesses wish to keep their customers' matters confidential. Banks, lending institutions, credit card companies, and department stores all strive to keep their records from getting into the hands of the curious. They avoid publicizing information in their possession about their customers. Nevertheless, a court of law could compel a company to produce its records if the records were relevant to a civil action. But if a communication is privileged, no person and no court can legally compel its disclosure for any purpose. It does not matter what the subject is as long as the client is seeking professional legal advice that is not for the purpose of committing an unlawful act.

The privilege applies to written communications as well as to oral communications. Whatever documents the client or lawyer prepares for the other concerning the legal problem are privileged. It does not matter which of them takes possession of the documents. Records and other documents a lawyer prepares in connection with the client's legal problem are similarly privileged. The principal requirement is that the communication or document is part of the client's effort to obtain legal advice or representation. Lawyers prepare numerous documents on behalf of clients with the intention of providing those documents to other persons. Usually, those documents are privileged until actually delivered to another person. Even drafts of the documents remain privileged until disclosed.

The privilege against disclosure belongs to the client, not to the lawyer. A lawyer must actively protect against any disclosure of the client's privileged information. Lawyers must assert the client's privilege when asked by another lawyer or court to disclose privileged documents or communications. The privilege is in effect forever or until the client waives it. A waiver may be intentional or inadvertent. A client may waive the privilege by simply telling a third person about the content of the document or communication. Therefore, a client must protect against unintentional disclosures. If a third person overhears a conversation between a lawyer and client, it is their fault, not the fault or responsibility of the third person. An inadvertent disclosure cannot be undone. The lawyer and client cannot avoid the consequences of disclosure by asserting that they did not expect anyone to overhear them. Because only the client may waive the privilege, a lawyer must have the client's consent to disclose privileged communications. If a lawyer mistakenly discloses a privileged communication or document, the lawyer is subject to civil liability to the client for any loss the disclosure causes. The lawyer is also subject to disciplinary action for unethical conduct.

In the following example, the client told her lawyer some facts: that the speed limit was forty miles per hour and that she was driving under the speed limit. Note, however, that the client's disclosure of these facts to her lawyer does not make those *facts* privileged. When the time comes, the client will testify that she was traveling

---

EXAMPLE

Suppose an automobile driver was injured in an accident and wants to make a claim for her injuries. Suppose during the initial interview she tells her lawyer she does not know how fast she was going when the collision occurred. But then she explains that she knew the speed limit was forty miles per hour, and that she was traveling well within the speed limit. When she said she did not know what her speed was she meant only that she did not know what her *exact* speed was at the moment of collision, because she was not looking at the speedometer at that moment. She was looking at the other car. Her statements to her lawyer cannot be discovered. The "admission" that she did not know what her speed was cannot be discovered and used against her. The privilege helps keep an adversary from using statements out of context. Otherwise, at court the opposing lawyer might ask: "Have you ever told anyone that you did not know what your speed was at the time of the accident?" A truthful answer would be, "yes." Then the client would have to explain the context of the statement, unduly compromising her case and discouraging candid lawyer-client conversations in the future.

---

less than forty miles per hour. However, her *statements to her lawyer* about her speed are not discoverable. Her lawyer could properly tell the opposing lawyer and the judge that his client was driving less than the speed limit. However, the lawyer should not say that the client *told him* she was driving under the speed limit. The lawyer's statement about what the client told him waives the privilege. Then the question becomes, "to what extent has the privilege been waived?"

Paralegals have the same obligation as lawyers to guard against any improper disclosure. For example, paralegals may expect to participate in lawyer-client conferences. These conferences may concern a client's wish to obtain a divorce, buy some land, bring a personal-injury lawsuit, obtain workers' compensation benefits, and so on. Regardless of the purpose, the communication is privileged. Most courts now recognize that lawyers must act through others, such as private secretaries and legal assistants. Consequently, the privilege has been extended in most jurisdictions to include lawyers' agents, such as paralegals. Courts should recognize that it is desirable and necessary for lawyers to disclose privileged information to paralegals assisting them. Of course, if the privilege is enlarged in this manner, paralegals must be subject to the same close controls that courts have over lawyers and to the same rigid professional ethics.

Not every communication between a lawyer and client is privileged. A communication is priviledged when it is for the purpose of obtaining legal advice. A client has no privilege to consult a lawyer about how to defraud a court or evade the law or commit a crime. For example, if a client were to consult a lawyer for the purpose of working out a plan to illegally evade taxes, the communication would not come within the privilege. Indeed, under those circumstances, the lawyer would be duty bound to try to persuade the client to comply with the law. Model Rules R.1.6(b).

In several recent cases, newspaper reporters have attempted to establish a rule that their "confidential" news sources should have privileged status. The law has been that reporters may be punished through contempt-of-court proceedings for refusing to divulge sources, assuming there was a good and sufficient reason for litigants to know the identity of the sources. The issue presented to the courts in the recent cases is whether the need for privileged news sources outweighs the need for identification of witnesses who have important evidence relevant to criminal and civil lawsuits. A second question is whether any story is newsworthy if the identity of the source is not subject to disclosure. Some reporters who have challenged the law in order to bring about a change have been forced to spend time in jail for refusing to comply with court orders directing them to testify. Their incarcerations were punishment for being in contempt of court.

If a client files an ethics complaint against a lawyer or commences a negligence action for malpractice against a lawyer, the client cannot claim the attorney-client privilege in an effort to keep the lawyer from using records and communications to defend herself or himself. The privilege is intended to be used as a shield for the client, never as a sword. A lawyer may use all the client's records and communications, whether written or oral, to defend herself or himself.

Attorney Fees

A lawyer's compensation is a matter of negotiation and agreement between the lawyer and the client. A lawyer may charge a fixed amount for a specified service or may charge an hourly rate. A lawyer's hourly rate usually depends on his or her experience and the complexity of the legal problems. When a lawyer represents a plaintiff in civil litigation to recover money damages, the lawyer's fee may be based on a percentage of the monies recovered. A client is always free to choose another lawyer if the proposed fee arrangement is unacceptable. There is some concern that lawyers are in a position to take advantage of clients who are in "desperate straits." Therefore, the Rules prohibit the charging of an unreasonable fee under the circumstances. Model Rules R.1.5(a). Consequently, it is desirable for lawyers to keep accurate records of the time they actually put in to a matter, even when working for a contingent fee.

When the fee is based solely on a percentage of monies recovered, it is called a **contingent fee.** The lawyer receives payment only if the client actually collects money damages. While some states regulate the percentage an attorney may charge, contingency fee percentages range between 20 percent and 50 percent. The percentage ordinarily depends on the size of the case, the possibilities of an appeal, and the likelihood and difficulty of obtaining a recovery. Lawyers justify high contingent fees on the basis that they may spend a lot of time on a case, forgoing other business, and end up with nothing. Historically, contingent fees were considered unethical, because they tended to foment litigation. Today, contingent fees are common.

When a lawyer undertakes to represent a client, she or he may be precluded from representing certain other persons or companies and, consequently, from obtaining other business. This limiting effect on a lawyer's business opportunities is another consideration in setting fees. In some types of cases, the amount of the fee or the contingency percentage may be limited by statute or court rule. For example, court rules may prohibit a lawyer from charging more than a certain percentage when representing a minor. In class actions, a lawyer's fee is subject to court approval for reasonableness.

contingent fee A fee for legal services based on an agreed percentage of the monies actually recovered. If the client does not recover any money damages in the litigation, the lawyer is not entitled to any fee.

If a client discharges a lawyer before the work is completed, the lawyer is entitled to be paid for services actually rendered. The usual basis for payment in such cases is for the value of the services the client received. The value may or may not be based on the original retainer agreement. If a client refuses to pay for services received, the lawyer may file a lien with the court in which the action is pending. The lien gives the lawyer a claim on any recovery of money the client obtains. The priority of the lawyer's claim depends on state law. The amount of the lien is subject to determination by litigation if the parties are unable to agree on the amount. A lawyer always has the right to bring an action in court for payment of a fee. Otherwise, lawyers would be at the mercy of unscrupulous clients.

If a lawyer handles a client's legal matters in such a way as to realize a profit, aside from a proper legal fee for services, the law presumes that the profit was obtained by undue influence or fraud. A lawyer has the burden of proving that any financial benefit he or she derived from the relationship, aside from reasonable fees, was not the result of undue influence.

Terminating the Relationship

A client must have complete confidence and trust in his or her lawyer. A client cannot be required to use a lawyer he or she does not want. For those reasons, a client may discharge his or her lawyer at will. A client does not need a reason to terminate the relationship. However, if a case is in progress, a court does not have to grant a continuance or delay because of the discharge. Otherwise, a client might discharge her or his lawyer as a mere tactic to stop a trial that is obviously going badly.

A lawyer has more difficulty ending the professional relationship. If a lawyer decides to withdraw merely because the client is difficult to work with, the lawyer probably forfeits the right to a fee.[4] If a lawyer is handling a case that is near trial, the lawyer's withdrawal could cause a hardship on the client and inconvenience the court. Consequently, some courts have special rules and procedures that lawyers must follow to withdraw from a pending case. Some courts have determined that a client's inability to pay a fee for legal services is not grounds for a lawyer to withdraw. This is especially true in criminal cases. Therefore, a lawyer may be constrained to obtain a substantial retainer at the outset.

A lawyer is permitted to withdraw from a case if the client refuses to follow court orders or other legal requirements. If a lawyer comes to believe that the client is using the lawyer's services to perpetuate a fraud, the lawyer has a duty to withdraw. Lawyers must be careful not to prejudice their clients' rights or interests by withdrawing. This means that a lawyer must provide reasonable notice to the client so the client can obtain a replacement lawyer and meet all deadlines.

A lawyer should carefully document his or her withdrawal from a case. The lawyer should send a letter to the client by registered mail formalizing the withdrawal. Otherwise, if problems develop with the case, the client may try to excuse himself or herself on the basis that the lawyer was still handling everything. In that event, the lawyer might face a malpractice action. A letter or formal **notice of withdrawal** helps to protect against such problems. You may be asked to prepare and send the letter, subject to review by the lawyer. If a lawyer is handling litigation that is pending in

notice of withdrawal   A notice an attorney files with the court and serves on all the parties, stating that he or she has withdrawn or will withdraw from the case.

court, a formal notice of withdrawal must also be filed with the court. In some states, lawyers must first obtain permission from the court to be able to withdraw. If the court order allows the lawyer to withdraw, the lawyer must send a copy to the client and opposing party.

Occasionally, a potential client discusses the merits of a claim with a lawyer, but the lawyer tells the person that his or her claim has no merit or, for other reasons, refuses to take the case. Before the want-to-be client is able to find another lawyer to take the case, the statute of limitations may run against the claim. The client may still want to pursue the claim but cannot because it has become time barred. The want-to-be client may contend that she or he believed the lawyer was working on the case and that the lawyer should not have let the statute of limitations run. To protect against this kind of scenario, the lawyer should make sure that the want-to-be client is told and understands (1) that the lawyer is not going to handle the case and (2) that the statute of limitations will run against the claim, making it important to pursue the claim promptly. The best procedure is to provide this information in a letter to the want-to-be client to reduce the possibility of a misunderstanding. It is also a good idea to establish proof of delivery of the letter.

Malpractice

Lawyers must exercise "due care" handling clients' matters. A failure to exercise due care is negligence. Negligence in rendering professional services is commonly called **malpractice.** A lawyer who commits malpractice is liable to his or her client for any consequential loss. A lawyer must possess the knowledge and skill ordinarily possessed by other competent lawyers. In addition a lawyer must exercise reasonable care in applying his or her knowledge and skill to the client's legal matters. However, if a lawyer advertises that he or she is a specialist in a particular field of law, the lawyer is held to the standards of specialists, which may require more knowledge and skill. The term *due care* includes due diligence. Lawyers must act in a timely manner.

In civil litigation, lawyers must exercise due care in gathering evidence and demonstrate ordinary ability in presenting clients' cases. However, the mere fact that a lawyer fails to win the case does not necessarily mean the lawyer is guilty of malpractice. Theoretically, lawyers are going to lose half the cases they try. There are too many uncertainties in litigation for lawyers to be right all the time. But if the mistake is the result of neglect, the lawyer is guilty of malpractice and is liable to the client for the consequential losses.

It seems that the biggest problem lawyers have, collectively, is the failure to be diligent. It is a problem that goes with being "too busy." It is easy to let deadlines slip by or wait too long to give necessary notices or fail to commence an action before the statute of limitations runs—especially when the particular matter seems to lack substance. As a paralegal, one of the most important things you can do is to make sure that all the cases you work on are handled in a timely manner. You should take the initiative; be proactive. With the help of conscientious paralegals, lawyers can do a better job of keeping current. You should initiate activity on files by preparing pertinent documents for the lawyers' approval and use. Keep a calendar for each case so that you know when things must be done and so that no deadlines are missed.

malpractice Negligence committed by a person while rendering professional services.

Maintenance

maintenance The practice of advancing monies to a litigant on the basis that the "loan" will be paid out of the verdict or settlement.

In most states, lawyers are not allowed to financially support clients by paying some or all of the clients' living expenses while the clients' cases are pending. To do so is called **maintenance.** Lawyers cannot even loan their clients money so that the clients can get by until their lawsuits are settled or tried. What is the problem? Consider the situation in which a self-employed family man is severely injured in an automobile accident and cannot work. He cannot pay his expenses. But he has a very good claim against another person to recover money damages for his injuries and loss of income. At first blush, it would be considerate, even charitable, for the victim's lawyer to support him until the case is concluded. Of course, the lawyer would expect to be paid back out of the case proceeds. That means the lawyer would have a financial stake in the outcome beyond the mere fee. The lawyer's need for repayment would create a conflict of interest. The danger is too great that a lawyer's professional judgment would be affected by his or her personal interest in the outcome of the litigation. In particular, a lawyer might be inclined to recommend for or against a settlement in light of her or his own needs rather than those of the client. A person who is personally involved is less likely to be able to provide the best advice. Furthermore, financing clients could become an expected practice—and most lawyers would find that to be an impossible burden. The lending of money is better left to financial institutions.

Some of the arguments against client maintenance are also used to attack the contingent fee. Lawyers are permitted to advance various litigation expenses on behalf of their clients. But that may be done only on the basis that the expenses will be paid by the client, regardless of the outcome of the case.

Champerty

champerty An agreement between an attorney and a client by which the attorney pledges to bear the cost of the client's litigation in return for a portion of the expected recovery of money damages.

When the owner of a claim enters into an agreement with a third person to share the recovery, the arrangement is called **champerty.** Champerty is unethical and may also be illegal. Therefore, lawyers may not invest money in their clients' lawsuits by buying interests in the expected recoveries. The law frowns on speculation in litigation for profit. The same principle was an obstacle to the use of contingent fees in civil litigation. Even today, contingent fees are unethical in criminal cases.

Champerty differs from maintenance in that a third person tries to buy an interest in the expected recovery. Again, maintenance concerns financing a litigant's nonlitigation expenses during the pendency of the litigation. Certain causes of action may be assigned, however. It is permissible to assign causes of action arising from transactions such as claims on contracts. However, assignment of personal-injury claims is contrary to public policy. The law distinguishes between such assignments because there is a real danger of champerty in the personal-injury field. An assignee of a cause of action must prosecute the action in her or his own name, so the assignee's interest in the outcome of the case is fully disclosed.

Solicitation and Advertising

Historically, lawyers were forbidden to advertise their services. They could not even permit others to advertise on their behalf. This prohibition was based, in part, on the concern that advertising would foment litigation and lawyers would unduly impose themselves on prospective clients at inappropriate times. But the United States Supreme Court determined that the prohibition on advertising unduly limited competition and that the public benefits from dissemination of information about where and how to locate lawyers, their specialties, backgrounds, and experience.

Today the principal limitation on lawyer advertising concerns the methods of advertising used. Lawyers may advertise in public media, including newspapers, television, billboards, radio, and directories. Lawyers may not advertise by direct solicitation, whether in person or by telephone. Lawyers may not pay or reward nonlawyers for recommending them to handle legal matters, but they may pay a referral fee to another lawyer. Model Rules R.1.5(e). Lawyers may provide information about themselves, such as age, date admitted to practice, law school attended, offices held in bar associations, teaching positions held, and certification in any specialties in the law. The information must be accurate and factual. For example, it would be unethical for a lawyer to advertise that he or she is a Harvard graduate if the lawyer's only degree from Harvard was an undergraduate degree. Obviously, such an advertisement is misleading.

A public advertisement may state the lawyer's address and telephone number and describe the basis for charges. For example, it may state flat rates for certain types of representations such as adoptions and uncontested divorces, or hourly rates for defending against a drunk driving citation. An advertisement may state that the lawyer handles civil litigation claims for a contingent fee and that the lawyer will advance court costs. An advertisement must be worded not to create unjustified expectations about the results the lawyer will obtain. For example, it would be unethical for a lawyer to advertise that the lawyer "wins all" of the cases he or she tries or that the lawyer has a reputation for obtaining "large" verdicts—large being a relative term. Lawyers may permit their names to be listed in professional directories. These directories are particularly useful to lawyers who need to refer clients to other lawyers in other communities. The principal such directory is called *Martindale-Hubbell*, which is published in several large volumes each year. A bare-bones version is available on-line at http://www.martindale.com.

Attorney Pro Se

A person may choose to represent himself or herself in a civil action; the law does not require litigants to hire lawyers. A person who elects to represent himself or herself is referred to as an **attorney pro se.** Usually, judges try to discourage laypersons from representing themselves, because they often become lost in the maze of procedural rules and substantive law. Sometimes the self-represented person feels that a lawyer's fee is too much to be affordable given the value of the case. Other times an attorney pro se has consulted with several lawyers who have told the pro se that the claim or defense is not valid, but the pro se wants to proceed anyway.

attorney pro se   A person who acts as his or her own attorney in a civil action.

TECHNOLOGY NOTES

Useful ethics Web sites include http://www.law.cornell.edu and http://www.legalethics.com. The National Federation of Paralegal Association (http://www.paralegals.org) maintains a Legal Resources page with extensive links to, among others: federal agencies and departments; federal laws, codes and statutes; state agencies and departments; state laws, codes and statutes; information about state supreme courts and the federal supreme court. It lists Internet directories and search engines.

The American Association for Paralegal Education (http://aafpe.org) is a national organization serving paralegal education and institutions that offer paralegal education programs. It maintains a "Useful Links" page and link list for software products and services.

Summary

The practice of law entails giving advice about the law, its application and representing another person in a court. Only a person licensed to practice law may do these things. A lawyer must possess and exercise ordinary ability (for a lawyer) in giving advice and handling the client's legal matters. However, if a lawyer holds herself or himself out to the public as a specialist in the law, the lawyer is held to the higher standard of a specialist. A lawyer must follow the clients' lawful directives in handling litigation, even when the lawyer believes the client should take a different course.

Communications between a lawyer and a client are privileged, whether oral or written. Records of communications are also privileged. The privilege extends to members of the lawyer's staff. The privilege belongs to the client, not to the lawyer. The client may elect to waive the privilege and disclose a communication. A lawyer cannot object to the client's disclosure. If a client makes a claim against the lawyer, the lawyer may disclose privileged communications to the extent necessary to defend himself or herself.

A lawyer must avoid any conflict of interest with a client. Also, a lawyer must not serve two clients where those clients have conflicting interests. This rule even precludes a lawyer from representing a client against a former client. However, if the lawyer makes a full disclosure of the conflict of interest, the clients may elect to waive the right to object. If a problem arises, the burden is on the lawyer to show that a full disclosure was made and that the client made an informed choice to waive the conflict. When a lawyer is faced with an ethical question, the lawyer may seek the advice of a board of professional responsibility for guidance.

A lawyer owes the duty of a fiduciary to protect any property and money the lawyer holds for a client. A fiduciary must put the client's interests ahead of his or her own. If property is lost or damaged while under the control of a fiduciary, the fiduciary has the burden of proving that the loss was not his or her fault.

A lawyer is the client's agent when handling civil litigation. When a lawyer acts within the scope of her or his authority, the lawyer binds the client the same as if the client had acted. A client has the right to control her or his civil litigation. A client may refuse to commence an action. A client may refuse to settle a claim or may insist that a claim be settled. A client may insist that a lawyer dismiss a claim. A client may insist that a lawyer withdraw a defense. A client may discharge a lawyer at any stage of the proceeding. However, if a case is in progress, a court does not have to grant a continuance or delay because of the discharge.

Champerty is an agreement between a plaintiff and a lawyer by which the lawyer acquires an interest in the outcome of the case for purposes of profit. The practice is unethical. Nevertheless, contingent fees are permissible and common in personal-injury litigation.

Historically, lawyers were strictly forbidden to solicit business, and they could not advertise. Today, advertising is permitted within certain prescribed limits. Those limits vary from state to state. The limits are designed to keep lawyers from imposing on the public and giving potential clients unreasonable expectations about what the lawyer can do for them.

When a lawyer handles a civil action on behalf of a client, the lawyer must serve the client, but the lawyer's highest duty is to the court. This principle requires lawyers to actively prevent a client from perpetrating a fraud on the court. The matter of duty should not be confused with the matter of privileged communications. A court cannot require a lawyer to disclose a client's privileged communications.

If a lawyer realizes a profit from the client's business, aside from a proper legal fee for services, the law presumes that the profit was the result of undue influence or fraud. A lawyer has the burden of proving that any extra financial benefit he or she derived was not the result of undue influence.

A client may discharge her or his lawyer at will. A client does not need a reason to terminate the relationship. A lawyer may terminate the relationship but not under circumstances that leave the client's litigation in a precarious position. Lawyers must not prejudice clients' rights or interests by withdrawing. A lawyer must provide reasonable notice to the client so that the client can obtain another lawyer and meet all deadlines. Courts have special rules and procedures that lawyers must follow to be able to withdraw from a pending case. Some courts have determined that a client's inability to pay a fee for legal services is not grounds for a lawyer to withdraw. A lawyer may withdraw from a case if the client refuses to follow court orders or other legal requirements. If a client is using the lawyer's services to perpetrate a fraud, the lawyer is under a duty to withdraw. A lawyer should document her or his withdrawal to protect against any claim that the withdrawal was without notice or was prejudicial.

The amount of a lawyer's fee and the basis for the fee are a matter of contract between the lawyer and the client. However, it is unethical for a lawyer to charge an unconscionable fee. If a fee is unconscionable, a court may modify it. Historically, contingent fees were unethical. Today such fees are common, especially in personal injury cases. Lawyers are not allowed to share fees with nonlawyers.

When a person represents herself or himself in court, the person acts as attorney pro se. An attorney pro se does not need a license to practice law or permission from the court to act on his or her own behalf.

KEY TERMS

affidavit	integrated bar
agent	maintenance
alternative dispute resolution	malpractice
arbitration	mediation
attorney pro se	principal
champerty	privileged communication
conflict of interest	notice of withdrawal
contingent fee	unauthorized practice of law
fiduciary	

Review Questions

1. What is the difference between confidential information and privileged information?

2. Is a paralegal subject to the direct control of the court system?

3. What is the cause of action that encompasses legal malpractice?

4. In what ways does the relationship between a lawyer and client differ from that between a typical agent and principal?

5. If a court orders parties to a civil action to arbitrate their dispute, may a paralegal handle the examination of witnesses in the arbitration hearing?

6. What are the considerations for setting the amount of a lawyer's fee?

7. What does a lawyer have to do before withdrawing from a civil case?

8. Why does a lawyer owe her or his highest duty to the court?

Case Assignment

Laura Raskin contacted attorney Ted Brown and asked him to take the case against Bradley Harper. But Brown is a very close friend of John Griffin and is afraid that Griffin might get involved, so he has declined to take the case. He did talk to Ms. Raskin at some length about the accident and the family's hardship caused by Mr. Nordby's death. You are a paralegal in attorney Brown's office. He directed you to write a letter to Ms. Raskin confirming that he will not be handling the case. Prepare the letter. It should not be more than one page. Be sure to confirm for her that your firm will not represent the next of kin and recommend steps she should take to preserve their rights.

Endnotes

1. Moral turpitude is characterized by vileness or dishonesty of a high degree.
2. A lawyer may prepare interrogatories, schedule depositions, prepare requests for admissions, issue demands for documents, attend calendar calls, attend pretrial conferences, and make representations to the court about the case's state of the readiness, all without first obtaining the client's permission. A lawyer may enter into stipulations with opposing parties concerning the evidence and trial procedures. A lawyer's implicit authority includes the right to object or not object to evidence and to present or not present certain evidence. Many of these responsibilities may be performed or assisted by paralegals.
3. Subornation of perjury is to induce or procure false testimony. It is a crime.
4. The fee is set by contract between the lawyer and client. But a contract that allows a lawyer to collect a fee after withdrawing from a case would probably violate ethical guidelines and be considered unconscionable.

 For additional resources, visit our Web site at www.paralegal.delmar.cengage.com

COURT ORGANIZATION

CHAPTER OUTLINE

Chapter Objectives

Chapter 3 describes the organization and interrelationship of state and federal courts. It also explains some important concepts, such as jurisdiction, venue, and the role of juries.

Introduction

There are two judicial systems in every state: a federal court system and a state court system. (See Exhibit 3.1.) In many ways the systems are similar. The two systems function independently of each other. However, the state and federal courts recognize each other and defer to one another in some situations. Each state has several courts that are integrated into a state court system, including district courts (also called trial courts), probate courts, and small claims courts. The federal system also has several courts, including District Courts, Bankruptcy Courts, the Court of Federal Claims, and the Court of International Trade.

    The state and federal systems have two levels of courts: (1) the trial courts where parties must first present their claims and defenses; and (2) the appellate courts, which determine whether the trial court followed proper procedures and correctly applied the law. The state appellate courts usually have two levels: an intermediate appellate court and a supreme court. The federal appellate courts have the United States Circuit

47

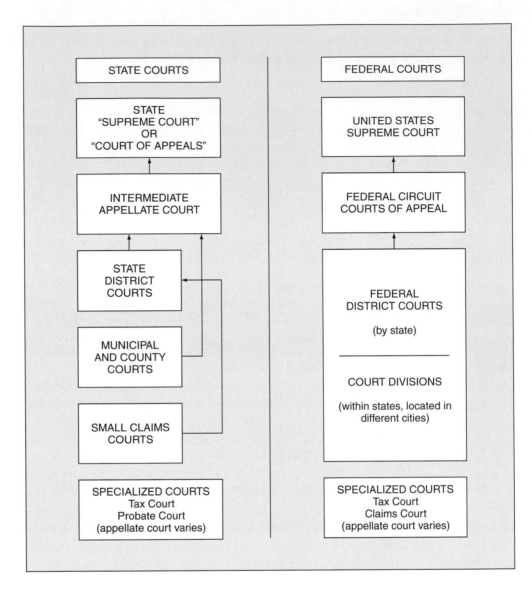

Courts of Appeal and the United States Supreme Court. We will focus on the federal judicial system—both trial and appelate courts—because it functions in all states and because many states pattern their court systems after the federal system.

District Courts

District courts are trial courts. Their function is to resolve disputes about the facts (i.e., what happened) and then to apply the law to those facts to resolve the dispute according to legal standards. When the parties disagree about what the facts are, the court must receive evidence about the alleged facts for the purpose of determining the truth. The parties may choose to have the judge determine the facts or to have a jury make the determination.[1] If the case is tried before a judge without a jury, the judge must make "findings of fact." Then the judge must apply the law to those facts. If the case is tried to a jury, the jury will find the facts by a general verdict (a general declaration of the case outcome) or by a special verdict (a written answer to a particular question(s)).

When a case is tried before a jury, the judge may choose one of three methods of having the jury resolve fact issues. The judge may direct the jury to make findings of fact by answering written interrogatories (a fancy word for questions), or make general findings of fact in a special verdict, or resolve all fact issues in a general verdict by orally declaring their verdict in favor of one party or the other. If the judge decides to use interrogatories in a special verdict, the judge must then apply the law to the jury's findings. The judge does this by making an order that contains the "court's conclusions of law." Courts greatly favor using special verdicts.

Congress has authorized each federal district court to appoint one or more **magistrate judges** to assist with the court's business. Each judge has at least one magistrate judge to assist him or her with the court's business. The judges select and hire the magistrate judges. A magistrate judge must have been admitted to practice in the state for at least five years before the appointment and cannot be related to any of the judges by blood or marriage. A magistrate judge exercises many of a judge's powers. Specifically, magistrate judges may hear and decide pretrial motions. They may preside over scheduling conferences and pretrial conferences. A magistrate judge may conduct hearings and make proposed findings for a judge to consider and adopt. For example, a party's motion to exclude evidence may require a hearing. A magistrate judge could conduct the hearing, make findings, and make recommendations to the judge, but the ultimate responsibility for deciding the issue remains with the judge. Parties may even stipulate to have their case tried by a magistrate judge with or without a jury. In that event, the magistrate judge may handle every aspect of the case, including posttrial motions and entry of judgment.

After the verdict has been rendered and the judge rules on the posttrial motions, the judge must order entry of a judgment. The judgment resolves the parties' legal rights and obligations concerning the transaction or occurrence in question. The trial court's order for entry of a judgment is usually its last act in the case. A trial court's judgment is final, unless one or more of the parties appeal from the judgment to an appellate court.

magistrate judge A federal magistrate judge has authority to hear and determine pretrial motions, to conduct hearings, including evidentiary hearings, and to submit to the supervising judge proposed findings of facts, conclusions of law, and recommendations for disposition of pending matters.

Appellate Courts

An appellate court's role is to supervise trial courts and make sure that trial courts follow the law, apply the law correctly, and do not abuse their discretionary powers. Once in a while, an appellate court may have to rule on the constitutionality of a law or procedure. Trial court judges have great latitude in deciding how to conduct trials because there are so many unique problems that require a judge to be creative and use judgment. An appealing party—the **"appellant"**—may not have any difficulty identifying the alleged errors that occurred in the trial but may have considerable difficulty persuading the appellate court that the error did not fall within the trial court's broad discretion. Furthermore, the appellant must show that the alleged error was prejudicial to the outcome of the case. Because appellate courts have the ultimate power to determine questions of law and the trial courts have sole responsibility for resolving fact issues, an appellate court will not set aside a jury's verdict or judge's findings of fact if there is some evidence to support the findings. Appellate courts never take testimony to resolve issues before them—in other words, witnesses are never allowed to testify. Only rarely will an appellate court receive new evidence in the form of exhibits.

appellant An aggrieved party who appeals to a higher court to review the proceedings of the trial court's order or judgment on the grounds that the trial court committed an error of law or procedural errors that adversely affected the outcome.

The overriding principle for appellate courts is the so-called unitary appeal (i.e., a one case, one appeal). Without such a rule, cases in the district court might never be concluded because one party or the other might choose to appeal each of the judge's dozens or even hundreds or thousands of individual rulings. Therefore, although there are limited exceptions, parties must wait to the final conclusion in the district court—usually the entry of a judgment that finally resolves all issues— before they may appeal to an appellate court. Even when a party (lawyer) knows that the district court has made a serious error and duly objects to the error, the trial must proceed to a conclusion. Then, after the trial is over and a judgment has been entered in the judgment book, the complaining party may appeal.

Appellate courts reverse trial judges for an abuse of discretion only when the abuse is clear and prejudicial to the outcome of the case. For example, trial judges have broad discretion in determining whether a witness qualifies to testify as an expert. It is common for appellate courts to state in their published opinions that the appellate court might have ruled differently than the trial court did on the admissibility of the evidence but that the trial judge's ruling is affirmed because it was not clearly wrong.

appellee A party against whom an appeal is taken. The party who seeks to sustain the trial court's order or judgment.

The appellant and **appellee** (respondent) must submit briefs that discuss the legal issues raised by the appeal. The format for briefs is strictly structured. A brief must contain a clear statement of each legal issue, a concise, accurate statement of the facts that gave rise to the issues, and an argument on the law. A brief should conclude with a statement that tells the court what relief or result the party wants. An appellate court's rules may or may not provide for oral argument to supplement the written briefs. An oral argument gives the appellate judges an opportunity to have a dialogue with the attorneys.

Appellate procedures are quite technical and discourage laypersons from attempting to prosecute their own appeals. Many appellate court decisions are published so that other litigants may obtain guidance from the precedent they establish. The publication of appellate court decisions, called opinions, is another check within the judicial system to keep courts responsible to the parties and to all citizens.

Jurisdiction

The term *jurisdiction* is synonymous with the "authority" and "power" of a court. A court's authority to determine legal rights and to enforce its decrees is limited to its jurisdiction. A court can act only within the scope of its jurisdiction. The government that created a court prescribes the court's jurisdiction. But, of course, a court cannot have power any greater than the government that created it. Jurisdiction is a very pragmatic concept that limits and shapes litigation. Every court is subject to some jurisdictional limits, including the United States Supreme Court. When a court acts beyond its jurisdiction, its orders, legal process, judgments, or decrees are void and unenforceable. Therefore, before a lawyer commences a civil action, the lawyer must determine which courts have jurisdiction over the subject matter of the dispute. Then the lawyer must determine whether the court can obtain jurisdiction over all the necessary parties. A defendant's lawyer must consider whether the court the plaintiff chose really does have jurisdiction and whether to challenge the court's jurisdiction. Frequently, more than one court could have jurisdiction. If so, the plaintiff's lawyer has the option of choosing the "best court" for the case. There are rules and guidelines for doing that.

Jurisdiction may generally be divided into two categories: **personal jurisdiction** over the parties and **subject matter jurisdiction.** A court must have jurisdiction in both respects to have jurisdiction over a case. Jurisdiction over the subject matter is a primary concern. When a case is commenced, the judge who handles it has a duty to review it for the purpose of determining whether his or her court has jurisdiction to proceed. If it appears the court does not have jurisdiction, the judge must order the parties to show cause why the court should not dismiss the case for lack of jurisdiction over the subject matter. For example, a suit based upon the subject matter of federal Social Security rights would not be within the jurisdiction of a state's probate court. The probate judge should recognize this—in the unlikely event that the parties do not—and dismiss the case. When a court raises the issue and acts on it, the court is said to act sua sponte, which means "of itself, without being prompted."

A court's jurisdiction is also subject to some territorial or geographical limitations. The usual territorial limits is a state's borders. As a general rule,[2] a court may obtain jurisdiction over a defendant only if the defendant is served with a summons and complaint within the state in which the court functions. One of the important exceptions is that a defendant may be served outside the state if the lawsuit arises out of the defendant's activity within the state, such as doing business there, or if the defendant was involved in an occurrence within the state, or is a citizen of the state. The territorial limitation on a court's jurisdiction also may concern the subject of the lawsuit. For example, a court cannot determine the legal rights of parties to property located in another state. Also, a court could not determine the voting rights of citizens in another state, or the constitutional rights afforded by the constitution of another state. A court obtains limited jurisdiction over a person who has been served with a summons and complaint outside the court's territory and that person comes to the jurisdiction solely to contest the court's jurisdiction. If the person succeeds in objecting to the court's jurisdiction, the court has no jurisdiction, and the plaintiff cannot use the person's presence in the state as a basis for obtaining jurisdiction.

Exhibit 3.2 illustrates that a court must have jurisdiction over the parties' persons, jurisdiction over the subject matter, and the matter must be within the courts territorial limits for a court to have jurisdiction over a case.

personal jurisdiction A court's jurisdiction or authority over a person, obtained through due process.

subject matter jurisdiction Jurisdiction over the type case and the subject of the litigation.

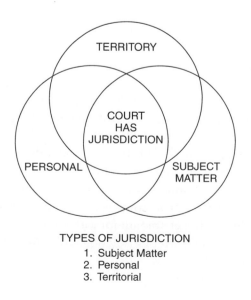

TYPES OF JURISDICTION
1. Subject Matter
2. Personal
3. Territorial

EXHIBIT 3.2

Jurisdiction Requirements

Subject Matter Jurisdiction

Subject matter jurisdiction is an esoteric concept. In general, subject matter jurisdiction relates to the type of case. As mentioned, the authority that created the court may decide what kinds of cases the court may handle. By way of example, most small claims courts may handle cases involving claims for about $15,000 or less. Therefore, if the plaintiff claims a loss in excess of the allowed amount, the small claims court does not have subject matter jurisdiction to decide the case. Similarly, probate courts that deal with trusts and estates do not have subject matter jurisdiction to handle personal-injury cases.

A court has subject matter jurisdiction if the parties' claims are the type that the court is authorized to handle and the dispute concerns something over which the court has power to make a determination. All courts have some limits on the types of cases they may handle. Factors that may affect a court's jurisdiction over a case include the type of dispute, the amount of money damages claimed, the kind of remedy the plaintiff seeks, or whether the cause of action is within the court's territorial limits. There can be other factors too, but these are the principal ones. State district courts ordinarily have the broadest subject matter jurisdiction. Consequently, they are often described as **courts of general jurisdiction.** They may handle actions to recover money damages in any amount, actions to determine ownership of land, marital dissolution actions, and so forth. But state courts do not have jurisdiction over the United States government or any of its agencies. And state courts are not authorized to handle some causes of action created by federal statutes. All civil actions involving the United States must be brought in a federal court, usually a federal district court. For example, the United States government permits individuals to sue the government to recover money damages for some torts perpetrated by federal employees, but those cases must be brought in federal court. Nor may state courts litigate disputes between states. For example, North Carolina cannot sue South Carolina in a state court. One state may obtain jurisdiction over another state only in a federal court. Federal courts, however, do not have jurisdiction over divorce cases, adoptions, actions to determine title to real estate, or probate contests.

A defendant cannot do anything to give a court jurisdiction over the subject matter of the case. Subject matter jurisdiction may be challenged at any time, even after entry of judgment. Yes, it has happened that the parties have gone all the way through a trial and an appeal only to discover the trial court did not have jurisdiction, and its judgment was a nullity.

The amount of money damages claimed in the plaintiff's complaint may affect a court's subject matter jurisdiction. We have seen the example of small claims courts, where the exact dollar limit is prescribed by statute and varies from state to state. Another example is federal district court diversity-of-citizenship cases,[3] where the amount in controversy must *exceed* $75,000. Federal district courts do not have jurisdiction to handle claims for $75,000 or less, even if the parties are not from the same state. Congress decided it did not want federal district courts to spend time on smaller cases. And the parties cannot avoid the jurisdictional requirement by agreement or otherwise. If the amount in controversy is $75,000 or less, it would be a fraud on the court to feign a larger amount for the purpose of trying to give the federal court jurisdiction. Subject matter jurisdiction is discussed later as part of the discussion of court organization.

courts of general jurisdiction Courts that have the broadest subject matter jurisdiction. They may handle actions to recover money damages in any amount, actions to determine ownership of land, marital dissolution actions, and so forth.

Personal Jurisdiction

Personal jurisdiction concerns a court's jurisdiction over the parties, whether individuals, partnerships, corporations, trusts, governmental agencies, or other legal entities. Normally, there is no issue about a court's jurisdiction over a plaintiff, because the plaintiff voluntarily submits to the court's jurisdiction by commencing an action in the court. Personal jurisdiction depends on two factors. First, the defendant must be within the territorial limits of the court in which an action is brought or be subject to extraterritorial jurisdiction. With a few exceptions, courts do not have authority beyond their territorial limits. Second, the plaintiff must serve[4] a summons and complaint, or other legal process, on the defendant in the manner provided by law.

A court has jurisdiction over everyone who is physically within its territory, which is usually a state. A state court has jurisdiction over the citizens of the state—even while the citizens are absent from the state. Federal courts have jurisdiction over United States citizens even when they are in a foreign country. A corporation is subject to personal jurisdiction in the state where it is incorporated. A corporation is also subject to jurisdiction of courts in states where it conducts its business. A corporation does business in the states where it has factories, offices, and other facilities. So state district courts and federal district courts have jurisdiction over everyone who is in the state while in the state. In addition, a court has jurisdiction over anyone who consents to jurisdiction whether or not the person is in the state.

There are two interesting exceptions to the general rule that a court has personal jurisdiction over anyone who is within the state (district). First, a defendant who has been served with process outside the state or by publication may *appear specially* in the state to contest jurisdiction. In the previous example, if the process server failed to follow proper procedures, Smith could go back to Minnesota and present evidence to show that the Minnesota court does not have jurisdiction. Being within Minnesota for that special purpose would not subject Smith to Minnesota's jurisdiction. Similarly, a witness who is appearing in court under compulsion of a court order or subpoena is not subject to the state's jurisdiction for any other purpose while in the state.

Second, a person may knowingly consent to a court's jurisdiction, as where a corporation registers to do business in a state, or may give implied consent to jurisdiction.

EXAMPLE

The Tasty Pork Company is a Minnesota meat processor. Smith is a farmer and resident of Iowa. The Tasty Pork Company claims Smith defaulted on a contract to sell some hogs to it. The contract was made in Iowa and the hogs were to be delivered in Iowa for shipment by truck. Tasty Pork would have to go to an Iowa court to obtain jurisdiction over Smith. But suppose that Smith traveled to Minnesota to show some prize hogs at the Minnesota State Fair. If Tasty Pork's process server could find Smith in Minnesota and serve a summons and complaint on Smith in Minnesota, a Minnesota district court would have jurisdiction over Smith.

EXAMPLE

Suppose two Californians are traveling in an automobile through Nevada when they are involved in a collision. The passenger is injured. The driver returns to California immediately after the accident, but the passenger decides to remain in Nevada. The passenger may bring the personal injury action in Nevada. The Nevada courts have jurisdiction because the driver consented to jurisdiction by using Nevada's highways. The lawsuit could also be brought in California where the driver lives.

Implied consent to jurisdiction is a little esoteric but very pragmatic. We already discussed the situation where a corporation consents to jurisdiction because it has chosen to do business in the state. All states provide by statute that when a person from another state uses its highways and has an accident in the state, the nonresident consents the state's courts jurisdiction. Consent to jurisdiction is by operation of law and meets all the due process requirements. The practical effect is that the plaintiff may have the court's summons and complaint served on the nonresident in his or her own state. And the nonresident is subject to the court's jurisdiction.

The cause of action originates in the territory where the accident occurred, Nevada, but it follows the defendant when the defendant goes to another jurisdiction. Consequently, the plaintiff can sue the defendant driver in any state where he can be found.

Causes of action in tort and breach of contract follow defendants to other jurisdictions. When the plaintiff follows the defendant to another state and brings the action there, the defendant may counterclaim against the plaintiff for any claim the defendant has that arose from the same transaction or occurrence. But the defendant is not permitted to counterclaim for some unrelated cause of action.

In the previous illustration, the nonresident motorist appoints the state commissioner of highways to be the motorist's agent to receive service of process for any motor vehicle accident in which he or she is involved within the state. All states have such statutes. So the plaintiff passenger may serve the summons and complaint on the Nevada Commissioner of Highways. Due process requires the plaintiff to mail a copy of the summons and complaint to the nonresident motorist at that person's last known address. Through this procedure, state courts obtain jurisdiction over nonresident drivers.

A court obtains jurisdiction over the person of the defendant through service of a summons and complaint upon him or her. This is called *service of process*. The summons informs the defendant that the lawsuit has been commenced and instructs the defendant to appear in the case by serving and filing an answer to the complaint. The summons and complaint identify the court. If the defendant fails to appear by answering the complaint, the plaintiff may take a default judgment against the defendant. The most common method of service is to hand the summons and complaint to the defendant. Depending on circumstances, process may be served using other methods. Service of process is discussed in Chapter 6.

When an attempted service of process is defective, the court fails to obtain personal jurisdiction over the defendant. The defendant may ignore the defective service, challenge the court's jurisdiction by making a motion for dismissal, or voluntarily submit to the court's jurisdiction. If the defendant ignores the aborted service, it is likely the plaintiff will take a default judgment against the defendant. Then the defendant will have to challenge jurisdiction when the plaintiff tries to enforce the judgment. Meanwhile, the judgment becomes a matter of public record and may cause the defendant some inconvenience. If service of process proves to be valid, however, the defendant will be bound by the default judgment. Needless to say, it is risky to ignore service of a summons and complaint. It is better to resolve jurisdictional issues at the outset.

Unlike a defect in subject matter jurisdiction, which can never be waived or ignored, the lack of personal jurisdiction is an affirmative defense, which the defendant may waive. The waiver may be intentional or inadvertent. A defendant submits to a court's jurisdiction by appearing in the case without objecting to jurisdiction. Defendants often waive personal jurisdiction defects resulting from improper service of process because the technical defects that impaired jurisdiction usually can be cured, and there is no sense in making the litigation more complicated or expensive.

In recent years, the concept of due process of law has been expanded to permit states to enact so-called long-arm statutes for protection of its citizens. Long-arm statutes give states the power to reach persons in other states and exercise jurisdiction over them when nonresidents commit torts within the state. Under the long-arm statutes, courts obtain personal jurisdiction over manufacturers and vendors who commit torts within the state even though they do not do business in the state. Process may be served on a foreign corporation by serving the Secretary of State. Generally, whether a person from another state is subject to service of process under a so-called long-arm statute—thereby coming within a court's personal jurisdiction over him or her—depends on whether the circumstances giving rise to the suit make it fundamentally fair for the person to defend himself or herself in that other state. This fundamental fairness is another term for due process.

EXAMPLE

Suppose two Californians are traveling in an automobile through Nevada when they are involved in a collision. The passenger is injured. The driver returns to California immediately after the accident, but the passenger decides to remain in Nevada. The passenger decides to bring a personal injury action in Nevada. The passenger arranges for service of a summons and complaint on the Nevada Commissioner of Highways but provides the Commissioner with the wrong address in California. Nevertheless, the driver does receive the copy in California. Service is defective. The Nevada court does not have jurisdiction, because service of process is defective. But the driver may waive the jurisdictional defect by interposing an answer to the complaint without objecting to jurisdiction.

Example

The XYZ Corporation made a defective part that went into a snowmobile engine. The engine was installed in a snowmobile by the Fast Track Snowmobile Company, which is located in Wisconsin. The snowmobile was shipped to Wyoming and sold to the plaintiff there. Soon after purchasing the snowmobile it exploded and injured the plaintiff. The plaintiff wants to sue the XYZ Corporation in Wyoming. The tort occurred where the injury occurred. Even though the XYZ Corporation does not do business in Wyoming, it is subject to Wyoming service of process under Wyoming's long-arm statute.

The plaintiff could serve the summons and complaint on the Wyoming Secretary of State who, in turn, would mail a copy to the XYZ Corporation at the address given by the plaintiff. In addition, due process requires the plaintiff to mail a copy of the summons and complaint to the XYZ Corporation at its registered office or principal place of business. In that way, the foreign corporation can be required to defend itself in the state where the consumer's injury occurred. If the plaintiff consumer moves to another state, the cause of action does not follow the consumer. The suit must be brought in the state where the product was sold or the injury occurred or where the defendant corporation conducts its business as of the time of service.

In this section, we have been talking about state district courts obtaining personal jurisdiction in various ways. Federal district courts have statewide jurisdiction. Therefore, if a federal court has subject matter jurisdiction, the plaintiff may be able to obtain personal jurisdiction over the defendant in federal court on the same bases discussed above.

Subpoenas

A court cannot require a nonparty to do anything until the court obtains jurisdiction over him or her. To give a court jurisdiction over a nonparty, someone must serve a subpoena on the nonparty. A subpoena gives the court personal jurisdiction over a nonparty. But jurisdiction is limited to the one case and is further limited in time, scope, and purpose. The subpoena must state the name of the action in which the nonparty is to appear, the purpose for the nonparty's appearance, the time, and place. A subpoena may require a nonparty to appear at a trial to give testimony and/or to produce exhibits. A subpoena may be used to require a nonparty to appear for an oral deposition for purposes of discovery or to preserve the person's testimony for use at trial at a later date. A subpoena may be used to require the custodian of documents to produce the documents for the parties to inspect and copy. It may be used to require the possessor of real estate to allow the parties to examine and photograph the real estate. Of course, this assumes the real estate and documents are relevant to the parties' civil action. Usually it is not necessary to subpoena an actual party because parties are already subject to the court's jurisdiction. However, a party must comply with a subpoena, the same as anyone else.

A signed subpoena form may be obtained from the clerk of the federal district court where the trial is to be held, the deposition taken, or the inspection conducted. The clerk will sign the subpoena but, otherwise, it is in blank. You will have to complete it for service. An attorney who is admitted to practice in the court may issue a subpoena by signing it instead of the clerk of court.

A subpoena must identify the court from which the subpoena is issued and state the title of the action in which the nonparty is to appear. When the court that issues the subpoena is not the same as the one in which the action is pending, the latter must be identified.[5] A subpoena must state the case number and the time, place, and purpose for the nonparty's appearance. The purposes may include the following:

1. To testify at trial.
2. To testify at a hearing.
3. To testify in an oral deposition.
4. To testify in a deposition on written questions.
5. To produce documents for inspection and copying.
6. To produce tangible things for inspection and nondestructive testing.
7. To provide entrance to real estate for inspection and photographing.

A subpoena may combine a mandate for inspection and copying with a mandate to testify. But if the events are to take place at different times and places, it is better to serve two subpoenas. A subpoena must advise the nonparty that any failure to comply with the subpoena subjects him or her to the penalties of law.

The procedure for obtaining and serving a subpoena is simple. As a paralegal, you may prepare the notice for taking the nonparty's deposition, but an attorney must sign it. You must serve a copy of the notice on each party, as described previously. You must file the original notice with the clerk of court with a proof of service. The clerk of court will give you a subpoena form to complete. (See Exhibit 3.3.) Rule 45(a)(3) provides:

> The clerk shall issue a subpoena, signed but otherwise in blank, to a party requesting it, who shall complete it before service. An attorney as officer of the court may also issue and sign a subpoena on behalf of (A) a court in which the attorney is authorized to practice; or (B) a court for a district in which a deposition or production is compelled by the subpoena, if the deposition or production pertains to an action pending in a court in which the attorney is authorized to practice.

When a nonparty corporation is subpoenaed, the subpoena must clearly inform the corporation of its duty to respond by designating someone to appear at the deposition on its behalf. The person who appears must be able to speak for the organization concerning the subject matter clearly described in the subpoena. The subpoena may cite and quote the rule.

Any person who is not a party and is not less than 18 years of age may serve a subpoena. It must be delivered to the deponent along with a witness fee for one day's attendance and a mileage fee as set by statute. A subpoena is served by *delivering* it to the person named in the subpoena. Delivery is tantamount to handing it to him or

EXHIBIT 3.3 *Subpoena Form*

AO 88 (Rev. 1/94) Subpoena in a Civil Case

Issued by the
UNITED STATES DISTRICT COURT

DISTRICT OF _____

SUBPOENA IN A CIVIL CASE

V.

CASE NUMBER:[1]

TO:

☐ YOU ARE COMMANDED to appear in the United States District Court at the place, date, and time specified below to testify in the above case.

PLACE OF TESTIMONY	COURTROOM
	DATE AND TIME

☐ YOU ARE COMMANDED to appear at the place, date, and time specified below to testify at the taking of a deposition in the above case.

PLACE OF DEPOSITION	DATE AND TIME

☐ YOU ARE COMMANDED to produce and permit inspection and copying of the following documents or objects at the place, date, and time specified below (list documents or objects):

PLACE	DATE AND TIME

☐ YOU ARE COMMANDED to permit inspection of the following premises at the date and time specified below.

PREMISES	DATE AND TIME

Any organization not a party to this suit that is subpoenaed for the taking of a deposition shall designate one or more officers, directors, or managing agents, or other persons who consent to testify on its behalf, and may set forth, for each person designated, the matters on which the person will testify. Federal Rules of Civil Procedure, 30(b)(6).

ISSUING OFFICER SIGNATURE AND TITLE (INDICATE IF ATTORNEY FOR PLAINTIFF OR DEFENDANT)	DATE

ISSUING OFFICER'S NAME, ADDRESS AND PHONE NUMBER

(See Rule 45, Federal Rules of Civil Procedure, Parts C & D on Reverse)

[1] If action is pending in district other than district of issuance, state district under case number.

continued

PROOF OF SERVICE

	DATE	PLACE
SERVED		

SERVED ON (PRINT NAME)		MANNER OF SERVICE

SERVED BY (PRINT NAME)		TITLE

DECLARATION OF SERVER

I declare under penalty of perjury under the laws of the United States of America that the foregoing information contained in the Proof of Service is true and correct.

Executed on _____
                    DATE

_____
SIGNATURE OF SERVER

_____
ADDRESS OF SERVER

_____

Rule 45, Federal Rules of Civil Procedure, Parts C & D:

(c) PROTECTION OF PERSONS SUBJECT TO SUBPOENAS.

(1)   A party or an attorney responsible for the issuance and service of a subpoena shall take reasonable steps to avoid imposing undue burden or expense on a person subject to that subpoena. The court on behalf of which the subpoena was issued shall enforce this duty and impose upon the party or attorney in breach of this duty an appropriate sanction, which may include, but is not limited to, lost earnings and a reasonable attorney's fee.

(2)(A) A person commanded to produce and permit inspection and copying of designated books, papers, documents or tangible things, or inspection of premises need not appear in person at the place of production or inspection unless commanded to appear for deposition, hearing or trial.

(B) Subject to paragraph (d)(2) of this rule, a person commanded to produce and permit inspection and copying may, within 14 days after service of the subpoena or before the time specified for compliance if such time is less than 14 days after service, serve upon the party or attorney designated in the subpoena written objection to inspection or copying of any or all of the designated materials or of the premises. If objection is made, the party serving the subpoena shall not be entitled to inspect and copy the materials or inspect the premises except pursuant to an order of the court by which the subpoena was issued. If objection has been made, the party serving the subpoena may, upon notice to the person commanded to produce, move at any time for an order to compel the production.   Such an order to compel production shall protect any person who is not a party or an officer of a party from significant expense resulting from the inspection and copying commanded.

(3)(A) On timely motion, the court by which a subpoena was issued shall quash or modify the subpoena if it

(i)   fails to allow reasonable time for compliance;

(ii) requires a person who is not a party or an officer of a party to travel to a place more than 100 miles from the place where that person resides, is employed or regularly transacts business in person, except that, subject to the

provisions of clause (c)(3)(B)(iii) of this rule, such a person may in order to attend trial be commanded to travel from any such place within the state in which the trial is held, or

(iii) requires disclosure of privileged or other protected matter and no exception or waiver applies, or

(iv) subjects a person to undue burden.

(B) If a subpoena

(i)   requires disclosure of a trade secret or other confidential research, development, or commercial information, or

(ii) requires disclosure of an unretained expert's opinion or information not describing specific events or occurrences in dispute and resulting from the expert's study made not at the request of any party, or

(iii) requires a person who is not a party or an officer of a party to incur substantial expense to travel more than 100 miles to attend trial, the court may, to protect a person subject to or affected by the subpoena, quash or modify the subpoena, or, if the party in whose behalf the subpoena is issued shows a substantial need for the testimony or material that cannot be otherwise met without undue hardship and assures that the person to whom the subpoena is addressed will be reasonably compensated, the court may order appearance or production only upon specified conditions.

(d) DUTIES IN RESPONDING TO SUBPOENA.

(1) A person responding to a subpoena to produce documents shall produce them as they are kept in the usual course of business or shall organize and label them to correspond with the categories in the demand.

(2) When information subject to a subpoena is withheld on a claim that it is privileged or subject to protection as trial preparation materials, the claim shall be made expressly and shall be supported by a description of the nature of the documents, communications, or things not produced that is sufficient to enable the demanding party to contest the claim.

her. A person cannot evade service by turning his or her back on the process server. If that were to happen, the process server should just leave the subpoena and fee in the named person's presence. When a respondent fails to appear, some remedial action may be necessary. The first step is for you to prepare and file with the court a "proof of service." A proof of service is titled the same as the subpoena. It states the time, place, and circumstances of service. The process server must sign the proof of service under oath. The subpoena gives the court jurisdiction over the named person, so the court can order a United States marshal to arrest the violator and bring him or her before the court for punishment.

A subpoena may be served on a nonparty anywhere within the federal court district (state) that issued the subpoena. In addition, a federal subpoena may be served "at any place without [outside] the district that is within 100 miles of the place of the deposition, hearing, trial, production, or inspection specified in the subpoena" [Rule 45(b)(2)]. Subject to the "100 mile rule," the court in which the inspection or deposition is to take place must issue the subpoena.

Litigants must be careful not to abuse nonparties. Indeed, courts are particularly protective of nonparties. Rule 45(c)(1) provides for the following:

> A party or an attorney responsible for the issuance and service of a subpoena shall take reasonable steps to avoid imposing undue burden or expense on a person subject to that subpoena. The court on behalf of which the subpoena was issued shall enforce this duty and impose upon the party or attorney in breach of this duty an appropriate sanction, which may include, but is not limited to, lost earnings and a reasonable attorney's fee.

When a person is subpoenaed to produce records for inspection and copying, the person must produce the records in the form and condition in which they are ordinarily kept. But if the subpoena asks to have the records organized and categorized in a particular manner, so as to make them easier to use and understand, the respondent should try to comply. A respondent has fourteen days in which to serve a written objection to a subpoena's requirements for production. If the subpoena has allowed less than fourteen days, the written objection should be served before the time scheduled for production. The written objection may state generally the grounds for objecting. Grounds include the need for protection of privileged communications, protection of trade secrets, protection of unretained expert[6] opinions, or a requirement that a nonparty travel more than 100 miles for the production. The written objection automatically stays enforcement of the subpoena. The party who caused the subpoena to be served may then move the court for an order compelling the respondent to comply with the subpoena. If the court does order production, the court should make sure the order provides appropriate protections to the nonparty-respondent.

If the person named in the subpoena finds the subpoena's requirements too burdensome, he or she may move the court to quash the subpoena. Some of the grounds for quashing a subpoena include the following: (1) it has not given the deponent sufficient time to comply; (2) it requires the nonparty to travel more than 100 miles from his or her place of residence or employment; (3) it requires disclosure of matters that are privileged or otherwise protected; (4) it is simply too burdensome. The fourth factor is a "catchall" that gives courts broad discretion and power to help nonparties. A motion to quash should be scheduled as soon as possible. The parties should try to meet a nonparty's concerns whenever a nonparty complains about litigation proceedings.

No one wants to be subpoenaed for a deposition or a trial. Subpoenas tend to scare people. Consequently, a lawyer runs a significant risk of alienating a witness by serving a subpoena on her or him. It is a good idea to personally explain to the witness before the subpoena is served why the subpoena is being used. If a better reason cannot be found, the witness can be told that the Federal Rules of Civil Procedure require it. A witness may be more comfortable if you explain that, in case of an emergency, she or he can obtain a release from the subpoena by contacting the lawyer who issued it. The lawyer's name and address are on the subpoena. If the witness has cogent reason for being unable to appear, other arrangements can be made.

Federal Court Organization

The United States Constitution created the United States Supreme Court and established that Court's jurisdiction. Congress cannot abridge the Supreme Court's jurisdiction. Congress created all other federal courts and determined their authority and powers. State legislatures created state courts and thus may change the structure and functions of state courts through legislation. For example, a state legislature may add more judges, may redefine judicial districts, may abolish courts, and may establish new courts—such as a new intermediate appellate court. In most states, the highest appellate court was created by the state's constitution, and therefore the state legislature cannot modify the powers of that court. A "constitutional" court usually has been given authority to supervise lower courts in its state, including propounding rules and disciplining judges.

The United States Constitution, Article III, provides that the judicial powers of the United States are vested in the Supreme Court and in such lower courts as Congress establishes through the legislative process. As authorized, Congress created two levels of lower courts. Congress created a district court for each state and for each United States territorial possession. Congress structured the district courts and established their jurisdictions. Each district court has one or more divisions, and each division is located in a different city and has its own courthouse. Almost all federal cases originate in the district courts. The district courts conduct trials, and the trials lead to entry of a judgment that determines the parties' ultimate legal rights and obligations. Most cases conclude at the district court level.

The second level of courts created by Congress consists of eleven circuit courts of appeal, and the Circuit Court of Appeals at Washington, D.C. Exhibit 1.1 shows the circuit courts' territories. Each circuit court serves as an intermediate appellate court for several district courts. By way of example, the Ninth Circuit serves the federal district courts in Alaska, Arizona, California, Hawaii, Idaho, Montana, Nevada, Oregon, and Washington. The circuit courts of appeal handle appellate matters; they do not handle trials. A party who believes that the district court committed error may appeal from the district court judgment to the circuit court of appeals for that jurisdiction.

Federal Jurisdiction

The federal judicial system has the power (i.e., subject matter jurisdiction) to hear and decide civil lawsuits that arise under the United States Constitution, treaties, and federal laws. Federal courts also have the power to adjudicate cases between two or more states. Federal courts have authority to interpret the meaning and scope of federal laws, including the United States Constitution. The Supreme Court may determine whether a federal statute was properly enacted so that it may become law. Federal courts have authority to determine whether state statutes comport with the United States Constitution and whether the manner in which a state statute has been applied is constitutional. Congress decided that the Supreme Court should participate in establishing the Rules of Civil Procedure by which the lower courts conduct their business. Congress, therefore, enacted enabling legislation authorizing the Supreme Court to promulgate the Federal Rules of Civil Procedure.

Any action against the United States government or any of its agencies must be brought in a federal district court. In addition, federal district courts may be used to bring actions against foreign governments, against the government of another state, or against a corporation incorporated in a foreign country. If the case is not subject to federal jurisdiction, the plaintiff must resort to a state court.

Federal Diversity-of-Citizenship Jurisdiction

In addition to the types of jurisdiction discussed above, federal district courts are authorized to hear cases between citizens of different states if the amount in controversy exceeds $75,000, without regard to the type of case. Such cases are commonly referred to as "diversity cases." Because diversity-of-citizenship jurisdiction can bring some atypical matters into federal court—a car accident case, for example—a large body of law has developed concerning **diversity of citizenship** requisites to federal jurisdiction. As an illustration of diversity, suppose two Texans are involved in an automobile accident in Texas and decide to sue each other to obtain money damages for personal injuries. They cannot bring their actions against each other in the federal district court for Texas. But if one of the parties were from Arkansas, then there would be diversity of citizenship, which would permit an action in federal district court, assuming the amount in controversy exceeds $75,000. Remember, even though a diversity of citizenship exists, if the claim is for a sum of $75,000 or less, a federal district court does not have subject matter jurisdiction. This limitation is imposed by federal statute, not by the Constitution.

In cases arising from transactions, such as an action on a contract or promissory note, there is no problem determining whether the controversy involves more than $75,000. However, cases that arise from personal injury and property damage claims are more difficult to evaluate for purposes of jurisdiction. As a rule of thumb, courts and parties look to the amount of special damages[7] and the "apparent" seriousness of the injuries. If there is evidence of a significant permanent disability caused by a personal injury, federal courts usually accept jurisdiction. However, individual federal judges may differ on how stringently they apply this limitation on jurisdiction. If a case goes through trial and the jury determines that full compensation should be less than $75,000, federal district courts allow entry of judgment for the amount of the verdict, even though the award is below the jurisdictional amount. The monetary limitation does not cause the court to lose jurisdiction retroactively, because it

diversity of citizenship   A basis for federal district courts to obtain jurisdiction of a civil lawsuit when the amount in controversy exceeds $75,000. The plaintiff and the defendant must have their domiciles in different states at the time the action is commenced.

is the amount in controversy, not the amount ultimately awarded—which can be zero—that confers diversity jurisdiction.

Venue

Occasionally, more than one district court has jurisdiction of a case. In that event, the courts and parties must decide which court is the best **venue** for the case. The term *venue* refers to the geographic area from which the jury is selected, such as a county, municipality, or state. The term *venue* identifies the jurisdiction or place where a case is to be tried. The rules for determining the proper venue center on which venue is most convenient for all the parties and the witnesses. Usually, an action should be brought in the venue in which the cause of action accrued. In tort actions, the cause of action usually accrues where the injury or loss occurs. In contract cases, the cause of action accrues where the breach occurred—usually the place where the contract was to be performed. If the contract was not performed at all, the cause of action may accrue in the venue where the contract was made. Also, contracts may anticipate the possibility of litigation and designate what state's laws will apply and where any action on the contract shall be brought.[8] In cases involving title or possession of real estate, the cause of action accrues in the venue in which the real estate is located.

The plaintiff selects a venue when he or she commences the action by filing the complaint. If the defendant believes the plaintiff selected the wrong venue, the defendant must make a demand for a change of venue within the time specified by law—usually before the answer is due. Otherwise, the defendant waives the right to have the case heard in the proper venue. Some of the factors that determine jurisdiction and the proper venue may be similar, but the two terms involve quite different concepts. The basic difference is that jurisdiction relates to the court's authority, and venue relates to the physical place for trial of the action.

Federal Circuit Courts of Appeals

An aggrieved party may appeal to a federal circuit court of appeals from a district court judgment or final decision. The appeal is taken to the circuit court of appeals that serves the area in which the trial court is located. The mere fact that the appellant is unhappy with the judgment and thinks that the jury misunderstood the evidence is not a basis for an appeal. Instead, the appellant must demonstrate that the trial court committed an error of law that may have affected the outcome of the case. The error of law may have been in using the wrong rule of law, in misapplying a rule of law, or in committing some procedural error. An error is considered prejudicial only if it adversely affected the outcome of the case. An error must be prejudicial to be the basis of a successful appeal. A federal district court case cannot be appealed to a state court.

United States Supreme Court

The Supreme Court is an appellate court. Nevertheless, it has original jurisdiction in a few kinds of disputes.[9] Relatively few cases are appealed to the Supreme Court. There are very few cases in which a party has a right to have the United States Supreme Court take the appeal. Most of the cases that do reach the Supreme Court are accepted as a matter of discretion (i.e., by the Court's choice) pursuant to

venue The judicial district in which an action is brought for trial and that is to furnish the panel of jurors.

writ of certiorari A writ issued by a superior court to a lower court that requires the lower court to transmit its record to the superior court so that the superior court can inspect the proceedings and determine whether any irregularities occurred.

petition for a **writ of certiorari.** The procedure requires the petitioning party to file a brief that explains what the lower courts did, why they were wrong, and why the legal issue has significance beyond the particular case. For example, the petitioner may be able to show that there is disagreement among the lower courts about how a particular rule of law is applied; therefore, the Supreme Court should take the appeal so that it can review the rule of law and resolve the conflict in the lower courts. In that way, the Supreme Court can keep the eleven circuit courts of appeals from developing separate and inconsistent bodies of law. When the Supreme Court deems the issue to be significant to society or to the law in general, it may grant the application by ordering the lower court to send up its file for review. In the vast majority of cases, the Supreme Court declines further review, and the result stands as decided in the circuit court of appeal.

State Court Organization

Most state judicial systems are similar to the federal system. They have a district court that has general jurisdiction and one or more appellate courts. A majority of states have an intermediate appellate court like the federal circuit courts of appeal. In addition, most states have some lower courts that deal with "lesser" cases.

District Courts

State district courts have general jurisdiction. A court of general jurisdiction has authority to grant all remedies available in law and equity. Each district court has power to hear almost any kind of case, regardless of the amount of money in controversy or the type of remedy being sought. In addition to awarding money damages in unlimited amounts, these courts have authority (i.e., subject matter jurisdiction) to issue decrees for adoption, divorce, injunctions, specific performance, and change of name, and to issue judgments determining title to real estate. Courts of limited jurisdiction are not able to provide some of these remedies.

Each district court has statewide jurisdiction; so its subpoenas, orders, and decrees may be enforced anywhere within the state. Nevertheless, each district court operates within a specified territory, usually a county or group of counties. Venue considerations are the same for state district courts as in federal district courts. District courts are courts of record. That means the proceedings are recorded, including all the testimony, the lawyers' arguments and comments, and the judge's orders and comments. The record is public, unless the judge has good reason to order the record "sealed." Each county or parish has a district court with general jurisdiction.

A losing party may appeal directly to an appellate court. Some district court rules provide that if the plaintiff is the prevailing party but recovers a judgment for an amount within the monetary jurisdiction of a small claims court or a county court, the *losing* party may recover her or his costs against the prevailing party. The purpose of the rule is to encourage parties to use the lower courts when possible, and to save the courts of general jurisdiction for the more significant cases. Taxable costs may include the filing fee, witness fees, and charges for service of process.

Small Claims Courts

Small claims courts provide a speedy, inexpensive forum. They are not well suited for cases that involve difficult legal issues. Small claims courts are limited to cases in which the claim is for money damages. Small claims courts vary, but typically are limited to claims of $15,000 or less. They handle a large volume of cases involving claims for property damage, wages, rent, contract damages, and even personal injuries. But the only remedy the small claims courts can provide is an award of money damages. Usually the rules of small claims courts preclude parties from having lawyers represent them, because the objective is to keep trials short and inexpensive. But companies and corporations cannot appear in person, so they must send lawyers to appear on their behalf, if the rules permit it. In some states, a corporation cannot have a lawyer unless it moves the case from small claims court to district court. Most small claims courts have subpoena power, but subpoenas are seldom used. Service of process in small claims courts is kept simple and inexpensive.

The usual procedure is that the plaintiff prepares a sworn complaint in the clerk of court's office. The complaint should contain a short narrative of the plaintiff's version of the facts. The clerk often helps the plaintiff frame the allegations. In particular, the complaint must state the time and place of the occurrence or transaction. The filing fee is nominal. The plaintiff must provide the defendant's mailing address. The clerk mails a copy of the complaint to the defendant along with a notice that directs the defendant to appear in court at a specified time to defend against the allegations. The notice states that if the defendant fails to appear and defend, the plaintiff may take a default judgment against the defendant in the amount specified in the complaint. If the last known address proves to be incorrect, that would be grounds for setting aside a default judgment obtained against the defendant. The defendant is not required to prepare and serve an answer to the complaint. The judge simply assumes that the defendant denies everything. Of course, if the defendant wishes to make a counterclaim, the defendant has to follow the same procedure.

Specialized Courts

Each state has a variety of specialized courts, such as a tax court, probate court, family court (for divorces and adoptions), and workers' compensation court. Each of these courts handles only one type of case. A state's rules may provide for an appeal from those courts to a district court or to an appellate court. The specialized courts do not authorize jury trials and may provide for only limited discovery. Otherwise, their proceedings are conducted much like a district court.

Juries

Courts must have a means for resolving disputed facts. Only then can a court apply the law to resolve the parties' dispute according to law. Courts require parties to present evidence about the facts. The problem is to determine what the evidence proves or what it fails to prove. Judges may also act as fact finders. When a judge tries a case without a jury, the judge decides what evidence to believe and what facts have been proved by the evidence. But if the parties have a jury trial, the jury decides what evidence to believe and determines what facts have been established by the evidence. A jury never decides legal issues or questions of law.

Most litigants seem to want juries to decide their cases, rather than a judge. Many litigants are suspicious of decisions made by one person, regardless of the person's qualifications and apparent conscientiousness. Some lawyers worry that judges may be influenced by their past experience with similar cases or past experience with the lawyers or parties. By contrast, jurors' inexperience allows them to approach a case with a fresh perspective. Jurors do not know the parties or lawyers. Jurors will have little or no experience with particular types of cases. Jurors will probably find the dispute and proceedings to be more interesting than a judge would. Also, most lawyers prefer decisions by group's consensus, rather than by one person. It has been said that the jury system is for losers, because a loser usually finds a jury verdict more palatable than a judge's adverse decision.

Right to Trial by Jury

The United States Constitution and all state constitutions guarantee the right to trial by jury whenever the claim is for money damages. The United States Constitution, Seventh Amendment, states this guarantee:

> In Suits at common law, where the value in controversy shall exceed twenty dollars, the right of trial by jury shall be preserved, and no fact tried by a jury shall be otherwise re-examined in any Court of the United States than according to the rules of the common law.

The constitutional mandate means that parties have a right to *request* a trial by jury whenever the claim is for money damages. If a party fails to request a jury trial, the right to a jury trial is waived. The Constitution does not give parties a right to a jury trial when parties seek **equitable relief,** such as specific performance of a contract or **injunctive relief.** A jury that tries a case, whether criminal or civil, is called a **petit jury.** A petit jury is distinguished from a grand jury, which is an investigatory body that determines whether a crime has been committed and whether a person should be indicted for the crime.

Veniremen

A petit jury is drawn from a panel of **veniremen.** The panel of veniremen is drawn at random from the community as a whole. The veniremen must come from a fair cross section of the community. The method of obtaining veniremen must not discriminate against any class of potential jurors. However, a person must be able to hear and see the evidence to qualify to be a juror. This means a person must be able to understand the English language. Each potential juror must fill out a juror qualification form. Jurors must be citizens of the United States, at least eighteen years of age, able to read and write, able to understand the English language, physically capable of participating, and mentally competent. A person may be disqualified from service if he or she has been convicted of a crime punishable by imprisonment for one year or more or has criminal charges pending against him or her for such a crime. A juror's term of service may not exceed thirty days, unless more time is needed to finish a trial that commenced within the thirty-day period. Federal courts may not call persons for jury duty more than once during any two-year period.

The Jury's Role

A jury's function is to resolve fact issues from the evidence. A jury does not decide questions of law. Jurors are supposed to use their common knowledge and experience to evaluate the evidence. They must determine what the facts are from the evidence.

equitable relief   Redress provided by a court other than money damages. Equitable relief includes remedies such as specific performance, rescission of a contract, reforming a contract, and injunctive relief.

injunctive relief   An order issued by a court ordering someone to do something or prohibiting some act after a court hearing.

petit jury   A jury that tries the facts in a civil action.

venireman   A person who has been selected to undergo questioning to determine whether she or he may qualify to sit on a petit jury.

They may not speculate about the facts. They may not supplement evidence with information they have. For instance, a juror may not assume what happened or how something happened on the basis that he or she had a similar experience. Jurors must find from the evidence that a fact is probably true; otherwise, the fact has not been proved. A jury's verdict is based on the facts that the jurors found from the evidence.

After determining the basic facts concerning the transaction or occurrence, the jury must determine the ultimate questions of fact. In a negligence action, the ultimate facts are determined by asking questions like these: Were the parties negligent? Was a party's negligence the proximate cause of the loss? If both parties were causally negligent, what are their percentages of causal negligence? What sum of money would provide full compensation? In a contract case, the ultimate facts are whether the parties had a valid contract, whether the defendant breached the contract, whether the plaintiff breached the contract, and what sum of money would fairly compensate the plaintiff for loss of the benefits of the contract. The ultimate fact issues are conclusions of fact that are drawn from the basic facts.

The Constitution makes the jury's determination of facts final. The jury's determination, as reflected in its verdict, cannot be set aside merely because the trial judge or the appellate judges disagree with it. The verdict is final, provided there is competent evidence to support it and the verdict is consistent with the law. The trial judge or reviewing judges may be required to determine whether there is sufficient evidence to support the verdict concerning one or more material facts. It takes more than a scintilla (trace) of evidence to prove a fact before a court can sustain a jury's verdict. Furthermore, if, after going through a trial, there is no dispute concerning some controlling fact or facts, there may be nothing for the jury to decide, and the judge can apply the law to resolve the dispute.

A verdict cannot be based on evidence that leaves a disputed fact subject to mere speculation. Suppose the plaintiff's decedent is found dead in a railroad switching yard and was probably struck by a train, but no one knows when or just how the accident happened. If those facts were presented to a jury, the jury could not find that the railroad was negligent or otherwise liable for the accident, because the verdict would be based on mere speculation that the railroad did something wrong. By the same token, a judge's determination that certain evidence is inadmissible may have the effect of keeping an essential fact from being proved. The parties have a right to have the jury decide a fact only when credible evidence supports the fact. Otherwise, the court must resolve the facts against the party who has the burden of proof, usually the plaintiff.

When a case is tried to a judge without a jury, the judge is obligated to make Findings of Fact, Conclusions of Law, and Order for Judgment. (See Exhibit 3.4.) A judge may take months to decide a case and issue the order; whereas, a jury usually decides critical fact issues within a matter of hours or days. Juries help expedite litigation and the court's business by relieving judges of the very taxing function of remembering, reviewing, and evaluating evidence before making a decision. When a case is submitted to a jury on a special verdict, the judge must accept the jury's findings of fact as stated in the verdict. The judge must use those findings as the basis for preparing his or her conclusions of law and order for judgment.

EXHIBIT 3.4   *Sample Findings of Fact, Conclusions of Law, and Order for Judgment*

STATE OF MINNESOTA   **DISTRICT COURT**
COUNTY OF HUBBARD   **THIRD JUDICIAL DISTRICT**

Laura Raskin, Trustee for the heirs
and next of kin of William Nordby,
decedent,

        Plaintiff,   FINDINGS OF FACT
                          CONCLUSIONS OF LAW
    vs.   and
                       ORDER FOR JUDGMENT

Bradley Harper,
        Defendant.

On December 12, 2001, the above entitled matter came before the undersigned for trial by the court without a jury. Attorney Donald Smith, Esq. appeared on behalf of the plaintiff. Attorney William Hoch appeared on behalf of the defendant. The parties rested on December 16, 2000.

The court having heard the evidence and considered the arguments of counsel, and being fully advised in the premises, here by makes its:

FINDINGS OF FACT

1. Laura Raskin was duly appointed trustee to represent the heirs and next of kin of decedent William Nordby who died on April 5, 2001.
2. He was sixty-nine years of age. His wife and his adult daughter, Laura Raskin, survived him. They incurred $115,345 in medical expenses for Nordby's care and $4,772 for funeral and burial expenses. The Chevette was not repairable. It had a fair market value of $4,500.
3. The decedent William Nordby and defendant Bradley Harper were involved in a motor vehicle accident on October 17, 2000 on Hubbard County Road 13, 200 yards west of County Road 118 in Minnesota.
4. The highway was straight. The weather was clear. There were no obstructions to either driver's view.
5. County Road 13 is an east and west, two-lane, asphalt, secondary highway with one lane in each direction. County Road 118 forms a T intersection with County Road (CR) 13 to the north.
6. Decedent Nordby was driving his Chevette automobile in an easterly direction on Country Road 13. He slowed to make a left turn to go north on CR 118. He did not signal his intent to turn.
7. Defendant Harper was then driving his pickup truck in an easterly direction on CR 13 some distance behind the Nordby Chevette. Harper was driving at least fifty-five miles per hour and proceeded to pass the Chevette by moving into the westbound lane. Both driver's were west of the intersection and approaching it.

(continued)

Demand for Jury

Rule 38 of the Federal Rules of Civil Procedure prescribes the procedure a party must follow to obtain a jury trial. A plaintiff may demand a jury trial by noting the demand on his or her pleading. The jury demand is usually made at the bottom of the complaint or answer and labeled as such. Or, either party may serve a separate

EXHIBIT 3.4   *Sample Findings of Fact, Conclusions of Law, and Order for Judgment (continued)*

8. As defendant Harper proceeded to pass the Nordby Chevette, Nordby turned left to cross the westbound lane to go north on CR 118. The left front corner of Nordby's Chevette struck the front right fender of Harper's pickup truck.
9. Both drivers lost control of their vehicles and crashed.
10. Decedent Nordby was injured. On April 5, 2001, Nordby died as a result of his injuries.
11. Nordby was sixty-nine years of age. Nordby was retired at the time of his death. His only income was social security and income from his properties which were in joint tenancy with his wife, Mary Nordby. His wife and his adult daughter, Laura Raskin, survived him. They incurred $115,345 in medical expenses for Nordby's care and $4,772 for funeral and burial expenses. The Chevette was not repairable. It had a fair market value of $4,500.

CONCLUSIONS OF LAW

1. Defendant Harper was negligent for driving at an excessive speed for existing conditions, including approaching an intersection and moving vehicle that was slowing.
2. Defendant Harper was negligent for attempting to pass another vehicle at a rural intersection without giving warning.
3. Defendant Harper's negligence was a direct cause of the parties' motor vehicle accident.
4. Decedent Nordby was negligent for failing to signal his intent to make a left-hand turn on to CR. 118.
5. Decendent Nordby was negligent for failing to keep a proper lookout for other motorists when attempting to make a left-hand turn.
6. Decedent Nordby's negligence was a direct cause of the parties' motor vehicle accident.
7. The parties' combined causal negligence was:

Harper's causal negligence		40%
Nordby's causal negligence		60%
Total	100%	

8. Defendant is entitled to judgment of dismissal.
9. Defendant is entitled to recover statutory costs.

ORDER FOR JUDGMENT

The clerk of court is directed to enter judgment of dismissal in favor of the defendant. The defendant is allowed statutory costs against the plaintiff.

February 20, 2002

    /s/_____
                (District Judge)

demand for jury in writing. The written jury demand must be served and filed within ten days after service of the last pleading, whether the pleading is an answer to the complaint or an answer to a cross-claim or an answer to a third-party complaint.

The party who serves and files a demand for jury may specify particular fact issues to be tried to the jury, leaving all nonspecified fact issues to be determined by the judge as the fact finder. If a party receives a demand for jury that is limited to specific issues, she or he has ten days in which to serve a counterdemand for jury that specifies additional fact issues or makes an unqualified demand for jury. Usually a party makes a general demand because he or she can always waive the right to a jury later—assuming the other party does not object [Rule 38(d)]. One party's demand for a jury protects the adverse party's right to a jury, and vice versa. The defendant could not withdraw his or her jury demand so as to preclude the plaintiff from having a jury, even if the plaintiff did not file a demand.

Failure to Demand Jury

If neither party demands a jury in the manner prescribed by Rule 38, the judge may, nevertheless, order a jury trial if she or he believes that is preferable. The judge may order a trial by jury on the basis of a party's motion or make the order sua sponte, that is, on the judge's own initiative.

Why would a judge want the parties to have a trial by jury? The role of a fact finder is often difficult, stressful and time consuming, whether the fact finder is a jury or judge. When a judge acts as a fact finder, the judge must prepare Findings of Fact, Conclusions of Law, and Order for Judgment. It is a single document that has three parts. The judge must specify the material facts that he or she found from the parties' evidence, must articulate his or her conclusions of law, and must order the clerk of court to enter a judgment in the form the judge specifies. Judges commonly attach a memorandum of law to their orders to explain the legal analysis and basis for the decision. This is a time-consuming process.

Advisory Jury

advisory jury In cases where the plaintiff seeks equitable relief and the judge is responsible for determining the facts, the judge may empanel an advisory jury which is selected and acts like any other petit jury, except the judge is not required to accept or use the verdict.

Occasionally, a judge may choose to have an **advisory jury** even in cases where the parties have not requested a jury or the parties do not have a constitutional right to a jury. For example, parties do not have a right to a jury trial in actions to reform a written contract, to obtain an injunction, or to obtain a divorce. A judge need not accept the findings of an advisory jury. The judge remains ultimately responsible as the fact finder in such cases.

Number of Jurors

The United States Constitution does not specify the number of jurors to sit on a case. But, historically, the number has been twelve. That number has been maintained in criminal cases to the present time. Rule 48 provides that federal district courts will seat not fewer than six and not more than twelve persons for the jury. There is no provision for a party to ask for a particular number of jurors. The Rules Advisory Committee believes there is an implied constitutional right to have at least six persons on a jury. The committee has observed that courts should avoid allowing verdicts by fewer than six jurors because smaller juries tend to be erratic. Most lawyers and judges who remember working with twelve-person juries believe that twelve-person verdicts were less likely to go to extremes. Twelve-person juries are more predictable. Nevertheless, the trend is to use smaller juries. The preference for smaller juries is primarily a matter of economy. The government has fewer jurors to pay and trials may be somewhat shorter. Of course, the more jurors there are, the harder it is to obtain a consensus. Consequently, parties who have the burden of proof tend to prefer smaller juries.

Most civil actions are now tried to six jurors and one or two alternates. Judges commonly impanel more than six jurors, because jurors cannot be added once trial begins. If one or more jurors were to become ill or otherwise unable to return a verdict, the judge might have to declare a mistrial. A judge must declare a mistrial whenever an irreparable problem arises that prevents the parties from having a fair trial. If the number of jury members became less than six, that would be an irreparable problem. For example, if the court seats eight jurors but subsequently releases two from service because of illness, the remaining six jurors can decide the case. If the court seats only seven jurors, however, and two become ill so that they cannot complete the trial, the judge must declare a mistrial. Having additional jurors provides a measure of protection against a mistrial. If none of the jurors became ill or otherwise unavailable, they all deliberate.

Alternate Jurors

Most state courts have six-person juries, but, like federal courts may have twelve. Most state courts are authorized to empanel one or more alternate jurors. Alternate jurors are usually the last ones called to the jury box. The alternate jurors participate in the trial, the same as other jurors. However, they are allowed to deliberate only if they replace a regular juror who becomes sick or otherwise unable to participate. Usually, alternates are not told they are alternates. There is some concern they might not pay as close attention to the evidence if they knew they are alternates. They participate to the very end of the trial. They hear the final arguments. They listen to the judge's instructions on the law. They are excused from further service when the other jurors are sent to the jury room to deliberate. Consequently, if a juror becomes ill during the deliberations, there is no alternate juror to take over that juror's responsibilities.

In some states, the parties may stipulate that the alternate jurors may participate in the deliberations the same as the regular jurors. In that event, the case is decided by a seven- or eight-person jury. The verdict must be unanimous, unless the parties stipulate on the record that a fraction of the jurors may return the verdict. The party who has the burden of proof may be reluctant to have alternate jurors deliberate because he or she has more minds to persuade. For the same reason, defendants usually want larger juries. The principal reason a plaintiff may agree to have an alternate deliberate is that he or she may feel the alternate is the "best" juror and will favorably influence the others. There are no alternate jurors in federal courts. If seven or more jurors are impaneled, to make sure at least six are available to return a verdict, all of them deliberate and participate in the verdict.

Types of Verdicts

In civil actions, courts may use any one of three types of verdicts. The three types of verdicts are: general verdict, **general verdict with interrogatories,** and special verdict. The judge decides which type to use. The type of verdict does not depend on the kind of case. Rather, the choice is based on the complexity of issues and the desirability of identifying specific facts and issues. The type of verdict that is used may affect how the attorneys argue the case, how the judge instructs the jury about the law and the procedure for entering judgment. The judge may wait until the end of the trial before deciding which type of verdict to use. The judge is responsible for preparing the verdict form.

general verdict with interrogatories
A general verdict in which the jury finds for the plaintiff or defendant and, in addition, must answer specific questions about the facts of the case. The judge decides what questions to ask and how to word the questions.

Historically, general verdicts were the most common. They are simple in form and easy to employ. The verdict form simply asks the jury to indicate whether they find for the plaintiff or the defendant. If the jury finds for the plaintiff, they must state the amount of money to which the plaintiff is entitled. If the defendant prevails on a counterclaim, the amount of money must be stated. To arrive at a general verdict, the jury must first resolve the fact issues and then apply the substantive law to those facts. In effect, the jurors have a lot of leeway and the opportunity for compromising in arriving at their decision. The clerk of court enters judgment on the verdict.

General verdicts with interrogatories require the jury to find "for the plaintiff" or "for the defendant." But in addition, the jury is required to answer specific fact questions. The fact questions must be phrased so that the jury can answer each question with a short, specific answer, such as "yes" or "no." Rule 49(b) recognizes that one or more of the jury's answers may result in an inconsistency with the general verdict or that interrogatory answers may, themselves, be inconsistent. The Rule instructs the court how to deal with inconsistencies. The court may tell the jury that the answers are inconsistent and ask the jurors to deliberate further and try to make the answers consistent. Or, the court may declare a mistrial and try the case again with a new jury.

Currently, the most common type of verdict is the special verdict. A special verdict asks questions concerning disputed facts and ultimate questions of fact. The jury must apply substantive law to arrive at the ultimate issues of fact. The court then applies the law to the facts as determined by the jury and issues an order for judgment. The verdict form allows the jury to decide issues by giving short, one-word, answers. For example

1. Did plaintiff sign the "Release" (defendant's exhibit A)? (yes or no) _____
2. Was the defendant negligent? (yes or no) _____
3. If your answer to question 2 is yes, was the defendant's negligence a direct cause of the accident? (yes or no) _____
4. If your answer to question 3 is yes, what amount of money would fairly compensate the plaintiff? $ _____

In state courts, which allow less than unanimous verdicts, all concurring jurors must agree to all answers. The clerk of court does not enter judgment on the verdict. The court uses the jury's findings of fact as the basis for making conclusions of law and ordering entry of a judgment.

A special verdict may omit one or more fact issues. The omission may be intentional or inadvertent. The rule prevents the omission from becoming prejudicial error by providing that the judge shall act as the fact finder concerning the omitted item. The parties waive their right to a jury concerning any omitted fact issue unless, before the jury begins its deliberations, the complaining party asks the court to submit the question to the jury. The request should be in writing, and the request must clearly appear on the record. Otherwise, the fact issue, if material to the judgment, can be determined by the judge as the finder of fact [Rule 49(a)]. One reason for using a special verdict is that if an error occurs in the trial but it can be determined from the jury's answers that the error did not affect the outcome of the case, the error is not prejudicial and cannot be used as grounds for an appeal.

Unanimous Verdict

Rule 48 says a verdict must be unanimous unless the parties stipulate that some designated lesser number may agree on a verdict: "Unless the parties otherwise stipulate, (1) the verdict shall be unanimous and (2) no verdict shall be taken from a jury reduced in size to fewer than six members." Suppose that after five days of trial, the case is submitted to a jury that has eight members. After a full day of deliberation, the jury forewoman tells the judge the jury is deadlocked. Seven jurors are able to agree on a verdict, but one is holding out. The parties could stipulate that they will be bound by a verdict rendered by the seven who do agree.

The Rules Advisory Committee clarifies this issue:

> In exceptional circumstances, as where a jury suffers depletions during trial and deliberation that are greater than can reasonably be expected, the parties may agree to be bound by a verdict rendered by fewer than six jurors. The court should not, however, rely upon the availability of such an agreement, for the use of juries smaller than six is problematic for reasons fully discussed in *Ballew v. Georgia*, 435 U.S. 223 (1978).

A stipulation to a verdict by less than six is not inconsistent with the rule that requires that at least six jurors consider the case. If the parties do not stipulate, they have a right to a unanimous verdict.

TECHNOLOGY NOTES

The Internet provides information about the courts of almost all states. If you need information about your local courts to do legal research or to compare rules of procedure, you can obtain it through the following Web sites: http://www.uscourts.gov/; http://www.LLRX.com/; and http://www.findlaw.com.

Cornell Law School sponsors the Legal Information Institute which provides access to almost any facet of the law. You can obtain information about your state's courts, and your state's rules of civil procedure and statutes. It provides access to federal and state court opinions. The Web site is http://www.law.cornell.edu. See also the federal court's home page at http://www.uscourts.gov/; and the federal court locator at http://www.law.vill.edu.

SUMMARY

Parties must allege and prove their claims and defenses in a trial court. They must present evidence to prove the facts on which they base their claims and defenses. Either or both parties may appeal the trial court's judgment to an appellate court. An appellate court's function is to determine whether the trial court correctly applied the law and followed proper procedures. Occasionally, an appellate court must decide whether the prescribed rule or law is constitutional. An appellate court does not receive evidence or even pass judgment on what the evidence proves. An appellant may obtain relief in an appellate court only if the appellant can show that the trial court committed an error of law that likely affected the outcome of the case.

A court must have jurisdiction over the subject matter and the parties to be able to adjudicate the case. If the court lacks jurisdiction, its judgment is a nullity. A party may voluntarily grant jurisdiction over his or her person. And, if a defendant fails to interpose a timely objection to a court's lack of personal jurisdiction, the defendant waives the jurisdictional defect. Parties cannot waive or grant subject matter jurisdiction to a court. A judge must dismiss a case whenever it appears that the court does not have jurisdiction.

Each state has one federal district court. Each federal district court may have several divisions. Federal district courts have original jurisdiction. They are trial courts, not appellate courts. They adjudicate cases that involve federal questions and may litigate "diversity cases" in which the parties are residents of different states whether or not a federal question is involved; however, in "diversity cases" the amount in controversy must *exceed* $75,000.

A court may have jurisdiction of a case even though it is the wrong venue. The defendant has a right to have the case prosecuted in a reasonably convenient venue. The term *venue* refers to the forum in which a case is set for trial. If the case was brought in the wrong venue, the defendant may move the court for an order that changes the venue. But the defendant waives the venue defect by failing to make a timely motion. Venue statutes list the factors that a court must consider in determining which venue is the correct one.

The federal court system has two levels of appellate courts. An aggrieved litigant has a right to appeal from a federal district court judgment to one of the eleven circuit courts of appeals. The appeal may be based on procedural errors or errors of law concerning the parties' substantive rights. The appeal must be prosecuted within the time and in the manner prescribed by the Federal Rules of Appellate Procedure. The circuit court of appeals' decisions are published in "opinions," which are available to the public. The opinions are replicated in books and are available on the Internet. The decision of a court of appeals is usually final. With few exceptions, a party does not have a right to appeal to the United States Supreme Court.

Relatively few cases are appealed to the United States Supreme Court. To obtain review by the Supreme Court a party must petition the Supreme Court to accept review. The petition must show that the court of appeal's decision is wrong, that the decision has broad application, serious ramifications and that the issue(s) is likely to recur. One good basis for obtaining review is to show that several of the circuit courts of appeal have considered the issue and have reached different, inconsistent results.

Every state has a system of trial courts, often described as district courts, that have general jurisdiction statewide. Those courts handle all kinds of cases, involving any sum of money. States also have a variety of lesser trial courts, including small claims courts, justice courts, municipal courts, and county courts. The latter courts are limited in the kinds of cases they may adjudicate and the amount of money damages they may award. The jurisdiction of a small claims court is usually limited to the city or county in which the court is located. The only remedy a small claims court may provide is money damages in a limited amount. Workers' compensation courts, probate courts, family courts, and bankruptcy courts are specialized courts. Each handles only one kind of case. The specialized courts usually function in a manner similar to trial courts. An appeal from a specialized court may be to a district court or directly to an appellate court, depending on what the legislature has provided by statute. Paralegals may work with lawyers in those courts just like in trial courts.

Parties have a right to a jury trial in most civil actions. A jury resolves controverted fact issues. A jury finds the facts from the evidence presented by the parties. Jurors may not substitute their own experience or information for the evidence. But they may use their experience and knowledge to evaluate the evidence. The jury's determination of the facts is reflected in the jury's verdict. The verdict is the basis for entering a judgment. A judgment is a permanent public record that declares the parties' legal rights and obligations in the matter.

A party requests a trial by jury by making a demand for jury on the party's pleading or by serving and filing a written demand for a jury. The written demand must be served within ten days after the last pleading has been filed. A party may request a jury trial on specified fact issues, leaving the remaining fact issues to be determined by the judge as the fact finder. A party waives the right to a jury trial by failing to make a timely demand for a jury. Parties do not have a right to a trial by jury when the plaintiff seeks equitable relief. When a judge acts as the fact finder, the judge must prepare a written Findings of Fact. A "Findings of Facts" is suppose to detail the judge's determination of the material facts and ultimate facts. Then the judge must apply the substantive law to those facts. The judge determines the parties' legal rights and obligations by applying the law to the facts. The judge must set forth his or her legal determinations in a written Conclusions of Law. The latter then becomes the basis for the judge's Order for Judgment. The clerk of court prepares the judgment in compliance with the Conclusions of Law and Order for Judgment.

A petit jury is drawn from a jury panel of veniremen. The panel of veniremen is drawn from the community as a whole. To qualify as a juror, a person must be able to hear the evidence, be able to speak and understand the English language, and not have a felony conviction. A jury may be composed of any number of jurors between six and twelve. The jury must have at least six members when the case is decided. Often more than six jurors are selected to serve to make sure that when the trial is finished six or more jurors are available to decide the case. Federal courts do not use alternate jurors. Most state courts do use alternate jurors.

In civil actions, courts may use a general verdict, a general verdict with interrogatories, or a special verdict. The judge decides which type to use. The type of verdict does not depend on the kind of case. Rather, the choice is based on the complexity of issues and the desirability of identifying specific facts and issues. The judge is responsible for preparing the verdict form.

General verdicts simply ask the jury to indicate whether they find for the plaintiff or the defendant. If the jury finds for the plaintiff, they must state the amount of money to which the plaintiff is entitled. To arrive at a general verdict, the jury must first resolve the fact issues and then apply the substantive law to those facts. General verdicts with interrogatories require the jury to find "for the plaintiff" or "for the defendant." But in addition, the jury is required to answer specific fact questions. The fact questions must be phrased so that the jury can answer each question with a short, specific answer, such as "yes" or "no." A special verdict asks questions concerning disputed facts and ultimate questions of fact. The jury must apply substantive law to arrive at the ultimate issues of fact. The court then applies the law to the facts as determined by the jury and issues an order for judgment. The court uses the jury's findings of fact as the basis for making conclusions of law and ordering judgment. A special verdict may omit one or more fact issues. The parties waive their right to a jury concerning any omitted fact issue.

KEY TERMS

advisory jury	magistrate judge
appellant	personal jurisdiction
appellee	petit jury
courts of general jurisdiction	subject matter jurisdiction
diversity of citizenship	veniremen
equitable relief	venue
general verdict with interrogatories	writ of certiorari
injunctive relief	

REVIEW QUESTIONS

1. What happens if the defendant fails to object to the court's lack of jurisdiction? Does it matter whether the jurisdictional defect involves the subject matter or the defendant's person?

2. When may the parties waive a jurisdictional defect?

3. What is the difference between venue and jurisdiction?

4. If a party loses a case in a federal district court, to what court may that party appeal?

5. In what federal circuit is your federal district court located?

6. Does a party have a right to prosecute an appeal to a federal circuit court of appeals? If so, under what conditions? If not, why not?

7. Does a party have a right to appeal to the United States Supreme Court? If so, under what conditions? If not, why not?

8. What happens if the defendant fails to object that the court the plaintiff selected is the wrong venue?

CASE ASSIGNMENT

Ms. Raskin has retained your law firm to prosecute a wrongful death action against Bradley Harper. She was told at the initial conference that the firm would commence an action in the Hubbard County District Court after the litigation team obtains a copy of the police accident report, interviews the sheriff, and talks to Griffin and Harper if they will talk. That will take about one week. In the meantime, people have been telling Ms. Raskin that she should sue in federal court, because she would get a larger award. And she wants a twelve-person jury, because that would give the case more importance. You have been asked to prepare a one-page letter to her that explains why the case cannot be brought in federal court and that civil actions only have six-person juries. She is threatening to go to another firm if we do not put the case in federal court.

Endnotes

1. Parties do not have a right to a trial by jury in some types of cases.
2. There are a number of important exceptions to this general rule. Some of those exceptions are discussed later in the book.
3. Federal statutes authorize citizens to sue in federal court if the plaintiff and defendant are residents of different states.
4. The plaintiff must arrange to have the United States marshal or other suitable person serve the summons and complaint. The law forbids the plaintiff from serving the papers, because there is too much danger of physical violence and the possibility of fraud.
5. A subpoena commanding attendance at a trial or hearing shall issue from the court for the district in which the hearing or trial is to be held. A subpoena for attendance at a deposition shall issue from the court for the district designated by the notice of deposition as the district in which the deposition is to be taken. If separate from a subpoena commanding the attendance of a person, a subpoena for production or inspection shall issue from the court for the district in which the production or inspection is to be made. Rule 45(a)(D)(2).
6. An "unretained expert" is one who has made studies independently of the litigation. Courts protect unretained experts from having their work pilfered by litigants.
7. Special damages are out-of-pocket expenses that the claimant incurs because of the alleged wrongful conduct of the defendant.
8. But note that the parties cannot confer subject matter jurisdiction on a court through an agreement or otherwise.
9. Article III provides, in part, "In all cases affecting ambassadors, other public ministers and consuls, and those in which a State shall be party, the Supreme Court shall have original jurisdiction. In all other cases before mentioned, the Supreme Court shall have appellate jurisdiction, both as to law and fact, with such exceptions, and under such regulations as the Congress shall make."

 For additional resources, visit our Web site at www.paralegal.delmar.cengage.com

CHAPTER 4

CAUSES OF ACTION AND REMEDIES

Chapter Objectives

Chapter 4 explains that only certain kinds of disputes may be brought to court for resolution. It explains how to determine whether a claim is the type that is proper for suit. It also discusses the kinds of relief or remedies the courts may grant.

Introduction

A court can and will provide a remedy—where appropriate. Contrary to the popular aphorism that "for every wrong there is a remedy," courts cannot undo every wrong. Nor can courts provide a remedy for every perceived loss or inconvenience. But some disputes are significant and have serious consequences for the parties. Based on centuries of experience, courts have determined that only certain kinds of wrongful conduct, which cause certain kinds of losses, should be "actionable," that is, be the subject of a lawsuit. A claim that is actionable states a "cause of action" or is a "cause of action." You need to know about the requirements that must be met to establish a cause of action and why they exist, because they are the basis for making claims and asserting defenses.

Not every wrongful act and loss gives rise to a cause of action. A claim for relief must have a legal theory to support it or a court will disallow it. A "cause of action" is a legal theory on which a court will grant relief to a plaintiff against a defendant. A man may call his neighbor "stupid" or say he is a "jerk." As unflattering and hurtful as these remarks are, they do not give rise to a cause of action. A saleswoman may spend many hours helping a customer with the selection of a car and then lose the sale to another saleswoman who spent only a few minutes with the customer. The first saleswoman may feel that she has been wronged, her time and help abused, but she does not have a cause of action. There are many causes of action, and each applies to a specific type of dispute. A lawyer must determine which cause of action, that is, which legal theory, to assert as the basis for the client's claim. Sometimes, more than one cause of action may apply to make a claim. The chapter outline lists some of the more common causes of action.

Causes of Action in General

Judges and lawyers are able to analyze and discuss claims in a causes-of-action context, much like physicians are able to communicate about diseases by naming them, rather than by describing their symptoms and consequences. When a lawyer says a claim is for "trespass," other lawyers and judges immediately know the nature of the claim, what the elements of proof must be, what kind of remedy is allowed, and what defenses may be applicable. The more a legal assistant knows about causes of action, the better equipped the legal assistant is to communicate with lawyers and understand the reasons for assignments. The critical aspects of causes of action are that each cause of action

- is fashioned to give effect to a particular legal duty.
- has specific requirements that must be met.
- affords a particular remedy or remedies.
- is subject to certain defenses and time limitations.

Although there are many different causes of action, all have some elements in common. Specifically, to prove a claim on which a court will grant relief, regardless of which cause of action is involved, a plaintiff must prove each of the following:

- The defendant breached a legal duty that the defendant owed to the plaintiff.
- The plaintiff sustained an injury or property damage or a monetary loss.
- The defendant's breach of the legal duty was a proximate (direct) cause of that injury, damage, or loss.

Some legal duties are prescribed by our legislatures in statutes. Some legal duties are voluntarily assumed by the parties, as when they contract with each other. Some legal duties have been created by our courts as part of the common law. The plaintiff's complaint must specify the particular legal duty that the plaintiff claims the defendant breached and state the time and place that the defendant breached that duty.

A plaintiff's lawyer must determine whether the plaintiff's alleged facts support all the elements of at least one cause of action. In other words, is there a basis for a lawsuit? If even one of the necessary elements is missing, the claim/dispute cannot succeed in court. Rule 12(b) of the Federal Rules of Civil Procedure provides that the case must be dismissed if the complaint fails to state *a claim on which relief can be granted.* Another way of saying this is that the case must be dismissed if the complaint fails to state a cause of action. Usually, the requirement is easily met by the following:

- Identifying the time and place of the transaction or occurrence that gave rise to the dispute.
- Identifying the time and place of the defendant's alleged breach of duty.
- Identifying the cause of action on which the claim is based, such as a "breach of contract," "trespass," "assault and battery," or a statute.

Each cause of action has its own remedy, and each remedy has its own measure of damages. Consequently, the amount of compensation a plaintiff may seek depends on the legal theory (cause of action) the plaintiff pursues. For example, a claim for breach of contract allows compensation based on the plaintiff's loss of the bargain, that is, a loss of profits. A claim for fraud, however, may allow compensation only for the plaintiff's out-of-pocket expenses. The two legal theories have different elements and different measures of damages. Even though a plaintiff may allege more than one cause of action as alternatives, it is important to choose and prove the most advantageous one.

affirmative defense A defense that is usually based on the plaintiff's act or conduct or consent.

Each cause of action is subject to certain **affirmative defenses.** Affirmative defenses are usually based on some wrongful conduct on the part of the plaintiff—but not always. Like a cause of action, each affirmative defense has certain elements. But in this instance the defendant has the burden of proving those elements. An affirmative defense completely defeats the plaintiff's cause of action or, in certain cases, reduces the amount of the plaintiff's money damages. Ordinarily, the defendant's burden of proof is by a fair preponderance of the evidence.

A party's investigation, discovery procedures, and trial preparation are prompted by the legal issues, and the legal issues are prompted by the elements of the plaintiff's cause of action. The plaintiff has the burden of proving all the elements of the cause of action; the burden is not on the defendant to disprove the claim. The customary burden of proof is to establish the elements of the cause of action by a fair preponderance of the evidence. The evidence preponderates (weighs) in favor of a particular fact when all the evidence, taken as a whole, shows that the fact is more likely true than not true. If a client does not have a cause of action—a claim on which a court can grant a remedy—he or she should be told that as soon as possible because the time, effort, and money spent prosecuting a deficient claim are wasted.

A paralegal is not expected to know everything about every cause of action and all affirmative defenses. But when working on a particular case, a paralegal should become familiar with the elements of the cause of action and any affirmative defenses alleged. Most lawyers are eager to have paralegals show an interest in the technical aspects of litigation. The more knowledgeable a paralegal is about the law and legal procedures, the more effectively he or she can handle assignments in litigation. The balance of this chapter provides an introduction to some of the more common causes of action.

Breach of Contract

A breach of contract is a failure to comply with the terms or conditions of an agreement. A cause of action for breach of contract arises—what the law calls accrues—when the defendant fails to perform his or her part of the contract. The defendant's legal duty to the plaintiff comes from the promises the parties made to each other in their contract. There is no need to show that the breach was willful or the result of fault. Culpability (blameworthiness) is not a factor or an issue. The usual remedy is an award of money damages to compensate the plaintiff for the loss of the benefits the contract would have provided. The plaintiff must plead and prove that

- There was a contract between them.
- The defendant breached the contract by failing to comply with one of its material terms or conditions.
- There was a loss resulting from the defendant's breach—including the nature and extent of the loss.

At trial the proof must establish each of these elements by a preponderance of the evidence.

Of course, a cause of action for breach of contract presupposes that the parties have an enforceable contract. In its most simple form, a contract is merely a legally enforceable promise. A contract may be written or oral, or both. The parties voluntarily enter into a contract expecting that each will benefit from their mutual commitments. The benefits may be monetary or the acquisition of something desired, such as land, personal property, or even an idea. The type of remedy afforded by the law depends, in part, on the purpose of the contract, the parties' objectives, and their reasonable expectations. Usually, the plaintiff seeks money damages as compensation for a loss of the bargain, such as a loss of profits, that the plaintiff would have realized if the defendant had fully performed his or her side of the contract.

Some contracts are implied by the parties' conduct, and some are implied by operation of law. Despite the variety of contracts, certain elements are essential to all contracts. An enforceable contract requires all of the following:

- The parties are competent to enter into a contract.
- An offer and acceptance that results in a meeting of the parties' minds concerning the essential terms of the contract.
- An exchange of **consideration.**
- Compliance with particular formalities imposed by statutes for certain types of contracts.

consideration Consideration is an essential element to an enforceable contract. It is something of value that is given in exchange for a contracting party's performance or promise of performance.

A contract is not enforceable if the object of the contract or the means for performance is unlawful.[1]

Each party to a contract must have the capacity to enter into a contract. For example, a person who is a minor, insane, under a guardianship, or intoxicated lacks

voidable Capable of being voided.

the mental capacity to make an enforceable contract. If a person lacks capacity to contract, any purported contract he or she makes is **voidable** at that person's election. For example, a minor may back out of a contract to purchase a car.[2] And a business that is not incorporated has no separate legal existence and cannot contract for itself. An unincorporated company may contract only through its owners as individuals. Partnerships are legal entities that may contract through one or more partners. In effect, the partners are each other's agents. Similarly, corporations are legal entities and may contract through its officers and agents.

Assuming capacity, there must be contract formation through one party's offer and the other's acceptance. An offer to contract ordinarily specifies the essential terms and conditions of the contract. Acceptance of the offer must be communicated to the offeror in compliance with any conditions imposed by the offeror. If the acceptance is qualified, or changes any of the essential terms of the offer, the acceptance is a counteroffer, which does not create a contract unless accepted by the original offeror. A contract is made only if the parties reach a meeting of minds concerning the subject matter. For example, if the seller offers to sell an automobile to the buyer, they must have in mind the same automobile or a valid contract cannot result from their negotiations.

A contract also requires an exchange of consideration between the parties. Generally, consideration can be understood as value. In this respect, a contract differs from a simple promise. Unless consideration (value) is given, there is nothing between the parties but a base promise. And a mere promise—even if made under oath—is not a contract and cannot be enforced by law. The most common consideration given to support a contract is money. But even a promise given in exchange for the other party's promise may be a legal consideration that will support the existence of a contract. If a contract recites that consideration has been paid, but in fact it was not, the alleged contract is defective and unenforceable. Absent a fraud, courts do not consider the value or fairness of the consideration. The pleadings in Exhibits 4.1 and 4.2 are illustrative for a typical breach-of-contract case.

Only certain contracts must be in writing and signed in order to be enforceable. The statute that identifies such contracts is commonly referred to as the **statute of frauds.** The statute specifies what kinds of contracts must be in writing and the necessary elements to each written contract. The most common of these contracts is one for the sale of land. If a contract is required to be in writing but is not, it is unenforceable. Failure to meet the requirements of the statute of frauds gives the defendant a complete defense.

statute of frauds A body of law that precludes certain types of contracts from being enforceable unless the contracts are in writing and are signed by the person to be bound.

When a breach of contract occurs, the parties may elect to continue performance of the remainder of the contract. That may be the only realistic choice in some cases. If a party elects to proceed with the contract knowing that the other party has breached it, the election to proceed may constitute a waiver of the breach. It would be unfair for the plaintiff to sue on the contract after waiving a breach. The parties may formalize the waiver by preparing a writing in which the extent of the waiver is described and the consequences of the waiver stated. Ordinarily, a waiver is a complete defense that the defendant must allege in the answer and prove. An alternative would be for the parties to make a new contract that sets forth the change of circumstances and the parties' modified agreement. Such written modifications frequently occur on construction projects.

An action for breach of contract is subject to certain affirmative defenses. An affirmative defense defeats the plaintiff's action even though the plaintiff proves all of the elements of his or her claim. Usually an affirmative defense is based on the plain-

EXHIBIT 4.1

Complaint for Breach of Contract

COMPLAINT

Comes now plaintiff and for its cause of action against defendant alleges:

1. [Jurisdictional allegations.]
2. On August 2, 2006, defendant contracted to sell and deliver to plaintiff ten tons of newsprint-quality rolled paper.
3. The terms and conditions of said contract between the parties were reduced to writing; a copy of said written contract is attached hereto and incorporated by reference as Exhibit A.
4. Said written contract was signed by defendant's representative at the time and place specified in the contract.
5. Plaintiff paid to defendant the sum of $3,000 as a partial payment as recited in the written contract.
6. All conditions precedent of said contract have been performed or have occurred.
7. Defendant did not deliver said newsprint paper to plaintiff as required by the terms of said contract, and defendant is in default.
8. Plaintiff has necessarily sought and obtained other newsprint paper to meet its needs and requirements.
9. As a direct consequence of defendant's failure to perform on said contract, plaintiff has suffered damages as follows:
   a. Plaintiff is entitled to recover the $3,000 initially paid to defendant as a down payment, together with interest at the rate specified in the written contract [or the legal rate provided by law].
   b. Plaintiff's printing business was necessarily interrupted for a period of ten working days, causing plaintiff to suffer a loss of profit in the amount of $10,000.
   c. Plaintiff was required to purchase similar newsprint from another supplier at an additional cost of $6,000.

Wherefore, plaintiff prays for judgment against defendant in the sum of $19,000, together with plaintiff's costs and disbursements herein.

[date]

Attorney for Plaintiff

[Attorney signature]

tiff's own wrongful conduct or neglect. The defendant has the burden of proving all of the elements in an affirmative defense. A partial list of affirmative defenses appears in Rule 8(c), and includes the following:

- Accord and satisfaction
- Arbitration and award
- Assumption of risk

Exhibit 4.2

*Answer to Complaint for
Breach of Contract*

Answer

Comes now defendant and for its answer to plaintiff's complaint:

1. Denies each and every allegation, statement, and matter in plaintiff's complaint, except as hereinafter expressly admitted or alleged:
2. Admits the allegation of paragraphs 1 through 8 of the complaint.
3. Admits that defendant is liable to plaintiff in the amount of $3,000 for money had and received, but denies defendant is liable for interest thereon.

Defense 1
Alleges that paragraph 9(b) of the complaint fails to state a claim upon which relief can be granted.

Defense 2
Alleges that on August 7, 2006, defendant's entire plant and warehouse were destroyed by fire through no fault of defendant, and that the loss of the plant and warehouse made impossible defendant's performance of the contract.

Wherefore, defendant prays that plaintiff take nothing by reason of its alleged cause of action and that defendant have judgment for its costs and disbursements.

[date]

Attorney for Defendant

[Attorney signature]

- Contributory negligence
- Discharge in bankruptcy
- Duress
- Estoppel
- Failure of consideration
- Fraud
- Illegality
- Injury by fellow servant
- Laches
- License
- Payment
- Release
- Res judicata
- Statute of frauds
- Statute of limitations
- Waiver

Affirmative defenses are discussed in detail in Chapter 5.

A plaintiff's own breach of the contract provides an affirmative defense to the defendant. The defendant must prove the breach, but the defendant does not have to prove any loss resulting from the breach.[3] If the defendant can prove that the plaintiff obtained the contract through fraud, the contract is voidable at the election of the defendant. If the parties made a new agreement to replace an old one and fully performed the new agreement, the old one is a nullity and unenforceable. The new agreement and its performance are called an **accord and satisfaction.** The accord and satisfaction is a complete defense to an action on the original contract. A plaintiff's failure to sue within the time specified by the contract to which the parties have agreed (contract condition) or within the time specified by the statute of limitations provides an affirmative defense. Once in a while, after a contract is made, circumstances develop making performance of the contract impossible. Impossibility is a defense, but it is a difficult defense to prove and subject to stringent limitations. Many other affirmative defenses are potentially available in contract actions.

accord and satisfaction   An *accord* is an agreement that replaces a disputed claim or prior disputed contract. A *satisfaction* is the execution or fulfillment of the new agreement.

Specific Performance

In the vast majority of cases, a plaintiff's remedy is to recover the economic value (i.e., money) of the consequences resulting from a breach of contract by another. **Specific performance** is a remedy that is available in a very limited number of breach-of-contract actions where the award of money is an inappropriate or inadequate remedy. Specific performance means that the breaching party is required to complete the actions (i.e., perform) as he or she promised in the contract. Such a remedy is available only when one party's breach of contract causes the other party to suffer "irreparable harm." In those cases, a court of general jurisdiction has the authority to require (force) a party to perform the contract. "Specific performance" of a contract is both a cause of action and a remedy. The most common use of a specific performance action is to force the defendant to sell real estate as he or she contracted to do. Because the law presumes that each parcel of land is unique and irreplaceable, money damages are not adequate to replace the loss of land. Therefore, the law allows a court to require the seller to sign a deed or order the transfer.[4] Specific performance may also be available to the buyer of a unique work of art. The buyer may force the seller to deliver the artwork and title. If the buyer breached the contract, however, the seller could not compel the buyer to take the art work but could obtain money damages for loss of the bargain. That's because the payment of money is an adequate remedy for the seller in that circumstance even though the same is not true for the buyer. A sample complaint for specific performance and its answer appear in Exhibits 4.3 and 4.4, respectively.

specific performance   A remedy provided by a court that has equity powers.

Similar to, but to be distinguished from, specific performance, courts may enjoin (command) parties to perform or not perform certain activities. For example, a court may order a union not to strike or not to picket. A court may order a corporation to undertake negotiations to settle a labor dispute. Actions to enjoin conduct may involve the use of restraining orders, temporary injunctions, and permanent injunctions. Courts cannot order an individual to perform personal services, however, for that would constitute involuntary servitude and would be unconstitutional.

COMPLAINT

Comes now plaintiff and for his cause of action against defendant alleges:

1. [Jurisdictional allegations.]
2. On or about August 3, 2006, plaintiff and defendant, through his duly appointed agent, entered into a written contract by which defendant agreed to sell and plaintiff agreed to buy certain specific real estate. A copy of said contract is attached hereto as Exhibit A.
3. As provided by said written contract plaintiff duly tendered to defendant the purchase price for the land as provided for in Exhibit A.
4. Defendant wrongfully refused to accept tender of the purchase price.
5. Defendant wrongfully refused to convey title of said land to plaintiff.
6. Plaintiff is ready, willing, and able to perform on the contract and hereby offers the full purchase price to defendant.
7. Plaintiff cannot obtain similar land, similarly situated, that would meet plaintiff's requirements.
8. All conditions precedent have been performed or have occurred.

Wherefore, plaintiff prays that court issue its decree ordering defendant to perform the contract by providing plaintiff with a warranty deed to said land.

If specific performance is not granted, plaintiff prays for judgment against defendant in the sum of $50,000 as damages for defendant's breach of contract.

Plaintiff further prays for his costs and disbursement herein.

[date]

Attorney for Plaintiff

[Attorney signature]

Fraud

Fraud is the intentional misrepresentation of a fact made with the expectation that another person will rely on the misrepresentation. The law recognizes, however, that many people make statements, both written and oral, that are not true or are only half-true but for which no legal liability should result. If a woman tells her friends that she is five years younger than she is, should that misrepresentation create a cause of action? Of course not. But if she misrepresents her age on an application for a life insurance policy and the insurer relies on the misrepresentation to its detriment, the misrepresentation is actionable as a fraud. If a car owner tells friends that his car gets fifty miles per gallon, but it actually gets only fifteen miles per gallon, the misrepresentation is amusing, but it is not actionable.

EXHIBIT 4.4

Answer to Complaint for Specific Performance

ANSWER

Comes now defendant and for his answer to plaintiff's complaint:

1. Denies each and every allegation, statement, and matter in said complaint contained, except as hereinafter expressly admitted or alleged.
2. Admits that he is the owner of the land described in Exhibit A.
3. Denies that he executed the contract identified as Exhibit A attached to the complaint.
4. Denies that any person had authority to sign said contract for him or to act on his behalf concerning said land.
5. Denies that he received any consideration for the alleged contract.

Wherefore, defendant prays that plaintiff take nothing by reason of his pretended cause of action and that defendant have judgment for his costs and disbursements herein.

[date]

Attorney for Defendant

[Attorney signature]

In contrast, if the seller of an automobile makes a similar misrepresentation to a buyer, the misrepresentation is actionable.

Courts and legal scholars have variously stated the elements for a cause of action for fraud. The following comprehensive list has been used by more than one court.

1. There must be an oral or written representation.
2. The representation must be false.
3. The misrepresentation must have to do with a past or present fact (i.e., not a future prediction).
4. The misrepresented fact must be material to the contract or transaction.
5. The representation must be susceptible of knowledge.
6. The defendant must know the representation is false or, in the alternative, must assert the fact as of his or her own knowledge without knowing whether it is true or false.
7. The defendant must intend to induce the other person to act, and the plaintiff must be justified in acting on the misrepresentation.
8. The plaintiff must justifiably act in reliance on the misrepresentation.
9. The plaintiff must suffer a loss by relying on the misrepresentation.

Suppose that the seller has never had a wet basement, but after the buyer acquires possession, she discovers water in heating ducts under the basement floor. Assume that the seller was unaware of the water below the floor. Is the seller's

EXAMPLE

Suppose the seller of a house represents that he has never had a "wet basement," but for as long as the seller has had the house in fact significant amounts of water collected on the floor after every rain. All the elements of a fraud are present. The measure of damages is the difference between the value of the house as it is and the value that the house would have had with a dry basement. That is the buyer's out-of-pocket loss. In this kind of case, the difference in value usually approximates the cost of making repairs.

statement actionable as a fraud? No, the seller did not have a legal duty to know whether there was water under the basement floor, and the buyer's question did not impose a duty on the seller to investigate. The seller's statement was consistent with his knowledge and based on his experience with the house. However, if the buyer had asked the seller whether there had ever been water in the heat ducts, the seller must respond that he does not know. If he says "No," without knowing, and is wrong, he has *negligently misrepresented* a material fact, and that gives rise to a different cause of action against him.

The plaintiff must rely on the defendant's false representation, and the defendant must have reason to believe that the plaintiff will rely on it. If the seller of a parcel of land represents that the parcel is 200 feet deep, but before the sale, the buyer measures the length and determines it is only 190 feet deep, the buyer cannot later sue for fraud, because he did not rely on the misrepresentation. Suppose an art dealer misrepresents a certain painting to be an original, and the painting is purchased by a knowledgeable collector who knows that it is not an original. Does the collector have a claim for fraud? No, because the collector did not *rely* on the false representation.

A statement of a mere opinion usually is not actionable. For example, "This is a very good car" is a mere expression of an opinion. Ordinarily, a representation concerning a future event is not actionable as fraud. For example, "This business is going to make a $500,000 profit next year" is not actionable, because the future event is not a past or existing fact. Of course, the rule is subject to qualifications and exceptions. For example, if the seller of a parcel of land knows that an aircraft flight pattern is going to be established over the land in the near future, a representation to the contrary is a fraud, because the defendant has made a misrepresentation about an existing plan. But usually a prediction is not actionable as a fraud.

The plaintiff must prove that the misrepresentation caused a loss. Suppose that the seller of a used automobile misrepresents that it is a 1988 model, knowing that it is a 1987 model; suppose that 1988 models have an average value that is $300 more than that for comparable 1987 models; suppose further that the buyer ends up paying no more for the automobile than she would have paid for a good 1987 model. In other words, suppose the buyer received full value for what she paid, but believed she was getting a better bargain. Has the buyer really sustained a loss because of the misrepresentation? By contract standards, the answer would be "yes." She did not get the benefit of the bargain. But she has not sustained an out-of-pocket loss, as required in fraud actions. Note, however, that a few states do allow loss-of-the-bargain damages in fraud actions. In such a state, the buyer's damages would be $300. In an out-of-pocket-damages state, the buyer has not sustained a loss.

Rule 9(b) requires that the plaintiff plead fraud and misrepresentation with particularity, whether asserted as a claim or as a defense. This means that fraud and negligent misrepresentation must be pled by alleging detailed facts relevant to each element of the cause of action. Exhibits 4.5 and 4.6 are examples of a complaint and answer in fraud. The answer in Exhibit 4.6 does not undertake to raise all possible defenses to an action in fraud. It merely illustrates a proper way of alleging denials and defenses.

EXHIBIT 4.5

Complaint in Fraud

COMPLAINT

Comes now plaintiff and for her cause of action against defendant alleges:

1. [Jurisdictional allegations.]
2. On or about June 1, 2006, plaintiff and defendant entered into an agreement by which defendant agreed to sell to plaintiff a certain 1995 Buick automobile, and plaintiff agreed to buy said automobile.
3. The parties' agreement was reduced to writing, and a copy thereof is attached hereto as Exhibit A and is incorporated herein by reference.
4. Defendant represented to plaintiff that said automobile had a "new" engine, as appears more fully in Exhibit A.
5. Defendant intended plaintiff to rely upon said representation, and plaintiff did so rely.
6. Defendant's said representation was false; the engine is not new, and the original engine was never replaced or overhauled before the sale.
7. Plaintiff paid to defendant the sum of $7,500 for said automobile in reliance upon defendant's false representation.
8. The cost of a new engine for said automobile is $1,500, and the fair market value of the automobile without a new engine is not more than $7,000.
9. Plaintiff has sustained a loss due to defendant's fraudulent misrepresentations in the amount of $1,500.

Wherefore, plaintiff prays for judgment against defendant in the sum of $1,500, together with her costs and disbursements herein.

[date]

Attorney for Plaintiff

[Attorney signature]

Answer

Comes now defendant and for her answer to plaintiff's complaint:

1. Denies each and every statement, matter, and thing in said complaint contained, except as hereinafter expressly admitted or alleged.
2. Denies that the court has jurisdiction over the subject matter of plaintiff's claim and that the controversy exceeds the threshold requirement of $10,000.
3. Admits that the parties did enter into a sales agreement for the sale of an automobile about the time and place specified in the complaint.
4. Specifically denies that the automobile engine, referred to in the complaint, was misrepresented and puts plaintiff to her strict proof of the alleged misrepresentation.
5. Denies that plaintiff did not receive full value for the purchase price of said automobile.
6. Alleges that Exhibit A, attached to the complaint, is incomplete and does not set forth the full agreement of the parties.

Wherefore, defendant prays that plaintiff take nothing by reason of plaintiff's pretended cause of action, and that defendant have judgment for her costs and disbursements herein.

[date]

Attorney for Defendant

[Attorney signature]

Negligent Misrepresentation

negligent misrepresentation A statement made as a fact when the person making it does not know whether it is true or not true, and has reason to know that the person to whom it is made may rely on it.

A **negligent misrepresentation** is the misrepresentation of a fact expecting that another person will rely on the misrepresentation but without knowing whether the fact is true. A cause of action for negligent misrepresentation lies when the circumstances are such that the defendant had a duty to speak the truth, knowing that the plaintiff would rely on the statement. For example, suppose a real estate agent tells a prospective buyer that the seller's house never had a wet basement without knowing the basement's history. Even though the agent did not *know* his statement was false, he was negligent in making the statement. The buyer could reasonably assume that the agent knew the basement's history. The buyer had a right to rely on the statement. The agent had reason to know that the buyer would rely on the statement. A negligent misrepresentation is actionable whether the statement is oral or written. Again, the plaintiff must prove that she or he relied on the misrepresentation to her detriment. The measure of damages is the same as in an action for fraud. The fundamental difference between negligent misrepresentation and fraud is that fraud requires proof that the declarant knew the misstatement to be false.

Trespass

A trespass is an entry on real estate without the possessor's consent and without legal authority. The early common law focused on property rights and exalted those rights. In that vein, courts created trespass as a cause of action. The law's concern is that a person who has lawful possession of real estate has a right to the peaceful, quiet,[5] possession of the property. The occupant or person who is entitled to immediate possession of the property at the time of the trespass is the person who owns the cause of action (claim) against the trespasser. A trespass is a tort against property, not against a person. The trespasser is responsible for any harm the property sustains because of the trespass. The cause of action allows the plaintiff to obtain money damages to compensate for the damage. The owner may not be the possessor. For example, a tenant may be the possessor.

A possessor who brings an action in trespass against a trespasser is entitled to compensation for damage to the property, including damage to crops, trees, loss of minerals, damage to buildings, or damage to other features of the land. Even if the trespasser did not cause any actual damage, the trespasser may be liable to pay nominal money damages. On that basis, the law affirms the possessor's right to be exclusive, and the occupant's right to peaceful[6] possession. When the possessor is not the owner, the possessor ordinarily is obligated to return the property to the owner in good condition; therefore, the possessor may hold at least some of the damages award for the benefit of the owner.

A trespasser is liable for the damage caused by his or her wrongful entry. Moral fault is not an element. A wrongful entry may be involuntary, as where a ship is forced ashore by a storm. A trespass may be inadvertent, as where a person honestly believes that the land is hers or his but is mistaken. Or a trespass may result from negligent conduct on the part of the defendant. For example, suppose a drunken person drives a car off the road and into the plaintiff's house. The unauthorized entry is a trespass even though accidental. A trespass may be malicious, as where the trespasser enters for the purpose of taking water, trees, crops, or minerals, or to damage a structure. However, an involuntary entry caused by a third person's wrongful conduct is not a trespass. For example, if a third person negligently drove a vehicle so as to force the entrant onto the plaintiff's property, the entrant is not a trespasser. The negligent motorist who caused the accident and entrance is, in effect, a trespasser. A trespass may be committed by throwing articles on the plaintiff's land or across the land. For example, the wrongful placement of utility lines over property may constitute a trespass and shooting bullets over land is a trespass.

A trespasser is liable for any harm caused by a voluntary but wrongful entry, even if the entry was unavoidable. If an airplane accidentally crashes on the plaintiff's land, causing damage to the land, the airplane's entry is a trespass. The pilot is liable for the damage caused by the trespass even though he could not have prevented the crash.

If the trespasser enters for the purpose of stealing crops, trees, or minerals, he or she is liable for the value of the materials taken or for the resulting diminution in the value of the real estate. For example, if a trespasser cuts down an ornamental tree for the wood or as a matter of spite, the damage to the land (diminution in value) may exceed the worth of the tree or the cost of a similar tree. If the trespasser wrongfully removes a mineral such as gravel, however, the gravel may be worth more than the land's diminution in value. In this instance, the occupant may elect to recover the value of the gravel. In many states, the occupant is allowed by statute to recover three times the value of the trees, crops, or minerals taken by the trespasser. These so-called treble damages are a civil penalty for the benefit of the victim. The penalty is to act as a deterrent. A penalty is necessary because if trespassers had to pay only for the value of the property taken, the trespasser could, in effect, force the property owner to make a sale of the trees, minerals, or crops. That would be intolerable.

In common law, the possessor or occupant of property is allowed to use such force as is reasonably necessary to eject a trespasser from the premises. The possessor owes the trespasser a duty not to intentionally kill or injure her or him. The law now places a higher value on "life and limb" than on the protection of real estate. Therefore, a trespasser does not subject herself or himself to being intentionally shot or injured just because she or he is trespassing. Nor may the possessor set a "trap" for trespassers without being liable in tort for compensation for personal injuries the trespasser sustains. Of course, the possessor has a common-law right to self-defense. The possessor's best alternative, when practicable, is to call on local authorities to remove trespassers.

Historically, the common law permitted a landlord to use reasonable force to eject a holdover tenant, that is, a tenant who, without the permission of or agreement with the landlord, stays in possession of the premises after the lease has expired or otherwise is terminated. Many states have enacted laws against self-help and now require landlords to bring an action for unlawful detainer or an action in ejectment to remove the holdover tenant. After the owner's right to possession has been established, the court orders the sheriff to evict (remove) the holdover tenant. The plaintiff-owner has a right to have an expedited hearing to have the tenant removed. Often the owner can obtain possession within thirty days or less. Of course, if there is a dispute about whether the alleged trespasser has a right to be on the property, the litigation will take much longer.

If an owner of real estate does not register his or her title in the manner provided by state law, it is possible for a trespasser to obtain ownership to the real estate by what is known as adverse possession. This means the trespasser becomes the owner by simply occupying and using the property as his or her own for a statutorily prescribed number of years, usually ten or fifteen years. The trespasser's occupancy and use of the real estate must be open, notorious, and hostile to anyone else's rights in the property.[7] A tenant cannot acquire title from the landlord through mere occupancy and use, because a tenant's occupancy is not hostile to the rights of the landlord. The law tends to assume that a person who has possession of property, whether personal property or real estate, owns it and has a right to use it. Therefore, when a person is not in possession but claims a right to possession, the onus is on that person to prove a higher right to the property.[8]

The possessor's consent to an entrant's use of the property or to an entry to the premises is an affirmative defense. Consent may be expressed orally or in writing or implied by the circumstances. Also, entry under authority of the law is an affirmative defense. Authority is implied when the entrant has a legal duty to enter. Police officers and firefighters who enter on a property in the line of official duty have implied authority to enter. They are not trespassers.

The defendant has the burden of proving consent or authority. These defenses must be pleaded in the defendant's answer. Exhibits 4.7 and 4.8 illustrate the documents that are filed to open a trespass suit.

COMPLAINT

Comes now plaintiff and for his cause of action against defendant alleges:

1. [Jurisdictional allegations.]
2. At all times material herein plaintiff was and is the owner and in possession of Lots 1–5, Block 4, Townsend Addition, Clay County, State of Iowa.
3. On August 4, 2006, defendant wrongfully entered and trespassed upon said premises and damaged plaintiff's buildings, removed gravel from the premises, and destroyed three trees, all to plaintiff's damage in the sum of $26,000.

Wherefore, plaintiff prays for judgment against defendant in the sum of $26,000, together with his costs and disbursements herein.

[date]

Attorney for Plaintiff

[Attorney signature]

EXHIBIT 4.7

Complaint in Trespass

ANSWER

Comes now defendant and for his answer to plaintiff's complaint:

1. Denies each and every allegation, statement, and matter in said complaint contained, except as hereinafter expressly admitted or alleged.
2. Admits the allegations contained in paragraph 2 of the complaint.
3. Admits that defendant entered upon said premises on August 4, 2006, but specifically denies that the entry was wrongful or a trespass.
4. Denies that defendants caused any damage to plaintiff's buildings and puts plaintiff to his strict proof of same.
5. Admits that defendant cut down three trees that had been located upon the premises, but denies that said trees had any value to the premises.
6. Alleges that defendant entered the premises with consent of the owner and/or possessor of the premises, and that he was duly authorized and directed to remove the trees from the premises.

Wherefore, defendant prays that plaintiff take nothing by reason of his pretended cause of action and that defendant have judgment for his costs and disbursements herein.

[date]

Attorney for Defendant

[Attorney signature]

EXHIBIT 4.8

Answer to Complaint in Trespass

EXHIBIT 4.9

*Complaint for Assault
and Battery*

COMPLAINT

Comes now plaintiff and for her cause of action against defendant alleges:

1. [Jurisdictional allegations.]
2. On August 6, 2006, in the city of Smithville, Ohio, defendant assaulted plaintiff by pointing a rifle (weapon) at plaintiff, and defendant verbally threatened to shoot plaintiff.
3. Plaintiff was put in great fear for her life and was fearful of severe bodily injury.
4. Defendant struck plaintiff with a blunt portion of her rifle, thereby breaking plaintiff's jaw and rendering plaintiff unconscious.
5. As a direct consequence of the battery, plaintiff suffered severe and painful injuries that may be permanent in nature.
6. Plaintiff incurred medical expenses, will incur future medical expenses, has suffered a loss of income, and will suffer a loss of earning capacity as a direct consequence of the battery.
7. The assault and battery perpetrated by defendant upon plaintiff was intentional and malicious.
8. Plaintiff is entitled to recover punitive (exemplary) damages from defendant.

Wherefore, plaintiff demands judgment against defendant in the sum of $50,000 for compensatory damages and $10,000 as punitive damages, together with plaintiff's costs and disbursements herein.

[date]

Attorney for Plaintiff

[Attorney signature]

Battery

A battery is an intentional, unpermitted physical contact of an injurious nature or an intentional physical contact with a person that is offensive to ordinary sensibilities. The contact must be intentional to be actionable as a battery. Most physical contacts incidental to living in a society are considered permissible and not actionable. Typically, batteries include such wrongful acts as an intentional punch in the face; an intentional shooting; an intentional tripping, spanking, or rape; or a tackle in the course of a non-contact recreational activity. A more esoteric example is a medical operation on the wrong part of the body. The surgeon did not have consent to operate on that part and caused harm. The physical contact was intentional. It does not matter that the surgeon did not intend to "harm" the patient. Too often practical jokes end up being batteries. For example, if during a pool party the defendant throws the plaintiff into the pool as a joke, but the plaintiff sustains a broken leg, the defendant's wrongful act is a battery.

Some contacts are batteries, not because they are harmful, but because they are offensive to most people. An allegedly obnoxious contact is not actionable unless the

EXHIBIT 4.10

Answer to Complaint for Assault and Battery

ANSWER

Comes now defendant and for her answer to plaintiff's complaint:

1. Denies each and every allegation, statement, and matter in the complaint, except as hereinafter expressly admitted or alleged.
2. Admits the allegations of paragraphs 1, 2, 3, and 4 of the complaint.
3. Alleges that defendant is without sufficient knowledge or information upon which to form a belief concerning plaintiff's claims of injuries and damages and, therefore, puts plaintiff to her strict proof of same.
4. Alleges that plaintiff trespassed upon defendant's premises and entered defendant's dwelling for the purpose of burglarizing the dwelling.
5. Alleges that when defendant discovered plaintiff in defendant's home, plaintiff was armed with a knife and carrying off personal property belonging to defendant.
6. Alleges that defendant then and there arrested plaintiff and held plaintiff until the police could be summoned.
7. Specifically denies that defendant used more force than appeared necessary to protect herself and her property and to effectuate the arrest.

Wherefore, defendant prays that plaintiff take nothing by reason of her pretended cause of action and that defendant have judgment for her costs and disbursements herein.

[date]

Attorney for Defendant

[Attorney signature]

---

plaintiff actually experiences emotional distress. Mental suffering is not presumed. An obvious example of a battery without any actual physical harm is contact that is sexually oriented, such as an unwanted kiss or grope. Merely touching a person with a knife in a threatening manner would constitute a battery. Even throwing a pail of dirty water on a plaintiff could give rise to an action for a battery.

A cause of action for battery requires proof of all of the following items:

- Proof of a physical contact.
- Proof that the contact was without actual or implied consent.
- Proof that the contact was intentional.

The intent to make contact may be implied from the nature of the contact and surrounding circumstances. Compensatory money damages are allowed for any physical injury and emotional distress caused by the battery. Punitive damages are allowed in many states where the battery is malicious, that is, where there is an intent to cause harm as a result of the impermissible contact. Exhibits 4.9 and 4.10 illustrate a complaint for assault and battery and an answer to the complaint.

Assault

An assault is any intentional *threat* of death or serious bodily harm that actually puts the victim in fear of imminent physical harm. An assault does not require any physical contact. The cause of action for assault accrues when the victim experiences apprehension of imminent death or serious bodily harm. The wrongful conduct must cause the victim to be in fear of *immediate* bodily harm, or there is no assault. A plaintiff is entitled to compensatory damages for mental suffering caused by an assault. The threat of injury or death may come from words or a physical gesture or both. The tortfeasor need not use or have a weapon, but it must reasonably appear to the plaintiff that the tortfeasor has the ability to carry out the threat of harm. For example, if the defendant threatens to beat up the plaintiff "next year," there is no assault. Only if a contact occurs is there a battery in addition to the assault.

The tortfeasor must have a specific intent to cause the victim to be fearful or apprehend immediate harm. It is not enough that the alleged tortfeasor should have known that the plaintiff would become fearful. The defendant commits an assault if he or she puts the victim in fear while unsuccessfully trying to commit a battery. For example, if the defendant intentionally shoots a gun at the plaintiff but misses, an assault has occurred if the plaintiff was put in fear of being shot. The apprehension of injury must occur while the defendant is in a position to cause harm, not subsequently. If the plaintiff did not know that the defendant tried to shoot her with a gun but found out about the event later, no cause of action will lie for assault.

Some people are fearful of even innocuous or ordinary conduct. But the victim's apprehension of injury is judged on the basis of whether an ordinary, reasonable person would feel threatened. Stated another way, the plaintiff must have been put in fear, and the fear must have been reasonably justified. Mere swear words or foul language uttered in the presence of the victim or uttered at the victim do not constitute an assault. The words must convey a threat of harm with an apparent ability to do harm. An assault may be by a gesture, such as a "cocked fist" held close to the victim's face.

Consent to an assault is an affirmative defense. When people voluntarily enter into some games and athletic contests, by implication they consent to conduct which, under other circumstances, would constitute an assault. Another defense is that the alleged tortfeasor has a privilege to conduct herself or himself as an authority figure, as when a parent disciplines her or his own child or when a police officer makes an arrest.

Negligence

Legal Duty in General

To understand the basis for a negligence action, it is necessary to understand the underlying legal duty of reasonable care. Every person has a legal duty to use reasonable care not to injure others or damage another person's property. Negligence is failure to use reasonable care where significant harm is a foreseeable consequence. In determining whether a person's conduct was negligent, it is necessary to weigh the utility of the conduct against the foreseeability of harm and the seriousness of that harm. Ordinarily, a jury must decide whether a person was negligent by applying the "community standard" of reasonableness—another subjective concept. The law does not demand perfection. What is reasonable care depends on the circumstances that are known or should have been known at the time. A person's conduct is not judged on the basis of hindsight. Adults are charged with knowledge ordinarily possessed by members of the community and knowledge of natural laws such as gravity.

A cause of action in negligence requires proof that the defendant was negligent and that the defendant's negligence directly caused the plaintiff's injury or loss. Reasonable care is care that a reasonable person would use under like circumstances. Said another way, negligence is doing something that a reasonable person would not do, or failing to do something a reasonable person would do where there is an undue risk of significant harm. In the case of a child, reasonable care is care that a reasonable child of the same age, intelligence, training, and experience would use under like circumstances. A higher duty is imposed on common carriers such as airlines, railroads, and bus companies. They must exercise the highest degree of care for the protection of their passengers.

State and federal statutes prescribe the standard of care (i.e., what is reasonable) for many activities, such as driving speed limits. A violation of the statute makes the conduct unreasonable as a matter of law, and therefore negligent. When a statute has been violated there is no need to weigh the utility of the act against the foreseeability of harm and the gravity of the harm. The following typical jury instruction illustrates the application of such a statute: "If the statute was violated, the violation is negligence unless you, the jury, find evidence tending to show reasonable excuse or justification or evidence from which a reasonable person, under the circumstances, could believe that the violation would not endanger any person entitled to the protection of the statute."

Most state highway codes provide that traffic violations are merely prima facie evidence of negligence. This means that proof of a violation is enough to justify a finding of negligence, but it does not compel a finding of negligence. Highway codes generally regulate conduct, rather than prohibit. A technical violation may be excused or justified. A violation is to be judged on the basis of all the other circumstances surrounding an accident, including the known risks and the risks that reasonably should have been anticipated and the reasons for the violation. A jury has the task of weighing the reasons for the violation against the gravity of the violation and the foreseeability of harm resulting from the violation. Could a jury be justified in excusing a father's unlawful speed if he is driving his seriously injured child to a hospital to obtain medical care? Perhaps. Suppose he collides with a car that violated a stop sign—the father being on a through street. The jury would be entitled to weigh the reasons for the violation against the reasons for the statute.

There is an important but difficult distinction between an act that is regulated and an act that is prohibited. A prohibited act cannot be justified or excused. For example, a statute that prohibits the sale of liquor to a minor establishes a legal duty, not a mere standard of care.

In the hierarchy of culpability, the next level above negligence is reckless misconduct, which is conduct intentionally perpetrated in the face of substantial and obvious danger to other persons or property without specific intent to injure anyone. For example, driving on a crowded city street at a speed slightly over the speed limit is negligence, but driving on a city street at eighty miles per hour is reckless misconduct. Some states recognize degrees of negligence such as ordinary negligence, gross negligence, and willful and wanton negligence. The distinctions are quite esoteric and beyond the scope of this text.

The plaintiff must prove negligence by a fair preponderance of the evidence. Said another way, negligence must be established by the greater weight of the evidence. The mere fact that an accident happens does not necessarily mean that anyone was negligent. If the evidence fails to prove all of the elements of negligence, the court must direct a verdict against the party who has the burden of proof. A directed verdict means that the claim or defense is disallowed by the judge, because the evidence failed to prove certain facts that are essential to the cause of action.

Legal Duty Based on Relationships

The concept of legal duty is easily understood where a person committed an act that injured another person or someone else's property. The concept's application is less clear where the person allegedly failed to act or failed to protect another person from harm. The relationship between persons may be critical in determining whether a duty of care exists and whether the duty requires some affirmative action to protect. The following examples illustrate this concept of legal duty and the basis for it.

1. Suppose a person sees a neighbor using a metal ladder very near an uninsulated electric power line and recognizes that the neighbor is in danger of being electrocuted. Does that person have a legal duty to warn or stop the neighbor from going near the line? No. Failure to warn or stop the neighbor would not result in legal liability if an injury occurred. The law does not require ordinary individuals to act to protect fellow citizens, whether or not neighbors. But if a homeowner has a friend helping with some house painting and sees the friend near a power line, the homeowner has a duty to stop the dangerous activity. The duty arises from the special relationship between the owner of the property and the friend's status on the property as an entrant or invitee.

2. Suppose a pedestrian discovers a trench in the road and realizes that motorists may not be so fortunate as to see and avoid it. If a vehicle were to run into the trench, the vehicle would be damaged and its occupants injured. Does the pedestrian have a legal duty to warn approaching motorists of the danger or to stop motorists or to fill in the trench? Is there negligence toward the motoring public for a failure to take these precautions? No, because the pedestrian does not have a legal duty to act for the benefit of the public. However, the person who excavated the trench or failed to erect barricades is negligent. By creating the "trap" in the public highway, he or she breached a legal duty to members of the public using the highway. Suppose the trench exists in an area of highway that is under the control of a construction contractor. The contractor may have a duty to protect the public from the trench, even though he or she did not create the trench. The contractor's duty arises from a contractual relationship with the government to protect the public in the construction zone.

3. Suppose a woman invites people to her home for a social gathering. She knows that most of the guests will use the front sidewalk but is unaware that several bricks in the sidewalk are dangerously loose. One of the guests trips on a loose brick, falls, and is injured. A negligence action may lie against the hostess as the occupant of the premises. Because she owes a

legal duty of reasonable care to make the premises reasonably safe for people that she expects to enter the premises. The duty arises from the relationship created when one invites another onto his premises. In some states, the duty of reasonable care includes an obligation to conduct reasonable inspections to discover potential dangers to her guests and to take preventive action such as to give warnings or correct the danger. Conversely, the law in other states provides that the occupant of a house does not owe a legal duty of inspection and preparation to mere social guests. The occupant's only duty is to correct known defects or hazardous conditions or to warn social guests of known dangers. So if the hostess was unaware of the loose bricks, she would not have a legal duty to repair the walkway or warn her guests. In all states, however, the law imposes a legal duty on the part of a business to inspect and prepare the premises for business invitees.

4. Suppose a man dug a hole in his backyard for planting a tree. During the night a thief entered the premises to steal a motorboat engine. As he was leaving the premises with the engine, he fell in the hole and was injured. Did the property owner have a duty to keep the premises reasonably safe for the intruder? Should the property owner be liable to the thief for leaving the hole unguarded? Does the thief's malevolent purpose insulate the property owner from liability? In most states, thieves are treated as trespassers. A thief has no right to be on the premises; the property owner does not owe any duty of care to the thief. However, property owners may not set traps for the purpose of catching or injuring trespassers—even thieves. In negligence actions it is often necessary to determine whether there is a special relationship between the injured plaintiff and the defendant that imposes a legal duty on the defendant to protect the plaintiff.

So-called malpractice cases are really just actions in negligence. They are claims against professional people based on their alleged failure to comply with the standards of their profession. Of course, the substandard performance must have caused some harm to the plaintiff for an action to lie. Malpractice actions may be brought against physicians, lawyers, nurses, accountants, pharmacists, engineers, architects, and so on. The gravamen of the claim is that (1) A duty arises by reason of the relationship formed between physician and patient, attorney and client, and so on; (2) the professional failed to have the necessary education or skill to practice in the profession; or (3) the professional failed to perform in accordance with professional standards. In either event, the standard of the profession dictates the minimum standard of care and what it requires.

Laypersons are presumed to be unfamiliar with professional duties and the applicable standards. Consequently, the law requires other professionals, who are familiar with professional standards, to establish the applicable standards in court. This usually is done through expert testimony. Expert testimony also may be necessary to determine whether the standards have been violated. An untoward or disappointing result from the professional's services is not, in itself, a sufficient basis for a malpractice action in court. For this reason, a patient who sues his or her physician usually must find another qualified physician who will testify that the treating physician's conduct deviated from acceptable professional standards. Otherwise, the patient's case must be dismissed for failure to prove a prima facie case.[9]

The preceding examples illustrate that even though negligence is simple in theory, its application may be complex. To make the whole subject even more difficult, the law of negligence is constantly changing. The study of negligence involves a study of the interrelationships between people, public institutions, and governments. Each special relationship creates a different duty. For example, a bus driver must exercise the *highest degree* of care for the protection of passengers, but only *reasonable care* for the protection of other motorists or pedestrians using the roadways. The difference in the duty of care is based on the difference in the relationships.

Causation

In a negligence action, the plaintiff must prove that the defendant's conduct was negligent and that the defendant's negligence was a **proximate cause** of the plaintiff's injury or property damage. If the defendant's negligence was not a proximate cause of the loss, the defendant is not liable even if he or she was negligent. The term **direct cause** may be used interchangeably with proximate cause.

The term *proximate cause* is simple in theory. There must be some significant nexus between the defendant's alleged wrongful act or omission and the plaintiff's loss. A proximate cause is a cause that significantly contributes to the cause of the parties' accident and injury or other loss. By way of illustration, suppose a motorist parks an automobile two feet from the curb when local law requires her to park within one foot, and another motorist runs into the back of the parked automobile. It is unlikely that the technical violation of parking two feet from the curb actually caused the accident. The cause may be immediate or through a series of events that naturally follow one after another. For example, suppose that a workman is required to use hand signals to guide a delivery truck that is backing up through a construc-

proximate cause   A cause that has a direct and substantial part in bringing about an occurrence, injury, loss, or harm for which a party seeks a remedy in court.

direct cause   The term is synonymous with proximate cause. A direct cause is a cause that had a substantial part in bringing about an accident, loss, or injury either immediately or through happenings that follow one after another.

EXAMPLE

Suppose a motorist is traveling on a through highway at five miles per hour over the posted speed limit and is "broadsided" by a vehicle that failed to stop for a traffic light. The motorist's excessive speed is merely coincidental; it does not matter how fast the motorist was traveling on the through highway if hit by a car on a cross-street that failed to stop for a stop light or stop sign. The stop light violation was the sole cause of the collision. The effect of the victim's excessive speed was too remote to be considered a proximate cause. Violation of the statutory speed limit is negligence, but it is not a proximate cause of the collision. A stop sign violation would have caused the collision even if the other motorist had been traveling well within the speed limit. The speed limit is designed to reduce the risk that a driver will lose control of his or her vehicle. It also is designed to make it easier for other vehicles to enter the highway. But a speed limit is not designed to prevent a collision with a driver who violates a stop sign.

tion site, and the workman misdirects the truck causing it to go into a trench; the truck tips and material falls out of the truck; the material hits a cart that is propelled and strikes the plaintiff injuring him. The example shows a series of events that "naturally" flowed from the original negligent act—misdirecting the backing truck. At some point, an act or omission becomes too remote in time, place, or effect to be considered an operative cause of the loss.

But suppose the motorist is traveling twenty-five miles per hour over the speed limit. It is reasonable to believe that a passenger's injuries will be greater because of the excessive speed? Speed limits are established to reduce the severity of injuries as well as to prevent accidents. Again the question arises, did the excessive speed cause the accident or consequential injury? Usually, the issue of proximate cause is a question of fact for a jury to decide.

An accident may have more than one proximate cause. When the effects of the negligent conduct of two or more persons actively work at substantially the same time to cause the accident, the conduct of each may be a proximate cause of the accident. If two defendants contribute toward a plaintiff's loss, they are jointly and individually liable for the entire loss. For example, if two motorists collide in an intersection because both failed to keep a proper lookout, their concurrent negligence makes both of them liable for *all* their passengers' injuries. Each motorist is individually liable to the passengers in both cars for all of the passengers' injuries, but both motorists have the right to contribution from the other in proportion to their relative share of the fault. If one of the negligent motorists has no insurance and no money to pay for the loss, the entire loss could fall on the motorist who is financially responsible.

Another facet of causation is the principle of **superseding cause.**[10] A superseding cause insulates a negligent person from liability for prior negligent conduct. The elements of a superseding cause are very specific. For a cause to be a superseding cause, its harmful effects must have occurred after the original negligence, and the superseding cause must not have been brought about by the original negligence. For example, if the driver of an automobile sees a truck unlawfully stopped on the highway ahead and has sufficient time in which to avoid a collision but negligently fails to do so, the automobile driver's negligence is a superseding cause of the collision. The superseding negligence of the automobile driver insulates the truck operator from liability for the collision, even though the truck created the dangerous condition.

superseding cause An independent cause of an injury or loss that insulates or relieves the defendant from liability for his or her negligence. Superseding cause is often referred to as efficient intervening cause.

Affirmative Defenses to Negligence Actions

In addition to the numerous affirmative defenses that are applicable in most cases, two defenses have special application in negligence actions: contributory negligence and assumption of risk. Contributory negligence is not a special kind of negligence. It is simply the plaintiff's own negligence that directly contributed to the plaintiff's loss. The common law rule was that if the plaintiff was negligent and that negligence was a proximate cause of the plaintiff's loss, the plaintiff's contributory negligence entirely defeated the plaintiff's claim. For example, suppose a merchant negligently left a large hole unguarded at his store and a customer fell into the hole and was injured. If a jury concluded that the customer was negligent for not keeping a proper lookout for her own safety, the customer's negligence was a complete defense to her claim against the negligent merchant. The common law viewed negligence and causation as absolutes and did not compare fault between the parties. Any causal negligence was sufficient to support a claim or to provide a defense. As seen below, the law has evolved to replace this harsh all-or-nothing rule with a more equitable rule of comparative negligence.

In common law, a plaintiff's assumption of risk also gave the defendant a complete defense to a negligence action. The plaintiff assumed the risk if she or he voluntarily placed herself or himself in a position to chance a known hazard. To prove assumption of risk, the defendant had to prove that the plaintiff had actual knowledge of the specific risk (danger), that the plaintiff appreciated the risk, that the plaintiff had a choice or opportunity to avoid the risk, that the plaintiff voluntarily chose to incur the risk, and that the assumed risk materialized to cause the plaintiff's injury or harm. As the law has evolved, this rule too has narrowed so that it applies to limited factual circumstances.

Contributory Negligence

Under the old system of contributory negligence, each defendant who was liable for the plaintiff's injury or loss would be liable jointly and individually for the whole loss and the entire award of compensatory damages. If the action involved two defendants, they would be equally liable to each other for one-half of the award made to the plaintiff. If each of three defendants were liable, their share would be one-third. And so on.

Comparative Negligence

In most states, the law concerning contributory negligence and assumption of risk has evolved into the law of comparative negligence. Many states adopted comparative negligence through legislation. Some state supreme courts adopted the doctrine through judicial decisions and thereby modified the states' common law rule. Because comparison of wrongful conduct can apply to actions other than garden-variety negligence (product liability, for example) the modern doctrine often is referred to as **comparative fault.** The comparative fault doctrine encompasses almost any type of wrongful acts or omissions—except intentional wrongs—that are actionable.

comparative fault An expanded concept of comparative negligence that includes strict liability in tort, breach of warranty, dram shop liability, and other causes of action not based on intentional wrongful conduct.

Comparative negligence and comparative fault is more fair. The objective is to provide some compensation to a plaintiff even though he or she also was negligent and contributed to the injury or loss. When a case is tried pursuant to the law of comparative negligence, the jury is required to evaluate each party's causal negligence and apportion the parties' negligence on a percentage basis.

For example, assume the jury determined that the plaintiff was 20 percent at fault, defendant A was 10 percent at fault, defendant B was 30 percent at fault, and defendant C was 40 percent at fault, and the amount of money damages awarded to the plaintiff is $10,000; the plaintiff's recovery will be $8,000. The plaintiff's recovery is reduced by 20 percent, which is the amount of her or his causal negligence. The plaintiff cannot recover any damages from defendant A because the plaintiff was more negligent than defendant A. Defendants B and C are jointly and separately liable to the plaintiff for the entire $8,000. Therefore, if defendant B cannot pay any portion, C must pay the entire $8,000. Nevertheless, as between defendant B (30 percent) and defendant C (40 percent), they are obligated to pay the $8,000 award proportionately. Defendant B is obligated for $3,428.57, and defendant C is obli-

EXAMPLE

Suppose that two defendants and the plaintiff were found causally negligent. Suppose that the jury allocates causal negligence as follows: 50 percent to defendant A, 10 percent to defendant B, and 40 percent to the plaintiff. If the jury set the plaintiff's money damages at $10,000, the plaintiff would actually recover 60 percent, or $6,000. The plaintiff could collect the entire $6,000 from either defendant, because they are jointly liable. But defendant A would be entitled to receive contribution from defendant B for 10 percent, which is $1,000. Or, defendant B would be entitled to receive contribution from defendant A for 50 percent, which is $5,000.

gated for $4,571.43. The proportionate amounts are easily calculated by converting the 30 percent to 30/70, or 3/7, and converting the 40 percent to 40/70, or 4/7.

$3/7 \times \$8,000.00 = \$3,428.57$
$4/7 \times \$8,000.00 = \$4,571.43$

There is **pure comparative negligence** and **ordinary comparative negligence.** In states that have adopted *pure comparative negligence*, the plaintiff's recovery of money damages is reduced by her or his percentage of causal negligence even if that percentage is 80 percent, 90 percent, or even 95 percent. Each joint or concurrent tortfeasor is liable to the plaintiff for the full amount of the damage not attributable to the plaintiff's fault. As between the joint or concurrent tortfeasors, they must share on the basis of their percentages of causal negligence. Of course, the practical problem arises for the defendants when one of them lacks the ability to pay his or her share.

In states that have adopted *ordinary comparative negligence*, the plaintiff's award is reduced by his or her percentage of causal negligence, as it is under pure comparative fault, but if the plaintiff's causal negligence is *greater* than the defendant's

pure comparative negligence The plaintiff may recover money damages from a defendant who was causally negligent, regardless of the fact that the plaintiff may have been much more negligent than the defendant.

ordinary comparative negligence Comparative negligence in which the plaintiff's claim is barred if the claimant's causal negligence is more than the defendant's causal negligence.

EXAMPLE

Suppose that two defendants and the plaintiff were negligent. Suppose that the jury allocates causal negligence as follows: 50 percent to defendant A, 10 percent to defendant B, and 40 percent to the plaintiff. If the jury set the plaintiff's money damages at $10,000, the plaintiff would actually recover only 60 percent, or $6,000. The plaintiff could collect the entire $6,000 from defendant A, because the plaintiff was not more negligent than defendant A. The plaintiff could not collect any money from defendant B, because the plaintiff was more negligent than B. In effect, defendant A becomes liable for defendant B's share.

causal negligence—51 percent to 49 percent in a two-party case—the plaintiff is not permitted to recover any damages at all. In that event, the plaintiff's greater comparative negligence is a complete defense to the plaintiff's action.

The law of comparative negligence can be fairly complex and difficult to apply where several parties are involved.

Sample Complaint and Answer

The documents in Exhibits 4.11 and 4.12 are typical of those filed in negligence actions. The answer in Exhibit 4.12 admits the occurrence of the accident, but denies liability by denying negligence. Plaintiffs are put to their proof to establish their damages. The answer raises two affirmative defenses: contributory negligence and assumption of risk. Note that Maria Gallegos's claim is based on what is called a derivative cause of action. Therefore, her claim is defeated by any affirmative defense that defeats her husband's claim.

Product Liability

Product liability law includes several causes of action for people who are injured by defective products. Historically, the injured consumer had to prove an action in negligence against the manufacturer or vendor to recover money damages for an injury caused by a defective product. The consumer had to prove that the product was negligently designed or fabricated and that the defect was the proximate cause of the plaintiff's injury. This can be a daunting task. Under product liability law, a product is considered to be defective if it is unreasonably dangerous for use in the ordinary manner. A product may be unreasonably dangerous because of its design, fabrication, lack of instructions for safe use, or inadequate warnings about dangers of use.

While the law had long recognized the right of the parties to create *express* warranties concerning the quality and fitness of goods sold in the marketplace, the next step in the evolution of product liability law was the imposition of *implied* warranties from merchants to buyers. At first, a buyer could only allege a breach of warranty against the person from whom he or she purchased the product. Eventually, the law extended implied warranties from the manufacturer to anyone in the chain of sale of a new product. The result is that a buyer now may bring a breach-of-warranty claim against the retail vendor, the distributor, and/or the manufacturer. The retailer may seek indemnity from the distributor and manufacturer. The distributor may seek indemnity from the manufacturer. The manufacturer who merely assembled the product may have a right to indemnity from the supplier of a defective component. However, the common law recognized various common-law affirmative defenses to implied-warranty actions, such as contributory negligence and/or assumption of risk on the part of the user. The law also required the buyer to give a timely notice of the injury and defect to preserve the right to make a claim. Furthermore, vendors were able to avoid liability by making warranty disclaimers part of the sales contract.

Legal scholars and writers began to believe that the law should make compensation for the harm caused by defective products a cost of doing business. Gradually, many of the restrictions on implied-warranty actions were abrogated by court decision and statute. For example, an implied warranty was extended to members of the buyer's family. They reasoned that most products in modern society are manufactured

COMPLAINT

EXHIBIT 4.11

Complaint in Negligence

Comes now the plaintiffs and for their cause of action against defendants allege:

1. [Jurisdictional allegations.]
2. Plaintiffs are and at all times material herein have been husband and wife, and they reside in the state of Wisconsin.
3. Defendant Shawn and Associates, Inc., is and at all times material herein was a Wisconsin corporation having its office and principal place of business in Spencer, Wisconsin.
4. Defendant Drake Apartments, Inc., is and at all times material herein was a Wisconsin corporation having its office and principal place of business in Spencer, Wisconsin.
5. Defendant Barton and Associates, Inc., is and at all times material herein was a Minnesota corporation having its office and principal place of business in Madison, Minnesota.
6. On or about July 19, 2006, Shawn and Associates contracted with Drake Apartments, the owner of premises located at 724 South Fifth Street, Spencer, Wisconsin (hereinafter the job site), to act as general contractor for the construction of an addition to said premises, and in connection therewith Shawn and Associates agreed to assume responsibility for providing a safe place to work for all persons working at the job site, including all subcontractors and their employees.
7. On or about October 26, 2006, Drake Apartments entered into a contract with Barton and Associates whereby Barton and Associates agreed to provide certain services, including architectural services, to Drake Apartments. On or about the 28th day of July, 2006, Shawn and Associates, as general contractor, entered into a contract, attached as Exhibit A, with Johnson Construction, a subcontractor, for erection by Johnson Construction of the structural steel frame for the addition to said premises. In connection therewith Shawn and Associates agreed to assume responsibility for providing a safe place to work for Johnson Construction and all Johnson Construction employees at the job site, and Johnson Construction agreed to indemnify Shawn and Associates from all claims for damages and injury in connection with the work.
8. Plaintiff Juan Gallegos at all times material herein was employed by Johnson Construction as a steelworker.
9. Drake Apartments negligently and in violation of its legal obligations failed to employ a competent and careful contractor to do the work and to perform the duties that Drake Apartments owed to third persons, including the plaintiffs, and to take precautions against the risk of physical harm to persons on the premises.
10. Prior to and on February 7, 2006, defendants negligently and in violation of federal and state OSHA standards and in breach of their contractual obligations failed to provide plaintiff Juan Gallegos with a safe place to work at the job site; failed to use proper construction procedures and failed to

continued

properly supervise the work at the job site; failed to properly inspect the job site and failed to correct unsafe conditions; failed to erect proper barricading to protect plaintiff at the job site; failed to adequately warn plaintiff of unsafe conditions and hazards existing at the job site; and failed to fulfill its nondelegable contractual and legal responsibilities with respect to working conditions at the job site.

11. Defendant Barton and Associates negligently and in breach of contractual duties to plaintiff failed to provide general administration of the construction contract; failed to properly represent the owner; failed to determine, in general, if the work was proceeding properly and in accordance with contract documents; and failed to advise and consult with Drake Apartments regarding safety on the job site.

12. On February 7, 2006, as a direct consequence of the negligence of the defendants, and each of them, plaintiff Juan Gallegos, while working at the job site, fell in a stairwell at the job site and suffered permanent injuries and permanent disability.

13. Because of his injuries, plaintiff Juan Gallegos has been prevented from transacting his business and has lost wages in the approximate amount of $50,000; he has incurred expenses and obligations for medical attention, hospitalization and related care, and miscellaneous items in the approximate amount of $100,000; he has been and will in the future be totally physically disabled and totally dependent upon others for his care; he has lost all future earning capacity and will lose all future wages; he will incur substantial medical expenses, and additional living and miscellaneous expenses in the future; and he has suffered and will in the future suffer great pain of body and mind.

14. Owning to the injuries sustained by Juan Gallegos, plaintiff Maria Gallegos has been and in the future will be required to provide care for her husband; she has permanently lost the services of her husband; and her comfort and happiness in his society and companionship have been permanently impaired.

Wherefore, the plaintiffs, and each of them, demand judgment in their favor and against the defendants, and each of them, jointly and severally, as follows:

1. Money damages for plaintiff Juan Gallegos in a fair and adequate sum as proved at trial.
2. Money damages for plaintiff Maria Gallegos in a fair and adequate sum as proved at trial.
3. Reimbursement for plaintiffs' costs and disbursements herein.

[date]

Attorney for Plaintiffs

[Attorney signature]

EXHIBIT 4.12

Answer to Complaint in Negligence

ANSWER

Comes now defendant Drake Apartments, Inc., and for its answer to plaintiffs' complaint:

1. Denies each and every allegation, statement, matter, and thing in said complaint contained, except as hereinafter expressly admitted or otherwise alleged.
2. Admits that plaintiff Juan Gallegos sustained injuries about the time and place mentioned in the complaint, but specifically denies that Drake Apartments was negligent.
3. Alleges that this answering defendant does not have sufficient knowledge or information upon which to form a belief concerning plaintiffs' claims of injuries and damages; therefore, plaintiffs are put to their strict proof of same.
4. Alleges that plaintiff Juan Gallegos was negligent so as to cause his alleged injuries and damages.
5. Alleges that plaintiff Juan Gallegos assumed the risk of his alleged injuries.

Wherefore, defendant Drake Apartments prays that plaintiffs take nothing by reason of their pretended cause of action, and that this answering defendant have judgment for its costs and disbursements herein.

[date]

Attorney for Defendant

[Attorney signature]

and marketed by large, well-established companies that could easily spread out the cost of damage claims by simply increasing the cost of their products. This rationale led to the creation of a new cause of action commonly known as strict liability in tort.

Now all states have adopted the strict-liability-in-tort cause of action in one form or another as an additional means of providing compensation to persons injured by defective products, regardless whether the injured person was the purchaser of the particular product. All an injured person has to prove is that the product was defective at the time it left the vendor's possession and that the defect was the proximate cause of the plaintiff's injury. A cause of action for strict liability in tort lies against manufacturers, distributors, wholesalers, and retailers. But no action will lie against a seller of a product who is not in the business of selling that kind of product. In other words, implied-warranty actions and strict liability actions can be maintained only against merchants who are in the business of selling the particular product.

As originally conceived, contributory negligence and assumption of risk, and comparative negligence were not supposed to be defenses to strict liability tort actions. Nevertheless, the current trend is to use comparative fault as a basis for reducing the plaintiff's recovery of damages. The need for comparative fault arose out of a string of cases where consumers were grossly abusing products—using them in ways that were totally improper. The law gave the vendor the burden of proving that the product was not being used for its intended purpose or was being used in such a dangerous manner that the vendor had no duty to warn against it. Once the courts recognized product abuse as a defense to strict liability claims, it was relatively easy to move to the comparative fault doctrine for allocating damages in product cases.

Nowadays, the plaintiff's claim may be based on negligence, breach of warranty, or strict liability in tort. The alleged facts may permit the plaintiff to pursue all three legal theories (causes of action) in one case. The theory on which recovery is sought determines what facts must be proved, what evidence is necessary, and even what damages are recoverable. Defenses applicable to a negligence action may not apply to a warranty action or to a strict liability action, and defenses that apply to a warranty action may not apply to a negligence action. The amount of damages recoverable under one theory may be significantly more than those recoverable under another theory. Therefore, the plaintiff's lawyer must choose the cause or causes of action carefully. In some states, the plaintiff is required to elect between a negligence claim and a strict liability claim before the case is submitted to the jury. This development has occurred because, on occasion, some states have found that the submission of both theories in the same case leads to inconsistent verdicts.[11]

A brief review and example should be helpful to understand the interplay of these causes of action in products cases. Manufacturers owe a duty to purchasers and users to apply due care to make products that are not unreasonably dangerous when used in the ordinary manner and for a proper purpose. But a manufacturer is not liable for the consequences of a product's failure if the manufacturer used ordinary care in making the product. By way of example, if a manufacturer builds an automobile that has a defective axle and the defect could not have been prevented or discovered by the exercise of reasonable care, the manufacturer is not liable to the purchaser or occupants who are injured in an accident caused by the broken axle. The retail vendor of the automobile is not liable. Very often, reasonable care is perceived as the care that other manufacturers use in making similar products.

The same example may be used to illustrate a breach-of-implied-warranty theory for recovery. An automobile with a defective axle is not of merchantable quality and certainly is not fit for use as a motor vehicle. Therefore, a recovery in favor of the purchaser and members of his or her family may be possible under the breach-of-implied-warranty theory. But passengers who are not members of the purchaser's family could not maintain a warranty action—at least not in some states. The law permits the vendor to qualify and limit implied warranties. Indeed, the contract of sale may exclude all warranties by making the sale "with all faults" or "as is." Furthermore, contracts often limit the time during which a warranty may be claimed. Assume, for purposes of this example, that the axle broke twenty-five months after the automobile was purchased and the contract eliminated all warranties after twenty-four months. The sales contract effectively negated the implied warranties.

The owner and occupants of the automobile in the preceding example could maintain an action in strict liability in tort for their personal injuries caused by the defective axle. They would need to prove that the axle was defective when it left the manufacturer's plant. One might wonder why a negligence action is ever pursued in a products case, because a strict liability case is easier to prove. In certain cases a jury has determined that the product in question was not defective, but the vendor's negligence caused the accident.[12]

Each vendor in the chain of sale is liable to the plaintiff consumer for the full amount of the plaintiff's damages. But each vendor whose liability is based on mere warranty or strict liability in tort is entitled to indemnity from the preceding vendor or vendors in the chain. Therefore, a negligent vendor is precluded from obtaining indemnity but may be allowed to obtain contribution from other negligent vendors in the chain of sale. Sample documents for initiating an action in strict liability in tort appear in Exhibits 4.13 and 4.14.

Liquor Vendors' Liability

Historically, vendors of intoxicating liquors were not liable at common law for the accidents caused by inebriated customers, because an inebriated person's wrongful conduct was considered the sole proximate cause of a resulting accident. The consumer was held responsible to know when he or she had had enough alcohol; the vendor was not the consumer's guardian. The law did not impose liability on a person merely because he or she was intoxicated at the time the person was involved in an accident. For instance, if a defendant driver collided with the rear end of the car ahead, the defendant's negligence would be based on his or her failure to keep a proper lookout, not having control of his or her car, and driving too close to the car ahead. The driver's intoxication would tend to explain why the driver was negligent, but it would not, in itself, constitute negligence.

In the early 1900s, state legislatures began making it illegal to sell intoxicants to minors and to obviously[13] intoxicated adults. In addition, state legislatures enacted liquor liability laws that made liquor vendors liable for harm an intoxicated person caused if the vendor made an illegal sale to the intoxicated person. Most or all states now have so-called **dram shop** legislation, which imposes civil liability on liquor vendors in favor of persons who have been injured as the result of an illegal sale of intoxicants. The intoxicated person does not have any claim against the liquor vendor for injuring herself or himself. Nevertheless, if the intoxicated person is killed or disabled, the spouse and children of the intoxicated person have a claim against the vendor for loss of support. Liquor vendors have considerable difficulty defending such cases, because the allegedly intoxicated person is all too willing to testify that he or she was very drunk so that the family will get some money from the vendor.

In these dram shop actions, an illegal sale does not have to be a proximate cause of the plaintiff's injury. The law only requires that the illegal sale and intoxication *contribute* to the accident and injury.

A victim who participated in an illegal sale of an intoxicant is guilty of **complicity.** Most states recognize complicity as an affirmative defense to a dram shop action. The defendant liquor vendor must allege complicity in the answer. The vendor has the burden of proving complicity. Complicity is a complete defense, even in states that have comparative fault statutes. For example, suppose two men spend several hours in a liquor establishment buying each other intoxicants and become obviously intoxicated. An illegal sale of liquor is made to them, and one of the intoxicated men attempts to drive his car with the other as a passenger. They have an accident that was contributed

dram shop A civil action against liquor vendors and in favor of persons, other than the inebriate, who suffer harm as the result of an illegal sale of intoxicants.

complicity An affirmative defense to a dram shop action. For example, complicity is established by showing that the plaintiff bought the intoxicants for the intoxicated person.

Exhibit 4.13

Complaint in Strict Liability in Tort

COMPLAINT

Comes now plaintiff and for her cause of action against defendant alleges:

1. [Jurisdictional allegations.]

Count 1

2. At the times herein mentioned, defendant Dawn Company, Inc., was engaged in the manufacture of a chemical oven cleaner called Sparkle. Said cleaner was manufactured for sale to the general public.

3. During the month of February 2006, plaintiff purchased a can of defendant's oven cleaner identified by the marking 5M142D, which was manufactured and sold by defendant for retail sales to the general public.

4. At all times following the purchase of the oven cleaner, plaintiff reasonably and properly handled the product.

5. Defendant sold and delivered the oven cleaner to retailers knowing that in the regular course of business it would be resold to a customer for use as an oven cleaner.

6. Defendant failed to provide plaintiff with a warning concerning the hazards of using the oven cleaner.

7. The oven cleaner was negligently designed, manufactured, tested, and inspected by defendant, and the oven cleaner was dangerous to the physical health of users when it left defendant's control or possession.

8. Defendant was negligent in failing to provide adequate instructions for the oven cleaner's use and failing to warn of the product's dangers.

9. On March 12, 2006, plaintiff used the oven cleaner for the first time and in accordance with the printed instructions on the can, for the purpose of cleaning her oven in her home located at 5606 Lawndale Lane, Spencer, Illinois.

10. Defendant's negligence directly caused plaintiff to suffer severe itching, swelling, dizziness, restricted breathing, and an anaphylactic reaction, all to plaintiff's general damage.

11. Plaintiff incurred expenses for medical attention, hospital care, and medicines in the sum of $500.

Count 2

12. Plaintiff realleges paragraphs 1 through 10 of count 1 as if those allegations were set forth in full in this count.

13. In marketing the oven cleaner product, defendant impliedly warranted that the product was of merchantable quality and was fit for the purpose for which it was intended.

14. In fact, the product was not of merchantable quality and was unsafe and unfit for the purpose for which it was sold, purchased, and used.

15. Defendants breach of said implied warranties caused plaintiff to suffer serious bodily injuries.

Count 3

16. Plaintiff realleges paragraphs 1 through 14 of counts 1 and 2 as if those allegations were set forth in full.

17. Defendant expressly warranted that the oven cleaner contained no caustic or choking fumes or chemicals to irritate eyes or nose.

continued

18. The oven cleaner did not conform to the express warranties made by defendant and printed on the product container.

19. As a result of defendant's breach of the express warranties, plaintiff suffered serious bodily injuries.

Count 4

20. Plaintiff realleges paragraphs 1 through 18 of counts 1 through 3 as if those allegations were set forth in full.

21. The oven cleaner manufactured and sold by defendant was unreasonably dangerous for use in the ordinary manner and, therefore, was a defective product.

22. Plaintiff used the product in the intended manner for the proper purpose.

23. As a result of the defective and injurious character of the oven cleaner, plaintiff suffered injuries as described above.

24. As a result of the defective condition of the oven cleaner, defendant is strictly liable in tort to plaintiff for the injuries sustained and losses suffered as described above.

Wherefore, plaintiff prays for judgment against defendant in a fair and adequate sum as proved at trial, together with her costs and disbursements herein.

[date]

Attorney for Plaintiff

[Attorney signature]

to by the driver's intoxication. The passenger's complicity in the illegal sales is a defense to his claim against the liquor vendor who illegally sold liquor to the driver. Similarly, if a person participates in a sale of intoxicants to a minor and is injured as a result of the minor's intoxication, that person cannot recover compensation from the liquor vendor who made the illegal sale. Note, however, that some states may not recognize complicity as a defense.

Dram shop statutes typically require the plaintiff to give the liquor vendor notice of the illegal sale, occurrence, loss, and intent to make a claim. The notice must be delivered within a specified time limit, typically 120 days after the occurrence. Failure to give the statutory notice is a bar to any action against the liquor vendor. The notice requirement gives the vendor an opportunity to investigate and evaluate the claim before the evidence disappears. If a notice is required by state law, the plaintiff must allege in the complaint that he or she complied with the notice requirement. If the vendor denies receiving a notice of claim, the burden is on the plaintiff to prove that notice was duly delivered. The plaintiff's lawyer should be careful to establish and preserve proof that the notice was delivered in a timely manner.

Unless specified in the dram shop statute, negligence on the part of the injured plaintiff is not a defense. The law seems to be moving toward application of

EXHIBIT 4.14

Answer to Complaint in Strict Liability in Tort

ANSWER

Comes now defendant and for its answer to plaintiff's complaint:

1. Denies each and every allegation, statement, matter, and thing in said complaint contained, except as hereinafter expressly admitted or alleged.
2. Admits the allegations of paragraphs 1 and 2 of the complaint.
3. Alleges that defendant is without sufficient knowledge or information upon which to form a belief concerning plaintiff's claims of injuries and damages and, therefore, puts plaintiff to her strict proof of same.
4. Alleges that if plaintiff sustained injuries and damages as alleged in the complaint, they were caused by the negligence of plaintiff.
5. Alleges that plaintiff did not serve defendant with notice of breach of warranty as required by law.
6. Alleges that plaintiff assumed the risk of injury.[1]

Wherefore, defendant prays that plaintiff take nothing by reason of her pretended cause of action and that defendant have judgment for its costs and disbursements herein.

[date]

Attorney for Defendant

[Attorney signature]

[1] It is not necessary to allege that plaintiff misused the product, and that was the cause of injury, because misuse is not an affirmative defense even though misuse by plaintiff would prevent plaintiff from recovering money damages. Plaintiff has the burden of proving that she used the product in the ordinary, intended manner.

comparative fault principles in these cases, however. If comparative fault or negligence is applicable, the plaintiff's recovery of money damages is reduced by her or his percentage of causal negligence.

Exhibits 4.15 and 4.16 are a typical complaint and answer in a dram shop action.

Nuisance

nuisance   A cause of action in tort to recover money damages for the unreasonable interference of an occupant's use or enjoyment of real property. The harm must be substantial.

A **nuisance** is any inappropriate activity that unreasonably interferes with an occupant's use or enjoyment of her or his land. Included would be such things as creating disturbing odors, noise, or vibrations. An activity may be a nuisance without being illegal or even negligent. The interference must be substantial in its effect and duration, not minor. The law allows an occupant to bring a civil action in nuisance to obtain money damages as compensation for the loss of use and enjoyment of her or his land. If the nuisance is likely to continue, courts have the power to enjoin a nuisance, that is, order an abatement of the nuisance. A nuisance differs from a trespass in that a trespass involves a wrongful entry on a premise; whereas, a nuisance is caused by an activity somewhere off the property. In an action for trespass, the plain-

EXHIBIT 4.15

Complaint in Dram Shop

COMPLAINT

Come now the plaintiffs and for their cause of action against defendants, and each of them, allege:

Count 1

1. [Jurisdictional allegations.]
2. Joy Peterson is the personal representative for the estate of James William Peterson.
3. On June 1, 2006, defendant Kenneth Roberts was operating his motor vehicle on Constance Boulevard at or near the intersection of Highway 65 in Tampa, Florida.
4. At said time and place, James Anderson was operating his motor vehicle on Highway 65 at or near the intersection with Constance Boulevard in Tampa, Florida.
5. Plaintiffs Christine Peterson and James Peterson were passengers in the automobile owned and operated by James Anderson.
6. At the above time and place, defendant Kenneth Roberts and the intestate James Anderson operated their respective vehicles in such a negligent, careless, and unlawful manner that they caused their vehicles to come into violent collision.
7. As a direct result of said collision, Christine Peterson and James Peterson suffered serious and permanent injuries and were prevented from transacting their business, sustained great pain of body and mind, and have incurred and will in the future incur expenses for medical attention and hospitalization in a sum not presently known but believed to exceed $50,000.
8. As a direct and proximate result of defendants' negligence, plaintiffs Christine Peterson and James Peterson have each sustained and will sustain in the future a loss of earnings and loss of earning capacity in a sum not presently capable of determination.

Count 2

Plaintiffs reallege all paragraphs set out in count 1 as if fully set forth herein.

9. On May 31 and June 1, 2006, defendant Happy Hour Tavern illegally sold, furnished, and/or bartered intoxicating liquors to Kenneth Roberts in violation of [dram shop statute] and by this violation of statute and by the illegal

continued

tiff seeks damages for harm to the property. In an action for a nuisance, the plaintiff seeks damages for the plaintiff's loss of use or enjoyment of the property.

In determining whether an activity is a nuisance, the law weighs the value of the activity and the character of the area against the effect on the plaintiff's use and enjoyment of her or his premises. For example, if the defendant sets up a creosote plant near an established residential area, the unpleasant smell and fumes may be too overpowering for the residents. The residents may have a cause of action in nuisance for damages and grounds for obtaining an injunction to abate operation of the creosote plant. But suppose the plaintiff buys a house near a creosote plant that has been operating without

EXHIBIT 4.15

Complaint in Dram Shop (continued)

sale, furnishing, or bartering caused and/or contributed to the intoxication of Kenneth Roberts.

10. On May 31 and June 1, 2006, defendant Happy Hour Tavern illegally supplied, furnished, or gave alcoholic beverages to defendant Kenneth Roberts, thereby causing or adding to the intoxication of said Kenneth Roberts. [In most states an allegation of a negligent sale of intoxicants would not state a cause of action.]

11. As a direct and proximate result of the illegal selling, furnishing, bartering [or negligence in supplying] on May 31 and June 1, 2006, Kenneth Roberts collided with a motor vehicle owned and negligently operated by James Anderson, in which plaintiffs Christine Peterson and James Peterson were passengers, thereby causing severe and permanent injuries to Christine Peterson and James Peterson as alleged above.

12. As a direct and proximate consequence of said collision, plaintiffs Christine Peterson and James Peterson suffered injuries of which they herein complain.

13. As a further direct and proximate consequence of said collision, plaintiffs Christine Peterson and James Peterson have incurred hospital expenses and medical expenses and will require medical attention in the future.

14. Plaintiffs Christine Peterson and James Peterson have been damaged in their ability to earn income and will suffer an inability into the future.

Wherefore, plaintiffs, and each of them, pray for judgment against defendants, and each of them, in a fair and adequate sum as proven at trial, together with their costs and disbursements herein.

[date]

Attorney for Plaintiffs

[Attorney signature]

EXHIBIT 4.16

Answer to Complaint in Dram Shop

ANSWER

Comes now defendant, Happy Hour Tavern, and for its separate answer to plaintiffs' complaint.

1. Denies each and every allegation, statement, matter, anything in said complaint contained, except as hereinafter expressly admitted or alleged.

2. Alleges defendant is without sufficient knowledge or information upon which to form a belief concerning plaintiffs' claims of injuries and damages and, therefore, puts plaintiffs to their strict proof of same.

3. Alleges that plaintiffs failed to serve notice of claim upon defendant as required by law. Wherefore, defendant prays that plaintiffs take nothing by reason of their pretended cause of action and that it have judgment for its costs and disbursements herein.

[date]

Attorney for Defendant

[Attorney signature]

problems for fifty years. Or suppose the plaintiff buys real estate for a house near an airport in the path of the runway. Even though noise may constitute a nuisance, the necessity of having the airport near town justifies some impairment of plaintiff's right to the quiet enjoyment of her or his property. Also, the courts tend to protect the existing character of an area, so if an airport or railroad or sanitary landfill or paint factory was in the area first, the newcomer is usually expected to accept the status quo. Nevertheless, being there first is no guarantee of prevailing in a nuisance action. A complaint for an action in nuisance may take the form illustrated in Exhibit 4.17, and its answer in the form in Exhibit 4.18.

EXHIBIT 4.17

Complaint for Nuisance

COMPLAINT

Comes now plaintiff and for his cause of action against defendant alleges:

1. [Jurisdictional allegations.]
2. At all times material herein plaintiff was the owner and in possession of the premises commonly known as 3908 East Ninth Street, Bakersville, Ohio.
3. Plaintiff occupied said premises as his homestead with his family.
4. During the period of June 1, 2006, to the date of the commencement of the above entitled action, defendant has occupied and used the premises at 4000 East Ninth Street, Bakersville, Ohio, as a meat-cutting plant and for the preparation of various meats for sale in commerce.
5. During said period of time defendant has allowed meat products, meat by-products, and various chemicals to create toxic and offensive-smelling fumes and odors.
6. Said fumes and odors significantly reduce the plaintiff's use, comfort, enjoyment, and value of said property.
7. Before commencement of this action, plaintiff notified defendant of the adverse effect that defendant's activities have had on plaintiff's premises.
8. Defendant's activities could be conducted in a manner so as not to endanger and impair the use of other properties in the area.
9. Defendant's present activities create and permit the noxious and toxic odors and fumes that damage plaintiff's property and impair its use.
10. Plaintiff has suffered damages in the amount of $15,000 for the loss of enjoyment and impaired use of his property.
11. Unless defendant is enjoined from continuing to create the noxious fumes and odors, plaintiff's property will continue to suffer damage.

Wherefore, plaintiff prays for judgment against defendant permanently enjoining defendant from creating toxic and noxious fumes and odors that escape from defendant's premises to adjoining properties, and further prays for damages in the sum of $15,000, together with plaintiff's costs and disbursements herein.

[date]

Attorney for Plaintiff

[Attorney signature]

Exhibit 4.18

Answer to Complaint for Nuisance

ANSWER

Comes now defendant and for its answer to plaintiff's complaint:

1. Denies each and every allegation, statement, and matter in the complaint contained, except as hereinafter expressly admitted or alleged.
2. Admits the allegations of paragraphs 1, 2, 3, 4, and 7.
3. Specifically denies that defendant's use of defendant's land has created a nuisance.
4. Alleges that defendant is without sufficient knowledge and information upon which to form a belief concerning plaintiff's alleged damages and puts plaintiff to his strict proof of same.
5. Alleges that defendant's plant and operations have been conducted in essentially the same manner for twenty-five years and that plaintiff acquired his premises knowing the existence of defendant's facilities.
6. Alleges that defendant purchased an easement[2] from plaintiff's predecessors in interest, which easement and covenant[3] runs with the land and binds plaintiff, precluding plaintiff from suing defendant for the alleged nuisance.
7. Alleges that plaintiff's pretended cause of action is barred by laches.[4]
8. Alleges that plaintiff's pretended cause of action is barred by the easement and covenant, a copy of which is attached hereto as Exhibit A and incorporated by reference.
9. Alleges that plaintiff's cause of action is barred by the applicable Ohio statute of limitations.

Wherefore, defendant prays that plaintiff take nothing by reason of his pretended cause of action and that defendant have judgment for its costs and disbursements herein.

[date]

Attorney for Defendant

[Attorney signature]

---

[2]An easement is a right created by an agreement, express or implied, to use a certain area of land for some specified purpose. The purpose may be general or limited. An easement is considered a right to use, rather than an ownership interest in, the land.

[3]A covenant is an agreement or promise to do or not to do something and is commonly made part of a real estate transaction that affects or limits the buyer's use of the land. For example, the buyer could covenant not to sell liquor on the premises.

[4]Laches is a doctrine that precludes a person from asserting a right where that party has let the claim become stale with the passage of time. It is analogous to a statute-of-limitations defense.

Ultrahazardous Activities

An activity is ultrahazardous if it is incapable of being conducted without a significant likelihood of damage to property or injury to persons. A person who engages in ultrahazardous activity is said to be absolutely liable for damage caused by the activity. This means the defendant is liable even though he or she conducts the activity with great care. Culpability is not an issue. Nor is the utility or necessity of the activity an issue. The only real question is whether the activity is appropriate for the locale in which it is conducted.

Pile driving and dynamiting for construction projects are two examples of ultrahazardous activities. If the pile driving causes vibrations in the earth that damage nearby structures, the contractor is liable even though pile driving may be necessary. Similarly, the owner of a dam may be liable to other properties damaged by percolation of water through the soil. If the dam should break, the owner could be absolutely liable for harm to persons and property caused by the escaping water. A person who keeps a wild animal, as opposed to domestic animals, is engaged in an ultrahazardous activity. The owner is liable for any injury caused by a wild animal that escapes from the keeper's premises. Crop spraying is another ultrahazardous activity. If some of the chemical escapes onto a neighbor's property and causes damage, the person who allowed the chemical to escape is absolutely liable for the damage. Conversely, a crop sprayer would not be absolutely liable to a customer for damage to *other* foliage on the *customer's* property (though the crop sprayer could be liable in negligence).

In each of the preceding examples, the defendant acted reasonably to promote his or her own business or other legitimate interest. In each instance, the party acted for a proper purpose. But because the activity is considered to be ultrahazardous, the actor is strictly liable for harm caused to others. In this way the law encourages property owners and contractors to be as careful as possible when engaging in such hazardous activities. In effect, the law precludes one landowner from using his or her land to the detriment of another landowner.

Intentional Infliction of Mental Suffering

To recover for intentional infliction of mental suffering, the plaintiff must prove the defendant had a specific, subjective intent to cause the plaintiff mental suffering. Mere negligence does not support this cause of action. Unlike an action for assault, there is no need to put the plaintiff in fear of bodily harm. The means or method the defendant uses to inflict mental suffering is not material. It may involve words or conduct or both. Not only must the defendant intend the plaintiff to experience mental suffering, the defendant's conduct must be outrageous in its character. The conduct must be of the type that is not intolerable in a civilized society. Mere insults, swearing, foul language, even verbal threats do not give rise to this cause of action. The jury must find the defendant had an actual, wrongful intent to cause the plaintiff to suffer. It is not enough for the jury to find that the defendant should have known that his or her conduct could cause mental suffering. The plaintiff must prove that the wrongful conduct was the proximate cause of her or his suffering. It is not necessary for the plaintiff to show physical symptoms manifesting the mental suffering. Nor is medical treatment a necessary element to obtain damages.

The cause of action accrues when the plaintiff experiences the mental suffering. In the following example, the cause of action accrues when the statement is made to the plaintiff. Furthermore, this cause of action may be available in situations where actions for assault and defamation would not lie—although the actions certainly could overlap.

EXAMPLE

The defendant maliciously tells the plaintiff that the plaintiff's spouse has just been killed in an accident at work. In fact, the statement is not true. The defendant's motive for uttering the false statement was to upset the plaintiff, and the plaintiff suffers an emotional breakdown. These facts would meet the requirements for an action for intentional infliction of mental suffering. An action for defamation would not lie because the statement, even though false, is not damaging to the plaintiff's reputation. An action for assault would not lie because the plaintiff was not put in fear of bodily harm. A cause of action for invasion of privacy would not lie because the statement has not been made public and because other elements are missing also.

Negligent Infliction of Mental Suffering

Negligent infliction of mental suffering is a relatively new cause of action. In most states the plaintiff must prove the following:

- The defendant was negligent.
- The defendant's negligence caused the plaintiff to believe that he or she was in danger of being killed or of sustaining serious bodily injury.
- The plaintiff's belief was reasonable on an objective basis.
- The plaintiff developed physical manifestations caused by his or her mental suffering.

The law imposes these limits on the cause of action because, as social beings who live in communities, we are going to upset, irritate, and bother each other inevitably. Courts simply cannot concern themselves about such problems. But where the defendant's negligence subjects the plaintiff to a genuine threat of grievous bodily harm and the plaintiff suffers a serious emotional reaction as a result, the law gives the plaintiff a right to claim money damages.

As part of the burden of proof, the plaintiff must show that he or she was in a "zone of danger." For example, suppose the plaintiff is a tenant in an apartment building that explodes because the local utility negligently failed to turn off the gas. A fire ensues, and many people are burned and killed. Suppose the plaintiff escapes without physical injury, but after the fire the plaintiff develops an ulcer because of the experience. The plaintiff has the basis for making a claim for negligent infliction of mental suffering. But suppose the plaintiff arrives at the scene of a terrible motor vehicle accident and becomes ill because of what she saw. She was not in the zone of danger and has no claim.

Courts require a physical manifestation of the emotional upset in order to provide some independent corroboration of the mental suffering. Mere headaches, sleeplessness, and loss of weight are not sufficient physical manifestations of mental suffering to establish a claim. Furthermore, it appears that an aggravation of a pre-existing physical condition does not support the cause of action.

False Imprisonment

False imprisonment is a cause of action that allows the plaintiff to recover money damages for mental suffering and physical harm. The plaintiff must prove that the defendant intentionally confined the plaintiff to a specific area without authority in law to do so. The confinement must be real and significant in duration. The plaintiff must be aware that he or she is being confined. It is not sufficient for the plaintiff to discover, after the alleged confinement, that she or he would not have been permitted to leave the premises had she or he wanted or attempted to leave. The cause of action, however, does not require physical restraints such as handcuffs, walls, or a fence. The defendant can effectively confine the plaintiff through mere threats of force or false assertions of authority. The defendant may be liable for a false imprisonment where the defendant merely forces the plaintiff to accompany the defendant. In criminal law, it would be the same as kidnapping. The law makes a careful distinction between confining a person and preventing a person from entering a restricted area. For example, an action for false imprisonment will not lie against a theater for not allowing certain customers to enter.

The defendant must intend to confine the plaintiff by limiting or controlling the plaintiff's freedom of movement. Parents have legal authority to limit their children's freedom of movement. A parent may delegate such authority to a baby-sitter or neighbor under some circumstances and for some purposes. For all persons, the confinement must be intentional and not merely inadvertent or even negligent. For example, if a store owner closes and locks the store for the night and a customer is accidentally locked in the store, the customer does not have an action against the storekeeper for false imprisonment. But that would not necessarily preclude an action in negligence.

The restriction on the plaintiff's movement must be complete and not voluntary. If the plaintiff remains in a certain area because he or she is merely *asked* to do so, no cause of action will lie. The confinement must be against the plaintiff's will. The cause of action accrues as soon as the plaintiff becomes aware that his or her freedom of movement has been wrongfully restricted. No physical injury or symptoms are required. A defendant can defeat a claim of false imprisonment by proving that she or he had authority to confine or restrain the plaintiff, or that the plaintiff consented to the restrictions.

Malicious Prosecution

Malicious prosecution is the use of criminal court proceedings for an improper purpose. For example, if the defendant files a criminal complaint against the plaintiff merely to damage the plaintiff's reputation or to cause inconvenience and expense, an action for malicious prosecution will lie. The plaintiff must prove that the defendant instituted the criminal proceedings or wrongfully caused the proceedings to continue and that the defendant lacked probable cause to believe that the criminal proceedings were justified. In other words, the defendant must have acted out of malice against the plaintiff and not to serve the ends of justice. The criminal proceedings must be resolved in the plaintiff's favor by dismissal or verdict.

malicious prosecution A cause of action in tort to recover money damages for personal injury caused by the defendant's intentional wrongful use of criminal court proceedings, without justification, for an improper purpose.

The cause of action allows the plaintiff to recover money damages for loss of time spent in defending against the criminal proceedings, expenses incurred in the defense, loss of income, damaged reputation, and mental suffering. A cause of action for malicious prosecution does not accrue until the criminal proceedings have terminated in the plaintiff's favor. There is no special affirmative defense to a malicious prosecution action. The cases are usually defended on the basis that the defendant reasonably believed that the plaintiff committed a crime or that the defendant acted without malice.

Abuse of Judicial Process

abuse of process   A cause of action in tort to recover money damages for personal injury caused by another person's willful misuse of the civil or criminal legal process.

Abuse of process is somewhat similar to malicious prosecution, but it involves the unjustified use of civil procedures for a wrongful purpose. Again, the plaintiff must prove that the defendant was motivated to use the courts for an improper purpose. The cause of action does not accrue until the plaintiff obtains a dismissal of the underlying civil action. Therefore, the defendant cannot file a counterclaim against the plaintiff to obtain money damages for abuse of process. An abuse-of-process claim must be brought as a separate, new action. The burden of proof is difficult. The cause of action conflicts with the philosophy that people should freely use the courts to resolve their significant disputes.

Defamation

defamation   The publication of a false statement, oral or written, that damages another person's reputation. See *libel* and *slander*.

Defamation is the publication of a false, defamatory statement to a third person about the plaintiff that harms the plaintiff's reputation. Publication simply means to make something known to the public. The law recognizes two types of defamation, libel and slander. Each is discussed separately, but the ideas of the one generally apply to the other as well.

Libel

libel   A cause of action in tort for injury to a person's reputation caused by the publication of a false statement in writing.

Libel is the publication of a false, defamatory statement *in writing* to a third person about the plaintiff that harms the plaintiff's reputation. The purpose of a libel action is to protect the plaintiff's reputation. A writing may consist of any kind of documentation such as a letter, memorandum, news article, photograph, motion picture, or painting. A statement is defamatory if it would cause the plaintiff to suffer a loss of esteem in the community or the eyes of those who know her or him. A statement is "published" when it is communicated to a third person. The cause of action gives the plaintiff the opportunity to hold the defendant accountable for publishing defamatory statements. The plaintiff benefits by being exonerated from the falsehood and obtaining compensation for damage to his or her reputation and for mental suffering.

Unless the false, defamatory statement is published to a third person, there is no cause of action, but publication to even one other person is sufficient to establish a claim. Therefore, an action for libel will not lie where the defendant writes a letter to the plaintiff and says in the letter that the plaintiff is a crook. An action will not lie no matter how much the plaintiff's feelings are hurt by the letter. There is no claim for libel unless the false statement is communicated to a third person. The plaintiff cannot create a cause of action by voluntarily telling other persons about the false statement. However, the defendant is liable for any republications by a third person or any republications that authorities required the plaintiff to make.

Some statements are obviously defamatory. They include allegations of criminal conduct, sexual misconduct, professional incompetence, and affliction with a loathsome disease. But almost any statement may be considered defamatory if it would tend to cause other people to lose confidence in the plaintiff's abilities, trustworthiness, or reliability. Some statements may be defamatory only because of the plaintiff's particular circumstances, position, or relationships. For example, it could be defamatory to write that the plaintiff is inclined to have an alcoholic drink on occasion if the plaintiff is a leader in a church that has abstinence as one of its tenets. Statements that merely reflect the defendant's *opinion* about the plaintiff are not considered to be defamatory. Such statements are understood to reflect on the defendant as much as, or more than, on the plaintiff. The distinction between fact and opinion is sometimes difficult to ascertain. However, a defendant could not avoid liability by qualifying the statement by adding, "In my opinion, the plaintiff is a crook." In determining whether a statement is defamatory, the words are given their ordinary meaning. However, the plaintiff has the right to prove that the words used by the defendant contain innuendo which, when taken in context, is understood by others to be defamatory. An action for defamation cannot be brought on behalf of a deceased person for the benefit of the decedent's reputation or to assuage the feelings of the survivors. A corporation can be defamed, but only if the defamatory statements reflect adversely on the corporation's honesty, integrity, or credit. A corporation is not defamed by a statement that its products or services are bad.

The cause of action accrues when the defamatory statement is published. The plaintiff has the burden of proving the statement, publication of the statement to a third person, and consequential harm. However, in libel actions and certain slander actions, the law infers some harm even if no specific damage can be shown. Truth is a complete defense. For example, if the defendant states that the plaintiff is a crook, the statement is obviously defamatory. If the defendant can prove that the defendant committed a crime, the defendant's proof defeats the claim for libel. The defendant's proof of the truth of the statement need only be by a fair preponderance of the evidence. Even if the plaintiff was previously tried in a criminal action and found not guilty, the defendant in the libel action has the right to try to prove that the plaintiff is, in fact, a crook.

A defendant may avoid liability for defamation by showing that the publication was subject to a privilege or a qualified privilege. Statements made by officers of the court and by parties in pursuit of proper legal proceedings are clothed with a privilege. Therefore, statements made in pleadings or testimony in depositions, testimony at trial, and legal opinions are clothed with a privilege. Legislators acting in their official capacity are clothed with privilege. Newspapers and other publishers are given a qualified privilege that allows them to print information about public persons when that information is newsworthy, provided the publisher acts in good faith. The plaintiff must prove that the news media acted out of malice; otherwise, the cause of action will fail. A member of the news media may mitigate damages by printing a timely retraction.

Slander

slander A cause of action in tort for injury to a person's reputation caused by the publication of a false statement made orally.

Slander is the oral publication of a defamatory statement. The dichotomy between libel and slander exists because, in the eyes of the law, libel is somewhat more serious. People tend to believe written statements. Furthermore, defamatory statements in documents appear to be more calculated and have a potential for greater distribution. Generally speaking, damages are easier to obtain and are larger in actions for libel. Otherwise, the preceding discussion about libel applies to slander.

Invasion of Privacy

invasion of privacy A cause of action in tort for personal injury for wrongful publishing of a person's likeness or private information about the person in a manner that is outrageous.

An action for **invasion of privacy** may take one of four forms. "Intrusion upon seclusion" occurs when a person intentionally intrudes upon the plaintiff's solitude or private affairs in a highly offensive manner. This occurs, for example, when one person makes repeated harassing telephone calls to another person's home. "Appropriation" protects one's identity. A violation occurs when a person uses the plaintiff's name or likeness for their own benefit, as would occur if an advertisement used Michael Jordan's basketball highlights to imply the endorsement of a product. "Secrecy" protects against public disclosure of information about the plaintiff's private life if the matter disclosed would be highly offensive and not of legitimate public concern. "False light" protects against publicity that places the plaintiff in the public in a false light. The classic example is a newspaper headline that proclaims "Man Arrested in Massive Fraud Scheme," accompanied by a picture of the plaintiff that is actually meant to accompany an article somewhere else on the page. The casual reader associates the picture with the headline, thus placing the plaintiff in a false light. But many courts have refused to recognize false-light privacy claims because they are so similar to defamation and because they usually involve First Amendment speech and press issues but with fewer protections than exist in the law of defamation.

Other Causes

Many, many other causes of action exist to provide various forms of relief. They include actions for dissolution of a marriage, dissolution of a partnership, damages caused by domestic animals, damages for United States patent infringements, damages for unfair competition and violation of civil rights, and so on. Each action has specific requirements or elements and is subject to certain affirmative defenses.

TECHNOLOGY NOTES

Lawyers do a great deal of their legal research through computer-assisted research services such as Westlaw and Lexis. These legal services are a study in themselves. You must be a subscriber to use the services, although many colleges and universities are given free access for their students, presumably to gain brand loyalty for the future.

American Law Sources On-line provides a comprehensive list of practice aids and commentary from governmental and nonprofit organizations without charge.

The Web site can be accessed at http://www.lawsource.com/also/. See also US-Law.com; and http://www.law.cornell.edu/. These sites allow keyword searches.

SUMMARY

A cause of action is a claim for which a court is able to provide a remedy, that is, some form of relief. There are many causes of action. Each cause of action is designed to cover a particular kind of claim. A plaintiff's complaint must state a cause of action against the defendant or a court will not consider the claim. Some causes of action come from the common law, some have been created by statute, and some arise from contracts between the parties. All causes of action have certain basic requirements. For a cause of action to exist the following must hold true:

1. The defendant must owe a legal duty to the plaintiff.
2. The defendant must have breached the legal duty.
3. The defendant's breach of the legal duty must be the proximate cause of the plaintiff's injury, loss, or other harm.
4. The harm must be of a type the law recognizes as real and substantial.

The plaintiff has the burden of proving each element to an alleged cause of action. Some causes of action, such as fraud, must be pleaded with particularity. In other words, the facts supporting each element of the claim must be stated. Each cause of action is subject to a particular standard of proof, such as a fair preponderance of the evidence or clear and convincing evidence. Each cause of action is limited in the kinds of remedies a court can grant. Each remedy has particular items for which damages may be awarded. Consequently, a litigation team must make sure that they have found the best cause of action for the client.

A transaction or occurrence may give rise to more than one cause of action. A plaintiff may pursue two or more causes of action at the same time against the defendant. On occasion, the law requires a party to choose between causes of action. That decision should be made by a lawyer. When more than one cause of action is alleged in the complaint, each should be set forth as a separate count. The plaintiff's complaint must identify the transaction or occurrence that gave rise to the claim by stating the time and place of the defendant's alleged breach of legal duty. A complaint should set forth allegations and facts in convenient, numbered paragraphs. The plaintiff's lawyer or paralegal should draft the complaint in such a manner as to encourage the defendant's lawyer to admit, by paragraphs, the facts that are not really contested.

The elements of the cause of action determine what facts are material to the case. The plaintiff must prove all the facts material to the cause of action. When assisting the plaintiff or plaintiff's attorney, a paralegal should focus on gathering evidence to prove the material (controlling) facts. When assisting the defendant, the paralegal should focus on gathering evidence to show that the facts, in truth, do not support the cause of action alleged by the plaintiff.

In a contract case, the usual measure of damages is the loss of the bargain, which may include a loss of expected profits. In a fraud case, the usual measure of damages is the out-of-pocket loss. In most tort cases, the usual measure of damages is an amount of money that will fully and fairly compensate the plaintiff for the loss.

Rule 11 requires lawyers and parties to believe there is good basis in law and fact for any cause of action asserted in a complaint. A party or lawyer who alleges a claim that does not have merit is subject to disciplinary action by the court.

KEY TERMS

abuse of process	malicious prosecution
accord and satisfaction	negligent misrepresentation
affirmative defenses	nuisance
comparative fault	ordinary comparative negligence
complicity	proximate cause
consideration	pure comparative negligence
defamation	slander
direct cause	specific performance
dram shop	statute of frauds
invasion of privacy	superseding cause
libel	voidable

REVIEW QUESTIONS

1. How does a common law civil battery differ from a civil assault?

2. How does a nuisance differ from a trespass?

3. What elements give rise to the legal duty to act with reasonable care?

4. What elements give rise to a dram shop action?

5. When is specific performance awarded, rather than money damages?

6. How does fraud (deceit) differ from negligent misrepresentation?

7. How does an action for invasion of privacy differ from an action for defamation?

8. How does a cause of action for malicious prosecution differ from a cause of action for abuse of process?

CASE ASSIGNMENT

Negligence is the failure to exercise reasonable care in light of a foreseeable risk of harm to another person or to oneself. The standard of care is determined by a jury or judge based on community standards, except where the standard of care is prescribed by statute. For example, a highway code may establish duties for drivers. There are statutes that prescribe speed limits, when to pass, when to give warning to motorists, where motorists may pass. In addition, there are common-law rules that require motorists to keep a proper lookout for actual and potential hazards and maintain control over their vehicles. What is Griffin's duty to Harper? What is Brandt's duty to Griffin?

1. Describe the duty of care that Harper owed to Nordby and how Harper may have breached that duty.
2. Describe the duty of care that Griffin owed to Harper and how Griffin may have breached that duty.
3. Describe the duty of care that Brandt owed to Griffin and how Brandt may have breached that duty.

Endnotes

1. Lawyers usually use the term *illegal* to describe conduct that is criminal in nature. The term *unlawful* may include conduct that is illegal, but it tends to be used more broadly to include any conduct that is contrary to the civil law or criminal law. The word *unlawful* is used here to describe conduct that is in violation of common law standards or standards established by statutes.
2. A minor is liable to pay the reasonable value of necessities that he or she has received, such as food, clothing, and shelter.
3. Of course, if the defendant has asserted a counterclaim and seeks a recovery of money damages, the defendant must prove a loss. But the defendant's alleged breach of the contract would provide a complete defense to the plaintiff.
4. This is not to say that every breached contract for the sale of land is enforced by an action for specific performance.
5. Note that the term *quiet* refers to a state in which there is an absence of threats to the ownership and/or possession of the property. It does not refer to noise or the loudness of sound.
6. Note that the term *peaceful* is similar to the term *quiet*, both of which serve as legal "terms of art." So, *peaceful*, in this instance, does not connote the absence of armed conflict.
7. Meaning the trespasser is claiming and acting as if she or he owns the property.
8. This is one of the reasons we have laws that allow owners to register with the government items of property such as automobiles, real estate, patents, and so forth. The registration makes proof of ownership easy and inexpensive.
9. A prima facie case is one that has sufficient facts to support all the elements to the cause of action. There must be sufficient evidence to establish all the necessary, material facts. When determining whether a prima facie case has been established, there is no consideration given to the persuasiveness of the evidence.
10. This is sometimes called an "efficient intervening cause."
11. See *Hauenstein v. The Loctite Corp.*, 347 N.W.2d 272 (Minn. 1984).
12. See *Bigham v. J. C. Penney Co.*, 268 N.W.2d 802 (Minn. 1978).
13. A person is obviously intoxicated when he or she manifests outward symptoms of intoxication such as loss of coordination, slurred speech, incoherence in thinking, loss of balance, emotional volatility, and so on. The determination is made on an objective basis.

 For additional resources, visit our Web site at www.paralegal.delmar.cengage.com

CHAPTER **5**

AFFIRMATIVE DEFENSES

CHAPTER OUTLINE

Chapter Objectives

Chapter 5 explains the bases for defending against civil actions, how a defense is raised and how a defense is presented. A defense that is available in one type of case may not be available in another. This chapter explains why.

Introduction

There are two bases for defending against a civil lawsuit. First, the defendant may deny that the plaintiff's claim has any merit. Second, the defendant may prove an affirmative defense. The first approach forces the plaintiff to prove the claim by disputing the alleged facts and challenging the plaintiff's evidence. The defendant's objective is to prevent the plaintiff from proving a cause of action. Simply stated, the plaintiff claims, "You did it," and the defendant responds, "No, I didn't." The second approach to defending against any civil action is to allege and prove an affirmative defense that avoids or defeats a plaintiff claim. An affirmative defense overcomes the claim without regard to whether the claim is true and could be fully proven. Simply stated, the plaintiff says, "You did it," and the defendant replies,

"Maybe, I did it, but I win anyway, because you did (or failed to do) something too." The "something too" is the affirmative defense that is the subject of this chapter. You may think of affirmative defenses as a counterpart to causes of action. A defendant must plead an affirmative defense to use it. Each affirmative defense applies only to certain causes of action. A defendant must prove each element of the defense or it fails.

Defenses in General

Whatever a defendant's strategies, the answer must admit allegations in the complaint that the defendant knows are true. Rule 8(b) is very specific, "Denials shall fairly meet the substance of the averments denied." In other words, any denial must be made in good faith. Every allegation in the complaint that is not denied is deemed admitted. The defendant's admission of a fact in the answer precludes the defendant from disputing the truth of the allegation. In other words, an admitted fact is removed from contention. Therefore, it is common for a defendant to begin the answer by stating, "The defendant denies each and every allegation, statement, matter, and thing in the complaint, except as expressly admitted or alleged in the answer." Then the answer admits specific allegations in the complaint. A defendant may admit allegations by stating the facts or by identifying the paragraphs of the complaint that state those facts. If a party admits paragraphs in another party's pleading, he or she must be sure the paragraphs are clear. A plaintiff should encourage the defendant to make admissions by keeping controversial allegations separate from non-controversial allegations of fact.

In the first approach—defending the merits—the defense strategy is simple. The defendant disputes and refutes one or more of the essential facts on which the plaintiff's case depends. The defendant may deny that the transaction or occurrence happened or that the occurrence happened in the way plaintiff claims. If the plaintiff has evidence that tends to prove the facts denied, the defendant may try to exclude the evidence by making appropriate objections. If the evidence is admissible, the defendant may try to impeach or discredit the plaintiff's evidence. If the evidence cannot be impeached, the defendant may try to negate its persuasiveness by offering other evidence to refute, explain, or qualify it. For example, in a breach-of-contract action, the plaintiff must prove that a contract existed, that the defendant breached the contract, and that the breach of contract caused the plaintiff to sustain a loss. Suppose there was a contract and the defendant breached it. The defendant must admit those facts. However, if the defendant honestly believes that the plaintiff did not sustain any loss, the defendant may challenge the plaintiff's evidence concerning the alleged loss. The defendant's strategy is to prevent the plaintiff's evidence of a loss from being heard or, if it is received, to keep it from being believed. The defendant may discredit the evidence by showing it comes from an unreliable source or is unreliable in its nature. If the plaintiff cannot prove a loss caused by the breach, the plaintiff's claim for money damages necessarily fails, and the defendant wins, despite having breached the contract.

The rest of the chapter explains some affirmative defenses commonly asserted in civil actions. Rule 8(c) provides a partial list of affirmative defenses. All causes of action (claims) are subject to various affirmative defenses. The Rules require the defendant to allege all affirmative defenses in the answer. A defendant has the burden of proving an affirmative defense, just as a plaintiff has the burden of proving a cause of action. Most affirmative defenses must be proved by a fair preponderance of the evidence. Specifically, the jury must find that the affirmative defense is more likely true than not true for the defense to prevail. A few affirmative defenses, such as some causes of action, require proof by evidence that is clear and convincing. For example, proof of a **mutual mistake,** which is grounds for reforming a written contract, must be established by evidence that is clear and convincing. Even then, the burden of proof is less than "beyond a reasonable doubt," which is the government's burden of proof in prosecuting criminal actions.

Pleading Affirmative Defenses

Pleading an affirmative defense is much like pleading a cause of action. The defendant's answer must contain a short, plain statement of the facts on which the affirmative defense is based. Each affirmative defense should be pled in a separate paragraph for clarity and convenience of the parties. The time and place of the acts or omissions that give rise to each affirmative defense must be stated. See Rule 9(f). The defendant's failure to plead an affirmative defense in the answer results in a waiver of the defense. Usually, it is sufficient for the defendant to allege a defense as a legal conclusion. For example, a defendant's answer may allege, "Plaintiff's cause of action is barred by plaintiff's assumption of risk." The material time and place were sufficiently stated in the plaintiff's complaint, so the defendant need not reiterate them in the answer. However, when an affirmative defense relates to a new transaction or occurrence, it must be identified by time and place. For example, if the defendant pleads a **release** as an affirmative defense, she or he must allege the time and place at which the release was given, along with the terms of the release.

The Rules assume that the plaintiff denies the defendant's affirmative defenses, so the plaintiff is not required to respond to them. However, if the plaintiff has an affirmative defense to the defendant's affirmative defense, the plaintiff must plead it in a reply to the answer [see Rule 7(a)]. For example, if the plaintiff alleged an action in negligence to obtain money damages for personal injuries and the defendant alleged a release as a defense, the plaintiff could allege fraud as an affirmative defense to the release. Because the allegation of fraud raises a new legal theory and new fact issues, the claim of fraud must be pled. Note, fraud must be pled with particularity whether as a claim or as a defense [Rule 9(b)].

A defendant's answer must state every affirmative defense. Any affirmative defenses not alleged are waived. Paragraph 5 in Exhibit 5.1 is an affirmative defense.

mutual mistake   A basis for reforming a written contract. The party who wishes to reform the written contract must prove that both parties agreed on the terms, but they made a mutual mistake in expressing the terms in the writing.

release   A contract by which a person releases a legal claim or right against another person. A release is usually made in writing.

EXAMPLE

First Defense
Plaintiff's alleged cause of action is barred by the release plaintiff executed in defendant's favor on May 31, 2006, at Memphis, Tennessee. A true and correct copy of the written release is attached hereto as Exhibit A and incorporated by reference. (Releases are discussed later in the chapter.)

STATE OF MINNESOTA	**DISTRICT COURT**
COUNTY OF HUBBARD	**THIRD JUDICIAL DISTRICT**

Laura Raskin, Trustee for the heirs
and next of kin of William Nordby,
decedent,

      Plaintiff,

  vs.   ANSWER

Bradley Harper,
        Defendant.

Comes now defendant, and for his answer to plaintiff's complaint:

1. Denies each and every allegation, statement, matter, and thing contained in the complaint, except as expressly admitted or alleged herein.
2. Admits the allegations in paragraphs 1, 2, and 5 of the Complaint.
3. Admits defendant and William Nordby were involved in a motor vehicle accident about the time and place specified in the complaint, but specifically denies that defendant was negligent.
   [Note, by making this admission, all of the facts in paragraphs 1, 2, and 5 are taken out of issue. The defendant would have to obtain permission from the plaintiff or the court to withdraw the admissions. Unless the admissions are withdrawn, the plaintiff does not have to present evidence to prove those facts.]
4. Alleges defendant is without sufficient knowledge or information upon which to base a belief concerning the allegations in paragraphs 7 and 8; therefore, plaintiff is put to her strict proof of same.
5. Alleges said motor vehicle accident was caused by the negligence of William Nordby, and his negligence is either a bar to plaintiff's claim or reduces plaintiff's claim by Nordby's percentage of causal negligence.

    Wherefore, defendant prays that plaintiff take nothing by reason of her alleged cause of action and that defendant have judgment for his costs and disbursements.

[Date]

Attorney for Defendant

/s/ _____
            William Hoch

[Address]
[Telephone]

Form 20 in the Appendix of Forms for the Rules of Civil Procedure suggests how defenses may be pled. The form's "First Defense"[1] is a procedural defense. It denies the adequacy of the plaintiff's complaint. The adequacy of a complaint should be determined by a motion that the defendant may make at any time before the case reaches trial. The "Second Defense"[2] is a procedural defense. It contends that the plaintiff has failed to include a necessary party in the lawsuit. The "Third Defense"[3] is neither a procedural defense nor an affirmative defense. It simply clarifies that the defendant admits certain allegations in the complaint and that the defendant will require the plaintiff to prove the remaining allegations. Many lawyers provide similar paragraphs at the beginning of their answers. The "Fourth Defense"[4] is an affirmative defense. It invokes a statute of limitations. It would be better if the paragraph specified the statute on which the defendant relied.

Release

A release is a type of contract by which a person voluntarily relinquishes a claim or legal right. A release ends the right of the plaintiff to sue on the claim in question. Parties usually reduce a release to a writing, but the law does not require a writing. The parties to a release must have a meeting of minds concerning the essential terms and conditions. As in any contract, the parties must exchange consideration. Therefore, the party who obtains a release of a claim must give something for the release. Sometimes both parties agree to give up claims or rights against each other. In that event, the release is called a mutual release. In a mutual release, the exchange of promises is the consideration, although one party may pay some additional money.

If a defendant asserts a release as an affirmative defense, the terms and conditions of the release must be pled in the answer. If the release was in writing, a copy may be attached to the answer and incorporated into the answer by reference. If the release is valid and pertains to the plaintiff's claim, it provides a complete defense even though at one time the plaintiff had a valid claim. The plaintiff may dispute the validity or application of a release. Affirmative defenses to the claim of release include mutual mistake, lack of consideration, duress, and fraud. (See Chapter 22 for a more detailed discussion of releases.)

Accord and Satisfaction

Accord and satisfaction is similar to a release. It arises from the parties' decision to replace their former dispute with a new agreement. The new agreement is an "accord." Full performance of the accord is a "satisfaction" of the accord. Accord and satisfaction is a complete defense to an action on the prior obligation. The defendant must present evidence proving that the parties had a bona fide dispute over the terms or application of their original agreement and both sides intended the new agreement to be a compromise and to replace the original. The existence of the bona fide dispute and compromise provide the necessary consideration to make the accord an enforceable contract. Proof of the satisfaction, such as payment, is essential to the defense. If the defendant defaulted on both the old agreement and the new accord, the plaintiff may elect to sue on either.

When a dispute arises over a transaction, a party may tender a check in a reduced amount as "payment in full." If the drawer makes clear that the check is tendered to resolve a disputed claim (not a partial payment of a disputed obligation) and if the check is accepted by the payee on that basis, the disputed obligation is fully discharged. The payee must accept the check on the terms and conditions tendered or return the check uncashed. A payee accepts a check by cashing it or refusing to return it. However, the payer's purpose to create an accord and satisfaction must be manifest to the payee.

Arbitration and Award

Parties to a dispute may contract to submit their controversy to a third person or tribunal for a determination and resolution. The process is called arbitration, or **arbitration and award.** When the dispute is duly decided by the arbitrator(s), the award is binding on all parties.[5] The disappointed party cannot subsequently litigate the controversy in court. The prevailing party may assert the award as an affirmative defense to a civil action. Arbitration usually is a relatively simple and inexpensive procedure. Only if fraud or some other defect occurred in the arbitration procedure can the losing party dispute the award. See Chapter 23 for a detailed discussion about arbitration.

arbitration and award An arbitration tribunal's award. The award may be binding or nonbinding between the parties, depending on the agreement under which the arbitration was conducted.

Statutes of Limitations

The mere passage of time may create or end legal rights. A **statute of limitations** establishes a time limit by which a plaintiff must commence suit or forfeit the claim. Each state has a statute that prescribes a limitation on various causes of action such as contract, trespass, battery, slander, negligence, and so forth. Ordinarily, a statutory cause of action specifies its own time limitation. Congress determines what time limitations are applicable to rights created by federal statutes. On occasion, parties have to litigate which statute of limitations applies to their matter. In some states, the applicable statute may be as short as one year for a particular cause of action. In other states, the same cause of action may be subject to a much longer statutory period, such as six years.

The purpose of a statute of limitations is to bar old, stale claims. Circumstances change. Evidence disappears. Memories fade. If a person has disregarded or overlooked a claim for a long time, he or she should not disturb the status quo by resurrecting it. There is value in maintaining the status quo. For example, if two motorists were involved in a minor accident, it would be unfair for one to sue the other ten years later claiming that the accident caused serious bodily harm. The passage of time would impair the defendant's ability to obtain evidence with which to defend against the claim. The same is true for contract actions. Therefore, state and federal legislatures have established various time periods within which actions must be commenced. Statutes of limitations help prevent fraud.

The general rule is that the statute of limitations begins to run against a claim when the cause of action accrues. Ordinarily, a cause of action accrues when the injury or loss

statute of limitations A statute that limits the time during which a lawsuit may be brought against a person. The time period provided by a statute of limitations usually begins to run at the time the cause of action accrues.

occurs. The rule has a simple, clear application in automobile accident cases, where the cause of action accrues the day of the accident even if the victim is unaware of the injury. The time period allowed by statutes of limitations begins to run the same day. The day of the event is counted. In a defamation case, the statute begins to run the day the defamatory statement is published, though the actual harm to the plaintiff's reputation may not occur until later; the law presumes that some harm occurred at the time of publication. The same is true in most tort actions, where the plaintiff seeks money damages for personal injury or property damage. An action for breach of contract accrues the day the breach occurs and the statute of limitations begins to run the same day.

But it is not always easy to figure out when a cause of action accrued. For example, suppose the plaintiff alleges that a medical doctor was negligent for exposing the plaintiff to excessive radiation over a period of weeks. It may be difficult to determine just when the treatment became injurious and when the cause of action accrued. Consequently, in medical malpractice actions the limitation period usually begins to run when all treatment for the condition ceases. In some states, the statute does not begin to run until the patient discovers the injury and "should have known" it was caused by malpractice. States that take that approach have what is commonly called the "discovery rule." For example, if the surgeon inadvertently leaves a surgical sponge in the patient, the patient's claim for injury does not begin to run until the harm becomes apparent to the patient. Postponement of the running of the statute of limitations in medical malpractice cases is justified on the basis that the time limitation is relatively short and the physician has a fiduciary relationship to the patient.

If the plaintiff's cause of action is based on fraud, the cause of action does not accrue until the plaintiff discovers the fraud or should have discovered it. If the defendant acts to conceal the fact that the plaintiff has a claim, the statute does not begin to run until the plaintiff discovers that he or she has a claim. In other words, the defendant's fraud keeps the statute of limitations from running, but once the fraud is discovered, the statute begins to run.

A statute of limitations does not run against a minor during her or his minority. A minor plaintiff is always allowed the time granted by the statute. If that time runs out during the plaintiff's minority, the plaintiff is allowed another year, after reaching legal age, in which to bring the action. For example, if a six-year statute of limitations applies to a negligence action, and the plaintiff is age sixteen at the time the cause of action accrues and will attain majority at age eighteen, the statute runs against the plaintiff's claim when the six-year period expires, or during the plaintiff's twenty-second year. If the minor plaintiff is only ten years old when the cause of action accrues, the six-year period would end during the plaintiff's sixteenth year. However, the law provides that the statute of limitations is "tolled"[6] during the plaintiff's minority. Furthermore, a minor has one more year after reaching majority, in which to assert the claim. In this example, the statute runs against the minor's claim when the minor attains the age of nineteen. A statute of limitations is also tolled by legal disabilities such as insanity.

Laches

laches Laches is a court-made doctrine that resembles a statute of limitations. Laches is an affirmative defense that is similar to a statute of limitations defense, but applies only when there is no applicable statute of limitations.

Laches is a court-made doctrine that resembles a statute of limitations. Laches is an affirmative defense that is similar to a statute-of-limitations defense, but applies only when there is no applicable statute of limitations. It applies to actions in equity, such as an action to reform a written instrument or an action to enjoin the defendant's conduct. At some point a claim becomes so stale it must be time-barred. Courts created laches as a defense to these equitable actions because ordinarily no statute of limitations applies to them. When applying laches, courts determine whether the delay prejudiced the defendant. The delay may prejudice a defendant because he or she no longer has access to witnesses and evidence that would have been available if the claim had been timely. Delay may prejudice a defendant because he or she has changed his or her legal position believing no dispute existed.

Statutes of Repose

Statutes of repose are another form of time limitation. In situations where a cause of action may accrue many years after the transaction or occurrence—for example, a construction defect that manifests in a wet basement fifteen years after a house is completed—a statute of repose provides that a cause of action may not *accrue* after a specified time.

The time period under a statute of repose is typically ten years or more. Its purpose is to provide an outside limit for all conceivable suits. For example, if the statute of limitations is three years and accrual is at the time of discovery, a wet-basement suit could be commenced ten, fifteen, or even thirty years after the home was built (so long as discovery was within the previous three years). A ten-year statute of repose would prevent accrual after the ten years, thus preventing all suits commenced more than thirteen years after completion of construction.

statute of repose A statute that has the effect of barring a claim because the act that gave rise to the claim took place many years ago, and even if the injury is recent, the actor should not be held accountable at such a late date.

Assumption of Risk

Assumption of risk is an affirmative defense that applies to actions in negligence and to some breach-of-warranty claims in product liability cases. The defendant must prove that the plaintiff's injury or property damage was the result of a danger that was open and apparent to the plaintiff, that the plaintiff appreciated the risk of harm created by the condition, that the plaintiff voluntarily chose to incur the risk, and that the injury resulted from the risk assumed. For example, suppose the defendant negligently spilled a slippery liquid on the floor, making the floor dangerous. If the plaintiff sees the liquid and understands that the floor is slippery but voluntarily chooses to walk on the floor, the plaintiff assumes the risk of slipping, falling, and being injured. But suppose the defendant has a duty to maintain a sidewalk that the plaintiff must use, and the sidewalk is dangerously slippery. Although the plaintiff uses the sidewalk knowing the danger, the plaintiff does not assume the risk of injury if the sidewalk is the only practicable means of ingress or egress. Under the circumstances, the plaintiff does not *voluntarily* incur the risk.

As another example, spectators at baseball games should know that some baseballs will be hit into the stands. That is a normal occurrence. If a spectator has the opportunity to sit in a protected area but voluntarily chooses to sit in an open area, the spectator can hardly complain about getting hit by a home run ball. The spectator has chosen to be where the action is. Though the ballpark could have provided more protection for more spectators, it is not liable if a spectator assumes the risk of being hit by a ball. The same rules apply to hockey pucks. Although these rules have been in place for decades, some recent and highly publicized tragedies at sporting events may be changing society's expectations about ballpark and arena safety. And with changed societal expectations comes change in the law, so this may be a developing area of the law over the next decade.

Often the defense of contributory negligence or comparative fault overlaps that of assumption of risk. With the advent of comparative fault, some states have mostly abolished assumption of risk as a defense. In those states, assumption of risk is looked on as being merged with negligence. In other words, a plaintiff who assumes the risk of an obvious danger is negligent, but the plaintiff's causal negligence must be weighed against the defendant's causal negligence. Other states, such as Minnesota, have made it even more complex. They have fashioned two types of assumption of risk. One type is *primary assumption of risk*. It remains as an affirmative defense. The baseball fan who is hit by a fly ball or the participant in an inherently dangerous event are still classic examples. The other is *ordinary assumption of risk*. The latter is merged into comparative negligence. Courts have had great difficulty articulating a difference.

Contributory Negligence

Contributory negligence is negligence attributable to the plaintiff. The common-law rule was that contributory negligence is a complete defense to the plaintiff's claim. For example, if the plaintiff's vehicle and the defendant's vehicle collided in an intersection, and the jury determined that both were negligent, the plaintiff could not recover damages from the defendant. It did not matter that the plaintiff may have been far less negligent than the defendant. Contributory negligence was not a defense to some other tort action, such as trespass, assault, battery, strict liability in tort, and a liquor liability claim. It is important to note that the defense of contributory negligence has been abolished in states that have adopted the comparative-negligence doctrine. See Chapter 4. Instead of barring recovery, comparative negligence (also known as comparative fault) reduces the plaintiff's recovery by his or her percentage of fault in causing the accident.

Discharge in Bankruptcy

Federal law provides that individuals and corporations may voluntarily file for bankruptcy if they cannot meet their current obligations. Creditors can also force an individual or corporation into involuntary bankruptcy. The effect of the court's determination that the petitioner is bankrupt is to discharge the petitioner from all disclosed and declared debts as of the date of the petition. The debtor must give notice to creditors of the petition for bankruptcy so they have an opportunity to challenge the petition and to share in the debtor's assets. Defects in the proceedings, such as a failure to give a creditor notice, preclude the debtor from being discharged.

Certain kinds of debts are not dischargeable in bankruptcy. These include debts created by the petitioner's fraud, willful conversion (theft) of property, and intentional tortious acts that cause injury to persons or damage to property such as assault, battery, murder, and fraud.

In personal-injury litigation, the plaintiff most often looks to the defendant's liability insurance for payment. Because such insurance could never pay for any of the defendants' other debts—unpaid credit cards, for example—bankruptcy does not discharge a tort obligation to the extent the defendant has applicable liability insurance.

Duress

A commitment that would be legally enforceable is not binding if obtained through **duress.** Duress is the threat of death, bodily harm, or damage to property. The defendant must believe that he or she was subject to some harm if he or she did not make the commitment.

duress A threat of death, bodily harm, or damage to property.

Estoppel

Estoppel is an esoteric concept that has a variety of applications to actions in tort and in contract. It originated in equity, but it is now firmly recognized as a legal defense. The defense of estoppel precludes the plaintiff from recovering money damages for a loss that resulted from the defendant's mistake where that mistake was induced by the plaintiff's wrongful conduct in the first place. For example, suppose a corporation replaces its outstanding stock certificates with new certificates but fails to collect the old certificates from one shareholder. If that shareholder subsequently sells the old certificates to a bona fide purchaser, the corporation could be estopped from denying the old certificates' validity. The purchaser would be entitled to dividends and to having her or his ownership recorded on the stockholders' register. Also, for example, where an insurance company holds out an agent as authorized to sell its insurance policies, it cannot subsequently avoid a policy on grounds the agent was not licensed. The insurer is estopped from denying the agent's lack of qualifications. By way of another example, if a plaintiff represented to a defendant that the plaintiff's car is owned by another person, who has possession of the car, and the possessor sold the car to the defendant, the plaintiff could be estopped from denying that the possessor was the owner. The law would give effect to the sale because of the plaintiff's misrepresentation on which the defendant reasonably relied. Does this example seem far-fetched? Look at the hypothetical case. John Griffin had indicated to agent Burns that Griffin's son was the owner of the pickup truck, and the agent dealt with the son accordingly.

estoppel An affirmative defense that precludes the plaintiff from recovering money damages for a loss that resulted from the defendant's mistake where that mistake was induced by the plaintiff's wrongful conduct in the first place.

Waiver

Waiver is an affirmative defense that has application to actions in contract and in tort. Waiver is the intentional relinquishment of a known legal right under circumstances in which the defendant would be prejudiced if the plaintiff were allowed to reassert the right. A waiver may be formal and even reduced to writing. Or, a waiver may result from the parties' conduct. For example, suppose an automobile insurance application and policy provide that the policy will be void if the applicant has had an accident within the year preceding the application. Suppose an applicant misrepresents in the application that he or she has not had any accidents, but the insurer learns about the misrepresentation within a month after the policy is issued and does

waiver An intentional, voluntary giving up of a legal right. A waiver may be in writing, oral, or implied from circumstances.

nothing about canceling the policy. The insurer's failure to promptly take steps to revoke or cancel the policy after discovering the misrepresentation could result in a waiver of the right to cancel.

Suppose a store lease provides that the landlord may terminate the lease if the tenant sells liquor on the premises, and to the landlord's knowledge, the tenant does sell liquor for a couple of years. The landlord's acquiescence in the tenant's violation may constitute a waiver of the right to cancel the lease for future violations.

Fraud

Fraud and its elements are discussed in Chapter 4 as a cause of action in tort that gives rise to a claim for money damages. The same elements will give rise to an affirmative defense to actions in contract and in tort.

Consent

consent Voluntary acquiescence. Consent is a complete affirmative defense to most tort actions. Consent may be expressed in words or acts, or implied from circumstances.

Consent is an affirmative defense to actions for assault, battery, trespass to real estate, and conversion of personal property. Consent is a manifestation, either verbal or conduct, that shows the plaintiff agrees to or acquiesces in the defendant's conduct, which otherwise would be wrongful. For example, if the plaintiff sues the defendant in battery to obtain money damages for personal injuries caused by a punch in the nose, the defendant may avoid civil liability by proving that the plaintiff agreed to fight. When professional boxers enter the ring, they consent to be battered. Consent is different from assumption of risk. Consent requires actual agreement to the defendant's conduct and the bodily contact. A plaintiff may give consent before or during the wrongful act. The defendant has the burden of proving that the plaintiff duly consented. A person who suffers from a legal disability, as being under age, cannot consent to another's wrongful acts.

Consent may be inferred from the circumstances. Express consent is easy to understand and apply. But an implied consent may be more problematic. Suppose, for example, the plaintiff and defendant are well acquainted with each other and the defendant asks the plaintiff for permission to use the plaintiff's car. The keys are lying on the table. The defendant picks up the keys, goes to the car, enters it, and drives away without any objection from the plaintiff. Permission to use the car is implied by the circumstances. The plaintiff should not be allowed to claim that the defendant stole (converted) the car. There was implied consent.

Procedural Affirmative Defenses

Some affirmative defenses are based on the plaintiff's failure to comply with the Rules of Civil Procedure. One consequence of violating procedural mandates can be dismissal of the lawsuit. A defendant may assert the defense in a motion to dismiss or in the defendant's answer. But if the defendant fails to raise the defense in a timely manner, it is waived. The defendant has the burden of proving the plaintiff's procedural error. When a court dismisses the plaintiff's action because of a procedural error, the dismissal is often without prejudice, so the plaintiff may bring the action again. But then another defense may arise, such as the statute of limitations.

Insufficiency of Process

A plaintiff's failure to follow prescribed procedures when commencing an action may result in an **insufficiency of process** or insufficiency of service of process. Either results in a lack of personal jurisdiction. The defendant may raise lack of jurisdiction as a defense in a motion or in the answer. For example, if the plaintiff served a complaint without a summons attached to it, the service would be defective, and the defendant would be entitled to a dismissal. If the process server left the summons and complaint at the defendant's residence with a person who did not reside in the house, service would be defective, and the defendant would be entitled to a dismissal. Incredible but silly mistakes such as these do occur, often with serious consequences.

insufficiency of process A failure to follow the procedures prescribed by law for serving process on another party.

Absence of Necessary Party

If the plaintiff fails to include a necessary party to the lawsuit, the defendant is entitled to a dismissal. The absence-of-necessary-party defense may be raised by motion or in the answer. For example, if the plaintiff brings an action to enforce a real estate purchase agreement for real estate owned by two persons in common, the plaintiff must join both persons to obtain a full adjudication of the matter.

Res Judicata

Res judicata means "the matter has been adjudicated." The plaintiff may prosecute his or her claim only once. If the plaintiff brought the same claim in a prior action, perhaps as part of another claim, and lost, the prior result is binding and prevents the claim from being prosecuted again. Res judicata is an affirmative defense that the defendant must allege in the answer or it is waived.

Collateral Estoppel

When a plaintiff prosecutes a claim and fact issues are determined against the plaintiff, another party in a subsequent action may be able to assert the prior determinations as defenses where the plaintiff attempts to relitigate those same facts. In effect, the plaintiff is estopped from denying the truth and effect of the prior determination. Suppose the plaintiff was a passenger in a two-car collision and brought a lawsuit against only one driver to recover money damages for her alleged injuries; suppose the jury determined that the plaintiff did not sustain any injury. If the plaintiff were to bring a subsequent, separate lawsuit against the other driver, the latter could show that the plaintiff litigated the injury issue in the first lawsuit. The prior determination is an adjudicated fact that she cannot deny or relitigate. In other words, the plaintiff is collaterally estopped from avoiding the fact of no injury that was duly established against her in her first lawsuit. The principle depends on the plaintiff having the opportunity and incentive to fully prove the claim in the first action.

Note that res judicata applies to a previously litigated claim, while collateral estoppel applies to previously litigated issues litigated in a separate claim. The effect is the same, but the circumstances giving rise to the defense are slightly different.

Ethical Consideration

A lawyer is subject to disciplinary action for asserting a claim or defense that is frivolous. A claim or defense is frivolous if it has no apparent basis in fact or in law. This is another important difference between criminal law and civil law. In criminal law, a defendant and the defendant's lawyer may put the state to its burden of proving every element of the crime, although they know the defendant did what they accuse him or her of doing. They know that no defense exists; nevertheless, they may put the state to its proof. In a civil action, a party has no right to remain silent or to force an opposing party to prove facts a party knows are true. Besides professional ethics, Rule 11 provides that a lawyer's signature on a pleading is the lawyer's certification that the lawyer has made reasonable inquiry into the matter and believes that the claims and defenses alleged in the pleading have basis in fact and are justified by law. A lawyer also certifies that he or she is not asserting the claim or defense for an improper purpose, such as harassment or delay.

SUMMARY

An affirmative defense defeats the plaintiff's claim, even if the claim is true and has a basis in law. Most causes of action are subject to some type of affirmative defense. Only certain affirmative defenses, however, are available to certain causes of action. Rule 8(c) contains a partial list of affirmative defenses.

The defendant must allege his or her affirmative defenses in the answer. Some procedural affirmative defenses may be raised by motion. A defendant waives defenses not alleged, except for subject matter jurisdiction. The defendant may allege more than one affirmative defense to a claim. The plaintiff does not have to serve a reply to the defendant's affirmative defenses, because an affirmative defense is not a counterclaim.

The defendant has the burden of proving all the facts on which an affirmative defense is based, by a fair preponderance of the evidence. Whenever possible, a defendant's two-prong defense strategy should be to attack the merits of the plaintiff's claim while also attempting to establish whatever affirmative defenses are available.

The defendant's answer must assert his or her affirmative defenses by providing a short, plain statement of the facts on which each defense is based. Each affirmative defense should be pled in a separate paragraph for the clarity and convenience of the parties. The time and place of the events that give rise to each affirmative defense must be stated as provided by Rule 9(f).

A release is a type of contract by which a claim or legal right is voluntarily relinquished. It ends the right of the plaintiff to sue on the claim that is released. A release usually is reduced to a writing, but no law requires it. A release must meet all the requirements of a contract to be enforceable, including a meeting of the minds on the essential terms and an exchange of consideration between the parties.

An accord and satisfaction is an agreement to replace a prior contract with a new one, which, if fully performed by the defendant, precludes enforcement of the prior agreement. An accord and satisfaction is a complete defense to an action on the original contract.

An arbitration and award resolves a dispute and precludes litigation of the same dispute. An arbitrator's award is binding, and a court may enforce it by confirming it. A losing party cannot appeal an arbitration award or take the matter to court unless the prevailing party or tribunal committed a fraud or exceeded the scope of submission. The parties' arbitration agreement may prescribe the procedures the parties must follow, or the parties may adopt a procedure provided by statute. The parties must agree on the scope of the submission to arbitration, and the scope should be reduced to writing. No rule of law prohibits laypersons from handling arbitration procedures.

A statute of limitations establishes the time within which a plaintiff must commence action on the claim; otherwise, the claim is time-barred. The statute of limitations begins to run against a claim when the cause of action accrues, and that is usually, but not always, when the injury or other loss occurs. States differ in their use of the statute of limitations. In some states, a statute of limitations does not begin to run until the plaintiff discovers the tortious act or injury, or should have discovered it. This so-called discovery rule almost universally applies to claims for fraud, but its application varies widely among states for other causes of action like medical negligence and construction defects. A statute of limitations does not run against a minor during his or her minority. A statute of limitations is also tolled by legal disabilities such as insanity.

Laches only applies to actions in equity, such as an action to reform a written instrument or to enjoin the defendant's conduct. Courts created laches as a defense to these equitable actions because ordinarily no statute of limitations applies to them. When applying laches, courts look to see if the defendant was prejudiced by the delay.

A statute of repose bars a claim because the act that gave rise to the claim took place many years ago and, even if the injury or its discovery is recent, the actor should not be held accountable at such a late date. Statutes of repose apply most commonly to actions against building contractors and manufacturers of products.

Assumption of risk applies to actions in negligence and some products cases. The defendant must prove that the plaintiff's injury or property damage was the result of a danger that was open and apparent to the plaintiff, that the plaintiff appreciated the risk of harm created by the condition, that the plaintiff voluntarily chose to incur the risk, and that the injury resulted from the risk assumed. With the evolution of comparative fault, some states have abolished assumption of risk as a defense. In those states, assumption of risk is perceived as merged with negligence.

Contributory negligence is negligence attributable to the plaintiff. The common law rule was that contributory negligence was a complete defense to the plaintiff's claim. Contributory negligence was not a defense to other tort actions such as trespass, assault, battery, strict liability in tort, and dram shop claims. The defense of contributory negligence has been abolished by states that have adopted the comparative fault doctrine.

The comparative-fault doctrine allocates legal responsibility between parties and apportions their financial responsibility in proportion to their causal negligence. The critical difference from contributory negligence is that the latter completely bars a plaintiff's recovery, while comparative fault merely reduces the plaintiff's recovery by his or her own share of fault. For this reason, comparative fault is always measured in percentages.

Discharge in bankruptcy eliminates the legal obligation on which a claim is based, whether in contract or tort. Certain kinds of debts are not dischargeable in bankruptcy, including debts based on fraud, willful conversion (theft) of property, and intentional tortious acts that cause injury to persons or damage to property. The existence of liability insurance mutes the bankruptcy defense in personal-injury litigation to the extent of applicable coverage.

Duress is a defense to any contractual obligation. It is the threat of death, bodily harm, or damage to property. The defendant must believe that she or he was subject to some harm if she or he did not make the promise.

Estoppel precludes the plaintiff from recovering money damages for a loss that resulted from the defendant's mistake where that mistake was induced by the plaintiff's wrongful conduct in the first place. The wrongful conduct may be verbal or behavioral.

Waiver is the intentional relinquishment of a known legal right under circumstances where the defendant would be prejudiced if the plaintiff were allowed to reassert the right. Waiver applies to actions in contract and in tort.

The same elements that give rise to a cause of action for fraud make fraud an affirmative defense to actions in contract and in tort.

Consent is an affirmative defense to actions for battery, trespass to real estate, and conversion of personal property. The defendant must show that the plaintiff knew exactly to what he or she was consenting. Consent does not have to be expressed to be effective. It may be implied from the circumstances of the occurrence.

Some affirmative defenses are procedural in nature. That is, they arise from the prosecution of the litigation. These include insufficiency of process, where the plaintiff fails to follow the prescribed procedures for commencing an action; absence of necessary party, where the plaintiff fails to include a necessary party to the lawsuit; res judicata, which precludes the plaintiff from prosecuting the claim more than once; and collateral estoppel, which precludes the plaintiff from prosecuting the same issue a second time, even against another party, where that issue has been decided against the plaintiff.

KEY TERMS

arbitration and award
consent
duress
estoppel
insufficiency of process
laches

mutual mistake
release
statute of limitations
statute of repose
waiver

REVIEW QUESTIONS

1. How does an affirmative defense affect the plaintiff's cause of action?
2. How many affirmative defenses may a defendant raise?
3. How may the defendant raise (assert) an affirmative defense?
4. Does Rule 8(c) contain a complete list of all affirmative defenses?
5. Which type of comparative fault is used in your state?
6. Which type of comparative fault is applied by the federal district courts?
7. How does collateral estoppel differ from res judicata?
8. How does consent differ from assumption of risk as an affirmative defense?
9. What are the essential elements of a release?

CASE ASSIGNMENT

Bradley Harper retained attorney William Hoch to represent him in the action brought by trustee Raskin. You are employed by attorney Hoch's law firm and on his litigation team. He has asked you to determine what affirmative defenses are available to Harper and advise him in an intraoffice memorandum. Because Harper has a potential claim against John Griffin and the Security Insurance Company, he wants your analysis to identify any affirmative defenses they may have against Harper's claim for breach of contract and fraud. If you find that you need more information or have some specific suggestions for Mr. Hoch, include them in your memorandum. Remember, sometimes it is a good thing to go beyond the specific assignment.

Attorney Hoch has asked you to prepare an intraoffice memorandum concerning the statutes of limitations that might apply to the various causes of action in this matter. You should use the statutes of limitations that apply in your state, not Minnesota. The causes of action that potentially apply are negligence, breach of contract, estoppel, and fraud.

Endnotes

1. First Defense: The complaint fails to state a claim against defendant upon which relief can be granted.
2. Second Defense: If defendant is indebted to plaintiffs for the goods mentioned in the complaint, he is indebted to them jointly with G.H. G.H. is alive, is a citizen of the State of New York. [The state in which the action has been brought.] and a resident of this district, is subject to the jurisdiction of this court, as to both service of process and venue; can be made a party without depriving this court of jurisdiction of present parties, and has not been made a party.
3. Third Defense: Defendant admits the allegation contained in paragraphs 1 and 4 of the complaint; alleges that he is without knowledge or information sufficient to form a belief as to the truth of the allegations contained in paragraph 2 of the complaint; and denies each and every other allegation, contained in the complaint.
4. Fourth Defense: The right of action set forth in the complaint did not accrue within six years next before the commencement of this action.
5. Unless otherwise provided by law, parties may contract for nonbinding arbitration. The parties expect to abide by the arbitrator's award but are not legally obligated to do so.
6. To toll the statute of limitations is to stop the statute from running against the cause of action for a period of time.

 For additional resources, visit our Web site at www.paralegal.delmar.cengage.com

INTRODUCTION TO FEDERAL PROCEDURE: PARTIES AND PLEADINGS

Chapter Outline

Chapter Objectives

Chapter 6 describes the process and procedures a plaintiff uses to start a civil action in federal district court. It also describes how a defendant appears in a case to defend. The chapter explains collateral litigation, which involves additional claims and additional parties. The emphasis is on pleadings, how they are used, and how they are prepared.

Introduction

Laypersons tend to see civil litigation as a labyrinth, too involved, encumbered, slow, and expensive. Clients want to know, "Why can't I just go to court and tell my story?" There are good reasons why the civil justice system operates as it does. As a paralegal, you must understand how the system works and what makes it work. In part, this means understanding civil procedure. You must understand the difference between a fact issue and a legal issue, how a lawsuit is commenced, how the legal issues are framed, and what lawyers do. You need to understand the time parameters for getting things done and the consequences of missing a deadline. This chapter gives you an overview of federal procedure.

Commencing a Civil Action

The first step in commencing a civil action is to prepare a complaint. The plaintiff's complaint states the plaintiff's claim and describes the basis for the court's jurisdiction. Although the plaintiff's attorney is responsible for a complaint's preparation and content, paralegals may draft them. Rule 11 requires the plaintiff's attorney to sign the complaint.[1] The signature certifies that the attorney has read the complaint, that there is a good basis for the allegations, and that the pleading has not been filed for the purpose of harassment, delay, or some collateral purpose. The attorney's signature certifies that the attorney has made due inquiry about the claims or defenses; the attorney must believe that the claims or defenses have a good basis in law and there is evidence to support them.[2] An attorney cannot justify any omission or improper allegation by contending that she or he did not actually draft it or was in a hurry when she or he read it. Any allegation that is redundant, incompetent, or insufficient to state a claim or defense is subject to being stricken by court order [Rule 12(f)]. Parties must not use pleadings to malign another party or person [Rules 11 and 12(f)]. A court may order stricken any allegation that is scandalous, impertinent, or immaterial to the claim or defense. All pleadings become public records when they are filed. Anyone may read them, including the news media. Consequently, pleadings may engender publicity that could hurt a party or even third persons.

In addition to the complaint, a plaintiff's attorney or paralegal must prepare a summons. A summons is a court mandate to the defendant to appear in the action. Rule 4(a) prescribes the form and content of a summons. You may obtain summons forms from the clerk of court or on-line. You only have to fill in the blanks, supplying the title of the action, the court's name, the defendant's address, and the plaintiff attorney's address. You must present the prepared summons to the clerk of court when you file the complaint. The clerk is required to examine it. If it is proper in form, the clerk will date and sign it and apply the court seal. You may arrange to have a United States marshal serve the summons and complaint. Or, any adult other than the plaintiff may serve them. The Rules forbid the named plaintiff to serve the summons and complaint, because there is too much danger of violence or fraud.

The back of the summons is a "Return of Service" form, which must be completed by the person who serves the summons and complaint on the defendant. If you serve the summons and complaint, you will complete the Return of Service after serving the defendant. The summons directs the defendant to serve an answer on the plaintiff's attorney within twenty days, excluding the day of service. The summons advises the defendant that if he or she fails to answer within twenty days, the plaintiff may take a default judgment against him or her. Defendants usually serve their answer by mail. They mail the original copy to the clerk of court and a copy to the plaintiff's attorney.

An action is commenced by filing the summons and complaint with the clerk of court. The date of commencement is important because that is the date that determines whether the statute of limitations has been met. Many federal and state district courts permit the parties to file their pleadings by fax or e-mail. But the named defendant does not become a party and is not subject to the court's jurisdiction until the summons and complaint are actually served on the defendant. The plaintiff's complaint and the defendant's answer frame the issues to be litigated. Most pleadings do not have to be notarized, but there are exceptions. For example, some states require notarization of plaintiffs' signatures in complaints seeking dissolution of marriages.

The clerk does not decide whether the complaint is adequate. The clerk assigns a file number to the case and signs a summons, which the litigation team has prepared (see Rules Appendix of Forms, form 1). A summons is not a pleading. The summons uses the title of the action and the court's file number. The number may be similar to this: 06 Civ. 532. The 06 means the case was filed during the year 2006. Civ. means it is a civil action. The last number indicates the case's place on the calendar. All subsequent pleadings, motions, orders, affidavits, and depositions must use that file number. The clerk must sign and date the summons at the bottom.

The clerk must issue a separate summons for each defendant. The summons is attached to a copy of the complaint. The clerk gives the summons to the plaintiff's lawyer, who is then responsible for arranging to serve the summons and a copy of the complaint on each defendant [Rules 4(a) and (d)]. A plaintiff's lawyer may arrange for the United States marshal to serve the summons and complaint. The plaintiff's lawyer must provide the defendant's last known address. It is helpful to supply the defendant's employment address as well. A summons includes the address where the defendant may serve the answer. An answer may be served by mail or in person.

The summons and complaint must be served on the defendant within 120 days after the action was commenced. Otherwise, the action is subject to dismissal without prejudice.[3] A summons informs the defendant that he or she has 20 days in which to **appear** and defend against the plaintiff's action [Rule 4(b)]. The 20-day period begins to run the day after service.[4] If the defendant fails to appear in the action within 20 days, the defendant is in default. Note that the 20-day period does not begin to run on the same day that the action is commenced. Indeed, the summons and complaint may not be served for many days after the action is commenced. The United States has sixty days in which to answer a complaint.

The defendant does not have to actually appear in court. A defendant appears in the action by serving and filing an answer, by filing a motion contesting the sufficiency of the complaint, by contesting service of process (Rule 12), or by obtaining an extension of time in which to do these things. In federal courts, a party should not assume that an extension will be granted, even if the other attorney agrees. If more time is necessary, don't wait to pursue an extension.

A defendant who has liability insurance should immediately deliver the summons and complaint to his or her insurance company. Unfortunately, sometimes defendants delay contacting their insurers. Sometimes, insurance companies have difficulty determining whether a claim is covered and whether to undertake the defense. The insurer may need extra time in which to make a "corporate decision."

State courts usually give lawyers more control over deadlines. More often than not, the plaintiff's lawyer will readily grant additional time for answering. An informal extension of time for answering helps everyone. The plaintiff's lawyer actually retains a little more control over the situation by stipulating to enlarge the time for answering. The lawyer decides how much time to give the defendant, rather than the court. Both sides should try to avoid spending unnecessary time and money on procedural matters. An attitude of goodwill and cooperation benefits everyone.

appear A party appears in an action when he or she serves or files a pleading or motion.

Laypersons are often surprised at how much and how often lawyers, who are adverse in a case, accommodate each other. If the defendant acts promptly to consult a lawyer or to deliver the summons and complaint to the defendant's liability insurer, the twenty-day period provided by the Rules should be sufficient.

Complaints

A complaint states the plaintiff's claim against the defendant and describes the relief the plaintiff wants the court to award. A complaint must clearly describe all the plaintiff's claims, so the defendant can admit or deny them. Rule 8(a) states the criteria for a complaint:

> A pleading which sets forth a claim for relief, whether an original claim, counterclaim, cross-claim, or third-party claim, shall contain (1) a short and plain statement of the grounds upon which the court's jurisdiction depends, unless the court already has jurisdiction and the claim needs no new grounds of jurisdiction to support it; (2) a short and plain statement of the claim showing that the pleader is entitled to relief; and (3) a demand for judgment for the relief the pleader seeks. Relief in the alternative or of several different types may be demanded.

Elements of a Complaint

The top of the complaint identifies the court in which the action is being brought. The complaint's title identifies the plaintiff(s) and defendant(s). However, a person does not actually become a defendant until duly served with a summons and a copy of the complaint. The complaint must allege the court has jurisdiction over the case and set forth the basis for its jurisdiction. The complaint must specify one or more legal theories (causes of action) on which the plaintiff bases her or his claim for relief. For each cause of action, the complaint must (1) allege facts showing the court has jurisdiction over the subject matter, (2) identify the transaction or occurrence in question, (3) describe generally the manner in which the plaintiff claims defendant breached a legal duty owed to the plaintiff,[5] and (4) allege that the breach was a direct cause of the plaintiff's injury or loss. If the action involves a contract, lease, deed, or other document, a copy of the document may be attached as an exhibit.

A complaint identifies the transaction or occurrence by describing its type, date, and place [Rule 9(f)]. The time element not only identifies the occurrence, it also determines whether the statute of limitations applies and whether the parties have complied with all notice requirements. Because laws may change, the time alleged helps identify what law applies. The place of the occurrence is important in determining whether the court has jurisdiction. The place may also determine which state's laws apply.

The complaint must describe, in general terms, the nature and extent of plaintiff's loss or injury. When two or more plaintiffs are named in the complaint and each has a separate loss, the losses should be stated separately. Losses take various forms, such as lost profits, expenses, damage to property, destruction of property, personal injury, pain, mental anguish, disfigurement, disability, loss of reputation, loss of use, and loss of support. A claim may be for future losses, such as future pain, future loss of income, and future loss of profits. The list of compensable losses is almost without a limit.

special damages Out-of-pocket expenses that a party has incurred because of another party's wrongful conduct.

A complaint must specifically identify all items of **special damages** [Rule 9(g)]. Special damages are out-of-pocket expenses the plaintiff sustained because of the defendant's wrongful conduct. In a personal-injury action, the plaintiff's medical expenses, loss of past income, and property damage are items of special damages. In a breach-of-contract action, the amount of the lost profits, loss of the bargain, and consequential expenses should be stated as special damages. A monetary value need not be assigned to each item of special damage—though it frequently is. A complaint closes with an **ad damnum clause.** It is sometimes called the "Wherefore clause," because it frequently begins with the word *Wherefore.* It is also described as the plaintiff's "prayer for relief." The ad damnum clause tells the defendant the total amount of money damages the plaintiff is claiming and describes any other relief plaintiff wants the court to award. The amount of the ad damnum is important when jurisdiction is affected by the amount in controversy. If the ad damnum is too much, a county or municipal court cannot have jurisdiction. In diversity cases, United States district courts do not have jurisdiction unless the plaintiff, in good faith, demands judgment in excess of $75,000, exclusive of costs and interest.

ad damnum clause The "Wherefore" clause at the end of a civil action complaint, in which the plaintiff specifies the relief or recovery the plaintiff wants the court to award.

If the defendant fails to serve an answer to the complaint within the time specified, she or he is in default. The plaintiff may move the court for entry of judgment (Rule 55). In a default setting, the judgment may not exceed the amount of the ad damnum. There is a legal presumption that the defendant acquiesced in obligation and the amount, as stated in the complaint, is correct. The plaintiff's recovery is limited to the amount of the ad damnum even though she or he is able to show more damages when "proving up" the default judgment. A plaintiff "proves up" a default judgment by presenting in an uncontested hearing evidence of the default, a prima facie case of liability, and damages. When a defendant duly appears and defends against a claim, however, the defendant's obligation may be determined to be more than the amount demanded in the complaint.

Nothing but a sense of professional responsibility prevents the plaintiff's attorney from asking for an excessively large amount of money. Unfortunately, the news media is unduly impressed by large money demands that are, in reality, just random figures chosen by the plaintiff's attorney. Consequently, a few states have laws or rules that prohibit plaintiffs from stating a specific dollar amount in excess of $50,000. When a claim is for a larger amount, the ad damnum clause merely states the claim is for "more than $50,000."

A complaint should state each allegation in a short, separate paragraph [Rule 8(a)]. Because attorneys are prone to admit and deny allegations by referring to complaint paragraphs, a plaintiff's attorney encourages a defendant to admit allegations by limiting each set of circumstances to a single paragraph. For example, where the plaintiff's complaint sets forth indisputable facts in paragraphs 1, 2, and 5, the defendant's answer may state, "Defendant admits the truth of the allegations contained in paragraphs 1, 2, and 5 of the complaint." If a paragraph contains some facts the defendant could admit and some that defendant denies, the defendant's attorney will not admit the paragraph. Because a plaintiff wants a defendant to admit as many of the complaint allegations as possible—admitted allegations do not have to be proved at trial—it is important to limit the facts alleged in any given paragraph. The facts and legal conclusions a defendant admits in the answer cannot be controverted. A defendant would have to obtain the court's permission to amend her or his answer to contest facts previously admitted. Similarly, a plaintiff cannot deny facts that he or she alleges in the complaint. For example, suppose a plaintiff's complaint alleges she was employed by the defendant at the time of an accident, but as the case develops she concludes her case would be better if she were not an employee.[6] She cannot deny her employee status for purposes of the lawsuit without amending her complaint.

Counts

There are times when a complaint should be divided into parts or **counts** to make the claims more clear. In particular, a complaint should treat each transaction and each occurrence separately by using a separate count for each. Whereas a complaint paragraph should relate to a single subject, each count should relate to a separate claim. Each count should be independent from other counts and be able to stand alone. Nevertheless, a count may incorporate by reference paragraphs in another count.[7] When two or more plaintiffs have claims arising from the *same* transaction or occurrence, they may join as coplaintiffs in a single action (Rule 20). A complaint should clearly segregate the plaintiffs' claims by using separate counts. See Exhibit 4.13 for an example of counts in a complaint.

counts Separate statements of a claim within a complaint, counterclaim, or cross-claim.

Signature

A lawyer's signature is her or his certification that the claim has a good basis in fact and law and that the action has not been brought to harass, embarrass, or delay (Rule 11). A lawyer may have to subject the client to some aggressive interrogation and investigate facts, however, to make sure the claim is not fraudulent or groundless. Litigants must comply with the letter and spirit of Rule 11. If a lawyer or a client violates Rule 11 by starting a groundless lawsuit, he or she is subject to court sanctions. For a lawyer, it could even mean disbarment. A client could be found in contempt of court and put in jail or fined. You may need to explain to a client the seriousness of Rule 11 and its application. You have an obligation to keep clients honest.

Sample Complaint

Exhibit 6.1 identifies the contract, the place of its performance, the time and place of the breach, the nature of the breach, and the nature and extent of the loss claimed. The contract document is fully identified by attaching a photocopy to the complaint. The use of photocopies eliminates the possibility of introducing error into documents where the wording may be critical. This complaint provides the defendant with enough information to determine whether to deny the claim or admit liability.

Amended Complaint

A plaintiff may amend a complaint as a matter of right, without leave of the court, if the plaintiff serves the amended complaint *within* twenty days after service of the original complaint or before the defendant serves an answer [Rule 15(a)]. Otherwise, the plaintiff must move the court for leave to amend. A defendant may agree (stipulate) to accept service of an amended complaint after expiration of the time provided by Rule 15(a). The easiest way to amend is to ask the defendant's lawyer to

admission of service A party's formal acknowledgment that he or she received service of process or documents or court order. An admission of service must be in writing, dated, and signed by the party or party's attorney.

admit service on the original amended complaint. Or, the defendant's lawyer may accept service by signing an **admission of service.** An admission of service can be similar to the following example:

Example

Due and proper service of the amended complaint is admitted this first day of April, 2006.

/s/ _____

Attorney for Defendant

An amended pleading should be identified as "Amended." If another amendment becomes necessary, it should be called "Second Amended Complaint."

There are many reasons why a party may agree to accept an amended pleading and not force the opponent to seek the court's permission. Courts liberally permit amendments, so most lawyers choose not to waste time and money resisting motions that will likely be granted. Usually, a party who wants to amend a pleading agrees to allow opponents to conduct whatever discovery they need to prepare for the new issues.

A party who opposes an amendment must show that he or she would be prejudiced by the amendment (Rule 15). An amendment may significantly help the plaintiff establish a claim against the defendant, but that does not constitute prejudice to the defendant. A party is prejudiced only if the party's ability to defend against the new allegation was, in some way, impaired by the delay. For example, critical evidence may no longer be available because a witness died or documents have been destroyed.

A defendant has at least ten days in which to answer an amended complaint. But if the amended complaint was served fewer than ten days after the original complaint was served, the defendant must answer within the time period for answering the original complaint. In other words, the defendant's answer to the amended complaint is due at the same time as it would be due for the original complaint or within ten days after service of the amended complaint, whichever time period is longer.

Amendments "relate back" to the date of the original pleading. This means that the suit is deemed commenced—even the amendment—at the time it was originally commenced. Obviously this is important for statutes of limitations. For example, suppose the plaintiff brings an action to recover compensation for damage to real estate, and the original complaint alleged only a cause of action in negligence. Assume that after the suit was started, the statute of limitations ran on all tort claims. If the plaintiff is allowed to amend the complaint to allege a cause of action in trespass too, the amendment is deemed to relate back to the date on which the action was originally commenced. By amending the original complaint, the plaintiff avoids the statute of limitations defense.

When a party needs more time in which to prepare a pleading and the opposition will not agree to an extension of time, the party must make a notion to the court

(Court)

(Title of Cause)

For his cause of action against the defendant, plaintiff alleges:

1. Plaintiff is a resident of the state of New York, and defendant is a resident of the state of New Jersey; the amount in controversy exceeds $10,000, not including costs and interest.
2. On May 10, 2006, plaintiff and defendant entered into a written contract in which plaintiff agreed to purchase from defendant and defendant agreed to sell a certain XYZ computer bearing manufacturer's serial number 54321 and then located at defendant's plant at 33 Hart Street, Newark, New Jersey.
3. The agreed purchase price for the computer to be delivered at defendant's plant was $30,000.
4. A copy of the contract is attached hereto as Exhibit A and incorporated herein by reference.
5. Defendant promised to deliver the computer to plaintiff at defendant's plant in Newark, New Jersey, on June 15, 2006.
6. Defendant failed to deliver the computer to plaintiff at that time and place, although plaintiff has made demand upon defendant to do so.
7. Plaintiff tendered to defendant the agreed purchase price of $30,000, and all other conditions precedent have occurred or have been performed by plaintiff.
8. By reason of defendant's breach of contract, plaintiff has been required to purchase another electronic computer, similar in type, at a cost of $50,000; therefore, defendant's breach of contract has caused plaintiff to sustain a loss in the amount of $20,000, plus interest thereon at the legal rate of 8 percent per annum.

Wherefore, plaintiff prays for judgment against defendant in the sum of $20,000, together with interest thereon at the legal rate of 8 percent per annum from the date of defendant's breach, together with plaintiff's costs and disbursements herein.

Plaintiff demands trial by jury.

[date]

Attorney for Plaintiff

[Attorney Signature]

for an extension. Such a motion may be made with or without notice to the opposing party if it is made before the prescribed time period expires [Rule 6(b)]. The moving party must show the court that she or he has good reason (grounds) for making the request. The reasons ordinarily are set forth in an affidavit that must be filed with the motion.

If the defendant fails to appear in the action by serving a motion or serving an answer to the complaint within the time specified by the summons, the plaintiff may obtain a judgment against the defendant by default [Rule 55(a)]. A defendant may later move the court to set aside the default judgment [Rule 55(c)], but the defendant must show the court that the default was the result of **excusable neglect** or inadvertence [Rule 60(b)]. "Excusable neglect" covers a lot of litigation sins. The Rules do not attempt to define circumstances that constitute excusable neglect. A party's failure to comply with the Rules, a court order, or time limitation may be excused if there is some justification and the consequences would be out of proportion to the neglect. Courts have broad discretion to grant or disallow such motions. Courts consider the moving party's excuse, the effect on the moving party if the motion were denied, the merits of the parties' claims and defenses, the prejudice to the opposing party, and costs the opposing party incurred by reason of the moving party's delay.

excusable neglect Ordinarily, to be excusable, neglect must not be more culpable than mere inadvertence or oversight. The neglect must not be willful.

Supplemental Complaint

The plaintiff has a right to serve and file a **supplemental complaint** to state a new cause of action against the defendant if a new claim accrues in favor of the plaintiff after the original complaint was served. A supplemental complaint uses the same title and court number as the original complaint, assuming the plaintiff wants to have the new action heard with the first action. However, if the second claim is unrelated to the first, it may be preferable to keep the matters separate.

supplemental complaint A complaint that alleges a new, additional claim that arose from a transaction or occurrence that took place after the initial complaint was filed.

State Practice for a Complaint

Some courts authorize the plaintiff's lawyer to sign the summons as well as the complaint. Also, some states allow the summons and complaint to be served on the defendant before actually filing the summons and complaint with the court. In those states, the cause of action is commenced either (1) when the summons and complaint are delivered to a proper public officer, such as a sheriff, for service or (2) when the summons and complaint are served on the defendant. If the action is commenced at the time of service and there are several defendants, the action may commence against them on different days. There is no rule to require the plaintiff to file the summons and complaint. However, as soon as either party wants the court to become involved, the party must file a pleading (complaint or answer) with the clerk of court, and the case then proceeds as it would in federal court. Other states operate like the federal courts from the beginning. It is important for a paralegal to know the rules for commencement of suit in the state where he or she practices.

Defendant's Response to a Summons and Complaint

A defendant appears in the case by serving an answer to the complaint, by serving and filing a motion challenging jurisdiction, by moving the court for an order striking the complaint, by moving the court for judgment on the pleadings, or by moving the court for an order compelling a more definite statement of the allegations in the complaint [Rule 12(a)]. If the defendant elects to appear in the case by serving a Rule 12 motion, an answer need not be served while the motion is pending. After the court rules on the motion, the answer is due within ten days of the ruling—unless the court dismisses the complaint or sets a different time for answering [Rule 12(a)]. Unlike the summons and complaint, the answer or motion may be served by mail.

Answers

The answer uses the same title as the complaint, even if the defendant's name is misspelled. The correct spelling of the parties' names may be set forth as a separate allegation in the answer, but the title in the complaint must be used until amended by court order. When a case has two or more plaintiffs or defendants, the answer and all subsequent pleadings may abridge the title by using just the name of the first plaintiff and first defendant. The abbreviation "et al." follows the names to indicate there are additional parties.

Unless denied, a complaint's allegations are presumed to be admitted [Rule 8(d)]. Consequently, an answer usually begins with a general denial, such as "Defendant denies each and every allegation, statement, matter, and thing contained in the complaint, except as hereinafter expressly admitted or alleged." A defendant must admit all of the plaintiff's allegations that the defendant knows are true. The plaintiff does not have to prove allegations that the defendant admits are true. An admission takes the admitted fact out of contention. When appropriate, the court informs the jury the admitted facts are not disputed. An answer must deny all allegations the defendant believes are not true. A general denial, standing alone, is improper and insufficient, unless the defendant disputes that he or she was even involved in the transaction or occurrence. If the defendant does not have sufficient knowledge on which to form a belief concerning an allegation in the complaint, he or she may so state. The claimed lack of knowledge has the same effect as a denial.

An answer uses numbered paragraphs, just like a complaint, to separate each set of circumstances and each affirmative defense. It is common practice to use one paragraph to set forth all admissions. For example,

> 2. Defendant admits the allegations contained in paragraphs 1, 2, and 3 of the complaint, and further admits that the motor vehicle accident occurred about the time and place specified in the complaint.

An admission that an accident occurred is not an admission of fault or legal responsibility for the accident. Nevertheless, some lawyers feel constrained to add a statement, such as "specifically denies that the defendant was negligent," after admitting that the defendant was involved in the accident or other occurrence. When the defendant admits an alleged fact that is part of a paragraph that contains many facts, the defendant must be careful to clearly delineate the scope of the admission.

Allegations and denials in the answer do not have to be consistent with one another [Rule 8(e)]. For example, an answer may deny the plaintiff and defendant entered into a contract. At the same time, the answer may allege that the plaintiff's claim on the contract is barred by affirmative defenses such as accord and satisfaction, release, fraud, and waiver, which apply only if the contract had been made. See Rules Appendix of Forms, forms 20 and 21, for examples of answers and their responses to allegations.

An answer must allege all the affirmative defenses the defendant has [Rule 8(c)]. Affirmative defenses not asserted are waived. An affirmative defense is a fact or set of circumstances that defeats the plaintiff's claim even if the plaintiff were able to prove her or his cause of action. Rule 8(c) provides a partial list of affirmative defenses. Also, see Chapter 5. Each affirmative defense should be set forth in a separate, numbered paragraph for the convenience of the parties and the court. See Rules Appendix of Forms, form 20.

An answer concludes with a "wherefore" clause in which the defendant states his or her request for relief. The following is a typical wherefore clause.

> Wherefore, defendant prays that plaintiff take nothing by reason of her alleged cause of action, and that defendant have judgment for her costs and disbursements herein.

Amended Answer

After serving an answer, a defendant has twenty days in which to amend the answer as a matter of right. After the twenty-day period expires, the answer may be amended only by stipulation or by court order [Rule 15(a)]. An answer may be amended to correct mistakes in the original answer, to allege new facts or to allege new affirmative defenses. A defendant could amend the answer simply to admit allegations in the complaint that the defendant had denied. An admission that is duly corrected or withdrawn by an amendment cannot be used against the defendant.

Unless an amendment prejudices the plaintiff, it should be allowed.[8] For example, a plaintiff is not prejudiced if the defendant amends the answer to allege the statute of limitations as an additional defense, even though the new defense could defeat the claim. The defense is one about timing and the evidence about when things occurred would very likely be unaffected by the delay in pleading the defense. On the other hand, if the defendant admitted in the answer that the defendant's stairway was unlighted at the time of plaintiff's accident, withdraw of the admission may well prejudice the plaintiff if the scene has changed and evidence the plaintiff would need to prove the absence of lighting is no longer available due to the issue of lighting seeming to be admitted.

Procedure

An answer must be served within twenty days after the complaint is served. The twenty-day period begins the day after the summons and complaint are served. All the time periods prescribed by the Rules exclude the day of the act or event, so it makes no difference whether the defendant was served at 9:00 A.M. or 4:00 P.M., the time period begins to run the next day. The answer is due on the twentieth day, not after twenty days. If the twentieth day falls on a Saturday, Sunday, or legal holiday, the time period is extended to the next business day [Rule 6].

A defendant or defendant's attorney may ask the plaintiff for additional time in which to serve the answer. The defendant's lawyer simply may telephone the plaintiff's lawyer and ask for a specified number of days. If an informal extension is granted, one of the lawyers should confirm the extension by letter. A confirmation letter helps to prevent misunderstandings and provides good evidence of the lawyers' intent if a disagreement develops. A formal stipulation is not necessary, but could be used.[9]

If a plaintiff cannot or will not grant an extension voluntarily, the defendant may move the court for an order extending the time for answering [Rule 6(b)]. If the defendant makes the motion within twenty days after service of the complaint, the motion may be made ex parte—that is, without notice to the other party [Rule 6(b)]. (See Exhibit 6.2.) Motions to lengthen time periods are granted routinely. However, if the time period has expired, the party in default must show the court his or her failure to act was the result of excusable neglect.

If a plaintiff takes a default judgment against a defendant, the defendant must show his or her neglect is excusable to warrant setting aside the default judgment. A court considers the defendant's explanation, whether the defendant has a meritorious defense, whether the defendant is merely stalling, and whether the plaintiff will be prejudiced by setting aside the judgment. The defendant who gets a default judgment set aside usually has to pay all costs the plaintiff incurred in obtaining the judgment. These costs may include reasonable attorneys' fees.

Motion Defenses

Motions are discussed in detail in Chapter 17. The following discussion is limited to motions a defendant may make instead of serving an answer. Paralegals may prepare these motions and supporting documentation. However, the lawyer who is handling the case must read, approve, and sign every motion. A motion is an application to a court for an order that assists the moving party or provides guidance. Rule 7(b) provides for the following:

(1) An application to the court for an order shall be by motion which, unless made during a hearing or trial, shall be made in writing, shall state with particularity the grounds therefore, and shall set forth the relief or order sought. The requirement of writing is fulfilled if the motion is stated in written notice of the hearing of the motion.
(2) The rules applicable to captions and other matters of form of pleadings apply to all motions and other papers provided for by these rules.
(3) All motions shall be signed in accordance with Rule 11.

A written motion ordinarily has four parts. The parts are not always separated into numbered paragraphs as is customary with pleadings. Part one tells the court what assistance and what order the moving party wants. Part two should identify any legal authority that the moving party relies on, such as a Civil Procedure Rule. Part three should state the grounds for the motion. The grounds are the reasons the moving party believes he or she is entitled to the court's assistance or needs the court's directions. Part four should identify the supporting documents on which the motion is based, such as records, affidavits, and exhibits. The special rules of some courts require parties to serve and file a memorandum of law to support the motion. Exhibit 6.3 is illustrative of a properly drawn motion.

When serving a motion, a party must include all supporting documents, except those previously served and filed. Those documents may be incorporated by reference. A respondent must serve copies of all documents the respondent relies on to oppose the motion. Opposing documents must be served and filed at least one day before the motion is heard [Rule 6(d)].

Exhibit 6.2

Ex Parte Motion for Extension of Time to Answer

(Court)

(Title of Cause)

Plaintiff hereby moves the court for an order extending the time in which plaintiff may answer defendant's interrogatories, which were served upon plaintiff on [date].

This motion is made pursuant to Rule 6(b).

The grounds for this motion are that plaintiff was out of the country on business from October 6, 2006, to October 21, 2006, and has not been able to gather the evidence requested by defendant's interrogatories. Plaintiff believes that an additional ten days would provide sufficient time in which to prepare the necessary answers. The case is currently one year away from trial. Therefore, defendant will not be prejudiced by a ten-day extension.

This motion is supported by plaintiff's affidavit, which is attached hereto, explaining that plaintiff was unable to attend to the preparation of answers to interrogatories while on his business trip.

A proposed order extending the period of time for answering is attached hereto.

[date]

Attorney for Plaintiff

[Attorney Signature]

Address
Telephone

Motion for Judgment on the Pleadings—Rule 12(c)

If a complaint fails to state a cause of action, the defendant may move to strike the complaint and judgment on the pleading. A plaintiff might respond to the motion by seeking to amend the complaint. If the complaint is stricken, the dismissal would not preclude the plaintiff from trying to bring the action again.

Motion for More Definite Statement—Rule 12(e)

Sometimes complaints are ambiguous. The defendant has a right to know what is being claimed against him or her. One way of forcing the plaintiff to be specific and more descriptive is to move the court for a more definite statement. For example, a complaint that attempts to allege a cause of action for defamation and merely alleges that the defendant has made various false statements about the plaintiff over a period of time is not technically adequate. The time and place of each defamatory publication should be stated in the complaint [Rule 9(f)]. The defendant is entitled to have the court order the plaintiff to specify each defamatory statement: what was said, when it was said, where it

EXHIBIT 6.3

Motion for Dismissal

(Court)

(Title of Cause)

Defendant moves the court for an order dismissing plaintiff's complaint.

This motion is made pursuant to Rule 12(c) of the Federal Rules of Civil Procedure.

The grounds for this motion are that the complaint fails to state a claim upon which relief can be granted. The complaint fails to allege the claim of fraud with particularity as required by Rule 9(b).

This motion is based upon the allegations of plaintiff's complaint, which is on file with the court; the allegations and denials set forth in defendant's answer, which is on file with the court; a copy of the parties' contract upon which plaintiff's claim is based; and the affidavit of John Sutherland, which is attached hereto.

[date]

Attorney for Moving Party

[Attorney Signature]

---

was said, and to whom it was published. The court should not force the defendant to obtain the information through answers to interrogatories, because the missing information is fundamental to the cause of action. A motion for a more definite statement may be made as an alternative to a motion for judgment on the pleadings.

Motion to Strike—Rule 12(f)

If an attorney pro se or attorney improperly makes a derogatory, impertinent, or scandalous remark about the opposing party in a pleading, the opponent may move the court to strike the allegation.

Counterclaims

Lawsuits frequently run in both directions. A defendant states his or her claim against the plaintiff in a counterclaim. All the requirements for stating claims in complaints apply to counterclaims, except that many of the essential allegations are already provided in the complaint and answer. Allegations in the complaint and answer may be incorporated into the counterclaim by reference. Counterclaims commonly contain a paragraph similar to the following:

> Defendant hereby incorporates the allegations of paragraph 1 of the complaint and all the allegations of defendant's answer as though fully set forth herein.

compulsory counterclaim A defendant's claim against the plaintiff that arises from the same transaction or occurrence as the plaintiff's claim.

permissive counterclaim A counterclaim that does not arise from the transaction or occurrence that is the subject of the plaintiff's complaint but that may be prosecuted in the same action.

A counterclaim must be served with the answer. Usually, the two pleadings are combined into one document, called an "answer and counterclaim." A counterclaim may be separately stated but must be served with the answer. If the defendant's claim arises from the same transaction or occurrence as the plaintiff's claim, the counterclaim is compulsory. A **compulsory counterclaim** must be asserted in the plaintiff's action or the right to make the claim is waived [Rule 13(a)]. If the claim arises from a different transaction or occurrence, however, the counterclaim is called a **permissive counterclaim.** That is, the defendant has the option whether to pursue it in the plaintiff's action or separately [Rule 13(b)].

If the defendant inadvertently fails to serve a counterclaim with the answer, the defendant may move the court for an order allowing service of the counterclaim. Possible grounds for the motion include oversight, inadvertence, and excusable neglect [Rule 13(f)]. The defendant must obtain permission to serve a counterclaim separately because a late pleading may cause a delay in the normal progression of the case to trial. Because a counterclaim inevitably raises new issues of fact and law, the parties may need additional time to investigate and conduct discovery. But courts often place heavy burdens on delinquent parties to expedite the necessary discovery procedures and trial preparation. A court may impose costs and other sanctions as a condition to allowing a late counterclaim. Some lawyers believe counterclaims may be served anytime within twenty days after service of the answer, because the answer may be amended without a court order during the twenty-day period [Rule 15(a)].

A defendant may not assert a counterclaim concerning a matter over which the court does not have jurisdiction. But in federal courts, a counterclaim may seek relief that is more or different in kind than what is claimed in the complaint [Rule 13(c)]. This difference may preclude jurisdiction over some counterclaims in state courts that have limited jurisdiction, however. For example, if the plaintiff's claim was brought in a municipal court and that court's jurisdiction is limited to $20,000 and the counterclaim is for more, the usual procedure is to transfer the whole case to a court of general jurisdiction.

If a counterclaim requires the presence of a third person who is not subject to the court's jurisdiction, the claim need not be asserted; it is not then compulsory. For example, if a plaintiff sues for breach of contract, and the defendant claims that the plaintiff and the plaintiff's partner defrauded the defendant in the same transaction, and that the partner is not subject to that court's jurisdiction, the counterclaim is not compulsory. The defendant may assert her or his claim for fraud against both persons in another action in another court that has jurisdiction over both persons.

A counterclaim has obvious application when the defendant in an automobile accident case sues for personal injury and property damage—claiming that the plaintiff is liable. A counterclaim may also be used by the defendant to make a claim against one plaintiff for contribution to the claim of another plaintiff. For example, suppose two plaintiffs are husband and wife. Suppose they sustained injuries when their automobile was struck by the defendant's truck. If the plaintiff husband was driving and he was partially at fault, the defendant could counterclaim against the plaintiff husband for contribution to the wife's claim—assuming that the lawsuit is brought in a state that does not recognize interspousal immunity.[10]

As a general rule, courts favor consolidating claims so they can be determined in a single trial. Consolidation usually leads to a speedy, more economical determination by avoiding duplication of effort. But if trial of a counterclaim with the main action would unduly complicate the proceedings, a court may order a severance of the claims for purpose of trial [Rules 13(i) and 42(b)].

A counterclaim for a cause of action that accrued after the answer was served can be brought by a **supplemental counterclaim** [Rule 13(e)]. Supplemental pleadings are permitted only by court order on showing that the cause of action accrued after service of the original pleading [Rule 15(d)]. A court order that allows a supplemental pleading should specify whether a responsive pleading is necessary—that is, an answer, reply to counterclaim, or answer to cross-claim.

supplemental counterclaim A counterclaim filed for a cause of action that accrued after the answer was served.

Reply to Counterclaim

Because a counterclaim asserts a claim against the plaintiff, the plaintiff must be given the opportunity to admit or deny the allegations and plead affirmative defenses. A plaintiff responds to a counterclaim by serving and filing a reply to counterclaim [Rule 7(a)]. The reply is tantamount to an answer, so the requirements are the same as those for an answer. A reply to counterclaim must be served within twenty days after service of the counterclaim [Rule 12(a)]. When the counterclaim is served by mail, as it usually is, three days are added to the time allowed for the reply [Rules 12(a) and 6(e)].

Cross-claim and Answer to Cross-claim

Two or more persons who are liable to the plaintiff for injury or property damage may be joined as codefendants (Rule 20). Codefendants may have claims to make against each other for injuries or losses they sustained or for contribution to the plaintiff's claim. A defendant may make a claim against a codefendant by serving and filing a cross-claim. A cross-claim is, in effect, a complaint that states one or more causes of action against a codefendant. The rules and guidelines for drafting complaints apply to preparing cross-claims. Exhibit 6.4 is typical of allegations found in cross-claims.

A cross-claim is usually served as a separate document. If a defendant has appeared in the case by serving an answer or a Rule 12 motion, the cross-claim may be served on the defendant's lawyer by mail [Rule 5(b)]. Usually, the cross-claim cannot be served with the answer because the identity of the codefendant's lawyer is not yet known. If a named codefendant has not yet been served with a summons and complaint, a cross-claim may be served in the manner provided by Rule 4, as an original summons and complaint.

The rules do not state a time limit for serving and filing cross-claims. Nevertheless, common sense dictates that a cross-claim shall not be served so late as to delay the trial of the main action, that is, the plaintiff's case. A defendant who has been served with a cross-claim must respond by serving and filing an answer to the cross-claim within twenty days [Rule 12(a)]. If the cross-claim was served by mail, three days are added [Rule 6(e)]. The answer to cross-claim serves the same function as an answer to complaint, and the same general rules apply.

Usually a defendant's lawyer can obtain the identity of a codefendant's lawyer by contacting the plaintiff's lawyer. Otherwise, it may be necessary to contact the codefendant directly, but the facts of the case must not be discussed with the codefendant if she or he is represented by a lawyer.

(Court)

(Title of Cause)

Defendant B and for her cross-claim against defendant C alleges:
1. Plaintiff has commenced the above entitled action against each defendant above named. Plaintiff alleges that defendants are jointly and severally liable to plaintiff for money damages, as more fully set forth in the complaint, a copy of which has been served upon each defendant.
2. Defendant B has denied liability to plaintiff as set forth more fully in her answer, which has been served on all parties and filed with the court. A copy of the answer has been served upon each party.
3. Defendant C's negligence was the proximate cause of the accident described in the complaint.
4. If defendant B is determined to be liable to plaintiff, as alleged in the complaint, or otherwise, defendant B is entitled to contribution from defendant C on the grounds that C's negligence was a proximate cause of the accident and concurred with defendant B's alleged negligence to cause plaintiff's alleged loss.

Wherefore, defendant B prays for judgment of contribution from defendant C to any sums awarded in favor of plaintiff against defendant B, together with her costs and disbursements herein.

[date]

Attorney for Defendant B

[Attorney Signature]

Cross-claims establish technical adversity between defendants. This may be important at trial in determining whether a defendant's lawyer has the right to cross-examine another defendant and whether the defendants are required to share peremptory challenges in the jury selection. See Chapter 20.

Third-Party Practice

A "third" party is someone who is not yet a party to an action. Third-party actions are very common because the same facts that give rise to the plaintiff's cause of action against the defendant also may create rights in favor of the defendant against some third person who has not been sued. For example, if a plaintiff consumer was injured by a defective product, the consumer has a cause of action against the retailer and against the manufacturer. If the plaintiff chooses to sue only the retailer, the retailer may commence a third-party action against the manufacturer to obtain indemnity and/or contribution. Frequently, the manufacturer has the ultimate responsibility for the injury. If the retailer shows that the manufacturer was responsible for the defect and injury, the retailer may obtain full reimbursement (indemnity) from the manufacturer for any money damages the retailer is obligated to pay to the plaintiff consumer.

Third-party actions are most often used to seek contribution, a concept that simply means "fair shares." For example, if two negligent motorists collide, causing injury to a passenger, and the passenger sues only one driver, that defendant driver may bring a third-party action against the other driver for contribution. This situation occasionally arises when one family member is injured in an automobile accident while another family member is driving. The injured family member may elect to sue only the non-family driver. The defendant may bring a third-party action against the family member for contribution. Generally, however, most plaintiffs choose to sue every potentially liable defendant.

A defendant has a right to commence a third-party action without leave of the court any time within ten days after serving his or her answer to the complaint [Rule 14(a)]. Otherwise, the defendant must apply to the court for leave to commence the third-party action. Again, the time is limited because the defendant must not cause the plaintiff's case to be unduly delayed, and the act of bringing in an additional party has the potential for causing some delay. A third-party plaintiff must serve a third-party complaint on the third-party defendant in the same manner Rule 4 requires for service of the original complaint. A third-party complaint can be used only to obtain indemnity or contribution. It cannot be used to assert a new or separate claim. Third-party actions are not compulsory.

A third-party defendant may serve a claim against the plaintiff if that claim arises from the same transaction or occurrence. The plaintiff also may serve a claim on the third-party defendant. When that is done, the third-party defendant is then treated as a direct defendant. The two or more defendants are referred to as codefendants.

A third-party action complicates the plaintiff's case. Nevertheless, it is preferable to consolidate claims for indemnity or contribution with the plaintiff's case, because consolidation prevents inconsistent determinations. Because a person who could be joined as a third-party defendant is not bound by the results of a trial if the person was not made a party, the defendant runs a risk that she or he may be held liable to the plaintiff and not be able to prove the plaintiff's loss in a second action for contribution. Also, the defendant who seeks indemnity or contribution in a separate action has the burden of proving the plaintiff's damages, and that can be awkward. For example, if the defendant had to bring an entirely separate lawsuit against a joint tortfeasor to obtain contribution, the first jury might award more damages than a second jury in the contribution action, and that would reduce the amount of contribution the third-party plaintiff could obtain. But a third-party action, the third-party plaintiff can force the alleged joint tortfeasor to participate in the plaintiff's case, and both are bound by the result.

A third-party plaintiff (i.e., a defendant who wishes to join a third party) must commence the third-party action within ten days after serving the answer to the plaintiff's complaint. The defendant may move the court for an extension if more time is needed. If the motion for an extension is made within the ten-day period, the motion may be made and heard ex parte. If the defendant is unsuccessful in a belated effort to commence a third-party action, the defendant may, nevertheless, start a separate lawsuit to obtain contribution or indemnity. The time limit is to protect the plaintiff from undue delay, not to protect the proposed third-party defendant.

Third-party Complaint

A third-party complaint should allege the date on which the plaintiff commenced the action against the defendant. A copy of the plaintiff's complaint should be attached as an exhibit. It should reiterate the gist of the plaintiff's claim and that the defendant denies liability. It should allege that the defendant duly interposed an answer on a specified date. The Rules do not specifically require the third-party plaintiff to attach a copy of the answer, but it is preferable to do so. The third-party defendant will need a copy eventually. Finally, the third-party plaintiff must allege that he or she is entitled to indemnity or contribution from the third-party defendant for any sums that may be awarded to the plaintiff against the third-party plaintiff. The third-party complaint uses an ad damnum clause to specify the relief sought. The prayer for relief is for indemnity or contribution, not for a sum of money.

Third-party Answer

A third-party defendant has twenty days in which to serve her or his answer to a third-party complaint. The third-party answer must be served on the plaintiff and on the third-party plaintiff. In turn, the third-party defendant may commence a so-called fourth-party action for indemnity or contribution against anyone who is liable to her or him because of the transaction or occurrence in question. The third-party defendant would then have the additional title of fourth-party plaintiff. Theoretically, any number of parties may be joined in this manner.

A third-party defendant's answer must assert whatever defenses the third-party defendant has to the third-party plaintiff's claim. In addition, the third-party defendant may allege defenses that the third-party plaintiff has against the plaintiff's claim. For example, if the defendant (third-party plaintiff) has a statute of limitations defense to the plaintiff's claim, the third-party defendant may raise that defense in his or her answer, even if the third-party plaintiff failed to raise it. This is important because the third-party action is, by its nature, predicated entirely on the defendant's liability to the plaintiff. If the third-party plaintiff is not liable to the plaintiff, the third-party defendant cannot have any liability to the third-party plaintiff for indemnity or contribution. In other words, if the third-party defendant keeps the plaintiff from recovering against the original defendant, the third-party defendant wins too. The rule helps to prevent any collusion between the plaintiff and the third-party plaintiff against the third-party defendant.

Severance

Any party may move the court to sever a third-party action from the main action (Rule 42). Although consolidation of claims is generally favored, there are situations when claims should be severed.

Cross-claims Between Third-party Defendants

If there is more than one third-party defendant, each third-party defendant may serve a cross-claim against the others, just as codefendants may cross-claim [Rule 14(a)]. A third-party cross-claim requires an answer to cross-claim.

Joinder of Claims and Consolidation of Cases

One objective of the Rules of Civil Procedure is to keep civil litigation as inexpensive as possible (Rule 1). The joinder of two or more claims into one lawsuit may make the overall handling of several disputes more efficient and less expensive. Similarly, the consolidation of two or more lawsuits into one trial may provide a significant savings for the parties and the court. Not every party always benefits, however. There are circumstances that mitigate against consolidation of claims and cases, including untoward delay, added complexity, and confusion about legal issues and evidence issues. Therefore, courts have broad discretion in determining whether to join claims and whether to consolidate cases for trial.

Joinder of Claims

A plaintiff may include in one lawsuit all the claims he or she has against the defendant, even if some of the claims arose from unrelated transactions or occurrences. Rule 18(a) provides for this:

> A party asserting a claim to relief as an original claim, counterclaim, cross-claim, or third-party claim may join, either as independent or as alternate claims, as many claims, legal, equitable, or maritime, as he has against an opposing party.

Each separate claim should be stated in the complaint as a separate count.

The possibility that a plaintiff has several claims against a defendant may seem remote, but it is not. By way of example, suppose the plaintiff company has been purchasing bolts of cloth from the defendant company for many years, but for the past three years the defendant's deliveries have been late, frequently causing the plaintiff to experience down time. The bolts of cloth are increasingly defective, and orders are being misplaced. Finally, the defendant company makes a major error that causes the plaintiff to suffer a large loss. Their business relationship is at an end. Once the plaintiff company has decided to sue, it might as well sue for all the breaches of contract and warranties that occurred during the past several years All the claims may be included in the one lawsuit. Again, each transaction should be pled as a separate count.

The preceding example involves a series of transactions between two parties. A series of occurrences that give rise to multiple claims in favor of a plaintiff is a little more difficult to envision. Nevertheless, it can happen. Suppose the defendant is a large contractor who has overall responsibility for the construction of a large interstate freeway interchange next to a large shopping center owned by the plaintiff. The highway construction work may cause damage to the plaintiff's property at various times by use of explosives, pile driving, and trespasses by large machinery. The contractor may have blocked access to the shopping center, causing a loss of business. Dust and noise from the project might have created an actionable nuisance. Each of these events may be the basis for a separate cause of action against the unfortunate contractor. Again, each cause of action should be stated in the complaint as a separate count.

Suppose the defendant offers his house for sale, the plaintiff likes the house, and the two enter into a purchase agreement. Suppose the plaintiff returns to the house to inspect it and is injured by a defect on the premises. As a result of the plaintiff's accident, the defendant refuses to sell the house. The plaintiff could sue for breach of contract and bodily injury in the same lawsuit, even though one claim is based on a transaction and the other on an unrelated occurrence. It might be quicker and more economical for the parties to have just one trial. However, the defendant may want to have the claims tried separately because his liability for one claim might adversely affect his defense of the second.

Suppose the plaintiff was injured in two automobile accidents that occurred one year apart. The plaintiff may not want the cases consolidated for trial, especially if one of the accidents was her fault. The defendants may try to show that most of the plaintiff's injury was caused by the accident that was her fault. If neither accident was the plaintiff's fault, however, the plaintiff may want the two cases consolidated to avoid having the first jury conclude that her injuries were caused by the second accident and the second jury conclude that her injuries were caused by the first. If the two cases are tried together, the plaintiff can let the defendants worry about how the jury will allocate the injuries between the two accidents.

The defendant also has the right to join two or more claims into one lawsuit. The defendant may assert multiple claims in the counterclaim [Rule 18(a)]. Or the defendant may start a separate lawsuit, as a plaintiff, against the original plaintiff, and then seek a court order consolidating the two actions. The two cases may be tried as one [Rule 42(a)]. When two claims accrue in the same jurisdiction and the same venue, consolidation is a relatively simple process. But consolidation is not possible when a party's venue rights are impaired or the court lacks jurisdiction over one or more of the claims or parties.

Severance of Claims

Even when a plaintiff properly joins several claims against the defendant in one suit, the court may order some claims tried separately [Rule 42(b)]. The severance may be based on the defendant's motion for a severance or on the court's own motion (Rule 42). A severance of claims is desirable when consolidation makes a trial too complicated, too long, or too cumbersome. Even the plaintiff may decide, when the case reaches trial, that a trial of two or more claims before the same jury would be inconvenient, expensive, or a bad tactic, and move for a severance. Sometimes the resolution of one claim makes it possible for the parties to settle the remaining claims.

Severance of Issues

Rule 42 allows a court to order a severance of legal issues as well as a severance of claims. For example, a negligence action in which the plaintiff seeks money damages for a personal injury involves at least three major issues: negligence, proximate cause, and damages. Pursuant to Rule 42, a trial court could order that the issues of negligence and causation be tried together and that the damages issue be tried separately. The damages issue is material only if the plaintiff prevails on the negligence and causation issues. Severance may be a good option if the liability part of the case is simple and the damage part of the case is complex and expensive to present. Note that lawyers who represent plaintiffs in personal-injury cases usually want the injury (damages) issue presented at the same time as the liability issues, because they believe that the sympathy engendered by the plaintiff's injuries helps to carry the liability portion of the case.

Consolidation of Cases

Federal district courts have authority to consolidate cases for trial whenever cases involve common questions of law or common questions of fact [Rule 42(a)]. This is true even though the cases involve different parties. Cases are never consolidated for trial merely because they coincidentally involve common questions of fact or law. For example, the fact that two automobile accident cases happen to involve stop sign violations is no reason to consolidate those cases. Even if the two automobile accidents involved the same intersection and the same stop sign, a trial judge would not consolidate them. Some underlying, unifying circumstance must make consolidation convenient for the court without unduly complicating or prolonging the trial for the parties.

Suppose five people sustain injuries in the crash of a small airplane. Suppose each injured person sues the pilot, the manufacturer, and the airplane maintenance company. Assume legal responsibility is unclear. The court may elect to consolidate the five cases for trial, at least to determine the liability issues. If the plaintiffs are able to establish liability, some of them might be able to settle the damages issues. The defendants gain by having to defend only once rather than five times. The basis for consolidation is that there are common questions of the facts surrounding the single accident. Another example of cases involving common questions of fact is where a plaintiff has been injured in two separate accidents and has two separate claims. Each defendant is likely to contend that the plaintiff's injuries occurred in "the other" accident. The parties may determine that they would prefer to consolidate both cases because they involve a common question of fact: What injuries were sustained in which accident? Consolidation is useful in cases involving business transactions as well as in accident cases. Suppose a corporation sells franchises for fast-food stores, and a problem develops with ten of the franchisees. Their contracts with the franchiser are all the same. The parties may want to have the cases consolidated for one trial.

Many cases have common questions of law but would not be helped by consolidation. For example, suppose that during a three-month period, five pedestrians fell on city sidewalks at separate locations, sustained injuries, and sued the city. These five cases involve common questions of law. The questions of law are not a major consideration; they are pretty well settled. Could the cases be consolidated? Perhaps. Should they be consolidated? No. A consolidation of the cases for trial will be of no value if no genuine dispute exists about the application of legal principles common to the several cases. But suppose a statute requires plaintiffs to notify cities of accidents within thirty days as a condition precedent to bringing a lawsuit against a city. Suppose there is an issue in all five cases whether the plaintiffs gave due notice of the accidents, and the plaintiffs challenge the constitutionality of the statute. The legal issue is important and common to all cases. The cases may be consolidated for the purpose of determining the legal issue. If the legal issue is resolved in the plaintiffs' favor, the cases subsequently would be tried separately.

As another example, suppose numerous property owners have sued an airport commission, claiming that airplane noise resulted in an involuntary, partial condemnation or "taking" of their property for which they should be compensated. The legal theory is novel. Consolidation of those cases would permit the property owners to participate in a trial of the legal issue—that is, whether a cause of action for condemnation exists. The property owners would be able to minimize legal expenses by hiring one lawyer for all cases. If the legal issue were resolved in favor of the plaintiffs, clearing the way for an award of money damages to each property owner, each plaintiff could prove her or his damage in a separate trial (Rule 42).

Intervention

intervention   A procedure by which a person may join in a lawsuit to protect a related interest or legal right. A person who seeks to intervene may align with one of the parties or take a position adverse to all the existing parties.

Intervention is a procedure that permits a person to join in a pending lawsuit by applying to the court for leave to become a party (Rule 24). He or she may apply to be a defendant or a plaintiff. A person may intervene as a matter of right if his or her interests in the subject matter will be affected by the outcome of the litigation [Rule 24(a)]. For example, suppose the defendant damaged real estate by creating a nuisance, and the real estate is owned by three joint tenants, and two of the joint tenants sue for damages. The third joint tenant will be allowed to intervene in the case as a matter of right [Rule 24(a)]. If a trustee sues or is sued, the beneficiary may elect to intervene to protect his or her interest in the trust. If an agent is sued for a wrongful act committed in the course and scope of the agency, the principal, who is vicariously liable for the agent's acts, may intervene to make sure the defense is adequately presented (Rule 24). The right to intervene is granted whenever a person could properly be joined as a party or his or her claim or defense could be consolidated as involving common questions of law or fact.

An intervener *must* show the court that he or she will be affected by the outcome of the case. The criteria are the same as for consolidating cases under Rule 42. An intervener's motion must show that his or her claim or defense involves an important common question of law or fact and intervention will conserve the court's time, save the parties' expense, and not prejudice anyone. Some statutes expressly encourage consolidation and direct courts to order consolidations. Certain federal civil rights actions are typical of those encouraging consolidation and intervention. In those instances, a party may intervene as a matter of right [Rule 24(a)]. This means the party does not have to convince the court of the desirability of an intervention.

The intervener must serve the motion on all parties. The motion must state the moving party's interest in the subject matter. The moving party may also show that she or he has a special relationship to the parties to the action or that there are common questions of law or fact that permit the intervener's matter to be joined with the pending action. The motion must include a proposed pleading (complaint or answer), with the proposed new title. The pleading must set forth the claims or defenses [Rule 24(c)]. The motion must give the parties at least five days' notice of the hearing (Rule 5). The original parties have a right to object to a motion to intervene. They could oppose intervention on the grounds that intervention would unduly delay or complicate the case.

Class Actions

A class action under Rule 23 is the most ambitious consolidation of claims, defenses, and parties. If the difficult requirements are met an entire class, or group, of persons may be plaintiffs or defendants in an action in which the class is represented by just one or a few litigants. Courts have to exercise close supervision over the representatives of the class to make sure the class is adequately represented. This supervision starts with deciding whether to allow the case to even proceed as a class action—a process called "class certification"—and continues throughout the case. In recent years there has been a public backlash to what is perceived as abuses in the use of class actions. Many perceive class actions as frequently used to benefit only lawyers. An example could be a class action against a major industry for price fixing, but a settlement that provides members of the class only coupons with significant restrictions, while class counsel obtains significant fees in actual dollars. In response to these perceived problems, Congress passed legislation in 2005 that allows for class actions to be removed from state court to federal court if more than $5 million is in controversy—not an especially large sum in class-action litigation—and there are some parties from more than one state. Congress presumably believes that the federal courts will supervise for potential abuses better than state courts. In addition, Congress sought to end the practice of filing class actions in a few obscure state court counties that had become known for treating such actions favorably.

The following example illustrates the criteria and management of class actions. Suppose a large commercial bank contracted to pay interest on money it collects from mortgagors to hold in escrow to pay real estate taxes as they come due. Suppose a dispute arises whether the bank has calculated the interest properly or has made questionable charges against the escrow accounts. The number of mortgagors may be a thousand. They can be identified easily. If an action is brought by just one or several mortgagors to recover their losses caused by overcharges, it would be best for the class (all mortgagors) and for the bank to have a resolution of the problem in one lawsuit and one trial. The active participation of every mortgagor should not be necessary if the class is adequately represented. If liability exists, the damages for each mortgagor would be easy to calculate. The amount in dispute may be fairly small for each member of the class, so having a large number of claimants may help justify the cost of the litigation. The total recovery could be substantial. The bank avoids the expense of multiple lawsuits. A court decision would be binding on all the mortgagors. If the case were not certified as a class action, the bank's successful defense against the initial plaintiff would not be binding on other plaintiff mortgagors. Theoretically, if the prerequisites of Rule 23 are met so that a class action is permissible, everyone benefits.

Sometimes a defendant may want to keep a case from becoming a class action. If the potential recovery by each member of the proposed class would be very small, the plaintiffs, as individuals, might have no interest in pursuing their claims. If the defendant can keep the court from certifying the case as a class action, the claims may go away. The promoters of a class action are usually the representatives of the class. Class actions are often very lucrative for the lawyers who handle them.

If a party wants to move the court for an order certifying a case as a class action, the party must show the court that all of the following elements are present:

1. The class is so large that it is not practical for its members to sue or defend as individual parties with a consolidation of cases or as parties joined in a single action.
2. Common questions of law or fact have the same effect on the rights or obligations of all members of the class.
3. The party or parties applying for class certification are truly representative of the proposed class.

4. Separate suits by or against individual members of the proposed class might result in varying or inconsistent determinations for the members.
5. A class action can effectively dispose of all the legal and fact issues that exist between members of the proposed class and the adverse party.
6. The individual members of the proposed class do not have a superior interest in controlling the handling of the litigation.
7. No other pending litigation would be adversely affected by certifying the class action.
8. Commencement of a class action would not unduly burden the court and would not cause prejudice to persons who might choose to have their case presented in another forum.

If a class action is allowed, the court must make sure the members are given notice about the case, that they are informed about their obligations in the action, and that their rights are protected by the representative. A class action cannot be compromised or dismissed without court approval [Rule 23(e)].

One type of class action has been given special treatment by the Rules: a shareholders' derivative action to enforce rights of their corporation against a party when the board of directors wrongfully refuses or neglects to do so (Rule 23). Because the board of directors—not the shareholders—is charged with the responsibility for running the business, the shareholders may institute actions on behalf of the corporation only in extreme circumstances. The shareholders must show the court that they tried to get the directors to take appropriate action and that the directors refused. A shareholder who tries to institute a derivative action must show that he or she was a shareholder at the time the transaction or occurrence in question took place and that he or she adequately represents the other shareholders. As in other class actions, a shareholders' derivative action cannot be compromised or dismissed without court approval.

Substitution of Parties

There are several situations in which a person should be substituted for a party in a pending civil action: death of a party, incompetency of a party, or transference of a party's interest in the subject matter to another person. Of course, if the law holds that a particular cause of action dies with the party, there is nothing for the court to do but dismiss the case. For example, if a person suffers an injury in a car accident but later dies of cancer, the cause of action for the injury dies with the person. No one may pursue a cause of action to recover damages for injury to someone else's body. But if the cause of action survives the death of a party, someone must arrange to have the party's representative substituted as the party. In the hypothetical case, Mr. Nordby died months after his automobile accident. If he had started a personal injury action against Mr. Harper, the trustee could have been substituted to continue with the suit. The suit may continue because death was caused by the accident. And the damages will not be for Nordby's injuries but instead for the survivors' lost means of support, lost companionship, and so on. Any party may move the court for an order directing a substitution. If a representative has been appointed by a probate court, that representative may move the court for an order substituting herself or himself for a deceased party. If a party moves the court for a substitution, and a probate court already has appointed a representative to handle the estate, that representative must be served with the motion and notice of hearing. The motion must be served in the manner provided in Rule 4 for service of a summons. The motion may not be served on a nonparty by mail.

Once the parties and the court receive notice of a defendant's death, the remaining parties have ninety days in which to act to obtain a substitution for the deceased party. Otherwise, the action against the decedent will be dismissed [Rule 25(a)]. The rule implies that the court shall order the dismissal on its own motion. Suppose the defendant dies one week before trial of a personal injury action. The defendant's lawyer should notify the court. The trial will have to be postponed. If the plaintiff fails to take steps to have the decedent's personal representative substituted as the defendant, the court must dismiss the action ninety days after receiving notice of the defendant's death. Under these circumstances, the burden does not lie with the defendant's lawyer to obtain the substitution, or with the decedent's estate.

If a party becomes incompetent to handle his or her legal matters, a representative party must be appointed and substituted. For example, if a party becomes senile, a guardian should be appointed by a probate court having jurisdiction. The guardian must replace the senile party in the manner discussed previously.

If an action is brought by joint tenants of real estate and one tenant dies before a determination is reached, the action will continue in the name of the survivor. One characteristic of joint ownership of property is that title passes to the survivor. (Tenants in common do not have a similar right of survivorship.) The title of the action may be amended by an order of the court showing that the surviving joint tenant is the only plaintiff [Rule 25(c)].

Service of Process

"Legal process" or "process" refers to procedures courts use to obtain jurisdiction over persons or property. The term is also used in reference to the documents used in the procedures. A summons is a process. A subpoena is a process. Service of a summons is service of process. Anyone who is not a party and is at least eighteen years of age may serve a legal process [Rule 4(c)]. Where a special need exists, a party may move the court to appoint a United States marshal to serve a summons and complaint or subpoena. Under no circumstance may a plaintiff personally serve a summons and complaint on the defendant. The Rule is designed to keep parties separated to reduce the possibility of fraud and violence.

There are several methods for serving legal process. Each method is simple, quite inexpensive, and reasonably effective to inform the person about the court's jurisdiction, the nature of the legal proceeding, and what the person must do. Rule 4 governs the methods of serving legal process. Process may be served on a person who is not yet an adult. However, to be effective, the person must be old enough to understand the significance of the process.

Personal Service

Personal service is the traditional and surest method of serving process. Personal service may be made by handing a copy of the summons and complaint to the defendant or by leaving a copy of the summons and complaint at the defendant's *usual place of abode* with a person of *suitable age and discretion who also lives there.* The summons and complaint may not be left "with a suitable person" at a place where the defendant is staying temporarily, such as a vacation house or a hotel room. Process may be left at the defendant's usual place of abode with a person who is not yet an adult so long as that person is of suitable discretion. Historically, anyone fourteen years of age or older is presumed to meet the age and discretion requirements. A younger person may qualify, but if any question should later arise as to whether service was valid, the burden rests with the plaintiff to show that the recipient was of suitable age and discretion. Suppose the defendant's adult sister is visiting at the defendant's home for a few days. Could the summons and complaint be served on the defendant by leaving the papers with the sister? No, because she is not a resident of the household.

If a defendant decides to be uncooperative and "turns her or his back" on the process server, the server may leave the summons and complaint in the defendant's presence. There is no need to touch the defendant as if playing a game of tag. The law does not require that service of process be made at any particular time of the day, but service must be made at a reasonable hour considering the circumstances. Service may be in the middle of the night if the defendant ordinarily works nights and sleeps days. There is no prohibition against serving process on Sundays or legal holidays.

A proof of service of process must be filed with the clerk of court before the time for answering expires [Rule 4(g)]. If the server was a United States marshal, the marshal makes a record of the service of process in a document called the marshal's return. If a person other than a United States marshal serves the summons and complaint, he or she prepares an affidavit of service. A marshal's return and a process server's affidavit must show the date, time, place, and manner of service, and the identity of the person to whom the papers were delivered. The back of the summons has a "Return of Service" form, which the process server should use.

Service by Mail

The federal rules do not per se provide for commencement of an action by mail; they provide a mechanism by which the defendant is encouraged to waive the right to personal service. The waiver rules apply to individual and corporate defendants (not governmental bodies or agencies). The plaintiff obtains a waiver by mailing the summons and complaint to the defendant by first-class mail along with Form 1A from the Federal Rules, Appendix of Forms. The plaintiff must allow the defendant at least thirty days to waive service by signing and returning the waiver that is provided in Form 1A. The plaintiff must provide prepaid return postage. If the defendant fails to waive service, he or she must pay the plaintiff's costs of effectuating personal service upon that defendant. A domestic defendant who accepts the waiver has sixty days from the time the plaintiff sent the request to answer the complaint. This extra time to answer provides additional incentive to accept a waiver.

But you must use caution when considering whether to commence your action via a waiver. If the statute of limitations on your client's cause of action is about to expire, choosing to commence suit by waiver can be fatal. That's because in the waiver process it is the *defendant* who controls whether commencement of suit will be successful. If the statute of limitations expires before you realize that the defendant will refuse to waive personal service, the costs you may recover for effectuating (untimely) personal service will be no consolation. The case will be dismissed, and the defendant's refusal to waive personal service will not be a defense.

After the summons and complaint have been served, most litigation documents are served by mail. Service by mail is complete when the document is deposited at a post office for delivery or put in a United States mailbox. The date of mailing is the date of service. Whenever a pleading, motion, or notice is served by mail, the addressee is given an extra three days in which to respond—that is, three extra days from the date of mailing [Rule 6(e)].

Although mail is still widely used, postcommencement service by electronic means is rapidly increasing [Rule 5(b)(2)(D)]. Note, however, that service in this manner is a matter of written consent between the parties, usually as agreed to among the lawyers. Making such an agreement is usually one of the first things experienced counsel like to do. Then service of things like interrogatories and so on can be accomplished by facsimile or by e-mail, again as agreed. And even through electronic transmission is usually immediate (unlike mail), Rule 6(e) provides that three days are added to response deadlines when service is effectuated electronically.

Of course, the agreement among counsel (or lack thereof) governs unless a court order provides a procedure, which will control. For materials that will be filed with the court as well as served upon all parties (a summary-judgment motion, for example), most federal courts are moving toward, or have already implemented, mandatory electronic filing and service. It is likely that all federal courts will have electronic filing by 2007. Electronic filing may differ from district to district, but it is generally accomplished through the court's Web site. Access is limited by password for each case. Documents produced on your word-processing system—a memorandum of law or affidavit, for example—are converted to Adobe and sent to the court electronically through its Web site. Documents not produced on your system—supporting documents like a loan agreement that is the subject of the action, for example—are scanned and then sent to the court in similar fashion. Once the system accepts your filing, all other parties receive notice of an electronic court filing (an "ECF notice") via e-mail. Those parties use the ECF notice to link to each filed item. Typically, each party will save those items to their own system and then make hard copies at their leisure. The filing must mail or deliver one hard copy of all materials to the presiding judge's chambers.

Once filed, all documents become part of the so-called PACER system. PACER is a system for Public Access to Court Electronic Records. It is a portal to the federal courts. The system allows the attorneys (indeed the public) to review all documents on file in any given federal case. When parties access a document via PACER—as opposed to via the initial ECF notice—there is a downloading charge.

Service on an Agent

Service on business organization may be made by delivering the summons and complaint to a managing officer or agent [Rule 4(d)(3)]. A company cannot restrict the method of service by limiting its officers' authority. But a company may appoint a nonofficer, or even a nonemployee, to be an agent to receive service of process. Some companies are frequently involved in litigation, so it is convenient for them to appoint a particular person or agent to receive service of process for them.

The law may designate an agent who may receive service of process for certain defendants. Most, if not all, states provide for service of process on the secretary of state as an agent for domestic and foreign corporations. By state statute, the commissioner of highways or the secretary of state is an appointed agent to receive service of process on behalf of nonresident motorists who have been involved in accidents within the state. The state commissioner of insurance is appointed by statute to receive service of process on behalf of any insurance company that does business within the state. Service is made by delivering a copy of the summons and complaint to the official's office. The official stamps the original summons and complaint, thereby acknowledging receipt and admits service. The office records the time of service. The plaintiff must provide the agent with at least one additional copy of the legal process, which the agent can send to the defendant's registered address or last known address. In addition, the plaintiff may be required to mail a copy of the summons and complaint to the defendant's last known address. Ordinary first-class mail will suffice. A plaintiff's lawyer must file an affidavit of compliance with the court showing that the mailing requirements have been met. The affidavit is prima facie evidence of compliance.

Service on a Guardian

If the defendant is a minor, service must be made in the manner prescribed by the laws of the state in which she or he resides. Usually, service must be made on one of the minor's parents or on a legal guardian. The plaintiff may cause a guardian to be appointed if the child does not have one. A guardian who is appointed for the sole purpose of the lawsuit is called a guardian ad litem. Some states authorize service directly on minors who are at least fourteen years of age. A guardian ad litem may be appointed later for the minor.

Age is only one type of legal disability that may affect service of process. If a defendant has been adjudged mentally incompetent to handle his or her own legal matters, the plaintiff must serve a copy of the summons and complaint on the defendant's guardian. The guardian must act to protect the ward's legal interests. A guardian does not actually conduct the litigation. The guardian's responsibility is to select a lawyer to represent the ward and make decisions that are ordinarily reserved to a party, such as whether or not to settle the claim. Some states require guardians to be bonded so as to guarantee faithful performance on behalf of the ward.

Service on a Government

A plaintiff cannot sue the United States government per se, but only its agencies as authorized by law. Service of process on a United States agency requires at least two steps. The summons and complaint must be served on the United States district attorney or assistant district attorney for the particular district in which the action is commenced. A copy must be mailed to the United States attorney general in Washington, D.C., by registered mail or certified mail. First-class mail does not suffice. In addition, copies of the papers must be mailed to the United States agency affected by the litigation. The statute that created the agency designates the manner for service of process on the agency and specifies the official who may receive service within the agency. Service is not effective until all the requirements are met, but the action is commenced by filing the complaint with the clerk of court. The local United States district attorney may designate a nonlawyer to accept service for him or her at the district attorney's office. When that is done, a letter or notice must be filed with the clerk of court, naming the administrative employee who has been designated.

Service may be made on a municipality by serving the chief executive officer or in any other manner prescribed by local law.

Service of Process by Publication

If the defendant has left the state or is in the state but hiding to evade service of process, service may be made by publishing the summons in a newspaper having substantial circulation in the area. The methods prescribed are intended to give the defendant actual notice of the litigation, especially if she or he is more or less expecting to be sued. Most state laws require the summons to be published for three weeks. As part of the publication procedure, the complaint must be filed with the clerk of court and be available for inspection. The plaintiff is required to mail a copy of the summons and complaint to the defendant's last known address. The plaintiff's lawyer and the publisher must each file an affidavit stating that the notice was duly published and mailed. The plaintiff must file copies of the published notice. If the defendant can be found in another state, personal service in the other state may be tantamount to service by publication and may give the local court personal jurisdiction. In divorce actions, where the defendant is not a resident of the state, service of process may be made by publication.[11]

Service in an Action in Rem

An action against property, rather than a person, is called an **action in rem.** No person is designated as a defendant. Nonetheless, anyone who claims an interest in the property must assert his or her claim by filing an answer; otherwise, he or she will forfeit any interest in it. In this kind of case, the local court has jurisdiction over the subject matter, and anyone claiming an interest in the property, even nonresidents, can be compelled to submit to the court's jurisdiction or forfeit his or her interest in the property. Service of a summons and complaint must be made on each person known to claim an interest in the subject matter. Furthermore, the "world" must be given notice through publication of a notice of the action.

action in rem An action against property, rather than a person.

Service on a Party's Lawyer

Once an action has been commenced and a party is represented by a lawyer, all pleadings, orders, motions, and so forth must be served directly on the lawyer. This is the most convenient arrangement for the parties and the lawyers. A lawyer is a buffer between the protagonists. Service is typically made by mailing the litigation documents to the lawyer at his or her last known address [Rule 5(h)]. On occasion, it is necessary to serve motions, interrogatories, demands for documents, orders, and other documents by personal service on the opposing lawyer. Personal service is complete when the papers are delivered to the lawyer, wherever she or he may be. If the lawyer cannot be found, personal service may, nevertheless, be made by handing the papers to the lawyer's clerk or secretary or to a person who is in charge of the lawyer's office. Otherwise, the papers may simply be left in a conspicuous place at the lawyer's office during regular business hours. Personal service on a lawyer may be ordered by a court whenever time is critically short. The process server must make an affidavit describing the manner, time, and place of service.

As previously explained, however, service by electronic means is increasingly popular. But unlike mail and personal service, electronic service is a matter of agreement among the parties [Rule 5(b)(2)(D)]. It is not a matter of agreement, however, when the particular district court has a system of mandatory electronic filing. Then the parties must follow the procedures (details provided above) for their particular district court. Service will be automatic via an ECF notice, which the opposing parties will receive on e-mail. All federal district courts will likely have some form of electronic filing within a few years. Once that is in place, look for the systems to be made uniform throughout the federal district courts. State courts will undoubtedly follow suit as they are able, but funding for such systems is a major roadblock to their implementation.

Service to the Clerk of Court

If neither the opposing party nor his or her lawyer can be found so that service can be made by mail or personally, service may be made by leaving the documents with the clerk of court. The process server must make an affidavit stating that the party and his or her lawyer could not be found. The affidavit should contain a brief description of the efforts made to locate them [Rule 5(b)].

Service of Subpoenas

The United States marshal or any person who is eighteen years of age or older and who is not a party to the action may serve a subpoena. A civil subpoena may be served only by delivering a copy of the subpoena to the person named in the subpoena.[12] A subpoena may not be served by leaving the subpoena at that person's usual place of abode. It must be tendered to the person along with a witness fee and mileage, as provided by statute. A subpoena may be served anywhere within the territorial jurisdiction of the court. In addition, a subpoena to testify at a federal district court trial may be served on a witness outside the judicial district, provided the witness is not required to travel more than 100 miles from the place where he or she resides, works, or was actually served with the subpoena [Rule 45(e)]. A subpoena that is used to compel a witness to give deposition testimony cannot be served outside the jurisdictional limits of the court that issues the subpoena. Furthermore, a deposition witness cannot be compelled to travel more than 100 miles from his or her home, his or her place of employment, or the place at which he or she was served with the subpoena.

A couple of examples may help illustrate the application and limitations imposed by Rule 45. Suppose the plaintiff needs to have a witness testify at trial in New York City, but the witness resides in Newark, New Jersey. Because Newark is less than 100 miles from the federal district court in New York City, the New York federal court could issue a subpoena for service in Newark. However, the New York federal district court could not issue a subpoena to require the witness to travel from Newark to New York City for a deposition. The party who wants to depose the witness would have to travel to New Jersey to take the deposition there, and if a subpoena were necessary, the proponent would have to obtain the subpoena from a federal district court for the state of New Jersey.

A subpoena could be used to require a witness to travel from Rochester, New York, to New York City to testify at a trial, a distance of 369 miles. However, a witness could not be compelled to travel that distance for a deposition, even though the federal district court for the state of New York has jurisdiction covering the entire state of New York. Depositions are supposed to be taken at a place that is reasonably convenient for the witness. But if a resident of Rochester is found in New York City, perhaps on a shopping trip, and served with a subpoena to appear in New York City for a deposition, the service would be valid.

If a subpoena has been served for an improper purpose, the person who is named in the subpoena has the right to move the court to **quash** the subpoena. If a subpoena requests production of documents or other things that the person named in the subpoena wants to protect, that person may file and serve an **objection to inspection.** The objection precludes the lawyer from enforcing the subpoena. Instead, the lawyer must obtain a court order requiring the person to produce the documents or things for inspection. The person who objects must serve the notice of objection within ten days after service of the subpoena, unless a shorter time has been specified by the subpoena [Rule 45(d)]. If the party still wants to inspect the documents in question, the party must make a motion to the court for an order for production. The moving party must give notice of the motion to the person who objected to the inspection. Any person who wrongfully disobeys a subpoena may be held in contempt of court [Rule 45(f)]. Only the court that issued a subpoena may impose sanctions.

quash To annul, cancel, rescind a court order or judicial decision.

objection to inspection A formal statement of disagreement to a judge in an attempt to quash a subpoena of documents.

Demand for Jury Trial

A plaintiff may demand a jury trial by "endorsing" a **jury demand** on the complaint. See Exhibit 6.1. This simply means that the plaintiff may state on the complaint, in some conspicuous place, that "plaintiff demands trial by jury." If the plaintiff fails to make the demand in the complaint, she or he may still make the demand within ten days after service of the last pleading directed to the issues to be tried. For example, the plaintiff's demand may be made ten days after the defendant serves the answer. The defendant may demand a jury trial during the same ten-day period. If the defendant demands a jury trial in her or his answer, the plaintiff need not make a separate or additional demand. A third-party defendant may demand a jury trial by endorsing the demand on her or his third-party answer, or in a separate document served within ten days after the third-party answer was served. Failure to demand a jury trial in the manner prescribed by Rule 38(b) results in a waiver of the right to a jury trial, and all the issues shall be tried to a judge without a jury [Rule 38(b)].

jury demand A notice on a pleading or separate statement served and filed by a party, indicating that the party wants a trial by jury.

Continuance

Sometimes a case is not ready for trial as scheduled. If a continuance of the trial is necessary, the parties may stipulate to a continuance or show the court good cause why the court should order a continuance. But a motion to delay a trial is not always granted, even when both parties want a continuance. Scheduling is discretionary with the court. Federal courts are especially aggressive in managing their trial calendars, so moving for a continuance should never be considered to be just a matter of form. In a system of ever-increasing numbers of cases a continuance only adds to the problem. And although time may be a natural healer, the passage of time can only detract from a good claim or a good defense. Counting on a continuance can be a costly mistake.

TECHNOLOGY NOTES

Web site useful for federal practice include http://www.uscourts.gov; http://www.findlaw.com; and http://www.law.cornell.edu.

SUMMARY

In federal court, a lawsuit is commenced when the plaintiff files the complaint. A complaint must show that the court has jurisdiction. It must contain a short, plain statement of the plaintiff's claim, showing the plaintiff is entitled to relief. It must state the time and place of the transaction or occurrence and describe it. A complaint must describe the relief the plaintiff wants. When an action is predicated on a written contract, promissory note, or other document, it is desirable to attach the document or a photocopy of the document to the complaint and incorporate the document into the complaint by reference. A lawyer must sign the complaint. If the plaintiff is acting as her or his own attorney, the plaintiff must sign it. A lawyer's signature certifies that the lawyer has made due inquiry and believes there are good grounds for the action.

A plaintiff may amend the complaint as a matter of right during the first twenty days following service. Thereafter, the complaint may be amended only by leave of the court or by stipulation of the defendant. The plaintiff may serve a supplemental complaint to allege new facts or claims that accrued after service of the original complaint.

A defendant must serve his or her answer within twenty days after service of the complaint, unless the plaintiff grants more time or the defendant obtains a court order extending the time. If a defendant fails to serve an answer in a timely manner, the plaintiff may take a default judgment against the defendant. The answer must admit the allegations in the complaint that are true and may deny the rest. It must allege all the defendant's affirmative defenses. It must specify the relief the defendant wants. A defendant has a right to amend the answer within twenty days after serving the initial answer.

If the complaint is vague or ambiguous, so that the defendant's lawyer is uncertain about the nature or scope of the plaintiff's claim, the lawyer may move the court for an order compelling the plaintiff to state the allegations more particularly, more specifically, or more definitely [Rule 12(e)]. If a complaint fails to state a cause of action, the defendant may move to strike the complaint and for judgment on the pleading. If a pleading contains any scandalous or impertinent allegation, the opposing party may move the court to strike the allegation.

A defendant may assert her or his claims against the plaintiff in a counterclaim. If the counterclaim arises from the same transaction or occurrence that gave rise to the main action, it is compulsory; in other words, it must be asserted with the answer or it is lost. If the defendant has a claim against the plaintiff that arose from another transaction or occurrence, the counterclaim is permissive—it can be prosecuted in a separate suit. The plaintiff must respond to a counterclaim by serving and filing a reply to the counterclaim. The reply must assert the plaintiff's affirmative defenses to the counterclaim.

One defendant may assert claims against a codefendant by serving a cross-claim on the codefendant. A cross-claim must be based on the transaction or occurrence that is the subject of the plaintiff's complaint. A defendant who is served with a cross-claim must serve an answer to the cross-claim. The answer to the cross-claim must assert the defendant's affirmative defenses to the cross-claim. A cross-claim may seek a remedy for a loss that the defendant sustained, unrelated to the loss or losses claimed by the plaintiff.

A defendant may bring a third-party action against another person to obtain indemnity or contribution toward the claim the plaintiff has asserted against the defendant. A third-party claim cannot be used to assert a new, unrelated claim against a third person.

A plaintiff may include two or more claims in the complaint even though the claims arise from separate transactions or occurrences. The purpose of joining claims is to reduce costs and promote efficiency. Alternately, either party may move the court for an order joining two or more claims between the parties into one lawsuit. Separate lawsuits may be consolidated for purposes of discovery or trial if they involve common questions of fact or law. The purpose of consolidating lawsuits is to promote economy and efficiency for the parties and the court. Various factors may mitigate against consolidating cases, including untoward delay, increased complexity, and confusion about issues and evidence. Therefore, courts have broad discretion in deciding whether to join claims and whether to consolidate cases for trial. Not every party always benefits from a joinder or consolidation.

Class actions are not generally favored. Courts have to exercise close supervision over the representatives of the class to make sure the class is adequately represented. The prerequisites for a class action are difficult to meet. When a party moves for an order certifying a case as a class action, the party must persuade the court the class is so large it is not practical for parties to sue or defend individually. Common questions of law or fact must exist that affect the rights or obligations of all members of the class the same. The moving party must persuade the court he or she is truly representative of the proposed class. The court considers whether separate suits might lead to varying or inconsistent results. Individual members of the proposed class must not have a superior interest in controlling the handling of the litigation. The court considers whether other pending litigation would be affected adversely. When a class action is allowed, the court makes sure that the members of the class are given notice about the case and that they are informed about their obligations. A class action cannot be compromised or dismissed without court approval [Rule 23(e)].

When a court receives notice of a party's death, the remaining parties have only ninety days in which to obtain a substitution for the deceased party. Otherwise, any action against the decedent will be dismissed [Rule 24(a)]. Any party may move the court for an order making the substitution. If a personal representative has been appointed in a probate proceeding, the representative may seek the substitution. If a party becomes incompetent to handle his or her business, a representative party must be appointed and substituted.

A plaintiff may have the summons and complaint served upon a defendant by having a process server deliver them to the defendant or by leaving them at the defendant's usual place of abode with a person of suitable age and discretion. Any person who is eighteen years of age or older, except the plaintiff, may serve the summons and complaint. The process server must make an affidavit of service or a return of service, which describes the date, place, and manner of service.

A plaintiff may try to serve a defendant by mail. However, the service is not complete or effective unless and until the defendant accepts service by acknowledging service. If the defendant refuses to acknowledge a service by mail, the plaintiff's only recourse is to arrange for personal service. If the plaintiff prevails, he or she is entitled to recover the costs for making personal service.

A party who wants a jury trial must make a timely demand.

A party may compel a nonparty to appear in the case and provide evidence by serving a subpoena on the nonparty. A subpoena may be served by any adult other than the party. The subpoena must be delivered to the nonparty. No rule or statute defines "suitable age." A person who does not comply with a subpoena's mandates is subject to being held in contempt of court.

KEY TERMS

action in rem	jury demand
ad damnum clause	objection to inspection
admission of service	permissive counterclaim
appear	quash
compulsory counterclaim	special damages
counts	supplemental complaint
excusable neglect	supplemental counterclaim
intervention	

REVIEW QUESTIONS

1. What functions does the complaint serve?

2. Why is is important that an amendment to a pleading relate back to the date of the original pleading?

3. What is the difference between a supplemental complaint and an amended complaint?

4. How does a defendant appear in a civil action?

5. What is the effect of a waiver of a legal right?

6. When is a counterclaim compulsory?

7. In what way is a third-party claim tied to the plaintiff's claim?

8. May a cross-claim be based on a transaction or occurrence unrelated to the plaintiff's claim?

9. Who may serve a subpoena?

10. How are a summons and complaint served?

CASE ASSIGNMENT

Your litigation team represents defendant Bradley Harper. The summons and complaint were served on him two weeks ago. Attorney Hoch will serve Harper's answer next week, within the twenty-day period. Attorney Harper has asked you to prepare a third-party complaint for Harper to bring John Griffin into the case as a third-party defendant. You do not need to prepare a paragraph alleging jurisdiction. Harper has two possible causes of action: breach of contract and fraud.

Prepare an intraoffice memorandum to the firm's investigator, who is also the firm's process server. He is new to the firm. Instruct him to serve the third-party complaint on Mr. Griffin. Explain to him what to do and how to do it. Be sure to identify any deadlines that may apply.

Endnotes

1. A party who appears in an action as attorney pro se (i.e., a party who is self-represented) must sign the complaint.
2. The law recognizes that, on occasion, a party may have good reasons and arguments to challenge an existing law. In that event, Rule 11 provides that a party may assert a claim or defense that is contrary to the existing law if the legal contention is warranted by a nonfrivolous argument for the extension, modification, or reversal of existing law or the establishment of new law.
3. Without prejudice means that the action may be recommended later. But if the statute of limitations runs out in the meantime, the failure to accomplish service within 120 days of filing will prove fatal. The complaint will need to be refiled, thereby establishing a new (and potentially untimely) commencement date. Thus, getting an action properly commenced is extremely important.
4. For example, if the summons and complaint were served on Tuesday, the twenty-day period begins to run on Wednesday.
5. The Rules do not require the plaintiff to make the allegations in a formal, legalistic manner.
6. An employee's right to recover money damages for work-related injuries may be severely limited by a state's workers' compensation laws.
7. This is another reason to keep paragraphs short, concise, and limited to one subject.
8. The plaintiff is prejudiced by a late amendment only if the delay impairs the plaintiff's ability to deal with the new matter raised.
9. A stipulation is a written, dated agreement signed by the lawyers in which the parties make commitments concerning the case.
10. Interspousal immunity means spouses cannot sue each other for money damages for torts. Most states have done away with interspousal immunity.
11. Federal courts do not handle divorce actions or other domestic relations cases.
12. Rule 45(b) provides, "Service of a subpoena upon a person named therein shall be made by delivering a copy thereof to such person and, if the person's attendance is commended, by tendering to that person the fees for one day's attendance and the mileage allowed by law."

 For additional resources, visit our Web site at www.paralegal.delmar.cengage.com

CHAPTER **7**

GATHERING EVIDENCE

Chapter Objectives

Chapter 7 is an introduction to the methods parties may use to obtain information and evidence. Specifically, there are two principal means for gathering evidence: (1) a party's own investigation and (2) discovery procedures authorized by court rules. Although the two processes are separate, they should dovetail. This chapter describes how parties may conduct investigations. It introduces discovery procedures prescribed by court rules for obtaining information and evidence from other parties and witnesses. Chapter 7 prepares you for the detailed discussions in subsequent chapters about obtaining, organizing, preserving, and using evidence.

Introduction

When a party retains a lawyer to prosecute a claim or conduct a defense, the lawyer assumes responsibility for gathering and presenting the evidence. Lawyers act on the premise that the party who does the best job of collecting, preserving, and presenting the evidence will prevail. Certainly, a party who fails to prepare and present a good case will lose. The more information and evidence a party obtains, the better he or she can evaluate the case, prepare for trial, and present a convincing case. Even the most skilled advocate cannot expect to win if all the evidence favors the opponent. Parties are not under an obligation to present all the evidence they have or to assist the opposing party. But the adversary nature of civil litigation does not permit a party to conceal or misrepresent evidence. Through discovery procedures each party can require an opposing party to disclose the evidence the party has and knows about. Gathering the evidence includes determining what evidence is needed, locating the evidence, obtaining it, and preserving it. Paralegals perform all these functions for clients.

Information and Evidence

Having a strong theory on the law is no good without having the facts to support the legal theory. Parties need evidence to prove the facts on which they base their claims and defenses. They need evidence to disprove the opponent's contentions. Unless a party has evidence that is admissible and more persuasive than the opponent's evidence, he or she will probably lose. Parties obtain evidence through their investigations and through discovery procedures. Each party is required to obtain her or his own evidence. They should begin as soon as possible.

Each party conducts his or her own investigation without involving the opposing party or using court procedures. An investigation is the simplest and most economical means of obtaining information and evidence.

By contrast, discovery involves the use of court procedures to obtain information and evidence. Discovery procedures, prescribed by court rules and supervised by courts, are designed to give both parties equal access to all the evidence, including evidence that is under the control of the opposing party or possessed by persons who are not parties. Discovery is not limited to evidence that is admissible at trial. Parties may use discovery procedures to compel another party to disclose evidence that is adverse to his or her position. When a party responds to another party's discovery request, the response must be served on all parties. A litigation team should coordinate its investigation and discovery procedures for effectiveness and economy.

As parties gather information and evidence, they gain a better understanding of the case and can evaluate their respective legal positions more accurately. This is important, because at some point each party must decide whether to abandon the case, settle, or go to trial. The sooner parties determine what course to take, the better for everyone. While gathering evidence, the litigation team should consider how best to preserve it, organize it, and use it. The process may be very simple when dealing with a small, routine case, or very complex in a large, involved case. This chapter is an introduction. Subsequent chapters cover many of the topics in greater detail.

Investigation

An investigation is a methodical search for information and evidence. By definition, mere information about facts is not evidence and cannot be used to "prove" facts at trial. Nevertheless, information is important. It leads to evidence and more information. Information is useful for evaluating evidence. The primary sources of evidence and information are the client, witnesses, official investigation files, and the place of the occurrence or records concerning the transaction.

Like vapor, evidence vanishes. Disputes involving business transactions often turn on records and key personnel. It seems that businesses are always in a state of flux because of personnel changes, supervisory changes, procedural changes, and the like. Documents get misplaced. Witnesses to an accident usually have an acute interest in the accident and its consequences during the first few days, but then their interest wanes. So the sooner a party begins to investigate, the more effective and efficient the investigation will be. Witnesses who are "independent" or "nonaligned" often develop empathy with the party whose representative contacts them first. This does not always happen, but it occurs often enough to be a reason to try to be the first to meet and interview nonaligned witnesses. But even if no empathy develops, the party who investigates first generally obtains the most cooperation of independent sources. By way of example, if a witness was contacted by the other side and treated poorly, the witness may try to avoid other investigators. Even if treated well, a witness simply may get tired of talking to investigators. Soon witnesses, who originally were sympathetic and eager to help, do not want to be involved in someone else's litigation. They refuse to cooperate.

Ordinarily, paralegals are not able to force witnesses to cooperate. Therefore, a paralegal must learn to cultivate cooperation and maintain contact with witnesses. You can conduct an investigation with little or no involvement of the opponent. The less the opponent knows about your efforts, the less the opponent can take advantage of them. However, as explained later in the chapter, an opponent can use discovery procedures to obtain the product of a party's investigation.

The authority and reliability of evidence also lessen with the passage of time. For example, photographs of skid marks taken at the scene of a motor vehicle accident, while the vehicles are in their at-rest position, are much more authoritative than photographs taken three days later. Original records are more usable than copies. The originals may have colors that do not show up in photocopies, or information in the margins may not show up on copies, or copies may be difficult to read.

There is no one formula for conducting investigations. You build on information as you obtain it. Be thorough and pay attention to detail. Have a theory, but do not assume too much. An investigation usually begins with a client interview. Usually, the client can provide a good description of the transaction or occurrence and significant background information. Usually, the client can identify important witnesses who have evidence and information. You should never assume that the information a client volunteers is all she or he has. All too often, clients fail to appreciate the value of evidence they already have. Consequently, you should ask clients searching questions about information they probably have but did not volunteer. You must keep asking, "then what happened; why; when, where, who?" Encourage the client to write down any additional thoughts he or she may have before the next conference. If they do not write down their thoughts, the stress causes them to forget, and forgetting causes more stress. As you obtain information and evidence, examine it objectively, make a record of it, and preserve it.

After the client interview, a paralegal should formulate a theory about the facts—about what happened, how it happened, and why it happened in the manner that it did. The theory may be little more than the client's version of the transaction or occurrence, but it should not be limited to the client's version. A theory often suggests what facts and evidence ought to exist, and that in turn helps an investigator focus the search. Also, a theory helps an investigator evaluate other theories by testing one against the other. For example, the client contends she slowed before the collision; she applied her brakes really hard. There should have been skid marks, but the police report says there are no skid marks. The amount of vehicular damage suggests that she did slow down. How can we explain the absence of skid marks? By talking to a mechanic you might learn that the client's car had "antilock brakes," and they would not leave skid marks under those conditions. An apparent anomaly has been solved. The theory pushes you to find an answer. A theory is like a physician's working diagnosis. It provides a basis for action and will be the premise on which the physician provides treatment until a better diagnosis can be made. The theory must be tested against the evidence as the evidence accrues and modified when the evidence is against it.

Lawyers and paralegals must never forget that their communications with witnesses are not privileged. Anything you write or say may be disclosed to the opposition. Therefore, a paralegal should never say anything to a witness that could betray a confidence or embarrass anyone. Witnesses should be assured that it is proper, even expected, for them to meet and talk with paralegals about the transaction or occurrence. Tell witnesses they are free to acknowledge the meeting and discussion. If handled properly, an interview should make the interviewee feel comfortable.

An investigator must remain objective and not presume the truth of "apparent" facts, not even the facts claimed by the client. Presumptions may deter investigators from being thorough. An investigator must pay strict attention to detail and look for patterns and inconsistencies. An investigator must remain flexible in thinking. Investigations can be ongoing. You may continue investigating even while the case is in trial. An investigation should be coordinated with discovery. Indeed, a party's investigation and discovery should complement each other.

Discovery

Overview

An underlying premise of the Federal Rules of Civil Procedure is that parties can resolve their differences without a trial if they have equal access to all the evidence. Discovery procedures are designed to help each party obtain evidence from the other parties and witnesses. Nevertheless, consistent with the adversary nature of civil litigation, the onus is on each party to actively seek the evidence and information. Neither party can make a blanket demand on the other to "tell me all you know about the case." Discovery procedures enable parties to ask each other and witnesses specific questions relevant to the case. Parties can obtain access to documents held by other parties and witnesses, inspect the documents and copy them. They can inspect property in another party's custody or witness's custody. Parties can even obtain an independent medical examination of an adverse party concerning a medical condition that is in issue. Each discovery procedure is designed to meet a particular need. Each procedure may be used independently, but to be most effective and economical, discovery procedures should be coordinated and combined with a party's own investigation. As a paralegal, you may prepare discovery requests and draft discovery responses. The only proscription is that you may not sign requests or responses.

scheduling conference   A court-ordered conference convened to create a schedule that will keep the case moving toward trial and meet the needs of the case and of the parties.

discovery conference   Rule 26(f) requires the parties' attorneys to meet at least fourteen days before the court's mandatory scheduling conference to prepare a discovery plan. The conference is informal and usually conducted at one of the attorneys' offices.

discovery plan   The discovery plan must state the parties' respective proposals or agreements for making initial disclosures and conducting discovery.

Discovery Conference

Federal district courts and many state district courts conduct **scheduling conferences.** Ordinarily, a scheduling conference is held soon after commencement of the action. In preparation for the conference, the attorneys must meet for a **discovery conference** to discuss the "nature" and "basis" of the claims and explore settlement. A party who is not represented by an attorney must attend the meeting in person. The parties should meet as soon as feasible but at least twenty-one days before the court's scheduling conference. If the parties do not settle the case, they must develop a formal **discovery plan.** The plan must be reduced to writing. Usually, one party drafts the plan according to agreements reached during the meeting. The parties circulate a draft, modify it, and then adopt a final version. The ratified discovery plan must be submitted to the court within ten days after the meeting. The parties' plan is subject to court modification. Obviously, the parties must act quickly. Paralegals may draft discovery plans. If the parties cannot agree on a discovery plan, they must submit a detailed explanation to the court, and the court will impose a plan. Lawyers must conduct the discovery conference in "good faith." In other words, when the lawyers fail to agree on a required item, they must have justification for their respective positions [Rule 26(f)].

A discovery plan must identify the legal and fact issues to which discovery will be directed. The parties must establish parameters for discovery, including the methods of discovery. They must establish a time table with deadlines for all aspects of discovery. They must agree on limits for the number of interrogatories and depositions. A discovery plan may provide for discovery phases and apply the time table to phases. For example, the first phase may be to exchange interrogatories and documents; the next phase may be to take depositions of independent witnesses; the next phase may be to take the parties' depositions; the next phase may be to obtain independent medical examinations. If a party has a concern about the scope of inquiry, the plan requires the parties to discuss the problem and state any limitations on which they can agree. If parties disagree about the scope of discovery, the written discovery plan must note the disagreement, and the court will decide the issue when it finalizes the plan. For example, a party may claim that certain information is a trade secret. The trade secret may not be discoverable, or the court may impose limitations on the parties' use after disclosure. As an assist to the court, the discovery plan must identify (list) the subjects on which discovery is needed. A discovery plan may provide for the allocation of expenses, such as expert witness fees. Whether prepared by the parties or by the court, the plan may be modified from time to time as circumstances require, but once established, it must be followed.

The Rule's limitations on discovery apply unless the parties stipulate to a change or the court finds a good reason for deviating. For example, Rule 33(a) limits a party to twenty-five interrogatories to each other party. Absent a stipulation or court order, twenty-five is the limit. Rule 30 limits parties to ten depositions. Absent a stipulation or court order, a party may not take more.

The parties are jointly responsible for the discovery plan. They should agree who will initiate a written proposal for the other's consideration. The plan must be submitted to the court within fourteen days after the meeting. It should bear the case caption and is called "Report of Parties' Planning Meeting." It must relate the time and place of the meeting and who attended. Exhibit 7.1 is a sample of a written plan.

As a paralegal, you can play a major role in preparing the discovery plan and working out its details.

Initial Disclosures

Within fourteen days after the discovery plan meeting, the parties must make an **initial disclosure** of witnesses, documents, computation of damages , and liability insurance. (See Exhibit 7.2.) Each party must disclose all the evidence and information that is then available to him or her. In other words, lawyers and paralegals have an obligation to actively seek out and collect the evidence that is in the client's possession, under the client's control, and within the client's knowledge. A party cannot avoid disclosure by claiming he or she has not been able to complete the investigation. A party

initial disclosures Rule 26(a) requires parties to disclose to each other, in writing, the following information: (1) the name, address, and telephone number of each known witness; (2) a description of each document that is or contains evidence and the identity of the custodian of each; (3) a compilation of damages claimed; (4) relevant insurance policies; and (5) expert witnesses and experts' reports.

EXHIBIT 7.1

Discovery Plan

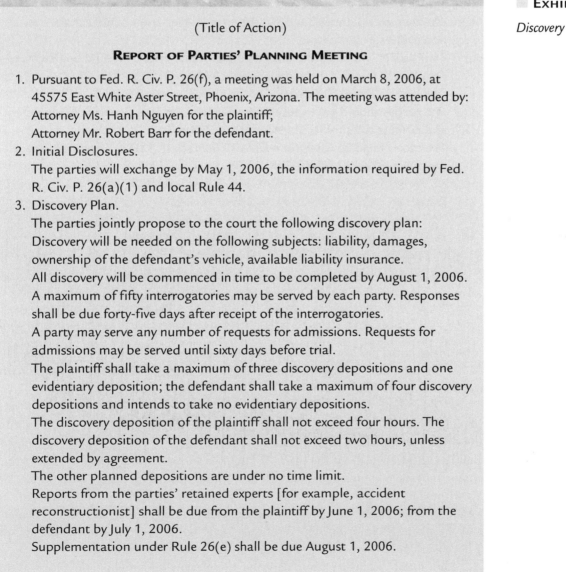

(Title of Action)

REPORT OF PARTIES' PLANNING MEETING

1. Pursuant to Fed. R. Civ. P. 26(f), a meeting was held on March 8, 2006, at 45575 East White Aster Street, Phoenix, Arizona. The meeting was attended by:
   Attorney Ms. Hanh Nguyen for the plaintiff;
   Attorney Mr. Robert Barr for the defendant.
2. Initial Disclosures.
   The parties will exchange by May 1, 2006, the information required by Fed. R. Civ. P. 26(a)(1) and local Rule 44.
3. Discovery Plan.
   The parties jointly propose to the court the following discovery plan:
   Discovery will be needed on the following subjects: liability, damages, ownership of the defendant's vehicle, available liability insurance.
   All discovery will be commenced in time to be completed by August 1, 2006.
   A maximum of fifty interrogatories may be served by each party. Responses shall be due forty-five days after receipt of the interrogatories.
   A party may serve any number of requests for admissions. Requests for admissions may be served until sixty days before trial.
   The plaintiff shall take a maximum of three discovery depositions and one evidentiary deposition; the defendant shall take a maximum of four discovery depositions and intends to take no evidentiary depositions.
   The discovery deposition of the plaintiff shall not exceed four hours. The discovery deposition of the defendant shall not exceed two hours, unless extended by agreement.
   The other planned depositions are under no time limit.
   Reports from the parties' retained experts [for example, accident reconstructionist] shall be due from the plaintiff by June 1, 2006; from the defendant by July 1, 2006.
   Supplementation under Rule 26(e) shall be due August 1, 2006.

continued

EXHIBIT 7.1

Discovery Plan (continued)

4. The parties have not been able to agree on the discoverability of the plaintiff's hospital records concerning a prior accident and injury.

The parties request a conference with the court before entry of the scheduling order, because of the plaintiff's claim of privilege concerning the hospital records.

The parties request a pretrial conference to be held in September or October 2006.

The parties wish to reserve the right to amend pleadings until the time of the pretrial conference.

The parties do not intend or expect to add parties to the action.

All potentially dispositive motions must be filed by the date of the Rule 16 Pretrial Conference.

Settlement cannot be evaluated before August 1, 2006.

Alternative dispute resolution in the form of mediation could enhance the possibilities of settlement.

Final lists of witnesses and exhibits under Rule 26(a)(3) should be due from the plaintiff by the date of the pretrial conference;

from the defendant by the date of the pretrial conference.

The parties should have thirty days after service of the final lists of witnesses and exhibits to list objections under Rule 26(a)(3).

The case should be ready for trial by November 1, 2006. The parties expect the trial will require four full days.

Dated:

/s/ _____

/s/ _____

---

must make initial disclosures though the opposing party's disclosures are inadequate or late. Withholding information or being late in making disclosures subjects a party to court sanctions [Rule 26(a)].

A party must disclose all witnesses, including expert witnesses. A disclosure must include the witness's name, address, and telephone number. It must describe the subject about which each witness has knowledge. For example, a treating physician has knowledge about the plaintiff's injuries and medical expenses. An auto mechanic may have knowledge about the condition of the defendant's automobile. An eyewitness to the accident has knowledge about the facts and circumstances of the accident. Police have knowledge about the facts and circumstances of the accident and the plaintiff's injuries. The disclosure need not go beyond the subject matter. There is no need to provide a summary of the expected testimony.

The initial disclosure must describe all relevant documents and things using categorical descriptions, such as location, custodian, and type of data contained. As

United States District Court for the
Southern District of New York
Civil Action, File Number _____

A. B. Plaintiff

vs.

C. D. Defendant

To: Defendant C. D. and his attorney, James Smith, 1310 East Highway 96,
Suite 204, Albany, New York, 12232

PLEASE TAKE NOTICE that plaintiff makes the following initial disclosures
pursuant to Rule 26(a)(1) of the Federal Rules of Civil Procedure.

a. Witnesses

Name	Address	Telephone	

b. Documents

Categorical Description	Custodian	Address

c. Damages Computations

Description of Loss	Amount Claimed	Basis or Calculation

d. Liability Insurance

Name of Insurer	Amount of Applicable Coverage	Policy Custodian and Address

[date]

Blake & Brown Law Firm
Attorneys for Plaintiff
By _____
309 East Ninth Street
Suite 4434
New York, New York 00245

an alternative, a party simply may provide copies of the documents, but production is not required at that point. The description must be meaningful so that the recipient can appreciate what is included and what is excluded. The disclosure need not summarize contents of documents or even describe why the documents have probative value. For example, a party may disclose the existence of witness statements, including the name of each witness, the date of each statement, and the custodian of each statement, but she need not summarize the statements. The recipient should be able to decide from the disclosures how to obtain the documents and tangible things through discovery procedures. A party must disclose the identity of documents and things that are relevant though privileged. The rule requires disclosure of the existence of documents and things so that an opposing party can decide whether to challenge the claim of privilege or work product [Rule 26(b)(5)].

Plaintiffs and defendants who have counterclaims, must state the amount of money claimed for each alleged loss. The claimant must provide a compilation that explains how the damages are computed and identify all supporting documents. The compilation is supposed to be by category. For example, an automobile accident victim may claim damages for pain, disfigurement, loss of wages, medical expenses, future disability, and property damage. Each item is a separate category. The supporting documentation must include the materials "bearing on the nature and extent of the injuries suffered."

A defendant's initial disclosure must identify all liability insurance policies that may be available to respond to the claim for money damages. Although the rule seems to require production of the insurance policy, if there is no coverage issue or dispute about the amount of coverage, most lawyers are satisfied to have the name of the insurers, the amount of coverage, and the contract number. If the defendant's lawyer assures the plaintiff's lawyer that the insurer has not denied coverage, the plaintiff has no need for the policy. The defendant could provide a copy of the policy's declaration page. It shows the policy period, type, and amount of coverage. The defendant has as much interest in establishing coverage as the plaintiff.

Stipulations

The parties may stipulate to modifications of the initial disclosure requirements. A stipulation must be in writing and signed by the lawyers. The stipulation may modify time parameters and even procedures. However, the parties may not stipulate to extend the time for discovery if an extension disrupts the court's schedule. For example, if the court has ordered the parties to complete discovery by a particular date, the parties may not avoid that order through a stipulation. If the court has scheduled a motion for a particular date, the parties cannot make a discovery stipulation that interferes with the hearing. The parties should make their stipulation and then seek court approval. In practice, courts generally allow the parties to do whatever the parties want or believe they need to do.

Discovery Methods

Parties may use discovery procedures to obtain information about any relevant matter, whether related to a claim or defense of the party seeking discovery or to the claim or defense of any other party. However, a party may not use discovery procedures to obtain information about privileged matters. Parties may use discovery procedures to ascertain the existence, description, nature, custody, condition, and location of any books, documents, or other tangible things and the identity and location of persons having knowledge of any discoverable matter. The mere fact that the information sought will not be admissible at trial does not preclude discovery. The information sought must pertain to the case, or it must appear the information could lead to the discovery of admissible evidence.

Parties may obtain discovery by one or more of the following methods: depositions on oral examination or written questions; written interrogatories, demand for production of documents or things, demand for inspection of land or other property, demand for physical and mental examination of a party, and requests for admissions. Each discovery procedure was designed to meet a particular need. Each procedure may be used independently. Each party decides what discovery procedures to use and when. All discovery requests must be served on all parties to keep them informed. Similarly, when a party responds to a discovery request, he or she must send a copy of the response to all parties.

- Interrogatories are written questions that parties ask each other. They are usually served in sets. Each **interrogatory** should be specific, clearly stated, and succinct. Answers to interrogatories are made under oath. They must be responsive, candid, and complete. See Chapter 11.

- An **oral deposition** is a method of questioning a party or witness where all parties are present or represented by attorneys. The witness—the "deponent"— must testify under oath and is subject to cross-examination. The deponent may have an attorney to advise him or her. The questions and answers are recorded, usually stenographically. A **deposition transcript** is the typed, verbatim record of the questions and answers. Oral deposition testimony is often used at court in place of a person's live testimony. Court rules require parties to submit for at least one deposition. Parties may use subpoenas to compel witnesses to appear for depositions. See Chapter 12.

- A deposition on written questions is a method of requiring a party or witness to respond to written questions, including cross-examination. The answers must be written and are under oath. They may be used at trial to provide evidence through the deponent.

- A demand for production of documents is a written request to a party to provide access to specified documents at a specified time and place. The proponent may inspect and copy the documents, but does not obtain custody of them. The respondent does not have any obligation to discuss or explain the documents; therefore, a demand for production of documents is often combined with an oral deposition. See Chapter 15.

- A demand for inspection of land or property is a written request for the opportunity to enter land or gain access to personal property for the purpose of inspecting, photographing, or testing the subject. When the proponent's testing procedures are destructive, the procedure must be carefully monitored and, sometimes, limited.

- A party who puts his or her physical or mental condition in issue may be required to submit to one or more independent medical examinations by physicians selected by the opponent. The physician must prepare a written report. The party who was examined may demand a copy of the report, but waives his or her medical privilege by making the demand. See Chapter 14.

- Request for admissions are written statements that a party asks another party to admit are true. The purpose of a request is to take the stated fact out of issue and narrow the scope of the controversy. A respondent may admit the request or deny the request or make a qualified denial. If a party fails to respond to a request for admissions within the time provided, the request is deemed admitted. This feature makes requests for admission a potentially very harmful device for the party on the receiving end. If you

interrogatory   A written question to another party to a civil action that must be answered under oath.

oral deposition   A procedure, established by Rule 30 of the Federal Rules of Civil Procedure, that enables any party to obtain the testimony of any other party or witness for the purpose of obtaining information and evidence or to preserve the testimony for use at trial.

deposition transcript   A verbatim copy of an oral deposition, either typed or printed in a booklet form.

are assigned to prepare responses to requests for admissions, never overlook the deadline or assume that late responses will not matter. When a request is "deemed admitted" against your client, it can have serious consequences. Requests for admissions are often combined with interrogatories. See Chapter 16.

These discovery tools are used to obtain information and evidence and to preserve evidence for use at trial. If a party or witness refuses to cooperate with a proper discovery request, that person is subject to the penalties provided by law. Some discovery procedures may be used even before an action has been commenced, where a special need exists and that need can be shown by petition to a district court that has jurisdiction over the subject matter.

Scope of Discovery

The philosophy underlying the rules for discovery is that all parties should have access to all the information and evidence. The premise is that if the parties have access to all the evidence, they will understand the material facts, and that will lead to settlement of most cases. Therefore, discovery is favored; concealment is punished.

A discovery inquiry must seek relevant evidence or be *reasonably calculated to lead to evidence that will be admissible at trial.* Otherwise, the inquiry is beyond the scope of authorized discovery and subject to objection. Evidence is relevant if it tends to prove or disprove a fact that is material to a claim or defense raised by the pleadings. The relevancy requirement helps keep parties from using discovery for ulterior purposes. Thus, where a customer slips and falls in a store and commences a negligence action to recover money damages for bodily injuries, the customer is not permitted to conduct discovery about the store's financial condition, business operations, trade secrets, or the like. The scope of the customer's discovery is limited to determining whether the store was negligent in the manner in which it maintained the premises.

Discovery procedures may not be used to harass another party. The frequency or extent a party uses discovery may be limited by court order if the court determines that discovery requests are cumulative or duplicated, or if the information is obtainable from another source that is more convenient, less burdensome, or less expensive. In determining whether the discovery is unduly burdensome or expensive, courts consider the needs of the case, the amount in controversy, limitations on the parties' resources, and the importance of the issues at stake in the litigation.

A defendant's liability insurance, which may pay the plaintiff's damages, is irrelevant as evidence in most civil lawsuits. However, the availability of liability insurance may be a very important consideration in determining whether a case should be settled and for how much. Consequently, Rule 26(b)(2) allows parties to discover the existence of liability insurance, the scope of coverage, the amount of coverage, and even a copy of the insurance policy. On occasion, a problem develops between the defendant and her or his liability insurer, because they do not agree on whether the claim is covered. The plaintiff may need a copy of the policy to determine who is correct.

Rule 26(b)(2) appears to refer only to liability insurance, which is insurance that will be available to pay a judgment or otherwise indemnify a party for liability. Nevertheless, there is general agreement that the defendant may discover whether the plaintiff has direct-loss insurance that covers all or part of the loss in question (e.g., health insurance). One reason for this is that a direct-loss insurer who has made payments to the insured plaintiff may have subrogation rights. The defendant is entitled to know all the circumstances affecting an insurer's interest in the case, and such information is most conveniently obtained through interrogatories. Furthermore, the direct-loss insurer may have relevant information about the amount of the loss and the measure of damages. A defendant should be able to discover whether the plaintiff in a personal injury action has medical insurance to cover some of the expenses.

Limitations on Discovery

Discovery procedures may not be used to obtain information, communications, or documents that are privileged. The matter of what is privileged is determined by state law and federal statute. Ordinarily, privileged matters include communications between a physician and a patient, and the patient's medical records; communications between a lawyer and a client, their written communications and records. Presumably, your state extends the attorney-client privilege to paralegals. Also privileged are communications between a cleric and a penitent concerning matters of religious counseling and communications between a husband and a wife during marriage. However, the privilege relates to the documents and communications, themselves, not their existence. So it would be appropriate to inquire whether a party discussed the party's accident with his spouse, but not to ask what he or she said. The privilege is forfeited if the party lets someone hear the communication or tells someone else about the subject of the communication. A party must preserve and protect the privilege, or it is lost.

Discovery procedures may not be used to obtain information about the opposing party's trial preparation, such as the attorney's mental impressions, conclusions, opinions, or theories about the case [Rule 26(b)(3)]. This limitation on discovery is commonly referred to as the **attorneys' work product** rule. The limitation protects from discovery the work product of a party's employees, agents, and other representatives, including insurance representatives. For example, a party may not use a discovery procedure to ask an opposing party how he or she will conduct his or her investigation or what significance the opposing lawyer places on certain evidence or what facts the lawyer believes the evidence tends to prove. A party may not use discovery to find out what the opposing party has done to prepare for trial. A party may inquire about the names and addresses of all witnesses, but a party cannot use discovery to find out what the party's investigator concluded from the witness interview. Rule 26(a)(1)(A) requires parties to disclose the subject matter to which any known witness will testify, however. The respondent may state the subjects as categories, such as "accident," "breach of contract," "damages."

A party may demand and obtain a recorded statement he or she gave to another party. The statement is not protected by the work product rule. Similarly, a person who is not a party has a right to obtain a copy of statements given to a party. However, a party cannot require an opposing party give up recorded statements obtained from witnesses.[1] Witness statements are considered the work product of the party who obtained them. Many states, however, have adopted a different approach by requiring parties to disclose and produce for copying all witness statements that they

attorneys' work product A doctrine, predicated on Rule 26 of the Federal Rules of Civil Procedure, that prevents one party from discovering what another party's attorneys have done or have accomplished in preparing for trial.

have obtained. There is considerable controversy over the discoverability of recorded statements obtained from parties by their own insurance company. The general rule is that the statement is not discoverable if it was prepared in anticipation of litigation.

Sequence and Timing

As a general rule, the parties cannot initiate discovery until after they have conducted a discovery conference and made their initial disclosures. The disclosures help the parties to know what information they need to obtain and how to obtain it. No party has a right to go first or second. No party may delay discovery on the basis that the other party has been dilatory or uncooperative or obstructive. In other words, each party must comply with the Rules and court orders regardless of the other party's conduct. Parties may stipulate, as provided by Rule 29, to different time parameters. But they may not stipulate to extend the time for discovery if doing so changes the court's discovery plan or conflicts with a court deadline.

Some courts actually cut off the use of requests for admissions with "discovery deadlines" even though that is when a party should prepare and serve requests for admissions, because that is when the facts are known and the admissions should be made. This problem should be considered at the time the parties prepare and submit their discovery plan.

Supplementation of Discovery Responses

A party is under a continuing duty to supplement and correct his or her initial disclosures and discovery responses. The duty arises when a party becomes aware that a prior disclosure or response is incomplete or incorrect. The duty is to make a response "complete," not just technically correct [Rule 26(e)].

Compelling Disclosures

If a party wrongfully fails to comply with discovery demands, the proponent may move the court for an order compelling the party to comply (Rule 37). This is termed a motion to compel discovery. If the court orders the delinquent party to answer interrogatories or testify by oral deposition, the court may require the culpable party to pay the moving party's costs [Rule 37(a)(4)]. If the court determines that the respondent was correct in refusing to comply with discovery demands, however, it may require the proponent to pay costs the deponent respondent incurred. A court may determine that both parties had reasonable grounds for their respective positions and acted in good faith. On that basis, the court could decide to let each party bear her or his own costs.

Sanctions

sanctions   Penalties a court imposes on a party who fails to comply with the court's order or rules.

Discovery demands and disclosures must be signed by a lawyer or by a party. A person who signs a disclosure that is not "complete and correct as of the time it is made" is subject to court **sanctions** [Rule 26(g)(1)]. In addition, a party has an obligation to correct and supplement previous responses in a timely manner (Rule 37). A party or lawyer may justify a nondisclosure only by showing "substantial justification" and "harmless" error. In the language of Rule 37(c)(1)

A party that without substantial justification fails to disclose information required by Rule 26(a) or 26(e)(1) or to amend a prior response to discovery as required by Rule 26(e)(z), shall not, unless such failure is harmless, be permitted to use as evidence at a trial, at a hearing, or on a motion any witness or information not so disclosed. In addition, . . . on motion and after affording an opportunity to be heard, [the court] may impose other appropriate sanctions.

Additional sanctions include payment of costs and attorneys' fees. At trial, the judge may inform the jury about a party's failure (lawyer's failure) to make proper disclosures. Obviously, such a statement would adversely affect the party's entire case.

If a party refuses to disclose certain facts, a court may order that the facts are established against the delinquent party, prohibit the party from denying the opponent's claim or defense, or preclude the party from presenting certain evidence at trial. A case in point would be where the plaintiff claims damage to personal property but will not permit the defendant to examine the property. The court could issue an order that provides, for purposes of the pending action, that the property was not damaged. A court may strike all or part of the delinquent party's pleading, leaving that party in default. For example, suppose the plaintiff in a personal injury action refuses to disclose his past employers or refuses to produce copies of his or her income tax returns. The refusal would significantly impair the defendant's ability to contest the plaintiff's claim for loss of income. The court could strike the paragraph of the complaint that alleges damages for loss of income and loss of earning capacity.

A court may find a party to be in contempt of court for failing to comply with a discovery order [Rule 37(b)(D)]. The right to discovery includes the right to have one or more **independent medical examinations** of a party who has put his or her physical, mental, or blood condition in issue; however, a party who refuses to submit to an independent medical examination cannot be held in contempt of court even though ordered to submit. Some other sanction must be used. The most severe penalty that a court may impose is to enter judgment against the disobedient party [Rule 37(b)(C)].

independent medical examination A medical examination of a party to an action conducted by a physician selected by an adverse party for the purpose of evaluating the party's physical, mental, or blood condition.

Analyzing and Organizing Evidence

Parties usually do not present all the evidence that is available to them, but instead present only the evidence they need to prove their claims or defenses. Parties have no legal or ethical duty to present all the available evidence. Indeed, courts do not want parties to inundate the jury with cumulative evidence. However, a party must not take evidence out of context or manipulate evidence to present a false picture. Furthermore, a lawyer must not conceal, suppress, or tamper with evidence. If lawyers disregard these proscriptions, the judicial system would collapse. Lawyers must conduct themselves on the basis that the truth is sacred. The litigation team must sort through the evidence and decide what to use and how to present it.

The litigation team should organize the evidence and present it in a manner that makes the evidence authoritative, interesting, and persuasive. The first step is to revisit the legal issues. The pleadings establish the legal issues and should contain the basic facts; therefore, a good place to begin the trial preparation is to review the pleadings. The legal issues determine what facts are material to the case. The fact issues determine what evidence is relevant to the parties' claims and defenses. This process is discussed in detail in Chapter 17 concerning the preparation of a "fact brief." Some lawyers begin trial preparation by constructing a final argument, because a final argument should bring the case together for the jury. A good argument explains how the evidence proves the client's version of the facts and how the law applies to those facts. When a lawyer decides what to tell the jury in the final argument, he or she knows what evidence to present. They work backward, making sure they have evidence to prove the facts they need. So the final argument can provide a basis for organizing the evidence. If the lawyer discovers the evidence does not support the argument, it's back to the drawing board. The evidence should be consistent and logical. It should make sense. Discrepancies must be resolved as soon as possible. Otherwise, a lawyer and paralegal may pursue an invalid theory and lose the case.

A litigation team must make certain that the client's theory of the case is consistent with physical facts and scientific principles. The physical facts are demonstrable. They include time, place, sequence, size, measurements, color, and so forth. In automobile accident cases, the physical facts include skid marks, position of debris on the road, point of impact on each vehicle, the amount of damage caused by the impact, lighting conditions, road configuration, road surface, weather, and so on. If photographs show both cars are red, "red" is a physical fact. If the client or a witness remembers a different color, the discrepancy must be resolved as soon as possible. Perhaps you should confront the witness about the physical facts. Present the photographs. Take witnesses back to the accident scene. Require witnesses to reread the documents. But *do not mislead a client or witness!*

Where specific facts have been established by the pleadings or responses to requests for admissions, the parties are committed to those facts, unless a court releases them from the commitment. The rest of the case and evidence should be consistent with those irrefutable facts. If there are inconsistencies, they must be resolved, and the sooner, the better.

Thorough trial preparation includes helping witnesses and the client to fully understand what they observed, refreshing witnesses' recollections, and helping them appreciate all the facts that are relevant to their testimony. In other words, witnesses should be given the opportunity to see how each witness's testimony fits into the case as a whole. However, lawyers and paralegals must not tell witnesses what to say. A witness's testimony must come from what the witness knows from his or her own observations and knowledge, not what the witness hears from others. Nevertheless, sometimes a witness's observations must be put into perspective. For example, a witness may have a valid estimate of the width of an intersection by reason of the witness's own observations, but it is not wrong to tell the witness what the exact measurement is to assure the witness that her or his estimate is reasonable. If a witness's estimate is not valid, the witness ought to examine the roadway again and measure the distance in question (assuming nothing has changed since the time of the accident). If the witness changes her or his estimate as a result of a subsequent measurement, the reason for the change is a matter that is subject to cross-examination. It is perfectly proper to help a witness to be accurate with estimates and recollections. It is never improper to help a witness find the truth and understand why it is the truth.

Documentary evidence, such as business records, should comport with the judicial admissions, physical facts, and anticipated testimony. If they do not, the reason for any inconsistency must be determined so that evidence can be reconciled and/or a proper explanation provided.

Preserving Evidence

It is not enough to find favorable evidence. The evidence must be preserved so that it is available for trial. For example, suppose that you have found the perfect witness. She is totally supportive of your client's version of the facts; she was in a good position to observe the occurrence; she is empathetic with the client; she is articulate and makes an excellent appearance; she is independent but cooperative. But it will be a year before the case will reach trial. What can be done to preserve this evidence? There are several options. You could make a detailed memorandum of the interview and the witness's expected testimony.[2] You could obtain a signed statement from the witness that details the information she has. You could have a court reporter record the interview in which the witness uses her own words. You could make an audio recording, so the witness can hear herself. When it comes time for her to testify she can refresh her recollection from her own words. Or, you could arrange for a stenographically recorded deposition or videotaped deposition. That would preserve the witness's testimony so it could be used at trial even if the witness were not available. But that would expose the witness to a cross-examination by the other side. The best choice for preserving a witness's evidence depends on the purpose, importance of the evidence, costs, and cooperativeness of the witness.

When you locate documents that are evidence or contain evidence, there are several methods of preserving them. You could make a memorandum to the file that states or summarizes the documents' contents, identifies the custodian and their location. If you do that, you should make sure that the custodian will not lose or destroy the documents. You could take possession of the documents. But if the owner of the documents will not release them, you must find an alternative. You could photocopy the documents and keep the copies. But that would not provide the necessary foundation for using them at trial. You could photocopy them and submit them to the other party with a request for admission that the documents are genuine. You could take the custodian's deposition and have the custodian identify the original documents. In that event, copies could be substituted for the originals. Again, the choice for preserving the evidence depends on various factors. How important are the documents? Is the custodian cooperative? How many documents are there? What is the cost of copying? How long before the documents will be needed? Are there other documents to be gathered?

Role of Paralegals in Gathering Evidence

Paralegals may handle any aspect of an investigation, including client interviews, obtaining witness statements, and taking photographs. You may obtain, organize, analyze, and summarize documents. You may meet with experts and assist with experts' reports. You may handle most aspects of discovery, subject to a lawyer's supervision. Court rules only permit lawyers and parties to sign discovery requests and responses, but paralegals may prepare the documents. About the only discovery function a paralegal may not handle is the taking of oral depositions.

The evidence must be admissible, understandable, and persuasive. Sometime before trial, the trial lawyer and paralegals must carefully analyze all the evidence they have collected, and organize it. They need to make sure they have all the evidence they need to prove the client's version of the disputed facts. They must make sure that their evidence is admissible and persuasive. They must decide on the best methods of presenting the evidence. Most courts now require the parties to "mark" their exhibits for identification before the trial starts, including a list of all proposed exhibits. A legal assistant needs to understand the evidence, how it may be used, and its limitations.

SUMMARY

The elements of the plaintiff's causes of action and the defendant's affirmative defenses determine what facts are material. The evidence that tends to prove a material fact is relevant evidence. Most relevant evidence is admissible in a civil trial. The parties to a civil suit must gather their own evidence. They may obtain evidence through their own investigation efforts and through discovery procedures. The methods of gathering evidence should be used to complement each other.

The advantages of an investigation are that a party need not wait until a lawsuit is commenced or depend on the cooperation of the opposing side. Obtaining evidence and information through an investigation is relatively economical. A party need not share her or his investigation efforts with another party. However, a party may be required to disclose the products of her or his investigation, depending on application of discovery rules. A party (lawyer) has more control over the development of evidence when conducting her or his own investigation.

The Federal Rules of Civil Procedure provide several methods for conducting discovery: initial disclosures, interrogatories, oral depositions, depositions on written questions, demands for inspection and copying, independent medical examinations, and requests for admissions. Each procedure has a specified period of time in which the respondent must comply with the proponent's discovery request. The procedures may be used to inquire about any relevant (material) fact or relevant evidence or to obtain information that may lead to the discovery of admissible evidence. Discovery procedures are particularly useful for obtaining information from an opposing party and uncooperative witnesses. A party should use discovery procedures to complement her or his own investigation.

The court will schedule a discovery conference as soon as practicable after the defendant has appeared in the case. The parties must use the conference to prepare a discovery plan. The plan must provide a time table and identify the methods of discovery that the parties will use. The discovery rule limits apply unless the parties stipulate to different parameters. Parties may make any stipulations they want concerning discovery unless the stipulation interferes with the court's schedule.

Each party must make an initial disclosure of witnesses, documents, damages computations, and liability insurance after the discovery conference. The parties must disclose all witnesses and documents they know about whether favorable or unfavorable. They may initiate discovery after the discovery conference and initial disclosures. Parties may not avoid the initial disclosure by claiming the opposing party is delinquent or not cooperating.

All discovery demands and disclosures must be signed by a party or a lawyer. A person who signs a disclosure that is incomplete or incorrect when made is subject to court-imposed penalties. A party cannot resist discovery on grounds that the opposing party is delinquent or uncooperative in conducting discovery. A party must keep his or her discovery disclosures correct and complete by supplementing them on a timely basis. A party cannot use discovery to obtain privileged information or privileged documents. A party cannot use discovery to obtain another party's work product or the work product of another party's lawyer.

Parties are limited to ten depositions, twenty-five interrogatories, and one independent medical examination, unless the parties stipulate to more or the court orders more. If the parties cannot agree on discovery parameters, the court will establish the parameters for them. Use requests for admissions to reduce the number of fact issues and to establish the genuineness of documents.

An investigatory interview should make the interviewee feel comfortable with the interviewer and the process. A paralegal should assure witnesses that it is proper to talk with them and attorneys about the case. It is unethical to mislead a witness into believing that the witness should not talk to the opposing side. Anything a lawyer or paralegal says to a witness may be discovered and used by the opposition. Therefore, a paralegal should never say anything to a witness that could embarrass anyone. Witnesses should be informed that they are free to tell others about the meeting, but they are not required to do so.

Parties can compel witnesses to appear for oral depositions by serving a subpoena on the witnesses. A court can compel a witness to testify by finding a noncompliant witness in contempt of court. If a party fails or refuses to allow discovery, the proponent may move the court for an order compelling discovery. If the delinquent party disobeys the court order, the court may impose sanctions.

A party who fails to comply with an order for discovery is subject to a variety of court sanctions. A court may strike the delinquent party's pleading, leaving that party in default. A court may instruct the jury that the omitted facts are established, or prohibit the delinquent party from denying the opponent's claim or defense affected by the nondisclosure. A court may preclude the party from using the nondisclosed evidence at a trial. A delinquent party may be required to pay the other party's costs and attorney's fees. A court may inform the jury about a lawyer's failure to make disclosures required by law.

If a party wrongfully refuses to make admissions pursuant to Rule 36, the only penalty that a court may impose against that party is an award of costs in favor of the proponent of the request for admissions. The recoverable costs are those the proponent incurred to prove the facts, which should have been admitted by the respondent.

A litigation team must preserve the evidence for use in trial preparation and the trial. There are many methods of preserving evidence, including memorandas, statements, oral depositions, recordings, photographs, and copying documents. The choice depends on the cooperativeness of the witness, cost, volume, importance of the evidence, and other factors. Preserved evidence may be used to prepare for trial by refreshing witnesses' recollections, helping the client and witnesses to fully understand what they observed, and helping them appreciate all the relevant facts so they understand how their testimony fits into the case as a whole. It is proper to help a witness to be accurate with estimates and recollections. However, lawyers and paralegals must not tell witnesses what to say—only how to say it. It is always proper to help witnesses find the truth and understand why it is the truth.

The legal issues determine what facts are material to the case. A party must organize and present evidence in a manner that makes it probative, authoritative, educational, interesting, and persuasive. A party has no legal or ethical duty to present all of the evidence, but a party must not take evidence out of context or use the evidence to present a false picture. Lawyers and paralegals must believe the truth is sacred. A party's evidence should be consistent with facts established by the pleadings, the laws of nature, physical facts, and judicial admissions. If the evidence does not comport, the reason for the inconsistency must be determined so that evidence can be reconciled and/or a proper explanation provided.

KEY TERMS

attorneys' work product
deposition transcript
discovery conference
discovery plan
independent medical examination

initial disclosures
interrogatory
oral deposition
sanctions
scheduling conference

REVIEW QUESTIONS

1. Why should an investigator develop a theory about the accident or transaction?

2. What is the one discovery procedure that a paralegal may not conduct?

3. Name three advantages that an investigation has over discovery procedures.

4. When does the task of gathering the evidence end?

5. What are the principal limits on the scope of discovery?

6. When is a party required to supplement discovery responses?

7. When is evidence or information relevant for the purpose of discovery procedures?

8. What is a discovery plan?

9. How do requests for admissions differ from discovery procedures?

10. What sanction may be imposed on a party who wrongly fails to admit a fact pursuant to a Rule 36 request for admission?

11. Why is evidence preserved?

12. Name three methods of preserving a witness's expected testimony.

13. What is the most serious sanction a court may impose on a party who refuses to allow discovery?

CASE ASSIGNMENT

1. Prepare the Trustee's Initial Disclosure for service on defendant Harper. The action's title is:

STATE OF MINNESOTA   **DISTRICT COURT**

COUNTY OF HENNEPIN   **FOURTH JUDICIAL DISTRICT**

PERSONAL INJURY

Laura Raskin, Trustee for next of kin   File No. PI-93-0000145
of William Nordby, deceased,
                    Plaintiffs,

          vs.   **INITIAL DISCLOSURE**

Bradley Harper,
                    Defendant.

   Plaintiff makes this Initial Disclosure, pursuant to Rule 26 of the Minnesota Rules of Civil Procedure.

2. Prepare an intraoffice memorandum to the litigation team head, Donald Smith, with your suggestions for an investigation plan. *Hint:* Consider the facts your team needs to prove; consider the evidence you know exists to prove those facts; consider what evidence might be available to prove the facts; determine how you should preserve the evidence; identify the source for each item of evidence, such as a witness, a document, or a record; then establish a pragmatic and efficient order for going to the sources.

   Fact:
          Available evidence
          Potential evidence
          How to preserve
          Sources
   Fact:
          Available evidence
          Potential evidence
          How to preserve
          Sources

          * * *

   Order of investigation
          Client
          Accident report
          Interview sheriff
          Interview Harper's passenger

Endnotes

1. Nothing prevents a witness from obtaining her or his statement and then providing copies to parties.
2. An unsigned witness statement is sometimes described as a memorandum of interview. Because the witness has not signed it, the witness has no right to obtain a copy of it. The memorandum is treated as the attorney's work product.

 For additional resources, visit our Web site at www.paralegal.delmar.cengage.com

CHAPTER 8

EVIDENCE

CHAPTER OUTLINE

Chapter Objectives

Chapter 8 explains what evidence is and why courts have rules that exclude some kinds of evidence. The chapter describes many of the exclusionary rules of evidence and how they apply. Chapter 8 prepares you to find, obtain, and preserve evidence, as discussed in subsequent chapters.

Introduction

Most lawsuits involve a dispute about what happened, how it happened, or why it happened. In other words, the parties disagree about the facts concerning their transaction or occurrence. Each party remembers or interprets the facts differently. Courts hold trials to determine the truth concerning disputed facts. Each party has the opportunity to present evidence to prove her or his version of the facts and refute the opponent's version. Evidence is anything that tends to prove or disprove a fact. To be effective, the evidence must be admissible at trial and should be persuasive.

A lawyer assumes a responsibility to a client to gather the evidence, preserve it, organize it, and present it in its most persuasive form. Paralegals help with these responsibilities. As a paralegal, you will have a major role in obtaining evidence for your team's clients. You will conduct investigations and assist with various discovery procedures authorized by court rules. You may investigate accident scenes, interview witnesses, examine records, and prepare summaries of facts for use at trial. Your objective is to obtain evidence that can be used in trial, that is, **admissible evidence.** Also, the

admissible evidence Evidence that tends to prove a material fact and which is not subject to any exclusionary rule of evidence.

199

evidence must be organized and preserved in such a way as to keep it admissible. To effectively gather evidence, organize it, and preserve it you must understand what evidence is, whether a court will receive it, and how it can be used. When you conduct an investigation and assist with discovery you will obtain facts, admissible evidence, inadmissible evidence, and mere information. You will deal with each category differently. Each has a separate value. Therefore, before considering how to obtain evidence, we are going to examine what evidence is and why some evidence is not admissible evidence. This chapter provides an overview of evidence that should help you deal effectively with evidence. Chapter 9 discusses the process of gathering and preserving evidence.

The difference between a "fact" and "evidence of a fact" is not always clear. A **fact** is a truth, an absolute, something that happened or exists or did exist. Some facts can be determined with certainty, such as your present height and weight. But seldom can a disputed fact in a civil lawsuit be demonstrated with such certainty. Usually, the best that parties are able to do is present evidence of the fact. In an accident case, the speed of a party's automobile immediately before the collision may be a controverted, material fact. A person who observed the car's speed may testify about that fact. The witness's testimony is evidence of the fact. Once a fact is proved, that fact may become evidence of another fact. For example, the existence and length of skid marks may be a fact issue. A witness's testimony concerning his or her observations about the skid marks is evidence of that fact. In addition, the existence and length of skid marks may be circumstantial evidence of the automobile's speed, because they may make a certain speed more or less probable. Therefore, the skid marks (a fact) may be evidence of speed, evidence that the motorist applied the brakes, and evidence of where the vehicle was when the brakes were applied.

Parties and their attorneys usually want to tell courts and juries more than they need to know. To maintain efficiency, economy, and clarity, courts restrict the parties' evidence to the **material facts.** Facts are material if they affect the parties' legal rights and obligations. Facts are material if they affect the outcome of the case. All other facts are considered immaterial. A fact does not have to be disputed to be material. A party should not be allowed to present evidence about immaterial facts, because such evidence merely confuses and prolongs the case. Nevertheless, parties persist in wanting to present collateral, immaterial facts to embellish their own cases or to prejudice the opponents. Evidence about immaterial facts is subject to objection by the other party and exclusion by the court.

A party's evidence must relate to a material fact. As mentioned previously, evidence is anything that *tends* to prove or disprove a material fact. But there are limits on what is meant by "tends." For evidence to be admissible in a trial, the evidence must be **relevant.** Irrelevant evidence is not admissible in a trial. Evidence is relevant if it tends to make the existence of a fact more probable or less probable. This is called probative value. Relevant evidence is admissible in a trial, unless the evidence conflicts with an exclusionary rule of evidence. The exclusionary rules prevent courts from considering evidence even if it is relevant. Each exclusionary rule is grounded in notions of fairness or sound public policy. The rules of evidence help courts and lawyers to determine when relevant evidence should be excluded from consideration in determining the facts. Because reasonable minds may differ on whether a fact is material and whether evidence is relevant, trial judges have broad

fact   A truth; something that happened; something that exists or did exist.

material fact   A fact that directly relates to an issue in the case.

relevant   Means there is a logical relationship between proposed evidence and the fact for which the evidence is offered to establish the fact.

discretion in ruling on the admissibility of evidence. The tendency of most judges is to err on the side of receiving doubtful evidence.

Evidence varies greatly in its reliability and persuasiveness. Consider, how would you prove how much you weighed three years ago? Your weight three years ago cannot now be measured or demonstrated. Of course, you could *testify* concerning your past weight. But would your testimony be based on a present recollection of a specific weight or would it merely be an estimate. Perhaps your driver's license recorded your weight three years ago, but was the recorded weight a mere estimate at the time? Maybe you could produce medical records that recorded a measured weight.[1] All these sources *tend* to prove what your weight was three years ago. But if each source leads to a different answer, which would be most reliable?

What is a court to do when there are conflicts in the evidence? The correctness and acceptability of a court's judgment depend on the quality of the evidence the court receives. Courts must have a rational basis for allowing and disallowing evidence. The evidence must have some guarantee of trustworthiness. Therefore, only competent witnesses are allowed to testify. Most evidence is presented under oath and is subject to **cross-examination.** The evidence must not be repetitious or cumulative. Evidence must not be disruptive to the proceedings. It must not create "unfair prejudice." Courts must be pragmatic about what evidence is reasonably available to parties. It would be unfair to require the parties to present only the very "best" evidence. The jury must consider the evidence as a whole.

The admissibility and uses of evidence are highly technical subjects, but also very interesting ones. Certain kinds of evidence may be used in some cases but not in others. Some evidence must be presented in a particular manner. Some kinds of evidence are more persuasive than other kinds and, therefore, are preferable. Lawyers and paralegals must consider what evidence is admissible and its probative value when evaluating clients' cases and when preparing cases for trial. Also, lawyers must consider how best to present each item of evidence and how the presentation will influence the jury to believe about the client and the client's claim or defense.

Every civil lawsuit involves at least one "ultimate question of fact" that a **fact finder** must decide. An **ultimate fact,** such as negligence or proximate cause, is the fact finder's conclusion drawn from all the underlying, proven facts. An ultimate fact is a fact that in itself may determine the parties' legal rights and obligations. For example, if the evidence shows that one of the motorists in the preceding example drove over the speed limit and did not have control of his vehicle, those two facts would be the basis for finding, as an ultimate fact, that the motorist was negligent in the operation of the vehicle. The fact finder also may determine that the excessive speed and lack of control were the direct cause of the parties' accident. A determination that the motorist was *negligent* and that the motorist's negligence *caused* the accident is a basis for concluding that the motorist is legally liable for the accident.

Jurors must use their experience in life to evaluate the parties' evidence. They may draw inferences from facts established by the evidence. But jurors may not speculate (guess) about facts that are not supported by any evidence. Jurors may only determine the facts based on the evidence.[2] Jurors may not, through their own independent knowledge, supply any apparent missing fact or use their own knowledge about facts to reject evidence. For example, if the witnesses to an accident cannot remember whether the roadway in question had a painted centerline, jurors who are familiar with

cross-examination The examination of an adverse party or hostile witness in which the examiner may ask leading questions and may seek to limit answers by asking very narrow, circumscribed questions.

fact finder The fact finder must consider and weigh the evidence to resolve disputed facts and determine the ultimate questions of fact.

ultimate fact The facts to which the rules of law are applied so that a judgment can be rendered by the court.

the roadway may not use their independent knowledge of the roadway to make that determination. Suppose the witnesses testified that there was no stop sign at the intersection in question, but a juror remembers that there was a stop sign. The other jurors are supposed to disregard their fellow juror's recollection in favor of the witnesses' testimony. But suppose the witnesses are evenly divided on the issue, what is the likely effect of a juror's personal knowledge? For this reason, lawyers are inclined to avoid having jurors who profess familiarity with facts material to the case. Lawyers want to be able to control the case by controlling the evidence as much as possible.

The rules of evidence are designed to promote truth, fairness, and efficiency. The common law developed a battery of exclusionary rules of evidence to promote justice and make evidence reliable. Congress promulgated the Federal Rules of Evidence on July 1, 1975. They codify most of the common law exclusionary rules of evidence. The Federal Rules of Evidence apply to all judicial proceedings in our federal courts. Many states have adopted similar codifications following the federal rules to keep laws and procedures uniform.

Categories of Evidence

Evidence is anything that tends to prove or disprove a fact. Most evidence is admissible in a trial. There are various kinds of evidence. No one kind is more important than another. The following categories are derived mostly on the basis of the source of the evidence. The categories do not, in themselves, have any legal significance.

Testimony

Testimony is verbal evidence. It may be oral or written in form. By definition, testimony is given under an oath and is subject to cross-examination. A statement that is not made under oath or is not subject to cross-examination is not testimony. It is commonly described as "hearsay." Hearsay may be received into evidence for some purposes, but a hearsay statement is not testimony. A witness's oath serves several purposes. It adds to the solemnity of the proceedings. It makes clear that the witness is not merely having a conversation with the jury. It emphasizes the court's commitment to the truth and the witness's legal duty to tell the whole truth. A witness who makes a false statement under an oath is subject to criminal prosecution for perjury, which is a felony. If a judge believes that a witness has testified falsely, the judge may ask the prosecuting attorney to investigate and bring charges against the witness.

A witness must be mentally competent to testify. A witness must not be under the influence of intoxicants or drugs when in court. But a witness who was intoxicated at the time of an occurrence may, nevertheless, testify concerning his or her observations about the occurrence or transaction. The witness's state of intoxication goes to the witness's credibility[3] but not to the admissibility of the witness's testimony. Even a child of tender years may testify to facts that she or he observed if the court is satisfied that the child appreciates the duty to tell the truth, had an opportunity to make a reasonably reliable observation, and comprehended the facts. A witness must have a **foundation** for her or his testimony. Foundation is merely preliminary evidence that shows the witness had an opportunity to observe the facts and now has an adequate memory to make the testimony reasonably reliable.

foundation A body of evidence that tends to establish either that a witness is competent to testify on a certain matter or that other evidence is relevant, thus making the testimony or evidence potentially admissible and usable in the case.

To illustrate foundation, when an automobile accident case reaches trial the skid marks are no longer available for the jury to inspect. But the skid marks' existence, point of beginning, and length may be established through photographs, police records, someone's memory of their measurement, or someone's memory of their estimated length. Note that each form of evidence mentioned is weaker than the one before it. Nevertheless, if a proper foundation[4] is laid for the evidence, the court would allow the jury to consider any form. The photographer could lay foundation by testifying that he or she saw the skid marks and the photographs accurately depict them. A foundation for the police officer's record is that he observed the skid marks and recorded his observations. A witness provides foundation by testifying that he or she saw the skid marks and remembers them. The witness may then testify from memory. A jury must *weigh*, or evaluate, the evidence in the context of all the evidence. The foundation usually takes only a couple brief questions.

The examination of a witness takes either of two forms: **direct examination** or cross-examination.[5] The rules of evidence apply somewhat differently to each form. A direct examination is conducted by the lawyer who calls the witness for her or his side of the case. A direct examination is supposed to be conducted without using **leading questions.** A leading question is one that suggests the answer desired by the interrogator. The testimony is supposed to come from the witness, not from the lawyer. Consequently, leading questions on direct examination are subject to objection. However, leading questions are often used on direct examination to expedite a witness's testimony concerning necessary facts that are not controverted. For example, a lawyer may lead a witness by asking, "You are 25 years of age? You live at 425 Rose Street? You witnessed an accident on January 1, 1995? You are appearing in court today pursuant to a subpoena that my paralegal served upon you?" All the witness has to say is "yes." In effect, the lawyer is testifying even though it is the witness's testimony. The witness has merely adopted the lawyer's words. But the lawyer would not be allowed to ask, "Is it your estimate that the car was traveling at a speed of thirty miles per hour when the collision occurred?" After laying the necessary foundation, the lawyer could ask the witness only to state the car's speed.

A leading question does not make the answer less acceptable as evidence. Consequently, in the absence of an objection, the answer to a leading question will be received into evidence, and the possible objection is waived. Though a leading question does not make the answer **incompetent,** experienced trial lawyers know that leading questions used in a direct examination of a friendly witness tend to overprotect the witness and reduce the authority, effectiveness, and credibility of the witness. If a lawyer leads his or her own witnesses, the presentation lacks persuasiveness. Most students of trial strategy believe that the jury wants to hear the witnesses, not the lawyers.

A cross-examination is the examination of an adverse party, a hostile witness, or a witness who is aligned with the opposing party. A witness is considered to be aligned with an adverse party if she or he is related to that party by blood, marriage, or employment, or has some other close association with the party. Merely disagreeing with a party does not make a witness hostile or one who is aligned with the other side. As a general rule, a lawyer may cross-examine any independent witness who is called to testify by the opposing side. Furthermore, a lawyer may call an adverse party to the stand and cross-examine that party. Similarly, a lawyer may

direct examination The examination a lawyer conducts of the lawyer's own client or client's witness.

leading question A question that suggests the answer the interrogator wants to receive.

incompetent Lacking the capacity, fitness, qualifications, or ability to act.

cross-examine a witness who clearly is aligned with the adverse party even though the lawyer called the witness to the stand.

Unlike direct examination, leading questions are not only proper but necessary on cross-examination. Although witnesses have a tendency to simply agree with answers suggested by an interrogator, the law presumes that an adverse witness or adverse party will not permit herself or himself to be led by the opposing lawyer. Therefore, on cross-examination, leading questions are not subject to an objection. By asking carefully phrased leading questions, a lawyer can effectively circumscribe a hostile witness's responses, because a witness is not allowed to answer more than the question before her or him. There is general agreement that this limitation on witnesses is a good one. It keeps the proceedings from becoming a debate or shouting match. On redirect examination, the witness usually has an opportunity to give any explanation that is really necessary in light of the cross-examination. The redirect examination is the follow-up examination by the lawyer who called the witness to testify.

Witnesses are not allowed to give narrations about what they observed. A witness who is allowed to ramble may speak about matters that are not permitted by the rules of evidence. Therefore, witnesses almost always testify by answering specific questions the lawyers put to them. The lawyer who calls the witness to the stand is first to ask questions. A lawyer's questioning begins by having the witness identifying himself or herself. Then the lawyer asks questions to show the witness is competent to testify. The lawyer is supposed to keep the witness from interjecting statements that are irrelevant, unfairly prejudicial, or otherwise inadmissible. A witness has no responsibility to know what to talk about. The witness is supposed to listen to the question and respond to the particular question, nothing more. The procedure allows for a full development of the witness's testimony and prevents the witness from interposing improper evidence. Lawyers control testimony by selecting appropriate questions. Knowing what questions to ask, when to ask them, and how to ask them is part of the skill in good lawyering.

Facts and Opinions

As a general rule, a witness may testify only to facts that he or she observed through his or her senses. A witness is not allowed to go beyond the facts to explain the witness's impressions or feelings about the facts or tell what the witness considers significant about the facts. Witnesses are not allowed to testify about their impressions of what happened or about their **opinions** of why it happened. By way of example, a witness may be allowed to testify that a car was traveling at fifty-five miles per hour and describe the condition of the highway, weather, and traffic. But the witness would not be allowed to testify that the car was traveling "too fast." "Too fast" is an opinion. The jury must decide what is "too fast" for conditions. Furthermore, a witness is not allowed to testify to the *ultimate question of fact*, that is, who is right and who is wrong. By way of illustration, a witness who observed an automobile shortly before a collision would not be allowed to testify that the driver was "negligent." "Negligence" is the ultimate question of fact for the jury to determine from *all* the evidence. It is the jury's responsibility to draw conclusions from the facts and not be swayed by what the witnesses think the facts prove. However, courts make some very important exceptions to the general rule.

opinion (1) A written statement by an appellate court containing the court's decision and the reasons or analysis by which the court reached its decision. (2) A witness's judgment or appraisal concerning a particular matter.

In everyday situations, people tend to act and react more on the basis of their opinions, judgments, and conclusions than on the basis of facts. Many situations and many conditions simply cannot be described meaningfully by a factual account. For example, an experienced driver observes that an automobile ahead of her has stopped, so she knows she must stop before she reaches the other automobile. Most drivers would be able to bring their automobile to a smooth, complete stop at a reasonable distance behind the other vehicle without knowing the measured distance (number of feet) or the measured braking force. Similarly, a driver stopping in an intersection to make a left-hand turn knows he must yield to oncoming traffic that is close enough to constitute an immediate hazard. A motorist in this situation must make a judgment concerning the oncoming vehicle's distance and speed. These judgments are usually quite reliable even though the motorist could only guess at the number of feet involved. But should a jury make a finding on the basis of what a witness believed? If the driver cannot measure the distance or even estimate the distance, should the driver have to lose the case?

Rule 701 provides that a witness's opinion may be received into evidence when the opinion is based on the witness's personal observation and is "helpful to a clear understanding of the witness' testimony or the determination of a fact in issue." How does a person measure, factually, the slipperiness of a floor or the condition of lighting at dusk, except by expressing an opinion? How can an eyewitness ever know, factually, whether another person is intoxicated or the speed of a passing vehicle? At best, the witness can have an opinion about such facts. The law is a human institution. It was created by people to deal with human problems. It must, therefore, deal with human problems on human terms. When a condition or situation best can be described in the form of an opinion and is meaningful to most people, opinion evidence usually is admissible. So, ordinarily, a witness who has personal knowledge about the condition of a sidewalk is permitted to express an opinion that it was or was not slippery. But first, the witness would have to be able to describe the conditions or circumstances that caused the slipperiness. Lighting conditions may be described in common terms such as pitch-black or fairly dark or fairly light or bright.[6] These terms are probably more meaningful to a jury than would be scientific measurements of light. A lay witness who admits to some "worldliness" usually qualifies to express an opinion as to whether a person she or he observed was or was not intoxicated.

A witness cannot have a valid opinion unless he or she observed the occurrence, condition, person, or *fact* in question. Only after the witness has shown that he or she is capable of observing, did observe, and is able to recall the observations may the witness go on to render an opinion about what he or she observed. In other words, opinion evidence requires a foundation. A witness could not qualify to give an opinion that a sidewalk was slippery because of ice if he or she merely observed it at a distance. A witness would not qualify to give an opinion that another person was intoxicated unless he or she observed signs of intoxication such as slurred speech, unsteady gait, loud and inappropriate conduct, loss of inhibitions, flushed appearance, odor of alcohol, or red eyes. A witness may express an opinion about the speed of a passing vehicle only if he or she observed it long enough and has sufficient experience to form a valid opinion about speed in miles per hour. Exhibit 8.1 presents a comparison of facts and opinions. The typical jury instructions in the example contain guidelines for evaluating testimony.

The following list may be helpful in distinguishing between facts and opinions when dealing with evidence.

Facts	Opinions
Sixty miles per hour	Fast
One mile	Far or close
Ten thousand candle power	Bright
A specific color	Dark or light
No variation	Smooth
Many variations	Rough
Ten inches, feet, yards, meters	A block (as unit of measurement)
Ten inches, feet, yards, meters	Wide or narrow
Ten inches, feet, yards, meters	High, long, close, far
Twenty decibels	Loud or soft
Crying	Sad, depressed, unhappy, hurting
Grimace, muscle spasm	Pain
Able to lift or move 100 pounds	Weak or strong
Sixty watts	Dim or bright
Disfigured	Ugly
In compliance	Sufficient, adequate
Out of compliance	Wrong, mistaken

In the last analysis, rely on your own experience, good judgment, and common sense.

Expert Witness Testimony

expert witness   A person who has special education, training, and experience in a particular subject or field and whose opinions would help the jury to understand the evidence or facts relevant to the case.

Sometimes courts need the help of **expert witness** testimony to explain the significance of the available evidence. For example, a fingerprint may be available to identify a person, but how does the jury know that the fingerprint is being properly interpreted? An expert in fingerprinting can explain it. A blood sample may be available that has an alcohol content, but what is the significance of that amount of alcohol? A toxicologist can explain it to the jury. Sometimes courts need experts to explain the very facts of a case. For example, in a medical malpractice case, the patient may complain that her chiropractor should have taken an x-ray but failed to do so. The patient alleges that, consequently, she had a fracture that went undiagnosed for a year causing her to suffer a lot of pain and expense. How does a jury know whether chiropractic standards required the doctor to x-ray the plaintiff's injury? It does not matter what a layperson thinks, or even what a medical doctor thinks should have been done. The question is what an ordinarily competent chiropractor would have done under the circumstances. Did the defendant chiropractor fail to do what most chiropractors would have done? Only another chiropractor who has the necessary training and experience could testify to the chiropractic standard. The court needs a chiropractic expert to evaluate the facts.

EXAMPLE

You are the sole judges of whether a witness is to be believed and of the weight to be given to her or his testimony. There are no hard and fast rules to guide you in this respect. In determining believability and weight, take into consideration the following:

1. Interest or lack of interest in the outcome of the case
2. Relationship to the parties
3. Ability and opportunity to know, remember, and relate the facts
4. Manner and appearance
5. Age and experience
6. Frankness and sincerity, or lack thereof
7. Reasonableness or unreasonableness of the testimony in light of all the other evidence in the case
8. Any impeachment of the testimony
9. Any other circumstances that bear on believability and weight

A person who has special education, training, and experience in a particular subject may qualify to give expert opinion testimony concerning that subject. There are many kinds of experts, including scientists, accountants, physicians, engineers, and other professionals. But a person does not have to have a degree in higher learning to qualify as an expert witness. An auto mechanic, plumber, carpenter, electrician, or machine operator may qualify as an expert on the basis of training and experience. The author had Billy Martin, a former New York Yankee baseball manager, testify as an expert witness concerning batting a baseball.[7] Typical jury instructions are presented in the accompanying example. They provide guidelines on how to evaluate an expert witness and his or her opinion testimony.

A jury must consider the experts' opinions on the basis of all the other evidence in the case. The reasons each expert gives for her or his opinion is particularly important. A jury could conclude that none of the experts are believable. That has happened. When you are helping to select experts to testify, you should be careful to evaluate the reasons for the experts' opinions.

An expert opinion requires a foundation to establish that the witness has the necessary qualifications and experience about the subject in question to have a reasonably reliable opinion. This is called "laying a foundation" for the expert's opinion. The judge must decide, in each case, whether the foundation is adequate. A judge has broad discretion in deciding whether a witness qualifies as an expert. A person may qualify as an expert in one case and be rejected in another. Competent expert witnesses often reach different conclusions. The fact that experts differ in their opinions is not a concern for the judge. If there is sufficient foundation to show that a witness is an expert and there are facts to support the witness's opinions, the jury must decide the probative value of the opinions.

As parties have continued to employ experts to provide testimony on more and more matters, the federal courts have gotten increasingly vigilant as gatekeepers of allowable evidence. This gatekeeper function has led to many more instances where so-called expert witnesses are not allowed to provide their opinions to the fact finder, usually a jury. The concern that led to this increased vigilance was the practice of presenting so-called "junk science" to juries. In science, as knowledge evolves, we want to encourage researchers to hypothesize the next step and to seek advances in any number of fields. But in the law we are not prepared to impose liability upon someone on the basis of another's unproven theory. Generally speaking, it is this dilemma—science is always ahead of the law—that has led to stricter scrutiny of proposed expert testimony. When the basis for the expert testimony is too uncertain, courts will not allow a jury to be the prognosticators of scientific advancement while deciding the legal rights of parties to a given action.

Professionals are liable for any harm caused by their negligence. A professional is negligent if he or she fails to comply with professional standards. In malpractice actions, *expert witnesses* are allowed to testify whether a party's conduct comported with established applicable standards. The expert must explain what the professional standards are and then is allowed to opine whether the defendant violated those standards. A violation of professional standards is tantamount to negligence. In effect, experts are allowed to testify to the ultimate question of fact; that is, whether the defendant professional was negligent. Rule 704 expressly authorizes such opinion testimony.

Demonstrative Evidence

demonstrative evidence Physical or tangible evidence that can be brought to the courtroom and used to prove a fact or for illustrative purposes to help a witness explain testimony.

Demonstrative evidence *shows* facts, in contrast to verbalizing facts. Any tangible evidence (exhibit) is considered to be demonstrative evidence. Demonstrative evidence may involve the very heart of the controversy, such as the product in a products liability case. For example, an allegedly defective tire may be the subject of the lawsuit. The tire in question is demonstrative evidence that the jury may see and touch. If a similar tire is offered into evidence to make comparisons, it also is an item of demonstrative evidence. Photographs, diagrams, sketches, and models are common types of demonstrative evidence.

Tangible evidence that is directly related to the case is ordinarily received into evidence as exhibits. The jury may take those exhibits with them to their deliberations. Then jurors have the opportunity to examine the exhibits without the lawyers there to point out things or offer explanations. In the preceding example, the defective tire would be an exhibit that the jury could examine during its deliberations. If the jurors found something from the exhibit that the lawyers and witnesses had not noticed or mentioned, the jurors could, nevertheless, consider it. The alleged defective tire is, in itself, evidence that proves facts.

Not all demonstrative evidence (not all exhibits) prove facts. Not all tangible evidence is allowed to go to the jury. Some exhibits are received into evidence and used during the trial solely for *illustrative* purposes. This means that the exhibit, by itself, does not tend to prove any fact relevant to the case, but it helps a witness to explain his or her testimony. Exhibits commonly used for illustrative purposes include photographs taken after the scene of the accident has changed, products that are similar to the one in question but have some differences, and a freehand drawing that is not made to scale. A physician may use a model of the human spine to illustrate an injury to a vertebra or intervertebral disc or another model to show how a nerve injury occurred.

Illustrative exhibits need not be examined by the jury during its deliberations, because they are not evidence of anything. Indeed, they might actually mislead jurors who might come to think of them as evidence of a fact. In some cases, though, some judges allow illustrative exhibits to be used by the jury in its deliberations. For example, a photograph taken well after the scene of the accident has changed may show a particular feature of the scene that is relevant to the case, although other matters shown in the photograph may not pertain to the accident. The photograph would be received and not limited to an illustrative role. However, the jury would be instructed and cautioned about its limited application.

An engineer's scale drawings may be very helpful at trial to show sizes, relationships, and even functions. Often, one witness's drawings are used by several different witnesses to illustrate each witness's observations. The jury could not possibly absorb and remember all the detail shown in the drawings. Consequently, more often than not, such drawings become evidence that goes to the jury for consideration during deliberations.

Suppose a large machine has been made the subject of a lawsuit. It is much too large to bring into the courtroom. The plaintiff claims that the machine is defective in design because it is top-heavy and dangerously unstable. Photographs that fairly depict the machine are evidence of what the machine looks like. A motion picture or videotape could be used to show its operation. A model of the machine may show physical characteristics, including the alleged built-in instability. All these items could be received into evidence as exhibits. They are the best evidence because the machine is not available. The jurors could examine the photographs and model during their deliberations.

Forms of demonstrative evidence that are encouraged by courts as time-savers are summaries, charts, and graphs for the purpose of reducing voluminous documents down to the essentials (Rule 1006). The preparation of such summaries requires a thorough knowledge of the subject and the purpose of the evidence. Paralegals are often asked to prepare such documents.

Demonstrative evidence has the obvious value of psychological impact. Jurors are more likely to understand and remember evidence that can be seen and heard. Jurors are more likely to grasp a party's theory of the facts when demonstrative evidence is used. Lawyers are always looking for new and better ways of using demonstrative evidence. Paralegals who have a good appreciation for the role of evidence and who understand the client's case can be very helpful in locating and preparing demonstrative evidence. Do not hesitate to make suggestions for presenting evidence.

Photographs may show the material facts, such as a victim in pain and bleeding at an accident scene. A motion picture of an airplane crashing would be graphic evidence. However, such photographs also tend to incite passion and prejudice in juries. When that kind of demonstrative evidence is offered, the judge must decide whether the exhibit's probative value outweighs its prejudicial effect. If the prejudicial effect of the evidence outweighs its probative value, the evidence should be kept from the jury's view and consideration. Obviously, the trial judge must have broad discretion in ruling on such issues.

Direct and Circumstantial Evidence

A fact may be proved by **direct evidence** or **circumstantial evidence** or both. The law does not prefer one form over the other. Direct evidence is testimony from witnesses who observed the facts to which they testify. Direct evidence also includes exhibits that, in themselves, establish facts. A witness's testimony that she saw certain automobile skid marks is direct evidence proving the existence of the skid marks. A photograph showing skid marks is direct evidence proving the existence of the skid marks.

Circumstantial evidence is indirect proof that requires logic and deductive reasoning. Where one or more facts are established through direct evidence, it is permissible to infer, from them, the existence of other facts. For example, by proving through direct evidence the existence of skid marks, a party thereby proves, through circumstantial evidence the location of the vehicle when the brakes were applied and the course of the skidding vehicle as it approached the point of impact. Further, the skid marks tend to prove that the driver observed the danger at some point before she or he applied the brakes. Or suppose a construction worker spent two weeks working near an electric power line and then sustained an electrical burn by contacting the wire. The circumstantial evidence permits an inference that he or she knew the wire was there and considered it to be dangerous, because he or she successfully avoided it for two weeks. The inference is permissible and valid, even though the construction worker denies awareness of the power line. Circumstantial evidence is really a matter of using common sense.

Substantive Evidence

Substantive evidence is any evidence the jury is allowed to consider that is capable of supporting a verdict. It is separate and apart from **impeachment evidence** and **illustrative evidence.**

Impeachment Evidence

Impeachment evidence is received by a court for the purpose of testing the credibility of a witness. It is evidence that the witness has said something or written something or conducted herself or himself in a manner inconsistent with what the witness testified to in court. For example, if a witness testified that he observed the defendant enter the intersection without stopping for a red light, he would be impeached

---

direct evidence Testimony about a fact by an eyewitness who observed the fact, or an exhibit that tends to prove the existence or nonexistence of the fact.

circumstantial evidence Indirect proof that depends on the application of logic and common experience to infer the existence of a fact; evidence offered to prove one or more facts from which the existence of other material facts can then reasonably be inferred.

substantive evidence Evidence that will support a judgment that determines the parties' rights and obligations.

impeachment evidence Evidence offered solely to cast doubt on other evidence received by the court and that will not, in itself, support a verdict.

illustrative evidence Evidence that does not, in itself, have probative value, but that helps a witness to explain her or his testimony.

by the testimony of another witness who heard him say that he did not notice the color of the traffic light at the time of the accident or that the plaintiff was the one who went through the red light. The second witness's testimony is not substantive evidence, but merely impeachment evidence, because the first witness's out-of-court statement was not sworn testimony subject to cross-examination. The second witness's testimony is sworn testimony subject to cross-examination, but not as to the truth of the first witness's observations—only about what the first witness said. If the jury chooses to believe the sworn testimony of the first witness, it could determine that the defendant did violate the traffic light. But if the jury believes the second witness, the jury is left with no substantive evidence from these two witnesses about the color of the traffic light. Only the first witness claimed to see the color of the light, and he cannot be believed, so these two witnesses have provided no evidence on the point.

A prior inconsistent statement by a *party* may be received into evidence to impeach that party. In addition, a prior inconsistent statement by the *party* is evidence that a jury may use as substantive evidence. For example, if a witness heard the plaintiff admit that he went through a stop sign, but the plaintiff testifies at trial that he stopped for the sign, the party's admission would be received as impeachment and as substantive evidence. As substantive evidence it tends to prove the fact that the plaintiff did go through the stop sign.

Hypothetical Questions

An expert witness's opinion must be based on facts that he or she has observed or on facts that have been proved through other witnesses and exhibits. "Proved," in this sense, does not mean that the jury necessarily accepted those facts; it means that the facts are supported by evidence that the jury has heard so that the jury *could* determine that the facts exist. Because an expert witness usually does not have personal knowledge about the occurrence and many other important facts, the question arises, how can he or she qualify to render an opinion based on those facts? The answer is through the device of the **hypothetical question.**

A hypothetical question permits the expert to assume the facts are true, just as though the expert had personally observed the facts. The lawyer relies heavily on the jury to agree with those facts from the other evidence. Sometimes, hypothetical questions are very long and involve many exhibits. The longer the hypothetical question, the greater the risk that it might fail—either because it is technically defective, not entirely supported by the evidence, or because it lacks persuasiveness. The jury is instructed at the end of the trial that the expert's opinion assumes and depends on the truth of all the facts contained in the hypothetical question, and if the jury should determine that any one or more of the assumed facts is not true or not established, the expert's opinion based on the hypothetical question should be rejected. The cross-examination of an expert whose opinion is based on a hypothetical question is often designed to show that the hypothetical question is incomplete, or that with the addition of other facts, the expert's opinions would have to be different. A cross-examination also may try to show that the expert is assuming each fact in the hypothetical question to be true, and the cross-examiner may be able to show later that one or more of those assumed facts were false. Sometimes, the cross-examiner is able to show

hypothetical question   A question put to a witness that asks the witness to assume specified facts and render an opinion on the basis of those assumed facts.

that the hypothetical question contains facts that are contrary to the expert's own records or inconsistent with calculations or observations the expert has made. To some extent, the cross-examiner is also permitted to test the expert with additional hypothetical questions.

Hypothetical questions are almost always reduced to writing and previewed with the expert before she or he takes the stand. An experienced paralegal may help prepare hypothetical questions. Each lawyer develops her or his own form and approach. Usually, the shorter the hypothetical question is, the more reliable and effective it is.

Court Exhibits

To use any tangible item as evidence, a lawyer must lay a foundation for it. The foundation establishes what the exhibit is before it is used to prove a fact. A witness must identify the item, describe it, and a court reporter must give it an exhibit number or letter. Then the witness must show that the exhibit is relevant to the case. At that point the lawyer may *offer* the exhibit into evidence. The following dialogue is representative of the necessary foundation. In this scenario, the lawyer is questioning a personnel manager of a company to lay foundation for personnel records. The lawyer has had the exhibit marked by the court reporter for identification.

> **Q:** I am now showing you what has been marked as plaintiff's exhibit A. Can you identify that for us?
>
> **A:** Yes, that is Mr. Albin Moyers's personnel file with the XYZ Corporation.
>
> **Q:** Who has custody of these records?
>
> **A:** As personnel manager of the XYZ Corporation, I have custody of these records.
>
> **Q:** How long have you been the personnel manager?
>
> **A:** For the past ten years.
>
> **Q:** Did you bring these records with you to court pursuant to a subpoena served upon you yesterday?
>
> **A:** Yes.
>
> **Q:** Have you brought with you all of Mr. Moyers's personnel records that are kept in your custody and control?
>
> **A:** Yes.
>
> **Q:** Are these records kept in the ordinary course of the business of the XYZ Corporation?
>
> **A:** They are.
>
> **Counsel to the court:** Plaintiff offers plaintiff's exhibit A into evidence.
>
> **Court to defendant's counsel:** Is there any objection to the exhibit?

If the relevancy of the records is not apparent, it must be shown by indicating how the documents tend to prove controverted facts. When a party offers a record into evidence, he or she must have the entire record available so that any portions omitted from the offer can be examined, and perhaps offered, by the cross-examiner. Otherwise, facts might be taken out of context. Once the original records are made available for examination, the parties commonly stipulate that photocopies may be received into evidence in lieu of the originals. The originals are then returned to their custodian.

In the following scenario, the plaintiff's lawyer is questioning the plaintiff to lay a foundation for a photograph the plaintiff took of his automobile after an accident.

Q: I am now showing you a photograph marked as plaintiff's exhibit A. Can you identify it for us?

A: Yes, it is a photograph that I took of my automobile.

Q: When was the photograph taken?

A: On June 7, 2006.

Q: Where was it taken?

A: At the Anderson Chevrolet garage.

Q: What portion of your vehicle is depicted in the photograph?

A: The rear portion of my automobile.

Q: Does the picture fairly show the condition of your automobile as it appeared after the accident?

A: Yes.

Q: Is the damage that appears in the photograph entirely a result of the automobile accident on June 4, 2006?

A: No.

Q: What damage is shown in the photograph that, to your knowledge, did not occur in the accident?

A: The photograph shows the rear bumper pulled back on the right side. That happened at the garage—maybe when the car was towed in.

Q: Otherwise, does the photograph fairly show and represent the damage that the rear portion of the car sustained in the accident?

A: Yes.

Counsel to the court: Plaintiff offers plaintiff's exhibit A into evidence.

Court to defendant's counsel: Is there any objection?

At this point, the defendant's lawyer is allowed to ask questions only about the foundation for the exhibit, that is, questions concerning the admissibility of the exhibit. Any questions about its probative value will have to wait until the plaintiff's lawyer has finished direct examination.

When a photograph is offered into evidence, it is desirable to have the photographer available to explain the method of making the photograph as well as its subject matter. It is well-known that the type of lens used in a camera can significantly change the subject matter's appearance, especially its depth and apparent width. Distances between two points can be made to look quite different depending on the type of lens used. However, it is often sufficient, for purposes of laying foundation, to have a witness or party to the suit who is acquainted with the subject matter testify that the photograph accurately portrays the subject. Note that the photograph does not establish itself. It is just an extension of the testimony of the witness. The extent of the foundation that is required depends on the purposes for which the photograph is offered and whether it is actually disputed. As often as not, both sides want the photograph in evidence.

Judicial Notice

judicial notice A rule of evidence by which a court may recognize a fact that is capable of being known or determined to a certainty by consulting indisputable sources.

A trial judge may take **judicial notice** of certain facts, and those facts are binding on the parties and the jury. As stated in Rule 201(b)

> A judicially noticed fact must be one not subject to reasonable dispute in that it is either (1) generally known within the territorial jurisdiction of the trial court or (2) capable of accurate and ready determination by resorting to sources whose accuracy cannot reasonably be questioned.

For example, a judge may determine that December 25, 1999, fell on a Saturday or that a mile contains 5,280 feet. When the judge takes judicial notice of a fact, the parties do not have to present evidence to establish the fact. The judge simply tells the jury that it is an established fact that they must accept as true.

Suppose the plaintiff brought a negligence action for damage to certain property, and it becomes material to the case whether the accident occurred within the corporate limits of a municipality. If the precise location of the accident is not in controversy, the trial judge could take judicial notice of whether the conduct occurred inside or outside the corporate limits. However, any controversy over the location of the accident would have to be resolved by the jury from the evidence.

A court may take judicial notice of scientific facts. Examples might be that an object traveling at sixty miles per hour moves eighty-eight feet per second, water boils at 212 degrees Fahrenheit, or Los Angeles is in the Pacific time zone. By statute, in some states, a trial judge is authorized to take judicial notice of a person's normal life expectancy as established by approved actuarial tables. According to Rule 201, the court may take judicial notice of such facts whether or not the parties ask it to do so. In civil litigation, judicially noticed facts are to be accepted by the jury as conclusive. The judge may conduct a hearing in the absence of the jury to determine whether the fact in question is true and whether to take judicial notice of it.

Summaries

A civil action may involve thousands of records and documents essential to the parties' claims and defenses. More often than not, the parties do not have any real dispute about the contents, but differ on the application of the documents and conclusions to be drawn from them. The Rules of Civil Procedure provide the means for a party to obtain, review, and copy relevant documents. Evidence Rule 1006 authorizes a party to prepare summaries that reflect the contents of records and use summaries at trial. A summary may be received into evidence as an exhibit, but the originals must be available for comparison. The rule encourages parties to review all of the supporting documentation before the trial so as to reduce the amount of time needed for presentation of the summaries. The Rule provides

> The contents of voluminous writings, recordings, or photographs which cannot conveniently be examined in court may be presented in the form of a chart, summary, or calculation. The originals, or duplicates, shall be made available for examination or copying, or both, by other parties at a reasonable time and place. The court may order that they be produced in court.

Summaries that are prepared for use as provided in Rule 1006 are not part of a lawyer's work product. They are discoverable and should be disclosed to all other parties to avoid unnecessary delay at trial. The original documents must be available for inspection and comparison. Paralegals may prepare Rule 1006 summaries for use at trial.

Presumptions

Some facts can be established at trial by presumptions in law. For example, in cases involving a person's death, the law presumes the decedent did not commit suicide. In cases where the plaintiff delivers personal property to the defendant's custody and it is returned in a damaged condition, the law presumes that the damage was caused by negligence on the part of the defendant. Where a person has been missing for more than seven years, the law presumes the person to be dead.

Suppose the plaintiff must prove that a written notice of cancellation of a contract was delivered to the defendant. The plaintiff may prove delivery by showing the notice was sent to the defendant by United States mail. The plaintiff must offer evidence to show that the notice was put in an envelope that was properly addressed, that had the proper postage, and was deposited in a United States mailbox or delivered to a post office. By proving those facts and that the envelope was not returned to the plaintiff a presumption in law arises that the letter was delivered to the defendant addressee. This is true even though the defendant denies receiving the letter. The underlying facts concerning addressing and mailing the notice must be established by a witness who has personal knowledge, or through business records. A post office receipt is not necessary but is helpful. The jury must decide whether the presumption of delivery is more convincing or less convincing than the defendant's sworn denial. The presumption exists because of the necessity of such proof and the strong likelihood that it is true.

As described by Rule 301

> In all civil actions and proceedings not otherwise provided for by statute or by these rules, a presumption imposes on the party against whom it is directed the burden of going forward with evidence to rebut or meet the presumption, but does not shift to such party the burden of proof in the sense of the risk of nonpersuasion, which remains throughout the trial upon the party on whom it was originally cast.

Presumptions, unlike judicially noticed facts, are not binding on the parties and the jury. A jury may find for or against a presumed fact. There are many other presumptions in law. Some have been created by the courts as part of the common law; others have been created by statute.

Res Ipsa Loquitur

In a negligence action, the plaintiff must prove that the defendant was negligent. Ordinarily, the plaintiff does this with evidence that shows how the accident occurred. But when the instrumentality that caused the accident was under the exclusive control of the defendant at the time of the accident, there may not be any evidence available to the plaintiff to show how or why the accident occurred. The plaintiff's

res ipsa loquitur A legal doctrine by which one party may establish an inference of negligence on the part of another party.

problem of proving negligence in such cases has been given special treatment by the courts under the **res ipsa loquitur** doctrine. The Latin phrase means that the accident speaks for itself of negligence. The doctrine has its origin and justification in the probability that the accident was caused solely by the defendant's negligence, and the evidence concerning the occurrence is more readily available to the defendant, so the defendant should come forward with an explanation. In most states, the doctrine does not shift the burden of proof. The permissible inference, however, is sufficient in itself to carry the burden of proof even if the defendant has an explanation that exonerates him or her from fault.

Res ipsa loquitur is an evidentiary doctrine. The doctrine applies only to actions based on negligence. The doctrine's requisites are as follows:

1. The accident is of the type that does not ordinarily occur in the absence of negligence.
2. The defendant was in exclusive control of the instrumentality that caused the injury or property damage claimed.
3. The accident did not result from any voluntary act or negligence on the part of the plaintiff or some third person for whom the defendant would not be responsible.

The doctrine is designed to "level the playing field" by allowing the defendant, who had control of the instrumentality and the opportunity to explain why the defendant was not negligent. Although the doctrine allows a permissible inference that the defendant was negligent, the burden of proof remains on the plaintiff to convince the jury that the defendant was negligent. In other words, the jury must weigh the inference of negligence against the defendant's explanation. For example, if a passenger train derails and crashes, the inference is that railroad employees were negligent because trains do not ordinarily leave the tracks in the absence of negligence. The railroad has the right to try to explain why it denies it was negligent.

The doctrine has applicability where a restaurant customer is injured by a foreign object in her food, a commercial airliner crashes for no apparent reason, a passenger on a railroad train is injured when the train derails or crashes into another train operated by the same railroad, a patient undergoes surgery and sustains injury to a non-involved part of his or her body during the operation, an automobile inadvertently leaves the highway and crashes, an elevator falls, city gas escapes from utility pipes, electricity escapes from an appliance under the defendant's control, a dentist's drill slips and causes injury to the patient's mouth, a surgeon leaves a surgical instrument or sponge in the patient, and so forth.

Credibility and Persuasiveness

Certain evidence that supports the client's claim may be admissible, but should it be presented? Suppose that the plaintiff's lawyer needs to prove that the defendant went through a stop light and caused the parties' intersection collision. Suppose four people witnessed the occurrence. The most emphatic witness happens to be the plaintiff's best friend, who was riding in the plaintiff's car and who also has a claim against the defendant. The police determined at the accident scene that this witness was intoxicated. A second witness was a pedestrian who was not looking at the traffic lights when the collision occurred but did see that the light was red for the defendant immediately after the accident. He does not know any of the parties but is easily confused and has difficulty expressing himself. A third witness was driving another automobile that was approaching the intersection from the direction opposite that of the defendant. This witness does not specifically remember the color of the light at the time the vehicles entered the intersection or when they collided, but she recalls that she was intending to stop. The fourth witness is the defendant. He was charged with a traffic violation but pled not guilty to the charge in traffic court. The problem is, What witnesses should the plaintiff's lawyer have testify at trial? Who will the jury believe? Will the witnesses present conflicting versions? Will the witness enlighten or confuse the jury?

A lawyer must decide how much time and money should be spent to gather and present the evidence. Should the client have the benefit of one expert witness, or three? If the case involves a machine, should the trial lawyer ask an operator, an engineer, the vendor, or the manufacturer to explain its design and operation? Should a matter be illustrated on a blackboard or with an engineer's scale drawing or by photographs or by a simple model or by a working model or by all five? Should the "thing in question" be brought to the courtroom? Should the defendant be asked to try on the glove? The choice comes down to a judgment call based on several factors, especially time, expense, admissibility, persuasiveness, and risk. Besides technical considerations, a lawyer must be concerned with the likely effect the presentation will have on the judge and jury. Will too much evidence bore the jury? Will the jury feel that the evidence is trustworthy and, therefore, the party who presented it is trustworthy? What is the best order for presenting the evidence? Can a weak witness be "sandwiched" between two strong witnesses? The evidence should be presented so that it is understandable, interesting, and appealing. A lawyer must make many judgment calls concerning what evidence to use, when to use it, and how to use it.

Exclusionary Rules of Evidence

The Federal Rules of Evidence are designed to promote justice, economy, and the expeditious determination of lawsuits (Rule 102). Unless the parties' relevant evidence violates an exclusionary rule, it is admissible at trial. A party must make a timely objection to evidence when it is offered to keep a jury from hearing it and using it. Sometimes objections are made before the evidence is offered.[8] If a party fails to make a timely objection, he or she waives the right to complain that the jury should not have heard the evidence. Lawyers interpose objections simply by stating "objection" and the grounds. For example, a lawyer might say: "Objection, on the grounds of hearsay." If the objection is sustained, the evidence is not received. If the objection is overruled, the evidence is received. Only if a lawyer duly objects to evidence that should not be part of the case, may its admission be used as grounds for seeking a new trial or reversal. Of course, there is an exception. If the error is manifest and extremely likely to have brought about an unjust result, an appellate court may take notice of the "plain error" and grant relief even though the lawyer failed to object. This rule provides an "escape hatch" to correct grievous wrongs, but it is rarely available.

The exclusionary rules are premised on logic, practicality, and human experience, but they cannot be applied with mathematical precision. Trial judges have a great deal of discretion in determining whether to receive evidence. An appellate court will not reverse a trial judge's rulings on evidence where the judge has acted within her or his discretion. The tendency of trial courts is to receive evidence even if there is some doubt about admissibility.

offer of proof A procedure that may be used at trial to put in the record evidence that the trial judge disallowed. The offer of proof may be made by having the witness testify, out of the hearing of the jury, about the matters excluded by the judge's ruling.

If a lawyer believes that a trial court has erroneously excluded evidence, the lawyer has a right to make an offer or proof outside the hearing of the jury as to what the evidence is and what it would prove. An **offer of proof** is nothing more than testimony of a witness or a statement by the lawyer that shows an appellate court the facts that would have been established if the evidence had been allowed. An appellate court may consider the offer of proof in deciding whether the evidence was improperly disallowed and the importance of it [Rule 102(a)(2)].

Objections to evidence are supposed to be stated concisely without argument. An objection could be phrased, "The question is objected to on the grounds of hearsay." But an objection that is phrased as an argument is improper. For example, it would be improper for a lawyer to state, "The question is objected to because this witness doesn't have any personal knowledge about the subject matter and is only relying on some highly questionable statement she heard or read." The opposing lawyer would object to the objection. The trial judge might caution the lawyer. Lawyers are not supposed to argue the value, weight, or effect of the evidence until the final arguments [Rule 103(c)]. They may seek leave of the court to argue objections outside the hearing of the jury.

Materiality

The evidence must relate to facts that are material to the case as framed by the pleadings. Evidence is material if it tends to prove a fact concerning the parties' claims or defenses as pled. Evidence is immaterial if it does not relate to the parties claims or defenses. When a party attempts to inject evidence that does not relate to the issues as pled, the opposing lawyer should object on the grounds of materiality: "Objection, immaterial." If the opponent fails to object, the evidence will be received and the pleadings are deemed to be amended to conform to the evidence [Rule 15(b)]. A judge may exclude immaterial evidence on his or her own motion to keep the parties from digressing and to avoid abuses of the court's time. In recent years, courts and attorneys have blurred the distinction between materiality and relevancy. Technically, relevancy has to do with the probative value of evidence.

Relevancy

relevant evidence Evidence that tends to establish or negate a controverted fact (see Rule 401).

Evidence must be probative to be admissible; that is, the evidence must tend to prove or disprove a material fact. Rule 401 defines **relevant evidence** as "evidence having any tendency to make the existence of any fact that is of consequence to the determination of the action more probable or less probable than it would be without the evidence." If the evidence does not tend to prove or disprove a material fact, the evidence is subject to exclusion on the grounds that it is irrelevant: "Objection, irrelevant." Relevance is determined by such factors as time, distance, and the degree of the connection between the evidence and the fact to be proved. For example, if a witness observed a motor vehicle traveling ten miles per hour over the speed limit, but this occurred five miles from the accident scene, the question arises whether this evidence tends to prove excessive speed at the time of the accident? The answer is not always easy. If the observation was made on a freeway, so the driver had no occasion to change speeds during the five miles, maybe the evidence would be relevant. But if the driver had several stops during the five miles or had to contend with heavy traffic during the five miles, the prior excessive speed is probably irrelevant.

Consider whether evidence of a party's *past* bad driving record would be relevant to prove whether he negligently caused a recent accident. Most courts would hold that the past driving record is too remote and too weak to prove how or why an accident occurred. It does not prove what the driver did at any particular time. Nevertheless, the opposing party would love to get the past bad driving record into evidence and argue from it. For example, the law presumes that parties involved in an accident were sober. A claim of intoxication must be proved. Evidence that proves the defendant motorist is an habitual drunkard and that he was drunk on the day preceding the accident would not tend to prove he was drunk at the time of the accident. The evidence is too remote in time. However, if other competent evidence tended to prove that the defendant was drunk at the time of the accident, and the defendant controverted that evidence, perhaps the judge could be persuaded to rule that the defendant's habit of drinking and recent intoxication would be relevant (Rule 406—Habit; Routine Practice).

Proof that the defendant was found liable on other contracts, which she or he contested, does not tend to prove she or he is liable on the one in question. Evidence that the defendant was involved in a similar accident at the same place three years earlier does not tend to prove how or why the accident in question occurred. However, where the alleged cause of the accident, such as a defective step, has caused other accidents, proof of the prior accidents is relevant to prove that a condition was dangerous, known to the defendant, and could cause an accident of the type in question. Courts usually distinguish between animate and inanimate causes of accidents when determining relevancy of past accidents.

The absence of prior accidents may be relevant. Suppose a visitor in an apartment building falls on a stairway used by all the tenants. Suppose the visitor contends that the accident was because of inadequate lighting. The landlord would be allowed to present evidence that the stairway was frequently used; the lights in use at the time of the accident had been in use for ten years; and no one else ever reported a fall because of insufficient lighting.

Remember, evidence is *immaterial* if it goes to prove a fact that is not related to the case. The evidence is *irrelevant* if it is too weak to have probative value even though it relates to a material fact.

Best Evidence

Courts require parties to present the best evidence reasonably available. This means that a copy of a document should not be used if the original document is reasonably available (Rule 1002—Requirement of Original). A copy is subject to the objection that it is not the best evidence: "Objection, not the best evidence." If the absence of the original can be explained, then a copy is the best evidence and may be used. For example, if it can be shown that the opponent was the last person to have custody of the original or that the original is needed elsewhere, a copy may be used. Parties may stipulate to the use of copies, and that is often done in cases involving hospital, medical, and business records.

Parol Evidence

The so-called **parol evidence** rule precludes any evidence that is offered to vary or contradict the language of a written contract: "Objection, parol evidence." The rule applies to all contracts in which the parties have formalized their agreement in writing. When the parties reduce their agreement to a writing that is intended to be complete, it would be unfair to have either party change the terms by oral testimony or by some prior writing. The parol evidence rule gives real significance to the writing. Most people do accord special importance to any agreement that has been put into writing.

One exception to the parol evidence rule is that extrinsic evidence[9] may be received to clarify ambiguities in a writing. But a judge must first determine that the writing is ambiguous. A provision is ambiguous if it is reasonably subject to more than one meaning. Also, parol evidence may be used to prove that the opposing party induced or procured the writing by fraud. Parol evidence may be used to establish a subsequent change in the contract mutually agreed to by the parties. To avoid this exception, most written agreements expressly provide that any modification must be in writing and signed by all parties.

Parol evidence may also be used to prove that a written contract contains a mistake that both parties made. If a mutual mistake is proven, the contract may be reformed or rescinded.

Dead Man Statute

Some states have the so-called dead man statute, which provides that a party to a lawsuit may not testify concerning any oral statement she or he heard another person make if, at the time of trial, the person who made the utterance is deceased: "Objection, violates the Deadman's statute." The statute is intended to reduce the possibility that parties may fabricate evidence. If a party fails to object to such testimony when it is presented, the evidence will be received, and a verdict may be based on it. Note that the exclusionary rule applies only to prevent *parties* from testifying. It does not prevent independent witnesses from testifying about oral statements made by persons who died before trial. The dead man statute has no application to writings; it applies only to oral statements. The Federal Rules of Evidence do not have a rule similar to the dead man statute.

Settlement Negotiations

Some evidence is excluded because it would be contrary to public policy to allow its use at trial. A primary example is evidence of a party's statements made in the course of settlement negotiations (Rule 408—Compromise and Offers to Compromise): "Objection, privileged matters." Settlement negotiations are favored. Courts want parties to discuss their differences and settle their controversies whenever possible. If parties had to be concerned that their efforts to compromise would be used against them, negotiations would be sharply curtailed, if not impossible. Therefore, a jury is never told about the parties' settlement negotiations. The danger is much too great that a jury would infer that an offer to compromise is evidence of weakness.

Rule 409 specifically provides that a party's offer to pay another's medical expenses may not be used against the offeror as an admission of liability for the accident in question. A typical situation is where a person falls down on premises where he or she is visiting. The owner of the premises may suggest, even urge, the guest to have a medical checkup for which the owner will pay. The offer cannot be used against the offeror as an admission of fault or legal responsibility. Evidence of the offer may only be used to prove the offer and to hold the offeror to his or her promise.

Privileged Communications

All states provide in their common law or by statute that certain communications are privileged against disclosure whether oral or written. In particular, the law protects communications between spouses, between a patient and physician, between a client and attorney, and between a parishioner and clergy person. In addition, certain communications with governmental agencies are accorded a privilege status: "Objection, privileged." But a person who owns the privilege may voluntarily waive it. For example, when a patient signs a release/authorization for disclosure of medical records, the patient waives the privilege. Once waived, it is gone. The privilege must be claimed or asserted in a timely manner; otherwise, it is waived. The privilege does not belong to the physician, lawyer, or clergy person. They cannot keep the client from disclosing communications. Each has a professional obligation, however, to protect the client's privilege by not voluntarily disclosing privileged communications.

Remedial Measures

In a case where a plaintiff claims he or she was injured by a defective product or a dangerous premises, the **remedial measures** rule prevents the plaintiffs from using evidence that the defendant made improvements to the product or premises immediately after the accident: "Objection, remedial measures." Such evidence seems to be an admission on the part of the defendant that the product or premises was inadequate and needed the improvement or repairs. However, public policy is better served by encouraging defendants to correct problems without fear that the remedial measures will be used against them. If the courts were to allow evidence of remedial measures, defendants would be discouraged from making changes that may provide greater safety in the future. Furthermore, it is human nature to be extra careful about conditions once an accident has occurred. Remedial measures are often taken not because they are really necessary, but because they seem like an assurance against the accident happening again. Furthermore, a party's standard of care should not be judged on the basis of hindsight. If the product or premises is truly defective, the defect can be proved without resort to an inferred admission of fault—at least, that is the rationale behind the rule. (See Rule 407—Subsequent Remedial Measures.)

If repairs or improvements were made after an accident, the defendant's lawyer usually tells the court about them at the beginning of the trial[10] and asks the court to order the plaintiff's witnesses not to mention the modifications. Evidence of the changes could be so prejudicial as to require a mistrial.

remedial measures A party's activity to correct some danger or problem after an injury or damage has occurred.

Of course, there is an exception to the remedial measures exclusionary rule. If the defendant were to contend that the cost of making the product safe was prohibitive, evidence of subsequent safety improvements is allowed. Proof that the defendant made changes after the accident is very persuasive evidence that the expense was not prohibitive. Evidence of the remedial measures is received, in those cases, to impeach the defendant's claim that the cost was prohibitive. This exception to the remedial measures exclusionary rules does not come into effect unless put into issue by the defendant. The defendant can avoid any evidence of the changes in the product simply by not claiming that the cost of the changes would have been prohibitive before the accident.

Evidence of remedial measures is also allowed when the defendant alleges that it was not feasible to make the product or premises safer. For example, suppose the manufacturer of a drill press claims that it was not feasible to install a guard of the kind the plaintiff's expert says was needed. The plaintiff could present evidence that the defendant modified the product after the accident by installing such a guard. Again, the evidence of remedial measures is received on the basis that it impeaches the defendant's claim that the guard was not feasible.

There is yet another exception to the exclusionary rule. If the defendant contends that he or she did not own or have control over the premises where the plaintiff was injured, evidence that the defendant made subsequent repairs to the property is admissible to prove that the defendant was owner or did have control. The evidence is admissible to prove ownership only if the defendant who made the subsequent repairs denies that he or she was the owner (Rule 407).

Hearsay

hearsay   Evidence proceeding not from the personal knowledge of the witness, but from the mere repetition of what the witness has heard others say.

Hearsay evidence is any out-of-court statement, oral or written, that is offered to prove the truth of matters stated. The rule excluding hearsay is logical and goes to the very heart of the adversary system. Facts should be established through witnesses who have first-hand knowledge about the facts. The opponent should have the opportunity to cross-examine the witness. Juries should have the opportunity to assess the witness's ability to observe and remember the facts. But hearsay evidence does not come from the person who observed the fact. Hearsay evidence comes from a person who heard the observer talk about the fact observed. So the opponent has no opportunity to cross-examine the observer.

The rule against hearsay evidence is simple and fundamentally fair. But there are many important exceptions to the hearsay rule that create difficulties for lawyers and the courts. The exceptions are based on the necessity of having certain evidence and the usual reliability of some kinds of hearsay evidence.

Historically any statement made by an adverse party could be received into evidence against that party as an admission. Admissions were received into evidence as an exception to the hearsay rule. Rule 801(d)(2) provides that such admissions shall be received into evidence on the basis that they are not hearsay. An admission may be made by the party or by the party's agent who had authority to make such statements. The admission by an agent must be made during the agency relationship. Rule 801(d)(1) provides that prior out-of-court statements made by a witness may be received into evidence as substantive evidence, not merely as impeachment, if they were under oath and subject to cross-examination. Such prior statements would have to be part of a deposition or testimony at a hearing or a trial. Again, the rule declares such statements not to be hearsay.

Hearsay Exceptions

Rules 803 and 804 undertake to codify many of the exceptions to the hearsay rule. The hearsay definitions, rules, and exceptions are quoted here for convenient reference.

Definitions

The following definitions apply under this article:

	RULE 801

   (a)   **Statement.** A "statement" is (1) an oral or written assertion or (2) nonverbal conduct of a person, if it is intended by him as an assertion.

   (b)   **Declarant.** A "declarant" is a person who makes a statement.

   (c)   **Hearsay.** "Hearsay" is a statement, other than one made by the defendant while testifying at the trial or hearing, offered into evidence to prove the truth of the matter asserted.

   (d)   **Statements which are not hearsay.**

The Rule defines hearsay to exclude impeachment evidence and party admissions from its application. It provides that a statement is not hearsay if

   (1)   **Prior statement by witness.** The declarant testifies at the trial or hearing and is subject to cross-examination concerning the statement, and the statement is (A) inconsistent with his testimony, and was given under oath subject to the penalty of perjury at a trial, hearing, or other proceeding, or in a deposition, or (B) consistent with his testimony and is offered to rebut an express or implied charge against him of recent fabrication or improper influence or motive, or

   (2)   **Admission by party-witness.** The statement is offered against a party and is (A) his own statement, in either his individual or a representative capacity or, (B) a statement of which he has manifested his adoption or belief in its truth, or (C) a statement by a person authorized by him to make a statement concerning the subject, or (D) a statement by his agent or servant concerning a matter within the scope of his agency or employment, made during the existence of the relationship, or (E) a statement by a co-conspirator of a party during the course and in furtherance of the conspiracy.

Hearsay Exceptions; Availability of Declarant Immaterial

The following are not excluded by the hearsay rule, even though the declarant is available as a witness:

	RULE 803

   (1)   **Present sense impression.** A statement describing or explaining an event or condition made while the declarant was perceiving the event or condition, or immediately thereafter.

   (2)   **Excited utterance.** A statement relating to a startling event or condition made while the declarant was under the stress of excitement caused by the event or condition.

(3) Then existing mental, emotional, or physical condition. A statement of the declarant's then existing state of mind, emotion, sensation, or physical condition (such as intent, plan, motive, design, mental feeling, pain, and bodily health), but not including a statement of memory or belief to prove the fact remembered or believed unless it relates to the execution, revocation, identification, or terms of declarant's will.

(4) Statements for purposes of medical diagnosis or treatment. Statements made for purposes of medical diagnosis or treatment and describing medical history, or past or present symptoms, pain, or sensations, or the inception or general character of the cause or external source thereof insofar as reasonably pertinent to diagnosis or treatment.

(5) Recorded recollection. A memorandum or record concerning a matter about which a witness once had knowledge but now has insufficient recollection to enable him to testify fully and accurately, shown to have been made or adopted by the witness when the matter was fresh in his or her memory and to reflect that knowledge correctly. If admitted, the memorandum or record may be read into evidence but may not itself be received as an exhibit unless offered by an adverse party.

(6) Records of regularly conducted activity. A memorandum, report, record, or data compilation, in any form, of acts, events, conditions, opinions, or diagnoses, made at or near the time by, or from information transmitted by, a person with knowledge, if kept in the course of a regularly conducted business activity, and if it was the regular practice of that business activity to make the memorandum, report, record, or data compilation, all as shown by the testimony of the custodian or other qualified witness, unless the source of information or the method or circumstances of preparation indicate lack of trustworthiness. The term "business" as used in this paragraph includes business, institution, association, profession, occupation, and calling of every kind, whether or not conducted for profit.

(7) Absence of entry in records kept in accordance with the provisions of paragraph (6). Evidence that a matter is not included in the memoranda, reports, records, or data compilations, in any form, kept in accordance with the provisions of paragraph (6), to prove the nonoccurrence or nonexistence of the matter, if the matter was of a kind of which a memorandum, report, record, or data compilation was regularly made and preserved, unless the sources of information or other circumstances indicate lack of trustworthiness.

(8) Public records and reports. Records, reports, statements, or data compilations, in any form, of public offices or agencies, setting forth (A) the activities of the office or agency, or (B) matters observed pursuant to duty imposed by law as to which matters there was a duty to report, excluding, however, in criminal cases matters observed by police officers and other law enforcement personnel, or (C) in civil actions and proceedings and against the government in criminal cases, factual findings resulting from an investigation made pursuant to authority granted by law, unless the sources of information or other circumstances indicate lack of trustworthiness.

(9) Records of vital statistics. Records or data compilations, in any form, of births, fetal deaths, deaths, or marriages, if the report thereof was made to a public office pursuant to requirements of law.

(10) Absence of public record or entry. To prove the absence of a record, report, statement, or data compilation, in any form, or the nonoccurrence or nonexistence of a matter of which a record, report, statement, or data compilation, in any form, was regularly made and preserved by a public office or agency, evidence in the form of a certification in accordance with Rule 902, or testimony, that diligent search failed to disclose the record, report, statement, or data compilation, or entry.

(11) Records of religious organizations. Statements of births, marriages, divorces, deaths, legitimacy, ancestry, relationship by blood or marriage, or other similar facts of personal or family history, contained in a regularly kept record of a religious organization.

(12) Marriage, baptismal, and similar certificates. Statements of fact contained in a certificate that the maker performed a marriage or other ceremony or administered a sacrament, made by a clergyman, public official, or other person authorized by the rules or practices of a religious organization or by law to perform the act certified, and purporting to have been issued at the time of the act or within a reasonable time thereafter.

(13) Family records. Statements of fact concerning personal or family history contained in family Bibles, genealogies, charts, engravings on rings, inscriptions on family portraits, engravings on urns, crypts, or tombstones, or the like.

(14) Records of documents affecting an interest in property. The record of a document purporting to establish or affect an interest in property, as proof of the content of the original recorded document and its execution and delivery by each person by whom it purports to have been executed, if the record is a record of a public office and an applicable statute authorizes the recording of documents of that kind in that office.

(15) Statements in documents affecting an interest in property. A statement contained in a document purporting to establish or affect an interest in property if the matter stated was relevant to the purpose of the document, unless dealings with the property since the document was made have been inconsistent with the truth of the statement or the purport of the document.

(16) Statements in ancient documents. Statements in a document in existence twenty years or more the authenticity of which is established.

(17) Market reports, commercial publications. Market quotations, tabulations, lists, directories, or other published compilations, generally used and relied upon by the public or by persons in particular occupations.

(18) Learned treatises. To the extent called to the attention of an expert witness upon cross-examination or relied upon by him in direct examination, statements contained in published treatises, periodicals, or pamphlets on a subject of history, medicine, or other science or art, established as a reliable authority by the testimony or admission of the witness or by other expert testimony or by judicial notice. If admitted, the statements may be read into evidence but may not be received as exhibits.

(19) Reputation concerning personal or family history. Reputation among members of his family by blood, adoption, or marriage, or among his associates, or in the community, concerning a person's birth, adoption, marriage, divorce, death, legitimacy, relationship by blood, adoption, or marriage, ancestry, or other similar fact of his personal or family history.

(20) Reputation concerning boundaries or general history. Reputation in a community, arising before the controversy, as to boundaries of or customs affecting lands in the community, and reputation as to events of general history important to the community or state or nation in which located.

(21) Reputation as to character. Reputation of a person's character among his associates or in the community.

(22) Judgment of previous conviction. Evidence of a final judgment, entered after a trial or upon a plea of guilty (but not upon a plea of nolo contendere), adjudging a person guilty of crime punishable by death or imprisonment in excess of one year, to prove any fact essential to sustain the judgment, but not including, when offered by the government in a criminal prosecution for purposes other than impeachment, judgments against persons other than the accused. The pendency of an appeal may be shown but does not affect admissibility.

(23) Judgment as to personal family or general history, or boundaries. Judgments as proof of matters of personal, family or general history, or boundaries, essential to the judgment, if the same would be provable by evidence of reputation.

(24) Other exceptions. A statement not specifically covered by any of the foregoing exceptions but having equivalent circumstantial guarantees of trustworthiness, if the court determines that: (A) the statement is offered as evidence of a material fact; (B) the statement is more probative on the point for which it is offered than any other evidence which the proponent can procure through reasonable efforts; and (C) the general purposes of these rules and interests of justice will best be served by admission of the statement into evidence. However, a statement may not be admitted under this exception unless the proponent of it makes known to the adverse party sufficiently in advance of the trial or hearing to provide the adverse party with a fair opportunity to prepare to meet it, his intention to offer the statement and the particulars of it, including the name and address of the declarant.

Hearsay Exceptions: Declarant Unavailable

RULE 804

(a) **Definition of unavailability.** "Unavailability as a witness" includes situations in which the declarant:
   (1) is exempted by ruling of the court on the ground of privilege from testifying concerning the subject matter of his statement; or
   (2) persists in refusing to testify concerning the subject matter of his statement despite an order of the court to do so; or

(3) testifies to a lack of memory of the subject matter of his statement; or

(4) is unable to be present or to testify at the hearing because of death or then existing physical or mental illness or infirmity; or

(5) is absent from the hearing and the proponent of his statement has been unable to procure his attendance (or in the case of a hearsay exception under subdivision (b) (2), (3), or (4), his attendance or testimony) by process or other reasonable means.

A declarant is not unavailable as a witness if his exemption, refusal, claim of lack of memory, inability, or absence is due to the procurement or wrongdoing of the proponent of his statement for the purpose of preventing the witness from attending or testifying.

(b) **Hearsay exceptions.** The following are not excluded by the hearsay rule if the declarant is unavailable as a witness:

(1) **Former testimony.** Testimony given as a witness at another hearing of the same or a different proceeding, or in a deposition taken in compliance with law in the course of the same or another proceeding, if the party against whom the testimony is now offered, or, in a civil action or proceeding, a predecessor in interest, had an opportunity and similar motive to develop the testimony by direct, cross, or redirect examination.

(2) **Statement under belief of impending death.** In a prosecution for homicide or in a civil action or proceeding, a statement made by a declarant while believing that his death was imminent, concerning the cause or circumstances of what he believed to be his impending death.

(3) **Statement against interest.** A statement which was at the time of its making so far contrary to the declarant's pecuniary or proprietary interest, or so far tended to subject him or her to civil or criminal liability, or to render invalid a claim by him or her against another, that a reasonable man in his position would not have made the statement unless he believed it to be true. A statement tending to expose the declarant to criminal liability and offered to exculpate the accused is not admissible unless corroborating circumstances clearly indicate the trustworthiness of the statement.

(4) **Statement of personal or family history.** (A) A statement concerning the declarant's own birth, adoption, marriage, divorce, legitimacy, relationship by blood, adoption, or marriage, ancestry, or other similar fact of personal or family history, even though declarant had no means of acquiring personal knowledge of the matter stated; or (B) a statement concerning the foregoing matters, and death also, of another person, if the declarant was related to the other by blood, adoption, or marriage or was so intimately associated with the other's family as to be likely to have accurate information concerning the matter declared.

(5) **Other exceptions.** A statement not specifically covered by any of the foregoing exceptions but having equivalent circumstantial guarantees of trustworthiness, if the court determines that (A) the statement is offered as evidence of a material fact; (B) the statement is more probative on the point for which it is offered than any other evidence which the proponent can procure through reasonable efforts; (C) the general purposes of these rules and the interests of justice will best be served by admission of the statement into evidence. However, a statement may not be admitted under this exception unless the proponent of it makes known to the adverse party sufficiently in advance of the trial or hearing to provide the adverse party with a fair opportunity to prepare to meet it, his intention to offer the statement and the particulars of it, including the name and address of the declarant.

Evidence of Conduct

As seen, a party's admissions may be received into evidence against him or her even though the out-of-court statement would otherwise be hearsay. But an admission may be made through conduct or silence as well as in a statement. For example, immediately following an automobile accident, one driver might accuse the other of failing to stop for a stop sign. If the person accused of wrongdoing fails to respond and deny the accusation, her or his silence, under some circumstances, may be considered to be an admission that the accusation was true. The test is whether, under the circumstances, one would ordinarily expect a denial if the accusation were false. Perhaps the party was hard of hearing or incapacitated because of injuries—then silence could not be considered to be an admission of fault.

If a party's "admission" is offered into evidence against him or her and came from a written statement, deposition, or oral conversation, the party who made the admission has a right to introduce into evidence the entire conversation or entire statement insofar as it relates to the "admission" in dispute. The Rules of Evidence do not allow parties to take alleged admissions out of context.

TECHNOLOGY NOTES

Some cases involve thousands of documents. Bar codes now provide a means for storing and instantly retrieving the documents for use at trial. Each document is given a bar code. When the document is needed as evidence at trial, the attorney or paralegal scans the code to retrieve the document onto a computer screen. The judge, jury, witness, and attorneys have separate screens on which to view the documents. Bar codes now provide a means for storing and instantly retrieving the documents for use at trial. Each document is given a bar code. When the document is needed as evidence at trial, the attorney or paralegal scans the code to retrieve the document to a computer screen. The judge, jury, witness, and attorneys have separate screens on which to view the documents. This method has proven especially useful for impeachment. When a witness gives testimony at odds with the content of a document or his or her deposition testimony, the attorney or paralegal scans the bar code for the impeaching document. Suddenly juries can actually visualize the inconsistency, sometimes with devastating results for the witness.

SUMMARY

Paralegals should be able to gather evidence, preserve it, prepare it for use at trial, and assist at trial. You need to have a basic understanding of evidence and how it is used at trial.

A lawyer must use professional judgment in deciding what evidence to offer, when to use it, and how to use it. The evidence must be admissible. But also the evidence should be understandable, interesting, and persuasive. Many factors affect the persuasiveness of the evidence, including the relationship of the witness to the parties and motives the witness may have. Witnesses who appear sincere and authoritative are the most persuasive. Lawyers must decide how much time and money to spend preparing and presenting an item of evidence. The presentation of some evidence may adversely affect other items of evidence. A party should strive to present evidence that is wholly consistent. A lawyer may chose to forego evidence he or she believes is not reliable even though the lawyer believes the evidence to be true. Of course, lawyers are forbidden to offer false evidence.

Civil litigation is an adversarial process. Each party has the opportunity and responsibility to make timely objections to evidence the party wants to exclude. When a party fails to object to improper evidence, the evidence probably will be received. If evidence is received, it will be considered by the court and jury and could affect the outcome of the case.

The parties' pleadings identify the parties' legal theories, that is, their claims and defenses. The pleadings frame the legal issues. The legal theories and legal issues determine which facts are material to the case. A fact is *immaterial* if it has no relationship to the parties' claims and defenses. Evidence that is offered to prove an immaterial fact is subject to objection and should not be received. If a party fails to object to immaterial facts, the pleadings are said to be amended to conform to the evidence, an event that may result in a new legal theory.

Evidence that is too remote or too weak to prove a fact for which it is offered is *irrelevant* and subject to objection.

The fact finder (jury) must sort through the evidence and determine what facts the evidence proves. Then the jury must apply the law to those established facts to determine the *ultimate facts* in the case. Every civil action involves at least one ultimate fact. Examples of ultimate questions of fact include a determination that a party was negligent, breached a contract, breached a warranty, trespassed, assumed a risk, was defamed, or was defrauded. A jury may draw inferences from facts established by the evidence, but jurors must not speculate about facts not supported by evidence. The jury must not supply missing evidence by speculation, conjecture, or on the basis of information the jurors obtained outside the trial. Jurors may not, through their own independent investigation, supply additional evidence.

Testimony is a statement, oral or written, made under oath, subject to the right of cross-examination. Lawyers are supposed to keep witnesses from interjecting statements that are irrelevant, unfairly prejudicial, or otherwise inadmissible. The procedure for examining witnesses allows for the full development of a witness's testimony and, at the same time, prevents the witness from injecting improper evidence. A lawyer controls a witness's testimony by carefully crafting questions and limiting the witness's answers to the questions asked. Ordinarily, a witness may only testify to facts that he or she observed or experienced. In other words, testimony is usually limited to the witness's personal knowledge.

Demonstrative evidence is anything that is tangible and is ordinarily received into evidence in the form of an exhibit. An exhibit may be the subject of the dispute, such as the written contract in an action concerning an alleged breach of the contract. An exhibit may be evidence of a fact in issue, such as a photograph of skid marks. An exhibit may be offered for illustrative purposes. An illustrative exhibit is not, in itself, evidence of a fact. Illustrative exhibits are used to help witnesses explain their testimony. An illustrative exhibit is not substantive evidence. For that reason, courts usually do not allow the jury to take illustrative exhibits into their deliberations.

When a layperson cannot possibly describe a set of circumstances on a factual basis, the law allows opinion evidence. For example, a layperson could describe a floor as slippery or not slippery, because the condition cannot be described factually. Experts are allowed to state their opinions to the jury when it appears the opinion evidence will help the jury to understand a material fact or to understand other evidence.

A person who has special education, training, knowledge, or experience in a particular subject or field may qualify to give expert opinion testimony about it. Expert opinion evidence requires a foundation to establish that the witness has the necessary background and is sufficiently knowledgeable about the subject in question to have a reasonably reliable opinion.

A fact may be proved by direct evidence or circumstantial evidence or both. The law does not prefer one form over the other. Direct evidence is testimony by witnesses who observed the facts to which they testify. Circumstantial evidence is indirect proof that depends on principles of logic and common experience and deductive reasoning. By determining that one or more facts are true the fact finder concludes that certain other facts are also true.

Substantive evidence is any evidence the jury is allowed to consider that is capable of supporting a verdict. The form of the evidence makes no difference.

Impeachment evidence is considered only for the purpose of testing the credibility of a witness. It is evidence that a witness has said something or written something or conducted himself or herself in a manner inconsistent with what the witness testified to in court.

A hypothetical question assumes the truth of facts that are supported by evidence and allows an expert to give an opinion based on those assumed facts just as though the expert had personally observed them. The jury is instructed, at the end of the trial, that the expert's opinion assumes and depends on the truth of all the facts contained in the hypothetical question. If the jury determines that any one or more of the assumed facts is not true or not established, the expert's opinion based on the hypothetical question should be rejected. As a general rule, the shorter a hypothetical question is, the more reliable and effective it is. An experienced paralegal may help with the preparation of hypothetical questions.

A judicially noticed fact must be one not subject to reasonable dispute in that it is either (1) generally known within the territorial jurisdiction of the trial court or (2) capable of accurate and ready determination by resorting to sources whose accuracy cannot reasonably be questioned.

Parties may prepare charts and summaries of detailed or lengthy records and offer the summaries into evidence in lieu of the records. The parties should conduct a thorough review of all the relevant documentation before the trial and thereby reduce the amount of time needed for presentation of the essential evidence from the documents. Paralegals may prepare summaries of evidence and charts for use at trial.

Some facts may be established at trial by presumptions in law. Presumptions, unlike judicially noticed facts, are not binding on the parties and jury. A jury may find for or against a presumed fact.

Res ipsa loquitur is a legal doctrine that permits a jury to infer that the defendant was negligent when the evidence shows that (1) the accident is of a type that would not ordinarily occur in the absence of negligence; (2) the defendant was in exclusive control of the instrumentality that caused the injury; and (3) the accident did not result from any voluntary act or negligence on the part of the plaintiff or some third person for whom the defendant would not be responsible. The defendant has the opportunity to explain why he or she denies the negligence. In most states, the doctrine does not shift the burden of proof. The permissible inference, however, is sufficient to carry the burden of proof even if the defendant presents an explanation that exonerates him or her from any fault.

Parol evidence is any evidence that attempts to modify or interpret a written agreement between the parties. Parol evidence may not be used to vary or contradict the clear language of a writing that formalizes the parties' agreement. The rule does not apply unless the writing fully integrates the parties' agreement. Parol evidence is admissible to explain ambiguities in a written agreement.

Courts prefer that the parties present the best evidence that is available concerning any material fact. The best evidence is the evidence that is most directly connected to the fact. For example, the original of a document is better than a photocopy, and a photocopy is better than a person's summary of the document.

A party may not offer evidence about settlement discussions in an effort to show the jury that the opposing party made concessions or admissions. This exclusionary rule is based on the public policy that favors settlement and settlement negotiations.

Communications between spouses, between a patient and physician, between a client and attorney, and between a parishioner and clergy person are privileged. A court cannot require a party to disclose a privileged communication. The professionals are obligated to protect the client's privilege by not voluntarily disclosing privileged communications. A party must claim or assert the privilege in a timely manner; otherwise, it is waived. Once waived, it is gone.

Evidence is subject to objection. In accident cases, the plaintiff is not allowed to use evidence of remedial measures to prove that a condition was dangerous. The remedial measures rule arises from a public policy to encourage people to make their properties and products as safe as possible. However, if the defendant contends that the cost of making the product safe is prohibitive or that modifications were not feasible, evidence of remedial measures is allowed for the purpose of impeaching the defendant's contention. When ownership or control of property is in issue, evidence that the defendant made repairs may be received in evidence to show that the defendant exercised control over the property.

Hearsay evidence is any out-of-court statement, oral or written, that is offered to prove the truth of matters referred to in the out-of-court statement. Hearsay evidence is subject to objection, but there are many exceptions to the exclusionary rule.

KEY TERMS

admissible evidence	incompetent
circumstantial evidence	judicial notice
cross-examination	leading question
demonstrative evidence	material facts
direct evidence	offer of proof
direct examination	opinion
expert witness	parol evidence
fact	relevant
fact finder	relevant evidence
foundation	remedial measures
hearsay	res ipsa loquitur
hypothetical question	substantive evidence
illustrative evidence	ultimate fact
impeachment evidence	

REVIEW QUESTIONS

1. How does a fact differ from a material fact?

2. When is evidence relevant?

3. How does illustrative evidence differ from demonstrative evidence?

4. Why is evidence of a remedial measure inadmissible at trial?

5. Describe an accident that would permit the plaintiff to use the res ipsa loquitur doctrine.

6. May a paralegal prepare an evidence summary for use at trial?

7. Give an example of circumstantial evidence.

8. What circumstances determine whether a person qualifies as an expert witness?

9. When may a witness testify to an ultimate question of fact?

10. When a lawyer attacks a witness's credibility, is the lawyer challenging the ability of the witness to testify? Explain.

CASE ASSIGNMENT

Trustee Raskin will have to prove defendant Harper was negligent and his negligence was a direct cause of the accident. In an intraoffice memorandum, attorney Smith has identified several "apparent facts" on which the Trustee will base her claim that Harper was negligent: (1) Harper was driving at an excessive rate of speed considering the circumstances and conditions; (2) Harper did not warn Nordby that he intended to pass; (3) Harper was attempting to pass at an intersection; (4) Harper failed to keep a proper lookout for potential dangers; (5) Harper did not have control over his pickup. Attorney Smith has asked you to prepare an intraoffice memorandum in which you identify evidence that tends to prove each of the four facts, respectively. For each item of evidence, identify the potential objections that may be raised to keep the evidence from being received at trial.

Hint:

Fact: Harper did not warn Nordby he was about to pass Nordby.

Evidence: Harper did not tell deputy sheriff Smith that he sounded his horn. Harper could not have used his lights to give warning because it was daylight. Presumably, Harper will admit in his deposition that he did not give warning. Passenger Patner can testify that no horn was sounded.

Possible Objections: None.

Endnotes

1. The records would have to be relevant, that is, close enough in time to the event to have probative value.
2. If there is no jury, the presiding judge determines the facts.
3. Lawyers often describe such factors as affecting the "weight" to be given to the testimony.
4. When the jury cannot see the evidence for themselves, court requires a party to show that the evidence is reasonably reliable by having a witness explain the source and its nature.
5. Once in a great while a judge may elect to ask the witness a question, usually for the purpose of clarification.
6. One convenient way of describing lighting conditions is to have the witness say whether there was sufficient light to be able to read a newspaper.
7. The fact issue was whether a batter is necessarily negligent if the bat slips out of the batter's hand and strikes a teammate in the face.
8. A party may make a motion at the beginning of the trial to exclude certain items of the other party's evidence. It is called a motion in limine.
9. Extrinsic evidence is any evidence, oral or written, that is outside the contract as written.
10. This is another example of a motion in limine.

 For additional resources, visit our Web site at www.paralegal.delmar.cengage.com

CONDUCTING AN INVESTIGATION

Chapter Objectives

Chapter 9 explains how an investigation should be planned and conducted, including interviews, obtaining recorded statements, making photographs, and using experts.

Introduction

An investigation is an active, hands-on process. No amount of education or experience can equip an investigator to gather evidence by sitting in the office. Like a news reporter, an investigator must try to be at the right place at the right time. An investigator must pay close attention to the details, because so often, that is where inconsistencies show up, in the client's version as well as the opponent's version. An investigation should be conducted aggressively but not in a disagreeable manner.

Investigation Plan

The client's version of the transaction or occurrence should provide a basis for developing a theory about what happened and how it happened. A fact theory is the predicate for developing an investigation plan. An investigation plan is a kind of road map that helps an investigator prioritize steps in the investigation to focus on the material facts, and avoid duplication and false starts. An investigation plan considers what evidence ought to exist and where it is probably located. The plan may be as simple as preparing a list of things to do and things to find or it may be a detailed schedule and outline. One item of evidence often leads to another, so a plan must be flexible to allow the evidence to build. An investigation usually provides stepping stones for discovery. Lawyers act on the premise that the party who does the best job of collecting, preserving, and presenting the evidence will prevail.

An investigation plan should be developed as soon as possible. It should

1. Identify the material facts—the facts the client needs to prove to prevail.
2. Determine which facts are disputed and which are not.
3. Determine what evidence is needed.
4. Identify the witnesses and other likely sources of evidence.
5. Decide on an order for the steps in the investigation, including an order for contacting witnesses.
6. Decide how best to preserve the evidence you expect to collect, including the types of statements to obtain from witnesses.
7. Coordinate the investigation with discovery procedures.

An investigation is not complete until the investigator knows what happened, how it happened, and has the means for proving the facts in court. If you ask experienced lawyers about their investigation plans, the lawyers would probably reply, "What plan?" Lawyers do not write investigation plans. But if you ask them whether the seven considerations are important or whether they do these things, they would say, "yes." They do them intuitively.

A good investigation builds in a natural progression. For example, suppose you have to investigate an automobile accident. You can obtain information from the client, who was one of the drivers, from one independent eye witness, from a police officer, and from the other driver who is represented by an attorney. The most efficient and effective order is to interview the client driver first. The client should be readily available. You need to know what she claims happened. The client can provide an authorization to obtain a copy of the police report. Go to the police headquarters and order a copy of the report as soon as possible. Do not delay other phases of the investigation while waiting for it. You should inspect the **accident situs.** The "situs" is the place where it occurred—whether or not the circumstances or conditions have changed. Take photographs and make a diagram to reinforce your memory and to use when interviewing the independent witness. Next, interview the police officer. Officers usually are experienced in these matters and are very matter-of-fact. You will be fully prepared to ask the right questions because you have the report and have inspected the situs. Now you are in a position to interview the independent witness. The witness is probably at work or home. Usually, there is no need to make an appointment. The independent witness is not likely to be as matter-of-fact as the officer. So you may need to help the witness to focus on the material facts, to be specific, avoid guessing, and get him or her pinned down. If the witness has some negative information for you that conflicts with what the client and officer say, you are in a position to "challenge" the witness's false

accident situs The place where an accident occurred, but the physical conditions and circumstances may have changed.

impressions. You have been to the situs, you have photographs, a diagram, and police report, so the witness will be impressed with your authority. It is unlikely that the witness will be able to mislead you. You have not wasted any time backtracking or obtaining clarification.

The hypothetical case scenario gives us an opportunity to construct an investigation plan. Attorney Donald Smith's initial concern is whether he can establish a negligence action against Bradley Harper. He will take the case only if there is some likelihood of prevailing. If he can obtain evidence that Harper was negligent and caused the accident, his next concern is whether Nordby was negligent and whether Harper will make a claim against Nordby. At the outset Smith has no reason to assume there is going to be a problem about insurance and ownership. Attorney Smith's litigation team's investigation plan could be similar to the outline in the accompanying example.

EXAMPLE

INVESTIGATION PLAN

1. Interview Nordby
   a. Can he give us any information?
   b. If he is incapacitated, determine when, if ever, he might be able to help us.
   c. Have Laura Raskin talk with the doctors and report back as soon as possible.
   d. Obtain authorization from Nordby or Raskin to get police report.
2. Inspect and photograph location of accident.
   a. Is there any remaining physical evidence relevant to the accident?
   b. Measure roadway.
   c. Any traffic control signs?
   d. Any lines or markings on the highway?
   e. Verify speed limit.
3. Interview deputy sheriff with or without the official report.
   a. Has he been interviewed by anyone else?
   b. Does he have any photographs?
   c. What have the drivers said to him?
   d. Were there any witnesses?
   e. Were there any passengers?
4. Make "cold call" on Harper at home or work.
   a. Does he have a lawyer?
   b. Who is his insurer?
   c. Has he been interviewed?
   d. Has he given a statement? Get a copy.
   e. Does he have photographs?
   f. What is his version?
   g. Take recorded or written statement—which ever seems best.

Interviewing the Client

Most likely, the attorney who is handling the case will conduct the initial client interview. More and more, attorneys are seeing the wisdom of including a legal assistant at the beginning. If the attorneys you work with have not discovered the importance of early involvement yet, you should suggest it. Team work promotes efficiency and effectiveness. During the initial interview you will learn about the client's assumptions about the case and expectations. If the attorney is wise enough to include you in the initial conference, your role is to be an observer. Do not make comments unless requested. You may be expected to take notes and prepare a summary of the meeting, including significant disclosures, decisions affecting the further handling of the case and your investigation assignments. You will not be expected to make a record of the discussion like a stenographer would. After the initial interview, you probably will meet with the client alone to begin the investigation. The meeting may be immediately after the initial interview or sometime later, depending on circumstances. Ordinarily, time is of the essence! If you meet with the client later, you should have your investigation plan already prepared.

An investigator usually begins with the client's version of the transaction or occurrence. Clients often have more information than they realize. Encourage the client to narrate the transaction or occurrence, not just answer "yes" or "no." Draw out as much information as you can. Do not stop or correct the client until you have obtained the whole story from the client's perspective. Of course, you may need to interrupt occasionally to ask, who, where, when, what, and how. But the more the client talks, while you listen sympathetically, the more open he or she will be. Take notes so that you can review significant items with the client *after* you have obtained the client's story. Many clients do not want the interview tape recorded, but they understand the necessity of note taking. While listening to the client's version, try to understand the client's perspective. Is the client being overemotional, exaggerating to obtain sympathy, or relying on guesses instead of facts? Not every client is wonderful.

After you have obtained the client's version, begin the process of questioning the client about apparent omissions, errors, and inconsistencies. Try not to be critical but press gently for details and the truth. Your job is to serve the client, and you cannot do that if you make the client uncomfortable or unhappy. But likewise, you cannot serve the client if you fail to be objective about the facts and the client's version of them. Listen carefully to the client's explanations about apparent mistakes in his or her story. You may be the one who has made the mistake. Even if the client does not know what happened, find out what the client believes happened. That may provide a starting point for the investigation. The client's beliefs about the transaction or occurrence influence the client's expectations concerning your performance.

If the investigation concerns an accident, you must examine the accident situs as soon as possible. It is a matter of judgment and feasibility whether to include the client on your first visit to the situs. At some point, you will have to examine the accident situs with the client to develop a mutual frame of reference. The same frame of reference improves communication. For example, when you talk about the tree that blocked the client's view, you must be sure that you are talking about the same tree. If you conduct an initial inspection alone, you can make measurements, take photographs, and prepare for a subsequent inspection with the client. Your familiarity with the situs will make you appear authoritative. But if you do not have the client accompany you on your first visit to the situs, you may lose precious time. You are making two trips when maybe one would really do.

While at the situs, ask the client to demonstrate what she or he did leading to the accident. If you can simulate the accident by driving the same path, you may be able to refresh the client's memory or help the client make critical estimates. Once the relevant speed, time, and distance factors are established, they can be calculated, analyzed, and made consistent. Where that is not feasible, ask the client to illustrate what happened. Concentrate on the details. Even if the client did not witness the accident, it may be useful to meet at the accident situs to develop the same frame of reference. Most clients appreciate being included in the early preparation. They know that their matter is being pursued.

In accident cases, the physical features of the situs are often important in explaining why and how the accident happened. You should position yourself to obtain the perspective each party had and each witness had. The features should be photographed. If the situs is the same as it was at the time of the accident, the photographs will be evidence of its condition. In other words, the photographs are, in themselves, evidence. But if the situs has changed, photographs can only be used as "illustrative evidence" to assist witnesses to explain what they observed. Aside from their value as evidence, photographs are useful aids for interviewing witnesses and refreshing memories.

The accident situs should be measured and diagrammed with special attention to the physical features, so your diagram complements your photographs. Diagrams should note directions, widths, lengths, heights, traffic controls, landmarks, any obstructions to the parties' views, point of impact, and so on. The measurements and related information can be kept on a diagram and/or on a data sheet. Diagrams are useful even if they are not to scale. The mere act of preparing a diagram will help your orientation and memory. Your diagram is an attorney work product. It is not discoverable, unless your side chooses to use it. An investigator who has been to the situs cannot help but feel more authoritative when speaking with witnesses and can better understand photographs and diagrams prepared by others. As the investigation progresses, you should try to form a mental picture, even a mental motion picture, of the occurrence. The mental picture should be based on the evidence you have. Where there are voids in the mental picture, you need more evidence to fill the voids.

Interviewing Witnesses

An investigation plan should consider how to locate and deal with each witness. Look for a logical order in which to contact the known witnesses. The order should allow you to build on the information as it is obtained so you will not have to return to ask more questions. That is important because witnesses are less likely to be accommodating on second and third contacts. Indeed, repeat visits may lead to hostility. Good planning helps you to remain focused, so witnesses do not become impatient and annoyed.

Consider where and how each interview should be conducted. Can the interview be conducted over the telephone? Should the telephone conversation be recorded? Is it necessary to see the witness in person? Should the client attend the witness interview? If the witness is particularly friendly to the client, it may be very useful to have the client attend the interview. If the witness is neutral or hostile, it would be counterproductive to have the client attend. Should the witness be contacted at home or at work, during lunch time or at another time? Would the witness consider meeting at the scene of the accident? Because you are not in a position to force witnesses to cooperate, you must do your work when and where it is convenient for them. Is it going to be necessary to compensate the witness for her or his time? On what basis? Ordinarily, the basis for compensation is the value of the witness's time and out-of-pocket expenses, not the value of the information provided. In what form should the payment be made? Cash? Check? The other side is entitled to know about any payments and bring them up in court. Would a jury feel that the payment has compromised the witness?

Some witnesses do not want to become involved because they do not understand the process. They fear criticism and personal involvement. You need to be able to allay the witnesses' concerns about the process and assure them that their cooperation will not harm them. If a witness's reluctance to cooperate has some other basis, your task may be more difficult. For example, a witness who has a criminal record may shy away from interviews and refuse to give statements. Witnesses who have been involved in litigation of their own that did not go well for them may be reluctant to help in another person's case. They will avoid you, refuse to give a statement, and be evasive when they do talk to you. Try to make witnesses feel they are important to the investigation, to the case, and to you. A witness who believes that his or her contribution is unique and really important will be more interested and motivated to help. Most witnesses derive a feeling of satisfaction from being part of the civil justice system and doing their duty.

You should assure witnesses that it is proper to meet with you. Although there is no formula for dealing with all witnesses, some guidelines should be considered. Be polite, respectful but not solicitous. Be forthright, sincere, and concerned about discovering the truth. Your manner should gain the witnesses' respect and trust. You represent the client, so whatever you do reflects on the client. The manner in which you approach a witness must be comfortable for you and the witness. Your approach depends, in part, on your own personality. If you are not comfortable, you will appear to lack sincerity and authority. That will make the witness feel uncomfortable too. You may be able to obtain the witness's cooperation by developing his or her interest in the case. At the same time, try to develop the witness's empathy for the client's position. Your approach may depend on the witness's relationships to the parties. If a witness is known to be friendly to the client, the interview should be relatively easy. If the witness is aligned with the opposing party, however, he or she may be evasive, contrary, and even belligerent. In response, emphasize that you are seeking the truth. Interviews should be conducted in a relaxed manner, and you should not be overbearing.

A witness may identify with your client because of what the witness observed, or knows about the event, or because of the witness's relationship to the client. Of course, these same factors may cause a witness to be antagonistic toward the client. As part of the investigation plan, determine whether you can say something to make the witness have some concern for the client or the client's problem. When representing a plaintiff, it may be useful to explain to the witness how serious the accident was for the client or how serious the injury is. When representing the defendant, it may be useful to explain the defendant's position and that without the witness's help, a serious injustice may result. It may be useful to tell the witness that his or her evidence is important to the case as a whole. These suggestions are made to obtain cooperation and reliable evidence, not to mislead or to twist the facts.

You have no right to conceal your identity from witnesses. However, investigators occasionally choose not to identify their clients. You may begin interviewing a witness by explaining you need information about the transaction or occurrence. You can set the stage with an overview to catch the witness's interest and help the witness to understand how his or her evidence fits into the case. An overview may help a witness recall additional facts that the witness might otherwise overlook. An overveiw may describe the entire transaction or occurrence. Or, an overview may simply describe bits and pieces as the interview progresses. Either way, the purpose is to focus the interviewee's attention and lead the interviewee into an adoption of facts favorable to the client. It is not unethical to emphasize the facts that tend to favor your client. It is unethical to misrepresent the facts or evidence or mislead a witness. An overview may help clear up misconceptions the witness may have. However, if the witness disagrees with your overview, the witness may be deterred from discussing the case with you because he or she may not want to argue with you. So the "overview approach" is potentially useful but also problematic.

The "overview approach" is quite different than the approach in which the investigator simply asks questions, such as, "who, when, where, how, why, then what happened." The overview educates the interviewee. This may be good, counterproductive, or bad. Whether to use it is a matter of judgment.

When recording a statement, you may use leading questions to support the client's version of the facts. For example, if you believe the client was traveling only twenty-five miles per hour at the time of the accident, then say to the witness, "Wouldn't you agree that Ms. Fredericks was driving only twenty-five miles per hour?" Do not ask, "Was Ms. Fredericks traveling more than twenty-five miles per hour or in excess of the speed limit?" Another approach is to lead the witness through the facts. You can make brief statements about a fact and ask the witness about his or her version. Then move to the next fact. For example, "The police report says the blue car was going fifty miles per hour as it entered the intersection. What do you think?" Witness, "Yes, that seems right." Paralegal, "My client says that he tried to stop. He applied his brakes and left some skid marks. Did you see the skid marks?" Witness, "Yes, I believe I did, but I wasn't looking, at the time." One problem with leading the witness is that you could lead the witness away from important information. Of course, you can ask questions without trying to direct the discussion, and that is how most interviews are conducted.

Knowing something about the witness's background and position in the community can help the investigator evaluate the witness's evidence. You need to find out the witness's age, address, employment, education, experience with courts, and whether the witness has had similar experiences. For example, in automobile cases, it is useful to know whether the witness is a licensed driver, whether the witness has

EXAMPLE

THE OVERVIEW APPROACH

Suppose your litigation team represents insurance agent Fredrick Burns in the hypothetical case, and you have a chance to interview Carl Griffin. Burns says that Carl told him Mr. John Griffin had sold the pickup truck to Harper. Burns says that Carl told him he bought a new Camero. Carl instructed him to allocate the unused insurance premium to the new Camero. These facts are helpful to Burns. They show that the pickup was sold, so John Griffin could not continue to insure it in his name. They show that Burns had good reason to rely on what Carl told him. It was appropriate to transfer the insurance coverage to the Camero, because the Camero had to be insured and Griffin did not have any need for insurance on the pickup. Also, Burns says that Carl did not mention Griffin's agreement to insure the pickup until he could find the certificate of title. You want to obtain a statement from Carl, if you can, that corroborates Burns's contentions.

You could begin by telling Carl that you are looking for information about Harper's accident with the pickup truck. Of course, Carl has no knowledge about the accident, so he will be less concerned about talking to you. At this point, he feels he is not really involved. Then you could mention that you know Harper bought the pickup from Griffin. You could point out that Carl bought a Camero about the same time as Mr. Griffin sold the pickup to Harper. You could suggest that he probably used the money from the sale of the pickup to buy the Camero. He probably knew he had to have insurance on the Camero and did not need insurance on the pickup any more. You could suggest that Carl asked Burns to insure the pickup. But Carl did not pay any money to insure the Camero. Instead, he asked Burns to transfer the pickup insurance to the Camero. Then you would suggest that he probably told his father, John Griffin, what he had done about the insurance. If Carl agrees, his father is in big trouble.

---

been directly involved in any motor vehicle accidents, whether the witness has ever testified in court or given a deposition. If the case involves an industrial accident, you need to find out if the witness has engaged in similar work and is familiar with certain types of equipment.

You need to find out whether the witnesses have been interviewed by anyone else and whether they have given statements to anyone else. If so, the witness may have a copy of the statement and may be willing to let you copy it. Indeed, a witness who has given one statement may feel that one is enough and refuse to give more. If a witness does not have a copy of his or her statement, the witness has a right to obtain a copy from the party. You can so inform the witness. Some state court rules make witness statements discoverable, but only after an action has been commenced.

What can you do about a witness who is mistaken about the facts due to a defect in memory or perception? To what extent is it legal and ethical to challenge the witness? Again, you cannot control the witness. If you cannot obtain her or his co-operation, the last resort is to subpoena the witness to appear for a deposition.[1] You should be guided by the premise that it is never wrong to earnestly seek the truth, but it is unethical to mislead a witness or to induce a witness to falsify evidence.

You may explain to a witness that his or her mistaken version of the facts is not physically possible or conflicts with observations of other witnesses who had a better view. It is proper to ask a witness to reconsider and analyze his or her version in light of other known circumstances or other evidence. The witness may or may not appreciate such help. A witness's response usually depends, in part, on how he or she is approached about the problem. If a witness feels that the investigator is applying pressure to improperly influence him or her, the witness will be, and should be, resistant, upset, and uncooperative. If the witness believes that he or she is being treated fairly and helped to avoid making a mistake, however, the witness will be receptive. So much of what you do with witnesses is a matter of judgment. And sometimes you do not have much time in which to decide what to do.

Usually, your best approach is to get the witness's whole story before challenging his or her facts. Then suggest to the witness that "there is a little problem." Then explain why you are having trouble understanding how the mistaken facts could be true. Do not tell the witness that he or she is wrong. Do not try to dictate to the witness. Instead, solicit the witness's help to resolve the problem. You should manifest a desire to help the witness to resolve the problem. You do this by raising innocuous questions and offering suggestions that lead the witness to the truth. You may lead the witness through a reasoning process that helps the witness recognize the truth. Hopefully, when the witness understands the big picture and understands how her or his evidence fits into it, the witness will see that her or his information was mistaken. Hopefully, the witness will be willing to abandon false beliefs in favor of the truth. These suggestions have no application where the witness is simply lying.

Suppose the witness mistakenly recalls that the accident occurred during daylight. You could explain to the witness that the police report shows the time of the accident as 9:00 P.M., and the dispatcher's records corroborate the time. The United States Weather Bureau records show that the sun set at 6:15 P.M. By 9:00 P.M., the **accident scene** would have been dark, except for artificial lighting. The witness may feel as though he or she has a very good recollection of the accident, and, consequently, believes that he or she had a good view of it. Artificial lighting may have made the scene seem as bright as day. Consequently, that is how the witness remembers the scene—as daylight. Witnesses do not want to make mistakes. Indeed, they are afraid of making mistakes. They usually do not resent being helped.

accident scene The situs of an accident while conditions are the same as they were at the time of the accident.

Witness Statements

A recorded witness statement is a written recital verified by the witness's signature or a verbatim recording that duly identifies the witness. Verbatim recordings may be electronic or stenographic. You may use a recorded witness statement to preserve a witness's *expected* testimony.[2] A **recorded statement** becomes part of the investigation file, so the investigator may compare it with other information and evidence. A statement preserves the information a witness has. A statement may be used to refresh the witness's recollection when preparing for trial. It may also be used to

recorded statement A witness's statement that is a verbatim record of the witness's words made by an electronic means, shorthand, or other means.

impeach the witness if the witness changes his or her version. A statement may be shown to the opposing party as part of a settlement negotiation effort. A lawyer is much more comfortable preparing for trial knowing that the witnesses have committed themselves to facts as recorded in their statements. If a lawyer has made claims about what a witness will say and the witness changes his or her testimony, the recorded statement shows the lawyer's good faith.

As a general rule, lawyers want recorded statements from the witnesses whether or not the witnesses are favorable to the client's case. An adverse witness will hurt the client's case no matter what. A lawyer who has a recorded statement to work with can cross-examine a witness more effectively. Nevertheless, it is always a matter of judgment whether to obtain a recorded statement from a witness and to select the kind of statement. In states where a party must disclose witness statements to adverse parties, it may be better not to have a recorded statement from a person whose version of the facts is totally adverse and clearly not truthful. It might be better to have a **memorandum of interview** about the witness's expected testimony. A memorandum of interview is a work product and does not have to be disclosed to the opposing side [Rule 26(b)(3)]. It is merely the interviewer's notes. Although the memorandum of interview is protected from discovery, the identity of the witness and the subject of expected testimony are not protected against discovery. When you interview a witness, you must decide whether to obtain a recorded statement and what to include in it.

Recorded witness statements are hearsay and cannot be used as evidence to prove the facts in the statements, unless an exception to the rule against hearsay applies. Some of the possible exceptions include the following: (1) a party's recorded statement may be put into evidence as substantive evidence *against* that party as an admission; (2) a recorded statement may be used as a trial exhibit to impeach a witness;[3] (3) a recorded statement may be used to prove facts contained in the statement when the witness is "unavailable" and the court is satisfied that the statement is trustworthy. Rule 807 covers these exceptions and provides:

> A statement not specifically covered by any of the foregoing exceptions but having equivalent circumstantial guarantees of trustworthiness, [may be admitted] if the court determines that (A) the statement is offered as evidence of a material fact; (B) the statement is more probative on the point for which it is offered than any other evidence which the proponent can procure through reasonable efforts; and (C) the general purposes of these rules and the interests of justice will best be served by admission of the statement into evidence. However, a statement may not be admitted under this exception unless the proponent of it makes known to the adverse party sufficiently in advance of the trial or hearing to provide the adverse party with a fair opportunity to prepare to meet it, the proponent's intention to offer the statement and the particulars of it, including the name and address of the declarant.

Each method of recording a witness statement has its own advantages and disadvantages. Therefore, you must carefully consider which type of statement to obtain from each witness. When deciding whether to make a recorded statement, keep in mind it may become evidence at trial. Make the statement clear, concise, and accurate, and limit it to relevant matters. Do not include anything that is scurrilous.

impeach To cast doubt on the credibility of a witness or exhibit by showing inconsistencies in what the witness says or in the use of the exhibit.

memorandum of interview An investigator's memorandum of his or her interview with a witness. The memorandum contains the same information that would be in a witness statement, but the memorandum is not signed by the witness.

Types of Witness Statements

The most frequently used type of witness statement is a written statement signed by the witness. The witness's signature provides the foundation for offering the statement into evidence to impeach the witness if the witness's testimony is inconsistent with the statement. If the witness denies that the signature is his or hers, the investigator must testify that the witness did read and sign the statement at the time and place shown on the statement. Then it is up to the jury to decide whether the investigator or witness is telling the truth. The statement may be written at the time of the interview, or it may be prepared from the investigator's notes, typed, and subsequently signed. A written statement may or may not be notarized. If it is notarized, it becomes an affidavit that can be used to support motions. Some written statements are witnessed by one or two persons. The person who conducts the interview may be a witness.

A witness statement may be electronically recorded using an audiotape or a videotape. The witness does not sign the recording. Instead, at the beginning of the interview, the witness is asked to state her or his name and address and give other identifying information. To some extent the value of an audio tape depends on voice recognition to verify the witness's identity. Ordinarily, a typed transcript is made of the recording, because a transcript is more convenient and easier to use than a recording. If the witness reads and signs the transcript, it may be used in the same manner as a signed written statement. If the statement is obtained from a witness who becomes a party to an action, the custodian of the statement may use requests for admissions to force the party to admit to the interview and that the transcript is accurate.

A witness statement may be prepared from a recording made during a telephone interview. Some states have laws that require the interviewer to disclose to the interviewee that the recording is being made. A telephonic recording may be used like any other electronic audio recording.

A witness statement may be stenographically recorded. A stenographer must attend the witness interview and make a verbatim record using shorthand notes or a stenographic machine. The notes are not self-authenticating and are not evidence of the interview. The notes may be used by the stenographer to testify to what she or he heard the witness say during the interview. Again, if the witness reads and signs the transcript made from the shorthand notes, it may be used in the same manner as a written statement that is signed by the witness. If the written statement is notarized, it may be used to support motions.

The manner in which you approach a witness depends, in part, on whether you are going to try to obtain a statement and how that statement will be recorded. For example, if there is reason to believe that a particular witness is not going to be cooperative, it may be desirable to employ a stenographer to observe and record the interview, because the witness is not likely to sign a written statement and may avoid a tape recorder. An experienced stenographer is capable of being unobtrusive during the interview. Also, a stenographer may be a helpful witness for the investigator if the interviewee challenges the statement or makes a complaint about the investigator's conduct.

Written Statements

The procedure for obtaining a written, signed statement is simple. The investigator almost always prepares it for the witness to sign, because most witnesses will not make the effort to prepare their own statements. You may tell the witness that you are preparing a statement for him or her to sign. Or, you may simply start asking the witness a series of questions and write down the answers in a statement format, which, at the end of the interview, you ask the witness to read and sign. In other words, your notes become the witness's statement. Use the witness's own words as much as possible. You may elect to use your notes to prepare a typed statement and ask the witness to read and sign it later. Either way you have quite a bit of control over what goes into a written statement. Remember, you do not have to include everything the witness says. But a witness may, and should, refuse to sign a statement if the witness feels that it omits important information. A witness cannot be impeached with a statement unless the witness has verified it by signing it.

One example of a statement that a witness does prepare is the form statement insurance companies mail to witnesses. (See Exhibit 9.1.) Witnesses are asked to fill

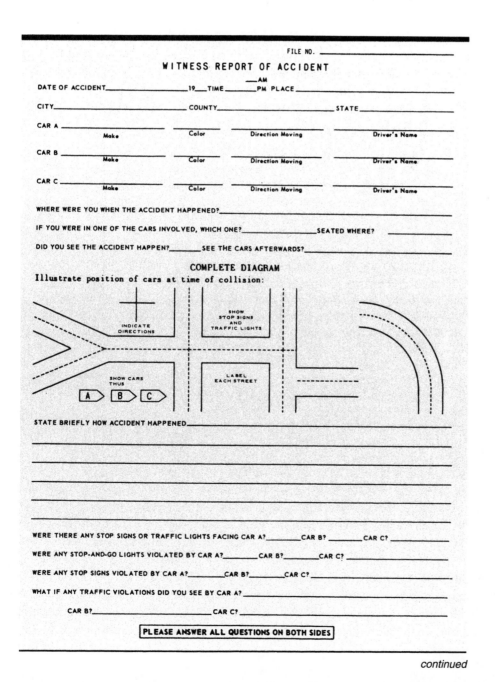

EXHIBIT 9.1

Witness Statement Form

continued

WERE ALL LIGHTS BURNING ON CAR A?_____ CAR B?_____ CAR C?_____

WHAT, IF ANY, SIGNALS WERE GIVEN BY CAR A?_____ CAR B?_____ CAR C?_____

WHAT WAS THE SPEED OF CAR A?_____ CAR B?_____ CAR C?_____

WHAT WAS THE SPEED LIMIT?_____

WAS VISIBILITY RESTRICTED FOR DRIVER OF CAR A?_____ CAR B?_____ CAR C?_____
(Indicate whether rain, snow, fog, dust, trees, shrubs, buildings, parked cars)

CONDITION OF ROAD OR STREET: DRY_____ ICE_____ SNOW_____ WET_____ MUDDY_____

WHERE WAS POINT OF IMPACT ON CAR A?_____

    CAR B?_____ CAR C?_____

WHAT DEFECTS DID YOU SEE IN THE CONDITION OF CAR A?_____

    CAR B?_____ CAR C?_____

WHAT MARKS OR DEBRIS DID YOU SEE ON THE ROAD?_____

WHERE WERE THEY WITH REFERENCE TO THE CENTER OF THE STREET AND WITH REFERENCE TO THE CARS INVOLVED?

_____

_____

LENGTH OF SKID MARKS, IF ANY, FROM CAR A?_____ CAR B?_____ CAR C?_____

WHAT WAS THERE ABOUT THE POSITION OF THE CARS, OR THE MARKS ON THE ROAD, OR OTHER FACTS THAT YOU

OBSERVED, TO INDICATE WHO WAS TO BLAME FOR THE ACCIDENT?_____

_____

WAS EITHER CAR ON THE WRONG SIDE OF THE ROAD?_____

WHAT DID YOU HEAR THE DRIVERS SAY AFTER THE ACCIDENT?_____

_____

WERE YOU INJURED?_____ DID ANYONE ELSE APPEAR TO BE INJURED?_____ IF SO, IN WHAT CAR?_____

WHO ELSE WAS A WITNESS TO THIS ACCIDENT?

    NAME _____ ADDRESS_____

    NAME _____ ADDRESS_____

            YOUR NAME HERE: _____ AGE: _____

            ADDRESS: _____

    TELEPHONE: RESIDENCE _____ BUSINESS:_____

            DATE: _____

in the blanks and make diagrams that show what they observed. They are asked to sign, date, and return the statements in envelopes the insurer provides. Some law firms use a similar approach where many witnesses are involved, such as with a hotel fire or an airplane crash. Such statements usually are considered to be preliminary contacts and are used to identify witnesses who might have significant information and are cooperative.

A written statement ought to be single spaced to reduce the possibility of interpolation. A witness statement ought to conclude with an acknowledgment that the witness has read it. The witness should be asked to sign each page. The witness's signature is the witness's assurance that this is the statement he or she gave and it is accurate. If the witness is reluctant to sign the statement, you may offer to give a copy to the witness. Explain that the copy will be a valuable reference when other lawyers and investigators contact him or her. It is fair to point out that in one or two years, the witness's memory may not be as clear as it is currently, so signing the statement provides assurance that it was true and correct when made. In other words, signing the statement is for the witness's own benefit and protection. If a copy is provided, that should be noted in the statement. It is easy to make a copy for the witness to keep.

If the witness's signed statement is totally beneficial to your client, you may suggest to the witness that by signing it and retaining a copy, the witness can use the same statement when other investigators contact him or her. The laws of some states require investigators to give witnesses copies of all signed statements. Rule 26(b)(3) requires a party to give a witness a copy of his or her statement if and when requested *by the witness*. Some courts require parties to provide copies of witness statements to the opposing parties when requested. Those states do not recognize the preparation of witness statements to be part of a party's work product or attorney's work product.

Electronically Recorded Statements

Electronically recorded statements are increasing in popularity as recording devices become smaller and more reliable. Tape recordings are inexpensive, unobtrusive, and less cumbersome than hand written statements. Tape-recorded interviews eliminate the chore of writing the statement. Tape-recorded interviews take less time than preparing a written statement. However, it takes more preparation to get ready for a recorded interview. A tape recording allows you to enter into a dialogue with the witness. Some witnesses develop "stage fright" when they see a tape recorder. They are afraid they will make a mistake and the recording will "trap" or embarrass them. Some witnesses simply refuse to be interviewed when told the interview will be recorded. You have less control over what goes into a recorded statement than a written statement. A written statement can be "edited" as it is prepared.

You may want to conduct a preliminary interview with the witness to prepare both of you for the recorded interview. The preview gives you an opportunity to determine exactly what the witness knows, what the witness is willing to say, and how you should ask your questions. You will do a better job of framing questions and avoiding matters that are sensitive or counterproductive. When you have obtained a good overview of the witness's information, you tell him or her that you would like to cover this *same* material in a recorded statement. "Would that be all right?" The recorder should be ready. You should state your name, the name of the witness, the date, and the time of the interview. Ask the witness to state his or her name and spell it. Ask the witness to give his or her address. It is fine to ask leading questions. A leading question suggests the answer you want. Witnesses do not mind, and leading questions do not impair the usual uses of recorded witness statements. Answers given to leading questions, however, are never as persuasive as statements in the witness's own words.

Stenographically Recorded Statements

You may hire a stenographer to make a verbatim transcript of the interview. The stenographer may make notes in shorthand or use a stenographic machine. Lawyers typically refer to stenographers as "court reporters" even though they do not necessarily work in a courtroom or for a court. Stenographic statements are not made under oath, but they may be. You should choose a stenographer who is authorized to administer oaths. After the interview, the stenographer uses her or his notes to prepare a transcript. The transcript provides a verbatim record of the interview—questions and answers. The transcript resembles an oral deposition transcript.

The transcript may be used to refresh the witness's recollection when preparing for trial, but not when testifying.[4] If the witness is willing to read the transcript and adopt its contents by signing the transcript, it may be used to impeach the witness if the witness testifies to something different. If the witness declines to sign the transcript, the court reporter may testify from his or her notes concerning the witness's prior statements. The stenographer testifies to what he or she heard during the interview and may use the stenographic notes to "refresh" and confirm his or her recollection. Technically, a stenographer's transcript cannot, by itself, impeach the witness; it is the stenographer who impeaches the witness. But a written statement that the witness has signed is, itself, evidence that can impeach a witness. Stenographically recorded statements are particularly useful when dealing with a witness who is uncooperative. A stenographer is an independent witness to the interview, and that may provide some protection if the witness should later claim that the investigator applied undue pressure to obtain the statement.

Telephone Interview Statements

A telephone interview can be recorded, and a transcript can be made from the recording. In some states, a witness must be told that the conversation is being recorded. Telephone interviews are easy to make, quick, and inexpensive. Very little time and effort are needed to set up and conduct a telephone interview. A telephone interview causes the witness the least amount of inconvenience. Telephone interviews, however, are difficult for investigators to do well. A witness can easily terminate the interview. The investigator cannot see the witness, and so cannot fully evaluate the witness's appearance. Too often, telephone recordings are garbled. The audiotapes of telephone conversations are difficult to use at trial. One solution that sometimes works is to prepare a transcript of the recording, but the witness may object even if the transcript tracks the recording perfectly.

Contents of Statements

A recorded statement, regardless of the type, should commit the witness to his or her version of the occurrence or transaction. It should clearly set forth the information, evidence, and facts that the witness knows, and identify the sources of the witness's knowledge. For example, it is not enough to state that the witness saw a vehicle traveling at a certain speed. The statement must also show that the witness had an opportunity to accurately observe the vehicle's speed. The statement should note where the witness was when he or she saw the vehicle, where the vehicle was, how long he or she observed it, and the direction of travel. The statement should establish that the witness has good eyesight and has sufficient experience to make a reasonably accurate judgment concerning the speed of the vehicle. The more details a lawyer has to work with, the more effectively he or she can cross-examine witnesses.

A good statement should also record the witness's lack of knowledge about important facts. For example, it could properly note that the witness did not look for skid marks, does not know of any other witnesses, did not talk to any of the parties, is not acquainted with any of the parties, did not hear a horn sounded before the collision, did not see the traffic light, and so forth. Some signed statements are purely **negative statements.** A negative statement provides that the witness does not have particular information or know any facts about the transaction or occurrence. A good negative statement neutralizes the witness, making it unlikely that he or she will come forward at a later date with evidence that is harmful to the client's case. If a witness indicates that he or she does not have the information you want, but will not give a statement to that effect, the witness's reluctance is a red flag that the witness may be hiding information or be aligned with the other side.

You must use common sense in determining what to include in a recorded statement and what to omit. There is no rule that requires a statement to be complete in every detail. You may try to keep out things that the investigator knows are wrong and will cause the witness problems later on. Keep in mind that if a statement is used at trial for any purpose, the whole statement is likely to be received into evidence.

A recorded statement usually begins with the date, time, and place, as shown in Exhibit 9.2. At the outset, you must decide whether to tell the witness that your notes will be a written statement that you will ask him or her to sign. It may be best to talk with the witness for a while, to find out what the witness knows and to assess the witness's attitude. After you have developed some rapport with the witness and understand the witness's perspective you should start writing the body of the statement.

Investigators commonly make minor mistakes, such as spelling errors, in written statements. If you make an error, identify it, make the necessary correction and ask the witness to initial the correction. The witness's initials in the body of the statement are evidence that the witness has read and corrected the statement. The inference is that the final product is correct and specifically approved by the witness. Indeed, some investigators make it a point to make at least one mistake so that the witness has the opportunity to make at least one correction in the body of the statement. Ask the witness to sign each page. That makes the statement more reliable, authoritative, and easier to use. It may be a year or more before the witness looks at it again, and having his or her signature on all pages assures the witness that it is his or her statement. It also protects the party who is relying on the statement.

Witnesses will be most cooperative if they feel the investigator is being fair and sensitive to their concerns. If a witness is reluctant to give a signed statement, you may point out that, like it or not, the witness is already involved in the matter. It will be easier for everyone if the witness cooperates by "doing the right thing." Advise the witness he or she ought to have a record of his or her observations, and the proposed statement can be that record. The statement will be a convenient reference for him or her if the case goes to trial.

As a last-resort kind of argument, you may tell a reluctant witness that if he or she will not give a signed statement, the lawyers will have to arrange to take the witness's deposition. An uncooperative witness may be subpoenaed. The deposition will be at some time and place convenient for the lawyers. The witness will have to give the information, probably in greater detail, and under oath. The choice is the witness's. Usually, depositions may not be taken until after the matter has been put into suit [Rule 30(a)]. However, if good cause is shown, a deposition may be taken before suit [Rule 27(a)]. Unlike like an oral deposition, taking a written statement does not subject the witness to a cross-examination.

negative statement A signed or recorded witness statement relating that the witness does not have any knowledge about the transaction or occurrence.

Exhibit 9.2

Written Witness Statement

(handwritten witness statement)

Statement of Jasmine E. Carter
August 20, 2006
Vicksburg, Virginia

I live at 2245 North Tenth Street. I am 20 years of age. I am employed at Brown and Mann Company in Vicksburg. I also attend college. My parents are Martin and Susan Carter. They live at 8525 Second Avenue South in Columbus, Ohio. Telephone 554/555-4466. They usually know where I am if I have to travel. On August 10, 2006, I was at the home of Robert Wheeler in Vicksburg attending a party. The party began about 7:00 P.M., but I did not arrive until 7:30. There were at least fifty people there when I arrived. Alcoholic drinks were being served by the host. To my knowledge all the guests were over eighteen years of age. We were celebrating Robert Wheeler's girlfriend's birthday. The weather was warm. People were gathering on the deck, which is one story above the ground level. About 8:00 P.M. I got a sandwich and a beer and was walking toward the screen door to the patio when I heard a loud noise. Then I heard screaming. Then I saw the deck slowly pull away from the house and go down. There were thirty or more people on the deck. There was nothing they could do. There was nothing I could do. I ran down the stairs. Someone called 911. No one told me that the deck was not safe. No one said anything about limiting the number of people on the deck. I have not talked with Robert Wheeler about the accident. I have not seen any pictures of the deck before or after the accident. I do not know why the deck collapsed.

I have read the above statement consisting of one page. Yes
The statement is true and correct. Yes
I have received a copy of this statement. Yes

/s/_____

Witness signature (Date)

Paralegal signature (Date)

Memorandum of Interview

In states where parties are required to exchange witness statements on demand, lawyers are reluctant to obtain statements except for very specific and compelling reasons. They do not want to share their work product with the opposition. In those states, a practice has evolved of making a memorandum of interview. A memorandum contains all of the witness's information but is not considered a recorded statement, because it is not a verbatim recording and has not been verified or adopted by the witness. A lawyer may supply a copy of the memorandum of interview to the witness, so that the witness can refer to it, but then the witness is free to disclose it to anyone else. Rule 26(b) defines witness statements:

> For purposes of this paragraph, a statement previously made is (A) a written statement signed or otherwise adopted or approved by the person making it, or (B) a stenographic, mechanical, electrical, or other recording, or a transcription thereof, which is a substantially verbatim recital of an oral statement by the person making it and contemporaneously recorded.

Preserving Evidence

Documents and other physical evidence must be preserved for use during the rest of the investigation and at trial. This is called **preserving the evidence.** You must provide safe, convenient storage with easy access. Sometimes the quantity of relevant documents is so small that they can be kept in your filing cabinet, but sometimes there are so many documents that lawyers have to obtain warehouse space for them. Physical evidence may be large, such as a truck, or small such as a medical instrument or a piece of glass. The method and manner in which physical evidence is stored must ensure the evidence's admissibility and maintain the evidence's authority, that is, its credibility. For example, suppose that a hospital instrument is the subject of a medical malpractice action and your law firm represents the hospital. As part of the investigation, you have taken custody of the instrument and kept it in an envelop in your filing case. When the instrument is offered into evidence at trial, the court will require the hospital to show that *this* is the instrument that was used in plaintiff's treatment; that it has not been repaired or changed. If the plaintiff makes alteration of its condition an issue, the hospital might have to prove the "chain of custody," that is, identify each person who had custody of it since it was used on the patient and through those persons try to establish that its condition has not changed. You would be part of the chain. You would have to testify. Are you going to be able to assure the court that no one tampered with the instrument while it was in your custody? Yes, because you are now aware of the problem, and you and your law firm will adopt a procedure that will prevent any problems and embarrassment.

You may have to decide whether to take possession of some physical evidence or leave it with its usual custodian (i.e., keeper). If the custodian is not a party and not subject to the court's control, you can only rely on the custodian's good faith to ensure proper care.[5] If the custodian will not part with the evidence, consider using a deposition as a means for giving the court custody. Otherwise, offer the custodian help to preserve the evidence. If there is some expense to storing the evidence, you may need to cover it. Make sure the custodian understands the importance of keeping the evidence secure. Explain that the case might not be resolved for many, many months, and the evidence must be kept until the case is fully resolved. Tell the custodian you will notify him or her if the case is resolved, so he or she must presume the evidence is needed until you notify him or her to the contrary. Send follow-up letters that reiterate your instructions, the status of the case, and the importance of the matter. (See Exhibit 9.3.)

preserving the evidence Following procedures to ensure that evidence will be available when it is needed. The choice of method for preserving evidence depends on the importance of the evidence, the likelihood that it will not be available when it is needed, and the cost of preserving it.

Exhibit 9.3

Sample Letter

Dear Mr. Jones:

Thank you for meeting with me yesterday and showing to me the Starcraft Boat that was involved in Mr. Gallop's accident of June 7, 2006. I understand that the boat was towed to your facility directly from the accident. The owner is considering whether to repair the boat. If the owner decides to repair it, you probably will be the person who will supervise the repairs.

As I told you yesterday, the boat is the subject of litigation. The parties may need to inspect it and photograph it. I realize that you cannot keep the boat indefinitely. At some point, you will no longer be able to store it. Please let me know if you decide to release the boat or otherwise dispose of it. I will help you to make arrangements for transferring it or storing it. The litigation may not reach trial for another year. The boat must be kept available to the parties until the case is concluded.

Please telephone me if you have any questions or concerns. I may telephone you from time to time to obtain information about the status of the boat. I hope that will be all right with you. Thank you for your kind cooperation.

Sincerely,

/s/ _____

Photography

You may use photography to capture and preserve evidence. Lawyers like photographs because most juries are interested in them. Through photographs jurors can visualize things and conditions that cannot be brought to the courtroom. Use photographs during your investigation as aids for interviewing witnesses. Witnesses can be more specific when they have photographs to look at while describing conditions. Sometimes you can use photocopies of a photograph in your investigation work. They are easy and cheap to make. Photographs help witnesses recall facts. Photographs will help you to avoid being misled by a witness whose perspective is wrong or whose memory is bad or who is biased. Obtain as many photographs as possible from the client, authorities, and witnesses. Take as many additional photographs as you may need. Err on the side of taking too many pictures, rather than not enough. You can have copies made from photographs; you do not need negatives. The guidelines for gathering, preserving, and using photographs apply to motion pictures and videotapes.

A photograph that depicts a fact, such as a skid mark, defective stairway step, or body wound, is evidence of that fact. The jury sees the fact by looking at the photograph. To be evidence of the fact, the photograph must show the subject matter in the same condition as it was at the time of the occurrence. A witness must lay a foundation for use of the photograph by identifying when the photograph was taken and explaining that it shows the subject matter in the condition it was at the time in question. With that foundation, the jury may use and rely on the photograph as a basis for determining the truth. For example, a photograph of an accident scene that shows conditions as they were at the time of the accident is evidence of those conditions (e.g., ice on the roadway surface). If the photograph shows a car parked near the situs of the accident, the jury may conclude that the parked car was present, even though some witnesses testify that they do not remember a car parked there.

Police officers often make photographs of accident scenes to preserve the facts. Always check to see if the police or other authorities have photographs. Usually, they will supply copies at a nominal cost. Although you may not be able to be at the scene, photographs made after the fact are still useful. It is surprising how long valuable evidence remains at an accident situs, whether an airplane crash, a shooting, a slip-and-fall accident, or other. Even when skid marks and debris have disappeared from an automobile accident scene, good photographs of the situs may be used to illustrate conditions that did exist. For example, photographs taken within hours of an accident may show skid marks on the pavement, but a witness may be able to use the photographs to illustrate the location of skid marks and debris as the witness observed them at the scene. A photograph taken days after an intersection collision may not show the scene, but may accurately show the location of street signs, the width of the road, and traffic markings on the road surface.

Photographs that show a material fact are not work product and are not protected from discovery. Consequently, photographs that contain evidence must be disclosed and made available to other parties if and when requested. Furthermore, such photographs must be protected from loss or destruction. A party who loses material evidence is subject to all of the sanctions provided by Rule 37(a)(4) (see Chapter 8).

Photographs that are taken for *illustrative* purposes are useful because they show similar objects or similar scenes or similar circumstances. Illustrative photographs may be used at trial to help a witness describe what the witness observed. The photographs are not, in themselves evidence, but they support a witness's testimony, which is evidence. Consequently, jurors see the illustrative exhibits only while they are being used by the witness in the courtroom. They are not allowed to take illustrative photographs into their deliberations. There is too much danger the jury may forget that illustrative exhibits are not proof of anything. If a judge does allow the jury to take illustrative photographs into their deliberations, the judge should instruct the jury concerning the photographs' limited application. Jurors must rely on the testimony, not on the illustrative exhibits.

Photographs you take during your investigation that do not show material facts are work product. At most, they might be used for illustrative purposes. The litigation team does not have to disclose such photographs in the initial disclosure, unless you expect they will be used at trial. In general, the existence of illustrative photographs a party does not intend to use at trial must be disclosed pursuant to discovery requests, but because they are work product they need not be produced. Illustrative photographs a party intends to use at trial must be produced if requested. If you were to lose an illustrative photograph, it is not as though you lost material evidence.

Suppose that a month after the plaintiff's slip-and-fall accident on the defendant's stairway, the defendant's investigator took photographs of the stairway but realized, after the photographs were developed, that they show some debris on the steps. They are prejudicial to the defense. They do not, in themselves, contain evidence relevant to the accident. What should the investigator do? They should be destroyed, and new photographs should be taken without debris on the steps. However, if the photographs had been taken immediately after the accident and showed the condition of the stairway as it was at the time of accident, they would have to be preserved and disclosed. They would be evidence and irreplaceable.

When taking photographs, consider how they probably will be used. Will a photograph be illustrative or evidence? As mentioned, just because a photograph is taken long after the accident does not mean that it will not become evidence. For example, a photograph taken of a dented fender six months after the accident may still be evidence of the dent as it looked immediately after the collision. Once the fender is repaired, that photograph is the best evidence of the dent.

Protect photographs, plats, diagrams, and similar items from corrupting marks. If you find it necessary to make marks on a photograph during the investigation or while preparing for trial, be sure to use a copy. Do not contaminate a photograph that you expect to be used as evidence. Any marks you or a witness make may disqualify a photograph from being received into evidence. For example, if witness A has drawn skid marks on a photograph and witness B attempts to use the photograph at trial, A's markings could be considered "leading" witness B. It is safest to have more than one set of photographs and other graphics, and mark only on expendable copies.

Taking Photographs

Use a good 35mm camera. A 50mm lens is usually best, because it is neither wide-angle nor telephoto. A 50mm lens tends to show the subject in the most natural configuration. Any lens that is less than 50mm is a wide-angle lens. Any lens that is more than 50mm is a telephoto lens. If you were to photograph a highway curve, you might feel that a wide angle is best because it gives you the whole curve. But a photograph taken with a 28mm, wide-angle lens will greatly distort the curve's appearance. The photograph might be kept out of evidence for that reason.

You should nicely frame the subject in the picture, but you must note who and what are in the background. You do not want your assistant to appear in the picture. You may have to wait until the scene is set. Help the jury to visualize the subject by starting with an overview, "big picture." Then take photographs in a sequence that moves closer and closer to the critical matters. As the jury looks at the photographs, they will feel truly acquainted with the subject. They will feel that you have been forthright with them. You did not take anything out of context.

Here is an example of series photography. Suppose your case concerns the condition of the bottom step of a stairway in an apartment house. You should begin the sequence by taking photographs of the entire front of the building and each side. Then you should take photographs showing the front entrance, then the entrance and foyer, then the foyer and stairway, then the stairway, and finally the bottom step. You continue moving closer and closer to the bottom step. Then you will need a series of photographs of the step to show the riser, tread, and tread surface. The step should be photographed from every angle. You can use a ruler to show the dimensions in some of the photographs. A set of photographs taken in this manner makes the jurors feel as though they have visited the scene. You must make a record of the date and time the photographs were taken, the direction of each view, relevant measurements, relevant colors, and who was present.

Lawyers may have difficulty deciding which photographs to use. In the preceding example, although the photographs of the back of the apartment house may be "interesting" and may help the jurors feel familiar with the accident site, are they relevant? What if they show a lot of debris and disrepair? The apartment house owner will want to keep those photographs out of evidence, because they might prejudice the court and jury against him. For that reason, the plaintiff wants the jury to see the photographs. The photograph of the back of the apartment building would not have to be disclosed, because it is not relevant evidence of a material fact. It is no more *relevant* than a photograph of your grandmother.

You cannot always know the value and purpose for which a photograph will be used. By way of illustration, suppose you took a photograph of the street where an accident occurred to show the location of the stop sign. The photograph might become important because it shows there were no skid marks on the street at the time the photograph was made. Sometimes the absence of something may be as important as the presence of something. But how do you know what is missing and that the missing thing is important? You don't.

Records

Most transactions and occurrences that become the subjects of civil litigation involve some records. The records may have been generated as part of a business transaction that has gone sour. The records probably reflect the parties' contentions about the transactions. The records may be part of an occurrence, as in a medical malpractice case where records concerning the patient's care and treatment are routinely prepared by the physicians and hospital staff. The records may have been generated directly as the result of an untoward occurrence, as when the federal transportation board investigates and reports on an airplane crash. In personal injury cases, the plaintiff's past employment records, tax records, and medical records are relevant.

Records that are under a party's control are readily available. Many records are public documents and are available for the asking. Official records and reports that were generated by the transaction or occurrence often provide the names and addresses of important witnesses and should be obtained as soon as possible.

Some records cannot be obtained without a party's signed authorization, such as tax returns, hospital records, medical records, police reports, employment records, school records, and official death records. Each law office has its own forms for obtaining such records. The custodians of such records may have preferred forms, and the custodians' preferences should be honored. If a custodian's requirements become too unreasonable, the records may be obtained by taking the custodian's deposition and having the records subpoenaed for inspection and copying at the deposition [see Rule 45(a)]. For example, in some communities, physicians decided to charge several dollars per page for photocopies of records. Photocopying became a profit center. The solution was to compel the physicians to appear for depositions, have them produce their records, copy them, and pay them only a witness subpoena fee. The price of photocopying came down dramatically.

At your initial meeting with the client, you should have him or her sign the necessary authorizations so you can obtain relevant records. Leave the authorization undated until you use them. If there is some delay before the authorizations are used, they will appear to be current. If an authorization is signed by someone other than a client, it should be dated when signed, even though it is not convenient to use the authorization right away. A party's authorization should be dated and specify who may use it. Otherwise, an authorization becomes similar to a blank check. When an injured plaintiff gives the defendant an authorization to review the plaintiff's records, the defendant may prefer to wait until the plaintiff stops treatment and returns to work before obtaining the records. But the defendant should not wait so long that the authorization becomes outdated or stale. The decision concerning when to review and obtain records is influenced by whether the defendant can obtain another authorization at a later date.

Using Experts

You should always consider hiring experts to assist with the investigation. For example, if a plaintiff is considering a medical malpractice action against a physician or hospital, it is useful—and in some states required—to have a physician or nurse review all the patient's records to determine whether a lawsuit would be justified. A party may hire an accident reconstructionist to assist with the investigation of an accident. Reconstructionists are available to help with all kinds of accidents, including automobile, airplane, and industrial accidents and explosions. In an accountant malpractice action, the plaintiff should retain an accountant to review the records and advise whether they were prepared properly and whether proper procedures were followed. An expert can help locate important publications concerning the subject matter. Some publications may establish standards applicable to the profession. If so, the publications can be used as evidence, as provided in Rule 803(18). Professional publications are often useful to a lawyer in preparing to cross-examine opposing expert witnesses.

There are several national organizations that act as clearing houses for obtaining expert witnesses for litigants. Paralegals often assist with the search for experts who are willing to provide timely assistance. You may be asked to prepare letters to experts outlining the nature of the case, the issues and describing the kind of help the client needs. Ultimately, you will need a letter that states the scope and terms of the expert's engagement. You may be asked to collect data for the expert to review. You may be the expert's principal contact for additional information about the case.

Ethical Considerations

Suppose that immediately before trial, the client confesses that the information she or he supplied to you in a written, signed statement is false. Your firm has been relying on the information in preparing the case for trial, but the statement has not been disclosed to anyone else. What course of action should be taken? Your firm cannot allow a client to use fraud or deceit against an adverse party. As officers of the court, lawyers have a duty to prevent clients and witnesses from testifying falsely. Because the false information has not been communicated to anyone else, the firm does not need to disclose the fact that the client has lied. If false information has been supplied to the opposing side, through answers to interrogatories or in some other manner, you must immediately inform the opposing party about the error, but not necessarily how the error occurred. The opposing party may insist on an explanation, and a court may determine that he or she is entitled to an explanation. That probably would depend on how adversely the opposing party is affected by the false information.

If the client is unwilling to allow corrections to be made to discovery responses, the firm is faced with a dilemma. The lawyer must not disclose privileged communications. However, the lawyer must not permit the client to perpetrate a fraud upon the court. The lawyer would have to withdraw from the case if the client persists with the lie. If the client continues to lie, the court can order a lawyer to disclose the privileged information to the court.

TECHNOLOGY NOTES

The Internet gives access to maps of most towns and cities in the United States. You can examine these maps by going to Yahoo or Google and choosing "Maps." And there are map Web sites like Mapquest that provide driving directions as well as area maps. Of course there are also software map programs that may provide even more detail.

You can conduct "People Searches" through most of the Internet search engines, including Yahoo and Google. These search engines are not interrelated, so if you do not find the person for whom you are looking at one site, try another. There are also Web sites that charge a fee to do a person search, but they purport to be more effective.

SUMMARY

An investigation usually begins with the client's version of the transaction or occurrence. The client's version provides a basic theory of what happened and how it happened. The client's theory of the facts is the predicate for developing an investigation plan. An investigation plan helps you to focus on the issues and prioritize the investigation. It helps you to focus on the material facts, avoid false starts, and avoid duplication. It forces you to consider what evidence ought to exist and where it is most likely to be found. The plan may be as simple as preparing a list of things to do. A plan must be flexible to allow the evidence to build. Your role in the initial conference with the client is to be an observer. Do not make comments unless asked.

An investigation plan should (1) identify the material facts—the facts the client needs to prove to prevail; (2) determine which facts are disputed and which are not disputed; (3) determine what evidence is needed; (4) identify the witnesses and other likely sources of evidence; (5) decide on an order for the steps in the investigation, including an order for contacting witnesses; (6) decide how best to preserve the evidence you expect to collect, including the types of statements to obtain from witnesses; (7) coordinate the investigation with discovery procedures. You must try to be at the right place at the right time. Pay close attention to the details, because that is where inconsistencies show up—in the client's version as well as in the opponent's version.

Build on the evidence as it is obtained. Test claims and assumptions against physical fact. An investigation should be conducted aggressively, but never be obnoxious.

An investigation is a party's work product. You do not have to tell the opposing party what efforts you have made or what you have not done. You do not have to share mere information that you have obtained. Although you may be required to share some of the products of the investigation, unlike discovery procedures, you have complete control over when, where, and how to conduct your investigation. An investigation is a stepping stone for discovery. As you collect evidence you must make sure it is preserved. You preserve it by providing safe storage that maintains the evidence's admissibility and credibility.

Make witnesses feel that you are being fair with them. Establish good communication with them. Make witnesses feel appreciated. Stress civic duty. Show witnesses why their information is important so they are motivated to help. Determine whether the witnesses will be available when needed and how to find them if they were to move.

A written statement ought to be single spaced to reduce the possibility of interpolation. A witness statement ought to conclude with an acknowledgment that the witness has read it. The witness should be asked to sign each page. The witness's signature is the witness's assurance that this is the statement he or she gave and it is accurate. Use the witness's own words insofar as possible. You have some control over what goes into a written statement. You do not have to include everything the witness says. It is difficult to keep extraneous matters out of electronically recorded statements. A witness cannot be impeached with a written statement unless the witness has verified it by signing it. It is best to have the witness sign all pages and initial corrections. A witness can be impeached with an electronically recorded statement if the witness's identity is duly established. The laws of some states require investigators to give witnesses copies of all signed statements. Rule 26(b)(3) requires a party to give a witness a copy of his or her statement if and when requested *by the witness*. Some courts require parties to provide copies of witness statements to the opposing parties when requested. Those states do not recognize the preparation of witness statements to be part of a party's work product or attorney's work product.

Electronically recorded interviews take less time than preparing a written statement. However, recorded interviews take more preparation. A tape recording allows a dialogue with the witness. You have little control over what goes into a recorded statement. You may interview a witness to prepare both of you for a recorded interview. The preview gives you an opportunity to determine exactly what the witness knows, what the witness is willing to say, and how you should ask your questions. Ask the witness to state his or her name and spell it. Ask the witness to give his or her address. It is fine to ask leading questions, but answers to leading questions are never as persuasive as statements in the witness's own words.

You may hire a stenographer to make a verbatim transcript of a witness interview. You should choose a stenographer who can administer an oath. The stenographer's transcript provides a verbatim record of the interview—questions and answers. The transcript may be used to refresh the witness's recollection when preparing for trial, but not when testifying. If the witness is willing to read the transcript and adopt its contents by signing the transcript, it may be used to impeach the witness if the witness testifies to something different.

A telephone interview can be recorded, and a transcript can be made from the recording. In some states, it is illegal to record a telephone conversation without consent. Telephone interviews are easy to make, quick, and inexpensive. They cause witnesses the least amount of inconvenience. But telephone interviews are difficult for investigators to do well. A witness can easily terminate the interview. You cannot see the witness, so you cannot evaluate the witness's appearance. Too often, portions of telephone recordings are garbled. The audiotapes of telephone conversations are difficult to use at trial. Consider recording a telephone conversation on the second contact, so that you know the right questions to ask and avoid the wrong questions.

You should decide at the outset whether your notes will be a witness statement or a memorandum of interview. It may be best to talk with the witness for a while, to find out what the witness knows and assess the witness's attitude. A memorandum of interview contains all the witness's information but is not verified or adopted by the witness. You may supply a copy of the memorandum of interview to the witness, so that the witness can refer to it, but then the witness is free to disclose it to anyone else.

A witness statement usually begins with the date, time, and place. It should commit the witness to his or her version of the facts and show that the witness had an opportunity to observe the facts. A statement should be as factual as possible, but opinions may be used when that is the only way to express information. The more details a lawyer has to work with, the more effectively he or she can cross-examine witnesses. Details help make a pattern and point to additional facts. A good statement should record the witness's lack of knowledge about important facts. A negative statement, in effect, establishes that the witness does not have particular information or know any facts about the transaction or occurrence. A negative statement neutralizes the witness. Investigators commonly make minor mistakes in written statements and use the mistakes as an opportunity to have witnesses initial their corrections. The initials of a witness are evidence that the witness has read and corrected the statement. The inference is that the final product is correct and specifically approved by the witness.

Keep the "big picture" in mind while collecting and evaluating evidence. Evaluate evidence for completeness. Examine records and other documents volunteered by the opposing party. There should be no need to verify records supplied pursuant to discovery rules by a lawyer, but it never hurts to be thorough. Watch for unsigned copies of affidavits, statements, and documents. Be alert to "negative evidence" and the absence of evidence, such as the absence of skid marks, absence of physical complaints, symptoms, medical findings, and property damage. Do not let appearances mislead you or cause you to make false assumptions. Evidence that, at first, may seem irrelevant may become critical as the investigation continues, and evidence that at first seems detrimental may turn out to be very helpful.

Start with the client's version. Visit the scene of the occurrence. Collect all the documents relevant to the transaction. Obtain official records and documents. Locate and interview eyewitnesses. First, interview friendly witnesses, then interview neutral witnesses. Interview hostile witnesses last. Interview a potential adverse party only if she or he is not represented by a lawyer. An adverse party's statements should be accurate and all-inclusive; do not omit anything, whether good or bad.

Photographs that show facts are evidence. Illustrative photographs may be used to help witnesses testify to the facts. Form a mental picture of the critical events of the occurrence. Any voids in the picture point to a need for more evidence. Preparing diagrams helps people to orient their thinking and reinforces the memory about conditions.

It is better to take too many pictures than not enough. Take pictures of the entire scene or situs though the relevance may not be evident yet. Use a camera with a 50mm lens. Subjects should be photographed from several angles to obtain several perspectives. Photographs should be taken in sequence, from a distance leading up to the subject, so that the viewer can see the subject in context. Do not "clean up" the accident scene before taking pictures. Do "clean up" the accident situs when taking photographs for illustrative purposes. To be admissible evidence photographs must be a reasonably accurate portrayal of subject matter. Distorted and/or prejudicial photographs should not be received into evidence. A witness must lay a foundation for photographs to use them at trial. When you make photographs, record the date, time, type of camera, lens, direction, distance, and subject matter.

Use experts to help conduct the investigation. Experts are very useful for identifying problems, and for preserving information and evidence. Experts may be able to suggest additional areas of inquiry and use of scientific literature.

KEY TERMS

accident situs

accident scene

impeach

memorandum of interview

negative statement

preserving the evidence

recorded statement

REVIEW QUESTIONS

1. Why should you prepare an investigation plan?

2. List at least five considerations for preparing an investigation plan.

3. Of what use are photographs during the investigation?

4. Can you ever use photocopies of photographs during the investigation?

5. Under what circumstances should a memorandum of interview be used rather than a witness statement?

6. Under what circumstances is it all right for a paralegal to try to have a witness change her or his version of an occurrence?

7. Why is it important to obtain background information about independent witnesses?

8. What advantage does a tape-recorded witness statement have over a handwritten, signed witness statement?

9. What advantages does a handwritten, signed statement have over a tape-recorded statement?

10. Why is it significant that a witness statement is hearsay?

11. Are you required to give the witness a copy of the witness's signed statement?

12. How does a typical signed witness statement differ from an affidavit?

13. What should you do about a substantive error you make in a written witness statement?

CASE ASSIGNMENT

Attorney Donald Smith heard that Bradley Harper was interviewed by Griffin's insurance company. He asked you to contact the company and interview the insurance claims person and obtain a copy of any statement the claims person obtained from Harper. You contacted Diane Kaplan. She gave you a copy of the telephone interview transcript, but she would not let you hear the recording. Prepare a half-page, intraoffice memorandum to attorney Smith giving him the essential information. After the summary, make recommendations for further investigation in light of the information in the statement.

Endnotes

1. The threat of being served with a subpoena makes some witnesses cooperative.
2. As discussed previously, a recorded statement is not admissible as testimony. Testimony can be preserved only by using a deposition where the witness is placed under oath and is subject to cross-examination.
3. To impeach is to challenge a witness's testimony by showing the witness said or did something inconsistent with his or her present testimony.
4. When testifying, a witness may refresh his or her recollection only from a document that the witness has prepared himself or herself.
5. Obviously, the fewer custodians, the shorter the chain of custody. And that makes it easier to establish the necessary foundation for use of the evidence at trial.

 For additional resources, visit our Web site at www.paralegal.delmar.cengage.com

CHAPTER 10

EXPERT WITNESSES

CHAPTER OUTLINE

Chapter Objectives

Chapter 10 describes what an expert is and how lawyers use experts to obtain evidence, evaluate cases, and prepare for trial.

Introduction

An expert is a person who has special education, training, and experience concerning a technical subject that, ordinarily, lay persons do not understand well. The law recognizes experts in almost all fields, such as medicine, engineering, law, weather, ballistics, brake systems, toxicology, and so forth. A list of all the subjects would be endless. A person does not have to have "higher" education to be an expert. A machine operator who does not have a high school diploma could qualify as an expert concerning a certain machine or type of machines. Experts are allowed to testify to their **expert opinions.** Expert witnesses are allowed to explain the application and effect of evidence. They add another dimension to litigation. You will work with experts. You may help to locate experts your trial team needs. You may help with retainer agreements. You probably will have occasion to work with experts to investigate accidents and transactions. You can help experts prepare their reports. Working with experts is always interesting, often challenging, and sometimes fun.

expert opinions Opinions of a person who has special education, training, and experience in a subject not ordinarily known or understood by laypersons.

262

Experts

As you already know, witnesses usually are not allowed to testify about their opinions.[1] The premise is that juries should decide cases on the basis of facts, and not on the basis of opinions. Furthermore, the prejudicial effect of witness opinions ordinarily outweighs their probative value. The proscription against opinion evidence promotes objectivity and fairness. But the law allows expert opinion evidence, when the opinions will help the jury find the truth and avoid confusion. An expert's opinion takes on the aura of a fact. Rule 702 of the Federal Rules of Evidence provides the following:

> If scientific, technical, or other specialized knowledge will assist the trier of fact to understand the evidence or to determine a fact in issue, a witness qualified as an expert by knowledge, skill, experience, training or education may testify thereto in the form of an opinion or otherwise.

Experts are allowed to state opinions when their opinions help the jury to understand evidence material to the case and when their opinions provide information that is not ordinarily available in any other form. Courts should not allow an expert to act as an advocate and argue the facts of a case. Experts are not allowed to testify to what the law is or how the law applies to the facts of the case.

A mechanic with less than a high school education may qualify concerning matters with which the mechanic is familiar through on-the-job training and experience. A machine operator may qualify solely by reason of experience. A truck driver may qualify on the basis of experience concerning the proper methods of loading and operating a particular type of truck. The author retained Billy Martin, former manager of the Minnesota Twins and the New York Yankee baseball teams, to testify as to why a batter, who is being careful, might inadvertently lose control of a baseball bat and let it fly, even though the batter gripped the bat firmly.

Parties need experts for more than just testifying. Experts can analyze a party's claim or defense on the facts and make recommendations about obtaining evidence. They are familiar with pertinent literature and can recommend articles and books to study. They can help locate other experts. They can analyze and interpret relevant documents, such as medical records. They can help attorneys gather evidence. They can educate lawyers and paralegals concerning technical subjects. In medical malpractice cases, it is not enough for the plaintiff to prove a bad outcome. The plaintiff must prove that the physician deviated from accepted medical standards or procedures. The plaintiff's attorney usually consults another physician (expert) to ascertain how the diagnosis should be made and how treatment should be administered. An expert can identify the factors that might cause a bad outcome—some malpractice and some not. An expert can review the patient's medical records to determine whether they show anything improper about the patient's care and treatment. So experts may be brought into a matter even before a lawsuit is started. Their input is usually ongoing as new information is obtained. Lawyers keep finding new ways to use experts.

When one party hires an expert to testify, it is almost mandatory for the other parties to obtain experts to explain and contain the first expert's testimony, or contradict the testimony. The mere presence of an expert on one side tends to weight the case in favor of that side. In all probability, if a party looks hard enough, she or he can find an expert to support a theory helpful to the case. But the use of experts substantially adds to the cost of preparing and trying cases.

You can expect to work with experts. But first, you must understand what they contribute to litigation and how they do it. Your firm or company may ask you to select experts, engage their services, help them to prepare their reports, and help prepare them for trial. You may be the principal conduit between the expert, your firm, and the client. Some experts make their livelihood in litigation. For others, litigation is a sore spot, and they allow themselves to become involved only out of a sense of duty. You will soon learn the reputations of the experts in your community and how to work with them.

Opinions and Conclusions

conclusion A determination about a fact obtained by reasoning from evidence and other known facts.

There is a fundamental difference between an opinion and a **conclusion.** Understanding the difference will help you work with experts and evidence. Experts are allowed to testify to opinions based on the evidence, but not to conclusions drawn from the evidence. Drawing conclusions from the evidence is the jury's function. The Federal Rules of Civil Procedure and the Federal Rules of Evidence do not define opinions or conclusions, probably because the subject is too esoteric and any definitions that could be devised would be riddled with exceptions. For our purposes, an opinion is an informed judgment about facts. The expert's *informed judgment* comes from the witness's education, training, and experience and the expert's familiarity with the facts in question or similar facts. Consider the accompanying example.

EXAMPLE

EXPERT OPINION

A patient has a sudden onset of nausea with abdominal pain. The pain begins to localize in the right, lower quadrant of the abdomen. A low-grade fever begins. The physician probably will make a differential diagnosis that includes the possibility of appendicitis. The physician will probably elect to check the patient's abdominal reflexes, order a white blood count, and observe the patient for a short while. If the patient's condition worsens and the white blood count is greatly elevated, the physician may form an opinion that the patient probably has appendicitis. Only then will the physician elect to operate. The opinion must be reasonably certain before the physician will act on it. The opinion cannot be confirmed and made a "final diagnosis" until the operation is performed and the physician can actually see the inflamed appendix. Until then, the opinion has the possibility of being mistaken even though it is very reasonable and well supported. The patient would not want the physician to wait until she or he knows for sure that the appendix is inflamed before operating, because then it would be too late. But neither does the patient want the physician to operate on the basis of a mere guess that the appendix *might* need to be removed.

The physician called on education, training, and experience to make the diagnosis. The diagnosis is a medical opinion. The opinion is a product of the physician's experienced judgment.

A conclusion does not require judgment. A conclusion is reached through a process of deductive reasoning from the evidence. A conclusion may require skill in reasoning through the facts to reach the right conclusion, but it does not require an expert's informed judgment. When it is necessary to draw conclusions from the evidence, the jury is supposed to go through the analytic steps and draw the conclusions. This is one of the purposes of the attorneys' final arguments—to help the jury reason through the evidence to make conclusions about what the evidence proves or does not prove. Experts should not be allowed to do the jurors' reasoning for them by making deductions from the evidence or to advocate certain conclusions. They should be allowed to explain technical evidence and facts the jury could not understand without their input.

In the preceding example, the physician had a number of facts to consider: nausea, presence of pain, location of pain, type of pain, elevated temperature, elevated white blood count, change in abdominal reflexes, and so forth. The physician could actually observe some of these facts, such as the elevated temperature. Some of the facts were merely reported to the physician, such as the pain. Some of the facts were observed by others, such as the elevated white blood count, which was determined by a laboratory technician.[2] In court, it works the same way. An expert is allowed to take into consideration all such evidence, but the jury has a right to know what evidence the expert has relied on and what evidence the expert has disregarded. An expert is subject to cross-examination concerning the factors on which his or her informed judgment is based, including education, training, and experience.

Foundation

An expert opinion must have a **foundation** to be received in evidence. A foundation is established by preliminary evidence. There are two parts to a foundation. First, the preliminary evidence must show that the expert has the necessary qualifications (competency) to form an opinion on the subject. Second, there must be sufficient evidence of facts on which an expert can reasonably base an opinion. In addition to the foundation, the expert must affirm that his or her opinion is based on probability or on **reasonable certainty,** not speculation.

A witness lays the foundation through testimony in which the witness shows that she or he has the necessary education, training, and experience in the field. Lawyers place great importance on the witness's credentials: the extent of the witness's education, training, and experience. The better the expert's qualifications, the more persuasive her or his testimony will be. Just how much education and experience are required is a matter left to the **sound discretion** of the trial judge. This means that the trial judge has a great deal of latitude. The witness qualifies if the judge concludes that the witness's opinions probably would help the jury to understand facts or evidence (Rule 702).

In the past, the tendency was for trial judges to resolve doubt on the side of allowing a particular expert to testify, to provide wide latitude for cross-examination, and to let the jury sort out the weight it would give to the expert's opinions. As explained above, however, the federal courts have gotten increasingly vigilant as gatekeepers of allowable expert evidence. This gatekeeper function has led to many more instances where so-called expert witnesses are not allowed to provide their opinions to the fact finder, usually a jury. The concern that led to this increased

foundation   A body of evidence that tends to establish either that a witness is competent to testify on a certain matter or that other evidence is relevant, thus making the testimony or evidence potentially admissible and usable in the case.

reasonable certainty   A high degree of probability that the opinion is correct or the expectation will materialize.

sound discretion   The power to make a decision based on knowledge and experience. A presiding judge has a great deal of discretion or latitude concerning the admissibility of evidence and trial procedures.

vigilance was the practice of presenting so-called "junk science" to juries. In science, as knowledge evolves, we want to encourage researchers to hypothesize the next step and to seek advances in any number of fields. But in the law we are not prepared to impose liability upon someone on the basis of another's unproven theory. Generally speaking, it is this dilemma—science is always ahead of the law—that has led to stricter scrutiny of proposed expert testimony. When the basis for the expert testimony is too uncertain, courts will not allow a jury to be the prognosticators of scientific advancement while deciding the legal rights of parties to a given action.

It is now quite typical for a district court to hold a so-called pretrial *Daubert* hearing—named after the case that expanded the role of the district courts as gatekeepers—to probe the admissibility of the proposed expert opinions. The outcome of these hearings can be decisive in cases where a plaintiff must use expert testimony to prove a prima facie case. In a medical-malpractice case, for example, a plaintiff cannot establish a doctor's negligence without another doctor—an expert— to explain to the lay jurors the standard of medical care applicable to the particular medical condition at issue. If the court rules that the plaintiff's expert testimony is inadmissible, there will be no basis upon which the plaintiff can prove her or his case. Then the ruling will lead to a corresponding order for dismissal of the case. For example, suppose the defendant doctor negligently failed to diagnose the plaintiff's genetic disease. But suppose further that the disease at issue has proven fatal in an overwhelming number of cases without regard to when it was diagnosed or what treatment is given. Will the plaintiff be allowed to prove causation (i.e., that a delay in diagnosis caused or will cause his or her death) with the testimony of a leading expert, who would testify that an effective treatment for the disease will probably be found? In all likelihood, no. Jurors are not prognosticators of scientific advancement. There are a multitude of other situations where proposed expert testimony may be challenged, from engineering to physics to hydrology, the list of possibilities is virtually endless. And in those cases where the exclusion of evidence does not lead directly to dismissal, such a ruling can still drastically affect that party's chances of persuading a jury to her or his theory of the case.

The testimony concerning qualifications is usually provided directly by the expert. Some courts allow experts to supply a written **curriculum vitae** as evidence of their qualifications. A curriculum vitae—a fancy word for résumé—is a written description of the witness's education, work experience, publications, membership in professional associations, and professional awards or recognition. If a party elects to offer a curriculum vitae into evidence to establish the expert's qualifications, the expert should not be allowed to reiterate the contents when testifying, because the evidence is cumulative. Cumulative vitae evidence may be given undue emphasis by the jury. There are advantages to having the expert testify to his or her qualifications and some benefits from using a curriculum vitae. The trial lawyer must decide which is best for the case. By the way, some courts allow juries to consider both the curriculum vitae and testimony to establish the expert's qualifications.

As part of the foundation, a lawyer will ask the expert on direct examination what the expert did to familiarize himself or herself with the problem. The expert responds by identifying the documents the expert has reviewed and the inspections and tests the expert conducted. At some point the expert must identify the facts that he or she has relied on to conduct his or her analysis. The facts must have support in the evidence or the foundation fails.

curriculum vitae   A written description of a witness's background, education, training, associations, and publications.

Finally, the foundation must be based on the expert's belief that his or her opinion is probably correct, not merely speculation. An expert's assumption, speculation, or guess is of no value to the court and jury. But if an expert expresses an opinion concerning a future fact, the opinion must be stated in terms of reasonable certainty. For example, a physician may testify that the plaintiff's injury was caused by the accident in question. The opinion deals with a past or present fact and must be based on probability. The same physician may testify that the plaintiff's injury will require medical treatment for the rest of the patient's life. That opinion deals with a future fact and must be based on reasonable certainty. Reasonable certainty is a degree of certainty on which an expert would rely to make important decisions in his or her specialty. It is a higher standard of belief than probability. An opinion that is reasonably certain is not subject to serious doubt.[3] The court dialogue may be similar to the following:

Q: Do you have an opinion based on reasonable [medical][4] certainty?
A: Yes.
Q: What is your opinion?
A: My opinion is that. . . .

Again, experts may disagree about what is reasonably certain. It is not uncommon for one surgeon to recommend an operation but another surgeon to recommend trying medication first. Patients often obtain second medical opinions before submitting to treatment, because of an honest disagreement between competent physicians. Juries are entitled to hear the experts and to choose from among the experts' opinions. Juries usually make their choices on the basis of the relative competence of the experts and the reasons they give for their opinions. So we often have two opposing opinions, both of which are based on reasonable probability or certainty.

Expert Opinion Evidence

Some kinds of litigation, such as professional malpractice cases, require expert testimony to prove liability. For example, suppose a bridge collapses and a malpractice action is brought against the structural engineer who designed the bridge. The collapse does not, in itself, establish that the engineer failed to use due care in the bridge's design or specifications. Similarly, the mere fact that a lawyer loses a case does not mean the lawyer was negligent in preparing for the trial or in presenting the evidence. And a poor outcome from medical treatment does not necessarily mean the physician was negligent. To prove malpractice, the plaintiff must prove that the professional failed to comply with standards, practices, or procedures applicable within the profession. The plaintiff also must prove that the defendant's deviation from established professional standards was a direct cause of the loss. But a jury does not have the collective experience to determine what the professional standards are. Therefore, they cannot determine whether the professional violated the standards. Nor can they use their own experience to determine the cause. Therefore, someone who is familiar with the standards of the profession, usually a member of the profession, must describe the standards for the jury. A defendant in a malpractice action usually qualifies as an expert witness to testify whether there are standards, what the standards are, and whether he or she violated the standards.

Some cases do not require expert testimony, but expert testimony is allowed because it helps the jury to understand other evidence and its application to disputed facts. For example, if two automobiles have a head-on collision on a two-way highway and no one survives and no one sees it happen, expert witnesses may be allowed to reconstruct the accident. The experts have to show they have special training and experience in reconstructing automobile accidents. The experts would have to examine the accident scene and photographs, talk to witnesses, read depositions, examine the damaged vehicles, review scientific tables, and then explain, in the form of opinions, how and why the accident occurred. Reconstructionists testify in many kinds of accident cases, including accidents involving construction sites, automobiles, airplanes, and even slip-and-fall accidents.

An expert on arson may qualify to testify concerning the source of the fire and its point of origin based on evidence found at the scene of the fire. But an expert should not be allowed to take the next step and say who started the fire. There is question whether reconstructionists truly add informed judgment or merely draw conclusions. The parties probably could present the same evidence to the jury that the reconstructionist considers. Perhaps the jurors could use their own knowledge and experience and do just as good a job of concluding what happened. Some courts hold that if eyewitnesses can testify to what happened, no experts should be allowed to "reconstruct" the accident for the jury.

Equally qualified experts may come to diametrically opposed opinions or conclusions. Some experts engage in a good deal of sophistry. Nevertheless, experts play an important role in civil litigation. Do not be cynical about them. But do not be overwhelmed by them either. Your experts must be able to persuade you that their opinions are valid. If you are not convinced, a jury probably will not be convinced either. Always look to the reasons that the expert gives for his or her opinion. An expert's analysis and opinions are no better than the information (evidence) on which the expert relies. As the computer worlds says, "garbage in, garbage out." For example, if your expert opines that your client was driving less than thirty miles per hour, because the client's skid marks were only ten feet long, but the opponent's "better evidence" shows the skid marks were thirty feet long, the expert will not be believed. What is worse, on cross-examination, the expert may be asked to assume the truth of the opposing party's evidence and end up supporting the opposing party's version. Almost as important to persuasiveness are the reasons an expert gives for his or her opinions. The reasons are the explanation part of the analysis. For example, suppose there is a dispute about whether an orthopedic surgeon set a bone in plaintiff's leg in proper alignment. The patient contends the surgeon must have erred because she still has pain. But the defendant's expert has x-rays that show the bone is in perfect alignment. The defendant's expert's opinion is that the bone was properly set. The x-ray is a reason for the opinion.

Although courts allow experts to testify concerning a broad range of subjects, some limits have been well established. Expert witnesses may not testify what the law is or how the law applies to the facts of a case. That is the judge's role. An expert may not testify to whether the defendant had a legal duty to the plaintiff. An expert may not interpret contracts or statutes for the jury. An expert may not give opinion testimony about how the law applies to a certain set of facts. These are the judge's functions. For instance, an expert in insurance law would not be allowed to testify, as an expert, concerning the meaning and application of an insurance contract. The court (judge) must interpret the contract and tell the jury how it applies. Similarly, the judge must interpret applicable statutes and tell the jury how the statutes apply to the case. An expert who testifies to his or her analysis of the evidence and then renders a conclusion about what the evidence proves is merely making the attorney's final argument. It should not be allowed.

More often than not, each party is able to find an expert who will contradict the opposing expert's opinion. The jury has to choose between two or more opinions. The jurors cannot disregard the opinions entirely and form their own "expert opinion." They are limited to choosing, although they may be able to combine the opinions in some fashion.

An expert is not allowed to tell the jury how to decide the case. The rule is captured in the phrase that an expert must not "invade the province of the jury." However, the rule has some gray areas and is "bent" from time to time. For example, in medical malpractice cases, the parties' experts usually are allowed to testify that the defendant did or did not comply with standards of care. In effect, the expert is saying that the defendant was or was not negligent. The problem is addressed by Rule 704 of the Federal Rules of Evidence. It provides, in part, that "testimony in the form of an opinion or inference otherwise admissible is not objectionable because it embraces an ultimate issue to be decided by the trier of fact." Therefore, where opinion testimony is essential to help the jury, it is admissible even though the opinion may, in effect, tell the jury how the expert thinks the jury should decide the case. Otherwise, a court should not allow experts to influence the jury by testifying how the jurors should answer verdict questions or otherwise decide the case. As a general rule, an expert witness is not allowed to testify that the plaintiff or defendant was "negligent."

After a lawyer and expert have consulted, the expert may decide, for one reason or another, that she or he cannot or does not want to help. Or, the lawyer might decide against using the testimony of a particular expert even if she or he is willing to help. If their communications were subject to discovery, the disclosures could be problematic, even embarrassing. The theories advanced and rejected in the course of their frank discussions might be used against the party. Statements of facts and assumptions about facts made only tentatively might be used against a party in an effort to suggest a lack of certainty or apparent inconsistency. But if the expert has not yet been "retained," you don't have to disclose the expert. Therefore, care should be taken when soliciting and retaining experts.

Discovery of Experts' Opinions

With some difficulty, the Federal Rules of Civil Procedure have steered a course that preserves the adversary nature of civil litigation and yet allows each party to obtain all the essential information about the opposing party's experts and their opinions.[5] Rule 26(a) requires parties to disclose their expert witnesses as part of the initial disclosure. The expert must prepare a signed report that contains the expert's *complete* opinions, the basis and reasons for the opinions, the "information" and "data" the expert considered in deriving his or her opinions. The report must identify all exhibits the expert will use to support the opinion. The report must describe the expert's qualifications, including any publications the expert authored within the previous ten years. The report must identify all cases in which the expert has testified during the preceding four years, whether in trial or by deposition. In addition, the expert must disclose the payments he or she received to study the problem and the basis on which the expert will be paid for testifying. The disclosures must be supplemented in a timely basis as new information is obtained. The party who retained the expert must pay the costs incurred to prepare the report.

The effect of Rule 26 is to create three categories of experts: (1) experts who have been retained to testify at trial; (2) experts who have been retained to assist on the case, but not selected to testify at trial; (3) experts who have been consulted but who have not been retained. A party does not have to disclose experts who have not been retained. A party does not have to disclose in the initial discovery report experts who have been retained but will not testify at trial. Those experts, however, are subject to being identified through interrogatories. Another party cannot take their depositions or otherwise discover their opinions without a showing of exceptional circumstances. An attorney's consultation with such experts is treated as the attorney's work product. As part of the initial disclosure, a party must identify all experts whom the party retained to testify at trial. In addition, the party must provide other parties with a report from those experts. An opposing party may take the oral depositions of those experts without obtaining permission from the court.

When a party takes the deposition of another party's expert the proponent should pay for the expert's time and necessary expenses connected with the deposition. Otherwise, courts would be encouraging "fishing" for expert opinions, trying to secure such opinions through "admissions." However, the proponent should not have to pay for time the expert spends with the lawyer who retained the expert to prepare for the deposition. That is time the expert spends for the benefit of the party who hired him or her.

A Rule 26 initial disclosure need not identify experts with whom the attorney has consulted but who have not been retained to testify. Because parties need not voluntarily disclose such experts, the question arises, how does the opposing party find out about them? The answer is that a party may serve interrogatories that ask for information about experts who have been consulted but who are not expected to testify. That would seem to be "work-product" information. But according to Rule 26(b)(5):

> When a party withholds information otherwise discoverable under these rules by claiming that it is privileged or subject to protection as trial preparation material, the party shall make the claim expressly and shall describe the nature of the documents, communications, or things not produced or disclosed in [a] manner that, without revealing information itself privileged or protected, will enable other parties to assess the applicability of the privilege or protection.

Therefore, when asked, a party must disclose the existence of experts who have been consulted but who are not expected to testify. Interrogatories may inquire properly about the experts' identity, field of expertise, dates of consultations, the existence or reports, the date of each report, the number of pages in each report, who prepared each report, and the subject of each report. A proponent may not ask the deponent about the contents of the reports, why the deponent has elected not to have the expert testify, what the expert's opinions are, or what facts the expert has considered. So there is still a place for expert witness interrogatories in federal court.

On rare occasion, a party may be entitled to discover the opinions of another party's expert who is *not* going to be called to testify at a trial. There must be "exceptional circumstances" that make it impracticable to obtain facts or opinions on the same subject matter by other means. For example, suppose a woman buys a bottle of soda, consumes about half of it, and becomes ill an hour later. She assumes that the soft drink caused her illness. Her husband has a local chemist analyze the remaining soda. The chemist finds nothing unusual in the sample. Two months later, the husband takes the remaining soda to another chemist, who purports to find a toxin in it. The foreign substance is not ordinarily found at the bottling plant but is common to households. When an action is commenced months later, none of the soda is left for the defendant vendor to have analyzed. For obvious reasons, the plaintiffs may elect not to ask the first chemist to testify. Would it be fair to deny the defendant vendor the right to have the information that is available through the first chemist? No.[6]

Suppose some of the soft drink is still available for an independent analysis by a chemist to be chosen by the defendant. Should the defendant, nevertheless, be entitled to the first expert's opinion, analysis, factual data, and records? Probably, yes. The soft drink may have been contaminated after the first chemist completed the analysis. Therefore, the *same* subject matter is not necessarily available for analysis.

Most state courts preclude discovery of experts' reports, except in rare circumstances. A lawyer's consultation with experts for advice and guidance is treated as the lawyers' work product. Experts' reports are similarly treated as the attorney or party work product. The protection afforded to experts' reports allows candid discussion between lawyers and their experts. Notwithstanding the limitations on discovery of expert opinions and reports in state courts, parties commonly give their opponents a copy of an expert's report. There are various reasons for disclosing an expert's report. A report may be very persuasive and offered in the hope of obtaining a settlement. The parties may agree to exchange reports for, in effect, an even trade. Or, by producing an expert's report, a lawyer may seek to avoid the inconvenience of answering interrogatories about the expert's opinion.

The interrogatories in Exhibit 10.1 may be useful in state courts to obtain basic information about an opponent's experts. The first two interrogatories in Exhibit 10.1 should be easy to understand. The answer to the second interrogatory should describe fully each expert's education, training, and experience. Interrogatory 3 asks for each expert's opinion. In the example of the patient who presents symptoms of appendicitis, the physician would testify that in her or his opinion the patient had appendicitis and was in need of surgery to treat the problem.

A party should not take too much comfort in obtaining an opposing party's experts' report. The report may not contain or provide as much information as properly answered interrogatories would provide. A report may not contain all the information the expert has. The report may be selective and especially prepared for submission to the opposition. You must guard against diversionary tactics, even though it would be unethical for a lawyer to supply a false report. Willful use of a false report is **grounds** for disbarment.

grounds   A basis or foundation for a claim, motion, cause of action, or allegation.

■ Exhibit 10.1

Expert Witness Interrogatories

For each expert witness you intend to call to testify at the trial, do the following:

1. State the name, age, address, and employment of each such expert.
2. Describe in detail the qualifications of each expert with particular reference to the subject matter on which each expert may testify at trial.
3. State fully the opinions to which each expert is expected to testify.
4. Describe in detail the facts on which each expert relies for each opinion, respectively.
5. State a summary of the grounds for each opinion to which each expert is expected to testify.
6. Identify by author, title, publication date, and publisher all writings that your experts may use at trial as learned treatises.
7. Identify separately any document that you intend to call to the attention of any expert witness on cross-examination.

In state courts that do not follow the federal rules, parties may obtain much of the same information by serving interrogatories. Interrogatories can be used to obtain an expert's identity, a description of the subject matter about which the expert will testify, a statement of the facts the expert relies on, and the reasons for the expert's opinion. Only on a showing of exceptional circumstances and need will a court order a party to present his or her expert for an oral deposition or provide a written report. State rules may distinguish between experts who will testify and those who have merely been consulted. State courts seem to be a little more protective of a party's "work product" by limiting discoverability of contacts with experts.

Lawyers need time to prepare to deal with an opposing expert. A court may prohibit a party from using any expert witness whom the party failed to disclose in a timely manner. A party will not be allowed to obtain an advantage by failing to comply with disclosure or discovery requirements, even when the nondisclosure is inadvertent. But sometimes, as an alternative to exclusion, courts order the delinquent party to produce the secreted expert for an oral deposition. Needless to say, the scope of examination may go even beyond what would be covered in an initial disclosure report. Ordinarily, the parties determine how expense should be apportioned before the discovery is conducted. But if the parties cannot agree, the court will decide the allocation for them [Rule 26(b)(4)(C)].

Expert Witness Interrogatories

How should interrogatories be used in the typical case? Suppose the plaintiff suffered an injury when a five-year-old metal extension ladder collapsed while he was on it; he was carrying a heavy object and was near the top when the ladder's tread and side rail bent and gave way; and the ladder and the plaintiff fell to the ground. The plaintiff claims that the ladder was defective and that the manufacturer is strictly liable in tort because of the alleged defects. The complaint may or may not specify the defects claimed. Many kinds of defects are possible, including defects in

EXHIBIT 10.2

Expert Witness Interrogatories

For each expert witness you intend to have testify at trial, please do the following:

1. State the name, age, address, and position of employment of each expert.
2. Describe in detail the qualifications of each expert with particular reference to the issues about which he or she may be called to testify at the trial.
3. Describe in detail the subject matter on which each expert is expected to testify.
4. State fully the opinions to which each expert is expected to testify.
5. Describe fully the facts each expert relies on to support his or her opinions.
6. State in detail the grounds (reasons) for each opinion given in your answers to item 4.
7. Identify by author, title, copyright date, and publisher any writing that may be used as a "learned treatise" on which your expert may rely at trial in rendering his or her opinion.
8. Identify separately all documents you intend to call to the attention of any other expert witness on cross-examination, including the exact language of the documents that you claim can be read into evidence.
9. Set forth all data on which your expert will base his or her opinions that he or she claims is relied on by experts in his or her particular field even though such facts or data may not be admissible in evidence.
10. Identify each model, plat, diagram, or other tangible item used by the expert to verify or demonstrate his opinions, including
    a. A description of the item and its subject matter.
    b. The date of its preparation.
    c. The name and address of the current custodian.

materials, a defect in the metal (fissures) causing a weakness, a defect in design such as the side rails being too narrow or too thin or inadequate fasteners being used, or defects in instructions and failure to warn the user about foreseeable dangers, such as the need to position the ladder at certain angles or about the danger of overextending or overloading the ladder.

Assume that the plaintiff discloses that he has an expert who will testify that the ladder is defective. What information can the defendant obtain through written interrogatories directed to the plaintiff? The plaintiff's answers must specify the defect or defects claimed. The defendant is entitled to a summary of the grounds for the expert's opinion. The grounds are the expert's reasons, calculations, and the application of any relevant industry standards. The interrogatories should demand disclosure of all tests the expert conducted, such as analyses of cross sections of the side rail, any microscopic examinations, and any x-ray studies conducted to show the presence of fissures. The expert presumably determined the load strength by doing tests and making calculations. The defendant may ask for all such tests, the methods by which the tests were conducted and all calculations used to determine strength.

The defendant's interrogatories to the plaintiff could be similar to those presented in Exhibit 10.2. Interrogatories 1 and 2 are relatively simple to answer. Interrogatory 3 asks for the subject matter about which the expert will testify. An appropriate answer could be, "The design and construction of the ladder, including the materials out of which it is made." Interrogatory 4 asks for the plaintiff's expert's opinion. This is the "bottom line" question. The remaining interrogatories relate to the answer the expert gives to this question. A possible answer to Interrogatory 4 is "The ladder was defective when sold to the plaintiff because it was made out of an alloy that does not have sufficient strength to bear the weight ordinarily expected of a ladder. The design of the ladder leaves it without sufficient strength considering the materials used in its fabrication." The answer identifies two problems for the defendant: improper materials and/or improper design.

Interrogatory 5 asks for the facts the expert relied on to form the opinion. An appropriate answer could be, "The plaintiff weighs only 180 pounds. He was carrying a widget that weighed only 70 pounds. Their combined weight was only 250 pounds. A ladder has a useful life expectancy of more than five years, but this ladder failed after only five years of use. A close examination of the ladder shows that it has not been abused. There is no evidence of prior damage. The ladder's side rails are made out of an alloy of aluminum and manganese. Tests showed the metal in the side rails have a strength of only 200 pounds per square inch. No other ladder manufacturer uses such an alloy in side rails. There was no warning on the ladder that it would not support 250 pounds."

Interrogatory 6 asks for the grounds for the opinions. An appropriate response could be, "A ladder sold for use in construction work must be able to support 500 pounds at any rung. This ladder failed when supporting only 250 pounds. The side rails are made out of an "I" beam that is only 2.5 inches high and .25 inches thick. As constituted, the ladder has a strength of only 200 pounds per square inch. The ladder could be made stronger by having thicker side rails; otherwise, a different metal was required. The ladder should have tested at twice the strength to be adequate for use in construction work. If that metal were to be used in a ladder, the side rails would have to be twice as thick as the side rails in the ladder in question." The grounds for an opinion are the same as the reasons for the opinion. If the expert were relying on any governmental or industrial standard, it should be mentioned as a ground for the opinion.

Interrogatory 7 requires disclosure of publications on which the plaintiff's experts rely as authorities to support their opinions. Experts commonly justify their opinions by looking to published regulations, textbooks, and professional journals that seem to agree with them. Because the Rules of Evidence allow experts to use learned treatises to support and justify their opinions,[7] it is a good idea to find out, in advance, what publications an expert might use. Apparent support from one or more publications may be additional grounds for an expert's opinions.

Interrogatory 8 is not directed to the plaintiff's expert. That is information the defendant wants from the plaintiff's attorney so that the defendant can prepare its expert witnesses for trial. Interrogatory 9 asks for the "data" on which the plaintiff's expert relies. "Data" is one of those words that lawyers use very loosely. It includes almost anything that is in writing, such as reports, governmental statistics, industrial guidelines, official publications, and so forth. It is a catchall term. In our hypothetical case, if the ladder industry has published any standards or criteria for materials, design, fabrication, testing, or warnings, it should be mentioned—assuming the plaintiff's expert intends to use it to support his opinion.

Interrogatory 10 asks about any demonstrative evidence that the plaintiff's expert might use at trial to explain or support his opinion. An appropriate response is

A: Expert [name] will use the ladder in question, an identical ladder that is in new condition for comparison; a sample of the metal; a similar ladder manufactured by the XXX Company that is able to support 500 pounds. There is no date of preparation. Expert [name] has custody of the items at his laboratory.

Notice that the answer does not use the interrogatory subparts. Unless the answer is absolutely clear, as stated, it is preferable to use the subparts and show that the answers are truly responsive.

In an ordinary case, answers to interrogatories provide sufficient information about an opponent's expert to make additional discovery unnecessary. Even though a lot of information can be obtained through carefully drawn interrogatories, discovery of expert opinions through interrogatories does have significant limitations. The answers do not give the proponent an opportunity to evaluate the expert's personal appearance. Does the expert appear authoritative? Does the expert express himself or herself well orally? Does the expert recognize that other formulas or other methods of calculating are used in the industry and give different results? In the example, can the expert rule out the possibility that fissures developed in the side rail at some time after the ladder was sold to the plaintiff? To what extent have comparisons been made with other ladders? Can the expert rule out consumer misuse? If so, how? Is he aware of any weaknesses in his theory? What tests did the expert conduct that do not support the opinions expressed in the answers? With whom has the expert consulted for advice and guidance in forming the expressed opinions? These are the kinds of questions that would be raised if the court ordered the expert to submit to an oral deposition.

A state court may order a delinquent party to produce his or her expert for an oral deposition. If an expert refuses to appear for a deposition after a court has authorized it, the proponent can compel the expert to appear by serving a subpoena upon him or her. The same subpoena may be used to require the expert to produce records for inspection at the deposition. If the expert violates the subpoena, he or she is subject to being found in contempt of court and punished by fine or imprisonment. A party is presumed to be able to control a hired expert, so ordinarily subpoenas are not necessary. If a party cannot control the expert, she or he should notify the other side so that the expert can be placed under a subpoena.

Experts' Reports

After you have outlined the case to the prospective expert, the expert will examine the evidence that you have provided. The expert will form some preliminary opinions about your theory and the case as a whole. The next step is to have a meeting or obtain a *preliminary* report from the expert. That report is not the report that Rule 26(a)(2) requires as part of the initial disclosures. It is for your information. It helps to establish a meeting of the minds between the litigation team and the expert on how the case should be developed and what further information is needed. In this regard, you should instruct the expert to open two files. One file is for correspondence between the expert's office and yours. The other file should be a "work file." The work file should include everything that the expert has examined and considered in forming his or her opinions, including the engagement letter or retainer agreement, data, calculations, exhibits, and final reports. It should contain minimal correspondence.

When the expert's deposition is taken, as provided by Rule 26(b)(4)(A), the expert must produce the work file. Of course, the proponent's attorney will be interested in obtaining access to the "correspondence file" too. Keeping him or her from having access to it is problematic. It is not always clear what constitutes a report or whether a report is discoverable. So-called preliminary reports are work product and should be protected against discovery, but courts do not always agree. Whether the solicitation letter and preliminary report are discoverable depends on local customs and practices in your jurisdiction. You need to find out what is typical in your community.

The federal rules assume that after the attorney, paralegal, and expert have done their homework, they will have a consensus on what the **initial disclosure report** should say and how it should be worded. Although the rule refers to reports "written and signed" by the expert, you may be asked to *draft* the report. The final draft will be the expert's report. Preparing the report is not a formidable task. By this time all the real work has been done. You can obtain the information you need from the pleadings, correspondence, conferences, and preliminary reports. All you have to do is put the pertinent information into the appropriate section. The initial disclosure report should use the section headings suggested by Rule 26(a)(2), namely

> a. Expert's Identity
> b. Expert's Qualifications
> c. a. Background
>   b. Publications
>   c. Other Cases
>   d. Compensation
> d. Statement Of Opinions
> e. Data Considered
> f. Summaries [used by expert] or Exhibits (if any)
> g. Signature

The report will need to be approved and signed by the expert.

Party as an Expert

The federal rules treat parties who are experts the same as any other expert witness. If a party intends to testify as an expert, he or she must make an initial disclosure, provide a report, and submit to a deposition. Expert witnesses who are employees of parties are treated similarly. The work-product limitation only applies to "outside" experts who are retained to assist with the particular litigation.

---

initial disclosure report   Rule 26(a) requires parties to disclose to each other, in writing, the following information: (1) the name, address, and telephone number of each known witness, (2) a description of each document that is or contains evidence, (3) a compilation of damages claimed and all supporting documentation, (4) relevant insurance policies, (5) expert witnesses and experts' reports.

What if a party serves notice of the depositions of another party's employees who are experts but who have nothing to do with the particular occurrence? May the proponent's lawyer ask them questions about the occurrence and ask for opinions about design, materials, fabrication methods, and so forth? Rule 26 does not address this situation. Probably a court would quash the notice for taking their depositions if the defendant showed by affidavit that the employees had no connection with the project. If they were deposed, they probably could elect to have no opinions concerning the subject matter. Unless an expert is an employee of a party, the expert's concessions and admissions are not party admissions.

In any malpractice litigation, the defendant will hire another professional to review the case to determine whether the defendant committed malpractice. In a medical-malpractice case, the physician hired to evaluate the treatment may conduct a Rule 35 independent medical examination of the plaintiff. Thus, one expert may have two distinct roles. Each role must be handled separately. If the plaintiff asks for a report on the independent medical examination, Rule 35 requires the examiner to provide a complete report. This report is available through the party who requested the examination—not directly from the independent medical examiner. The Rule 35 report should discuss the patient's medical history, the findings, diagnosis, and so forth. However, the medical report should not discuss the malpractice issues. The expert witness should prepare a separate report concerning the malpractice allegations. The plaintiff's attorney may take the expert's deposition concerning the expert's opinions on the malpractice issue, but not concerning the independent medical examination. See Rule 35. The defendant should consider having separate experts for these tasks. The same problem is presented in engineering and architect malpractice cases. A party may want to hire one expert to evaluate the malpractice claim and other experts to evaluate the alleged loss.

Retaining Expert Witnesses

There are lots of experts in every field. The problem is finding an expert who agrees with your theory of the occurrence, *and* who has good credentials, makes a good appearance, is cooperative, and is affordable. Most lawyers have their preferred experts and sources for obtaining experts. You will find that many experts advertise their services in the classified sections of attorneys' publications. Many advertise by direct mail. Large consulting firms active in construction, accounting, utilities, transportation, and the like advertise that they have specialists who assist lawyers. You may find experts through a local college or university. There are many sources.

Once you have found an expert who seems qualified, you have to bring him or her into the case. The first contact should be in person or by telephone to keep the initial meeting "work product" and not discoverable. Assuming the expert is willing to help, he or she will want a detailed written description of the case and an outline of his or her role.[8] If you chose to write a letter to the expert, the letter should clearly assert at the top of each page that the letter is a "PRIVILEGED COMMUNICATION." Maybe it is and maybe it is not, but it is best to claim the privilege. At least it shows that the document was prepared in anticipation of litigation. Notwithstanding the assertion, the letter should be drafted in light of the possibility that someday it will be discovered by the other side. You and the attorney will have to confer about the letter's contents to make sure that enough information is provided but not "too much." If after receiving your letter, the expert decides against helping, is your contact with the expert and your letter discoverable? Probably not, because the expert has not been *"retained in anticipation of litigation or preparation for trial."* See Rule 26(b)(4)(B).

There is no reason why a party should be limited to the opinions of the first expert the party happens to consult. If the first expert with whom you consult decides not to work on the case or you decide to discontinue the relationship, you have to continue your search. It is perfectly reasonable and proper for a party's representatives to consult with several experts before choosing one to testify. You do not have to disclose an expert with whom you have consulted but who has not been retained. But if the expert is retained and does some work on the case, there may be a question whether the expert was "retained" within the meaning of the Rule. If so, the next question is whether the expert formed any opinions. If so, your letter may be one of the items on which the expert relied to form an opinion, and that would make your letter discoverable.

Good trial preparation requires each side to find out as quickly as possible about the other side's expert witnesses, their opinions, and the grounds for their opinions. It usually takes quite a bit of time to fully analyze an expert's rationale, check the expert's data, and check on the expert's background. In addition, it usually takes time to locate opposing expert witnesses who are knowledgeable, authoritative, and persuasive. The rules balance the need for such information against the principle that each party must obtain his or her own evidence. You will have lots of opportunities to work with experts and their reports.

Costs

The use of experts adds considerably to the cost of litigation. Experts must be paid for time they spend reviewing the facts, analyzing the problem, conferring, preparing reports, testifying in a deposition, preparing for trial, and appearing in court. Experts should charge by the hour or day, but never as a percentage of the money damages recovered. Resist any such suggestion! Of course, the party who retains the expert is obligated by contract to pay the expert's fees and expenses. In the event a court orders another party to pay the expert's fees, still, the party who retained the expert remains responsible until the expert has been paid.

The Rules provide guidelines for determining who pays an expert for time spent in discovery proceedings. When an expert's opinion is sought through interrogatories, the party who hired the expert must pay the expert's fees for the time spent helping to answer the interrogatories. If an oral deposition is ordered, the proponent must pay a *reasonable* fee for the time the expert spends testifying. If the expert charges more, his or her employer will have to pay the difference. If the parties and the expert cannot agree on what amount is reasonable, the issue may be submitted to the judge for determination. If the judge awards a fee smaller than is acceptable to the expert, the expert's remedy is to obtain the balance from the party who retained him or her. The amount the expert actually charges is subject to discovery, because it may reflect on the expert's credibility. The party who retained the expert must pay for any preparation time. The expert's preparation time is not for the proponent's benefit, and the proponent has no control over it.

Sanctions

If a party fails to disclose an expert before trial, the expert may not be allowed to testify. If the consequences of excluding the expert are too severe and if the prejudicial effect of the nondisclosure can be eliminated by postponing the trial or allowing the opponent to take the expert's oral deposition, or both, a court may choose those options. The delinquent party usually has to pay all the opposing party's expenses in connection with the deposition. A court always has the more severe options available, such as striking the delinquent party's pleading, excluding the delinquent party's evidence and assessing costs.

TECHNOLOGY NOTES

Your firm will probably have a list of expert witnesses who have been effective and reliable on subject matters the firm regularly litigates. If you need to search out a new expert, the Internet provides access to experts in almost every field. Use "expert witness" as a key word, and you will find hundreds of expert-witness directories. This should tell you that a referral will probably produce more effective and reliable expert assistance than a search of a large directory. In other words, be selective in your search for expert assistance.

SUMMARY

When scientific, technical, or other specialized knowledge will help the trier of fact to understand the evidence or to determine a fact in issue, a witness qualified as an expert by knowledge, skill, experience, training, or education may testify thereto in the form of an opinion or otherwise. Trial court judges have broad discretion in deciding whether the "expert" is qualified and whether the "opinions" may be helpful to the jury. A person does not have to have a strong academic background to be an expert where the subject in question does not involve higher learning. An automobile mechanic who did not finish high school might qualify as an expert concerning automobile repair work. A person may qualify to be an expert solely through experience in the field. Generally speaking, lawyers like to use expert witnesses. Experts can make almost any subject more understandable. But experts add significantly to the cost of litigation.

Expert opinions are admissible in evidence when the jury needs experts' experienced judgment to understand or resolve esoteric fact issues. An expert provides a perspective that jurors could not have because of their limited knowledge or experience. An expert opinion is a form of evidence that a jury may consider in rendering a verdict. An expert's opinion must be based on facts that are supported by evidence in the case. An expert must apply the standards of his or her profession to those facts and use his or her experienced judgment to form the expert opinion. The opinion goes a step beyond the facts on which it is based and becomes evidence in itself. As part of the foundation for an expert opinion, the expert must testify that he or she is reasonably certain that the opinion is correct. That means the expert, being intellectually honest, must believe that the opinion is one on which he or she would act. An opinion that is reasonably certain is not subject to serious doubt in the expert's mind. The expert's belief that the opinion probably is correct does not give the opinion sufficient credibility to allow it to be evidence.

An expert witness's conclusions from the facts are not evidence. A witness reaches a conclusion merely by reasoning through the evidence and concluding what the evidence proves. It may require skill and expertise to do the reasoning and to reach the right conclusion, but a conclusion does not add to the evidence. An opinion may require the same reasoning, but, in addition, it requires the application of experienced judgment. An opinion is additional evidence, which a jury may consider. A conclusion is merely a deduction or argument and something a jury should not consider in resolving a fact issue. Only the attorneys are allowed to argue what the evidence proves. That is the purpose of an attorney's final argument.

A witness must qualify as an expert before the court will allow the witness to express any expert opinions. An expert qualifies by testifying to his or her own education, training, and experience in the particular field. Some courts allow the expert to supply a curriculum vitae as evidence of his or her qualifications. If the expert intends to provide a curriculum vitae, a copy should be attached to the initial disclosure report. In malpractice actions, the defendant usually qualifies as an expert witness and may express an opinion concerning the correctness of his or her own conduct.

Certain types of litigation, such as a professional malpractice, require expert opinion testimony to establish a prima facie case of liability. It requires an expert to identify the professional standards the plaintiff claims the defendant violated. Without expert testimony, a jury could only guess whether the defendant acted according to the standards of his or her profession. An expert's opinions are persuasive when the expert has good credentials and has good reasons for her or his opinions.

An initial disclosure report need not identify experts whom a party has consulted but who has not been retained to testify at trial. However, parties may serve interrogatories to obtain the identity of experts who were hired to provide advice or information for the case but will not be called on to testify at the trial. But such experts' opinions cannot be discovered unless a court authorizes discovery. A court will authorize the discovery only on a showing of exceptional circumstances that make it impractical for the opposing party to obtain *facts* or *opinions* on the same subject by other means.

Experts who have been retained to testify at trial are subject to being deposed. A party must show the court exceptional circumstances to obtain leave to depose another party's expert who was retained but not chosen to testify. You do not have to disclose an expert with whom you have consulted but who has not been retained to assist with the case.

In state courts that have not copied the federal rules, parties may use interrogatories to obtain an opponent's experts' opinions. A proponent may inquire about the identity of experts, the subject matter about which the experts will testify, any statements on which the experts rely, and the grounds (reasons) for the expert's opinions. Interrogatories do not give the proponent an opportunity to evaluate the expert's personal appearance or ability to express himself or herself orally. Nor is there an opportunity to cross-examine the expert. If a party fails to disclose experts in a timely manner, the court may prohibit the expert from testifying or may order the delinquent party to produce the expert for a deposition at the latter party's expense.

Notwithstanding the proscriptions on discovery of expert opinions and reports, parties often give their opponents their experts' reports. In federal court, as part of the initial disclosure, each party must provide to the others reports by the experts who will testify at trial. Each report must contain the expert's identity, qualifications, background, publications, other cases, compensation, opinions, data considered, summaries used by the expert, exhibits used by the expert, and signature of the expert. If the expert's testimony deviates from the report, the report could be used to impeach the expert. The party who hired the expert must pay for the initial disclosure report.

A party who is an expert is treated the same as any other expert witness. If a party intends to testify as an expert, he or she must make an initial disclosure, provide a report, and submit to a deposition. A party's employees who are experts are treated similarly. The work-product limitation on discovery only applies to "outside" experts who are retained to assist with the particular litigation. If an expert has not been disclosed before trial, the expert may not be allowed to testify, but the trial judge has broad discretion in how to handle the problem.

KEY TERMS

conclusion	grounds
curriculum vitae	initial disclosure report
expert opinions	reasonable certainty
foundation	sound discretion

REVIEW QUESTIONS

1. What factors determine whether a court will allow the parties to present expert witness testimony?

2. What factors determine whether a person qualifies to testify as an expert witness?

3. When is an expert's opinion discoverable in federal court?

4. When is a party required to disclose the expert opinion of a consultant whom the party does not intend to call on to testify at trial?

5. What elements determine whether a person has sufficient competence to testify as an expert witness?

6. Is expert testimony limited to matters involving science and engineering?

7. Is an expert required to disclose the fact that he or she has testified in other cases?

8. May the parties define the scope of discovery for expert opinions as part of their discovery plan?

9. Is a detrimental statement by a party's expert witness an admission of the party?

10. What is meant by the grounds for an expert's opinion?

11. If a party elects to take the deposition of another party's expert witness, who must pay the expert's fee?

12. If a retained expert refuses to issue a written report, what remedy does the opposing party have?

CASE ASSIGNMENT

You are working on attorney Donald Smith's litigation team representing the plaintiff trustee. He has decided to retain Dale Peterson to "reconstruct" the accident and provide a supporting plat if it would help the trustee's case. Mr. Peterson has already told attorney Smith that he will help if he can. Mr. Smith has asked you to write a letter to Mr. Peterson that explains what you know about the accident and what the litigation team needs from him. Mr. Peterson has done work for the firm in the past. He is well qualified. Because you may not have all the information he needs yet, you should ask what more he needs.

Endnotes

1. Laypersons may provide opinion evidence in some situations. By way of example, an experienced driver may testify concerning the speed of a moving vehicle in terms of miles per hour, but not whether the vehicle was going "too fast" or "too slow" or at "an unsafe speed." Speed in miles per hour is a fact. In effect, the witness has an opinion about a fact. In this example, a layperson qualifies to give an opinion based on his or her training and experience with motor vehicles. The law has had to compromise and allow opinion evidence because sometimes it is the best evidence available.

2. The facts upon which an expert bases an opinion may have been observed by the expert or merely communicated to the expert.

3. There is nothing in law that prevents an expert from claiming even higher degrees of certainty. Specifically, an expert might be willing to testify that her or his opinion concerning a past or present fact is based on reasonable certainty or absolute certainty. Now we are getting into legal strategies.

4. Insert whatever the particular field of endeavor is.

5. Rule 26(a)(2) provides

   (A) . . . [A] party shall disclose to other parties the identity of any person [expert] who may be used at trial to present evidence under Rules 702, 703 or 705 of the Federal Rules of Evidence. (B) Except as otherwise stipulated or directed by the court, this disclosure shall, with respect to a witness who is retained or specially employed to provide expert testimony in the case or whose duties as an employee of the party regularly involve giving expert testimony, be accompanied by a written report prepared and signed by the witness. The report shall contain a complete statement of all opinions to be expressed and the basis and reasons therefor; the data or other information considered by the witness in forming the opinion; any exhibits to be used as a summary of or support for the opinions; the qualifications of the witness, including a list of all publications authored by the witness within the preceding ten years; the compensation to be paid for the study and testimony and a listing of any other cases in which the witness has testified as an expert at trial or by deposition within the preceding four years.

   Rule 26(b)(4)(B) limits discovery with regard to experts who will not testify at trial: A party may, through interrogatories or by deposition, discover facts known or opinions held by an expert who has been retained or specially employed by another party in anticipation of litigation or preparation for trial and who is not expected to be called as a witness at trial only as provided in Rule 35(b) or upon a showing of exceptional circumstances under which it is impracticable for the party seeking discovery [the proponent] to obtain facts or opinions on the same subject by other means.

6. This hypothetical situation also shows why a party is required to disclose the identity of witnesses whose testimony is protected against discovery as "work product" without disclosing the privileged subject matter. How else could the defendant find out about the first chemist, except through discovery. So the plaintiff must disclose the fact of the prior test and the identity of the first chemist, but may refuse to disclose what the chemist found—until a court orders it.

7. [Rule 803(18)].

8. Experts are inclined to want all of the information in writing. Lawyers are reluctant to put such communications in writing, however, because the writing may be subject to discovery.

 For additional resources, visit our Web site at www.paralegal.delmar.cengage.com

CHAPTER **11**

INTERROGATORIES

CHAPTER OUTLINE

Chapter Objectives

Chapter 11 explains what interrogatories are, how they are used to obtain information and evidence, and how to prepare them. It also discusses how to answer interrogatories and how to deal with improper interrogatories.

Introduction

Interrogatories are formal, written questions that one party poses to another party to obtain information and evidence concerning their litigation. Interrogatories are the most basic and economical method of discovery. You can expect to work extensively with interrogatories. You will prepare interrogatories for service on opposing parties. You will prepare answers to other parties' interrogatories. You will search for information and documents with which to answer interrogatories. You can identify problem interrogatories to which objections should be interposed. You may prepare objections. You may prepare motions for challenging interrogatories or insufficient answers to interrogatories. Interrogatories will be an important part of your practice.

Preparing Interrogatories

Rule 33 authorizes party interrogatories. We will refer to a party who propounds interrogatories as a **proponent,** and a party who must answer interrogatories as a **deponent.**[1] Although interrogatories are inherently questions, they may be stated either as questions or imperatives. For example, an interrogatory may be phrased: "What is the date of your birth?" Or, "State the date of your birth." The scope of inquiry is prescribed by Rule 26(b). But in addition, interrogatories may be used to require a deponent to explain more fully and clearly the legal theory on which the party's claim or defense is based. Also, interrogatories may be used to require another party to explain how he or she contends the law applies to particular facts. Interrogatories may be used in this way because the answers are prepared by the deponent's attorney and paralegals. Interrogatories may be served only on other parties, not on witnesses. Each question must be stated separately. Interrogatories should be drafted to be clear and concise.

In federal court, parties are allowed to serve only twenty-five interrogatories on each other. If the case involves two defendants, the plaintiff may serve up to twenty-five interrogatories on each. And if there are several plaintiffs, each defendant may serve up to twenty-five interrogatories on each plaintiff. Parties do not have to be adverse to be able to serve interrogatories on each other. Thus, codefendants who have not cross-claimed may serve interrogatories on each other. Plaintiffs who do not have claims against each other may serve interrogatories on each other. A party may move the court for leave to serve more. The motion must explain why more interrogatories are needed. If a deponent believes that the proponent's interrogatories are excessively burdensome or constitute harassment, he or she may move the court for a protective order limiting the interrogatories or limiting their scope [Rule 26(c)].

The limitation forces parties to ask only important questions. It reduces abuse of interrogatories, as where a party serves hundreds of them. Also, parties' initial disclosures provide information that routinely had been obtained through interrogatories. Some state courts limit the number of interrogatories, although the limit is more likely to be larger, such as fifty.

Timing

Rule 26(d) precludes parties from serving interrogatories until they have participated in a discovery planning meeting:

> Except . . . when authorized under these rules or by order or agreement of the parties, a party may not seek discovery from any source before the parties have conferred as required by Rule 26(f).

One of the purposes of the meeting is to obtain agreement on the number of interrogatories the parties may use and other appropriate limits. A deponent has thirty days in which to prepare and serve his or her answers to interrogatories. But when a

proponent A party who makes some demand or request on another party or who actively seeks some action by a court.

deponent A person who gives testimony under oath in an affidavit, in an oral deposition, in a written deposition or in court.

proponent serves interrogatories by mail, the deponent has three more days in which to serve the answers [Rule 6(e)]. Rule 6(b) allows a party to move the court, ex parte, for an order that increases the time for answering, but the motion must be made before the prescribed limit has expired. If discovery is needed before a suit can be brought, the proponent must resort to an oral deposition as provided by Rules 27 and 30.

State Court Parameters

In most state courts, discovery is not tied to *initial disclosures* or *discovery conferences*. A plaintiff may serve interrogatories with the complaint or any time after the action has been commenced. A defendant may serve interrogatories on the plaintiff even before the answer is due. If a plaintiff serves interrogatories before the defendant has answered the complaint, the interrogatories cannot be served by mail. But the defendant may serve interrogatories by mail on the plaintiff's attorney. The usual length of time for answering interrogatories is thirty days after service. But in most states the period is extended by fifteen days if the plaintiff serves interrogatories on the defendant before the answer is due. Defendants commonly serve interrogatories with their answers to the complaints to obtain the kind of information provided in federal initial disclosures. When interrogatories are served by mail, the prescribed periods are increased, usually by three days.

Format

Federal rules do not prescribe a format for interrogatories. Of course, like any other litigation document, interrogatories must bear the title of the action, court file number and the title: "INTERROGATORIES." An introductory sentence is often used to make clear the parameters. Example: "Plaintiff demands that defendant answer the attached interrogatories as provided by Rule 33 of the Federal Rules of Civil Procedure." An interrogatory may refer to the deponent by name or as "you" or by party designation—"defendant" or "plaintiff." In the example in Exhibit 11.1, the requirement that the deponent describe periods of employment for each job does not keep the question from being singular.

Each interrogatory must be separately numbered. When appropriate, interrogatories may include subparts. But each subpart counts as an individual interrogatory. In this example, question 1 asks five questions. Otherwise, lawyers and paralegals could circumvent the limitation by creatively using subpart questions. Can you

---

EXAMPLE

1. For each witness statement obtained by the defendant, state the following:
   a. The name and address of the person who interviewed the witness.
   b. The date on which the statement was obtained.
   c. The means by which the statement was recorded.
   d. The name and address of each person who was present when the statement was obtained.
   e. Whether the witness has been given a copy of his or her statement.

EXHIBIT 11.1

Format for Interrogatories

United States District Court for the
                    Southern District of New York
                    Civil Action, File Number _____

A. B., Plaintiff,
        vs.   SET ONE
                                    INTERROGATORIES TO
C. D., Defendant.   Defendant C. D.

To: Defendant C. D. and his attorney, James Smith, 1310 East Highway 96,
Suite 204, Albany, New York, 12232

PLEASE TAKE NOTICE that plaintiff demands answers to the following interrogatories, under oath, pursuant to Rule 33 of the Federal Rules of Civil Procedure.

1. State the names and addresses of all persons and companies that have em-
    ployed you during the past ten years, and identify the period of each em-
    ployment respectively.

DATED: February 7, 2006.   By _____
                                              Plaintiff

                                      By _____
                                      W. S. Hutton [State License No.]
                                      4200 High Tower
                                      39 North Sixth Street
                                      Indianapolis, IND. 35402
                                      [Telephone]

                                      Attorneys for Plaintiff

make one question by combining the subparts? How about asking: "Describe each witness statement you have obtained by identifying fully the date on which it was obtained, the identity of the interviewer, how the statement was recorded, whether the witness has been given a copy?" You can see that reasonable people might differ as to whether it is a single question.

Parties who have a limited number of interrogatories must consider ways of conserving them. Suppose a husband and wife bring an action to recover money damages for the wife's injuries sustained in an automobile accident and the defendant wants to serve more than twenty-five interrogatories to obtain information about the accident, wife's injuries, plaintiffs' background, exhibits, and so forth. The defendant could serve twenty-five interrogatories on the wife and another twenty-five on the husband. In effect, the defendant can ask fifty questions. Of course, none of the interrogatories served on the husband should duplicate interrogatories served on the wife. Duplication wastes time and effort and irritates deponents.

Parties often serve interrogatories in groups or "sets." The first set of interrogatories should be labeled "Set One." As a party has a need to ask more questions and serve more sets, each set should be identified consecutively as "Set Two," "Set Three," and so on. Whenever additional sets are used, the better practice is to continue numbering the interrogatories consecutively. To illustrate, if Set One ends with interrogatory "8," Set Two should begin with interrogatory number "9." This makes it simpler and easier to refer to the interrogatories. A set of interrogatories contains all the questions that the party needed to ask at the time the set was served. Parties never group interrogatories into sets on the basis of subject matter or some other classification. For instance, when a defendant serves initial interrogatories on a plaintiff, the defendant does not serve one set concerning liability and another set concerning damages.

A proponent should keep interrogatories from being unduly burdensome. In the past, some lawyers had no compunction against serving hundreds of interrogatories covering all aspects of the litigation. The respondent was forced to spend lots of time and effort trying to answer the questions—some of which was really needless. Federal courts reacted to the problem by limiting the number of interrogatories one party may serve on another. Many state courts have taken a similar approach. The relevancy and importance of the questions should be weighed against the burden and inconvenience to the deponent. Some lawyers try to ensure specificity and clarity by using a list of definitions at the beginning of each set of interrogatories. The set of definitions should help to keep the interrogatories concise. But some definitions are too long and merely complicate the process. Each interrogatory should be drafted to facilitate an easy answer. For example, if it is possible, phrase an interrogatory so that it can be answered with a "yes" or "no." The interrogatory will not be burdensome and the answer cannot be misinterpreted.

Law firms that specialize in particular types of litigation usually have form interrogatories to cover common issues. Form interrogatories are perfectly acceptable, but they must be applicable to the case. It is unprofessional to serve form interrogatories that were drafted for another type of case and are not directly pertinent to the current issues. If your office uses form interrogatories, be careful to select from the forms only those interrogatories that truly are relevant.

You should avoid using two interrogatories where one would suffice. For example: (1) "Do you know of any witnesses to the accident?" (2) "If your answer to the preceding interrogatory is yes, state the name and address of each witness." A better approach is to use one interrogatory stated as an imperative: "State the name and address of all witnesses to the accident."

Do not propound an interrogatory without having a specific purpose and a reasonable need for the information. It is all too easy for proponents to serve a myriad of questions that require the respondent to spend days collecting useless information. If interrogatories are served just to make the file look substantial or to satisfy the client's curiosity or to harass the deponent, the proponent has abused the process. Poorly drafted interrogatories frustrate and irritate the deponent, the deponent's attorney, and the court. Carefully drafted interrogatories encourage appropriate responses. A deponent cannot easily circumvent carefully drawn interrogatories. If an interrogatory is poorly phrased, the deponent has good grounds for objecting or not answering it. Or the deponent may provide a nonresponsive answer, knowing the proponent will be too embarrassed to ask the court for an order compelling the deponent to give a better one. The proponent may serve a replacement interrogatory, but he or she has reduced the allowed number. You must use interrogatories properly. You must act responsibly, with restraint.

Interrogatory Uses

Interrogatories may ask whether the deponent knows of any witnesses to the occurrence or transaction. But the question should be phrased as an imperative: "State the names and addresses of all persons whom you claim witnessed the parties' accident." Stated as an imperative, the answer must disclose the identity of witnesses instead of merely answering "yes" or "no." The answer will not be evidence but may lead to the discovery of evidence.

Interrogatories may be used to determine the existence or nonexistence of records and documents and information about their contents and location. They can be used to obtain copies of documents.

EXAMPLE

Interrogatory Concerning Documents

1. In regard to all business records and other documents relevant to the above-entitled action, state:
   a. The nature and subject matter of each document.
   b. The date on which each document was prepared.
   c. The names and addresses of the persons who prepared the documents, respectively.
   d. The name and address of the custodian of each document.

A deponent must answer by identifying each document and providing the appropriate information concerning each document. A deponent would be subject to sanctions if he or she provided the information without keeping it relevant to each document, respectively.

Interrogatories are used to ascertain the existence or nonexistence of tangible evidence, its location, and custodian.

EXAMPLE

Interrogatory Concerning Tangible Property

1. If you claim any tangible item is evidence or contains evidence relevant to the above matter, state:
   a. The description of each item fully.
   b. The names and addresses of the custodian of each item.

A party may use interrogatories to force another party to reveal sources of information, such as witnesses who have knowledge about a particular subject.

EXAMPLE

Interrogatory Concerning Witnesses

1. State the names and addresses of all persons you claim have any knowledge of or information concerning the accident described in the complaint.

Note, the only witnesses to be identified are those who have information about the accident. The interrogatory may not ask what each witness knows. That information will have to be obtained by interviewing the witnesses or taking their depositions.

Interrogatories may require a deponent to identify witnesses by categories, such as "all persons who witnessed the accident," or "all witnesses who arrived after the accident," or "all witnesses who have information concerning damages." A deponent is not required to summarize each witness's expected testimony or the information the deponent believes each witness has. Interrogatories that ask the deponent to summarize a witness's expected testimony are objectionable. Once a respondent has disclosed the identity of a witness, the proponent can contact the witness to interview the witness or obtain a statement or take the witness's deposition—whatever the situation requires. Similarly, a party may use interrogatories to force another party to reveal sources of information, such as witnesses who have knowledge about a particular subject; the existence of witness statements, photographs of a particular subject, and specific documents; or the subject matter of conversations.

A party may use interrogatories to obtain information about the contents of specific documents and conversations.

EXAMPLE

1. Describe fully any conversation you had with police officers about the accident, including:
   a. The date, time, and place of each conversation.
   b. What you stated to each officer; if you cannot recite the statement verbatim, state the substance.
   c. What each officer stated to you; if you cannot recite the statement verbatim, state the substance.

Note, there is a difference between asking what a witness has said and what the witness knows or to what the witness would testify. Interrogatories that ask about conversations should request the deponent to repeat the exact words in the conversation. Of course, it is almost impossible to repeat exact words unless the conversation was recorded, so the interrogatory should provide, in the alternative, for disclosure of the substance of what each person said. It is also important to find out who was present, whether a record or memorandum was made of the conversation, who prepared it, and who has custody of the recording or memorandum. The deponent's answers to such interrogatories provide groundwork for further inquiry when the deponent's deposition is taken.

Interrogatories are used to obtain basic background information, such as a party's previous addresses, employment history, claims history, medical history, litigation history, criminal convictions, educational background, use of aliases, social security number, and marriages. Interrogatories are used to ascertain the existence or nonexistence of tangible evidence, its location, and custodian. They are the best discovery procedure a party may use to force another party to explain in more detail the basis for the party's claims or defenses. Similarly, they are the best discovery procedure a party may use to ask another party to explain how that party contends the law applies to given facts. Example: "State the facts on which you base your claim that the defendant was negligent." And "Describe fully the facts on which defendant bases his allegation that plaintiff assumed the risk of his injuries." And "State fully why the lawn mower manufactured by defendant 'is not of merchantable quality' as alleged in plaintiff's complaint." Of course the answers to such interrogatories will be prepared by the party's attorney. These kinds of questions would not be useful in a deposition, because the attorney would not be allowed to testify.

Also, obtaining a more specific statement of the opponent's claim or defense does not conflict with the rule against disclosure of attorney's work product. The deponent is not required to disclose what his or her side has done to develop or substantiate the legal theories. For example, the plaintiff and her lawyer must answer the interrogatory about negligence with specific allegations such as unlawful speed (specifying miles per hour), failure to yield right-of-way, driving on the wrong side of the highway, failure to signal a turn, failure to keep a proper lookout, and so forth. If the plaintiff's answer only specifies the defendant's excessive speed as the negligent act, and, at trial, the plaintiff attempts to prove the defendant's brakes were negligently maintained, the defendant may be able to exclude any evidence about brakes, or to obtain a postponement of the trial to allow the defendant to prepare on the new issue. Similarly, in a product liability case, the complaint may allege generally that the defendant's product is defective in its design, fabrication, warnings, and instructions. The defendant's interrogatories may ask the plaintiff to specify the alleged defects. The plaintiff's answers should specify the problems. The defendant can focus on those alleged problems. The plaintiff may pose the same type of interrogatory to the defendant concerning affirmative defenses asserted in the answer. In this way, interrogatories allow the parties to concentrate on specific issues.

The defendant's initial interrogatories usually ask about the plaintiff's version of the transaction or occurrence and plaintiff's evidence. In addition, defendants ordinarily inquire about factors affecting the plaintiff's claim for damages, including the nature and extent of the alleged loss. In personal-injury actions, defendants ask questions about plaintiffs' medical expenses, prior income, and loss of income. Any matter concerning a plaintiff's claim for money damages is a proper subject for interrogatories. Suppose the plaintiff is claiming $20,000 in damages for his damaged automobile. The defendant needs to know the original cost of the automobile; when and from whom it was purchased; whether it can be repaired or has to be replaced;

the estimated or actual cost of repair; the availability of supporting documentation such as repair bills, invoices, and receipts; and more.

A proponent may ask whether the deponent has any liability insurance that will pay any judgment against the deponent. The proponent is entitled to discover the name of the insurer, the identity of the particular insurance policy, the amount of available coverage, and whether there is any dispute over the coverage [Rule 26(b)(2)]. If there is a dispute over coverage, the proponent should consider making a demand for the policy in question, pursuant to Rule 34. Technically, the availability of liability insurance is not relevant to accident cases because insurance does not affect issues of liability or damages. Nevertheless, discovery of insurance is allowed, because it may affect the parties' willingness or ability to settle their dispute. The most efficient means of obtaining insurance information is through written interrogatories.

A defendant served the interrogatories in Exhibit 11.2 on a plaintiff who was injured in an automobile accident. As you study the interrogatories and answers, consider the effect of using the conjunctive "and" or the disjunctive "or." Consider whether the information sought will lead to admissible evidence. Consider how questions can be made more succinct. Are any of the questions multiple but disguised to be singular? Illustrative answers are provided in the recommended form in Exhibit 11.2, that is, stated after reiterating each question. You will notice that a narrative answer was given to a question with subparts. Consider whether the narrative answer is fair. Are any of the answers really useful to the defendant? Has the plaintiff said more than she should in any of the answers? Note the date in Exhibit 11.2 is not necessarily the date on which the interrogatories are served. The date provides a convenient means of identifying the interrogatories.

A deponent's answers to interrogatories may merely provide the proponent with information or the answers may be evidence that the proponent can use at trial. For example, if the deponent describes his or her conversations with the police about how the accident happened, the proponent may offer the interrogatory answer into evidence as a party's admission.

Interrogatories may be used to establish that an opponent does not have evidence concerning a particular fact. For example, when the defendant serves interrogatories requiring the plaintiff to disclose the identity of witnesses to the accident, the plaintiff may answer that she or he does not know of any witnesses. This disclosure allows the defendant to avoid spending effort and money to locate witnesses who do not exist. The interrogatory answer has served to narrow the scope of the defendant's investigation. As another example, suppose the proponent did not have any conversation with the police but wants to make sure that the deponent does not claim a conversation did occur. The proponent may ask the deponent to describe any conversation she or he heard between the proponent and the police. The answer should be "none." In another example, a plaintiff might ask a defendant, "Identify any evidence you know about that reveals that the injuries plaintiff claims preexisted the parties' accident." If the defendant has no evidence that the plaintiff was injured in a prior accident, that fact must be disclosed.

Interrogatories may be used to require an opponent to explain how he or she contends the law applies to facts of the case. According to Rule 33(c), an interrogatory otherwise proper is not necessarily objectionable merely because the answer to the interrogatory involves an opinion or contention that relates to fact or the application of

EXHIBIT 11.2

Answers to Interrogatories

[Title of Cause of Action]

Defendant makes the following answers to plaintiff's interrogatories pursuant to Rule 33 of the Federal Rules of Civil Procedure:

1. Describe fully how the accident occurred.
   ANSWER: I was proceeding north on Highwood Avenue at twenty-five to thirty miles per hour. When I was still 200 feet from the intersection, I noticed defendant's automobile coming south on Highwood. It was somewhat closer. As I was about to enter the intersection, defendant made a left-hand turn directly in front of me. I slammed on my brakes. The front of my car unavoidably struck the right side of defendant's car.

2. Identify and describe each negligent act and omission you allege against defendant(s).
   ANSWER: Defendant was negligent for failing to signal for a left-hand turn in violation of statute [cite]. Defendant was negligent for failing to keep a proper lookout for oncoming traffic. Defendant may not have had control over his car. He may have been under the influence of drugs or an intoxicant.

3. State the names, addresses, and telephone numbers of all persons you claim have any knowledge or information concerning the accident described in the complaint.
   ANSWER: 1. John Jones, 2244 Main Street, . . .
              2. . . .

4. State the names, addresses, and telephone numbers of all persons you claim have any knowledge or information concerning the injuries alleged in the complaint.
   ANSWER: 1. Dr. Mark Smith, 2005 Medical Arts Building
              2. Mrs. Plaintiff, [address]
              3. Investigating Police Officers
              4. Ambulance attendants and paramedics
              5. St. Mary's Hospital emergency personnel

5. List all expenses [special damages] you claim you sustained by reason of the alleged accident and show how they have been calculated.
   ANSWER: 1. Ambulance $175.00
              2. St. Mary's Hospital $550.00
              3. Dr. Mark Smith $690.00
              4. Automobile repairs $4,875.00
              5. Lost wages $3,555.00
              6. Mileage—130 miles @ 30¢ $39.00

6. List the dates on which you were examined and treated at any hospital, whether as an inpatient or outpatient, since January 1, 2004.
   ANSWER: March 5 to March 9, 2005.
              I was examined at St. Mary's Hospital in the emergency room on the date of the accident and kept overnight for observation.

continued

7. List the dates on which you received any medical treatments and medical examinations at any physicians' offices since January 1, 2004, giving the name and address of the physician(s).

   ANSWER: I have had annual physical examinations at Dr. Mark Smith's office. The examinations are in March of each year. I have not required any medical treatment, except in March 2005 I suffered a bowel obstruction and required surgery for that condition. I do not remember the name of the surgeon. It should be in Dr. Smith's records.

8. List all other accidents of any kind whatsoever in which you have been involved by answering the following:

   a. Dates and places.

   b. Type of accident, such as automobile, work, or otherwise.

   c. Names and addresses of all persons involved.

   d. Nature of injuries.

   e. Doctors and hospitals rendering care and treatment.

   f. Names of all persons, corporations, employers, and insurance companies against whom claims were made.

   ANSWER: None.

9. State the names and addresses of all persons, including parties, from whom you have obtained statements or reports concerning the above-entitled matter; give the date on which the respective statements and reports were obtained.

   ANSWER: I have obtained a copy of the police accident report. I expect to obtain a statement from John Jones.

10. If you have any insurance which covers any of the expenses or losses you claim resulted from the accident in question, state the name of the insurer and the amount of the coverage afforded.

    ANSWER: Mammoth Insurance Company of Bellview, New York. I have $300,000 of liability coverage for personal injuries and $25,000 of liability coverage for property damage.

11. State the date and place of your birth.

    ANSWER: March 3, 1968 at Walker, New York.

12. State your social security number.

    ANSWER: 407-39-2467

13. Describe fully the nature and extent of your alleged injuries.

    ANSWER: I do not know the full extent of my injuries yet. X-rays indicate I have a herniated intervertebral disc at the C5-C6 level. I had multiple soft tissue injuries on my right side. I may have suffered a concussion. I had severe headaches for a week following the accident.

14. If you know of any photographs relevant to the above-entitled action, state:

    a. The subject matter of each photograph.

    b. The name and address of the custodian of each photograph.

    c. The date the photograph was taken.

    d. The name and address of the photographer.

EXHIBIT 11.2

*Answers to Interrogatories
(continued)*

ANSWER: My attorney has eight (8) photographs, which he obtained from the police department. My attorney also has 24 photographs of the intersection and my damaged automobile. I took the photographs one week after the accident.

15. For each expert witness you intend to call on to testify at trial:
   a. State the expert's name, home address, and business address.
   b. State the expert's occupation.
   c. Describe the extent of the expert's education, training, and experience in his or her particular field of expertise.

   ANSWER: As of this time, I have not retained an expert. However, if defendant denies that he was traveling within the speed limit, I expect to retain an accident reconstructionist.

16. As to each expert witness identified in your answer to interrogatory number 15:
   a. State the subject matter on which the expert is to testify.
   b. State the substance of the facts which have been determined (or assumed) by the expert, which facts have become the basis for the expert's opinions relevant to the above action.
   c. State the expert's opinions and conclusions and a summary of the grounds for each opinion and conclusion.

   ANSWER: Not applicable.

17. State the name, address, and occupation of each person who has assisted the expert in gathering facts and information relevant to the above action.

   ANSWER: Not applicable.

18. State the date and number of pages of each report issued by each expert in connection with the above action.

   ANSWER: Not applicable.

19. Identify each photograph obtained or used by the expert by stating:
   a. Its subject matter.
   b. Date on which it was taken.
   c. Person who took the photograph.
   d. The name and address of the current custodian.

   ANSWER: Not applicable.

20. Identify each model, plat, diagram, or other tangible item used by the expert to verify or demonstrate his or her opinions, including:
   a. A description of the item and its subject matter.
   b. The date of its preparation.
   c. The name and address of the current custodian.

   ANSWER: Not applicable.

21. Set forth in detail an itemized list of all payments plaintiff has received pursuant to:
   a. A federal, state, or local income disability or workers' compensation act; or other public program providing medical expenses, disability payments, or similar benefits.

continued

Exhibit 11.2

Answers to Interrogatories (continued)

b. Health, accident, and sickness insurance; automobile accident insurance; or liability insurance that provides health benefits or income disability.

c. A contract or agreement or a group, organization, partnership, or corporation to provide, pay for, or reimburse the costs of hospital, medical, dental, or other health care services.

d. A contractual or voluntary wage continuation plan provided by employers or any other system intended to provide wages during a period of disability except benefits received from a private disability insurance policy where the premiums were wholly paid for by the plaintiff. With respect to each such payment, identify the name and address of the payor of such payments, the amount of the payment made, and the name of the insured or policyholder under the contract that provides for the making of payments.

ANSWER: a. None.

b. Blue Cross has paid all my medical and hospital bills, except for a $150 deductible applicable to medical expenses and $200 deductible applicable to hospital expenses. Defendant's liability insurer has offered to pay the deductibles.

c. Not applicable.

d. My employer has paid me during the time I was off work. However, the expense may be charged to my sick leave benefits.

22. With regard to any of the payment referred to in your answer to the preceding interrogatory, identify all such payments for which a subrogation right exists and/or has been asserted. If the subrogation right has been asserted, set forth the facts that establish that it has been asserted and the name and address of all persons with information concerning those facts. If a subrogation right exists or has been asserted, identify all documents that evidence that subrogation right.

ANSWER: I understand that Blue Cross claims a right of subrogation, so the damages I receive from defendant will be used, in part, to repay Blue Cross.

23. With regard to the payments described in your answer to Interrogatory No. 21 above, set forth a specific and detailed list of all amounts that have been paid, contributed, or forfeited by, or on behalf of, the plaintiff or members of the plaintiff's immediate family for the two-year period immediately before the date of the accident to secure the right to any such benefits that the plaintiff is receiving as a result of losses caused by the accident in question. Indicate the name and address of the person or entity to whom such payments have been made.

ANSWER: None.

24. Identify each witness from whom you have obtained a signed or recorded statement, and for each witness state:

a. The name and address of the witness.

b. The date on which the statement was obtained.

c. The name and address of the person who obtained the statement.

d. The number of pages.

  e. The subject matter of the statement.
  f. The name and address of the current custodian.
  ANSWER: Plaintiff does not have a witness statement from the defendant.
  Plaintiff objects to the remainder of interrogatory 24 on the grounds that
  the question calls for trial preparation materials.

25. Have you ever been convicted of a traffic violation?
  ANSWER: Plaintiff objects to the interrogatory on the grounds that it calls
  for information that is irrelevant and will not lead to the discovery of admissible evidence.

26. Have you been convicted of a felony within the past ten years?
  ANSWER: No.

DATED: February 7, 2006.   By _____
                                                 Plaintiff

                                         By _____
                                         R. D. Higgens   [State License No.]
                                         4200 High Tower
                                         39 North Sixth Street
                                         Indianapolis, IND. 35402
                                         [Telephone]

                                         Attorneys for Defendant

law to fact. However, a party may not be able to provide a definitive answer to that kind of question until all or most of the discovery has been completed. Therefore, the rule goes on to provide that such interrogatories need not be answered until after designated discovery has been completed or until a pretrial conference has been conducted or another time is set by court order. The deponent should explain that the interrogatory cannot be answered now and indicate when he or she expects to be able to respond. By way of illustration, suppose a plaintiff contends that Bart Smith is the defendant's employee, but the defendant denies any employment relationship. The defendant may serve an interrogatory that requires the plaintiff to state "all the facts upon which you base your claim that Bart Smith is defendant's employee." The plaintiff may have to examine the defendant's business records, organization charts, and tax records, and take depositions before the plaintiff can answer the interrogatory. The law recognizes that first things should come first.

Interrogatories are also used to obtain information about the existence of business records and their contents. Rule 33(d) gives the deponent the option to extrapolate the requested information or to produce the records for inspection and copying. In deciding how to proceed, the primary considerations are time, expense, and convenience. If the parties cannot agree on which procedure to use, the court will decide for them. Usually parties try to make their best deal with each other and avoid imposing on a judge.

A deponent may not refuse to answer an interrogatory on the grounds that he or she does not know the answer. A deponent has a duty to make a reasonable effort to find the information or documents that answer the proponent's questions. But a deponent is only required to search for information that is *reasonably* available. A party cannot use interrogatories to force another party to do his or her investigation.

In federal courts the parties' initial disclosures provide the kind of information that parties otherwise obtain through interrogatories, including the names, addresses, and telephone numbers of witnesses. In addition, initial disclosures must specify the nature of the information each witness is believed to have. Parties also must disclose documents, their location, and the subject of their contents. A party who has asserted a claim for damages must provide a description of the loss and computations supporting the claim for damages.

Scope

Interrogatories must be relevant to the case. They are relevant if they are designed to obtain evidence or designed to *lead to* admissible evidence. Otherwise, they are subject to objection as irrelevant. If a plaintiff's interrogatory asks for the names of all persons who work in the defendant's shipping department, the fact that they are not likely to testify at trial is not a reason for the defendant not to disclose them. If the shipping department was even tangentially involved in the transaction in question, the interrogatory is proper. A proponent must have some expectation of obtaining admissible evidence. Otherwise, an inquiry is nothing more than harassment or the proverbial "fishing expedition." Mere "fishing"[2] for evidence is impermissible; it is an abuse of the discovery process. A party "fishes" by asking questions that, on their face, have nothing to do with the lawsuit and the proponent has no legitimate purpose for asking.

Interrogatories should not ask about matters that are privileged against disclosure, whether communications, documents, attorney's work product, or a party's work product. Therefore, an interrogatory is objectionable if it asks a defendant, "What did you tell your wife about the accident?" Communications between a husband and wife are privileged. But the matter of privilege becomes a little ambiguous when the proponent asks about the existence of evidence that is privileged. The deponent does not have to disclose the privileged material, but does have to disclose that it exists.

EXAMPLE

Interrogatory—Did you have a conversation with your wife about the accident?
Answer—Defendant objects to Interrogatory on the grounds of privilege.
Subject to the objection, defendant states he discussed the accident with his wife, but the content of the conversation is privileged.

The proponent may agree with the deponent's claim of privilege, and that ends the inquiry. Otherwise, the proponent may move the court for an order compelling the deponent to disclose the substance of the conversation. The motion puts the claim of privilege in issue. The same approach applies to privileged documents. They must be identified, but the contents remain protected from discovery.

Interrogatories may not be used to inquire into a party's work product or an attorney's work product [Rule 26(b)(3)]. Again, there are exceptions as discussed in Chapter 8.

Expert Witnesses

The scope of inquiry through interrogatories is the same as for other discovery procedures, with one important exception. In many states, interrogatories are the only means for obtaining information about expert witnesses whom an opposing party expects to have testify at trial. A proponent may serve interrogatories to obtain information about the identity of the deponent's experts, the subject matter to which an expert will testify, and the grounds for the expert's opinions. Only if the proponent can show exceptional circumstances to the effect that the proponent cannot obtain facts or opinions on the same subject, then, upon motion and court order, the proponent may be allowed to take the deposition of the deponent's expert. Most states do not require disclosure of experts who were consulted but whom the deponent or deponent's lawyer does not intend to have testify. Consultation with an expert who is not selected to testify is considered part of the attorney's work product and not discoverable. Suppose the deponent's expert conducted tests on something that is no longer available to be tested, the party seeking discovery has a right to know about the details of the test. The only practical and fair way to obtain the information is to cross-examine the deponent's expert in a deposition. The party who consulted the expert cannot keep the expert from being deposed. The fact that the party does not expect to call the expert to testify at trial is not grounds for not disclosing the expert or keeping the expert from being deposed.

Interrogatory Answers

A deponent's answers should use the same format and numbering system as the interrogatories. Indeed, most state courts now require a deponent's answers to repeat each question and state the answer immediately after each question. The procedure makes using answers more convenient for everyone. Answers should use the same wording and form as the interrogatories when it is reasonable to do so. Answers should be made with short, declarative sentences. Sometimes a single word suffices, such as "yes" or "none" or a date. If an interrogatory is not relevant to the particular facts, the answer may be "not applicable." A deponent must answer each interrogatory separately. In other words, the deponent may not prepare a lengthy narrative that seems to cover all the questions, and leave it to the proponent to separate the information and apply it to the interrogatories. Each answer must be complete as of the time it is served. When the deponent obtains additional or new information that makes a prior answer incomplete or wrong, the deponent must supplement the prior answer in a timely manner.

Answers may be made based on information and belief as well as on personal knowledge. A corporate officer or authorized agent may sign for a corporation. When a deponent signs answers under oath, though he or she does not have personal knowledge about some of the matters stated, the notary clause should state that the answers are "made upon information and belief." By way of example, when the president of a corporation signs answers on behalf of the corporation upon information gathered by various employees, the answers should so state. Rule 33(a) does not require the deponent to identify the sources of the corporation's information, but if sources are not disclosed, the proponent may ask for them in another set of interrogatories. If specifically authorized by the corporate party, the lawyer handling the case may sign on behalf of the corporation.[3] The deponent's lawyer must sign as an attorney of record, including his or her address and telephone number.[4] Most state courts also require lawyers to sign their clients' answers to interrogatories. A lawyer's signature verifies that he or she has read them and believes them to be accurate and supported by facts.

An interrogatory may ask the deponent about the contents of certain business records. The amount of time and effort required to examine the records to obtain the information could be substantial, even unreasonably burdensome. Rule 33(d) authorizes the deponent to respond to the interrogatory by simply offering to produce the records for the proponent to examine. The rule says that "the specification [interrogatory answer] shall be in sufficient detail to permit the interrogating party to locate and identify . . . the records from which the answer [information] may be ascertained." The deponent must allow the proponent to have reasonable access to the records and must permit copying. The deponent must provide the records in the same condition and same order in which they are ordinarily kept. The burden shifts to the proponent to review the records and decide what information is relevant. If the proponent cannot understand the records or it would be unreasonably expensive for the proponent to examine the records, a court could require the deponent to answer the interrogatory by preparing a compilation, abstract, or summary and could charge the proponent for the reasonable cost of doing so.

Objections

If an interrogatory is improper for any reason, the respondent may state an objection in lieu of an answer. The objection must state the reasons (grounds) for the objection. The principal grounds are privilege, work product, repetition, and undue burden. Interrogatories are unduly burdensome when they exceed the authorized number, call for information that is more readily available to the proponent, or call for information that more properly could be obtained through another mode of discovery. If the proponent's interrogatories and subparts exceed the authorized number, the deponent may refuse to answer any of them or choose the twenty-five interrogatories that he or she prefers to answer. Courts that limit the number of interrogatories also provide a means for obtaining a court order authorizing more interrogatories when more are necessary. Sometimes deponents simply should accommodate the proponent and answer the extra interrogatories. Everyone needs special consideration occasionally, and it is easier to ask for consideration if consideration has been extended previously.

A respondent may answer an improper interrogatory "subject to objection." The purpose is to preserve the objection, but give the proponent enough information to convince him or her that the subject is not worth pursuing. For example, suppose the plaintiff's interrogatory asked the defendant to reiterate any conversation that the defendant had with his wife about the parties' automobile accident. The defendant could properly answer: "Defendant objects to Interrogatory on the grounds it calls for privileged information. Subject to the objection of privilege, defendant states that he told his wife the plaintiff violated the stop sign and the accident was entirely plaintiff's fault." By making the objection and claiming the privilege, defendant has preserved the privilege and indicated that any further inquiry will not be useful. However, if the defendant has any concern that a limited statement about the conversation "opens the door" to broader inquiry, the voluntary disclosure should not be made. Another example: Suppose an interrogatory asked whether the deponent had ever been convicted of a crime. The deponent may answer that he has not had any convictions in the past ten years and object to the question insofar as it applies to convictions before that time [see Rule 609(b)].

When a deponent objects to an interrogatory, the proponent has the right to move the court for an order compelling the deponent to answer. There is no time period within which the objection must be scheduled for hearing. However, if a discovery plan is in effect, it may provide a time limit. In any event, discovery must be completed within the prescribed time, and a party who delays pursuing discovery will lose out. If a deponent objects to an interrogatory and the proponent does not make a motion to compel an answer, the law presumes the proponent concurs in the deponent's objection.

Preparing Answers

The deponent's answers must be based on the collective information available to the deponent, the deponent's lawyer, employees, and agents. A deponent has a duty to make reasonable inquiry to obtain the information requested by the interrogatories. However, if the information is unknown to the deponent and is equally available to the proponent, the deponent is under no duty to do the proponent's work. An interrogatory that requests such information is subject to objection.

As soon as a deponent's lawyer receives interrogatories, he or she must review them to determine which can be answered, which should be deferred, which are subject to objection, and who has the information necessary to answer each question. That information should be shared with his or her paralegal, and the paralegal should assume immediate responsibility for preparing answers. A good practice is for you to send a copy of the interrogatories to the client and explain what they are. Advise the client that the interrogatories must be answered within thirty days. Identify the interrogatories that you can answer on the basis of information in the file. Tell the client which interrogatories the client must answer. Recommend that the client write answers to those questions and send the answers to you. Explain that you will edit the answers and put them into a proper legal form for the client's signature. Mention that the answers must be made under oath. Invite the client to telephone you about any questions the client might have. Instruct your client to fully answer each question. You will edit the client's responses and remove information that should not be disclosed. If time is short, you may need to meet with the client to make sure the responses are proper.

The answers to interrogatories are due thirty days after being served. But if served by mail, the period is extended by three days from the date of mailing. For example, if the defendant serves interrogatories on the plaintiff by placing them in a United States mailbox on June 1, the thirty-day period begins to run on June 2. Add three more days because service was by mail [Rule 6(e)]. Therefore, the answers to interrogatories must be served on July 5. The time period actually ends on July 4, but that is Independence Day, a legal holiday, so another day must be added. If the legal holiday were not the last day of the time period, it would not extend the time for answering [Rule 6(a)]. A deponent must serve objections to interrogatories within the same time period. On occasion objections are served with the deponent's answers to interrogatories.

Parties often accommodate each other by voluntarily extending the time in which to answer interrogatories. As between the parties, an extension may be oral or simply confirmed by a letter. But to be enforceable, Rule 29 requires that any stipulation that amends the application of discovery rules be in writing and signed by the attorneys of record. If a party needs an extension of time in which to answer interrogatories, the party may move the court for an order granting an extension. If the motion is made before the time period expires, the motion may be made ex parte [Rule 6(b)]. If a proposed extension conflicts with the court's discovery plan or trial schedule, either party may move the court for an order modifying the schedule. The customary procedure for obtaining a court-ordered extension of time is for the parties to enter a stipulation in writing that sets forth a reasonable extension and the reasons the extension is necessary. The stipulation is then made the basis for a motion in which the court is asked to issue an order that comports with the stipulation. Courts generally encourage the parties to accommodate each other on discovery matters and grant extensions freely, but the latter is changing as courts struggle to manage ever-increasing case loads.

Uses of Interrogatory Answers

Proponents use the deponent's answers to determine what additional investigation and discovery is necessary. By way of illustration, if the answers identify new witnesses, the proponent must decide whether to interview them and whether to try to obtain statements. Similarly, if the answers disclose new documents or tangible items, it may be necessary to arrange to inspect and copy them. The answers may prompt the proponent to send additional interrogatories focused on the deponent's most recent disclosures. The answers may indicate a need to take depositions to obtain information. Very often, answers lead the way to preparing requests for admissions, which are discussed in Chapter 16. The deponent's answers should be reviewed in preparation for trial and coordinated with other evidence and information.

A party's answers to interrogatories may be used at trial "to the extent permitted by the rules of evidence" [Rule 33(c)]. Generally, we do not think of interrogatory answers as evidence. Nevertheless, they may be used insofar as they tend to prove disputed facts or impeach deponents who have been inconsistent in their testimony. A party-deponent may not put into evidence his or her own answers to interrogatories to prove a fact. This is true even if the party-deponent has personal knowledge of the facts and the facts are relevant. The legal analysis is (1) interrogatory answers are self-serving hearsay; (2) but a proponent may put a deponent's answers into evidence *against* the deponent as a party admission, which is an exception to the hearsay rule; (3) a party admission may be received as substantive evidence or impeachment evidence or both; (4) the proponent should make clear the purpose for which the evidence is offered. A deponent has the right to explain, justify, or even retract an answer at trial when an answer is put into evidence; (5) the fact finder (jury) must weigh the explanation or retraction in light of all the other evidence in the case. A proponent cannot use an interrogatory answer to impeach the deponent unless the deponent testifies at trial. A possible exception is that answers to interrogatories might be received into evidence at trial on behalf of the deponent if the deponent dies before trial [see Rule 804(b)(5)]. A few examples may be helpful.

EXAMPLE 1

The deponent claims that he was driving only twenty-five miles per hour at the time of the accident. Suppose he offers into evidence his own interrogatory answer to show he has been consistent and to buttress his testimony. His answer is self-serving hearsay and will not be received into evidence.

EXAMPLE 2

Suppose there are two defendants and one of them states in his answers that the other defendant was driving in excess of the speed limit. The interrogatory answer is hearsay. The deponent may testify on the stand to what he saw, but the interrogatory answer cannot be received into evidence.

EXAMPLE 3

Suppose the deponent answers that he was driving twenty-five miles an hour in a thirty-five-mile-per-hour zone just before the accident. Even though the statement does not admit to culpability, another party may offer the answer into evidence *against* the deponent. The answer is hearsay, but comes within the "party admission" exception to the hearsay rule. The answer would be substantive evidence[5] to prove the deponent's speed. In most courts, the proponent could read the answer into evidence without calling the deponent to the stand.[6]

EXAMPLE 4

Suppose the deponent testified at trial that his speed was twenty-five miles per hour, but his answers to interrogatories stated thirty miles per hour. Suppose further that the proponent wants to offer the interrogatory answer into evidence solely for the purpose of impeaching the deponent's trial testimony. The proponent would have to have the deponent on the witness stand and ask about the inconsistency. The interrogatory answer would not be offered into evidence, unless the deponent denied making the interrogatory answer. In that event, the proponent could offer the answer into evidence solely for impeachment purposes.

Interrogatory answers are put into evidence by reading the answers to the jury. The answers are merely testimony. The discovery document is not put into evidence, because that would give the document undue significance. So juries do not have occasion to read the answers to interrogatories as part of their deliberations.

Would a proponent always try to impeach the deponent with inconsistent answers to interrogatories? Not necessarily. Suppose the deponent states in her answers to interrogatories that her speed was twenty-five miles per hour as she entered the intersection, but, at trial, she admits to a speed of thirty miles per hour. Should the proponent show the jury that the deponent's prior answer is inconsistent and impeaching? Perhaps, but maybe not. Like so many things about trial strategy, it depends on how the evidence fits into the big picture and the overall strategy. The proponent's lawyer is going to have to make a judgment call, and she or he may not have much time to consider all the ramifications. What may be lost by not showing the inconsistency? Perhaps the deponent will recall that the speed was only twenty-five or twenty miles per hour after all, and the jury may believe the deponent's correction.

Suppose the defendant served interrogatories that asked the plaintiff to fully describe all personal injuries she sustained in an accident, and the plaintiff described only head and neck injuries in her answers. Then, at trial, the plaintiff testifies that she has had a lot of low-back pain since the accident. Her failure to refer to low-back pain in her answers to interrogatories may be used to impeach her and her claim of a low-back injury. It may be substantive evidence tending to show that she did not have any back injury, at least as of the time she answered the interrogatories. However, the deponent's answers to interrogatories are not judicial admissions, which means that they do not conclusively establish the facts indicated in the answers against the deponent. This is an important difference between Rule 33 answers to interrogatories and Rule 36 responses to requests for admissions. In this example, the plaintiff's answers to interrogatories merely affect the weight the jury gives to the deponent's testimony.

Continuing with the preceding example, the proponent-defendant could move the court to preclude any evidence or claim of a back injury, but it is not likely that the motion would be granted. Or, suppose the independent medical examiner mentioned back pain, the defendant could hardly claim surprise on the basis that the interrogatory answer fails to mention a back injury. You will be surprised how often this kind of problem arises.

Abuses and Sanctions

A proponent has a right to rely on the deponent's answers to interrogatories. If the deponent wrongfully withholds or conceals information by giving incomplete or misleading answers, the deponent is subject to sanctions (Rule 37). Courts have several options for dealing with deceitful deponents. The court's choice probably will depend on whether the violation was intentional, the effect on the proponent, consequential costs, fair play, and justice. If a deponent fails to disclose a witness, the proponent may move the court to exclude the witness at trial, limit the witness's testimony, take a discovery deposition before the witness takes the stand, or seek a postponement of the trial to give the proponent additional time to prepare. If the court orders the deponent to produce the witness for an oral deposition so the proponent can find out everything about the witness and the witness's expected testimony before the witness takes the stand, the deponent may have to pay all the expenses involved. This procedure gives the "surprised party" an opportunity to find out whether he or she really needs more time to prepare for trial, and, if so, how much. A deponent's disclosure that he or she is not aware of any relevant documents, photographs, or other tangible evidence gives the proponent grounds for excluding the nondisclosed items from evidence or obtaining a postponement of the trial. Other options include assessing costs, imposing penalties, postponement and "remedial discovery."

SUMMARY

Written interrogatories are the most basic and economical discovery procedure. You will be expected to prepare interrogatories for clients and analyze opponents' interrogatory answers. Interrogatories are particularly useful for obtaining basic information from other parties. The answers may help to identify the parties' theory of the facts and law. The answers provide a basis for additional investigating and discovery. They are especially helpful in forcing an opposing party to explain how he or she contends the law applies to particular facts. They may be used to obtain clarification of the deponent's pleadings. A proponent may serve an interrogatory that asks the deponent about the contents of business records and other documents. A deponent may elect to make the records and documents available for inspection and copying rather than describe the contents. The records and documents must be produced in the condition in which they are maintained by the custodian. If the proponent cannot understand the records or it would be unduly burdensome for the proponent to examine the records, a court may order the deponent to prepare a compilation, abstract, or summary of them at the proponent's expense.

In federal court, parties' initial disclosures must provide reports describing their experts' findings, analyses, and opinions. The reports must be complete and signed by the experts verifying the contents. The initial disclosures need not identify experts with whom a party has consulted but who has not been chosen to testify. The best way to obtain that information is through interrogatories.

In federal court, interrogatories may not be served until after parties have made their initial disclosures. A party may not serve more than twenty-five interrogatories, including subparts, on another party, unless the parties agree in the discovery plan to a greater number or unless a court order allows more. In state courts plaintiffs commonly serve interrogatories with their complaints, and defendants ordinarily serve interrogatories with their answers. Where court rules limit the number of interrogatories, the limitation treats each subpart as an interrogatory. Each interrogatory must be separately numbered. When two or more sets of interrogatories are used, interrogatories in a following set should continue with the numbering used the previous set. When you prepare answers to another party's interrogatories, repeat the question before each answer.

You must draft each question carefully, making sure it is clear and within the scope of permissible discovery. Do not use two interrogatories where one will do. You may use form or "pattern" interrogatories when they are relevant. If your office has form interrogatories, use only those that are pertinent. You must keep the questions from being overly burdensome. Do not ask questions to obtain information you already have. If it is necessary to pin down a deponent concerning facts you already know, use requests for admissions. Do not harass another party by serving interrogatories concerning issues in which you have no real interest.

You will prepare interrogatory answers for your client. You do not have to use the client's thoughts or words. The opponent expects that your client's answers will be phrased to be as self-serving as possible. There is no proscription against it. But your answers must be forthright and complete. The answers must be complete in light of the information that is available to the deponent, attorney, and paralegals, not just what they already know. In other words, deponents have a duty to make reasonable inquiry to obtain information with which to answer interrogatories. Answers must be supplemented in a timely manner as new information is obtained. Do not embarrass the client or cause the client to get trapped by providing answers that fail to meet the spirit of discovery. The deponent and deponent's attorney of record must sign the answers. The deponent signs under oath. The deponent must serve the answers to interrogatories within thirty days after being served.

Interrogatory answers cannot be used in lieu of the deponent's live testimony at trial unless the deponent is unavailable for trial. Even then the judge must conclude that the answers are reasonably reliable and there is no other way to prove the matter in question. Answers to interrogatories may be used to cross-examine the deponent. It does not matter that the answers' wording was that of the deponent's lawyer or paralegal; the deponent is stuck with the answers as written.

An adverse party may offer a deponent's interrogatory answers into evidence as admissions by the deponent. However, the deponent may explain or even contradict an answer to an interrogatory. The answer may be impeaching or even used by the jury as substantive evidence, but the answer is not conclusive against the deponent in the way that a Rule 36 admission is. Interrogatories are often combined with requests for admissions, which are discussed in Chapter 16.

If the deponent believes that the proponent's interrogatories are too burdensome or harassing, he or she may move the court for a protective order limiting the interrogatories in number or in scope. If an interrogatory is improper for any reason, the respondent may state an objection in lieu of an answer, or the respondent may answer the interrogatory subject to an objection. If a deponent objects to an interrogatory, the objection must be supported by "reasons." Objections to interrogatories must be served within the same time period as the answers. If the deponent fails to object to an improper interrogatory by the time the answer is due, the deponent waives the right to object.

KEY TERMS

deponent   proponent

REVIEW QUESTIONS

1. When may interrogatories be served on a nonparty?

2. When may the plaintiff first serve interrogatories on a defendant?

3. Under what circumstances may the deponent offer her or his interrogatory answers into evidence?

4. How may the deponent try to obtain additional time in which to answer interrogatories?

5. Interrogatories are particularly valuable for obtaining what kind of information?

6. When is the deponent's lawyer required to sign the answers to interrogatories?

7. How many sets of interrogatories may one party serve on another?

8. When is a party able to discover the opinions of an expert with whom the opponent has consulted but whom the opponent does not expect to have testify at trial?

9. If a deponent does not have information with which to answer an interrogatory, what must the deponent do to comply with the spirit of the discovery rules?

10. How does an admission in an interrogatory differ from an admission made in the party's pleading or a Rule 36 admission?

CASE ASSIGNMENT

Attorney Donald Smith sent an intraoffice memorandum that asks you to prepare a set of interrogatories to Bradley Harper concerning the accident and the availability of insurance. Label these interrogatories as "Set One." Because attorney Smith is concerned that the litigation team may need to serve additional interrogatories later, he asks that you limit this set to fifteen.

Endnotes

1. A deponent is a person who testifies under oath.
2. *Fishing* is a term often used by courts when describing impermissible discovery.
3. But that could become a problem for the lawyer if the lawyer is cross-examined at trial about the answers. A lawyer is not supposed to testify in a case where he or she is an attorney of record.
4. Rule 26(g) provides

   > (1) Every disclosure made pursuant to subdivision (a)(1) or subdivision (a)(3) shall be signed by at least one attorney of record in the attorney's individual name, whose address shall be stated. An unrepresented party shall sign the disclosure and state the party's address. The signature of the attorney or party constitutes a certification that to the best of the signer's knowledge, information, and belief, formed after a reasonable inquiry, the disclosure is complete and correct as of the time it is made. The court must strike any response or objection that is not duly signed.

5. Substantive evidence is any evidence that supports a verdict. Not all impeachment evidence is substantive evidence. Some impeachment evidence is heard by the jury only for the purpose of discrediting a witness but cannot be considered by the jury as proof of any facts in dispute.

6. The proponent party may elect to treat the statement as an admission. Perhaps the plaintiff's theory is that even twenty-five miles per hour was too fast for existing conditions. The point is that an opposing party has a right to use interrogatory answers as evidence against the deponent.

 For additional resources, visit our Web site at www.paralegal.delmar.cengage.com

CHAPTER 12

ORAL DEPOSITIONS

CHAPTER OUTLINE

Chapter Objectives

Chapter 12 is a detailed explanation about oral depositions, how they are scheduled, how they are conducted, and how depositions transcripts are used. The emphasis is on what paralegals may do to assist with depositions. It explains how to prepare deposition summaries and how the summaries are used.

Introduction

An oral deposition is a procedure prescribed by court rules in which a party or non-party may be interrogated about matters relevant to a pending action. A deposition may be used to preserve testimony or to discover evidence or both. Every party has a right to attend all depositions and to be represented by an attorney. The deponent has a right to be represented by an attorney during the deposition even if the deponent is not a party. A party may be required to submit to at least one deposition. The interrogation is conducted as it would be in a trial using a question-and-answer format. The deponent is subject to cross-examination. The questions and answers are recorded stenographically or electronically. Nonparties may be subpoenaed to appear for their depositions. A party's deposition is requested and scheduled simply by serving a notice for taking the deposition.

Paralegals assist attorneys to prepare to take depositions. They attend important depositions to help with the evidence. They prepare reports on depositions. They may prepare clients and witnesses for their depositions. You must have a good understanding of deposition procedures and uses.

Definitions

At the outset, we need to define some terms connected with discovery. The terms sharpen and facilitate communication. In *Litigation and Trial Practice*, we have been referring to the party who initiates or conducts discovery as a proponent—as in the proponent of discovery. A proponent serves or makes a discovery request.[1] A deponent is a person who gives evidence by testifying under oath. The word **depose** means to give evidence. But it also has come to mean to interrogate a deponent, as in, "I will depose the witness next week." The term **deposition** is synonymous with testimony—to make a statement under oath subject to cross-examination. It has come to mean the procedure in which a deponent is interrogated. The word *deposition* also is sometimes used to refer to a transcript of a deponent's testimony. A deposition transcript is the typed, verbatim record of the questions and answers. An oral deposition is a discovery procedure prescribed by court rules. In an oral deposition a lawyer asks a deponent questions relevant to the action, and the deponent must answer the questions under oath. All parties have a right to attend the oral deposition and put questions to the deponent. A verbatim record is made of all the questions and answers.

Deposition on written questions is another discovery procedure (very rarely used) prescribed by court rules. At a scheduled time and place, a person authorized to administer oaths, reads the questions to the deponent. The officer records the deponent's response to each question. The officer files the responses and provides a copy to each party. See Rule 31.

When a deposition is taken to preserve testimony of a person who cannot be available to testify at the trial, the deposition is referred to as a **testamentary deposition.** When a deposition is taken to find out what the deponent knows, the deposition is referred to as a **discovery deposition.** Oral depositions are the mainspring of discovery. They provide direct access to adverse parties and independent witnesses. The interrogator can obtain detailed information, test the deponent's version of the facts by cross-examination, and evaluate the deponent's appearance. Whether a deposition is testamentary or discovery, it is scheduled and taken in the same manner. Indeed, a discovery deposition may end up being used as a testamentary deposition. Depositions are often used to support or oppose motions, such as motions for summary judgment. Our concern in this chapter is with discovery depositions.

---

depose (1) to give testimony in an affidavit, in a deposition, or in court. (2) To take a person's deposition by asking the person questions (see Rule 30).

deposition The procedure for taking a person's testimony for discovery or to preserve testimony. The transcript of a person's testimony.

testamentary deposition An oral deposition taken for the specific purpose of using the recorded testimony in place of the deponent's live testimony at trial.

discovery deposition A deposition of a party or witness taken for the purpose of obtaining information and evidence relevant to the case.

Paralegals' Responsibilities

Taking an oral deposition is tantamount to eliciting testimony in court. The transcripts may be used at trial as evidence. Consequently, only lawyers may take depositions and make objections at depositions. Although paralegals are not authorized to interrogate deponents, they may make the arrangements for depositions. You may schedule depositions, prepare the notice for taking depositions, make arrangements for the place where a deposition will be conducted, collect and organize the exhibits to be used, and prepare outlines concerning facts and opinions to be covered. You may be asked to attend depositions to observe the deponent and help with the exhibits. You may be asked to prepare a report on the deponents' testimony for the client or client's insurance company. If your client or friendly witness is the deponent, you may prepare him or her to testify. You may be asked to prepare a summary of the testimony or index the transcript to make it more usable at trial. After your client's deposition has been taken, you may assist the client to correct errors or make additions in the transcript as authorized by Rule 30(e).

Scheduling Depositions

Obtaining a person's oral deposition is simple. A party may take the deposition of any other party or nonparty without first obtaining permission from a court. A party (proponent) begins the deposition process by serving a notice for taking the deposition. The notice must state the name and address of the deponent and the date, time, and place at which the deposition will be taken. In many communities, the proponent contacts the other parties' lawyers before serving the notice to get a consensus for a mutually convenient time. Again, professionalism is an important key to the success of the civil justice system. The notice does not have to name the officer before whom the deposition will be taken. The officer must be authorized to administer oaths or be especially appointed by the court. The officer is usually the stenographer who records the testimony. A copy of the notice must be served on each party and the original copy filed with the court. Service is almost always by mail. The notice may be served on any party, including a deponent, by mailing it to the party's attorney. The proponent must subpoena any deponent who is not a party. If a party does not receive due notice of a deposition, the deposition transcript cannot be used against that party for any purpose. In other words, the evidence in the deposition cannot be used against that party.

Where an organization, such as a government, corporation, or partnership, is a named party, any other party may schedule the deposition of the organization's employees and agents by designating the organization as the deponent and describing in the notice the subject matters to which the organization's personnel must testify. The burden is on the organization to select the employees and agents who can provide the information. The subjects must be identified with "reasonable particularity." The rule does not contemplate a broad brush approach. The designated deponent may have to seek out and obtain information to prepare for the deposition. Corporate parties are expected to be forthcoming in discovery proceedings. Of course, corporate personnel may be identified by using their names, if known. Parties should use interrogatories to obtain the identification of witnesses to facilitate scheduling witnesses' oral depositions.

notice of deposition   A notice that one party serves on all other parties, scheduling the deposition of a person who may have knowledge, information, or evidence relevant to the case.

court reporter   A person who is authorized to administer oaths and to record testimony in court or in oral depositions.

The **notice of deposition** must bear the title of the action and be signed by a lawyer. (See Exhibit 12.1.) An extra copy of the notice of deposition should be made for the **court reporter** to keep. The notice provides the reporter with most of the information she or he needs, including the title of the action, court file number, correct spelling of the deponent's name, names of the lawyers who are appearing, and identity of the lawyers' respective clients. The notice must state the method by which the testimony will be recorded, that is, by stenography, sound, or sound and visual. Rule 30(b)(7) authorizes parties to take oral depositions by telephone or other remote electronic means. The party who noticed the deposition must pay the cost of recording the testimony. When an audio or video recording is made, a written transcript is not necessary, but any party has the right to arrange for a transcription to be made from a recording made by nonstenographic means [Rule 30(b)(2)]. The party who orders the transcription must pay for it. A party may want a written transcript of an audio recording because transcripts are easier to use in trial preparation and at trial. If the deposition is electronically recorded, the recording must not distort the appearance of the deponent or lawyers.

When a proponent wants to take the deposition of an organization's employee or agent, the proponent may not know the person's name but can describe her or

EXHIBIT 12.1

Notice of Deposition

United States District Court for the

Southern District of Illinois
Civil Action, File Number CV01-00783

Roberta Jones, Plaintiff,

     vs.   Notice of Deposition

William Smith, Defendant.

    PLEASE TAKE NOTICE that the oral deposition of Roberta Jones will be taken on the eighth day of May, 2006, at 10:00 A.M. at 2205 Parkway South, Chicago, Illinois, before [name of officer or court reporter]. The deposition will be recorded electronically by video. Roberta Jones shall present herself at said time and place for the purpose of her oral deposition. She shall bring to the deposition all photographs she has relevant to the accident and her alleged injuries.

[date]

Gary W. Hoch

/s/ _____
Attorney for Defendant
33 South Fifth Street
Chicago, Illinois

him. In that event, a description will suffice. For example, the notice could describe the deponent as "president of the defendant corporation." The notice may require a party to bring documents or other tangible items to the deposition for inspection, copying, and photographing. If there is any error, deficiency, or irregularity in the notice, a party must immediately serve a written objection on the proponent or the defect is waived. In other words, courts do not want mere technical errors to interfere with the discovery process.

Parties may not serve a notice for taking a deposition until they have their discovery plan in effect. The notice must give the other parties and deponent a reasonable amount of time in which to prepare for the deposition. A deponent who receives less than reasonable notice has the option of proceeding with the deposition *or* filing a motion for a protective order that sets a different time or place for the deposition. Depositions are usually taken at an attorney's office—usually the proponent attorney's office. But they may be taken almost anywhere that is convenient, such as a courthouse, hospital, hotel, airport meeting room, or private home.

Attendance

Parties have a right to attend all depositions. Clients should be asked to attend other parties' and witnesses' depositions. The experience may help the client to prepare for her or his own deposition. It may give the client a better appreciation for problems in the case. The client may be able to suggest additional questions to put to the deponent. An opponent's presence can also make a difference, psychologically, for the deponent. An opposing party's presence tends to keep deponents from exaggerating and minimizing. Psychologists might say that it is easier to lie about a person than it is to lie to a person. Notwithstanding the numerous benefits of having clients attend depositions, they often do not.

A deponent is entitled to have her or his own lawyer attend the deposition and advise, even if the deponent is not a party. The lawyer who noticed the deposition must attend. If the proponent party fails to take the deposition as scheduled, he or she may be required to pay the costs incurred by the parties who did appear [Rule 30(g)(1)]. Consequently, if a party decides to cancel or postpone a deposition, he or she must make sure that everyone is notified about the change. Similarly, a party whose deposition has been noticed must appear or pay the costs of those who do. Other parties are not required to attend. However, if a party has received notice and elects not to attend, the deposition may be used against that party just as though he or she had attended. For example, the deposition testimony could be used to support a motion or be used as substantive evidence at trial if the deponent were unavailable to testify in person. A party who elects not to attend a deposition may, nevertheless, use the deposition transcript or recording for any proper purpose. A nonparty deponent who fails to appear for his or her deposition is subject to sanctions only if he or she was subpoenaed.

If a party is not served with a deposition notice, but the party or party's lawyer attends the deposition anyway, the deposition may be used against that party the same as if notice had been served. The party's or lawyer's appearance at the deposition constitutes a waiver of any defect in the notice or in the service of the notice. A party who did not receive notice of a deposition and did not attend may buy and use a copy of the deposition transcript and seek to take the deponent's deposition at another time. Of course, this is not fair to the deponent who is not responsible for serving the notice and who rightfully expects that his or her deposition will be taken only once.

A party may avoid the expense and inconvenience of obtaining and serving a subpoena when a witness is willing to appear for a deposition without being subpoenaed. However, if the witness fails to appear at the scheduled time and place, the proponent is required to reimburse the other parties for their time and expense, including attorneys' fees, incurred by reason of the aborted deposition. If the proponent serves a subpoena on the witness, the proponent cannot be blamed for the witness's nonappearance, and costs cannot be assessed against the proponent [Rule 30(g)(2)]. In addition, the witness is subject to being held in contempt of court.

A party's lawyer may elect to appear at an oral deposition by submitting written questions through the party or lawyer who scheduled the deposition. The written questions and the deponent's answers are incorporated into the reporter's stenographic notes and the deposition transcript. This procedure is seldom used but can be very valuable. Suppose a third-party plaintiff schedules the deposition of a witness to be taken halfway across the country, but the testimony is going to be relevant only to the third-party claim against the third-party defendant. The plaintiff's lawyer may avoid the expense of traveling to the deposition by submitting a few questions in writing. The written questions must be served on the lawyer who noticed the deposition and who will be taking it. The written questions must be placed in a sealed envelope, which is not opened until the deposition begins. The lawyer gives the written questions to the deposition officer (court reporter), who then presents the questions to the witness. This procedure lacks flexibility and allows no opportunity for follow-up questions for clarification or to develop a point that suddenly appears to be more important than previously believed.

Deposition Procedure

A deposition must be taken before an officer who is duly authorized to administer oaths. The officer is not a judge. The officer begins the deposition by stating her or his name; business address; the deposition's date, time, and place; the deponent's name; and that the oath was administered to the deponent. The officer is required to note the names of all persons in attendance and which parties are represented. Objections to the qualifications of the officer are noted by the officer on the record, but the deposition proceeds subject to the objections. The officer does not have authority to exclude anyone. When a deposition is recorded by a stenographer, he or she is usually the deposition officer, and usually is referred to as a "court reporter." The court reporter must make a verbatim record of the entire proceedings.

A party has a right to attend all depositions and to have an attorney attend. A court cannot exclude a party or a party's attorney. An organization has the right to have a designated person attend on its behalf, in addition to the organization's attorney. The parties may agree to allow observers (Rule 29). For example, a representative from the defendant's liability insurance company might want to observe the plaintiff's deposition to evaluate the claim. No party can demand that any witness or other party be excluded. If a party wants to **sequester** witnesses—to keep them from hearing each other's testimony—the party must obtain a court order before

sequester To keep a witness apart from other witnesses and outside the courtroom to prevent the witness from being influenced by the testimony of others. To keep a jury together and out of communication with the rest of the world while the jury hears a case or deliberates.

the depositions begin. A witness who hears someone else's testimony may be induced to change her or his testimony in some way. Suppose two bartenders were witnesses to a fight in the bar. Inconsistencies in their versions of the fight are more likely to develop if neither hears the testimony of the other. However, if witnesses are trying to be honest and helpful to the court, it is probably better to let witnesses hear each other. Consequently, sequestration of witnesses is the exception. Usually, the parties can agree on who should be excluded. A deposition is not a public meeting. Reporters from the news media do not have any right to attend. It would be inappropriate for a lawyer to invite news media reporters.

If problems arise during a deposition being conducted away from the home district, the parties may apply to the federal district court in which the deposition is being taken for a resolution. For example, if it appears to one or more of the parties that the deposition is being taken so as to embarrass or oppress the deponent, either he or she or another party may stop the deposition and move the court in that district for an order terminating the deposition or limiting the scope of the deposition or directing the manner of the taking of the deposition [Rule 26(c)]. It would be inconvenient for everyone to have to return to the home district court, obtain a ruling, and then journey once again to the place where the deposition is being taken. Rule 30(c) gives the home district court the obligation of ruling on the admissibility of the evidence at trial. If the deposition is terminated by order of a court other than the home district, the deposition cannot be resumed until ordered by the home district court, that is, the court in which the action is pending. The deponent or party has an absolute right to demand that the deposition be suspended until the court rules on his or her objection. The party or lawyer at fault may be required to pay the expenses of the motion and deposition [Rules 30(d) and 37(a)(4)].

At the request of a party, any documents and things produced for inspection during a deposition must be marked for identification and attached to the deposition transcript. The parties may inspect and copy the documents during the deposition. The parties are entitled to a fair opportunity to verify the copies by comparison with the originals. Lawyers may question the deponent about documents and tangible evidence while they are looking at it. If the custodian wants to retain the documents, he or she may offer copies to be attached to the transcript. The custodian may retain them after the deposition. The copies may be used as originals for purposes of the case. As an alternative, the custodian may give to each party copies of the documents. The original must be marked for identification, but the custodian may retain them. After the deposition, the copies may be used in the same manner as if annexed to the deposition. Of course, the parties must have a reasonable length of time in which to inspect the copies and compare them against the originals.

Rule 30(f) requires that the party who noticed the deposition shall take custody of the transcript and safeguard it. The party who "owns" the exhibits used by the deponent may retain them, or the exhibits may be kept with the deposition transcript.

Scope of Examination

The scope of permissible examination in discovery depositions is broader than in a trial. The examination may encompass any matter that reasonably could lead to the discovery of admissible evidence. Because it is difficult to know what information will lead to evidence, there is a tendency to allow almost any question, as long as the questioning does not become abusive or unreasonably burdensome. For example, in a case where the plaintiff is seeking money damages for personal injuries caused by an accident, the plaintiff's lawyer is likely to ask questions about the defendant's background, including such things as the defendant's past employment, education, past residences, military service, and criminal convictions. A court should not preclude such inquiry even though it has very little to do with the facts of the accident. A court would not condone a line of questioning that is calculated to harass or embarrass the deponent; however, it would be unfair, and thus not permissible, to question the defendant about details of a divorce or other personal matter. As part of discovery, it is proper to ask whether the deponent has given a deposition in any other case, and in what cases. Sometimes it is difficult to determine where relevant discovery ends and witness abuse begins.

Examination of Deponent

Before any testimony is taken, it is common for the lawyers to make preliminary statements for the record, including any stipulations they have made concerning the deposition. Then the officer administers the oath to the deponent. Examination and cross-examination proceed as in a trial. The attorney who noticed (scheduled) the deposition usually begins questioning the deponent. The first questions usually concern the witness's identity and background: name, address, age, marital status, birth date, birthplace, employment, and criminal record. Other areas of questioning relate to the transaction, occurrence, liability, causation, and damages. Each question is supposed to be singular and clearly stated. The deponent should give a responsive answer that does not go beyond the question. They have a dialogue. The attorney may ask follow-up questions that force the deponent to respond fully. Lawyers give careful attention to the context and meaning of their words and the words used by the deponent. For example, consider the question: "Did you make a left-hand turn?" and the answer "Right." Does "right" mean "a right turn" or "correct?" A lawyer must make sure that the deponent's answers are meaningful, clear, and responsive. A lawyer may ask leading questions and cross-examine a deponent if there is adversity or if the deponent is hostile [Rule 611(c)]. A hostile witness is one who is aligned with another party or who is recalcitrant while testifying. There is no set limit on the number of questions that a lawyer may ask. Nor is there any time limit. The questions must not be repetitious or irrelevant. A deponent does not have the right to "go off the record to talk to an attorney."

When the first lawyer finishes asking questions, the other lawyers ask their questions in turn. Lawyers seldom have any dispute about the order in which they interrogate. When more than one lawyer questions the deponent, it is common to have a second round of questioning, because others' questions prompt more questions. When all the interrogators are through asking questions, the deponent's own lawyer may ask questions. However, usually a deponent's lawyer does not ask questions in a discovery deposition, except to clarify testimony already given. Only if the lawyers agree to an intermission may the court reporter stop recording the dialogue.

The attorneys are primarily interested in obtaining information from the deponent. But they also are interested in finding out whether the deponent will be an effective witness. Attorneys watch the deponent's demeanor. They listen to how the deponent expresses himself or herself. They make judgments whether the deponent is able to understand questions and whether the deponent is easily lead. They gauge how well the deponent knows the subject and how the deponent feels about it. A cross-examination usually reveals the strengths and weaknesses of the deponent's testimony. A lawyer is able to assess the deponent's authority and credibility. A lawyer's and paralegal's impressions about the witness are important to any report made concerning the deposition.

The deponent and parties have the right to object to a lawyer's improper questions, but there is no judge to rule on the objections. The officer notes objections in the record so they are preserved for subsequent resolution if and when necessary. Attorneys should state their objections concisely, in a nonargumentative and non-suggestive manner. The proscription against "suggestive objections" is to prevent lawyers from using objections to suggest to the deponent how to answer questions. Objections concerning the manner in which the deposition is handled, a participant's conduct, and other aspects of the proceedings are noted in the record, but the examination of the deponent proceeds, subject to the objections [Rule 30(d)].

On some few points an attorney or party may object and instruct a deponent not to answer questions. A deponent need not answer questions concerning privileged matters or questions that have a limitation previously ordered by the court. Also, a deponent or party, or attorney for either, may demand that the examination be *suspended* so that he or she can move the court for an order that terminates or limits the deposition. The moving party must show that the deposition was being conducted in bad faith or in such a manner as to unreasonably annoy, embarrass, or oppress the deponent or a party. The motion may be brought in the court in which the action is pending or in a court in the district where the deposition is being taken. The court may order the deposition terminated or limit the scope or manner in which the deposition is taken [Rule 30(d)]. The provisions of Rule 37(a)(4) apply to the award of expenses incurred in relation to the motion. So, if the motion is denied, the moving party must pay the costs other parties incurred in resisting the motion. If the motion is granted, the other parties must pay the costs the moving party incurred in bringing the motion.

Objections

There are several reasons why lawyers object to questions or answers during a deposition. Objections are made to ensure that decorum is maintained. Another reason is to "protect the record" by making and recording objections, so a judge can rule on the objections later. In that regard, a lawyer's decision to object or not object usually is affected by whether the deposition is for discovery or is testamentary. There is no judge to rule on the objections, so the testimony is taken subject to the objection. The information is disclosed regardless of the objection.[2] Lawyers are disinclined to make objections during a discovery deposition. Objections merely take up time and may cause frustration. Furthermore, usually there is no reason to seek a ruling on an objection after a discovery deposition has been completed, because the information has been disclosed. If a witness answers notwithstanding an objection, the lawyer who objects might discover the answer is actually helpful to his or her theory and withdraw the objection. Or, the lawyer might conclude the answer is innocuous and not worth fighting about.

When a deposition is taken to use at trial, objections play a more important role. The court will have to rule on the admissibility of the evidence to which objections were made. One of your roles, as a paralegal, may be to identify the parts of deposition testimony that your client will offer at trial and the parts to which your client objects. A question may be objectionable because of the form or because the evidence the question asks for is inadmissible. The rules treat these two bases for objecting differently. A question is objectionable because of its form when there is a better way in which to ask the question. If answered, such questions are capable of eliciting admissible evidence. An objection to the form of a question must be made during the deposition; otherwise, the right to object is waived. The waiver puts substance over form. Questions may be objectionable because of form if they are leading, argumentative, confusing, or prejudicial.

Most objections may be made for the first time when the deposition evidence is offered at trial. The rules provide that objections to the competency of a witness[3] or to the competency,[4] relevancy,[5] or materiality of testimony are not waived by failure to make them before or during the deposition, unless the ground for the objection is one that could have been obviated or removed if presented during the deposition [Rule 32(d)(3)(A)]. At trial, the proponent may argue that the grounds for objecting could have been obviated had the objection been made during the deposition and the witness was available to supply the missing information. It is a difficult showing. This is a matter for the lawyers to handle, but an example might be helpful for you to understand the principle. Suppose a witness testified in a deposition that he did not hear the train whistle for the railroad crossing where the train struck a car. Suppose the witness is not available for trial, so one of the parties offers the deposition testimony as evidence but there is no foundation for the witness's "negative inference" that the engineer did not sound the whistle. In other words, there is no evidence that the witness possessed adequate hearing and was in a position to hear a whistle if sounded. Because other people could be called to testify that they know the witness, knew that he had good hearing, and could establish where the witness was located at the scene, the deposition testimony will probably be admissible.

When an objection is made, the interrogator may rephrase the question or abandon the question or insist on an answer. If the interrogator insists on an answer, the deponent's lawyer has to decide whether to let the deponent answer, or *answer subject to the objection*. By making the objection, the lawyer has protected the record and a judge can rule on it later. However, if the deponent answers notwithstanding the objection, the objectionable question gets answered and the interrogator obtains information to which the interrogator may not be entitled. The alternative is to suspend the deposition and ask the court to rule on the objection before proceeding. On occasion, lawyers agree to finish the deposition on all other matters and suspend the deposition to obtain a court ruling on the objection. If the court sustains the objection, the deposition is concluded. If the court overrules the objection, the parties must reconvene the deposition. The deponent may be allowed to respond to the specific question by answering it in writing under oath. That would be more convenient and more economical than resuming the deposition. But it is an unsatisfactory alternative if the answer leads to more questions. The court is authorized to award costs and attorneys' fees in favor of the party whose position on the objection was correct [Rules 30(d) and 37(a)(4)]. The judge has broad discretion in deciding what costs should be allowed and how much the attorney's fee should be.

Hypothetical Questions

A hypothetical question asks a witness—usually an expert witness—to assume the truth of specified facts and render an opinion on the basis of those facts. Hypothetical questions are primarily used as a means of obtaining opinion evidence from a witness who does not have sufficient personal knowledge of the facts to give an opinion. As discussed earlier in the text, it is for the court to determine whether a legal duty exists, not for any witness and not for the jury. However, customs and practices in an industry or profession may be relevant to the legal issue. If the facts can be proved through other witnesses, an expert is permitted to assume the truth of those facts and, relying on them, give an opinion concerning their effect. There must be evidence to support the assumed facts; otherwise, the question would be irrelevant and disallowed. The witness is not required to validate the assumed facts. Indeed, in a cross-examination situation, the witness may strongly disagree that the assumed facts are correct. Hypothetical questions are not common in discovery depositions. They are not useful as a means of discovering facts or evidence of facts. Nevertheless, hypothetical questions are used to obtain an adverse party's expert opinions, especially in malpractice actions.

Sometimes lawyers try to use hypothetical questions to try to force the witness to establish a legal duty owed by one party to another.[6] This is especially true in tort actions involving professional malpractice, in construction accident cases, and in products liability cases. Suppose a question arises whether a general contractor is responsible for erecting restraints around the floors of a multilevel building. Suppose an ironworker fell from the second structural level while the steel beams, columns, and flooring were being installed. He was an employee of the steel erection company that subcontracted to do the work. No other subcontractors were on the job. Only ironworkers were allowed on the steel framework while it was being erected. Suppose the plaintiff's lawyer asks the general contractor's superintendent to assume those facts and asks whether he would ordinarily take action to prevent an ironworker from engaging in an unsafe act. Suppose the lawyer asks the superintendent what action he would ordinarily take? What is his authority to act? Suppose the lawyer asks the superintendent, hypothetically, if he saw an ironworker on the second floor who was repeatedly throwing down objects in a pedestrian area, would he, the superintendent, speak directly with the ironworker to stop him? Could he cause the ironworker to be taken off the job? Does the superintendent's authority to act come through the contract, subcontractor union contract, or customs and practice? The probable answers, in this example, are that the superintendent has no authority or power to stop the ironworker's misconduct. But if the superintendent were to answer that he could stop the ironworker's misconduct, the plaintiff's lawyer would try to use the answer to show a legal right/duty to protect the ironworkers from themselves.

The lawyer may try to use the deposition at trial to cross-examine the superintendent to establish that the general contractor has a legal duty to put up perimeter restraints for the protection of ironworkers. If the superintendent recognizes some authority or responsibility, the superintendent's statement will be used against the general contractor as an admission at trial. A hypothetical question in a discovery deposition is frequently a "heads I win, tails you lose" effort to get admissions from another party. Rarely is a hypothetical question used to actually discover facts or evidence.

A deponent's lawyer can avoid the problems created by hypothetical questions by instructing the deponent not to answer or by preparing the deponent to cope with hypothetical questions. Of course, a deponent can avoid answering a hypothetical question on the grounds that he or she has no opinion. You may be asked to prepare your client-deponent by explaining the adverse party's objectives and going through some examples and solutions. You should discuss this subject thoroughly with the supervising lawyer to determine how to handle it. Lawyers differ on the approach to take. You may be assigned the task of preparing hypothetical questions for use in a deposition or at trial. This is not an easy assignment. Some lawyers have considerable difficulty preparing intelligible, effective, and admissible hypothetical questions.

Correcting Deposition Transcript

The court reporter is required to submit the transcript or electronic recording to the deponent or deponent's lawyer as soon as it has been prepared. The deponent must review the transcript or recording within thirty days from the date received or waive the right. A deponent has the right to make corrections and changes. The deposition may not be used by anyone until the deponent has exercised the right to make changes or has waived the right. The changes may affect the "form or substance" of the testimony [Rule 30(e)]. A change in "substance" affects the meaning, application, and/or effect of the deponent's testimony. For example, if the transcript shows that the deponent testified he was driving forty miles per hour and the deponent changes his testimony of the speed to thirty miles per hour, that is a change in substance. A change in form does not affect the integrity of the answer. For example, the deponent's birth year may have been recorded as 1980 and should have been 1981 or a name may have been misspelled. The change is not going to affect how the deposition is used at trial.

Usually, the deponent and paralegal review the transcript separately. Each notes apparent errors and proposes corrections. Then they discuss the matter. The paralegal then prepares an addendum or "errata sheet," which the deponent must sign under oath. Only the deponent can make changes and corrections. There is no provision in the rules that allows a lawyer to correct the stenographer's record. The deponent must sign a certification and verify that she or he has read the deposition and that, as changed, it is correct. The deponent must give a reason for every change, whether it affects form or substance. Reasons for making changes include (1) court reporter error; (2) deponent misunderstood the question; (3) deponent misspoke; or (4) deponent reconsidered the question and concluded the first answer was wrong. There is no set form for errata sheets. Most lawyers use a form that has at least four columns: deposition page, testimony, corrected testimony, and reasons for change. (See Exhibit 12.2.) The addendum is then mailed or delivered to the court reporter, who must append the corrections to the end of the transcript.

A deponent must make the changes within thirty days after it is made available to his or her attorney. If the deponent makes changes, he or she must sign the transcript and errata sheet under oath. If the deponent does not sign the transcript, the court reporter is supposed to make a statement in the transcript explaining why the deponent was unable or unwilling to sign it. The transcript then may be used as though it has been signed by the deponent.

EXHIBIT 12.2

Deposition Errata Sheet

TITLE:　　Roberta Jones, Plaintiff, vs. William Smith, Defendant

WITNESS:　　[name]

PAGE	LINE	CHANGE FROM	TO	REASON
3	6	The light was true green.	The light was turning to green.	Court reporter didn't understand my answer.
10	2	My skid marks were 50 feet.	My skid marks were approximately 50 feet.	I want to clarify that I did not measure skid marks. I only estimated the length.
32	18	right	left	I was confused and misspoke. The left side of my car was damaged.
40	7	$12,000	$8,500	I recalculated my loss of income from my payroll receipts after the deposition.
45	5	Johnson	Johnsen	Court reporter error. The witness spelled his name as Johnsen.
47	9	1998	1997	I was mistaken about the date of my previous accident.

A deponent may waive the right to make corrections to the transcript or recording if the parties agree (Rule 29). The deponent does so by stating at the conclusion of the deposition that he or she waives the right to read and sign the transcript. If the deponent waives the right to review the transcript, he or she necessarily relies on the accuracy of the stenographer (court reporter). In some cases, lawyers recommend to their client that they waive the right to read and sign because no substantive changes are needed. The changes concerning form (such as spellings) are obvious and do not really affect anyone's legal rights. It is easier to simply rely on the accuracy of the reporter. Most court reporters are very capable, conscientious, and reliable. A deponent automatically waives the right to review and correct the transcript if she or he fails to make the corrections within thirty days after the transcript is submitted by the reporter. The thirty-day period begins to run the day after the deponent or deponent's lawyer receives the transcript [Rule 6(a)].

Deposition Record

When a deposition is recorded by electronic means, the audiotape is the record. When a deposition is recorded by stenographic means (shorthand or stenotype) the stenographer's notes are the record. Regardless of the type of record, a printed transcript can be made from it. The proponent of a stenographically recorded deposition must pay the court reporter for making an original transcript. A transcript is a typed or printed booklet. It is a verbatim statement that duplicates the record. It bears the title of the action. Each party who wants a copy of the transcript must pay for it. A party who did not schedule the deposition may elect to use an *additional* method of recording the deponent's testimony. Of course, that party must bear the cost of the additional record.

Stenographic depositions are the most common. Usually the parties want transcripts. But if the deponent's testimony proves to be useless, the parties may elect not to order a transcript. Transcripts are easy to work with. When used to cross-examine a witness or as a testamentary deposition a transcript can be read to the jury. As a paralegal, you may be asked to take the witness's role at trial, sit in the witness chair and read the witness's testimony. The lawyers read their parts. With a little "play acting" the presentation can be quite effective. The procedure simulates a live witness testifying.

Video recordings have the advantage of allowing the jury to see and hear the actual witnesses. A witness who is authoritative and who makes a good physical appearance usually makes a good presentation in a video deposition. Like making a motion picture, a video deposition requires extra careful preparation. They require a room large enough to accommodate the lights, camera, and other paraphernalia. All participants must wear microphones. At trial, the proponent must supply monitors for the jury, court , and other attorneys. Video depositions are fine when the parties want an entire deposition presented, but any electronic recording is a nuisance when only excerpts of the testimony are needed. They are difficult to edit. For example, if the court upholds ten of the objections made when the deposition was taken, the sound will have to be turned off when those questions and answers are reached. It is not impossible, but it is awkward and inconvenient. You will notice a video recording seems to magnify problems a witness has articulating answers. The pauses between questions seem eternal. Some witnesses are more nervous on camera than when testifying in court in person. Discussions between the lawyers seem more argumentative.

Some lawyers choose to present expert testimony by video because of the difficulty of scheduling experts for court. Also, it may be less expensive, because using a video presentation conserves the expert's time. This is especially true when the expert resides far away. Making a good video deposition requires experience and careful planning. If a law firm has its own video equipment, the firm may want its paralegals to develop expertise in operating the equipment and be the "movie-directors" when depositions are taken.

The court reporter may sell copies of the transcript to anyone who wants them—whether or not a party to the action. Lawyers commonly search for and obtain copies of depositions given by an adverse party in other cases. They may be able to find out about a party's other litigation by examining the litigation indexes kept by the clerk of court. Court files are open for public inspection. The clerk also keeps a list of all documents filed in connection with each case, so it is relatively easy to determine whether a person's deposition was taken in a case. The easiest way for a nonparty to obtain access to a deposition transcript is to contact one of the lawyers who was involved in the case and review her or his copy. The transcript is not a privileged document. It is easy to make a photocopy of a transcript. If for some reason it is not desirable to contact one of the lawyers, the court reporter who took the deposition can make a copy from her or his stenographic notes. Usually reporters do not retain copies of transcripts, so it is cheaper and more convenient to try to find an existing copy.

Using Depositions at Trial

Rule 32(a) allows the parties to use a deposition for any purpose at trial if the deponent is not available. A deponent is not available if the deponent is dead, is more than 100 miles from the place of trial, is ill, for some reason cannot be subpoenaed, or is in prison. A lawyer usually makes an affidavit to show that the deponent is unavailable. If a paralegal has made the investigation and tried to subpoena the witness, the paralegal's affidavit is used. A party must not procure the witness' unavailability so that the deposition can be used. Rule 32(c) provides that the deposition transcript may be used to impeach the witness at trial. But if the deposition is used at trial when the deponent is not available, the testimony must be presented orally. In other words, someone must read the testimony to the jury. If the testimony was electronically recorded, the recording may be played to the jury. The court cannot allow the jury to take the deposition testimony into its deliberations, because that would place an undue emphasis on the recorded testimony.

Motion to Suppress

A party may move the court for an order suppressing the use of a deposition, or any part of it, because of an irregularity in the proceedings. The burden rests on the moving party to persuade the court that the deposition is invalid or that its use would cause prejudice outweighing its value to the court and jury. A motion to suppress must be made promptly after the error or irregularity has been discovered [Rule 32(d)(4)].

Constraints on Depositions

A deposition may not be noticed until the parties have met to prepare their discovery plan. The parties may agree to earlier discovery or, if some exigency exists, a court may authorize depositions to be taken earlier. A party may not take more than ten depositions, unless the other parties agree or the court authorizes more [Rule 30(a)(2)(A)]. A deponent may be required to appear for only one oral deposition. However, a deponent may voluntarily appear more than once and a court may order a second deposition. If the deponent makes substantive changes in his or her deposition testimony, that would be grounds for obtaining a second deposition. A deposition transcript may not be used against a party who was not given notice of the deposition.

A court order or local rule may limit the amount of time for taking a deposition. But if good cause is shown a court may allow additional time when needed to conduct a fair examination of the deponent. If the deponent or another party impedes or delays the examination, that is grounds for extending the time allowed. If the court finds such an impediment, delay, or other conduct that has frustrated the fair examination of the deponent, it may impose on the persons responsible an appropriate sanction, including the reasonable costs and attorney's fees incurred by any party.

State Court Procedures

State courts generally do not require *initial disclosures* of the kind prescribed by Rule 26(a). The parties must seek discovery and not rely on an opponent to provide evidence or information. Parties usually begin discovery using interrogatories to obtain basic information that helps them prepare to take depositions. A plaintiff may not be permitted to take the defendant's deposition during the first thirty days following service of the summons and complaint. Courts recognize that the defendant and his or her lawyer would have difficulty preparing for a deposition that soon. Furthermore, the legal and fact issues are not framed until the defendant serves an answer to the complaint. However, if a compelling reason exists, the plaintiff may move the court for an order granting leave to depose the defendant or nonparty witness sooner. The plaintiff must show good cause to obtain an accelerated date. Grounds include the deponent's intent to leave the state permanently, a progressive illness, impending death, or call to military service. This list is not exhaustive.

The procedure for taking an oral deposition in a state court is very similar to that in federal court. One difference is that a party may not have a right to record testimony by electronic means. Instead, a party may have to obtain the other parties' agreement or obtain a court order to use a video or audio recording. Stenographic records are standard everywhere. A state court may not require nonparty deponents to travel outside the county in which he or she lives or is regularly employed to give a deposition.

Subpoenaing a Nonparty Deponent

A deposition notice cannot compel a nonparty to appear for a deposition. A court cannot require a nonparty to do anything until the court obtains jurisdiction over him or her. A subpoena must be served on a nonparty to give the court personal jurisdiction over him or her.[7] See Chapter 3. A subpoena must state the name of the action in which the nonparty is to appear, the purpose of the appearance, the time, and place. It must inform the deponent that failure to comply with the subpoena subjects him or her to the penalties of law.

If the sole purpose of a subpoena is to have the nonparty produce documents for inspection, the nonparty may have someone else deliver the documents at the designated time and place. A subpoena that requires the production of documents, records, or other tangible things is called a subpoena duces tecum. A subpoena must clearly identify all the items the deponent is to produce at the deposition. If the purpose of the subpoena is to have the nonparty allow an inspection of real estate, the nonparty need not even attend the inspection. Of course, if the nonparty is subpoenaed to testify, he or she must appear in person.

A subpoena may be served on the deponent anywhere within the district (state) of the court that issued the subpoena. A federal district court's subpoena may be served "at any place without [outside] the district that is within 100 miles of the place of the deposition, hearing, trial, production, or inspection specified in the subpoena [Rule 45(b)(2)]. When the nonparty lives in another district (state), you must file the notice of deposition with the clerk of court in that district. Subject to the "100 mile rule," the court in which the deposition is to be taken must issue the subpoena. Whenever a nonparty is required to travel more than 100 miles to attend a trial, deposition or inspection, the nonparty is entitled to additional compensation for expenses.[8] It is often desirable to serve a subpoena on a nonparty deponent though he or she is cooperative, because then the proponent cannot be held responsible for the nonparty's failure to appear. These concerns do not apply to a party's deposition.

If scheduling or other conditions of the deposition are too inconvenient, the deponent may serve and file a written objection to the inspection. The grounds for objecting may be stated generally. If more than fourteen days' notice has been given, the objection must be served within the fourteen-day period. The written objection relieves the respondent from any obligation to produce the documents or things specified in the subpoena. The party who served the subpoena has the right to move the court for an order compelling production. Otherwise, by electing to proceed with the deposition, notwithstanding the objection, the parties must assume that the deponent will not produce the documents or things. A motion to compel a nonparty to produce things for discovery must be served on the nonparty personally, not by mail, because the nonparty has not appeared in the case.

A nonparty deponent must not be allowed to believe he or she can avoid the deposition, inspection, or trial. A witness may have a hundred reasons why he or she cannot be available. Some witnesses hide themselves when they have advance warning that they may be served. Therefore, legal professionals should be careful about telling others about plans to subpoena someone. Counsel a nonparty deponent against trying to put off the inevitable. When a person disobeys a subpoena, he or she may be held in contempt of court. A person who is found to be in contempt of court may be punished by imprisonment. Civil contempt is not a crime. A court uses incarceration as one means of enforcing its rules and orders.

Deposition Summaries

You will have the opportunity to prepare summaries of discovery depositions. Clients, expert witnesses, and insurance companies often need summaries to evaluate the case. Corporate management and legal department heads need detailed reports on the status of litigation. The reports may include summaries of depositions. Lawyers use summaries to abstract essential information to prepare for trial and to prepare to take other depositions. You may prepare a summary from the transcript or from notes that you made while attending the deposition or both. Of course, it is always beneficial to see and hear the deponent, especially if you comment on the deponent's credibility. Preparing a good summary requires an understanding of what is important. To know what is important requires an understanding of the legal issues, fact issues, and parties' theories.

There is no one format for a deposition summary. Indeed, the format of choice depends on the purpose for which the summary will be used. A deposition may be summarized in outline form or as a narrative. A narrative summary may be in the form of a formal report, memorandum report, or a letter. A summary may use transcript page references and even a system of cross-referencing. A summary may be chronological to reflect the evolution of the case and the deponent's involvement. Or, a summary may parallel the transcript from beginning to end. Or, a summary may discuss the testimony by categories. The categories may be general, such as (1) deponent's background, (2) occurrence, (3) loss and damages, (4) deponent credibility. Or, the categories may be very specific, such as, deponent's education, deponent's work history, deponent's traffic record, deponent's litigation history, deponent's prior hospitalizations. A summary may paraphrase testimony and even quote critical testimony. You may interpolate commentary to highlight the significance of the testimony. Or, your summary may be Spartan—just the facts. A summary may have a wide margin to allow readers to make notes. Regardless of the form, a summary should provide an overview and quick reference. It should always be authoritative.

Clients, department heads, and insurance companies usually prefer narrative summaries. They want to know the gist of the deponent's testimony, your impression of the deponent, and the significance of the testimony to the case. A good narrative provides this information. If a lawyer intends to use the summary to prepare for trial, however, the information must be focused and have references to the transcript pages and lines. The tendency, at first, is to provide too much information. That makes it more difficult to find the important information. Soon you will learn what to include and what may be omitted. Most court reporters have stenographic machines that "plug in" to their computers so they can supply a CD-ROM of the transcript for you. The disk may have a key word index. Taking advantage of the disks and your computer will make preparing summaries relatively easy.

Narrative Summaries

A narrative summary is informational; it is not for use at trial or to prepare for trial. Appendix I at the end of this chapter is a summary a legal assistant prepared for the defendant's insurance company, which was paying the cost of defending the claims against her. The plaintiff's lawyer took the treating doctor's deposition to use at trial. This was not a discovery deposition. Information may be categorized and put into paragraphs, not necessarily in the order questions were asked. Page references are not used, because the insurance company does not need to refer to the transcript. The legal assistant minimized use of expressions such as, "The witness testified that. . . ." The entire report is about Dr. Ellen Wales's testimony and need not be reiterated. The summary properly relates the testimony to the parties' theories of the case. The commentaries are quite apparent, so they do not require disclaimers. The summary is authoritative. When the insurance company asks the lawyer to evaluate the case, he can rely on this summary to expedite the process.

Some background information will help you to follow the summary. A sixteen-year-old girl brought a malpractice action against her chiropractic doctor alleging that the doctor failed to diagnose her slipped capital femoral epiphysis. The epiphysis is a growth plate at the end of the femur in the hip socket. When it "slipped," it detached from the femur. The condition is quite painful. It can be corrected by surgery if performed promptly. The longer the delay, the worse the expected outcome. In this case, there was a dispute about when the slippage occurred. The plaintiff's condition was eventually diagnosed by a medical doctor and surgically repaired. The plaintiff claimed that if the diagnosis had been made earlier, while being treated by the chiropractor, she would have recovered fully. Instead, she was left with a disability and the prospect of having to have a hip replacement in the future. The chiropractor contended that he treated her for a different problem, and she never presented symptoms associated with a slipped epiphysis. He contended that she fully recovered from the problem for which he treated her, and she terminated her treatment. During the ensuing year the plaintiff was seen by a medical doctor for some problems, including leg pain. He did not observe any hip problem. Then she returned to the chiropractor with symptoms of back and leg pain that he attributed to a new injury. After three weeks of treatment, he realized that she was not improving and referred her to an orthopedic surgeon who immediately diagnosed the problem.

Trial Preparation Summaries

The deposition summary in Appendix II for this chapter was prepared by a paralegal for the trial lawyer's use. It provides page numbers from the transcript where the information may be obtained or verified. The subject matter is identified by a generic topic. The information is reviewed in the same order as in the deposition transcript. The legal assistant has been careful to provide all the pertinent names and dates. She has not provided any commentary on the merits of the testimony or related the testimony to the parties' legal theories.

In the example, the plaintiff was involved in two motor vehicle accidents and one work-related injury, but claimed that his treating chiropractor twisted his neck and ruptured a cervical intervertebral disc. He brought suit against the chiropractor to obtain money damages for the disc injury. He claimed that the December 1999 automobile accident caused a minor neck strain but permanently injured his right shoulder and right elbow. He claimed that the January 1997 accident did not cause any injury; however, the other driver did make a claim against him for injuries. He received a traffic ticket for that accident. He injured his lower back at work in March 2002. He started treatment with the defendant chiropractors for that injury. He alleged that on April 9, 2003, Dr. Anne Jackson adjusted his neck in such a manner that she caused the intervertebral disc at C6-C7 to herniate and press on the nerve root at that level. The pressure on the nerve caused pain in his neck and weakness and numbness in his left hand. In April 2003, his treating neurologist referred him to a neurosurgeon, who arranged for a magnetic resonance imaging (MRI) scan of his cervical spine. The scan showed that he did not have a herniated disc at all, but had a large bone spur that predated even the first automobile accident.

Using Depositions to Prepare for Trial

A trial has many facets. Preparing for trial is a building process. There are many pieces, and they must fit together. The pieces must establish the client's legal theory. The pieces must reflect the client's theme. If any piece seems to be at odds with another piece, the inconsistency must be resolved. Lawyers scrutinize deposition summaries and transcripts to organize and reconcile the evidence. For example, lawyers can use depositions to identify all the witnesses who have evidence concerning a particular issue or disputed fact. Then they can abstract what each of those witnesses has said relative to the issue or disputed fact. Lawyers look for collateral evidence that will help them to bolster each witness who has helpful evidence and collateral evidence to attack the witnesses who are adverse. Lawyers strive to reduce harmful inconsistencies.[9] It is a difficult balancing act to deal with a witness whose testimony is helpful on some facts and harmful on other facts. Knowing what each witness has said under oath and, presumably, will say at trial is very helpful to the building process. So deposition transcripts and summaries are invaluable for organizing the evidence and evaluating the probable probative value of each item of evidence.

A person who will testify at trial can use his or her deposition transcript to prepare. In all probability, the lawyers asked all the important questions in the deposition, so the transcript provides a nice review. It should refresh the deponent's memory. The time that the deponent spent preparing for the deposition will pay a second dividend, because the trial testimony *should be* consistent with the deposition testimony. It is like having perfect notes to review in preparing for a test. Everything is there! When a lawyer takes a discovery deposition of an opposing party, the lawyer's questions tend to reflect the lawyer's theory. So when a deponent reviews his or her own transcript, it may help the deponent to understand how the opponent is going to develop the case at trial. A deponent should not be reluctant to acknowledge that he or she reviewed his or her transcript before testifying at trial. Any inconsistency between a deponent's deposition testimony and his or her testimony at trial may be brought to the jury's attention. The inconsistency is called impeachment. A jury may consider impeachment when considering whether to believe a witness. A deponent can avoid impeachment by studying the deposition before trial.

A witness may study the deposition testimony of other witnesses to learn what they have to say about subjects of concern. That may help a witness's recall or help a witness to clarify a disputed fact. Lawyers study deposition transcripts to help them prepare to examine a deponent and to prepare to examine other witnesses who will be testifying on the same issue or disputed fact. By knowing what a witness is likely to say, a lawyer can better phrase questions and avoid asking questions that will prompt damaging answers.

Using Testamentary Depositions at Trial

Testamentary depositions are taken to preserve the deponent's testimony so it can be presented at trial in lieu of the deponent's live testimony. A testamentary deposition is taken because the proponent expects the deponent will not be available for the trial. But, as noted earlier, a deposition that was originally taken for discovery may be used as a testamentary deposition if the deponent is unavailable for trial. A deponent is considered unavailable for trial if he or she died, is more than 100 miles from the place of trial, is ill, infirm, in prison, or has not responded to a subpoena. Other reasons may be accepted by a court to establish a witness's unavailability [Rule 32(a)(3)].[10] Deposition testimony may be read at trial and used against a party only if that party attended the deposition or had due notice of it. Under certain circumstances, a deposition taken in one case may be used in another case [Rule 804(b)(1)]. Of course, the deposition testimony remains **subject to objection** as provided by the Federal Rules of Evidence.

A party's deposition may be used *against* him or her by another party for any purpose. In other words, a party may offer into evidence a portion of another party's deposition even though the party is available to testify in court and the deposition testimony is not impeaching. The deposition testimony is received into evidence as a party admission. A lawyer may take this approach when he or she is particularly pleased with the way the deponent said something in the deposition. But a party may not offer his or her own deposition testimony to support the party's own case.

A deposition may be used at trial to cross-examine and impeach the deponent. The deponent does not have to be a party to be subject to impeachment. A deponent is impeached when his or her trial testimony concerning a material fact differs from what the deponent said in his or her deposition. The inconsistency may be brought to the jury's attention by reading the deposition testimony to the jury. The procedure is simple. At this point, the lawyer simply reads the relevant deposition questions and answers. To put the matter in context, it may be necessary to read a whole page or even more. Then the cross-examiner usually concludes the impeachment by stating:

Q: Those questions were put to you, and those were your answers, weren't they?

EXAMPLE

Q: Mr. Smith you will recall that you came to my office on [date] and gave a deposition. You testified under oath concerning this case?

A: Yes.

Q: You will recall that I asked you this question and you gave the following answer in your deposition. Let the record show that I am reading from page 2, beginning at line 7 of Mr. Smith's deposition.

Often the witness responds with a rather weak answer, such as, "If that is what it says." The safeguards against abuse are in the court reporter's certification that the transcript is accurate and in the witness's right to read and correct the transcript before it is used. The cross-examiner does not ask the witness for any explanation. An adverse party may require the cross-examiner to read other parts of the transcript to keep the impeachment evidence in context. But the witness is not given any opportunity to explain or justify the apparent inconsistency until the direct or redirect examination is conducted. The transcript is not made an exhibit and the jury does not get to read it. Even testamentary depositions are not made exhibits. The relevant parts are merely read to the jury. To have testimony submitted to the jury in writing would tend to emphasize it over oral testimony.

Inconsistencies can be extreme. For example, in a personal injury case a plaintiff was claiming a neck injury that caused pain and weakness in her arm and hand. She claimed the symptoms began immediately after the automobile accident. In her deposition she claimed the right arm and hand were affected. At trial she forgot and testified that it was the left hand and arm that were affected. Of course, the im-

subject to objection Controlled by the rules of governing objections. Evidence or procedure that is in violation of a court rule or standard is subject to an objection.

peachment was devastating to her case. The jury is instructed, at the end of the trial, to consider any impeachment when evaluating a witness's credibility.

Impeachment only affects the witness's credibility, not the admissibility of testimony. Impeachment does not disqualify a witness from testifying or even subject the witness to penalties, because the witness may not have lied intentionally. More often than not, the inconsistency that results in impeachment is due to a simple mental lapse, not intentional deception. An example may be helpful. Suppose the plaintiff in a personal injury action testified at trial that all her aches and pains began immediately after the accident. But the testimony is at variance with her deposition testimony, in which she admitted that her lower-back discomfort did not begin until two months after the accident. A delay of two months in the onset of pain suggests that the accident did not cause the problem. The impeachment might occur as presented in the accompanying example during cross-examination.

It is difficult to believe that the witness lied, that is, committed perjury in either her deposition or her court testimony. Nevertheless, she was inconsistent; both answers could not be correct. She elected to yield her recollection to that of her husband. But she cannot testify as to his recollection, because that would be hearsay testimony. Perhaps her husband will be allowed to testify concerning his observations of her condition, and such testimony would help to rehabilitate the witness. The jury will be instructed that they may and should consider impeachment of the witness or of the witness's testimony when weighing the believability of the testimony. The deposition testimony concerning the onset of the plaintiff's back pain is substantive evidence, because it is the prior statement of a party. Based on the deposition testimony, the jury could decide that the plaintiff's back pain did not begin until two months after the accident. As part of trial preparation, you should make sure that all depositions that may be used at trial have been filed properly.

A witness also may be impeached in other ways, without using deposition transcripts. If, for example, a witness testifies that he saw that the traffic light was green for the plaintiff, another witness would be allowed to testify that she heard the first witness state she was not looking at the traffic light when the collision occurred. The impeaching witness must come to court and testify under oath. A witness may be impeached by her or his recorded statement if the contents of the statement differ from the witness's testimony in court. The necessary foundation for using a recorded statement to impeach a witness is more difficult than that for using a deposition transcript (see Rule 613). If the statement is in writing and is signed by the witness, the cross-examination may be conducted as in the accompanying example.

A signed statement has almost the same impeachment effect as a deposition. But the statement is more cumbersome to use because it must be identified and the witness must acknowledge that it is his or her statement. If, in the preceding example, the witness had continued to deny that the signature was his, the person who took the statement would have to be called as a witness to identify the statement and relate the circumstances under which it was obtained. Then it becomes the paralegal's word against that of the witness. If the statement had been secured by the attorney who was examining the witness, a further problem would be introduced because ethics preclude an attorney from testifying in a case that he or she is trying. It would be very difficult for the attorney to put the statement into evidence if the witness remained adamant that he did not sign it.

EXAMPLE

Q: You will recall, Ms. Johnson, that on May 10, 2006, you appeared, with your attorney, at my office for your deposition?

A: Yes.

Q: At that time, you testified concerning your accident and the injuries you sustained?

A: Yes.

Q: Before testifying, you took an oath to tell the truth, the whole truth, just as you did before testifying here in court?

A: Yes.

Q: Ms. Johnson, you will recall that during your deposition I asked you the following questions, and you gave the following answers.

A: Well, I don't know!

Q: Please listen. Beginning at page 24, line 10, you testified as follows:

> **Q:** Right after the collision occurred and the cars came to rest, how did you feel?
>
> **A:** Shook up; kind of sick.
>
> **Q:** Well, did you have any specific aches or pain?
>
> **A:** Yes. My neck began hurting, and I had a headache.
>
> **Q:** Where was your headache located?
>
> **A:** In the back of my head.
>
> **Q:** When did the headache begin?
>
> **A:** Right away.
>
> **Q:** Did you have any other pains while at the accident scene?
>
> **A:** No.
>
> **Q:** Are you claiming any other injuries to your person besides your head and neck?
>
> **A:** Yes.
>
> **Q:** What?
>
> **A:** My back hurts.
>
> **Q:** Where does your back hurt?
>
> **A:** In the lower part, here [indicating].
>
> **Q:** When did that begin to bother you?
>
> **A:** It came on kind of gradual.
>
> **Q:** Well, when did you first become aware of the problem? What were you doing?
>
> **A:** I'm not too sure.
>
> **Q:** So you can't say whether it was two months, six months or any particular time after the accident?
>
> **A:** I know it wasn't six months—maybe two months.
>
> **Q:** That's your best recollection?
>
> **A:** Yes.
>
> **Q:** Do you remember what you were doing when you first noticed that your lower back was uncomfortable?
>
> **A:** No.

continued

> **Q:** Now, just where in the lower back do you have this pain?
>
> **A:** Here [indicating].
>
> **Q:** Let the record show that the witness has pointed to an area just below the waistline, directly over the spine. Have I accurately described the location to which you were pointing?
>
> **A:** Yes.
>
> [End of deposition]

Q: Now, that was your testimony when your deposition was taken, wasn't it?

A: Yes.

Q: And that was the truth—your testimony under oath?

A: Yes, but after the deposition I talked with my husband about it, and he said I complained about my back hurting the same day of the accident.

Attorney: Your honor, I move that the witness's last answer be stricken as not responsive and on the grounds that it is hearsay.

Court: The last answer is stricken, and the jury is instructed to disregard it.

Q: Certainly your memory about the accident and related events would have been better when your deposition was taken than now.

A: I don't know.

Q: You do not have any current recollection as to when your back started hurting, do you? That is, of your own memory.

A: Well, we talked about it, and I'm just trying to remember—it's been so long, and I've seen so many doctors.

Attorney: I move to strike the last answer as not responsive.

Court: The last answer is stricken, and the jury is instructed to disregard it.

[End of trial testimony]

Presenting Deposition Testimony to a Jury

Deposition testimony may be presented to the jury in various ways. A lawyer chooses a method on the basis of the importance, amount of testimony, costs, and personal preference. The simplest and most economical method is for the lawyer to read the pertinent parts to the jury. Depending on local court rules, the lawyer may stand in front of the jury or sit in the witness box and read the transcript. The lawyer or court introduces the procedure by explaining that the lawyer is going to read a witness's testimony and why the deposition is being read. The judge's explanation should mention when and where the deposition was taken, who was present, that the witness testified under oath, and was subject to cross-examination. Then the lawyer should state for the record which pages and lines he or she will read. While the lawyer reads the questions and answers, the other lawyers watch their copies of the transcript to make sure it is read accurately. When the lawyer finishes reading, the other lawyers may read any other portions they feel are relevant. This method of presenting deposition testimony is satisfactory if the reading is short;

EXAMPLE

Q: Do you recall that on [date] you were interviewed by a Ms. Chin [a paralegal] about this accident?

A: No. Well, maybe. I'm not sure. I've talked to so many people, and it has been a long time.

[Counsel has the statement marked as defendant's Exhibit 1 for identification.]

Q: I am now showing you a document marked as defendant's Exhibit 1. Can you identify it?

A: No.

Q: I am showing you the bottom of the second page. Is that your signature?

A: It appears to be.

Q: Do you now recall that on the date shown here, [date], you were interviewed at your home concerning this accident?

A: Could be.

Q: At that time you were asked about your version of the accident as you saw it.

A: Perhaps.

Q: Please take the exhibit now and read it to yourself.

A: Yes, I seem to recall it.

Q: This is your signature?

A: Yes.

Counsel: I offer defendant's Exhibit 1 into evidence.

Court: For what purpose, Counsel? I don't see the connection yet.

Counsel: The exhibit is being offered for impeachment purposes.

[At this point the plaintiff's counsel would probably demand to see the statement, as provided in Rule 613.]

Court to witness: Is that your signature and your statement?

A: Yes.

Court to plaintiff's counsel: Is there any objection?

Counsel: Yes. No foundation has been laid for the exhibit, and it is not impeaching.

Court: Objections overruled. Exhibit received.

[Note that the contents of the document cannot be referred to until after the exhibit is received into evidence.]

Q: You stated, at the time you gave this statement, that you did not see the traffic light before the collision.

A: I don't specifically remember saying that.

Q: Please read with me. Now referring to defendant's Exhibit 1, "I was standing at the southwest corner waiting for a bus which would be coming from the west. I was looking westerly when I heard the collision behind me. I turned around right away. The southbound car (white convertible) was stopped in the middle of the intersection. The eastbound car (Ford) slid sideways and came to rest at the northwest corner of the intersection. It was turned almost 180 degrees around. I could see the driver of the Ford was slouched over. As soon as I was sure that no other cars were coming, I ran over to the Ford."

continued

Example   *continued*

Q: Now, that is what your signed statement said, isn't it?

A: That's what it says.

Q: And when you gave that statement, you were trying to be truthful—to give a truthful account of what you observed?

A: Yes.

Q: And you did not intend to claim that you saw things that you didn't see?

A: But the statement doesn't say everything I saw . . .

Q: When you signed it you considered it to be accurate, didn't you?

A: Yes.

Q: If an important point had been left out of the statement, you would have brought that to the attention of Ms. Chin when she took the statement, wouldn't you?

A: Well, I didn't know what she thought was important.

Q: We're talking about what you think is important.

A: [No response]

Q: No further questions.

At this point the lawyer who put the witness on the stand and initially examined the witness is allowed to conduct a redirect examination to try to rehabilitate the witness.

Redirect Examination

Q: Is this written statement, defendant's Exhibit 1, in your handwriting?

A: No.

Q: But the signature is yours?

A: Yes.

Q: Did you choose the wording used in this statement?

A: No.

Q: Did you choose the things to be said or included in the statement?

A: No.

Q: Were you told when this statement was being written down that you would be asked to sign it?

A: No.

Q: Were you given a copy of the statement?

A: No.

Q: Did you read it before signing it?

A: Well, I just sort of glanced over it, and it looked OK, so I signed it. I think she told me I had to.

Q: Did you, in fact, look at the traffic light?

A: Yes, I did.

Q: What color was it?

Counsel: Objection. The question is objected to for lack of foundation—there is no showing of just when the observation was made, and the witness has disqualified himself.

Court: Perhaps a little more foundation should be laid.

EXAMPLE   *continued*

Counsel: Yes, I was just about to do that, Your Honor.

Q: You say you did take notice of the traffic signal light?

A: Yes, sir.

Q: Just when did you make this observation of the light?

A: Soon as I heard the crash and turned around—when I looked to see if any other cars were coming; that's when I saw that the light was green for east–west-bound traffic.

Q: No further questions. Thank you.

At this point the lawyer who impeached the witness is allowed to follow up on new matters injected by the prior redirect examination.

Re-cross-examination

Q: Let's see now. On direct examination this morning, you said that you saw the light before the crash, but now you say you saw it after the crash. Is that right?

A: I guess the statement refreshed my memory.

Q: Are you familiar with the intersection? Do you catch a bus there every day?

A: No. I go that way to see my sister sometimes.

Q: Where is the traffic light located—the one you observed after the collision?

A: There is only one. It sorts of hangs on a wire over the center. I saw the light that faces west, and it was definitely green.

Q: But you said that you saw the Ford sliding sideways and turning around and coming to rest at the northwest corner.

A: Yes.

Q: You saw all that, and then you saw the driver of the Ford slumped over?

A: Yes.

Q: And you felt that you should get over to help him?

A: Yes.

Q: You realized that there might be an emergency right there in front of you?

A: I don't know if I. . . . Well, yeah, sort of.

Q: As soon as you could see that no cars were coming, you dashed right over to the Ford?

A: Yes.

Q: Isn't it true that you could not see the color of the light by looking from the place where you were standing, the bus stop?

A: I don't know. I saw the light, and it was green.

Q: But after hearing the crash, seeing the Ford slide to a stop, and looking for other traffic in the area—about five or six seconds lapsed before you could have looked at the light?

A: I didn't time it. You don't have a stopwatch.

Q: It would have been at least five seconds, wouldn't it?

A: Four, maybe five, I suppose. Something like that.

Q: You didn't tell Ms. Chin when she interviewed you on [date], when this statement was given, that you saw the light, now did you?

continued

EXAMPLE   *continued*

A: No.

Q: Why not?

A: She didn't ask.

Q: And you didn't think she was interested or needed that information from you?

A: If she'd asked, I would have told her. I talked to a lot of people. And I was getting kind of tired of it all.

Q: You didn't tell the investigating police, either, that you saw the light, did you?

Counsel: Objection. That's irrelevant and calls for hearsay.

Court: Overruled.

Q: You may answer. Did you tell the police that you saw the light?

A: They were too busy. I gave them my name.

Q: I have no further questions of this witness.

The lawyers have the right to continue examining the witness only as long as new points have been brought up by the other side. Unfortunately, too often, lawyers try to get "the last word." Here is what usually happens.

Re-cross-examination

Q: There is no doubt in your mind about it, is there? You did see the light?

Counsel: The question is objected to on the ground that it is repetitious, leading, and suggestive.

Court: Sustained.

Q: Thank you, Mr. [Witness]. That will be all for now. You are excused.

---

it is not satisfactory if a substantial portion of the deposition is to be read. It is too monotonous. Also, it is difficult for the jury to follow questions and answers when one person reads both.

Another method of presenting deposition testimony is for the lawyers to read their parts and someone, such as a paralegal, to sit in the witness chair and read the deponent's answers. This method gives the appearance of a dialogue. It is much easier for the jury to follow and understand. An effective reader can imitate the deponent. Occasionally, a reader makes a better appearance than the deponent would have made.

Because you may be asked to be a reader, here are some guidelines for making the deposition testimony effective. Read slowly. Inject a brief pause between sentences. This helps the jury to assimilate the evidence. Natural pauses occur when a witness testifies in person, which too often are omitted in a reading. Jurors are supposed to look for conflicts in the evidence. They must have a moment to reflect on what they are hearing. Look at the jury as much as you can to see if they are listening and understanding. If they look blank or puzzled, you have to make some changes. Also look for body language that lets you know whether they are accepting what you are reading. A juror may subconsciously nod in agreement or shake his head negatively. A juror may roll her eyes or look around the room. When you are done, you should have a feeling about whether the jury was receptive.

You must be appropriately dressed and well-groomed for the role you assume. You must be prepared to pronounce all the words correctly, especially medical terms. If the deponent used exhibits while testifying, you should use the exhibits in the same way. This may require rehearsing. You should not just say, "Here, the deponent pointed to the photograph." You should put yourself into the role and do the pointing. Do not change the presentation when a different lawyer asks questions.

Finally, a videotaped deposition may be played for the jury. The proponent must arrange to set up the electronic equipment in the courtroom. The monitors must be arranged so that the judge, jury, and lawyers can see the screen. A video allows the jury to see and hear the witness, so video is particularly valuable when a deponent makes an especially good appearance or uses exhibits while testifying. When an objection is made, the whole production must be stopped until the court can rule on it. For this reason, many courts require the lawyers to make their objections and obtain a ruling before the video begins. Usually a video shows only the deponent and the exhibits. After a while, the picture of one person tends to become tedious. The witness may become quite uncomfortable being on camera for a long time. It is like having someone constantly staring at you. Notwithstanding these problems, the trend is toward more and more use of video depositions.

TECHNOLOGY NOTES

Modern stenotype machines have electronic recorders that enable stenographers to make almost-instant transcripts from their shorthand notes. Stenographers (or, court reporters) can also use their electronic notes to index transcripts. A deposition index is usually based on proper names, dates, places, and specific material facts. This allows attorneys and paralegals to quickly find specific testimony subject matter in a large transcript. Stenographers can use their electronic notes to make deposition summaries. But their summaries are in a generic form and usually cannot meet your litigation team's requirements. Nevertheless, a stenographer's summary may be helpful to you in preparing your own summary. A stenographer can supply a CD-ROM with the transcript. You can use the disk with your computer's word processing program. That will help you to put the transcript on your computer for analysis and assist you in making your deposition report.

SUMMARY

Paralegals help lawyers prepare for depositions. You may prepare clients for their depositions. You may collect and organize exhibits. You may prepare outlines that identify critical facts and opinions to be covered. You may obtain and prepare subpoenas to compel nonparties to appear and give oral depositions. Paralegals often attend and assist at depositions. You may observe deponents, make notes, and prepare reports on depositions. You may make indexes for depositions to make them easy to use. You may prepare deposition summaries. You may review deposition transcripts with clients to help them make corrections and additions in the transcripts. You may outline and index deposition transcripts to make them more usable at trial. On occasion, paralegals attend depositions for lawyers who intend to ask no questions but want reports on what the deponent said and the kind of appearance the deponent made.

Each party is limited to taking ten depositions, unless the other parties agree to more or the court authorizes more. A lawyer schedules a deposition by serving a notice of deposition on all parties. A notice commands parties to attend. No court order is necessary. Depositions must be conducted at places that are reasonably convenient for all concerned. A notice must specify the time, place, and officer before whom it will be taken. All parties have a right to attend any deposition, whether of a party or of a nonparty. A corporate entity has the right to have a designated person attend in addition to the corporation's lawyer. The news media has no right to attend. Parties may stipulate to exclude nonparties from a deposition or the parties may agree to allow observers. When the party who serves the notice fails to appear and take the deposition, he or she is required to pay the costs of the parties who did appear. A party's appearance at a deposition constitutes a waiver of any defect in the notice or defect in the service of the notice. Because a deponent's deposition may be noticed only once, a party who did not receive notice and did not attend must apply to the court for an order for leave to take a second deposition. Any person, even a nonparty, may buy a copy of the deposition transcript from the court reporter.

A nonparty can be required to appear for a deposition only by serving a subpoena on him or her. You can obtain a subpoena from the clerk of court in the district where the deposition is to be taken. As a paralegal, you may complete the subpoena for service, but it must be signed by the issuing officer. The issuing officer may be an attorney or the clerk of court. A nonparty deponent is entitled to have a lawyer attend the deposition and give advice.

A subpoena may be served on the deponent anywhere within the district (state) of the court that issued the subpoena, but the person subpoenaed cannot be required to travel more than 100 miles from home or work to give a deposition. A federal district court's subpoena may be served "at any place without [outside] the district that is within 100 miles of the place of the deposition, hearing, trial, production, or inspection specified in the subpoena." A subpoena may be used to compel a nonparty to produce documents for inspection and copying or other tangible things, or to permit an inspection of real estate that the nonparty controls. If a deponent finds that the demand for documents, things, or an inspection is too burdensome, the deponent may serve and file an objection stating the grounds. The objection stays the deposition until the court rules on the objection.

The scope of permissible inquiry in depositions is broader than at trial. A lawyer may examine the deponent about any matter that is relevant to the case and any matter that may reasonably lead to the discovery of admissible evidence. Each deposition question is supposed to be singular and clearly stated. Questions concerning privileged communications and records and questions concerning an attorney's work product are improper. When the deponent objects on those grounds and the interrogator insists on an answer, the deponent's lawyer may stop the deposition (walk out), or the lawyers may agree to proceed with other questions and finish the deposition. They can obtain a ruling on the objection at a later time. By making objections, lawyers protect the record in the sense that if the deposition is used at trial, a judge will have to rule on the objections before the question and answer may be read to the jury. A party may move the court for an order suppressing the use of a deposition, or any part of it, if there was some irregularity in the proceedings. The burden rests on the moving party to persuade the court that the deposition is invalid or that its use would cause prejudice outweighing its value to the court and jury. A motion to suppress must be made promptly after the error or irregularity is discovered.

An oral deposition may be taken stenographically or in a video or audio recording. The recording must be a verbatim record of the entire proceeding. The party who noticed the deposition does not have to order a transcript for the court, for himself or herself, or for anyone else, but if any party orders a transcript, the court reporter must file the original deposition transcript with the clerk of court.

The court reporter is required to submit the transcript to the deponent so he or she can make corrections before it is filed with the court. The changes may affect the form or substance of the testimony. The transcript may not be used for any purpose before the corrections are made, unless the deponent waives the right to make corrections. A deponent automatically waives the right to review and correct the transcript if she or he fails to make the corrections within thirty days after it is submitted by the reporter. Day one of the thirty-day period begins on the day after the deponent or deponent's lawyer receives the transcript. The deponent must justify each correction with a written statement giving a reason or explanation for each change.

Depositions have various uses at trial. A party may offer any part of an adverse party's deposition testimony into evidence. Depositions are used to provide evidence through a deponent who cannot be available for trial. Depositions may be used to impeach a deponent whose testimony at trial differs from what he or she said in the deposition. Deposition testimony is presented to a jury by reading from the transcript. When the portion to be offered is short, the lawyer may read it. But if the testimony is long, it is better to establish a dialogue by having someone, such as a paralegal, sit in the witness stand and read the deponent's answers while the lawyers read their questions. A videotaped deposition allows the jury to see and hear the deponent. A video deposition is desirable when the deponent makes a particularly good appearance or when the deponent effectively uses exhibits to explain his or her testimony.

KEY TERMS

court reporter	notice of deposition
depose	sequester
deposition	subject to objection
discovery deposition	testamentary deposition

REVIEW QUESTIONS

1. List four reasons for taking a person's oral deposition rather than using interrogatories.

2. How many oral depositions do the Federal Rules of Civil Procedure allow?

3. Under what circumstances may a paralegal take a deposition?

4. Why would a deponent waive the right to read and correct a deposition transcript before it is filed with the court?

5. What kinds of changes may a deponent make in a deposition transcript?

6. How does the deponent makes changes in a deposition transcript?

7. Can the deponent's original answers have any role in the trial even though they were duly changed as authorized by the court's rules?

8. For what reasons might a party take another person's oral deposition by video rather than have a court reporter make a stenographic record?

9. What advantages does a deposition transcript have over a video-recorded deposition?

10. May a paralegal handle the mechanics of making a videotaped deposition?

11. How much notice must a party give for taking a witness's deposition?

12. On what grounds may a party object to questions asked of him or her in an oral deposition?

CASE ASSIGNMENT

You are a member of attorney Donald Smith's litigation team representing the plaintiff trustee. He has decided to take Bradley Harper's deposition. He has asked you to prepare a notice for taking the deposition. He also wants your suggestions for ten questions he can ask Harper about how the accident happened. Please prepare the notice and list of questions.

Endnotes

1. *Proponent* is not a common term, but the authors have not been able to find a generally recognized term that works as well.
2. A lawyer may instruct his or her client not to answer questions to protect a privilege or to enforce a previously made court order.
3. Rule 601.
4. Rules 602, 701, 702, and 703.
5. Rules 401–411.
6. As discussed in Chapter 3, the court determines whether a legal duty exists.
7. Note, parties are not allowed to personally serve pleadings or subpoenas. Any personal contact might lead to a confrontation, so the law wisely keeps parties away from each other and away from nonparties who are forced to become involved in litigation.
8. Rule 42 (c)(3)(B)(iii).
9. Lawyers are not allowed to mislead witnesses or encourage false testimony.
10. Rule 32(a)(3)(E) provides that a person's deposition may be read at trial "upon application and notice, that such exceptional circumstances exist as to make it desirable, in the interest of justice and with due regard to the importance of presenting the testimony of witnesses orally in open court. . . ."

APPENDIX I
DEPOSITION SUMMARY, NARRATIVE

DR. ELLEN WALES'S DEPOSITION SUMMARY

Dear Mr. Insurance Supervisor:

Dr. Ellen B. Wales's videotaped deposition was taken on July 30, 2006. The following is a summary of her testimony.

Deponent's Background

Dr. Wales is a board certified orthopedic surgeon. Orthopedic surgery deals with the skeletal system and all supporting structures, including muscles and ligaments. She practiced general medicine from 1962 to 1968. She became board certified in orthopedic surgery in 1973. She has practiced orthopedic surgery since then. Dr. Wales is an assistant professor of orthopedic surgery at the University of Minnesota. Since 1976 she has supervised in the Knee Clinic at the local veterans' hospital. She is affiliated with Superior Orthopedics, a medical group, located in St. Paul. Superior Orthopedics has nine orthopedic surgeons. The group serves St. Joseph's, St. John's, Midway, and Divine Redeemer Hospitals. All members of the group are on the staff of the University of Minnesota Hospital and of the local veterans' hospital. Dr. Wales travels to Forest Lake, Hastings, and Grantsburg, Wisconsin, to provide consulting services to the smaller communities. Dr. Wales has had a great deal of experience diagnosing and treating slipped capital femoral epiphyses.

Slipped Epiphysis

A slipped capital femoral epiphysis is most common in children who have not yet reached their full growth. Children who are eleven to fifteen years old and obese are particularly vulnerable to injury. The slip (break) may be caused by trauma, or there may be no history of any apparent trauma. The condition usually goes through four discrete stages. The symptoms and patient presentation vary depending on the stage. In the first stage the patient has some knee and hip pain. In stage 2 the patient has increased hip pain, thigh pain, groin pain, and a distinct limp. In the third stage the patient has more pain, and the affected leg may turn out or rotate outward. In the fourth stage the patient has an emergency condition. In each stage the slippage has advanced. In the fourth stage the epiphysis has completely separated from the head of the femur.

Plaintiff's Diagnosis

Dr. Wales first saw Susan Smith on May 3, 2006, at the Orthopedic Clinic located in Hastings. She happened to see Smith walk on the sidewalk to the front door and into the office. Her mother helped her sit down because she was limping. Dr. Wales says she could have made the diagnosis from just seeing how Susan walked. She noted that Susan was somewhat obese. On examination she found that Susan had groin and thigh pain and pain that went into her knee. Susan walked with a "short-leg" gait. Her left leg was shortened several centimeters and externally rotated outward. Susan could not flex her hip up or bring it out straight. She could bring it out laterally, but the movement caused a great deal of pain. She had little or no rotation of her left hip. The diagnosis of slipped capital femoral epiphysis was clear even without x-rays. Nevertheless, Dr. Wales took "frog-leg" views of the plaintiff's pelvis and hip point to confirm the diagnosis. The x-rays showed a grade 3 slipped capital femoral epiphysis.

Dr. Wales testified that there are grades of slippage. A preslippage condition could last as long as one year. It may or may not be symptomatic. The patient's condition would be expected to progress to a grade 1. Dr. Wales opined that it did not take long for Smith to go from a preslip to a grade 3. She was not blaming Dr. Marcus Santos [the chiropractor] for Smith's slipped capital femoral epiphysis.

Plaintiff's Treatment

Dr. Wales had Susan admitted to United Hospital for surgery. Dr. Wales drilled the pins across to hold the joint from slipping further. She tried to have the growth center closed so that it would not be vulnerable to more slippage or injury. Because of the surgery, Smith's growth center has prematurely closed and completely fused. The plaintiff's ball and socket are not matched.

Causation

Dr. Wales opines that a direct relationship exists between the symptoms Smith presented to Dr. Santos in February 2005 and Dr. Wales's diagnosis of a grade 3 slipped capital femoral epiphysis in May 2006. She believes the slip began in February 2005. She bases her opinion on the fact that children with slipped capital femoral epiphysis who have come in early, before the actual slip, experience groin and thigh pain. They may or may not have a normal gait. They sometimes complain of knee pain. This is called the preslip stage, and if the condition is caught at this stage, surgery usually restores full function. The epiphysis is surgically nailed in place, and normal growth continues. Dr. Wales believes the diagnosis of slipped capital femoral epiphysis could have been made in February 2005 by exam and x-rays. If x-rays were taken in February 1998, yielding the diagnosis of early slippage, it would have been a grade 1 slippage. Appropriate orthopedic care would have included a surgical pinning of the hip.

If the slipped capital femoral epiphysis had been diagnosed in February 2005 when she was under the defendant's care, Susan would now have a normal hip. She would not have any restrictions. In Dr. Wales's opinion, Dr. Santos's chiropractic adjustments did not provide any "medical" benefit for her limp. Dr. Wales knows that chiropractors are not licensed or qualified to treat slipped capital femoral epiphysis. She believes that Dr. Santos's treatment harmed Smith's hip condition by keeping her from seeing a qualified medical doctor.

Factors

Dr. Wales's opinion takes into consideration the fact that Susan did not have pain in her hip from February 2005 [when Dr. Santos discharged her from his care] until

March 2006. She testified that sometimes children who have initial slippage can settle down and will not slip any further for a significant period of time. Children who have slippage continue to have synovitis. That is an inflammation of the hip joint. They produce excess fluid and have pain from the distension of the sack around the hip joint. If Susan had a quiescent period during which no slippage occurred, then the fluid could have been reabsorbed, and she would not have had as much pain as she had in the recent past. Dr. Wales testified that Susan's development of a significant limp in March 2006 indicates that the epiphysis slipped again, to change her condition to a grade 3. Dr. Wales could not obtain a good alignment because of the delay and increased slippage. The delay of almost a year in diagnosis caused a repairable problem to turn into a permanent problem.

Injury

Susan will experience untoward wear and tear on her hip joint during her early adult years, and this will lead to the need for at least one hip replacement. During her lifetime, she may need two or three hip replacements. Her leg is externally rotated and is somewhat shorter. This will lead to degenerative arthritis and increased pain. A new hip joint will cost approximately $25,000. A hip joint replacement is considered to be a temporary procedure. If the procedure is performed on a patient in his or her forties, one can pretty well guarantee that a second total hip replacement will be needed eight to twelve years later. Susan can no longer partake in any sporting activities or running. She has difficulty riding a bicycle.

Cross-examination

Dr. Wales knew Susan fell while playing in gym class, and hurt her knee. That is the problem for which she originally consulted Dr. Santos in February 2005. Although the chiropractor's records show that Susan progressively recovered to the point that she was symptom free, Dr. Wales feels that she was not in fact symptom free. In other words, she disagrees with the records. She has no explanation why the plaintiff did not return to Dr. Santos or see another doctor if she was continuing to have symptoms during the year. It appears that neither she nor the plaintiff's attorney is aware of the record that the plaintiff did see another medical doctor during the year, and that doctor did not observe symptoms of a slipped epiphysis. Dr. Wales talked to Smith's mother at great length. The mother told Dr. Wales that Susan had been having a great deal of difficulty over the past three months and was having trouble in gym class. Dr. Wales concluded that Dr. Santos's confidential history indicated that Susan was limping on the left leg and had fallen during her gym class. He believes that Susan had a grade 1 slip at that time. She had a sheering force to her hip when she fell on her knee in gym. The limp indicated that she had an effusion and pain in her hip.

Comments

Dr. Wales makes a good appearance. She is articulate and very knowledgeable. She obviously believes Dr. Santos was negligent for not referring Susan to a medical doctor in February 2005 so that her hip could have been evaluated medically. Dr. Wales has her mind made up. Her version and explanations do not fully account for Susan's lack of symptoms after February 2005 even though she was fully, normally active. Dr. Wales's testimony raises a dilemma for the medical doctor who did see Susan for leg pain in March of 2006.

We will continue to keep you advised of any further developments.

Very truly yours,

_____

Carol Manson
Legal Assistant

Read and approved by

_____

Attorney

APPENDIX II
DEPOSITION SUMMARY, TRIAL PREPARATION

DEPOSITION SUMMARY OF
Michael Strike
Taken on April 26, 2004
Office File No. 7777

FORMAT
> Page
> Topic
> Description

1

Personal

Deponent is now single. He was married from 1979 to July 1999. He was divorced in Spencer. His former wife's name is now Paula Jean Lund. She resides at 801 Ninth Avenue SE. They have a daughter, Jennifer, who is eighteen and a son, Jonathon, who is seventeen. His son lives with him at 2285 Ahrens Hill Road North. His daughter is a junior at Moorhead State.

9

Occupation

Deponent is a recreational therapist for the state of Iowa. He has had that job for eight years. Before that he was a recreation program assistant for the state. He worked at Spencer Regional Treatment Center for one or two years. Before being a program assistant he was a human services technician for the state at Spencer Regional Treatment Center. Before that, when he was eighteen, he worked for Viking Coca-Cola Company.

10

Recreational Therapist

Recreational therapists program recreational activities for developmentally disabled persons. They write programs, implement programs, do one-on-one training, provide leisure counseling, and so forth.

11

Recreational Therapist

Recreational therapists have professional responsibilities for the implementation of a program. They direct the line staff to implement the programs they write. They counsel, observe, do quality assurance tasks, and so forth.

11

Physical Requirements of a Recreational Therapist

Recreational therapists "model" the activities they teach their clients. In other words, they demonstrate and participate in the activities. They may include any kind of aerobic activity, lifting weights, playing baseball, anything that involves socialization and physical activity.

12

Education

The deponent has a bachelor of science degree in physical education and a bachelor of science in art education, K through 12. He obtained the degrees from St. Cloud University from 1978 through 1982. He graduated from Spencer High School in 1971.

12

Weight

He has weighed approximately two hundred pounds since June 1999. He did take off some extra weight the year he was getting divorced, in 1999, by bicycling, lifting weights, and running.

13

Self-defense Courses

Occasionally, he conducts seminars for women in self-defense through the school system. The last time he conducted a seminar was in March 2002. In that month he made approximately $220 from the self-defense classes. He was unable to conduct one seminar because of his arm and shoulder injuries. He would have made approximately $300.

15

Certification in Therapeutic Intervention

Instructors are certified in therapeutic intervention every year through the state of Iowa. Therapeutic intervention is the method the state has authorized for control of residents who become aggressive and assaultive. The deponent is an instructor. He was picked by his supervisor and then trained by state certified instructors through a one-week workshop.

16

Decoy Business

He believes he started his duck decoy work in the mid-1980s. He started it as a hobby and turned it into a business. A friend of the family, John Bale, thought a market existed and asked him if he was willing to do it for money, and he responded, "Sure." He is no longer in the decoy business. He got out of the business about the same time he was involved with the neck injury. His wife helped him for a period of time. He is now able to do the basic rough shapes, but he is unable to do detailing, as it requires a steady hand. His tax returns show that he earned $122 in 1999 in the decoy business. He earned only that much because he did not have his wife's assistance in the business. In 2001 and 2002 he did not sell any decoys. Since his automobile accident of 2002, he has been able to partially complete only one decoy. In some years he made $5,000 in this business. The decoys sold for $350 to $450 each. They were sold to the Harris Gallery in Storm Lake.

21
Loss of Feeling in Fingers/Decoy Business

He does not have any feeling in his index finger, the finger next to it on the left hand, and his thumb. He says that if you do not have feeling in your fingers when you are wood burning, you dig too deep. You have to have dexterity to do symmetrical lines. At this point in time, he does not have plans to continue with the decoy business unless something turns around as far as the numbness in his hand.

23
Treatment Since January

At the beginning of the year, he went through a bout of bronchitis and started having trouble with his neck because of the heavy coughing. He saw Dr. Peter Fowler, who referred him to Physical Therapist Greg Phillips. Phillips gave him a grip test, which revealed that he had 120 pounds of grip strength in his right hand and 50 pounds in his left. He is left-handed. The physical therapist was happy that he showed up because his condition was deteriorating. Phillips put him in traction and performed massage and had him do exercises to strengthen his left hand. Now his grip strength is back up. He has an appointment to see Dr. Fowler this week.

24
Appointment with Dr. Fowler for Right Shoulder

He scheduled an appointment to see Dr. Fowler, as his shoulder has been giving him a lot of trouble. He is losing mobility and strength in it. It is painful to lift heavy objects. Because this is a problem that was dealt with before, he is going to ask that he be referred back to Phillips for physical therapy for his right shoulder.

24
Podiatrist

He saw a podiatrist for a bone spur on his right heel that aggravated the Achilles tendon.

24
Right Shoulder

His right shoulder feels as if it is stretching away from the socket. Dr. Fowler managed to resolve some of the problems the last time the doctor worked on it. He has trouble lifting heavy objects, twisting, turning, swinging anything, sleeping, and so forth. It is very painful.

25
Physical Activities

He walks and sometimes jogs. However, he cannot jog too much because "it shakes things around" and he stiffens quickly. He is not able to do any other body strengthening things that he was able to do before. Any strenuous midsection exercises seem to affect his neck.

26

Lifting Weights

He is not now on a weight training program. Occasionally, he would go in and lift weights with the clients. He would occasionally demonstrate the use of weights at his job, but he has a recreational assistant who generally will take over those duties.

26

Recreational Assistant Moser

His recreational assistant is Randy Moser, who lives in Spencer.

26

Strength Training

Before the accident, he did have a strength training program. He would lift weights three times a week at the Spencer Regional Treatment Center. There was a universal gym. He has not worked with the universal gym since the accident in 2002. He has done limited amounts of strength training. His shoulder has been bothering him for the past two months, so he has not lifted.

28

Current Complaints

He is concerned the numbness in his hand is getting worse. He is worried that when he was able to do repetitive activities, like shoveling snow, he had a lot of pain in his left elbow. Also, his right shoulder has gotten weaker. He wonders what the longevity of the treatment is going to be. He has lost flexibility in his neck. One of the problems he has as an instructor of therapeutic intervention is that a lot of times he is not able to demonstrate some of the techniques and has to defer to the other instructor, Karen Stuneck, who lives in Spencer.

29

Neck

He used to be able to move his neck a lot more. Now when he moves his neck beyond a certain point it is very painful. He is not receiving treatment for his neck problem currently. He was treated for it in February.

29

Medications

He is not taking any medications.

30

Neck

He has not been given any home exercises to do for his neck problem. In the past year, his neck has stayed about the same.

30

Left Hand Complaint

He has loss of sensation in his thumb and first two fingers since April 2003. He has lost some dexterity.

30

Left Arm Complaint

If he does anything repetitive, he has a burning, painful sensation across his elbow, which is like lateral epicondylitis. He was given cortisone by Dr. Fowler after the accident in the joint. Anything repetitive causes problems. That is why he does not lift weights anymore.

32

Prior Neck Problem

He denies any neck problem before 1990. Medical records indicate he fell off a ladder in 1987, hurting his neck. When questioned, he remembered falling off the ladder and testified that he might have had a stiff neck. He probably saw a doctor one time, but he does not recall any continuing symptoms from that fall.

33

Prior Right Shoulder Problems

He initially did not recall having any right shoulder problems before 2002. When questioned, he remembered that he did separate his shoulder while skiing at Ski Gull. He was going down a hill too fast and leaned into the hill and separated his shoulder. At the time of the 2002 automobile accident, his shoulder was not bothering him from the separation. He was lifting weights and was in good shape before the car accident.

34

Reason for First Seeing a Chiropractor

In March 2002, he stopped a resident from dropping weights on the resident's chest. He hurt his lower back, which led him to see the defendant chiropractors. He does not recall treating with chiropractors before that.

35

First Visit to Dr. Frazee's Office/Neck Problems

His lower-back pain was acute and he was unable to see his orthopedic surgeon. He had heard from Janet Wagner at work that she had good luck with Moira Frazee's office. Any neck symptoms he had as a result of the accident had resolved themselves before he went to the chiropractor. He did not have any big problems with his neck. He was very satisfied with the treatment he received at St. Joseph's Medical Center.

36

Neck Problem

Right after the automobile accident of 2002, he did have a stiff neck, for which he saw Dr. Fowler.

36

Prior Elbow Problems

Before the automobile accident of 2002, he does not recall having any left elbow problems.

37
Golfing
He did not golf last year or the year before. It was one of the things he enjoyed doing. He will not be able to play golf in the foreseeable future. He attempted to play twice with some friends but gave it up, as it was too frustrating. He is a certified golf coach. That is part of his teaching certificate. He was a very decent golfer, and it was frustrating to play badly. He does not have the necessary rotation to play golf. Golfers need grip strength and dexterity in their fingertips, he says. When he tried to golf, he experienced shoulder and elbow pain. He used to play golf four times a month.

39
Waterskiing
He has had to give up waterskiing. He tried it once last year and could not rise out of the water because he did not have the arm or shoulder strength to hold himself up.

39
Running and Walking
He walks and runs approximately two and a half to three miles three times a week. Physical problems depend on the road surface, how he slept, or how he feels during warm-up stretching. Stretching is a necessity. His hip will hurt, and his shoulder will hurt from holding his arms. When that happens, he starts walking. He runs less than he did before.

40
Subject Accident
On December 21, 1999, he had been visiting his girlfriend Wagner, for a week at Christmas in Bayfield, Wisconsin. He was on Interstate 35 heading south at 2:45 in the afternoon when the accident occurred. He had just crossed the bridge across Lake Superior and was approaching an incline. The visibility was bad, and all the traffic had slowed and eventually stopped because of a snowplow ahead. The roadway was slippery. As soon as he stopped, he looked in his rearview mirror because some of the traffic had been moving at a higher rate of speed than he would have deemed safe. He saw Alfred Walker's car approaching from the rear. Walker had his lights on, and the deponent stated, "I think we're going to be hit." He grabbed onto the steering wheel and reached across Wagner. Walker's car hit him with enough impact to break his seat back and total out the back of the car. The back end of the car was pushed to the windshield.

42
Walker's Vehicle
Walker's vehicle was a 1978 Thunderbird. Walker could not open the doors and had to crawl out the window.

42
Highway 35
Interstate 35 is a four-lane highway. Two lanes are northbound, two are southbound. Both southbound lanes were stopped before the accident.

42

Subject Accident

The deponent did have his lights on. He was stopped for maybe two minutes before he was hit. He was wearing his seat and shoulder belts. On impact he was pitched forward and felt a burning sensation in his left arm from hanging onto the steering wheel. He then pitched back, and the seat back broke. He was concerned about his passenger. Wagner banged her head against the window. She had not been ready for the impact, and by the time he told her they were going to be hit, she was not braced. His left hand had been holding on to the steering wheel; he had put his right arm and hand in front of his passenger. He does not know if his left elbow hit anything inside the car. He just knew they were going to be hit and hit hard.

44

Theory of Stopped Traffic/Plow

His theory in regard to why the traffic was stopped was that a blue light was flashing from a road plow up ahead that was not moving. He believes it was a wing plow, which stopped traffic in both lanes.

44

Vehicle Trajectory

His car was pushed forward into the guardrail in the left-hand lane.

44

Conversation at the Scene

After the impact, the deponent got out and looked at the damage. He and Walker agreed that it was better that they both get off the road so that someone else would not get hit. Because both of their cars were operable, they decided to drive a quarter mile and use an off-ramp to get to a grocery store. There they exchanged numbers and called the highway patrol. Walker appeared to be shaken up and said it was hard to see. The traffic started to move right after the accident.

45

Treatment After the Accident

The deponent received treatment from a doctor at the Spencer Medical Center after the accident.

45

Prior Accident

He was involved in another accident on January 18, 1997, near Spencer. He had stopped at a stop sign at a pile of snow. He could not see traffic coming from the north because of the snow. Most of the traffic comes from the south, so he looked that way. He was hit from the north. His back quarter panel was hit. The police investigated the accident. He does not have a claim against the other driver, Harlan Olson. His left rib cage was bruised. He believes he bruised his ribs on the armrest. The deponent had been driving a 1995 Honda Accord.

49

Claim Against Him

Olson is suing him for the second accident. Notification his attorney received said that Olson was hurt. However, Olson did not seem hurt at the scene.

49

Damage to Deponent's Vehicle

His vehicle sustained substantial damage to the rear quarter panel and was repaired. He was surprised that they would fix it. The damage was probably in excess of $3,000. Horace Mann Insurance Company would know the cost of repair.

50

Incident Resulting in Chiropractic Treatment

On March 13, 2002, he was spotting for a resident on an incline bench press. The resident pushed the bar up and dropped it. The deponent grabbed it before it came down too hard. He was concerned that the weight might hit the patient, and the bar might break if it was dropped from any distance. He was not in a good position to stop the downward motion of the weight. He was some-what bent over. The deponent immediately felt a pinch in his lower back. He reported the incident to his employer. The next day he went to get chiropractic treatment.

53

Conversation with Chiropractor

He told the chiropractor he injured his back in a weight lifting incident at the state hospital. He did not tell the chiropractor about the automobile accident, as he felt that he had recovered from that accident.

53

Time Lost from Work

His answers to interrogatories state he missed 137 hours of work. This was covered by workers' compensation. He knows he received a check from somebody in February 2003. He does not recall from whom it came.

55

Medical Bills

He believes he submitted his medical and chiropractic bills to Mann.

56

Other Injuries

Other than the two automobile accidents and the incident where he hurt his lower back, he has not been involved in any other automobile accidents or hurt himself in any other way.

57

Income from Decoys

The most money he has ever made in one year from making decoys was $5,000 or $6,000. He sold the decoys for $350 to $400 in Storm Lake.

57
Education
He has a four-year bachelor's degree in physical education and art education.

58
Girlfriend
His girlfriend is Janet Wagner. She resides at 6047 Fourth Street North, Nisswa. She is thirty-nine years old.

58
Income from Decoys
He earned $5,000 or $6,000 in 1987 and 1988.

59
Fall from Ladder
He believes it was 1987 when he fell off the ladder and developed a stiff neck. He does not recall what treatment he might have had as a result of the fall. He saw whoever was on call at the Spencer Medical Center.

60
Loss of Feeling in Left Thumb
He has a loss of feeling in his left thumb. It began in April 2003 after manipulation. It occurred at the same time he lost feeling in his left hand. The deterioration of his condition took place over a period of time. He does not recall specifically when he noticed it.

61
Medical Bills
He has submitted his medical bills to Mann. He does not believe he has any medical bills outstanding.

61
Olson's Claim
Olson has made a claim against him. Olson is being represented by the Van Drake Law Firm in Spencer.

62
Wagner's Injuries/Conversation
After the accident, the deponent asked Wagner how she was. She said she got a bump on the side of her head from hitting the door window. She might have complained of a headache. He does not recall. Wagner asked the deponent how he was. The deponent said he was shaken up but seemed to feel OK. He cannot recall if he said he had a headache.

63
Neck Discomfort
He did have neck discomfort following the accident, but he did not tell that to Dr. Anne Jackson [the chiropractor he saw at Dr. Frazee's office on March 14, 2003].

63

Numbness

He had numbness in the front of his left hand in addition to his index finger and middle finger. Basically the numbness was along the perimeter of the hand.

64

Recommended to Dr. Frazee

He went to Dr. Frazee's office on March 14, 2003. He had hurt his lower back the previous day. The individual who recommended Dr. Frazee's office had problems between her shoulder blades. She is currently a patient of Dr. Frazee's. She has never complained about Dr. Frazee. She likes him.

65

First Visit to Dr. Frazee

He does not recall any adjustment on his first office visit on March 14. He received massage and heat. X-rays were taken. He saw Dr. Jackson. He does not recall Dr. Jackson's diagnosis.

65

Second Visit

His second visit to Dr. Frazee's office was on March 19. He saw Dr. Jackson. His neck was not adjusted.

66

Third Visit

At his third visit on March 21, he saw Dr. Jackson. On that day he told Dr. Jackson he was having some headaches. Dr. Jackson asked if he had ever had adjustments on his neck for headaches. He had not. Dr. Jackson suggested that he try an adjustment to see if it would help his headache. A cervical adjustment was administered. He does not recall any problem following the adjustment. He was shocked how loud it was. He did not experience an increase of discomfort in his neck following the adjustment.

67

Fourth Visit

The next chiropractic treatment took place on March 26. He was still having headaches. Dr. Jackson suggested that he try a cervical adjustment. When the doctor finished the adjustment, he felt no worse. He felt that he was being taken care of professionally and his condition was being treated appropriately.

69

Fifth Visit

His next treatment at the Frazee Clinic was April 2. He again had treatment to his lower back. He does not recall if he had treatment to his neck.

69

Sixth Visit

His sixth visit to the chiropractor was on April 9. His back seemed to be getting better. He was not doing anything for his back aside from getting chiropractic adjustments. He had been able to continue working notwithstanding his back discomfort. He was feeling better than he had when he first came in on March 14. He believes he had a cervical adjustment. Other than his lower-back pain, he still had recurring headaches. He believes Dr. Jackson indicated that she was going to try cervical adjustments at different levels to see if she could find a trigger point for the headaches. When he left, he felt the treatment was a little more vigorous than the prior treatments. He made no complaints to the doctor. He scheduled another treatment.

72
Seventh Visit
His seventh visit was on April 11.

72
Subsequent to the April 9 Adjustment
After the April 9 adjustment, which occurred on his lunch break, he went back to work. He felt funny, so he basically did paperwork. He worked until 8:30 in the evening. He went home after work. He was with his son. He took ibuprofen.

73
Injuries from December 21, 1999, Accident
He is not aware that he struck his left elbow against anything. He was braced against the steering wheel. He might have had some slight swelling of the left elbow. He went to see a doctor for his left elbow.

74
Asleep on Couch
On the night of April 9, 2003, he watched television while lying on the couch with two pillows. The next day, April 10, his neck was very sore.

74
Neck Pain
On April 10, after he got out of bed, his neck was very sore. His head was tipped toward his shoulder. He could not move in any direction comfortably. The pain was very severe. He had used two pillows to support his shoulders and neck while lying on the couch.

76
Contact with Dr. Frazee's Office
On April 10, in the morning, he contacted Dr. Frazee's office to see if he could be examined by Dr. Jackson. He was told that Dr. Jackson was not in but Dr. Frazee was in his Storm Lake office. He made arrangements to be examined by Dr. Frazee at Storm Lake. He did go to work on the tenth.

78
Others Who Had Knowledge of Neck Problems/Medication
His recreational assistants and his secretary showed concern. He probably took some Advil.

78

April 11 Visit

He saw Dr. Frazee in Storm Lake on April 11. He drove himself to the doctor's office, which was approximately twenty-two miles away.

79

Conversations with Dr. Frazee

He told Dr. Frazee that he last had an adjustment from Dr. Jackson on April 9. He also told the doctor that he had slept on the couch for a while with two pillows and later had severe neck pain. Dr. Frazee examined his neck. Dr. Frazee probably explained to him that a chiropractic adjustment could not be given to him because of the pain. The deponent thought maybe Dr. Jackson had messed up and Dr. Frazee could straighten out his problem. It was his original intention to see Dr. Frazee because that is to whom he was referred.

81

Treatment with Dr. Frazee

He continued treatment with Dr. Frazee for several office visits. He does not recall if Dr. Frazee gave him any type of chiropractic adjustment.

81

MRI

He and Dr. Frazee discussed an MRI. Dr. Frazee felt it would be a good idea. The deponent made arrangements to have an MRI on April 29, 2003.

82

Physical Therapy/Traction

After the MRI he received physical therapy prescribed by a medical doctor. Along with physical therapy treatments, he had traction to his neck. The traction seemed to make it feel better when he was having it. He also had a home traction unit. Along with the traction, he received massage and heat. It was the same treatment he was receiving for his lower back at the chiropractor's office. He does not recall having any discomfort during his physical therapy. Traction felt good.

83

Medical Attention After December 21, 1999, Accident

The first treatment he received following the automobile accident on December 21, 1999, took place at the Spencer Medical Center on December 26. He gave a history of having stiffness in his neck immediately following the automobile accident. He complained of recurring headaches. He experienced a slight discomfort when the therapist worked on his elbow. He let the doctor know. He told the doctor of the changes and sensations he was experiencing in his left arm, fingers, hand, and shoulder. Dr. Kenneth Galbraith released him to return to work without any restrictions as of July 11, 2000. The doctor told him he was very happy with the progress being made in physical therapy. The doctor told him that if he did not straighten out his problems, he would probably be a candidate for surgery. However, he progressed.

85

First Medical Doctor Seen After Development of Wryneck Condition
The first medical doctor he saw after the development of the wryneck condition was
Dr. Phyllis Thomas. He explained to Dr. Thomas that the pain began in his neck
the day after the chiropractic treatment.

86

April 15, 2003, Visit to Dr. Thomas
In addition, he was having pain in his left shoulder and down to his elbow.

86

April 25 Visit
On April 25 he saw Dr. Thomas and reported having shoulder and neck pain that
radiated into his elbow.

87

May 8 Visit
On May 8 he reported to Dr. Thomas, for the first time, having problems with tin-
gling down into his hand and fingers. The day of his MRI was the day he went on
vacation. He was suffering a few symptoms of this during his vacation.

87

Vacation
He and Wagner went on vacation to New York City to see some shows and visit the
Statue of Liberty. He was suffering symptoms at this time. The second day there, he
was not sure if he should hop a flight back to Spencer and check himself into the
hospital. Since the automobile accident of December 21, 1999, he had also gone to
Michigan skiing in February. In addition, he had just returned from Arizona. He did
a lot of walking there.

89

Additional Visits to Dr. Jackson
Before discontinuing his chiropractic care, he saw Dr. Jackson for his back and neck.
He did not complain to Dr. Jackson that she had done something unusual to his
neck. He usually does not complain.

90

Traction to Neck
The therapist usually does manual traction where she places her hands basically un-
derneath the deponent's whole back. At that time she would ask the deponent how
he felt. When using the mechanical device, the doctor gave him the stirrup to hang
on to. The deponent would be in control and would not go beyond what was comfortable for him. He was reclining on the treatment table when the traction was administered to his neck.

90
Current Problems
Currently, his left elbow is better. He can use it normally although he has to avoid repetitive motions. Shoveling snow is very hard on it, as is lifting repetitively. He experiences problems with his elbow first and then his shoulder.

92
Causation of Problems
He does not know what the causation of his problems is. All he knows are the results. He argues that he is not a neurologist or orthopedic surgeon. He does not have any judgment as to what incident or incidents have caused his problems.

92
Dr. DeKoster
He has not personally been examined by Dr. David DeKoster. Dr. DeKoster only reviewed his records. [Dr. DeKoster is a chiropractor whom plaintiff retained to render an opinion that the defendant chiropractor was negligent.]

93
Complaint Regarding Headaches
He did not complain to the chiropractors about headaches before they did the first adjustment to his neck. He had a cold, and they discussed the possibility he had a sinus infection.

94
Deponent did not waive the right to read and make corrections to the transcript.
End of Deposition Transcript

 For additional resources, visit our Web site at www.paralegal.delmar.cengage.com

CHAPTER 13

PREPARING CLIENT FOR DEPOSITION

CHAPTER OUTLINE

Chapter Objectives

Chapter 13 describes the process for preparing a client for his or her oral deposition. It identifies some of the problems paralegals may encounter and proposes some solutions.

Introduction

The preceding chapter explained what oral depositions are, how they are conducted, and their value as a discovery tool. In this chapter we are approaching the subject from the perspective of the deponent. As a paralegal, you can play a vital role in preparing clients for depositions. The fact is that most clients need more time for preparation than many lawyers are willing to give. You can make the difference. But you must thoroughly understand the purposes for which each client's deposition is being taken, the issues, theory of the case, and potential uses of the deposition. You cannot expect to assume responsibility for client preparation until you have had some on-the-job experience and the opportunity to observe some depositions. Each lawyer tends to have a different approach and emphasis. You must honor the lawyer's preferences, but this chapter should help you to prepare for the opportunity to work with clients in this important area.

　　The opposing lawyer will take your client's deposition to obtain more than just evidence and information. The lawyer wants to evaluate your client and your preparedness. The lawyer will evaluate your client by what the client says and how he or she says it. By the time the deposition is through, the lawyer will have opinions about whether your client understands the case, whether the client is an effective witness, and whether he or she has the fortitude to go to trial. And, of course, a lawyer looks for possible impeachment. Any mistakes can severely damage the client's ability to prove a claim or defense. Even minor mistakes tend to alter the settlement value of a claim or defense. If the client is able to be comfortable with the procedure and has a good deposition, you will have the undying gratitude of a happy client.

There is no one formula for preparing a client for an oral deposition. Some steps may change or be omitted, depending on the circumstances. Nevertheless, certain objectives are generally applicable, whether the client is a plaintiff or a defendant and regardless of the type of case. As always, good preparation is essential. You should make the client comfortable with the process. Impress on the client the necessity of being truthful. Strive to keep the client's deposition testimony consistent with the client's anticipated trial testimony. Keep the client from making inadvertent admissions by putting the expected testimony into context. Help the client choose the right words to make the testimony clear. Try to anticipate problems and take steps to avoid them. You must not lead the client into error or cause any mistakes.

Preparing to Meet a Client

Make sure you have the parties' *legal theories* well in mind. Start by reviewing the pleadings to identify the legal theories. The legal theories frame the legal issues, which in turn determine what facts are material to the case; the material facts (also thought of as controlling facts) determine what evidence is relevant to prove those facts. Relevant evidence is anything that tends to prove or disprove a material fact.

Make sure you understand your legal team's *theory of the facts*. Review the investigation and discovery files. You must understand what happened, why it happened, and how it happened. You must concentrate on making the client's version truthful and, hopefully, consistent with your team's theory of the case. Lawyers and paralegals have a duty to the courts and society to prevent clients from testifying falsely. Your zeal to develop consistency between the theory of the facts, testimony, and other evidence must not denigrate the truth. If the client's version of the facts does not agree with the team's strategy, the conflict must be resolved before the client's deposition is taken. Clients really appreciate competent guidance, especially by a person whom they believe is sincerely interested in their welfare.

While studying the investigation materials, initial disclosures, answers to interrogatories and depositions already taken, you should:

1. Determine what facts are indisputable and what facts are not disputed. The evidence should be marshaled around those facts.
2. Focus on the material facts. Decide which disputed facts are really important to the parties' theories of the case. The disputed material facts require the most attention and detail. For example, in an automobile

accident case, speed, condition of the highway, and positions of traffic controls are material facts. But whether the client had military service or has been divorced are only collateral facts, not really material.

3. Determine whether the client's expected version is consistent with the laws of nature and the physical facts. For example, if the client's privileged-file-statement says he just "tapped" the other automobile, but he caused $5,000 of damage, there may be a problem with the client's version. The client's version must be modified. But be careful! Strange things have happened, so be concerned that the client's version might still be correct.

4. Consider whether the client's expected testimony is consistent with probability, common experience, and common sense.

5. Consider whether the client's contentions are believable. Is there an explanation for the client's version that needs careful development?

6. Determine whether the client's version requires testing. For example, if the client claims she found a foreign object in her soda is there any way the object could have gotten into the bottle after it left the bottling plant? Did the client's children have access to the bottle before she drank from it?

7. Consider whether you need additional photographs to work with to prepare the client for the deposition.

8. Decide whether any of the photographs and documents in the file will be used as exhibits. You may want to make extra copies to use during preparation and copies to use in the deposition. You must not make marks on exhibits that may be used at trial. If an exhibit has marks on it and the witness merely adopts the position suggested by those marks, the exhibit may be objected to as "leading." Leading questions are objectionable and lack persuasiveness.

9. Consider duplicating photographs and documents for the opponent to use during the deposition so that your original exhibits are not marked or used during the deposition and "messed up" by the other lawyer.

10. Consider whether the client should be allowed to make drawings or sketches during his or her deposition. Making a sketch often is a problem for deponents, especially if they are not prepared. Even though a sketch made during a deposition is expressly not to scale, it may be used at trial to cross-examine the deponent. You may want to prepare an acceptable sketch and have the client practice, using your sketch as a guide.

11. Examine original documents in the file and become very familiar with the critical language, dates, and names.

12. Often, the client is the only source for some critical evidence, so that evidence must be stressed in the preparation. The details become even more important.

13. Decide whether the client's spouse should or should not attend. Ordinarily, most lawyers prefer to exclude the client's spouse from the preparation and deposition. However, if the client needs the spouse's support, that is all right. If both spouses are going to testify, they should

be prepared together. However, a client and an independent witness should not be prepared together, because communications with the independent witness are not privileged. The independent witness could be compelled to testify to anything and everything you and the client said.

14. Meet with the trial lawyer to review your preparation and intended approach.

If the case involves an accident, before meeting with the client, you may need to view the situs[1] to obtain a better understanding about how the accident occurred. Consider meeting the client at the situs if you did not do so during the investigation. Make and verify relevant measurements. Make sure all speed, distance, and time factors correlate with your legal team's theory. Your fact theory should fully accommodate all the known facts. Of course, the theory may change as new information and evidence is obtained.

The importance of facts and the admissibility of evidence about them dictate how much time you should spend on them. Suppose both drivers survived, and immediately after the accident the opposing party admitted the accident was his or her fault. If no one else heard the admission, the client must be prepared on this point with great care. You must prepare the client to testify in great detail about the circumstances, such as where the parties were standing when the admission was made, the circumstances leading to the admission, and the parties' subsequent conduct that confirmed the admission. But if several witnesses heard the opposing party make the admission, it will be enough to prepare the client to relate the statement and its context without so much detail. Of course, you cannot tell the client what to say. When you do make suggestions about how to say something, you must make sure the client is comfortable with the suggestions and understands that they are only suggestions. In the final analysis, the testimony must be that of the client. You must anticipate problems and develop a plan for dealing with each of them. Consider preparing a list of items to discuss in the order of their importance.

Some lawyers spend only an hour preparing their clients for depositions. An hour is not enough. When the deposition goes poorly, they blame the client for giving dumb answers. The lawyer thinks that he or she told the client how to answer, but the lawyer did not spend enough time reinforcing the client's memory and understanding. Ideally, the client should be prepared in two sessions. A client is more comfortable during the first meeting knowing she or he does not have to testify right away. The first session should be used to bring the client up to date, explain the deposition procedure, discuss the legal issues, discuss problems that you have identified, and go through a mock cross-examination. The second meeting should focus on the client's anticipated testimony. Between sessions, you can spend some time on solving problems. The client has time to reflect on what you have taught him or her. It also gives the client time in which to check on facts and clear up uncertainties. For example, the client may review a journal for dates, look for repair bills or an insurance form, make measurements, examine the car, and so forth. The deposition preparation meeting should be at your office. You should have the file organized, exhibits organized, and a calendar available. Have your telephone calls held. Determine whether the attorney you are working with is available if needed.

Try to make the client feel the deposition will be beneficial and a positive experience. The deposition gives the client an opportunity to *practice* testifying. He or she can use the transcript as an aid to prepare for the trial. Explain that after the parties' depositions have been taken, the lawyers will evaluate the case for purposes of settlement. That is good news to both plaintiffs and defendants. Be positive. You may tell the client that the opposition is entitled to only one deposition, absent unusual circumstances.[2] Your joint preparation should help the client feel confident about the case.

Impress on the client the importance of the deposition to the case without making the client unduly nervous. You can do this by being fully prepared, relaxed, and confident. Conduct yourself in a professional manner; try to be authoritative in a pleasant, caring way. Show concern for the client's needs and comfort. Do not be casual or try to be funny. Take charge. For most of us, the unknown is the principal cause of apprehension. The more apprehensive or nervous the client is during the deposition, the more likely she or he is to make mistakes. So do what you can to make the client feel comfortable about testifying. But, the client must appreciate it is the client's lawsuit, not yours or the insurance company's. The problems are the client's, not yours. You are there to help him or her, not vice versa.

Some clients need to be assured that it is proper to prepare for a deposition. They worry that you are going to try to put words in their mouths, and they know that is wrong. They wonder why they can't just tell what they saw. Suppose an insurance company has retained your office to defend the client. The client may worry about your loyalties and motives: that you might wrongly put the insurance company's interests ahead of the client. Your approach must show that you are there to help the client. In that regard, you also may have to explain that the case is against the client, not against the insurance company, and the insurance company is not your client. It merely pays the litigation expenses.

Your client must testify truthfully. Testimony is given under oath. A deponent must not fabricate or twist the facts. There is no surer way to lose a case than for a party to be caught in a lie. Telling the truth means testifying accurately—without exaggerating or minimizing. A witness's opinions must comport with what the witness actually believes. A deponent who testifies falsely commits perjury and is subject to criminal prosecution. Perjury is a felony. Jurors are instructed that if they conclude that a witness has testified falsely, they may disregard everything the witness said. If a party tries to win a case on the basis of false testimony, that party is fighting against heavy odds and faces severe penalties. If a client indicates that she or he wants to be told what to say, you must be firm that she or he is to tell the truth and only the truth. If the client does not know the answer to the question, the client must be instructed to say he or she does not know.

The truth is not always clear or discernable. The adversary system permits each party to give herself or himself the benefit of any honest doubt concerning a disputed fact. For example, if a motorist honestly believes she was not exceeding a thirty-mile-per-hour speed limit, but did not look at her speedometer to determine her actual speed, she should testify to what she believes her speed was. She should be prepared to deny driving any faster. However, she must be candid that she did not look at the speedometer. Her opinion is only an estimate. But she should refuse to speculate that she may have been going faster than she truly believes she was. Nor should she speculate that her speed might have been less.

Never lead a client into error. By this time, your legal team has its theory of the facts. But be sure that you also understand the client's version of the facts. Hopefully, your theory and the client's theory are in agreement. But if not, you must consider the client's explanations before making any suggestions about reconsidering his or her version. Try to understand the client's perspective and explanations, because the client could be right, and your team might be wrong. If the client loses the case, it should be for the right reasons. However, when a client's belief about certain facts clearly is wrong, you must help the client to find and understand the truth. You do this by determining the source of the client's false belief. Put the fact issues into context for the client. Work through the evidence in a systematic manner by asking simple questions that help the client to discover the truth for himself or herself.

Let us take an example of a hypothetical discussion with a client who is mistaken about an important fact. Suppose you are assisting a plaintiff with a personal injury claim that arose from an automobile accident. Both cars entered an uncontrolled intersection at the same time. The client was on the right and had the statutory right-of-way. The client claims the defendant was going fifty miles per hour and made no effort to stop, but photographs show only minimal damage to both cars. The defendant admitted to the police that she was going ten miles per hour at contact, and you believe the defendant was going between ten and fifteen miles per hour. The combined speeds of the two cars could have caused the injury the client sustained. You could use the approach outlined in the accompanying example.

Try to keep the client from becoming emotionally committed to a mistaken view of the facts. You should try to make it easy for the client to let go of false beliefs about the facts. A client will become resentful if the client thinks you are trying to lead her or him into error. Your responsibility is to help the client avoid making mistakes.

EXAMPLE

Q: I have talked with your doctor. He says your injury could have resulted from the combined speeds of your car and the defendant's car, even if the defendant was going only ten miles per hour. The damage to the cars suggests the defendant was traveling about ten to fifteen miles per hour when the collision occurred. Why do you think the defendant might have been going faster?

A: The collision was such a shock. There was a tremendous noise. She must have been way down the block, because I looked and there was no car near the intersection as I approached. Suddenly, there she was.

Q: The police report and these photographs show two vans parked along the curb. They could have momentarily obstructed your view of the defendant's car. Her car could have been behind them. She admitted traveling ten miles per hour. Don't you think it is possible, just possible, her car was blocked from your view when you looked to your left and then back to your right?

continued

EXAMPLE   *continued*

A: The way she was going, she must have been farther back.

Q: Neither car had much damage. If she were moving fifty miles per hour, wouldn't you expect more damage?

A: I don't know. Maybe.

Q: Her car didn't move after the point of collision, did it?

A: No, not that I remember.

Q: How far does a car move in one second if it is going fifty miles per hour?

A: I don't know; I never figured it.

Q: Well, the charts show it moves seventy-seven feet per second. You were traveling ten miles per hour as you entered the intersection. At ten miles per hour, you traveled fifteen feet per second. She must have been about the same distance back. In three seconds you traveled forty-five feet to the point of impact. If she was going fifty miles per hour, she would have traveled 225 feet in three seconds. It hardly seems possible that she could have been that far back when you were only forty-five feet from the point of collision.

A: What about it?

Q: Well, if she was going ten to fifteen miles per hour, we can see how your view was blocked, but if she was 150 feet back, the parked trucks would not have blocked your view.

A: But if she was going faster, doesn't that mean the accident was her fault?

Q: No. Speed isn't our concern. You had the right-of-way. Our concern is whether the defendant's lawyer can contend that you didn't keep a proper lookout. He will argue that you didn't see that which was in plain sight. You told the police that you didn't see the defendant's car until it was about to enter the intersection.

A: Do you think that my estimate of her speed is off?

Q: Yes. I think the shock of the collision made you feel that the defendant was traveling faster than she really was.

A: Could be. I never thought about it that way. Maybe she could have been going ten or fifteen miles per hour.

Scheduling a Meeting

A meeting may be scheduled using a letter like the one in Exhibit 13.1. Depositions are usually taken at the office of the lawyer who noticed it. However, it could be taken almost anywhere—a courtroom, airport, hotel, hospital, or the deponent's home. The primary consideration is availability of the deponent and convenience of a majority of the people involved.

EXHIBIT 13.1

*Letter for Scheduling Meetings
with a Client*

Dear Ms. Alice Rose:

Today, we received a notice from the defendant's lawyer demanding that you appear for a discovery deposition in his office on [date] at [time]. The defense lawyer has a right to ask you questions about the accident. You may recall that when we first undertook to prosecute this case on your behalf, we discussed the likelihood that the lawyer would exercise his right to take your deposition.

The deposition procedure is fairly informal. Only the defendant's lawyer, Mr. Robert Anderson, [the client's lawyer], a court reporter, and I will be at the deposition. The defendant has a right to attend, but it is likely he will choose not to be there.

You will have to answer the lawyer's questions under oath. The lawyer will try to find out what you know about the accident and what you do not know. He will also inquire into your background. A verbatim transcript will be made of his questions and your answers.

I want to help you prepare for the deposition. It would be best if we could plan on two meetings in which to conduct our preparation. The first meeting should be as soon as your convenience will permit. I have blocked out the morning of [date] on my calendar, hoping that time may fit into your schedule. We shall need at least two hours so that I can bring you up to date on your case, explain the issues, explain the deposition procedure, and discuss your testimony. Please let me know whether the date I have chosen is good for you.

Our second meeting should be on the day before the deposition. At that time we shall actually go through a mock examination, much like the procedure we expect the defense lawyer to use. I am sure that by the time we complete our preparation you will feel completely confident about testifying and about your case. This deposition gives us an opportunity to show the defense that our case has merit. I fully expect that after the defense lawyer has heard your testimony, the defense will be interested in discussing settlement with us.

Please telephone me. I look forward to hearing from you soon.

Sincerely,

Shawna Montgomery
Paralegal

Meeting to Prepare for Deposition

If possible, the lawyer should meet with the client first and then introduce the client to you. The lawyer should bring the client up to date about the status of case. Then preparation may be turned over to you. Some lawyers begin by explaining the deposition procedure. Others prefer to begin with an overview of the case—legal theories, issues, facts, evidence, and strategy. Then they discuss deposition procedures. The "big picture" provides a frame of reference, which helps clients to put questions into context. You want the client to understand how his or her testimony fits into the case as a whole. The explanations will help the client to understand the interrogator's questions and their relevancy. Also, the client will understand the consequences of her or his answers. Encourage the client to ask you questions, because the client's questions tell you whether the client understands what you are saying. Strive to have a dialogue with the client, rather than lecture. The client will understand and retain much more if he or she actively participates in the preparation. When the client starts asking irrelevant questions, redirect the focus. Do not let the conference get sidetracked. Do not allow the client's extraneous concerns to disrupt preparation.

Make sure the client understands the attorney-client privilege. Neither of you can be required to disclose what was said during your discussions. The client may acknowledge meeting with you, but the client cannot be required to relate the matters discussed. Keep in mind, the client has the right to disclose your discussions, and if the client subsequently becomes unhappy for some reason, he or she could choose to do so.

When you prepare a witness for a deposition, assure him or her that it is proper to meet. If asked during the deposition whether you had a meeting, he or she should freely acknowledge meeting. The witness should be prepared to give innocuous answers to questions like, "What did the paralegal tell you to say?" The witness should be prepared to answer, "I was told to tell the truth" or "I told him the same things I'm telling you," or "She just said that you would ask questions about the accident and that I should listen carefully to the questions and answer the questions truthfully. We talked about the basketball game and so forth." A savvy witness will try to steer to another subject. The worst thing that the witness could do is give a narrative about the meeting.

Preparing a Client to Testify

Explain the trial team's theory of the claim and defenses. Identify what facts are controverted and what facts are not disputed. Tell the client why the opposing party wants the client's discovery deposition. Explain, in a general way, the purposes of a deposition and uses of a transcript. The opposing lawyer's objectives are to get acquainted with the client by listening and observing her or him testify. The lawyer wants to evaluate the client's appearance, authority, and believability. The lawyer wants to find out what the deponent knows and does not know about the occurrence or transaction. In addition, the lawyer wants to force the deponent to commit to a particular version of the facts, so that the lawyer knows what she or he must deal with at trial. The lawyer will look for inconsistencies in the testimony. The lawyer will seek to obtain additional sources of information. Finally, the opposing lawyer may try to intimidate the client to make the client fearful about testifying at trial. Through all of this, the opposing lawyer will evaluate the client's preparedness and, consequently, the preparedness of your legal team. Did you do your job? The client's presentation reflects on the lawyer and paralegal who prepared him or her for the deposition.

Clients naturally want to justify themselves by fully explaining what happened and the reason. That is exactly what the opposing lawyer wants. You must instruct the client not to volunteer information. *Just answer the question.* There is no need to help the opponent any more than the law and ethics require. The more the opposing lawyer can find out about your client and what your client knows, the better the lawyer can prepare his or her case against your client. It follows that your client's best answer is a short answer, but the answer must be sufficiently complete to be truthful. In most cases, the parties' legal rights and obligations are determined by a few key points. You must identify the key points for the client. Explain how the opponent will try to develop a version of those key points to fit the opponent's claim or defense. Then explain to the client how the opponent's lawyer may try to pursue that version in the client's deposition.

There are exceptions to the general rule that the client should not volunteer information. Your team's overall strategy may require disclosure of certain facts (information) in the deposition. Consequently, you may want the client to volunteer that information. In that regard, the deponent's lawyer may elect to ask questions that the other lawyer failed to ask. Those questions and the client's answers should be carefully rehearsed. For example, the plaintiff in a personal injury action may want to settle before trial, but the defendant will not know the full monetary value of the injuries unless the defendant's lawyer finds out all about the injuries. The plaintiff's deposition strategy may be to provide a full picture of the injuries. The plaintiff may have to volunteer information about her injuries to present that full picture. Consequently, plaintiffs often volunteer information about their pains and disabilities. Another example is when the deponent's lawyer has in mind making a motion for summary judgment, and the client's testimony on a certain point is essential to support the motion. The client should be prepared to provide the correct information.

On occasion the deponent's lawyer needs to ask clarifying questions to protect the deponent. A witness may think she or he said one thing, but it came out quite differently. The deponent's lawyer must decide whether to explain and correct the mistake before the deposition is concluded. It is easy to do on the record. The deponent's lawyer may be able to use leading questions to avoid augmenting the mistake. The alternative is to correct the mistake when the transcript is submitted for review. A significant correction to a transcript may require the client to submit to another deposition. If the lawyer is not quite sure how the client will respond to the attempt to correct the mistake, the better practice is to correct the mistake as provided by Rule 30(e).[3] Either way, a mistake may subject the client to impeachment.

A deponent must be prepared to deal with estimates of time and distance. You may educate or remind the client about natural laws so the client makes estimates, judgments, and approximations that are accurate and authoritative. For example, it does not take one minute to travel 100 feet. You and the client may need to visit the situs to put everything in perspective. Good estimates can be very important in accident cases. Decide whether an estimate should be a single figure or a range. For example, depending on the legal team's theory and strategy, the client may estimate speed as a range of forty to fifty miles per hour or as a single figure of forty-five miles per hour. The estimate must comport with other physical facts and what is reasonable. It must not be a mere guess. Once selected, the range or figure should be firm even though the client must acknowledge that it is only an estimate. For example, if the client estimates a speed of thirty miles per hour, the client should not acknowledge that it could have been thirty-two or twenty-eight miles per hour. Instead, the client should respond that thirty miles per hour is the client's best estimate, and he or she is not going to argue about possibilities.

Sometimes a client has difficulty remembering some details and needs help to determine how to deal with the questions that are expected. Again, the client must not be led into error and must not testify falsely. With that caveat in mind, here are some suggestions. The client may give herself or himself the benefit of any honest doubt. You should determine what is consistent with physical fact and with other established facts. You should consider what probably happened. Once the client has reconstructed the situation and is confident that she or he is correct, the client should testify confidently from that belief. The client should avoid using qualifying expressions, such as "to tell you the truth" or "to be honest" or "as best as I can recall." Such phrases are hackneyed and take away from the witness's authority. The client must not plan on having any "aside" conferences during the deposition. Nevertheless, if necessary, a lawyer usually can interrupt the deposition to have a conference with his or her client.

Warn the client that the lawyers have a right to ask questions about almost anything, but when improper questions are asked, his or her lawyer will object. When an objection is interposed, the interrogator has several options. The interrogator may adjourn the deposition and seek a court order compelling the deponent to answer the question. Or, the interrogator may complete the deposition on other matters and seek a court order that requires the witness to answer.

You and the lawyers you work with must have a strategy for dealing with objectionable questions. As a general rule, when the deponent's lawyer objects to a question, the deponent should remain silent until the lawyer tells the deponent what to do. The lawyer who asked the question may decide to rephrase the question or go to another question. But if the interrogator insists on an answer, the lawyer who objected will have to decide whether to let the deponent answer subject to the objection. An answer is made subject to an objection when the client's lawyer objects to the question and states the grounds for the objection but allows the deponent to answer.[4] When the lawyer allows the client to answer the question subject to the objection, the client should ask the court reporter to read the question so the client can make sure he or she understands it. The lawyer's objection may contain a clue to the problem, so the client should listen carefully to the objections and grounds. The client should listen carefully to any discussion the lawyers have about the question and objection, because the discussion might help the client to understand the dangers. In the accompanying example, the questions were put to a landlord in an action brought by a tenant.

EXAMPLE

Q: How long had the stairway light been burned out before the plaintiff fell on the stairway?

Objection: The question is objected to on the grounds that it assumes facts not in evidence and is argumentative in form. The defendant does not know that the plaintiff fell on the stairway.

Q: You don't deny that the plaintiff fell on the stairway, do you?

A: I don't know that he fell.

Q: Well, how long was the light out?

A: I don't know that it was burned out. I heard from the plaintiff's wife that she changed the bulb in the stairway after the plaintiff went to the hospital. I understood that she put in a *brighter* lightbulb.

This witness was adequately prepared on the points in issue. The objection helped the witness to focus on the problem in the question.

Guidelines for Testifying in a Discovery Deposition

The following guidelines help deponents to testify in discovery depositions. These guidelines are not rules or regulations. You will not find them in any statute. They are mostly common sense, but they also take into consideration some of the peculiarities of the Rules of Evidence and court procedures. These guidelines do not necessarily apply to testifying at trial, because the objectives and purposes are different. Specifically, in trial a party must testify to educate and persuade the jury. In a discovery deposition, the deponent's objective is to disclose only what needs to be disclosed.

Tell the Truth

For the reasons stated previously, you must see to it that your client testifies truthfully. Lying not only is wrong, but the probability is that the client who lies will be caught in his or her web of deception.

Be Sincere

Sincerity is one hallmark of a persuasive witness. Second to sincerity is authority. A witness appears sincere when the witness appears to believe what she or he says. A witness appears authoritative when the witness is able to remember and describe details about the facts to which she or he testifies. To gain the appearance of sincerity and authority a client should be confident, thoughtful, and direct. The client should be polite toward everyone, including the opposing lawyer, before, during, and after the deposition.

A lawsuit is a serious matter for all concerned. Seldom is there occasion for wisecracks or jokes. Advise the client to avoid poking fun at another person—even if the client sees an opportunity to "put the opposing lawyer in his place." As often as not, someone will be offended. A joke may boomerang. If a duel of sharp-tongued wit develops, the forum favors the lawyer, because only the lawyer is authorized to initiate questions.

Listen Carefully

A witness should feel certain he or she understands the question before answering. The burden is on the lawyer to make each question clear and understandable. If the witness does not understand a question, it is not the witness's fault or problem. The lawyer must repeat or rephrase the question when asked to do so. A witness has the right to ask for clarification. Your client will be a lot less nervous when he or she realizes that the onus is on the lawyer to help the deponent understand the questions. The client should not be reluctant to admit that she or he did not hear a question or understand it.

Take Time

A deponent should reflect on each question for a moment and silently phrase the answer before responding aloud. Unless cautioned, some deponents are inclined to answer before a question is completed. They want to show the lawyer that they are listening and know the answer. Reflection keeps the witness from interrupting the lawyer's questions. More important, when a deponent answers quickly, he or she is likely to make mistakes. In addition, the deponent complicates the court reporter's task, because it is nearly impossible to record the statements of two people talking at the same time.

When a witness takes a moment to reflect on a question and to think through the answer, the witness's lawyer has an opportunity to object if the question is improper. Lawyers know that a thoughtful witness is less likely to be tripped up and may try to pressure the witness to answer quickly by showing impatience or irritation. You should caution the client against permitting the interrogator to rush her or him. A witness can hardly be too thoughtful or deliberate—at least, when testifying in a deposition. Testimony at trial presents a little different situation. There, excessive hesitancy or delay may be interpreted, rightly or wrongly, as uncertainty or a lack of authority or even a lack of candor. Pauses and little delays do not show up in a deposition transcript, unless a video is used. Even then, it is better to be thoughtful and deliberate.

Answer Only the Question

The more information the interrogator obtains, the better the interrogator can prepare for trial. In a discovery deposition, the deponent should not help the interrogator by volunteering information or by providing explanations not specifically requested. The answers should be responsive, direct, and specific. Succinctly stated, the deponent's best answer is the shortest answer, provided it is truthful. Short answers help to make the witness appear polite, authoritative, and nonargumentative. A verbose deponent tends to gravitate to the problems that are most bothersome to him or her. Some deponents are inclined to volunteer information when they want to emphasize their importance. Sometimes deponents feel constrained to explain why they know the answer. A talkative deponent opens new subjects and areas for questioning. The more the deponent talks, the greater the opportunity for inconsistencies.

A deponent should feel as though she or he is a well of information, and the interrogator dips into the well with each question. If the deponent feels as though the information is being *pulled out*, then the client is handling the discovery deposition correctly. The deponent should not feel like a fountain that gushes forth information. This does not mean that the client should be uncommunicative, stubborn, or difficult.

Each question is supposed to be singular, not multiple. A deponent should have to think about only one question at a time. A deponent can help to keep his or her answers short by declining to answer multiple questions. Although the deponent's lawyer is responsible for objecting to multiple questions, advise the client to watch for vague and multiple questions. Tell the client that if he or she senses that a question is multiple, the client should respond by saying, "Can you be more specific?" or "It seems you have asked two questions." The lawyer should be on top of the situation, but a client may ask for clarification without waiting for his or her lawyer to object. This kind of problem points out the importance of rehearsing for an oral deposition.

Do Not Guess

A witness should admit not knowing the answer to a question rather than guess at the answer. In general, a wrong guess can do more harm than a lucky guess can help. What is worse, a wrong guess may be interpreted as false testimony. If jurors determine a witness is prone to guessing, they are inclined to discount the witness's testimony. The authority of a witness can be severely diminished by guessing. The rule against guessing does not mean that a witness should refrain from making estimates or judgments or giving opinions and best recollections. By way of example, a witness may not know the exact width of the roadway but may be able to make a reasonably accurate estimate. A reasonably reliable estimate is not a mere guess. The law seldom requires exactitude or perfect recall. The law does require a witness to believe that his or her memory is reliable and estimates reasonably accurate.

To express some degree of uncertainty without guessing, witnesses often use expressions such as "to the best of my memory," "as best as I recall," "I believe," or "I'm not certain, but . . . ." Whenever a witness is constrained to qualify an answer in this manner, he or she loses some authority and persuasiveness. The client should be told that everyone assumes the client is testifying to what the client believes is true. Therefore, the client need not qualify answers by saying she or he does not know the answer with certainty but believes the answer to be true. For example, when the client is asked for a time, distance, or location, the client may respond with the answer that she or he believes is true by just stating it. The client need not volunteer that the answer is only an estimate. If asked whether the testimony is merely an estimate, the answer is yes. If the interrogator asks whether the time was clocked or the distance measured, the answer is a simple no. Again, the best answer is the shortest answer. Otherwise, a witness is inclined to say something like "I don't know what it is, but I'd guess that it's about fifteen feet." Such an answer may disqualify the witness from having and giving a reasonable estimate of the distance simply because the witness used the word guess. But if the witness has no estimate of the time or distance the only proper answer is, "I don't know."

If a party testifies that he or she does not know the answer to a particular question, that gives the opponent an opening to present evidence on the subject that cannot be challenged. For example, if the plaintiff testifies in his deposition that he cannot recall whether he talked with the defendant at the scene of the accident, he is in a difficult position at trial to refute the defendant's testimony that the plaintiff admitted at the scene that the accident was his fault.

Tell the client that if she or he cannot remember a certain fact but believes the fact or information can be obtained, the client should so indicate. We all have mental blocks now and then. Perhaps the information is available in records or a diary or is subject to recall later. A statement to that effect keeps the door open to supply the information after the deposition is completed. The subsequent production of the evidence will not be looked on with suspicion. By agreeing to try to obtain the information, the client keeps from being discredited by producing the information at a later date.

Be Respectful

A deponent should show respect for the lawyers and the process. A deponent should be polite but reticent. A deponent should exhibit a positive attitude about testifying, whether in a deposition or at trial. A positive attitude reflects confidence. A deponent should not assume an attitude of hostility, suspicion, or defensiveness. A deponent should not presume that the opposing lawyers will be abusive or sneaky. A deponent's hostility tends to mitigate against his or her appearance of sincerity and, therefore, against her or his effectiveness as a witness. If the opposing lawyers are overbearing and abusive, the deponent should make a conscious effort to remain polite but reserved. A deponent should never try to be clever or humorous.

Answer Out Loud

We regularly communicate by signs and gestures, such as a nod of the head or a shrug of the shoulders. But a court reporter may not see gestures and is not required to record them. So each answer must be stated orally and loud enough for everyone in the room to hear. Deponents should use the word "correct" rather than the word "right." They should say "yes" or "no" rather than "uh-huh" or "uh-uh."

Do Not Show Anger or Impatience

A deponent must avoid anger and impatience. Once a feeling of anger takes over, it is likely to grow and fester. It seldom goes away spontaneously. A display of temper reflects adversely on the deponent even when anger is justifiable. A deponent may feel like the star of the show because of his or her righteous indignation. But the deponent is much more subject to making avoidable errors. A display of temper creates the risk of being offensive and increases a possibility of becoming confused. An angry deponent loses perspective, forgetting the big picture. An angry deponent is likely to forget the other guidelines for testifying. When in trial, a lawyer usually tries to obtain a recess when his or her client shows signs of anger and is not thinking clearly. But it is not easy to obtain a recess for a party who is under cross-examination. A deponent should try to respond to each lawyer the same way, in a polite, courteous, reserved manner.

Keep Opinions Reasonable

Many conditions, situations, and "facts" only can be described in the form of opinions. Courts recognize this. When a witness describes a street as "slippery" or a room as "fairly dark" or rainfall as "heavy" or a streetlight as "dim" or an embankment as "steep" or elevator doors as "fast," he or she is giving an opinion. But how else can an ordinary person describe such conditions? There is no other practical way. Opinions cannot be tested against facts, because they are not facts. Maybe that is why witnesses tend to overstate their opinions when testifying. If opinion evidence is admissible, the witness should be sure that it is reasonable in light of the experience of the witness and in the experience of most people. If a floor is slippery because of water, the witness should not exaggerate by comparing it to oil or grease.

Witnesses seldom determine the speed of a motor vehicle in an accident by seeing the speedometer or obtaining a radar reading or clocking the vehicle. A witness who is reasonably familiar with motor vehicles and who observed a vehicle travel long enough to form an estimate about its speed is allowed to state the estimate in miles per hour. A witness is not permitted to state an opinion that the automobile was going "fast" or "slow." Also, a witness is allowed to estimate a distance in some unit of measurement: feet, yards, miles, and so forth. Again, she or he may not state an opinion that the object was "close" or "far."

A witness's opinion should be tested against physical facts. Remember that a witness must not guess. A witness may have the opportunity to revisit the accident situs to make comparison observations to help make an accurate estimate about a speed or distance. If a moving object is involved, the correlation between time and distance should be considered, as in the following:

Miles per hour	Feet per second
5	7
10	15
20	29
30	44
40	59
50	73
60	88

When a witness is questioned about a speed, distance, or time, the witness should first determine whether he or she has a valid estimate or judgment. If so, then decide whether to express an opinion in terms of a range or a precise measurement. For example, a witness could estimate skid marks to be forty to fifty feet long, or forty-five feet long. Either estimate is legitimate and reasonable. However, tactics or strategy may determine that one approach is preferable in a particular case.

A witness must be prepared to stay with an estimate if challenged. The interrogator usually begins by forcing the witness to "admit" that the figure given is only an estimate, not a measured quantity. Next, the interrogator may ask the witness to admit that, for instance, the estimate could be off (slower or faster) by one, two, or three miles per hour, and later the lawyer may suggest the estimate could be off by even five miles per hour. Again, the interrogator will resort to the phrase "Isn't it possible?" If the estimate could vary by five miles per hour more or less, there is a spread of ten miles per hour. Pretty soon, it appears that the estimate is of no value at all. Not only is the estimate likely to be rejected as unreliable, but the witness's authority—if not credibility—has been impaired.

The solution is for the witness to refuse to speculate about the possibility that the estimate could be slightly off. When asked if she could have been traveling one mile per hour slower or faster than estimated, the witness should respond that her best estimate is as previously stated, and she will not speculate about mere possibilities. Even if the questioner persists, the witness should continue in her refusal to go beyond the original estimate. She avoids weakening her testimony. The same principle applies to any type of estimate involving measurements.

Ensure That Memory and Observations Comport with Physical Laws

Estimates and memory should be tested against natural laws and physical or scientific fact. For example, if a witness has the impression that a motor vehicle collision occurred at thirty miles per hour, but the property damage is slight, the witness's observation or memory is in error. When preparing the witness to testify, you must gently show the witness that his or her present recollection or estimate is not possible. Then try to determine what the facts are. If the witness's recollection cannot be refreshed, and if in fact he or she has no valid estimate or recollection, he or she must not try to fabricate evidence.

Do Not Overemphasize Honesty

A witness should avoid using expressions such as "to be honest with you," "to tell you the truth," "if I remember right," "to the best of my recollection," or "it seems to me that." These expressions weaken the witness's authority and credibility. Testimony should be given without equivocation and without qualification except when absolutely necessary.

Avoid Hypothetical Questions

Hypothetical questions relate to fact situations that merely are assumed to be true for the purpose of having the witness render an opinion or otherwise comment on the assumed facts. The facts used in hypothetical questions must be supplied by other testimony or exhibits. Hypothetical questions have a legitimate and important role in trials. However, it is questionable whether they may be used properly in discovery depositions. Deponents must answer questions about the facts of a case. They must tell what was done and what was not done. They must tell what they know. A deponent must admit to a lack of knowledge when she or he really does not know. But a deponent should not speculate about what she or he would do or not do in hypothetical situations. The basic reason for this is that it is nearly impossible to prepare adequately for all conceivable hypothetical situations. A second reason is that many hypothetical questions that are used to test a witness's knowledge, judgment, or expertise are irrelevant to the case at hand. Suppose a witness is asked, "How many feet would you need to stop your automobile when traveling at ten miles per hour? Twenty miles per hour? Fifty miles per hour?" Most people would have to guess at the answers. On occasion, a question is phrased as a hypothetical question but is actually based on the facts of the present case. In that event, the witness must be prepared to answer. Of course, the deponent's attorney may object to any improper question.

Follow Instructions

Instruct the client to remain silent when her or his attorney objects to a question. Let the interrogator ask a new question or rephrase the question. Or, the deponent's attorney may instruct the deponent to answer the question *subject to the objection.*

Whenever the lawyers disagree about the propriety of a question, they must decide what to do. The witness has no responsibility to do anything until his or her lawyer provides specific directions.

A deponent's lawyer might object to a question but immediately follow with a direction to answer the question "if you understand it." The usual purpose of such an objection and instruction is to warn the witness that the question is dangerous and potentially confusing. The deponent should be particularly careful of this question.

A deponent may elect to read the deposition transcript to make corrections concerning form and substance. Often deponents are advised that they may waive the right to review and sign the transcript. However, if either the deponent or the lawyer thinks the transcript should be reviewed, the right to review and make changes should not be waived. The witness should be told during the preparation about the right to review and correct the transcript before it is certified and filed. If the lawyer decides at the end of the deposition that it is all right to waive the right to read and sign, the lawyer may ask his or her deponent whether he or she wishes to waive the right. That is a *signal* to the client that the lawyer believes a waiver is acceptable. The witness may still indicate that he or she prefers to review it. If the lawyer wants the witness to review the transcript, he or she will tell the reporter to make the transcript available for review.

Common Problems Deponents Encounter

In a typical personal injury case, the plaintiff's deposition lasts between one and three hours, depending on how many lawyers question the plaintiff. A defendant's deposition typically lasts one to two hours. But a deposition could last several days. No time limit is prescribed unless the Rule 26 "discovery plan," court order, or local rule imposes a time limit. Tell the client the court reporter is not allowed to stop recording the proceedings, unless the attorneys agree to go off the record. The client does not have a right to stop the reporter, or video camera, to make statements "off the record." If it is necessary to interrupt the deposition, the lawyers will agree on suitable arrangements.

Exhibits

Explain how exhibits may be used in the deposition, including the procedure for marking (identifying) exhibits, laying a foundation, and offering exhibits into evidence. Remember that the purpose of a foundation is simply to show that the exhibit is what it purports to be. The client may be asked to make sketches relevant to the occurrence or particular facts. The client should practice, not to improve artwork, but so that the client understands what to do. Some lawyers take the position that a deponent does not have to *create* evidence in a deposition, so they do not allow their clients to make drawings or sketches. Some judges might order the deponent to comply with a request for a sketch. Some lawyers make sketches in advance of the deposition and produce a prepared sketch if and when the client is asked to make one. Your legal team must decide what is acceptable in your community and works best for your clients.

Preparation Materials

The client will be asked what she or he has reviewed to prepare for the deposition. The opposing attorney will probably ask to see any document or thing the client has reviewed to prepare for the deposition. In particular, the attorney is interested in trying to obtain a copy of any statements that the client gave to you or to his or her insurance company. The statements are privileged, but some courts have held that the opposing lawyer has a right to look at any document a witness has used to refresh her or his recollection to testify in a deposition or at trial. In effect, the deponent waives the privilege by using the statement—so goes the rationale. To avoid this potential problem, you should not allow the client to review any document that the legal team does not want to share with the opponent. You can prepare the client fully without having the client look at privileged statements or work product documents.

Aggressive Interrogation

Advise the client to be polite but reticent, regardless of whether the interrogator is aggressive, abusive, or personable and pleasant. A personable interrogator is really the more dangerous, because the interrogator makes the deponent feel that he or she understands the deponent's side, and the deponent becomes much more willing to talk. The danger is that the deponent tends to talk too much. The antagonistic interrogator is likely to upset the deponent. When upset, a deponent may tend to forget the guidelines and get into trouble. The best way of avoiding these problems is for the deponent to be polite, reserved, and reticent. As explained elsewhere, the deponent's lawyer can protect the deponent from questions that are improper by making objections. When the deponent's lawyer objects, the deponent should not answer until the lawyer authorizes him or her to answer. By way of illustration, after an objection, the interrogator will ask the deponent to answer the question. At that point the deponent's lawyer is going to have to instruct the deponent not to answer or answer subject to the objection or withdraw the objection.

Negative Evidence

Some questions may relate to **negative evidence.** This happens when one of the parties is trying to prove that something did not happen. For example, a party may testify, "I didn't see any turn signal," or "I didn't hear any horn," or "I didn't hear anyone shout a warning," or "I didn't hear any gun," or "I didn't see any light in the hallway." The deponent must be prepared to explain that he or she would have heard or seen the event if it had happened. Furthermore, there is a better way of describing the absence of a fact or event. The deponent will be more authoritative if he or she states, for instance, "I could see that the other car did not have any turn signal flashing." This is a positive statement about the absence of a turn signal.

negative evidence Evidence that tends to negate or disprove the existence of an alleged fact, such as testimony by a witness that a train did not sound a whistle at a railroad crossing.

Problematic Words

You must help the client choose the words that best describe the facts. The paralegal may ask the client to repeat significant words. She or he may even ask the client to write the words to reinforce memory of them. Some important words in an accident case are *impact, contact, bump, tap, moment, second, split second,* and *instantaneous.*

The client should avoid the word *guess*, and instead use the word *estimate* or *approximately*. In a personal injury case, the plaintiff should be helped to explain the nature, location, and type of pain she or he has been experiencing. For example, pain may be described as sharp, dull, an ache, shooting, burning, and so forth. Instruct the client to be careful in answering questions that contain the words *duty* or *responsibility*, because the interrogator may be trying to obtain an admission to some legal duty that the client really does not have.

Denials

A client must be prepared to "deny" facts, assertions, and allegations that are not true. Sometimes interrogators ask questions in a manner that indicates they have evidence that the deponent said or did something the deponent actually did not say or do. For example, the interrogator may ask the client whether the client denies making a certain statement to an investigating police officer. The way in which the question is phrased may cause the client to worry that somebody claims she or he did make the statement. Consequently, the client may be reluctant to deny having made the statement. Failure to deny reduces the client's authority. Similarly, the client must be prepared to deny facts that may seem reasonable but are devastating in their effect, such as when the interrogator says, "You may have been going thirty-one miles per hour in this thirty-mile-per-hour zone."

Not Knowing the Answer

A deposition is not like a test in school where the student is expected to know the answers because the subject matter has been covered in the book or in class. A deponent can testify only to the things that he or she observed and now remembers. A deponent should never guess about anything when giving sworn testimony. A client should be cautioned, however, against saying he or she does not know the answer merely because that is an easy way to avoid controversy. Once a deponent admits he or she does not know something, the deponent is effectively disqualified from providing evidence on that point. If the deponent later tries to testify on the point, he or she will be impeached.

Sometimes a witness does not realize that she or he does not know the facts. The witness believes that certain facts are true because she or he has read about them or heard about them from someone. Do not let the client affirm a statement about a fact if the client does not have personal knowledge about the fact. The deponent should say that she or he does not know the answer when she or he really does not know. But once the deponent states that she or he does not know or remember the particular fact, the deponent is at the mercy of the other parties and witnesses. Again, the client must not say "I don't know" or "I don't recall" merely because that is an easy out.

The problem of saying "I do not know" is illustrated in the following hypothetical situation. Suppose the client testifies she cannot recall whether she discussed the accident with the other party. The other party may contend that the two did talk and that the client admitted that the accident was her fault. The client will have difficulty refuting the other party's claim because the client is on record saying that she does not remember whether they discussed the accident. Similarly, if a client says he does not recall how fast he was going, the other side may come up with some very damaging figures from unreliable witnesses. But the client cannot dispute the figures because he has admitted he did not recall the speed. Sometimes a deponent believes that a question about speed or distance requires an exact answer, so the client is inclined to say, "I don't know." The deponent may expect the lawyer to ask the deponent to estimate the speed or distance, which the deponent could do with reasonable reliability. However, the interrogator has the answer he or she wants and may not ask any follow-up questions. The client must be prepared to cope with such questions. On occasion a client may leave herself or himself some room by saying, "I cannot recall right now, but I can obtain that information for you." When asked where the deponent will search for the information, the deponent need not pin himself or herself down, "I'm not too sure just where I need to look, but I will look!"

Privileges

You should explain the application of any legal privileges, such as the physician-patient privilege, attorney-client privilege, the privilege against disclosing communications with the client's spouse, and the privilege against self-incrimination. In addition, the lawyer should explain any applicable statutory privileges.

The interrogator will ask questions from records prepared by the client and others. You must determine whether any of the client's records or reports are privileged or otherwise protected from discovery. You should caution the client against voluntarily referring to documents that are not discoverable. The Federal Rules require parties to disclose the existence of privileged documents, but not the contents.

Guessing

One of the guidelines for testifying is do not guess. Even to use the word "guess" creates problems. Prepare the client to use "estimate," "recollection" or "opinion" instead of "guess." A client might inadvertently disqualify himself or herself from testifying to crucial facts by misusing the word "guess." Explain the difference between a guess and an estimate or judgment. For example, suppose the client is the defendant who survived a collision at an intersection controlled by a traffic light. The other driver did not survive. There are no eyewitnesses other than the client. The client must know where the traffic light was located. If there were more than one light, he must know which one he watched. He must know where his car was when he first saw the green light, and when he last noticed the color of the light. He must know that the red light is at the top and the green light is at the bottom of the signal. He should know how long the light was green for him; the time sequence for the light, to keep him from being confused by time factors; the location of the other car when he first noticed it; at what point he applied his brakes; the point of collision on the cars; the point of collision on the roadway. What did he tell the police? What has he told other people about the accident? If the client were to testify that he could only *guess* at these facts or cannot remember them, he will not be able to help himself at trial.

Visit Situs

If you and the client need to visit the situs together, take a camera and a measuring tape. Hopefully, most of the essential information is already in the file, because the legal team has conducted a good investigation and documented all the findings. Nevertheless, sometimes it is useful to verify and document the accident location. For one thing, the scene may have changed significantly, and any changes should be documented. Then if the opponent testifies on the basis of the way the scene looks now, as opposed to how it looked at the time of the accident, the client's side is well on its way to a win.

Foundation Issues

Whenever a witness provides opinion evidence, there must be a foundation for the opinion. The foundation is preliminary evidence that shows a witness is qualified to have a reliable opinion. The witness had an opportunity to observe, understand, and recall the facts on which the opinion is based. Failure to make the necessary showing makes the opinion inadmissible. Presenting opinion testimony through a deposition is worrisome and risky, because there is no judge to rule on whether sufficient foundation has been laid. The proponent will not have a final ruling on the admissibility of the opinion until trial. It may be difficult or impossible to provide the foundation then. Suppose a nonexpert witness is asked for her or his opinion about the speed of a vehicle she or he observed. She or he saw the automobile for two seconds (or five seconds or fifteen seconds). Was the length of time sufficient to make a valid observation? The judge must decide. Fair-minded judges may differ on the ruling—hence, a lawyer's concern about the adequacy of foundation. In all probability, two seconds is not enough time to form a valid opinion about a vehicle's speed. Five seconds is probably enough time, depending on the witness's age and experience. Ten seconds certainly is ample time for a qualified witness. But suppose the deponent is only fourteen years old; would the deponent qualify to form an opinion of speed? Or suppose the deponent is sixteen but has no experience driving. Is there enough foundation? The decision ultimately will be made by the trial judge. Until then, the proponent's lawyer can only worry whether the opinion will be received into evidence.

Lawyers must provide foundations for their experts' opinions. If a lawyer fails to show his or her expert is qualified, the expert's opinion testimony is inadmissible. Again, the court will not rule on the adequacy of the foundation until the case reaches trial. A lawyer lays the foundation presenting evidence that shows the expert has special training and experience in the field and sufficient knowledge and information to have an opinion that will help the jury to understand the case. If the necessary foundation is not laid during a testamentary deposition, the expert's opinions cannot be used.

Mock Cross-Examination

Do not assume that talking about problems and explaining what to do ensures that the client will handle the problem correctly. After you have instructed the client concerning the guidelines for testifying and worked through the client's particular problems, you should test the client by interrogating him or her as though you were the opposing lawyer. A deponent needs to practice using the guidelines and phrasing answers. As questions and problems arise, you should stop the interrogation to resolve them.

A mock cross-examination should not be conducted in a hostile manner. Instead, unless you know to the contrary, you should assume the opposing lawyer will be very personable and will try to induce the client to volunteer information. The cross-examination should be well focused, searching, and calculated to raise problems for the client. Begin with background questions. Ask about the client's marital status, past employments, previous addresses, prior accidents, education. Ask about members of the client's family. These background questions will help the client to develop a feel for listening, reflecting, and answering. Try to establish a cadence that includes a significant pause after each question. By the way, this gives you an opportunity to find out more about your client. Really dig into his or her background during the mock cross-examination.

Then you may move to more difficult subjects, such as past criminal convictions, conversations with the opposing party, speeds, distances, and so forth. You should try jumping from one subject to another and back to see if the client is able to cope with changes. Test the client's recall for critical dates, times, distances, and words. If the client has trouble remembering them, try having him or her write down the words to reinforce his or her memory. The act of writing is a great aid to recall. Use repetition until the client overcomes problems with recall. The client must rehearse until the problems are extinguished—even if you have to schedule another session.

Help the client deal with questions that call for narrative answers, such as "Then what happened?" or "Tell me about everything you saw" or "How did the accident occur?" The client should not give narrative answers, only short answers. To prevent a narrative answer to the last question, the client could state, "Your client struck my car." The examiner should be forced to pursue the interrogation by using specific questions.

You must prepare the client for standard questions.

Example

Q: Have you read any documents, records, statements, or reports to prepare for this deposition?

A: No.

Q: Have you given any recorded statements to anyone?

A: Yes.

Q: To whom have you given statements?

A: To my attorney and to my insurance company.

Q: What did you tell [the police officer] about the accident?

A: The same thing I have told you. [Or] I told him that your client struck my car.

Try asking some questions that are improper in form, so the client develops a sense for them. Questions are improper in form if they are multiple, argumentative, abusive, or wrongly assume facts that are not true. You may object to your own questions, taking the role of the client's lawyer in the deposition, so the client experiences the objection procedure in operation. Explain that if the opposing lawyer conducts the cross-examination in bad faith, the deponent may terminate the deposition. This will make the client feel more comfortable. Deponents may worry about being abused by the opposing attorney.

Follow up after the Deposition

After the deposition, clients usually want to know if there were problems and whether they did all right. They need assurance. You should plan to spend some time with the client to review and plan. You can initiate the review by asking the client whether he or she has any concerns about the deposition. Try very hard to be positive. A client is entitled to your help to gain peace of mind. You want to increase the client's confidence about the case.

This is a good time to discuss possible additions and corrections to the transcript and confirm arrangements for reading and signing the deposition transcript. By making corrections in the manner provided by Rule 30(e), a lawyer may avoid subsequent problems, such as malpractice or client dissatisfaction. The corrections may be changes or additions. Corrections may relate to form, such as spelling; or to substance, as where the deponent testified that he was driving forty miles per hour and changes the transcript to state he was driving twenty-five miles per hour [see Rule 30(e)]. The corrections and reasons must be made in writing and are added to the end of the transcript.

Most courts allow the opposing party to present to the jury the deponent's original answer notwithstanding a proper correction. In effect, the court allows the deponent to be impeached by the inconsistent statement even though Rule 30(e) expressly reserves the right to make changes. The point is that the right to make corrections and changes is not a panacea for poor preparation. Still, a correction reduces the effects of impeachment, because the Rules specifically provide for making corrections in this manner.

Changes may be necessary because the court reporter made a mistake in recording the testimony, the deponent misspoke, the deponent had a memory lapse, or the deponent simply changed his or her mind. If, during the deposition, the deponent agreed to investigate the availability of additional information, the information may be supplied in the correction sheet.

SUMMARY

When a lawyer interrogates an opposing party in a discovery deposition, the lawyer tries to find out what the party knows, what the party does not know, whether the party will be an effective witness, whether the party is willing to go to trial, and how well the party is prepared. Furthermore, the interrogator will make some judgments about whether the deponent's legal team understands the case and is prepared.

You must not tell the client what to say, other than to tell the truth. You may assist a client to find and understand the truth and you may advise a client about how to testify. Your objective is to keep the client from making mistakes. To accomplish this, you should educate the client about the guidelines for testifying. Testifying is such a unique and problematic experience, a client cannot adequately prepare for it in a single one-hour session. There is too much to consider and too much to learn.

You must prepare before meeting with the client. You must familiarize yourself with the legal issues, fact theories, investigation, and particular concerns that your legal team has about the case. Determine what facts are indisputable and what facts are not disputed. The case and the client's testimony should be built around those facts. You should determine which disputed facts are really important. Spend time on the evidence and develop the details of those facts. Your team's theory about what happened and how it happened must accommodate the applicable law and known facts.

When you meet with the client, obtain the client's version of the facts. Is the client's version consistent with established facts, physical laws, probability, common experience, common sense, and the team's theory of the case? You must decide whether to test or correct some aspect of the client's version and, if so, how to do that. Try to relieve the client's natural apprehensions about the lawsuit and about testifying. An apprehensive deponent is doomed to mistakes and failure. When the client understands the big picture, the client has a frame of reference that helps him or her to understand individual questions and to answer with confidence.

Even though the client's version of the facts is highly questionable, you must listen to the client's explanation before making any suggestions about possible errors. She or he must try to understand the client's explanations, because the client may be right. You must not lead the client into perjury or errors, or induce discomfort. The client's deposition testimony must be consistent with the client's testimony at trial.

You must decide whether any of the photographs and other exhibits on file likely will be used as exhibits during the deposition and how they might be used. Consider making copies of documents so that the originals are not marked during the client's deposition. Make enough copies so that every party can have one. Consider whether the client should be allowed to make drawings or sketches. If so, have the client practice so he or she is comfortable with the process.

Some photographs are, in themselves, evidence, not merely illustrative. They must be protected against loss and alteration. When demanded they must be disclosed to other parties. Photographs of an accident scene are evidence. Photographs of an accident situs that do not show conditions that prevailed at the time of the accident are merely illustrative and not, in themselves, evidence. Therefore, such photographs are attorney's work product and need not be disclosed unless you expect they will be used at trial.

Ideally, you can prepare a client in two sessions. The first meeting should cover all the issues, with an emphasis on identifying and solving problems. The latter part of the meeting could include a mock cross-examination to help the client use guidelines. During the hiatus between meetings, you and the client have time in which to locate documents, pin down additional facts, and resolve problems that you identified. The second meeting should focus on the client's anticipated testimony with extensive cross-examination. You should interrogate the client in a personable manner and then in an abusive manner. Show the client why being polite, reserved, and reticent works best, regardless of how the interrogator conducts himself or herself. The client must not plan on having any "aside" conferences during the deposition. Nevertheless, if necessary, a lawyer can interrupt the deposition to have a conference with his or her client. Prepare the client to answer basic questions, such as the following:

What have you reviewed to prepare for the deposition?
What has your insurer told you to say?
Have you given a statement to anyone?
Have you ever said anything different?
Do you deny that . . . ?
What did you tell the police officer or investigator?
Where would you go to find out the answer to the last question?

Explain to the client the use of exhibits, including the procedure for identifying exhibits, marking exhibits, laying foundation for exhibits, and offering exhibits. The examiner will want to inspect and copy any document or thing the client has used to prepare for the deposition. In addition, the examiner will ask if the client has relied on the document (such as a statement) to refresh his or her memory and whether it did refresh his or her memory. Therefore, you should not allow the client to review any document that you and the legal team do not want to share with the opponent.

If the deponent's lawyer objects to a question, the deponent should remain quiet until instructed what to do. The interrogator may rephrase the question, go on to another question, or insist on an answer. If the interrogator insists on an answer, the deponent's lawyer will have to decide whether to let the deponent answer, answer subject to the objection, or refuse to answer. If the lawyer allows the client to answer the question subject to the objection, the client should have the court reporter read back the question to make sure the client understands it *in light of the objection.*

The following guidelines are helpful to deponents in discovery depositions:

1. Tell the truth.
2. A deponent should try to appear sincere, that is, appear to believe what he or she is saying by being thoughtful, deliberate, polite, and responsive.
3. A deponent should strive to appear authoritative by being direct and specific, and paying attention to details.
4. The deponent should listen to each question carefully and make sure he or she understands the question. The question must be meaningful to the deponent or the deponent does not understand it.
5. The deponent should avoid volunteering information and giving explanations that are not specifically required by the question. Be reticent.
6. The deponent should not guess about anything. Estimates and opinions should comport with what is probable, or, at least, with what is possible.
7. The deponent should not be defensive.
8. The deponent must answer each question out loud.
9. The deponent should avoid showing impatience or anger.
10. The deponent should consciously avoid hurrying to give his or her lawyer an opportunity to object to improper questions.

These same guidelines do not necessarily apply to testifying at trial.

A deponent has the right to read the deposition transcript to make sure that it has been accurately recorded. The deponent has thirty days in which to make corrections. The corrections may be changes or additions. The corrections may relate to form, such as spelling errors, or to substance, such as where the deponent testified that something was "black" but changes the answer to "white."

You and the client have an obligation to correct any misstatements as soon as they are discovered. Even if a misstatement is corrected in the manner provided by the Rules, the opposing side may use it against the client as an admission or for impeachment. Therefore, careful preparation is essential.

KEY TERM

negative evidence

REVIEW QUESTIONS

1. May a paralegal conduct a mock cross-examination of the client? Explain.

2. Why should the client be cautioned against giving narrative answers in a discovery deposition?

3. What can you do to help a client who is obviously confused about the facts about which she or he will be questioned by the opposing lawyer in a discovery deposition?

4. Is it better to correct the client's deposition testimony by asking clarifying questions at the end of the deposition or by making corrections in the errata sheet provided by the court reporter?

5. How many times may a party take the deposition of another party?

6. Why might a lawyer allow his or her client to answer an improper question subject to an objection?

7. What options does the deponent have where she or he believes that the interrogation is being conducted in bad faith?

8. Why should the deponent not review her or his privileged, written statement in preparing for a discovery deposition?

9. Why should you instruct a client not to guess when testifying?

10. Why do lawyers sometimes try to use hypothetical questions in discovery depositions?

11. Name at least eight of the guidelines for testifying in a discovery deposition.

12. Why are the guidelines that are used in a discovery deposition not necessarily useful for testifying at trial?

CASE ASSIGNMENT

The plaintiff trustee has scheduled Bradley Harper's deposition to be taken in attorney Donald Smith's office in thirty days. You are working on attorney William Hoch's litigation team defending Harper. Attorney Hoch has given you an intraoffice memorandum directing you to notify Mr. Harper about the deposition and to prepare him for it. Prepare a letter to Mr. Harper and schedule two meetings with him to prepare. Identify the things he should bring with him to the meetings. Preface your letter with "Privileged Communication."

Prepare an intraoffice memorandum to attorney Hoch to inform him about your plans for preparing Harper for the deposition. Be specific, but do not reiterate all the guidelines for testifying. Mention any specific problems on which you want his advice.

Endnotes

1. The situs or simply "site," is the place where the accident occurred; situs and location are to be distinguished from accident scene, which implies that the conditions are exactly the way they were at the time the accident happened.
2. For example, if a plaintiff is involved in another accident before trial, that could be a reason for having a second deposition.
3. The deponent may correct mistakes in his or her testimony by preparing a transcript correction sheet. The correction sheet identifies the page, line, and item that needs correction. The deponent must state the correct answer and the reason why the error occurred.
4. A lawyer preserves the objection by making an answer "subject to an objection" [Rule 30(c)]. At some later time the parties can ask a judge to rule on the objection. A lawyer does not protect against disclosure of the information required by the question, but may prevent subsequent use of the information. Also, the lawyer avoids the expense and inconvenience of stopping the deposition and obtaining a court ruling on the objection.

 For additional resources, visit our Web site at www.paralegal.delmar.cengage.com

CHAPTER 14

MEDICAL EXAMINATIONS AND RECORDS

CHAPTER OUTLINE

Chapter Objectives

Chapter 14 explains how a party may obtain an independent medical examination of an adverse party when the adverse party's medical condition is material to the case. It contains suggestions for making arrangements with physicians for examinations. It describes the adverse party's obligation to undergo an examination and the limits on such examinations. It makes suggestions for dealing with improper demands for medical examinations.

Introduction

Many civil actions involve disputes about parties' physical, mental, or blood condition. Actions to obtain money damages for personal injuries are probably the most common type. Others include actions to determine whether a party is able to work, whether a party is entitled to disability insurance benefits, whether a party is mentally competent, whether a party's disability was caused by his or her work, and whether a person is emotionally stable and fit to have custody of a child. In each, the fact issue is basically a medical question. Fairness requires that each party have access to the necessary evidence. But in these kinds of cases the subject matter is under the control of one party and that party has a legal privilege against disclosure. All of the party's medical records, hospital records, and communications with her or his physicians are privileged.

You will have the opportunity to arrange for Rule 35 medical examinations. You may schedule examinations. You may make the arrangements with the examiner and opposing attorney. You will review and comment on examination reports. You may help examiners to clarify their reports when they are ambiguous or do not meet the parties' needs or needs of the court. You will become familiar with medical terms, tests, and procedures.

Medical Examinations

How can a defendant evaluate a plaintiff's bodily injury claim and defend against it without a medical examination of the plaintiff? How can a court provide equal access to the evidence? Rule 35 attempts to balance the parties' need for evidence, protect parties' privacy and prevent undue intrusions. The Rule does this by requiring a party who has a medical condition that is in issue submit to a medical examination. A Rule 35 examination is an adversarial discovery procedure. Provisions for it must be made in the parties' discovery plan. Parties who must submit to an examination sometimes refer to it as an *adverse medical examination*. Discovery proponents often call it an *independent medical examination*. A judge is more likely to refer to it as a *Rule 35 examination*.

Medical conditions are often very personal. A medical examination may cause some embarrassment. Some medical tests are invasive, that is, they may pierce the skin or otherwise enter the patient's body. Some medical tests are painful; some may subject the patient to a risk of harm. It is perfectly understandable that a party may be reluctant to undergo such tests. Rule 35 requires a proponent to move the court for an order that requires the opponent to submit to a medical[1] examination concerning whatever mental, physical, or blood condition is in issue. The court may impose limits on a Rule 35 examination to protect the examinee. The proponent is entitled to select the examiner. The examiner must be a duly licensed professional. The examinee may demand a copy of the examiner's report from the proponent. However, by requesting a copy, the examinee becomes obligated to provide to the proponent copies of all of his or her reports concerning the same conditions. The examinee's obligation to provide reports is ongoing.

Some states require an examinee to submit to an examination only if the examinee has placed her or his medical condition in issue. In other words, a proponent cannot raise a question about the adverse party's condition and, on that basis, require the party to submit to a medical examination. Suppose the plaintiff claims that the defendant negligently transmitted a disease to her. The plaintiff does not have a right to obtain an independent medical examination of the defendant to determine whether the defendant has the disease because the defendant did not put his physical condition into issue. It is not clear how Rule 35 would handle that situation.

Reasons for Rule 35 Examinations

A Rule 35 examination is inconvenient and expensive. An examination should not be requested unless reasonably necessary. If an injured plaintiff gives the defendant access to the plaintiff's medical records and reports, the defendant's lawyer may be able to rely on them to evaluate the case, especially if the treating physician has a reputation for being capable, objective, and candid. Many personal injury cases are settled by liability insurance companies without having medical examinations. Nevertheless, there are many circumstances that make Rule 35 examinations necessary. Here are some of them:

- The proponent believes the treating physician's records and reports do not portray fully or accurately the claimant's condition, or the claimant will not provide copies of his or her records and reports.
- The treating physician may have obtained an inadequate or erroneous *medical history*. For example, the treating physician's report may describe the accident, the plaintiff's back injury, the treatment, and so forth, but fail to consider the plaintiff's preexisting back condition.
- The treating physician may have an incomplete or erroneous *accident history*. The defendant's lawyer often has more details about the accident and information about the plaintiff's conduct following the accident than the treating physician obtains. For example, the plaintiff may have indicated to the physician that the defendant's automobile was traveling forty miles per hour when it struck the rear of the plaintiff's truck, whereas the evidence shows that the impact was minor and did not even move the plaintiff's vehicle. This makes the treating physician's diagnosis of a serious injury very questionable.
- The findings recorded by the treating physician may be inconsistent with the plaintiff's subjective complaints. For example, the plaintiff may have testified in her deposition that she had severe low-back pain immediately after the motor vehicle accident and was disabled because of it. The treating physician's records, however, report some neck pain but no low-back pain and no treatment for low-back pain. The symptoms may vary from time to time, in an inexplicable way, to raise a doubt about their validity.
- The treating physician may not have sufficient expertise in the particular area. For example, in one case a general practitioner concluded that the plaintiff had a back strain following an automobile accident. But the defendant's independent examiner was an orthopedic surgeon who concluded that the symptoms and examination findings were not typical of a muscle strain. He ordered x-rays that showed that the plaintiff had a kidney stone. The stone was removed, and the plaintiff had no more back pain. Because the plaintiff had associated his back pain with the accident, so had his family doctor.
- The plaintiff may not have a treating physician and both parties want to make sure there is no latent injury before entering into a final settlement.
- A defendant's lawyer may believe that the plaintiff's treating physician's evaluation is inadequate, slanted, or wrong.

■ Occasionally, a defendant suspects collaboration between the patient and the treating doctor. Collaboration is rarely outright falsification, but, rather, a pattern of exaggeration and minimizing.

These considerations are not *grounds* for obtaining a Rule 35 examination, merely considerations.

Obtaining Rule 35 Examinations

good cause Some basis in fact and law; substantial compliance with a legal requirement or legal standard.

A motion for a Rule 35 examination must be made to the court in which the action is pending. The moving party must show **good cause,** that is, a substantial need for the examination. Ordinarily, it is enough to show that the party's medical condition is material to the case and there is a good faith dispute about the nature, extent, or cause of the condition. The burden is on the moving party to show that the proposed examination is appropriate. The examination is appropriate if it is designed to deal with the kind of medical condition(s) in issue and ordinarily performed by licensed professionals. The good cause requirement prevents parties from making unjustified and unreasonable demands for medical examinations. When there is more than one moving party, the court has discretion to allow each to have an examination or to require parties to share an examination. Rule 35 does not limit the number of examinations. However, it must appear that an additional examination is reasonably necessary before a court will require a party to submit to more than one.

Most examinations are conducted by medical doctors (physicians). But Rule 35 does not require the examiner to be a medical doctor. When appropriate, Rule 35 examinations may be conducted by psychologists, osteopaths, chiropractors, and professionals licensed in the healing arts. The proponent is entitled to select the examiner. The choice depends on the type of condition in issue, the kind of treatment the party-examinee has received, the seriousness of the condition, the availability of professional examiners in the locality, and costs. Some mental and some physical conditions require more than one examination. For example, a serious head injury may require a neurologist and an eye specialist. Again, courts have broad discretion to define the parameters and extent of a Rule 35 examination.

A court may require a party who has legal control over another person to require that person to undergo a Rule 35 examination. For example, a parent-party may be required to have a child submit to an examination. However, if a corporation is a party, the proponent cannot use Rule 35 to obtain an independent medical examination of the corporation's employees or agents. The rules of civil procedure in many states provide that when a plaintiff commences an action to recover money damages for personal injuries, the plaintiff partially waives his or her medical privilege. The extent of the waiver varies from state to state. The waiver may be total, or it may be limited to obtaining copies of the plaintiff's medical records. Federal courts follow the laws of the state concerning medical privilege and its waiver. Therefore, the application of Rule 35 and its procedure is subject to and qualified by state law. However, state law cannot be so narrow as to preclude a federal court from granting an independent medical examination when appropriate under the parameters established by Rule 35.

Suppose the parties were involved in an automobile collision at an intersection. The plaintiff wants to have the defendant's eyes examined because he contends that the defendant's vision is defective and that condition prevented the defendant from keeping a proper lookout and caused the accident. The eye condition is physical, and the best way of evaluating it is to have a medical examination. But is the defendant's eyesight a material fact? Is the acuity of defendant's eyesight a fact that is determinative of the outcome of the case? No, it is merely evidence that might influence a jury's view of other evidence to determine the outcome. A jury could agree that the defendant's eyesight was poor, but, nevertheless, find he kept a proper lookout. He saw what he should have seen. The material fact is whether the plaintiff exercised a proper lookout. Will a court order the defendant to submit to an eye examination? Courts differ on the answer. In most state courts, the defendant would not have to submit to an examination because he did not put the condition of his eyes in issue. When a defendant puts her or his physical condition into issue as a defense, the defendant may be required to submit to an examination. For example, a man had a sudden, unexpected heart attack while driving his car. He went off the road and killed some children. He claimed that the heart attack made the accident unavoidable. The issue is whether he knew or should have known the risk of having a heart attack and taken appropriate steps to avoid the risk of endangering others. He would be required to submit to an independent medical examination.

A party may request a Rule 35 medical examination at any stage of the litigation, subject to the court's scheduling order. Usually, a party takes the other party's deposition to find out as much as possible about the physical or mental condition before making a Rule 35 motion. A party may not use a request for an examination to delay the trial. Nevertheless, the court has in some cases ordered the plaintiff to submit to a medical examination during the trial where the plaintiff has asserted a new claim since the independent examination. More often than not attorneys avoid the expense and inconvenience of a motion and stipulate to Rule 35 examinations. They recognize the requesting party has the right to choose the examiner. They try to accommodate the examiner's schedule and the party's schedule. Usually they can agree on the scope of the examination. The stipulation may be formalized or be set forth in the attorneys correspondence. Rule 35(b)(3) recognizes that parties often stipulate to independent medical examinations. If any dispute arises, the agreements are construed to comport with the basic requirements of Rule 35.

If a plaintiff refuses to submit to a Rule 35 examination, the defendant may move the court for an order compelling him or her to submit to an examination. (See Exhibit 14.1).

If the party to be examined opposes the motion, she or he should serve and file an objection to examination. The objection should state the grounds and be supported by appropriate affidavits. The grounds may concern the time, place, examiner, number of examinations, scope of an examination, particular tests, or manner in which an examination is to be conducted. A judge must decide whether the examination should go forward as scheduled or impose limitations. For example, a plaintiff may want her spouse, attorney, or treating physician to attend the examination with her. As a rule, courts do not allow anyone to monitor or observe a Rule 35 examination. It unnecessarily complicates the process. Only if unusual circumstances exist will a court permit someone to attend the examination of an adult. For example, if the party examined is suffering from Alzheimer's disease a court might

United States District Court for the
Southern District of New York
Civil Action, File Number _____

A. B., Plaintiff,

    vs.

C. D., Defendant.

Motion to Compel Rule 35 Examination

Defendant C. D. moves the court for an order requiring Plaintiff A. B. to submit to an independent medical examination for the purpose of diagnosis and evaluation of plaintiff's alleged injuries. Specifically, defendant has arranged for Dr. Carol Ellingboe to conduct the examination on March 4, 2006, at 2:00 P.M. at Dr. Ellingboe's office at 2050 Abbott Street, Suite 657, Boston, Massachusetts. Dr. Ellingboe is licensed by the state of Massachusetts to practice medicine and specializes in neurology. The scope of the proposed examination is a complete physical and neurological examination to evaluate the plaintiff's claim of head, neck, and back injuries.

This motion is made pursuant to Rule 35 of the Federal Rules of Civil Procedure.

The grounds for this motion are that plaintiff put her physical and mental condition in issue by alleging in her complaint that her head, neck, and back were injured in the occurrence described in the complaint. Defendant needs an independent medical examination and medical opinion for the purpose of evaluating the plaintiff's claim and preparing his defenses.

This motion is based on the plaintiff's complaint and the attached affidavit of counsel.

[Date]

/s/_____
Attorney for the Defendant

allow someone to monitor the examination. The lawyer who represents the examined party does not have a right to interview the examiner. Rule 35 does not authorize the plaintiff to take the deposition of the independent examiner. But many courts have authorized either side to use audiotapes to record the discussions during examinations.

If a party refuses to submit to a medical examination in spite of a court order, the court has two options. One, the court may dismiss the plaintiff's lawsuit. Two, the court may resolve the disputed medical facts against the plaintiff by taking the medical condition out of issue. If the defendant is the disobedient party, the court may strike (disallow) his or her answer and find the defendant in default. If a party is in default, judgment may be entered against him or her without having a trial. A court may not hold a party in contempt of court for refusing to submit to a Rule 35 examination. This means the party who refuses to be examined cannot be fined or incarcerated for violating the court order.

Although Rule 35 provides that a proponent must move the court for an order to compel an adverse party to submit to a medical examination, usually that is not necessary. The attorneys know what a court will do, so the attorneys make their own arrangements. Professional examiners understand that the scope of an independent examination should be limited to what is reasonably necessary. They know they must conduct examinations in a way that comports with the standards of their profession.

The proponent must give the examinee sufficient notice to prepare for the examination. The examinee may have to take time away from work, arrange for baby-sitting, or make special arrangements for transportation. If the examinee does not have suitable transportation, the proponent may want to provide it. Generally, however, the examinee must pay her or his own expenses in traveling to and from the examination. Typically, the proponent's paralegal obtains one or two dates from the examiner's office. The paralegal then telephones the opposing attorney or paralegal and asks him or her to arrange to have the party appear for the examination. The opposing attorney contacts the client to make sure the client is available. If not, a new date is selected. The proponent then confirms the arrangements by letter. A proponent should schedule an examination at a time and place convenient for the examiner and examinee. The appointment is usually obtained through the physician's secretary. Although Rule 35 does not impose any geographic limitations, courts are inclined to require the proponent to have examinations in the county where the examinee resides or works. If the parties cannot agree, the court will determine the time and place for them. If the examinee fails to keep the appointment, he or she may be responsible for the physician's charge for reserved time. This is true whether the examination was scheduled by agreement or by court order.

Treating Physician's Role

A treating physician does not have any responsibility to establish the patient's claim. He or she is expected to obtain the information needed to make an accurate diagnosis and to prescribe the proper treatment. The Rules of Evidence presume that patients are candid with their physician when they seek medical treatment. The Rules assume that the plaintiff fully believes that the information she or he gives to the physician is for the purpose of obtaining the correct diagnosis and correct treatment. A physician is not expected to cross-examine the patient concerning the patient's accident history, **past medical history,** and symptoms. A patient's statements to a treating physician are admissible into evidence as an exception to the rule against hearsay evidence because of its probable reliability. Although a treating physician may be partial toward his or her patient, the physician is not an advocate. It is perfectly proper for the patient's lawyer and treating physician to meet, confer, and exchange information about the patient and the litigation.

past medical history A patient's past medical history that may have some relevance to a current medical problem or its cause.

Rule 35 Examiners' Role

Lawyers who schedule Rule 35 medical examinations need to have accurate, objective, candid reports. Examiners do not help the parties who retained them by providing reports that unfairly minimize an examinee's condition, injury, or disability. The proponent needs a correct diagnosis, evaluation, and useful recommendations. The examiner may be more skeptical about an examinee's accident history, prior medical history, subjective complaints, and symptoms than a treating physician. Indeed, the examiner should look for inconsistencies between the symptoms, symptoms and history, and symptoms and medical findings. The examiner should also look for medical improbabilities, such as a claim of permanent injury or permanent disability where there are no objective findings. But the examiner is not an advocate. The examiner must not provide any treatment to the examinee or even recommend a different course of treatment, except in his or her report to the proponent. It is perfectly proper for the proponent's lawyer/paralegal to meet with the examiner and discuss the patient and the litigation.

The examiner's role is illustrated in an extreme but true case, where the plaintiff was a forty-eight-year-old homemaker who had stopped her automobile at a traffic light. The defendant's semitruck "bumped" the rear of her car. Photographs showed a scratch on the rear fender. She saw her physician two days later. She told him that her car was struck forcefully and she was thrown about. She was dazed, and soon her neck, left arm, and shoulder began to hurt. The physician diagnosed a muscle and ligaments strain of her neck and shoulders. He treated her with medications and physical therapy for *several years*. At one point the physician called in a psychiatrist for consultation. He determined that the plaintiff was neurotic and a hypochondriac. Her psychiatric problems were deep seated and had existed long before the automobile accident. All of this was in her records, and the records were supplied to the defendant's attorney.

The defendant arranged for a Rule 35 examination by an orthopedic surgeon. The surgeon could find no objective evidence of injury or disability, but based on the plaintiff's medical history and symptoms of pain in the neck and left shoulder, he necessarily concluded the accident caused a musculoligamentous strain but no permanent disability. The surgeon was constrained to assume the correctness of the plaintiff's **subjective symptoms** and medical history. After the examiner testified in accordance with his report, the defendant's lawyer asked him to assume as true certain additional facts to which the defendant truck driver testified. Specifically, the truck was almost stopped at the moment of contact; and the contact merely caused a scratch on a chrome strip on the right rear fender, as shown by photographs. The car was not moved by the contact. The car was not repaired. No repair estimates were sought. According to the truck driver, the vehicles remained together after the contact. The plaintiff stepped out of her automobile immediately after the accident. She did not appear injured and did not complain of any injury.

The Rule 35 examiner testified that if the additional accident history were true, he would have to conclude the plaintiff was not injured in the accident. The contact would have to move the plaintiff's car some; otherwise, she could not have experienced any overstretching of her musculature. Her subjective complaints could not be attributed to a physical injury.

subjective symptoms A patient's description of pain or limited motion that a physician is not able to observe or verify apart from the patient's own statements or voluntary presentation.

The psychiatrist's **diagnosis** then provided the logical explanation for the plaintiff's overreaction to the accident and for her continued symptoms. The Rule 35 examiner had the psychiatrist's records available and was able to use them when he testified. The jury determined that the plaintiff was not injured at all. The accident provided her with an opportunity to obtain **secondary gains,** including money, help with her housework, sympathy, and an opportunity to "get out of the house" to visit her doctors periodically. The potential recovery of money damages may have been less important than the other considerations. The defendant trucker would not have prevailed without a Rule 35 medical examination, evaluation, and opinion. The examiner was not obligated to accept the plaintiff's version of the facts in the way her treating physicians were. He could be suspicious of the plaintiff's presentation.

diagnosis A physician's determination concerning the nature, and sometimes, the cause of a patient's apparent medical problem.

secondary gain A term used to describe psychological factors that cause a person to have physical complaints. The factors are characterized by benefits the person has from being ill, injured, or impaired.

When to Have a Rule 35 Examination

A proponent must decide when to have the opposing party examined. Sometimes the examination should be conducted as soon as possible. Other times the examination should be delayed as much as a year. The primary consideration is the purpose for the examination. For example, if a plaintiff is claiming only minor injuries, the defendant should obtain a Rule 35 examination as soon as convenient. An early examination can establish an early date for the plaintiff's medical recovery. The examiner probably can opine that the plaintiff is ready to return to work or will be able to return to work within a few weeks. An early examination is adequate when the proponent is only concerned about the nature and extent of the examinee's injury. An early examination is usually sought when an insurance company expects to cancel benefit payments to an insured. But sooner is not always better. When the plaintiff has sustained a serious, long-term injury, the primary purpose of the examination is to evaluate the extent of the plaintiff's medical recovery and residual problems, not the nature and extent of the initial injury. If the examination is conducted soon after the injury occurred, a subsequent examination may be necessary.

Selecting a Rule 35 Examiner

The proponent must decide what kind of examination should be conducted. Should the examination be conducted by a medical doctor (physician), osteopath, psychologist, chiropractor, or other practitioner? Because these practitioners are from different schools of the healing arts, they may have different theories about the problem and apply different standards for evaluating the plaintiff's condition. If a medical doctor is selected, should the examiner be a specialist? If so, which specialty is most directly related to the case? The type of treatment the plaintiff has selected often helps determine who should conduct an independent examination. For example, many states have no-fault insurance laws that require automobile insurers to pay their own insureds' medical expenses for treatment to the extent that the treatment is reasonably necessary. A question may arise as to whether the insured's continued treatment is necessary. If the patient is being treated by a doctor of chiropractic, the automobile insurer may want to have the opinion of another chiropractor. The same question may be presented in a workers' compensation case where the employer contends that the employee has received too much treatment.

The examiner must be qualified to evaluate the mental and physical conditions in issue. Courts do not require examinees to be the "best" in their fields. Indeed, any medical doctor is likely to qualify to evaluate and testify concerning any medical condition. But a proponent should try to retain a professional who has outstanding credentials, who appears authoritative, who is articulate, and who is willing to do the examination at a time and place that comport with the requirements of the litigation. An examiner should understand the medical problems in the context of the lawsuit—as the examiner in the preceding example understood the plaintiff's drive for secondary gain. An examiner should be able to recommend additional tests by other examiners when appropriate. An examiner must be willing to prepare a comprehensive, written report and submit it promptly. He or she must be willing to testify in support of his or her report and opinions. Some examiners are willing to testify by way of a deposition but are unwilling to set aside time to appear in court. If you need to have him or her to testify in court, that fact should be made clear at the outset and part of the engagement. Another consideration is the cost of the examination, report, and court appearance. Some experts are simply too expensive for the ordinary case. Many physicians simply refuse to do medical examinations for litigants. Lawyers have some difficulty finding examiners who are able to fulfill all these requirements.

If a proponent wants more examinations than the examinee is willing to undergo, the proponent's remedy is to make a motion and show good cause why additional examinations are necessary. If the examinee sustained multiple injuries and has been treated by several specialists, a court is likely to allow the proponent to have similar specialists examine. The proponent can strengthen the motion by having the first examiner provide an affidavit stating he or she recommends an additional examination by a particular specialist. When a long delay occurs between an examination and trial, the proponent may be entitled to a repeat medical examination to cover the interim period and prepare for trial, especially if the examinee has continued to receive treatment and is claiming a permanent injury.

The law gives lawyers a great deal of leeway in selecting Rule 35 examiners. An examinee could not disqualify the proponent's choice on the grounds that the examiner knows the proponent, knows the proponent's lawyer, has a reputation for testifying in a particular type of case, or always testifies for a particular side or corporation. The fact that the examinee does not like the examiner or does not trust the examiner is not a basis for disallowing the proponent's selection. The proponent's choice cannot be disallowed on the grounds that the examinee's lawyer thinks the examiner is not fair or honest. If the examinee wants to challenge the examiner's integrity, the challenge must be made by showing specific acts of dishonesty or wrongdoing. For example, a professional licensing board's findings of wrongdoing could be used for that purpose. It takes a compelling reason to disqualify the proponent's choice, such as the examiner has treated the examinee in the past. Lawyers like to work with expert witnesses who, based on past experience, they know will do a good job for the client. Most law firms have relationships with professionals who qualify to do Rule 35 examinations, so it is unlikely that you will have to find examiners. But if that should happen, there are organizations that specialize in locating expert witnesses, including Rule 35 examiners, for litigants.

Rule 35 does not impose any time limit. An examiner may take as much time as the particular type of examination ordinarily requires. But it is bad form for the examiner to make an examinee sit and wait for his or her turn. The examiner should schedule the examination so as not to interfere with his or her regular practice. Nevertheless, some inconveniences are common, and lawyers should prepare clients to be tolerant and accepting of the procedure. Consider asking the examiner to schedule the examination as the first appointment after the noon break or as the last examination of the day.

Confirming a Scheduled Examination

You should send a letter to the examiner confirming the arrangements for the examination. Your letter should inform the examiner about relevant details of the occurrence, the nature of the examinee's claims, the treating physician's diagnosis and prognosis, and the type of treatment the examinee has received. You should include copies of the treating physician's reports and records. Instruct the examiner that the enclosures are for background information, to help focus the examination. Make clear that the examiner should base his or her report on the history he or she obtains from the examinee and the examiner's own findings. The evaluation and conclusions must be the examiner's own. The letter to a Rule 35 examiner in Exhibit 14.2 is illustrative. It points up the value of an independent medical examination. Notice that the writer carefully has developed relevant details.

Paralegals regularly prepare this type of letter to Rule 35 examiners. The letter gives the examination context so examiners can give special attention to any unique problems, such as inconsistencies in the medical records. The letter gives the examiner the proponent's perspective. Remember that the examination is part of the discovery process. The examiner is not an independent expert appointed by the court. Your letter should ask whether additional examinations are appropriate. Sometimes the plaintiff may have multiple medical problems, but only one or two problems are really debatable.

Examination Procedure

A bodily or mental condition usually involves several separate but related medical questions that affect the litigation. Typically, the questions are, Did the occurrence cause any injury? If so, what injury? What is the extent of the injury? Has the injury resulted in any physical impairment? If so, what is the nature and extent of the physical impairment? Is the impairment temporary or permanent? Has the physical impairment caused any disability? A disability is a loss of ability to function in employment or loss of function in daily living activities caused by a physical impairment. Is the disability temporary or permanent? A physical impairment could be permanent but, the resulting disability may be only temporary if the examinee can be retrained or otherwise compensate for the impairment. Was the examinee's medical treatment reasonably necessary? Did the examinee obtain the proper medical treatment? Does the examinee require future medical care? If so, for how long? What is the fair and reasonable cost of the past and future medical care? Did the bodily injury cause any pain? Is the pain subject to control by medication? Will the

EXHIBIT 14.2

Letter to Rule 35 Examiner

February 2, 2006

Adam Goldes, MD
Medical Arts Building, 1000 Fifth Street
Dallas, Texas

Re: Diersen vs. Machacek
OUR FILE: 37610
Accident Date: September 25, 1999

Dear Dr. Goldes:

This letter will confirm the arrangements we have made for an independent neurological examination of Elizabeth Diersen to be conducted by you at your Medical Arts office at 9:00 A.M. on March 4, 2006. Mrs. Diersen is represented by Attorney Thomas Rice. His telephone number is 612/555-1555. The arrangements for this examination were made through his office. There is no need for you to contact him, unless an emergency were to require you reschedule the appointment.

Mrs. Diersen is claiming neck and back injuries, which she attributes to a rear-end-type automobile accident. She complains of headaches, dizziness, and pain in her right thigh. Mrs. Diersen was born on January 21, 1979. She is now twenty-seven years of age. She is married to Paul Diersen, who is thirty-three years of age. They have one child. Mrs. Diersen completed high school. Her past employments have been light assembly work. She worked with hand tools and circuit boards. She states that she has not been involved in any other motor vehicle accidents. She broke a couple of ribs many years ago when she fell in a school parking lot. Otherwise, she has enjoyed good health.

The automobile accident in question occurred Monday, March 6, 2004, about 7:00 A.M. on State Highway 5 in Eden, Texas. Mrs. Diersen stopped her Ford Mustang for a traffic light. She was in a line of traffic backed up from the light. Without any warning, she suddenly felt her car pushed ahead an undetermined distance. She did not strike the car in front of her. She did not hear any contact at the rear of her car. Her car seats had high backs. She was not wearing her seat belt. Her head struck the back of the seat. She did not strike anything else within the car. She did not sustain any cuts, bumps, swelling, or bruises.

Apparently my client, Mr. Robert Machacek, bumped the rear of an automobile driven by Ms. Rhea Bellman, and Ms. Bellman's car was pushed against the rear of Mrs. Diersen's automobile. Photographs show very minor damage to the back of the Diersen car. All three cars could be driven after the accident. Neither Ms. Bellman nor Mr. Machacek was injured. Mrs. Diersen denies feeling injured at the scene. She continued to work, called her husband, found herself feeling very upset about the accident, and started crying. Her husband was off work that day. He came to the plant, examined the car, and drove it home. Mrs. Diersen left work early and drove their camper vehicle home. At her husband's

EXHIBIT 14.2

Letter to Rule 35 Examiner (continued)

suggestion, she saw Dr. F. P. Ekrem that same afternoon. He is a general practitioner at the Spencer Clinic. Mrs. Diersen's complaints then included a headache and slight thigh tenderness. On examination, Dr. Ekrem found the reflexes in Mrs. Diersen's upper and lower extremities to be normal, and she had an "excellent" range of motion in her neck with minimal tenderness at extremes. She had slight occipital tenderness at the left, minimal vertebral tenderness in the neck, and no muscle spasm. No x-rays were taken. Tylenol and Valium were prescribed.

Mrs. Diersen returned on March 17 complaining of neck discomfort. Dr. Ekrem records the following:

> While working she has her head in one position looking downward, causing some neck strain. She also has to cut wire, and there is associated bending. She has constant pain with bending down, then straightening up.

He found a good range of motion in her neck with tenderness at the extremes of motion. His diagnosis was neck and lower-back strain and sprain. He felt she could return to work, gave her a booklet on back care, and prescribed outpatient physical therapy.

Mrs. Diersen returned April 12, complaining of more back pain, especially while doing household activities and picking up her child. She was having pain in her thigh and calf on the left side. These symptoms worsened toward evening. Dr. Ekrem found a full range of motion of the neck with no muscle spasm. The straight-leg-raising test was negative. Her back pain was identified as being at the insertion of the paraspinal muscles at the iliac crest posteriorly. Dr. Ekrem notes that Mrs. Diersen felt she could not go back to work.

Dr. Ekrem last saw Mrs. Diersen on August 15, 2005, but in the meantime, she started seeing Chiropractor Jane Zimmerman. When Mrs. Diersen saw Dr. Ekrem in August, she was complaining of dizziness and continued pain, the location of which is not specified. He felt she might benefit from physiotherapy. He suspected that the dizziness was caused by postural hypotension.

Chiropractor Zimmerman's first examination was April 28, 2000. She treated Mrs. Diersen's neck and lower back with chiropractic manipulation. Sometimes the adjustments were painful. Chiropractor Zimmerman told her that her spine was out of alignment and that was causing her symptoms. She referred Mrs. Diersen to Chiropractor James Brandt for a consultation. She last saw Mrs. Diersen in July 2000. Her services were discontinued because Mrs. Diersen was unable to pay her bill and because the Diersens moved from Eden to Crystal, Texas.

On July 28, 2005, Mrs. Diersen started treatment with Chiropractor Donna Wahlen. Chiropractor Wahlen felt she had myocytis of the cervical, dorsal, and lumbar spine. She was treated with chiropractic adjustments, ultrasound, and so forth. It appears that Chiropractor Wahlen referred Mrs. Diersen to D. L. Anderson

continued

and Dr. Anna Schut for a neurological evaluation. She was examined by one of them on September 6, 2005, when she was complaining of dizzy spells, neck pain, and lower-back pain. Dr. Anderson records that the lower-back pain did not begin until about a week after the accident. According to her history, the physical therapy she had received at Methodist Hospital as prescribed by Dr. Ekrem had not provided any help. The problem with dizziness began while she was under Chiropractor Zimmerman's care. The neurological examination was essentially normal. Specifically, testing of muscle strength and reflexes in the extremities was normal. Sensation was normal throughout the body. No Hoffman or Babinski signs were present. Gait and leg swinging were negative. The Romberg test was negative. However, she demonstrated some limitation in the range of motion of her neck. In this regard, Dr. Anderson states the following:

> However, the patient has a long, thin, angular neck probably capable of more range of motion than is elicited at this time. She has palpable muscle spasms in the cervical muscles bilaterally as well as the upper trapezius muscles, particularly on the left side.

He found the motion in the dorsal and lumbar spine to be within normal limits. However, again, he describes "palpable muscle spasms bilaterally over the lumbosacral spine." The straight-leg-raising test was negative at ninety degrees. The cause of her dizziness was not determined.

Dr. Anderson eventually had Mrs. Diersen admitted to the Eden Health Center for testing. She was also evaluated by Dr. Schut. An electromyogram dated September 20, 2005, was negative for both lower extremities. Ms. Sylvia Rush, psychologist, conducted an evaluation. A Minnesota Multiphasic Personality Inventory [psychological test] showed Mrs. Diersen to be significantly neurotic. In addition, Ms. Rush felt she sought secondary gain by obtaining financial benefits from her insurance coverage and other benefits that exceeded her wage loss. She also felt that Mrs. Diersen wanted to remain at home with her child rather than work. Though Mrs. Diersen states her home and family life is good and satisfying, the indications are to the contrary.

During the September 2005 hospitalization, a myelogram was performed and interpreted by radiologist L. O. Campbell. His conclusion is as follows:

> Congenital partial sacralization of L5. Bilateral small extradural defects at L4–L5 suggesting central bulging disk at this level.

Dr. David Olson, who was called in for consultation by Dr. Anderson, concluded that surgery was not appropriate at the time, but he does not rule it out for the future.

More recently, Mrs. Diersen has come under the care of a psychologist named Stanley Baker at Clifton Court in Dallas. He is putting her through various physical stress activities that cause her to shake. The purpose is to release her tensions. He massages her neck. They talk. So far she has gone through seven such sessions at $100 per session. She thinks Mr. Baker is helping her a lot. She intends to continue seeing him.

Mrs. Diersen's medical expenses now exceed $11,000. She remains off work. She apparently is seeking social security disability benefits. She appears highly motivated to cling to her symptoms.

Please provide me with a narrative report on your examination, including the history you obtain, your findings, diagnosis, and evaluation. Psychiatric and psychological evaluations seem indicated. Thank you for your able assistance in this matter.

Very truly yours,

Constance McKenzie
Paralegal

pain continue into the future? If so, for how long? Are the examinee's current symptoms explainable on a basis other than the occurrence/injury in question? Is the examinee's past medical history contributory? An examiner has a right to ask the examinee about almost anything relevant to the examinee's bodily condition. The same types of questions would be relevant to a mental condition in issue.

To answer these questions, an examiner needs to ask the examinee about his or her recent medical history. The recent history includes the examinee's version of the occurrence. What happened? The examiner should not be concerned with why it happened. Could the occurrence have caused the alleged injury or any injury? What are the probabilities? The examiner must inquire about the examinee's past medical history. Is it contributory in any way?

The examiner should compare the examinee's descriptions of his or her history, symptoms, and complaints with the descriptions in the examinee's medical records to determine whether the examinee is being consistent. Do the examinee's complaints comport with the type of injury claimed? If the symptoms recur (come and go), what causes them to improve and worsen? When do they recur? Is there a pattern? Is there evidence of normal progressive healing? The examiner must try to determine whether the subjective symptoms are corroborated by **objective medical findings.** Objective findings are those that the examiner can observe by sight, touch, or sound. A symptom is subjective when it is evidenced merely by the patient's statement or voluntary response. A scar on the face is objective. An atrophied

objective medical findings Evidence concerning a person's medical condition that a physician can observe.

limb is objective. A headache is subjective. Muscle pain is subjective. A limited range of motion in the body may be objective or subjective. A lack of consistency suggests the plaintiff's complaints and symptoms may be exaggerated or even fabricated. If the diagnosis is based solely on the patient's history and subjective complaints, there is no actual medical corroboration of the injury, impairment, or disability.

Scope of Rule 35 Examinations

After obtaining a complete medical history, the examiner must conduct a physical examination to evaluate the injury and any impairment. Courts are pragmatic about the scope of independent medical examinations. They are not inclined to impose specific limitations. They much prefer to defer to the examiners' professional judgment. A Rule 35 medical examination may exceed the scope of the examinee's claim of injury, because the examination is used to establish a baseline concerning the examinee's condition. A good examination should establish the outside limits of the examinee's claim of injury, so that if later the examinee makes new complaints, the examiner can rule out those complaints as not related to the occurrence. Furthermore, an examinee could be injured in another accident after the examination, in which case the examination should be useful in separating the injuries and quantifying any aggravation of a prior injury. For example, suppose an examinee's claim is limited to his or her lower back. Nevertheless, the examination properly may include the examinee's legs, upper back, neck, and more to confirm the absence of any related problem.

Sometimes proponents arrange for psychometric tests though examinees are claiming only bodily injuries. The mental testing is relevant because some bodily complaints may be caused by a person's mental state. Probably the most common example is the person who has neck pain and occipital headaches that recur daily and do not improve with the passage of time. The symptoms could be caused by a physical injury to the musculature of the neck, but tension and anxiety because of stress at work or home may cause the same symptoms.

Courts have authorized "independent examinations" for more than fifty years, and during that time there has been almost no evidence of abuse by the examiners. Lawyers generally select highly qualified professionals to conduct independent examinations, because they have to rely on the examiners to be persuasive. If an examiner were to do anything improper during the examination, he or she would harm the defense and the examiner's professional reputation. In addition, litigation teams prepare clients for examinations by carefully explaining the procedures and the limitations on the examinations. A plaintiff has the right to end an examination if the examiner exceeds the boundaries.

If a party has agreed to submit to a Rule 35 examination but a dispute arises over some aspect of the proposed examination, the examinee should move the court for a protective order. The court may limit the scope of an examination and prescribe the manner in which it must be conducted. For example, if the examinee is pregnant and should not be subjected to x-rays, she should identify the problem and suggest the limitation. A court will protect an examinee from impertinent medical tests and procedures. For example, if the plaintiff is claiming neck pain and headaches because of an automobile accident, there is probably no reason to require the plaintiff to submit to tests for venereal diseases. A court may impose conditions and limitations to protect the plaintiff's privacy and sensibilities. The examinee should obtain an affidavit from her or his treating physician to support any motion to limit the scope of a Rule 35 examination.

Risky and Painful Medical Tests

If the treating physician has failed to conduct or obtain appropriate tests, the Rule 35 examiner may want to do them. However, if the tests are painful or subject the patient to some risk of harm, the examinee cannot be required to submit to them. For example, courts do not require examinees to undergo angiograms. An angiogram is a diagnostic study in which a physician injects dye into the patient's bloodstream and then takes x-rays to determine whether there is some defect or obstruction in a blood vessel. The test carries some risk of a stroke and even death. The test may be well justified when the patient is seeking diagnosis and treatment for a serious problem, but it generally is not justified for purposes of litigation. Similarly courts do not require parties to submit to **invasive testing,** that is, testing that enters the body, such as laparoscopy or arthroscopy. However, courts routinely require examinees to submit to electromyograms to test muscle and nerve function, and electroencephalograms to test electrical activity of the brain. Both tests require the insertion of small needles into the patient's skin. The tests are considered uncomfortable but not painful. The tests do not put the examinee's health at risk.

> **invasive testing** Medical procedures that require the examiner to penetrate the examinee's skin or otherwise enter the examinee's body, such as drawing blood.

If the plaintiff will not submit voluntarily to a risky, painful, or invasive test, the test may not be done. Furthermore, courts do not allow the defendant to cross-examine the plaintiff about her or his refusal to submit to the tests. The proponent's lawyer, however, may cross-examine the treating physician about the tests and the physician's failure to conduct them to make a **definitive diagnosis.** The physician then can explain why she or he has not recommended the tests. If the examinee's physician recommended the tests but the examinee declined, the jury can decide why he or she declined. On occasion, the examinee voluntarily submits to the tests because they are useful and the proponent has to pay their cost. The examinee may agree to the test hoping to find out more about her condition at the defendant's expense. For example, the examinee's physician may not have ordered an MRI because of its cost. But the proponent may be happy to pay the cost to try to prove that the examinee is not as badly hurt as the examinee's lawyer is claiming. A definitive diagnosis is reasonably certain and is usually the final diagnosis. A **working diagnosis** is merely the physician's best judgment about the patient's condition in light of the information available. It is tentative diagnosis that is subject to change as the physician obtains more information. It gives the physician a basis for beginning treatment.

> **definite diagnosis** A diagnosis that specifically eliminates other possible diagnoses.

> **working diagnosis** A physician's diagnosis that is made on the basis of the patient's current symptoms so that treatment can be initiated.

Rule 35 Reports

Rule 35 provides that the examiner's report shall contain "the examiner's findings, including results of all tests made, diagnoses and conclusions." This provision is for the benefit of the examinee, because the examinee is entitled to request a copy of the report. The Rule helps to ensure that the report is complete, not illusory. Rule 35 does not prescribe the form of the report. An examiner's findings include whatever he or she noted about the examinee's condition, whether normal or abnormal, concerning the medical conditions in issue. A diagnosis is the physician's expert opinion about the plaintiff's medical condition. The term *conclusion*, as used in Rule 35, is the examiner's evaluation of how the medical condition relates to the subject of the litigation. For example, the examiner may diagnose a herniated intervertebral disk. Rule 35 requires the examiner report to explain how the herniated disk affects the patient with regard to pain, physical impairment, disability, whether additional treatment is necessary, and, if so, what kind of treatment.

SOAP An anagram made from the parts of a medical examination: **S**ubjective, **O**bjective, **A**ssessment, and **P**lan.

Physicians commonly use the **SOAP** format to prepare their records, and that format tends to guide the way in which they prepare their medical reports. **S** stands for subjective. Subjective information includes the patient's relevant history and relevant complaints or symptoms. **O** stands for objective. Objective information includes the physician's findings on examination and tests. **A** stands for assessment. Assessment information is the physician's diagnosis and prognosis. **P** stands for plan. The physician's plan is his or her prescription for treatment and observation. As part of the subjective section, examiners usually relate the examinee's current medical history, past medical history, complaints, and symptoms. The current history includes such things as the examinee's description of the occurrence, onset of symptoms, treatment, and improvement or lack of improvement. The past medical history describes the patient's prior accidents, injuries, illnesses, and treatments. The complaints and symptoms describe how the examinee is feeling, according to the examinee.

The next section describes the physician's examination and what the examination discloses about the examinee's condition. It also describes medical tests the physician may order, such as blood tests, x-rays, and electromyograms and their results. The following section contains the physician's diagnosis and evaluation with particular emphasis on the factors the proponent identified, such as causation, impairment, and disability. Exhibit 14.3 is a sample medical report. Exhibits 14.4 and 14.5 are attachments. These reports illustrate the type of medical inquiries and considerations involved in Rule 35 medical examinations. They also show why parties may have differences concerning the medical aspects of personal injury cases. Though the sample reports have been modified by changing names, dates, and places, they are based on an actual case. The physician who prepared the examination report appreciated the importance of thoroughness and detail. Of course, those qualities lend authority to the physician's opinions.

A proponent's legal team should review the examiner's report as soon as it is received. On occasion, the team finds that the report is ambiguous, confusing, fails to comment on critical matters, or simply is poorly done. When that happens the proponent's lawyer or paralegal must confer with the examiner about his or her report and arrange to have the report upgraded. The proponent's lawyer may provide guidance and suggestions to make the report comport with the requirements of Rule 35 and otherwise meets the parties' needs. After all, physicians are not expected to know what is required by the Federal Rules of Civil Procedure. If the examiner agrees to issue another report to replace the first, there is no need to refer to the first report. You may consider it a draft that was inadequate.

EXHIBIT 14.3

Rule 35 Medical Report

Dear Ms. McKenzie:

On March 4, 2006, I examined this twenty-seven-year-old female whom you so kindly referred for a neurological and psychiatric evaluation.

Family History

The patient's mother is sixty and well. Her father is sixty-two years of age and well. She has two brothers and one sister. Her husband is thirty-five years of age and presently is unemployed. She has one boy, age three. The patient graduated from Eden High School in 1997.

Personal History

This patient denies any serious illnesses. She had a tonsillectomy at the age of five. Her appendix was removed in 1983. In December 1989 the patient had a pyelonephritis and some bladder polyps removed by Dr. Walonick at the Eden Hospital. She denies any other automobile accidents before or since the one with your client.

Present Illness

The patient was involved in an automobile accident on March 6, 2004. It occurred about 7:00 A.M. on Highway 5 at Mitchell Road. She was driving her car and was struck from the rear. At the time of the impact, she said that her head hit the back of the seat but that nothing else happened to her. She was not knocked unconscious and actually did not feel very much. The police came, and information was exchanged. She went on to work. She said she rested in the ladies' room and after an hour went home.

At about 2:00 in the afternoon she saw her family physician, Dr. Ekrem. He examined her but did not take any x-rays. He gave her some Valium and told her to go home, rest, and take a couple of days off work. At that time she said her left leg was aching.

The patient rested at home, and, according to the patient, her neck started to bother her later in the day. Two days later she attempted to go back to work, and a few days after this she developed some soreness in her back. She went back to Dr. Ekrem, who sent her for some physiotherapy on an outpatient basis at the Methodist Hospital. She went there two or three times a week for about five weeks, and kept working off and on. Finally, on March 21, 2005, she was put on medical leave. According to the patient, the physiotherapy did not help.

The patient then went to Jane Zimmerman, a chiropractor in Eden, who took x-rays and adjusted her neck and back. Chiropractor Zimmerman also gave her a neck-and-back brace. Chiropractor Zimmerman sent her to a Dr. James Brandt, a chiropractor, for a consultation sometime in June 2005. Later the patient moved to Crystal, Texas, where she went to Dr. Donna Wahlen, a chiropractor. She took adjustments from Dr. Wahlen, starting out three times a week and now sees the doctor as necessary.

continued

The patient was having some dizzy spells, so she went to a Dr. Malmoud, who apparently is a partner of Dr. Ekrem. He felt that she possibly was having hypotension, but when he examined her, her blood pressure was all right.

The patient was referred to Dr. Anna Schut and Dr. D. L. Anderson. They examined her and gave her physiotherapy in their office, and on two occasions she has been hospitalized. The first time was in April 2005, when she was given in-hospital physiotherapy for two weeks, and rehabilitation for her neck and back. This was at the Eden Hospital. In September 2005, Dr. Anderson put her back in the Eden Hospital, where a myelogram was done. Dr. David Olson, who looked at the myelogram, said she might have a low midline ruptured disk. She was put on an exercise program and given a better back brace, but this did not cure her.

The patient also has been seen by Dr. Hammond for an insurance examination. About a year ago she went to a doctor in Kellogg Square, who examined her, but she cannot remember his name. She had a social security examination at the university but does not know the doctor's name. In addition, she has been to Dr. Walonick for her kidney problems, at the request of Dr. Anderson. She is still seeing Dr. Anderson about once a month.

The patient was sent to a psychologist, Mr. Stanley Baker, at Clifton Court. He has his wife, Sandy Baker, help him. They talk with the patient, and, according to the patient, they talk about the lawsuit, the attorneys involved, and letters that are coming to her. They try to get her to relax. They give her neck massage and put her in unusual positions. According to the patient, she will stand or bend over for a long period of time, or they may have her stand against the wall or even on her head. She has seen Mr. Baker about ten or twelve times, and she thinks he might be helping her. According to the patient, the Bakers are giving her advice about what to do about the examinations.

The patient has been seen by people from rehabilitation. Two names are Betty Johnson and Maddy Boll. They have told her how to fill out the application forms for rehabilitation benefits. They have told her she will continue to be paid as long as she earns less money than she earned in the job she had when she was injured. They got her a job at the Spa Petite in Eden, which she has been on for three days. She said she shows the members how to use the equipment, and she is on a running and exercise program with the members of the club. The patient volunteered to me that she will continue to be paid by rehabilitation as long as her compensation from Spa Petite is less than she had when she was working for EMT Electronics. The patient presently takes only ampicillin for a strep throat, which was prescribed by Dr. Ekrem. If her headaches become too bad, she takes Excedrin or Tylenol 3.

Prior to her employment with EMT Electronics, she did electronic soldering for Ross Shadow. After this, she had a child and at one time worked for Kentucky Fried Chicken preparing food and waiting on customers at the counter.

According to the patient, she had a cortisone shot in her left hip at one time for bursitis. When she was in the hospital, as well as having a myelogram, she had an electromyogram of her left leg. According to the patient, she does not think she is getting much better. She said all the therapy she has taken has really not helped very much as far as her neck, leg, and back are concerned. She said the doctors might think she is better, but she really is not.

Present Complaints
1. Daily headaches. These are bioccipital and bifrontal. They last a couple of hours and are relieved by Excedrin. The headaches are not associated with any nausea or vomiting and generally come on about noon.
2. Dizzy spells. She gets these approximately once a day. They consist of a light-headedness rather than a vertigo.
3. Some stiffness and discomfort in her neck and shoulders (primarily left). This is brought on by anything, and any type of paperwork or keeping her neck in one position bothers her.
4. Pain in the lower back. This is a stiffness and soreness and is always present. She wears a brace from time to time, particularly when driving or if she is going to sit for a long time.
5. Aching in her left leg, primarily in the thigh or hip region. This is worse in the evening. It is bothered by cold. Coughing and sneezing do not produce pain.

At this point, the patient has no blurred vision or double vision. She does not have any complaints as far as her chest and abdomen are concerned. She has had no syncope or convulsions. She is sleeping better on a water bed. The patient's appetite is good. She does a lot of exercises but does not play tennis, golf, or any sports. She does a fair amount of walking.

Physical Examination
The patient is five-feet-five-inches tall and weighs 123 pounds. She is well developed and well nourished. Blood pressure is one hundred over seventy; pulse is sixty-six; respirations are eighteen. Teeth and gums are normal. Eardrums are normal. Throat is negative. The chest is clear to auscultation and percussion, and there are no cardiac irregularities or murmurs. The abdomen reveals no masses, tenderness, or scars, except for appendectomy.

Neurological Examination

Cranial Nerves
The patient can smell test odors. The visual acuity is 20/20-2 bilaterally without correction. The visual fields were normal. The ophthalmoscopic examination did not reveal any evidence of any increased intracranial pressure, hemorrhages, or exudates. No optic atrophy. Good pulsation of the veins. The third, fourth, and sixth cranial nerves were normal. The pupils were equal and reacted to light. No nystagmus. No facial asymmetry. No hypesthesia of the face or cornea. Hearing revealed to be normal.

continued

Sensory Functions

The examination of the body to cotton, pinprick pain, and vibration and position sense was normal.

Motor Functions

The patient has a good grip bilaterally, and there is no atrophy, hypertrophy, twitching, or tremor of the musculature.

Body Measurements (in Inches)

Parts	Right	Left
Biceps	9 3/4	7 1/2
Forearm	5 3/4	7
Wrist	14 1/2	12 1/2
Hand	9 1/2	7 1/4
Thigh	5 3/4	7
Calf	14 1/2	12 1/2

Movements

The patient's neck goes through a full range of motion in all directions without any complaint of pain or evidence of spasm. The patient bends over to ninety degrees and comes about one inch from her toes. Straight-leg-raising tests go to ninety degrees. She is able to walk on her heels and toes and do a deep knee bend.

The patient has some tenderness over the left intertrochanteric bursa, indicating a bursitis in this area.

Coordination

The patient's gait is normal. The finger-to-finger, finger-to-nose, and heel-to-knee tests were done normally.

Reflexes

All the reflexes were present and equal. The toe signs were negative. She does not have any bowel or bladder dysfunction, and speech is normal.

X-rays

Roentgenograms were made of the cervical spine in the anteroposterior, lateral, and both oblique directions.

Diagnosis

Negative for evidence of old or recent fracture or other bone or joint abnormality. A normal curvature is seen in flexion and extension.

Conclusion: Negative cervical spine study.

Roentgenograms were made of the lower back.

Exhibit 14.3

Rule 35 Medical Report (continued)

There is no old or recent fracture. There are no productive or destructive changes and the disk spaces are maintained. The fifth lumbar vertebra is transitional. The sacroiliac joints and hips appear normal. A few droplets of contrast material are seen in the spinal canal as the result of a previous myelogram. An IUD is identified and appears to be normal in location.

Electroencephalogram

Basic alpha rhythm is ten per second. This is an awake record with some eye blink artifact, movement, and tension artifact. Some low-voltage and low-voltage fast activity. No evidence of any localized or diffuse spiking, slow waves, or delta activity. No amplitude asymmetry. No seizure discharges of any sort. Photic stimulation did not produce any driving response. Hyperventilation did not produce any buildup or slowing.

Impression: Within normal limits.

Electromyogram

An electromyogram was done by Jane E. Wilson, MD, on March 6, 2006. She found the entire left leg to be normal. A copy of her entire report is included with this letter.

Echoencephalogram

This echoencephalogram demonstrates a normal position for the midline echo complex.

Minnesota Multiphasic Personality Inventory

This was a valid test. There was a marked evaluation on hysteria or conversion reaction. Some mild depression and hypochondriasis were noted. This profile indicated the patient had tension within herself that was being converted to psychosomatic or psychophysiological symptoms. The symptoms undoubtedly have a secondary gain.

Psychological Examination

This patient was evaluated by Patrick Noble, PhD, Licensed Consulting Psychologist, on March 7, 2006. A copy of his entire report is included with this letter. His summary is as follows:

The testing reveals an immature, dependent person who has a basic personality that is in keeping with an individual who could easily siphon off her psychological conflicts into physiological manifestations. This type of personality develops over the years and is closely related to the fact that she apparently lived in a situation where she felt she was being controlled by a rather overpowering mother figure. Thus, her only out is to develop symptomatology to blame her psychological difficulties on some medical problem.

continued

EXHIBIT 14.3

*Rule 35 Medical Report
(continued)*

Conclusions

If one considers the mechanism of the accident, it is very difficult to imagine that really very much did occur to this patient. She had no symptoms at the time of the accident, and the back pain did not come on for several days. She could have had a very minimal strain of her neck, but one would expect that this would have disappeared within a few days. She has been overexamined and overtreated, and has had a tremendous number of chiropractic appointments. She has been going from doctor to doctor in an attempt to be cured, and this is not possible because 95 percent of her symptoms are psychological in nature. She has recently returned to work as a demonstrator at the Spa Petite. The patient's complaints are of headaches, light-headedness, pain in the neck and both shoulders, lower-back pain, and aching in her left leg. The physical examination is entirely normal for any abnormality as a result of this accident.

A complete neurological examination is negative. She does have bursitis in the left intertrochanteric bursa, and this is probably producing discomfort in the left leg. This is a degenerative affair and not related to the accident. She has had an injection of hydrocortisone in this area in the past.

X-rays of the cervical spine were normal. An x-ray of the lumbosacral spine was negative. A few droplets of contrast material were seen in the spinal canal, which was the result of a previous myelogram.

The electroencephalogram was normal.
The echoencephalogram was normal.
An electromyogram of the left leg was entirely normal.
The Minnesota Multiphasic Personality Inventory shows definite evidence of a conversion reaction with secondary gain. This secondary gain is obviously that the patient does not have to go to work, but can stay home and receive more compensation than she would get if she were working. In this respect a compensation neurosis is present.

The psychological testing showed an immature, dependent person who has a basic personality that is in keeping with an individual who could easily siphon off her psychological conflicts into physiological manifestations. This type of personality develops over the years and is closely related to the fact that she apparently lived in a situation where she felt she was being controlled by an overpowering mother figure. Thus, her only out is to develop symptomatology to blame her psychological difficulties on some medical problem.

A great number of the patient's symptoms are very close to consciousness. She has been told that a lot of her symptoms are based on tension and that they are not organic in character. A lot of this is very close to being a conscious mechanism, particularly with her desire not to return to work and to enjoy life at home as long as she can obtain financial rewards. The financial reward is paramount in her mind. This mechanism is so close to consciousness that it is

█ **EXHIBIT 14.3**

Rule 35 Medical Report (continued)

really not far from malingering. These mechanisms have been investigated by psychologists who have treated her and have been disregarded by her physicians and chiropractors. I find no evidence, from a clinical standpoint, of a herniated lumbar intervertebral disk. There is no weakness, reflex disturbance, or atrophy, and movements are excellent. The pain, I believe, is a result of the bursitis, which is not attributable to the accident.

Sincerely yours,

Adam Goldes, MD

█ **EXHIBIT 14.4**

Attached Electromyography Report

ELECTROMYOGRAPHY REPORT

PATIENT: Mrs. Elizabeth Diersen

DATE: March 6, 2006

Nerve Conduction Studies

Nerve	Motor Conduction Velocity	Distal Motor Latency	Motor Response Amplitude
Left peroneal	46.5 meters/second	5.0 milliseconds	5.0 millivolts

Left Lower Extremity Needle Electrode Studies

Muscle	Insertional Activity	Motor Unit Activity
Iliopsoas	Normal	Normal
Rectus femoris	Normal	Normal
Vastus lateralis	Normal	Normal
Vastus medialis	Normal	Normal
Tibialis anterior	Normal	Normal
Extensor digitorum longus	Normal	Normal
Peroneus	Normal	Normal
Medial gastrocnemius	Normal	Normal for strength of contraction
Soleus	Normal	Normal
Gluteus maximus	Normal	Normal
Lumbar paraspinal	Normal	Normal

Normal
Normal
Normal

continued

Exhibit 14.4

*Attached Electromyography
Report   (continued)*

Summary
The motor conduction velocity, distal motor latency, and action potential are normal in the left peroneal nerve.

The needle electrode examinations reveal no significant variation from normal.

Impression
The above electromyographic studies are within normal limits.

Jane E. Wilson, MD

Examinee's Right to a Report

The examinee is entitled to a copy of the written report. But the examinee must obtain the report through the proponent, not directly from the examiner. Indeed, the examinee's attorney should not have any contact with the examiner, except to assist with scheduling the examination. The proponent must deliver or mail a copy to the examinee's attorney promptly after the request. By requesting a copy of the report the examinee waives his or her medical privilege concerning the condition in issue. Rule 35(b)(2) states

> By requesting and obtaining a report of the examination . . . or by taking the deposition of the examiner, the party examined waives any privilege the party may have in that action or any other involving the same controversy, regarding the testimony of every other person who has examined or may thereafter examine the party in respect of the same mental or physical condition.

The waiver applies only if the examinee receives the report or takes the examiner's deposition.[2]

Examinee's Duty to Provide Reports

When an examinee demands a copy of a Rule 35 medical report and receives it, he or she becomes obligated to provide the proponent with a similar report from the treating physician(s). If the treating physician fails to provide such a report, the court may preclude the treating physician from testifying. In most state courts, a party's waiver of medical privilege extends to the party's medical records. Access to the opposing party's medical records is a trade off for the Rule 35 examination report. Usually, the examinee's lawyer obtains copies of the examinee's records from the treating physician and supplies additional copies to the proponent. If the treating physician charges the patient for reproducing the records, that expense cannot be passed on to the proponent—just as the proponent cannot charge the examinee for obtaining a copy of the Rule 35 report. An examinee is under a continuing obligation to produce new reports as she or he continues to receive treatment.

EXHIBIT 14.5

Attached Psychological Evaluation

PSYCHOLOGICAL EVALUATION

RE: Elizabeth Diersen

TESTS ADMINISTERED: Hillside Short Form of the Wechsler
Belleview Examination
Rorschach
Kahn Test of Symbol Arrangement
Sentence Completion

This woman indicates that she was in an accident 3-6-04. She states she was not unconscious and was not hospitalized, and her only symptom was a headache. At the present time she states her symptoms are "headaches and dizziness, left leg aches, neck and lower-back aches." Currently she is on no medication except Tylenol 3 for headaches. In the past she apparently has had various medications. She states she does not smoke, drinks occasionally, and does not use drugs. She indicates she started a job last week, working at a health club. In terms of social activity, she states they don't do much because it is too expensive and they tend to sit around home and watch TV, although they do some camping.

The patient states she comes from a family of four children, where she is the oldest. Her father is a truck driver, and her mother is a waitress. She has been married four years. Her husband currently is unemployed and has worked for the Milwaukee Railroad in the past and has been laid off for about eight or nine weeks. There is one child of this marriage, a boy age three. The patient states she completed high school. She indicates she has had no serious illnesses except for appendicitis resulting in an appendectomy. She has no history of any other serious accidents. The patient is a rather stoic-faced individual who has very little expression on her face. Speech is coherent, relevant, under good control, and shows no loose associations. Affective responses are felt to be somewhat flat at this time, and one gets the impression she may have some feelings of depression. There are no evidences of psychotic ideation. The patient is considered to be of average intelligence, is oriented in contact, and shows good comprehension, good attention span, and no loss of recent or remote memory.

This patient has been tested previously. The evaluation done in March 1998 indicated she was immature and had some self-esteem problems, with a diagnosis as an immature woman in stress with a self-esteem issue, unexpressed anger, and some sadness in relationship to her heterosexual life.

Testing at this time reveals a woman of average intelligence with a prorated IQ of 109. She continues to show the same type of immaturity and dependency that she apparently showed when she was tested previously. It would appear that she has been unsuccessful in separating from parental figures in the past and has more or less been living in a situation where the mother figure assumed

continued

Exhibit 14.5

*Attached Psychological
Evaluation (continued)*

a very domineering and controlling role. As a result of this, the patient has developed a very passive, dependent, and somewhat negativistic approach in dealing with her interpersonal life. She has problems also in attaining an adult heterosexual relationship and apparently will have some marital problems if this is not cleared up in the near future. The unresolved hostile feelings are still seen, although they may very well relate to her resentments over how she has been treated in the past. The testing also indicates that she more than likely tends to siphon off her emotional problems into this accident as a way of attempting to resolve her psychological problems. It may also very well be, even at the present time, that her financial conditions intensified her symptomatology, for she knows no other way of coping with the current changes except to maintain her symptomatology.

In summary, the testing continues to reveal an immature, dependent person who has a basic personality that is in keeping with an individual who could easily siphon off her psychological conflicts into physiological manifestations. This type of personality develops over the years and is closely related to the fact that she apparently lived in a situation where she felt she was being controlled by a rather overpowering mother figure. Thus, her only out is to develop symptomatology to blame her psychological difficulties on some medical problem.

Patrick Noble, PhD
Licensed Consulting Psychologist

If a party does not intend to call that physician as his or her own witness at trial and does not obtain his or her treating physician's report, the court may require the proponent to pay the cost of having the report prepared. Suppose the treating physician refuses to render a report until the patient pays for his or her treatment. The proponent's remedy is to take the physician's deposition.

Uses of Examination Reports

A proponent uses a Rule 35 report to evaluate the examinee and the case. Examiners often find it necessary to read from their reports when they testify at trial, because it would be impossible for them to remember all the details. A skilled lawyer can establish a dialogue with the physician although the physician is primarily reading from the report. The lawyer does this by having the physician read a sentence or paragraph and then asking the physician questions about what he or she just read. The questions may be similar to the following:

> Doctor, why do you obtain a "past medical history" from the patient?
> You just said that there was no "muscle spasm." What is muscle spasm?
> What is the significance of that finding for the patient?
> What do you mean by "subjective complaint?"

Was that complaint consistent with the plaintiff's history as recorded by her treating doctor?

Was the result of that test consistent with her other tests?

Was the result of that test consistent with the plaintiff's statement that she is unable to move her neck?

Doctor, you said that you did an electromyogram study. Please explain to the jury what that is and why you did that test.

The attorney can help the jury to understand the significance of the examination and make it relevant to them. The examiner is subject to cross-examination from the report, and the cross-examination may cover matters that the examiner failed to do or omitted from the report.

Preparing Clients for Rule 35 Examinations

You can help clients prepare for Rule 35 examinations. Presumably, when your law firm accepted the case, the client was told that the opposing party would request a Rule 35 examination. On receiving the request or order scheduling your client's examination you should send a letter to the client that explains the procedure. Most clients appreciate having information and instructions in a letter, which they can keep for reference. The letter should explain the purpose, scope, and manner of the examination. Exhibit 14.6 is a sample of the kind of letter you might use. It provides an overview of the procedure. It proposes a meeting to discuss preparation. You need to assure the client that the examination is routine for the type of case.

Study the report of examination in Exhibit 14.3 to learn about examination procedures. It is an actual report with only the dates, places, and names changed. The report is typical in form. The examination concerns a young woman (wife and mother) who was employed outside the home. She claimed neck, back, and head injuries from an automobile accident. The defendant's automobile slid on ice and bumped the car ahead. That car was pushed against the back of the woman's car. Photographs showed little damage to any of the cars. She admitted at the scene that she did not hear either contact and was not injured. She continued to work, called her husband who was home, and told him about the accident. After a couple hours her neck started hurting and she developed a headache. Her husband took her to her family doctor. There were no objective signs of injury. Her doctor thought that she might have a "soft tissue"[3] injury to her neck and expected a quick, full recovery. However, her subjective symptoms worsened. She went to many doctors for treatment. She did not improve with the passage of time. Her claim was placed in suit. The defendant's lawyer arranged for a Rule 35 examination by a neurologist, a medical doctor who specializes in diseases and injuries to the nervous system. The lawyer specifically asked the neurologist to arrange for psychometric testing, because the lawyer felt the woman's problems might be caused by an emotional problem.

An experienced examiner watches the examinee enter the examination room. The examiner notes how the examinee walks, stands, sits, moves his or her extremities, and the examinee's attitude. The examiner begins by taking a history concerning the occurrence, current condition, and past medical history. Sometimes examiners

■ EXHIBIT 14.6

*Letter to Client Confirming
Medical Examination*

Dear [client]:

As we anticipated, the defendant's lawyer has demanded a medical examination. The law allows the defendant to choose a licensed [type of practitioner, such as medical doctor, chiropractor, psychologist] to examine you at a reasonably convenient time and place. Ordinarily the defendant is entitled to only one examination, but sometimes circumstances require an additional examination. At this point the defendant is only asking for the one examination. The examination is scheduled for [date] at [time].

The defendant's purpose for requesting the examination is to determine the nature and extent of your injuries and the effect your injuries are having on you. The examiner will conduct a thorough physical examination, including standard medical tests. The examiner will submit a report to the defendant's attorney. The defendant's attorney will use the report to evaluate your claim. The report may be used at trial if the case cannot be settled.

The examiner is a licensed professional. She [or he] will treat you with respect and consideration. The examiner is not permitted to conduct any tests that pose a risk to you, and you are not required to submit to any tests that are painful. You may be asked to have some x-rays. Is there any reason why you should not undergo routine x-rays? If so, we want to make alternative arrangements.

We must assume the examiner selected by the defendant will look for weaknesses in our claim. We feel that it is important for you to understand how the examination will be conducted and what the examiner is likely to do during the examination. We want to explain to you your rights so that you can guard against any inadvertent intrusions into your privacy. Therefore, if you will telephone me, we can arrange to meet and prepare for the examination.

Please do not feel concerned about the defendant's request for the examination. It does not mean the defendant is aggressively contesting your injury claim. Indeed, it means the defendant is taking your claim seriously and wants to know more about it. We will be entitled to a complete report of the examination by the doctor who performs it. Usually the report helps both parties to evaluate the case and should help settlement negotiations.

I look forward to hearing from you soon.

Very truly yours,

[Paralegal]

include a "social history" and "family history." The examiner elicits the examinee's current symptoms and complaints. The complaints are usually listed in the order of importance to the examinee. The examiner takes notes. Your letter to the examiner will help him or her to identify and focus on the significant items.

The examiner looks for gross abnormalities and deformities. Then he or she examines body parts by palpating, measuring, and testing ranges of motion. By palpating soft tissue the examiner can determine whether there are tumors, muscle spasm, or focal pain. By measuring extremities the examiner can determine whether there is any wasting of muscles. Wasting may be caused by injury to nerves or simple disuse. The range-of-motion tests are designed to identify orthopedic and neurological problems. If an examinee's range of motion is limited, that warrants further studies of the affected part. An examiner will test the range of motion of the neck, back, extremities, and joints. A body part may have several different planes of motion to be tested. For example, the neck goes forward and backward (flexion and extension), it rotates left and right, and it tilts side to side. The examiner usually tests muscle strength of muscle groups, including hand squeezing. The examiner may repeat some of these tests during the examination to see if the examinee is consistent.

Medical Tests Commonly Used to Diagnose Injuries

Many medical tests are commonly used for diagnosing injuries, including the following:

- Ordinary x-rays show the condition of the bone.
- Computerized tomography (CT) scans show some bone conditions and soft tissue conditions, and their interrelationship.
- Magnetic resonance imaging (MRI) scans show the condition of soft tissue, including some brain injuries and diseases.
- Electromyograms (EMGs) test the electrical function of nerves and muscles.
- Electroencephalograms (EEGs) test brain wave function and may help to show whether the patient has a brain injury.
- Myelograms, which are a special type of x-ray of the spine, are useful in diagnosing injuries and abnormalities of the spinal nerve roots and spinal cord and intervertebral disk.
- Angiograms, which are a special type of x-ray, show the condition of blood vessels.
- Psychometric tests evaluate a person's mental and emotional status and functioning.
- Diskograms, which are a special type of x-ray, evaluate the condition of intervertebral disks in the spine; this type of test has come into disfavor and is being used with less frequency.
- Reflex tests indicate whether the peripheral nerves and/or the central nervous system have been injured or impaired.
- Range-of-motion tests test the movement of extremities (arms and legs) and all the joints in the body.

- Skin sensory tests indicate whether an apparent nerve injury corresponds with the expected nerve pattern.
- A coordination test is a clinical test that evaluates function of the central nervous system.
- A reflex test is a clinical test that evaluates peripheral nerves; there are many reflex tests, including the knees, elbows, and toe signs.

When the treating physician obtains such tests, the results ordinarily are available to the parties as part of the patient's medical-hospital records. The test results are quite objective and seldom need to be repeated. Even if physicians differ in their interpretation of the tests, the raw data usually is available to both sides for review and evaluation. The one significant exception is the interpretation of an electromyogram. Electromyography is a study of the electrical activity of nerves and muscle activity. The electrical activity is measured and evaluated by sound and by readings on an oscilloscope. No record is made of the measurements themselves during the testing. The examiner simply records his or her interpretation of the waves on an oscilloscope.

When you meet with the client, tell the client to treat the examiner with respect and to cooperate throughout the examination. Reiterate that the examiner will be professional and do nothing to harm him or her. Urge the client to be on time and to be patient if the examiner is a little late or seems to be a little slow. A client who exhibits a positive attitude while undergoing an independent examination makes a favorable impression on the examiner and, indirectly, on the opposing lawyer. Explain that the examination begins from the moment the client enters the physician's office, because the examiner will observe how he or she walks, sits, and moves. You should describe the examination procedure and tests the examiner is likely to conduct. Again, these examinations begin with the examinee's history, current and past. The clinical examination is designed to evaluate the patient's symptoms and physical condition. There are some excellent books that describe clinical examinations and medical tests physicians commonly use to evaluate patients. Some continuing legal education programs provide demonstrations and explain orthopedic, neurological, and chiropractic examinations. Some law firms have videotapes that demonstrate clinical examinations. You should try to obtain access to this kind of information. The examiner may repeat some tests during the examination to see whether the client's responses are consistent. If the results are not consistent, the examiner has reason to believe the client is trying to deceive the examiner. Help the client to avoid inconsistent responses by cautioning the client against exaggerating or minimizing symptoms.

Prepare the client to accurately relate the medical history, including accident history. You should identify the important items in the client's history and symptoms. You should explain that if the examiner goes beyond the scope of what is reasonably necessary, the client has the right to terminate the examination. For example, in the typical bodily injury case, a pelvic examination is not necessary. If the examiner proposes to do a pelvic examination, the client should know that it is all right to say "no!" On occasion, parties take diaries and notes to help answer the examiner's questions. When testifying, the examiner probably will mention the examinee's use of notes. No rule prohibits doing so, but juries often react negatively to a party who has an apparent need for such notes. The opposing lawyer will want to examine the diary to see what else might be in it. Diaries and notes tend to complicate the case for the examinee rather than help. You should prepare the client to answer examiner questions, such as the following:

Pain

Where is the pain located?

What causes the pain to increase? Coughing? Sneezing? Bowel movements? Walking? Standing? Sitting? Deep breathing?

Does the pain radiate to any other part of your body?

If so, what route does the pain take?

When did the pain start?

Can you relate the onset of the pain to an incident, activity, or time period?

Did the pain begin after some activity?

Have you experienced this type of pain before?

Has the pain increased in severity?

Has the pain increased in frequency?

Has the pain increased in the affected area?

At what time of the day is the pain the worst?

What activity increases the pain?

What movements increase the pain?

Does any activity reduce the pain?

Does rest relieve the pain?

Is the pain continuous, or does it come and go?

Does the intensity of the pain vary?

What medications help?

What medications have you tried that do not help?

Is the pain's intensity or duration improving with the passage of time?

It may help the client to know that everyone has a different pain threshold. People seem to feel pain differently. Nevertheless, most physicians try to grade pain on a scale of 1 to 5. The scale may be as follows:

1. Minimal
2. Mild or uncomfortable
3. Moderate or distressing
4. Severe or horrible
5. Excruciating

You should help your client to fully describe his or her condition. For instance, it may be a good idea to supply groups of adjectives that help to describe pain:

List of Pain Adjectives

Flickering	Dull	Penetrating	Hot
Quivering	Sore	Piercing	Burning
Pulsing	Hurting	Tight	Scalding
Throbbing	Aching	Numb	Searing

Beating	Heavy	Drawing	Tingling
Pounding	Tender	Squeezing	Itching
	Taut	Tearing	Smarting
Pricking	Splitting		Stinging
Boring		Pinching	
Drilling	Annoying	Pressing	Cool
Stabbing	Troublesome	Gnawing	Cold
Sharp	Miserable	Cramping	Freezing
Cutting	Intense	Crushing	Nagging
Lacerating	Unbearable		Nauseating
	Spreading	Tugging	Agonizing
Jumping	Radiating	Pulling	Dreadful
Flashing		Wrenching	
Shooting			

Physicians choose pain medication based on their assessment of the type and degree of the patient's pain. A physician tries to select an analgesic that is no more potent than necessary to minimize the harmful effects of the treatment. Thus the prescribed analgesic may not eliminate all the patient's pain. The objective is to make the pain tolerable.

Activities

How are your daily living activities affected?

How are your job activities affected?

Is there anything that you now cannot do at all? What?

What things can you do but suffer pain while doing them?

What things can you do but suffer pain afterward because you did them?

What activities had you given up but now resumed?

Help the client to understand what things she or he needs to tell the examiner and what things are privileged, such as the client's conversations with you, the lawyer, and the client's spouse. However, you are not to keep the examiner from discovering facts that are discoverable. The client should be much less anxious about the examination by being prepared for it.

TECHNOLOGY NOTES

You can obtain on-line help concerning medical issues at the following Web sites: http://webmd.com; http://drkoop.com; http://health.discovery.com; http://healthcentral.com; http://mayohealth.org; http://yoursurgery.com; http://ncbi.nim.nih.gov/PubMed/ (this is the National Library of Medicine site and regularly is used by physicians); http://medscape.com (use this site to find articles on particular medical conditions). There are software programs that provide descriptions of most prescription medications, anatomy, and medical terminology.

The *Physician's Desk Reference* provides a comprehensive review of all prescription drugs, including recommended dosages, side effects, contraindications, and history concerning the drugs. It provides Federal Drug Administration approved information. It may be obtained at http://medicalamazon.com. It is also available on CD-ROM.

SUMMARY

When a party's physical or mental condition is controverted, an adverse party may move the court for an order compelling that party to submit to a Rule 35 medical examination. A Rule 35 examination is part of discovery and adversarial. The moving party must show good cause for the examination. A party establishes good cause by showing the court that the condition is material to the outcome of the case and is controverted. The showing may be made by making reference to the pleadings, discovery documents, and filing affidavits in support of the motion. Usually, parties can agree whether an examination is appropriate. But sometimes parties disagree about the examination parameters or scope of an examination. When a court orders a party to submit to a Rule 35 examination, the court may impose conditions and limitations on the examination, including the number and kinds of tests that may be performed. Seldom, if ever, will a court order a party to submit to tests that are painful or expose a party to risk of harm. Only if there are unusual circumstances will a court allow another person to attend the examination of an adult. However, many courts have authorized either party to make an audio recording of the examination.

The examiner must be licensed in his or her profession and competent to do the examination. An examiner must be willing to prepare a comprehensive report that comports with Rule 35 and that the proponent can use to evaluate the case. You should send a letter to the examiner that confirms the engagement, outlines the problems, and focuses the examination. As soon as the examination has been scheduled, you should send letters to all other parties to confirm the arrangements and any special conditions. Parties should work together to make a Rule 35 examination as convenient as possible. If a party wrongly refuses to submit to a medical examination in spite of a court order, the court may dismiss the examinee's lawsuit, dismiss the claims involving the medical condition, or resolve the disputed medical facts against that party. A court cannot find the examinee to be in contempt of court and punish the examinee by fine or incarceration.

A proponent should request a Rule 35 examination of another party when the examinee's treating physician has obtained an inadequate or erroneous medical history, an incomplete or erroneous accident history, does not have sufficient expertise to make an authoritative determination, or both parties want to make sure there is no latent condition before entering into a final settlement. Suspected "collaboration" between a physician and patient is rare and usually a matter of exaggerating or minimizing.

Once the time and place for an examination have been established, the proponent should send a letter to the examiner confirming the arrangements. The letter should inform the examiner fully about details of the accident, the nature of all the examinee's complaints, the type of treatment received, and the treating physician's diagnoses and prognosis. It should provide a guide for taking the patient's history to make sure no critical facts are omitted. It should identify any unique problems, such as inconsistencies in the medical records, and help the examiner to focus the examination. Copies of the examinee's medical records, hospital records, and medical reports should be attached. But the examiner must base the report on the history the plaintiff gives to the examiner and the examiner's own findings, not the information supplied by the letter. The report should indicate whether the examiner believes that additional examinations are necessary.

A Rule 35 examiner must integrate the results of the examination with the examinee's past medical history, current medical history, subjective complaints, and findings. The process requires the examiner to compare the plaintiff's various statements about her or his history, symptoms, and complaints to determine whether they have been consistent and whether the plaintiff has been consistent in their reporting. The examiner must try to determine whether the subjective conditions are corroborated by objective medical findings. A Rule 35 examiner is entitled to be skeptical about the examinee's description of an accident, prior medical history, subjective complaints, and symptoms. The examiner is expected to look for inconsistencies between the symptoms, symptoms and history, and symptoms and findings. The examiner also looks for medical improbabilities, such as a claim of permanent injury where there are no objective findings. The examiner must be willing to stand by the report by testifying at trial when necessary. A proponent should select an examiner who can explain his or her findings, diagnoses, and prognosis to the jury. A proponent needs an examiner and report he or she can rely on. A report that is conservative to the point that it distorts the patient's condition or prognosis will cause the proponent to misevaluate the claim.

A Rule 35 examination may exceed the scope of the party's claim of injury because the examination also establishes a baseline concerning the plaintiff's condition. A good independent medical report should establish the outside limits of the plaintiff's claim of injury so that if new complaints develop after the examination, those new complaints cannot be attributed to the defendant. If the plaintiff were in a subsequent accident the examination will help separate the injuries and quantify any aggravation.

The examinee is entitled to a full, written report on the examination. Specifically, the report must describe the history the examiner elicited, the examiner's findings, test results, diagnosis, and medical opinions. The examinee must request the report through the proponent's attorney, not directly from the examiner. If the examiner fails or refuses to submit a report, the examinee's attorney may subpoena the examiner to appear for a deposition. A court probably would require the proponent to pay the costs the examinee incurred in taking the deposition. As an alternative, the examinee could move the court to exclude the examiner from testifying at the trial.

If an examinee demands a copy of the report of examination and receives it, the examinee becomes obligated to provide the proponent with copies of all the treating physicians' reports concerning the condition. The examinee's failure to provide the reports is grounds for precluding the treating physician(s) from testifying. The examinee's lawyer must obtain the examinee's records from the treating physician(s) for the proponent. If the treating physician charges the examinee for reproducing a report, that expense cannot be passed on to the proponent, just as the proponent cannot charge an examinee for a copy of a Rule 35 report. The examinee is under a continuing obligation to produce new reports if the examinee continues to receive treatment.

A Rule 35 examiner is considered an expert witness whose opinions must be disclosed. A party who retains an expert may be compelled under Rule 26 to reveal the substance of the expert's testimony. Rules 26 and 35 are not entirely exclusive of each other. Parties may agree among themselves to other methods of discovery to obtain medical reports, hospital records, and medical opinions.

As a paralegal, you may arrange for Rule 35 examinations. You may select the examiner; establish the criteria for the examination; negotiate the terms and conditions under which the examiner will do the examination; and negotiate with the opposing lawyers concerning the time, place, and scope of examinations. You may schedule examinations, and collect and assemble the documents the examiners need. You may prepare letters to examiners providing background information that will assist the examiner and help focus the examinations. You may prepare stipulations for the lawyers confirming the terms, conditions, and scope of examinations. Of course, sometimes a mere letter will suffice. When your litigation team represents the examinee, you may inform him or her about the results of the examination. If the client requests a copy of the report, you may handle those arrangements as well. When necessary, you can prepare motions and supporting documents to compel Rule 35 medical examinations. Or, you can prepare objections to proposed examinations and prepare supporting affidavits.

You should prepare clients to be tolerant and accepting of Rule 35 examinations. You may meet with clients to explain examination procedures and tell clients how to conduct themselves during the examinations. You should encourage clients to be forthright with examiners, and not conceal relevant history. An examinee should not exaggerate symptoms or complaints. But it is important to give the examiner the whole picture. Encourage clients to accept examinations as a necessary and positive development in the case.

In most states, a plaintiff waives her or his medical privilege when she or he commences an action to recover money damages for personal injuries. The extent of the waiver varies from state to state. At a minimum, the plaintiff's medical records and reports become discoverable.

KEY TERMS

definitive diagnosis	past medical history
diagnosis	secondary gain
good cause	SOAP
invasive testing	subjective symptoms
objective medical findings	working diagnosis

REVIEW QUESTIONS

1. Can the defendant move the court for an order requiring the plaintiff to submit to an independent examination to be conducted by a doctor of chiropractic?

2. How many independent medical examinations may a party request?

3. What information must the independent examiner include in her or his report?

4. Does a party have a right to take the deposition of the physician who conducted an independent medical examination on him or her?

5. Should you instruct your client to avoid volunteering information to the independent examiner? Why or why not?

6. Is it ethical to describe to the client what medical tests the independent examiner is likely to perform and the reasons for those tests?

7. What is the consequence of the plaintiff's request for a copy of the independent medical examiner's report?

8. Is the plaintiff required to pay for a copy of the independent medical examination report prepared by the defendant's examiner?

9. May the plaintiff's lawyer attend an independent medical examination conducted by the defendant's doctor?

10. May the plaintiff tape-record the independent medical examination that he or she is ordered to undergo?

11. What remedy does the defendant have if the plaintiff refuses to submit to an independent medical examination ordered by the court?

CASE ASSIGNMENT

You are working on Donald Smith's litigation team representing the plaintiff trustee against defendant Bradley Harper. Harper has interposed a counterclaim against the trustee to obtain money damages for his alleged personal injuries. Mr. Nordby's automobile insurance company has retained attorney Smith to defend the trustee against Harper's counterclaim. Attorney Smith believes Harper's injuries are minimal but has concluded he needs a Rule 35 medical examination. He talked with Harper's attorney and the attorney agreed. In an intraoffice memorandum, he asked you to schedule the examination with a local family practitioner, Dr. Stanley Farber, for sometime within the next four weeks. If Dr. Farber finds any significant problem, he is to recommend a specialist for a more thorough examination. Select a date for the examination. Notify attorney William Hoch, who represents defendant Harper, about the time and place. Prepare a letter to Dr. Farber outlining the problems and scope of the exam. Explain the report you will need from him and how the report will be used.

Endnotes

1. The term *medical* is used here in a broad sense. It includes all the licensed healing arts such as chiropractic, osteopathy, and therapeutic psychology.
2. An examinee does not have a general right to depose a Rule 35 examiner. The rule applies to situations where an examiner fails to write a report or the report is inadequate or incomplete. The examinee's attorney must subpoena the examiner for the deposition. A simpler solution might be for the examinee's attorney to move the court for an order precluding the examiner from testifying at trial.
3. Soft tissue injuries are injuries involving muscle strains and sprains or bruises and contusions that generally heal without problems.

 For additional resources, visit our Web site at www.paralegal.delmar.cengage.com

CHAPTER 15

INSPECTION OF PROPERTY, DOCUMENTS, AND THINGS

CHAPTER OUTLINE

Chapter Objectives

Chapter 15 describes the procedures provided by court rules for inspecting property that is in the custody of an adverse party or belongs to a person who is not a party. The procedures apply to documents, real estate, and tangible things. The chapter also discusses steps the legal team may take to protect against improper inspections.

Introduction

Parties must have equal access to the evidence; otherwise, litigation would not be fair. The truth would not be discoverable. Parties must not be able to hide evidence or even control access to it. Of course, evidence includes tangible things that tend to prove or disprove material facts. Property may contain evidence, or property may in itself be evidence. Either way, parties need access to property that is under another person's control. The property may be real estate, such as, land, structures, and fixtures, or it may be personal property. For our purposes, personal property is any tangible thing that is not real estate. Personal property includes such things as documents, business records, vehicles, instruments, recordings, even witness statements. Rule 34 provides a procedure that gives parties access to real and personal property under the control of another party. The procedure provides for inspections, photographing, measuring, testing, copying, and preserving it. The scope of the Rule is so broad that the terms "documents" and "things" are used to identify all forms of tangible property that contain evidence or are evidence. Therefore, the Rule not only applies to documents such as writings, but also to drawings, graphs, charts, photographs, audio recordings, and data compilations from which information can be obtained.

You may prepare formal inspection demands, but a demand must be signed by an attorney. You may arrange for inspections and conduct inspections on behalf of proponents. You may host inspections when the client is a respondent. You also may assist respondents to avoid inappropriate inspections and make sure that inspections are conducted properly. You may attend inspections conducted by an adverse party. You may make reports on inspections and recommendations for additional inspections. You may coordinate inspections with other discovery procedures.

Scope of Inspections

Rule 34 imposes very few limitations or conditions on inspections. It imposes a burden on all parties to accommodate each other. A proponent wants to find out what the respondent has. The proponent's interest in obtaining access to the respondent's property is obvious. A respondent, however, may have good reasons for not wanting a proponent to have access to the respondent's property. There may be matters of privacy, possible embarrassment, issues concerning relevancy, and concerns that the proponent might damage or lose the property. But then a respondent simply may want to keep opponents from having access to the evidence. When a dispute arises, a court must balance the parties' needs and concerns. Rule 34 seeks to provide that balance and keep the process inexpensive. Rule 34 gives courts broad discretion in how they resolve inspection disputes. But generally, the Rule operates with very little court involvement. Unlike a proponent who wants to obtain an independent medical examination, a proponent who wants to inspect another party's property does not have to make a motion and show good cause. Of course, to be subject to a Rule 34 inspection, property must contain evidence relevant to the litigation, or the inspection must be calculated to lead to the discovery of admissible evidence.

Rule 34 provides the means to obtain copies of a party's income tax returns when the party's income is relevant to the litigation. Even if a party does not retain copies of his or her tax returns, copies are available from the government, so the tax returns are under the party's "control." Income tax returns may be relevant to prove or disprove a party's claim for loss of income because of a personal injury or breach of a contract claim. Also, a defendant's tax returns may be relevant to a plaintiff's claim for punitive damages.

Demand for Inspection

demand for inspection A written demand served by one party on another party to schedule an inspection of any item of real or personal property that is in the control of the second party and relevant to the case.

A **demand for inspection** must be made in writing and specify a proposed time and place. It must identify the property to be inspected with "reasonable particularity." That means *clearly*. The Rule does not require that the demand use legal descriptions, serial numbers, or precise names or locations to identify the property. The demand may describe the property generically or by category. However, it must not be so broad or vague as to be a mere "fishing expedition." For example, a demand for inspection is objectionable if it merely says, "Produce for inspection and copying all the documents on which you base your claim." A demand for inspection could properly state, "Produce for inspection and copying all your payroll records for the year 2002." An attorney of record must sign the demand.

A demand for inspection must describe the manner of inspection, which includes its purpose and scope. The proponent must describe what he or she intends to do with the property during the inspection. An inspection may be as simple as looking at the property, measuring it, or photographing it. Or, an inspection might involve **destructive testing** in which part or all of the property is destroyed. If the proponent needs to make a video recording of an activity or machine working, the inspection demand should specify that a video recording will be made.

destructive testing Testing of property that causes or results in its destruction or a significant change.

The proposed time and place should be convenient for the people involved. The respondent is entitled to at least thirty days in which to respond to the demand. Consequently, a proposed inspection must not be scheduled sooner, unless the respondent agrees to an earlier date. A respondent must serve a written response within thirty days after service of the request. But if a plaintiff serves the demand with the complaint, the defendant-respondent may take up to forty-five days to serve a written response. When a proponent's demand for inspection is served by mail, add three days [Rule 6(e)].[1] A demand for inspection must be served on all parties even though it applies to property under the control of only one party.

If a proponent needs an inspection sooner and the respondent is uncooperative, the proponent may move the court for an order setting an earlier date. A motion to shorten the prescribed time period cannot be made ex parte (i.e., without notice to the other party or parties) [see Rule 6(b)]. The other parties must have an opportunity to object to any shorter period. Note that Rule 29 precludes parties from stipulating to increase the time for responding to a demand for inspection. Stipulations extending time limitations set by Rules 33, 34, and 36 may be made only with court approval. The reason for Rule 29's proscription against extending the time period is that an extension could delay other discovery procedures and the trial. Courts do not want to lose control over scheduling. Of course, parties may do almost anything they want to do to accommodate each other concerning discovery. But if cooperation breaks down, neither party may look to the court to enforce a stipulation that lengthens the time. A stipulation to shorten a time period for responding would not interfere with the court's schedule.

The time and place of an inspection should be practical and convenient for a majority of the people involved. For instance, if an inspection involves only a few documents, it should be conducted at the proponent lawyer's office or other lawyer's office. If there are only a few documents, the inspection may not even be necessary, because the respondent may be willing to send copies. But when an inspection is conducted to determine whether the opponent is hiding documents, you have to go to the source. If there are many documents to be copied, the proponent should schedule the inspection at the place where the documents are kept in the ordinary course of business. If the inspection is of a large machine, the inspection should be conducted where the machine is used or stored. If an inspection requires testing that can be done only in a laboratory, the laboratory must be designated. Timing is important. To illustrate, if the purpose is to photograph the interior of a manufacturing facility, it may be preferable to schedule the inspection after regular business hours.

If a proponent is uncertain about the existence or identity of property he or she thinks ought to be inspected, the proponent may serve interrogatories or take depositions to identify the property, its location, its owner, and custodian before making a Rule 34 demand. If a dispute develops over whether the respondent has produced the property specified in the demand, the burden lies with the proponent to persuade the court that the request duly specified or included the property in question. A demand does not have to be in any particular form. (See Exhibit 15.1.)

A demand for production of documents for inspection and copying is similar in form. See Civil Rules of Civil Procedure, Appendix of Forms, form 24.

EXHIBIT 15.1

Demand for Inspection[1]

1. See, form 24 of the Appendix of Forms of the Rules of Civil Procedure.

(COURT)

A. B., Plaintiff,

    vs.

C. D., Defendant.

Plaintiff A. B. requests defendant C. D. to respond within thirty-one (31) days to the following requests:

1. That defendant produce and permit plaintiff to inspect and to copy each of the following documents:

   [List the documents either individually or by category and describe each of them.]
   - All written statements signed or prepared or given by plaintiff.
   - All photographs to which you have access concerning the accident identified in the complaint.
   - All medical records and reports concerning plaintiff that you heretofore obtained.
   - All witness statements you have obtained or that are under your control.

[State the time, place, and manner of making the inspection and performing any related acts.]

Plaintiff proposes to inspect said documents at the defendant's attorney's office on Tuesday, July 11, 2006.

Plaintiff offers to pay the reasonable cost of reproducing which defendant selects.

2. That defendant produce and permit plaintiff to inspect and to copy, test, or sample each of the following objects:

   [List the objects either individually or by category, and describe each.]
   - Defendant's 2004 Chevrolet automobile.
   - The eyeglasses defendant was wearing at the time of the accident.

■ Defendant's automobile liability insurance policy that was in force at the time of the parties' accident.
■ Defendant's employment contract with the ABC Corporation.

3. That defendant permit plaintiff to enter [describe property to be entered] and to inspect and to photograph, test, measure, and sample [describe the portion of the real property and the objects to be inspected. A legal description is not necessary. An ordinary mailing address or full description will suffice.]

[State the time, place, and manner proposed for conducting the inspection and performing any related acts.]

Signed: [Must be signed by an attorney of record.]
Date:

Response to Demand for Inspection

A response to a demand for inspection must be in writing and signed by the respondent attorney. The respondent must state clearly whether the respondent will comply. A respondent may submit a counterproposal concerning the terms or scope of the proposed inspection [Rule 34(b)]. A counterproposal may provide conditions or limitations. It may suggest alternatives to the terms proposed in the demand. When a response proposes modifications, conditions, or limitations on an inspection, the proponent may accept or reject the counterproposal. Of course, the respondent's proposals must be stated clearly. A respondent's objections must be specific and supported by reasons. Blanket objections are inappropriate and subject the respondent to court sanctions. Rule 37(a)(2) provides, in part

> [I]f a party, in response to a request for inspection submitted under Rule 34, fails to respond that inspection will be permitted as requested or fails to permit inspection as requested, the discovering party may move for an order compelling an answer, or a designation, or an order compelling inspection in accordance with the request.

Exhibit 15.2 is a sample **written response to demand for inspection.** A respondent must produce requested documents in the form in which they are customarily kept in the respondent's business.

written response to demand for inspection A written response that must be served within thirty days of a demand for inspection. The written response must acknowledge the request and agree to the terms of inspection as expressed in the demand.

Informal Written Demand

Proponents commonly ask respondents to produce specified documents by mailing copies to the proponent. They may receive more documents than they would have selected at a formal inspection, but the savings in time may be worth the cost of

EXHIBIT 15.2

*Response to Demand
for Inspection*

(Court)

A. B., Plaintiff,

      vs.

C. D., Defendant.

    Defendant hereby responds to plaintiff's demand for inspection pursuant to Rule 34 of the Federal Rules of Civil Procedure:

1. Plaintiff's lawyer and the experts designated in the demand for inspection may enter defendant's plant at Des Moines, Iowa, for the purpose of inspecting the conveyor belt system on Thursday, October 5, 2006, between the hours of 2:00 P.M. and 5:00 P.M.
2. Plaintiff's representatives may take still pictures and motion pictures of the conveyor system in operation.
3. Plaintiff's experts may make measurements of the conveyor system and appurtenances.
4. Defendant objects to plaintiff's proposal to take sample swatches of the conveyor belt because that would seriously damage the integrity of the belt and conveyor system. Furthermore, B. F. Goodrich Company presumably has samples of the type of belt in question.
5. Defendant does not have any plans or specifications for the installation of the conveyor system. Therefore, defendant will not produce any plans or specifications at the scheduled inspection.
6. The only report of the accident in question was made for the defendant's liability insurer. The report was not made in the ordinary course of the defendant's business. It was made for the insurer in anticipation of litigation. The report is privileged and work product. It is not subject to discovery.

[Date]

Attorney for Defendant
/s/ _____
Address

some extra copies. If a respondent believes there are too many documents to copy, he or she should notify the proponent so they can make the discovery more focused. Proponents ordinarily pay the reasonable cost of having copies made. But before making the copies, the parties should be sure they have a meeting of minds concerning the probable cost. The respondent may state in his or her response the terms for making copies. Of course, paralegals may sign letters concerning informal arrangements.

Although many inspections are conducted informally, an informal approach is potentially problematic. Suppose you have an informal agreement that the opponent will provide "all the documents," and when the case comes to trial, it appears the opponent has not produced critical documents. What can your litigation team do? If you had conducted an inspection pursuant to Rule 34, you would be in a good position to move the court for an order requiring the opponent to produce the missing documents, monetary sanctions, and even a mistrial. You merely have to show that the inspection demand was clear and included the documents in question. But an informal arrangement gives the court less with which to work. All you can show is that you made a request for the documents in question, that the opposing party agreed to produce them, and a good faith response required production. The court may or may not be able to help your team. Ordinarily, a letter signed by the opponent is a sufficient commitment. The opposition's original production of some documents is strong evidence that there was an agreement and your team relied on it, so the real problem is to convince the court that the agreement included the documents or things in question.

You should never rely on an oral agreement concerning discovery. Rule 29 is specific that any modification of the discovery procedures must be in writing. If a party makes an oral agreement concerning discovery matters, she or he must send a signed letter confirming it as soon as possible. Make sure that stipulations and letters you prepare or receive concerning discovery expressly provide that they contain the entire agreement.

Objecting to an Inspection Demand

Objections to an inspection must be specific and supported by reasons. If the time or place of a proposed inspection is a problem, say so. If the scope of the examination is too burdensome, say so. Objections are not phrased as technical legal objections of the kind used to exclude evidence. An objection should identify and describe the problem. Explain why it is a problem. An objection should indicate what can be changed to make the inspection acceptable. Offer alternatives that would resolve the problem and still meet the proponent's legitimate needs, if you can. An objection must be served within thirty days after service of the demand. If the demand was served by mail, add three days from the date of mailing. If the demand is served with the summons and complaint, the defendant has forty-five days in which to serve objections. A proponent cannot require an inspection before the written response is due.

A respondent should decide, as soon as possible, whether the proposed inspection is acceptable and advise the proponent promptly. The thirty day time period is the outside limit. You may and should respond sooner when you can. The proponent will be preparing for the inspection. If you delay your objection, you may waste the proponent's time and effort. That may make your opponent angry. You never want to make an opponent angry, because then he or she works harder and meaner. The parties should extend themselves to be cooperative in arranging for inspections and conducting them. One thing courts always consider when they rule on discovery motions is whether the parties have been diligent and acted in good faith. Parties who are diligent and act in good faith are seldom penalized and seldom have to pay court costs.

Limitations on Inspections

A party may not use Rule 34 to compel another party to prepare a document that does not already exist. For example, the plaintiff could not use the rule to compel the defendant to make a summary of the defendant's business records. The defendant may offer to make and provide a summary of the records, however, and the plaintiff may accept the summary instead of inspecting voluminous records.

A party may not use Rule 34 to obtain documents that are privileged or a party's work product as defined by Rule 26(b)(3). Suppose a plaintiff brought an action to recover money damages for personal injuries, and the plaintiff's lawyer has obtained a copy of the plaintiff's hospital records. Could the defendant require the plaintiff to produce those copies for inspection and copying? Yes. The law in most states is that the plaintiff waives his or her medical privilege to records by commencing a personal injury action. A state's law concerning waiver of medical privilege is applied by the federal courts in that state. The fact that the party (lawyer) only has copies of the records is immaterial. Those copies are under the plaintiff's control and subject to inspection. The hospital records are not the plaintiff's work product.

If a paralegal takes a signed statement from an independent witness concerning the client's accident, the statement qualifies as attorney work product, because it was prepared in anticipation of litigation. Nevertheless, the witness has a right to obtain a copy of her or his own statement. But another party does not have a right, under Rule 26 or 34, to obtain a copy of the statement from the party who prepared it. If the witness obtains a copy, the witness could allow other people to see and copy the statement. Some states require parties to produce witness statements on demand. Again, the federal courts will follow the applicable state rule.

Inspection Procedure

A proponent usually has lots of preparations to make for an inspection, especially if an expert is going to assist. A proponent may have to make arrangements with expensive experts who will do the actual testing or photographing. The proponent should allow sufficient time between the date on which the written response is due and the date of the proposed inspection to make alternative plans. Suppose a proponent has demanded an inspection of a complex machine and needs the help of engineers to do the inspection. If the proponent receives the respondent's objection on the thirtieth day, he will need additional time to make other arrangements with the engineers. You should anticipate these kinds of problems by planning ahead.

When parties cannot agree on a mutually convenient time and place for the inspection or cannot agree on the manner in which the inspection should be conducted, the proponent may move the court for an order that specifies when, where, and how the proponent may conduct the inspection. The proponent has the onus of making the motion. If the court concludes that either party has acted unreasonably, the court may impose sanctions as provided by Rule 37. When the opponent serves a demand for inspection that arbitrarily designates a time and place for the inspection, a party may reply that the designated time is not convenient and suggest other arrangements. The party could save time and inconvenience by telephoning the lawyer for the opponent and explaining her or his intention to permit an inspection and work out an inspection program that the opponent subsequently can confirm in a new demand for inspection or letter. Or the party's written response may set forth the new terms of the inspection. Once an agreement has been reached on the particulars, either party may confirm the agreement by letter, but the letter must clearly specify all the terms and conditions of the inspection. Lawyers recognize that other discovery efforts may be delayed until the inspection is completed. Therefore, parties usually try to hasten inspections, rather than delay them.

Subpoena Duces Tecum

A subpoena duces tecum is an alternative method of obtaining access to property for inspections, copying, and photographing. Subpoenas duces tecum may be served on parties and nonparties. Neither procedure preempts the other. Rule 45(a) provides

> (1) Every subpoena shall
>
> . . .
>
> (C) command each person to whom it is directed to attend and give testimony or to produce and permit inspection and copying of designated books, documents or tangible things in the possession, custody or control of that person, or to permit inspection of premises, at a time and place therein specified;
>
> . . .
>
> A command to produce evidence or to permit inspection may be joined with a command to appear at trial or hearing or at deposition, or may be issued separately.

A subpoena duces tecum must be issued by a court that has jurisdiction over the custodian. A subpoena duces tecum must provide the same kind of information as a written demand for inspection. It must be served on the person who has custody of the property. It must describe the terms and scope of the proposed inspection. Because all other parties have a right to attend the inspection or the custodian's deposition, notice must be sent to all parties.

A proponent must serve a subpoena duces tecum in the manner provided by Rule 45. A court cannot authorize destructive testing of a nonparty's property. A court cannot order a nonparty to do something to his or her property, such as move it to another location for the convenience of the parties. A subpoena duces tecum merely provides access to the property. After obtaining access, a proponent may copy, photograph, and measure property. If the proponent schedules the nonparty's deposition to be taken at the same time, the proponent may ask questions about the property.

There are times when you may find it more advantageous to use subpoenas than a Rule 34 demand for inspection. Rule 34 does not apply to nonparties. If the property to be inspected or copied is under the control of a nonparty, you must use a subpoena to gain access. When you do not have enough time in which to make a Rule 34 demand, use a subpoena to require a party to provide access to property. When you want to take the custodian's oral deposition to ask the custodian about the property, use a subpoena. Even when the inspection of documents is merely secondary to taking a party's deposition, you may use a subpoena to require the party to produce the documents at the deposition.

Conducting Inspections

The generality of Rule 34 encourages parties to agree on inspection methods that meet the parties' needs and are reasonably convenient. Conducting an inspection is much like conducting an investigation. An inspection is not recorded in the way that an oral deposition is recorded. An inspection is more like a meeting, not even a conference.

Let us begin with an inspection of business records. When a large number of documents are involved, it is customary to conduct the inspection at the place where the documents are kept. Respondents must produce business records in the same form and condition as when used in the respondent's business. Rule 34 prevents parties from taking documents out of context. If taken out of context, documents may be difficult to understand and give the proponent a distorted picture of the facts. You and your assistants must carefully identify each item that the respondent produces pursuant to the demand. You ought to make note of items that you *expected* to be produced but that were not. You may discuss any apparent omission with the custodian-respondent. Presumably, you have already agreed on who will do the copying and the costs for copying. But make sure there is agreement concerning *when* the copies will be ready for you. As you go through the documents you should have some method of identifying which documents you want copied and how many copies of each. Ordinarily, respondents arrange to make duplicates for other parties so the respondents do not lose custody of the property. If you become involved in complex litigation, there can be hundreds of thousands or even millions of documents to manage. When the cost is justified, document-management systems are an essential part of complex litigation. Such systems allow each document to be scanned and coded. This allows for computerized searching on a desktop. The applications are endless. For example, you can use a laptop to access all documents relevant for preparing a particular witness to give deposition (or trial) testimony. This not only makes it convenient to prepare, it helps assure that the witness is ready to respond to questions on all key matters. Many systems allow the viewer to take personal notes on the document image that do no appear when the document is printed. This helps the lawyer while he or she is examining a witness about the document. These systems are easy to learn, and mastering them can be one of the more valuable assets a paralegal can bring to a complex-litigation team.

When you demand an inspection of a thing, such as a vehicle, machine, or medical instrument, you must determine in advance whether you need to observe it in use. If so, that should be made a "condition" of the inspection. Make sure you are inspecting the thing-in-question, or confirm it is one like the thing-in-question. Inquire about the availability of instruction manuals, owner's manuals, and recall notices. Typically, you will take photographs, make measurements and comparisons as discussed in Chapter 9.

Duplicate photographs can be made from negatives or from the original photographs. The party who requests copies usually pays the cost of duplicates. Film processors should always be cautioned that the photographs are evidence to be used in court, and they must protect the photos against loss or damage. Sometimes *photocopies* of photographs suffice, especially if the original photographs are available for comparison.

Sometimes the proponent needs to do destructive testing. For example, a proponent might need to enter a building and take concrete borings or samples of steel from the superstructure. Unless these invasive procedures would cause some significant harm to the structure, a court would require the respondent to allow the entry and testing. Suppose a case involves an airplane crash and there is reason to believe the crash was caused by metal fatigue. The proponent may need a piece of the metal to test in the laboratory; the piece cannot be returned in its pretested condition, and the test can be done only once. The respondent may resist testing or insist on doing the test or impose some limitations on testing. Sometimes only a court can resolve these disagreements.

You may wonder how destructive testing can be fair to all the parties? Won't the party who conducted the test always have the advantage? Over the years, some creative solutions have been devised. For instance, a court may order the parties to choose one or more "experts" who can document the property's appearance and condition before the test. The court may order the parties to agree on an expert to do the destructive test, so that all parties are confident about the validity of the test. If the parties cannot agree on an expert, the court has the power to appoint an expert to conduct the test, and each party may have his or her own expert observe the test. In addition, the court may allow the parties to make video recordings of the test while it is being conducted, including commentary.

The problem is most difficult when the proposed tests requires total destruction of the property. For example, suppose a controversy centers on the flammability of an article of clothing, and only a few small pieces of the clothing remain. The tests will destroy the remaining fragments. In all probability, all parties need the same test. The usual and best solution is to have the parties' experts agree on a testing procedure in which everyone participates. A paralegal may videotape the procedure and test results. If the parties cannot agree on how the tests should be performed, the court may appoint an expert to do the tests in the manner preferred by him or her. A judge should try to get the parties to agree on the selection of the expert, but if the parties cannot agree, the court has the power to appoint an expert without their agreement (see Rule 706 of the Federal Rules of Evidence).

TECHNOLOGY NOTES

You should schedule inspections so that you can make whatever photocopies are needed. You can copy documents directly into your computer by using an optical scanner. However, you must take time to carefully check the computer's interpretation against the original while you have it available.

SUMMARY

Parties must have equal access to all the evidence to prepare for trial, including the tangible evidence that is in an opposing party's custody or control. Rule 34 gives every party the right to examine any property under the control of an adverse party, whether the property is real estate; personal property; documents; or a thing, such as a machine or instrumentality. The right to inspect includes a right to measure, test, photograph, and make copies. Even destructive tests may be warranted. Property is subject to inspection whether it is relevant evidence or contains evidence or the inspection may lead to the discovery of admissible evidence. Rule 34 applies only to property that is under the control of another party. It cannot be used to obtain access to property that is under the control of a nonparty.

To initiate an inspection, a party must serve a written demand for inspection. A court order is not necessary unless the parties have a disagreement about the parameters or conditions of the inspection. The demand must clearly identify the property, state the time and place of the proposed inspection, and describe the manner in which the inspection will be conducted. The respondent has thirty days in which to serve a written response to the demand for inspection. The response must say that the inspection is permitted, as requested, except to the extent the respondent makes specific objections. Each objection must be supported by a stated reason. If the inspection must be made sooner than Rule 34 permits, the proponent may move the court for an order accelerating the time period. The motion may not be made ex parte (without notice to the parties).

If the respondent objects to an inspection or part of a proposed inspection, the burden is on the proponent to move the court to compel the inspection. Rule 34 cannot be used to obtain documents that are privileged. Rule 34 cannot be used to force another party to make charts or summaries or compilations or photographs. The party whose property is inspected has a right to observe the inspection. The sanctions provided by Rule 37 apply to inspection abuses.

KEY TERMS

demand for inspection
destructive testing

written response to demand for
   inspection

REVIEW QUESTIONS

1. For what purposes may a party demand the right to inspect real estate that is under the control of another party?

2. What determines the place of the inspection?

3. What information must be contained in a demand for inspection?

4. Why must the demand for inspection be in writing?

5. When can you use a subpoena duces tecum to obtain access to real estate in order to photograph the property?

6. When might you choose to subpoena a party's records rather than use a written demand for inspection?

7. What is one good reason why a proposed inspection should not go forward at the time and place scheduled in the inspection demand?

8. What right does a respondent have to the results of the proponent's inspection of the respondent's property?

9. What action may a respondent take to a demand for inspection of documents that the respondent would have to create from other documents that do exist?

10. How should the respondent answer a written request for inspection if the respondent does not have the specified property but knows where the property is?

CASE ASSIGNMENT

You are a member of Donald Smith's litigation team representing the plaintiff-trustee. The team is concerned that defendant Harper's hand controls on the pickup truck may have had something to do with how and why the accident occurred. The team wants to see whether they were properly installed and whether they operate properly. Attorney Smith has already talked with attorney Hoch about having an inspection, and Hoch appears agreeable. He also contacted an expert in the field, Duane Everett, to assist with the inspection. Prepare an inspection demand specifying a general inspection of the pickup and its hand controls. Schedule the examination to be conducted at Harper's address at 10:00 A.M. forty days from now. Prepare a letter to Mr. Everett informing him about the time, place, and purpose of the inspection. Be sure to ask if he needs any special preparation or input from you before the inspection.

Endnote

1. Always remember that when service is by mail you add three days to the triggering event. In this instance, the written response would be due thirty-three days after the demand was mailed. You do not count the day of mailing. You do not count from the day on which the respondent received the demand. You know the date of mailing because the person who mailed the demand must provide an affidavit of service.

For additional resources, visit our Web site at www.paralegal.delmar.cengage.com

CHAPTER **16**

REQUESTS FOR ADMISSIONS

CHAPTER OUTLINE

Chapter Objectives

Chapter 16 explains when and how a party may conclusively establish a fact and/or that a document is genuine by serving a request for admissions on an adverse party. It also makes suggestions for dealing with improper requests for admissions. The emphasis is on the paralegal's role in dealing with requests for admissions.

Introduction

In civil litigation, we tend to focus on areas of disagreement. Pleadings are designed to identify the disagreements and frame the issues. Although defendants are supposed to admit all of the allegations in a complaint that are true, often defendants do not have sufficient information to make all the appropriate admissions before the answers are due. But as the parties investigate and conduct discovery, they may find they agree on many aspects of the case. Once parties determine which facts are undisputed, they can focus on the real issues. But it is not enough to have an opponent acknowledge a material fact. To be useful, the fact must be established. To that end, Rule 36 provides a means for parties to conclusively establish facts. A party may serve **requests for admissions** on another party. The respondent's admissions establish the admitted matters for all purposes of the case. Once the admission is made, it becomes conclusive and may be withdrawn only with the court's permission. Whereas, a respondent may contradict[1] his or her interrogatory answers at trial, a respondent cannot contradict a Rule 36 admission.

While gathering evidence and preparing for trial, you may identify subjects that would be appropriate for requests for admissions. You may prepare requests for admissions, draft responses to requests, and prepare objections to requests. But the litigation team attorney must sign them. Many lawyers and courts perceive requests for admissions as an aspect of discovery. They are not discovery. You should know that a request is true and accurate before you serve it on another party. Some courts preclude parties from serving requests for admissions after discovery is closed, though that is the ideal time to determine what facts and evidence should be admitted.

> **request for admissions** A party's formal written demand to another party to admit the existence of a particular fact or the genuineness of a particular document (see Rule 36).

Scope of Requests for Admissions

A proponent may request admission of any fact, opinion, or document that *might* be admissible as evidence at the time of trial. In other words, there is no requirement that the fact or opinion be, on its face, admissible as evidence. The parameters for requests for admissions are succinctly stated in Rule 36:

> A party may serve upon any other party a written request for the admission, for purposes of the pending action only, of the truth of any matters within the scope of Rule 26(b)(1) set forth in the request that relate to statements or opinions of fact or of the application of law to fact including the genuineness of any documents described in the request. Copies of documents shall be served with the request unless they have been or are otherwise furnished or made available for inspection and copying.

A proponent may serve a request for admission even though she or he knows the respondent strongly disagrees with the request. The request places an onus on the respondent to verify her or his position. If a respondent wrongly denies the request, he or she may be required to pay costs the proponent incurs to prove the fact. The good faith test simply requires the proponent to know that the fact is true, not that the respondent knows it is true.

Clearly, any material fact is within the scope of Rule 36. The other areas in which Rule 36 operates need some explanations. A respondent's admission that a document is "**genuine**" is an admission that it is what it purports to be. If the respondent admits the document is genuine, the proponent may use the document at trial without providing further foundation. However, the document might be subject to exclusion on other grounds. A request may concern the application of law to specified facts. For example, a buyer of a product could ask the seller to admit that (1) the seller "sold" the product to the buyer; (2) the transaction was not a lease; (3) the seller provided the attached warranty document; (4) the document is genuine; (5) the document is a warranty as defined by the State's Uniform Commercial Code; and (6) the parties' rights and obligations are subject to the provisions

> **genuine** Actually being what it purports to be, as in the case of a document.

of the Uniform Commercial Code. All but item 3 involve the application of law to facts. This is important because parties often disagree about what law applies, what the law is, and how the law applies.

There is no limit on the number of requests that may be served. A proponent must give the respondent at least thirty days after service in which to respond to requests for admissions.[2] A proponent may designate a longer period, but not shorter. Parties may stipulate to a shorter period, but the agreement must be in writing. For good cause shown, a court may shorten the period to less than thirty days. If the proponent subsequently grants additional time in which to respond, the proponent must confirm the extension in writing. The time period is critical, because if the respondent does not serve the response or an objection within the allotted time, the requests are deemed admitted. A request for admissions must be served on all parties even though only the respondent party is asked to make admissions.

Facts

When a proponent wants a respondent to admit several related facts, the proponent should state each fact separately. Separation makes each request clear and difficult to avoid. Suppose the plaintiff alleges that the defendant taxicab company's taxicab struck the plaintiff and then left the scene. Suppose a witness identified the taxicab by its color and number. Suppose the driver of the taxicab that evening was John Smith, and he has left the state. The taxicab company denies that its taxicab was involved in the accident. The plaintiff could serve the following requests for admissions to strengthen her case.

> Please admit the defendant owns a taxicab that uses the identification number 222 painted on it.
> Please admit the defendant's taxicab, number 222, is painted yellow with black trim.
> Please admit the defendant's taxicab, 222, was in service on [date].
> Please admit defendant entrusted taxicab 222 to John Smith from 4:00 p.m. until 12:00 midnight on [date].
> Please admit the intersection of Fourth Street and Third Avenue is located within John Smith's operating territory.
> Please admit on or about [date], the defendant had the right, front fender of taxicab 222 replaced or repaired.
> Please admit the attached photograph fairly depicts taxicab 222 as it appeared immediately before the right, front fender was repaired.
> Please admit John Smith is no longer employed by the defendant.
> Please admit you do not know where John Smith currently resides.
> Please admit John Smith terminated his employment with the defendant on [date].
> Please admit that John Smith was employed by defendant on [the date of the accident].
> Please admit that defendant has not interviewed John Smith concerning plaintiff's claim that he was driving the taxicab that struck plaintiff.

The facts raised in these requests for admissions may have been discovered by taking the deposition of the company's employees, such as the dispatcher, payroll supervisor, and service supervisor. But it would be easier to prove the facts by simply reading the defendant's admissions to the jury than it would be to bring all the defendant's employees into court to testify. The requests will be useful in developing the case though the admissions do not, in themselves, establish the plaintiff's case against the taxicab company. Each fact is material and important to showing that the defendant's taxicab could have been involved in the accident.

On occasion a party may testify in a deposition in one case to facts that are adverse to that party in a second case. The party deponent may be asked in requests for admissions to admit that she or he made the statements in the prior case and that the statements were true. The following examples of requests for admissions relate to specific facts of various kinds:

1. Please admit that defendant did not stop before entering the intersection in question.

   [This request might be prompted by a notation in a police accident report that the defendant admitted to the investigating officer that she did not stop for the stop sign. The admission to the officer is evidence of the defendant's fault but is not conclusive on the fact. Obtaining the admission pursuant to a request makes the violation indisputable. Perhaps a follow-up request should be used, as in request 2.]

2. Please admit that defendant stated to Officer Burt Jones that defendant did not stop for the stop sign in question.

   [This request involves the same subject matter but a different fact, that is, the fact of a conversation. The defendant's admission that the conversation took place is not an admission that the stop sign violation occurred.]

3. Please admit that defendant was acting in the course and scope of her employment for the ABC Corporation at the time and place of the accident described in plaintiff's complaint.

   [The existence of an agency relationship is a common fact issue. An employer (principal) is legally responsible for an agent's torts committed in the course and scope of the agent's employment. The matter of agency may be a mixed question of law and fact.]

4. Please admit that defendant delivered four tons of wheat to plaintiff on September 5, 2006.

   [Though the request is a single, simple sentence, it contains a request for admission of five separate facts. Each fact is underlined. If the controversy centers only around the value of the wheat delivered, the plaintiff may be able to admit all five of the facts without any difficulty. But if a dispute exists over how many tons were delivered, all the facts but the quantity should be admitted by the plaintiff. This same request could be directed by the plaintiff to the defendant to establish that the defendant delivered less wheat than was contracted to deliver.]

5. Please admit plaintiff was not wearing her eyeglasses at the time of the accident described in the complaint.

6. Please admit the accident referred to in the complaint occurred at 6:04 P.M.

7. Please admit defendant executed the signature that appears on the attached promissory note (copy).

8. Please admit plaintiff was familiar with the stairway on which she fell.
   [A respondent might quarrel with the word "familiar." It is a conclusion. The request would be better if it asked the respondent to admit he used the stairway ten times or more before the accident. Then the inference of familiarity follows.]

9. Please admit that on [date] defendant received written notice of a defect in the pipe in question.

10. Please admit that the sidewalk on which plaintiff fell was
    a. four feet wide
    b. made of cement
    c. dry
    d. used by plaintiff at least three times a month for one year before plaintiff's alleged accident

11. Please admit that defendant negligently caused the accident described in the complaint.
    [Although negligence and causation are issues of fact, they are also the ultimate questions of fact, which establish a defendant's legal liability. If a defendant is constrained to admit that he was negligent and that his negligence caused the accident or injury, he is one step away from admitting liability. Requests for admissions may relate to ultimate questions of fact.]

12. Please admit that defendant breached the contract described in plaintiff's complaint.
    [Breach of the parties' contract is another ultimate fact issue. If the defendant is constrained to admit breaching the contract, she still may not be liable to the plaintiff if she can prove some affirmative defense.]

Statements

The reference in Rule 36 to "statements" is not a reference to recorded or signed witness statements. Instead, it concerns utterances and remarks made by someone orally or in writing. A common example is a party's comment at an accident scene that he or she was not injured. In another example, a party in an automobile accident may have exclaimed, "It's all my fault! I didn't see you coming!" The party may be asked to admit he or she made those statements at the accident scene. Requests for admissions could be phrased in the following ways:

Please admit you spoke to the defendant at the accident scene.
Please admit you stated to the defendant that the accident was your fault.
Please admit you made the statement, "It's all my fault."
Please admit you stated to the defendant that you did not see the defendant's car coming.
Please admit you stated to the defendant, "I didn't see you coming."
Please admit you told the investigating police officer that your speed was forty miles per hour.

Note, in any of these forms, the request only requires the party to admit that he or she made the statement. The party may admit having made the statement, but at trial deny that the statement was true. Consequently, there should be a follow-up request, such as, "Please admit that your statement was true." If the respondent denies the statement was true, you may ask for the respondent's explanation by serving an interrogatory.

Whenever a proponent believes a respondent should admit particular facts but suspects the respondent may refuse, the proponent may follow each request for admission with interrogatories that ask "discovery" type questions. For example, a request for admissions could be framed, "Please admit that you are the owner of the vehicle bearing state license plate number XYZ-333." The interrogatory that complements the requests could be, "If you deny the foregoing request for admission, state the name and address of the person you claim is the owner of said vehicle." This is another example of using the discovery tools to complement each other.

Documents

Requests for admissions may relate to the genuineness of documents. The kinds of documents that regularly are made the subject of requests for admissions include contracts, lease agreements, bank checks, legal notices, business letters, records of accounts, warranties, even recorded witness statements. Rule 36 does not define "genuine," but there is not much disagreement about its meaning. A document is genuine if it is what it purports to be. By admitting a document is genuine a respondent admits the document exists and that it was prepared on the date shown. The signatures were made by the persons who purported to sign the document. If a document is genuine, it is not a forgery or an imitation. It is not bogus. Usually, it is obvious from the face of a document what it is. After genuineness is admitted, the proponent may request admissions concerning collateral facts such as the date of execution, place of execution, date of performance, authority of signatories, and the exchange of legal consideration.

But if the proponent asks the respondent to admit that a witness statement is genuine, the respondent's admission establishes only that the witness statement was made, dated, and signed as appears on the document, not that the respondent is committed to the truth of the contents of the statement. If the proponent wants the respondent to admit facts contained in the statement, the proponent must submit additional requests concerning those facts.

A proponent may ask a respondent to admit the genuineness of documents possessed by either the proponent or the respondent. If the proponent has possession, the proponent must "furnish" the document to the respondent by delivering it or at least making it available for inspection. A strict reading of Rule 36 places the burden on the proponent to provide the original to the respondent. In practice, however, the procedure is to attach a good, clear photocopy of the document in question to the request and ask the respondent to admit that the document represented by the photocopy is genuine. For example, if the proponent wants the respondent to admit that a certain bank check was prepared, signed, endorsed, and negotiated as those facts appear on the face of the check, the proponent may attach to the request for admissions a clear photocopy of the check and incorporate the photocopy by reference. Proponents commonly ask respondents to admit that a photocopy attached to the request is a true and correct copy of the original; however, that should not be necessary. If any question is raised about the accuracy of the photocopy, the proponent has the obligation to produce the original for inspection—unless the respondent has the original. Although the Rules long provided that the original copy of the request for admissions (and all forms of written discovery, for that matter) must be filed with the clerk of court, the oppressive volume of materials filed with the clerk led to the current Rule, which prohibits filing such materials until they are actually used in the action.

When a party admits that a document is genuine, he or she does not thereby admit that it is also admissible in evidence. For example, a defendant may admit that a photograph of the plaintiff's decedent at the accident scene is genuine and accurately shows his mutilated body. However, the photograph is still subject to the objection that it is inflammatory, and, therefore, its prejudicial effect outweighs its probative value. Or, a document that is admittedly genuine nevertheless may be excluded from evidence because it contains statements that are hearsay.

Requests for admissions may be used to establish the necessary foundation for a document. By way of illustration, the following requests may be directed to a plaintiff in a tort action where the defendant is claiming that the plaintiff previously executed a release:

1. Please admit that the attached "release of all claims" is genuine.
2. Please admit that plaintiff signed the attached release on the date specified therein.
3. Please admit that plaintiff received the money described in the release as the consideration.
4. Please admit that the monies plaintiff received in exchange for the release have not been tendered or returned to defendant.

The plaintiff's admissions to these requests should facilitate the defendant's use of the release at trial. The plaintiff still could contend the release was obtained by fraud or duress.

Once a document is shown to be genuine, the document probably will speak for itself. In other words, the contents of the document will provide the relevant information and can be read to the jury or by the jury. Nevertheless, a party should consider asking additional requests for admissions that provide foundation for the document to be received into evidence. For example, suppose a party has a ten-page hospital record he or she wants to put into evidence but does not want to incur the expense of having a hospital administrator come to the trial to provide the foundation for the record. The party may request the respondent to admit that the hospital record is genuine; that the ten pages attached to the request are true and correct copies of the originals; that if the proper person were called to testify, that person would testify that the record was prepared and kept in the ordinary course of the hospital's business; and that the record was prepared and maintained for the purpose of providing medical care and treatment to the proponent. The proponent might even ask the respondent, the defendant in this instance, to admit that the amount of the hospital's charges for the proponent's treatment was fair and reasonable. The treating physicians can testify that the hospital care was necessary as a result of the accident in question.

Suppose the lawsuit centers around a counterfeit document and both parties know the document is counterfeit, but a dispute exists over who prepared the document and who signed it. The concept of genuineness would be difficult to use in this situation. Neither party would ask the other to admit that the document is what it purports to be. Nevertheless, a proponent may request the respondent to admit that a copy is a true copy of the counterfeit document; that the document in question is a counterfeit; that the opponent has possession of the original counterfeit document; and that the opponent knows (or does not know) who actually signed the counterfeit document.

Opinions

Requests for admissions may relate to opinions of laypersons and experts. Requests for admissions of opinions are useful when the proponent finds some admissions in the respondent's expert's reports that tend to favor the proponent. Each opinion must be clearly stated in a separate request so that the respondent knows exactly the scope and extent of each admission. The proponent establishes those favorable opinions by obtaining the respondent's admission. Again, there are two benefits: The proponent does not have to spend time and money proving those particular opinions, and the opinions become irrefutable. The opinions are taken out of controversy.

The following examples of requests for admissions relate to various kinds of opinions that could be relevant and admissible at trial:

1. Please admit that when you observed defendant at the scene of the accident in question, you observed that defendant was *not* intoxicated.
   [The request could be phrased to establish the defendant was intoxicated. Either way, the matter of sobriety is an opinion and subject to admission.]
2. Please admit that at the time plaintiff fell on defendants' sidewalk, the sidewalk had ice on it.
3. Please admit that at the time plaintiff fell on defendants' sidewalk the ice on it made it slippery.
   [The presence of ice is a simple fact. "Slippery" is an opinion.]
4. Please admit that Dr. Sawra Karimi's charges in the amount of $500 for services to plaintiff were reasonable.
   [This type of request frequently is used by plaintiffs in personal injury actions, especially if the lawyer does not intend to have the physician or hospital administrator testify. However, if the plaintiff refuses to permit the defendant's lawyer to talk with the physician, the defendant probably will not have the necessary information available to confirm the truth of the request. The value of the physician's services depends on many factors, including the physician's experience, skill, and time spent. Such information usually is not available in the records. Therefore, unless the plaintiff permits the defendant to interview the attending physician, the defendant may deny the request on the basis that she or he lacks sufficient information on which to make the admission.]
5. Please admit that the lumber delivered by defendant to plaintiff according to the contract in question complied with the specified grades and qualities.
   [The grade or character of products is often a matter of opinion.]
6. Please admit that the fair market value of plaintiff's automobile before the accident was $4,000.
   [The market value of personal property is usually a matter of opinion, unless the property is the kind that has a regular market, such as stock that is traded on a stock exchange.]

7. Please admit that the ignition point for natural gas is 3,300 degrees.
    [The ignition point of any material is a scientific fact, but the fact ordinarily is proved through expert opinion testimony. It is doubtful that a court would take judicial notice of such a scientific fact. A court would probably require the parties to present evidence to prove the fact, absent a stipulation or Rule 36 admission.]
8. Please admit that rust caused the steel bar joists to fail.
    [The cause of the joists' failure is a matter of fact. However, the fact would have to be proved by expert opinion testimony, unless the court determined a layperson could see that the steel joists were weakened by rust and gave way because of the weakened condition.]

Application of Law to Facts

When a request for admissions concerns the application of law to certain facts, the court takes judicial notice of the admission. The admission becomes part of the **law of the case.** That means the parties have agreed it is a controlling rule of law and determines their legal rights and obligations in this case. They have accepted it as the applicable rule, and it is controlling law even if they happen to be wrong. The same consequence flows when parties try a case and an error occurs to which no one objects. The following examples of requests for admissions involve the application of law to facts:

law of the case   The law according to which the parties tried their case without objection, so that the rules of law are considered controlling even though they might not be correct.

1. Please admit that at the time Joseph Linder signed the contract he was acting within the course and scope of his agency for plaintiff.
    [The existence of an agency and the scope of the agency depend on the existence of a legal relationship that may be created in various ways. The ultimate determination of whether the relationship exists depends on applying law to a set of facts.]
2. Please admit that defendant was negligent in the operation of his airplane.
    [The admission may be directed to the ultimate question of fact, which requires the application of law to a collage of facts. If the admission is made and negligence is thereby established, the issues of causation and damages still need to be established.]
3. Please admit that on October 1, 2006, plaintiff was an employee of defendant who is entitled to benefits under the terms of defendant's contract with the teacher's union dated August 1, 2006.
4. Please admit that at the time plaintiff was discharged from her employment by defendant, she was a tenured teacher within the meaning of the contract referred to in the complaint.
    [If certain conditions must be proved to establish tenure, the admission may save considerable time and effort proving those conditions.]
5. Please admit that defendant's failure to stop for the stop sign was a proximate cause of the automobile accident in question.
    [Proximate cause is probably the most subjective legal conclusion in tort law. Appellate courts are reluctant to hold, as a matter of law, that any set of facts necessarily establishes that an alleged cause is a proximate cause of an accident.]

Effect of Rule 36 Admissions

A deponent may admit a fact in answers to interrogatories or in a deposition. However, the deponent subsequently may deny or qualify the admission when testifying at trial. The only consequence for the deponent is that the change may be impeaching. Impeachment affects the believability of the witness or the witness's evidence. A respondent's admission that a specified fact or opinion is true, however, makes that fact or opinion conclusive for purposes of the case. The respondent is not allowed to refute or change it. It cannot be explained away, assuming the request and the admission were drafted clearly. For example, in a personal injury case a defendant could ask the plaintiff to admit that the plaintiff did not sustain any loss of income as a result of the accident. The plaintiff's admission precludes the plaintiff from offering evidence of lost income. Therefore, the defendant does not have to prepare against a loss-of-income claim. Or an admission may replace the need for evidence at trial. For example, a plaintiff could request a defendant to admit that the cost of the plaintiff's medical expenses ($500) is reasonable. If the defendant admits the request, the plaintiff can simply read the admission to the jury and into the record instead of offering evidence to prove the fact. The jury cannot reject admissions and stipulations. That is a good reason for using Rule 36 requests as often as possible.

Though the Rules do not specifically say so, an admission is not binding on a party who did not propound the request or was not required to respond to the request. Therefore, if a request for admissions is served by the plaintiff on one defendant and admitted by that defendant, the admission does not affect any other defendant.

A respondent is under a duty to correct a response that was true when given but subsequently became incorrect. What if the respondent denied a fact is true but subsequently discovered the fact to be true? Does the respondent have a duty to correct the response? Yes. What if a party erroneously makes an admission? Does it make any difference whether the error was technical or inadvertent or now clearly demonstrable or always subject to some doubt? Yes.

The purpose of Rule 36 admissions would be thwarted if a party easily could avoid an admission once it had been made. Consequently, Rule 36 prevents a respondent from withdrawing or changing an admission, unless the respondent can obtain the proponent's agreement or a court order allowing the change. The respondent must show the court good cause for allowing a withdrawal or change. As part of the good-cause requirement, the respondent must show that the withdrawal or amendment will not cause **unfair prejudice** to the proponent. A party is unfairly prejudiced if the party has relied on the admission and the evidence is no longer available to prove or disprove the fact that was admitted. A proponent cannot be unfairly prejudiced if the respondent can show to a certainty that the admission is wrong! As part of the good-cause showing, the respondent should show that the admission is not only wrong, but was made inadvertently and because of excusable neglect. In this regard, a respondent is in a much better position to obtain relief from the court if the admission was made in writing rather than as a result of letting the deadline expire. Where a party can show that an admission is clearly a mistake, the court should allow the respondent to correct the error, but a respondent has a heavy burden when he or she tries to avoid a Rule 36 admission.

unfair prejudice The unacceptable consequences of some procedure or improper evidence that a party has wrongly injected into the case.

A Rule 36 admission conclusively establishes the admitted fact for the purposes of the "pending action only." To encourage parties to sue requests for admissions, the rule precludes anyone from using an admission against a respondent in connection with another lawsuit or legal proceeding.

Consequence of Not Responding

If a respondent fails to serve a response within the allotted time, the request is admitted by operation of law. If a respondent inadvertently makes admissions by failing to respond, the respondent's only recourse is to move the court for leave to withdraw the admissions—even though no admissions actually have been made. As a rule, courts will not allow delinquent respondents to avoid admissions unless the respondent can show that the failure was because of excusable neglect *and* that the admission is wrong. Furthermore, Rule 36 directs courts to consider whether the proponent will be prejudiced by setting aside the admission. A proponent is prejudiced if necessary evidence is no longer available to the proponent. Therefore, you must never fail to meet a request-for-admission deadline. If you need more time in which to respond to a request for admission, you should obtain an extension of time in writing before the deadline expires. If the proponent will not voluntarily extend the time period for responding, your team must move the court for an order extending the time. Rule 6 permits the respondent to make an ex parte motion[3] for an extension of time.

affidavit of no response An attorney's affidavit that shows an opposing party has failed to perform an act required by a court order or court rule.

When a respondent defaults, Rule 36 does not require the proponent to do anything to show that the respondent is in default. The proponent's affidavit of service of the request for admission is sufficient to establish service of the request and due date. Nevertheless, the better procedure is for you to prepare and serve on the respondent an **affidavit of no response.** The affidavit should state the date on which the request was served; that no extension of time in which to answer was granted; that the respondent has not served a response as of the date of the affidavit; and that the request is deemed admitted for purposes of the pending action, as provided by Rule 36. When the respondent's lawyer receives the affidavit of no response, the lawyer will have to accept the fact that the admissions are made or take immediate steps to withdraw the admissions inadvertently made. The affidavit is useful because it prevents the defaulting party from claiming excusable neglect or inadvertence at trial.

Preparing Requests for Admissions

Requests for admissions resemble interrogatories. Requests may be served in sets. Requests may have subparts. They must identify the court at the top of the document, state the title of the action, and be labeled "Requests for Admissions." Requests must instruct the respondent to make admissions and explain that if the respondent fails to deny or object to the requests within the time allowed, the requests will be deemed admitted. Each request must be singular and deal with just one subject. A request should be phrased to allow the respondent to answer with a

EXHIBIT 16.1

Request for Admissions Form

United States District Court for the
Southern District of New York
Civil Action, File Number _____

A. B., Plaintiff,

    vs.

C. D., Defendant.

Plaintiff A. B. requests defendant C. D., within thirty days after service of this request, to make the following admissions for the purpose of this action only and subject to all pertinent objections to admissibility which may be interposed at the trial. Each request shall be deemed admitted pursuant to Rule 36 of the Federal Rules of Civil Procedure, unless specifically denied within the time specified above.

    I. Please admit that each of the following documents, exhibited with this request, is genuine.
      1.
      2.
      3.

    II. Please admit that each of the following statements is true.
      1.
      2.
      3.

[date]

/s/ _____
Attorney for Plaintiff
Address
Telephone

simple "admitted" or "denied." If a request uses a word that requires a specific definition, the definition should be stated separately. Exhibit 16.1 is a typical form used to make requests for admissions.

Ambiguities in requests for admissions are construed against the proponent, because the proponent is the drafter. The respondent should not have to worry that a request may contain some hidden problem. The more specific and clear a request, the more difficulty the respondent will have avoiding it. Requests lose their value when they are overly broad or ambiguous. A misuse of requests increases the cost of litigation and creates friction between the parties.

The requests for admissions in Exhibit 16.2 illustrate each type of request authorized by Rule 36. Notice that the requests are short, singular, and specific, except for number 4, which is poorly drafted. These requests are directed to a contested issue: ownership and legal responsibility for the operation of an automobile that allegedly caused the plaintiff's accident and injuries. The proponent wants to show that Raoul Esteban, who is a party to the case, was the owner of the automobile. Theresa Pavoloni was driving when it struck the plaintiff's automobile. Esteban claims he was not the owner because he sold the automobile to Pavoloni shortly before the accident. Esteban is Pavoloni's father. Defendant Esteban responds to the plaintiff's request for admissions as shown in Exhibit 16.3.

■ **EXHIBIT 16.2**

Request for Admissions

[1]The law of most states places the burden of proof on the registered owner to show that he or she no longer owns the vehicle. Other states provide that registration is conclusive on the issue of financial responsibility for an accident.

United States District Court for the
Southern District of New York
Civil Action, File Number _____

Evan Schmidt, Plaintiff,

      vs.

Raoul Esteban, Defendant.

TO: Defendant and John Jones, his attorney,

Plaintiff Evan Schmidt requests defendant Raoul Esteban, within thirty days after service of this request, to make the following admissions:

1. You owned the automobile that Theresa Pavoloni was operating at the time of the motor vehicle accident described in the plaintiff's complaint.
     [The plaintiff has requested admission of a fact. The fact is ownership of the automobile. In most cases, there is no dispute over the ownership of vehicles, but in this case there is.]
2. As owner of the automobile that Pavoloni was driving at the time of the parties' accident, you are vicariously liable for any legal liability that Pavoloni may have for the accident.
     [The plaintiff has requested admission of the application of law to a given fact. Again, ownership is the fact. The plaintiff wants Esteban to admit that an owner is liable for the legal liability of the driver. That is the current law in all states. It is a simple legal proposition.]
3. Pavoloni deposition exhibit 1 is a true and correct copy of the state certificate of title[1] to the automobile that Pavoloni was operating at the time of the accident described in the plaintiff's complaint.
     [The plaintiff has requested admission of the genuineness of a document. A document is genuine within the meaning of Rule 36 if it is what it purports to be.]

---

4. While riding as a passenger in the automobile being driven by Pavoloni when the accident occurred, you observed the plaintiff's automobile before the collision and formed an opinion that the plaintiff's automobile was traveling at less than thirty miles per hour at the moment of the collision. [The plaintiff has requested Esteban to admit to an opinion that he stated in his deposition taken at an earlier date. Rule 36 allows the proponent to request the respondent to admit lay opinions and expert opinions when relevant. In this case, Esteban had already expressed the opinion in his deposition. The request will keep Esteban from subsequently changing the opinion. Note that this request is too lengthy and too involved to be a good one.]

[Date]

/s/ _____
Attorney for Plaintiff
Address
Telephone

Exhibit 16.2

Request for Admissions (continued)

[1]The law of most states places the burden of proof on the registered owner to show that he or she no longer owns the vehicle. Other states provide that registration is conclusive on the issue of financial responsibility for an accident.

Serving Requests for Admissions

The plaintiff may serve requests for admissions with the summons and complaint or any time thereafter until the court establishes a cutoff date. A plaintiff may serve requests for admissions on the defendant's lawyer as soon as the defendant serves an answer or motion. After the defendant appears in the action, requests may be served by mail. A defendant may serve requests for admissions any time after the complaint is served. Requests and admissions must be served on all parties.

Limitations on Requests for Admissions

Requests for admissions may be served only on parties. Requests are not a substitute for interrogatories and depositions. A proponent should serve requests for admissions only when the proponent knows the fact is true or the document is genuine. The test is whether the proponent, not the respondent, knows the fact is true or the document is genuine. As part of a discovery plan or by court order, the time for serving requests for admissions will end. A party must be careful to avoid the deadline if he or she intends to make use of requests for admissions.

Of course, a respondent may refuse to admit a request that is improper for some reason. But the respondent must give reasons for objecting and not answering. The mere fact that the admission would not be admissible into evidence is not grounds for objecting. A respondent may object on grounds that the request is outside the scope of discovery as provided by Rule 26(b)(1), is too vague, or is ambiguous. A

Exhibit 16.3

*Response to Request for
Admissions*

United States District Court for the
Southern District of New York
Civil Action, File Number _____

Evan Schmidt, Plaintiff,

vs.

Raoul Esteban, Defendant.

TO: Plaintiff and William Smith, his attorney,

For defendant's responses to plaintiff's requests for admissions, defendant states:

REQUEST NO. 1. "You owned the automobile that Theresa Pavoloni was operating at the time of the motor vehicle accident described in the plaintiff's complaint."

RESPONSE: Denied.
 Reasons for denial: Although defendant Raoul Esteban was the registered owner of the automobile, Theresa Pavoloni was operating it at the time of the accident. The automobile in question had been sold to Pavoloni one week before the accident, as explained more fully in Esteban's deposition.
  [Ownership is a fact. The fact will turn on the validity of the purported sale. The proponent has not succeeded in eliminating ownership as a fact issue.]

REQUEST NO. 2 "As owner of the automobile that Pavoloni was driving at the time of the parties' accident, you are vicariously liable for any legal liability that Pavoloni may have for said accident."

RESPONSE: Denied.
 Reasons for denial: Defendant Esteban objects to the request as hypothetical and not a request for application of a law to an admitted fact. The defendant denies that he is vicariously liable for punitive damages claimed by the plaintiff even if it is determined that Esteban is vicariously liable for the automobile accident in question.
  [Request 2 depends on how the respondent answered request 1. If request 1 had been admitted, presumably request 2 would have been admitted, except for the punitive damages issue that the respondent raised. The respondent found the request to be too broad and challenged the request even while denying it. It is proper and desirable for the respondent to point out defects in a request. The respondent called the requested fact hypothetical because he denies that it is true, but it still might be true.]

REQUEST NO. 3. "Pavoloni deposition exhibit 1 is a true and correct copy of the state certificate of title to the automobile that Pavoloni was operating at the time of the accident described in the plaintiff's complaint."

EXHIBIT 16.3

Response to Request for Admissions (continued)

RESPONSE: Subject to response 2, admitted, that deposition exhibit 1 is genuine. [The respondent has not admitted ownership by admitting that the document is genuine. The admission means that the proponent will not have to have a witness come to trial and testify in order to lay foundation for the use of the document.]

REQUEST NO. 4. "While riding as a passenger in the automobile being driven by Pavoloni when the accident occurred, you observed the plaintiff's automobile before the collision and formed an opinion that the plaintiff's automobile was traveling at less than thirty miles per hour at the moment of the collision."

RESPONSE: Admitted.
[Suppose the request had been framed, "Please admit that in your deposition you testified the plaintiff's automobile was traveling less than thirty miles per hour at the time of the collision." What would be the effect or value of such a request? If the respondent admitted the request, would that prevent the respondent from giving a different opinion of speed at trial? If the respondent tried to change his testimony at trial to opine that the plaintiff's speed was forty-five miles per hour, would the change be in violation of Rule 36, or mere impeachment? A good argument could be made that the admission, as phrased, simply affirms what was stated in the deposition but does not commit the respondent to the less-than-thirty-miles-per-hour speed.]

request is "vague" when the request is incomprehensible. A request is ambiguous when it can be construed two different ways. A party may object to a request on the grounds that it is too vague to be intelligible, but the safer course is to make a **qualified admission** by stating what is admitted, using the respondent's own words.

A proponent cannot require the respondent to admit a matter that is privileged. For example, the plaintiff in an automobile accident case could not request the defendant to admit that the defendant told his wife he went through the stop sign, because conversations between spouses are privileged.[4] One well-publicized privilege is the Fifth Amendment privilege against self-incrimination. If the proponent serves a request on the respondent to admit that the respondent committed an act that was criminal, and the respondent and his or her lawyer know that he or she did commit the criminal act, the respondent cannot avoid the request for admissions by asserting the Fifth Amendment privilege. If he or she refuses to admit or deny on that ground, the request stands admitted. Admission by silence, however, could not be used against the respondent in a subsequent criminal action.

A request is objectionable if it is made for an improper purpose. For example, it is not proper to request the respondent to admit that she or he cannot or will not present evidence about a certain subject. Such a request is directed at discovering the respondent's trial strategy, and that is not authorized.

qualified admission An admission, made in response to a Rule 36 request for admissions, that is limited or qualified by the respondent.

qualified denial   A denial, made in response to a Rule 36 request for admissions, that provides an explanation or some information notwithstanding the party's denial.

reasonable inquiry   An inquiry or investigation that a reasonably prudent person would make to ascertain facts in light of the potential harm and the difficulties of making the inquiry or investigation.

Responses to Requests for Admissions

A respondent has several options for responding to requests for admissions: (1) deny the request, (2) admit the request, (3) assert an inability to admit or deny the request and explain in detail his or her reasons, (4) make a **qualified denial,** (5) make a qualified admission, or (6) object to the request. An objection has the effect of a denial. When a respondent decides to admit the request, he or she may intentionally let the time for responding expire, so that the request stands admitted; or serve a response that simply states the request is "admitted"; or repeat the request in a statement form. When the last approach is used, the response says, "[Name of party] admits that [request repeated word for word]."

A respondent may not evade a request for admissions by stating he or she does not have sufficient information to know whether the request is true. The respondent is obligated to make "**reasonable inquiry**" to obtain the information. A respondent makes reasonable inquiry if he or she contacts people and reviews documents that are available to the respondent to obtain the information. Rule 36 states:

> A denial shall fairly meet the substance of the requested admission, and when good faith requires that a party qualify an answer or deny only a part of the matter of which an admission is requested, the party shall so specify so much of it as is true and qualify or deny the remainder.

The document or people who have the information need not be under the respondent's control to be reasonably available. If the respondent makes contact, and the people who have the information will not provide it, that explanation is a sufficient response. If the information is obtainable through another party, the respondent may be under an obligation to consult with the other party. The respondent, however, does not have to travel, incur significant expense, or conduct an investigation to determine where the information is or who has it.

Suppose a proponent requests the respondent to admit that Third Avenue is forty-eight feet wide from curb to curb at its intersection with Sixth Street. The intersection is in the same town as the respondent's residence. The respondent will have to drive to the intersection, measure it, and admit or deny the fact. However, suppose the accident in question occurred three years ago, the roadway has been reconstructed, and the request asks the respondent to admit that at the time of the accident Third Avenue was forty-eight feet wide. If the respondent does not know, she or he does not have to conduct an investigation to determine who might know or what old records might provide the information. The proponent cannot shift to the respondent the obligation of investigating the facts. May the proponent ask the respondent to admit that the respondent does not know the width of Third Avenue as it was at the time of the accident? Yes. If the respondent does not have that information and cannot obtain it, the respondent should admit the fact that he or she does not know the width. More than likely, the respondent would provide an answer that contains an estimate of the width. The estimate constitutes a qualified denial.

When a request is partially correct, Rule 36(a) requires the respondent to identify that portion of the request that is true and deny the rest. For example, a plaintiff's request that defendant admit he occupied certain real estate during the year 2006 may draw a response that the defendant occupied the premises only during the month of January 2006. If he occupied the premises only in 2005, he could deny the request without qualifying the answer. He would not have to "admit" that he occupied the premises in 2005. The difference of an entire year is not a minor discrepancy. To qualify the response by going to another year is to change the substance of the request. The qualification would be outside the scope of the request.

If the request is essentially true but flawed in some respect, the respondent should "admit" by stating the fact or facts in a manner that meets the spirit of Rule 36(a). To illustrate, suppose a request asks the respondent to admit that he was driving a red automobile at the time of the accident. If the respondent's automobile is maroon, the response should state, "I was driving a maroon automobile at the time of the accident." The respondent should not deny the request in total merely because the shade of color was not correct. A denial would imply that the respondent was not even driving a car at the time of the accident. If a request asks the respondent to admit that the accident occurred at 9:00 in the morning, but there is a slight dispute about the exact time, the respondent could give a qualified response. The respondent could state, "Admits the accident occurred at 9:10 A.M."

When a plaintiff serves requests for admissions with the complaint, the defendant must serve a response within forty-five days. Otherwise, all parties have at least thirty days in which to respond. A proponent may grant more than thirty days or more than forty-five days, but cannot unilaterally grant less. When service is by mail, add three days [Rule 6(e)]. If the respondent fails to meet the deadline, the request is admitted by operation of law. Rule 36 is very clear on this, and the Rule is strictly applied. Each request must be answered separately—just as the requests are separate. Requests for admissions should not be used as a substitute for a trial concerning fact issues over which there is a bona fide dispute.

Paralegals may prepare responses to requests for admissions, but the respondent or the respondent's lawyer must sign it. The response does not have to be signed under oath; it is not testimony. Nevertheless, a response may be used at trial in the place of evidence. Suppose the respondent admits she or he was the owner of the automobile at the time of the accident. Instead of questioning the respondent about that fact during the trial, the proponent could stand before the jury and read the request and the response. When the judge instructs the jury at the end of the trial, the judge may tell the jurors they must accept as true the fact of ownership admitted in the response. The jury may not find otherwise.

Rescinding a Rule 36 Admission

A Rule 36 admission is not irrevocable. The party who mistakenly made an admission should first request the opponent for permission to withdraw or correct the admission. If the parties can resolve the problem by agreement, that is the quickest and easiest way of handling it. The agreement must be reduced to writing in the form of a stipulation. Otherwise, an admission may be withdrawn or modified only by court order.

Rule 36(b) provides that a court may allow withdrawal or amendment of an admission "when the presentation of the merits of the action will be subserved [promoted]" and the proponent fails to show that a withdrawal or amendment will prejudice him or her on the merits of the action. A motion to rescind a Rule 36 admission should (1) specifically request permission to withdraw or amend the admission, (2) state precisely how the proposed amended admission would read, (3) explain the reason for the amendment or withdrawal, and (4) explain why the other parties will not be prejudiced by the correction. The motion should be supported by affidavits to establish facts supporting the motion. Again, a party who has acted in good faith and with due diligence usually finds judges to be considerate.

Withdrawal of an admission may affect adversely another party's claim or defense in a significant manner. That does not mean the party has been prejudiced. Truth does not prejudice a party. However, if a party's ability to prove the truth has been prevented or hindered, as when a witness has died or other evidence has been lost, that party has been prejudiced. Also, a party is prejudiced if he or she is deprived of time in which to investigate or conduct discovery to gather evidence that, presumably, was available. A motion to withdraw or amend an admission ought to anticipate these issues and the availability-of-evidence problems.

Consequences of Denying Requests for Admissions

Rule 37(c) provides that a proponent who proves a fact or the genuineness of a document that the respondent denied may move the court for an order allowing the proponent to recover costs the proponent incurred to prove the truth, including reasonable attorneys' fees. The Rule provides that the court "shall" grant the proponent's motion for recovery of costs, unless the court finds that the request, as drafted, was objectionable; the request did not concern a matter that was really important to the case; or the respondent had reasonable grounds to believe the fact was not true or the document was not genuine. Rule 37(c) leaves a nice catchall exception by allowing the respondent to show "other good reason for the failure to admit." The respondent can help himself or herself, in this regard, by carefully detailing in the response the reasons why he or she cannot admit the request. These criteria are very subjective and give trial judges a great deal of latitude. The wording implies that judges should lean toward disallowing costs, unless the respondent acted in bad faith. However, bad faith is not the test or standard.

If a proponent believes a response is evasive, the proponent may move the court for an order "to determine the sufficiency of the answers [responses] or objections" [Rule 36(a)]. If the court determines that the respondent's response or objection is without merit, the court may order the respondent to answer the request. If the court determines that a response or objection is specious, the court may deem the request to be admitted. The court will issue an order to that effect. An alternative is for the court to give the respondent a specified period of time in which to amend the response or face the consequences of an erroneous response. Exhibit 16.4 contains a sample of negative responses to requests for admissions.

EXHIBIT 16.4

Negative Responses to Request for Admissions

United States District Court for the
Southern District of New York
Civil Action, File Number _____

A. B., Plaintiff,

vs.

C. D., Defendant.

TO: Plaintiff and John Jones, her attorney,

Comes now defendant C. D. and for his response to plaintiff's request for admissions, states:

REQUEST NO. 1. That the reasonable value of the medical expenses incurred by plaintiff as a result of the injuries received by plaintiff in the accident of September 15, 2005, are as follows:

Dr. Jerome Cowan
9-15-05 through 9-22-05
$92.00
Dr. Marilyn Berwin
9-22-05 through 12-5-05
$308.00
Midwest Medical Center
9-21-05 through 9-27-05
$1,082.60
Prescriptions
10-3-05 through 7-15-06
$421.00

RESPONSE: Denied.

Reasons for denial: Defendant objects to the request for admissions on the grounds that plaintiff failed to provide adequate documentation and information concerning the requests and is imposing on defendant the burden of securing copies of plaintiff's medical records and reviewing those records at defendant's expense. Defendant has been unable to make reasonable inquiry of plaintiff's physicians because plaintiff has not provided authorizations permitting defendant's attorney to interview them. Therefore, the only information readily obtainable to defendant is insufficient to enable him to admit the request for admissions.

As of this time, plaintiff has not authorized defendant's counsel to interview the attending physicians and hospital personnel. Therefore, defendant cannot verify the matters set forth in the various bills attached to plaintiff's request for admissions. Nor is defendant able to determine the qualifications, experience,

continued

Exhibit 16.4

Negative Responses to Request for Admissions (continued)

or expertise of the various providers of health care to determine whether their charges for medical services are reasonable. If plaintiff would specify the amount of time spent by each provider of health care for each service rendered, defendants would be in a better position to evaluate the truth of the requests. Also, plaintiff should supply copies of all hospital and medical records that are the bases for making the charges reflected in the bills attached to the request for admissions.

REQUEST NO. 2. That if the proper parties were called to testify, they would testify that each of the aforementioned expenses for medical care and attention referred to in request for admission 1 was reasonable.

RESPONSE: Denied.

Reasons for denial: Please refer to response 1.

REQUEST NO. 3. That in the event you deny either request for admission 1 or request for admission 2, supra, state the name, address, age, occupation, and employer of every person whom you will call to testify to dispute the reasonableness of such medical expenses.

RESPONSE: Denied.

Reasons for denial: Please refer to response 1. Plaintiff's request no. 3 is not a request for admissions, but in the form of an interrogatory that has no basis.

Dated: November 10, 2006

/s/ _____
Attorney for Defendant
Address
Telephone

SUMMARY

Request for admissions is a procedure parties may use to obtain admissions from other parties concerning facts, evidence, opinions, documents, and the application of law to facts. The scope of requests is similar to discovery procedures. An admission may be withdrawn only with the proponent's consent or by a court order. Requests may be used in conjunction with interrogatories. An admission may be read to the jury but not submitted to the jury as an exhibit. Rule 36 admissions cannot be used against the respondent in another civil action.

A respondent must answer a request for admission or object to it. If a respondent fails to respond to a Rule 36 request within the allowed time, the request is admitted by operation of law. Rule 36 requests must be relevant to the lawsuit. They cannot be used to obtain privileged information or a party's work product. These are grounds for objecting to Rule 36 requests. An admission does not automatically make the fact, document, or opinion admissible into evidence at trial. A respondent does not admit relevancy by admitting a requested fact, opinion, or document.

A respondent has at least thirty days in which to respond to requests for admissions. The proponent may allow more time and a court may extend the time. But if the respondent fails to answer within the allotted time, the request is admitted by operation of law. In other words, a default results in an admission. Rule 36 does not require an affidavit of default, and the proponent's choice to serve an affidavit of default is a matter of strategy.

A respondent has a duty to make reasonable inquiry to obtain information with which to answer a request for admissions. If a respondent does not have the information with which to admit or deny and has made reasonable inquiry, the respondent may answer by stating that he or she "cannot admit or deny" the request, and then state the reasons why. A response is treated as a denial. A respondent may not deny a request merely because it contains a minor, technical defect. A denial must "fairly meet the substance of the requested admission." A respondent may qualify an admission by identifying problems in the request or providing certain parameters that limit the scope and application of a response.

If a party wrongfully refuses to make admissions pursuant to Rule 36, the only penalty a court may impose is an award of costs in favor of the proponent of the request for admissions. The recoverable costs are those the proponent incurred to prove the facts that should have been admitted by the respondent. A court may disallow the costs of proving the fact, however, when it appears that the respondent had reasonable grounds to believe that the request for admission was not true or justifiable [Rule 37(c)].

KEY TERMS

affidavit of no response	qualified denial
genuine	reasonable inquiry
law of the case	requests for admissions
qualified admission	unfair prejudice

REVIEW QUESTIONS

1. Describe the consequences of a respondent's erroneous admission that she or he does not have a recorded witness statement from a particular witness.

2. How many requests for admissions may be served on any one party?

3. State two reasons for serving requests for admissions concerning a fact that the proponent already knows is true.

4. What is the criterion for determining whether a party may properly serve a request for admissions?

5. What is the consequence of mistakenly denying a request for admission that was correct?

6. What is the consequence of failing to respond to a request for admissions within the time allowed for the response?

7. If a party realizes before trial that he or she mistakenly admitted a request for admission, what course of action should the party take to avoid the effect of the admission?

8. May requests for admissions be used in conjunction with interrogatories?

9. When may a respondent refuse to respond to a request for admissions on the grounds that the admission may violate a right not to incriminate oneself?

10. How is a request for admission and its response presented to a jury during the trial of a civil action?

11. To what extent is a respondent required to seek out information he or she needs in order to admit or deny a requested fact?

CASE ASSIGNMENT

You are a member of attorney William Hoch's litigation team representing defendant Harper. Harper has commenced a third-party action against John Griffin alleging that Griffin is required to provide insurance or pay the trustee's claim. Prepare a set of requests for admissions for service on Griffin. Request admissions concerning the sale of the pickup, Griffin's agreement to provide insurance, Griffin's neglect and failure to obtain insurance for Harper, and the application of Harper's policy with the Security Insurance Company to the trustee's claim. Allow Griffin thirty days in which to respond. Consider supplementing some requests for admissions with interrogatories.

Endnotes

1. Of course, the respondent who contradicts his or her answer to an interrogatory is impeached and the respondent's credibility is affected adversely.
2. If service of the request is by mail, add three days per Rule 6(e).
3. An ex parte motion is made to the court without giving notice to the other parties in the case. Most motions are invalid unless duly served on all parties as provided by Rule 5.
4. However, if a party says something to her or his spouse and the remark is overheard by another person, the remark is not privileged. A privileged communication retains its privileged status only as long as the owner of the privilege protects the privilege.

 For additional resources, visit our Web site at www.paralegal.delmar.cengage.com

CHAPTER 17

MOTIONS

CHAPTER OUTLINE

Chapter Objectives

Chapter 17 describes what motions are and how they are made. A party makes a motion to obtain the court's help in dealing with a problem. The problems are usually procedural in nature, but sometimes motions deal with the substantive law. This chapter is primarily concerned with written motions. The discussion about motions has been postponed until this point when you are aware of the kinds of problems parties may encounter in preparing for trial.

Introduction

A **motion** is an application to a court for an order granting some kind of relief, guidance, help, or protection. When parties are in court for a trial or other proceeding, they may make oral motions concerning anything relevant to the proceeding. If they are before the court for a special proceeding, the oral motion must concern that proceeding. If they are in trial, the motion may concern anything that relates to the trial. Motions made during trial are usually oral. If the parties are not then in court, a moving party must make his or her motion in writing. The moving party must give notice to the other parties about the nature of the motion, and the time and place the motion will be heard by the court. Motions are often categorized as pretrial, trial, or posttrial. They are also categorized as **procedural** (nondispositive) or **dispositive.** Parties usually support their motions with arguments. Arguments may be made orally or in writing, depending on the circumstances. A written argument is submitted to the court in a memorandum of law that accompanies the written motion. If the

motion An application to a court for a ruling or order concerning a matter of procedure or law.

procedural motion Any motion by which a party seeks a court's assistance or guidance.

dispositive motion Any motion a party uses to obtain resolution of a claim or part of a claim or resolution of any alleged defense.

argument concerns the law, each party usually serves and files a memorandum of law, which provides legal analysis and authorities. If the argument concerns a fact issue or is based on facts, the parties usually submit affidavits, deposition transcripts, and exhibits to support their motions. Of course, the same kinds of materials may be submitted in opposition.

Paralegals play an important role in motion practice. Paralegals may identify the need to make a motion. They may draft written motions, prepare supporting affidavits, and assemble documents and other exhibits to support or oppose written motions. They may schedule motions for argument. Rule 11 provides that a lawyer of record must read, approve, and sign every motion, but that does not mean a lawyer must draft the motion. There must be a good basis for a motion. A motion must not be made for an improper, ulterior purpose. A court acts on a party's motion by issuing an order to the parties [Rule 7(b)].

There are a number of common motions. The federal rules refer to some motions by name, but there is no all-inclusive list. If your client or trial team needs help from the court, you simply devise a motion that gets the matter before the court. Rule 7(b) provides

> (1) An application to the court for an order shall be by motion which, unless made during a hearing or trial, shall be made in writing, shall state with particularity the grounds therefor, and shall set forth the relief or order sought. The requirement of writing is fulfilled if the motion is stated in a written notice of the hearing of the motion.
> (2) The rules applicable to captions and other matters of form of pleadings apply to all motions and other papers provided for by these rules.
> (3) All motions shall be signed in accordance with Rule 11.

Motions are a significant part of the adversary process. A routine procedural or discovery motion must be served at least five days before the hearing. A motion for summary judgment must be served at least ten days before it is heard [Rule 6(d)].[1] However, most courts have detailed rules—called local rules—that significantly alter these times. For dispositive motions (i.e., those that will dispose of part or all of the case, if granted) the time is usually at least twenty-eight days. You must familiarize yourself with local rules in every case. The rules are typically available on a court's Web site and cover myriad subjects about discovery, motion practice, and trial. When a motion is supported by affidavit, the affidavit shall be served with the motion. Opposing affidavits must be served at least one day before the hearing, unless otherwise ordered by the court. All affidavits are supposed to be based on personal knowledge. Otherwise, the affidavit should state that it is made on "information and belief."[2]

A motion may be scheduled in the manner provided by the local court's rules or by special arrangements made directly with the judge or the judge's clerk. A **notice of motion** must be served with every written motion, unless the motion may be heard ex parte. However, the notice may be combined into one document with the motion. The notice tells the nonmoving party when and where the motion will be heard. A notice of motion must use the case caption and "Notice of Motion." A motion may be scheduled as provided by the local court's rules or by special arrangements made directly with the judge or the judge's clerk.

notice of motion A notice that accompanies a motion and sets the time and place at which the motion will be heard by the court.

Parts of a Motion

Although not stated in any rule, a motion should have four parts. The parts are not necessarily separated into numbered paragraphs as is customary with pleadings. The first part should tell the court what assistance and what order the moving party wants. The second part should identify any legal authority that the moving party relies on, usually one of the Rules of Civil Procedure. The third part should state the grounds for the motion. The grounds are the reasons why the moving party is entitled to the court's assistance and the court's authority to provide that assistance. The fourth part should identify the supporting documents on which the motion is based, such as records, affidavits, and exhibits. Supporting documents must be served with the motion, unless previously served and filed. If filed, they may be incorporated into the motion by reference. If the opposing party relies on additional documents to oppose the motion, they must be served and filed no later than one day before the motion is heard [Rule 6(d)].

Motion Format

Exhibit 17.1 illustrates the structure of a properly drawn motion. A motion may specify the type of motion in the caption or may simply be titled "Motion." The motion must be made before the time period expires. The motion must be in writing and must conform generally with the four-part format required for all motions.

A motion identifies the problem and places the issue before the court. If the motion is predicated on certain facts that are subject to dispute, the motion must be supported by evidence of those facts. In motion practice, the support is provided in the form of affidavits, not oral testimony. (See Exhibit 17.2.) One or more supporting affidavits may be attached to the motion and should be identified in the motion. An affidavit is supposed to recite facts, not opinions or arguments. The affidavit must show that the affiant (i.e., the person who will sign the affidavit under oath) has personal knowledge of the facts. In other words, an affidavit is supposed to contain testimony that would be admissible in evidence at trial. An affidavit may incorporate additional documents if the affidavit has provided foundation for those documents. Any document that has been filed with the court may be incorporated by reference. An opposing party always has the right to serve and file opposing affidavits. Conflicting affidavits pose problems for judges, because they do not take testimony and hear evidence to resolve the factual dispute.

Affidavits are not supposed to contain arguments on the facts or arguments on the law. A party may make an argument on the law by filing a **memorandum of law** with the motion. Most local rules require parties to serve and file memoranda of law before the hearing. A memorandum of law is a written argument that provides the court with legal authorities and analysis to persuade the court to grant or deny a motion. The usual memorandum has the case caption and is entitled "Memorandum of Law." A memorandum of law typically has four parts: (1) a clear statement of the issues, (2) a succinct statement of the material facts, (3) an argument or discussion of the applicable law, and (4) a conclusion. The conclusion should state exactly what the party wants the court to hold or to do. Some lawyers prefer to state the legal issues after the facts and before the argument. An issue may be stated as a question or

memorandum of law A memorandum a party submits to a court to identify the law the party claims is relevant and in which a party argues how the law applies to the particular case.

■ Exhibit 17.1

Notice of Motion and Motion

United States District Court for the
Southern District of Illinois
Civil Action, File Number CV06-00783

Roberta Jones, Plaintiff,

vs.

William Smith, Defendant.

NOTICE OF MOTION

PLEASE TAKE NOTICE that on the 2nd day of February, 2006, at 10:00 o'clock in the morning defendant will bring the attached motion for hearing at the United States Federal Court House before the Honorable James Johnston, courtroom 505, or as soon thereafter as the matter may be heard.

Motion to Dismiss

Defendant hereby moves the court for an order dismissing the above entitled action.

This motion is made pursuant to Rule 12 of the Federal Rules of Civil Procedure.

The grounds for this motion are that the complaint fails to state a claim on which relief can be granted. The complaint fails to allege the claim of fraud with particularity as required by Rule 9(b).

This motion is based upon the allegations of plaintiff's complaint, which is on file with the court; the allegations and denials set forth in defendant's answer, which is on file with the court; a copy of the parties' contract upon which plaintiff's claim is based. The contract is attached to plaintiff's complaint and incorporated by reference.

[date]

Attorney for Defendant

/s/_____
John Smith
1996 First Avenue North
Smithville, Virginia
(555) 333-2222

an imperative. The argument is the body of the memorandum. It provides an analysis of the facts and applies legal authorities to the facts. The legal analysis explains how the authority relates to the current problem. The conclusion should state exactly what the moving party wants the court to hold or to do. Even when there is no rule requiring parties to file memoranda, they usually do.

EXHIBIT 17.2

Affidavit

United States District Court for the
Southern District of Illinois
Civil Action, File Number CV06-00783

Roberta Jones, Plaintiff,

    vs.

William Smith, Defendant.

William Smith, being first duly sworn, deposes and says:

    I am the defendant in the above-entitled action. I make this affidavit in support of defendant's motion to dismiss.

    The plaintiff's claim is based in part upon the contract between the plaintiff and defendant. Plaintiff attached to the complaint a purported copy of the contract. However, the purported contract failed to include two amendments which the parties executed. True and correct copies of the two amendments are attached hereto and submitted to the court so that the court may consider them in connection with defendant's motion to dismiss.

[date]

/s/ _____
John Smith

[Notary Seal]

Ex Parte Motions

A motion that may be made without notice to opposing parties is called an ex parte motion. Ex parte motions are limited to procedural matters. Rule 6(b) specifically authorizes parties to make ex parte motions to obtain an extension of the time provided by other rules for doing something or relief from a prior court order. But an ex parte motion for additional time must be made *before* the original deadline expires. If a party moves to extend the time *after* expiration of the prescribed time period, the motion cannot be made ex parte. The most common ex parte motion is a motion to obtain an extension of time in which to comply with a court rule or court order. An ex parte motion is addressed to the judge's sound discretion. The motion may be granted subject to terms and conditions that the judge believes are appropriate. When a party seeks an extension of time in which to act, the grounds may include impossibility or justification for being unable to comply with the rule or order in question or excusable neglect. As additional grounds for the motion, the moving party should promise compliance within a reasonable period of time and show the absence of prejudice to the opposing party.

    Exhibit 17.3 is an ex parte motion to obtain an extension of time in which to answer interrogatories. A copy of the ex parte motion could be sent to the opposing

Exhibit 17.3

Ex Parte Motion

United States District Court for the
Southern District of Illinois
Civil Action, File Number CV06-00783

Roberta Jones, Plaintiff,

    vs.

William Smith, Defendant.

Plaintiff hereby moves the court for an order extending the time in which plaintiff may answer defendant's interrogatories, which were served upon plaintiff on June 1, 2006.

    This motion is made pursuant to Rule 6(b).

    The grounds for this motion are that plaintiff was out of the country on business from May 25, 2006, to June 15, 2006, and has not been able to gather the evidence requested by defendant's interrogatories. Plaintiff believes that an additional ten days would provide sufficient time in which to prepare the necessary answers. The case is currently one year away from trial. Therefore, defendant will not be prejudiced by a ten-day extension.

    This motion is supported by plaintiff's affidavit, which is attached hereto, explaining that plaintiff was unable to attend to the preparation of answers to interrogatories while on his business trip.

    A proposed order extending the period of time for answering is attached hereto.

[date]

Attorney for Plaintiff

_____

John Smith
1996 First Avenue North
Smithville, Virginia
(555) 333-2222

party as a courtesy. If the prescribed time for acting has lapsed, the moving party may move for an extension, but the motion cannot be made ex parte.

Types of Motions

A few of the more common motions deserve special mention. The first four are dispositive motions prescribed by Rule 12. See also Chapter 6.

Motion for Judgment on the Pleadings

If a complaint, answer, or other pleading is insufficient to state a claim or defense, the opposing party may make a motion for judgment on the pleadings. In effect, the opposing party's pleading is stricken and the moving party obtains judgment by default [Rule 12(c)]. For the moving party to prevail, it must be clear from the pleading itself that it is defective or insufficient. Therefore, the moving party may not submit documents to support the motion. As provided in Rule 12(h), this motion may be brought at any time, even at trial. It may be brought even before the defendant's answer is due.

For example, if a complaint merely alleges that the defendant said he would sell his business to the plaintiff someday and that the defendant now refuses to do what he "promised" to do, that allegation does not state a claim of an enforceable premise. The defendant could not have breached a contract with the plaintiff, because there was no contract. The offer was too vague, and there was no consideration for the alleged promise. The defendant is entitled to judgment on the pleadings and should move for dismissal.

Motion to Dismiss for Lack of Jurisdiction over Subject Matter

A court must have subject matter jurisdiction over a case to be able to decide it. A party may move to dismiss a case if the court does not have subject matter jurisdiction. For example, a federal court has diversity-of-citizenship jurisdiction only if the amount in controversy exceeds $75,000. If a given diversity case has less in controversy, the federal court lacks subject matter jurisdiction. The case must be dismissed. The sooner the case is dismissed, the better for everyone. A motion to dismiss for lack of subject matter jurisdiction may be made at any time—even after trial. This defense cannot be waived. The motion may be supported by affidavits and other documents.

Motion to Dismiss for Lack of Personal Jurisdiction

A party may move to dismiss an action if the court has not obtained jurisdiction over him or her. But if a party fails to raise the defense by way of a motion or in the answer, the defense is waived. There are several grounds for finding a lack of jurisdiction over the person. The summons may have been defective or the summons and complaint may not have been served in a proper manner. For example, the process server may have left the summons and complaint at the defendant's home with a person who did not reside there. The motion may be supported with affidavits and other documents that show why service was defective. For example, a defendant could provide an affidavit that the person to whom the summons and complaint were delivered was not a resident in the defendant's usual place of abode.

Motion to Dismiss for Failure to State a Claim

A party may move to dismiss a claim, whether in a complaint, counterclaim, cross-claim, on the grounds that the pleading's allegations fail to state a claim on which relief can be granted. If the claimant has alleged several claims and only one is defective, this is the motion to use. Otherwise, if the claimant has alleged only one cause of action and it is defective, the moving party should move for judgment on the pleadings. If the moving party uses documents to support the motion, the motion is treated as a motion for summary judgment or partial summary judgment. Summary judgment motions are discussed later in the chapter.

Motion for More Definite Statement

Pleadings tend to be very general. Sometimes they are too general, and that leads to ambiguities and uncertainties. Because parties have a right to know what is being claimed against them, one way of forcing an opponent to be specific and descriptive is to make a motion for a more definite statement. By way of example, a complaint that alleges a cause of action for slander by merely alleging the defendant made various false statements about the plaintiff over a period of time is not adequate. The complaint must identify each defamatory statement and indicate the time and place of each publication [Rule 9(f)].

The defendant is entitled to a court order requiring the plaintiff to specify each defamatory statement: what was said, when it was said, where it was said, and whether it was published. The court should order a more definite statement. The court should not force the defendant to obtain the information through interrogatories, because the missing information is fundamental to the cause of action. The probabilities are that the court would allow the plaintiff to amend the complaint to make it comply.

Motion to Strike

A party may move the court to strike an "insufficient defense" from an answer or reply [Rule 12(f)]. It must appear on the face of the pleading that the allegations do not establish a viable defense. For example, an answer that merely alleges that the parties' contract is unfair does not state a defense to an action on the contract. The purported defense should be stricken as insufficient.[3] It does not happen very often, but on occasion a lawyer or party pro se may use a pleading to make a derogatory, impertinent, or a scandalous remark about the opposing party. If any pleading contains such allegations, the allegation is subject to being stricken on motion [Rule 12(f)]. A motion to strike must be made before any responsive pleading is interposed. If no responsive pleading is authorized, the motion must be made within twenty days after the pleading is served.

If a party elects to make any of the three motions just described and the motion is denied, the moving party *cannot* go back to court on the same issue by making either of the other two motions. Specifically, a party may combine any or all three of the motions but cannot make the motions sequentially.

Motion in Limine

motion in limine A motion made at the beginning of a trial for an order allowing or disallowing certain evidence. A motion in limine may be used to resolve some procedural issue.

The phrase *in limine* means "at the threshold" of the trial. Therefore, a **motion in limine** deals with problems concerning the admissibility of evidence and procedural issues. The Rules do not prescribe or regulate motions in limine. Depending on local rules and customs, they may be made when the parties appear for trial or with court-ordered pretrial submissions. Motions in limine are not supposed to deal with substantive legal issues. Lawyers usually think of them as motions to prevent an opposing party from presenting particular evidence at trial. Motions in limine prevent evidentiary problems from complicating the trial and eliminate or minimize surprises. If the parties are before the court for trial, a motion in limine may be made orally on the record without notice. Ideally, they should be made in writing and filed with the court before the parties report for the trial. The judge will be much more sympathetic to the motion if notice is given. A written motion in limine should be supported with a memorandum of law.

Often the context in which evidence is offered affects its admissibility. Judges do not like to rule in advance. There is too much opportunity for error. But on occasion an opposing party's offer of inappropriate evidence may be so damaging or prejudicial that even the offer should be prevented. Also, if certain evidence is critical to the opponent's evaluation of the case and that evidence should not be allowed, a ruling in advance will help. It is inappropriate to challenge anticipated evidence without having strong grounds.

Suppose the plaintiff is trying to build a case around the theme that the defendant was intoxicated at the time of their automobile accident, but the defendant only had one beer, and the police investigation shows he had a nominal blood alcohol content. By making a motion in limine and obtaining an order that the plaintiff shall not attempt to offer any evidence of intoxication and shall make no reference to possible intoxication during the voir dire examination or during the opening statements, the defendant has helped himself greatly. The in limine order may even preclude the plaintiff's attorney from mentioning the one beer that the defendant admits drinking. Suppose the defendant has evidence that the plaintiff was intoxicated at the time of the accident in question. However, because the plaintiff was a passenger in the defendant's vehicle at the time of the accident, his intoxication has nothing to do with the cause of the accident or injuries. The plaintiff may make a motion in limine to prevent the defendant from offering evidence of the plaintiff's intoxication. The grounds for excluding this evidence is that it is irrelevant and the prejudicial effect of the evidence outweighs its probative value.

Motions in limine commonly are used when the plaintiff has vivid photographs showing her or his injuries. The prejudicial effect may outweigh the photographs' probative value. The judge has discretion to exclude such photographs or to limit the number the plaintiff may put into evidence. Similarly, a court may limit the number of photographs dealing with a particular subject to avoid repetition and the cumulative effect.

A party may make a motion in limine to exclude an opponent's expert witness or an expert opinion. Of course, the opponent's case will be damaged if he or she loses the expert. Indeed, the case may be dismissed for lack of critical evidence. By raising the evidentiary issue before trial the moving party has given the court time in which to adequately consider the issues. When parties wait until trial to challenge experts' qualifications or opinions, the judges are inclined to disallow arguments that may delay trial. Instead, they will allow the testimony on the premise that they can deal with the problem later—perhaps in a posttrial motion. Then the tendency is to allow the evidence.

Attorney Smith's affidavit in Exhibit 17.4 should explain in greater detail why the plaintiff will be prejudiced and why it would not be sufficient for the court simply to allow the plaintiff to take Burger's deposition at this late date.

United States District Court for the
Southern District of Illinois
Civil Action, File Number CV06-00783

Roberta Jones, Plaintiff,

　vs.

William Smith, Defendant.

Plaintiff hereby moves the court for an order precluding William Burger from testifying in the trial of the above-entitled action.

This motion is made pursuant to Rules 26, 33, and 37 of the Federal Rules of Civil Procedure.

The grounds for this motion are that defendant did not name William Burger as a witness in his initial disclosures; did not name William Burger as a witness in his answers to interrogatories; and did not disclose William Burger at the pretrial conference. Plaintiff has been precluded from conducting any discovery or investigation concerning William Burger so as to be able to prepare to deal with his anticipated testimony. Plaintiff has been prejudiced by the late disclosure.

This motion is supported by the affidavit of attorney John Smith, which is attached hereto, and the court's files and records.

A proposed order precluding William Burger from testifying is attached hereto.

[date]

Attorney for Plaintiff

_____

John Smith
1996 First Avenue North
Smithville, Virginia
(555) 333-2222

Motion for Judgment as a Matter of Law

A party may make a motion for judgment as a matter of law as soon as the opposing party rests, and the motion is renewable when both parties have rested finally. Rule 50(a)(1) provides the standard for granting such motions:

> If during a trial by jury a party has been fully heard on an issue and there is no legally sufficient evidentiary basis for a reasonable jury to find for that party on that issue, the court may determine the issue against that party and may grant a motion for judgment as a matter of law against that party with respect

to a claim or defense that cannot under the controlling law be maintained or defeated without a favorable finding on that issue.

A motion for judgment as a matter of law is often called a motion for a directed verdict.

Summary Judgment Motions

A motion for summary judgment is a specialized litigation procedure designed to identify cases that do not need to go to trial. Instead, such cases can be decided by a judge merely by applying the law. Before we study the summary judgment procedure, we need to review the civil litigation process. When parties litigate their dispute, a court resolves the dispute by applying the law. The law determines the parties' legal rights and obligations. Judges determine what the law is and how the law applies to establish those legal rights and obligations. But when the parties' dispute involves a disagreement about the *facts* of their transaction or occurrence, those facts must be resolved before a judge can apply the law and determine their legal rights. Courts hold trials to resolve factual disputes. The two steps or processes are so intertwined that they often seem to be one process.

The summary judgment motion procedure allows parties to circumvent a trial when there is no dispute concerning any *material* fact. The procedure makes it possible for either party to apply to the court for an order determining that the case does not require a trial. The threshold is a showing that all material facts are undisputed. Then the judge may apply the law to the undisputed facts, determine the parties' rights and obligations, and enter a judgment accordingly. It is called a "summary judgment" because the parties have avoided going through a trial. However, the judgment has the same legal effect as any other judgment. It is an adjudication on the merits and leads to a final judgment. In other words, a summary judgment is not merely a dismissal of a claim or the striking of a defense.

A party may move for summary judgment on the grounds that his or her claim or defense is conclusive as a matter of law. Or, the moving party may move for summary judgment on the grounds that the opposing party's claim or defense is insufficient as a matter of law. Motions for summary judgment have four principal applications: (1) to determine whether there is a material fact issue; (2) to determine what the law is and how it applies to a particular matter; (3) to determine how the law applies to a given set of facts; and (4) to interpret and apply a legal document, such as a contract. The summary judgment procedure may be used to resolve a case as a whole or only part of the case. Though motions for summary judgment are commonly thought of as a defense tactic, plaintiffs may use them effectively to eliminate nonmeritorious affirmative defenses [Rule 56(a)].

Grounds for Summary Judgment Motions

A party's motion for summary judgment must show the court it may grant a summary judgment only if the case can be decided by resolving an issue of law. If there are material fact issues, the case must go to trial. Rule 56 provides that a court shall order summary judgment "if the pleadings, depositions, answers to interrogatories, and admissions on file, together with the affidavits, if any, show that there is no genuine issue as to any *material fact* and that the moving party is entitled to judgment as a matter of law."[4] A material fact is one that can affect the outcome of the case.

Summary Judgment Procedure

The first steps are to determine whether there are any disputed facts and, if so, whether those disputed facts are material to the legal issues. A party who desires to make a motion for summary judgment has the burden of showing the court there is no disputed material fact that prevents the court from granting a summary judgment. The moving party must present evidence to the court that shows he or she is entitled to judgment in his or her favor. The evidence must qualify to be admissible in trial, if there were a trial, but the evidence must be in documentary form. The evidence may come from "admissions" in the pleadings, responses to requests for admissions, answers to interrogatories, affidavits, deposition transcripts, and exhibits. Rule 56(e) explains

> Supporting and opposing affidavits shall be made on personal knowledge, shall set forth such facts as would be admissible in evidence, and shall show affirmatively that the affiant is competent to testify to the matters stated therein. Sworn or certified copies of all papers or parts thereof referred to in an affidavit shall be attached thereto or served therewith. The court may permit affidavits to be supplemented or opposed by [transcripts of] depositions, answers to interrogatories, or further affidavits.

Affidavits made in support of or in opposition to a motion for summary judgment must be made on personal knowledge and show the affiant is competent to testify concerning the facts. Parties may not submit oral testimony; otherwise, a summary judgment hearing would turn into a trial. A party may not use statements from his or her own pleadings to establish facts but could use admissions in an opponent's pleading to show that a fact is not disputed. The foundation for exhibits may be established through affidavits. For example, a corporate officer could provide an affidavit that an exhibit contains corporate records kept in the ordinary course of the corporation's business. All evidence offered in support of a summary judgment motion must be served and filed with the motion.

stipulation of facts A stipulation by which the parties express their agreement that a fact or a body of facts is true and may be relied upon by the court.

cross-motions for summary judgment Motions for summary judgment made by adverse parties against each other.

Parties may enter into a **"stipulation of facts"** that details relevant facts on which they agree. Indeed, parties may enter into a stipulation that provides *all* the facts the court needs to rule on the motion. Stipulations are often used when parties make **cross-motions for summary judgment.** District courts accept stipulations of facts even though Rule 56 does not expressly authorize their use. A stipulation is conclusive for and against the parties, so the parties must make certain the stipulation is accurate. Sometimes a party is willing to concede a disputed fact to facilitate summary judgment but intends to contest the fact if the case goes to trial. Courts have been willing to accept "conditional stipulations," which provide that the stipulation is made solely for the purpose of the summary judgment motion.

A party cannot avoid summary judgment by merely denying the truth of the moving party's evidence. A party who defends against a motion for summary judgment must present evidence that shows there is a dispute concerning material facts. Of course, the evidence must be proffered in good faith [Rule 56(e)].

Occasionally, attorneys try to use their own affidavits to support or oppose a summary judgment motion. Such affidavits are seldom appropriate, especially when they are in the form of an argument or recite facts about which the attorney has no personal knowledge. More than one summary judgment has been lost because the lawyer did not make the effort to provide proper evidence in affidavit form. However, an "attorney's affidavit" or "paralegal's affidavit" is appropriate when it deals with a material fact concerning a procedural matter. Of course, lawyers and paralegals may make affidavits concerning facts they have developed in the course of their investigation, because they have personal knowledge of the facts.

Suppose John Jones made an oral offer to sell certain real estate at a specified price and William Smith orally accepted the offer. Suppose that Jones subsequently refused to convey the property as promised. If Smith sued to enforce the oral contract, Smith could move for summary judgment of dismissal on the grounds that an oral contract for the sale of real estate is unenforceable. This is true even if Jones admits making the offer and Smith accepted the offer. A contract to sell real estate must be in writing to be enforceable. The material (controlling) fact is that the purported contract was not in writing. Whether other facts are disputed, they become immaterial to the application of a dispositive rule of law.[5] The judge can apply the law to the two undisputed material facts: The contract was for the sale of land, and the contract was not in writing. Based on those facts, the defendant is entitled to summary judgment of dismissal.

A fact issue must be material to prevent summary judgment. In the preceding example, if the parties disagreed on the time and place and the land's description, the disagreements would not preclude summary judgment, because those facts are not material to the controlling rule of law. For example, in the typical automobile accident case, the cause of action accrues and the statute of limitations begins to run when the accident occurs. Suppose the applicable statute of limitations is two years. Suppose the date on which the action was commenced is easily determined from the clerk of court's records. If indisputable evidence shows that the action was commenced after the claim was barred, the action should be dismissed as a matter of law. It does not matter that there is a dispute concerning liability and damages, because the statute-of-limitations defense is dispositive of the entire case. For purposes of the summary judgment motion, the material facts are those relevant to the statute-of-limitations defense—that is, the date of the accident and the date on which the action was commenced. The defendant is entitled to an order granting summary judgment of dismissal.

Sometimes parties do not know what facts are material until they complete discovery, so motions for summary judgment are seldom made until the parties have completed discovery. Because the moving party has the burden of showing there is no dispute on the material facts, if an opponent contests a fact, the moving party must show that the alleged disputed fact is not material to the grounds for summary judgment. The court should resolve any reasonable doubt against the moving party.

A plaintiff must wait until at least twenty days after commencement of the action to serve a motion for summary judgment. A defendant may serve a summary judgment motion any time after commencement of the action[6] [Rule 56(a)]. However, if the defendant serves a motion for summary judgment within the first twenty days, the plaintiff may immediately serve a cross-motion for summary judgment. A defendant may not serve a motion for summary judgment on his or her counterclaim or cross-claim until twenty days after serving the counterclaim or cross-claim. As a practical matter, most summary judgment motions are made only after both parties have had an opportunity to conduct sufficient discovery to support or oppose such a motion. Otherwise, the court will often postpone the motion until all parties have had a fair opportunity to conduct discovery. A summary judgment motion and all supporting documents must be served at least ten days before the hearing [Rule 56(c)]. When a motion is served by mail, add three days to the allotted time. Though Rule 56(c) does not clearly say so, it contemplates that the moving party will receive the opposing affidavits at least one day before the hearing. But remember, most courts have local rules that expand these time requirements.

A moving party must serve all supporting affidavits and documents with the motion. All documents offered to support or oppose a summary judgment motion must be of a kind that would be admissible into evidence at trial. A party may not establish or challenge a material fact with evidence that would not be received in a trial. However, the form in which the evidence is presented does differ. In other words, a witness's testimony must be presented by affidavit, deposition, or in answers to interrogatories. At trial, the witness would give oral testimony.

When parties agree that no fact issue exists and work together to submit the case to the court, the parties usually make cross-motions for summary judgment.[7] A court may still determine, notwithstanding the parties' mutual desire to obtain a summary resolution, there is a disputed material fact and deny the cross-motions for summary judgment.

A party incurs some risk in making a motion for summary judgment. The risk is that the court will agree no fact issue exists but award summary judgment in favor of the nonmoving party. The court has authority to do so, and courts have done so. Even though the court denies a summary judgment motion, the court may determine, and provide in its order, that certain facts are conceded and, therefore, for purposes of the trial, established [Rule 56(d)]. The effect is like that of a Rule 36 admission. Also, a motion for summary judgment may force both parties to disclose some of their strategies.

Needless to say, a summary judgment motion is a serious step. The motion may end the case. When a court is confronted with conflicting affidavits and believes the parties have acted in good faith, the court should deny the summary judgment motion and let the case proceed to trial. A judge may not weigh the credibility of the affidavits or the quantity of evidence offered to support and oppose a summary judgment motion. But the court should analyze the evidence for admissibility and disregard any inadmissible evidence.

Partial Summary Judgments

A summary judgment may resolve a part of a case leaving the rest to go to trial. A summary judgment may dismiss one of several causes of action or one of several affirmative defenses or one of several parties. Suppose the plaintiff brought an action against the defendant for injuries caused by a product the defendant sold. Suppose the plaintiff's action is based on breach of warranty and negligence. Suppose the breach-of-warranty claim is subject to a four-year statute of limitations, and the negligence claim is subject to a six-year statute of limitations. If the plaintiff commenced the action five years after the causes of action accrued, the defendant is entitled to a partial summary judgment dismissing the warranty claim. A summary judgment may determine that a defendant is liable to the plaintiff, but leave for trial the issue of damages. Exhibit 17.5

EXHIBIT 17.5

Notice of Motion and Motion for Summary Judgment

United States District Court for the
Southern District of Illinois
Civil Action, File Number CV06-00783

Roberta Jones, Plaintiff,

   vs.

William Smith, Defendant.

NOTICE OF MOTION

PLEASE TAKE NOTICE that on the 2nd day of February 2006 at 10:00 o' clock in the morning defendant will bring the attached motion for hearing at the United States Federal Court House before the Honorable James Johnston, courtroom 505, or as soon thereafter as the matter may be heard.

MOTION

The plaintiff hereby moves the court for an order granting summary judgment to plaintiff holding that defendant is liable to plaintiff for money damages, in an amount to be determined by trial, for defendant's wrongful trespass upon plaintiff's real estate and destruction of plaintiff's trees.

This motion is made pursuant to Rule 56 of the Federal Rules of Civil Procedure.

This motion for partial summary judgment is made upon the grounds that defendant's answer admits that defendant entered plaintiff's property by mistake and mistakenly cut down plaintiff's trees and denies only the amount of plaintiff's loss. Defendant's mistake is not a defense to an action in trespass. There is no dispute concerning any material fact that would prevent the court from holding defendant liable in trespass as a matter of law.

This motion is made upon plaintiff's complaint, defendant's answer, and plaintiff's affidavit, which identifies the trees, their location upon plaintiff's property, and plaintiff's ownership. Further, plaintiff's affidavit shows that defendant did not have plaintiff's consent to enter upon plaintiff's land.

[date]

Attorney for Plaintiff

/s/_____

is an example of a motion for partial summary judgement. A summary judgment may be awarded to a plaintiff on the question of liability and damages against one defendant, but leave for trial the plaintiff's claims against another defendant in the same case.

As an example of a summary judgment that defeats an affirmative defense, suppose a property owner brought an action in trespass against the defendant for entering upon the plaintiff's property and removing trees. Suppose the defendant alleges in his answer that he had the plaintiff's consent to cut and remove the trees. The plaintiff could support a summary judgment motion with his affidavit that states he did not consent to the entry or removal of any trees. If the defendant does not refute plaintiff's affidavit in good faith, the plaintiff would be entitled to a partial summary judgment eliminating the affirmative defense of consent, leaving only the issue of damages to be litigated [Rule 56(c)].

Uses and Limitations of Summary Judgments

Interpreting a Legal Document. Contracts, wills, mortgages, deeds, leases, and similar legal documents establish legal rights and obligations. The parties and a court often are able to determine those rights and obligations by simply referring to the document. But occasionally parties disagree about what a document means. Sometimes a document is ambiguous; sometimes the document seems incomplete; sometimes a party contends the document does not express the real agreement. If the parties' disagreement centers on the meaning or application of a legal document, they may ask the court to look at it and decide what it means or how it applies. *Juries do not interpret legal documents.* That is a judge's responsibility.[8] After the court determines what the document means, the court can determine what the parties' legal rights and obligations are and enter judgment accordingly.

Negligence Actions. Negligence actions are not well suited for summary judgment motions, because the ultimate questions in such cases are questions of fact. Even when there is no significant dispute about the underlying facts, usually a jury must decide whether a party's conduct was reasonable under the circumstances and whether the negligence was a proximate (legal) cause of the plaintiff's injury or loss. The criterion for determining whether a person was negligent is what a reasonable person would do or would not do under the same circumstances. Because a jury must decide what the hypothetical reasonable person would or would not have done, the jury must determine whether the party was negligent. If the jury decides a party did what a reasonable person would have done, then the jury finds that the party was not negligent. Similarly, proximate cause of an injury or other harm is an ultimate question of fact. For example, if a landlord in an apartment building used a "small" 60 watt bulb to light a stairway and the plaintiff fell on the stairway allegedly due to inadequate lighting, it would be a question of fact for the jury to decide whether the lighting was reasonable, whether the plaintiff used due care for his own safety, and whether the dim light was the proximate cause of plaintiff's fall. This is true even though there is no dispute about the light and that the plaintiff fell. Rarely can the question of reasonable care be decided as a matter of law. Consequently, in most negligence cases, even if the parties agree on what happened and how it happened, a jury has to decide whether the act or omission was negligent.

Legal Duty. Nevertheless, there are a few issues of law in negligence actions that permit a court to order summary judgment. When a dispute exists whether the defendant owed a legal duty to protect the plaintiff from the risk that caused the plaintiff's injury or loss, the issue may be decided as a matter of law. Consider, does a motorist have a legal duty to stop and warn other motorists about a hole in the road? No. Does a swimmer have a legal duty to try to save another swimmer who appears to be drowning? No. Does a subcontractor on a construction project have a duty to warn another subcontractor's employees about work site hazards it did not create? No. Does the owner of a boat have a duty to warn people who dive from the boat about the possibility of rocks under the water? No.[9] A person incurs a duty to assist or protect another from harm only if there is a **special relationship** between them and the nature of the special relationship creates a legal duty to assist or protect.

Suppose the plaintiff was a customer in a gas station and slipped on a small puddle of oil, fell, and was injured. Because business owners have a legal duty to protect patrons from dangerous conditions on the premises, the gas station will not succeed if it moves for summary judgment on the basis of duty. A jury would have to decide whether the station attendant was negligent for failing to discover the puddle of oil before the plaintiff fell and for not cleaning the floor to prevent the accident. The question of whether the attendant—the gas station's agent—used reasonable care (i.e., was negligent) is a question of fact. But suppose the plaintiff was injured by a robber as the plaintiff was leaving the gas station, and the plaintiff alleges that the station was negligent for failing to protect him from the robber. A court could examine the undisputed facts and determine, as a matter of law, that the plaintiff and the station did not have a special relationship that required the latter to protect the plaintiff from the robber. The issue whether a business has a legal duty to protect a customer from a robber is a question of law. If a business does not have a legal duty to protect a customer from a robber, the station could not be found negligent for failing to protect the plaintiff. The case could be resolved on a motion for summary judgment. If the court concluded that the law did impose a legal duty on the station to provide some protection, a jury would decide whether the station provided adequate protection.

When Expert Testimony Is Required.   When the standard of care must be established by expert testimony, as in a medical malpractice action, the plaintiff's failure to have the necessary expert testimony is a basis for summary judgment. If the plaintiff's answers to interrogatories state that the plaintiff does not have any experts to testify to the standard of care, that would be a basis for moving for summary judgment. The judge would have the option of dismissing the case or giving the plaintiff a specified period of time in which to find an expert to testify that the defendant violated the applicable standard of care when treating the plaintiff.

Application of Statutes or Ordinances.   Summary judgments may resolve cases concerning the application of an ordinance or statute. Suppose a city adopts an ordinance that provides all property-line fences must have a two-foot setback. Suppose the plaintiff's fence is on the property line shared with a neighbor and was in existence long before the ordinance was adopted. The plaintiff could use the summary judgment procedure to obtain a court declaration that the ordinance does or does not apply retroactively to her fence. The facts are not in dispute; the issue concerns how the law is to apply to uncontested facts.

Interpreting Legal Documents.   Suppose the plaintiff brought suit on a written contract in which the plaintiff claims that the defendant agreed to sell a certain parcel of land to the plaintiff and a dispute exists concerning one of the terms of the contract. If the parties agree they have a contract and the only issue concerns the

special relationship   A term or phrase used by courts to identify a relationship between persons that gives rise to legal rights and obligations (duties) between them.

proper interpretation of the contract, the matter can be determined by summary judgment. However, if the court determines that the contract is ambiguous and controverted evidence outside the written document is necessary to properly construe the contract, there is an issue of fact that precludes the court from granting summary judgment.

Opposing Summary Judgment

A party who opposes a motion for summary judgment has a right to adequately prepare for it. If the opponent needs more time, he or she has a right to a postponement of the hearing to prepare. The opposing litigation team must prepare and file an attorney's affidavit stating he or she needs more time to obtain evidence with which to oppose the motion [Rule 56(f)]. The affidavit must identify the missing evidence and state when and how he or she expects to obtain it. For example, suppose the defendant asserted a release as an affirmative defense, and the plaintiff takes the position that the release is void because it was obtained by fraud. Nevertheless, suppose the defendant proceeds to base a summary judgment motion on the release. The plaintiff is entitled a reasonable amount of time to take depositions of witnesses to prove the release was obtained by fraud. When an attorney serves and files an affidavit to obtain a postponement of a summary judgment motion, the moving party usually agrees but seeks agreement to a new date. If the parties cannot agree, they may appear at court for the summary judgment motion as scheduled, but the opponent's request for postponement will be considered first. If the court finds the request for postponement reasonable and properly documented, the court will order a postponement. The court will decide how soon the opponent must complete discovery. The order may specify exactly what additional discovery may be conducted and set a new date for hearing the summary judgment motion.

The most common grounds for avoiding a summary judgment motion is to show the court there is a fact issue that requires a trial. But a summary judgment opponent cannot create a fact issue by merely denying that the moving party's evidence is true. An opponent has the burden of presenting documentary evidence that shows a fact dispute exists [Rule 56(e)].

> When a motion for summary judgment is made and supported as provided in this rule, an adverse party may not rest upon the mere allegations or denials of the adverse party's pleading, but the adversary's response, by affidavits or as otherwise provided in this rule, must set forth specific facts showing that there is a genuine issue [of fact] for trial. If the adverse party does not so respond, summary judgment, if appropriate, shall be entered against the adverse party.

This provision cannot be applied literally to all cases. Suppose the plaintiff is a business invitee on the defendant's premises and claims that she fell because of a small accumulation of water in the hallway of the defendant's building. Suppose the incident was not reported until a week later, and the defendant's management has no information about the puddle. If the defendant has no knowledge about the water or about the plaintiff's alleged accident, how can the defendant present "specific facts showing that there is a genuine issue for trial"? The defendant's affidavits will have to show that no one else reported any slippery condition or accumulation of water on the premises at the time of the plaintiff's accident and the plaintiff did not give the defendant notice of the alleged accident until days later. These are merely general denials, not specific facts that mitigate against the plaintiff's accident. Nevertheless, the affidavit's allegations are sufficient to create a fact issue and preclude summary judgment in the plaintiff's favor. A jury will have to decide whether there was a puddle of water; whether it existed for such a period of time that the defendant should have discovered it and removed it; whether the plaintiff actually fell on the premises; and whether the puddle caused the plaintiff to fall. Courts recognize that trying to prove a negative is very difficult. But a party is entitled to a summary judgment when the opponent cannot produce any evidence to prove a claim or defense. That is the reason for having summary judgments. The summary judgment procedure helps courts to get rid of cases that lack merit.

Attorneys' Fees and Costs

Rule 56(g) authorizes a court to award attorneys' fees and costs against any party who files an affidavit to delay a summary judgment without having grounds. Suppose the plaintiff moves for summary judgment and the defendant interposed affidavits in bad faith to prevent summary judgment. Suppose the plaintiff spends $5,000 for attorneys' fees and other costs preparing for trial. The plaintiff is entitled to recover those costs because of the improper affidavits. The costs could be added to the plaintiff's judgment or made the subject of a separate order. Furthermore, an affiant who gives a false affidavit is subject to criminal prosecution for perjury.

Posttrial Motions

A trial and jury verdict do not always end the litigation. A party who is dissatisfied with the outcome may try to obtain relief from the verdict or judgment through one or more posttrial motions. Occasionally, both parties consider the verdict to be unsatisfactory and both may make posttrial motions. There are several kinds of posttrial motions. They may be combined or made in the alternative, depending on what the moving party sees as the problem. The most common posttrial motions are prescribed by court rules. The moving party must comply with the strict time requirements prescribed by the rules. The time constraints are designed to keep a losing party from delaying justice. The trial lawyer must decide which posttrial motions to make and identify the grounds for the motions. Paralegals may be asked to prepare the posttrial notice of motion and motion, and to assemble the supporting documentation. The trial lawyer must sign the motion papers.

There are countless opportunities for error in a trial. Errors may occur in the procedures, rulings on the evidence, party misconduct, juror misconduct, judge's misconduct, misstatement of the substantive law in the jury instructions, and so forth. Regardless of the type of error, the moving party is entitled to relief from the jury's verdict if the error was *preserved* by a timely objection and the error was *prejudicial*.

Preserving Error

A timely objection gives the trial judge an opportunity to consider the problem, deal with it, and correct it. If a party fails to object to an error, the error is waived. A party may not ignore an error and wait to see the outcome before complaining about the error.

Posttrial motions give the trial judge another opportunity to consider errors already brought to the judge's attention. In addition, a few errors, called **plain errors** or **fundamental errors,** may be noted for the first time in a posttrial motion. Plain error is very basic error that goes to the heart of the case. By characterizing an error in this manner, an appellate court acquires some discretion in deciding whether to deal with the problem. If the court concludes that a serious miscarriage of justice occurred, it may call the error "plain error," using that characterization as a basis for setting aside the lower court's judgment even though the error was missed during trial. One factor courts consider is whether the party who committed the error did it with design. The system provides many checks and balances in an effort to ensure a fair trial and proper result according to law.

Prejudicial Error

As a human endeavor, trials will have errors. But if the trial was conducted without any *prejudicial* error, there is no basis for changing the result. Otherwise, trials would never be final. The system requires lawyers to work to keep errors from becoming prejudicial. For example, when a lawyer objects to improper evidence but the jury has already heard the witness's answer, the lawyer must ask the court to instruct the jury to disregard the answer. The error does not warrant a new trial, unless it is very serious.

Error is considered prejudicial only if it adversely affects the outcome of the case. Rule 61 provides guidelines for identifying **prejudicial error:**

> No error in either the admission or the exclusion of evidence and no error of defect in any ruling or order or in anything done or omitted by the court or by any of the parties is ground for granting a new trial or for setting aside a verdict or for vacating, modifying or otherwise disturbing a judgment or order, unless refusal to take such action appears to the court inconsistent with substantial justice. The court at every stage of the proceeding must disregard any error or defect in the proceeding which does not affect the substantial rights of the parties.

A large body of case law focuses on what constitutes a substantial right and when error is considered to be prejudicial. The important point to appreciate is that unless the trial court's errors likely affected the outcome of the case, it will not warrant posttrial relief.

For example, suppose the plaintiff and defendant were involved in a motor vehicle accident. The plaintiff was injured and brought an action in negligence. The judge mistakenly allowed the plaintiff to present evidence that suggested the defendant was intoxicated at the time of the accident, and the defendant objected to the evidence. The jury returned a verdict in favor of the plaintiff, awarding damages in a large amount but not so large as to be shocking. Suppose the defendant makes a posttrial motion for a new trial on all issues, claiming that the evidence of his intoxication was improperly allowed. Assume further that the judge concludes there was insufficient foundation to raise the issue of intoxication. The judge must decide whether the jury might have found the defendant negligent because of intoxication and whether the evidence about intoxication could have affected the amount of damages awarded; otherwise, the evidence was not prejudicial. The judge should consider the following issues: (1) Intoxication is not, by itself, a basis for imposing civil liability. The defendant did not breach any legal duty to the plaintiff when he became intoxicated. However, the defendant's state of intoxication is evidence that tends to explain why he drove his car improperly or might have driven improperly.

People, including jurors, are inclined to believe that a drunk person has or will be negligent. In this case, the plaintiff had to prove that the defendant did something wrong, such as failed to keep a proper lookout, drove on the wrong side of the road, or drove at an excessive speed. Without proof of some such act or omission, the plaintiff fails to prove a prima facie case of negligence against the defendant, regardless of whether or not the defendant was intoxicated. So, presumably there was some evidence the defendant committed a wrongful act. (2) Was the jury more likely to find that the defendant committed the wrongful act if they found that he was intoxicated? If so, the evidence of intoxication was prejudicial, because it could have affected the outcome of the case. Here, if the evidence concerning the defendant's speed was conflicting, a jury might be more inclined to find the defendant was speeding if he were intoxicated. (3) Did the evidence prejudice the amount of the verdict? If the verdict was within an acceptable range, but high, the evidence may have affected the jury's evaluation. Jurors tend to award higher damages, almost as a penalty, against drunk drivers. If the award was low, however, the judge has to decide whether the jury might have made a compromise between awarding some damages and awarding none. If the judge concludes that the amount of the verdict was a compromise, the judge should award a new trial on damages as well as liability.

Motion for New Trial

Where the alleged error may have affected the outcome of the case, but the court cannot ascertain how the case would have been decided if the error had not occurred, the remedy is to order a new trial. Hopefully, the error will not be repeated. A new trial on all issues is often called a **trial de novo.** Any error in procedure, evidence, or substantive law that could have affected the jury's verdict is grounds for a motion for new trial. The new trial may be on all issues or only those issues that could have been affected by the error. The moving party does not have to prove that the error did in fact affect the outcome. That would be impossible.

trial de novo A second trial that is a new trial in all respects. A trial de novo is totally unaffected by rulings or determinations made in the first trial.

A motion for a new trial must be served on all parties within ten days after the entry of judgment (Rule 59). To illustrate, if judgment was entered on Monday, the ten-day period begins to run on Tuesday. The tenth day would be the second Thursday. The motion must be filed on or before the second Thursday.

A motion for a new trial must state the precise grounds for the motion. Proof of the error may be established by having a partial transcript of the proceedings prepared by the court reporter. The motion may be supported by affidavits of persons who have knowledge of the claimed errors. In addition, the motion is almost always based on the facts as recorded in the **judge's minutes**—official notes—made during the trial.

judge's minutes The notes a judge keeps concerning the evidence and proceedings in a trial.

The Rules provide that a trial judge may order a new trial within ten days after the entry of judgment even though neither party has made a motion for a new trial. The same power permits the trial judge to order a new trial on grounds that were not raised by the moving party's motion for a new trial. The court must give the parties notice and an opportunity to be heard, and the order for a new trial must state the reasons or grounds for granting a new trial. An order denying the motion for a new trial needs no explanation.

A motion for a new trial is the first step to an appeal. In some state courts a motion for a new trial is a prerequisite to an appeal. It gives the trial judge an opportunity to consider and correct the alleged errors. It also gives the judge an opportunity to specify his or her reasons explaining away the alleged errors.

Common Grounds for a New Trial

There are many possible grounds for seeking a new trial. Most of the grounds fit into one of the following categories.

Misconduct on the Part of One or More Jurors.   If a juror were to conduct an investigation of the case outside of the courtroom, that would constitute misconduct that could require a new trial. If a juror were to have contact with a party or witness before or during the trial and not disclose the contact to the court, that could give the appearance of favoritism or worse. A juror's false statement in the voir dire examination would be juror misconduct. A jury also engages in misconduct by returning a **quotient verdict**.[10]

quotient verdict   A verdict for money damages arrived at by having each juror select an amount, adding the amounts together, and dividing the total by the number of jurors. The jurors then agree on the quotient amount as the amount for the verdict.

Misconduct on the Part of the Prevailing Party.   If the prevailing party concealed evidence, concealed witnesses, suborned perjury, made an improper, prejudicial remark during the final argument, or engaged in some other form of misconduct, the trial court should order a new trial. The misconduct must be substantial, prejudicial, and not corrected during the trial. Even though an attorney may have committed the wrongful act, the wrong is characterized as "party misconduct."

Newly Discovered Evidence.   The moving party must show the court that the newly discovered evidence did not exist, was unavailable, or could not have been found through the exercise of due diligence. The party must show the new evidence could have changed the outcome of the case. Parties must diligently gather their evidence *before* trial. If a party finds that more time is needed to secure important evidence, the party should move the court for an order postponing trial. It would be unfair for a party to neglect to gather or present evidence and then use the omission to obtain a new trial. This rule illustrates the adversarial nature of civil litigation. It manifests the duty each party has to be self-reliant in obtaining and presenting evidence. The verdict is final, even if wrong, where the parties have had a full, fair opportunity to present their claims and defenses. If a party finds new evidence after expiration of the time for making posttrial motions, too bad. If all parties have had a fair opportunity, there must be finality to every dispute.

Inappropriate Award of Damages.   The amount of compensation to be awarded is peculiarly a question of fact for a jury. Nevertheless, courts have developed a sense of proportion about the adequacy or inadequacy of money damages for most types of cases. If an award does not shock the judge's conscience as either too high or too low, it must stand. But an award that is manifestly unfair should be set aside and a new trial should be ordered. The new trial may be limited to the issue of damages only.

A party who moves the court for a new trial on the issue of damages usually combines the motion with a request for an **additur** to the verdict if the award is too little or a **remittitur** to the verdict if the award is too much. An order for an additur increases the award to a specified amount. An order for a remittitur reduces the award to a specified amount. The trial judge may determine that a certain amount of money added to or taken away from the verdict will do substantial justice, and by ordering a change in the award, the expense of a new trial is avoided. The judge must condition his or her order for a new trial on the basis that if the plaintiff will accept a remittitur a new trial is denied. Or, if the award is unconscionably small, the judge

additur   A court-ordered increase of money damages awarded by a jury.

remittitur   A court-ordered reduction in the amount of money damages awarded to a party by a jury.

may order a new trial on damages but provide that if the defendant will agree to pay an additur, the new trial motion is denied.

Suppose the jury returns a verdict for $1,000,000, and the judge concludes that amount is excessive. If the judge decides that an award of $250,000 would be fully adequate, the judge may order a remittitur. If the plaintiff accepts the reduction, the defendant's motion for a new trial on damages is denied. If the plaintiff refuses to accept the reduction, the defendant's motion for a new trial is granted. Similarly, a judge may order an additur for the plaintiff on the condition that the defendant agrees to pay the increased amount. If the defendant refuses to pay the additur, the plaintiff is given a new trial, and the defendant runs the risk of having to pay even more.

Additurs and remittiturs are very rare. A verdict must be out of all proportion to a reasonable amount before a judge will consider one. Were it otherwise, trial by jury would end up being trial by judge, and that would cause a breakdown in our system.

Jury Instructions.   If a lawyer believes that the court misstated the law in the jury instructions, she or he is required to bring that error to the judge's attention *before* the jury commences deliberations. Ordinarily, as soon as the judge finishes instructing the jury on the law, she or he asks the lawyers whether there were any errors or omissions in the instructions. The lawyers must speak then or waive the right to complain. It is unnecessary to repeat objections about errors in the instructions that were fully discussed on the record, in chambers, before the judge undertook to instruct the jury. Also, a lawyer preserves her or his objections by filing written requested instructions that correctly cover the rule in question.

Verdict Not Supported by the Evidence.   If a party believes that no evidence supported the particular claim or defense, he or she may make a motion for a new trial on that ground. Usually, it is very difficult to obtain a new trial on this ground, because almost any believable evidence on a fact issue is enough. The trial court, in effect, has a duty to sustain the verdict if reasonably possible. The court must resolve reasonable doubt in favor of the verdict. This motion is always accompanied by a motion for judgment as a matter of law.

Motion for Judgment as a Matter of Law

The grounds for making a motion for judgment as a matter of law are that the determinative issue must be decided as a matter of law, or the evidence is insufficient to establish the opponent's cause of action or affirmative defense, even though the jury has found in favor of the opponent. The verdict should be set aside if no competent evidence reasonably tends to support the verdict. The grounds for granting judgment as a matter of law are similar to those for granting a Rule 56 summary judgment, except the judge has had the opportunity to hear and consider the evidence.

This posttrial motion is useful when the trial judge denied a summary judgment motion believing the jury would not find as it did and the judge wanted the parties to have their case decided by a jury. Because the jury did the unexpected thing, the judge must now correct the error. Another situation that may give rise to a successful posttrial motion is when the judge does not have time to fully consider the applicable law and, rather than make the jury wait for the court and lawyers to fully consider the law, submits the case in line with the prevailing party's theory. After further consideration, the judge may conclude that the legal theory was wrong or unsupported by the evidence. To correct the problem, the judge may grant judgment to the losing party as a matter of law. This motion is usually combined with a motion for new trial. (See Rules 50,59).

Motion for Amended Findings

When a jury returns a special verdict, the judge must make findings of fact and conclusions of law based on the answers to the special verdict questions. If the case was tried to a judge without a jury, so the judge made findings of fact, conclusions of law, and an order for judgment, the moving party may move the court for amended findings of fact or amended conclusions of law or both.

Posttrial Motion Format

As stated earlier, a motion should have four parts. The motion should state what relief the moving party wants the court to provide, the procedural rule (if any) under which the motion is made, each of the grounds for the motion, and it should specify the documents the party used to support the motion.

The following motion is similar to one made by a defendant landlord who was held liable in negligence for the rape of a tenant committed by an intruder who entered the apartment through a ground-floor window. The landlord contended that he did not have a legal duty to protect the tenant from a break-in and that the tenant had left the window open. The plaintiff tenant contended that the window lock was defective, and that consequently she was unable to lock the window. The landlord argued that if the tenant knew the lock was defective, which he denied, she had a duty to repair the lock or take other action to secure the window. Furthermore, the lease provided that the landlord was not responsible for repairing or maintaining the premises. The law is that if the tenant knew the lock was defective, the landlord had no further duty to warn or repair. In addition, there was a question whether a landlord could be held liable for the criminal acts of the intruder. The jury returned a **special verdict** for the plaintiff tenant. The judge made findings of fact, conclusions of law, and an order for judgment for the plaintiff based on the jury's verdict. The defendant landlord moved for judgment as a matter of law, and, in the alternative, for a new trial. The defendant also moved for amended findings and conclusions of law. Two or more posttrial motions may be combined into one document. See Exhibit 17.6.

special verdict   A verdict form in which a jury answers specific questions about the facts of the case.

SUMMARY

A motion is an application to a court for an order granting some kind of relief, guidance, help, or protection. When parties are before the court they may make oral motions concerning anything relevant to the matter under consideration. If they are in trial, the motion may concern anything that relates to the trial. If they are before the court for a special proceeding, the oral motion must concern that proceeding. Otherwise, a motion must be in writing. Then the moving party must give notice to opposing parties about the nature of the motion, and the time and place the motion will be heard. Parties usually support their written motions with written arguments

EXHIBIT 17.6

*Notice of Motion and
Combined Motions*

Butler County District Court for the
State of Illinois
Civil Action, File Number CV06-00783

Roberta Jones, Plaintiff,

    vs.

William Smith, Defendant.

NOTICE OF MOTIONS

PLEASE TAKE NOTICE that on June 28, 2006, at 9:00 A.M., or as soon thereafter as counsel can be heard, defendant will move the court for judgment as a matter of law, or amended findings, or, in the alternative, for a new trial. Said motions are scheduled to be heard by the Honorable Ann Balton in room C751 of the County Government Center, Smithville, Illinois.

MOTION FOR JUDGMENT AS A MATTER OF LAW

The defendant hereby moves the court for an order granting judgment as a matter of law to the defendant.

This motion is made pursuant to Rules 50.02 and 59 of the Illinois Rules of Civil Procedure.

The grounds for the defendant's motion are that the defendant was entitled to a directed verdict at the conclusion of the plaintiff's case-in-chief and at the close of all the evidence. Specifically, the plaintiff's claim and testimony that she knew the "shell lock" on the window in question could not be engaged so as to keep the window from being opened from the outside, precluded the defendant landlord from having any legal duty to warn the plaintiff about the lock or to repair the lock in question.

The plaintiff's second theory of negligence contradicted her first theory and was unsupported by the evidence. Specifically, the plaintiff testified that the window lock could not be engaged, and the plaintiff's counsel was allowed to argue that the assailant was able to force the window open from the outside because the shell lock used washers as spacers and that the defendant was negligent for having spacers in the lock.

The great weight of the evidence showed that the window lock in question was operable and the plaintiff failed to use the lock.

The jury's determination that the plaintiff sustained a loss of earning capacity in the amount of $250,000 is contrary to the great weight of the evidence and was the result of passion and prejudice. The award is excessive as a matter of law.

continued

The grounds for these motions are stated more fully in the defendant's memorandum of law, which is served herewith.

This motion is made on the court's minutes, court's files, exhibits, and records, including deposition transcripts used at trial, a partial transcript of the plaintiff's testimony, and the defendant's memorandum of law.

MOTION FOR AMENDED FINDINGS OF FACT, CONCLUSIONS OF LAW, AND ORDER FOR JUDGMENT

The defendant hereby moves the court for an order amending the court's findings of facts, conclusions of law, and order for judgment so as to determine that the defendant was not negligent and his alleged negligence was not a proximate cause of the plaintiff's injury.

This motion is made pursuant to Rule 52.02 of the Illinois Rules of Civil Procedure.

The grounds for this motion are that the findings of fact are contrary to the evidence and contrary to the great weight of the evidence and contrary to law.

This motion is made on the files, exhibits, deposition transcripts used at trial, trial transcripts, and minutes of the court.

MOTION FOR NEW TRIAL

The defendant hereby moves the court for an order granting to the defendant a new trial on all issues.

This motion is made pursuant to Rule 59 of the Illinois Rules of Civil Procedure.

The grounds for the defendant's motion are as follows:

1. There were irregularities in the proceedings of the court that deprived the defendant of a fair trial, including the following:
   a. The plaintiff was permitted to argue that an event is foreseeable if it is a mere possibility.
   b. The plaintiff was permitted to argue two theories of liability that were in direct conflict with each other and that were contrary to the great weight of the evidence.
   c. The plaintiff did not offer evidence to rebut the legal presumption that an intentional criminal act is not foreseeable by the parties and is to be treated as a superseding cause of the plaintiff's harm.
2. There were irregularities in the proceedings by the prevailing party that prevented the defendant from having a fair trial.
3. Plain errors of law concerning admissibility of evidence occurred at trial, to which objections were made at the time.

EXHIBIT 17.6

Notice of Motion and Combined Motions (continued)

4. The special verdict answers 1, 2, 3, 8, and 10 are not justified by the evidence.
5. The court's decision and order for judgment based on the special verdict answers are not justified by the evidence.
6. The special verdict answers 1, 2, and 3 are contrary to law.
7. The court's decision and order for judgment are contrary to law.
8. The awarded damages for loss of earning capacity, future pain, and emotional distress are excessive in amount and appear to have been rendered under the influence of passion and prejudice.

These motions are made on the court's minutes, files, exhibits, and records, including deposition transcripts used at trial and partial transcripts of testimony at trial.

JOHNSON AND JOHNSON

DATED: April 3, 2006

By _____

B. L. Bogat
Mary M. Cleary
Attorneys for Defendant
4200 Trenton Tower
333 South Sixth Street
Springfield, Illinois 55402
(555) 555-5555

in the form of memoranda to the court. When the argument concerns the law, parties' memoranda provide the court with legal authorities and legal analysis. When the argument concerns a fact issue or is based on facts, the parties usually submit affidavits, deposition transcripts, and exhibits to support or oppose motions. Paralegals may identify the need to make a motion. They may draft written motions and prepare supporting affidavits. They may draft affidavits, and assemble documents and other exhibits to support or oppose a written motion. They may schedule motions for argument. Paralegals may not make oral motions, sign written motions, or appear in court to argue motions.

A written motion should contain four parts: (1) a statement that identifies the help or relief that the moving party wants; (2) the legal authority the moving party is relying on as a basis for the motion; (3) the grounds, or reasons, why the court should grant the motion; and (4) identification of the supporting documentation. Many motions are time limited. It is important to check the Rules and the local rules to make sure the motion is timely and that sufficient notice is given.

When the dispute can be reduced to one or two dispositive legal issues, a summary judgment motion may be appropriate. Motions for summary judgment are used to resolve issues of law and to apply the law to a given set of facts. Defendants may use motions for summary judgment to obtain dismissal of a plaintiff's cause of action. Plaintiffs may use summary judgment motions to eliminate nonmeritorious affirmative defenses. A summary judgment may end the entire case, or only a part of the case. A dispute over some facts does not preclude a summary judgment if the disputed facts are not material to the dispositive legal issue. A fact is material if it affects application of the law to the case. Motions for summary judgment are seldom made until after the parties have completed their discovery procedures.

Only documentary evidence may be used to support a summary judgment motion. Oral testimony may be used only if it has been reduced to a deposition transcript or affidavit and served and filed with the motion. Other documents that may be used to support a summary judgment include pleadings, exhibits, written stipulations, interrogatory answers, and Rule 36 admissions. A party can not use statements from his or her own pleadings to establish facts but can use admissions in an opponent's pleading. The affidavits may only recite facts that would be admissible in evidence. The affiant must show he or she is competent to testify and has personal knowledge about the facts. All documents referred to in an affidavit must be attached to the affidavit or served with it.

A party who moves for summary judgment has the burden of showing that no material fact is in dispute. When a court determines a material fact is in dispute, the court must deny the motion for summary judgment. This is true even if both parties have moved the court for summary judgment. When parties mutually agree no fact issue exists, they may enter into a written stipulation of facts and submit the case to the court on cross-motions for summary judgment. District courts accept stipulations of facts even though Rule 56 does not expressly authorize their use. A written stipulation of facts is conclusive for and against the parties, so the parties must make certain the stipulation is accurate.

A party may not defend against a summary judgment motion by merely contending the moving party's evidence is incorrect or incomplete. A party must come forward with documentary evidence of the type admissible in court to show that a dispute exists concerning one or more material facts. A party may obtain more time in which to oppose a summary judgment motion by submitting an affidavit to the court, explaining why the allotted time is insufficient and that the necessary evidence can be obtained within a reasonable period. The affiant must state what evidence he or she expects to obtain, from whom, when, and in what form it will be presented to the court. A person who gives a false affidavit is subject to criminal prosecution for perjury. A party who wrongly uses an affidavit to avoid summary judgment may be required to pay attorneys' fees the moving party incurred in preparing for a trial that was not necessary.

A defendant may serve and file a motion for summary judgment any time after commencement of the action. A plaintiff may not serve a motion for summary judgment until twenty days after commencement of the action. However, if the defendant serves a motion for summary judgment sooner, the plaintiff may immediately serve a cross-motion for summary judgment. A summary judgment motion must be served at least ten days before the hearing. When any motion is served by mail, three days are added to the allotted time. A summary judgment is a dispositive motion; therefore, a party may need additional days or weeks to prepare to resist the motion.

There are several types of posttrial motions. They may be combined with one another and may be presented in the alternative. The most common posttrial motions are motion for a new trial, motion for judgment as a matter of law, motion for additur, motion for remittitur, and motion for amended findings of fact or amended conclusions of law or both. An error must be prejudicial to be grounds for obtaining posttrial relief. Error is prejudicial only if the error could have affected the outcome of the case. Rule 61 provides guidelines for identifying prejudicial error. Plain error is very basic error that goes to the heart of the case. Even plain error must be prejudicial to be grounds for a new trial. Paralegals may prepare posttrial motions and notices of motion. Paralegals may prepare and assemble supporting documentation. It is the responsibility of the trial lawyer to determine which motions to make and the grounds for each motion. An attorney of record must sign the motion papers.

A motion for a new trial must be served on all parties within ten days after the entry of judgment. The motion must identify and verify the error. The moving party may use a trial transcript, affidavits, exhibits, or the judge's minutes to show the error occurred. A new trial may be granted on all issues or only on the issues that might have been affected by the error. The moving party does not have to prove that the error did in fact affect the outcome, merely that the error could have affected the outcome. A trial judge may order a new trial on its own motion within ten days after the entry of judgment even though neither party made a motion for a new trial. The same power permits the trial judge to order a new trial on grounds that were not raised by the moving party's motion for a new trial. The powers are almost never used.

The most common grounds for posttrial motions are jury misconduct, misconduct on the part of the prevailing party, discovery of new evidence, excessive or inadequate damages, unrectified errors of law at trial, and the verdict is not supported by the evidence. The grounds for obtaining judgment as a matter of law are that the determinative issue can be decided as a matter of law, or the evidence is insufficient to establish a cause of action. The standard for challenging the sufficiency of the evidence is that the verdict is contrary to all the evidence in the case and reasonable minds could not differ as to the correct outcome.

KEY TERMS

additur	plain error
cross-motions for summary judgment	prejudicial error
dispositive motion	procedural motion
fundamental error	quotient verdict
judge's minutes	remittitur
memorandum of law	special relationship
motion	special verdict
motion in limine	stipulation of facts
notice of motion	trial de novo

REVIEW QUESTIONS

1. How soon must a posttrial motion be made?

2. What are the criteria for deciding whether the court should order an additur?

3. What role may a paralegal have in handling a posttrial motion?

4. What is meant by plain error, and how does it differ from other error?

5. In the absence of plain error, what two circumstances must be established to justify an order for a new trial?

6. What four parts should every motion contain?

7. What are the criteria for granting a motion for judgment as a matter of law?

8. When does a party move for amended findings rather than a new trial?

9. Who decides whether an error was prejudicial to the moving party?

10. What are the potential benefits to a party who makes a motion for summary judgment?

11. In what form must the evidence be presented to support a motion for summary judgment?

12. At what point in a civil action may a defendant make a motion for summary judgment?

13. When is a disputed fact considered material so as to preclude a summary judgment?

14. Could a moving party use an opposing party's signed, unsworn statement to establish a fact to support a motion for summary judgment? If so, how?

15. May a party move the court to order a partial summary judgment?

16. May a party use admissions in pleadings to support a motion for summary judgment?

17. May a party use her or his own answers to interrogatories to oppose a motion for summary judgment?

18. May a party use the opponent's responses to requests for admissions to support a motion for summary judgment?

19. May a court grant summary judgment against the moving party?

CASE ASSIGNMENT

You are on attorney Catherine Dolan's litigation team and are helping agent Burns to defend against the fourth-party action that John Griffin brought for indemnity or contribution toward the plaintiff trustee's claim. Attorney Dolan has determined that the bill of sale and Harper's use of the pickup truck as his own are conclusive on the issue of ownership. Harper was the owner-in-fact at the time of the accident even though he did not have a certificate of title. Because Griffin did not own the pickup truck at the time of the accident, he could not buy liability insurance on the pickup to protect the owner-in-fact. He did not have an insurable interest. Otherwise, motorists could use subterfuge to obtain cheap insurance for high-risk motorists by pretending an insurable person was the owner. Attorney

Dolan has asked you to prepare a notice of motion and motion for summary judgment dismissing the fourth-party action. She will prepare a supporting memorandum of law. She believes that the only supporting documents you need to mention in the motion are the sale agreement between Griffin and Harper and Harper's recorded statement. They may be incorporated by reference. Give at least thirty days notice.

Endnotes

1. If service is by mail, add three days.
2. Information and belief may not be a sufficient basis to support some motions, such as a motion for summary judgment. However, it is usually sufficient for procedural motions.
3. In this example, damages still might be an issue so the plaintiff would not be entitled to a default judgment.
4. Emphasis added.
5. A rule of law is dispositive if it controls to resolve the entire case.
6. An action is commenced when the complaint is filed with the clerk of court, even though the summons and complaint may not be served until days later.
7. Cross-motion means that each party has moved the court for the same order in his or her favor.
8. For an excellent explanation about the judge's duty to construe legal documents, see *Otten vs. Stonewall Insurance Company,* 511 F.2d 143 (8th Cir. 1975). Even if the document is ambiguous, the judge must construe it, not the jury. The matter goes to a jury only if the document is ambiguous *and* evidence is admissible to clarify the ambiguity *and* there is a conflict in the evidence.
9. In *Harper vs. Herman,* 499 N.W.2d 472 (Minn. 1993), there is an instructive discussion about legal duties in negligence actions.
10. A quotient verdict is a compromise by which jurors agree to total damages that each one would award and then divide the sum by the number of jurors. The vice of a quotient verdict is that jurors are all supposed to agree that the amount awarded is based on their own evaluation.

 For additional resources, visit our Web site at www.paralegal.delmar.cengage.com

CHAPTER **18**

PREPARATION FOR TRIAL

Chapter Objectives

Chapter 18 explains the intricacies of preparing for trial, beginning with a case analysis and development of a trial strategy. It explains the importance of organizing the evidence and selecting the best evidence to promote a party's strategy. It describes the use of a trial notebook and the contributions a paralegal may make to it. The chapter makes suggestions for organizing the evidence, making appropriate disclosures, and dealing with witnesses who will be needed at trial.

Introduction

When a case is filed in federal court, it automatically moves toward trial along with many other cases. Some cases are accelerated on the trial calendar, and some are delayed because of special circumstances. Usually, cases progress according to the court's schedule and the presiding judge's preferences. Parties must be ready for trial when their case is called. A few state courts do not place a case on the active trial calendar until one of the parties certifies the case is ready for trial. You should find out what procedure the courts in your community follow.

Although a litigation team begins trial preparation with the initial meeting with the client, in this chapter we are concerned with "final preparation." At this point the litigation team has collected all the evidence. The issues have been narrowed through admissions, stipulations, and court orders. Nevertheless, the parties have been unable to settle their dispute. The case is going to trial. Now you must determine what evidence to use and how to use it. Now is the time to anticipate and solve problems. Now is the time to organize the evidence and put it in its most persuasive form. A trial is like a game of chess; a "move" that seems to benefit your client may cause problems. When your team offers evidence to prove a fact, you might unintentionally prove another fact that hurts the client's case or impairs the usefulness of other evidence. Your team may have a month in which to prepare or only a few days. Do not leave final preparation to the last minute. There is never enough time to do everything that could be done. Trial preparation has a collateral value. It may help the parties to reevaluate the case for purposes of settlement.

Paralegals can assemble and organize the evidence. You may prepare witnesses to testify and prepare documents for presentation. You can prepare illustrative exhibits and summaries to supplement the evidence. You can get the team ready to go! But first, the team must agree on the trial strategy. A trial strategy helps lawyers make decisions as a case develops. The first step to developing a trial strategy is to conduct a legal analysis. You want your client's evidence to prove facts that form a seamless web. The web should enfold the case. In other words, everything should fit together.

Case Analysis

A **case analysis** puts on paper the mental analysis a trial team must go through to prepare for trial. Airplane pilots use checklists to make sure they have addressed each pre-flight item before takeoff. A case analysis is a custom-made checklist that helps your team to determine whether it has all the evidence needed to prove every material fact, the best way to use the evidence, and the best way in which to present the evidence. A case analysis requires the team to review the legal issues in context of the facts and review the facts in context of the evidence. The trial team must be objective when evaluating their own evidence and the opponent's evidence. The analysis helps the trial team to maximize the persuasiveness of their evidence. It provides a basis for a winning strategy. More than anything else, a case analysis tells the trial team what more needs to be done to get ready for trial. Its value is in conducting the analysis, not the written product.

The term "case analysis" is not commonly used by lawyers, but it is convenient for our purposes. Some law schools require students to prepare written case analyses as part of their trial advocacy courses. Some continuing legal education courses teach lawyers how to handle new types of cases using case analyses. Although lawyers seldom prepare written analyses, they must go through each step. With experience, the process becomes intuitive. You will be more effective when working with trial lawyers if you understand how to make a case analysis. An analysis may deal with the entire case in great detail, like Exhibit 18.1, or it may deal with only one aspect of the case.

case analysis   A process a party may use to determine whether his or her care is ready for trial. It begins by comparing the pleadings against the known facts and available evidence.

Exhibit 18.1

Case Analysis

Abstract of Pleadings

Complaint	Answer
On June 7, 2004, plaintiffs and decedent entered into a contract in which plaintiffs agreed to give up their home and to move into decedent's house, and to take care of the decedent and his house until his death.	Denied. (Plaintiff did not agree to care of the decedent.)
In consideration of the agreement, the decedent promised to convey his house and lot at 74 Golf Terrace, Edison, Minnesota, to plaintiffs.	Denied.
Plaintiffs gave up their home, moved in with William Brown, and fully performed their part of said agreement.	Denied—that plaintiffs performed their part of the agreement.
Decedent devised his house to Edward Bordon in his will dated July 20, 2006, instead of devising his real property to plaintiffs as required by the agreement.	Denied—the existence of the agreement to devise decedent's property to plaintiffs.
Plaintiffs performed personal services valued at $50,000.	Denied—the performance of the services. No cause of action exists. Agreement is unenforceable because it is within the statute of frauds. Plaintiffs have been fully compensated by the salary of $100 a month, free rent and utilities, and the $2,000 bequest in the decedent's will.

Analysis

Issues

1. No agreement existed between the decedent and the plaintiffs whereby the decedent agreed to devise his real property at 74 Golf Terrace, Edison, Minnesota, to the plaintiffs in return for their services.
2. The services were not satisfactorily performed by the plaintiffs; therefore, they breached the contract, if there was one.
3. The alleged contract is voidable, because it violates the statute of frauds.

EXHIBIT 18.1

Case Analysis (continued)

DEFENDANT'S CASE-IN-CHIEF

1. No agreement was made between the plaintiffs and the decedent whereby the decedent promised to convey his real property at 74 Golf Terrace, Edison, Minnesota, in return for the performance of services by the plaintiffs, for the facts are as follows:

   a. The complaint states that only one arrangement was made between the plaintiffs and the decedent.

   b. This arrangement was allegedly made on June 7, 2006, during a dinner party at the decedent's home, given in honor of Dr. Carl Olson.

   c. Negotiations and statements concerning the arrangement were made during a card game in the presence of Dr. Carl Olson, William Mitchell, John Hughes, and William Brown, the decedent.

   d. The terms of the alleged arrangements were substantially these:

      1. The Hughes agreed to move into the upstairs apartment of the decedent's house.

      2. Take care of the yard and walks and perform other external maintenance on the house.

      3. Decedent agreed to pay the Hughes $100 a month and to provide the apartment and utilities at no cost.

   e. At no time during the negotiations or the ensuing arrangement was any reference or mention made concerning the decedent's house, or any agreement to devise said house to the plaintiffs at the decedent's death.

   f. The decedent made the proposal to John Hughes, and after a short discussion with Mrs. Hughes, the plaintiffs accepted these terms.

   g. No mention was made by either party that the plaintiffs would be personally caring for the decedent. The decedent was not then in need of any personal care.

THE LAW

1. Whether a contract was made is a question of fact to be determined by the jury. The burden is on the plaintiff to prove a contract was made and all its material terms. The terms of the contract must be specific, definite, and certain. This type of contract must be established by clear and convincing evidence, not merely by a preponderance of the evidence.

2. Because it is an oral contract, it is within the statute of frauds. The statute of frauds is a complete defense.

3. The plaintiffs failed to provide satisfactory care for the decedent's house and yard as provided by the contract, specifically as follows:

   a. The plaintiffs failed to rake the leaves, as a result of which the yard usually appeared unkept in the fall and spring and aroused ill will among several of the neighbors.

   b. The plaintiffs failed to cut the grass at reasonable intervals, causing large portions of the lawn to become infested with crabgrass and other noxious weeds.

continued

c. The plaintiffs were normally several months late in changing the storm windows and screens and failed entirely to change the storm windows in 2005.

d. The plaintiffs never shoveled the snow from the sidewalks.

e. The plaintiffs failed to remove an accumulation of ice from the front sidewalk, the accumulation having occurred from the runoff of an eaves spout. As a result, a passing neighbor fell and broke his ankle, and under threat of an action at law, the decedent paid $750 to the claimant as a settlement.

f. The reason for the lack of care given to the maintenance of the yard and house, besides irresponsibility, may be that the plaintiff was gainfully employed as a paintbrush salesperson and, in carrying on his business, had little time to devote to the property.

g. The decedent did some of the outside work himself, when it became apparent that it would not otherwise be done.

h. The plaintiffs sporadically helped the decedent clean the lower floor of the house, and the decedent normally did his cleaning himself.

i. The decedent did his own cooking, laundry, and other personal chores.

j. The plaintiffs, although friendly with the decedent, remained aloof from the decedent in both their daily living activities and social activities. Mrs. Hughes was often out with her friends and often entertained in the apartment.

k. Robert Burger, the decedent's attorney, acted as the decedent's financial adviser and kept all his accounts.

l. As compensation for the arrangement, the plaintiffs received $100 a month, free rent, and utilities. They also received a bequest of $2000 in the decedent's will.

m. The decedent was at all times in good physical condition and capable of caring for himself.

The law is as follows: When an oral agreement is made unenforceable by the statute of frauds and does not merit specific performance, the plaintiff may recover only damages for services actually rendered under the agreement. The theory of recovery is "quasi-contract." The measure of damages is the value of the services to the decedent, less the benefits the plaintiffs received under the contract. The plaintiff cannot recover damages for any breach of the *oral* contract. The value of the property to be devised is not a measure of recovery.

To obtain specific performance of an oral contract, the terms of the contract must be definite and certain. The services must be performed under the terms of the contract. To merit specific performance, the services must be of a peculiar and personal nature. If the partial performance of the contract is as beneficial to the plaintiff as to the deceased, specific performance will not be allowed.

EXHIBIT 18.1

Case Analysis (continued)

Plaintiffs' Anticipated Case-in-Chief

1. They made an oral contract with the decedent. The decedent promised to devise his house and lot to the plaintiffs. They will testify the terms of the contract were stated, "If you come and live with me and care for me and my house until I die, I will bequeath my house to you." Mr. Hughes, "I accept."

   Meet this by disputing the terms of the alleged contract and by contending that these terms do not specify that the plaintiffs were to assume a "peculiar" domestic relationship with the decedent.

2. The plaintiffs are entitled to recover $50,000 for the value of the services they performed.

   Meet this by showing the services were not performed adequately and, sometimes, not performed at all. Show what the proper measure of recovery is, and show that the plaintiffs have been fully compensated. Show the plaintiffs' failure to present their claim in probate court. Show the actual value of the services the plaintiffs allegedly performed.

3. The decedent made statements to neighbors to the effect that the plaintiffs were to receive the property when the decedent died.

   Meet this by showing that the witness is a friend of the plaintiffs and is biased. Show that the plaintiffs never objected to the will. Show that the plaintiffs made statements adverse to their pecuniary interest: They did not know what they were going to do or where they were going to go if the decedent were to die.

4. The plaintiffs will testify as to their close relationship with the decedent.

   Meet this by showing that the decedent addressed the plaintiffs by their last names and was not informal with them at the party on June 7, 2006. Show that the decedent was interested in activities with his own friends, that he was independent and capable, and that the relation was merely friendly. Show that Mr. Hughes worked a large number of hours each week and that Mrs. Hughes was absorbed with her friends and community interests.

5. The plaintiffs will testify that they gave up a lease at a loss of $100, a $5,000-a-year job, and friends by moving from Anoka, Wisconsin.

   Meet this by showing that the plaintiffs moved into a nice apartment and had many new friends, and that the plaintiffs appeared to be fully employed.

Testimony-in-Chief for Defendant

1. William Mitchell, witness
   a. As to relationship with the decedent—
      Was a longtime friend.
      Worked for same railroad. Is now retired.
      Lives at 72 Golf Terrace.
      Was hunting and fishing companion of decedent.
      Had conversation with decedent about getting someone to help him.

continued

Exhibit 18.1

Case Analysis (continued)

Suggested calling minister.
Decent told him of the minister's suggestion.
  b. As to the oral agreement—
  Was invited to the dinner party of the decedent on June 7, 2006.
  Knew purpose of the party.
  Was with decedent when Dr. Olson asked if he could bring plaintiff to
  the party.
  Was member of the card game and heard negotiations.
  Heard the terms: $100 a month, apartment, and utilities for services.
  Was with decedent at all times during evening and helped straighten up.
  c. As to the will—
  Was present when drawn.
  Will was made on July 20, 2006, in evening.
  Will was drawn in presence of the plaintiffs.
  d. As to the quality of the work performed—
  He always had his seasonal work done well before plaintiffs.
  William Brown did some of the yard work.
  Plaintiffs painted porch, but it had to be repainted.
  Noted specific items of disrepair and unperformed or misperformed
  services.
  Decedent did his own cooking, and enjoyed it.
  Decedent did his own housecleaning and laundry personally.
  e. As to the decedent's health—
  Decedent's health was excellent for his age.
  Accompanied decedent on hunting and fishing trips.
  Decedent's illness of 2002 was a mild heart attack.
  Decedent recovered in one and one-half months with a two-week con-
  finement to house.
  Subsequent to illness, decedent was as sound as before—fishing, officer
  in church.
  f. As to the plaintiffs' living quarters—
  Complete apartment in second floor of decedent's house.
  Originally furnished for Paul Smith and wife while going to college.
  Outside entrance.
  2. Robert Burger, witness
  a. As to the will of decedent—-
  Was called to hospital on July 20, 2006, to draw up will.
  Reads the will to the court after identifying signature.
  Plaintiffs were present when will was made.
  All persons were in position to hear provisions—read provisions to
  decedent.
  Plaintiffs did not object to provisions and have not to date.
  Decedent was specific and clear on provisions he desired.

Exhibit 18.1

Case Analysis (continued)

    b. As to the decedent's financial matters—
        Decedent was a client for ten years.
        Took care of all monthly expenses, as decedent did not wish to be bothered.
        Paid taxes, utilities, and other monthly bills.
        Paid the plaintiffs $100 a month by check.
        Canceled checks were sent to decedent—does not know their where-
        abouts.
        Paid threatened claim in amount of $750 as a settlement.
        Thought claim valid because of unnatural condition.
        Took over decedent's investments in 2005.
        Was told by decedent that plaintiff was incompetent to invest and had
        lost money.
        Now has stable securities.
    c. As to the upstairs apartment in decedent's house—
        Knew of the previous occupancy by Smith and wife.
        Had advised what kitchen equipment to buy.
        Has gone through it—five rooms and bath, all necessary facilities.
        Is an expert in real estate—sells, buys, has made many leases.
        Is familiar with decedent's neighborhood and price of apartments.
        Rental value is $100 plus utilities.
    d. As to the decedent's health—
        Saw him every month or two during the past six years.
        He was as alert and active after the illness as before.
 3. Allen Anderson, witness
    a. As to the quality of work done by the plaintiffs—
        Went by decedent's house every day on way to the bus.
        Grass was never cut on time—crabgrass and noxious weeds set in.
        Storms and screens were never changed on time.
        Storms were never removed in 2005.
        Sidewalks were never shoveled, except for a few times when decedent did it.
        Leaves were never raked unless decedent did it—heard neighbor complain.
        Saw plaintiff painting porch, later saw another painter doing it.
        Fell on sidewalk and fractured left ankle.
        Was off work for three weeks.
        Told attorney to start action, but settled with decedent for $750.
        Fall occurred from hump of ice that had accumulated from eaves spout.
    b. As to the plaintiff's hours away from home—
        Many times saw plaintiff leaving house at 8:00 A.M.
        Often noticed him driving into the yard at about 5:00 P.M.
        Was given a ride to work by plaintiff several times.
        Plaintiff told him business was good and he was working long hours.
        Business was rushing during spring, summer, and fall, according to
        plaintiff.

continued

c. As to the plaintiff's statements adverse to his interest—
During one ride, plaintiff said he hated to leave house when old man died.
During another ride, said too bad the old man had relatives.
Stated that witness had nothing against plaintiff; thought him OK.

Memo of Anticipated Testimony for Plaintiff

1. Raymond Quin, friend of the decedent's, probably will be called to testify to the terms of the oral agreement.
   a. Ensure that he testifies only to facts within his own knowledge.
   b. Determine his relation with the plaintiffs. Impeach by use of friendly witness by showing intimacy with the plaintiffs.
   c. Test his certainty of the agreement.
   d. Have him corroborate the purpose of the party.
2. John Hughes, plaintiff, probably will be called to testify to the extent of his services and also to the oral agreement.
   a. Ensure that he testifies only to facts within his own knowledge.
   b. Ensure that he does not testify to any part of the oral agreement.
   c. Bring out the fact that he is an interested party.
   d. Impeach on investments and personal services by friendly witnesses.
3. George Robb, friend of the decedent's, probably will be called to testify to the quality of services performed by the plaintiffs, and subsequent statements of the decedent indicating his obligation to the plaintiffs.
   a. Ensure that he testifies only to facts within his own knowledge.
   b. Determine how he observed the performance of the services.
   c. Counter subsequent admissions by the plaintiffs' statements to Anderson.

Steps in Preparing a Case Analysis

The pleadings provide basic information about the transaction or occurrence. So that is where you begin.

1. Set the pleadings side by side and compare the allegations and admissions.
2. Identify each of the plaintiff's causes of action.
3. Under each cause of action, identify the elements to the cause of action.
4. Identify each affirmative defense.
5. Under each affirmative defense, identify the elements to the defense.
6. Under each element describe the facts that must be proved to establish those elements.
7. Identify the facts that have been conclusively established by admissions in the pleadings, by Rule 36 admissions, by stipulations between the parties, and by the court's pretrial order. Those facts are conclusively established. No evidence will be needed to prove them. The remainder of the analysis will focus on the controverted facts.

8. Describe the disputed facts. By expressing the fact issue, you will ensure that you understand the problem. You sharpen your thinking. The value of checklists is that they force you to do what you should.

9. Now examine the evidence that has been gathered through investigation and discovery procedures. Determine whether you have evidence for each disputed material fact. Determine whether your team can prove your causes of action or affirmative defenses. Determine whether you can meet the opponent's evidence that will be offered on the same facts. Be objective, not merely wishful.

10. For purposes of economy, to avoid duplication, to make your client's presentation uncluttered and persuasive you will have to leave out some of the evidence you have gathered. The trial team must select the best evidence to prove the client's version of the material facts.

11. The team must consider the form in which the evidence should be offered. In this regard, consider the sources. For example, your team may have the option of proving a medical diagnosis through medical records, one physician, two physicians, or a Rule 35 examiner. What would be best? Perhaps the evidence should be presented through more than one source.

12. Anticipate what evidence the opponent has on each material fact that your team intends to prove.

13. Consider how your team is going to counter the opponent's evidence. Can the evidence be kept from the jury by making a motion in limine?[1] Can the evidence be excluded by making a legal objection to its admissibility? Can the source of the evidence be discredited as unreliable? If the source is a witness, is the witness subject to impeachment on a collateral issue? Is there other evidence with which to contradict the opponent's evidence? Is there other evidence with which to explain or qualify the opponent's evidence? Should that evidence be saved for rebuttal? All these questions should be considered for each item of evidence relevant to each material fact.

The trial team must anticipate the opponent's objections and prepare to meet them with arguments and legal authorities. A team must consider how to protect favorable witnesses just as much as how to attack adverse witnesses. You can help the trial team by making sure the evidence is available, organized, and its integrity is maintained.

The case analysis in Exhibit 18.1 is concerned with an action to enforce a decedent's oral contract to make a will. The plaintiffs claim they contracted with the decedent. They claim he promised to bequeath his house to them if they would take care of him for the rest of his life. Unfortunately for the plaintiffs, the decedent's will left the house to the defendant. This case analysis has been prepared by the defendant's trial team to guide their trial preparation. The defendant wants to sustain the will and keep the house for himself.

The defendant's lawyer decided to challenge the plaintiffs' claim that the decedent made a contract to devise the property to the plaintiffs. This means he must find ways to avoid and discredit the plaintiffs' evidence. In addition, he claims that even if the plaintiffs did have a contract with the decedent, they cannot enforce the contract because they breached it by not providing the services they now allege they provided.

Abstract of Pleadings

Even in a simple case, lawyers go through the mental process of coordinating the facts, evidence, and law. Although you will not have occasion to prepare a case analysis, you may be asked to prepare an analysis of the facts and evidence concerning a particular issue. When that happens, try using the case analysis approach.

A case analysis provides a basis for organizing evidence and devising a trial strategy. Some attorneys use trial notebooks to implement the analysis and strategy.

Trial Strategy

trial strategy A lawyer's plan for presenting a case at trial to make his or her theory about the facts and the evidence persuasive.

Trial strategy is not technical stuff. It is the team's plan for presenting the case to the court and jury. The plan is constructed around the litigation team's legal theories, theory of the facts, and available evidence. The plan should be the product of common sense and careful preparation. A good strategy allows a party to gain full benefit from the evidence. Whereas a case analysis ensures that you have the evidence to deal with disputed facts, trial strategy determines how your trial team will use that evidence to obtain maximum advantage. For example, if the opponent has a strong witness concerning a crucial fact, the strategy must deal with the witness. Your team must find a way to neutralize the witness and/or the witness's evidence. The strategy considers whether there is a basis in law to keep the witness from testifying. If not, is there a technical objection that will exclude the crucial testimony? If not, can the witness be impeached? If not, can the evidence be impeached? If not, is there circumstantial evidence that contradicts the witness? If not, how can the harmful testimony be "deflected?" How can the team bolster opposing witnesses? Can the team obtain other testimony from the adverse witness that is favorable for the client? If so, would the team's use of that evidence enhance the witness's credibility and hurt your overall position? Trial strategy looks at all the alternatives, and usually there are many. There is no one best strategy. Lawyers may strongly disagree over strategy. After all, strategy is a matter of judgment. Furthermore, a strategy that works for one lawyer may not work for another. As in a game of chess, you must plan your moves, but your plans have to change as the opponent makes moves and the court makes rulings. A strategy must remain flexible.

In forming a trial strategy, the team must give consideration to how the legal theories impact on one another. For example, assume your team represents a plaintiff who is probably entitled to recover punitive damages from the defendant. At first blush, it seems logical to seek punitive and compensatory damages. However, suppose the defendant has no assets with which to pay punitive damages; that his liability insurance policy does not cover punitive damages; and that any evidence that proves the defendant acted intentionally to injure your client might preclude insurance coverage.[2] In that event, the plaintiff would likely never collect the punitive damages awarded. That fact must be considered in light of the common belief that juries may award less compensatory damages when they award substantial punitive damages in the same case. By pursuing a punitive damages claim, the consequence might be to reduce the client's net recovery of damages. Therefore, the better strategy may be to abandon the punitive damages claim. The decision is not driven by the law or the facts—just strategy.

Suppose your client was a passenger in the defendant's car when the defendant drove off the road into a tree injuring the plaintiff. The evidence shows that the defendant had consumed several beers shortly before the accident and may have been intoxicated. That could explain why the defendant lost control of the car and help to establish that the defendant was negligent. However, suppose the defendant's theory of defense is that his being intoxicated was obvious; the risk of riding with him was apparent. In other words, the plaintiff was negligent for riding with him.[3] The plaintiff's strategy should focus on the accident, the injuries, and why the plaintiff did not know the defendant was not in a condition to drive. The plaintiff does not want to magnify the defendant's intoxication. The trial team must look at the case as a whole—the big picture. When your evidence proves one fact, it may disprove another fact you need. An overall strategy will guide your efforts, including your final preparation.

Trial Notebooks

A litigation team prepares a trial notebook for use as a convenient reference during trial. A **trial notebook** is not a litigation document. It is more like a script for a theatrical play. There is no set format for trial notebooks. They are typically loose leaf binders, so materials can be easily added, relocated, or removed. The sections are tabbed for quick access. The notebook sections are organized chronologically. A very complete notebook contains outlines of the direct and cross-examinations the trial attorney expects to use. Notebooks contain copies of exhibits that will be put into evidence. The size and content of a notebook depend on the complexity of the case and the trial lawyer's preferences. Trial notebooks are particularly useful in dealing with complex cases.

trial notebook A notebook that a lawyer prepares for her or his own use as a reference for handling a case during trial. Paralegals may help to prepare trial notebooks.

A trial notebook is not a **trial brief.** Lawyers prepare trial briefs to inform the judge about the law applicable to the case. A trial brief discusses the facts only insofar as is necessary to provide a basis for discussing or arguing points of law. A trial brief does not discuss how the party intends to prove the facts. A lawyer would never share her or his trial notebook with an opponent. A trial notebook is the ultimate attorney's work product. But any trial brief submitted to the judge must be provided to an opponent.

trial brief A brief that a party prepares for the court to identify legal issues, supply authorities, and argue contested points of law.

Customary Notebook Sections

Trial Schedule. Identify all the trial schedule particulars: judge's name, courtroom, judge's clerk's name, trial date, and time to report for trial. Leave space for a "things to do list." Note any special arrangements you need to make such as transportation for witnesses, subpoenas, contacting witnesses' employers, making hotel reservations, and so on.

Directory. The directory has several parts. It lists all the witnesses, their home addresses, business addresses, telephone numbers, and the names and telephone numbers of persons who know how to contact the witnesses, such as relatives, employers, coworkers. It lists the people with whom the trial team must deal, including the client, opposing trial team members, and court personnel. Another section lists the names, addresses, and telephone numbers of custodians of documents and other exhibits.

Pleadings. Notebooks contain copies of the pleadings. You may highlight significant items in the copies. Most lawyers prefer to keep the original pleadings in the office file. Make sure that all original pleadings, motions, affidavits, and so on have been filed.

Witness List. Make a list of your team's witnesses and a list of the opponent's witnesses. For each witness, identify the issues and subjects the witness will cover. Note the exhibits that you associate with the witness. Some lawyers write out the questions they intend to ask the witnesses. Do not include the deposition transcripts, because they make the notebook too bulky. But you can identify deposition subjects and their page numbers. Lawyers must be careful to avoid becoming too dependent on a script, because they must be flexible. A lawyer must be ready to pursue other lines of inquiry as they open. Also, a lawyer must be prepared to move to a different subject when a line of inquiry proves to be counterproductive.

Exhibit List. Make a list of the exhibits in the order in which your trial team expects to use them. Now that you know about "case analysis," you might want to identify the critical facts that each exhibit proves. You should identify the witness through whom each exhibit will be offered and identify alternative conduits for getting the exhibits into evidence. Also note the names of other witnesses who will have occasion to use or refer to an exhibit. Make an Exhibit Tracking Sheet. Consider using the following headings and columns:

EXHIBIT LIST

IDENTIFICATION	DESCRIPTION	WITNESS	OFFERED	RECEIVED	DENIED/GROUNDS
1	Contract	Plaintiff	✓	✓	
2	Sales receipt	Johnson	✓		✓ No foundation

Motions. A trial notebook is a convenient place to keep copies of all the pretrial motions, whether served by your trial team or the opponent. Again, most attorneys prefer to keep the original motions in a separate file. You may highlight significant portions of a motion and make notations in the margins. This is what the trial lawyer probably will use when it comes time to argue the motion. Certainly, a notebook should contain all the motions in limine.

Voir Dire Questions. The first phase of a trial is jury selection. The judge and lawyers conduct a voir dire examination of potential jurors to determine their qualifications to be on a particular case. The judge and lawyers ask questions about each potential juror's background, interests, experiences, familiarity with the parties and witnesses, and their knowledge about the case. In federal courts, judges usually ask all the questions, but attorneys are allowed to suggest questions and may be allowed to supplement the judge's interrogation. It is helpful to have questions prepared in advance. The trial attorney probably has a set of questions that can be tailored to fit any case. Consider making a seating chart to help you identify jurors. The trial team probably will talk about the jurors as the trial progresses.

Opening Statement.   A notebook may contain the trial lawyer's opening statement, either as a narrative or as an outline. Lawyers try to avoid reading their opening statements and final arguments. However, by writing down statements, they know they have covered all the important points and it helps them to select just the right words and phrases.

Investigation Memoranda.   A notebook is a good place to keep your memoranda concerning contacts with witnesses; notes on the accident scene; and notes on visitations to premises, such as a factory, construction site, or house. Consider including the expert witnesses' reports, medical records, and police reports.

Memoranda of Law.   A notebook may contain copies of the parties' memoranda of law. The memoranda may concern issues that already have been argued and decided, because old issues have a way of popping up again.

Direct Examinations.   Trial notebooks may contain the direct examination for each witness your trial team intends to have testify. The questions may be in outline form or verbatim. The trial lawyer may not use the notebook to examine witnesses, but near the end of an examination he or she may look to you to let him or her know whether anything was omitted. Your reference is the notebook. Lawyers usually prefer to have your suggestions in notes they can read rather than have whispered conversations in front of the jury.

Cross-examinations.   A notebook should contain the cross-examination for each witness the opponent is expected to have testify. Also, the trial team may have occasion to cross-examine hostile witnesses whom your side is constrained to have testify. This section does not lend itself to verbatim questions. But it should at least identify the subjects to be covered and could use an outline form.

Jury Instructions.   A notebook is a good place to keep the proposed jury instructions—yours and the opposition's. They will be handy when needed.

Pretrial Conferences

Rule 16(c) authorizes district courts to conduct pretrial conferences to facilitate trial preparation and trial management. A pretrial conference is a meeting between the presiding judge and lawyers. Sometimes parties are allowed to attend. The conference may be conducted in the courtroom or in the judge's chambers. The Rule even authorizes judges to conduct pretrial conferences by telephone. There could be two pretrial conferences: one conducted weeks before the trial and a second immediately before trial. The judge may order the pretrial conference **sua sponte,** or a party may ask the judge to schedule a conference. A party's request may be made by letter with a copy to all other parties. A motion is not necessary. Sometimes judges have their court reporters make verbatim records of the conferences. The record is an easy way to preserve the parties' stipulations, commitments, and any oral orders the judge makes during the conference. However, the significant decisions should be reduced to a written order.

sua sponte   Voluntarily, as when a court takes some action or step without the request of a party to do so.

Pretrial Conference Functions

Deal with Legal Issues.   The judge may believe that the case raises particularly difficult legal issues concerning jurisdiction, evidence, jury instructions, constitutionality, or other matters. The judge may order the lawyers to file memoranda of law to help the court deal with such issues. The memoranda may be due at the time of trial or days before. Or, the court may schedule another pretrial conference to deal with problematic legal issues.

Simplify the Legal Issues and Amend the Pleadings.   The simpler a case can be made, the better for everyone. By narrowing the legal and fact issues, the parties shorten the trial and reduce the possibility of error. Judges encourage parties to agree on what the law is and how the law applies to the case. For example, if at the time the defendant interposed the answer she believed that the plaintiff's claim would be barred by the statute of limitations, but new information shows that the statute of limitations is not applicable, the defense should be withdrawn. Where agreement is not possible, judges may eliminate claims and defenses that do not seem to have any merit by ordering them stricken. A pretrial conference gives the parties an opportunity to take care of such "housekeeping" matters, and, perhaps it is the last opportunity to do so. When parties appear before the court on a motion, it is unlikely that any other matter will be discussed, and the court should not issue any order that is outside the purview of the motion. But when the parties appear for a pretrial conference, *everything* is "on the table" and subject to a dispositive ruling.

A judge could ask a lawyer how he or she intends to prove a particular claim or defense, or what evidence he or she has to support the claim, or what rule of law justifies the claim. The judge's questions may persuade the lawyer to voluntarily dismiss a claim or defense. Or, a lawyer's response may be so ineffective that the judge strikes the claim or defense. Similarly, a **pretrial order** should strike **frivolous** claims and defenses. A claim or defense is frivolous if there are no facts to support it or the legal theory is contrary to established law.[4] The disappointed party can raise the issue on appeal, but the issue will not be part of the trial. If the court's order goes to the heart of a claim or defense, the order should state how the pleadings are amended to comport with the court's order.

Simplify Fact Issues.   A pretrial conference gives the judge and the lawyers an opportunity to discuss the facts and how the parties intend to prove the facts. The court's pretrial order should identify material facts that are not controverted. The effect of the order is similar to that of a signed stipulation or a Rule 36 admission. The agreement saves time and expense and reduces some of the uncertainties of litigation. Although parties may agree on certain facts, they may not agree about the effect of facts on the case.

Obtain Stipulations Concerning Evidence.   The parties may agree on the admissibility of certain evidence and exhibits. Again, a parties' agreement that certain evidence may be received by the court does not prevent the parties from disagreeing about what the evidence proves. Parties often stipulate to the foundation for exhibits.[5] For example, parties commonly stipulate to the foundation for hospital records, so medical record librarians do not have to come to court to identify the records. Parties commonly stipulate that copies of records may be used in place of originals. Parties may stipulate to the reasonableness of charges for medical care without agreeing that the medical care was necessary or even necessitated by reason of the accident.

Limit the Number of Expert Witnesses.   Lawyers are using more expert witnesses. They are finding new ways in which to use them. They are tending to use

pretrial order   An order a court issues following a pretrial conference that embodies the court's rulings and plan for managing the progression of the case to trial.

frivolous   Not supported by facts, or contrary to law. Any party who prosecutes a frivolous claim or defense is subject to sanctions and disciplinary action.

experts on subjects that do not really require experts. Experts have become "window dressing" for cases. It does not seem to matter that expert testimony is expensive and time consuming. Lawyers have found that experts make cases more authoritative. When one expert is needed, lawyers tend to use two or three. So far, courts have not imposed arbitrary limits on the number of experts who may testify to an issue or in a case. However, courts have the right to limit the number of experts. Suppose the plaintiff brings a medical malpractice action against his physician, a hospital, and a medical products manufacturer, alleging that each was negligent and caused his injury. The plaintiff will need an expert witness to testify to the medical problem, another to testify that the defendant violated the standard of care of medical doctors, and another to testify to the alleged product defect. Clearly, the plaintiff will be entitled to have three expert witnesses. But suppose the plaintiff wants to have three expert witnesses testify that the physician did not comport with medical standards and four expert witnesses to testify about the alleged product defect. A party might want to use many experts to overwhelm the jury. A judge would seriously question whether so many experts should be allowed. Of course, the opposing party would feel compelled to hire a similar number of experts. A court must be pragmatic about the number of experts a party may call, and keep the presentation fair to both sides.

Consider Referring Matter to Arbitration, Mediation, or a Referee. Courts and lawyers are showing increased interest in alternative dispute resolution, sometimes called ADR. It is useful when both parties want to conclude the dispute as quickly and economically as possible. The special rules of some courts now require parties to go through nonbinding ADR before the case may be tried. The parties may accept the ADR award, the parties may convert the ADR award to a judgment and dismiss the case, or a party who disagrees with the award may insist on going ahead with a jury trial. The jury would not be told about the parties' use of ADR or the ADR award. Local rules may provide that the party who insisted on the trial may have to pay the opposing party's trial expenses if he or she does not obtain a "better result" in the trial.

Explore Other Ways to Facilitate a Disposition of the Case, Including Settlement. Approximately 90 percent of all cases settle before or during trial. Because so many cases do settle, the civil justice system is trying to devise ways to help the parties settle earlier. Sooner is better. Rule 16(c)(9) expressly authorizes the presiding judge to use her or his position to encourage settlement negotiations. A judge may even assume the role of a mediator or appoint a magistrate to mediate.

Amend Pleadings to Add Claims or Defenses. A pretrial conference provides what may be the last opportunity for a party to add a claim or defense. A party who wants to add a claim or defense should notice a motion for leave to amend the pleading pursuant to Rule 15. The motion should explain why the amendment could not have been made earlier and why the adverse parties will not be prejudiced by the late amendment. When appropriate, the moving party usually offers to submit to additional discovery. The court has authority to allow amendments to pleadings at the pretrial conference even if no motion was served.

Consider Appropriateness and Scheduling Summary Judgment Motions. A judge may feel that a correct application of the law would dispose of an issue or the case as a whole. In that event, the judge should initiate summary judgment proceedings by framing the issue(s) and setting a time for the motion to be argued. The court's time parameters should comport with the requirements of Rule 56. The parties should have at least thirty days in which to prepare and submit memoranda of law. The judge can decide whether or not to have oral arguments.

Pretrial Conference Attendance

Every party who is represented by an attorney must have at least one attorney of record attend the conference. Parties who represent themselves must appear in person. Otherwise, courts differ on whether the parties should attend in person. If the judge intends to pursue settlement discussions during the conference, he or she will probably insist that the parties attend. The lawyers who attend must have authority to make stipulations and to make admissions of the type discussed previously. A lawyer cannot refuse to admit a fact or dismiss a claim or defense on the grounds that he or she does not have authority. If the lawyer does not have the client's authority, the client must attend the conference in person. A lawyer does not have to commit to unreasonable agreements or admissions, however. Sometimes a lawyer's fortitude is tested when the judge applies pressure to obtain concessions.

When an insurance company has an interest in the outcome of the case, although not a named party, the insurance company's representative may attend the conference, especially if the insurance company has retained authority to make stipulations and admissions. An insurance company's interest may come from its obligation under a liability insurance policy or a right to some of the litigation proceeds by reason of a right of subrogation.

Alerting the Client and Witnesses

As soon as the trial team receives a trial date, you must notify the client. You should telephone the client, so he or she knows you are concerned about his or her welfare. A trial date may be good news or the worst kind of news. Be prepared to answer the client's questions. The client is going to have to make arrangements to leave work, get baby-sitters, and so on. Even if you do not have a day-certain setting, you should be able to estimate when the trial will start and how long it will last, so the client can plan accordingly. A surprising number of clients wonder why they have to attend the entire trial. They still think that the trial is the lawyer's responsibility, but the trial belongs to the client. The lawyer is there to help the client. The client must be there every minute. The client must be there to help with problems as they occur and to see how the case is developing and why it is developing as it does. Furthermore, the legal team does not want the jury to infer that the client is not interested in the case. When a corporation is the client, you should have an officer personify a company. You need a person to whom the jury can relate.

You must notify your side's witnesses. You should be able to estimate when the trial will start and how long it will last. Witnesses do not have to attend the entire trial. You may want to telephone some witnesses. You must send a letter to each witness, giving the witness the date on which the trial will begin, the date and time when the witness will be needed, courthouse address, courtroom, court hours, probable starting time each day, and information about parking. You may confirm the arrangements for expense reimbursement. The letter should be written so that it will not be a problem if the opposition were to read it.

Subpoenaing Witnesses

The only way in which a party can compel a witness to come to court is to subpoena the witness. A subpoena gives a court jurisdiction over the person who has been duly served, just as service of summons and complaint gives the court jurisdiction over a party. However, a court's authority is limited to requiring the witness to appear and testify. A party who has taken the precaution of subpoenaing a reluctant or forgetful witness cannot be blamed or penalized for the witness's failure to appear. The court may order the sheriff or marshal to find the witness and bring the witness to court for an explanation and possible punishment. A lawyer has no recourse against a witness who fails to show but was not subpoenaed. A person who fails to comply with a subpoena may be held in contempt of court. The penalty could be incarceration or fine or merely a stern lecture. Even more important to the trial team, the client can obtain a recess or delay in the proceedings until the United States marshal brings the witness to court.

The onus is on the lawyer to have his or her witnesses in court and ready to testify when needed. However, that onus switches to the witness if the lawyer has served a subpoena on the witness. Consequently, it may be prudent to subpoena even cooperative witnesses, because if a witness were to become unavailable, the subpoena would justify a recess or even a continuance of the trial. Subpoenas should be served as soon as possible on the witnesses. Do not leave anything to chance.

A subpoena must designate the time and place the witness is to appear to testify. But lawyers may not know precisely when the witness will be needed. This problem can be handled by designating in the subpoena the earliest probable time that the witness will be needed and asking the witness to cooperate by staying near a telephone so that she or he can be reached on very short notice. In this way, the witness may wait at home or work until contacted. The alternative is for the witness to sit in the courtroom and wait for her or his turn. The wait could be hours or even days. A party takes a bit of risk by accommodating witnesses in this manner. But a lawyer incurs a greater risk by not subpoenaing witnesses. Only the court or the lawyer who caused the subpoena to be served may release the witness from the subpoena. It takes only a simple, oral statement, "you are released."

Any person eighteen years of age or older, who is not a party to the suit, may serve subpoenas in civil cases [Rule 45(c)]. The process server must pay a witness fee in the amount provided by statute. Also, the witness must be paid a fee based on the mileage from his or her home to the courthouse. If there is any doubt about the mileage, the process server should be sure to tender enough. Failure to tender an adequate payment makes service defective. The process server's affidavit of service must state the time, place, manner of service, and fees paid. The affidavit is a party's proof that the witness was served. The affidavit must be filed with the court. Also, parties may use United States marshals to serve civil subpoenas.

There are times when an independent witness prefers to be subpoenaed to come to court so that his or her appearance is viewed as involuntary. A subpoena protects the witness from appearing to be aligned with one side against the other. Public officials and police officers often ask to be subpoenaed for that reason. Another example is when the testimony of the plaintiff's treating physician favors the defendant, but the physician does not want to appear to be voluntarily testifying against his or her patient. The physician may be more comfortable about testifying if placed under a subpoena.

A witness may want you to serve a subpoena so the witness can show it to his or her employer to get off work. Some public officials and some hospital personnel have rules that prevent them from going to court without a subpoena. Sometimes people only need the subpoena for their records, so they do not insist on actually being served. You could send the subpoena by mail to these people. However, if the subpoena is not served, it is unenforceable. If the witness does not appear as requested, the lawyer has no recourse through the subpoena. The lawyer cannot tell the judge the witness was subpoenaed if the witness was not served. If a witness must appear at a particular time and if there is any doubt about whether the witness will come to court when needed, it is best to serve the subpoena as provided by Rules 4 and 45.

Parties are under the court's jurisdiction, but no rule says a party has to attend the trial. That could be a real problem if the opposing party has evidence that is critical to your client's claim or defense. If your trial team wants to be sure the opposing party will attend the trial at a particular time, so that she or he can be called for cross-examination, your team may ask the court to provide in the pretrial order that the opposing party must make herself or himself available for cross-examination. Or, you may compel the party to come to trial by serving a subpoena on him or her.

Organizing the Evidence

You know what the facts are. You know what facts you need. You have gathered the evidence. You have preserved it so it is available. Your litigation team has put together a trial strategy. Now you must determine that the witnesses are available. You must review your evidence to make sure it is admissible. For example, do you have foundation for the photographs, business records, medical records, and so on. Will the expert witness's opinions be admissible? The trial team must decide, in light of the trial strategy, how to present the evidence to be most persuasive. For example, the foundation for hospital records could be established by the hospital administrator, a medical record librarian, or by stipulation. Having testimony from the hospital administrator or librarian may favorably impress the jury, but that adds another witness and increases the client's expenses. Is the witness worth the time and expense if the opponent will stipulate? Suppose the opposition is willing to stipulate that your expert's resume and report may be received into evidence, so you do not have to have the expert testify at trial. The resume establishes the expert's qualifications. The report is adequate to prove the facts your client needs. The stipulation would save time and expense. However, the report would be boring. The expert would not be available to answer additional questions. The jury could not fully appreciate your expert's authority. So your team probably will choose to have the expert testify anyway. There are similar choices to be made concerning most of the evidence.

Of course, your evidence should be consistent and dovetail. But, in addition, look for ways to make each item of evidence your team offers complement other items of evidence. For example, in a personal injury action, a Rule 35 examiner can describe the plaintiff's injury, but the examiner's testimony will be more effective, more persuasive, if the examiner coordinates her or his testimony with the medical records and hospital records. It does not matter that the examiner did not make any of the entries in those records. As another example, if you have good photographs of an intersection where your client's accident occurred, the attorney will put them into evidence, probably, through the person who took them. But plan on having other witnesses who are familiar with the intersection use the photographs too. They will give the photographs authority, and the photographs will strengthen the witnesses' testimony. Try to keep the evidence interesting for the judge and jury.

You should begin organizing the evidence around the facts that have already been established by admissions in pleadings and admissions in responses to Rule 36 requests. The judge will instruct the jury, at the beginning or end of the trial, that they must accept those facts as true. Make sure your client's evidence does not conflict with those established facts. Any evidence that is inconsistent with them is, in effect, impeached. Similarly, your team should make sure that all the client's evidence comports with natural laws and incontrovertible physical facts. For example, if your client was involved in an intersection collision and testifies that "suddenly the other car appeared in front of me," the necessary inference is the client was not keeping a proper lookout. Cars do not "suddenly appear" in intersections. Or, if the client says she just "bumped" the plaintiff's car, but photographs show $5,000 worth of damage, the client's description of the accident is not consistent with demonstrable physical facts. The client's testimony of a "bump" will be rejected. Furthermore, the jury has a right to be suspicious of any other evidence your client and team offers. The trial team's strategy must deal with these kinds of problems.

Your trial team must be objective about the evidence. Just because you have a witness who will testify favorably on an important point does not mean the jury will believe the witness. You must do what you can to support the witness and the witness's testimony. Consider how you can make the witness's testimony interesting and persuasive. Because most evidence is introduced through witnesses, it is logical to organize the evidence around witnesses—yours and the opponent's. Begin by identifying the remaining fact issues, and determine what role each witness can play in proving the facts. Consider how each witness's testimony can complement other evidence your team will present. For example, if you decide to have a hospital administrator testify to lay foundation for hospital records, try to have the administrator comment favorably on your client's physician. Have your physician comment favorably on the quality of the nursing staff and their records.

Your trial team should consider whether the client's physical evidence is in its most persuasive form. For example, consider whether to make enlargements of some of the documents and photographs. Should you show documents to the jury by using a projector? Or, should you have a photocopy of the documents for each juror so jurors can look at the copies while your side's witnesses testify? If the trial attorney has not considered this approach, you may want to suggest it. Consider preparing illustrative exhibits to help witnesses explain the facts to which they will testify. If your client is going to have difficulty explaining how the accident occurred, you could prepare a scale drawing for the client to use. Maybe you should make or obtain some model cars to use with the diagram. Pay attention to the details. Careful development of details gives evidence authority, credibility, and persuasiveness.

Identify impeaching evidence to discredit adverse witnesses. Look to answers to interrogatories, deposition transcripts, witness statements, and photographs. Consider how you can use adverse witnesses to help the client's case. Or, identify some innocuous facts that adverse witnesses will concede are true. Such facts may include the time, place, arrival of police, point of contact of the vehicles, photographs, and so on. The evidence is not important. It is the appearance of agreement with "your facts" that is important. If experts are going to be used, you should abstract the important points from the experts' reports, records, answers to interrogatories, deposition testimony, and treatises. Organize the points for convenient reference. As mentioned earlier, you should try to find the areas where the opposing expert agrees with your team's theory and bring out those points in the cross-examination. You can facilitate the trial lawyer's efforts by finding what he or she needs.

You should look for potential conflicts in your evidence and resolve them. Begin by determining whether a conflict is actual. Sometimes apparent conflicts arise because of a misunderstanding of the evidence or false assumptions about the evidence or even false assumptions about the facts. In accident cases, you may need to reinspect the accident situs. An inspection may show why one witness could make an observation that another witness at another location could not make. The phenomenon is known as a parallax.[6] If the case involves a transaction, such as breach of a contract to construct a building, it may be necessary to examine the building—not just the written contract and specifications. By inspecting or reinspecting, you will have a better feel for the evidence as a whole and that will help you to communicate with the client and witnesses. Experienced trial lawyers know they must have personal knowledge about the subject to be able to effectively examine witnesses. The evidence should build as the evidence tells the client's story.

Preparing the Client to Testify

You can have a major role in preparing a client for the trial. You can explain trial procedures and what will happen at the trial. You can describe the client's role. You will need at least two meetings to prepare him or her. Schedule the first meeting a week or two before the trial. The second meeting or third should be immediately before trial. Instruct the client to reread his or her deposition transcript before the meeting. Tell the client to bring his or her copy to the meetings.[7]

At the first meeting, tell the client about the status of the case. Hopefully, the status is good. Assure the client that all the evidence has been gathered, sorted, and organized. The trial team has confirmed the legal theories. The facts support your legal theories. You have analyzed the opponent's allegations and arguments, and you are confident that you can refute them. Emphasize that the trial team is ready. You have done your preparation. The client will be more comfortable knowing that the case is proceeding as it should. However, be candid about problems and the uncertainties of litigation. Tell the client about any additional steps the trial team is taking to prepare for the trial.

Before explaining the client's role at trial, describe trial procedures. The client will be more comfortable at trial if he or she understands what is happening. For example, tell the client that it is not uncommon for the judge to meet with the attorneys in chambers for a while before selecting the jury to discuss questions of law, scheduling of witnesses, preliminary motions, and the possibilities of settlement. Then, when you report to the courtroom, the client will not worry about an apparent delay while the lawyers are in chambers. Furthermore, the client will feel that the trial team knows the program.

Tell the client how to conduct herself or himself during the trial. Emphasize that he or she should be pleasant, polite, and on her or his best behavior. Discuss clothes and grooming. Tell the client to be positive about the trial and about the jury. He or she should presume that the jurors like her or him. The client should look on trial as an opportunity to obtain deserved justice. Explain to the client what he or she can do to help during the trial. The client should listen carefully to the voir dire examination and tell you his or her reaction to each of the potential jurors. The trial team should take the client's subjective feelings about the jurors into consideration during the selection process. Make it clear that the lawyer will decide which jurors to keep and which to strike. That is the lawyer's responsibility. Tell the client to listen carefully to witnesses as they testify and be prepared to discuss their testimony with the trial team during recesses. The client may make notes about important developments and raise questions for discussion during recesses. The client should appear attentive and sincere while at court. There is always the possibility of being observed by jurors, the opposing party or lawyer.

You should review the client's deposition transcript with the client. Explain that the opposing lawyer will study the transcript. Explain how the deposition transcripts will be used at trial. The opposing lawyer probably will want to know whether he or she reviewed the transcript before coming to court. The answer is "yes." It is perfectly proper to do so. If the client is asked to look at the transcript while on the witness stand, the opposing attorney may look at it and note anything that is written in the margins or highlighted. So you may want to give the client a fresh, unmarked copy to use at trial. The client must study the entire transcript, not just highlighted parts. He or she must be familiar with it. The opposing lawyer might test the client by asking, "Didn't you testify in your deposition that . . . ." If the client has not studied the entire transcript, the client will not be comfortable answering, "no." You may provide the client with a preview of the trial. Explain the legal theory of the claim and defense. Describe the evidence that is available to both sides. Identify the points that the client's testimony must address. These explanations will help the client to feel confident that the trial team knows what it is doing and is ready. Regardless of what happens during the trial, the client should try to appear calm and collected. The client must not overreact to evidence or anything else that happens. Explain to the client to be sure no one can hear them discuss the case. The attorney-client privilege is lost if a third person hears them or reads their notes.

If there is time in the first meeting, you may begin preparing the client to testify. At the close of the first meeting, determine what each of you needs to do to prepare for the next meeting. That is when you will finish preparing the client to testify. Encourage the client to write down questions as they occur during the preparation phase. Then you can answer the questions at your next meeting. If the client does not write down his or her questions, the client will forget some of them. When that happens, the client worries that there was something important to ask and become anxious about not being able to remember what it was. As you can see, there is a great deal to do at the first meeting.

Guidelines for Testifying at Trial

You may be asked to help prepare the client to testify. The trial team should put the client through a mock direct examination and cross-examination. Mock examinations help to identify problems and weaknesses in the client's testimony. The client should be asked some "trick" questions that assume facts favorable to the opposition.

You should help the client to deal with such questions. In preparing to testify, a client should write down the important facts and figures to reinforce recall. But the client must not take personal notes to the witness stand. The client may take a copy of the deposition transcript and will have access to the exhibits, but nothing else should be used as an aid to testify. The client should not memorize a "story," so that the testimony appears fabricated. Although the facts should be committed to memory, that is different from memorizing a "script." You should know generally what the other witnesses will say. If the anticipated testimony of other witnesses will conflict with the client's testimony in some significant respect, explain to the client why there is a conflict and how the trial team is dealing with it.

The client probably has already testified in a deposition. However, the guidelines for testifying in a discovery deposition do not necessarily apply at trial. In preparing for the deposition, you told the client to give a short answer to each question; do not explain the answer, unless asked; do not volunteer information. That was good advice for a discovery deposition but not for trial. In a trial, the client's reticence is not persuasive. It could alienate jurors. Short answers make the witness look evasive and defensive. The client's testimony should be informative, interesting, and persuasive. You want to educate and persuade the judge and jury. The client should look on every question as an opportunity to tell the jury what they need to know. It requires a lot of preparation to appear authoritative and sincere without being overbearing.

Most of the guidelines for testifying in an oral deposition, as described in Chapter 13, apply to testifying at trial, but there are some exceptions. Also, some guidelines need to be qualified. The following guidelines complement and qualify the deposition guidelines.

1. The hallmarks of a good witness are sincerity and authority. A witness appears sincere when the witness appears to believe what he or she is saying. The appearance of authority comes from an ability to remember and relate the facts, an ability to cope with details, and confidence without arrogance or being overbearing. A witness can enhance his or her appearance of sincerity by sitting up, looking at the lawyers and jury, and speaking in a thoughtful, deliberate manner.

2. A witness should answer questions using full sentences and explaining major points fully. This is true whether the questions come from your trial team or from the opponent. In other words, it is counterproductive for a witness to appear open and friendly toward his or her own lawyer but hostile and defensive when questioned by the opposing lawyer.

3. A witness must not argue, fence, or joke with the lawyers or be coy with the jury.

4. A witness must not lose his or her temper. Answers that suggest disagreement should not be made in a disagreeable manner.

5. If a witness becomes irritated, tired, confused, or physically uncomfortable, the witness should ask for a short recess or for a drink of water or bathroom privileges.

6. A witness should use the big picture as a frame of reference to keep his or her testimony consistent.

7. A witness appears more authoritative and credible when he or she reflects briefly on each question before answering.

8. A witness should look at the lawyer while the lawyer is asking a question, whether on direct examination or cross-examination. A witness should look at the jury at least two-thirds of the time while answering a question. It is all right to look at the lawyer a third of the time when answering. A witness must avoid looking at the ceiling, out the window, or at the floor.

9. A witness must not steal furtive glances at his or her lawyer, as if to say, "I really made a good point!" or "Please help me!"

10. A witness has the right to answer fully. An answer should provide relevant explanations. The opposing lawyer may object that a *full* answer is not responsive. If the judge sustains the objection and instructs the witness to "just answer the question," that should not concern the witness. The witness should not feel as though he or she did anything wrong. As long as the proffered explanation was relevant to the question and not blatantly self-serving, the jury will not be unhappy with the witness. The lawyer who put the witness on the stand will make a note to cover the point during the redirect examination.

11. If a witness realizes that he or she gave an incorrect answer, the witness should correct the mistake as soon as possible. The witness may indicate to the judge that he or she wants to correct something said earlier. The judge probably will ask what the correction concerns. The judge may confer with the witness out of the jury's hearing or tell the witness it can be taken care of when "your lawyer" has the opportunity to ask questions. The witness's request will be a signal to his or her lawyer that the witness has something more to say about a matter already covered. The jury will be interested and wait for the testimony. The jury is much less likely to think the witness has merely "changed" his or her story.

12. A witness should avoid expressions like, "to tell you the truth" or "to be honest with you" or "to the best of my knowledge." If a witness believes the testimony is true, there is no need or reason to qualify it. These phrases weaken the testimony and take away from the witness's authority. If a witness is dealing with an estimate or judgment, use those words. Remember that a mere "guess" cannot be received into evidence.

13. A witness should avoid exaggerating and minimizing anything.

14. If a lawyer tries to put a witness on the defensive by starting a question with "Do you admit that. . . ," it is appropriate to respond that you do not know what he or she means by "admit," but the witness "agrees" with the statement.

15. A witness should not deny that, while preparing for trial, he or she read the deposition transcript, viewed the accident situs, examined exhibits, or conferred with a lawyer.

16. A witness should not let an opposing lawyer suggest that he or she does not have an independent recollection of the facts to which the witness testified.

17. A witness should not refer to insurance unless specifically advised by a lawyer before taking the witness stand that insurance is a proper subject in the case. The judge, lawyers, and other witnesses carefully will avoid

mistrial (1) A trial that has been aborted because of some defect in the proceedings that prevents it from being valid or fair. (2) The presiding judge's order that cancels a trial, usually allowing the case to be tried again.

mentioning insurance, because there is the belief that jurors might be too generous if they think they are awarding insurance money. An improper reference to insurance could cause a **mistrial.**

Tell the client to listen carefully to the opening statements, as they provide a good preview and overview. Ask the client to note any misstatements the lawyers make in the opening statements. If your team's lawyer makes a misstatement and you tell him or her about it, the lawyer will be able to correct the misstatement later in the trial. Your suggestion will help motivate the client to listen carefully. The opposing lawyer's opening statement gives you a good idea about your case's strengths and weaknesses. Explain to the client that, as a party, he or she may be called for cross-examination by the opponent during the opponent's case-in-chief. A defendant may find he or she is the very first witness. It should not be a surprise.

Preparing Witnesses to Testify

As soon as the court gives your trial team a trial date, you must arrange for the witnesses to be available. You may write to the cooperative witnesses or telephone them. Ask them to confirm their availability. The sooner you address scheduling problems, the easier it is to solve them. Just as clients need help to prepare for trial, so do witnesses. You cannot tell a witness what to say, other than to tell the truth. Nevertheless, you can help a witness with how to present testimony and other evidence. If a witness is friendly and cooperative, you can prepare the witness in much the same way as you would prepare a client. However, there is one very important difference. With a mere witness, there is no legal privilege, so anything you say to each other is subject to disclosure.

Witnesses do not have a legal duty to cooperate. They do not have to come to your office to discuss the case. They do not have to visit the accident situs to refresh their memories. They do not have to review exhibits with you. So if a witness meets with you or even simply talks to you, the witness is doing you a favor. You may have to subpoena uncooperative witnesses. Once you have a witness in court, the witness can be compelled to answer questions under oath. However, always focus on cultivating a good relationship. Go out of your way to accommodate. Turn the other cheek when you are abused. Do the best you can. By cooperating, witnesses have the opportunity to find out what kinds of questions will be asked at trial and get help with how to answer questions. In addition, they have the opportunity to see the exhibits that will be used—diagrams, photographs, business records, summaries, and the like. You can explain the procedure for having exhibits put into evidence and how the witness may use them. Explain to the uncooperative witness how you can help if he or she will work with you.

Some witnesses require more preparation than others. For example, an experienced police officer who testifies in court regularly may not be interested in having help with his or her testimony. Nevertheless, you should make the effort to meet and discuss the officer's expected testimony. The better the officer understands the issues and problems, the better he or she can explain to the jury what the jury needs to know. And you can tell the officer about the stipulations and admissions that have narrowed the fact issues, so the officer can focus on what is at issue. Every case is unique, so even experienced witnesses benefit from a little preparation. The trial team always benefits from preparing a witness.

If a witness is a nice person who is well respected, the witness reflects well on the party. If for any reason a witness is bad, the witness will reflect adversely on the party. There is a natural tendency for jurors to associate a party with his or her witnesses. Therefore, a trial team needs to know as much as possible about their witnesses before putting them on the stand. If the team knows there is something unsavory about a witness, there are several things the team can do to avoid the "association problem." A lawyer may prepare the jury by explaining the problem in his or her opening statement. The explanation dissociates the client from the witness even before the testimony begins. The witness will not be present during opening statements to hear the lawyer's disclaimer. Or, when questioning the witness about his or her background, the lawyer can emphasize that the witness has no direct relationship to the client. This works well when dealing with a witness to an occurrence, because a party does not choose who is going to witness his or her accident. But it may be more problematic when dealing with witnesses to a transaction where parties have chosen their associates. The sooner the team knows about the problem, the better the team can deal with it.

Coping with Uncooperative Witnesses

Some witnesses are uncooperative because they are aligned with the opposition. Some are uncooperative because they do not want to be involved with courts. They think that by avoiding you, you will go away. An independent witness might misinterpret your contact as an illegal effort to tamper with evidence. Some witnesses are just mean spirited. The reasons a witness is uncooperative make a difference in how you cope with him or her. If a witness refuses to speak with you about the case, the witness's refusal may be brought out on cross-examination to emphasize the witness's bias. A manifest bias works against the witness's credibility, especially if the witness was verbally or physically abusive. If the witness is not aligned with the opponent, the witness's willingness to cooperate often depends on how you approach him or her. Common sense dictates that you should approach a witness in a friendly, open, respectful manner. You should try to develop the witness's interest in the case. Make the witness feel important, because he or she is. You may assure witnesses it is proper, even necessary, for lawyers and paralegals to contact them and discuss the case.

You may contact and interview a witness whom you know the opposing party intends to put on the stand, unless the witness is represented by a lawyer. Then your contacts must be through the lawyer. Remember that anything you say may be brought out through the witness against your client, so you must be extremely careful. For example, if you tried to ingratiate yourself with the witness by saying that you believe you have caught the opposing party in a lie, the witness might tell the opposing lawyer. The opposing lawyer might find some way of bringing that up during the trial in such a way as to reflect adversely against your trial team.

Suppose a witness has a different view of the evidence than your trial team. You must determine the reasons for the difference. Someone is mistaken. Try to get the witness to review the transaction or occurrence with you. Be prepared to ask questions as the witness explains what he or she observed. But ask your questions in such a way as not to challenge the witness, at least, not at first. Get the full story. Do not make the witness defensive. Unfortunately, the more a witness repeats an erroneous version, the more committed the witness becomes. So help the witness to resolve the errors in the witness's version as quickly as possible.

When you have to cope with an uncooperative witness, consider using exhibits, especially photographs, as bait to catch the witness's interest. Even hostile witnesses usually are interested in seeing exhibits relevant to what they intend to say at trial. Begin the discussion by minimizing disagreements. Identify areas of agreement; then, step by step, show the witness how her or his idea is wrong. Refer the witness to the laws of nature, physical facts, photographs, police reports, depositions, or statements by other witnesses. Show the witness how his or her version conflicts with other evidence. Explain how the testimony fits into the big picture or doesn't fit. Hopefully, once the witness senses that you are a sincere and pleasant person who appreciates the witness's cooperation, the witness will become more receptive and cooperative. Occasionally, a witness who harbors an erroneous belief will abandon it when the case is put in perspective. Even if the witness will not abandon the erroneous idea, she or he may be less adamant about it at the trial.

Interviewing Witnesses Together

You should try to interview a witness without anyone else around. Sometimes it is necessary to meet with two or more witnesses at the same time. They may be friends, co-workers, or related. Remember that your meeting is not privileged. The witnesses can be asked about anything you or they say in the meeting. Furthermore, if there is a problem, you may have to take the witness stand yourself to describe what was done and what was said. They may be able to help each other remember pertinent details and avoid unnecessary inconsistencies, however. It is best to begin with an overview of the case, so that they can appreciate how their evidence relates to the other evidence. They should be told to freely acknowledge this meeting. They should also be prepared to explain that you only told them to tell the truth.

Dealing with an Erroneous Version

Too often, parties encounter witnesses who have erroneous versions of the facts. Usually there is an explanation for the error, but sometimes not. If the case involves an accident, you should take the witness to the accident situs to visualize and discuss what happened and how it happened. When a witness is cooperative but persists with an erroneous version, you probably need to challenge the witness's memory or powers of observation. Again, the bases for challenge are the laws of nature, demonstrable physical facts, probability, and the weight of other witnesses' evidence. It is counterproductive to do this in an argumentative way. It must be handled as though the witness is doing you a favor to even speak with you. It is better to ask questions than to be demanding. If the witness's version conflicts with photographs of the accident scene, show the photographs to the witness. When the witness's version conflicts with another witness's deposition testimony, show the transcript to the witness. The witness may insist that the photographs or other witnesses are wrong. But once a witness has had an opportunity to see what other witnesses say, what the other evidence is, most are willing to correct an honest mistake. Conscientious witnesses appreciate help to avoid mistakes and embarrassment. They do not want unnecessary complications with the legal system. Consider telling the witness you can understand how she or he could have misinterpreted or incorrectly remembered the particular fact. Remember, you must not lead any witness into error.

Suppose a police accident report shows that the accident occurred at 9:30 P.M. The United States Weather Bureau's records show that the sun set at 8:45 P.M. and the weather was overcast. Nevertheless, a witness who has essential and reliable testimony about the collision has the mistaken idea that the accident happened in daylight. By taking the witness to the accident location under similar conditions, it may be possible to show the witness that the artificial lighting from the streetlights and stores made the area seem "bright as day." There should be no concern that this extra effort will hurt the client's case in any way. No undue influence has been applied. If your efforts with the witness come out at trial, it just shows your trial team has a sincere interest in establishing the truth. Once the reason for a witness's error in perception or recollection is identified, the witness's mistake can be explained and corrected. Of course, this approach is not helpful where the witness is simply lying.

You may investigate the availability of the opponent's witnesses. Contacting witnesses aligned with the opposition is ethical provided no privilege is violated. For example, it would be ethical for the defendant's lawyer to telephone the office of the plaintiff's treating doctor to find out whether the doctor will be in town during the week the case has been set for trial. If the doctor will be out of town for a convention, such information could be significant in evaluating the case. Furthermore, it is always useful to know whether the opposition is doing its homework and preparing for trial.

Compensating Witnesses

A party may properly reimburse a witness for expenses incurred in coming to trial to testify. You may offer to pay a witness for time off work, milage, parking, meals, and lodging. Whatever you pay or agree to pay is subject to disclosure on cross-examination. The witness should be told to acknowledge an agreement or payment when asked about it. Sometimes the exact amount of the witness's expenses cannot be determined until the trial is completed. In that event, the witness's best answer is to explain that the amount has not been set but the witness expects to be reimbursed for expenses. A party cannot offer to pay for testimony, only for time and expenses.

A different situation is presented when dealing with expert witnesses who do charge for their services, including testimony. Again, the amount of the fee is subject to disclosure. Indeed, the expert witness may be asked about the amount charged for testifying in other cases. If the fee is exorbitant, the jury has a right to infer that the witness is selling testimony—that the witness would say whatever the party asked if the price were right. When a jury learns that an expert witness charges a *contingent* fee, so that the expert gets paid only if the party who retained her or him wins the case, the expert's credibility is destroyed. Again, a jury properly may conclude that the witness is merely a "hired gun" who will say anything for a fee. If an expert appears reluctant to testify about her or his fee, that will reflect adversely against the witness and the party who retained the witness. Part of preparing the witness to testify is making sure that the matter of fees and expenses is appropriately handled.

Preparing Exhibits

The court's pretrial order may require the parties to have all their exhibits "marked for identification" before the trial begins. The parties are supposed to stipulate to the foundation for all marked exhibits, unless an actual dispute exists concerning the foundation. If a party fails to disclose and mark an exhibit as ordered, the court may not receive the exhibit into evidence. The Federal Rules do not establish a particular method for identifying exhibits. However, local court rules may mandate a method to maintain uniformity. The trend is to use numbers, rather than letters, to identify all exhibits.

Before exhibits are marked for identification, you must carefully examine them to make sure they do not contain inappropriate markings or notations. Once in a while photographs get marked up by a witness, or a sticker used for organizing the exhibits is left on an exhibit. Underlining passages in documents, notations in the margins, and *X*s used in photographs to pinpoint locations might cause the exhibits to be inadmissible or reduce their authority. For example, someone might have penciled the point of impact on a photograph during the investigation. A new photograph should be obtained from the negative so that an "undamaged" photograph can be used at trial. You may want to make photocopies of documents that will be put into evidence, because once an exhibit has been received into evidence, the clerk of court takes custody of it. The parties might not have access to it after court hours. Photocopies are useful for preparing witnesses, preparing the final argument, and preparing posttrial motions. Even photographs may be photocopied, and photocopies may be adequate for these collateral uses.

Pretrial Disclosures

At least thirty days before trial, each party must disclose in writing the identity of each witness the party intends to have testify, the identity of witnesses whose depositions will be used in lieu of live testimony, and each exhibit the party intends to offer into evidence. The pretrial disclosure form is similar to the initial disclosure form. On receiving a pretrial disclosure, a party has fourteen days in which to file objections to any of the exhibits. Failure to object may constitute a waiver of the right to object at trial.

Proposed Jury Instructions

Most courts require the parties to submit proposed jury instructions before the trial begins. Again, most law firms have a collection of jury instructions from which proposed instructions can be tailored to fit almost any case. You may help the trial lawyer by selecting and organizing the proposed instructions. With a little experience, you will be able to select and assemble them for presentation. If a party submits proper "requested instructions" and the court fails to give one of them, the court's omission may give the client grounds for a new trial or an appeal. Most judges have their own **boilerplate instructions** that they usually prefer despite the lawyers' requests. Nevertheless, it is always a good practice to submit requested jury instructions that reflect the trial team's theory of the case.

boilerplate instructions A colloquial term used to describe standard jury instructions generally used by a particular judge or all of the judge's at a particular court.

Proposed Verdict Form

There are three types of verdicts: general verdict, special verdict, and general verdict with interrogatories (Rule 49). When judges use special verdicts, they ordinarily ask parties to submit proposed verdict forms. Again, most law firms have a collection of special verdict forms that can be tailored to fit a new case. You may be asked to prepare a verdict form. (See Chapter 19 concerning types of verdicts and their applications.)

SUMMARY

A case analysis provides a method that lawyers and paralegals can use to determine whether the case is ready for trial. When you conduct a case analysis, you are forced to consider the facts in the context of the law and to consider the evidence in the context of the facts. A case analysis tells you whether your trial team can present a prima facie case. A case analysis identifies each material fact, the evidence that can be offered to prove each fact, and the sources of the evidence. A trial team must be objective. Resolve the conflicts. A completed case analysis provides a basis for developing a trial strategy. A trial strategy is a beacon that guides final preparation and the presentation of evidence. It helps the trial team to choose which evidence to present and the manner in which to present it.

The primary purposes for pretrial conferences are to settle cases, simplify cases for presentation, and make sure everyone is ready for trial. A court may simplify a case by encouraging the parties to agree on certain facts and the admissibility of certain evidence. A court may simplify the case by eliminating certains claims and defenses by obtaining party stipulations. A court can strike claims and defenses that lack merit. Because any legal and fact issue is subject to consideration at a pretrial conference, the court may raise a legal issue sua sponte[8] and make orders concerning any aspect of the case. A court may order that certain evidence will be excluded, allow amendments to the pleadings, or require parties to submit memoranda dealing with particularly difficult legal issues. A court may limit the number of expert witnesses each side may use. A court may require the parties to mark all their exhibits for identification under the supervision of a magistrate before the trial begins. The parties must be prepared to stipulate to the foundation for exhibits, unless there is an actual dispute concerning foundation. If a party has failed to disclose and mark an exhibit as ordered, the court may refuse to receive the exhibit into evidence. Local court rules usually mandate a method for marking exhibits to maintain uniformity.

When you prepare a client to appear and testify at trial, begin by explaining the big picture. Report on the status of the case, describe trial procedures, explain how each witness's testimony fits into the case as a whole. This will give the client a frame of reference the client can use when testifying. You cannot tell the client what to say, but you can tell him or her *how* to tell his or her story. Help the client and witnesses to appear sincere and authoritative. Each item of evidence should be consistent with all the other evidence your team will offer. The evidence must not conflict with facts established by stipulation or admissions. Your client's evidence must comport with the laws of nature and incontrovertible physical facts.

Examine your team's exhibits to make sure documents do not have highlighted passages, there are no notations in the margins, and the photographs are not marked up. Such markings could make the exhibits inadmissible or reduce their authority. You have time in which to make duplicates. Consider making copies of documents that will be exhibits at trial, because once the documents have been received into evidence, you will not have access to them during evening hours. Extra copies are useful for preparing witnesses to testify, and preparing the final argument and posttrial motions.

Courts usually require parties to submit proposed jury instructions before trial. Paralegals may help select and organize proposed instructions. If a party submits requested instructions and the court fails to give one, the court's omission may give the client grounds for an appeal.

The trial team must not be beguiled by its own evidence. You must be objective. If the trial team does not see any problems in the case, the team needs to look again and look harder. Something has been overlooked. Good trial preparation is detail oriented. It is sometimes tedious and frustrating, but necessary and worth the effort. There is logic to what must be done. As you gain experience, you can assume greater responsibility for initiating and conducting trial preparation.

KEY TERMS

boilerplate instructions   sua sponte
case analysis   trial brief
frivolous   trial notebook
mistrial   trial strategy
pretrial order

REVIEW QUESTIONS

1. Why is it important to develop the details when preparing for trial?

2. What must you do if you have two witnesses, each with a somewhat different version of a fact?

3. What is the first thing you should do in response to a trial alert?

4. What are the principal differences in how a party testifies in a discovery deposition and at trial?

5. How does trial strategy differ from a party's legal theory of the case?

6. Why might a party subpoena an opponent to come to the trial?

7. What kinds of matters may be covered at a pretrial conference?

8. Why does Rule 16 require the lawyer to have authority to make admissions and stipulations on behalf of the client at pretrial conferences?

9. May a party's liability insurer send a representative to attend the pretrial conference?

10. What are the hallmarks of a good witness at trial?

11. When is a claim or defense considered frivolous?

12. For whom does a paralegal or lawyer prepare a case analysis?

13. What is the principal purpose for preparing a case analysis?

14. Do the Federal Rules of Civil Procedure require the parties to prepare a preliminary case analysis as part of their discovery plan?

15. At what point in the development of a case is a case analysis most valuable to the preparer?

16. May a case analysis that is prepared for one case be used in another case?

17. To what extent does a case analysis contain citations of legal authority?

18. Would a lawyer commit malpractice if he or she did not compile a case analysis when preparing for a trial?

19. Does a case analysis have to encompass the entire case in order to be useful?

20. What action must a lawyer and paralegal take, if during the preparation of a case analysis, they discover that their client's answer to the opponent's interrogatory is incomplete because it fails to disclose information that they have and that was requested in the interrogatory?

CASE ASSIGNMENT

You recently started working in attorney Catherine Dolan's law office. Agent Burns's "errors and omissions" insurer retained her to defend Mr. Burns. Ms. Dolan mentioned that she was considering making a motion for summary judgment to get the case dismissed against Burns. She started to ask you whether you believe a summary judgment motion would work, but your conversation was interrupted by a telephone call. You know Ms. Dolan will bring it up tomorrow. Of course, you want to show her that you really know your job. So you have decided to take the file home and do a case analysis, so you will be ready to discuss it tomorrow. Share your analysis with your instructor.

To get you started, here are some suggestions. Harper's third-party complaint against Burns alleges he was negligent for transferring coverage from the pickup to the Camaro. Griffin will need expert testimony to establish the standard of care applicable to insurance agents. Burns is an expert because he is a licensed insurance agent, and he can give an affidavit that he complied with standards applicable to insurance agents. Although agent Burns can assert all the defenses asserted by the defendant Harper and third-party defendant Griffin, Ms. Dolan is only interested in arguing that Burns did not cause Griffin's problems and that he did not do anything wrong. Her answer to the fourth-party complaint alleged that when Griffin sold the pickup to Harper he no longer had an insurable interest in it.[9] Therefore, the issues are (1) Did Griffin own the pickup at the time of the accident? If he did not own it, he could not insure it. The question is one of fact. (2) Can a person buy a liability insurance policy in his or her own name to secretly insure another person? The issue raises solely a question of law. So the analysis has a fact question concerning ownership. What evidence do you have that Harper owned the pickup at the time of the accident? What is the evidence against it? The certificate of title was in Griffin's name, but under the state law, the certificate is not conclusive proof of ownership. By the way, in a similar case, Ms. Dolan made the motion and won in the district court. The Minnesota Supreme Court affirmed.

Endnotes

1. A motion in limine is used to exclude evidence that the moving party expects another party to offer during the trial. "In limine" literally means "at the threshold." The motion is made at the threshold of the trial out of the jury's hearing. The purpose is to prevent the jury from knowing anything about the objectionable evidence by keeping the opposing party from making any reference to the evidence. As a general rule, courts prefer not to rule on the admissibility of evidence until the evidence is actually offered, so the judge can assess the importance of the evidence in the context of the other evidence.
2. Most liability insurance policies do not cover injuries that an insured intentionally inflicts. However, coverage does apply to intentional acts as long as no injury was expected or intended.
3. Another way of expressing the defense theory is that the plaintiff assumed the risk of injury by riding with a person who was obviously intoxicated.
4. A party who prosecutes a frivolous defense or claim is subject to sanctions and possibly to disciplinary action. The sanctions may include an assessment of costs, an order striking the party's pleadings, or even an award of judgment in favor of the opposing party.
5. When parties stipulate to the foundation for an exhibit they agree that the exhibit is what it purports to be, or what they say it is.
6. The apparent displacement or difference in apparent direction of an object as seen from two different points.
7. Ordinarily, you would provide a copy to the client immediately after the deposition was taken so the client can make corrections.
8. A court acts sua sponte when it issues an order or initiates some activity without any motion or prompting from a party.
9. A person cannot buy automobile insurance on the basis of his or her good driving record to provide that insurance to another person who is not disclosed to the insurance company.

     For additional resources, visit our Web site at www.paralegal.delmar.cengage.com

CHAPTER 19

STRUCTURE OF A CIVIL TRIAL

CHAPTER OUTLINE

Chapter Objectives

Chapter 19 describes how a civil trial is conducted and how paralegals can assist. It covers each step in a trial, from selecting the jury to receiving a verdict. It shows how all the preparation is used and rewarded.

Introduction

A courtroom resembles a laboratory where the parties examine and test disputed facts. Like a controlled scientific study, a trial follows strict protocols, rules of procedure, rules of evidence, and rules of law. The structure and rules are designed to promote fairness and impartiality. As far as possible, courts treat parties equally. Each party has an opportunity to present his or her evidence. Each has an opportunity to argue for the result he or she seeks. Once the facts are established, the court must apply the law to the facts and resolve the dispute according to law. The outcome should be predictable within a reasonable range. If the outcome is extraordinary, some error probably occurred. When parties resort to a trial, they are constrained by legal standards. They lose the right to use their own standards and values to resolve their dispute.

Trial of a civil case is open to the public. There is room for spectators, including the news media. Local rules differ concerning where the parties may sit. Some courts allow parties to sit with their attorneys at the counsel table. Some courts have them sit in a designated area. Sometimes parties sit in the spectators' section. Although the parties have a constitutional right to observe the trial, witnesses do not. When good cause is shown, a court may **sequester** witnesses by keeping them out of the courtroom until they testify. The purpose is to prevent witnesses from being influenced by what other witnesses says.[1]

sequester To keep a witness apart from other witnesses and outside the courtroom to prevent the witness from being influenced by the testimony of others. To keep a jury together and out of communication with the rest of the world while the jury hears a case or deliberates.

A judge presides over all aspects of the trial, from the selection of the jury to entering judgment; from courtroom decorum to determining the substantive law. Lawyers are officers of the court. A judge has the right to expect lawyers to help manage the trial. Lawyers help by making objections and motions when they believe the opponent or court has made a mistake. If the mistake is promptly corrected, no one is harmed. Lawyers present evidence, provide guidance concerning the law, and argue the client's case. Lawyers must control their clients and witnesses by instructing them about procedures and their responsibilities to the court. Judges rely on lawyers to keep their clients and witnesses from testifying falsely. Paralegals help lawyers in these important functions.

Preliminary Conference

State court judges often hold preliminary conferences with the lawyers when they report to the courtroom to begin trial. Federal court judges seem less inclined to have preliminary conferences. Preliminary conferences are quite informal. They are held in the judges' chambers. A preliminary conference is not a pretrial conference. The lawyers may be in chambers less than ten minutes or all day. Usually, the judge wants to know whether the parties want a *little* more time to discuss settlement. Some judges want to know the amount of the plaintiff's last demand and the defendant's last offer. Other judges prefer not to know the amounts, but only whether the parties are still negotiating. The lawyers inform the judge about problems they anticipate, such as scheduling a witness. Parties often have scheduling problems, but planning and cooperation between the parties reduce the problems. This is also a time for arguing motions in limine, submitting proposed jury instructions, and submitting voir dire questions, if the judge is going to conduct the examination. Some state courts require parties to submit statements of case immediately before trial. A statement of case provides a summary of the claims, the witness list, and the exhibit list.

Juries

Selection of Jurors

The judge directs the clerk to bring twenty or more jury panel members to the courtroom. Traditionally, a panel member was called a venireman. The panel members sit in the spectators' section of the courtroom. As the clerk reads each panel member's name and address, he or she walks to the jury box and takes a seat. The process continues until the desired number of panel members has been seated. You should observe carefully how each panel member is dressed and what he or she carries, such as newspapers, books, lunch, or a briefcase. Try to see what members brought to read. A panel member who has comic books may not be much interested in your client's business transaction. When you are handling a personal injury or disability case, try to observe whether any panel members have physical impairments. Are the impairments of the type that might influence him or her for or against your client? For example, in a personal injury case, the defense lawyer ought to be concerned about a potential juror who limps as he or she walks to the jury box. Your observations may lead to additional questions that should be put to panel members. Trial lawyers usually want paralegals to write notes so they can quickly read your suggestions. They prefer to avoid whispered conversations in front of the panel.

The parties are entitled to impartial jurors who are competent to understand the evidence and will follow the law without favor or bias. Courts have voir dire examinations of panel members to determine whether they are qualified to sit on the particular case. A voir dire examination is a cross-examination under oath concerning a panel member's background, qualifications, and attitudes. The judge has broad discretion in deciding what questions may be asked. Rule 47 provides that the voir dire examination may be conducted by the lawyers or the judge or both:

> The court may permit the parties or their attorneys to conduct the examination of prospective jurors or may itself conduct the examination. In the latter event, the court shall permit the parties or their attorneys to supplement the examination by such further inquiry as it deems proper or shall itself submit to the prospective jurors such additional questions of the parties or their attorneys as it deems proper.

Some judges require the lawyers to submit proposed voir dire questions before the trial begins. Judges have broad discretion in deciding what questions may be asked. If a panel member is obviously biased or incompetent, a party may strike the panel member for cause. If a party simply does not like a panel member, the party may strike him or her by using a **peremptory challenge.**[2] But each party is allowed only three peremptory challenges.

At the end of the trial, there must be at least six jurors to render a verdict. The clerk must seat enough panel members to provide for the six, plus any alternates and to accommodate the parties' peremptory challenges and challenges for cause. To illustrate how the number of panel members is determined, assume the judge wants eight jurors to sit on the case. Two of the eight will be alternates. Therefore, even if two jurors became ill, the remaining six could return a verdict. Assume the case involves one plaintiff and two defendants who are adverse to each other. Each party is entitled to three peremptory challenges for a total of nine. The judge must empanel eight plus nine for a total of seventeen. But the judge may assume two panel members might be excused for reasons of health, bias, or extreme inconvenience, so two more should be added to the panel. Based on these assumptions, the judge needs to empanel at least nineteen to end with eight. The nineteen jurors are subject to a voir dire examination to determine their qualifications to sit on *this* jury. For one reason or another they might not qualify for this case, but can sit on another case.

peremptory challenge By law and court rule, the right of each party to remove a specified number of jurors, usually two or three, from the panel during the voir dire examination without explanation or justification.

Challenges for Cause

actual bias A state of mind that prevents a venireman, juror, or witness from being impartial.

All challenges for cause are determined by the court (28 U.S.C.A. § 1870). **Actual bias** exists when a panel member acknowledges that she or he cannot be fair or has a close relationship with one party or a close relationship with a material witness. Actual bias may be for or against a party. Or, a panel member may be biased because he or she has been in the same situation as one of the parties. If a venireman is related by blood or marriage to a party or one of the lawyers, or works for a party, or has some other close connection with the case, there is **implied bias,** and the court will excuse the member even if the member claims she or he can be fair. The problem is the appearance of unfairness.

implied bias Bias that is assumed to exist because of the relationship between the witness or juror and a party.

A judge may determine sua sponte that a potential juror should be stricken for cause because of bias or apparent bias. Or, a lawyer may move the court to strike a panel member "for cause." The motion usually is made at the judge's bench, out of the panel's hearing, because the motion might be denied and the lawyer's remarks might prejudice the juror against the lawyer or client. Furthermore, the discussion at the bench could unduly influence other members of the panel if they heard it. A panel member who has actual or implied bias is stricken before the next panel member is examined. Each party has an unlimited number of challenges for cause. When a panel member is stricken for cause, the court may add another member to the panel. Judges must keep potential jurors from feigning bias to evade jury service.

Peremptory Challenges

The law assumes parties have subjective, but important, reasons for not wanting certain persons on their juries. Therefore, courts give parties peremptory challenges that allow parties to strike up to three panel members without expressing any reason for the strikes. One method of selection requires the attorneys to accept or strike a panel member before questioning the next panel member. That is the procedure most commonly used in criminal cases. It is cumbersome and does not give lawyers an opportunity to compare all panel members before exercising their precious peremptory challenges. Also, the procedure may cause a little more embarrassment for panel members and lawyers because a peremptory challenge must be exercised before going on to the next juror. The other method permits the court and attorneys to question the panel as a whole before parties exercise their peremptory challenges. The jurors know that some will be stricken though all of them may be perfectly acceptable.

When two or more parties are aligned and have similar interests in the outcome of the case the court may treat them as a single party. For example, when the plaintiff sues the owner and the driver of an automobile to obtain money damages for injuries, the owner and the driver may have to share their peremptory challenges. If a husband and wife have brought an action to recover money damages for the wife's injuries, they are aligned and must share their peremptory challenges. Parties who are adverse to each other, however, do not have to share peremptory challenges. Parties are adverse if the pleadings raise issues between them. For example, cross-claims make codefendants adverse. The same circumstances determine whether plaintiffs must share peremptory challenges. A court may allow aligned parties to exercise their challenges separately or jointly. If jointly, they may confer with each other about using the strikes. Some state courts limit the number of peremptory challenges to two. A party should not "waste" a peremptory challenge on a panel member whom they can strike for cause. The lawyers may decide not to use a peremptory challenge on an alternate, because the court may excuse the alternate at the end of the trial.

Parties exercise peremptory challenges by noting their strikes on the clerk's jury list. The defendant's lawyer must exercise the first peremptory strike. Then the plaintiff strikes one. The process is repeated until the parties use all their strikes. Occasionally, a lawyer announces to the panel that she or he finds all panel members to be acceptable. Lawyers who engage in that kind of bravado are merely trying to ingratiate themselves with the jury. It is a tactic, but not a good one.

Although peremptory challenges are generally thought to be available to strike jurors for any reason or for no reason, lawyers are not entitled to use them to strike jurors on the basis of their race or other constitutionally protected status. But because lawyers are not required (or inclined) to announce the strategy behind their use of peremptory challenges, the law is faced with a dilemma. The answer is that a lawyer, if challenged for using a peremptory strike for an improper reason, must announce a protected-status-neutral reason for the strike. The trial judge must then rule whether the announced reason is acceptable or whether it is a sham for using an improper strike. The issue can be tricky, but it is important. The integrity of our system would be compromised if people could be excluded on an improper basis. Therefore, what is ordinarily a matter of lawyer discretion and strategy must yield to the system's need to prevent unlawful discrimination.

Judge's Introductory Remarks

Immediately before the voir dire examination, the judge usually introduces the parties' lawyers and gives the panel members an outline of the case. The panel members need this information so that they can answer the voir dire questions, such as "Do you know any of the parties?" A judge's introductory remarks may be similar to the following:

EXAMPLE

Members of the jury panel, you have been summoned to this courtroom so that of your number six may be selected to hear, try, and determine this case. You might be an excellent juror in ninety-nine out of one hundred cases; however, because you may be acquainted with one or more of the parties, lawyers, or witnesses, or because you have a present leaning one way or another about this case or this type of case, you may be considered to be biased or prejudiced concerning this case. What we need are six persons from varying walks of life who will diligently seek the truth; who will fairly and impartially and without fear or favor try the issues of fact; and who will decide this case on the evidence adduced here in the courtroom and on the law that will be given to you by me.

continued

EXAMPLE   *continued*

In order that we may ascertain if you are a proper or qualified person to sit as a juror in this case, first I, then counsel, will ask you questions about your qualifications. In so doing, it is not the lawyers' intention to pry into your private life, but it is their duty to select a jury of the quality and character indicated. Please be open, frank, and responsive to the questions put to you so that justice may be done between the parties.

So that you may intelligently respond to questions put to you testing your qualifications, I shall briefly state the identity of the parties, the nature of the case as reflected by the pleadings, the identity of the lawyers, the names of possible witnesses, and certain fundamental rules of law applicable to this case and all cases of like character.

At that point, the court introduces the parties and lawyers.

Voir Dire Examination

The judge and lawyers ask questions concerning age, occupation, family, education, past and present occupations, prior jury experience, experience with similar occurrences or transactions, experience with litigation as a party or witness, attitude toward the judicial system and the kind of lawsuit in question, attitude toward the parties, willingness to follow and apply the law, and willingness to set aside natural feelings of sympathy. This list is not all-inclusive. If the lawyers question panel members, the defense lawyer usually goes first. Some courts require the defense lawyer to question the first panel member until the lawyer challenges the member for cause, or exercises a peremptory challenge, or accepts the juror. Then the plaintiff's lawyer questions the panel member in the same fashion. They continue the process until all jurors have been questioned and accepted. Some courts require the defense lawyer to question all panel members before the plaintiff's lawyer examines them. They may challenge for cause during the questioning, but they do not use their peremptory challenges until both lawyers have finished questioning. They exercise their peremptory challenges by striking names from the clerk's jury list. The jurors do not know which lawyers struck them, but usually it is quite apparent.

Although the purpose of the voir dire examination is to obtain competent, impartial jurors, lawyers look for more. They try to build connections between themselves and jurors or between the client and jurors. In effect, a lawyer seeks jurors who will favor their client and disfavor the opponent. Because lawyers are not supposed to use the voir dire examination to indoctrinate the jury or ingratiate themselves with the jury, an inexperienced lawyer may get into trouble by overstepping the bounds. There is a fine line between being courteous and ingratiating one's self. Of course, a lawyer should have his or her trial strategy well in mind while conducting the voir dire examination. A well conducted voir dire examination is wonderful to see.

You should listen to the panel members' responses. Listen to what they say and how they say it. Consider whether panel members appear confident and respond appropriately. Or, are they easily confused? Do they look at you or at the parties? Do they avoid looking at you? Watch for body language. An obviously shy person may not contribute much to the jury's deliberations, no matter how strongly he or she feels about the facts. Maybe that is bad or good. Either way, it is a consideration. The more you can observe about the jury panel, the more helpful you can be in the selection process. Be sure to obtain the client's participation. The client may have subjective feeling about a potential juror that makes the client uncomfortable. You have the opportunity to discuss the panel with the client while the lawyers are conducting the voir dire examination. The trial team must consider the client's feelings. Indeed, make the client part of the team. The voir dire examination provides the only opportunity the lawyers have to speak with the jurors. Although some critics complain that lawyers spend too much time trying to sell their cases during the voir dire, most trial lawyers believe the voir dire examination is essential to obtain a fair-minded, qualified jury.

Preliminary Jury Instructions

After the six to twelve jurors have been selected, they are sworn to follow the court's orders and the law. The following is typical of oaths administered to jurors:

> You each do swear that you will impartially try the issues in this case and a true verdict give according to the law and the evidence given you in court; your own counsel and that of your fellows you will duly keep, you will say nothing concerning the case, nor suffer anyone to speak to you about it, and you will keep your verdict secret until you deliver it in court.

The court may remind jurors that they must act on reason and good judgment, not on the basis of feelings, emotion, or speculation. The judge may give some preliminary instructions, such as in the accompanying example.

EXAMPLE

At the appropriate time, I will instruct you concerning the law that applies to this case. You must take the law exactly as I give it to you. You must apply such law to the facts as you find them to be from the evidence. You must render your verdict accordingly to the facts and the law, despite the consequences. I do not make the law. I merely declare what it is in this case. The law comes from federal and state constitutions, from federal and state statutes, and from declarations contained in judicial decisions stating the public standards of rights and duties in matters not covered by the constitutions and statutes. If juries were not bound by these laws and juries could set up private and personal standards of rights and duties, people would never know in advance of a decision how they should have acted in a particular situation. No one would be safe from the courts. Cases must be decided on settled principles of law and not on the notions of a judge or of a jury. Accordingly, it must be apparent to you that even though you may

continued

EXAMPLE   *continued*

have an opinion about what the law is or should be, you must set that aside. You must accept and apply the law exactly and precisely as I give it to you. I cannot at this time instruct you concerning all the rules of law applicable to this case because I have not yet heard the evidence.

I have some general instructions that will help you. Our hours are generally 9:30 A.M. to 12:00 P.M., 1:30 P.M. to 5:00 P.M. Those hours may be modified or extended depending on circumstances. For example, should a witness's testimony be nearing completion at the customary recess time, we would continue so that the witness would not need to come back for the next session. Promptness, of course, is extremely important, and I am sure I need say no more about that.

About midway in the morning session and midway in the afternoon session, we will take a fifteen-minute recess. On those occasions, as well as during the noon hour and after hours, you will be among the public. Do not discuss this case or the subject matter of the case with anyone; not even with each other. Once the case is over and you have rendered your verdict and you have been discharged from the case, you may speak as fully and freely as you wish. You also may say, "I have done my best; I would rather not discuss it."

During the voir dire examination, I told you where the parties' accident occurred. Please do not go there and view the premises. You are not investigators. You are to determine the facts from the evidence submitted here in the courtroom, so keep that in mind. Besides there may be changes that you do not know about.

You must try to keep an open mind until all the evidence has been presented and until I have instructed you about the law. The plaintiff will proceed with his case first, followed by the case-in-chief of each defendant. If new materials are submitted, the plaintiff will have the right to make a rebuttal. If new material is submitted on rebuttal, the defendant will have a right of rebuttal. In that way, all of the evidence that is proper will be submitted to you without repetition. The rebuttal is limited to the new material.

After all the evidence has been presented and the parties have rested their case, you will have the opportunity to hear the attorneys' summations. The attorneys will review the evidence and draw conclusions about what facts the evidence proves or does not prove. They will discuss rules of law they believe apply to the facts for which they contend. The summations may be—and usually are—of assistance to you, but the responsibility of decision is yours, not that of the attorneys.

When you enter the jury room, you will have all the tools with which to determine the facts of the case and to apply the law. Meanwhile, do not jump to conclusions. You must keep an open and objective mind while the case is being presented. You should maintain that same objectivity when you commence your deliberations.

EXAMPLE *continued*

You may take notes if you wish. However, those notes are yours to refresh your own memory. If your notes help your memory so that you can say, "Now, of my own knowledge, I know this was said," then you may say that to your fellow jurors. But your fellow jurors should not use your notes to refresh their memory. Such notes are no more authoritative than another juror's memory. There is a danger that when writing notes, you will not hear other important evidence. Your observations and memory are more important than note taking.

From time to time I may conduct conferences at the bench with the attorneys. Those conferences are intended to be out of your hearing. They involve questions of law or procedure, not questions of fact. Do not attempt to overhear our conversation. Under no circumstances should you try to guess the subject of our conversations and permit that to bear on your determination of facts or the ultimate issues. If you were to do so, your decision or determination would be based not on facts and the law, but on speculation and conjecture—which is repugnant to good judicial administration.

If anytime during the trial something of a personal nature bothers you, come to me about it. I am sure I can handle it so that it will not be detrimental to any party. But do not ask me what the evidence is, because that is solely within your province. That is your responsibility. As I told you before, you should not consider or even know what I think of the evidence.

Sometimes, after the jury commences deliberations, a disagreement arises as to what a witness may have said—and it seems simple to call the court and say, "May we come back and have the court reporter read a witness's testimony?" I do not permit that except under unusual circumstances. In all probability, I will have started another trial. The attorneys have probably gone their respective ways and may be trying another lawsuit—even in another county. If you were to come back and have portions of the testimony read to you, I would have to contact the attorneys, get them back and recess my current case. And then, after I have permitted the reading of that one witness's testimony, the attorneys may be constrained to point out that, in fairness, the testimony of other witnesses who touched on that subject ought to be read; otherwise, one facet of the case may be overemphasized. By the time I complied, we would be trying the case again.

When you fail to hear an attorney's question or a witness's answer, speak up, raise your hand. I will make sure that it is read back at that time, in its proper context and without any fear of possible overemphasis. Do not wait until the end of the testimony or end of the trial. It will be too late then to go back.

The judge should caution jurors against discussing the case among themselves until they receive their instructions on the law and begin their deliberations. There is a danger that by discussing some facet of the case a juror might become an advocate for a particular position before hearing all the evidence and receiving instructions on the law. For the same reason, jurors should not make strong statements at the beginning of their deliberations.

Some courts allow, even encourage, jurors to take notes. However, a juror must not use her or his notes to influence other jurors. Notes are not necessarily more reliable or authoritative than another juror's memory. One reason for this is that a juror may be so busy writing that the juror may not be listening. The juror's notebooks are collected and kept by the clerk during evening recesses to prevent anyone from tampering with them and to keep them from being lost.

There is a trend in the courts for judges to give the jury some preliminary instructions concerning the substantive law that applies. The judge may repeat the preliminary instructions at the end of the trial. The preliminary instructions help jurors to appreciate the significance of the evidence. Most courts also give jurors preliminary instructions to help them evaluate evidence. The instructions on evidence may or may not be repeated at the end of the case. Instructions on evidence may be similar to the following:

Direct and Circumstantial Evidence

A fact may be proved by either direct or circumstantial evidence, or by both. The law does not prefer one form of evidence over the other. A fact is proved by direct evidence when, for example, it is proved by witnesses who testify to what they saw, heard, or experienced, or by physical evidence of the fact itself. A fact is proved by circumstantial evidence when its existence can be reasonably inferred from other facts proved in the case.

Evaluation of Testimony—Credibility of Witnesses

You are the sole judges of whether a witness is to be believed and of the weight to be given to the testimony of each. There are no hard and fast rules to guide you in this respect. In determining believability and weight, you should take into consideration, as to each witness, the following:

The witness's interest or lack of interest in the outcome of the case.
The witness's relationship to the parties.
The witness's ability and opportunity to know, remember, and relate the facts.
The witness's manner and appearance.
The witness's age and experience.
The witness's frankness and sincerity, or lack thereof.
The reasonableness or unreasonableness of the witness's testimony in the light of all the other evidence in the case.
Any impeachment of the witness's testimony.
Any other circumstances that bear on believability and weight.
You should rely on your own experience, good judgment, and common sense.

Expert Testimony

A witness who has special training, education, or experience in a particular science, profession, or calling is allowed to express an opinion. In determining the believability and weight to be given such opinion evidence, you may consider, among other things, the following:

The education, training, experience, knowledge, and ability of the witness.

The reasons given for the witness's opinion.

The sources of the witness's information.

Considerations already given you for evaluating the testimony of a witness. Opinion evidence is entitled to neither more nor less consideration by you than the other fact evidence.

Evaluation of Deposition Evidence

Testimony may be presented to you by way of videotaped deposition. The testimony of a witness who for some reason cannot be present to testify in person may be presented in this form. Such testimony is under oath and is entitled to neither more nor less consideration by you because it was so presented. You are to judge its believability and weight in the same manner as you would have had the witness been in court.

Impeachment

In deciding the believability and weight to be given the testimony of a witness, you may consider three types of evidence:

1. Evidence that the witness has been convicted of a crime. In doing so, you may consider whether the kind of crime committed indicates the likelihood of the witness telling or not telling the truth.
2. Evidence of the witness's reputation for truthfulness.
3. Evidence of a statement by or conduct of the witness on some prior occasion that is inconsistent with the witness's present testimony. This evidence may be considered by you only for the purpose of testing the believability and weight of the witness's testimony and for no other purpose. However, if the statement was given under oath or the witness is a party or an agent of a party in the case, the evidence of the prior inconsistent statement or conduct may be considered as substantive evidence bearing on the issues in this case as well as for testing the believability and weight of the witness's testimony.

Opening Statements

Lawyers have the right to make opening statements. Note that it is called a statement, not an argument. Opening statements are the lawyer's opportunity to tell the jury what he or she expects to prove during the trial. They are not a time to argue about what conclusions the jury should draw. They may describe the transaction or occurrence. They may provide an overview of the evidence. But they are not supposed to make arguments. Opening statements are like road maps that show the jury where the case is going and how the evidence will take them there. Opening statements help the jury to understand the evidence, why the evidence is relevant, and how the evidence interrelates. Lawyers may use opening statements to explain concepts, relationships, technical subjects, terms, and procedures. For instance, if the trial involves a medical procedure, the lawyers may prepare the jurors to hear about the procedure by describing it in a nonargumentative manner. In a case involving electricity, the lawyers might define some terms and explain some principles about which the experts will testify. Depending on local rules, the lawyers may be allowed to show exhibits during the opening statements.

Lawyers are not supposed to use opening statements to persuade jurors. It is one thing to describe the evidence that a lawyer intends to present, and quite another thing to argue what the evidence proves. Lawyers must not discuss evidence they know the court will not receive. They should not argue the consequences of a party's conduct or condemn a party's conduct. Lawyers are not supposed to discuss the law or its application to the facts during opening statements. But courts give lawyers latitude to identify the claims, facts, and evidence. Some lawyers preface their remarks with "The *evidence* will show. . . . " This preface helps them to focus on the evidence rather than argue the case. Furthermore, the phrase is disarming, because it makes an argument sound as though it is merely a preview of the evidence. Help the trial team watch for this tactic. For example, "The evidence will show that the defendant was driving much too fast for conditions" is a veiled argument and is objectionable. However, a lawyer may say "The evidence will show that the defendant was driving forty miles per hour in a thirty-mile-per-hour zone." The latter statement is fact based and comports with the evidence the lawyer intends to offer. A lawyer should not state the defendant was *negligent* for driving forty miles per hour in a thirty-mile-per-hour zone, because that statement involves the application of law to the expected evidence.

Most lawyers prefer to describe the facts chronologically with the supporting evidence. A chronological approach is the easiest for the jury to understand. Unfortunately, lawyers cannot always present evidence chronologically. They may have to present evidence in a disconnected fashion. So a chronological overview helps the jury to understand and appreciate the evidence as they hear it. A lawyer's opening statement should complement the final argument he or she intends to make. An opening statement may last five minutes or thirty minutes. The Rules do not impose a time limit, but some judges do. Most lawyers try to keep their opening statement to about thirty minutes. For most cases, an hour is too long. If a lawyer spends that much time, it suggests he or she is not prepared and not well focused. Furthermore, there is real danger in saying too much.

The party who has the burden of proof makes the first opening statement, because that party must present his or her evidence first. Usually, the plaintiff has the burden of proof. The defendant's lawyer may make an opening statement following the plaintiff's opening statement or after the plaintiff **rests.** The plaintiff rests when the plaintiff has finished presenting his or her case-in-chief. Usually, defendants' lawyers give their opening statements immediately after the plaintiffs', because they want the jury to appreciate, at the outset, that there are two sides to the case. They want jurors to know about the problems in the plaintiffs' cases. They try to prepare

rest   A party's formal announcement that he or she has no more evidence to offer in support of a claim or defense.

jurors to follow the cross-examinations of the plaintiffs' witnesses. If the jurors appreciate that there really is a legitimate dispute, they are more likely to keep an open mind until they have heard all the evidence. A defense lawyer who waits to make an opening statement until the plaintiff has rested may have some surprise evidence or impeaching evidence that he or she does not want to discuss until the plaintiff is fully committed to a position.

An opening statement educates the opposing party as well as the jury. Consequently, no one listens more carefully to a lawyer's opening statement than the opposing lawyer. Your trial lawyer may ask you to take notes on the opponent's opening statement. If a lawyer makes an assertion in the opening statement that the evidence does not support, the inconsistency can be used against the lawyer in the final argument. The opponent's opening statement may flag some problems for you and your witnesses. While listening to the opponent's opening statement, you should consider whether the statement reflects the strategy your trial team anticipated. Listen carefully to your trial team's opening statement. If the lawyer makes a misstatement, let him or her know, because the lawyer can correct the mistake during the trial. For example, if the lawyer misstates an important date and you catch the mistake, the lawyer can emphasize the correct date while questioning witnesses. The same is true if the lawyer leaves out some important point. You should tell the client to listen carefully to the opening statements. The opponent's statement tells the client exactly what the opponent thinks is important and what the opponent is likely to ask during cross-examination.

Burden of Proof

A party who asserts a claim has the burden of proving the claim. In criminal cases, we recognize the burden of proof as the familiar "guilt beyond a reasonable doubt." In civil cases, a claim must be proved by a fair preponderance of the evidence. The evidence, taken as a whole, must cause the jury to believe that the claim is more likely true than not true. If the evidence leaves the jury in doubt about the claim, the claim has not been proved, and the verdict must be against the party who made it. Although the burden of proof in civil cases is not as great as in criminal cases, it is significant. Most defense lawyers believe they should have a theory of the case to show the jury what happened, and not merely raise doubts about the plaintiff's evidence. The judge defines burden of proof in the jury instructions.

> Whenever I say a claim must be proved, I mean that all the evidence by whomever produced must lead you to believe it is more likely that the claim is true than not true. If the evidence does not lead you to believe it is more likely that the claim is true than not true, then the claim has not been proved. Proof of a claim does not necessarily mean the greater number of witnesses or the greater volume of testimony. Any believable evidence may be a sufficient basis to prove a claim.

Although the instruction is in terms of *claims*, the instruction applies to each fact a party relies on to prove a claim. The jury must evaluate and weigh the evidence. The jury may decide that one witness is more believable than three other witnesses on a

EXAMPLE

Suppose the plaintiff brings a wrongful death action against her deceased husband's medical doctor on the theory that the doctor should have diagnosed a heart infection sooner than he did and that earlier treatment would have prevented the patient's death. Suppose further the plaintiff has three medical doctors who testify that a reasonably competent physician should have conducted the tests that would have disclosed the infection sooner and could have cured the patient, but the defendant physician testifies that the patient was so ill he would have died anyway. If the defendant's testimony leaves the jury in doubt about whether he was responsible for the patient's death, the plaintiff's three experts have not carried the plaintiff's burden of proof. The jury may be impressed with the defendant attorney's cross-examination or by the reasons the defendant gave for his opinion that the patient would have died anyway.

Suppose a plaintiff in a personal injury case testifies that he or she has had neck pain for two years following an automobile accident. The defendant may present evidence by an independent medical examiner and the plaintiff's own treating doctor that there is no objective evidence of any injury, impairment, or chronic problem. Nevertheless, a jury could choose to believe the plaintiff and award damages for her neck pain. In other words, meeting the burden of proof may be a very subjective standard.

particular point. Cases have been lost or won because the jury was not persuaded that a critical fact or claim was more likely true than not true.

In the rare case when the defendant has the burden of proof, the defendant has the right to present evidence first. As an example, if the plaintiff entrusted her fur coat to the defendant for storage and the coat was lost or damaged, the storage company would have the burden of proving it was not negligent. Therefore, the storage company would have the right to present evidence first. Without any evidence about how the loss occurred, the defense would fail. When an insured sues to recover benefits under the policy and the insurance company denies coverage because of a condition or exclusion in the policy, the insurer has the burden of proving facts that bring the claim within the condition or exclusion. Therefore, the insurer gets the first opening statement and presents its evidence first. However, if the insurance company denied coverage on the basis that the policy was not in force at the time of the insured's loss, the insured would have the burden of proving that the policy was in force and the loss is the type covered. The insured gets the first opening statement and must present evidence first.

Plaintiff's Case-in-Chief

The party who has the burden of proof must present all his or her evidence first. A good trial strategy might be to hold some evidence back until the opponent has put in his or her evidence. But that tactic is impermissible. The plaintiff may present evidence to defeat the defendant's affirmative defenses or wait until after the defendant has presented his or her evidence to present evidence against the affirmative defenses. A plaintiff may require a defendant to testify as part of the plaintiff's **case-in-chief.** Indeed, it is common for a plaintiff's lawyer to call the defendant as the first witness. There are several reasons for doing this. The plaintiff's lawyer can pin down the defendant's version of the facts and then attack that version. The plaintiff's lawyer may cross-examine the defendant about one or two matters where the defendant's credibility is weak. This approach is good strategy, because it makes the plaintiff's case appear strong at the beginning. The defendant has not heard the other witnesses, so the defendant may be a little less prepared than she or he will be later in the trial. A defendant's lawyer may follow with a direct examination of the defendant or wait until the defendant's *case-in-chief.* Most judges permit defendants' lawyers to ask a few questions to clarify points developed during the plaintiff's cross-examination that might be misleading if not promptly explained.

> **case-in-chief** The body of evidence a party presents to establish the party's claim or affirmative defenses before the party rests.

When the plaintiff's lawyer is finished, he or she indicates so by stating that "the plaintiff rests." At that point, the court and parties must determine whether the plaintiff's evidence has established a prima facie case. A prima facie requires some evidence on each element of the cause of action. Believability of the evidence is not a concern. If the evidence fails to prove a prima facie case, the claim should be dismissed as a matter of law [Rule 50(a)(1)]. See the next section. If the evidence is sufficient, the case proceeds and the defendant may present the defendant's case-in-chief. After resting, the plaintiff may present only **rebuttal evidence.** Of course, there is an exception. The plaintiff may move the court for leave to reopen the plaintiff's case-in-chief and present new evidence, but the judge must find there are extenuating circumstances. Trial tactics is not grounds for reopening. The defendant may cross-examine the plaintiff's witnesses and make objections. But, otherwise, the defense team must watch, listen, and be stoic.

> **rebuttal evidence** Evidence that a party offers to contradict or refute evidence previously offered by another party.

Motion to Dismiss

If the plaintiff's evidence fails to establish a prima facie case, the defendant may move for dismissal. The court must decide whether there is evidence to establish each element (essential fact) in the plaintiff's cause of action. If not, the case is over. Rule 50 provides

(a) Judgment as a Matter of Law
  (1) If during a trial by jury a party has been fully heard on an issue and there is no legally sufficient evidentiary basis for a reasonable jury to find for that party on that issue, the court may determine the issue against that party and may grant a motion for judgment as a matter of law against that party with respect to a claim or defense that cannot under the controlling law be maintained or defeated without a favorable finding on that issue.
  (2) Motions for judgment as a matter of law may be made at any time before submission of the case to the jury. Such a motion shall specify the judgment sought and the law and the facts on which the moving party is entitled to the judgment.

A defendant who previously made a motion for summary judgment would use the same arguments and authority to support a motion for dismissal. The grounds are the same. The only difference is that the court has now heard the plaintiff's evidence rather than simply seen it in documentary form. Also, this motion provides a predicate for making a postverdict motion for judgment as a matter of law. See posttrial motions in Chapter 17.

Defendant's Case-in-Chief

After the plaintiff rests, the defendant's lawyer takes charge. The defendant's case-in-chief is presented much like the plaintiff's case-in-chief. The defendant's lawyer has three objectives: (1) to present evidence to prove the facts that support the defendant's theory of the transaction or occurrence, (2) to counter the plaintiff's evidence on disputed facts, and (3) to prove the defendant's affirmative defenses.

The plaintiff cannot present evidence during the defendant's case-in-chief. The plaintiff may object to the defendant's evidence and test the evidence through cross-examination. The defendant's evidence must be sufficient to establish the elements of his or her affirmative defenses. Otherwise, the court will dismiss them. When the defendant's lawyer is finished, he or she states that "the defendant rests." The plaintiff may move for judgment as a matter of law, dismissing any affirmative defense not established by the evidence [Rule 50(a)(1)]. However, at this point, the court looks to *all* the evidence to decide whether the evidence is sufficient to establish the defense.

Plaintiff's Rebuttal

The plaintiff may present rebuttal evidence. Rebuttal evidence is limited to issues and facts covered by the defendant's evidence. The plaintiff may not offer rebuttal evidence on matters not raised or covered in the defendant's case-in-chief. A party may not use the rebuttal as a means to ambush an opponent. When the plaintiff's lawyer is finished, she or he again states, "plaintiff rests."

Defendant's Rebuttal

A defendant's rebuttal evidence is limited to the matters covered in the plaintiff's rebuttal. The defendant's lawyer must repeat, "defendant rests." When both parties have finally rested, the judge instructs the jury, "The evidence is closed." The clerk notes the date and time for the record.

Presenting Evidence

Parties may offer evidence in many forms. Again, evidence is *anything* that tends to prove or disprove a material fact. A court may receive evidence as Rule 36 admissions, through parties' stipulations, testimony, exhibits, summaries, and judicial notice. The evidence may be direct or circumstantial. The law does not prefer one kind of evidence over another. The challenge is to make the evidence admissible, understandable, interesting, and persuasive. Also, the trial team must keep the evidence from being unduly repetitious, cumulative, and inconsistent. A fact may be proved with more than one kind of evidence. For example, skid marks can be proved using testimony, photographs, diagrams, or a combination of them. How much evidence on any given fact is enough? What evidence should not be used? The trial team's strategy must deal with these problems.

A fact is proved by **direct evidence** when it is proved by a witness who testifies to what he or she saw, heard, or experienced. And physical evidence of a fact is direct evidence. **Circumstantial evidence** is evidence of one or more facts from which the existence of another fact can be inferred. Or, said another way, a fact is established by circumstantial evidence when its existence can be inferred from other facts. Some examples may help. The classic example is footprints in the sand or snow. Evidence of footprints is evidence that a dog, deer, or person had been there. A more relevant example is, if a witness saw the defendant's car skid to the point of impact, the witness has direct evidence of the skid. If the witness did not see the car skid but did see skid marks on the road, however, proof of the skid marks is circumstantial evidence that the car skidded. Similarly, a witness who observed and measured skid marks can provide direct evidence of their direction and length. From those facts a jury may infer that the driver saw danger and applied his or her brakes and that the driver was or was not keeping a proper lookout.

Although circumstantial evidence is indirect proof, it is not considered any less trustworthy or less credible than direct evidence of a fact. When a jury is confronted with circumstantial evidence that conflicts with direct evidence, the jury may elect to accept either. Circumstantial evidence requires some analysis and reasoning. Therefore, it is only as good as the jury's ability to analyze and reason or the lawyer's ability to explain it. Matters of intent, motive, and knowledge are often proved through circumstantial evidence. Suppose the plaintiff claims the defendant intentionally shot him, but the defendant claims the gun discharged accidently. If the plaintiff was shot three times, would you believe the direct evidence or the circumstantial evidence?

Witnesses

You may be the trial team's liaison with the witnesses. You would be responsible for having the witnesses available when needed. This may mean juggling schedules, solving transportation problems, and even serving subpoenas. Lawyers want their witnesses to testify in an order that tells the client's story. Usually, they want to present the facts chronologically. But each witness may have only a few pieces of the story, and those pieces may not fit the chronology. Often witnesses are not available when needed. If the trial team disregards a witness's convenience, the witness may be vindictive and less helpful. It is much better to accommodate witnesses. The chronological presentation must yield to the witnesses' availability. This is one reason the opening statements are so important, to tie evidence together. Lawyers have found it is very important to accommodate physicians' schedules. To avoid scheduling problems, parties may use videotaped depositions to present their testimony at trial. Witnesses usually do not come to court until the day on which they are to testify. Unless sequestered, they may sit in the spectators' section until their turn.

When a lawyer calls a witness to the stand, the clerk or judge administers an oath to the witness. The witness states his or her name and address for the judge,

direct evidence Testimony about a fact by an eyewitness who observed the fact, or an exhibit that tends to prove the existence or nonexistence of the fact. See, for contrast, *circumstantial evidence*.

circumstantial evidence Indirect proof that depends on the application of logic and common experience to infer the existence of a fact; evidence offered to prove one or more facts from which the existence of other material facts can then reasonably be inferred.

hostile witness   A witness who has demonstrated animosity toward one of the parties.

reporter, and jury. The lawyer must conduct a direct examination of the witness, unless the witness is an opposing party or aligned with an opponent as a **hostile witness.** The answers must come from the witness. The questions identify subjects but do not suggest answers. Each question should be clear to the witness and to the jury. Each should be singular and not ask for too much information. Each question should flow naturally from the witness's prior answer. To make testimony interesting and flow is an art.

Conversely, lawyers may cross-examine witnesses aligned with an opposing party, hostile witnesses, and any witness an opposing party calls to testify. In a cross-examination a lawyer may ask leading questions, because the witness is not looking to the lawyer to suggest the "correct" answer. Questions may be framed to keep the answer very specific—to keep witnesses from volunteering beyond the question. If a witness's answer does go beyond the question, the lawyer may move to strike the answer as nonresponsive. A cross-examination is supposed to be limited to the matters covered in the witness's direct examination, unless the witness is an adverse party. For example, if the plaintiff's lawyer called a witness to testify about the plaintiff's injuries, the defendant's lawyer could cross-examine the witness about the injuries. If the defendant's lawyer were to ask questions about the accident (a different subject), the plaintiff's lawyer could object that the cross-examination is outside the scope of the direct examination. The defendant could ask the court for leave to call the witness as his or her own witness and cover the new subject by way of a direct examination. The lawyer could cross-examine, however, if the witness is a hostile witness. A judge may determine that a witness is hostile because the witness is contrary and antagonistic or because of the witness's relationship with the other party.

A judge has control over the interrogation to keep lawyers from being repetitious, to avoid undue embarrassment, and to prevent lawyers from harassing witnesses (see Rule 611). A judge may ask questions for clarification for his or her own benefit or for the benefit of the jury. Witnesses should not take anything to the stand that the opposing side should not see. It is all right for witnesses to take their deposition transcripts. Medical doctors and expert witnesses take their business files and reports with them. Expert witnesses expect to have their files examined by the opposing lawyer.

Exhibits

An exhibit requires a foundation to be received into evidence. The foundation identifies the exhibit and shows its relevancy to the case. The foundation may be provided in a response to request for admissions or by a stipulation, but usually a witness provides the foundation. Judges have broad discretion in determining whether a witness's testimony is adequate to establish the necessary foundation. A witness's foundation testimony may be similar to the following:

Q: Mr. Harper, can you identify what has been marked as exhibit 2?
A: Yes, that is the agreement Mr. Griffin prepared when he sold the pickup truck to me.
Q: Can you identify the signatures on the exhibit?
A: Yes, that is my signature and that is Mr. Griffin's signature.

Q: How do you know that it is Mr. Griffin's signature?

A: Because I saw him sign it. I was there.

Q: On what date did you and he sign the exhibit?

A: We both signed it on April 6, 2000.

Q: Are there other parts to this written agreement that you both signed?

A: No, that is all there is. The one page.

Q: Third-party plaintiff offers exhibit 2 into evidence.

Court: Any objection?

Attorney Hoch: No objection.

If the other parties waive their objections to foundation, and that is common, the lawyer who wants to use the document states for the record what it is.

Expert Testimony

When technical or specialized knowledge is required to understand a disputed fact or other evidence, expert opinion evidence is admissible to help a jury. A witness can qualify to be an expert by showing he or she has special education, training, and experience with the subject. The foundation evidence may come from the witness, other witnesses, and documents. If the witness is licensed by a state in a profession, the licensure usually qualifies the witness to testify concerning matters within the ambit of the profession, provided he or she has experience with the subject. Educational degrees and official certifications help. But the primary consideration is the extent of the witness's experience with the technical subject. For example, a family physician holds the same license to practice medicine that a cardiac surgeon has, but a family physician may not qualify to testify to the intricacies of a particular phase of heart surgery.

Your trial team needs to do more than simply qualify the witness as an expert. Your trial team needs to make the expert interesting, authoritative, and persuasive. To do this, the team needs to present the witness's background in the subject, such as teaching, writing, and practical experience. If your expert has written several books and articles, you may want to prepare an attractive bibliography of the publications to put into evidence as an exhibit. It is nice to be able to show the witness has received awards and professional recognition by his or her peers. A witness may testify about his or her accomplishments. If your expert is listed in directories, consider getting copies to show the jury. The fact that a witness often has testified may be good or counterproductive. The witness must explain the nature and extent of his or her experience with the subject. The judge decides whether the foundation evidence is adequate. Assuming a witness qualifies to testify as an expert, the credibility and the weight to be given to his or her opinions is for the jury to decide. Again, the trial team has to decide how much background information is enough and what would be too much.

A party runs a risk of losing credibility by calling too many expert witnesses. Even two experts may be one too many. Experts often disagree with each other even when testifying for the same party. They might arrive at the same basic conclusion, but their assumptions, analyses, or reasons may differ. The inconsistencies can weaken the total impact. A skilled cross-examination may show that an expert witness would have reached the same opinion despite the underlying facts. Whoops! The expert is biased.

Objections

The Rules of Evidence determine what evidence is subject to exclusion. Evidence is admissible unless it violates an exclusionary rule. There is a technical objection for every situation. A lawyer objects by stating, "Plaintiff objects on the grounds of hearsay." Or, "Defendant objects on grounds of lack of foundation." Or, "Plaintiff objects, no foundation." The objection does not have to be phrased in a particular way, but should include the grounds. The jury is not supposed to hear anything more than the grounds. An objection is not supposed to be an argument against the evidence. For example, an objection should *not* explain, "Plaintiff objects on the grounds the defendant has presented no evidence to show that the exhibit is authentic; on its face it appears to have been executed on a different date; and the signature is not verified." The technical objection is "lack of foundation." Or, "Defendant objects on the grounds of hearsay, because this witness only would be repeating what the witness heard from another person." The objection is "lack of foundation." Some judges strictly limit objections to the technical grounds and others do not. A judge's failure to limit lawyers to technical objections may result in each objection becoming a diatribe between the lawyers. If a question or exhibit is objectionable on several grounds, all grounds may be stated.

Each party is responsible to prevent the jury from hearing improper evidence offered by the other. A judge must disallow improper evidence when a timely objection is made. Without an objection, a court may receive evidence that was subject to exclusion. If improper evidence is received, it becomes part of the case, and a jury may use it and base their verdict on it. For example, hearsay evidence may prove a claim or defense if it is received without objection. Jurors may use the improper evidence to discount or discredit other evidence that was properly received. If evidence is offered but not received, it may not be used by the court or jury for any purpose.

A lawyer must state the grounds for his or her objection. That helps the judge to identify the problem. If a lawyer states the wrong grounds for an objection and, therefore, the objection is overruled, the lawyer cannot complain that the evidence should have been excluded. The lawyer failed to help the judge identify the problem with the evidence. A judge may **sustain** an objection, however, on grounds other than those stated. In that event, the judge should state the ground on which he or she excluded the evidence. At the end of the trial, the judge usually instructs the jury that evidence that was received over an objection should not be given any greater or less weight than other evidence.

A lawyer should object before the witness answers but without interrupting the question. If the witness answers before the court rules, the lawyer who objected may ask the court to strike the answer and instruct the jury to disregard the answer. Evidence that is **stricken** cannot be used for any purpose. Of course, the problem is that parties never really know whether the jury was influenced by the evidence that was stricken. If they heard the improper evidence and are likely to be influenced by it, the judge may order a mistrial. This occurs very rarely and only when the improper evidence is especially inflammatory. When a judge disagrees with an objection, the judge states, "Objection overruled." The witness may answer. When a judge agrees with an objection, the judge states, "Objection sustained." The lawyer who offered the evi-

sustain   To accept or admit. A party's objection to another party's evidence or conduct is sustained when it is accepted by the court and is allowed.

strike   Take out. For example, to *strike* a word is to remove it from a document.

dence must decide whether to go on to something else or find another way of offering the evidence. On occasion a lawyer may strongly disagree with the judge's ruling and ask for permission to approach the bench to discuss the ruling. They do not require the judge to allow discussion. Sometimes the judge and attorneys leave the courtroom to have their discussion. If the judge allows a discussion, all lawyers must participate. The court reporter should record the discussion to make it part of the record. The record may be important for purposes of appeal. On further consideration, a judge may reverse his or her previous ruling and allow the evidence. A lawyer may quickly wear out his or her welcome by asking for too many "bench conferences."

The objection establishes error in the record, which may entitle the objecting party to a new trial. However, an error justifies a new trial only if it is prejudicial. In other words, the wrongful exclusion must have the potential for affecting the outcome. Some nonprejudicial errors occur in almost every trial. When the court sustains an objection, the proponent has a right to make an "offer of proof" to show what the evidence is and what it would prove. The proponent must make the offer out of the jury's hearing. The judge cannot prevent a party from making an offer of proof. An offer of proof helps the appellate court to appreciate the significance of the excluded evidence. It also gives the trial judge an opportunity to reconsider the ruling.

Though a proponent's evidence is subject to an objection, the opposing lawyer may decide not to object. Lawyers are reluctant to object too often. They do not want to appear as though they are hiding information from the jury. If an objection is overruled, the objection may serve only to highlight the evidence in the eyes of the jury. Furthermore, why object to evidence that could be received if presented in another form, especially if it would be stronger evidence if properly presented? A lawyer must make a very quick analysis. It goes like this: Is the evidence harmful? If so, how harmful is it? If quite harmful, is the evidence subject to an objection? If so, is an objection counterproductive? Does the evidence "open a door" to evidence that might otherwise not be admissible? Is that good or bad? The analysis points out again the importance of a well-thought-out trial strategy. Do not be too concerned when your trial attorney elects not to object to some improper evidence. Making an objection should never be a mere reflex reaction.

Using Depositions

A deposition transcript may be used at trial to impeach the deponent while he or she is on the witness stand. Also, a deponent's transcript may be read to a jury instead of live testimony if the deponent is not available. This is true though the deposition was taken for discovery, not to preserve testimony for use at trial. Rule 32(a) provides:

> At the trial or upon the hearing of a motion . . . , any part or all of a deposition, so far as admissible under the rules of evidence applied as though the witness were then present and testifying, may be used against any party who was present or represented at the taking of the deposition or who had reasonable notice thereof, in accordance with any of the following provisions: (1) Any deposition may be used by any party for the purpose of contradicting or impeaching the testimony of deponent as a witness, or for any other purpose permitted by the Federal Rules of Evidence.

(2) The deposition of a party or of anyone who at the time of taking the deposition was an officer, director, or managing agent . . . of a public or private corporation . . . which is a party may be used by an adverse party for any purpose.

(3) The deposition of a witness, whether or not a party, may be used by any party for any purpose if the court finds:

(A) that the witness is dead; or

(B) that the witness is at a greater distance than 100 miles from the place of trial or hearing, or is out of the United States, unless it appears that the absence of the witness was procured by the party offering the deposition; or

(C) that the witness is unable to attend or testify because of age, illness, infirmity, or imprisonment; or

(D) that the party offering the deposition has been unable to procure the attendance of the witness by subpoena; or

(E) upon application and notice, that such exceptional circumstances exist as to make it desirable, in the interest of justice and *with due regard to the importance of presenting the testimony of witnesses orally in open court*, to allow the deposition to be used.

(Emphasis added) A witness is "unavailable" if the witness is dead, is outside the United States, is more than 100 miles from the place of trial, is ill or too infirm to appear in court, or is in prison. Otherwise, a party must show the court he or she tried to subpoena the witness and could not. The strong preference is to require witnesses to appear in person at trial.

The procedure for using a deposition transcript at trial varies depending on whether it is being used for impeachment or as testimony. For impeachment, the lawyer may call to the witness's attention the page and line of the deposition where the impeaching testimony appears. Then the lawyer may read the relevant questions and answers. Typically, the lawyer follows with a question, such as, "That was your testimony on [date] when you gave your deposition?" "You understood that you were testifying under oath, just as you are under oath here in court?"

There are two methods of using a deposition transcript to present testimony. The easiest, but least effective, way is for the lawyer to read the questions and the deponent's answers verbatim. The opposing attorney has the right to make objections as the testimony is read. That method is satisfactory if the evidence is short and routine. It gets the evidence to the jury and in the record. Another method is to have you sit in the witness chair and read the witness's answers. The opponent has the right to read other portions of the transcript to the jury to explain or clarify and put the testimony into context. The transcript is not an exhibit. The jury is not allowed to read it. But it is part of the court's record.

A party may put into evidence all or any portion of an opposing party's deposition. A party's deposition testimony is treated as a party's admission; therefore, it qualifies as substantive evidence. Also, it may be received as impeachment evidence. A party-deponent may or may not be on the witness stand when his or her deposition is read into evidence. The term "admission" does not mean the deponent admitted fault or responsibility. If deposition testimony is offered solely for impeachment, the jury uses it to evaluate the deponent's credibility. Suppose the plaintiff stated in her deposition that she never saw the defendant's car before the collision, but testified at trial she did see the defendant's car when it was still 100 feet away. The defendant could offer the plaintiff's deposition testimony into evidence to prove the plaintiff was not keeping a proper lookout, because she did not see the defendant's car before the collision. The jury could base its verdict on the deposition testimony.

A nonparty's out-of-court statement cannot be used as evidence if the witness is available to testify in court. The reason for this is that courts strongly prefer to have the jury *see and hear* the testimony. Seeing and hearing helps the jury to evaluate the credibility of the witness and the testimony. Therefore, nonparty deposition testimony is treated as hearsay. If a nonparty's testimony at trial differs from what he or she said in a deposition, in effect, the witness has retracted the prior out-of-court statement. Though the out-of-court statement is not substantive evidence, it may be brought to the jury's attention to help the jury evaluate the nonparty's testimony. If a nonparty's testimony in court is believed, that testimony will support a verdict though the witness was impeached by deposition testimony. Suppose a nonparty witness testifies in his deposition that he saw the defendant driving fifty miles per hour in a thirty-mile-per-hour zone, and at trial testifies the defendant's speed was twenty-five miles per hour. The witness's testimony is competent to prove a speed of twenty-five miles per hour. The deposition testimony of a higher speed casts doubt on the witness's credibility, but the jury cannot use the out-of-court testimony as a basis for finding, as a fact, that the defendant traveled fifty miles per hour. The fifty miles per hour testimony is impeached; the witness is impeached. But the impeachment does not prove the defendant's speed was fifty miles per hour. If the defendant (a party) testified in his deposition that he was driving fifty miles per hour at the time of the accident and testifies at trial to a speed of twenty-five miles per hour, however, the jury can accept the "admission" in his deposition as substantive evidence and find that his speed was fifty miles per hour.

At the end of the trial, the court instructs the jury to consider impeachment when evaluating the witnesses' testimony. Impeachment (a showing of inconsistency) does not necessarily mean the witness has lied. Nor is the witness disqualified from testifying. Impeachment evidence merely affects the weight and believability of testimony.

Final Arguments

Although you cannot deliver a final argument, you can assist if you understand the purpose and limitations. The trial strategy probably was built around the final argument. The argument brings everything together. Traditionally, lawyers make final arguments after the jury has heard all the evidence but before the judge instructs them on the law. A few courts instruct juries on the law before the lawyers make their final arguments. The rationale is that the court should tell the jury what the law is before the jurors hear the lawyers' arguments. But the consensus is that the jury instructions are much more important than the arguments and should be the last thing the jury hears before deliberating. Furthermore, the court's instructions serve as a "buffer" between the arguments and the jury's deliberations.

Courts differ concerning the order in which the parties may make their arguments. Some courts require the plaintiff's lawyer to argue first, because the plaintiff should explain his or her claim and the defendant should answer it. The defendant's lawyer argues second. He or she may argue against the plaintiff's claims and argue for application of the affirmative defenses. When the plaintiff's lawyer goes first, he or she is entitled to make a short rebuttal argument. The rebuttal may be limited to as few as five minutes. Furthermore, the rebuttal is limited to matters raised in the defendant's argument. Other courts require the defendant's attorney to argue first. The rationale is that plaintiff's lawyer should argue last, because the plaintiff has the burden of proof.[3] When the defendant argues first, there is no right to rebuttal. Consequently, the defense lawyer must anticipate the opponent's argument. That is a difficult assignment. Unlike opening statements, lawyers have a great deal of latitude in what they may say. Each attorney has his or her own style. We will examine some of the "do's" and "don'ts."

Attorneys describe the claims and defenses. They may postulate a theory about what happened and why. They may review the evidence. They may comment on the believability of witnesses, testimony, and exhibits. They may tell jurors why jurors should believe certain evidence and disbelieve other evidence. They may argue why a witness should or should not be believed. They may show the jury the exhibits and comment on their application. They may discuss the judge's instructions on the law and how the law applies to the evidence. In this regard, lawyers have a right to know, before they make their final arguments, exactly what the judge intends to tell the jury about the law. Attorneys must not misstate the evidence, facts, or law. They must not argue from evidence the court did not receive. They must not postulate an argument that has no evidence to support it. They must not ask the jurors to put themselves in the position of one of the parties. Lawyers must not invoke religious beliefs for or against a party. The jurors may not ask questions.

Lawyers often use charts to illustrate points, list items of damages, compute money damages, highlight items of evidence, and so forth. A lawyer has a right to know in advance about charts the opposing attorney intends to use, unless the charts have been received in evidence as exhibits. Lawyers may read from documents, such as hospital records, received into evidence but not from documents not received in evidence. Lawyers try to keep their argument to less than an hour. However, the length and complexity of the case determine the length and scope of the argument.

A lawyer may object to improper statements an opponent makes. If an objection is sustained, the judge tells the jury to disregard the statement. If a lawyer's argument is misleading, an opponent may be entitled to a corrective jury instruction. In that event, the judge not only tells the jury to disregard the improper statement but why the statement was wrong and what the evidence is or in what respect the law was misstated. After the arguments, the judge cautions jurors that they must rely on their own memories of the evidence and not on the lawyers' recollections. The judge tells them that if the lawyers said anything about the law that differs from his or her instructions, the jury must disregard it.

Jury Instructions

The judge instructs the jury concerning their duties, the procedures they must follow, and the law they must apply to decide the case. Judges always read the jury instructions to minimize the opportunity for error. Many judges give jurors copies of their written instructions to use in their deliberations. As part of the instructions, the judge explains the verdict form and how the jury is to use it. They are told to fully discuss the case before deciding anything.

Occasionally, jurors determine they need clarification on some point of law or procedure, so they notify the judge, through the bailiff, that they need additional instructions. The judge must summon the lawyers to the courtroom so they can hear the jury's question and help the judge answer it. The judge has ultimate responsibility to handle the problem. Ideally, the lawyers will agree on the solution. Their agreement precludes the problem from becoming a basis for an appeal. Usually, the problem can be solved by rereading the instructions already given to the jury. If the judge merely rereads the instructions previously given, the lawyers may elect not to return to the courtroom to participate. Sometimes, before signing a special verdict, the jury wants to know what effect the answers will have. For example, sometimes jurors ask judges what happens if they find the defendant was negligent but that he did not cause the accident. Judges customarily answer by telling the jury not to concern themselves with the consequences of the verdict. Some states expressly permit lawyers and judges to tell the jury about the effect of their answers in special verdicts. The instructions usually begin with an overview, such as:

> Your role is to determine the facts from all the evidence. Then you must apply the law to those facts to render a verdict. In a few minutes, I will tell you what the law is. You will follow and apply the law as I give it to you whether or not you agree with it. You must not be influenced by any personal likes or dislikes, opinions, or prejudices.
>
> I have given to you a verdict form containing several questions. You must answer these questions on the basis of the facts you find were established by the evidence and the rules of law I give you. Based on the answers you make in the verdict form, I must enter a judgment. The judgment will conclude the case.
>
> You must consider and apply my instructions as a whole. Do not single out some parts and ignore others; all parts are all equally important. In other words, parts may complement and explain other parts. The order of the instructions is not significant. Similarly, in determining what the facts are, you must consider all the evidence you have seen and heard no matter by whom produced. You should consider reasonable inferences which may be drawn from that evidence. Do not concern yourself about whether the answers seem to favor one party or the other. You must not read into these instructions, or anything I have said or done, a suggestion as to what I think your answers in the verdict should be.
>
> Attorneys are officers of the court. It is their duty to present evidence on behalf of their clients and to make such objections as they deem proper, and to

argue fully their client's cause. However, the arguments or other remarks of the attorneys are not evidence in the case.

If the attorneys have made, or if I have made or should make, any statement about the evidence that differs from your recollection of the evidence, then you should disregard the statement and rely solely on your own memory. If the attorneys' arguments contain any statements of the law that differ from my instructions on the law, you should disregard their statements.

You must decide whether a witness is to be believed and what weight to give to the witness's testimony. In this regard, you should consider the following:

1. A witness's interest or lack of interest in the outcome of the case.
2. A witness's relationship to the parties.
3. A witness's opportunity to know the facts.
4. A witness's ability to remember and relate the facts.
5. A witness's manner and appearance.
6. A witness's age and experience.
7. A witness's frankness and sincerity, or lack of it.
8. The reasonableness or unreasonableness of a witness's testimony considering all the other evidence in the case.
9. Whether a witness has been impeached.

Besides these guidelines, you should use your own experience, good judgment, and common sense to evaluate testimony.

I mentioned that you may consider whether a witness has been impeached to evaluate the witness's testimony. Impeachment consists of any of the following:

1. Evidence the witness was convicted of a crime.
2. Evidence that on some prior occasion the witness has made a statement or acted inconsistent with what the witness said here in court. The prior statement or conduct may be considered by you only for the purpose of testing the witness's believability. But a prior statement or act of a party may be considered by you as evidence to prove facts as well as for testing the witness's believability.

EXAMPLE

A person may assume every other person will use reasonable care and will obey the law until the contrary appears.

Negligence is the failure to use ordinary care. Ordinary care is that care that a reasonable person would use under like circumstances considering the foreseeability of injury or harm. Negligence is the doing of some act or failing to do something that a reasonable person would do under like circumstances. An act or omission is not negligent if an injury or other harm could not have been foreseen.

The preliminary instructions are followed by instructions on the substantive law. The accompanying example presents instruction on negligence.

The judge usually asks the lawyers whether they have any additions or corrections to suggest. They need not repeat the objections they have already made to the instructions. At this point, the judge is only interested in knowing whether he or she omitted something he or she intended to say or misstated something.

Jury Deliberations

After the instructions, the marshal or bailiff sequesters the jury. The jury is not allowed to talk with anyone, except the marshal or the bailiff who "guards" them. The jury must select a foreperson. There is no established procedure for making the selection. The foreperson is supposed to direct the jury's deliberations, keep the jury focused, decide when and how to vote, and sign the verdict form on behalf of the jury. A foreperson should encourage all the jurors to participate in the deliberations. There is no time limit on their deliberations. A jury may reach a verdict within minutes or hours. Or, a jury may deliberate as long as several days. They may deliberate into the night after regular court hours. In civil actions, jurors usually are allowed to go to their homes during the evening hours. While separated, they must not discuss the case with anyone, not even with other jurors. Suppose that the jury recessed for the night and two jurors rode home together. Suppose that one juror commented to the other that he did not believe a certain witness. That would be **juror misconduct** and be grounds for a mistrial. All discussion must be in the presence of all the jurors. An average length of time for a jury to deliberate is about six hours.

juror misconduct The intentional or willful participation by a juror in a forbidden act, disregarding his or her legal responsibility.

Verdict

Most courts do not require the parties and lawyers to wait at the courthouse for the verdict. The foreperson fills in the blanks, signs, and dates the verdict. In civil cases, the judge or clerk usually reads the verdict aloud. The lawyers may ask the judge to poll the jurors to make sure all jurors concur in the verdict. The judge merely asks each juror whether she or he concurs in the signed verdict. The juror must answer aloud and the court reporter records each juror's answer. Occasionally, a juror who had some reservation about the verdict decides to repudiate the verdict when polled. In that event, the jury is sent back to resume deliberations. If there is no hope in obtaining agreement, the judge may declare a mistrial.

Although the lawyers have a right to be present when the jury returns its verdict, some choose not to attend. The judge or clerk telephones them and informs them what the jury found. The lawyers have copies of the verdict, so they can fill in the blanks. The verdict is then filed with the clerk of court. If the court used a special verdict, which determines only questions of fact, the judge must use the verdict to prepare his or her own findings of fact, conclusions of law, and order for judgment. If the jury returns a general verdict—a rare procedure—it simply finds for the plaintiff for a specified sum of money, or for the defendant. The clerk enters judgment on a general verdict.

Posttrial Jury Contacts

After being polled in court, jurors do not have to talk to anyone about their verdict, their deliberations, or any other aspect of the trial. No law prohibits jurors from talking about the case to the parties, lawyers, news media or anyone else, however. In the course of interviewing jurors you might discover some misconduct. If you learn about or even suspect jury misconduct or misconduct of a juror, your trial team must notify the trial judge. The judge, not the parties, must investigate the suspected misconduct. Interviewing jurors after the verdict may not be used as a subterfuge to find error to obtain a new trial. Any contact parties or lawyers or paralegals have with jurors can result in a waiver of the right to complain about possible jury misconduct.

Jurors usually are enriched by the experience. They provide an important service to their government and community. They derive a better understanding of the judicial system and have a better appreciation for its value. They help to maintain a system that has been instrumental in preserving domestic tranquility for more than 200 years. Within a few days, jurors set aside the worries and anxieties they may have had about their responsibilities, but their new respect for the justice system continues. It is the responsibility of judges, lawyers, and paralegals to help make jury service a satisfying experience.

Taxation of Costs

The prevailing party is entitled to recover certain costs and disbursements incurred in the prosecution of the case. The recoverable costs are specified by statute or court rule. See Rule 54(d). The prevailing party must prepare a bill of costs and disbursements that itemizes the various costs claimed. The losing party has the right to object to the costs and the amounts claimed. As to the amount recoverable, the guideline is *reasonableness*. If an objection is made, a hearing must be held on the objections. Otherwise, the clerk of court accepts the costs as claimed and adds them to the judgment. When the defendant is the prevailing party, the defendant obtains a money judgment against the plaintiff for taxable costs. Before a judgment may be filed, the prevailing party must file an **affidavit of identification,** which fully describes the judgment debtor. Each court has a form or recommended form for this.

affidavit of identification An affidavit, usually prepared by an attorney or paralegal, to establish the identity of a judgment debtor so the court may issue an order to a sheriff or marshal to seize the judgment debtor's property to satisfy the judgment.

TECHNOLOGY NOTES

A litigation team may use portable computers to obtain a "real time" transcript of testimony during a trial. The court reporter must have a stenotype machine that is capable of producing an instant copy. By making arrangements with the court reporter, the legal team can connect a computer into the court reporter's stenotype-computer system. The testimony appears on the team's portable computer almost as it is being given. A member of the team can even edit and annotate the transcript as it is produced.

Other technological innovations have made the courtroom more effective for the lawyers and more attention-grabbing for the jurors. Many up-to-date courtrooms have individual monitors for jurors to view documents as they are discussed with a witness. Documents can appear on screen from a hard copy placed on an

Elmo Visual Presenter or by a computer document image. Documents that have bar codes can be called up instantly to help the jury understand the witness's testimony or to visualize the witness's impeachment. The computer can even enlarge key words or lines on the screen, much like television news reports do when reporting on the contents of some important document like an indictment or a piece of controversial correspondence. Another effective use for bar-coded documents is to have them synchronized with a witness's video deposition testimony. Then a cross-examining lawyer can show the deposition testimony on screen followed by a document that contradicts it. The jurors see these things on a screen, and it really has an impact. If your litigation team regularly uses this type of technology, your ability to master it will provide great value to the team's trial efforts.

SUMMARY

Some judges have preliminary conferences with the lawyers immediately before starting trial. Judges use the conferences to deal with witness problems, settlement negotiations, and motions in limine.

Courts ensure the parties' right to an unbiased, competent jury by subjecting the panel members to a voir dire examination. The judge and lawyers conduct voir dire examinations of jury panel members to determine whether the members qualify to sit on the particular case. The questions must relate to the panel members' qualifications. The veniremen must answer the questions under oath. If the judge asks all voir dire questions, the lawyers have a right to submit written questions to the judge to ask. A panel member may be stricken for cause or because of actual or implied bias. Actual bias exists when a panel member acknowledges that he or she cannot be fair. Implied bias exists if a panel member is related to a party or to one of the lawyers, has some connection with the case or works for a party. Panel members will be excused for cause for actual bias or implied bias. Each party has an unlimited number of challenges for cause. Whenever a panel member is stricken for cause, the court adds another member to the panel. Each party has three peremptory challenges. A party usually does not have to justify or explain a peremptory challenge, but if a challenge may have been used to exclude a juror for an improper reason—rare, for example—a lawyer may be required to provide a neutral explanation for the strike. As a member of a trial team, you should watch and evaluate panel members so you can help with the selection.

Lawyers use opening statements to tell juries about the evidence they intend to present to prove the facts on which they base their claims or defenses. They are not supposed to argue the case. They are not supposed to discuss the law or its application to the facts. The defendant's lawyer may make his or her opening statement immediately after the plaintiff's opening statement or wait until the plaintiff rests. An opening statement helps the jury appreciate and understand the evidence. Opponents capitalize on any misstatements or inadequacies in a lawyer's opening statement. A lawyer must not overstate the client's case but tell the jury enough to make the jurors believe the client has a strong and just position. Like a good witness, a lawyer should strive to appear sincere and authoritative.

The party who has the burden of proof presents her or his evidence first. If a party fails to present a prima facie case, it will be dismissed as a matter of law. Rule

50(a)(1) provides guidelines for motions for judgment as a matter of law. In determining whether a prima facie case has been proved, the court looks to see if the party has presented evidence to support each element of the party's cause of action. A court does not consider the believability of the evidence or whether the evidence has been contradicted by other credible evidence. While the plaintiff presents his or her case-in-chief, the defendant may object to the plaintiff's evidence and test the evidence through cross-examination, but the defendant is not allowed to offer evidence. The plaintiff may require the defendant to testify as part of the plaintiff's case-in-chief. At the end of the plaintiff's case-in-chief, the plaintiff's lawyer states, "Plaintiff rests." After that, the plaintiff may offer only rebuttal evidence. Rebuttal evidence is limited to issues an opponent has raised. Good strategy requires the defendant to have a theory about the case and develop that theory in her or his case-in-chief. A defendant must prove all the elements of her or his affirmative defense; otherwise, the defense will be dismissed.

A lawyer must conduct a direct examination of witnesses aligned with his or her client and any independent witness the lawyer calls to testify. Direct examination question must not suggest the answer the examiner wants. A lawyer may cross-examine any witness whom an opponent calls to testify, unless the witness has been called to the stand for cross-examination. A lawyer may cross-examine any witness who is aligned with any opposing party or who is hostile toward the lawyer. A judge must determine from the circumstances whether the witness is hostile. On cross-examination the lawyer may ask leading questions. The questions should be phrased to keep the witness's answers very specific to keep the witness from volunteering testimony. When an answer goes beyond the question, the lawyer may move to strike the answer as nonresponsive.

A fact is proved by direct evidence when it is proved by a witness who testifies to what she or he saw, heard, or experienced, or by physical evidence of the fact itself. A fact is proved by circumstantial evidence when its existence can be inferred from other facts proved in the case. Circumstantial evidence is not considered any less trustworthy than direct evidence. Circumstantial evidence may require some analysis and reasoning. Therefore, it is only as good as the jury's ability to analyze it or a lawyer's ability to explain it. Matters of intent, motive, and knowledge are often proved by circumstantial evidence.

Judges occasionally ask witnesses questions for clarification for the judge's own benefit and for the benefit of the jury. Federal judges have unlimited authority to ask questions of witnesses. Lawyers and paralegals may talk with an opposing party's witnesses, unless a witness is represented by a lawyer.

Expert witnesses may testify to their opinions to help jurors understand facts and other evidence. A person may be an expert witness without having a strong academic background. Experience in the subject is the most important consideration. The weight to be given an expert's testimony is a matter for the jury to decide. Usually, an expert's persuasiveness depends on the reasons he or she gives and the reliability of the information. The mere fact that the evidence comes from an "expert" does not mean the jury can or should give more weight to the evidence. Experts are never allowed to testify to what the law is or how the law applies to the facts of the case, except in legal malpractice actions.

If a party fails to object to an opponent's evidence, it will be received. The jury may consider the evidence though it would have been excluded if an objection had been made. An objection states the grounds without arguing. If a lawyer states the wrong grounds for an objection and the objection is overruled, the lawyer cannot complain that the evidence should have been excluded. If an objection is sustained, the interrogator must rephrase the question or move to another subject. An objection duly made and erroneously overruled establishes error in the record, which may entitle the objecting party to a new trial. When an objection is sustained, the lawyer who offered the evidence has a right to make an offer of proof to show what the evidence is and what it would prove. An offer of proof helps the appellate court appreciate the significance of the excluded evidence. It also gives the trial judge an opportunity to reconsider the ruling.

A party may put into evidence any part of an adverse party's deposition. A party's admissions are substantive evidence, not merely impeachment. Deposition testimony may be received into evidence at trial if the deponent is unavailable to testify in person. A deponent is "unavailable" if the deponent is dead, out of the country, incapacitated because of illness, or not subject to subpoena. The deposition testimony is received as though the deponent were in court. If a deponent testifies at trial, his or her deposition only may be used to impeach him or her.

Lawyers may use final arguments to summarize the evidence, to explain their theories about the facts, and to argue why jurors should believe certain evidence and disbelieve other evidence. Lawyers may use any of the exhibits that were received in evidence. They may preview the law and argue how the law applies to the facts. Lawyers have a right to know, before they make their final argument, exactly what the judge intends to tell the jury about the law. Lawyers may not ask the jurors to put themselves in the place of a party. If a lawyer's argument misstates the evidence or misstates the law or is otherwise misleading, the opponent may object and is entitled to have the court correct the lawyer.

The jury instructions inform jurors about the verdict form, substantive law, and the procedures they should follow. The court sequesters jurors during their deliberations. If they need anything, they must communicate through the marshal or the bailiff. Jurors are usually allowed to go to their homes during the evening hours. They are given strict instructions not to discuss the case with anyone, not even other jurors, until they reconvene. A violation would be jury misconduct that could cause a mistrial. If jurors take notes during the trial, they may use them to refresh their own memories but not to persuade other jurors what the evidence is. Each juror must rely on his or her own memory.

The judge decides which type of verdict to use. In a general verdict, the jury finds for the defendant or plaintiff and awards an amount of money damages. The clerk may enter judgment on the general verdict. In a special verdict, the judge poses fact questions, usually ultimate fact questions. The jury answers each question. The judge applies the law to the facts as determined by the jury. The judge then makes conclusions of law. The judge orders entry of a judgment based on his or her conclusions of law. Special verdicts are used most often. In a general verdict with interrogatories, the jury finds for the plaintiff or the defendant and answers questions about particular facts. The jury's answers to the interrogatories may help resolve some collateral problem or merely assure the judge that the jury understood the issues. If the answers seem inconsistent, the judge may require the jury to resume deliberations so they can resolve the inconsistency.

The judge receives the jury's verdict in open court. The lawyers and parties have a right to be present. The parties have a right to poll the jury to determine whether each juror concurs in the verdict as read. No rule prohibits jurors from talking to the parties, lawyers, media reporters, or anyone else about the case after they are discharged. Occasionally, lawyers and paralegals contact jurors to find out what they thought about certain aspects of the case. Lawyers may not contact jurors for the purpose of finding jury misconduct. If your contact with a former juror uncovers some jury misconduct, you must not investigate. Instead, a lawyer must report the matter to the court and let the court investigate.

The prevailing party is entitled to recover costs and disbursements as provided by statute. The prevailing party must prepare, serve, and file a bill of costs and disbursements. The losing party can object to items listed and amounts claimed. Each court has a form for this.

KEY TERMS

actual bias	juror misconduct
affidavit of identification	peremptory challenge
case-in-chief	rebuttal evidence
circumstantial evidence	rest
direct evidence	sequester
hostile witness	stricken
implied bias	sustain

REVIEW QUESTIONS

1. What subjects are usually covered in a preliminary conference?

2. When does the court hear motions in limine?

3. What is the general purpose of any motion in limine?

4. How may a paralegal help the trial lawyer with jury selection?

5. What are the primary purposes of an opening statement?

6. What are the limitations on a lawyer's opening statement?

7. Which party makes the first opening statement?

8. Why is the formality of "resting" important?

9. What is a prima facie case?

10. What is meant by a fair preponderance of the evidence?

11. What are the limitations on rebuttal evidence?

12. Why do courts require lawyers to use formal, technical objections when they want to exclude improper evidence?

Mr. Hoch's theory on the facts is that Mr. William Nordby was driving slowly, too slowly for a rural highway. But many elderly people do that, so Mr. Harper had a right to pass Nordby's slow moving car. Mr. Harper would not have attempted to pass if he had known Nordby was going to make a left turn at the intersection. Mr. Nordby did not signal a turn, so it was reasonable for Harper to pass by using the oncoming lane. Nordby caused the accident by "swerving" into the oncoming lane and striking the right front of Harper's pickup truck. He is concerned some jurors may be prejudice against Harper, because he must use hand controls to operate the pickup. With regard to the third-party action against John Griffin, the theory is that Griffin is a lawyer. Harper reasonably assumed that Griffin had assumed responsibility for providing insurance. Otherwise, Harper would not have paid for the pickup truck without getting a certificate of title.

You are a member of attorney William Hoch's trial team and representing defendant Harper. Mr. Hoch is concerned about obtaining jurors who do not have any connections with John Griffin who is an attorney and who is engaged in numerous civic organizations in the county. He has held some minor public offices too. Mr. Hoch has asked you for an intraoffice memorandum that gives him suggestions for questions to ask the panel members in the voir dire examination. About eight questions relevant to the accident and seven questions relevant to Griffin will suffice.

Endnotes

1. Rule 615 provides that a party may move the court for an order excluding a witness from the courtroom so that the witness cannot hear the testimony of any other witness. The purpose is to keep a witness from being influenced by what some other witness says. However, a party cannot be excluded. A government or business organization has the right to have a representative present and that representative may not be excluded.
2. A peremptory challenge is one that a party may make as a matter of right without giving the court any reason or justification for it.

 For additional resources, visit our Web site at www.paralegal.delmar.cengage.com

JUDGMENTS

CHAPTER OUTLINE

Chapter Objectives

Chapter 20 describes what a judgment is, the process for entering a judgment on the judgment roll, how to tax costs against the losing party, and how a judgment is enforced against a judgment debtor. The emphasis is on how a paralegal can help with the process. It also discusses how to protect judgment debtors from abuse.

Introduction

A judgment is a court's ultimate declaration of parties' legal rights and obligations. Once a party has obtained a judgment, the party is entitled to have the state's executive branch help enforce the judgment. A judgment also prevents either party from prosecuting the same litigation again. A judgment is a valuable property right. As a paralegal, you may help clients to obtain enforcement of their judgments and cope with judgments against them.

The terms *judgment* and *decree* are often used interchangeably. Historically, a decree was a determination made by a court in equity that required a party to do something or not do something. In contrast, a judgment was an award of money or property by a court of law, or a determination that a party did not owe money. Today, the distinction between decrees and judgments is not important.

Judgments

When a case is tried to a jury, the verdict is the basis for the court's judgment. If a special verdict is used, the judge must order entry of a judgment based on the verdict. When a case is tried to a judge, he or she must make written findings of fact and conclusions of law. The conclusions of law are the basis for a judgment. The judge must make an order that directs the clerk how to prepare the judgment. If the plaintiff is entitled to money damages, the judgment states the amount. The plaintiff becomes a **judgment creditor,** and the defendant is a judgment debtor. A judgment is a lien against the defendant's property. If the defendant is found not liable, the judgment provides that the plaintiff's claim is dismissed. A judgment for the defendant may include taxable costs. In that event, the defendant becomes a judgment creditor. A court's order for judgment may be similar to Exhibit 20.1.

judgment creditor A party who has obtained a judgment in his or her favor against another party for a sum of money.

The clerk of court enters the judgment in a **judgment book.** The clerk must send to the parties a notice of entry of the judgment "immediately" after entering the judgment. State law determines how long a judgment remains enforceable. The federal courts follow and apply state law in this regard. In most states, a judgment remains in force for ten years. Unless renewed before expiration, it automatically expires and becomes a nullity. Renewing a judgment is a simple, administrative act. The cost is nominal. Interest accrues on the verdict from the day the jury returns

judgment book A public record containing civil judgments. It is maintained by the clerk of court.

United States District Court for the
Southern District of Illinois
Civil Action, File Number CV06-00783

Roberta Jones, Plaintiff,

    vs.

William Smith, Defendant.

The above-entitled action came on for trial before the court and a jury, the Honorable Russell A. Smith, United States District Judge, presiding, and the issues have been duly tried, and the jury has duly rendered its verdict.

It is ordered and adjudged that the plaintiff, Roberta Jones, recover from the defendant, William Smith, the sum of twenty-five ($25,000.00) thousand dollars and his taxable costs. Let judgment be entered accordingly.

Dated at Chicago, Illinois,
this 18th day of October, 2006.
/s/ Raymond A. Johnson
Clerk of Court

EXHIBIT 20.1

Order For Judgment

the verdict. The clerk adds the interest to the judgment. Once the judgment is entered, interest accrues on the judgment at a rate prescribed by state statute.

A judgment is a public record. Credit searches always include the local judgment books to determine whether the subject (person) is a judgment debtor. A judgment is a lien against the debtor's property. Therefore, a judgment debtor may have difficulty obtaining credit or more credit. If a judgment debtor owns a house or land and wants to sell it, most buyers require debtors to satisfy the judgment before the sale. Or, the buyer might arrange to pay the judgment by deducting the amount of the judgment from the sale price. The judgment debtor must prepare a "satisfaction of judgment" for the creditor to sign. The debtor should file the satisfaction with the clerk of court. The satisfaction discharges the legal obligation.

A judgment may provide that the plaintiff is entitled to recover specific property or that she or he is the owner of certain property. When litigation concerns ownership of property, the judgment declares which party is the owner. A judgment may declare that a party must abstain from specified conduct that has been deemed wrongful and injurious to another party's person or property. A judgment may require a party to execute a deed or bill of sale to evidence ownership or the transfer of ownership. A judgment may declare that a party must do a certain act, such as vacate a parcel of real estate. Rule 70 provides guidelines for enforcing the judgment:

> If a judgment directs a party to execute a conveyance of land or to deliver deeds or other documents or to perform any other specific act and the party fails to comply within the time specified, the court may direct the act to be done at the cost of the disobedient party by some other person appointed by the court and the act when so done has like effect as if done by the party. . . . If real or personal property is within the district, the court in lieu of directing a conveyance thereof may enter a judgment divesting the title of any party and vesting it in others and such judgment has the effect of a conveyance executed in due form of law.

If the judgment debtor refuses to sign a deed or transfer title, the court may appoint someone to act in place of the debtor. The court cannot send the debtor to prison. A judgment for money may be assigned or transferred to another person. A transfer must be in writing and filed with the clerk of court. There are legal forms for transferring judgments.

Execution and Attachment

writ of execution (1) A writ that directs the sheriff or marshal to seize certain property that belongs to the named judgment debtor and to hold or sell the property for the benefit of the judgment creditor. (2) Any writ that puts into force the court's judgment.

attachment A proceeding by which a judgment debtor's property is seized to satisfy the debtor's legal obligation to the judgment creditor.

A judgment is a lien against the judgment debtor's property, insofar as the property is not exempt from seizure as provided by state law. If a judgment is for a sum of money and the debtor cannot or will not pay it, the court may issue a **writ of execution,** which directs the executive branch of the government, usually a sheriff, to locate the defendant's property, seize it, and sell it in the manner prescribed by law. The procedure is called **attachment.** Usually a debtor's property is sold at a public auction with due notice given to the public and to persons who have special interests in the property. However, the sheriff may hold the property for a designated period of time during which the judgment debtor has an opportunity to redeem it by paying the judgment. Rule 69(a) provides for these actions:

Process to enforce a judgment for the payment of money shall be a writ of execution, unless the court directs otherwise. The procedure on execution, in proceedings supplementary to and in aid of a judgment, and in proceedings on and in aid of execution shall be in accordance with the practice and procedure of the state in which the district court is held, existing at the time the remedy is sought, except that any statute of the United States governs to the extent that it is applicable.

A judgment creditor may be required to post a bond protecting the judgment debtor against any errors or improprieties that might occur when the property is seized and sold. The sheriff probably does not know the exact location of the judgment debtor's property. Therefore, it behooves the judgment creditor to provide the sheriff with whatever information she or he can about the identity and location of nonexempt property to be seized. The sheriff charges the creditor for her or his time and expenses, but these expenses ultimately become the responsibility of the judgment debtor.

Rule 62(a) precludes the judgment creditor from enforcing the judgment during the first ten days after entry in the judgment book. The ten-day period gives the judgment debtor an opportunity to decide whether to pay the judgment, make a post-trial motion, appeal, or take some other action to protect his or her interests. Rule 62(b) authorizes a court to stay enforcement of a judgment during the pendency of a motion for new trial or a motion for judgment as a matter of law. A party may seek an order staying enforcement of the judgment by making a separate motion or as part of the posttrial motion. However, the party who seeks a stay against enforcement of the judgment should not wait for the posttrial motion to be heard before securing the order staying enforcement of the judgment, or it may be too late.

Rule 64 provides that the parties to a federal civil action are subject to the post-trial remedies provided by the laws of the state in which the federal district court functions:

> [A]ll remedies providing for seizure of person or property for the purpose of securing satisfaction of the judgment ultimately to be entered in the action are available under the circumstances and in the manner provided by the law of the state in which the district court is held. . . . The remedies thus available include arrest, attachment,[1] garnishment, replevin, sequestration, and other corresponding or equivalent remedies, however designated and regardless of whether by state procedure the remedy is ancillary to an action or must be obtained by an independent action.

When a judgment declares that the debtor should transfer property to the judgment creditor, the court may order the judgment debtor to execute (sign) a quitclaim deed in favor of the judgment creditor. If the debtor refuses to do so, the court may appoint a trustee to act for the judgment debtor. In some jurisdictions, courts are empowered to declare, "That which the judgment debtor should have done, is done." In other words, the judgment has the effect of a deed. The judgment is accepted for filing by the local registrar of deeds. Judgment creditors ordinarily prefer to have an actual deed, rather than a judgment; therefore, creditors apply to courts to transfer title only when debtors refuse to act.

Supplementary Proceedings

Sometimes the judgment creditor and sheriff cannot find the debtor's property or money, but the creditor believes the debtor does have assets. In that event, the judgment creditor is allowed to conduct **supplementary proceedings** to try to locate the debtor's assets. A judgment creditor can move the court for an order that compels the debtor to appear at a specified time and place for an oral deposition in which creditor's lawyer may interrogate the debtor about earnings, properties, past transfers of property, future income, and future acquisitions. The debtor may be asked about current and recent employments, salary, mode of payment, checking accounts, savings accounts, accounts receivable, and so forth. The debtor's testimony is under oath, so she or he is subject to the penalties of perjury. Rule 69(a) authorizes these proceedings:

> In aid of the judgment or execution, the judgment creditor or a successor in interest when that interest appears of record, may obtain discovery from any person, including the judgment debtor, in the manner provided in these rules or in the manner provided by the practice of the state in which the district court is held.

Some courts authorize creditors to serve interrogatories on debtors to obtain the information, but they are less useful. If the debtor refuses to answer questions about the nature and extent of his or her property and finances, he or she may be held in contempt of court. If held in contempt, the debtor may be incarcerated until he or she agrees to cooperate with the civil justice system. Note, the debtor is not being penalized for failure to pay the debt.

Armed with new information obtained through the supplementary proceedings, the judgment creditor can obtain a new writ of execution. The sheriff can try again to locate, seize and sell the debtor's properties. If the sheriff is able to find cash, the sheriff may deliver it to the judgment creditor. Again, the sheriff deducts her or his fees and expenses before the creditor is paid. However, the judgment creditor's total recovery is not reduced by the sheriff's fees. If enough money or property can be found, the judgment debtor ends up paying those costs.

State law governs when and how creditors may engage in supplementary proceedings. Judgment creditors must obtain leave of a court to take debtors' depositions and to serve interrogatories. Creditors are allowed only a certain number of depositions a year. Judgment creditors must not harass debtors by conducting unnecessary supplementary proceedings. A debtor may move the court for a protective order to stop an overly aggressive creditor from abusing the process.

Garnishment

Garnishment is a statutory process that allows a judgment creditor to attach money or property that belongs to the debtor but a third person has possession. A judgment creditor commences a garnishment action by serving a garnishment summons on the third person, who is designated a **garnishee.** The summons informs the gar-

---

supplementary proceedings Legal proceedings that a judgment creditor may use to discover what property the judgment debtor has with which to pay the judgment.

garnishment A procedure by which a judgment creditor may attach property or money that is in the hands of a third person and belongs to the judgment debtor.

garnishee A person who holds money or property belonging to a debtor and who is subject to a garnishment proceeding by a creditor.

nishee about the judgment debtor's obligation and the amount. The summons directs the garnishee to disclose to the judgment creditor the amount of money, if any, the garnishee is holding. The third person may be an employer who is holding money for wages, a bank in which the debtor has an account, or a business that owes money on an account. The garnishee must prepare, serve, and file a garnishment disclosure. The disclosure is under oath. There are standard disclosure forms. Creditors frequently use garnishment actions to attach wages. All states have laws that partially exempt wages, so only a fraction of a debtor's take-home pay can be seized.

If a garnishee discloses it does not hold any money or property belonging to the judgment debtor, the judgment creditor may challenge the disclosure by moving the court for leave to serve a supplemental complaint on the garnishee. The judgment creditor must show the court that there is **probable cause** to believe that the garnishee does have property or money that belongs to the judgment debtor and should be available to pay the debt. A litigant shows probable cause by producing evidence that would cause a reasonable person to believe the garnishee *may* have property that could be used to satisfy the judgment. It is a preliminary showing. But the evidence must be of a type that would be admissible at a trial. If probable cause is shown, the court allows the judgment creditor to start a garnishment action against the garnishee. The garnishee cannot relitigate the judgment debtor's liability, except to challenge the court's jurisdiction to render the judgment. Ordinarily, the only issue is whether the garnishee has any property or money that belongs to the judgment debtor. When the plaintiff obtains a judgment against the defendant in a personal injury action and the defendant contends that he has liability insurance that covers the loss, but the insurer wrongly denied coverage, the plaintiff, as a judgment creditor, can serve a garnishment summons on the insurance company to force the insurance company to litigate the coverage issue. There is an example of that in the hypothetical case.

probable cause A standard or degree of proof required before a garnishor may proceed with an action against a garnishee who denies that the garnishee is holding any money or property belonging to the judgment debtor.

Transfer of a Judgment

What does a judgment creditor do if the judgment debtor moves to another state? How does a judgment creditor enforce a judgment if the debtor's money and property are in another state? A judgment creditor can have the judgment transferred to a court in another jurisdiction for enforcement. The procedure is relatively simple. The creditor can obtain an authenticated copy[2] of the original judgment from the clerk of court and file it with the second court. The transferred judgment establishes the nature and extent of the debtor's obligation. As provided in the United States Constitution, states must give full faith and credit to each other's judgments. The judgment is presumed to be valid. The judgment debtor may contest the transferred judgment on the grounds that the original court lacked jurisdiction[3] or that he or she has paid the judgment. Either of these defenses requires a trial to establish the truth. The judgment debtor has the burden of proving facts in avoidance of the judgment. However, the judgment debtor cannot relitigate the merits of the case in which the judgment was obtained. For example, the judgment debtor cannot challenge the sufficiency of the evidence or the court's rulings on objections. Assuming the judgment debtor fails to prove a lack of jurisdiction, the local court renders its own judgment, which may be enforced like any other judgment within the jurisdiction.

Relief from Judgment

Although our system is good, it is not perfect. Occasionally, a court enters a judgment that ought to be modified or even set aside. Rule 60(a) provides that a court may correct clerical errors in a judgment at any time. The court may act on its own initiative or on a party's motion. A clerical error is any statement in the written judgment that does not comport with the court's actual intent. It may concern a number, name, omitted fact, or other similar mistake.

A judgment may be set aside or modified on the grounds that the prevailing party obtained it through a fraud. The fraud may have been on the court or on the losing party. A judgment may be set aside on the grounds of newly discovered evidence. The moving party must show that the evidence was not available to him or her before the trial was completed [Rule 60(b)]. In addition, Rule 60(b) contains a catchall provision that allows a court to set aside or modify a judgment on the grounds of "mistake, inadvertence, surprise, or excusable neglect." If a party seeks to vacate a judgment for any of the reasons stated in this paragraph, the motion must be made within one year after the judgment was entered in the judgment book.

Rule 60 does not limit the time in which a judgment may be challenged on the grounds that the court lacked jurisdiction in the case. Also, a judgment may be set aside or modified because of subsequent events, as when the debtor shows that she or he paid the judgment, but the judgment creditor failed to provide a satisfaction of judgment.

Taxation of Costs

After a judgment is entered, a party may apply to the clerk of court to compute and add taxable costs to the amount of the judgment. The clerk determines what costs the court will allow, as provided by statute, and adds those costs to the judgment. The taxable costs may include the party's filing fee, deposition costs, subpoena fees, and expert witness fees within prescribed limits. If a party is entitled to recover his or her attorney's fees, the party must, within fourteen days after entry of the judgment, make a motion to obtain a court order allowing the attorney's fees and determining the amount [Rule 54(d)]. As discussed previously, only a few types of lawsuits permit the recovery of attorney's fees, and those are prescribed by statutes. A paralegal may be asked to prepare the client's bill of costs and disbursements for taxing costs against the opposing party.

Offer of Judgment

In almost every case that goes to trial, the parties have conducted some settlement negotiations, but the negotiations were unsuccessful. Consequently, the parties have been forced to incur the expense of a trial. Some costs may be taxed against the losing party. A defendant who is clearly liable to the plaintiff, but cannot settle because the plaintiff's demand is excessive, is at a disadvantage. Because the plaintiff is sure to win some award, the defendant will have to pay the plaintiff's litigation costs. However, Rule 68 provides some help to the defendant. The Rule allows a defendant to make a formal written offer to let judgment be entered against her or him for a specified amount. The offer of judgment must be made at least ten days before trial and must include agreement to pay plaintiff's taxable costs to the date of the offer. An offer of judgment may be served by mail in accordance with Rule 5. The plaintiff has ten days in which to accept the offer of judgment. More time may be granted by the offeror. When service is by mail, the offeree has an additional three days in which to accept. If the offer is not accepted before the deadline, it is rejected. There is no limit on the number of offers of judgment a defendant may make. But the last offer is controlling. If an offeree rejects the offer and obtains a larger award than offered, the offer of judgment has no effect.

Unless the offeree obtains a judgment that is more favorable than the offer, the offer precludes the offeree from taxing costs against the offeror. Furthermore, the offeror can tax all his or her costs against the offeree. An offer of judgment is not an offer to make an immediate payment of money. Therefore, even if the defendant does not have enough money to pay the judgment, he or she may still make an offer of judgment. As with settlement negotiations in general, neither the plaintiff nor the defendant may inform the jury about an offer of judgment. If the offeree accepts the offer of judgment, either party may file the offer and acceptance with the clerk of court, along with the proofs of service. The clerk is authorized to enter judgment as provided in the offer of judgment. The lawsuit is concluded by the judgment. An offer of judgment cannot be made unless a civil action is pending.

SUMMARY

A judgment is a court's ultimate declaration of the parties' legal rights and obligations. A judgment is a valuable property right. It is a lien against the judgment debtor's property. A judgment creditor can use the judgment to obtain a writ of execution from the court. The writ of execution directs the sheriff to seize the debtor's money and property. The money may be delivered to the creditor. The sheriff sells the property at public auction. Interest accumulates on the debt. The judgment remains in effect as a lien against the debtor's property until it expires. Most states provide that a judgment is good for ten years. The creditor can keep the judgment in effect for another ten years by paying a nominal fee.

After a judgment has been entered, the creditor may institute supplementary proceedings to find the debtor's money and property to use to pay the judgment. The creditor can require the debtor to appear for an oral deposition and testify about her or his financial condition, including assets, employment, ownership of property, and claims against other persons. State statutes limit the number of times a judgment creditor can force the debtor to testify.

A judgment is the predicate for a garnishment action to obtain money or property a third person holds that belongs to the judgment debtor. A judgment creditor starts the process by serving a garnishment summons on the third person. The summons informs the garnishee that the judgment debtor owes the creditor a certain amount of money and directs the garnishee to disclose to the creditor the amount of money, if any, the garnishee is holding. The money may be owed to the debtor as wages, bank accounts, accounts receivable, and the like. A garnishee complies with the summons by serving and filing a garnishment disclosure. In all states, wages are partially exempt from garnishment, so an employer can remit to the creditor only a portion of the debtor's wages.

If a garnishee's disclosure states that the garnishee does not have any money or property that belongs to the judgment debtor, the creditor may challenge the disclosure by moving the court for leave to serve a supplemental complaint on the garnishee. The creditor must serve the motion and the garnishee and debtor. The judgment creditor must show the court there is probable cause to believe the garnishee does have property or money that belongs to the judgment debtor, and it should be available to pay the judgment. If the creditor shows probable cause, the court allows the judgment creditor to start a garnishment action against the garnishee. The creditor commences the action by serving the garnishee. If the garnishee has already appeared in the matter to oppose the motion, the garnishment complaint may be served by mail. The garnishee cannot relitigate the judgment debtor's liability, except to challenge the prior court's jurisdiction to render the judgment. Ordinarily, the only issue in a garnishment action is whether the garnishee has any property or money that belongs to the judgment debtor.

A judgment may be transferred to another jurisdiction and enforced in the same manner as a local judgment. The only basis for challenging a transferred judgment is that the court that rendered the judgment lacked jurisdiction over the judgment debtor or the subject matter of the litigation.

KEY TERMS

attachment   judgment creditor
garnishment   probable cause
garnishee   supplementary proceedings
judgment book   writ of execution

REVIEW QUESTIONS

1. What is a judgment?

2. Of what value is a judgment for money damages if the judgment debtor will not voluntarily pay the obligation?

3. What procedure may a judgment creditor use to force a judgment debtor to disclose the existence of the debtor's assets?

4. What protection does a garnishee have against harassing-type claims?

5. What protection does a judgment debtor have against a judgment creditor who is overly aggressive in trying to discover the debtor's assets?

6. How does a defendant benefit by making an offer of judgment?

7. What is the difference between a judgment book and a judgment roll?

8. What are two grounds for setting aside a judgment?

9. What is the time limitation for vacating a judgment on the grounds of fraud?

10. What is the time limitation for setting aside a judgment on the grounds that the court that granted the judgment lacked jurisdiction over the subject matter?

CASE ASSIGNMENT

You are a member of attorney Donald Smith's trial team. He is very optimistic that the trustee can obtain a verdict against Mr. Harper for at least $200,000. But he is concerned about whether Harper has any money or assets. He is also concerned about the Security Insurance Company's denial of coverage for Harper. He has asked for an intraoffice memorandum from you that outlines what the team can do to check on Harper's assets and the insurance as soon as the judgment is entered.

Endnotes

1. Attachment is a proceeding in which a judgment debtor's property is actually seized by the sheriff or a United States marshal and held for the benefit of the claimant. A writ of attachment may be issued only after a hearing that provides due process protection and will be granted only where there is good reason to believe that the opposing party will dispose of the property to avoid paying his or her legal obligation.
2. It is sometimes called an exemplified copy.
3. A trial court may have lacked jurisdiction because it failed to obtain jurisdiction over the person of the defendant or over the subject matter, because it went beyond its power in granting a particular remedy, or because it acted beyond its geographic limitations.

For additional resources, visit our Web site at www.paralegal.delmar.cengage.com

CHAPTER **21**

APPEALS

Chapter Outline

Chapter Objectives

Chapter 21 explains how a party who lost at trial may appeal from the judgment to obtain a new trial or reversal. It describes the ground for appealing and the procedure the parties must follow. It explains how paralegals can assist in the appeal process.

Introduction

Some errors occur in every trial. The civil justice system does not require perfection. At most, the civil justice system can provide a fair trial that is unaffected by prejudicial error. An appeals court will not reverse a trial court's judgment unless there was an error of law or an error in the procedure that may have affected the trial's outcome. Appealable errors may occur in almost any phase of the trial, from jury selection through to the final arguments. A party who appeals is referred to as the **appellant.** The party against whom an appeal is taken is called the **appellee.**[1] Appellate courts do not retry cases. They do not decide whether the jury made the right or wrong decision. They do not evaluate the evidence to ascertain whether the evidence is credible or reliable. They do not judge the fairness of the jury's verdict. An appellate court will not reverse on the grounds that the appellate court would have come to a different conclusion from the evidence or would have preferred a

appellant An aggrieved party who appeals to a higher court to review the proceedings of the trial court's order or judgment on the grounds that the trial court committed an error of law or procedural errors that adversely affected the outcome.

appellee A party against whom an appeal is taken.

different outcome. Appellate courts only decide issues of law and procedure. An appellate court corrects errors by vacating the lower court's judgment or modifying the judgment and, sometimes, by ordering a new trial. An appellate court can order the lower court to enter judgment as directed by the appellate court.

Appeals are governed by the Federal Rules of Appellate Procedure. Witnesses never testify in appellate courts. Legal issues and arguments are submitted in written briefs. After the briefs are filed, the lawyers are allowed to make oral arguments on behalf of their clients. An appellant has the burden of persuading the appellate court that there was an error and there is good reason to believe the verdict or decision would have been different had the error not occurred. A party has a right to appeal to the court of appeals in the circuit in which the district court is located. There are thirteen circuit courts of appeals, including a Court of Appeals for the District of Columbia. A map showing the circuits appears in Exhibit 1.1.

There are very few situations in which a party has a right to appeal to the United States Supreme Court. The usual method of appealing to the United States Supreme Court is to petition the court for leave to appeal. The system does not allow a party to appeal merely because he or she is disappointed in the outcome or strongly disagrees with the lower court's holding. With a few exceptions, the Supreme Court may choose which cases it wants to consider.

As explained in Chapter 1, our judicial systems have adopted the common law. That means courts have the power to make new rules of law to apply to society's ever-changing needs. Appellate courts have inherent power to overrule their own prior decisions and propound new rules of law. However, an appellate court cannot disregard a statute, unless the court determines the statute is invalid. An appellate court may determine that a statute is invalid because the statute violates a state constitution or the United States Constitution or was enacted by a procedure that was defective. A statute may be too vague to be enforceable, thus violating due process. Most changes in the law come through the legislative process. Although appellate courts cannot change statutes, they can change their *interpretation* of statutes, and that can have almost the same effect. To a large extent, the stability of our legal system depends on the reluctance of appellate courts to change rules of law once decided.

Relatively few cases are appealed. There are several factors that mitigate against appealing. Appeals are expensive. The amount of a judgment may not justify the cost and effort of an appeal. The system tends to favor appellees. A large majority of appeals are affirmed. The appeal process may take more than a year. Appellants are required to file an appeal bond that protects the judgment creditor against any loss because of the delay. Appeal bonds are expensive. Furthermore, interest accrues against the judgment while the appeal is pending. The appellate process is very exacting. Trial lawyers often prefer to have other lawyers handle their appeals.

Although appellate work is highly technical and tends to focus on legal issues, paralegals can help, especially when they have assisted in preparing the case for trial and attended the trial. You may be asked to search through the record to find testimony and exhibits bearing on the alleged error. You may outline portions of the trial transcript in the same way that depositions are outlined and summarized. You may proofread drafts, check citations, shepardize[2] cases and help assemble a brief's appendix. If you are familiar with the facts of the case and have good writing skills, there is no reason why you cannot help write the all-important statement-of-facts section of a brief.

Notice of Appeal

notice of appeal   A notice that the appellant files with the district court to start the appeal process. The notice must be served on all other parties.

cost bond   A bond that a party must provide to the court to guarantee payment of the adverse party's taxable costs and disbursements.

supersedeas bond   A bond that the appellant must file with the court to ensure that the judgment the appellee has been granted will be paid of the appellant does not obtain a modification of that judgment.

representation statement   A document filed with the court of appeals identifying the parties and attorneys who will appear in an appeal.

An appellant must serve and file a **notice of appeal** to start an appeal. The notice must be filed with the clerk of the federal district court within thirty days after entry of judgment. Exhibit 21.1 is an example of a notice of appeal.

The appellant must pay a filing fee to the clerk. The district court may require the appellant to file a **cost bond** or give other security to guarantee that the appellee's costs will be covered. If the appellee obtained a judgment for a sum of money, state courts require the appellant to file a **supersedeas bond** that protects the appellee for the amount of the judgment and taxable costs. Parties commonly stipulate to a waiver of appeal bonds. An appellant avoids the cost of a bond and the appellee benefits because, if the appellee loses the appeal, the appellant could tax the cost of the bond against her or him. Within ten days after filing the notice of appeal, the appellant must send to the court of appeals' clerk a **representation statement,** which identifies the parties and attorneys who will appear in the appeal.

■ **EXHIBIT 21.1**

Notice of Appeal

United States District Court for the
Southern District of Illinois
Civil Action, File Number CV06-00783

Roberta Jones, Plaintiff,

     vs.

William Smith, Defendant.

To: Plaintiff Roberta Jones and Angela Von, her attorney:

Notice is hereby given that defendant William Smith appeals to the United States Court of Appeals for the Seventh Circuit from the final judgment entered in this action on the 12th day of September 2006.

[date]

/s/ _____
Attorney for Defendant
Address
Telephone

Record on Appeal

The record on appeal consists of the litigation documents filed with the clerk of court, including the pleadings, motions, and exhibits; a transcript of the proceedings (trial); and a certified copy of the docket entries, which the clerk must prepare. The appellant must order a transcript of the trial within ten days after filing the notice of appeal. The appellant may order the entire transcript or only a portion. If the appellant orders only a portion, the appellee may order any additional part he or she deems necessary. The parties must arrange with the court reporter to pay the reporter's fee for preparing the transcript. The transcript may include all the testimony, oral motions, jury instructions, and discussions that were on the record. If the appeal is concerned only with a liability issue, the testimony concerning damages may be omitted, and vice versa. The reporter must file the original transcript with the clerk of court. The appellant must provide at least one copy of the transcript to each appellee. The clerk of the district court must send the record to the court of appeals' clerk for filing.

Appellant's Brief

The appellant's brief and appendix is due forty days after the record is filed. In many circuits, this time limit is replaced by a court-ordered briefing schedule that specifies the exact dates on which each party must file their briefs. Although forty days is not much time in which to write a brief, the appellant should have started that task even before he or she filed a notice of appeal. Similarly, the appellee has the opportunity to organize and start his or her brief before the appellant's brief is due.

A brief is a major production. Like a trial, it should be crafted artfully but strictly follow technical requirements. You can help with the preparation. You may begin by keeping an appeal calendar that notes all the deadlines. The calendar should begin by listing the date of the verdict and date on which judgment was entered. Then note the dates on which the notice of appeal was filed and the transcript ordered. From that point on, the deadlines will be based on each prior step in the appeal process or upon the appellate court's briefing schedule. It must contain the following:

1. A corporate disclosure if your client happens to be a corporation. The disclosure must list a parent corporation, if any, and the identity of any other corporation that owns as much as 10 percent of the corporate client's stock. You can obtain the necessary information from the client. No corporate certificates are required.
2. A table of contents with page references. Ordinarily a secretary prepares the table of contents, as a word processing function, after the brief has been prepared. However, you may be asked to prepare or check the table of contents for completeness and accuracy.
3. A table of authorities that lists cases alphabetically, statutes, and secondary authorities.

4. A jurisdictional statement that shows the district court had jurisdiction with supporting facts; a jurisdictional statement that shows the court of appeals has jurisdiction; a statement that shows the appeal is timely and based on a final order or a judgment. This requirement illustrates the importance placed on jurisdiction. It is a priority matter.

5. A statement of the legal issues raised by the appeal.

6. A statement of case that describes the nature of the action, the course of the proceedings, and the district court's disposition of the matter. The court of appeals wants a succinct statement about what happened in the district court. For example, was the case dismissed on a motion on the pleadings or a summary judgment or was there a trial? What did the trial court do? Only a very brief explanation is required. A short paragraph should suffice.

7. A statement of the facts that are relevant to the issues on appeal. The material facts must be supported by references to pages in the record and exhibits. The lawyer should outline the facts he or she needs. This is a priority item and should be started as soon as the notice of appeal is filed. As soon as the transcript is available, you can review the record to find support for those facts. Most lawyers consider preparation of the statement of facts to be the most difficult part of good brief writing. The statement must be candid, not argumentative, and yet support the client's version.

8. A summary of the arguments advanced in the body of the brief. The summary should be succinct and meaningful.

9. An argument of the issues. This, of course, is what most people think a brief is—just an argument. A lawyer must prepare the argument, using the authorities and statement of facts to show how the lower court erred and that the error was prejudicial. The lawyer must identify the standard of review applicable to each issue. A standard of review is the extent to which an appellate court must defer to the lower court's authority and discretion.

10. A conclusion that specifies the relief or ruling the appellant wants from the court of appeals. For example, the appellant may want judgment notwithstanding an adverse verdict, or the appellant may want a new trial on all issues or a new trial on one or two issues.

The rules provide a limit on the length of briefs. In the past, the limit was fifty pages. But as word processing systems made it increasingly easier to expand the amount of material that can fit on a given page—by unnoticeable adjustments in font size, line height, and margin width, for example—lawyers found it increasingly difficult to resist cheating on length. Therefore, the federal courts and most state courts have now converted to word-count limits. The federal limit is 14,000 words for principal briefs. All word processing systems are capable of counting the words. The lawyers must certify at the end of a brief that they have had the words counted and that the total is within the court's word limit. In practice, it should seldom be necessary to even approach the 14,000-word limit. Judges want to read concise, well-written briefs, not verbose, disjointed, and repetitious ones. Even though some lawyers cannot resist filling all the space allowed, shorter is usually better.

An appellant's brief must have an appendix. The appendix provides collateral information for the court of appeals and a convenient reference source. Specifically, an appendix must provide relevant docket entries, such as the date the complaint was filed, the date on which the verdict was returned, the date on which judgment was entered, and the date on which the notice of appeal was filed. It must contain relevant portions of the pleadings, jury instructions, and the lower court's findings. It must contain a copy of the judgment or order, which is the basis for the appeal.

The appellant's argument on the law is the body of the brief. The appellate court assumes that the verdict is consistent with the evidence that favored the appellee. Any evidence favoring the appellant, which is inconsistent with the verdict, is presumed to have been rejected by the jury. The fact that more witnesses and exhibits supported the appellant is of no importance on appeal. Suppose the plaintiff claims to have sustained a brain injury in an accident. Suppose he or she was attended by six physicians, only one of whom testified that the accident caused plaintiff's brain injury. Suppose one physician had no opinion and four were emphatic that the accident could not have caused a brain injury. Suppose an independent medical examiner testified that, to a reasonable medical certainty, the accident did not cause any brain injury. If the appellate court determined that the one physician, who supported the plaintiff's claim of a brain injury, was competent and there was adequate foundation for the physician's opinion, the verdict would stand. But suppose the only witness to opine that the plaintiff sustained a brain injury was a psychologist and the appellant contends the psychologist did not qualify to render a *medical* opinion. If the appellate court were to hold that the psychologist's opinion lacked foundation, the court would set aside the plaintiff's verdict. The error affected the admissibility of evidence, not merely the credibility of the evidence. If the appellant successfully established that the psychologist's opinion lacked foundation, there would be no evidence to support the appellee's claim. The appellate court would order the trial court to vacate the judgment and enter judgment for the defendant.

An appellant may disagree with the trial judge's application of a rule of law and make that the basis for an appeal. Suppose your state has a two year statute of limitations on actions against physicians and hospitals. Does the statute apply to claims against osteopaths and chiropractors? A court must resolve the uncertainty. The dispute may be over which of two laws applies to the parties' transaction or occurrence. The appellant may contend that state law applies but the judge applied federal law, creating disagreement about how a particular rule of law applies to the parties' transaction or occurrence. For example, the rule of law is that a liability insurance covers only accidental occurrences. But is an employer's wrongful discharge of an employee an "accident" where the wrongful discharge caused the employee to suffer emotional upset and become ill? In other words, is the terminated employee's illness an accidental occurrence that invokes insurance coverage for the employee's claim against the employer? The law is clear, but a court must determine how the law applies to the particular facts. It is not a jury issue.

The parties' arguments on the law usually rely heavily on statutes and precedent from other cases that have dealt with the same or similar problems. Prior cases decided by the court in which the appeal is pending are considered controlling. A court should follow the precedent of its own decisions until the court expressly overrules them. Parties look to the decisions of other jurisdictions as instructive and persuasive, but not controlling. Of course, opinions from other appellate courts are helpful when they contain clear, forceful rationale. An appellant may argue that an established rule of law in that jurisdiction is not workable and show other appellate courts have rejected the rule. Courts strive for uniformity in the law and are reluctant to render decisions that are in conflict with what other courts are holding. By way of example, many states have rules of civil procedure that use the same language as the Federal Rules of Civil Procedure. State courts are inclined to follow federal decisions that interpret and apply the federal rules. However, state courts are not bound by the federal court interpretations merely because the rules' language is the same.

The last section of a brief is the conclusion. Customarily, conclusions state the legal issue or issues in a positive way, indicating how the party wants the court to rule. For example, if the issue is whether a chiropractor is a "physician" within the meaning of a state statute of limitations, the conclusion might state, "Therefore, the statute of limitations applies to a doctor of chiropractic, the same as any other health care provider; otherwise, the statute unconstitutionally discriminates between persons in the same class." The conclusion must specify the relief the appellant wants, like a new trial or judgment as a matter of law.

Appellee's Brief

The format of the appellee's brief is the same as that of the appellant's brief. An appellee has thirty days from the date the appellant's brief is served in which to prepare and file his or her brief. However, an appellee can well anticipate what the issues and arguments will be, especially if the appellant made posttrial motions. So the appellee ought to begin working on his or her brief on receiving the notice of appeal. The appellee usually argues in support of the trial court's rulings or that the errors were not prejudicial.

If the appellee disagrees with the appellant's phrasing of the issues, the appellee may submit a different statement of the issues in her or his brief.

Appellant's Reply Brief

An appellant may file a reply brief, which is limited to 7,000 words. A reply brief may address only the arguments made in the appellee's brief. An appellant's reply brief may not be used to advance new issues or arguments already made.

Amicus Curiae

Once in a while, an appellate matter raises an issue of law that affects persons or companies who are not parties, and they may want to participate in the appeal. They may apply to the appellate court for leave to file an amicus curiae brief—a brief by a "friend of the court." No one has an absolute right to file an amicus brief. The court considers the nature of the applicant's interest and the importance of the issue in deciding whether to permit it. The parties have an interest in who will participate and to what extent, but they have no veto power over a motion for leave to file an amicus brief. An amicus party is not usually given the right to make an oral argument.

Oral Argument

Each circuit court of appeals has eight or more judges. Many cases are decided based only on the briefs, without oral argument. As the appellate courts' caseload increases, the number of cases orally argued decreases. Courts choose cases that are more difficult and raise questions for the attorneys to address. For cases chosen to be argued, the clerk of court schedules argument before three or more judges. If a case has unusual importance, all the judges may attend the oral argument and participate in the decision making. When all the judges participate, it is called an **en banc hearing.**

The clerk gives the parties at least thirty days' notice. An appellate court ordinarily hears three or four oral arguments during a morning's session. Each case is allotted one hour or less, often as few as thirty minutes total. The appellant may be allowed to save some of the allotted time for a rebuttal. The lawyers should have well-planned arguments. The judges may interrupt to ask questions. The judges never state what their decision will be, but they have no reason to conceal how they feel about the issues and law. Lawyers may be able to guess what the outcome will be on the basis of the judges' questions and apparent attitude toward the issues.

en banc hearing An appellate court hearing in which all the judges of the court participate.

Court's Opinion

The judges confer immediately after the oral argument and determine how the case should be decided. One of the judges writes the opinion for the court. A draft opinion is circulated among the judges for additions or corrections. As soon as they reach a consensus on a final draft, the judge who authors the opinion signs it. The opinion is filed with the clerk, who sends a copy to each party.

If one or more of the judges disagrees with the **majority opinion,** they may write a dissenting opinion. The **dissent** is published along with the majority opinion. On occasion, a judge may agree with the result reached by the majority but disagree with the reasons given for the majority decision. The judge may write and file a **concurring opinion,** in which he or she explains why and how the rationale of the majority opinion should be qualified. A unanimous decision is considered more forceful authority as precedent. If a court is closely divided in reaching a decision, the decision might be overruled the next time it comes before the court. On occasion, the appellate court judges are evenly divided on how the case should be decided. The consequence is that the trial court's decision breaks the tie: The trial court's judgment is affirmed. An appellate court usually issues its opinion within six months after the oral argument. The length of time depends on many factors. Some cases have taken more than a year.

majority opinion The opinion written or signed by a majority of the judges on an appellate court, when one or more other judges of the court file a separate dissent or concurring opinion.

dissent An opinion filed by an appellate court judge who disagrees with the holding and reasoning of a majority of the judges whose opinion becomes the law of the case.

concurring opinion An appellate court opinion written by an appellate judge to explain why the judge agrees with the decision or result reached by the majority of judges as expressed in their opinion, but disagrees with the reasons given by the majority for their decision.

Motion for Rehearing

When a party receives the appellate court's opinion, he or she might conclude that the appellate court overlooked some controlling fact or point of law. The remedy is to file a motion for rehearing, in which the moving party sets forth the reasons why a rehearing is necessary. If the written motion convinces the court that a rehearing is justified, a rehearing is ordered. More often than not, motions for rehearing are denied without explanation. If a court does grant a rehearing, that does not mean the court will hear another oral argument. A second oral argument is extremely rare. Whatever is to be done will normally be done in writing. A successful petition for rehearing is very rare.

Appeals to the United States Supreme Court

A very small percentage of cases reach the United States Supreme Court. Only a few types of cases may be appealed to the Supreme Court as a matter of right. Most cases are appealed to the Supreme Court by petitioning the Court for a writ of certiorari. The writ is an order to a lower court to transmit its record to the Supreme Court so it can review the proceedings and determine whether any irregularities occurred. Every year many petitions for writs of certiorari are filed, but the Supreme Court grants only a small percentage. At least four of the nine Supreme Court justices must vote in favor of granting the petition. A petitioner must try to persuade the Supreme Court that the case is unusually important—that it has ramifications beyond its effect on the parties. For example, the Supreme Court is likely to grant review if two circuit courts have reached opposite conclusions on the law, and a decision by the Supreme Court is needed to harmonize the law.[3] If an appeal raises significant constitutional questions or questions of general importance to the nation, the appeal is more likely to be accepted. The amount of money or property in question is not a major consideration.

Order for New Trial or Reversal

vacate   To declare that a judgment is of no force and effect; it is void.

When an appellate court determines that a trial court erred, the appellate court may **vacate** the trial court's judgment and order an entry of judgment in favor of the appellant. In that event the appellate court reverses the trial court. The vacated judgment is nullified. An appellate court may order the trial court to enter a different judgment or direct the trial court to provide a new trial. In that event the case is remanded to the trial court. A new trial may be ordered on all issues or on specified issues. For example, a court may determine that the error did not affect the jury's determination of liability in favor of the plaintiff, but did affect the jury's determination of the amount of damages awarded to the plaintiff. Under those circumstances, the appellate court could direct the trial court to have a new trial on the issue of damages only. In light of the appellate court's decision, the parties may be able to settle their dispute without actually going through another trial.

Extraordinary Appeals

writ of mandamus   A type of court order that directs a public official to perform his or her duty.

Ordinarily a judge's mistake cannot be appealed until a judgment has been entered. The usual appeal is from a judgment. But once in a great while a judge's mistake is very serious and prevents a party from being able to prepare for trial. That party must try to obtain help from an appellate court even before the case goes to trial. There is a procedure available. The aggrieved party may petition an appellate court for a **writ of mandamus.** The petitioner asks the appellate court to order the trial judge to change the ruling or to handle the case in a particular manner. If the judge is committing error by doing something and the aggrieved party needs to stop the judge, the party may seek a **writ of prohibition** from an appellate court. For example, the parties might disagree over the scope of discovery. If a deponent's lawyer objects to a line of questioning on the grounds of privilege and, on motion, the district court wrongly required the deponent to answer and if the disclosure would cause irreparable harm, the deponent's remedy is to petition for a writ of mandamus. The petition would ask the appellate court to order the trial judge to change his or her ruling. Appellate courts issue such writs only in extreme cases.

writ of prohibition A writ issued by an appellate court and directed to a judge in a trial court, ordering the judge not to enforce an order already issued.

Taxable Costs

Appellate courts have broad discretion in determining what costs should be awarded to the parties in connection with an appeal. An appellate court's decision specifies what costs, if any, are allowed and to whom the costs are awarded. Costs are not always awarded.

SUMMARY

Appellate courts are error-correcting courts. They determine whether trial courts followed correct procedures and whether they applied the law correctly. They do not decide fact issues. An appellate court will not reverse on the grounds that it would have preferred a different outcome. Appellate courts do not act as superjuries. Appellate courts correct trial courts' errors by vacating the lower court's judgments, ordering new trials, or ordering a different judgment. An appellate court examines the trial court's record to determine whether the trial court followed proper procedures and correctly applied the law. An appellate court will not set aside a trial court's judgment unless there was an error that may have affected the trial's outcome. In other words, the error must be prejudicial.

A paralegal may work on various aspects of an appeal. You may be asked to outline portions of the trial transcript in much the same way that depositions are outlined and summarized. You may prepare exhibits, assemble a brief's appendix, proofread drafts of the brief, and check citations. If you have a good understanding of the facts of the case and have good writing skills, you could help write the statement of facts. You may assist with legal research.

An appellant initiates an appeal by serving and filing a notice of appeal. The notice must be filed with the clerk of the district court within thirty days of the date on which the judgment was entered. The appellant must order a transcript of the trial from the official court reporter within ten days after filing the notice. The trial transcript, exhibits, and district court file make up the record on appeal. The appellant must supply at least one copy of the transcript to each party.

An appellant's brief must not exceed the 14,000-word limit. A brief contains a statement of the legal issues, a statement of the facts, an argument on the law, and a conclusion. The body of a brief is the argument on the law that relates the law to the facts in the case. An argument usually relies on statutes and case precedent of other cases that have dealt with the same or similar problems. A prior decision that was made by the same appellate court and is directly in point should be controlling. An appellate court should follow the precedent of its own decisions until it expressly overrules the prior decisions. Parties look to the decisions of other jurisdictions as instructive and persuasive but not controlling. Any evidence favoring the appellant, which is inconsistent with the verdict, is presumed to have been rejected by the jury. A conclusion should state what relief the appellant wants.

An appellee has thirty days from the date on which he or she receives the appellant's brief to file a responsive brief. The format of the appellee's brief is the same as that of the appellant's brief. An appellant's reply brief is limited to 7,000 words and may address only the arguments made in the appellee's brief. A reply brief may not be used to advance new issues or new arguments.

A person who may be affected by the appellate court's decision can petition for leave to file an amicus curiae brief. The court considers the nature of the petitioner's interest and the significance of the case in deciding whether to permit a nonparty to appear in a case. The parties have no veto power to keep a nonparty from appearing as a friend of the court. An amicus argument should be limited to the legal issues that directly affect his or her interests.

The United States Supreme Court is the highest federal appellate court. Most cases appealed to the Supreme Court come from the circuit courts of appeals. Subject to a few exceptions, parties do not have a right to appeal to the Supreme Court. A party initiates an appeal to the Supreme Court by petitioning the Court for a writ of certiorari. If the Supreme Court concludes that the case and issues are particularly important, it issues a writ of certiorari to the lower court, requiring the lower court to transmit the record to the Supreme Court for review. At least four of the nine Supreme Court justices must vote in favor of granting the petition; otherwise, the petition is disallowed.

When a party needs to appeal before a judgment has been entered, the party may ask an appellate court for a writ of mandamus to require the trial judge to do a particular act, or a party may seek a writ of prohibition to prevent the trial judge from doing a particular act. These writs are obtained to keep the judge from causing irreparable harm to a party. A party uses these appeal procedures while the case is still in the district court.

KEY TERMS

appellant	notice of appeal
appellee	representation statement
concurring opinion	supersedeas bond
cost bond	vacate
dissent	writ of mandamus
en banc hearing	writ of prohibition
majority opinion	

REVIEW QUESTIONS

1. What two circumstances must exist to successfully prosecute an appeal?

2. How does the appellant initiate an appeal?

3. What is the time limit for appealing?

4. What are the principal parts of an appellant's brief?

5. What are the principal limitations on an appellant's reply brief?

6. What are the grounds for filing an amicus curiae brief?

7. How does a party initiate an appeal to the United States Supreme Court from a circuit court of appeal's decision?

8. How does the United States Supreme Court decide whether it will review a case?

9. What is the purpose of obtaining a writ of prohibition?

10. How does a remand differ from a reversal?

CASE ASSIGNMENT

You are a member of attorney Donald Smith's litigation team representing the plaintiff-trustee. Assume the trustee's case against Harper was tried to a judge without a jury, and the judge ordered judgment for Harper as reflected in Exhibit 3.4. Attorney Smith has asked you to prepare a notice of appeal. Use the federal procedure, but appeal to the Minnesota Supreme Court.

Endnotes

1. Many state courts use the term *respondent*.

2. *Shepardize* is a colloquial legal expression. To shepardize a case is to use the Shepard's Citation system to find out whether other courts have considered the case and what the courts have said about the case. By using Shepard's Citations, one can determine whether the case has been overruled, questioned, followed, distinguished, approved, or ignored. Courses on legal research cover methods of using resources like Shepard's Citations.

3. When federal courts differ in how they handle a particular issue or type of case, litigants try to maneuver their cases to the more favorable forums.

 For additional resources, visit our Web site at www.paralegal.delmar.cengage.com

CHAPTER 22

SETTLEMENTS, RELEASES, AND DISMISSALS

Chapter Objectives

Chapter 22 explains the procedures for concluding cases where the parties have agreed on a resolution. The chapter explains how parties may settle part of a claim, leaving the remainder for trial. It describes a variety of settlement agreements that are designed to cover most situations. It provides samples of settlement agreements paralegals may use under the supervision of an attorney.

Introduction

Civil justice remedies cannot satisfy everyone. Indeed, a court-mandated solution may not satisfy any of the parties. Also, litigation is expensive. Consequently, parties often have good reasons to choose to settle their dispute even though a settlement may be disappointing. Although the parties may believe they know what a court's resolution would be, they may not want to gamble on the outcome. Litigants settle many more claims than go to trial and judgment.

The law favors voluntary settlements. Everyone benefits from an early, reasonable settlement. Parties avoid expense, delay, the uncertainties, and the inconveniences of litigation. The government and community avoid the cost of providing more courts for more trials. The parties make commitments that they can tolerate if not embrace. If parties go to trial, however, the plaintiff may recover little or nothing, leaving him or her in a desperate financial condition. Or, a large verdict in favor of the plaintiff might force the defendant to go into bankruptcy, so neither party benefits. Usually, a wise settlement is a better solution, even if neither party is happy with the terms. Indeed, it is often said that if neither party is happy with the settlement, it is probably a good settlement.

A party may elect to settle because a key witness has died. A party may choose to settle because he or she has a weak case and knows it. But the reason a party settles may be totally unrelated to the merits of the case. For example, a party may settle because she or he feels that a trial would be too strenuous. Or, a party may need some money right away. Or, the parties may be related and the relationship is more important than winning money in a lawsuit. When parties settle their dispute, they may use their own terms and make considerations not available in the law. For example, a claim does not have to be one for which a court can provide a remedy to be the subject of a settlement agreement. A settlement may be partial or full. A settlement may apply to all parties or only to some. A settlement may be contingent or absolute. Parties can settle before commencing an action or while an action is pending or even after a judgment has been entered.[1] If parties settle while their lawsuit is pending, court rules provide an easy method for dismissing it.

Paralegals may help clients to make settlements. You may be asked to prepare a written release for a client. You may have occasion to discuss settlement procedures with clients and the consequences of a settlement. However, you must not *advise* clients whether to give a release or which kind of release to use. That would be practicing law without a license. In this chapter, we will use the term *claimant*. Any person who asserts a claim is a "claimant" whether or not the claim is in suit.

Settlements and Releases

A settlement is a voluntary agreement (contract) that resolves a dispute. Settlement agreements are usually the product of a mutual compromise arrived at without a judicial order or decree. Where money is paid for a release, money is often called the settlement. The parties' agreement replaces the disputed claim. They exchange a disputed claim for clearly defined legal rights and obligations. In the most common settlement agreement the respondent pays an agreed sum of money to the claimant for a release of the claimant's claim. A release is a critical part of most settlement agreements. A "release" discharges the cause of action or claim. The party who pays money to settle a claim is said to have "bought her or his peace." As a contract, a "settlement agreement" is enforceable in court. The agreement must end the dispute or some specific part of the dispute to qualify as a settlement and release.

Because a settlement agreement is a contract, the agreement must have all the elements of a contract. The elements include an offer, acceptance of the offer, a meeting of the minds on the essential terms and conditions, and an exchange of consideration.

A naked promise is not a contract. A party must give legal consideration for the promise, but even another promise may suffice to make a contract. An agreement between two persons to mutually release each other is a valid agreement. The two promises are valid considerations, one for the other. But a promise to do what the promisor already is required by law to do is not legal consideration. The promisor has given nothing of value for the settlement.

Parties to a settlement agreement must have a meeting of the minds concerning the terms and conditions of their agreement. The importance of a meeting of the minds is highlighted by a personal injury case in which the claimant settles for a modest amount believing she had only minor injuries but subsequently discovers that she had other serious injuries. What if a claimant knows the extent of her or his injury but subsequently discovers an unanticipated consequence related to the injury? Suppose a young claimant's leg is broken in an automobile accident. The leg heals straight, strong, and without any loss of motion, and the claimant settles for a modest amount of damages. Suppose that two years after the accident, it is discovered that the injury damaged the bone so that it cannot grow anymore. Consequently, when the claimant obtains full growth, the injured leg is two inches shorter than the other leg. Should the "modest" settlement be "full and final?" Was there a meeting of the minds?

Because a claimant may have injuries the claimant and his or her doctors do not know about and because there may be unanticipated consequences of known injuries, most **full and final releases** in personal injury cases provide that the claimant releases his or her claims for all injuries, whether known or unknown. On that basis, there is a meeting of the minds about what the claimant has released. The defendant "buys" his or her peace, and the claimant assumes the risk of future problems. The parties may agree to settle their dispute on the basis that the claimant is releasing only known, specified injuries. However, for many reasons, the defendant or the defendant's liability insurer may refuse to settle unless the claimant gives a full and final release. Suppose that in the fractured leg example, the claim had gone to trial. The plaintiff's evidence would not have revealed the fact that the broken bone could not grow anymore, so the plaintiff would not have been compensated for that problem. The problem of unknown injuries and unknown consequences of known injuries points out the importance of not settling personal injury cases too soon.

A settlement agreement does not have to be in writing, but it usually is. Of course, there is an exception. The statute of frauds requires all contracts that, by their terms, cannot be performed within one year from the date on which they are made must be in writing and signed by the party against whom they are to be enforced. **Structured settlements,** which provide for periodic payments of a settlement, often fall into that category, so they must be reduced to a writing and signed. A written settlement contract should contain the entire agreement and state that it does. When parties reduce their agreement to a writing, they are forced to consider the details of the settlement. A writing helps to avoid subsequent disagreements about the terms, scope, and limits of the settlement. In particular, a settlement agreement should specify the consideration given for a release. The respondent actually must pay the consideration for a release to be enforceable. A mere recital of payment is not effective. A settlement agreement is not binding on a minor unless a guardian obtains court approval of it. Consequently, a person who must defend against a minor's claim ordinarily insists on negotiating through a guardian and having court approval of the settlement agreement.

full and final release   A release that discharges from liability the party who paid consideration for it and anyone else who might be liable to the claimant.

structured settlement   A type of settlement that allows the settling party to buy an annuity for the benefit of the claimant. The settling party pays a lump sum of money to a bank or insurance company, which provides scheduled benefits to the claimant over a period of years or over the claimant's lifetime.

A settlement agreement must be voluntary and not the result of duress or undue influence. If a party threatens to inflict personal injury or property damage, that is duress that would vitiate a settlement agreement. A party's desperate need for money, a compelling desire to end the dispute, or a party's threat to end settlement negotiations, however, are not duress.

In various ways, courts encourage settlements. Anything parties and their lawyers say during settlement negotiations cannot be used as evidence at trial. For example, if a defendant offered to pay $100,000 for a settlement, the plaintiff cannot use that offer as an admission that the defendant is liable or to prove the "reasonable" value of the claim. Suppose the defendant were to say, "For purposes of settlement, let us assume that I went through the stop sign; still, your demand is too high." Because the statement was made in the context of settlement negotiations, it could not be used against the defendant at trial. Statements made in settlement negotiations are not privileged. The information can be used if otherwise admissible. The Rules of evidence merely deem statements made during settlement negotiations are not relevant. For example, if a defendant admits during negotiations that he found some photographs that support the plaintiff's claim, the plaintiff could demand discovery of photographs. Similarly, if during settlement negotiations a defendant states, "I do not know whether I was going thirty or forty miles per hour," at trial the plaintiff could offer evidence to prove the defendant was traveling at the higher speed, but the plaintiff could not use the "admission" made during settlement negotiations as evidence of the higher speed. Some discretion must be used during settlement negotiations not to say too much. The guideline is to say only what you need to say to be honest and keep negotiations on track.

A release must identify all parties to the contract and specify all persons who are released. It must clearly identify the transaction or occurrence that led to the claim. This usually is done by identifying the nature of the transaction or occurrence, its time, and place. A release should describe the alleged harm or loss for which compensation is paid. A release should specify all special conditions and limitations that are part of the agreement. If the respondent pays money at the time the release is executed, the release should contain the releaser's acknowledgment that he or she received the money. The released party need not sign the release. However, if the agreement provides for a mutual release, then both parties must sign. It is customary to have the claimants' signatures witnessed and notarized though no rule or law requires those formalities. If the parties later disagree about the terms and conditions of the settlement, a court looks to the writing to decide the parties' intent. If the court were to find the written release to be ambiguous, the court could receive evidence concerning the parties' intent, including evidence about the nature of the claim and details of the parties' negotiations.

When parties settle their litigation, they must notify the court. They stipulate that the court may order a dismissal. The stipulation of dismissal may be with prejudice, meaning the claim cannot be brought again in any court. Or, it may be dismissed without prejudice, which means the claim could be asserted again if otherwise appropriate.

Historically, the sole purpose and effect of a settlement and release was to terminate the claim. The old common law gave a broad, inclusive effect to releases. A release terminated all the claimant's claims from the particular transaction or occurrence. It also released all persons who might have been liable to the claimant. Partial releases were considered an anathema to the law, because they did not put an end to the controversy.

partial release   A release of less than all the alleged tortfeasors. A release of part of a claim.

Historically, courts believed that partial releases led to uncertainty. Consequently, courts refused to enforce **partial releases.** In the alternative, some courts gave partial releases the effect of full and final releases. Since the early 1900s courts have come to accept and enforce partial settlements and partial releases. Experience has shown that when one facet of a case is resolved, the rest of the case is more likely to settle. Furthermore, courts now appreciate that having a portion of a dispute duly settled is better than no settlement. Therefore, the modern view is that partial settlements are valid, provided no secrecy surrounds the settlement and the settlement does not unduly prejudice the rights of other persons. However, unless very carefully drafted, a release used in a partial settlement can create uncertainty about the scope and application of the release. A variety of release forms have been devised to deal with various situations. We will consider some of them in the following sections.

General Releases

general release   A release that puts an end to all claims the claimant may have against the released parties for all transactions and occurrences between them as of the date of the release.

A **general release** is a full and final release. Ordinarily, the claimant agrees to release all claims he or she has against the payer-respondent from a particular transaction or occurrence. However, a general release can be even broader. A general release can even release everyone in the world who might be liable for the harm or loss the claimant sustained. A general release may release *all* existing claims the claimant *might* have against the payer-respondent. When parties want to resolve all their differences, they should use a general release. For example, suppose parties have several disputes pending after a long-term business relationship. Suppose the parties want to ensure that they have settled all matters between them—even problems they do not know about but that could arise from their past dealings. A general release could be used. But a general release could not settle and bar claims that arise after the release is executed. They could not have a meeting of the minds concerning losses that have not yet occurred.

When one of two joint tortfeasors (i.e., wrongdoers) pays for a general release, the law provides that the payer has also discharged the cotortfeasor's share. The cotortfeasor is then liable to the payer for contribution (i.e., for his or her fair share). For example, suppose the claimant is injured in an intersection collision while riding as a passenger. Suppose the claimant's driver is uninsured but the other driver has insurance. Suppose the claimant is willing to settle with the insured driver on a basis the insurer considers reasonable. The claimant can give the insured driver a full and final release, including any claim she may have against her driver. Now the settling driver has a claim against the nonsettling driver to recoup a fair share of what was paid to settle. This action is called contribution.

When a respondent brings an action for contribution, it is customary to attach the release to the complaint as an exhibit to show the respondent extinguished the joint tortfeasor's liability and is now entitled to contribution for that share. The respondent who paid for the release must prove by a fair preponderance of the evidence that the amount of the settlement is reasonable; that he or she settled the claim and paid the cotortfeasor's share. Exhibit 22.1 illustrates a typical general release.

Settling with Joint or Concurrent Tortfeasors

Joint and concurrent tortfeasors are jointly and severally liable for the claimant's whole loss. This means that each is liable to the claimant for the entire loss, but as

FOR AND IN CONSIDERATION of the payment to me/us at this time of the sum of dollars ($), the receipt of which is hereby acknowledged, I/we, being of lawful age, do hereby release, acquit, and forever discharge of and from any and all actions, causes of action, claims, demands, damages, costs, loss of services, expenses, and compensation, on account of, or in any way growing out of, any and all known and unknown personal injuries, developed or undeveloped, and property damage resulting or to result from the accident that occurred on or about the _____ day of _____ , 2006, at or near [location].

I/we hereby declare and represent that the injuries sustained may be permanent and progressive and that recovery therefrom is uncertain and indefinite, and in making this release and agreement it is understood and agreed that I/we rely wholly on my/our own judgment, belief, and knowledge of the nature, extent, and duration of said injuries, and that I/we have not been influenced to any extent whatever in making this release by any representations or statements regarding said injuries, or regarding any other matters, made by the persons, firms, or corporations who are hereby released, or by any person or persons representing him or them, or by any physician or surgeon by him or them employed.

I/we clearly understand that I/we are releasing and that this release includes all injuries now known to me/us and also all injuries now unknown, and I/we clearly understand that this release also includes all disabilities or results that may develop in the future from injuries now known or unknown to me/us.

It is further understood and agreed that this settlement is the compromise of a doubtful and disputed claim, and that the payment is not to be construed as an admission of liability on the part of _____, by whom liability is expressly denied.

This release contains the ENTIRE AGREEMENT between the parties hereto, and the terms of this release are contractual and not a mere recital.

I/we further state that I/we have carefully read the foregoing release and know the contents thereof, and I/we sign the same as my/our own free act.

WITNESS hand and seal this _____ day of _____ , 2006. In presence of

_____

_____

CAUTION! READ BEFORE SIGNING

_____

[Notary Seal]

between the cotortfeasors, they must share proportionately. Parties must consider the effect their settlement and release has on a cotortfeasor who does not participate in the settlement. The alternative to a full and final settlement is for the claimant to give the settling tortfeasor a partial release and keep the claim open against the nonsettling tortfeasor. The claimant retains the right to try to collect more damages from the nonsettling tortfeasor. The settling tortfeasor avoids further expense and involvement.

Settling Claims Involving Vicarious Liability

Claims involving vicarious liability (i.e., where the law makes one person liable for the acts of another) present unique problems. The most common vicarious liability relationship is that between a principal and agent. A principal who did nothing wrong is liable for his or her agent's negligence. A claimant cannot release the agent without automatically releasing the principal. By way of example, a full release of an automobile driver also releases the owner from any liability predicated on the driver's negligence. This is true, even if the claimant tried to give the driver a partial release, which expressly reserves a claim against the owner. Similarly, when a claimant releases a negligent employee, the claimant automatically releases the employer who was vicariously liable. There is only one quantum of fault, and that is released by releasing the agent/employee. Of course, a principal could remain liable for his or her own independent negligence.

Partial Settlements Involving Comparative Fault

partial settlement   A settlement that resolves only part of the claim arising from a transaction or occurrence.

A release of one of several negligent tortfeasors, in effect, releases a percentage of causal negligence attributable to the one released. The percentage of causal negligence is determined in the claimant's trial against the nonsettling tortfeasor.[2] When the case goes to trial against a nonsettling tortfeasor, the court informs the jury about the **partial settlement.** The jury needs to know why the tortfeasor who settled is not in court. But the judge does not tell the jury about the amount of the settlement or reasons for settling. At the end of the trial the court instructs the jury to determine whether the settling tortfeasor[3] was negligent and what percentage of causal negligence should be attributed to that tortfeasor when determining the percentage of causal negligence to be attributed to the plaintiff and the defendant-tortfeasors. The court may state this as follows:

> [Name of settling tortfeasor] is not a party to this lawsuit, because [name of settling defendant] and plaintiff have entered into a settlement agreement. You are not to concern yourselves with the reasons for the settlement. You are not to draw any conclusions from the fact that [name of person] settled with the plaintiff or from the fact that the defendants have not settled. The settlement agreement between plaintiff and [name of person] should in no way influence your judgment about the alleged negligence of the defendants and plaintiff.
>
> Even though [name of person] is not a party to this lawsuit, you will still be asked to determine whether [name of person] was negligent and whether that negligence was a direct cause of the accident. This is to ensure that the apportionment of negligence you make is fair and accurate.

The jury must determine the plaintiff's total money damages and the percentage of causal negligence attributable to each tortfeasor and the plaintiff. The court then calculates the amount of damages to which the plaintiff is entitled.

Suppose the plaintiff has claims against tortfeasors A and B, and settles with A. Suppose the case goes to trial. The jury awards the plaintiff damages in the sum of $200,000 and finds tortfeasor A's causal negligence is 10 percent and tortfeasor B's causal negligence is 90 percent. Defendant B receives a credit of 10 percent, or $20,000 against the amount of the verdict. Based on those findings, defendant B owes the plaintiff $180,000.

Settlements of Wrongful Death Actions

A court that has jurisdiction of a wrongful death action must appoint a trustee to represent a decedent's heirs and next of kin. A relative, probate representative, or other person may apply to be a trustee. A trustee must provide a bond guaranteeing performance of his or her responsibilities. A trustee must act to represent the best interests of all persons who stand to benefit from prosecution of the claim. If the representative is able to negotiate a settlement he or she believes to be in everyone's best interests, the proposed settlement must be submitted to court for approval. If approved, the court orders how the money damages are to be allocated to the surviving next of kin. The court discharges the trustee only after the settlement proceeds have been distributed and all costs paid. A court may approve a wrongful death settlement recommended by the trustee even if one of the next of kin disagrees with it. The trustee signs the release on behalf of all the next of kin.

Minors' Settlements

Minors cannot prosecute or defend against civil actions. Minors are under a **legal disability.** A minor must have a court appointed guardian to represent his or her interests. Parents cannot settle a child's claim without court approval. District courts have specific procedures for obtaining court approval of **minors' settlements.** A guardian may move the court for approval of a proposed settlement. If the court approves the proposed settlement, the guardian can give a full and final release that binds the minor. Though a minor cannot be bound by an ordinary release that she or he signed, such a release may become valid and binding if it is ratified after the minor turns eighteen. Also, a minor's release becomes binding if the minor fails to rescind it within a year after becoming eighteen.

legal disability   A want of legal capacity to make legally enforceable commitments. The lack of capacity may be due to a person's age, lack of mental competency, or lack of licensor.

minor's settlement   A settlement that must be approved by a court to be binding on the minor. The minor's parent or guardian must petition the court to approve the settlement and must show that the settlement is fair to the minor.

Structured Settlements

Structured settlements evolved from the need to provide periodic payments over a long period of time to individuals who might not be able to manage and/or conserve a large settlement. Structured settlements allow the tortfeasor to pay a lump sum of money to a bank or insurance company, which then provides a customized annuity for the claimant. The annuity provides scheduled benefits over a period of years or over the claimant's lifetime. Because the company that issues the annuity has the right to use or invest the money over the same period of time, the total amount the company pays is significantly larger than the amount the tortfeasor paid. Consequently, a settlement funded in the amount of $50,000 may result in payments of hundreds of thousands of dollars over a claimant's lifetime.

A structured settlement annuity must be purchased by the defendant, and the claimant must not be able to control the trustee's handling or investment of the funds. Customarily, structured settlements include immediate payments to cover past medical expenses, lost wages, attorneys' fees, and litigation expenses. Despite the many benefits of structured settlements, most personal injury claims are settled with single, lump sum payments.

Partial Releases in Workers' Compensation Cases

Employees who are injured in the course and scope of their employment are entitled to workers' compensation benefits, which include payment of medical expenses, lost wages, and disability benefits. Sometimes an employee's injury is caused by someone other than the employer. In that event, the injured employee has a right to receive workers' compensation payments *and* to pursue a common law tort action against the nonemployer tortfeasor. Automobile accidents and product liability accidents are most common. The employer who pays workers' compensation benefits is entitled, by law, to obtain reimbursement out of any monetary recovery the employee obtains from the tortfeasor. If the employee neglects or refuses to pursue a claim against the tortfeasor, the employer may bring what is called a subrogation action against the tortfeasor. Therefore, a tortfeasor who injures an employee in the course of the employee's work faces two claims. On occasion, a tortfeasor finds he or she can settle with the employee or employer, but not with both. A special type of partial release is used in these cases. The release allows the employee to retain his or her workers' compensation benefits and receive general damages for pain and suffering from the tortfeasor. The employer's subrogation rights are unaffected. The employer is left to pursue its subrogation rights. The subrogation claim may be settled later or go to trial.

Reverse Workers' Compensation Releases

A tortfeasor may negotiate a full and final settlement of the employer's workers' compensation subrogation claim and leave open the plaintiff employee's claim. The form of the partial release is similar to that used to settle the employee's claim.

High-Low Releases

high-low release An agreement between parties to settle their dispute by payment and acceptance of a sum of money within an agreed range, leaving to the court or tribunal the amount of money damages.

A **high-low release** is an agreement in which a tortfeasor agrees to pay a minimum amount to the plaintiff, and the plaintiff agrees to an upper limit on his or her recovery. If the verdict is against the plaintiff, the settling defendant nevertheless pays the minimum amount. If the plaintiff wins but receives a verdict for less than the minimum amount, the settling defendant must pay the full minimum amount. Usually, the defendant does not pay the claimant any money until the claim is litigated.

A high-low release can be advantageous when the claimant has a weak case, but the settling defendant risks a huge damage award if the claimant wins. Both parties reduce their risks. A high-low settlement reduces the likelihood of an appeal. A high-low release may misalign the parties when there are multiple defendants, however, and distort the eventual outcome. Your state's laws may require the parties to a high-low settlement agreement to inform the court and other parties about their arrangement.

Covenants Not to Sue

A **covenant not to sue** is not a release. It is a contract that allows the plaintiff and one of two or more tortfeasors to resolve their dispute without compromising the claimant's cause of action against the other tortfeasors. The settling tortfeasor pays the claimant a sum of money and the claimant covenants (i.e., promises) not to bring an action against the tortfeasor but does not release the tortfeasor from liability. The claimant may proceed against the other tortfeasors. Because the settling tortfeasor has not been released, the nonsettling tortfeasors may bring a third-party action against him or her for contribution. Suppose the claimant is a passenger in her husband's automobile when they collide with an automobile driven by the defendant. Assume the husband has only $10,000 of liability insurance and no assets. The husband's liability insurer may covenant with the claimant to pay its policy limits for a covenant that she will not sue her husband. The claimant receives the $10,000 and can prosecute an action against the other driver for the full amount of her claim. The other driver can bring a third-party action against the husband to obtain contribution, but if the husband has no more insurance and no assets, the contribution action is not worth very much. In this way, the "deep pockets" defendant may be maneuvered into paying more in a settlement or judgment than could be obtained if a partial release were used. There is some question about the fairness of covenants not to sue. Nevertheless, they are court approved. Exhibit 22.2 is an example of a covenant not to sue.

covenant not to sue A type of settlement agreement in which the plaintiff agrees not to commence or maintain an action against the defendant but does not release the defendant from liability for the occurrence.

EXHIBIT 22.2

Covenant Not to Sue

KNOW ALL PEOPLE BY THESE PRESENTS, that Daniel Trost, Paul Trost, and Thomas E. Trost, hereinafter referred to as plaintiffs, for and in consideration of the sum of four thousand dollars and no cents ($4,000.00), the receipt of which is hereby acknowledged, do hereby covenant and expressly agree with The Griff Company and Mutual Insurance Company, their successors and assigns (all of whom are hereafter referred to as "Settling Parties"), not to further prosecute the suit for damages by plaintiffs pending against The Griff Company in the District Court, Hennepin County, State of Minnesota, and agree to execute a stipulation for dismissal with prejudice in said action insofar as The Griff Company is concerned.

Plaintiffs further covenant and expressly agree with the Settling Parties to forever refrain from instituting any other action or making any other demand or claims of any kind against said Settling Parties for damages sustained by them as a result of an accident that occurred on June 22, 2005, in the City of Minneapolis at the intersection of Rowland Avenue and Mill Street.

The aforesaid consideration is not intended as full compensation for damages claimed by plaintiffs arising from said accident.

Plaintiffs reserve to themselves the balance of the whole cause of action, which they may have against Lloyd Koesling as a result of said accident. This covenant is not entered into nor in any way intended to release any claim or cause of action plaintiffs have against Lloyd Koesling as a result of said accident.

continued

Exhibit 22.2

Covenant Not to Sue
(continued)

The Settling Parties, in whose favor this covenant not to sue is executed, reserve and retain all claims and causes of action that they or any of them might have against others and, including without limiting the generality of the foregoing, any claim for contribution that they might have against Lloyd Koesling.

The payment of the consideration for this covenant is not to be construed as an admission on the part of any of the Settling Parties, of any liability whatsoever in consequence of said accident, to plaintiffs or to any other party.

IN WITNESS WHEREOF I have hereunto set my hand and seal this ___ day of May, 2006.

In presence of

_____   /s/ Daniel Trost

_____   /s/ Paul Trost

                                          /s/ Thomas E. Trost

STATE OF Minnesota
COUNTY OF Hennepin

On this ___ day of May 2006, before me personally appeared to me known to be the persons described herein, and who executed the foregoing instrument and acknowledged that voluntarily executed the same.

Notary Public [Seal]

My term expires: January 2, 2008

Loan Receipt Agreements

loan receipt agreement A contract by which a tortfeasor, or the tortfeasor's insurer, agrees to "loan" the claimant a specified sum of money and the claimant agrees not to pursue his or her claim against the lender, but both believe that another person has substantial liability and the claimant agrees to pursue the claim against that other person.

A **loan receipt agreement** is a contract between a claimant and settling tortfeasor by which they agree that one of them will prosecute the claim against another tortfeasor. The claimant stands to recover additional damages and the settling tortfeasor may get some of his or her money back by pursuing the claim. The settling tortfeasor, or his liability insurer, agrees to "loan" the claimant a specified sum of money, and the claimant agrees not to pursue the claim against the settling tortfeasor. The parties agree on some allocation of any recovery against the nonsettling tortfeasor. Usually, some stated amount goes to the party who finances the litigation against the nonsettling tortfeasor and the balance of the recovery is divided on some mutually satisfactory basis. If the claimant recovers nothing from the nonsettling tortfeasor, the "loan" need not be repaid.

As discussed in Chapter 1, a personal injury claim cannot be assigned and a claim must be prosecuted in the name of the real party in interest. If a settling tortfeasor or his or her liability insurer paid the claimant's damages and then tried to prosecute the claim against the nonsettling tortfeasor, it would be tantamount to an assignment of a personal injury claim and/or the claim would have to be brought in the name of the settling tortfeasor. The loan receipt device avoids those problems; as artificial as it may be, it is court approved. There are times when a loan receipt agreement provides the best strategy. The lender is not protected against claims brought by other tortfeasors for contribution. The loan receipt device, however, ordinarily is used only where the lender has paid most, if not all, the claimant's damages.

Mary Carter Agreements

A **Mary Carter agreement** (from *Booth vs. Mary Carter Paint Co.*, 202 So.2d 8 [Fla. Dist. Ct. App. 1967]) is similar to high-low and loan receipt agreements, with some important differences. A Mary Carter agreement is a secret or semisecret agreement between the claimant and one or more tortfeasors, but not all the tortfeasors. It provides that the settling tortfeasor must remain in the lawsuit. In addition, the settling tortfeasor can benefit from a verdict or judgment that is favorable to the claimant. A Mary Carter release is made up of three elements:

1. A clause that guarantees the claimant will receive a certain sum of money from the settling tortfeasor even if the claimant loses the case or receives a recovery less than the guaranteed amount. The claimant agrees to collect the amount of any verdict from a nonsettling tortfeasor. (In this situation, the settling party hopes the verdict will be larger than the amount she or he has guaranteed to pay.)
2. The settling party agrees to remain in the lawsuit until a judgment is reached or the claimant consents to its dismissal.
3. The settling parties agree to keep their settlement secret. In essence, the terms of the agreement are hidden from the court, the jury, and the nonsettling parties.

The third element, that of secrecy, is the most problematic aspect of Mary Carter agreements. Many people believe such secrecy permits the claimant and the settling party to manipulate the checks and balances in the civil justice system to the detriment of the nonsettling parties. Element 2, requiring the settling parties to remain in the lawsuit, is a matter of concern to many legal commentators. The arrangement perverts the adversarial system and amount to a fraud on the court. In light of the secrecy attached to Mary Carter agreements, some state courts have held them illegal. However, it is usually permissible for settling parties to remain in the lawsuit as long as the arrangements are not secret and the settlement agreement does not pervert the adversarial system.

Consent Judgment Against Liability Insurer

A stipulated consent judgment is a unique arrangement between a claimant and tortfeasor when the tortfeasor's liability insurer denies coverage for the claim. The problem is that the claimant may have a good cause of action and a right to substantial

Mary Carter agreement A secret agreement between parties to settle the case between them but to continue prosecution of the case against another party.

damages, but there is no one who can pay. Consider our hypothetical case of *Raskin vs. Harper.* Harper did not buy any insurance but claims coverage under John Griffin's policy with Security. Assuming that the insurer's denial of coverage may be wrong, the tortfeasor should be interested in pursuing an action against the insurer to establish coverage. But the claimant usually is interested more in establishing coverage than the tortfeasor is. Lawyers have found a way to give claimants the ability to prosecute the coverage claim and protect the tortfeasor from any personal liability. The arrangement requires you to use all your knowledge about civil litigation.

consent judgment   A judgment for which the parties to a civil lawsuit stipulate the terms and conditions.

The claimant and tortfeasor must enter into a settlement agreement in which the tortfeasor allows the claimant to have a judgment against the tortfeasor in a specified amount. This is accomplished by a **consent judgment** against the tortfeasor. The agreement provides that the claimant will look only to the liability insurance policy for payment of the judgment. The tortfeasor's personal assets are kept exempt from attachment. The claimant must obtain a settlement with the liability insurer or commence a garnishment action against the insurer. After the consent judgment is entered, the claimant serves a garnishment summons on the insurer, alleging the insurer holds money that it is obligated to pay on behalf of its insured—the tortfeasor and judgment debtor. The insurer responds to the garnishment subpoena by denying any indebtedness. The claimant, as a judgment creditor, is then in a position to move the court for leave to serve a supplemental complaint on the insurer to establish coverage.

An example may be helpful to show how a consent judgment is used. Suppose the tortfeasor was baby-sitting a six-year-old child and negligently failed to keep the child from touching a hot stove. Assume the tortfeasor's personal liability insurer denies coverage on the grounds that the occurrence comes within the business exclusion found in most homeowner's insurance policies. The defendant has no assets, other than the insurance policy, to pay the plaintiff's claim. If the plaintiff's lawyer believes the facts of the accident do not invoke the business exclusion, she or he may want to obtain control over the insurance coverage claim. The claimant and tortfeasor can stipulate that a consent judgment may be entered against the tortfeasor for a specified sum of money. The stipulated amount must be reasonable to be enforceable. The consent judgment eliminates the necessity of a trial of the personal injury claim. As a judgment creditor, the claimant can commence a garnishment action against the liability insurer. The claimant has control over the garnishment action and, therefore, obtains the right to prove the insurance policy provides coverage for the claimant's loss. As part of the garnishment action, the insurer has a right to challenge the reasonableness of the settlement. But the insurer cannot raise any issues concerning the tortfeasor's liability. The principal issue to be tried is insurance coverage.

bad faith claim   A willful failure to comply with a clear statutory duty or contractual duty.

A liability insurer derives some benefits from the arrangement. The insurer does not have the expense of defending the tort action. Because the consent judgment protects the tortfeasor from any claim against her or his personal assets, the tortfeasor cannot be harmed by the insurer's misguided refusal to settle the claim. Therefore, the insurer is insulated from any possible **bad faith claim.** The insurer avoids the cost prosecuting a declaratory judgment action to resolve the coverage issue.[4] Also, the amount of the claimant's recovery cannot exceed the amount of the insurance policy, so an insurer cannot be held liable for an excess verdict.

A consent judgment has some negative consequences for the insured. Some title insurance companies and mortgage companies do not appreciate the niceties of a consent judgment. They see a consent judgment as a cloud against the insured's title to real estate the insured may own. Consequently, the insured should take steps to have the judgment book show that the judgment is satisfied as soon as the coverage issue is determined. Indeed, the terms of the settlement agreement should specify who will take the necessary steps to satisfy or cancel the consent judgment after the coverage issue is resolved.

An insured tortfeasor would violate the insurance policy's cooperation clause by entering into a stipulation for a consent judgment, unless the insurer has denied coverage. A violation of the cooperation clause gives the insurer another coverage defense. So the claimant and tortfeasor must make sure that the insurer's denial of coverage is clear and unequivocal.

Rescission or Cancellation of Releases

A release is a contract that settles the dispute between parties. A release may be rescinded (set aside) if it was induced by fraud or the result of a mutual mistake concerning a significant term or condition of the release. Fraud in the inducement of the release is based on conduct and statements that precede execution of the release and have nothing to do with the terms and conditions as set forth in the written document. Fraud in the inducement may be proved by a mere preponderance of the evidence. The elements necessary to prove fraud are the same elements that apply to a cause of action in fraud. To prove a mutual mistake a party must challenge the language of the written release. Therefore, to avoid the release or to obtain reformation of the release, the claimant must present proof that is clear and convincing.

With regard to a claim of mutual mistake, courts consider several factors in deciding whether a release should be avoided:

1. The length of time between the injury and the settlement. (It is more likely that the parties did not really understand or appreciate the extent of the loss and the significance of the release if the settlement was made soon after the loss.)
2. The amount of time that elapsed between the settlement and the attempt to avoid the settlement. (The longer the delay, the less sympathetic the courts are to the claim of mistake.)
3. The presence or absence of independent medical advice of the plaintiff's own choice before and at the time of settlement. (If the plaintiff did not have competent medical advice concerning the nature, extent, and effect of his or her injuries, the claim of mistake is stronger.)
4. The presence or absence of legal counsel of the plaintiff's own choice before and at the time of settlement. (If the plaintiff had the advice of a lawyer concerning the terms of the release and concerning the settlement value, it is very difficult to claim a mistake.)
5. The language of the release itself.
6. The adequacy of the consideration paid for the release in light of the nature and extent of the injuries or other loss, and whether the settling party is likely to be found liable for the accident.

7. The general competence of the releaser. The plaintiff's education and experience may be considered by the court.
8. Whether the injury claimed by the releaser was a known injury at the time the release was signed or a consequence flowing from an unknown injury.

Generally, only mistakes of fact permit avoidance. However, when a claimant is not represented by an attorney, and the tortfeasor's liability insurer undertakes to advise the claimant of her or his rights, a "fiduciary" type relationship may be established. Such a relationship could convert a mistake of law into a mistake of fact making the settlement voidable.

Confession of Judgment

confession of judgment A person's written admission, made under oath, that he or she is indebted to the person named, and that the person named is entitled to have the court enter a judgment in his or her favor for a specified amount of money.

When a person against whom a claim is made acknowledges the obligation but has no money or other means by which to satisfy the obligation, the obligor may **confess judgment.** No lawsuit or other legal proceeding is needed. The obligor simply executes the necessary affidavits and forms, which authorize the clerk of court to enter a judgment pursuant to the parties' agreement. The laws of most states impose some strict formalities to confessions of judgment, including the requirement that they be notarized by two witnesses. The confessor must be an adult. A confession of judgment is binding only on the parties to the agreement. It would not be binding on a confessor's partner, spouse, heirs, assignees, or liability insurance company. The judgment remains a legally enforceable obligation for ten years, depending on the laws of the particular state.

Dismissals

A lawsuit may be terminated before a judgment is entered. A termination is called a dismissal. There are three types of dismissals: court-ordered involuntary, voluntary unilateral, and stipulated. The procedures for dismissing a case are controlled by Rule 41.

Court-ordered Dismissals

involuntary dismissal A court-ordered dismissal to which the claimant party did not consent.

When a plaintiff's case has a fatal defect, the court must order a dismissal. For example, if the defendant were to prevail on any of the motions authorized by Rule 12, the court must enter an order dismissing the case. A court may order dismissal as a sanction when the plaintiff fails to comply with a valid court order, such as an order to permit discovery pursuant to Rule 37. A court may dismiss the case if the plaintiff has been dilatory in prosecuting the action. A court may order an **involuntary dismissal** if the plaintiff's evidence fails to prove a prima facie case of liability against the defendant. Courts may order involuntary dismissals on many other bases as well, but these are the common ones.

An order of dismissal ends the case. Ordinarily, the dismissal does not result in entry of a judgment. However, if the plaintiff decides to appeal the court's order for dismissal, the losing party probably will arrange to have judgment entered against herself or himself to be able to appeal from the judgment. A court order for dismissal is without prejudice, unless it specifically states that it is with prejudice. If the dismissal is without prejudice, the plaintiff can bring the lawsuit again and try to avoid the problem that led to a dismissal the first time. If a dismissal is with prejudice, the suit cannot be brought again. The dismissal is res judicata.

Voluntary Dismissal on Notice

A plaintiff voluntarily may dismiss his or her claim. Rule 41(a)(1) imposes the following requirements:

> [A]n action may be dismissed by the plaintiff without order of the court (i) by filing a notice of dismissal at any time before service by the adverse party of an answer or of a motion for summary judgment, whichever first occurs, or (ii) by filing a stipulation of dismissal signed by all the parties who have appeared in the action.

Unless otherwise stated in the notice of **voluntary dismissal** or stipulation, the dismissal is without prejudice, except that a notice of dismissal operates as an adjudication on the merits when filed by a plaintiff who has once dismissed in any court of the United States or of any state an action based on or including the same claim. Though it is not stated expressly in the rule, the plaintiff should serve a copy of the voluntary dismissal on the defendant. Many state courts allow the plaintiff to voluntarily dismiss on notice at any time before the case is alerted for trial.

voluntary dismissal A dismissal of a cause of action or an action, given by a party without being subject to a court order.

Stipulated Dismissal

Parties are able to stipulate to a dismissal at any time on any terms. The **stipulated dismissal** may be the result of a settlement agreement and release, but not necessarily. A stipulated dismissal usually provides that all parties waive the right to recover costs from each other. A stipulated dismissal should be very specific about whether it is with or without prejudice. Rule 41 provides, in part, as follows:

stipulated dismissal A dismissal of a civil action by agreement of the parties.

> [A]n action may be dismissed by the plaintiff without order of court by filing a stipulation of dismissal signed by all parties who have appeared in the action. Unless otherwise stated . . . in the stipulation, the dismissal is without prejudice.

If the parties fail to be specific, the rule presumes the stipulation is without prejudice. Even though the rule specifies that the stipulation is to be signed by the parties, the rule is understood to authorize the parties' lawyers to sign the stipulation on behalf of the parties. The terms and conditions of the stipulated dismissal may be on whatever the parties agree. If the parties have negotiated a settlement of their controversy, the terms and conditions of the settlement need not be included in the dismissal. Exhibit 22.3 illustrates a stipulation for dismissal.

SUMMARY

Courts favor settlements. Parties avoid uncertainty, gain economies, and obtain a disposition that they know they can tolerate, if not embrace. Settlement agreements can be used to resolve contract disputes and tort claims. Parties settle for reasons that have nothing to do with the merits of the claims or defenses. A settlement agreement ordinarily releases a claim. A claim does not have to be one for which a court can provide a remedy to be the subject of a settlement agreement. A settlement

STATE OF MINNESOTA   DISTRICT COURT
COUNTY OF HENNEPIN   JUDICIAL DISTRICT TEN

Georgia Watson, Plaintiff,

          vs.

Alvin Johanson, Defendant.

The above-entitled action, having been fully compromised and settled,

     NOW THEREFORE, it is stipulated and agreed, by and between the parties hereto, through their respective counsel, that said action may be and hereby is dismissed with prejudice and on the merits, but without further costs to any of the parties.

     IT IS FURTHER STIPULATED AND AGREED that either party, without notice to the other, may cause judgment of dismissal with prejudice and on the merits to be entered herein.

[date]

_____
Attorney for Plaintiff

_____
Attorney for Defendant

agreement may provide for dismissal of an action or entry of a judgment. Because the law favors settlement negotiations, statements parties make in the course of negotiations are deemed not relevant evidence. However, any information disclosed in settlement negotiations is not protected against discovery or use at trial. Therefore, you must use discretion when conducting settlement negotiations.

     Settlement agreements must comply with all the requirements of contracts, and they are subject to all the defenses applicable to contracts. They do not have to be in writing but should be to avoid disagreement over the terms, scope, and limits. Your state's statute of frauds requires that all contracts that, by their terms, are not to be performed within one year from the date on which they are made, must be in writing and signed. A minor's settlement requires court approval. Usually, a settlement results in a release. A release must identify the parties, the transaction or occurrence, the type of injury or damage claimed, the consideration given, and any special conditions or limitations that are part of the settlement agreement. When the claim is for money, the amount ordinarily is paid at the time the release is signed. The party who is released usually does not sign the release. However, if the settlement agreement provides for a mutual release, both parties must sign. It is customary to have the signatures witnessed and notarized.

     A general release is designed to put an end to all claims as of the date of the release. A full and final release may apply to a particular transaction or occurrence or all past dealings. Parties may make partial settlements and use partial releases.

Partial releases are common in jurisdictions that have comparative fault. When one tortfeasor settles and the other does not, the court tells the jury about the partial settlement, but the court does not tell the jury about the amount of the settlement and is directed not to speculate about the reasons for the settlement.

A partial release cannot be used to preserve a claim against a person whose liability merely is vicarious. A release of an agent's liability necessarily releases the principal if the principal did not commit any separate wrongful act.

A special workers' compensation release allows an employee who has received workers' compensation benefits to enter into a settlement with the tortfeasor without affecting the employer's subrogation rights. The employer is left to pursue its own subrogation rights. The subrogation claim may be settled or go through a trial. A tortfeasor may negotiate a settlement of the employer's workers' compensation subrogation claim and leave open the plaintiff employee's claim. A high-low settlement agreement provides that the tortfeasor will pay an agreed minimum even if he or she prevails and the claimant agrees to a limit even though a jury might award more.

A covenant not to sue is a contract but not a release. It allows the plaintiff and one of two or more tortfeasors to resolve their dispute without compromising the plaintiff's cause of action against the other tortfeasors. The claimant agrees not to bring an action against the settling tortfeasor. But the claimant is free to pursue the claim against other tortfeasors who remain liable for the full amount of the plaintiff's damages. The settling tortfeasor remains subject to an action for contribution.

A loan receipt agreement is a contract in which a tortfeasor, or liability insurer, agrees to "loan" the claimant a specified sum of money. The claimant agrees to prosecute the claim against another tortfeasor. The claimant agrees to repay the loan out of any recovery he or she obtains against the tortfeasor. The claimant may retain any amount recovered in excess of the "loan." The claimant does not have to repay the loan if he or she does not make a recovery against the tortfeasor.

A Mary Carter agreement is a secret agreement between a claimant and one or more defendants. It provides that the settling defendant must remain in the lawsuit. In addition, the settling defendant may share in a verdict or judgment that is favorable to the claimant. These secret agreements are invalid in many states.

A stipulated consent judgment is used only when a liability insurer has denied coverage to its insured or denied that the tortfeasor is an insured. The insurer's denial of coverage raises an insurance coverage dispute. If the claimant believes the insurer is liable and wants to assume control over a claim against the insurer, the claimant may accept a consent judgment from the tortfeasor. The consent judgment precludes the claimant from attaching the tortfeasor's personal assets, but allows the claimant to bring a garnishment action against the insurer to establish coverage. After the insurer answers the garnishment summons by denying it holds funds belonging to the tortfeasor, the judgment creditor may move the court for leave to serve a supplemental complaint on the insurer to test the coverage issues. An insured violates the insurance cooperation clause by giving a consent judgment if the insurer has not denied coverage.

Structured settlements allow a tortfeasor to pay a lump sum of money to a bank or insurance company that provides scheduled benefits to the claimant over a period of years or over the claimant's lifetime. Because the company that issues the annuity has the right to use or invest the money over the same period of time, the total payout to the claimant may be much more than the amount of the settlement. The payments are not subject to income tax.

A wrongful death action must be prosecuted by a trustee appointed by the court. When a trustee settles the claim with a tortfeasor, the trustee must apply to the court for approval of the settlement. The court then determines how to allocate the proceeds to the decedent's heirs and next of kin. The court will not discharge the trustee until the settlement proceeds have been distributed. A court may approve the settlement over the objection of some next of kin.

Parents cannot settle their children's claims without court approval. Courts have specific procedures for obtaining approval of minors' settlements. If the procedures are followed, a release executed by a guardian on behalf of a minor is fully binding and enforceable against the minor. Although a minor's release that is not court approved does not bind a minor, the release may become binding if ratified once the minor gains legal capacity.

A release may be rescinded if it was induced by fraud or if a mutual mistake was made concerning a significant term. The elements necessary to prove fraud are the same elements that apply to a cause of action in fraud.

A person may avoid the expense and inconvenience of a lawsuit by confessing judgment. A confession of judgment binds only the person who confessed the judgment. A confession of judgment may be made even though a lawsuit is not pending.

The three types of dismissals are court-ordered involuntary, voluntary unilateral, and stipulated. The procedures are controlled by Rule 41. If a dismissal is without prejudice, the plaintiff can bring the lawsuit again and try to avoid the problem that led to dismissal the first time. If the dismissal is with prejudice, the suit cannot be brought again.

KEY TERMS

bad faith claim	loan receipt agreement
confession of judgment	Mary Carter agreement
consent judgment	minor's settlement
covenant not to sue	partial release
full and final release	partial settlement
general release	stipulated dismissal
high-low release	structured settlement
involuntary dismissal	voluntary dismissal
legal disability	

REVIEW QUESTIONS

1. What are some of the advantages the parties obtain by settling their case before trial?

2. Why should a settlement agreement and release be reduced to writing?

3. When is court approval of a settlement agreement necessary to make the agreement effective?

4. How does a covenant not to sue differ from a release?

5. Why are releases favored by the law?

6. In a comparative fault state, what kind of a release would a claimant propose for settling the claim against one defendant when several defendants are jointly liable?

7. If the parties' stipulation for a voluntary dismissal fails to state whether the dismissal is with prejudice, what effect will a court give to the dismissal?

8. What advantages may the defendant obtain by making an offer of judgment to the plaintiff?

9. Under what circumstances might the claimant and the tortfeasor agree that the tortfeasor should stipulate that a consent judgment may be entered against him or her?

10. Why would parties consider entering into a high-low agreement?

CASE ASSIGNMENT

You are a member of attorney Sandra Gillis's litigation team and represent John Griffin. At this point, agent Brandt has obtained a summary judgment dismissing Griffin's action against him. Griffin and Harper do not have any insurance, and Harper has few assets. He is "judgment proof." In other words, if a judgment were obtained against him, he could have it discharged in bankruptcy and would lose very little in the process. Attorney Donald Smith is very disappointed. It appears there is no "deep pocket" to pay his client's claim. He also is concerned that a court would find Mr. Nordby negligent, and his causal negligence might even be more than that of Harper. All of Nordby's medical expenses were covered by Medicare and insurance. Attorney Gillis and attorney William Hoch, who represent Bradley Harper, have told attorney Smith their clients would pay a total of $10,000 for a full and final settlement. Attorney Smith recommended to the trustee that she accept it, and she has agreed. Please prepare a full and final release for the trustee to execute in favor of John Griffin and Bradley Harper. The release also should resolve any obligations between Griffin and Harper.

Endnotes

1. For example, a plaintiff may recover a judgment that is much larger than even the plaintiff expected. The defendant may be so disappointed that he or she is prepared to have the debt discharged in bankruptcy. Under those circumstances, the plaintiff may be willing to accept less and the defendant may be willing to make payments over a period of time. The settlement may be conditioned on the defendant's performance, so if the defendant fails to make payments when due, the judgment can be enforced.

2. The burden falls on the nonsettling tortfeasor to try to show that the settling tortfeasor was negligent. At that point, the plaintiff usually tries to minimize the settling tortfeasor's involvement. This creates an interesting situation when the settling tortfeasor is a material witness.

3. Of course, the court refers to the settling tortfeasor by name and does not use the label "tortfeasor."

4. In most states, when a liability insurance company brings an action to determine whether its policy covers a claim against its insured, the company must pay the costs and attorneys' fees its insured incurs, if the court determines that the policy does provide coverage.

 For additional resources, visit our Web site at www.paralegal.delmar.cengage.com

ARBITRATION AND MEDIATION

Chapter Objectives

Chapter 23 discusses mediation and arbitration with an emphasis on what paralegals may do in these procedures. The chapter explains why parties should consider mediating their dispute, how the parties may initiate mediation, how to select a mediator, and a mediator's role and responsibilities. It also describes the limits as to what may be done in mediation. Mediation differs significantly from arbitration which more closely resembles litigation. The chapter explains how a matter is placed into arbitration, how an arbitration tribunal is selected, how an award is made, and how an award may be enforced. The discussion assumes that you have studied the prior chapters and understand litigation procedures.

Introduction

Alternative dispute resolution (ADR) includes any procedure that is designed to resolve disputes, except court procedures. Mediation and arbitration are the primary ADR procedures. ADR has become increasingly popular. ADR has some advantages over traditional civil litigation. The procedures are voluntary. They are less formal and relatively inexpensive. The parties have some control over the scope of the procedures, time requirements, and kinds of awards that can be made. The parties may design their arbitration to lead to a civil judgment, so the award is a final determination. However, ADR lacks the standards, constraints, and checks-and-balances of the legal system. ADR results tend to be less predictable. There is no ADR appellate procedure. A party may appeal to a court for relief from an arbitration award only when there is fraud or the tribunal has exceeded its authority. A court's power to review an arbitration award is very limited. ADR is growing in popularity because it tends to be faster, more economical, and simpler. In the recent past, lawyers assumed the role of mediators between the parties. They were more willing to encourage their own clients to compromise. It was part of being civil. However, as litigation has become increasingly adversarial in all aspects, lawyers have become more dependent upon others to facilitate settlement negotiations. Some scholars speculate that ADR has become necessary for society because attorneys have moved away from their roles as counselors, advisors and peacemakers to emphasize their role as advocates. Some attorneys need ADR as an initial step to settle cases.

Alternative Dispute Resolution

Arbitration and **mediation** are alternatives to civil litigation for resolving disputes. In current parlance, arbitration and mediation are referred to as forms of "alternative dispute resolution" or, simply, ADR. The ADR processes are as old as civilization. In mediation, the parties agree to have a third person (mediator) assist them to communicate and work through obstacles, so they can resolve their dispute. In arbitration, the parties present their evidence and arguments to a third person **(arbitrator),** who resolves the dispute for the parties. Unions, businesses, professional organizations, and religious organizations often use ADR to resolve disputes. ADR is flexible, speedy, and relatively inexpensive. ADR can be conducted in private, so the dispute and outcome are kept confidential. For this reason, ADR has increased appeal in malpractice claims against physicians, brokers, lawyers, and accountants. Parties may exercise some control over the process and its scope.

Unlike civil litigation, ADR may handle disputes for which there is no cause of action because the parties to ADR are not limited to legal remedies. Mediators and arbitrators do not have to be lawyers or judges. Persons who present evidence and make arguments to arbitrators and mediators do not have to be lawyers. Paralegals may handle any aspect of ADR. Of course, there is an important exception. If a dispute is already in litigation and the court orders ADR, the mediator or arbitrator is expected to follow the law. Then the mediator or arbitrator should be a judge, magistrate, or lawyer, and the advocates must be lawyers. But disputes that are not already in suit may circumvent legal procedures. For example, suppose a dispute arises between a hospital and physician where he or she admits patients. The hospital and physician may agree to arbitrate their dispute. They may agree on a three or five person arbitration tribunal consisting of physicians and hospital administrators. The petitioner-physician may be represented by another physician. The hospital-respondent may have its administrator represent its interests.

Terms and Definitions

In ADR a dispute is referred to as a **"matter,"** as "In the Matter of *Johnson vs. Smith*." The party who initiates ADR is a **petitioner.** The defending party is a **respondent.** An arbitrator is also a **tribunal.** An arbitration tribunal may have one, three, or five arbitrators. The number is odd to avoid ties. A **submission** is the parties' grant of authority to a tribunal to arbitrate their dispute. The **scope of submission** is the nature and extent of the tribunal's authority in the matter—similar to a civil court's jurisdiction. A tribunal's decision is an **award** whether or not money is awarded.

arbitration A procedure by which parties submit their dispute to another person or tribunal for decision. The submission may be voluntary, pursuant to a contract to arbitrate, or pursuant to a statute that requires arbitration.

mediation A dispute resolution procedure in which an intermediary facilitates communication between the parties, helps the parties overcome barriers in the negotiation process, and identifies the parties' real interests and needs so that they can make their own agreement.

arbitrator A person chosen by parties to a dispute to resolve their dispute.

matter The subject of a civil action or arbitration.

petitioner A person or corporation that files a petition with an arbitration tribunal.

respondent (1) The party against whom an appeal is taken; also called an appellee. (2) A party who must answer or respond to some formal demand in the litigation process.

tribunal A body, organization or person who has authority to adjudicate matters that are brought before it.

submission In arbitration, the parties' grant of authority to a tribunal to arbitrate their dispute.

scope of submission In an arbitration, the parties' agreement concerning the issues that the arbitrators may resolve and other limitations on the process or award.

award A decision or determination rendered by an arbitration tribunal.

binding arbitration Arbitration in which the parties must comply with the arbitration tribunal's award. The award may be filed with a court that has jurisdiction, for confirmation.

nonbinding arbitration Arbitration in which the tribunal's award is only advisory. A nonbinding award may be accepted, rejected, or modified by the parties.

Binding arbitration means the award is final and can be enforced against the parties. **Nonbinding arbitration** means the award is advisory only. A nonbinding award may become the basis for a settlement agreement.

Mediation

Mediation is a process in which parties engage a third person to help them negotiate a voluntary settlement of their dispute. The parties select their mediator. If the dispute is in litigation, a court may designate a mediator for the parties. There is only one mediator. He or she acts as a go-between. Because mediation is entirely voluntary, it requires some cooperation between the parties. They must have some interest in settling. They must be receptive to suggestions and willing to modify their positions. Even when a court orders parties to mediate, the court cannot order them to settle. A good mediator motivates reluctant parties and provides creative solutions the parties had not considered. But mediation cannot deal with disputes that require a resolution of controverted facts. Mediation does not resolve fact disputes or even allow for discovery. It is a negotiation process, not a trial. If mediation fails, the alternative is to arbitrate or litigate.

A mediator has no power to impose a solution or require a settlement. Parties cannot contract for binding mediation because that would be a contract to make a contract. That is impossible, because in a contract to make a contract there is no meeting of the minds concerning the essential terms. A mediator merely guides the parties' negotiations by helping them to see the ramifications of their dispute, keeping them from creating obstacles to negotiations, making suggestions, and encouraging them to be pragmatic. A settlement may be a compromise or a new "quid pro quo" undertaking, that is, an exchange of things or promises having similar value. A mediator may bring some special quality to the process by being a respected expert, a jurist, or a government official. Retired judges often are excellent mediators. Suppose two merchants have a dispute and both happen to have the same banker. They might agree to meet with the banker to obtain his or her advice about how to resolve the matter. The banker would be a mediator, a facilitator. The banker might be able to persuade the merchants to make a pragmatic settlement that maintains harmony in the community.

Although a mediator may be selected because of his or her special expertise, a party cannot claim he or she relied on the mediator's advice as a condition to the settlement or assert a claim that the mediator gave erroneous advice. Parties must settle on the basis of their own information and for their own reasons. They retain complete control over the terms of any settlement agreement. If a mediator understands how the matter would be handled and resolved in a court of law, his or her insights may be useful in directing settlement negotiations. There is the underlying premise that if the parties do not settle, their matter will be resolved according to the law.

One of the values of mediation is that the parties can pursue it as soon as the disagreement becomes manifest. The sooner a matter is mediated the better. The parties can avoid the expense of litigation. Even arbitration is more expensive and more time consuming. However, if there is serious disagreement about the underlying facts, mediation will not be useful. Mediation does not allow for the presentation of evidence. There is no one to persuade other than the parties themselves. If the dispute is already in litigation, a court may select a mediator for the parties. Then the parties have a right to expect a resolution that approximates what the law would do.

The mediator should be a magistrate or other person trained in the law. The parties should be represented by their lawyers.

Unfortunately, some lawyers seem reluctant to initiate mediation because they feel that any such move is an indication of weakness. Some lawyers and some parties need a little shove to get them to mediate. Consider the well-publicized disputes between airlines and pilot unions: Negotiations drag on for months, the pilots give notice they will strike, then the federal government steps in to provide mediation services to protect the public. The dispute is resolved in mediation. But neither party will initiate mediation on its own. Experience shows that litigants are often able to mediate their differences when a court orders them to mediate. When the parties or opposing lawyers know and respect each other, there is a better chance they can initiate mediation without being pushed into it. If you can find a way of getting your client's matter into mediation early, you will do him or her a great service. But your client should not enter mediation with the idea that the mediator will be on your side or, somehow, force the other side to your point of view.

A mediator may insist on a written contract that provides, among other things:

- The mediator shall have no responsibility to obtain a certain result.
- The mediator is not liable for the consequences of any agreement that is reached.
- The parties will not ask the mediator to be a witness in any subsequent trial—assuming the matter does not settle; the mediator's file and records are confidential.
- The parties will not use anything that is said by the other party or mediator as evidence.

The parties should agree on how the mediator is to be paid. The parties may be asked to affirm that they have come to mediation in good faith. The contract may provide a method of declaring that the mediation is ended. That is important, because mediation may go on for several days and arrive at a point where everyone is uncertain about the parties' positions, but it is clear the parties are not going to settle. The mediator determines when the process is concluded and then makes a formal declaration that the conference is ended. If the matter is already in litigation, the litigation process must resume. If the matter is not in suit, the parties are free to commence an action.

Mediation Procedures

There is no single prescribed procedure for mediating. A procedure that works in one matter may be useless in another. There are too many variables and, again, the process is voluntary. The following steps are intended to illustrate how a mediator could proceed. First, there is just one mediator, although a mediator may have a staff to provide assistance. The mediator may be appointed by a court if the matter is in litigation, or appointed by a governmental agency if the matter is subject to governmental regulation, or the mediator may be selected by the parties. Once selected, the mediator takes charge of the arrangements and procedures. The mediator must anticipate the probable length of the mediation conference. The mediator must schedule a conference for some time and place that is convenient for the parties.

A mediator may request each party to submit a position paper before the conference. A position paper should tell the mediator what he or she needs to know about the party's claims and defenses and suggest how to resolve the matter. Also, a party may comment on the opposing party's position. Mediators like position papers because position papers provide vital information and force parties to prepare. Usually mediators declare that they will keep the position papers confidential but they are free to use the information. Of course, in a court of law, a party could not submit anything to a judge without providing a copy to the opposing party. But mediation is not a court procedure. The parties may be more candid if they do not have to exchange their position papers. A mediator is not a judge and will not be making any decisions. A party may request the opportunity to exchange position papers if the party believes that will be helpful. But the mediator must decide on the best procedure and control the process. A position paper must be drafted carefully to advocate the client's cause but not disclose privileged information. It must be as accurate as possible. You may assist in drafting position papers.

A mediation may be conducted at the mediator's office, an attorney's office, conference center, courtroom, or hotel. Some business mediations are conducted at retreats, such as a resort. The conference room should be large enough to accommodate all the people who are involved. There should be a separate caucus room for each party, where they can talk without being overheard. The more conveniences the better: restrooms, telephones, fax machines, food, soda, coffee, comfortable chairs. The mediator is in charge. The mediator may make some preliminary remarks for the benefit of those who have not been through the process. Preliminary remarks are designed to make everyone feel comfortable and motivate the parties to negotiate. A mediator may describe the role he or she intends to take, the procedures to be followed, and what he or she expects of the parties. The mediator may outline the nature of the dispute and identify issues as he or she understands them. The mediator may allow opening statements from each side. The value is the parties get to say something in their own words and know the other side has heard it. But the mediator should have a clear understanding with each speaker that his or her opening remarks will not be argumentative and will not create obstacles to a compromise. Too many lawyers feel they have to take the offense—as they would at a trial. A mediator should disallow any opening remarks by the parties (lawyers) if the mediator senses the remarks would be counterproductive.

After the preliminaries, the mediator may ask the parties to adjourn to their respective caucus rooms. The mediator then meets with one of the parties to discuss the party's position and what the party could do to move the matter toward a settlement. If the matter involves a claim, the mediator usually starts with the petitioner. If the matter involves a union seeking a contract with a corporation, the mediator usually starts with the union to ascertain the union's current position and obtain a new proposal he or she can take to the corporation. The mediator may play the "devil's advocate" to get a party to modify his or her position in the initial proposal. The caucus may last fifteen minutes or several hours. In the meantime, the opposing party simply waits. Hence, the need for conveniences and comfort. You might even bring another file to work on during periods of "down time."

Next, the mediator meets with the other party to discuss the first party's current position and elicit a response, hopefully, a new proposal. The mediator might even make suggestions for a proposal. The mediator keeps going back and forth until the parties arrive at a settlement or an impasse. While caucusing with a party, a mediator may raise questions about the quality of the party's evidence, its admissibility, and credibility. If there is a problem, the party may be more inclined to settle. A mediator may look to solutions not provided by the law. For example, sometimes the mediator can obtain an apology for a party that is worth more than the money a court could award.

A mediator can play various roles. He or she may be a go-between who delivers messages between the parties. Sometimes a go-between is essential because the parties or their lawyers simply cannot communicate directly without being offensive and creating barriers to a settlement. A mediator may have experience and insight to share. For example, two lawyers who are dissolving their partnership may have some disputes about dividing the business, clients, and so forth. They may look to a third lawyer who has had a similar experience and whom they both respect to mediate their matter. They need someone who sees the big picture and can give friendly advice. Suppose an architect and a contractor have a dispute they want to resolve. They may need someone who understands the problem from both perspectives, someone who can communicate with them, someone who can see the big picture and is able to propose creative alternative solutions. They may chose someone in the building business whom they both respect. Sometimes parties just need to listen to someone for whom they have great respect but who can play the devil's advocate without being offensive. A mediator should not let negotiations become encumbered by details. A mediator needs to gauge the situation and use judgment in deciding how to proceed. Even then, the process should be kept flexible.

The mediator's job does not end when the parties "shake hands." The settlement agreement should be reduced to a writing while the parties are still there. The settlement agreement may require additional documents, such as a release, the revision of an existing contract, a confession of judgment, or the like. Questions may continue to arise. The mediator should remain involved, or at least available, until the concluding documents are executed. Of course, there is always the possibility that the parties might disagree about the terms of their settlement or how the settlement is to be accomplished. If that happens, the mediator could become a witness and his or her file become evidence. That is quite a different matter than trying to use the mediator as a witness concerning the original dispute.

Anyone who expects to engage in mediation should study the principles and advice in *Getting to Yes* (*Negotiating Agreement Without Giving In*), 2nd ed., by Roger Fisher and William Ury (New York: Penguin Books USA, 1991) and *Difficult Conversations*, by Douglas Stone, Bruce Patton, and Sheila Heen (Random House, Inc., 1999).

Arbitration

A matter may be placed in arbitration on any of three bases. (1) Statutes and regulations mandate arbitration of certain disputes. (2) Many contracts require parties to arbitrate disputes that arise between them concerning the contract. Some of the kinds of contracts that mandate arbitration are employment contracts, construction project contracts, insurance contracts concerning coverage issues, collective bargaining contracts, sale of real estate contracts, and sale of merchandise contracts. Automobile manufacturers ask dissatisfied customers to arbitrate warranty disputes and cost-of-repair disputes. (3) When parties agree they cannot resolve their dispute, they may voluntarily enter into a contract to arbitrate. Many organizations encourage members to resolve differences through arbitration. For example, some lawyers' associations encourage members to submit fee disputes to arbitration.

A contract to arbitrate should state whether the award is advisory or binding. It should provide for the number of arbitrators, specify how the arbitrators are to be selected, establish the scope of submission, and describe the kind of award the tribunal can make. The scope of submission delineates the dispute that the tribunal is to resolve. The tribunal's jurisdiction is limited by the scope of submission. The arbitrators must not decide matters beyond the scope of submission. Needless to say, it is a very important part of arbitration agreement. Parties may agree to arbitrate questions of fact and questions of law. This is true even though the arbitrator may not be a judge or lawyer.

Arbitration resembles civil litigation in various ways. Arbitration is designed to bring disputes to conclusion on an evenhanded basis, consistent with the parties' scope of submission. A tribunal is like a judge. It should be neutral, independent, and not caucus with either party. A tribunal hears evidence and resolves fact disputes. Parties may use subpoenas to compel witnesses to appear at an arbitration hearing and give evidence. Parties and witnesses must testify under oath. A tribunal determines the parties' rights and obligations and makes an award. In binding arbitration the award can be reduced to a judgment and enforced through legal procedures. Parties may reject a nonbinding award. If rejected, it still may be the basis for negotiating a settlement.

Arbitration differs from civil litigation in that it is less concerned with rules of law and legal standards. A tribunal does not have an official record (transcript) of the proceedings. However, a party may arrange with a court reporter for a private transcript. A tribunal has no power to add other persons as parties even if another person's participation is necessary to a full resolution. Many arbitrators tend to seek compromise solutions as a basis for their awards. Although parties may expect their tribunal to follow the law, a tribunal's misunderstanding about the law or misapplication of the law is not grounds for setting aside an award. There is no right of appeal from an arbitration award. The only grounds for voiding an arbitration award is that the tribunal exceeded its authority or perpetrated a fraud, or the prevailing party perpetrated a fraud. To contest a binding award, a party must bring a civil action against the prevailing party and tribunal. If the parties have a contract to arbitrate but one of them elects to commence a civil action, the civil action will control unless the defendant raises the right to arbitrate as an affirmative defense. The defendant may use the parties' arbitration agreement to support a motion for dismissal.

A number of attributes make arbitration attractive as an alternative to civil litigation. A tribunal is specially created to handle the one matter. The tribunal will be ready to proceed as soon as they are. Arbitration is not encumbered by rules of civil procedure and rules of evidence. Consequently, the parties' preparation for an arbitration hearing may be less extensive. Discovery is minimal if allowed. The parties' presentation of evidence may be streamlined. They may agree to submit their respective versions of the facts through affidavits, summaries, and experts' reports. They may elect to present their arguments in written form or orally. Depending on the scope of submission, a tribunal may select remedies not afforded by courts. Parties should consider the ramifications of arbitration before agreeing to it. For example, if a party's position is based on some rule of law, the tribunal's election not to apply that rule is not grounds for avoiding the arbitration award. If a party seriously questions the truth of the opposing party's evidence, arbitration may provide less opportunity to challenge the evidence. Technical defenses have less appeal. Parties may avoid the cost of discovery, but then they do not have the benefits of discovery. Nevertheless, arbitration usually produces reasonable results, albeit not the results a court would order.

Arbitration cannot be used to resolve probate matters, divorce, adoption, child custody, or to determine title to real estate, because the public has an interest in the proper disposition of such matters. A contract to arbitrate an illegal contract dispute is unenforceable. For example, if the parties agreed to arbitrate a dispute over a gambling debt and then one reneged, the reluctant party could not be compelled to arbitrate.

Scope of Submission

An arbitration agreement must define the scope of submission. The scope of submission is the grant of authority to the tribunal. The tribunal's authority is similar to a court's jurisdiction over the parties and over the subject matter. The agreement should clearly identify the transaction or occurrence to which the agreement applies. It should identify the nature of the dispute. If possible, it should state the issues to be resolved. It should instruct the tribunal concerning the type of relief it may award. It may identify the standards and measures the parties want the tribunal to apply. For example, the parties could establish high-low parameters for the tribunal's award, so the petitioner would receive at least something, but the respondent would not be at risk of a runaway award. Of course, the parties would not tell the tribunal about the parameters, because that might skew the process.[1] Parties may amend the scope of submission, and the tribunal is bound by the parties' amendments. Generally, an arbitration tribunal is not authorized to determine disputes concerning the scope of its power. A court of general jurisdiction that has jurisdiction over the parties can determine the scope of the parties' submission to arbitration.

Uniform Arbitration Act

At least forty states have adopted the Uniform Arbitration Act, or some version of it. The remaining states have statutes that are variations on the act. This act provides rules for conducting arbitration proceedings and defines the role of the civil justice system to support arbitration. Parties may incorporate the Uniform Arbitration Act procedures into their arbitration agreement by reference. Furthermore, parties may modify the procedures by agreement. For example, an arbitration agreement may specify whether the tribunal will have one, three, or five arbitrators. The agreement may specify how the arbitrators are to be chosen. However, in states that have adopted the Uniform Arbitration Act, written contracts to arbitrate are construed in light of that act. Therefore, if the contract to arbitrate has failed to provide guidance on how to manage some aspect of the arbitration, the arbitrators or the court may look to the Uniform Arbitration Act to supplement the contract or to help construe the contract. Agreements to arbitrate commonly incorporate by reference the provisions of the Uniform Arbitration Act.

The Uniform Arbitration Act, 1 section 6, expressly provides that any party has a right to be represented by an attorney at law. Nevertheless, the act does not exclude nonlawyers from participating. If the matter is already in litigation and being arbitrated pursuant to a court rule or order, paralegals may not sit as arbitrators or represent parties. If a dispute arises over whether the parties have an agreement to arbitrate, either party may commence a civil action in which the plaintiff asks the court to determine whether there is a contract to arbitrate and/or the scope of the submission to arbitrate and/or the scope of the arbitration tribunal's authority. Either party may commence an action to have a court determine their right to arbitrate or not arbitrate or the scope of the arbitration. Otherwise, an arbitration tribunal would have absolute power, and courts cannot permit that.

Suppose, for example, the XYZ Corporation sells many drill presses to the Star Tool Company, and the two companies have a contract to arbitrate any dispute that arises between them concerning quality and performance of the products. Suppose the Star Tool Company bought some parts from a subsidiary of XYZ and contends the parts are defective. Suppose Star Tool demands to arbitrate the matter in accordance with the arbitration agreement but the subsidiary refuses. Star Tool argues that the agreement with XYZ applies to the subsidiary. The dispute may be brought to court for resolution. Under the Uniform Arbitration Act, section 2, Star Tool may serve and file a motion in a court that has jurisdiction over the subsidiary for an order compelling the subsidiary corporation to submit to arbitration. Because the subsidiary denies it is obligated by the XYZ contract to arbitrate, the court will have to order a trial to determine whether the contract applies to the subsidiary.

The Uniform Arbitration Act provides that the court shall determine the issue in a summary manner. In other words, the case shall be accelerated on the trial calendar for an early determination. The court should allow discovery to the extent needed. Discovery should be limited to the existence of the contract to arbitrate. The court has authority to enjoin a tribunal from arbitrating while the litigation is pending. The only issue for the court is whether the arbitration agreement applies to the subsidiary.

Suppose that instead of asking for arbitration, Star Tool sues the subsidiary corporation for money damages, claiming a breach of contract because the parts were defective, and the subsidiary corporation defends against the suit by alleging that the parties must arbitrate under the agreement with XYZ. The subsidiary must allege the arbitration agreement in its answer as an affirmative defense. Either party has the right to move the court to determine the arbitration issue in a summary fashion, as a separate matter. If the court concludes that the contract with XYZ applies to its subsidiary, the court will order the parties to arbitrate and enjoin or dismiss the civil action. If the court concludes the arbitration agreement does not apply to the subsidiary, the civil action will proceed and the affirmative defense will be stricken. The point is, courts will litigate the issue of whether parties have a legal duty to arbitrate, and that issue should be scheduled for an early determination.

Arbitration Procedures

The arbitration agreement may prescribe hearing procedures. To the extent the agreement is silent or ambiguous, the arbitrators determine the procedure. Note, the arbitrators may construe the terms of the arbitration agreement as long as they are dealing with a matter that is within the scope of submission.

The petitioner must mail or deliver a demand for arbitration to the respondent. (See Exhibit 23.1.) The respondent must accept or reject the demand. If the respondent rejects the demand, the petitioner may file a civil action to compel arbitration. If the demand is accepted, the parties must begin the process of selecting arbitrators.

The number of arbitrators and manner of selecting them should be spelled out in the arbitration agreement. A tribunal may be composed of just one arbitrator or three or five. The process favors an odd number, because a mere majority may make

EXHIBIT 23.1   *DEMAND FOR ARBITRATION*   *Courtesy of the American Arbitration Association*

American Arbitration Association

_____**ARBITRATION RULES***
(Enter the name of the applicable rules.)

To institute proceedings, please send two copies of this demand *and the arbitration agreement*, with the filing fee as provided in the rules, to the AAA. Send the original demand to the respondent.

DEMAND FOR ARBITRATION

DATE: _____

TO: Name _____

Address _____
(of the Party on Whom the Demand Is Made)

City and State _____ ZIP Code _____

Telephone (   )_____ Fax (   ) _____

Name of Representative _____
(if Known)

Representative's Address_____

Name of Firm (if Applicable) _____

City and State_____ ZIP Code_____

Telephone (   ) _____ Fax (   ) _____

The below named claimant, a party to an arbitration agreement contained in a written contract dated _____ and providing for arbitration under the _____ Arbitration Rules of the American Arbitration Association, hereby demands arbitration thereunder.

THE NATURE OF THE DISPUTE:

THE CLAIM OR RELIEF SOUGHT (the Amount, if Any):

TYPES OF BUSINESS: Claimant _____ Respondent _____

HEARING LOCALE REQUESTED: _____
(City and State)

DOES THIS DISPUTE ARISE OUT OF AN EMPLOYMENT RELATIONSHIP?   ❏ Yes   ❏ No

You are hereby notified that copies of our arbitration agreement and this demand are being filed with the American Arbitration Association at its _____ regional office with a request that it commence administration of the arbitration. Under the rules, you may file an answering statement within fifteen days after notice from the administrator.

Signed_____ Title _____
(May Be Signed by a Representative)

Name of Claimant _____

Address (to Be Used in Connection with This Case)_____

Name of Firm (if Applicable)_____

City and State_____ ZIP Code_____

Telephone (   )_____ Fax (   )_____

Name of Representative_____

Representative's Address _____

City and State _____ ZIP Code _____

Telephone (   )_____ Fax (   )_____

MEDIATION is a nonbinding process. The mediator assists the parties in working out a solution that is acceptable to them. If you wish for the AAA to contact the other parties to ascertain whether they wish to mediate this matter, please check this box or list them on the back (there is no additional administrative fee for this service).

Form G2-5/99

* If you have a question about which rules apply or the address of the nearest regional office, please contact the AAA (1-800-778-7879).

the award, unless the contract to arbitrate requires unanimity. An even number of arbitrators may lead to a division without a majority. If there is just one arbitrator, the parties may go through a list of names until they can agree on one. There are various ways of making a list of potential arbitrators. One way is for each party to make a list. They review the lists together. Both lists may mention some of the same persons. Then the parties may choose from among those persons.

If the parties cannot agree on the selection, they may apply to a court to appoint an arbitrator. The Uniform Arbitration Act, section 3, provides that where the parties cannot agree on the selection of an arbitrator or arbitrators, a court may appoint the tribunal for them. Suppose a contract between a school district and the local teachers' union provides for arbitration of a wage dispute, and each party may nominate one arbitrator and the two nominees must select another. If the two nominees cannot agree on a third, the parties may move a court to appoint the third. The court must comply with the terms of the arbitration agreement in selecting arbitrators. For example, if the arbitration agreement specifies that at least one arbitrator must be a lawyer, the court should appoint a lawyer. If the agreement is silent or unintelligible or impossible to apply, the court may appoint arbitrators for the parties.

If the tribunal has more than one arbitrator, they must elect one to be chief. The chief manages the tribunal's calendar, sends notices, and communicates with the parties about the process. The chief should not have any communication with parties about the merits of the dispute. The tribunal must give a reasonable notice of the time and place of the hearing, so all parties have an opportunity to prepare and be heard. The Uniform Arbitration Act requires certified mail be used. The arbitrators may order a postponement, continuances, or recesses as they deem appropriate. If the notice was proper, the arbitrators may proceed with the hearing and make an award even though a party fails to appear. That party is considered to be in default and waives her or his right to object to any aspect of the proceedings, except to the scope of submission and fraud.

Parties do not have a right to conduct discovery, in the absence of an express agreement allowing discovery. They cannot serve interrogatories or demand records or require inspections. They cannot compel another party to undergo an independent medical examination. However, if some discovery is necessary, a party must move the tribunal for leave to do the discovery. If the motion is granted, the discovery will be limited. There is no right to take depositions to preserve testimony and present it in the form of a transcript.

Arbitration Hearing

A hearing allows each side to tell its story and provide supporting evidence. But the Rules of Evidence do not apply, not unless the arbitration agreement provides that they do. The proof does not have to meet legal standards. For example, an expert's opinion may not be based on reasonable certainty; proof of a fact may not be by a preponderance of the evidence. The procedures do not have to emulate those used by courts. The results or solutions are not limited to legal remedies.

To the extent that the scope of submission does not delineate how the hearing is to be conducted, a tribunal has broad authority to make its own rules. Arbitrators do not take an oath of office unless state law specifically requires them to do so.

However, when arbitration is mandated by statute, as where some insurance claims must be arbitrated, the law may impose an oath such as the following:

> I will act in good faith and with integrity and fairness. I have disclosed to the parties prior to this hearing any interest or relationship likely to affect impartiality or which might create an appearance of partiality or bias.

This statement highlights the expectation parties have of their arbitrators.

Arbitration hearings need not be recorded, but any party may arrange, at its own expense, to have a record made. In the absence of any record, problems in the hearing that require a court's intervention must be shown by way of affidavits from persons in attendance. Each party must be given an opportunity to present evidence to support his or her position and to challenge the opposing party's evidence. When the scope of submission provides that neither side will present live testimony, the evidence must be in the form of documents, as in a motion for summary judgment.

The Uniform Arbitration Act, section 7, authorizes duly constituted arbitration tribunals to issue subpoenas to compel witnesses to attend the hearing. Subpoenas may be obtained from the local court on due showing that the arbitration matter is pending. A subpoena must be served in the manner provided by court's rules. See Rules 4 and 45 of the Federal Rules of Civil Procedure. Note that petitioners and respondents should never be the ones to serve subpoenas. If a witness fails to comply with a subpoena, the arbitration tribunal cannot discipline him or her. The parties or the tribunal must move the court to take action against the recalcitrant witness. Parties must pay witnesses fees and mileage as provided by state statute. Evidence must be taken under oath; therefore, a tribunal must be able to administer oaths to witnesses. The Uniform Arbitration Act provides that the arbitrators have authority to administer oaths. The oath is an important safeguard. A person who violates the oath is subject to criminal prosecution for perjury.

The petitioner presents his or her evidence first. The Uniform Arbitration Act expressly preserves the right of cross-examination. Arbitrators have the authority to rule on objections to evidence. Even though the rules of evidence may not be controlling, some common sense limitations on evidence are required. Matters that are privileged may cause some difficulties. If the evidence offered is reasonably appropriate for the tribunal to consider, tribunals are prone to hear it. Consequently, objections are sometimes a matter of posturing or for pointing out the weaknesses. A tribunal that has more than one arbitrator must establish a procedure for ruling on objections. Usually, the chief arbitrator assumes that role or rulings may be by consensus. The respondent must wait until the petitioner rests to present evidence. The petitioner has a right to present rebuttal evidence, and so does the respondent. When the parties complete their presentations, the tribunal declares the matter is "submitted." Neither side may present evidence thereafter.

If the tribunal has more than one arbitrator, all must attend the entire hearing. The reason is that the decision process requires all the arbitrators to hear the same evidence and participate in the deliberations. Full participation is essential to the process. Each arbitrator's input and the opportunity to change the minds of other arbitrators is as important as their vote. Therefore, if one arbitrator of three is absent, the hearing cannot proceed. The parties could write a new contract to arbitrate and choose to have fewer arbitrators.

Arbitration Award

The arbitration award is the tribunal's decision. It must be made within the time specified in the agreement to arbitrate. If no time frame was specified, it must be within a reasonable time. The law does not impose a certain time period. The award may be unanimous or by a simple majority, unless the arbitration agreement provides otherwise. The award must be in writing but not in any particular form. The writing does not have to state reasons for the award. It does not have to be notarized. The award must make clear what has been decided, and describe the authority by which it was made. This is important so that the award can be filed with a court and converted into a court judgment. The award must be signed by all the arbitrators who concur in it. A dissenting arbitrator need not sign and is at liberty to submit a statement of dissent to the parties.

An award must comply with the scope of submission. It should be complete on its face. If the award is incomplete, it may nevertheless be enforced as far as it is within the scope of submission, but an award that is substantively incomplete is voidable. If the award goes beyond the scope of submission, the part of the award that is within the scope of submission is binding and enforceable. For example, a truckers' union and management agree to arbitrate a new payment schedule. The agreement's scope of submission provides that the payments are to be based on mileage. The arbitrator awards truckers eighty cents per mile and seventy-five dollars a day for any forced layovers because of weather. An award for layovers goes beyond the scope of submission. It is not binding. The arbitrator may have added it knowing the parties might consider it as a recommendation that would make the rest of the package more acceptable.

If an award requires the parties to take some action, the procedure they must follow should be made clear. An award should not require the parties to make any calculations to determine their obligations. The award binds the parties and anyone who is in privity with them. The award need not be filed with any court, unless the prevailing party wants to use it as the basis for obtaining a court judgment.

Unless the scope of submission provides otherwise, the award may determine which party is to pay the arbitrators' fees and expenses. The award may divide the fees and expenses between the parties. However, the tribunal is not authorized to award attorneys' fees to either party (Uniform Arbitration Act, section 10).

If a tribunal fails to make an award within a reasonable time, the parties may apply to a court for an order compelling the tribunal to act. The court may order the tribunal to issue an award by a certain date. If the tribunal fails to comply, a party may deliver an objection to the tribunal members. The objection has the effect of disqualifying the tribunal from making any award. The rationale for this rule is that after an unreasonable delay, the arbitrators probably have forgotten the evidence and arguments of the parties, so the delay has impaired the validity of the process. If a party fails to object to a delay until after the award is made, that party waives the right to object. A party may not wait to see if the award is favorable, and if not, then object.

The arbitrators may deliver the award in person or send it to the parties by certified mail (Uniform Arbitration Act, section 8). The award must be of the type authorized by the agreement to arbitrate. Suppose two companies agree to arbitrate a patent infringement dispute. The scope of the submission is for the tribunal to determine whether an infringement occurred and if so, what the petitioner's money damages are. Suppose the tribunal decides an infringement occurred and awards a small amount of money damages, but also awards the infringing party a license to use the patent in the future. The tribunal's award exceeds its authority. Insofar as the tribunal acts outside its authority, the award is invalid and may be set aside by a court.

Modifications of an Arbitration Award

If an award contains an apparent clerical error, misdescription, or miscalculation, a party may apply to the tribunal for clarification. Also, a party may apply for a modification of an award on the grounds the tribunal exceeded the scope of submission. To the extent the tribunal has exceeded its authority, it should grant the modification. A party may ask the tribunal to reword an award where the language creates some collateral problem for the party as long as the change does not affect the substance of the award. A motion to correct or modify an award limits the court's authority to that of giving effect to the tribunal's intent. A court does not have authority to change the substance or effect of the award.

An application for modification must be made within twenty days after the award is delivered to the party. Do not count the day on which it is delivered. Of course, a copy of an application for modification must be served on the other party. If an application for modification is duly made, the opposing party has a right to serve and deliver an objection to the modification. The objection must be delivered to the tribunal within ten days.

The Uniform Arbitration Act, section 13, authorizes either party to apply to a court within ninety days after delivery of the award for a correction or modification of the award on the same grounds as when applying to a tribunal. A party could resort to asking a court for corrections or modifications because the arbitrators are no longer available, the time for applying to the tribunal has expired, or the tribunal has refused to make corrections. Why would the arbitrators ever refuse to make corrections that should be made? They might try to use the refusal to force payment of their bills for services.

Vacating an Arbitration Award

Either or both parties have a right to move a court to vacate the arbitration award on the following grounds:

1. The award was procured by corruption, fraud, or other undue means.
2. An arbitrator appointed as a neutral was partial, an arbitrator was corrupt, or misconduct prejudicing the rights of a party occurred.
3. The arbitrators exceeded their powers.
4. The arbitrators refused to postpone the hearing even though sufficient cause was shown to justify a postponement, or refused to hear evidence material to the controversy, or otherwise conducted the hearing contrary to provisions of the Uniform Arbitration Act so as to prejudice substantial rights of a party.

5. No arbitration agreement existed, and the issue was not determined adversely in proceedings under the Uniform Arbitration Act, section 2, and the party did not participate in the arbitration hearing without raising the objection.

A motion to vacate must be made within ninety days after the party receives the award. If the parties receive the award on different days, the time period differs accordingly. When the ground for vacating the award is fraud or corruption, the ninety-day period does not begin to run until the party discovers the fraud or corruption or has reason to know about it. A motion to vacate may be combined with a motion to modify the award. The motion must be served on the opposing party in the manner in which the state courts allow a summons and complaint to be served. Ordinarily, that will be similar to Rule 4 of the Federal Rules of Civil Procedure.

If a court vacates an award, the court shall order a new arbitration hearing before a new tribunal. The court does not usurp the parties' agreement to arbitrate. Instead, it acts to enforce the agreement. The new arbitrators must be chosen in the manner provided by the agreement to arbitrate. If no agreement existed, the court may appoint the new arbitrator or arbitrators, or direct how the new arbitrators shall be selected by the parties. For example, a court could prepare a list of five persons and order each party to strike two, leaving one person who will be the arbitrator.

Enforcement of an Arbitration Award

A tribunal's arbitration award is not, in itself, enforceable against a party. If a party refuses to comply with a binding award, the prevailing party may move the court to confirm the award. A motion to confirm the award must state that the arbitration was duly conducted and the award duly made. The motion must be served on the opposing party in the same manner as a summons and complaint. The moving party must attach to the motion a copy of the arbitration agreement, arbitration award, and any modifications or corrections. If no objection is made or the opposing party's objections are overruled, the court adopts the award and orders an entry of judgment in the same words or to the same effect as the arbitration award. The clerk of court enters the award in the court's judgment book. At that point, the prevailing party has a civil judgment that may be enforced like any other judgment.

Arbitrators' Judicial Immunity

Arbitration is a quasi-judicial procedure. Arbitrators have to exercise judgment in deciding how to resolve the dispute. Arbitrators should not have to worry that if they decide the matter in a certain way, they will be sued by a disgruntled party. The concern is not that the arbitrator might be held liable, it's that people will not agree to be arbitrators if they are *subject* to being sued. Therefore, the law provides that arbitrators are immune from suits for malfeasance in the performance of their duties. They have no civil liability for negligence or even fraud. Proof of fraud on the part of an arbitrator is a basis for having the award set aside, but it will not subject the arbitrator to personal liability. An arbitrator who has committed fraud is not entitled to compensation for his or her services.

Arbitrators' Compensation

The agreement to arbitrate usually provides how the parties will pay the arbitrators for their service. If no agreement exists, the arbitrators may determine, as part of the award, how the parties shall pay the fees.

TECHNOLOGY NOTES

The American Arbitration Association (AAA) has a Web site: http://www.adr.org. The "adr" is a reference to "alternative dispute resolution." The Web site provides current versions of the federal Administrative Dispute Resolution Act of 1996 and the Federal Arbitration Act. The Web site also provides access to all the states' arbitration statutes. The AAA distributes various publications through the Web site.

SUMMARY

Arbitration and mediation are alternatives to civil litigation for resolving private disputes. ADR generally is fast and economical. Mediation is most useful when the dispute is new and the parties have not spent time and effort to buttress their positions. Paralegals may handle any aspect of the mediation and arbitration processes. A person does not have to be a lawyer to be an arbitrator or mediator, or to represent another person in these procedures.

When parties mediate their dispute, they retain control over the resolution of the matter. The premise of mediation is that the parties are willing to compromise for the purpose of resolving the dispute. If a party is not willing to compromise, she or he should not enter into mediation.

A mediator has no power to force a settlement. A mediator must rely on persuasion to bring the parties together. A mediator looks to the parties' positions in the dispute and tries to help the parties find a way of moving to a settlement, rather than making judgments about the parties' truthfulness or the persuasiveness of the evidence.

If a mediator helps the parties to arrive at a settlement, the settlement should be reduced to writing and accepted by the parties before the mediator withdraws. The parties' settlement does not have to comport with legal remedies.

Almost any dispute involving contract rights, property damage, or personal injury may be arbitrated. The parties' agreement determines the scope of arbitration and should address all matters of procedure that concern the parties. Most states have adopted the Uniform Arbitration Act. The act directs how the arbitration is to be conducted insofar as the parties' agreement to arbitrate is silent on any question that arises.

When parties submit their dispute to arbitration, they give up control over the resolution. They give to the arbitrators the right to decide how the controversy should be resolved. The arbitrators are supposed to base their award on the evidence and the law. However, an arbitration award cannot be set aside merely because the arbitrators made a mistake about what the law is or how the law applies. The parties' agreement to arbitrate must be contractual to be binding and enforceable. The contract may be made before or after the dispute arises.

The parties' agreement to arbitrate must define the scope of submission—that is, it should explain or define the matter that is to be arbitrated, how the arbitration is to be conducted, and what kind of award the arbitrators may make. The scope of submission determines the arbitrators' authority. If the agreement to arbitrate has prescribed a certain method for selecting arbitrators, the court should try to follow it. Otherwise, the court has broad discretion in selecting arbitrators for the parties.

Parties do not have a right to conduct discovery of the type provided by the Federal Rules of Civil Procedure. Parties may take depositions for the purpose of presenting the deponent's testimony in that form. Parties may obtain subpoenas from a court to compel a witness to appear and testify at an arbitration hearing. The parties may agree to present some or all of their evidence in the form of documentation. An arbitration tribunal is not required to follow rules of evidence. Nevertheless, a party may object to another party's evidence, and the tribunal decides for itself what evidence it should hear and consider.

A tribunal must make an award. The award must be in writing. The award need not explain the tribunal's rationale for the award. A binding arbitration award may be filed with a court of general jurisdiction and be confirmed and become the basis for a court judgment. The judgment then may be enforced like any court judgment. A court may order corrections to an arbitration award in order to make the award comport with the arbitrators' manifest intent, as when a clerical error or an error in calculations has occurred. A party may petition (move) a court of general jurisdiction to vacate an arbitration award on various grounds.

Arbitrators have an immunity from civil suit even if they engage in a fraud in making their award. The defrauded party's only remedy is to have the award set aside. Arbitrators who engage in fraud are not entitled to payment for their services.

Key Terms

arbitration
arbitrator
award
binding arbitration
matter
mediation

nonbinding arbitration
petitioner
respondent
scope of submission
submission
tribunal

Review Questions

1. Why does an agreement to arbitrate have to meet the requirements of a contract in order to be enforceable?

2. If the parties include an arbitration agreement in their contract for the sale of property, is the arbitration agreement enforceable even though the parties did not know at that time what disputes might arise under their sales agreement? Why or why not?

3. What value is it to the parties to contract for nonbinding arbitration?

4. How does nonbinding arbitration differ from mediation?

5. Will a court force two parties to arbitrate if they agree that they do not want to arbitrate their dispute and instead want to have a trial?

6. If a dispute arises over the scope of submission in an arbitration agreement, who resolves the dispute?

7. How may an arbitration award be enforced against a party who refuses to abide by the award?

8. What are the advantages of arbitration over civil litigation?

9. What are the advantages of civil litigation over arbitration?

10. What are the limitations on a paralegal's involvement in arbitration?

CASE ASSIGNMENT

You are on Sandra Gillis's legal team representing John Griffin. Ms. Gillis is concerned about agent Burns's legal defenses and thinks that Griffin might do better against Burns by arbitrating the fourth-party action. Furthermore, she would like to get the coverage matter resolved as soon as possible. A local retired judge, Paul Hoffman, is highly respected and might be available to be the arbitrator. Attorney Dolan might prefer to have him rather than the new district court judge. Ms. Gillis believes that she and Ms. Dolan could stipulate to the facts in writing, so arbitration would be very much like a summary judgment motion. Please prepare an arbitration demand letter to Ms. Dolan for Ms. Gillis's signature. Although it is called a "demand letter," your letter should be in the form of a proposal. The proposal should nominate Judge Hoffman to be the arbitrator; suggest binding arbitration; the scope of arbitration is to determine whether agent Burns was negligent in transferring coverage from the pickup to the Camaro without telling John Griffin. Ms. Gillis understands that if Burns could not provide insurance after the sale, the sale is what terminated coverage on the pickup, not Burns. Suggest that the arbitration be conducted at the courthouse in one month. Suggest that Ms. Gillis will prepare a proposed draft of stipulated facts. *Hint:* The letter only needs to be two paragraphs and less than one page.

Endnote

1. Parties could not make such an agreement in civil litigation. The agreement would be considered a fraud on the court. The difference is that the courts serve the public and arbitration is a private matter.

 For additional resources, visit our Web site at www.paralegal.delmar.cengage.com

APPENDICES

APPENDIX A

TIME TABLE FOR LAWYERS IN FEDERAL CIVIL CASES

2000 EDITION
FEDERAL CIVIL JUDICIAL PROCEDURE AND RULES

as amended to January 28, 2000

Rules of Civil Procedure
Rules of Judicial Panel on Multidistrict Litigation
Rules—Habeas Corpus Cases
Rules—Motion Attacking Sentence
Rules of Evidence
Rules of Appellate Procedure
Rules of the Supreme Court

Includes laws through the close of the 106th Congress, First Session (1999)

Title 28, Judiciary and Judicial Procedure
Act June 25, 1948, c. 646, §§ 2 to 39
Appendix:
    Judicial Personnel Financial Disclosure Requirements [Repealed]
    Development of Mechanisms for Resolving Minor Disputes [Codified]
Constitution of the United States
Title 5, Government Organization and Employees
    App. 4—Financial Disclosure Requirements of Federal Personnel
Consolidated Index

This Time Table, prepared by the Publisher's editorial staff as a guide to the user, indicates the time for each of the steps of a civil action as provided by the Federal Rules of Civil Procedure and the Federal Rules of Appellate Procedure. Certain steps governed by statute and by the 1997 Revised Rules of the Supreme Court are also listed. The user should always consult the actual text of the rule or statute. Usually the periods permitted for each of these steps may be

Source: Federal Rules of Civil Procedure, 2000 Educational Edition (St. Paul, MN: West Group, 19).

enlarged by the court in its discretion. In some cases no enlargement is permitted. Citations to supporting authority are in the form "Civ.R._____ " for the Rules of Civil Procedure; "App.R._____ " for the Rules of Appellate procedure; "28 U.S.C.A. § _____" for statutes; and "Supreme Court Rule _____".

ADMISSIONS

Requests for admissions, service of

On any other party after the parties have conferred pursuant to Civ.R. 26(f). Civ.R. 36(a).

Response to requested admissions

Answers or objections must be served within 30 days after service of the request, or such shorter or longer time as court may allow or as parties may agree to in writing. Civ.R. 36(a).

ALTERNATE jurors

The institution of the alternate juror has been abolished. Civ.R. 47, 1991 Advisory Committee note, subd. (b).

ANSWER

To complaint

See also, "Responsive Pleadings," this table.

Service within 20 days after being served with summons and complaint unless a different time is prescribed in a federal statute. Civ.R. 12(a)(1)(A). Service within 60 days after date request is sent for waiver of service of summons or within 90 days after that date if defendant was addressed outside any judicial district of the United States unless a different time is prescribed in a federal statute. Civ.R. 12(a)(1)(B).

Service within 60 days after service upon the United States Attorney, in action against the United States or an officer or agency thereof. Civ.R. 12(a).

The time for responsive pleading is altered by service of Civ.R. 12 motions. See "Responsive Pleadings," this table.

To cross-claim

Service within 20 days after being served with cross-claim. Civ.R. 12(a)(2).

60 days for United States. Civ.R. 12(a).

The time for responsive pleading is altered by service of Civ.R. 12(a) motions, see "Responsive Pleadings," this table.

To third-party complaint

Service of reply within 20 days after service of answer or, if reply is ordered by a court, within 20 days after service of order. Civ.R. 12(a)(2).

60 days for United States. Civ.R. 12(a)(3).

To notice of condemnation

Service within 20 days after service of notice. Civ.R. 71A(e).

Removed actions

20 days after receipt of pleading, or within 20 days after service of summons, or within 5 days after filing of removal petition, whichever is longest. Civ.R. 81(c).

Proceedings to cancel certificates of citizenship under 8 U.S.C.A. § 1451

60 days after service of petition. Civ.R. 81(a)(6).

ANSWERS (or objections) to interrogatories to party

Service within 30 days after service of the interrogatories. A shorter or longer time may be directed by the court or agreed to. Civ.R. 33(b)(3).

APPEAL

As of right

30 days from entry of judgment or order. App.R. 4(a)(1)(A).

District court may extend for excusable neglect or good cause upon motion filed not later than 30 days after expiration of time prescribed by App.R. 4(a); no extension to exceed 30 days past prescribed time or 10 days from entry of order granting motion, whichever occurs later. App.R. 4(a)(5).

60 days in cases in which the United States or its officers, agencies are parties. App.R. 4(a)(1)(B).

If any party files a timely motion of a type specified below, time for appeal for all parties runs from entry of order disposing of last such motion outstanding. App.R. 4(a)(4).

(1) motion for judgment under Civ.R. 50(b);

(2) Motion under Civ.R. 52(b) to amend or make additional findings of fact, whether or not granting the motion would alter the judgement;

(3) motion under Civ.R. 59 to alter or amend judgment;

(4) Motion under Civ.R. 54 for attorney's fees if time to appeal extended under Civ.R. 58.

(5) Motion under Civ.R. 59 for new trial.

(6) Motion for relief under Civ.R. 60 if motion filed no later than 10 days after entry of judgement.

App.R. 4(a)(4).

By other parties, within 14 days of filing of first notice of appeal, or within the time otherwise prescribed by App.R. 4(a), whichever last expires. App.R. 4(a)(3).

By permission	Petition filed with circuit clerk with proof of service within time specified by statute or rule authorizing the appeal, or if no such time is specified, within the time provided by App.R. 4(a) for filing a notice of appeal. App.R. 5(a).
Bankruptcy	If a motion for rehearing under Bankruptcy Rule 8015 is filed in a district court or in a bankruptcy appellate panel, time for appeal to court of appeals runs from entry of order disposing of motion. App.R. 6(b)(2)(A).
Class actions	Within 10 days after entry of order of district court granting or denying class action certification. Civ.R. 23(f).
Inmates	A notice of appeal is timely filed if deposited in the institution's internal mail system on or before the last day for filing. App.R. 4(c), 25(a).
Representation statement	Within 10 days after filing notice of appeal unless court of appeals designates another time, attorney who filed notice shall file with the circuit clerk a statement naming each party represented on appeal by that attorney. App.R. 12(b).
Entry of judgment or order, notice of	Lack of such notice by clerk does not affect time to appeal or relieve or authorize court to relieve party for failure to appeal within time allowed, except as permitted in App.R. 4(a). Civ.R. 77(d).
Record (Appellant)	Within 10 days after filing notice of appeal or entry of an order disposing of last timely remaining motion specified in App.R. 4(a)(4)(A), whichever is later: Appellant to place written order for transcript and file copy of order with clerk; if none to be ordered, file a certificate to that effect; unless entire transcript to be included, file a statement of issues and serve appellee a copy of order or certificate and of statement. App.R. 10(b).
Record (Appellee)	Within 10 days after service of appellant's order or certificate and statement, appellee to file and serve on appellant a designation of additional parts of transcript to be included. Unless within 10 days after designation appellant has ordered such parts and so notified appellee, appellee may within following 10 days either order the parts or move in district court for order requiring appellant to do so. App.R. 10(b).
Record (costs)	At time of ordering, party to make satisfactory arrangements with reporter for payment of cost of transcript. App.R. 10(b)(4).
Record (Reporter)	If transcript cannot be completed within 30 days of receipt of order, reporter shall request extension of time from circuit clerk. App.R. 11(b).
Stay of proceedings to enforce judgment	Effective when supersedeas bond is approved by court. Civ.R. 62(d). Supersedeas bond may be given at or after time of filing notice of appeal or of procuring the order allowing appeal. Civ.R. 62(d).

Briefs	Appellant must serve and file a brief within 40 days after the record is filed. Appellee must serve and file a brief within 30 days after service of the appellant's brief. A reply brief may be filed within 14 days after service of appellee's brief and, except for good cause shown, at least 3 days before argument. A court of appeals may shorten the times allowed for briefs either by local rule for all cases or by order for a particular case. App.R. 31(a).
Transcripts	See "RECORD," ante, this heading.
Tax Court decisions	Review must be obtained by filing a notice of appeal with the Tax Court clerk within 90 days after entry of decision. If a timely notice of appeal is filed by one party, any other party may take an appeal by filing a notice of appeal within 120 days after entry of decision by the Tax Court. If timely motion made to vacate or revise decision, time to file notice of appeal runs from entry of order disposing of motion or entry of new decision, whichever is later. App.R. 13(a).
APPEAL from magistrate judge to district judge under 28 U.S.C.A. § 636(c)(4) and Civ.R. 73(d)	
Notice of Appeal	[This Rule provided as follows, prior to its abrogation:] Filed with clerk of district court within 30 days of entry of judgment. Within 60 days if United States or officer or agency thereof is a party. Within 15 days after entry of an interlocutory decision or order. Civ.R. 74(a) [Rule 74 abrogated eff. Dec. 1, 1997].
	[This Rule provided as follows, prior to its abrogation:] When timely notice is filed by a party, any other party may file notice within 14 days thereafter or within time otherwise prescribed by Civ.R. 74(a), whichever period last expires. Civ.R. 74(a) [Rule 74 abrogated eff. Dec 1, 1997].
	[This Rule provided as follows, prior to its abrogation:] Upon showing of excusable neglect, time for filing may be extended on motion filed not later than 20 days from expiration of time for filing. Civ.R. 74(a) [Rule 74 abrogated eff. Dec. 1, 1997].
	Running of time for filing terminated as to all parties by timely filing of any of the following motions with the magistrate judge by any party, and the full time for appeal from judgment entered commences to run anew from entry of any of the following orders:
	(1) granting or denying motion for judgment under Civ.R. 50(b);
	(2) granting or denying motion under Civ.R. 52(b) to amend or make additional findings of fact;
	(3) granting or denying motion under Civ.R. 59 to alter or amend judgment;
	(4) denying motion for new trial under Civ.R. 59. Civ.R. 74(a) [prior to its abrogation] [Rule 74 abrogated eff. Dec. 1, 1997].
Joint statement of case	Parties could file in lieu of record within 10 days after filing of notice of appeal, under provisions of this rule prior to its abrogation. Civ.R. 75(b)(1) [Rule 75 abrogated eff. Dec. 1, 1997].
Transcript	Within 10 days after filing notice of appeal appellant to make arrangements for production. Unless entire transcript is to be included, description of parts appellant intends to present must be served on the appellee and filed by the appellant within the 10 day period. If appellee deems transcript of other parts to be necessary, designation of additional parts to be included must be served on the appellant and filed within 10 days after service of appellant's statement. Civ.R. 75(b)(2) [Rule 75 abrogated eff. Dec. 1, 1997].
Statement in lieu of transcript	If no record is available for transcription, parties must file a statement of evidence in lieu of transcript within 10 days after filing of notice of appeal. Civ.R. 75(b)(3) [Rule 75 abrogated eff. Dec. 1, 1997].
Briefs	Appellant to serve and file within 20 days after the filing of transcript, statement of case, or statement of evidence. Civ.R. 75(c)(1)[Rule 75 abrogated eff. Dec. 1, 1997].

Appellee to serve and file within 20 days after service of appellant's brief. Civ.R. 75(c)(2) [Rule 75 abrogated eff. Dec. 1, 1997].

Appellant may serve and file reply brief within 10 days after service of appellee's brief. Civ.R. 75(c)(3) [Rule 75 abrogated eff. Dec. 1, 1997].

If appellee files a cross-appeal, appellee may file a reply brief within 10 days after service of the reply brief of the appellant. Civ.R. 75(c)(4) [Rule 75 abrogated eff. Dec. 1, 1997].

Stay of judgments

Decision of district judge stayed for 10 days during which term a party may petition for rehearing. Civ.R. 76(b) [Rule 76 abrogated eff. Dec. 1, 1997].

APPEAL from magistrate judge under 28 U.S.C.A. § 636(c)(3)

Appeal to court of appeals in identical fashion as appeals from other judgments of district courts. App.R. 3.1. [Rule 3.1 abrogated eff. Dec. 1, 1998].

APPEAL from district court to court of appeals under 28 U.S.C.A. § 636(c)(5)

Petition for leave to appeal filed with clerk of the court of appeals within time provided by App.R. 4(a) for filing notice of appeal, with proof of service on all parties to action in district court. App.R. 5.1(a). [Rule 5.1 abrogated eff. Dec. 1, 1998].

Within 14 days after service of petition for leave to appeal, a party may file an answer or cross petition in opposition. App.R. 5.1(a). [Rule 5.1 abrogated eff. Dec. 1, 1998].

APPEAL to Supreme Court

Direct appeals

30 days after entry of interlocutory or final order, decree or judgment holding Act of Congress unconstitutional under circumstances provided by 28 U.S.C.A. §§ 1252, and 1253. 28 U.S.C.A. § 2101(a), as amended by Act May 24, 1949, c. 139, § 106, 63 Stat. 104. [28 U.S.C.A. § 1252 was repealed and 28 U.S.C.A. § 2101(a) was amended by Pub.L. 100–352, §§ 1, 5(b), June 27, 1988, 102 Stat. 662, 663, respectively. For effective date and applicability to cases, see section 7 of Pub.L. 100–352, set out as 28 U.S.C.A. § 1254 note.]

30 days from interlocutory judgment, order, or decree in any other direct appeal authorized by law from decision of district court. 28 U.S.C.A. § 2101(b).

60 days from final judgment, order, or decree in any other direct appeal authorized by law from decision of district court. 28 U.S.C.A. § 2101(b).

Other appeals and certiorari

90 days after entry of judgment or decree; justice of Supreme Court for good cause shown may extend time for applying for writ of certiorari for period not exceeding 60 days. 28 U.S.C.A. § 2101(c).

Briefs supporting certiorari

No separate brief supporting petition for certiorari shall be filed; see Supreme Court Rule 14.2.

Brief opposing certiorari

30 days after case is placed on the docket unless time is extended by Court or a Justice or by the Clerk; see Supreme Court Rule 15.3.

Brief on merits on appeal or certiorari

By appellant or petitioner, filed within 45 days of the order granting the writ of certiorari or the order noting probable jurisdiction or postponing consideration of jurisdiction; see Supreme Court Rule 25.1.

By appellee or respondent, filed within 30 days after receipt of the brief filed by the appellant or petitioner; see Supreme Court Rule 25.2.

Reply brief, if any, filed within 30 days after receipt of brief for appellee or respondent, but any reply brief to be received by Clerk not later than one week before the date of oral argument. See Supreme Court Rule 25.3.

Stay of mandate pending petition for certiorari

A stay of mandate pending a petition to the Supreme Court for certiorari cannot exceed 90 days unless the period is extended for good cause or unless during the period of stay, the party who obtained the stay files a petition for the writ and notifies the circuit clerk in writing in which case the stay will continue until final disposition by the Supreme Court. The court of appeals must issue the mandate immediately when a copy of the Supreme Court order denying the petition for writ of certiorari is filed. App.R. 41(d)(2).

ATTORNEY'S fees	See "Costs," this table.
BILL of particulars	Abolished. See Civ.R. 12(e), as amended in 1948. See, however, "More definite statement," this table.
CLASS actions	As soon as practicable after commencement court is to determine by order whether action is to be so maintained. Civ.R. 23(c)(1).
CLERICAL mistakes in judgments, orders, or record	May be corrected at any time; but during pendency of appeal, may be corrected before appeal is docketed in the appellate court, and thereafter while appeal pending may be corrected with leave of appellate court. Civ.R. 60(a).
COMPLAINT	Filing commences action—must be served with summons. Civ.R. 3.
	Service of summons and complaint within 120 days after filing. Civ.R. 4(m).
COMPUTATION of time	Exclude day of the act, event or default from which designated period of time begins to run. Include last day of the period so computed unless it is a Saturday, Sunday, or legal holiday, or, when act to be done is the filing of a paper in court, a day on which weather or other conditions have made the office of the clerk of the district court inaccessible, in which event period runs until end of the next day which is not one of the aforementioned days. Civ.R. 6(a).
	Intermediate Saturdays, Sundays, and legal holidays are excluded if the period is less than 11 days. Civ.R. 6(a).
	Exclude day of the act, event, or default that begins the period. Include last day of the period unless it is a Saturday, Sunday, or legal holiday, or, when the act to be done is filing of paper in court, a day on which weather or other conditions have made office of clerk inaccessible. App.R. 26(a).
	Intermediate Saturdays, Sundays, and legal holidays are excluded if the period is less than 7 days, unless stated in calendar days. App.R. 26(a).
	Service by mail is complete upon mailing. Civ.R. 5(b).
	Service by mail or by commercial carrier is complete upon mailing or delivery to the carrier. App.R. 25(c).
	Service by mail adds three days to a period of time which is computed from such service. Civ.R. 6(e). When a party is required or permitted to act within a prescribed period after service of a paper upon that party, three calendar days are added to the period unless the paper is delivered on the date of service stated in the proof of service. App.R. 26(c).
	Legal holidays are defined by Civ.R. 6(a) and App.R. 26(a)(4).
	Supreme Court matters—See Supreme Court Rule 30.
CONDEMNATION of property Answer to notice of condemnation	20 days after service of notice. Civ.R. 71A(e).
COSTS	Taxation on 1 day's notice. Motion to review taxation of costs 5 days after taxation. Civ.R. 54(d).
	Failure to comply with request for waiver of service of summons and to return waiver within time allowed which must be at least 30 days from date request is sent or 60 days from that date for a defendant addressed outside any judicial district of the United States. Civ.R. 4(d).
Attorney's fees and related nontaxable expenses	Motion filed and served no later than 14 days after entry of judgement. Civ.R. 54(d)(2)(B).
CROSS APPEAL Optional appeal from magistrate judge to district judge	Appellee may file reply brief within 10 days after service of reply brief of appellant. Civ.R. 75(c)(4) [Rule 75 abrogated eff. Dec. 1, 1997].

Appellate rules	Within 14 days of filing of first notice of appeal or within the time otherwise prescribed by App.R. 4(a), whichever last expires. App.R. 4(a)(3).
Inmates	Within 14 days after date when first notice of appeal was docketed by the district court. The 14 day period runs from date district court receives first notice of appeal. App.R. 4(c).

DEFAULT

Entry by clerk	No time stated. Civ.R. 55(b).
Entry by court	If party against whom default is sought has appeared, the party shall be served with written notice of application for default judgment at least 3 days prior to hearing on such application. Civ.R. 55(b).

DEFENSES and objections, presentation of

By pleading	See "Answer," this table.
By motion	Motion shall be made before pleading if further pleading is permitted. Civ.R. 12(b).
At trial	Adverse party may assert at trial any defense in law or fact to claim for relief to which such party is not required to serve responsive pleading. Civ.R. 12(b).
Motion affects time for responsive pleading	Service of motion under Civ.R. 12 alters times for responsive pleading. See "Responsive Pleadings," this table.

DEMURRERS   Abolished. Civ.R. 7(c).

DEPOSITIONS   See also, "Interrogatories," "Depositions on written questions," this table.

Notice of filing	Promptly. Civ.R. 30(f)(3) and Civ.R. 31(c).
Notice of taking	Reasonable notice to every party. Civ.R. 30(b).
Objections	As to admissibility, objection may be made at trial or hearing, but subject to Civ.R. 28(b) and 32(d)(3). Civ.R. 32(b).
	As to errors or irregularities in the notice, service promptly. Civ.R. 32(d)(1).
	As to disqualification of officer, objection made before deposition begins or as soon thereafter as disqualification becomes known or could be discovered. Civ.R. 32(d)(2).
	As to competency of witness or competency, relevancy, or materiality of testimony—not waived by failure to make such objection before or during deposition unless the ground might have been obviated or removed if presented at that time. Civ.R. 32(d)(3)(A).
	As to errors and irregularities at oral examination in manner of taking deposition, in the form of questions or answers, in the oath or affirmation, or in conduct of parties, and errors which might be obviated, removed, or cured if promptly presented—seasonable objection made at taking of deposition. Civ.R. 32(d)(3)(B).
	As to form of written questions submitted under Civ.R. 31—service within time allowed for serving succeeding cross or other questions and within 5 days after service of last questions authorized. Civ.R. 32(d)(3)(C).
	As to completion and return (transcription, signing, certification, sealing, etc.)—motion to suppress made with reasonable promptness after defect is or might have been ascertained. Civ.R. 32(d)(4).
Orders of protection	Subsequent to certification that movant has in good faith conferred or attempted to confer with other affected parties to resolve dispute without court action. Civ.R. 26(c).
Motion to terminate or limit examination	Any time during a deposition. Civ.R. 30(d)(3).
Perpetuate testimony pending appeal	Motion in district court upon same notice and service thereof as if action was pending in district court. Civ.R. 27(b).

Perpetuate testimony before action	Service of notice and petition 20 days before date of hearing. Civ.R. 27(a)(2).
Taking	Time specified in the notice of taking. Civ.R. 30(b)(1).
	Prior notice by a party to deponent and other parties to designate another method to record deponent's testimony in addition to method specified by person taking deposition. Civ.R. 30(b)(3).
Review of transcript or recording	Request by a party or deponent before completion of deposition. Deponent has 30 days after notice of availability of transcript or recording to review and to indicate changes. Civ.R. 30(e).
DEPOSITIONS on written questions	See also, "Depositions," "Interrogatories," this table.
When taken	After parties have met and conferred to discuss their claims, defenses and possibility of settlement and to develop a proposed discovery plan under Civ.R. 26(f). Civ.R. 26(d).
Cross questions	Service within 14 days after service of the notice and question. Court may enlarge or shorten time. Civ.R. 31(a)(4).
Redirect questions	Service within 7 days after being served with cross questions. Court may enlarge or shorten time. Civ.R. 31(a)(4).
Recross questions	Service within 7 days after service of redirect questions. Court may enlarge or shorten time. Civ.R. 31(a)(4).
Notice of filing of deposition	Promptly. Civ.R. 31(c).
Objections to form	Service within the time allowed for serving the succeeding cross or other questions and within 5 days after service of last questions authorized. Civ.R. 32(d)(3)(C).
DISCOVERY	See also, "Admissions," "Depositions," "Depositions on written questions," "Interrogatories," "Production of documents," this table.
	Discovery Conference
	Except in exempted actions or when otherwise ordered, as soon as practicable and at least 14 days before a scheduling conference is held or a scheduling order is due under Civ.R. 16(b), the parties shall meet to discuss their claims, defenses, and possibility of settlement, to make or arrange for disclosures, and to develop a proposed discovery plan. A written report outlining the plan is to be submitted to the court within 10 days after the meeting. Civ.R. 26(f); See also, Civ.R. 26(d).
	Without waiting for a discovery request and within 10 days after the Civ.R. 26(f) meeting of parties, a party must provide information specified in Civ.R. 26(a)(1). Disclosure of expert testimony under Civ.R. 26(a)(2), in absence of court direction or stipulation, is to be made at least 90 days before trial date or date case is ready for trial or if evidence intended as rebuttal of Civ.R. 26(a)(2)(B), within 30 days after disclosure of such evidence. Civ.R. 26(a)(2)(C). All disclosures are to be promptly filed with court. Civ.R. 26(a)(4).
	Identification of witnesses, documents, exhibits, including summaries of other evidence, and designation of witnesses whose testimony will be by deposition with a transcript of pertinent testimony if deposition is not taken stenographically to be provided to other parties at least 30 days before trial unless otherwise directed by court. Within 14 days thereafter, unless otherwise specified by court, a party may file objections. Civ.R. 26(a)(3).
DISMISSAL for want of subject-matter jurisdiction	Any time. Civ.R. 12(h)(3).
DISMISSAL by plaintiff voluntarily without court order	Any time before service of answer or motion for summary judgment. Civ.R. 41(a)(1).

DISMISSAL of counter-claim, cross-claim or third-party claim, voluntary	Before service of responsive pleading, or if none, before introduction of evidence at trial or hearing. Civ.R. 41(c).
DISMISSAL without prejudice	Service of summons and complaint not made within 120 days after filing of complaint. Civ.R. 4(m).
DOCUMENTS, Production of	See "Production of documents," this table.
ENLARGEMENT of time generally	
Act required or allowed at or within specified time by Civil Rule, notice thereunder, or court order	Court for cause shown may (1) with or without motion or notice order period enlarged if request therefor is made before expiration of period originally prescribed or as extended by previous order, or (2) upon motion made after expiration of the specified period permit act to be done where failure to act was result of excusable neglect; but court may not extend time for taking any action under Civ.R. 50(b) and (c)(2), 52(b), 59(b), (d) and (e), and 60(b), except to extent and under conditions stated in them. Civ.R. 6(b).
Affidavits in opposition, service	Time may be extended by court. Civ.R. 6(d).
Hearing of motions and defenses	May be deferred until trial. Civ.R. 12(d).
Mail, service by	Adds three days to a period that is computed from time of service. Civ.R. 6(e).
	When a party is required or permitted to act within a prescribed period after service of a paper upon that party, three calendar days are added to the period unless the paper is delivered on the date of service stated in the proof of service. App.R. 26(c).
Injunction—temporary restraining order	May be extended 10 days by order of court or for a longer period by consent of party against whom order is directed. Civ.R. 65(b).
Response to request for admissions	Time may be enlarged or shortened by court or as the parties may agree in writing subject to Civ.R. 29. Civ.R. 36(a).
Optional appeal from magistrate judge to district judge	Upon showing of excusable neglect, time to file notice of appeal may be extended upon motion filed not later than 20 days from expiration of time for filing. Civ.R. 74(a) [Rule 74 abrogated eff. Dec. 1, 1997].
Motion for judgment notwithstanding the verdict	No enlargement of the 10 day period except to the extent and under conditions stated in Civ.R. 50(b). Civ.R. 6(b).
Findings by the court, amendment of additional findings	No enlargement of the 10 day period except to the extent and under conditions stated in Civ.R. 52(b). Civ.R. 6(b).
Motion for new trial	No enlargement of the 10 day period except to the extent and under conditions stated in Civ.R. 59(b), (d), and (e). Civ.R. 6(b).
Motion for relief from judgment or order	No enlargement of the 1 year period except to the extent and under conditions stated in Civ.R. 60(b). Civ.R. 6(b).
Appellate rules	Court for good cause may extend time prescribed by App.Rules or by its order to perform any act or may permit act to be done after expiration of such time; but court may not extend time for filing notice of appeal, or petition for permission to appeal a notice of appeal from or a petition to enjoin, set aside, suspend, modify, enforce or otherwise review an order of an administrative agency, board, commission or officer of the United States, unless specifically authorized by law. App.R. 26(b).

Supreme Court matters	See Supreme Court Rule 30.
EXCEPTIONS for insufficiency of pleadings	Abolished. Civ.R. 7(c).

EXECUTION

Stay

Automatically: No execution to issue, nor proceedings for enforcement to be taken, until expiration of 10 days after entry of judgment; exceptions—injunctions, receiverships, and patent accountings. Civ.R. 62(a).

Stay according to state law. Civ.R. 62(f).

Motion for new trial or for judgment. Civ.R. 62(b).

Stay in favor of government. Civ.R. 62(e).

Supersedeas on appeal. Civ.R. 62(d).

Stay of judgment as to multiple claims or multiple parties. Civ.R. 62(h).

Stay of judgment pending appeal from magistrate judge to district judge. Civ.R. 74(c). Stay of decision of district judge for 10 days during which time a party may petition for rehearing. Civ.R. 76(b) [Rules 74 and 76 abrogated eff. Dec. 1, 1997].

FILING papers

Complaint must be filed at commencement of action. Civ.R. 3.

Service of summons and complaint within 120 days after filing of complaint. Civ.R. 4(m).

All papers required to be filed must be filed with clerk unless the judge permits them to be filed with the judge. Civ.R. 5(e).

Local court rules may permit papers to be filed by electronic means if consistent with standards of Judicial Conference of the United States, and clerk shall not refuse for filing any paper solely because it is not presented in proper form under Rules of Civil Procedure or any local rule or practice. Civ.R. 5(e).

All papers after the complaint required to be served upon a party, together with a certificate of service, shall be filed with the court within a reasonable time after service. Civ.R. 5(d).

FINDINGS
Motion to amend

10 days after entry of judgment. Civ.R. 52(b). Exception from general rule relating to enlargement. Civ.R. 6(b).

FINDINGS of master

See "References and Referees," this table.

FOREIGN law

Reasonable written notice required of party intending to raise an issue concerning the law of a foreign country. Civ.R. 44.1.

HEARING of motions

Unless local conditions make it impracticable, district court shall establish regular times and places for hearing and disposition of motions requiring notice and hearing; but judge may make orders for the advancement, conduct, and hearing of actions. Civ.R. 78.

Service of notice 5 days before time specified for hearing unless otherwise provided by these rules or order of court. Civ.R. 6(d).

Hearing of certain motions and defenses before trial on application of any party unless court orders deferral until trial. Civ.R. 12(d).

HOLIDAYS

New Year's Day, Birthday of Martin Luther King, Jr., Presidents' Day, Memorial Day, Independence Day, Labor Day, Columbus Day, Veterans' Day, Thanksgiving Day, Christmas Day, and any other day declared a holiday by the President, Congress or the state in which is located either the district court that rendered the challenged judgment or order, or the circuit clerk's principal office. Civ.R. 6(a); App.R. 26(a).

Exclusion in computation of time. Civ.R. 6(a); App.R. 26(a).

**INJUNCTION
(Temporary restraining order granted without notice)**

Order shall be indorsed with date and hour of issuance, filed forthwith in clerk's office, and entered of record. Civ.R. 65(b).

Expiration within such time, not to exceed 10 days, as court fixes, unless within time so fixed the order is extended for like period or, with consent of party against whom order is directed, for longer period. Civ.R. 65(b).

Motion for preliminary injunction shall be set down for hearing at earliest possible time—takes precedence of all matters except older ones of same character. Civ.R. 65(b).

Motion for dissolution or modification on 2 days' notice or such shorter notice as court may prescribe; hear and determine motion as expeditiously as ends of justice require. Civ.R. 65(b).

INSTRUCTIONS

Requests — At close of evidence or such earlier time as court directs. Civ.R. 51.

Objections — Before jury retires to consider verdict. Civ.R. 51.

INTERROGATORIES to parties — See also, "Depositions," "Depositions on written questions," this table.

Service after parties have met and conferred pursuant to Civ.R. 26(f). Civ.R. 33(a).

Answers or objections — Service within 30 days after service of the interrogatories. A shorter or longer time may be directed by the court or agreed to. Civ.R. 33(b)(3).

INTERVENTION — Upon timely application. Civ.R. 24(a), (b).

Person desiring to intervene shall serve a motion to intervene upon the parties as provided in Civil Rule 5. Civ.R. 24(c).

JUDGMENT or order

Alter or amend judgment, motion to — Shall be filed not later than 10 days after entry of judgment. Civ.R. 59(e). Exception to general rule, relating to enlargement. Civ.R. 6(b).

Clerical mistakes — May be corrected any time; but during pendency of appeal, may be corrected before appeal is docketed in the appellate court, and thereafter while appeal pending may be corrected with leave of appellate court. Civ.R. 60(a).

Default — See "Default," this table.

Renewal of motion for judgment after trial — Not later than 10 days after entry of judgment. Exception from general rule relating to enlargement. Civ.R. 6(b).

Effectiveness — Judgment effective only when set forth on a separate document and when entered as provided in Civ.R. 79(a). Civ.R. 58.

Entry of judgment — Upon general verdict of jury or upon court decision that a party shall recover only a sum certain or costs or that all relief shall be denied, entry forthwith and without awaiting any direction by court (unless court otherwise orders). Upon court decision granting other relief or upon special verdict or general verdict accompanied by answers to interrogatories, entry upon prompt court approval of form. Entry shall not be delayed for taxing of costs. Civ.R. 58.

Entry, notice of — Immediately upon entry, clerk shall serve notice thereof by mail in manner provided in Civ.R. 5 and make note in docket of the mailing. Any party may in addition serve a notice of such entry in manner provided in Civ.R. 5 for service of papers. Civ.R. 77(d).

Lack of notice of entry by clerk does not affect time to appeal or relieve or authorize court to relieve party for failure to appeal within time allowed, except as permitted by App.R. 4(a). Civ.R. 77(d).

Offer of judgment — Service more than 10 days before trial begins. Civ.R. 68.

Acceptance, written notice of—service within 10 days after service of offer. Civ.R. 68.

On pleadings, motion for judgment — After pleadings are closed but within such time as not to delay the trial. Civ.R. 12(c).

Relief from, on grounds stated in Rule 60(b)	Motion within a reasonable time and not more than 1 year after judgment, order, or proceeding entered or taken, for following grounds: (1) mistake, inadvertence, surprise, or excusable neglect; (2) newly discovered evidence; (3) fraud, misrepresentation, or other misconduct. Civ.R. 60(b). Exception from general rule relating to enlargement. Civ.R. 60(b).
	Motion within a reasonable time, for following grounds: (1) judgment void, (2) judgment satisfied, released, or discharged, (3) prior underlying judgment reversed or otherwise vacated, (4) no longer equitable that judgment have prospective application, (5) any other reason justifying relief. Civ.R. 60(b). Exception from general rule relating to enlargement. Civ.R. 6(b).
Stay	See "Execution," this table.
Summary judgment	See "Summary judgment," this table.
JURORS	The institution of the alternate juror has been abolished. Civ.R. 47, 1991 Advisory Committee note, subd. (b).
JURY trial Demand	Service any time after commencement of action and not later than 10 days after service of last pleading directed to the triable issue. Civ.R. 38(b).
	Adverse party may serve demand for jury trial within 10 days after service of first demand or such lesser time as court fixes. Civ.R. 38(c).
Removed actions	If at the time of removal all necessary pleadings have been served, demand for jury trial may be served:
	By petitioner, 10 days after the petition for removal is filed;
	By any other party, within 10 days after service on party of the notice of filing the petition. Civ.R. 81(c).
	Demand after removal not necessary in either of two instances: (1) prior to removal, party has made express demand in accordance with state law; (2) state law does not require express demands and court does not direct otherwise. Civ.R. 81(c).
LEGAL HOLIDAY	See "Holidays," this table.
MAGISTRATE JUDGES Trial by consent	Consent of parties to magistrate judge's authority to be exercised within period specified by local rule. Civ.R. 73(b).
Pretrial matters	Objections of parties to order disposing of matter not dispositive of claim or defense to be served and filed within 10 days after being served with copy of order. Civ.R. 72(a).
	Clerk to forthwith mail copies to all parties of recommendation of magistrate judge for disposition of matter dispositive of claim or defense of a party or prisoner petition. Specific written objections to recommended disposition may be served and filed within 10 days after service. Response to objections may be made within 10 days after being served with copy. Civ.R. 72(b).
MAIL	Service by mail adds 3 days to a period computed from time of service. Civ.R. 6(e).
	When a party is required or permitted to act within a prescribed period after service of a paper upon that party, three calendar days are added to the period unless the paper is delivered on the date of service stated in the proof of service. App.R. 26(c). A brief or appendix is timely filed if on or before the last day for filing it is mailed First-Class or other class at least as expeditious, postage prepaid, or dispatched for delivery within three calendar days by a third-party commercial carrier. App.R. 25(a)(2)(B).
MASTERS	See "References and Referees," this table.
MORE DEFINITE STATEMENT Furnished	Must be furnished within 10 days after notice of order or other time fixed by court or court may strike pleading. Civ.R. 12(e).

Motion for	Must be made before responsive pleading is interposed. Civ.R. 12(e).
MOTIONS, notices, and affidavits	See also, specific headings, this table.
In general	A written motion, supporting affidavits, and notice of hearing thereof—service not later than 5 days before time specified for hearing unless a different time is fixed by rule or by order of court. Civ.R. 6(d).
	Opposing affidavits may be served not later than one day before hearing, unless court permits otherwise. Civ.R. 6(d).
	Pleading, written motion, or other paper not signed by attorney or party shall be stricken unless omission of signature is corrected promptly after being called to attention of attorney or party. Civ.R. 11(a).
NEW TRIAL Motion and affidavits	Motion shall be filed not later than 10 days after entry of judgment. Civ.R. 59(b). Exception from general rule relating to enlargement. Civ.R. 6(b). If motion based on affidavits, they must be filed with motion. Civ.R. 59(c).
Opposing affidavits	Shall be filed within 10 days of service of motion for new trial; period may be extended up to 20 days either by court for good cause shown or by parties by written stipulation. Civ.R. 59(c).
Initiative of court	Not later than 10 days after entry of judgment, court may order new trial for any reason that would justify granting one on a party's motion. Civ.R. 59(d). Exception to general rule relating to enlargement. Civ.R. 6(b).
	After giving parties notice and opportunity to be heard, court may grant a timely motion for new trial, for reason not stated in the motion. Civ.R. 59(d). Exception to general rule relating to enlargement. Civ.R. 6(b).
Judgment as a matter of law	Party against whom judgment as a matter of law is rendered shall file a motion for a new trial under Civ.R. 59 no later than 10 days after entry of the judgment. Civ.R. 50(c)(2).
OBJECTIONS to orders or rulings of court	At time ruling or order of court is made or sought; if party has no opportunity to object to ruling or order at time it is made, absence of objection does not thereafter prejudice the party. Civ.R. 46.
Pretrial matters referred to magistrate judge	Objections of parties to order disposing of matter not dispositive of claim or defense to be served and filed within 10 days after being served with copy of order. Civ.R. 72(a).
	Specific written objections to recommended disposition of matter dispositive of claim or defense of a party or prisoner petition may be served or filed within 10 days after service. Response to objections may be made within 10 days after being served with copy. Civ.R. 72(b).
OFFER of judgment	Must be served more than 10 days before trial. Civ.R. 68.
	Acceptance must be served within 10 days after service of offer. Civ.R. 68.
ORDERS	See Judgment or order.
PARTICULARS, Bill of	Abolished. Civ.R. 12(e), as amended in 1948. See, however, "More definite statement," this table.
PLEADINGS Amendment of	Once as matter of course before responsive pleading served or within 20 days if no response is permitted and action has not been placed on trial calendar. Civ.R. 15(a).
	By leave of court or written consent of adverse parties, at any time. Civ.R. 15(a).
	During trial or after judgment to conform to evidence or to raise issues not raised in pleadings, but tried by express or implied consent of parties. Civ.R. 15(b).

Supplemental	Upon motion of party—court may upon reasonable notice permit service of supplemental pleading setting forth transactions, etc., which have happened since date of pleading sought to be supplemented. Civ.R. 15(d).
	Adverse party plead to supplemental pleading—if court deems advisable, it shall so order, specifying time therefor. Civ.R. 15(d).
Averments of time	Such averments are material and shall be considered like all other averments of material matter. Civ.R. 9(f).
Judgment on, motion for	After pleadings are closed but within such time as not to delay the trial. Civ.R. 12(c).
Striking of matter from	Motion made before responding to a pleading or, if no responsive pleading permitted, within 20 days after service of pleading. Civ.R. 12(f).
	On court's own initiative at any time. Civ.R. 12(f).
Signing of	Pleading, written motion, or other paper not signed by attorney or party shall be stricken unless omission of signature is corrected promptly after being called to attention of attorney or party. Civ.R. 11(a).
PLEAS	Abolished. Civ.R. 7(c).
PRETRIAL conferences	Scheduling order to issue as soon as practicable but in any event within 90 days after appearance of a defendant and within 120 days after complaint served on defendant. Civ.R. 16(b).
PROCESS	See "Summons," this table.
PRODUCTION of documents	
Request for, service of	Without leave of court or written stipulation, request may not be served before parties have met and conferred pursuant to Civ.R. 26(f). Civ.R. 34(b).
	May accompany notice of taking deposition. Civ.R. 30(b)(5).
Response to request	Within 30 days after service of the request. A shorter or longer time may be directed by court or agreed to. Civ.R. 34(b).
Time of inspection	The request shall specify a reasonable time. Civ.R. 34(b).
Subpoena	See "Subpoena," this table.
REFERENCES and Referees	
Order of reference	When reference is made, clerk shall forthwith furnish master with copy of order. Civ.R. 53(d)(1).
Hearings before master	Time for beginning and closing the hearings, as fixed by order of reference. Civ.R. 53(c).
Meetings	First meeting of parties or attorneys to be held within 20 days after date of order of reference. Civ.R. 53(d)(1). Upon receipt of the order of reference, unless order otherwise provides, master shall forthwith set time and place for such meeting and notify parties or their attorneys. Civ.R. 53(d)(1).
	Speed—either party, on notice to parties and master, may apply to court for order requiring master to speed the proceedings and make report. Civ.R. 53(d)(1).
	Failure of party to appear at appointed time and place—master may proceed ex parte or adjourn to future day, giving notice to absent party of adjournment. Civ.R. 53(d)(1).
Report of master	Filing of, time as fixed in order of reference. Master shall serve on all parties notice of the filing. Civ.R. 53(e)(1). Master, unless otherwise directed by the order of reference, shall serve a copy of the report on each party. Civ.R. 53(e)(1).
	Objections (in non-jury actions) may be served within 10 days after being served with notice of filing of report. Civ.R. 53(e)(2).

Court action on report and objections thereto—application (in non-jury actions) for such action shall be by motion and upon notice as prescribed in Civ.R. 6(d). Civ.R. 53(e)(2).

Speed—either party, on notice to parties and master, may apply to court for order requiring master to speed the proceedings and make report. Civ.R. 53(d)(1).

REHEARING

Petition for panel rehearing	Petitions for panel rehearings may be filed within 14 days after entry of judgement unless the time is shortened or extended by order or local rule. In all civil cases in which the United States or its agency or officer thereof is a party, the time within which any party may seek a rehearing shall be 45 days after entry of judgement unless the time is shortened or extended by order. App.R. 40(a).
Issuance of mandate	The mandate of the court must issue 7 days after the time to file a petition for rehearing expires, or 7 days after entry of an order denying a timely petition for panel rehearing, rehearing en banc, or motion for stay of mandate, whichever is later. The court may shorten or extend the time. The timely filing of a petition for panel rehearing, petition for rehearing en banc, or motion for stay of mandate, stays the mandate until disposition of the petition or motion, unless the court orders otherwise. App.R. 41(b), (d)(1).

REMOVED actions

Answers and defenses	Within 20 days after the receipt through service or otherwise of a copy of the initial pleading setting forth the claim for relief upon which the action or proceeding is based, or within 20 days after the service of summons upon such initial pleading, then filed, or within 5 days after filing of the petition for removal, whichever period is longest. Civ.R. 81(c).
Demand for jury trial	Demand after removal not necessary in either of two instances: (1) prior to removal, party has made express demand in accordance with state law; (2) state law does not require express demands and court does not direct otherwise. Civ.R. 81(c).
Notice of removal	Within 30 days after receipt through service or otherwise of a copy of the initial pleading setting forth the claim for relief upon which the action or proceeding is based, or within 30 days after service of summons if such initial pleading has then been filed in court and is not required to be served on defendant, whichever period is shorter. 28 U.S.C.A. § 1446(b).
	If the case stated by the initial pleading is not removable, a notice of removal may be filed within 30 days after receipt by the defendant, through service or otherwise, of a copy of an amended pleading, motion, order or other paper from which it may first be ascertained that the case is one which is or has become removable. 28 U.S.C.A. § 1446(b).
	A case may not be removed on the basis of jurisdiction conferred by 28 U.S.C.A. § 1332 more than one year after action's commencement. 28 U.S.C.A. § 1446(b).

REPLY

	See also, "Responsive pleadings," this table.
To answer or third-party answer	Only if ordered by court. Civ.R. 7(a). Service within 20 days after service of order, unless order otherwise directs. Civ.R. 12(a).
To counterclaim	Service within 20 days after service of answer. Civ.R. 12(a).
	United States or agency or officer thereof shall serve reply within 60 days after service upon U.S. attorney. Civ.R. 12(a).
Alteration of time by service of Civ.R. 12 motion	See "Responsive pleadings," this table.

RESPONSIVE PLEADINGS

	See also, "Answer," "Reply," this table.
To amend pleading	Within 10 days after service of amended pleading or within time remaining for response to original pleading, whichever is longer, unless court otherwise orders. Civ.R. 15(a).

To supplemental pleading	As ordered by court. Civ.R. 15(d).
Alteration of time by service of Civ.R. 12 motion	Service of motion permitted under Civ.R. 12 alters times for responsive pleadings as follows unless different time fixed by court: (1) if court denies motion, service of responsive pleading within 10 days after notice of denial; (2) if court postpones disposition until trial on merits, service of responsive pleading within 10 days after notice of postponement; (3) if court grants motion for more definite statement, service of responsive pleading within 10 days after service of the more definite statement. See "Injunction," this table.
RESTRAINING order, temporary, without notice RETURN	The court may allow a summons or proof of service to be amended. Civ.R. 4(a) & (*l*). The person effecting service shall make proof thereof to the court. Civ.R. 4(*l*).
SANCTIONS	Presentation to court of a pleading, written motion, or other paper is a certification under Civ.R. 11(b). If after notice and reasonable opportunity to respond, court determines that Civ.R. 11(b) was violated, sanctions may be imposed by a motion for sanctions which shall not be filed or presented to court unless, within 21 days after service of the motion, the challenged matter is not withdrawn or corrected. Civ.R. 11(c). Sanctions are inapplicable to discovery. Civ.R. 11(d).
SATURDAYS AND SUNDAYS	Exclusion in computation of time. Civ.R. 6(a); App.R. 26(a).
STAY or supersedeas	See "Appeal," "Execution," this table.
SUBPOENA Objection	Within 14 days after service of the subpoena or before the time specified for compliance if such time is less than 14 days after service, there be served upon the party or attorney designated in the subpoena written objection to inspection or copying of any or all of the designated materials or of the premises. Civ.R. 45(c)(2)(B).
Motion to compel production	If objection has been made, the party serving the subpoena may, upon notice to the person commanded to produce, move at any time for an order to compel the production. Civ.R. 45(c)(2)(B).
Motion to quash	The court by which a subpoena was issued shall quash or modify the subpoena on timely motion. Civ.R. 45(c)(3)(A).
Witnesses, documentary evidence, etc.	Subpoena specifies time for attendance and giving of testimony or to produce and permit inspection and copying of designated books, documents or tangible things in the possession, custody or control of that person, or to permit inspection of premises. Civ.R. 45(a)(1)(C).
SUBSTITUTION of parties	In cases of death, incompetency, or transfer of interest—motion for substitution, together with notice of hearing, served on parties as provided in Civ.R. 5 and upon persons not parties in manner provided in Civ.R. 4 for service of a summons. Civ.R. 25(a), (b), (c). Dismissal as to deceased party unless motion for substitution is made not later than 90 days after death is suggested upon the record. Civ.R. 25(a). Successor of public officer substituted automatically. Order of substitution may be entered at any time. Civ.R. 25(d).
SUMMARY JUDGMENT, motion for Claimant	May move at any time after expiration of 20 days from commencement of action or after service of motion for summary judgment by adverse party. Civ.R. 56(a).
Defending party	May move at any time. Civ.R. 56(b).

Service	Service of motion at least 10 days before time fixed for hearing. Civ.R. 56(c).
	Service of opposing affidavits prior to day of hearing. Civ.R. 56(c).
SUMMONS	Served with a copy of complaint. Civ.R. 4(c)(1). If not served within 120 days after filing complaint, court may dismiss action without prejudice, direct service be effected within a specified time, or extend time for service. Civ.R. 4(m).
	The person effecting service shall make proof thereof to the court. Civ.R. 4(*l*).
	Service by any nonparty at least 18, a U.S. marshal, deputy U.S. marshal, or other person or officer specially appointed. Civ.R. 4(c)(2).
SUPPLEMENTAL pleadings	See "Pleadings," this table.
SUPERSEDEAS or stay	See "Appeal," "Execution," this table.
TERM	The district courts deemed always open. Civ.R. 77(a).
	Terms of court have been abolished. 28 U.S.C.A. §§ 138–141, as amended by Act of Oct. 16, 1963, Pub.L. 88–139, 77 Stat. 248.
THIRD-PARTY practice	Third-party plaintiff need not obtain leave if third-party plaintiff files third-party complaint not later than 10 days after serving the original answer. Otherwise, must obtain leave on motion upon notice to all parties to the action. Civ.R. 14(a).
VERDICT Renewal of motion for judgment after trial	No later than 10 days after entry of judgment, motion for judgment as a matter of law may be renewed by filing the motion where motion made at the close of all the evidence is denied or for any reason is not granted. Civ.R. 50(b).
	Exception from general rule relating to enlargement. Civ.R. 6(b).
New trial where judgment as a matter of law rendered	Party against whom judgment as a matter of law is rendered shall file a motion for a new trial pursuant to Civ.R. 59 no later than 10 days after entry of the judgment. Civ.R. 50(c)(2).

Equity Rules Reference Table

The Federal Rules of Civil Procedure supplant the Equity Rules since in general they cover the field now covered by the Equity Rules and the Conformity Act (former section 724 of this title).

This table shows the Equity Rules to which references are made in the notes to the Federal Rules of Civil Procedure.

Equity Rules	Federal Rules of Civil Procedure	Equity Rules	Federal Rules of Civil Procedure
1	77	28	15
2	77	29	7, 12, 42, 55
3	79	30	8, 13, 82
4	77	31	7, 8, 12, 55
5	77	32	15
6	78	33	7, 12
7	4, 70	34	15
8	6, 70	35	15
9	70	36	11
10	18, 54	37	17, 19, 20, 24
11	71	38	23
12	3, 4, 5, 12, 55	39	19
13	4	40	20
14	4	41	17
15	4, 45	42	19, 20
16	6, 55	43	12, 21
17	55	44	12, 21
18	7, 8	45	25
19	1, 15, 61	46	43, 61
20	12	47	26
21	11, 12	48	43
22	1	49	53
23	1, 39	50	30, 80
24	11	51	30, 53
25	8, 9, 10, 19	52	45, 53
26	18, 20, 82	53	53
27	23	54	26

APPENDIX B

DEPOSITION TRANSCRIPT

The following is an actual discovery deposition transcript. The deponent was a plaintiff who claimed personal injuries as a result of an automobile accident. All names, addresses, and dates have been changed to protect privacy. The transcript illustrates the necessity of being persistent and detailed. Four major areas are covered, though the areas are not separated in any obvious manner: (1) the deponent's background, (2) the deponent's previous health and accidents, (3) the accident in question, and (4) the alleged injuries and expenses. Of particular interest is the deponent's obvious lack of preparation for the deposition. The transcript should be read in light of the various guidelines suggested for preparing a witness to testify. As an epilogue, the defendant's insurer was able to obtain a dismissal of the case with only a nominal settlement.

Duane Johnson, Plaintiff,

vs.

Clarence A. Souter, Defendant and Third-party Plaintiff,

vs.

Carolyn Jones, Third-party Defendant.

Appearances

Ellen Clarke, Esq., appeared on behalf of the plaintiff. John Fredricks, Esq., appeared on behalf of the defendant and third-party plaintiff. Lang & Spencer, by Robert L. Lang, Esq., appeared on behalf of the third-party defendant.

DISCOVERY DEPOSITION OF DUANE JOHNSON, taken under the Federal Rules of Civil Procedure for the district courts, at 700 Titan Building, Detroit, Michigan, on August 13, 2000, before John R. Nash, a notary public, commencing at approximately 11:10 A.M.

DUANE JOHNSON, plaintiff, called on behalf of the defendant and third-party plaintiff, having been first duly sworn, testified on his oath as follows:

Examination

By Mr. Fredricks:

> **Q:** Will you state your full name, please?
> **A:** Duane Anthony Johnson.
> **Q:** What is your birth date?

A: One-twenty-two-seventy.

Q: Where were you born?

A: Kansas City, Kansas.

Q: Where?

A: Kansas City, Kansas.

Q: Where do you currently reside?

A: You mean in Detroit.

Q: Yes.

A: South Detroit

Q: What is your address?

A: 1530 East 40th and a Half-Street.

Q: East 40th and a Half?

A: Yes. South Detroit

Q: How long have you lived there?

A: About nine months?

Q: Are you married?

A: No, single.

Q: Have you ever been married?

A: No, I haven't.

Q: Do you live with anyone at that address?

A: Friend.

Q: Who?

A: Catherine Baker.

Q: What's the name again?

A: Catherine Baker.

Q: You say you are friends.

A: Well, just two-bedroom apartment.

Q: I mean you are not related in any way.

A: No.

Q: How long has she been there?

A: About a year or two. About a year.

Q: Where did you reside before moving to your current address?

A: 16th Avenue. I forgot that apartment number. It was on 20—26th and 16th Avenue.

Q: How long did you live at that address?

A: About two months, three months.

Q: Where do your parents reside?

A: At the present time, 4245 Park Avenue South.

Q: And your father's name is what?

A: Donald Johnson.

Q: Are you presently employed?

A: Part-time.

Q: Where do you work?

A: Hearns Auditorium.

Q: I'm having a hard time hearing you.

A: Hearns Auditorium. That's on the Detroit campus.

Q: What do you do there?

A: Work in the office. Office work.

Q: How long have you worked there?

A: This summer. Started this summer. Summer work. That's for Model City.

Q: Who is your immediate supervisor?

A: Henry Hyslop.

Q: Will you spell the last name?

A: H-y-l—H-y-s-l-o-p.

Q: Do you intend to continue working there indefinitely?

A: No. That's just summer work, you know.

Q: Will that job end then in September?

A: It ends this month sometime.

Q: What other jobs have you had since August of 1995?

A: I was working at Honeywell on an assembly line, I think that was in '95.

Q: You work at Honeywell where?

A: In Detroit, Honeywell.

Q: What kind of work did you do for Honeywell?

A: Was just small work, just on an assembly line-like thing. It wasn't no kind of strenuous work.

Q: For what period of time did you work there?

A: That was summer work too.

Q: What was your pay rate while at Honeywell?

A: Ten dollars.

Ms. Clarke: You are going to have to yell a little bit louder, because I'm having a little bit of trouble hearing you, too.

The Witness: About ten dollars an hour.

Q: [By Mr. Fredricks] Did you take an employment physical, exam—

A: No I didn't.

Q: —before going to work for Honeywell—

A: No.

Q: —while working at Honeywell?

A: No.

Q: Did you make out an application for that employment?

A: Yes, I did.

Q: And was there any inquiry about the status of your health or physical condition in that application?

A: No, there wasn't.

Q: Okay. What was your condition, your physical condition, when you made your application to work at Honeywell? Were you having any problems?

A: The application wasn't like that, you know, as far as your health. The application wasn't—you know, it didn't ask about your health, you know, your background, nothing like that.

Q: I'm asking you now—what was your condition when you made out that application?

A: Back trouble and neck.

Q: Back and leg trouble?

A: Back and neck.

Q: And neck. Anything else?

A: That was the most—main thing at that time.

Q: Did you have to make out an application for your work when you started working for Hearns Auditorium.

A: No.

Q: Have you had any other employment since August of 1995?

A: No. I was working—last year I was working at the Children's Theatre and—

Q: Where?

A: Detroit, South Detroit. That was at—at the Mann. No, not the Mann, it's on Third Avenue, the Art Institute, Detroit Art Institute, and I was working for the Children's Theatre. That's combined together.

Q: How long did you work there?

A: That was summer work also.

Q: What was your pay rate at the time?

A: Ten dollars an hour.

Q: You worked forty hours a week, did you?

A: Yes.

Q: When you were at Honeywell, did you work forty hours a week?

A: Yes, it was.

Q: Did you work regularly at all of these jobs during the summer months? Did you work regularly, or did you have to miss a lot of time?

A: Well, I was getting hot pack treatments at Dr. Peterson's office.

Q: You mean after work?

A: Well, sometimes I have to go on work [time] because his office is only open in the afternoon.

Q: Other than the times you went for back treatments, did you have to miss any time from work?

A: Yes. A little, sometimes, yes.

Q: Do you have a record of what time you missed from work?

A: At home when I started I did, yes.

Q: Do you have that with you?

A: I don't have it with me, no.

Q: What chiropractor were you seeing?

A: Dr. Peterson.

Q: Thomas Peterson?

A: Thomas Peterson.

Q: I understand he is a chiropractor?

A: I beg your pardon.

Q: Do you understand that he is a chiropractor?

A: He was my doctor, I don't know what he was.

Q: I thought you said you were seeing a chiropractor. Did I misunderstand?

Mr. Lang: [Nods head]

Ms. Clarke: Maybe he was talking about the therapist. Were you talking about the guy that gave you the heat and all that stuff?

The Witness: I don't know his name.

Q: [By Mr. Fredricks] Bill Freeman?

A: Yes, something like that.

Q: William Freeman or something like that.

A: Yes, I believe so. You see, when I was going to Wahlstrom I was getting treatment too before I seen him.

Q: You completed high school?

A: Yes.

Q: What high school did you attend?

A: Central, Detroit Central.

Q: When were you graduated?

A: Ninety-three.

Q: Did you participate in sports in any school?

A: That was '98, I'm sorry. Sometimes, yes.

Q: What sports?

A: Basketball and just any—really any intramural thing. I didn't go out for—

Q: Were you ever injured in any sports?

A: No.

Q: Have you been involved in any other motor vehicle accidents other than the one of August 17, 1999?

A: No.

Q: At any time?

A: No.

Q: Have you ever been in a car when it has collided with another car, or object, or—

A: No. No.

Q: Even if you weren't hurt.

A: No.

Q: This is the only motor vehicle accident you have ever been in?

A: Yes it was.

Q: All right. Have you been injured in any other accidents of any kind at any time?

A: No, I haven't. Any other automobile accidents?

Q: No, no, any other accidents of any kind—

A: No.

Q: —at any time where you hurt yourself any way.

A: Well, I was just in an accident—

Q: All right.

A: —about two weeks ago, maybe a month ago.

Q: Where did the accident happen and—

A: On Traverse.

Q: What?

A: Traverse. Exact address I don't know. It was somewhere down Traverse Avenue.

Q: What happened?

A: Crossed the center line.

Q: Was this an automobile accident?

A: Yes.

Q: Oh. Well, you tell me, describe for me what—were you a driver?

A: Yes, I was.

Q: And what happened?

A: I was fixing a calendar watch and I was—the passenger was fixing my calendar watch, and she turned it—messed it up, and I looked down at it and went in the other lane.

Q: Was this a head-on type collision?

A: Yes.

Q: Did the police investigate?

A: Yes, they did.

Q: What time of the day did it happen?

A: In the afternoon, about twelve o'clock, one o'clock.

Q: It was daylight at that time?

A: Yes, it was.

Q: Who was your passenger?

A: Rebecca Parsons.

Q: Where does she live?

A: Cleveland.

Q: Cleveland?

A: North Cleveland.

Q: Where in North Cleveland?

A: I forget the address.

Q: Will you get that for me or get it to your attorney?

Ms. Clarke: No, I'm not going to get—why don't you find out if he got hurt. If he got hurt, then I will get you what you want, but you are dinging around on a fender bender, I suspect, and if that's where you are going—

Q: [By Mr. Fredricks] Were you hurt at all in the accident?

A: Just stitches on my lip.

Q: You struck your face against something inside the car?

A: Yes.

Q: Where did you get the stitches?

A: In the lip and also chin.

Q: Lip and chin.

A: Yes.

Q: Any other injuries in the accident?

A: And teeth, my teeth.

Q: What happened to your teeth?

A: They were all out, just about. Oh, they are all loose, you know.

Q: Lower-front teeth were loosened?

A: Lower and upper.

Q: Any other injuries?

A: That was about all. I just hit the steering wheel.

Q: Have any headaches following the accident?

A: No.

Q: You haven't had any headaches since that accident a month ago?

A: No I haven't.

Q: What doctors did you go to, for example?

A: General Hospital.

Q: Where else?

A: That was it.

Q: All of the treatment you have received was at General Hospital?

A: Yes.

Q: Have you been to Dr. Thomas Peterson since that accident?

A: No.

Q: Earlier I asked you about your other automobile accidents—

A: Yes.

Q: —and you didn't mention this.

A: Well, I didn't—you know, I really forgot about the accident. It didn't, you know, mean nothing.

Q: All right. Now, you search your mind: Are there any other automobile accidents?

A: No.

Q: Do you have a driver's license?

A: Yes, I do.

Q: What's the number on it? Would you get it out and check it for me? Now, have you been involved in any other accidents of any kind? I'm not referring—

A: You mean a passenger—no, I haven't, nothing.

Q: In no sports—you have never fallen down and hurt yourself, you have never burned yourself, you have never cut yourself, you have never had any other trouble?

A: No.

Q: All right. Have you been hospitalized at any time in your life other than for childbirth?

A: Just for asthma.

Q: When was that?

A: That was—I was born with it.

Q: When were you hospitalized for it?

A: I don't remember the exact date. Last year sometime. Two years before that. I stayed in the hospital with asthma.

Q: What hospital did you go to?

A: General Hospital.

Q: Have you ever made a claim against anyone for injuries other than this accident?

A: No.

Q: After completing high school you went to college.

A: Yes.

Q: What colleges have you attended?

A: Wahlstrom in Uhler, Michigan.

Q: What years did you attend?

A: Ninety-nine, 2000.

Q: Did you have a physical examination at that college?

A: Yes.

Q: Did you have any treatment for your back condition?

A: Yes, I did.

Q: What course of study did you pursue there? Liberal arts?

A: Liberal arts.

Q: All right. Did you complete one academic year at Wahlstrom?

A: It was more or less a program like for people who aren't capable of going to college but may, you know, learn something at college, you know, if they have the opportunity to go. Do you understand?

Q: Is there a name for that program?

A: It was called Demos.

Q: What?

A: Demos. D-e-m-o something. Demos. I don't know how to spell that.

Q: What month did you start then, September?

A: Yes.

Q: And—

A: Ninety-nine, 2000.

Q: What month did you complete the course?

A: I went the whole—full two years.

Q: Okay. Have you gone to another institution, college?

A: I'm going to the university at the present time.

Q: Well, you mean you have actually registered for class?

A: Yes.

Q: Will you be starting as a freshman?

A: Sophomore and junior, half and half now.

Q: Didn't you attend at Chicago?

A: No, I haven't. I seen it in the thing but I changed it. It was at Wahlstrom.

Q: I see. Did you live on campus when you were at Wahlstrom?

A: Yes, I did.

Q: Have you had your physical examination for the university?

A: Last year I did.

Q: When was that?

A: I don't know. It was at the beginning of the school year.

Q: Have you received any treatment for any physical condition or problems at the university health service?

A: No, I haven't.

Q: Or hospital?

A: No.

Q: All right. Now, referring to the accident of August 17th, 1999, that happened early on a Friday morning, didn't it?

A: Friday morning?

Q: Thursday night or Friday morning.

A: Yes.

Q: Do you recall what time it happened?

A: No, I can't. It was—I think it was about one, one o'clock.

Q: Okay. It was dark out at the time, wasn't it?

A: Yes, it was.

Q: And would it be consistent with your recollection that it was about 1:35 in the morning?

A: Probably so.

Q: Who were you with that night?

A: Carolyn Jones. She was driving. And a Ruby Watts, another girl, was in the back seat.

Q: Who was the other girl?

A: Ruby Watts.

Q: Ruby what

A: Watts, W-a-t-t-s.

Q: W-a-t-t-s? Where does she live?

A: I have no idea.

Q: Where were you going at the time?

A: Probably home.

Q: Probably?

A: Yes.

Q: Don't you remember?

A: It was probably my house. I'm pretty sure it was. See, I live about four blocks from the accident, and we were going in that direction. I believe we were. She was taking me home, I'm pretty sure.

Q: Where had you been?

A: Probably a dance or something. At a dance.

Q: Where?

A: Downtown. I forget the name of the club. I believe we went, you know, here and there. Let's see—

Q: Did you have anything—

A: No, no, no, this was a house party. I'm sorry. It was a house party, a get-together.

Q: Did you have anything alcoholic to drink?

A: No. They didn't have anything. I'm sure they didn't. No.

Q: How about Ms. Jones?

A: No, she doesn't drink.

Q: Were you dating that night? Was this a date with either of the two girls?

A: Well, I knew Carolyn from—we grew up together, just about. Well, we went to school together, high school, grade school. She just stopped and picked me up.

Q: All right. At the time of the accident, you were riding in a Buick automobile?

A: [Nods head]

Q: And you were traveling in an easterly direction on 38th Street.

A: Yes.

Q: And the other car was in a northerly direction on Second Avenue.

A: Yes.

Q: Do you recall whether Ms. Jones put on her turn signals as she approached this intersection?

A: We were going straight. We were going straight.

Q: Did she put on her turn signals, or don't you know?

A: I'm sure she didn't. I'm sure she didn't, because there wasn't no sense in turning, you know, that way.

Q: How far were you going to continue going straight ahead?

A: Oh, I would say we were going to my house, and I live about four blocks away on Park Avenue, and I believe it happened on Second Avenue. Well, I was staying at 38th and Park at that time.

Q: Well, all right. What happened? How did the cars come together, do you know?

A: No. I was hit on my side, on the right side of the car.

Q: Did you see the Souter car at any time before the collision?

A: No.

Q: How fast was Ms. Jones driving?

A: I didn't look at the speedometer. We weren't speeding or in a rush to go anywhere, you know. She normally drives slow anyways, the speed limit.

Q: Did anyone say anything before the collision occurred? Any exclamations?

A: No. Just hit. Surprised everybody.

Q: How would you describe the collision?

A: Sudden. Just happened, you know. I didn't—you know, surprised me.

Q: All right. What happened to the car in which you were riding, the Buick, when the collision did occur?

A: Seemed like it just pushed the car around in a circle, seemed like. Seemed like it just went around, you know.

Q: Are you saying the car was pushed sideways?

A: Yes. Like when it hit, seemed like I was—seemed like pain was just in my body, and I was just in pain, you know, for a second or two, and the car was just moving around.

Q: What was its position when the car came to rest?

A: It was in this way [indicating], turned like that all the way around.

Q: Well, the car had been traveling east, easterly?

A: [Nods head]

Q: What way was it facing when it came to rest?

A: South. It might even have spun the whole time, you know, one whole time. Seemed like it was spinning a long time and sliding.

Q: Now, the other car stopped right at the point of impact, didn't it?

A: I—I thought it was down—across the intersection, I'm sure. I'm pretty sure it did.

Q: Did Ms. Jones's car come to a stop outside of the intersection? Did it continue through the intersection and—

A: It was knocked past the intersection. Spun down, you know, like, towards west, east, went down. Like it spun and sort of pushed it forward down the street in a way and spun it too. Seemed like it happened—it did happen like that. Then it came to a stop.

Q: East of the intersection.

A: Yes.

Q: Is that your testimony?

A: It went past the intersection, a little way past it, I think.

Q: So that would be east of the intersection?

A: Yes. Going towards the river, that's—yes, right.

Q: All right. So that we are clear on this, you say that the Jones car came to rest east of the east curb line of Second Avenue.

A: It what? Pardon me.

Q: You say that the car came to rest east of the east curb line of Second Avenue.

A: Yes.

Q: Okay. Now, what happened to you when the collision occurred?

A: As soon as it hit?

Q: Right.

A: Seemed like I was in pain, and seemed like I was—seemed like I was just in pain for a short time, about a second or two, and like everything had blacked out for a second or two as I was in pain.

Q: Well, did you strike yourself against anything in the car, against the windshield?

A: Against the door, that side door I believe, or probably in the corner.

Q: You what?

A: Or probably in the corner of the—not the windshield. You know, like towards—kitty-corner over.

Q: Do you remember that clearly?

A: It was—I know it was on the side, what I'm saying. It wasn't the windshield. I didn't hit the windshield at all.

Q: Did you have any accident markings on your person, any cuts, bruises, bumps?

A: Yes.

Q: What?

A: Legs—well, like everything was sore, but it was—you know, like—seemed like this side [indicating], and my legs were sore, like they were bruised and stuff.

Q: Well, Mr. Johnson, you have told me you were sore, but I want to know if there were any bumps or bruises, anything that someone else could see or feel.

A: I think it was just skinned, more or less.

Q: Skinned?

A: Skinned like.

Q: An abrasion?

A: Pardon.

Q: You mean an abrasion or rubbing of the skin?

A: Yes, abrasion.

Q: Where the skin wasn't actually broken, but it was just an abrasion of the skin, is that what you are saying?

A: Yes, I guess abrasion, I don't know. It was like—you know, it was skinned.

Q: And you are indicating that this was someplace on your right arm.

A: It was on my—down here [indicating] on my chin.

Q: Now you are indicating your right chin.

A: Yes. Seemed like most of the pain was up here. Seemed like I hit the door, but my legs was hurting too.

Q: You are now indicating your right arm near your right elbow.

A: Well, seemed like my whole side was hurting, and my leg somehow was hurting too.

Q: Now you are indicating your whole right side was hurting.

A: Yes. Seemed it was a lot—I really don't know exactly—all I remember is something like my legs were hurting, too.

Q: Both legs? Is that what you are telling us?

A: I really don't remember. Just seems like it was hurting. My legs, they didn't—I didn't write it down or nothing what was hurting. It was a long time ago, and I don't remember exactly what was scratched or nothing like this.

Q: All right. You didn't notice any pain in your back or your neck immediately following the accident, did you?

A: No.

Q: The police came and investigated, didn't they?

A: Yes.

Q: And what did you tell the police about your condition?

A: Nothing. When I was walking around I thought I was all right.

Q: Did you seek any medical examinations or treatments right after the accident?

A: No.

Q: Well, didn't you go to General Hospital?

A: Yes. Well, like they were—they were busy like always, and they just took my temperature and told me to leave and—I could leave.

Q: Well, now you must listen to my questions carefully. I asked you if you sought any medical examinations. Well, you did—

A: The doctor—yes, I did—

Q: You went to General Hospital.

A: Yes.

Q: All right.

A: But I mean—go ahead.

Q: But they didn't do anything for you other than take your temperature, is that what you say?

A: No. Right.

Q: When did you next seek any medical examinations or treatment?

A: About a month or two after.

Q: Who did you see?

A: Dr. Peterson.

Q: How did you happen to go to Dr. Peterson?

A: Well, he is the only doctor that I knew over North, and I believe Carolyn told me about him because she was going there too.

Q: Who?

A: Carolyn Jones, the driver of the car.

Q: Okay. Had you ever been to Peterson before?

A: No.

Q: When did you first have any symptoms of neck problems, pains, or discomfort?

A: About a month or two after when I went to see Dr. Peterson.

Q: Okay. That's when you first really noticed any pain or problem in your neck.

A: Yes.

Q: Okay. All right. When did you first notice any pain or discomfort or any problem in your back?

A: About the time when I went to see him.

Ms. Clarke: You mean, you went for thirty days and you didn't have any trouble, and all of a sudden one day you had trouble with your back?

The Witness: Seemed like that.

Ms. Clarke: I don't believe that.

Mr. Fredricks: Pardon me.

Ms. Clarke: You mean, you didn't have any trouble the day of the accident or the day afterwards?

The Witness: No.

Mr. Lang: Objected to as leading and suggestive.

Mr. Fredricks: Ellen—

Ms. Clarke: Well, fantastic. I don't believe him.

Mr. Lang: Whether you believe him or not, that's what he said.

Ms. Clarke: I don't think he understands the question.

Mr. Lang: It's clear that he does.

The Witness: I mean, it didn't hurt just one month later. It was such a long time ago, like it—problems.

Ms. Clarke: Well, they are trapping you. The way you have answered these questions, that's the end of your lawsuit. That's basically what they have trapped you into here. Now, if you understand—

Mr. Fredricks: Now, that isn't true.

Ms. Clarke: That's true.

Mr. Fredricks: The word trap is not at all appropriate here, Ellen.

Ms. Clarke: Well, it is when it's obvious to me he doesn't understand your question, that's all. And if you understand what you are doing, then you can answer any way you want, but I want you to understand what you are saying here. That's why I'm here, to make sure you understand your questions.

The Witness: See, it was—

Mr. Fredricks: Let's see if we can't clarify this.

Ms. Clarke: Why don't you let him answer.

Q: [By Mr. Fredricks] About the time that you first had difficulties with your neck and lower back is when you went to see Dr. Peterson. Whether that was a week after or a month after, that's when you started having difficulty, and you went to see him at that time because you did notice that you were having difficulty.

A: Well, let me say—like I probably had some pain first. It was a long time ago, and I don't exactly remember how—how many days or what it was when I went to see Dr. Peterson after the accident or nothing like this. Like the pain probably came a week after, and I probably didn't think nothing of it, you know—

Q: All right.

A: —and it was probably there. I mean if a pain is just there, you don't go the same day, you see. I mean this is the way I looked at it. And from the questions you asked, you know, it was probably a month when I seen a doctor, a month or two months after when I went to see him to—

Q: But I'm asking you not when you went to see Dr. Peterson but when you first became aware of any discomfort in your neck or back, and you have said it was about a month, and now—

A: I mean I seen Dr. Peterson about a month or two after.

Q: That's what you meant.

A: I really don't even know exactly how long that was, exactly.

Q: But now it is your recollection that it was about a week or more after the accident before you first had any difficulty with your neck or your back, is that correct?

A: It was probably a week or so after I had trouble with my back?

Q: Yes.

A: I don't know exactly the—I really don't know. It probably was a week when I first felt pain somewhere.

Q: Now, do you recall if you were doing something particular, you were engaged in some activity when you first noticed this back pain, were you were walking up a stairway, or lifting something, or driving a car, or—

A: I really don't remember.

Q: By the way, when you had this accident about a month ago, were you driving your own automobile?

A: No, I wasn't.

Q: Whose car were you driving?

A: The girl's car.

Q: Ruby's?

A: No.

Q: What was her name?

A: Rebecca Ann Parsons.

Q: Rebecca. It was her car.

A: Yes.

Q: Do you know who she had her insurance with?

A: No, I don't.

Q: Well, you must have talked with some insurance man—

A: Yes.

Q: —since the accident.

A: I don't remember his name though.

Q: Did he give you a card or—

A: He called on the phone.

Q: Okay. Ellen, do you have a copy of that—did the police investigate that accident?

Ms. Clarke: No, but if you have any authorizations you want signed at all, why don't you give them to him now and I will have him check them.

Mr. Lang: What was the name of the person you had the accident with?

The Witness: I beg your pardon.

Mr. Lang: What was the name of the person you had the accident with?

The Witness: The other person. I forget her name. She was an elderly lady.

Mr. Lang: Do you know where she lives?

The Witness: South Detroit.

Q: [By Mr. Fredricks] All right. When you first noticed this pain in your back, or when you first noticed pain in your neck, what did it feel like? Describe it for me.

A: Just seemed like a sharp pain.

Q: Where was it located?

A: It was just a pain all over, seemed like. Seemed like I was paralyzed maybe—if that's the right term to use. Seemed like it was just—I can't even explain it.

Q: All right. Was this pain localized at any particular place in your back?

Ms. Clarke: You better explain what localized means, you know.

Q: [By Mr. Fredricks] You know—

A: I don't know—I really couldn't tell you.

Q: Was the pain in your neck localized or at any particular spot in your back? Was it on one side or the other?

Ms. Clarke: What he is trying to say is what part of your neck—when you talk about your back, he wants to know whether it's in the middle of your back, or in the lower back, or upper back. He wants to know what part of your neck or your back you are talking about.

The Witness: When I was going to say pain, it seems like a pain all over, I—you know, I didn't stop and think of where it was at, no, or nothing like this, because at the time I was being shook around at the same time.

Q: [By Mr. Fredricks] At the time you were being what?

A: At the time of the accident, you know. There was pain, and I was being shaken around at the same time, and I couldn't tell you exactly, you know, where the pain was. It was just a pain in the head all over.

Q: You have indicated that there was some period of time elapsed after the accident before—

A: Yes.

Q: —you became aware of pain in your neck and your back. Now I want to know when you did become aware of your neck pain or your back pain, where was it located?

A: Oh, you mean when I—after the accident.

Q: Yes.

A: Yes.

Q: It was a week or more after the accident, as I understand your testimony. Tell me what you felt.

A: It was in the lower back, pain in the lower back.

Q: All right. And was it on one side or the other? Was it on your left side or right side?

A: It was down the center of my back, the spinal cord.

Q: Right in the middle.

A: Yes.

Q: Was it below your belt?

A: It was down in the lower back.

Q: Below your belt line.

A: Lower part of my back.

Q: Was it below your belt line or above it?

A: Is this [indicating] below my belt line?

Q: This [indicating] is your belt.

A: Is this my belt [indicating], below my belt, or what?

Q: Yes, that's your—you have placed your hand well below your belt line.

A: That's where it was. That's where it was.

Q: All right, fine.

A: And my neck right here [indicating].

Q: Now, was there any particular activity, or were you doing something when you first noticed this pain in your lower back?

A: I don't remember.

Q: All right. When you first noticed this pain in your lower back, did it limit you in any way? Were your activities limited? Were your movements limited?

A: What do you mean, limited? What do you mean, was I limited? Could I walk?

Q: Did you have to go to bed because of the back pain, or did you have to stop swimming, or did you—is there anything that it did to affect you in any way?

A: Like when it hurt, I just—well, it was—it would hurt. Like when I'm sitting at school. For instance, when I first notice it I was in school or sitting in the chair.

Q: All right.

A: And it was just uncomfortable to sit in a chair.

Q: All right. Now, this would have been at Wahlstrom.

A: Yes, it was—well, like—it couldn't have been, because I seen Dr. Peterson before I went to Wahlstrom, and he said— let's see—I don't now how—I seen Dr. Peterson before I went to Wahlstrom, I was getting therapy at the clinic before I went to Wahlstorm, and now that—when I noticed it how it acted. Then I couldn't tell, but like when I was at school when I was sitting down in the chair, I remember that, you know, because I was always turning and stuff.

Q: How does your lower back feel right now?

A: Uncomfortable.

Q: Well, is there pain in it?

A: Just seemed like a slight—slight pain.

Q: Slight pain.

A: [Nods head]

Q: Does that keep you from doing anything?

A: No. I go—I still do what I do.

Q: How about your neck, how is that?

A: It's fair. It's all right.

Q: It's okay.

A: [Nods head]

Q: All right. You are not having any trouble with it now?

A: No.

Q: When is the last time you had any trouble with your neck?

A: I was in the hospital about last month or month—about two months ago, month and a half ago, for treatment.

Q: Which hospital?

A: Mt. Sinai.

Q: And you did have trouble with your neck at that time?

A: Yes. My neck and back.

Q: And is that Mr. William Freeman again who gave you therapy?

A: This was in the hospital.

Q: Yes. He worked at—or he—at least he did work at Mt. Sinai.

A: No, I was in traction, they put me in traction.

Q: All right. The heat packs and traction seemed to help.

A: It was all right. Like, after I got out of the hospital, well, last—about a week ago, I drove—well, rode down to Missouri, and it was uncomfortable sitting in the car.

Q: You were what?

A: It was uncomfortable sitting in the car, you know, long distance. Like, you know, drove to Missouri.

Q: Where in Missouri?

A: Monroe.

Q: Monroe?

A: Monroe.

Q: What did you go to Missouri for?

A: To see some people.

Q: Who?

A: Some people, some friends.

Q: Who did you go to see?

A: Some friends.

Q: What's their names?

A: I forget their last name.

Q: Who did you go with?

A: Some friends. Friend of mine and his family. See, they were—I just went for the ride, just to go, just to go out of town, and it was their cousins and things.

Q: Whose car?

A: Their car.

Q: And what is their name?

A: Cross. Cross.

Q: First name.

A: I forget their first name, lady's first name. I went with a family and a friend of mine my age.

Q: And what's his name?

A: Brian Cross.

Q: What?

A: Brian Cross. Does that make any difference who I go down there with?

Ms. Clarke: You tell him exactly what it was, that's all. You just tell him the truth, that's all I care about.

Q: [By Mr. Fredricks] Was it on that trip then—that was the last time you had any discomfort in your neck?

Ms. Clarke: I think he is talking about his back.

The Witness: My back. See, I—

Q: [By Mr. Fredricks] I thought you told me it was a month ago that you last had any problem with your lower back.

A: No. It was my neck.

Q: Your neck.

A: My neck is pretty much better now, but my back I still have some pain. Like I feel a slight pain now in my lower back.

Q: All right.

A: And during the trip down to Monroe, Missouri, I felt discomfort in my back on the way down and on the way back, and—

Q: And what month did you make that trip, July of 2000?

A: It was this month.

Q: August of 2000.

A: Yes.

Q: Did you seek any treatment for your back?

A: After this?

Q: While on that trip.

A: No.

Q: Did you take—

A: I was just taking hot baths and stuff.

Q: I see.

A: And I got a massage a couple times.

Q: You did.

A: Well, from, you know, his mother. She rubbed it down with Ben-Gay and stuff like that.

Q: After the trip.

A: Well, when I went down, got down to Monroe.

Q: Did you say your mother?

A: No, this—the dude's mother massaged my back when I was down there.

Q: Okay.

A: Mrs. Cross massaged my back.

Q: Have you had any military service?

A: No.

Q: Have you had a physical exam for military service?

A: No. See, I was going to school and they gave me a deferment for going to school.

Q: Do you have a military classification?

A: No, I don't.

Q: You don't have a military identification card or anything.

A: No.

Q: Have you ever been convicted of a crime?

A: No.

Q: Did you ever see or talk to this Souter after the night of the accident?

A: No.

Q: Did you talk to Mr. Souter at the scene of the accident?

A: No.

Q: Was there anyone in the car, Ms. Jones's car, besides you and Ruby?

A: No, just the three of us. Three of us.

Q: Do you have any plans to see Dr. Thomas Peterson again?

A: Well, I called him the other day, but he wasn't in, and I just wanted to talk to him because I didn't talk to him after I came out of the hospital. See, like, when I came out of the hospital, then I—he went into the hospital.

Q: He himself went in?

A: Yes. And, like, I sort of tried to avoid going over to—I have just been sitting in a hot bath, hot water.

Q: You can move your neck, and your back is all right now, as I understand your testimony.

A: Yes.

Q: And it's your lower back at this moment, you have slight pain in your lower back.

A: Yes.

Q: Does that get worse at times?

A: At night.

Q: At night.

A: Yes.

Q: What happens at night that causes your back to bother you?

A: Seems like there is a pain all down my back.

Q: Well, what are you doing, or what position causes your back problem?

A: I got a water bed, and it still hurts.

Q: You have a water bed?

A: Yes.

Q: How long have you had that?

A: About two months?

Q: Did it seem to help at all?

A: Not really. See, first I was sleeping on a mattress with a board up under, and that didn't seem to help it either.

Q: Did someone suggest that you try a water bed?

A: No.

Q: It was your own idea.

A: Yes.

Q: Does the water bed seem to hurt your back?

A: Not really. See, it hurts once in a while at night. It didn't hurt every night.

Q: I see. So usually your back feels better during the day than it does at night.

A: Sometimes I don't notice it during the day, sometimes I notice it during the day, sometimes at nights—

Q: What are you doing during the daytime that causes you to have back problems?

A: See, I sit down, I will be working in the office in Hearns Auditorium, and that's a lot of sitting, but I still walk around, you know, to—just to walk around, move my back around and stuff.

Q: The walking around seems to help.

A: Well, it's just moving around, if it—

Q: It does help.

A: It probably helps a little bit just to get up and move around.

Q: Does it?

A: Yes, it does. But when I sit down again for about five minutes, half hour again, I can feel the pain again.

Q: The pain in your legs cleared up quite soon after the accident?

A: Seemed like that came back little bit later too, pain in the other side of the leg.

Q: Your legs don't bother you now.

A: Not right now, no.

Q: When is the last time either of your legs bothered you? Been a long time?

A: Yes. About when I was seeing Dr. Peterson, getting therapy along in that time. Not the last—it probably was the last one. I haven't seen him—

Q: For about a year?

A: No, it hasn't been that long. About three—three or four months.

Q: Have you taken any drugstore medicines or—

A: Prescriptions?

Q: —prescription medicines?

A: Yes.

Q: When is the last time?

A: About four months ago.

Q: What drugstore do you get your medicine at?

A: I didn't get the medicine, this girl got it for me. It was just pain pills.

Q: Ms. Jones?

A: No, Cathy.

Q: The girl—

A: The one I'm staying with now, she went to the drugstore and got it. It was a pain pill though.

Q: Is it her prescription or yours?

A: Prescription Dr. Peterson wrote me.

Q: And when you had taken this medicine, why did you take it?

A: Why did I take it?

Q: Why?

A: For the pain.

Q: Where in?

A: My back pain.

Q: All right. Not your legs, not your neck, not for any headaches.

A: It was just—just a pain pill, Darvon. It's just for the pain. If you have pain in your leg, you know, supposed to knock it all out.

Q: The reason you have taken the Darvon is for your lower back.

A: Yes, sir.

Q: All right. And that's all.

A: Yes, sir.

Q: Okay. You haven't had any particular problem with headaches following this accident, have you?

A: Yes.

Q: You have.

A: Yes.

Q: For what period of time did you have headaches?

A: Sometimes I had it all evening. Well—

Q: I mean for—was it a month following the accident, two months, three months?

A: I couldn't—I couldn't tell you exactly. It's—it should be in Dr.—

Q: I'm not asking for an exact period of time, I'm asking for some—

A: I really couldn't tell you. It should be in Dr. Peterson's record, because I let him know when it happened.

Q: When is the last time you recall being bothered by a headache—long, long time ago, over a year ago?

A: I still have them. Well, like when I went on that trip I had headaches on the way down, something like a migraine headache. I remember the last time I had a terrible headache. Then again it was three, four months ago I was getting headaches, a headache, too.

Q: When?

A: About two or three months ago I was getting a headache.

Q: Did you have headaches while you were at Wahlstrom College?

A: I believe—I believe so.

Q: You don't recall now.

A: I'm pretty sure I did, because I remember getting a headache, you know, once in a while, serious headache.

Q: Like once a week?

A: No. I couldn't say exactly when—once a week or every two weeks. It was just a headache, you know, have a—a bad headache, you know, pain, headache.

Q: How often?

A: How often? What do you mean, how often?

Q: How often, when you were in college at Wahlstrom, did you have a bad headache?

A: Well, I can't answer that, you know, too perfect.

Q: Do you have any photographs about the accident, connected with the accident?

A: Do I have any pictures?

Q: Yes.

A: No.

Q: Do you claim that you have lost any income as a result of the accident?

A: Work?

Q: [Nods head]

A: Well, working, and taking the bus over there.

Q: Pardon me.

A: Taking the bus over from wherever I was at, taking a bus over to Dr. Peterson's office. And going too from Wahlstrom I was getting treatment, I had to—

Q: All right. You are claiming that you have lost some income.

A: Income and schooling too.

Q: Well, I'm not concerned about school time, I'm concerned about income right now. Do you file a tax return?

A: Did I this past one?

Q: Yes. Have you filed a tax return at any time since the August—

A: Yes.

Q: —accident?

A: Yes.

Q: Federal tax returns? You have.

A: [Nods head]

Q: All right.

Ellen, I will prepare authorizations for tax returns, and also an authorization for the accident report, and I will send them to you.

Ms. Clarke: Why don't you have him sign them now. Just sign any blank authorizations you have for any reason, because I would like to know about these things too. You can fill them in.

While you are looking, my notes show you were at the hospital for four hours.

The Witness: At General?

Ms. Clarke: Yes.

The Witness: I was there a long time just sitting.

Ms. Clarke: My notes also show you saw a doctor the next day. Who did you see the next day?

The Witness: A doctor.

Ms. Clarke: Yes, that's what this shows.

The Witness: I don't know. If it was anybody, it was Dr. Peterson, but I don't remember. I didn't see nobody at General.

[Whereupon a discussion was had off the record.]

Q: [By Mr. Fredricks] Have you ever had any injections in your neck or shoulders with a needle administered by any doctors?

A: No. No I haven't.

Q: Pardon me.

A: No, I haven't.

Q: Have you ever had any electromyogram tests where they put a needle in your muscles and—

A: Just in the head, scalp.

Q: You have had that in your scalp?

A: Yes.

Q: And when was that done?

A: When I went to the doctor.

Q: For what?

A: When I went to the hospital for Dr. Peterson, at Mt. Sinai Hospital.

Q: And was that soon after the accident then, or when?

A: No, this was recently when I just went to the hospital about two months ago, month and a half ago, for treatment, treatments in the hospital.

Q: That was at Mt. Sinai.

A: Yes, it was.

Q: And that's the only place you have had any such tests.

A: Yes.

Ms. Clarke: I notice there is a bill here for injection of something into your neck muscles; what's that for?

The Witness: What is it? What is it?

Ms. Clarke: Did it in the hospital, apparently.

The Witness: Which hospital?

Ms. Clarke: June 21st. It says injection, superior angles. Apparently into your neck.

The Witness: That was at Mt. Sinai.

Ms. Clarke: Yes.

The Witness: That's what it was then, at Mt. Sinai.

Ms. Clarke: You just told him you never had any injections. I want to know what you are talking about.

The Witness: I just seen it in the head and up here [indicating], but I don't know what he stuck down here [indicating].

Q: [By Mr. Fredricks] Do you know what I mean by a hypodermic needle, where you get a—

A: Blood thing?

Q: Yes. Needle that goes into your arm and they inject something under the skin or into the muscle.

A: All I remember is when they put pins all in the head and stuff, and—

Q: You don't remember Dr. Peterson ever injecting any needles into your neck or back?

A: No, I don't.

Q: Okay.

A: That one right there—they might have put some up here [indicating], but I don't remember.

Q: Sometimes he doesn't do it, Ellen, and he records it in his records, so I'm not surprised.

Ms. Clarke: He charged twenty bucks for doing it.

Mr. Fredricks: Yes.

Ms. Clarke: I got to know, if he didn't do it, I want to know about it.

The Witness: Where was it I said those pins were at?

Ms. Clarke: I don't have to tell. We are asking you the questions. You were there, I wasn't.

The Witness: I had pins up here [indicating]. Probably if they had some here [indicating], you know, I didn't feel it too much.

Q: [By Mr. Fredricks] You haven't had any problems or any discomfort in your throat area of your neck, have you? You never developed any pain in the front portion of your neck, did you?

A: Not that I recall.

Q: Okay.

A: Well, it was just—

Q: Just in the back of the neck.

A: You mean as far as strep throat or anything like this?

Q: No, I mean following the accident. Any injury to the front portion of your neck?

A: No, I can't—if it was, it was slight. It was just—what Dr. Peterson said it was, I don't know if it was here—you mean did I feel pain exactly right here [indicating] somewhere up in here [indicating].

Q: Yes.

A: No.

Q: Have you had strep throat or some problem like that?

A: One time, long time ago.

Q: Dr. Peterson didn't treat you for that?

A: No.

Q: You have been treated with some physical therapy at Mt. Sinai Hospital, and traction.

A: Yes.

Q: Have you had therapy or traction anywhere else?

A: At his office, at his clinic, and at Wahlstrom, downtown clinic.

Q: What clinic downtown? Was that Kennan's?

A: No. This was in Uhler, Michigan.

Q: Oh. What clinic?

A: It was at the hospital, at the Uhler Hospital down in Uhler, Michigan.

Q: But you said there was a clinic downtown in Uhler.

A: I meant Uhler Hospital, and there is a clinic there.

Q: At the hospital.

A: I believe so, yes.

Q: You saw some private doctors in Uhler.

A: Yes.

Q: Do you remember their names?

A: No, I don't.

Mr. Fredricks: Do you have that, Ellen?

Ms. Clarke: No, except it's on the—I sent your adjuster the bill for some x-rays down there, and I assume from that you can get a lead as to who ordered the x-rays. I don't even know that.

Q: [By Mr. Fredricks] Right. At the present time you are engaging in all of the activities that you used to participate in and enjoy before this accident.

A: Yes.

Q: You are not claiming that you are now handicapped or prevented from doing things that you would otherwise do due to this accident?

A: Well, I—you know, I know my back is hurting, I won't be picking up something that's heavy or something. I try to use some common sense what to do and what not to do with my back.

Q: All right. But you can throw a softball and you can—

A: Yes.

Q: If you enjoyed ice skating, you would go ice skating, or if you bowled you would go bowling, and if you want to take a trip like to Missouri, you go ahead and do it.

A: Yes.

Q: Okay. Have you made any other trips—

A: No.

Q: —out of the state or out of town since?

A: Yes. Yes.

Q: Where?

A: San Antonio.

Q: Texas?

A: Yes.

Q: When?

A: Right after school was out.

Q: And what was the purpose of that trip?

A: Just going down to San Antonio, Texas.

Q: Did you make this trip by car?

A: Yes.

Q: Who did you go with?

A: Some friends of mine. It was three in the car.

Q: Well, who were the friends?

A: Some friends I went to school with.

Q: I'm interested in names.

A: They were no kin or nothing like—

Q: Pardon me.

A: They were no kin to me or nothing like that.

Q: All right. But what were their names? Was it Ms. Jones? Was it Ruby?

A: No.

Q: Who?

A: Cooley. Cooley. They are from out of town. They are from out of town, from Des Moines.

Q: Oh, okay. Anyone else or any other trips?

A: No.

Q: How long were you gone to San Antonio?

A: Just down and back.

Mr. Fredricks: I believe that's all the questions I have.

Examination

By Mr. Lang:

Q: Have you ever worn any kind of belt, or brace, or collar?

A: Yes. Like when I went for my—on the trip to Monroe I wore a back brace.

Q: Where did you get that?

A: At Mt. Sinai. Well, see, it was a traction belt and I just cut the things off of it and used it, just used it as a belt.

Q: How wide is that?

A: This wide [indicating].

Q: About six inches wide?

A: Yes.

Q: How many times have you been hospitalized since this accident of August of '99?

A: Just that once.

Q: And how long a time was that?

A: A week.

Q: Did the hospitalization help you?

A: Not really. Not really.

Q: How long have you lived in the Detroit area?

A: About eleven or twelve years.

Q: Did you have headaches before this accident?

A: Not that I can recall, no.

Q: You referred to migraine headaches; now, have you been bothered with migraine headaches?

A: Not like that. Not no headaches like this one. I used to have just plain headaches, you know, like cold headaches, but like these headaches is something else.

Q: How often do you get those?

A: Once in a while.

Q: How often is that? Once a month?

A: Once a month, twice a month. You know, it isn't—

Q: How long do they last?

A: A long time; about three or four hours.

Q: Do you take anything for them?

A: Yes.

Q: What do you take?

A: Aspirins.

Q: Does that relieve them?

A: No.

Mr. Lang: I have no further questions.

Ms. Clarke: We will waive the reading and signing and the notice of filing of the deposition.

STATE OF MICHIGAN
COUNTY OF WAYNE

SS.

Be it known that I took the deposition of Duane Johnson, pursuant to agreement of counsel; that I was then and there a notary public in and for said county and state; that I exercised the power of that office in taking said deposition; that by virtue thereof I was then and there authorized to administer an oath; that said witness, before testifying, was duly sworn to testify to the truth, the whole truth and nothing but the truth relative to the cause specified above; that the deposition is a true record of the testimony given by the witness; that the reading and signing of the deposition was waived by the witness and pursuant to agreement of counsel; that I am neither attorney or counsel for, nor related to or employed by, any of the parties to the action in which this deposition was taken, and further that I am not a relative or employee of any attorney or counsel employed by the parties hereto or financially interested in the action.

WITNESS MY HAND AND SEAL this 13th day of August, 2000.

John R. Nash

Notary Public, Wayne County, Michigan
My Commission Expires November 25, 2004.

APPENDIX C

INTRAOFFICE MEMORANDA (PRIVILEGED)

TO: *Paralegal*

FROM: *Attorney*

DATE: _____

SUBJECT: *Trustee Raskin Case*
               Jurisdictional Issues

Ms. Laura Raskin's father, William Nordby, died as the result of an automobile accident that occurred on October 17, 2000 in Hubbard County, Minnesota. She has retained this Firm to represent her and the other next of kin in a wrongful death action. Bradley Harper was the other driver. Our action will be against him. Apparently, there is some problem about whether he has automobile liability insurance. The person he bought the car from agreed to provide insurance, but either neglected to obtain it or let it expire. There is some question in my mind whether the seller could contract to provide insurance, because the sale of insurance is a regulated business.

We will bring a negligence action in the Hubbard County District Court against Harper for Nordby's wrongful death. At least initially, we will let Mr. Harper figure out his insurance problems. He will have to look to the seller, Griffin, his agent, Burns, or the Security Insurance Company for coverage. But before we commence the action against Griffin, I want to be sure that we can eventually obtain jurisdiction over them in the same court or that Harper can obtain jurisdiction over them by bringing a third-party action.

Please prepare a short memorandum to me concerning whether jurisdiction is obtainable as to each potential party.

Thank you.

TO: *Attorney*

FROM: *Paralegal*

DATE: _____

SUBJECT: *Trustee Raskin Case*
               Jurisdictional Issues

FACTS
[In a narrative form, succinctly state the material facts.]

ISSUE
[State the legal issue as a question or as a declaratory sentence.]

SHORT ANSWER
[State your answer or conclusion.]
   All potential defendants and third-party defendants are subject to jurisdiction in the Hubbard County District Court.

ANALYSIS
[The analysis is your discussion that identifies the controlling rules of law and explains how those rules apply to the facts.]

RECOMMENDATIONS
[As a result of your analysis you may have information, comments, or suggestions for the attorney. Sometimes the recommendations go beyond the specific assignment. For example, you may have located a very similar case, a companion statute, or have some personal information about the parties, accident, witnesses, or the like. Provide all the input you can.]

GLOSSARY

abuse of process   A cause of action in tort to recover money damages for personal injury caused by another person's willful misuse of the civil or criminal legal process.

accident scene   The situs of an accident while conditions are the same as they were at the time of the accident.

accident situs   The place where an accident occurred, but the physical conditions and circumstances may have changed.

accord and satisfaction   An *accord* is an agreement that replaces a disputed claim or prior disputed contract. The new agreement relieves the parties from any obligations under the former agreement or disputed claim. A *satisfaction* is the execution or fulfillment of the new agreement. Together, an accord and satisfaction provide a complete defense to the prior claim or disputed contract.

action   A claim that has been placed in suit. A lawsuit. Also called an action at law.

actionable   An act or occurrence is actionable if it provides legal reasons for a lawsuit.

action in rem   An action against property, rather than a person. No person is designated as a defendant. Anyone who claims an interest in the property must assert his or her claim by filing an answer; otherwise, he or she forfeits any interest in the property. A district court in the state in which the property is located has jurisdiction over the subject matter (property), and anyone who claims an interest in the property, even nonresidents, must submit to the court's jurisdiction or forfeit his or her interest in the property.

actual bias   A state of mind that prevents a venireman, juror, or witness from being impartial. A predisposition or preconceived opinion about the issues, parties, or type of case that precludes a venireman from being fair. A witness who demonstrates actual bias against a party may be cross-examined by that party as a hostile witness.

ad damnum clause   The "Wherefore" clause at the end of a civil action complaint, in which the plaintiff specifies the relief or recovery the plaintiff wants the court to award. The clause at the end of the defendant's answer, cross-claim, or counterclaim that specifies the relief the defendant wants the court to award.

additur   A court-ordered increase of money damages awarded by a jury. A trial court has the authority to increase the amount of the award when the damages are manifestly inadequate. Usually, the trial court gives the defendant the option of paying an additur or going through a new trial where a new jury can determine the amount of damages. The trial court may order an additur even though no error of law or procedure explains the jury's inadequate award.

admissible evidence   Evidence that tends to prove a material fact and which is not subject to any exclusionary rule of evidence.

admission of service   A party's formal acknowledgment that he or she received service of process or documents or court order. An admission of service must be in writing, dated, and signed by the party or party's attorney.

adverse parties   Parties are adverse when their interests in the outcome of the litigation conflict. A party may cross-examine an adverse party. When adversity exists between parties, they cannot be required to share peremptory challenges for jury selection.

advisory jury   In cases where the plaintiff seeks equitable relief and the judge is responsible for determining the facts, the judge may empanel an advisory jury which is selected and acts like any other petit jury, except the judge is not required to accept or use the verdict.

affiant   A person who makes an affidavit.

affidavit   A written ex parte statement made under oath before an officer of the court or a notary public. A person who makes an affidavit is subject to prosecution for perjury for making a false statement under oath. Therefore, affidavits provide some assurance of truthfulness, but they lack the safeguard of a cross-examination.

affidavit of identification   An affidavit, usually prepared by an attorney or paralegal, to establish the identity of a judgment debtor so the court may issue an order to a sheriff or marshal to seize the judgment debtor's property to satisfy the judgment.

affidavit of no response   An attorney's affidavit that shows an opposing party has failed to perform an act required by a court order or court rule. An affidavit commonly used to show that an opposing party has failed to respond to a request for admission within the time allowed, thereby establishing that the request is admitted.

affirmative defense   A defense that is usually based on the plaintiff's act or conduct or consent. An affirmative defense bars the plaintiff's claim or cause of action even if the plaintiff proves all the elements of the claim to which the defense is asserted. The defense must be pled by the party who asserts it; otherwise the defense is waived. The party who asserts an affirmative defense has the burden of proving it.

agent   A person or corporation that has authority to act for another person, usually called a principal, and to make legally binding commitments on behalf of the principal. The agent's authority may be express or implied. The authority may be based on a contract between the principal and the agent, or it may be created by statute.

agreement to arbitrate   An agreement between parties to a dispute, which commits the parties to arbitrate the dispute. The agreement may be made before or after the dispute arises. The agreement to arbitrate ordinarily provides for the scope of submission.

alternate juror   A person who is selected to sit on a jury to hear and decide a case, but who does not participate in the jury's deliberations unless one of the regular jurors becomes unavailable. If the alternate is not needed, he or she usually is excused when the parties have completed their final arguments and the court has instructed the jury on the law. The parties may stipulate to let an alternate juror deliberate and participate in the verdict.

alternative dispute resolution (ADR)   Any procedure or method for resolving disputes between persons that does not involve the courts. The primary methods of alternative dispute resolution are arbitration and mediation.

amicus curiae   A "friend of the court." A nonparty may seek amicus curiae status to appear in a case for the limited purpose of presenting arguments and authorities on a question of law that, when decided, may affect the

nonparty in some way. The nonparty must first petition the court for leave to participate. The participation is limited to issues of law.

answer   A defendant's pleading in which the defendant admits and/or denies the plaintiff's allegations. A defendant's answer must allege all the affirmative defenses the defendant claims. A defendant may use the answer to raise procedural issues, such as improper service and jurisdictional issues. A defendant must serve a copy of the answer on the plaintiff within 20 days after the summons and complaint are served on the defendant. A defendant must file the original answer with the court in which the action is venued.

appear   A party appears in an action when he or she serves or files a pleading or motion. By appearing in an action, a person submits to the court's jurisdiction unless the appearance is "special" and limited to the purpose of challenging the court's jurisdiction.

appellant   An aggrieved party who appeals to a higher court to review the proceedings of the trial court's order or judgment on the grounds that the trial court committed an error of law or procedural errors that adversely affected the outcome.

appellee   A party against whom an appeal is taken. The party who seeks to sustain the trial court's order or judgment.

arbitration   A procedure by which parties submit their dispute to another person or tribunal for decision. The submission may be voluntary, pursuant to a contract to arbitrate, or pursuant to a statute that requires arbitration. Courts encourage parties to use arbitration even after an action has been commenced.

arbitration award   An arbitration tribunal's award. The award may be binding or nonbinding between the parties, depending on the agreement under which the arbitration was conducted.

arbitration tribunal   A person or persons appointed by parties to decide their dispute using an arbitration format. A tribunal may be composed of one or more persons; usually it is an odd number of people to avoid a tie vote. The individual members of an arbitration tribunal are called arbitrators.

arbitrator   A person chosen by parties to a dispute to resolve their dispute. An arbitrator's authority is limited to the parties' scope of submission. Otherwise, an arbitrator is free to decide a matter based on his or her own discretion. An arbitrator is not bound by legal procedures or rules of law, unless so provided in the scope of submission. The scope of submission is ordinarily part of the agreement to arbitrate.

arbitration and award An affirmative defense that arises when parties submit their dispute to binding arbitration. The tribunal's award replaces the dispute with an award. The award precludes either party from bringing an action against the other on the basis of the prior dispute.

assault A cause of action in tort that allows the victim to obtain money damages for personal injury, usually mental suffering, caused by an intentional threat of serious bodily harm or death even though no physical contact occurs. The threat may be made through acts or words that put the victim in fear of immediate bodily harm. However, words that are not accompanied by the apparent means of making good on the threat of bodily harm do not give rise to an action for assault. An assault may be accompanied by a battery.

assignment A transfer of one's property or legal rights to another.

assumption of risk An affirmative defense to an action in negligence and to some other tort actions. The defendant must show that the claimant voluntarily placed herself or himself in a position to incur a known risk of harm. Some courts recognize a difference between primary assumption of risk and secondary assumption of risk. A primary assumption of risk precludes the defendant from having any legal duty to the plaintiff. A secondary assumption of risk is treated as a form of contributory negligence or comparative negligence.

attachment A proceeding by which a judgment debtor's property is seized to satisfy the debtor's legal obligation to the judgment creditor.

attorney pro se A person who acts as his or her own attorney in a civil action.

attorneys' work product A doctrine, predicated on Rule 26 of the Federal Rules of Civil Procedure, that prevents one party from discovering what another party's attorneys have done or have accomplished in preparing for trial. The work that attorneys have performed for a client.

award A decision or determination rendered by an arbitration tribunal.

bad faith claim A willful failure to comply with a clear statutory duty or contractual duty. A cause of action

against an insurance company that wrongfully refuses to provide liability coverage to its insured.

battery A battery gives rise to an action in tort for personal injury. An intentional, impermissible physical contact of an injurious nature, or a physical contact that is offensive to ordinary sensibilities. The claimant must prove that the physical contact was intentional, although the claimant need not prove that an injury was specifically intended.

binding arbitration Arbitration in which the parties must comply with the arbitration tribunal's award. The award may be filed with a court that has jurisdiction, for confirmation. The court will enter a judgment on the basis of the confirmed award. The judgment may be enforced in the same manner as any civil judgment.

boilerplate instructions A colloquial term used to describe standard jury instructions generally used by a particular judge or all of the judges at a particular court.

breach of contract A cause of action to recover money damages, flowing from a person's violation of the terms of a contract.

breach of warranty A breach of an express or implied warranty relating to the title, quality, content, or condition of goods sold.

burden of proof A party's duty to present evidence to establish a claim, defense, or allegation. The burden of proof embodies two distinct concepts: One, it refers to the obligation to present sufficient evidence on all the elements of a claim or affirmative defense to establish a prima facie case. Two, it refers to the degree to which a party may have to convince the court or a jury to establish a claim or defense. In most civil actions, the proponent must prove a claim by a fair preponderance of the evidence. Some claims and defenses in equity require proof by clear and convincing evidence. In criminal cases guilt must be proved beyond a reasonable doubt.

calendar call A procedure in which a court requires the attorneys who have cases pending to appear at a specified time and state whether their case is ready for trial. The procedure allows the court to schedule cases for trial at a reasonably convenient time.

case analysis A process a party may use to determine whether his or her case is ready for trial. It begins by comparing the pleadings against the known facts and available evidence. A party can make sure he or she has all the evidence needed to establish a cause of action or affirmative defense. *See* fact brief.

case-in-chief   The body of evidence a party presents to establish the party's claim or affirmative defenses before the party rests. The plaintiff's body of evidence must establish a prima facie case or the claim will be dismissed. The defendant's body of evidence must establish a prima facie defense or the defense will be dismissed. A party's case-in-chief does not include the party's rebuttal evidence.

cause of action   A claim that is recognized by law and enforceable through the courts; a claim on which a court may grant relief. A cause of action presumes that the defendant has breached a legal duty and in doing so directly caused the plaintiff to sustain an injury or property damage or other loss. A cause of action is the basis for obtaining legal redress.

champerty   An agreement between an attorney and a client by which the attorney pledges to bear the cost of the client's litigation in return for a portion of the expected recovery of money damages.

chose in action   A claim or debt upon which a recovery can be made in a civil action. It is not a present possession. It is merely a right to sue. It becomes a possessory thing only if the litigation is successful.

circumstantial evidence   Indirect proof that depends on the application of logic and common experience to infer the existence of a fact; evidence offered to prove one or more facts from which the existence of other material facts can then reasonably be inferred. For example, a person's fingerprints on a glass are circumstantial evidence that the person handled the glass. The proof is by inference rather than by direct observation.

claim   A demand for compensation or restitution for personal injury, property damage, or loss of profits. A claim may be made without actually starting a lawsuit or having a lawsuit pending. A mere claim may or may not be based on a legal right. A claim may or may not qualify as a cause of action for which a court may provide relief. For a claim to be enforceable in court, it must be based on a breach of a legal duty owed to the claimant and constitute a cause of action.

claimant   A person who asserts a claim against another person, whether or not a lawsuit has been commenced.

clear and convincing   Creating a firm belief in the mind of the trier of fact. Clear and convincing proof is more than a fair preponderance of the evidence, which is the most common standard of proof applicable to civil

actions, but something less than beyond a reasonable doubt, which is the standard imposed on the government in the prosecution of criminal cases.

collateral estoppel   An affirmative defense that precludes the plaintiff from suing defendants not named in a prior case on the same cause of action, where the verdict against the plaintiff in the prior case held that the plaintiff either did not sustain a loss or was solely responsible for the loss. *See also* estoppel.

commencement of action   The date on which the plaintiff causes the action to begin against the defendant. In federal district courts, an action is ordinarily commenced at the time the plaintiff files the complaint with the clerk of court (see Rule 3). In many state courts, an action is not commenced until the summons and complaint are served on the defendant.

common law   A system of law that is based on precedent, rather than a civil code of laws. The law is derived from court decisions that evolve into rules of law that are followed as precedent unless or until the court that established them decides to replace or modify them. Most states rely on the common law to resolve disputes in civil litigation. The common law originated in England, both in concept and practice.

comparative fault   An expanded concept of comparative negligence that includes strict liability in tort, breach of warranty, dram shop liability, and other causes of action not based on intentional wrongful conduct. Liability is apportioned on the basis of the causal fault attributable to each party, including a plaintiff. In states that have comparative fault, a jury may be asked to compare one party's causal negligence with another party's liability and to apportion the causal fault on a percentage basis. The degree to which the breach of legal duty contributed to the loss, not the degree of culpability, is the basis for allocating damages. Comparative fault statutes include within their purview some torts that impose liability without fault, such as strict liability in tort.

comparative negligence   A legal doctrine that requires the fact finder (jury) in a negligence action to determine the percentage of causal negligence attributable to each person involved in the occurrence. A plaintiff's causal negligence does not necessarily bar the plaintiff from a recovery of compensatory money damages. If the plaintiff is found to be causally negligent, the amount of money damages recoverable is reduced by the amount of causal negligence. However, if the plaintiff is more causally negligent than the defendant, the laws of some states preclude the plaintiff from making any recovery against the defendant. If two or more defendants are found to be causally negligent, as between them, they must share the liability for money damages in proportion to their percentage of causal negligence; however, each defendant remains separately liable to the plaintiff for all the plaintiff's damages.

compensatory damages   A sum of money that is awarded to a person to reimburse her or him for personal injury or property damage. Compensatory damages are not intended to penalize the person who must pay them; they are intended to make up for the plaintiff's loss.

complaint   A document used in civil litigation to state a claim against a defendant. It must identify the parties, the court, and causes of action on which the plaintiff relies. It must describe the nature and extent of the plaintiff's loss and the remedy or compensation the plaintiff wants the court to award.

complicity   An affirmative defense to a dram shop action. The liquor vendor can avoid liability to the plaintiff who was injured by an intoxicated person, if the vendor can prove that the plaintiff was complicit in the illegal sale of intoxicants to the intoxicated person. For example, complicity is established by showing that the plaintiff bought the intoxicants for the intoxicated person.

compulsory counterclaim   A defendant's claim against the plaintiff that arises from the same transaction or occurrence as the plaintiff's claim. If the defendant fails to assert the claim in a counterclaim, it is waived by operation of law. The Rules make the counterclaim compulsory to avoid multiple trials based on a single occurrence.

conclusion   A determination about a fact obtained by reasoning from evidence and other known facts. An inference drawn by the jury or judge from the entire body of evidence provided by the witnesses as to the ultimate question of fact.

conclusions of law   Determinations judges make when applying the law to a given set of facts. For example, if the facts show that a motorist violated a traffic light and the law provides that a traffic signal violation is negligence, the legal conclusion is that the motorist was negligent. In an action decided by a judge without a jury, the judge must prepare a document that contains his or her findings of fact and conclusions of law. The conclusions of law determine the parties' rights and

obligations and are the basis for the court's order for judgment.

concurring opinion   An appellate court opinion written by an appellate judge to explain why the judge agrees with the decision or result reached by the majority of judges as expressed in their opinion, but disagrees with the reasons given by the majority for their decision.

condition precedent   A condition that must occur before a contract becomes effective, even though all the terms and conditions have been agreed on. A common example of a condition precedent is when a buyer agrees to purchase a new house on the condition that he or she can sell his or her present house.

confession of judgment   A person's written admission, made under oath, that she or he is indebted to the person named, and that the person named is entitled to have the court enter a judgment in her or his favor for a specified amount of money. A confession of judgment may be made without having an action pending against the confessor. Confessions of judgment are strictly regulated by statute in most states.

conflict of interest   A situation in which a lawyer's duty to a client to act or refrain from acting is or may be harmful to the interests of another client or a former client or to the lawyer's own interests. A lawyer must avoid conflicts of interests or obtain the client's express consent to act. To obtain the client's consent, a lawyer must make a full disclosure of the conflict. A client may voluntarily waive his or her right to object to a conflict of interest.

consent   Voluntary acquiescence. Consent is a complete affirmative defense to most tort actions. For example, the act of kissing a person is a battery, unless the person who is kissed consents to the physical contact. Consent may be expressed in words or acts, or implied from circumstances.

consent judgment   A judgment for which the parties to a civil lawsuit stipulate the terms and conditions. Occasionally, a defendant may stipulate that the plaintiff may enter a judgment against the defendant for a specified amount of money, with the provision that the plaintiff may collect the money only from the defendant's liability insurance policy. In that event, the plaintiff, who becomes a judgment creditor without having to go through a trial, covenants not to execute against the defendant's personal assets, other than the insurance policy. The plaintiff assumes the burden of establishing that the claim is covered by the insurance policy.

consideration   Consideration is an essential element to an enforceable contract. It is something of value that is given in exchange for a contracting party's performance or promise of performance.

contempt of court   A person's act or omission that interferes with a court's functions and for which a court may impose a punishment. The act or omission may be the person's refusal to comply with a court order or manifesting disrespect. If the wrongful act or omission occurs in the presence of the court, the court may summarily punish the offender. Otherwise, the court must hold a hearing to determine the facts. The court must give the alleged offender an opportunity to be heard, but the hearing is not a full trial.

contingent   Dependent on something else. An obligation or duty may be contingent on the occurrence of an event or performance of an act before it comes into being.

contingent fee   A fee for legal services based on an agreed percentage of the monies actually recovered. If the client does not recover any money damages in the litigation, the lawyer is not entitled to any fee.

contribution   A right or obligation between parties who are jointly liable to a third person, usually the plaintiff, for money damages recoverable in a civil action.

contributory negligence   Negligence on the part of the plaintiff that contributed to the accident and the plaintiff's injuries or other loss. Historically, contributory negligence provided the defendant with a complete defense to the plaintiff's action in negligence. The defense has been replaced in most states by the principles of comparative negligence and comparative fault.

conversion   The wrongful exercise of control of ownership over another person's personal property. A conversion of personal property is tantamount to a theft of the property.

cost bond   A bond that a party must provide to the court to guarantee payment of the adverse party's taxable costs and disbursements. An appellant may be required to provide a cost bond as a condition to prosecuting an appeal. Otherwise, some parties would appeal merely to delay payment of the judgment obtained against them.

counterclaim   A claim asserted by the defendant against the plaintiff to obtain compensation for a loss or damages suffered by the defendant, or the pleading in which such a claim is asserted. A counterclaim may be founded in tort or contract. It is attached to or made part of the defendant's answer.

counts   Separate statements of a claim within a complaint, counterclaim, or cross-claim. Counts may be used to state separate causes of action or to state claims arising from separate transactions or occurrences.

court reporter   A person who is authorized to administer oaths and to record testimony in court or in oral depositions. A reporter may record testimony by shorthand or by using a stenographic machine.

courts of general jurisdiction   Courts that have the broadest subject matter jurisdiction. They may handle actions to recover money damaged in any amount, actions to determine ownership of land, marital dissolution actions, and so forth.

covenant not to sue   A type of settlement agreement in which the plaintiff agrees not to commence or maintain an action against the defendant but does not release the defendant from liability for the occurrence. A tortfeasor who obtains a covenant not to sue avoids defending against the plaintiff's claim, and the plaintiff preserves the right to pursue the claim against a joint tortfeasor.

criminal   That which pertains to or is connected with the law of crimes or the administration of penal justice, or relates to or has the character of crime. Criminal justice and criminal procedures are quite distinct from civil justice and civil procedures. A criminal act is against the state as well as against the victim.

cross-claims   Claims by one defendant against one or more codefendants, arising from the same facts that support the plaintiff's claim against the defendants. An action to obtain relief in the form of indemnity or contribution from a codefendant.

cross-examination   The examination of an adverse party or hostile witness in which the examiner may ask leading questions and may seek to limit answers by asking very narrow, circumscribed questions.

cross-motions for summary judgment   Motions for summary judgment made by adverse parties against each other. The parties may assert or rely on different grounds for their motions.

curriculum vitae   A written description of a witness's background, education, training, associations, and publications.

damages   (1) The injury, loss, or other harm to a person or property that is proximately caused by another person's breach of a legal duty. (2) An abbreviation of the term *money damages*, which is compensation for the injury, loss, or other harm caused by another person's breach of a legal duty. In contract actions, money damages are paid in compensation for the loss of the bargain.

day certain   The date on which a trial has been ordered to begin. The court has cleared its calendar so that the case will definitely begin on that date. The parties must be ready to start the trial at the appointed time.

declaratory judgment action   An action to obtain a declaratory judgment.

defamation   The publication of a false statement, oral or written, that damages another person's reputation. *See* libel *and* slander.

defendant   The person against whom a legal action is brought. This legal action may be criminal or civil.

definitive diagnosis   *See* medical diagnosis.

demand for arbitration   *See* petition.

demand for inspection   A written demand served by one party on another party to schedule an inspection of any item of real or personal property that is in the control of the second party and relevant to the case. An action must be pending for a party to use the procedure. The demand may be made without first obtaining leave of the court. The procedure is prescribed by Rule 34.

demand for jury   A request made by a party on his or her pleading or in a separate document entitled "Demand for Jury," by which the party notifies the court and other parties of a request for a jury trial. The written demand for jury may specify only certain issues that the party wants tried to a jury; all other issues will be tried to the court, unless another party serves a demand for jury on those issues.

demonstrative evidence   Physical or tangible evidence that can be brought to the courtroom and used to prove a fact or for illustrative purposes to help a witness explain testimony. Demonstrative evidence may have been created by the transaction or occurrence in question, or it may be prepared specially by a party for use at trial.

deponent   A person who gives testimony under oath in an affidavit, in an oral deposition, in a written deposition, or in court.

depose   (1) To give testimony in an affidavit, in a deposition, or in court. (2) To take a person's deposition by asking the person questions (see Rule 30).

deposition   The procedure for taking a person's testimony for discovery or to preserve testimony. The transcript of a person's testimony. Lawyers commonly describe the interrogation process as taking the deponent's deposition. Deposition is synonymous with testimony. (1) A written deposition is a procedure established by Rule 31 of the Federal Rules of Civil Procedure. It enables a party to obtain written testimony of any party or witness for the purpose of discovering information or preserving the testimony for use at trial. The deponent may be compelled to testify by serving a subpoena on the deponent. The right to cross-examine the deponent is preserved. (2) *See also* oral deposition.

deposition transcript   A verbatim copy of an oral deposition, either typed or printed in a booklet form.

destructive testing   Testing of property that causes or results in its destruction or a significant change.

diagnosis   *See* medical diagnosis.

direct cause   The term is synonymous with proximate cause. A direct cause is a cause that had a substantial part in bringing about an accident, loss, or injury either immediately or through happenings that follow one after another. A direct cause is a cause that in a natural and continuous sequence produces an event, and without which the injury or loss would not have occurred.

directed verdict   An order by the trial judge that dismisses a claim or an affirmative defense on the grounds that there is insufficient evidence to prove the claim or defense or that the claim or defense is conclusively established by the evidence so there is nothing for a jury to decide. The order leads directly to an entry of judgment in favor of the prevailing party. The judge must determine that a reasonable jury could decide the facts only one way, therefore the judge is able to apply the law to the facts to resolve the litigation.

direct evidence   Testimony about a fact by an eyewitness who observed the fact, or an exhibit that tends to prove the existence or nonexistence of the fact. The evidence depends on the reliability of the witness or exhibit from which it comes. *See, for contrast,* circumstantial evidence.

direct examination   The examination a lawyer conducts of the lawyer's own client or client's witness.

The form of the examination precludes leading questions and impeachment, unless the interrogator can show surprise.

discovery conference Rule 26(f) requires the parties' attorneys to meet at least fourteen days before the court's mandatory scheduling conference to prepare a discovery plan. The conference is informal and usually conducted at one of the attorneys' offices. No record is made of the proceedings. The purpose is to search for ways in which the parties can narrow the issues and agree on procedures. The parties should take the opportunity to discuss settlement and the option of using some alternative dispute resolution procedure.

discovery deposition A deposition of a party or witness taken for the purpose of obtaining information and evidence relevant to the case.

discovery plan Rule 26(f) requires the parties' attorneys to meet at least fourteen days before the court's mandatory scheduling conference to prepare a discovery plan. The plan must state the parties' respective proposals or agreements for making initial disclosures and conducting discovery. If the parties desire to modify established time periods and limits on discovery, the proposals must be specified. The court may adopt, modify or reject the parties' proposals.

dismissal The termination of a lawsuit pursuant to Rule 41. The termination may be the voluntary act of the plaintiff, by stipulation of the parties, or by court order.

dismissal with prejudice A dismissal that precludes the plaintiff from bringing the claim at a later date against the party who has obtained the dismissal.

dismissal without prejudice A dismissal subject to the right of the claimant to bring the lawsuit again in the same court or another court at a later date.

dispositive motion Any motion a party uses to obtain resolution of a claim or part of a claim or resolution of an alleged defense. A motion for summary judgment is a dispositive motion. A motion for judgment on the pleadings is a dispositive motion. On the other hand, a motion to compel discovery or a motion for a new trial are procedural motions.

dissent An opinion filed by an appellate court judge who disagrees with the holding and reasoning of a majority of the judges whose opinion becomes the law of the case.

district court Trial courts of the United States courts system, and in some states, low-level state courts (or even appeals courts).

diversity of citizenship A basis for federal district courts to obtain jurisdiction of a civil lawsuit when the amount in controversy exceeds $75,000. The plaintiff and the defendant must have their domiciles in different states at the time the action is commenced. The parties are not required to be residents of different states at the time of the transaction or occurrence that gave rise to the lawsuit.

dram shop action A civil action against liquor vendors and in favor of persons, other than the inebriate, who suffer harm as the result of an illegal sale of intoxicants. A sale of intoxicants may be illegal and actionable because the customer was underage or obviously intoxicated.

duress A threat of death, bodily harm, or damage to property. If a person was under duress at the time he or she made a contract, will, or other legal commitment, a court will set aside the legal obligation. Duress is an affirmative defense that must be pled and proved by the party who claims to have been under duress.

efficient intervening cause An independent cause of an injury or loss that insulates or relieves the defendant from liability for his or her negligence. An efficient intervening cause must have occurred after the defendant's original negligence; must not have been brought about by the defendant's original negligence; must have actively worked to bring about a result that would not otherwise have followed from the original negligence. An efficient intervening cause relieves all prior negligent conduct of any liability for an accident. It is not a basis or grounds for allocating fault. Efficient intervening cause is often referred to as superseding cause.

en banc hearing An appellate court hearing in which all the judges of the court participate.

enjoin To order a person to stop or refrain from a particular activity or to abate a condition for which the person is responsible.

equitable relief Redress provided by a court other than money damages. Equitable relief includes remedies such as specific performance, rescission of a contract, reforming a contract, and injunctive relief.

equity (1) In its broadest and most general signification, the spirit and habit of fairness, justness, and right dealing that regulates the intercourse of persons—the rule of doing to all others as we desire them to do to us, or, as expressed by Justinian, "To live honestly, to harm nobody, to render to every man his due." Equity is, therefore, the synonym of natural right or justice. But, in this sense, its obligation is ethical rather than jural, and its discussion belongs to the sphere of morals. It is grounded in the precepts of the conscience, not in any sanction of positive law. (2) In a restricted sense, equal and impartial justice as between two persons whose rights or claims are in conflict; justice, that is, as ascertained by natural reason or ethical insight, but independent of the formulated body of law. This is not a technical meaning of the term *equity*, except insofar as courts that administer equity seek to discover it by these agencies, or apply it beyond the strict lines of positive law. (3) In a still more restricted sense, a system of jurisprudence, or branch of remedial justice, administered by certain tribunals, distinct from the common law courts and empowered to decree equity in the sense listed last in definition 2. Here equity becomes a complex of well-settled and well-understood rules, principles, and precedents.

estop To bar or prevent by estoppel.

estoppel An affirmative defense that precludes the plaintiff from recovering money damages for a loss that resulted from the defendant's mistake where that mistake was induced by the plaintiff's wrongful conduct in the first place. Estoppel has its origin in equity. To be able to invoke the doctrine, a party must show that she or he would be damaged if the doctrine were not applied. The doctrine precludes a party from denying the truth of a statement on which another person duly relied if the other person would be harmed by that denial. Estoppel also may arise from a party's conduct. It must be alleged as a cause of action or defense in order to be made an issue in a civil suit.

evidence Anything that tends to prove a fact, especially testimony and exhibits offered at a trial.

excusable neglect Ordinarily, to be excusable, neglect must not be more culpable than mere inadvertence or oversight. The neglect must not be willful. Excusable neglect is a basis for avoiding penalties for failure to comply with a court order or rule. The court allows the party to cure the omission.

ex parte On one side only; by or for one party; done for, on behalf of, or on the application of one party only. An ex parte judicial proceeding is one initiated on behalf of and for the benefit of one party, in which the opposing party does not participate and of which the opposing party receives no notice.

ex parte motion A motion made by one party without giving notice to another party. Ex parte motions are heard by the court with only one party in attendance. Ex parte motions are rarely made and are generally improper. However, a party may make an ex parte motion to increase the time period provided by an order or rule if he or she does so before the authorized period expires [see Rule 6(b)]. An ex parte motion may be made whenever the opposing party is in default.

expert opinions Opinions of a person who has special education, training, and experience in a subject not ordinarily known or understood by laypersons. The opinion may be about the existence of facts or the effect of facts material to the parties' controversy. For an opinion to be admissible in evidence, the presiding judge must determine that the opinion would help the jury to better understand the evidence in the case. The opinion must have a foundation in the evidence. As part of the foundation, the party who offers expert opinion testimony must show that the expert has the education, training, and experience to be an expert. Judges have broad discretion in determining whether a witness's background is adequate to make the witness an expert in a particular field.

expert witness A person who has special education, training, and experience in a particular subject or field and whose opinions would help the jury to understand the evidence or facts relevant to the case.

fact A truth; something that happened; something that exists or did exist. A fact is an absolute, something certain, but the existence of a fact may be far from clear. Parties establish facts in court through admissions and evidence. Courts may take judicial notice of certain, incontrovertible facts.

fact brief A brief a lawyer prepares as part of a case analysis to determine whether he or she has all the necessary evidence to prove the client's case and refute the adverse party's claims. A fact brief identifies the remaining issues, the facts to be proved, the evidence available with which to prove contested facts, the method of presenting the evidence, the use of evidence to defeat or contradict the opposing party's evidence, and the use of rules and procedures to defeat the opposing party's claims and defenses.

fact finder The fact finder must consider and weigh the evidence to resolve disputed facts and determine the ultimate questions of fact. When a case is tried by a jury, the jury is the fact finder. When there is no jury, the judge is the fact finder.

fiduciary　A person or corporation who assumes a special relationship with another person or another person's property, such as a trustee, administrator, executor, lawyer, or guardian. A fiduciary must exercise the highest degree of care to maintain and preserve the right or property within her or his charge. A fiduciary must place the interests of that charge ahead of her or his own. A lawyer is a fiduciary concerning any secrets, documents, and money given to her or him by the client for safekeeping as part of the professional relationship. A lawyer is not a fiduciary in the handling of the client's litigation.

final argument　The argument or summation that each party's lawyer may make at the end of the trial. The arguments are made after all the parties have rested but before the judge instructs the jury on the law. The arguments may be used to remind the jury what evidence was presented, why certain evidence should be believed or not believed, what the evidence proves or fails to prove, how the law applies to the facts of the case, and how the jury should answer questions in the verdict form.

findings of fact　A determination of facts made by the fact finder from the evidence produced in a trial. The trial court applies the law to those facts to reach conclusions of law.

foundation　A body of evidence that tends to establish either that a witness is competent to testify on a certain matter or that other evidence is relevant, thus making the testimony or evidence potentially admissible and usable in the case. Foundation is a legal requirement for a witness to testify, for a witness to qualify as an expert, or to show that evidence is relevant. Foundation is lacking when an exhibit is offered without proof concerning its source or authenticity.

fraud　An intentional misrepresentation of a material fact on which another person reasonably relies to his or her detriment. Fraud is a cause of action in tort and may be used as an affirmative defense. A statement of mere opinion is not usually actionable. However, if a false statement is rendered by an expert concerning a matter within the scope of his or her expertise, it may be actionable as fraud or negligent misrepresentation.

frivolous　Not supported by facts, or contrary to law. Any party who prosecutes a frivolous claim or defense is subject to sanctions and disciplinary action. The sanctions may include the assessment of costs, an order striking the party's

pleadings, or even an award of judgment in favor of the opposing party. A lawyer or party who prosecutes a frivolous claim or defense can be held in contempt of court (see Rule 11).

full and final release　A release that discharges from liability the party who paid consideration for it and anyone else who might be liable to the claimant. Unless expressly provided otherwise, the release applies only to the particular transaction or occurrence. It must identify the transaction or occurrence by type, time and place, and losses claimed. A full and final release is a predicate for settling the defendant's action to obtain contribution.

fundamental error　*See* plain error.

garnishee　A person who holds money or property belonging to a debtor and who is subject to a garnishment proceeding by a creditor.

garnishment　A procedure by which a judgment creditor may attach property or money that is in the hands of a third person and belongs to the judgment debtor. The judgment creditor serves upon the custodian (garnishee) a garnishment summons that requires the custodian to disclose what property she or he has that belongs to the judgment debtor and to hold it until further order.

garnishment disclosure　A document served and filed by a garnishee in which the garnishee discloses whether he or she is holding any money or property and the amount or particular items held.

general jurisdiction　A court's authority to adjudicate all controversies that may be brought before it within the legal bounds of rights and remedies, as opposed to special or limited jurisdiction, which covers only a particular class of cases, or cases where the amount in controversy is below a prescribed sum, or which is subject to specific exceptions.

general release　A release that puts an end to all claims the claimant may have against the released parties for all transactions and occurrences between them as of the date of the release. A release in which the claimant discharges all claims of any kind against the person or persons who obtained the release. It discharges all persons who might be liable for the injury or other loss the claimant may have sustained. If an action is pending, the plaintiff is required to stipulate to a dismissal of the action; nothing remains to be litigated.

general verdict　A verdict in which the jury simply finds in favor of the plaintiff by specifying an amount of money damages, or finds for the defendant. The jury does not have to make any specific findings.

general verdict with interrogatories   A general verdict in which the jury finds for the plaintiff or defendant and, in addition, must answer specific questions about the facts of the case. The judge decides what questions to ask and how to word the questions. The answers may help the court or parties decide whether an appeal would be useful or would help resolve some collateral problems raised by the case [see Rule 49(b)].

genuine   Actually being what it purports to be, as in the case of a document.

good cause   Some basis in fact and law; substantial compliance with a legal requirement or legal standard. A party may be required to show good cause in order to obtain an independent medical examination of an adverse party. The requirement is to show a substantial reason for the medical examination.

grand jury   A jury of inquiry that is summoned and returned by the sheriff to each session of the criminal courts, and whose duty is to receive complaints and accusations in criminal cases, hear the evidence adduced on the part of the state, and find bills of indictment in cases where it is satisfied a trial ought to be held. The jury issues an indictment if it determines there is good reason to believe that a crime has been committed and the accused is the perpetrator.

grounds   A basis or foundation for a claim, motion, cause of action, or allegation.

guardian ad litem   A guardian appointed by a court to help a minor to prosecute or defend a lawsuit in which the minor is a party. The minor may be the plaintiff or defendant. The guardian may or may not be a parent. A lawyer who represents a minor could not act as the guardian ad litem. A guardian ad litem has ultimate responsibility for making decisions about settlement and whether the action should be maintained or dismissed.

hearsay   Evidence proceeding not from the personal knowledge of the witness, but from the mere repetition of what the witness has heard others say. That which does not derive its value solely from the credibility of the witness, but rests mainly on the veracity and competency of other persons. The very nature of hearsay evidence shows its weakness, and it is received at trial only in limited situations owing to necessity. Hearsay evidence is competent to prove a fact and will be received by the court in the absence of an objection.

high-low settlement   An agreement between parties to settle their dispute by payment and acceptance of a sum of money within an agreed range, leaving to the court or tribunal the amount of money damages. The parties commit to be bound by the amount of the award if it is within the agreed range. If the award is for more than provided in the agreement, the parties settle for the high amount provided by the agreement. If the award is for less than provided in the agreement, the parties settle for the low amount provided by the agreement. The high-low agreement reduces the risk of an excessively high or low award. These agreements are used most often in connection with arbitrations.

hostile witness   A witness who has demonstrated animosity toward one of the parties. If the court declares a witness to be hostile toward a party, that party may cross-examine the witness even if that party called the witness to the stand to testify.

hypothetical question   A question put to a witness that asks the witness to assume specified facts and render an opinion on the basis of those assumed facts. The assumed facts must be supported by other evidence in the case; otherwise, the question would be irrelevant and disallowed. The witness is not asked or required to validate the assumed facts.

illustrative evidence   Evidence that does not, in itself, have probative value, but that helps a witness to explain her or his testimony. For example, a photograph or drawing that depicts the location of an accident may help a witness to explain what the witness observed. Illustrative evidence is received at trial solely as an aid for the witness. The jury may not be allowed to take a piece of illustrative evidence to its deliberations, because the exhibit's only value is to help the witness describe or explain her or his testimony; it is not, in itself, evidence of anything.

impeach   To cast doubt on the credibility of a witness or exhibit by showing inconsistencies in what the witness says or in the use of the exhibit. A witness also may be impeached by showing that the witness has been convicted of a crime of a type that indicates the witness is willing to disregard the obligations of the oath.

impeachment evidence   Evidence offered solely to cast doubt on other evidence received by the court and that will not, in itself, support a verdict. Prior inconsistent statements of a party may be both impeachment evidence and substantive evidence. Prior inconsistent statements of a witness who is not a party are usually impeachment evidence only.

implied bias   Bias that is assumed to exist because of the relationship between the witness or juror and a party.

incompetent   Lacking the capacity, fitness, qualifications, or ability to act.

independent medical examination   A medical examination of a party to an action conducted by a physician selected by an adverse party for the purpose of evaluating the party's physical, mental, or blood condition. The medical examination is not in itself an adversary proceeding. The physician is expected to follow professional practices and procedures in conducting the examination and in making an evaluation. The right to the examination is prescribed by Rule 35. In some communities this type of examination is referred to as an adverse medical examination. In this book, we have chosen to call it a Rule 35 examination.

initial disclosures   Rule 26(a) requires parties to disclose to each other, in writing:

- the name, address, and telephone number of each known witness
- a description of each document that is or contains evidence and the identity of the custodian of each
- compilation of damages claimed and all supporting documentation
- relevant insurance policies
- expert witnesses and experts' reports

The initial disclosures must be made within 10 days after the parties meet to plan their discovery.

injunction   A court order that prohibits a party from engaging in a specified activity. A prohibitive writ issued by a court of equity against a defendant, forbidding the defendant to do some act the defendant is threatening or attempting to commit or restraining the defendant in the continuance thereof. A court may enjoin a defendant's conduct where the harm to the plaintiff cannot be redressed adequately with money damages in an action at law.

injunctive relief   An order issued by a court ordering someone to do something or prohibiting some act after a court hearing.

insufficiency of process   A failure to follow the procedures prescribed by law for serving process on another party.

integrated bar   A state bar association that controls the right to practice law. All lawyers in the state must belong to the bar association.

interrogatory   A written question to another party to a civil action that must be answered under oath (see Rule 33).

intervention   A procedure by which a person may join in a lawsuit to protect a related interest or legal right. A person who seeks to intervene may align with one of the parties or take a position adverse to all the existing parties.

invasion of privacy   A cause of action in tort for personal injury for wrongful publishing of a person's likeness or private information about the person in a manner that is outrageous. The right to privacy is subject to the public's right to information about matters that have news value and are legitimately of public interest.

invasive testing   Medical procedures that require the examiner to penetrate the examinee's skin or otherwise enter the examinee's body, such as drawing blood.

involuntary dismissal   A court-ordered dismissal to which the claimant party did not consent.

irrelevant   Not related or not applicable to the matter in issue. Not tending to prove or disprove a material fact or issue.

joint liability   A condition in which two or more parties are concurrently liable to a claimant for the claimant's entire loss. Joint liability may arise from contract or tort. Tortfeasors may acquire joint liability by acting in concert for a joint purpose, or merely because their wrongful acts happen to be concurrent and contribute to an indivisible loss.

judge's minutes   The notes a judge keeps concerning the evidence and proceedings in a trial.

judgment   (1) A court's ultimate determination of the parties' rights and obligations concerning a particular matter. (2) The official decision of a court of justice on the respective rights and claims of the parties. (3) The clerk of court's record of the court's declaration of the parties' rights and obligations in a particular action.

judgment book   A public record containing civil judgments. It is maintained by the clerk of court.

judgment creditor   A party who has obtained a judgment in his or her favor against another party for a sum of money.

judgment debtor   A person against whom a judgment has been entered declaring he or she is indebted to the judgment creditor for a stated sum of money.

judicial notice   A rule of evidence by which a court may recognize a fact that is capable of being known or determined to a certainty by consulting indisputable sources. For example, a court may take judicial notice that Christmas falls on December 25, that water freezes at 0°C, or that there are 5,280 feet in a mile.

jurisdiction   The power and authority of a court. A court's jurisdiction depends on the court's following due process of law. Jurisdiction may be limited to a specific territory, to certain types of actions, to certain types of controversies, or certain classes of parties. A court's jurisdiction is necessarily limited by the authority of the body that created the court.

juror misconduct   The intentional or willful participation by a juror in a forbidden act, disregarding his or her legal responsibility.

jury demand   A notice on a pleading or separate statement served and filed by a party, indicating that the party wants a trial by jury.

laches   Laches is a court-made doctrine that resembles a statute of limitations. Laches is an affirmative defense that is similar to a statute of limitations defense, but applies only when there is no applicable statute of limitations. It applies to actions in equity, such as an action to reform a written instrument or an action to enjoin the defendant's conduct. At some point a claim becomes so stale it must be time-barred. Courts created laches as a defense to these equitable actions because ordinarily no statute of limitations applies to them. When applying laches, courts determine whether the delay prejudiced the defendant.

law of the case   The law according to which the parties tried their case without objection, so that the rules of law are considered controlling even though they might not be correct.

leading question   A question that suggests the answer the interrogator wants to receive.

legal disability   A want of legal capacity to make legally enforceable commitments. The lack of capacity may be due to a person's age, lack of mental competency, or lack of licensor.

legal duty   A duty that the law imposes on a person to act or refrain from acting. The breach of a legal duty gives rise to a cause of action against the violator to compensate the victim for any injury or damage caused by the breach. The legal duty may arise from a contract or by operation of the common law or by statute.

letters rogatory   A formal, written communication sent by a court in which an action is pending to a court or judge of a foreign country or state requesting that the testimony of a witness who resides within the latter's jurisdiction be taken under that court's direction and transmitted to the first court for use in a pending action. Letters rogatory is a means of obtaining jurisdiction over a witness for the purpose of obtaining the witness's deposition. The court to whom the request is directed can use its subpoena power.

liability   A legal obligation to make restitution or pay compensation. Liability may be contingent or absolute.

liable   To be legally responsible or obligated by law to another person.

libel   A cause of action in tort for injury to a person's reputation caused by the publication of a false statement in writing.

loan receipt agreement   A contract by which a tortfeasor, or the tortfeasor's insurer, agrees to "loan" the claimant a specified sum of money and the claimant agrees not to pursue his or her claim against the lender, but both believe that another person has substantial liability and the claimant agrees to pursue the claim against that other person. The claimant agrees that if he or she recovers money over a certain amount from that other person, he or she will repay all or part of the loan. If the claimant recovers little or nothing from the other person, the loan need not be repaid.

loss-of-bargain measure of damages   The amount of money a party duly expected to receive as a profit from the adverse party's full performance of the parties' contract.

magistrate judge   Federal law authorizes United States District Court judges to appoint magistrate judges. A federal magistrate judge has authority to hear and determine pretrial motions, to conduct hearings, including evidentiary hearings, and to submit to the supervising judge proposed findings of facts, conclusions of law, and recommendations for disposition of pending matters.

maintenance   The practice of advancing monies to a litigant on the basis that the "loan" will be paid out of the verdict or settlement.

majority opinion   The opinion written or signed by a majority of the judges on an appellate court, when one or more other judges of the court file a separate dissent or concurring opinion.

malicious prosecution   A cause of action in tort to recover money damages for personal injury caused by the defendant's intentional wrongful use of criminal court proceedings, without justification, for an improper purpose.

malpractice   Negligence committed by a person while rendering professional services.

mandamus   An order or writ that is issued by a court of superior jurisdiction and is directed to a governmental officer or to an inferior court, commanding the performance of a particular act. The basis for the writ is that the officer or judge has a duty to perform the act but has neglected or refused to do it. A writ of mandamus may direct a lower court to restore to the petitioner legal rights or privileges of which she or he was illegally deprived.

Mary Carter agreement   A secret agreement between parties to settle the case between them but to continue prosecution of the case against another party.

material   Important; more-or-less necessary; going to the merits; having to do with matters of substance, as distinguished from mere form. In civil actions, facts are material if they relate to a cause of action or defense. Evidence is material if it relates to the issues raised by the pleadings. Compare: Evidence is relevant if it tends to prove a material fact.

material fact   A fact that directly relates to an issue in the case.

matter   The subject of a civil action or arbitration.

measure of damages   The basis for assessing the monetary value of an injury, loss, or compensable harm. The rules of law by which courts determine the basis of compensation for various kinds of injuries and losses.

mediation   A dispute resolution procedure in which an intermediary facilitates communication between the parties, helps the parties overcome barriers in the negotiation process, and identifies the parties' real interests and needs so that they can make their own agreement. A mediator does not have authority to impose a solution on the parties.

medical diagnosis   A physician's determination concerning the nature, and sometimes, the cause of a patient's apparent medical problem. A diagnosis may be categorized as a "working diagnosis," which becomes the basis for providing treatment but subject to change as the physician obtains more information. A working diagnosis is distinguished from a "final diagnosis." A diagnosis may

be categorized as a "definitive diagnosis" when it specifically eliminates other possible diagnoses.

medical findings   The objective findings a physician makes while conducting a physical examination. The objective findings are distinguished from the patient's subjective symptoms.

memorandum of interview   An investigator's memorandum of his or her interview with a witness. The memorandum contains the same information that would be in a witness statement, but the memorandum is not signed by the witness. A memorandum of interview is work product and generally not discoverable, whereas many jurisdictions allow discovery of witness statements.

memorandum of law   A memorandum a party submits to a court to identify the law the party claims is relevant and in which a party argues how the law applies to the particular case. A memorandum of law usually contains a statement of facts, a statement of the legal issues, an argument that identifies the law the party claims is applicable, and a conclusion. The conclusion should describe how the party wants the court to rule and not be a summary of the argument.

minors' settlement   A settlement that must be approved by a court to be binding on the minor. The minor's parent or guardian must petition the court to approve the settlement and must show that the settlement is fair to the minor. In the absence of court approval, the settlement is not binding until the minor reaches majority plus one year. If the minor has not objected to the settlement by that time, it is automatically ratified and becomes binding.

misrepresentation   A false statement or representation concerning a fact that may give rise to a cause of action for fraud or negligent misrepresentation.

mistrial   (1) A trial that has been aborted because of some defect in the proceedings that prevents it from being valid or fair. (2) The presiding judge's order that cancels a trial, usually allowing the case to be tried again.

Model Rules of Professional Conduct   American Bar Association rules stating and explaining what lawyers must do, must not do, should do, and should not do. They cover the field of legal ethics (a lawyer's obligations to clients, courts, other lawyers, and the public) and have been adopted in modified forms by most of the states.

money damages   A sum of money awarded to a claimant as compensation for an injury, loss or other harm. *See also* damages.

motion   An application to a court for a ruling or order concerning a matter of procedure or law. The term *motion* is generally used with reference to all such applications, whether written or oral.

motion for directed verdict   *See* Motion for judgment as a matter of law.

motion for judgment as a matter of law   A dispositive motion that asks the court to apply the substantive law to the facts before the court and determine that the moving party is entitled to judgment in his or her favor. The motion is authorized by Rule 50. The moving party must persuade the judge that reasonable minds could not differ on the import of the facts, so all the court need do is apply the law to the facts clearly established by the evidence. The motion may be made by the defendant when the plaintiff rests, or by the plaintiff when the defendant rests. Either party or both parties may make or renew the motion after both parties have rested. The motion may be limited to a particular issue. In many jurisdictions this motion is called a motion for a directed verdict.

motion for more definite statement   A motion that is made by a defendant, usually before the answer is due, for an order requiring the plaintiff to state the claim or cause of action with more clarity and more detail.

motion in limine   A motion made at the beginning of a trial for an order allowing or disallowing certain evidence. A motion in limine may be used to resolve some procedural issue. It may not be used to obtain a ruling on the application of the substantive law to the case, such as a motion for summary judgment.

motion to confirm the award   A motion made in a court of general jurisdiction to have the court approve an arbitration award and convert the award into a civil judgment that can be enforced against the losing party.

motion to vacate the award   A motion made in a court of general jurisdiction to set aside or void an arbitration award. The motion must show that the award was procured through fraud or corruption or that the arbitration tribunal exceeded the scope of its authority.

mutual mistake   A basis for reforming a written contract. When people have a meeting of minds concerning the terms and conditions of a contract that they reduce to writing, but the written contract fails to express their mutual intent, the written contract may be reformed to comport with their intent. The party who wishes to reform the written contract must prove that both parties agreed on the terms, but they made a mutual mistake in expressing the terms in the writing. In most jurisdictions the mutual mistake must be proved by clear and convincing evidence.

necessary party   A person whose legal interests will be affected by the litigation or a person who must be a party if the court is to grant a remedy or complete relief according to law.

negative evidence   Evidence that tends to negate or disprove the existence of an alleged fact, such as testimony by a witness that a train did not sound a whistle at a railroad crossing. The foundation for such evidence requires a showing that, for example, the witness would have heard the whistle if it had been sounded.

negative witness statement   A signed or recorded witness statement relating that the witness does not have any knowledge about the transaction or occurrence. A statement that is obtained to make sure a potential witness does not have information or evidence that is adverse to the client's position. The statement eliminates the potential witness as a threat to the client's case.

negligence   A failure to exercise the degree of care that an ordinarily careful person would exercise considering the foreseeability of harm to persons or property. A person may be negligent toward another person or toward himself or herself. All persons have the legal duty to conduct themselves with reasonable care so as not to injure another person or another person's property. However, a person does not have a duty to act to protect another person from harm caused by a third person or forces of nature, unless that person has a special relationship recognized by law that imposes on him or her a duty to act and protect. The special relation may be based on requirements in the common law, a statute, or a contract.

negligence per se   An act or omission that is declared by statute to be wrongful and, therefore, is treated by the courts as negligence as a matter of law, without any reference to the reasonable person standard and without any reference to the foreseeability of harm that the act or omission may cause. For example, the violation of a statute that prohibits the sale of firearms to minors could be the basis for a court to hold that a vendor's sale to a minor constitutes negligence per se; the sale could be negligent even if the vendor believed that the buyer was an adult and that the firearm would be used properly. The illegal sale subjects the vendor to strict liability. The victim would have to be a person within the class of persons intended to be protected by the statute.

negligent misrepresentation   A statement made as a fact when the person making it does not know whether it is true or not true, and has reason to know that the person to whom it is made may rely on it. A negligent misrepresentation may be made in writing or orally.

nonbinding arbitration   Arbitration in which the tribunal's award is only advisory. A nonbinding award may be accepted, rejected, or modified by the parties. In no event may it be confirmed by a court order. The parties' scope of submission should state whether the award is binding or nonbinding. However, there is no requirement that the arbitration tribunal know whether the award will be binding.

notice of appeal   A notice that the appellant files with the district court to start the appeal process. The notice must be served on all other parties. In federal courts, the notice must be served and filed within thirty days after entry of the judgment from which the appeal is taken. On receiving the notice of appeal, the district court clerk must send the file to the clerk of the appellate court. The district court loses jurisdiction over the case once the appeal has been commenced.

notice of deposition   A notice that one party serves on all other parties, scheduling the deposition of a person who may have knowledge, information, or evidence relevant to the case. The person to be deposed may be a party or an independent witness [see Rule 30(b)(1)].

notice of motion   A notice that accompanies a motion and sets the time and place at which the motion will be heard by the court.

notice of withdrawal   A notice an attorney files with the court and serves on all the parties, stating that he or she has withdrawn or will withdraw from the case. The notice of withdrawal ordinarily informs the court and parties where to mail notices and orders after the withdrawal.

nuisance   A cause of action in tort to recover money damages for the unreasonable interference of an occupant's use or enjoyment of real property. The harm must be substantial. It does not matter whether the interference is negligent or intentional. The claimant must show that the harm greatly outweighs the utility of the defendant's conduct. The claimant may seek money damages and injunctive relief.

objection to inspection   A formal statement of disagreement to a judge in an attempt to quash a subpoena of documents. The objection precludes the lawyer from enforcing the subpoena, forcing him to obtain a court order requiring the person to produce the documents or things for inspection.

objective medical findings   Evidence concerning a person's medical condition that a physician can observe. The physician does not depend on the patient's descriptions or explanations to make the finding. A broken bone shown on an x-ray is an objective finding. A patient's complaint about a headache is subjective.

obviously intoxicated   Objectively manifesting signs of intoxication through personal conduct. Obvious intoxication is an ultimate question of fact and predicate for civil liability in a dram shop action. A liquor vendor may be liable in money damages caused by a patron to whom an alcoholic beverage was supplied while the patron was obviously intoxicated. The intoxicated person's inebriation must have been a contributing factor in causing harm to the claimant.

offer of judgment   A procedure authorized by Rule 68, by which a party may offer to let judgment be taken against him or her in a specified amount, together with accrued costs. If the offer is accepted, judgment may be entered forthwith according to the terms of the offer. If the offer is not accepted and the offeree fails to obtain a judgment that is more favorable, the offeror is entitled to recover the offeror's costs. The offeree is precluded from recovering costs even though otherwise the offeree would have been considered the prevailing party. If the offeree obtains a more favorable judgment by trying the case, the offer is without effect. The offer of judgment must be made at least ten days before the trial begins.

offer of proof   A procedure that may be used at trial to put in the record evidence that the trial judge disallowed. The offer of proof may be made by having the witness testify, out of the hearing of the jury, about the matters excluded by the judge's ruling. In some courts an offer of proof is sufficient if the attorney who offered the evidence merely states in the record what the evidence would have shown.

opening statement   A lawyer's statement to a jury made at the beginning of a trial in which the lawyer outlines the evidence that she or he expects to present on behalf of the client. The opening statement is not supposed to be an argument. Lawyers are not supposed to use opening statements to argue the effect of the evidence or the application of the law to the facts.

opinion   (1) A written statement by an appellate court containing the court's decision and the reasons or analysis by which the court reached its decision. (2) A witness's judgment or appraisal concerning a particular matter. An opinion differs from a mere conclusion in that an opinion requires application of the witness's experience to form the judgment; whereas, a conclusion is reasoned from facts. When a witness makes logical deduction from the evidence, the result is nothing more than a conclusion. As a general rule, the jury is supposed to make its own conclusions from the evidence without hearing conclusions of the witnesses. *See also* expert opinions.

oral deposition   A procedure, established by Rule 30 of the Federal Rules of Civil Procedure, that enables any party to obtain the testimony of any other party or witness for the purpose of obtaining information and evidence or to preserve the testimony for use at trial. Parties are required to submit to at least one oral deposition. A nonparty may be subpoenaed to appear for a deposition. The procedure allows parties to cross-examine the deponent. The deponent and parties have a right to be represented by counsel. A party may arrange for his or her own deposition to preserve testimony, but an attorney may not cross-examine his or her own client.

order for judgment   A trial court's order directing the clerk or administrator to enter a judgment in the judgment book, including the terms of the judgment.

ordinary comparative negligence   Comparative negligence in which the plaintiff's claim is barred if the claimant's causal negligence is more than the defendant's causal negligence.

original jurisdiction   The court in which an action may properly be commenced. A trial court has original jurisdiction. An appellate court does not have original jurisdiction.

out-of-pocket damages   The measure of damages allowed to the victim of a fraud. The out-of-pocket damages measure includes the victim's actual expenses and losses, but does not allow recovery for loss of the bargain, profits, or expectancies. It is to be distinguished from the loss-of-bargain measure of damages.

overrule   A court order that denies a party's objection to another party's evidence or acts committed in prosecuting an action.

parol evidence   Evidence that has the effect of changing or modifying the terms of a written contract. Parol evidence may be written or oral.

partial release   A release of less than all the alleged tortfeasors. A release of part of a claim.

partial settlement   A settlement that resolves only part of the claim arising from a transaction or occurrence.

party   A natural person, corporation, or other legal entity that is the plaintiff or defendant in a civil action.

party's work product   Documents and tangible things a party or party's agent have prepared in anticipation of litigation or for purposes of trial. A party's work product is commonly grouped with attorney's work product.

past medical history   A patient's past medical history that may have some relevance to a current medical problem or its cause.

peremptory challenge   By law and court rule, the right of each party to remove a specified number of jurors, usually two or three, from the panel during the voir dire examination without explanation or justification.

permissive counterclaim   A counterclaim that does not arise from the transaction or occurrence that is the subject of the plaintiff's complaint but that may be prosecuted in the same action.

person   In law, a natural person or a legal entity such as a corporation, unless otherwise defined.

personal jurisdiction   A court's jurisdiction or authority over a person, obtained through due process.

personal property   Tangible property that is not real estate. The term *personal property* does not include personal property that has been incorporated into a structure, such as a fixture in the structure.

petition   A formal request made in writing to a court that asks the court to take some specific action concerning a matter that affects the petitioner. A petition ordinarily recites the relevant facts, the nature of the petitioner's interests, concern, and the relief or assistance the petitioner requests.

petitioner   A person or corporation that files a petition with an arbitration tribunal.

petit jury   A jury that tries the facts in a civil action.

plain error   Very basic error that goes to the heart of the case. Plain error may be noted for the first time in a posttrial motion. An appellate court will consider plain error in an appeal even though no objection was made during the trial. By characterizing the error in this manner, an appellate court acquires some discretion to decide whether or not to deal with the problem. If the court concludes that a serious miscarriage of justice occurred, it may call the error "plain error" or "fundamental error" and use that characterization as a basis for setting aside the lower court's judgment even though the error was overlooked during the trial stage.

plaintiff   A person who brings (starts) a lawsuit against another person.

polling the jury   A trial procedure in which the judge asks each juror whether the juror agrees with the verdict after the verdict has been read in open court.

prejudicial error   Error that has adversely affected the outcome of the case.

preliminary evidence   Evidence to show that other evidence is relevant.

preponderance of evidence   The greater weight of the evidence as determined by its persuasiveness. Preponderance of evidence does not mean the greater number of witnesses or exhibits. It should cause the trier of fact to believe that a disputed fact is more likely true than not true.

preserving the evidence   Following procedures to ensure that evidence will be available when it is needed. The preservation of evidence requires the exercise of forethought and anticipation of problems or events that could cause the loss of evidence. If a witness may not be available when the case reaches trial, the witness's evidence may be preserved by taking an oral deposition, deposition on written questions, affidavit, recorded statement, or signed statement—in descending value of usefulness and persuasiveness. The choice of method for preserving evidence depends on the importance of the evidence, the likelihood that it will not be available when it is needed, and the cost of preserving it.

pretrial conference   A conference ordered by the court for the purpose of expediting a disposition of the case by securing admissions, securing stipulations, and narrowing the issues; establishing a plan for managing and moving the litigation toward trial and avoiding unnecessary delay; determining the state of preparedness of the parties and encouraging full preparation; and helping the parties to avoid unnecessary expense. The court may consider any aspect of the case in a pretrial conference and make orders accordingly (see Rule 16).

pretrial order   An order a court issues following a pretrial conference that embodies the court's rulings and plan for managing the progression of the case to trial.

prima facie case   A case in which a party presents sufficient evidence to establish all the elements of his or her cause of action, or in which the evidence is sufficient to support all the elements of an affirmative defense. The evidence is sufficient to support a verdict or a finding on a legal issue. A prima facie case may exist even though the evidence is in conflict or disputed. A court does not consider the credibility or persuasiveness of the party's evidence in determining whether a party has presented a prima facie case.

prima facie evidence of negligence   Sufficient evidence to establish all the elements of an action in negligence. Evidence of a violation of a statute is sufficient to establish a prima facie case of negligence unless the opposing party offers evidence that tends to excuse or justify the violation.

prima facie negligence   An act or omission that is, on its face, negligent. Proof of an act or omission that is specifically prohibited by law establishes that the applicable standard of due care has been violated. In the absence of some compelling excuse or justification, the fact finder (jury) must find that the conduct was negligent. The party against whom the claim of prima facie negligence is asserted may be permitted to explain and justify the violation, whereas an act or omission that is negligent per se may not be explained or justified.

principal   In the law of agency, a principal is a person who directed or permitted another person to act for him or her and is subject to his or her control.

privileged communication   A communication that is protected by law from disclosure. A court will not require a party to a privileged communication to disclose it to another party, another person, or even the court. A party may waive the privilege.

privity   A relationship between persons that gives rise to some mutuality of interest. The privity between an assignee and an assignor imposes the obligations of one on the other. The relationship between contracting parties is described as the privity of contract and is the basis for establishing legal rights and obligations between them.

probable cause   A standard or degree of proof required before a garnishor may proceed with an action against a garnishee who denies that the garnishee is holding any money or property belonging to the judgment debtor. Probable cause exists when reasonably trustworthy evidence indicates the garnishee might have property or money that is subject to garnishment. Probable cause cannot be established by innuendo or speculation. It may be established by using affidavits, oral testimony, and documents for which adequate foundation is provided.

procedural law   The rules of law that govern the conduct of a legal procedure or process, as distinguished from the law that determines the parties' substantive rights. Procedural rules govern the manner in which the substantive rights will be determined and enforced.

procedural motion   Any motion by which a party seeks a court's assistance or guidance.

process   Process refers to the means and procedures courts use to obtain jurisdiction over persons or property. The term is used in reference to documents used in the procedures by which courts obtain jurisdiction. A summons is process. Service of a summons is service of process. Service of a subpoena is service of process.

products liability   The liability that the manufacturer, vendor, or bailor for hire may have for supplying a product that is defective or is unreasonably dangerous for use. The liability may arise from a defect in the product, a defect in the design of the product, a failure to provide adequate instructions concerning the product's use, or failure to provide a warning concerning inherent dangers in its use.

proponent   A party who makes some demand or request on another party or who actively seeks some action by a court.

protective order   An order that limits the demands one party may make on the protected party. Protective orders are most commonly used in discovery procedures [see Rule 26(c)].

proximate cause   A cause that has a direct and substantial part in bringing about an occurrence, injury, loss, or harm for which a party seeks a remedy in court.

punitive damages   Money damages awarded to a plaintiff in a civil action to punish the defendant for willfully committing a wrongful act that injured the plaintiff or damaged the plaintiff's property. Punitive damages are recoverable in addition to compensatory damages. In determining the amount of punitive damages, the jury may consider the nature of the wrongful act, the seriousness of the plaintiff's harm, and the financial condition of the defendant. Some courts take into consideration whether the defendant has already been subjected to punitive damages to other plaintiffs for the same wrongful conduct.

pure comparative negligence   The plaintiff may recover money damages from a defendant who was causally negligent, regardless of the fact that the plaintiff may have been much more negligent than the defendant. However, the plaintiff's damages are reduced by his or her percentage of causal negligence.

qualified admission   An admission, made in response to a Rule 36 request for admissions, that is limited or qualified by the respondent. The qualification may limit the nature or scope of the admission or provide an explanation.

qualified denial   A denial, made in response to a Rule 36 request for admissions, that provides an explanation or some information notwithstanding the party's denial.

quash   To annul, cancel, rescind a court order or judicial decision. A court may quash a subpoena that has been issued improperly or for a wrongful purpose.

quotient verdict   A verdict for money damages arrived at by having each juror select an amount, adding the amounts together, and dividing the total by the number of jurors. The jurors then agree on the quotient amount as the amount for the verdict. A quotient verdict is improper because the jurors avoid discussing reasons for their differences and rely on the wrong basis for compromise.

real party in interest   A party who actually owns the cause of action and who is directly affected by the outcome of the litigation.

real property   Land and structures that are appurtenant to the land. It also includes fixtures that have been attached to the structures and are essential to the use of the structure.

reasonable certainty   A high degree of probability that the opinion is correct or the expectation will materialize.

reasonable inquiry   An inquiry or investigation that a reasonably prudent person would make to ascertain facts in light of the potential harm and the difficulties of making the inquiry or investigation. A person may have a duty to make reasonable inquiry when that person has a duty to know facts so that he or she can act with due care to protect himself or herself or another person or property. Parties have a duty to make reasonable inquiry before responding to another party's discovery requests.

reasonable probability   Something more than a 50 percent chance that the opinion is correct or the expectation will materialize.

rebuttal evidence   Evidence that a party offers to contradict or refute evidence previously offered by another party.

recorded statement   A witness's statement that is a verbatim record of the witness's words made by an electronic means, shorthand, or other means.

redeem   To regain possession of something by payment of an obligation, or to repurchase the item.

release   A contract by which a person releases a legal claim or right against another person. A release is usually made in writing.

relevant   Means there is a logical relationship between proposed evidence and the fact for which the evidence is offered to establish the fact.

relevant evidence   Evidence that tends to establish or negate a controverted fact (see Rule 401). Evidence must be relevant to be received in a trial.

relief   A remedy, redress, or assistance that a court awards to a party, other than money damages. Relief is often used to describe the protection a court orders against any future harm.

remand   To send back. An appellate court remands a case for a new trial or further consideration if it finds that the trial court committed an error that may have affected the outcome of the case.

remedial measures   A party's activity to correct some danger or problem after an injury or damage has occurred. Evidence of remedial measures is not admissible, as a public policy to encourage persons to make repairs and corrections without fear that the improvement will be used as evidence against them (see Rule 407).

remedy   The means by which a right is enforced or satisfaction is gained for a harm done. The means by which a violation of rights is prevented, redressed, or compensated.

remittitur   A court-ordered reduction in the amount of money damages awarded to a party by a jury. A trial court has the authority to reduce the award when the damages are manifestly excessive and apparently made as the result of prejudice or passion. A trial court may order a remittitur even though no error of law or procedure explains the jury's excessive award. Usually the trial court gives the plaintiff the option of accepting the remittitur or having a new trial where a new jury can determine the amount of damages.

representation statement   A document filed with the court of appeals identifying the parties and attorneys who will appear in an appeal.

request for admissions   A party's formal written demand to another party to admit the existence of a particular fact or the genuineness of a particular document (see Rule 36).

res ipsa loquitur   A legal doctrine by which one party may establish an inference of negligence on the part of another party. The inference of negligence comes from a showing that the accident in question was caused by an instrumentality that was in the exclusive control of the defendant, that the accident was not caused by any act of the plaintiff or some third person, and that the accident is of a kind that ordinarily does not occur in the absence of negligence.

res judicata   A matter adjudged; a thing judicially acted on or decided; a thing or matter settled by judgment. Res judicata is a legal doctrine that precludes a plaintiff from relitigating the same claim against the same defendant once the cause of action has been determined on its merits.

respondent   (1) The party against whom an appeal is taken; also called an appellee. (2) A party who must answer or respond to some formal demand in the litigation process.

rest   A party's formal announcement that he or she has no more evidence to offer in support of a claim or defense. At that point the opposing party may proceed with the presentation of evidence in rebuttal or make a motion for judgment as a matter of law.

restitution   The restoration of property or a legal right that was wrongfully taken, or the provision of its equivalent.

restraining order   An order a court issues to prevent a person from engaging in specified conduct until the court can hold a hearing to determine whether there is reason to believe the person is violating another person's legal rights. A restraining order is granted without a hearing. Consequently, the order provides an early date for a hearing. The person against whom the restraining order is issued is required to show cause at the hearing why the prohibition should not remain in effect until a trial can be held.

reverse   To overthrow, set aside, or invalidate. An appellate court reverses a lower court when the appellate court changes the outcome without ordering a new trial or other proceedings.

rules of evidence   Rules that govern the admissibility of evidence at trials.

sanctions   Penalties a court imposes on a party who fails to comply with the court's order or rules.

scheduling conference   A court-ordered conference convened to create a schedule that will keep the case moving toward trial and meet the needs of the case and of the parties [see Rule 16(b)].

scheduling order   An order containing the schedule that is the product of a scheduling conference [see Rule 16(b)].

scope of submission   In an arbitration, the parties' agreement concerning the issues that the arbitrators may resolve and other limitations on the process or award.

secondary gain   A term used to describe psychological factors that cause a person to have physical complaints. The factors are characterized by benefits the person has from being ill, injured, or impaired. The factors may be the expectation of monetary gain or avoiding work or avoiding a stressful relationship or avoiding a stressful activity. The secondary gain may be a factor in the patient's condition even though the patient is not aware of the connection.

self-help   An action conducted outside the court system to obtain revenge or payment for an injury; for example, the taking of another person's property because that person has damaged the actor's property.

sequester   To keep a witness apart from other witnesses and outside the courtroom to prevent the witness from being influenced by the testimony of others. To keep a jury together and out of communication with the rest of the world while the jury hears a case or deliberates. The purpose is to prevent improper contacts and to prevent the jurors from being affected by information they might obtain outside the courtroom.

sequestration   An exclusion of witnesses from a trial or hearing for the purpose of preventing them from hearing other witnesses and being influenced by them.

service of process   To deliver or communicate court papers to a person thereby giving the court jurisdiction over that person. The delivery or communication must be a reasonable means of providing actual notice to the person about the court matter. It must provide the person with a reasonable opportunity to appear and be heard on the matter.

settlement   An agreement between parties that results in a resolution of their dispute. Settlement agreements usually are made on the basis of a compromise between parties and arrived at without a judicial order or decree. Where money is paid as a result of a settlement agreement, the sum is often also referred to as the settlement. A jury verdict or arbitration award is not a settlement.

slander   A cause of action in tort for injury to a person's reputation caused by the publication of a false statement made orally. Whereas, a false, defamatory statement made in writing is a libel.

SOAP   An anagram made from the parts of a medical examination: **S**ubjective, **O**bjective, **A**ssessment, and **P**lan. The subjective part includes the patient's statements concerning the patient's complaints, symptoms, and history. The objective part includes the patient's immediate medical history, such as a recent accident and past medical history that may be relevant to the patient's current condition. The plan part includes the physician's diagnosis and plan for treatment.

sound discretion   The power to make a decision based on knowledge and experience. A presiding judge has a great deal of discretion or latitude concerning the admissibility of evidence and trial procedures. A judge's decision concerning such matters will not be disturbed by an appellate court, even if the appellate court disagrees with the trial court's handling, unless the ruling was palpably unfair. An appellate court would have to find that the trial judge clearly abused her or his discretion before finding that the trial court's actions constituted error that would require a new trial.

special damages   Out-of-pocket expenses that a party has incurred because of another party's wrongful conduct. In a personal injury action, the plaintiff's medical expenses, loss of past income, and property damage are items of special damages. Special damages must be listed in the complaint, although the dollar amount may be omitted. In a breach-of-contract action, the amount of lost profits and consequential expenses should be stated. The defendant needs to know about special damages at the outset; consequently, special damages must be specifically alleged in the parties' pleadings [see Rule 9(g)].

special relationship   A term or phrase used by courts to identify a relationship between persons that gives rise to legal rights and obligations (duties) between them. There are many kinds of special relationships. A list of special relationships would include principal-agent, landlord-tenant, husband-wife, land occupant-trespasser, merchant-consumer, physician-patient, attorney-client.

special verdict   A verdict form in which a jury answers specific questions about the facts of the case. A special verdict does not require the jury to apply rules of law to the determined facts for the purpose of deciding which party is entitled to the court's judgment. Instead, the court must apply the rules of law to the facts, as those facts are determined by the special verdict. The court then determines which party is entitled to judgment and to decide the terms of the judgment [Rule 49(a)].

specific performance   A remedy provided by a court that has equity powers. A remedy in which a court orders a party to perform a contract obligation because an award of money damages would be inadequate or because the measure of damages is without a basis in law.

splitting a cause of action   Dividing one cause of action or claim into two or more lawsuits. A party who splits a cause of action is bound by the result in the first trial and is barred from prosecuting the second part of the claim. Courts have a strong policy favoring the total resolution of a dispute in one action.

stare decisis   The doctrine of abiding by, or adhering to, decided cases. The principle that precedent should be followed unless and until compelling reasons occur to change the rule of law.

statement of case   An administrative document that some courts require parties to file to help the court manage the case. The statement of case may require information about the party, the party's evidence, witnesses, insurance, theory of the facts, theory of the law, and preparedness. Federal district courts do not use statements of case.

statute of frauds   A body of law that precludes certain types of contracts from being enforceable unless the contracts are in writing and are signed by the person to be bound.

statute of limitations   A statute that limits the time during which a lawsuit may be brought against a person. The time period provided by a statute of limitations usually begins to run at the time the cause of action accrues. The running of the statute may be tolled by a party's minority or other legal disability. The statute of limitations does not begin to run against an action based on fraud until the person discovers the fraud or reasonably should have discovered it.

statute of repose   A statute that has the effect of barring a claim because the act that gave rise to the claim took place many years ago, and even if the injury is

recent, the actor should not be held accountable at such a late date.

stipulated dismissal   A dismissal of a civil action by agreement of the parties [see Rule 41(a)].

stipulation   An agreement voluntarily entered into between the parties, concerning some aspect of their litigation. An agreement between the parties that the court will recognize and accept to facilitate judicial proceedings. Stipulations may go to matters of procedure or to substantive rights.

stipulation of facts   A stipulation by which the parties express their agreement that a fact or a body of facts is true and may be relied upon by the court. The most common uses for a stipulation of facts are to facilitate a trial or to support a summary judgment motion.

strict liability   A cause of action in tort in which liability is imposed upon a person without regard to fault, such as negligence.

strike   Take out. For example, to *strike* a word is to remove it from a document.

structured settlement   A type of settlement that allows the settling party to buy an annuity for the benefit of the claimant. The settling party pays a lump sum of money to a bank or insurance company, which provides scheduled benefits to the claimant over a period of years or over the claimant's lifetime. Because the company that issues the annuity has the right to use or invest the money over the same period of time, the company can add significantly to the initial payment from the tortfeasor. The annuity payments are structured to provide financial protection to the claimant and prevent other persons from having access to the funds. The claimant does not earn interest on the funds, so the claimant avoids a tax obligation. Nevertheless, the annuity has a total value to the claimant that exceeds the amount the settling party pays for it.

sua sponte   Voluntarily, as when a court takes some action or step without the request of a party to do so. When a court makes an order without either party having made a motion to obtain the order, the court has acted sua sponte.

subject matter jurisdiction   Jurisdiction over the type case and the subject of the litigation. A court must have jurisdiction over the subject of the litigation to be able to render an enforceable judgment. The parties cannot invest the court with jurisdiction over the subject matter.

subjective symptoms   A patient's description of pain or limited motion that a physician is not able to observe or verify apart from the patient's own statements or voluntary presentation. The term may be used to include a patient's subjective complaints concerning the patient's medical condition.

subject to objection   Controlled by the rules of governing objections. Evidence or procedure that is in violation of a court rule or standard is subject to an objection. If the objection is not made, the evidence may be received or the procedure used, and the party who failed to object cannot complain later.

submission   In arbitration, the parties' grant of authority to a tribunal to arbitrate their dispute.

subpoena   (1) A process commanding a party, witness, or deponent to set aside all pretenses and excuses, and appear before a designated court or magistrate at a specified time and place to testify. Failure to comply places the person under penalty by the court. A subpoena may be used in connection with motions, trials, and depositions. (2) A document that the court causes to be served on a person and that requires the person to appear before the court for the purposes of the particular case.

subpoena duces tecum   A subpoena that directs a witness to bring and present specified documents or things to be reviewed when the witness testifies at court or in a deposition.

subrogation   The substitution of one person in the place of another to make a claim or prosecute a cause of action. The subrogee acquires subrogation rights of the subrogor by paying the subrogor's loss under legal compulsion. The subrogee cannot acquire any greater rights than were possessed by the subrogor. For example, where a fire insurance company pays its insured for damage to property because of a fire, the insurer acquires the rights of its insured to bring a claim against the tortfeasor who caused the fire and loss. The insurance contract compels the insurer to pay the loss to the insured, so the insurer is not a volunteer in paying the loss. The insurer is limited to recovering damages in the amount it paid to its insured and is subject to any defenses the tortfeasor had against the insured.

substantive evidence   Evidence that will support a judgment that determines the parties' rights and obligations. Evidence adduced for the purpose of proving a fact in issue, as opposed to evidence given for the purpose of merely discrediting a witness.

substantive law   Law that creates, defines, and regulates legal rights between persons. Substantive law is distinguished from remedial and procedural law that prescribes the means for enforcing substantive legal rights or obtaining redress for the invasion of substantive rights.

summary judgment   A procedure by which a party may avoid a trial by showing the court that the material facts are not in dispute, so the court can apply the law to the facts without having a trial. The procedure allows the court to apply the law to the undisputed facts and order entry of a judgment. The procedure is initiated by a written motion filed with the court and served on all the other parties. A summary judgment may be dispositive of the entire action or resolve only part of the dispute. The motion deals with the parties' substantive rights and decides an issue or case on its merits (see Rule 56).

summons   A court mandate that informs a person that a civil action has been commenced against him or her and requires that person to appear in the case and defend; otherwise, the plaintiff is entitled to obtain a judgment by default for the relief specified in the complaint. The summons must be served with the complaint, except when service is by publication (see Rule 4).

supersedeas bond   A bond that the appellant must file with the court to ensure that the judgment the appellee has been granted will be paid if the appellant does not obtain a modification of that judgment.

superseding cause   *See* efficient intervening cause.

supplemental complaint   A complaint that alleges a new, additional claim that arose from a transaction or occurrence that took place after the initial complaint was filed.

supplemental counterclaim   A counterclaim filed for a cause of action that accrued after the answer was served.

supplemental pleading   A supplemental pleading, complaint or answer, adds to or corrects an original pleading to make the original technically accurate, complete, or more clear. A supplemental pleading may be used to allege facts that have occurred since the original pleading was filed.

supplementary proceedings   Legal proceedings that a judgment creditor may use to discover what property the judgment debtor has with which to pay the judgment [see Rule 69(a)].

sustain   To accept or admit. A party's objection to another party's evidence or conduct is sustained when it is accepted by the court and is allowed.

taxable costs   Costs of litigation that a prevailing party is entitled to recover from the losing party. The recoverable costs are set by statute and court rules.

territorial jurisdiction   The geographic area in which a court may function as determined by political boundaries. With some exceptions, courts have no authority beyond their territorial limits.

testamentary deposition   An oral deposition taken for the specific purpose of using the recorded testimony in place of the deponent's live testimony at trial.

third-party action   An action brought by a defendant against a person other than the plaintiff to recover money damages as contribution or indemnity to the obligation, if any, that the defendant has to the plaintiff. The defendant cannot seek damages for her or his own loss in a third-party action (see Rule 14).

tort   A private or civil wrong that causes injury to person or damage to property. A wrong independent of a contract. A violation of a duty imposed by general law or otherwise on all persons involved in a given transaction or occurrence. The violation must involve some duty owed to the plaintiff and, generally, must arise by operation of law and not by mere agreement of the parties.

tortfeasor   A person who commits any kind of a tort. For example, a person who was negligent and caused an accident or a person who committed a battery against another person may be called tortfeasors.

transaction   An act between two or more persons in which their legal relations are changed by their agreement or by operation of law concerning some identified, specific undertaking. The most common examples of transactions are the making of contracts, the sale of property, the making of loans, and the like. A transaction is never an accidental occurrence.

transitory cause of action   A cause of action that follows the defendant and, therefore, may be commenced in any jurisdiction where the defendant can be found.

trespass   A cause of action in tort to recover money damages for damage to real estate resulting from a wrongful entry on the land. A trespass occurs whenever the entry is made without consent of the possessor and without legal authority. An entry without consent of the occupant makes the trespasser liable for nominal damages even if no actual damage can be shown. The law affirms the possessor's right to exclusive, peaceful occupancy.

trial brief   A brief that a party prepares for the court to identify legal issues, supply authorities, and argue contested points of law.

trial de novo   A second trial that is a new trial in all respects. A trial de novo is totally unaffected by rulings or determinations made in the first trial.

trial notebook   A notebook that a lawyer prepares for her or his own use as a reference for handling a case during trial. It may contain an abbreviated fact brief in which the issues are identified and evidence is listed to support the client's version of the facts. A notebook is not prepared for the court or the other party to see. A trial notebook usually outlines the lawyer's trial strategy, lists important points concerning the substantive law and procedure, and lists authorities the lawyer may cite during the trial. Paralegals may help to prepare trial notebooks.

trial strategy   A lawyer's plan for presenting a case at trial to make his or her theory about the facts and the evidence persuasive. The manner in which a lawyer or party presents evidence and argues the case to make it persuasive. A lawyer's trial strategy is not to be confused with a lawyer's legal theory.

tribunal   A body, organization, or person who has authority to adjudicate matters that are brought before it. An arbitration tribunal may be created by law or by persons who voluntarily agree to submit to the tribunal's authority.

ultimate fact   The facts to which the rules of law are applied so that a judgment can be rendered by the court. A conclusion of fact made by the jury from all the evidence. Conclusions of fact are dispositive of the parties' claims and defenses. For example, in a negligence action, the ultimate questions of fact are whether the defendant was negligent, whether the defendant's negligence was a proximate cause of the harm, and what amount of compensation the plaintiff is entitled to receive.

ultrahazardous activity Activity that gives rise to strict liability in tort for money damages, because the activity is inappropriate to the place where it is conducted and necessarily involves a risk of serious harm to others or their property, and the risk cannot be eliminated by exercising the utmost care. Dynamite blasting and pile driving are examples of ultrahazardous activities that give rise to strict liability in tort.

unauthorized practice of law Nonlawyers doing things that only lawyers are permitted to do. Who and what fits into this definition is constantly changing and the subject of dispute. If, however, a clear case comes up (for example, a nonlawyer pretending to be a lawyer and setting up a law office), the practice may be prohibited and the person punished under the state's criminal laws.

unfair prejudice The unacceptable consequences of some procedure or improper evidence that a party has wrongly injected into the case. Almost anything a party does in the furtherance of his or her case is in some way prejudicial to the opposing party, but only certain wrongful conduct or improper evidence is unfairly harmful to the opposing party.

unilateral mistake A mistake concerning the terms or effect of a contract, made by only one of the parties.

vacate To declare that a judgment is of no force and effect; it is void.

venireman A person who has been selected to undergo questioning to determine whether she or he may qualify to sit on a petit jury.

venue The judicial district in which an action is brought for trial and that is to furnish the panel of jurors.

verdict The jury's decision based on its determination of the facts and its application of the law to those facts.

vicarious liability To impose legal liability on a person for the acts or omissions of another person.

voidable Capable of being voided. A contract is voidable when the contract's purpose is not contrary to law but is technically defective because of the wrongful conduct or inadvertence of one of the contracting parties. The party to the contract who did comply with all legal requirements has the option of enforcing the contract or voiding it. A contract that is void cannot be enforced by any party.

voir dire (1) The preliminary examination of jurors in which competency, interest, and so forth are tested. (2) A preliminary examination of a witness to determine whether the witness is competent to testify.

voluntary dismissal A dismissal of a cause of action or an action, given by a party without being subject to a court order [see Rule 41(a)(1)].

waive To intentionally and voluntarily give up a legal right. Under certain circumstances a person can inadvertently waive rights by failing to comply with court rules or a court order.

waiver An intentional, voluntary giving up of a legal right. A waiver may be in writing, oral, or implied from circumstances.

work product A doctrine that protects from discovery the impressions, mental processes, legal theories, and strategies that a party and the party's attorney formulated while preparing to prosecute or defend a civil action. The doctrine has been expanded to include the party's indemnitor or liability insurer. The doctrine is separate from but complements the attorney-client privilege against disclosure of their communications. It has express support in Rule 26(b) of the Federal Rules of Civil Procedure.

working diagnosis A physician's diagnosis that is made on the basis of the patient's current symptoms so that treatment can be initiated. A working diagnosis is subject to change as more information is obtained.

writ A written precept issued by a court and addressed to a person or officer of the government that commands the person to do something as described in the writ. A type of court order.

writ of certiorari A writ issued by a superior court to a lower court that requires the lower court to transmit its record to the superior court so that the superior court can inspect the proceedings and determine whether any irregularities occurred. If the superior court determines that there was some error that ought to be addressed, it will authorize the petitioning party to appeal.

writ of execution (1) A writ that directs the sheriff or marshal to seize certain property that belongs to the named judgment debtor and to hold or sell the property for the benefit of the judgment creditor. (2) Any writ that puts into force the court's judgment.

writ of mandamus   A type of court order that directs a public official to perform his or her duty. A court has authority to require public officials to perform ministerial acts. A court will not require an official to perform acts that are discretionary or require the exercise of judgment.

writ of prohibition   A writ issued by an appellate court and directed to a judge in a trial court, ordering the judge not to enforce an order already issued. A party may seek a writ of prohibition as an interim appeal to prevent the trial court from causing irreparable harm, as where a trial court has wrongly ordered a party to disclose privileged information.

written response to demand for inspection   A written response that must be served within thirty days of a demand for inspection. The written response must acknowledge the request and agree to the terms of inspection as expressed in the demand. If the respondent objects to any of the terms in the demand, the objections must be stated and reasons must be given for each objection [see Rule 34(b)].

wrongful death action   An action at law, created by statute, that permits the heirs and next of kin to recover money damages from a tortfeasor for the pecuniary losses resulting from the decedent's death. The elements of the cause of action are established by statute in each state. State statutes also declare what pecuniary losses are compensable and the limitation, if any, on the total amount of damages recoverable.

INDEX

Jerome Lawrence and Robert E. Lee. Photo copyright by Stathis Orphanos.

Selected Plays of

JEROME LAWRENCE and ROBERT E. LEE

SELECTED PLAYS OF

JEROME LAWRENCE AND ROBERT E. LEE

EDITED BY
Alan Woods

FOREWORD BY
Norman Cousins

OHIO STATE UNIVERSITY PRESS
Columbus

Publication, stock, and repertory rights for the works of Jerome Lawrence and Robert E. Lee, unless otherwise indicated below, are controlled by the Robert A. Freedman Dramatic Agency, Inc., 1501 Broadway, New York, NY 10036.

Inherit the Wind Copyright © 1951 by Jerome Lawrence and Robert Edwin Lee, as an unpublished work. Copyright © 1955 by Jerome Lawrence and Robert E. Lee. Copyright renewed 1979, 1983 by Jerome Lawrence and Robert E. Lee. Reprinted by permission of Random House, Inc.

Auntie Mame Copyright © 1957 by Jerome Lawrence and Robert E. Lee. Copyright renewed 1985 by Jerome Lawrence and Robert E. Lee.

The Gang's All Here Copyright © 1960 by Jerome Lawrence and Robert E. Lee. Copyright renewed 1988 by Jerome Lawrence and Robert E. Lee.

Only in America Copyright © 1960 by Jerome Lawrence and Robert E. Lee. Copyright renewed 1988 by Jerome Lawrence and Robert E. Lee.

A Call on Kuprin Copyright © 1962 by Jerome Lawrence and Robert E. Lee. Copyright renewed 1990 by Jerome Lawrence and Robert E. Lee.

Diamond Orchid Copyright © 1967, as *Sparks Fly Upward*, by Jerome Lawrence and Robert E. Lee.

The Night Thoreau Spent in Jail Copyright © 1970 by Jerome Lawrence and Robert E. Lee. Reprinted by permission of Hill and Wang, a division of Farrar, Straus & Giroux, Inc.

First Monday in October Copyright © 1979 by Jerome Lawrence and Robert E. Lee.

See p. 579 for further rights information.

Library of Congress Cataloging-in-Publication Data

Lawrence, Jerome. 1915–
    [Selections]
    Selected plays of Jerome Lawrence and Robert E. Lee / edited by
Alan Woods.
        p.   cm.
    Includes bibliographical references.
    ISBN 0-8142-0646-8 (alk. paper)
    I. Lee, Robert Edwin, 1918–1994.   II. Woods, Alan. 1942–
III. Title.
PS3523.A934A6   1995
812′.54—dc20   94-15894
                                                                          CIP

Text and jacket design by Donna Hartwick.
Type set in Caslon 540 by Huron Valley Graphics, Inc., Ann Arbor, Michigan.
Printed by Cushing-Malloy, Inc., Ann Arbor, Michigan.

9 8 7 6 5 4 3 2 1

CONTENTS

FOREWORD

Great playwrights are both teachers and social philosophers. They open the minds of people to important truths, enabling them to make useful connections with their fellow human beings. They put people in close touch not only with their own time but with past events that tend to lose reality in the history books. They help people to banish the terrors that disfigure life and to deal with their inner fears. Finally, they help people to come into more genuine possession of the joys of living.

Those qualities are quintessentially characteristic of the work of Jerome Lawrence and Robert E. Lee. They fulfill their obligation to entertain but they also enable people to leave the theatre feeling better about belonging to the human species than when they arrived. They transmit their own deep belief in the possibilities of human betterment—and they do this as storytellers and not as sermonizers. They don't superimpose; they share. When the curtain goes up on a Lawrence and Lee play, the theatregoer can expect an adventure in transformation, for Lawrence and Lee have discovered a way of transmitting their enthusiasm, concerns, apprehensions, and the possibilities of a more just social order without spotlights or special effects.

As human beings, Jerry and Bob are constantly involved in the drama of the surrounding world. The slightest vibrations are picked up on their antennae. They respond to whispers and not just to explosions. They are constantly on the lookout for the obscure ingredients that go into the making of great events. To paraphrase Winston Churchill, their work hangs on the hinges of history. And they are as involved in the human situation as are any of their characters.

Their success as collaborators is no accident. I have seldom known two human beings who are better suited intellectually, emotionally, and spiritually to the challenge of creative partnership. Each contributes different colors to achieve a rainbow effect over their stage. Their respect for each other has not wavered over half a century. The way they communicate with each other is one of the wonders of the world. The train of thought started by one has hardly begun to move when tracks are already being laid down by the other. Even more important perhaps than their joint creativity is their joint moral and social imagination. They have an instant and instinctive reaction to injustice—and the greater the effort of the perpetrator to conceal or justify the wrongdoing, the greater their skill in holding him to accounts. The result is that you feel connected to the injustice unless you do something about it.

Jerome Lawrence and Robert E. Lee are evolutionists—not in the sense of the central theme of their *Inherit the Wind*, but in the Jeffersonian sense. That is, they are constantly making the case for human perfectibility. Not for perfection but for the capacity of human beings to ascend to ever-higher levels of individual and collective growth. Like Hammerstein and Rodgers, they give a common touch to elegant ideas; they love the theatre and they satisfy the love of people for it. But they are first and foremost sensitive and compassionate thinkers, locked into the human procession with all its glory and pain, and determined to use their combined skills to advance that procession even as they make people proud to be part of it.

This collection of a cross section of their plays is long overdue and establishes them not just as important social critics but as architects and innovators—architects who know something about the design of a good society; innovators whose understanding of cause and effect enables them to define new causes and to produce remarkable new effects.

Norman Cousins

GENERAL INTRODUCTION

Jerome Lawrence and Robert E. Lee's partnership as dramatic writers, after five decades, serves as a reminder of the strength once possessed by the American theatre. The playwrights' joint work, represented by the plays in this volume, typifies the years in which the commercial theatre served as an arena for ideas of substance, presented through highly professional collaborations among writers, performers, directors, producers, and audiences. Lawrence and Lee's work recalls the achievements of that period before financial and other considerations reduced the commercial theatre to its current overwhelming reliance on lavishly entertaining spectacles.

Lawrence and Lee's plays were (and are), with one notable exception, intended for the commercial theatre: a professional, profit-making business enterprise. When successful, the plays reaped large profits for producers, performers, and playwrights alike. Perhaps for that reason, and others to be explored below, the plays of Lawrence and Lee have received little scholarly attention. Yet in sheer number of performances, audiences, and productions, the commercial theatre far outweighs the experimental art that receives the lion's share of scholarly criticism. As I have argued elsewhere,[1] the popular commercial theatre provides a rich source for comprehending the audience of the past in its broadest range. For that reason alone, Lawrence and Lee's work deserves examination.

But Lawrence and Lee are more than just popular commercial playwrights. At their most successful, their plays have become classics of the modern stage, far outlasting those "hits" by many other contemporary playwrights, which disappear after their initial Broadway run and subsequent productions in community, academic, and regional theatres. Lawrence and Lee's plays survive because they deal with ideas and provide more than an evening's entertainment: they provide food for thought as well, dealing with some of the major conflicts of our time.

Jerome Lawrence and Robert E. Lee have collaborated on more than twenty produced plays and musicals, several hundred radio and television scripts, and numerous films. Eight stage plays have been chosen for this selection of their work. Each represents at least one facet of their work that will be explored in greater length in the introductions to each play's text.

Three of these plays (*Inherit the Wind*, *Auntie Mame*, and *First Monday in October*) were commercial successes on the Broadway stage, while one (*The Night Thoreau Spent in Jail*) was a landmark success in the regional theatre movement.

The remaining four included in this volume had varying degrees of success in the commercial theatre. *Only in America* had a short life in New York but ran more than a year in Los Angeles. *Diamond Orchid* was a success in academic theatre after its premature Broadway closing. *The Gang's All Here* had a respectable run in New York without financial success but has been widely produced in the following years, its theme of political corruption remaining always current. *A Call on Kuprin*, despite high praise from most reviewers, is the only piece in this anthology that was unsuccessful commercially in its original production and has had little life since. The various reasons for its failure to attract an audience permit a different glance at aspects of the commercial theatre.

Lawrence and Lee routinely have used history to comment on contemporary events: both *Only in America* and *The Night Thoreau Spent in Jail* take actual figures from the history of the United States in order to reflect on topics ranging from racism and anti-Semitism to nonviolent civil disobedience. *Inherit the Wind* and *The Gang's All Here* take historic events (the Scopes "Monkey Trial," the corruption in the presidency of Warren G. Harding) and fictionalize them to allow the playwrights greater freedom in drawing modern parallels. In *Diamond Orchid*, the career of Evita Peron in post–World War II Argentina inspired Lawrence and Lee to create a fictional piece exploring the nature of demagoguery.

Two of the plays are dramatizations from fiction. *Auntie Mame*, taken from the best-selling sketches published in 1955 by Patrick Dennis, gave Lawrence and Lee the chance to celebrate the freedom of the individual, while noting—comically, to be sure—the need to maintain that freedom vigilantly. *A Call on Kuprin*, freely drawn from a 1959 novel by Maurice Edelman (then a member of the British Parliament), uses the Soviet-American space competition to explore questions of patriotism and the role of the scientist in the modern world.

First Monday in October is unique in this collection in that it forecast the future when it was first produced: what would happen, the play asks, if the first female Supreme Court justice were to be an archconservative in conflict with a politically liberal senior justice? Recent American history has proven much of *First Monday in October* to be prophetic—indeed, many drama editors termed the play "history before it happens."

The plays included here, then, are examples of the work of Jerome Lawrence and Robert E. Lee. As I hope to demonstrate, they are extremely well-crafted pieces. Responses to their initial productions have more to do with the nature of the commercial American theatre, its mode of production, and audience tastes than with the merits of particular scripts. This introduction will examine the lives and careers of Jerome Lawrence and Robert E. Lee, then explore the context of the American commercial theatre during their most active years, the period from the mid-1950s through the mid-1970s. Finally, I will attempt to explore some of the reasons for the lack of scholarly and critical examination of Lawrence and Lee's work: why this anthology represents the first attempt to explore the range and nature of their collaboration.

Both Jerome Lawrence and Robert E. Lee were born and educated in north-eastern Ohio, Lawrence in Cleveland on 14 July 1915, Lee some thirty miles west in Elyria on 15 October 1918. Ohio has served as a base for many of their later dramatic works, providing settings, origins for characters, and general backgrounds. Both men went to college in central Ohio, and both began individual careers in radio while in school. Lawrence became a Phi Beta Kappa graduate of Ohio State University in Columbus, where he won campus playwriting contests three times, wrote for the student newspaper as a columnist and drama critic (although not of his own plays), and gained radio experience by writing for the university station. He also acted extensively while a student and saw his first published play appear nationally in *Six Anti-Nazi Plays*.[2] Lawrence worked briefly for newspapers in Wilmington and New Lexington, Ohio, before moving into network radio on the West Coast as a writer and director.

Robert Lee's college education came at Ohio Wesleyan University in Delaware, Ohio, where he majored in astronomy and was active in the drama program. Before attending Ohio Wesleyan, he won a precollege summer scholarship at the school of speech at Northwestern University. Lee's deep voice got him continuous work as an announcer at radio stations in Columbus and Cleveland, and he was widely known as "Radio's Youngest Announcer": "I used to do all the big band remotes. . . . I really said 'Let's swing and sway with Sammy Kaye' more times than anybody else—his band used to have eight originations from Cleveland, and I did all of them."[3]

The two never met in Ohio, nor did their trails cross when each wrote and directed at KMPC in Beverly Hills, although at different times. Their careers paralleled in the late 1930s and early 1940s, with Lawrence writing and directing radio programs for CBS in both Hollywood and New York, while Lee was writing and directing on both coasts for the advertising agency Young and Rubicam, often at CBS.

By the early 1940s, Lawrence and Lee knew of each other's work; indeed, each had friends suggest that they meet. The meeting eventually took place at Colbee's Restaurant in the CBS New York headquarters building during January 1942, just after Pearl Harbor. The two decided to form a partnership and immediately began writing radio scripts together. Their first working session, at a Howard Johnson's in Manhattan with the pair writing on yellow pads, resulted in a script, "Inside a Kid's Head," produced on the experimental radio program, *Columbia Workshop*. "Inside a Kid's Head" was later widely anthologized in print.[4] The team's second joint script, "Brownstone Front," didn't carry the "Lawrence and Lee" credit: the sponsor of the *Manhattan at Midnight* series was a client of Young and Rubicam where Lee was still employed, so the script was credited to "Jerome Lawrence and Ulysses S. Grant."

The team of Lawrence and Lee succeeded so quickly with these and a number of other radio plays that by the spring of 1942, having completed other assignments—Lee at Young and Rubicam, Lawrence at CBS (where he was a writer on the wartime series *They Live Forever*)—they drove west to set up business in Los Angeles. Lawrence had been working on a proposed radio series about Amelia Earhart with publisher George Palmer Putnam, Earhart's widower. Putnam formed a partnership with the two writers and an editor, "Cap" Palmer (no relation), setting up offices in Hollywood as Lawrence, Lee, Palmer, and Putnam.

By the middle of 1942, World War II claimed the writers: in July, both went to Washington, D.C., as expert consultants to the secretary of war and became two of the founders of the worldwide network of the Armed Forces Radio Service, originating such programs as *Mail Call*, *Yarns for Yanks*, and contributing to *Command Performance*. They wrote and directed the major radio commemorations of World War II, including the official Army-Navy programs for D-Day, Victory in Europe Day, and Victory over Japan Day.

In what little spare time they could find, the partners also began writing for the live theatre. Their first effort, the comic *Madhouse on Madison*, was abandoned as too frivolous for the war years. Their second, *Top of the Mark*, took a more serious tone. Following a platoon through the war and ending with a reunion in San Francisco after the war's end, it treated serious social and political issues in the manner of their later successes. Despite support from such figures as playwright Marc Connelly, *Top of the Mark* was never produced. Connelly brought the play to agent Harold Freedman, a dominant figure in the commercial theatre of the day, who was impressed enough to take on Lawrence and Lee as clients. Freedman sent the play to the Theatre Guild,[5] whose cofounder, Theresa Helburn, wanted to discuss the play with the authors personally by telephone. By this time, however, both Lawrence and Lee were in uniform: Lawrence, a staff sergeant, was in Casablanca as a radio correspondent, en route to the Fifth Army Mobile Radio Station in Italy. Lee, an Air Force cadet stationed in Los Angeles with the Armed Forces Radio Services unit, was (as he put it), "guarding a cannon, protecting the Fox lot from enemy invasion."

Lee told Helburn the team couldn't work on the play until after the war. By that point, their interest (as well as that of the Theatre Guild) in *Top of the Mark* had waned. The play remains unproduced, while the promising connection with the Theatre Guild was never renewed.

Lawrence and Lee's first produced Broadway playscript was the book for the musical *Look, Ma, I'm Dancin'!* The team had met Hugh Martin, the composer of *Best Foot Forward* (1941) and the film *Meet Me in St. Louis* (1944), who was working on an idea for a musical with Jerome Robbins as a starring vehicle for comedienne Nancy Walker. (Walker had been a hit in a supporting role in *Best Foot Forward*.) Lawrence and Lee were asked to write a sample scene, about members of a traveling ballet troupe crowded into a single Texas hotel room. The writers accepted the task casually, turning out the scene within a week. To their delight, Oliver Smith and Richard Dorso, who were to produce the show, hired them to do the musical's book.

Elated, the team returned to New York to write the show, taking an apartment on Fifty-second Street between Fifth and Sixth Avenues, the block then known as Jazz Alley. But the production failed to materialize. Lawrence and Lee were still writing radio scripts, working at this point on the highly successful *Favorite Story* (starring Ronald Colman), *The Frank Sinatra Show*, and *Hallmark Playhouse*, among others. Lee eventually returned to Los Angeles to marry Janet Waldo, a radio actress then best known for playing Corliss Archer. As soon as Lawrence decided *Look, Ma, I'm Dancin'!* would never be produced and also returned to Los Angeles, the show was read by producer-director George Abbott, who took the project over and put it into rehearsal. Lawrence and Lee crossed the country again.

Look, Ma, I'm Dancin'!, starring Nancy Walker with Harold Lang and Herbert Ross in the cast, opened at the Adelphi Theatre in New York on 29 January 1948. The show traced the fortunes of an itinerant ballet company bankrolled by a beer heiress (Walker), who insisted on performing—turning into a comically bumbling ballerina in the process. With direction by Abbott and choreography by Robbins, *Look, Ma, I'm Dancin'!* garnered positive reviews and enthusiastic audiences. But it was what Lawrence termed "a nervous hit." Despite being housed in a large theatre away from Times Square, *Look, Ma, I'm Dancin'!* was among Broadway's top grossing hit musicals through the end of April 1948. An unusually hot May and June resulted in the box office figures dropping by more than fifty percent in those days before air conditioning, and the show closed on 11 July. (The heat also closed Rodgers and Hammerstein's *Allegro* and the long-running *Brigadoon*; the season's biggest hit, *High Button Shoes*, survived the heat wave.)[6] *Look, Ma, I'm Dancin'!* made a modest profit, however, and firmly established Nancy Walker as a star Broadway comic.

Look, Ma, I'm Dancin'! received a great deal of publicity, including a feature spread in *Life* magazine;[7] Lawrence and Lee's satirical thrust at Texas engendered a tongue-in-cheek response from one *Time* magazine reader, who threatened to cancel the company's "passports to Texas" because of the show's comic mockery of that state.[8]

Lawrence and Lee returned to their radio careers, continuing with the task of writing, directing, and producing 299 broadcasts of notable musical theatre works for the weekly series *The Railroad Hour* between 1948 and 1954, including the scripts and lyrics for sixty original musicals. Their next stage collaboration was *Inherit the Wind*, which would not be produced until 1955. With its success, first at Margo Jones's Theatre '55 in Dallas and shortly thereafter on Broadway, the partners moved firmly into the commercial theatre. Their timing was excellent: radio drama disappeared as a mass medium in the mid-1950s, buried by the competitive form of television. By then, however, Lawrence and Lee had become fixtures of the Broadway theatre scene and of the "road," the touring commercial theatre outside New York.

The partners wrote almost exclusively for the live theatre from 1955 through the late 1970s, with occasional projects for television and film being adaptations of their stage plays. Thus their 1956 Broadway musical, *Shangri-La*, hardly a utopia in its accident-prone Broadway production, had a far more salubrious presentation on television's *Hallmark Hall of Fame* in 1961. The film of *Auntie Mame* was an almost verbatim transfer of their stage play and remains vastly popular on videocassette into the 1990s. Notable films were also made of *Inherit the Wind* and *First Monday in October*. Their most recent collaboration, *Whisper in the Mind*, opened in October 1990 at Arizona State University in Tempe. *Whisper in the Mind* examines scientific rationalism and the power of the mind through Benjamin Franklin's confrontations with Dr. Anton Mesmer in 1784. As with many of their earlier works, *Whisper in the Mind* uses historic sources, adding fictional elements as a means to discuss contemporary concerns.

Lawrence and Lee's longevity as a writing team rests on the two partners' personal compatibility and on their careful nurturing of the collaborative process. The two have complementary personalities and interests: Lee, for example, is fascinated by how things work and possesses a photographic memory. Lawrence has been tirelessly active in professional associations, writers' conferences, symposia, and countless efforts aimed at national and international communication, joining delegations of writers on visits to the Soviet Union and the People's Republic of China in the 1960s and 1970s in efforts to encourage freedom of speech. Both teach (Lee at the University of California, Los Angeles, and Lawrence at the University of Southern California), lecturing extensively at colleges and universities across North America and at theatrical conferences and festivals.

From their earliest meetings in 1942, the two have avoided any set pattern of composition: one does not transcribe while the other dictates, the popular notion of how a writing partnership functions. (Lawrence and Lee's essay "Which One Can't Spell?"[9] explores some of the misconceptions about the collaborative process.) Rather, both write, discuss, revise, and, most importantly, read aloud. That both had theatrical performance experience is crucial; while neither writer pretends to high acting ability, they read all dialogue aloud, listening for words or phrases that sound false or are inappropriate to individual characters and situations. As Lawrence said, "When a play is really working, we become identified with the people we're writing about. We can easily play the roles of advocates in creating the dialogue. This way, the characters, if well fleshed-out, sit down alongside us and help us write the plays."[10] Lee adds, "Did Jerry write this? Did I write that? The point is, neither of us did. The play is really working when the character, whom we imagined, says, 'I've got to say this.'"

Most important for the collaborative process, the playwrights adopted what they term "the U.N. Veto" at the beginning of their partnership. "The whole theory is, either one of us has the absolute right to say 'no' . . . but then has the obligation to make his negative a positive, by coming up with something better—that the other will say yes to," Lawrence has explained. Both have written projects on their own, usually because the other wasn't fired by the idea—that was the case, for example, with Lawrence's one-act play, *Live Spelled Backwards . . .* (1966),

Lee's dramatization of John Reed's *Ten Days That Shook the World* (1973) and his chancel drama, *Sounding Brass* (1975).

Prose pieces are produced differently. "It's kind of impossible to do them jointly," according to Lee. The partners instead often write magazine articles and books separately. Lee authored *Television: The Revolution* in 1943, accurately forecasting that medium's future, while Lawrence published *Actor: The Life and Times of Paul Muni* on his own in 1974.

For articles published under the joint byline, the team collaborates on revisions after one has produced a first draft. "Then the other helps punch it up, changing. . . . So we're each other's editors," Lawrence says. In the period of their greatest activity in radio, during the run of *The Railroad Hour*, the partners often wrote (and directed) individual shows separately, although the writing credit was always to the partnership.

One result of their working pattern is that neither Lawrence nor Lee can identify which one originated lines, situations, or characters, except for rare instances. Perhaps their most quoted line of dialogue from *Auntie Mame*, for example, is Mame's "Life is a banquet and most poor sons-of-bitches are *starving* to death." Neither remembers who wrote it. Lee thought at first that the line came from Patrick Dennis's published book. But when asked for permission to quote it in books of popular quotations, Dennis pointed out that he first encountered the line in the original draft of Lawrence and Lee's play, "though he wished he had written it."

Similarly, the genesis for the plays, when not directly commissioned—as were *Auntie Mame* and *A Call on Kuprin*—remains lost in the collaborative process. Typical is Lawrence's description of starting work on *First Monday in October*: "One of us called the other and said, 'What would happen if there was a woman on the Supreme Court?'" *The Night Thoreau Spent in Jail* was a rare exception: the initial idea was Lawrence's. He roughed out an outline and began writing, using Thoreau's imagined trial of himself as the organizing point, but hit a snag. Lee came up with the idea of fluid, almost cinematic structure, "time awash," which solved the problem; so the play, originally to be Lawrence's sole work, became a collaborative effort.

The actual process of writing has varied with technology. When the partnership began in 1942, the writers used yellow legal pads, sometimes with Lee writing in his own shorthand; the writers then typed drafts from their handwritten copy. Over the years, they used whatever mechanical aids were available, speaking dialogue into tape recorders, transcribing the results on manual then electric typewriters, up to their present use of word processors linked by modems and fax machines.

Technology has permitted them to work together although geographically separated. Through much of the 1960s, Lawrence was based in New York, while Lee lived in Southern California. They worked over the telephone, meeting face-to-face only occasionally on one coast or the other.[11] More recently, with both in the

xv

GENERAL
INTRODUCTION

Los Angeles area but separated by some thirty miles of freeway, computer technology provides the link.

Whatever the equipment used, however, the process of writing, editing, and honing—what Lee terms "writing with an eraser"—has remained remarkably constant, as has the constant production of plays for all media, resulting in the enormous body of work, both realized and unrealized, of which this anthology represents only a fraction in a single form, the live theatre.

The commercial theatre world to which Lawrence and Lee aspired in the late 1940s and joined with such success in the mid-1950s, was to vanish by the early 1970s. When Lawrence and Lee became active, the "Broadway" theatre in New York City was the center of a national theatrical business: plays and musicals were developed during tryout tours (usually on the East Coast), then opened in New York. Successes toured across the North American continent after their Broadway runs, often for several years. Theatres in cities of even modest size provided venues for tours, termed the "road" in show business jargon, often with large subscription audiences. The Hartman Theatre in Columbus, Ohio, for example, offered its audiences eighteen touring productions in the 1947–48 season, when *Look, Ma, I'm Dancin'!* opened in New York.[12] Even moderately successful shows could, at least in the 1940s and early 1950s, recoup part of their investment on tour, billed as recent Broadway hits.

Stage stars—most notably such luminous figures as Alfred Lunt and Lynn Fontanne, Katharine Cornell, Maurice Evans, and Helen Hayes—routinely alternated seasons in New York with year-long tours of the road. The road tours in turn fueled the commercial theatre in New York: newspapers in such cities as Indianapolis, Columbus, and Pittsburgh regularly chartered "show trains" from railroads, taking hundreds of residents into New York for a weekend of sightseeing and theatregoing, often to see the same performers they had seen in touring productions at home.[13] Commercial theatre was a truly national one during this period: while centered in New York, its major stars and productions were visible across the continent.

Costs were low enough in the late 1940s that a production could recoup its investment in several months, rather than the several years that became necessary by the mid-1970s. Highly successful hits typically ran for a season or two; multiyear runs, although not unknown (*Tobacco Road* racked up seven years in the 1930s, while both *Oklahoma!* and *Life with Father* ran throughout the decade of the 1940s), were extremely rare. The relatively short runs of successes suggests that the audience was finite: after a season or so, the New York audience—even augmented as it certainly was by tourists and show trains—was exhausted. With runs for all but the most runaway hits limited, producers kept costs low in order to have some chance of repaying backers' investments.

Lower production costs, relatively rapid recovery of those production costs, and the possibility of high profits from adding a road tour to the Broadway run, all combined to create a high degree of activity in the commercial theatre: in the 1948–49 season, for example, seventy-six productions appeared in the commercial theatre. By 1955–56, the total had dropped to fifty-six; only twenty-nine productions constituted Broadway's 1988–89 theatrical season.[14]

The high level of production in the late 1940s and early 1950s also helped foster the existence of a professional theatre community based in New York: producers, directors, performers, and writers, all regularly working in the live theatre, and all collaborating on projects for production. By the mid-1950s, the theatre community—including performers, stagehands, designers, and so forth, was estimated to stand at twenty thousand people.[15] Jerome Lawrence and Robert E. Lee became part of that theatrical scene at a time when collaboration was normal, rather than exceptional, and when many of the theatre's workers regarded the creation of plays and musicals as the work of skilled craftspeople. Such collaborations were once common in the theatre, as Richard Hummler pointed out in *Variety*, the show business weekly.[16] Hummler is correct in finding such collaboration a function of "a more pragmatic and overtly commercial . . . era, when scripts were tailored more precisely for the marketplace, and for mass acceptance, than they are today."[17] While multiple authors are common in both commercial cinema and television, as Hummler writes, the common practice in those media is for writers to work separately on successive drafts. The true partnership process employed by Lawrence and Lee has become a rarity, as the modes and processes of theatrical production have changed to focus on the individual playwright, now nurtured through grants, workshops, and nonprofit theatrical venues. In the collaborative theatre community of the late 1940s and early 1950s, getting the show right for the individual star performer, or for the director/producer, was paramount, and with less attention paid to the theatre's "art" than became the case in later years.

Lawrence and Lee's most active years in the professional theatre are those of the theatre's most productive years, in terms of sheer activity at the very least, during the post–World War II period. As the plays in the present anthology make clear, the great activity of those years often resulted in masterworks of the theatre as well. Lawrence and Lee's contemporaries include Arthur Miller, Tennessee Williams, William Inge, Leonard Bernstein, Lerner and Loewe, Frank Loesser, the later works of Rodgers and Hammerstein, and the early works of Stephen Sondheim.

Although we tend to remember a period's theatre by the plays and their writers, and the major performers who attracted the audience, an integral part of the commercial American theatre's community were the producers, directors, and designers—the artists who created the physical productions. The commercial theatre in the 1940s and 1950s supported a number of major talents in each area. Producers such as Herman Shumlin, Kermit Bloomgarden, David Merrick, Griffith and Prince, Fryer and Carr, Robert Whitehead, Roger L. Stevens, George Abbott—all maintained permanent offices and mounted productions each season, often supported by "angels": the wealthy who regularly backed productions as a somewhat risky but always glamorous investment.[18] A major designer would work constantly; in the 1956–57 season alone, for example, Oliver Smith designed the scenery for four Broadway productions in addition to his work on *Auntie Mame*.[19]

The final component of the commercial theatre community was, of course, its audience. The theatregoing audience of the period consisted of people who attended with some regularity and saw more than just the major successes each season. Such an audience was sophisticated and experienced, discerning judges of talent in both the performance and writing of plays. Part of the high quality of the commercial theatre during the decades immediately following World War II is undoubtedly due to the presence of a regular and knowledgeable audience. That audience, and the activity that surrounded a theatre community in which large numbers of writers, performers, and production workers could make a living without needing constantly to seek employment in film and television, enabled the commercial American theatre to reach levels not attained before or since.

The regular theatre audience has, in large part, disappeared in New York City, as the city's population has fragmented into discrete communities. As Thomas Disch puts it in an examination of the decline of the commercial theatre, the "melting pot has been replaced by a mosaic, the separate components of which regard one another with apathy or contempt."[20]

By the mid-1960s, much of the creative energy of the Broadway theatre had dissipated. A new generation of playwrights was emerging, as the first of the generation born during the Depression and the early years of World War II reached maturity. But with the exception of Edward Albee, whose first full-length play, *Who's Afraid of Virginia Woolf?*, burst on the Broadway scene in 1962, many of the younger playwrights were produced not on Broadway, but in the burgeoning off-Broadway and off-off-Broadway theatre. As always in a commercial venture, costs underlay the shift: the Broadway theatre's steadily increasing costs in the early 1960s fostered steady increases in the prices charged for tickets. Increasing costs made theatregoers less willing to see plays other than those touted as hits by critics; increasing ticket prices also helped to scatter the regular theatre audience. By 1975, a small comedy such as *Same Time, Next Year* cost almost $154,000 to produce and charged $11 for the best tickets; in 1956, a similar comedy, *The Loud Red Patrick*, had cost $45,000 to produce and its best seats cost $5.75.[21] Increasing production costs also helped to kill off the touring theatre across North America. By the mid-1960s, the commercial American theatre was an industry in sharp decline, beset by apparently intractable problems.[22]

One response to the contracting American theatre was the establishment of professional regional theatres, intended to ensure that theatrical performances were available even if the commercial theatre no longer could supply enough productions to keep local theatres filled regularly. The Hartman Theatre in Columbus, mentioned above, housed only seven productions in the 1967–68 season and then closed permanently.[23] Founded at least in part as a response to the disappearance of the "road," those regional theatres frequently were established as nonprofit entities, intended as cultural institutions on the same level as art museums or symphony orchestras. The history of the nonprofit regional theatre movement of the 1960s and 1970s has been well documented and needs no repetition here.[24] One aspect of the regional theatre movement, in which Lawrence and Lee played seminal roles, does bear some discussion, however, as it provided a model for later developments.

Lawrence and Lee founded the American Playwrights Theatre in 1965 in hopes of bypassing the harshly commercial conditions then beginning to dominate the Broadway stage. Headquartered at Ohio State University, the American Playwrights Theatre (APT) created the first truly national theatrical production mechanism seen in the United States since a brief but intense period of activity by the American National Theatre and Academy (ANTA) in the late 1940s.[25] The APT provided original scripts by established playwrights to member theatres, who were in turn offered the exclusive rights to produce the scripts. In its fifteen-year history, the APT offered twelve scripts, nine of which received productions from member theatres.[26]

The most successful play in APT's history was Lawrence and Lee's own *The Night Thoreau Spent in Jail*, with more than two thousand performances at APT member theatres during its first two years alone.[27] By the end of the 1970s, the regional professional theatre had become so well established that the pattern of professional production changed: no longer were most commercial theatre plays and musicals rehearsed in New York, then tried out for several weeks in cities on the East Coast before opening on Broadway, the standard practice of earlier years. Now, many productions originated in nonprofit regional theatres and were either moved intact to the Broadway stage, as was the case with the 1990 winner of the Tony Award for best play, Frank Galati's adaptation of *The Grapes of Wrath*,[28] or were given new (and often more elaborate) physical productions before being transferred. Lawrence and Lee adopted that practice with *First Monday in October*, first presented at the nonprofit Cleveland Play House in 1975 before its 1977 commercial production at the Kennedy Center in Washington, D.C., and its 1978 move to Broadway, Los Angeles, and Chicago.

The team of Jerome Lawrence and Robert E. Lee has been active longer than any of their contemporaries other than Arthur Miller. Alone among theatre writers of the 1950s and 1960s, Lawrence and Lee moved freely—and successfully—from serious drama to comedy to musical comedy.

Despite their range and large body of work, Lawrence and Lee have not been the subject of much scholarly attention. Each of their plays was critically reviewed when first produced, of course, and new productions continue to gather reviews and publicity. Lawrence and Lee themselves have been frequently interviewed over the course of their careers. Accordingly, an enormous amount of printed material is available documenting the team's career.[29] The plays have not received a similarly extensive assessment, however. Given their success, such a lack seems odd. Some possible reasons for the critical silence suggest themselves, however, and may help to put these popular playwrights into closer perspective.

First, although Lawrence and Lee's major successes were popular with audiences and were highly praised by most of the New York reviewers, in several instances influential critics failed, on a first viewing, to recognize the playwrights' contributions. Lawrence and Lee were fortunate to have major stars in their first five Broadway productions, which also misled some of the reviewers. *Look, Ma, I'm Dancin'!* was regarded as a satisfactory vehicle for a new star, but there was little recognition of the structure and wit of the musical's book. Critical reaction to the other plays is discussed in detail below, in introductions to each text. Although positive, reviewers tended to focus on the productions rather than on the playwrights' contributions (with several notable exceptions). As the original reviews are widely available, either through microform editions of the *New York Times* or the collected volumes of *New York Theatre Critics Reviews*, later researchers find little to encourage further exploration of the plays.

A further reason for the silence regarding Lawrence and Lee's plays, ironically enough, is that they are too well crafted to attract the attention of major academic scholars of drama. The playwrights' penchant for fictionalizing historical events and characters in the interest of examining social issues frequently led careless reviewers to dismiss the plays as mere transcriptions of historic documents. That was especially the case with *Inherit the Wind* and *The Gang's All Here*: observers often congratulated Lawrence and Lee for including speeches and incidents that the playwrights had, in fact, created themselves.

Such responses were mistaken. Although *Inherit the Wind*, *Diamond Orchid*, and *The Gang's All Here* were based on actual events, Lawrence and Lee created what they have termed "factual fiction or fictional fact," inventing dialogue, characters, and incidents that do not exist in any public record. In *Only in America*, the team developed a plot based in part on Harry Golden's life, incorporating many of his pithy sayings while inventing more of their own.

Lawrence and Lee succeed in capturing the spirit of their subjects so well that often observers remain unaware of their contribution. Reviewers were unaware that many of the incidents and lines in *Auntie Mame* were not in Patrick Dennis's book but were created by the playwrights; in *Only in America*, Harry Golden received credit for proverbs minted by Lawrence and Lee. Supreme Court Justice William O. Douglas praised the writers for having the good sense to include Clarence Darrow's "famous speech" beginning "Progress has never been a bargain" in *Inherit the Wind*; Darrow never gave such a speech. "He could have said it," the playwrights observe, "he might have said it, he *should* have said it." But he didn't—the speech is the result of Lawrence and Lee's creative fictionalization of the Scopes trial.

The playwrights' very success in capturing the spirit of the characters and the events they choose to dramatize has thus worked against them. In every play, the partners are self-effacing: there is no readily apparent Lawrence and Lee style in structure or in diction. Instead, each play has a style appropriate to the dramatic action and character. This lack of an easily identifiable style makes the work of Lawrence and Lee difficult to categorize and makes it even more difficult to undertake critical analyses based on primarily literary concerns.

Finally, Jerome Lawrence and Robert E. Lee explore ideas, but do so in plays that either were enormously successful or which had limited Broadway runs. Perversely, either result can lead to dismissal by scholarly critics. The plays that were not box office smashes rarely are even read, while the major successes often still are regarded as star vehicles—certainly the fate of *Inherit the Wind*, *Auntie Mame*, and *First Monday in October*—despite the plays' continuing to hold the stage after more than three decades and after cast changes made the scripts' merits obvious belatedly even to the few initially negative New York reviewers.[30]

Lawrence and Lee's plays are linked by thematic concerns, however, even if dramatic structure and style vary individually from script to script. Throughout the plays included in this anthology, several themes remain constant. In all, the right of the individual to personal fulfillment and the expression of an individualized approach to life is explored—and frequently celebrated, as in *Auntie Mame*, *Only in America*, and *The Night Thoreau Spent in Jail*. In *Diamond Orchid*, the effects of societal oppression of individual development are explored, while in *Inherit the Wind*, *The Gang's All Here*, *A Call on Kuprin*, and *First Monday in October* the degree to which the individual can, should, or must exercise those rights is debated.

Individual rights often force characters to defy authority, always nonviolently, another constant theme running throughout the plays. That conflict is treated both comically, as in Mame's defiance of the Upsons and Mr. Babcock in *Auntie Mame* and Harry Golden's calm assertion of minority rights in *Only in America*, or more seriously, with Thoreau's incarceration in *The Night Thoreau Spent in Jail* or Kuprin's willingness to forego his own freedom so that his niece can escape in *A Call on Kuprin*.

Two of the plays published here present darker variations of the same themes. In *The Gang's All Here*, Hastings's lack of personal integrity and vision leads to governmental corruption; only when Hastings himself becomes aware of the widespread effect of his own failings can he redeem himself and set corrective forces in motion. In *Diamond Orchid*, Felicia's greed and her capacity for self-delusion is clearly shown to be a result of the crushing force exerted by a rigid and rapacious class system externally imposed. Alone among Lawrence and Lee's leading characters, Felicia never comes to self-knowledge. Although her final speech as she dies provides the audience with enough information ultimately to understand the character, Felicia herself never seems to understand that she has perpetuated the abusive patterns that created her implacable ambition. And the final scene in *Diamond Orchid*, with its implication that the social forces that created Felicia will produce new Felicias continually, suggests a less optimistic view of the world than is present in the other plays.

It is significant, of course, that the pessimism of *Diamond Orchid* is rare among the plays of Lawrence and Lee. While the playwrights are passionately involved with the ideas that motivate their plays, the plays celebrate the human potential for positive action and demonstrate their authors' optimistic belief that injustices can be overcome, that society's problems can be overcome. Just as Justices Dan Snow and Ruth Loomis attain a clearer understanding of, and sympathy for, their philosophical opposites in *First Monday in October*, most of Lawrence and Lee's characters learn and grow in the course of their plays. The ending of *Inherit the Wind*, with Drummond's weighing—and finding equal—Darwin's *Origin of the Species* and the Bible, provides the paradigm for Lawrence and Lee's plays. Issues are fully debated, and a new, more humane synthesis usually results.

In reaching those syntheses, Lawrence and Lee fully utilize the resources of the live theatre. The sheer theatricality of their plays, again varying according to subject matter, provides another constant in the work. The rapid whirlwind of Auntie Mame's personality, for example, is reflected in the structure of her play, composed of many fast-paced scenes with dizzying changes of scenery and costumes.[31] The orgiastic revival meeting vividly creates the atmosphere of intolerant religious bigotry in *Inherit the Wind*, while the fluid time and space of *The Night Thoreau Spent in Jail* mirrors Thoreau's dream-like examination of the sources of his moral stance in that play.

Lawrence and Lee's theatricality is present in smaller scenes as well. The interactions of the Supreme Court justices screening a pornographic film in *First Monday in October*, staged with the most minimal of stage devices, precisely encapsulates their conflicts, and Harry Golden's rehearsing the children in *Only in America* captures the essence of the character's response to racial prejudice. Similar instances could be cited from the other plays gathered here; in each case, Lawrence and Lee have found a theatrical metaphor that epitomizes the dramatic situation or conflict they wanted to address. Their choices of dramatic structure and the visual imagery of the stage precisely mirror the larger concerns of each play.

Jerome Lawrence and Robert E. Lee have supplied the American theatre with a string of major works stretching through much of the last half century. Through their founding of the American Playwrights Theatre, they provided a model for the development of new plays by the regional theatre movement, then in its fledgling state. As teachers of young playwrights (in addition to their university bases in California, both have taught in many other universities across the country and overseas at the Salzburg Seminar in American Studies), they have been instrumental in encouraging and developing new writers and in helping to provide a forum for their work. Both Lawrence and Lee have been highly active in encouraging international cooperation, leading ventures involving writers of different societies. Their major achievement, however, lies in their passionate belief that the theatre must be of consequence and must deal with ideas and issues of social significance. Their plays demonstrate how playwrights can write of major issues with passion, wit, and grace, avoiding the overtly didactic. The selected plays of Jerome Lawrence and Robert E. Lee collected here also demonstrate forcefully the achievements of the commercial American theatre during its period of greatest achievement, in the decades following World War II, and point to the establishment of new patterns of theatrical production with *The Night Thoreau Spent in Jail*.

As master craftsmen, Lawrence and Lee provide superb models in the plays printed here. This selection of their work provides a sampling of the range and breadth of their interests and concerns, as their collaboration continues actively on the fiftieth anniversary of their joint work.

NOTES

1. "Emphasizing the Avant-Garde: An Exploration in Theatre Historiography," in *Interpreting the Theatrical Past: New Directions in the Historiography of Performance*, ed. Bruce McConachie and Thomas Postlewait (University of Iowa Press, 1989), 166–76.

2. "Laugh, God!" in *Six Anti-Nazi One-Act Plays* (New York: Contemporary Play Publications, 1939).

3. Robert E. Lee, interviewed by the author, 28 December 1988, Malibu, California. Unless otherwise indicated, all direct quotations from Jerome Lawrence and Robert E. Lee are from this interview, a transcript of which is available at the Jerome Lawrence and Robert E. Lee Theatre Research Institute, The Ohio State University.

4. Some of the anthologies include Eric Barnouw, ed., *Radio Drama in Action* (New York: Farrar and Rinehart, 1945); Edwin Duerr, ed., *Radio and Television Acting* (New York: Rinehart, 1950); Ernest H. Winter, ed., *Happenings* (Toronto: Thomas Nelson and Sons, 1969); R. K. Sadler, T. A. S. Hayllar, and C. J. Powell, *Bring the House Down* (Sidney and New York: John Wiley and Sons Australasia Printing, 1976).

5. The Theatre Guild, founded by Lawrence Langner, Theresa Helburn, Phillip Moeller, Helen Westley, and Rollo Peters in 1919, was the single most prestigious producing organization in the American commercial theatre through the mid-1950s. Best known for its early association with playwrights Eugene O'Neill and George Bernard Shaw, the Guild offered regular subscription series both in New York and in major cities across North America. Its history is amply documented in Norman Nadel's *A Pictorial History of the Theatre Guild* (New York: Crown, 1969). An account of its most productive period is in Roy S. Waldau's *Vintage Years of the Theatre Guild* (Cleveland: Case Western University Press, 1972).

6. Box office figures are taken from the weekly listings of Broadway productions in issues of *Variety*, 4 February 1948 through 15 July 1948.

7. 23 February 1948.

8. 15 March 1948, p. 23.

9. *Theatre Arts* (June 1958): 63–65.

10. *W*, 31 October7–November 1975, p. 8; clipping in Billy Rose Theatre Collection, New York Public Library Research Center at Lincoln Center.

11. Whitney Bolton, "Lawrence and Lee Long Lasting Team," *New York Morning Telegraph*, 25 October 1966; clipping in Billy Rose Theatre Collection, New York Public Library Research Center at Lincoln Center.

12. Scrapbooks and business records in the Hartman Theatre Collection, Lawrence and Lee Theatre Research Institute, The Ohio State University.

13. One such show train, led by then–Columbus mayor Frank Lausche, allowed an onstage announcement of Melvyn Douglas's absence from a performance of *Inherit the Wind* to be turned into a celebration rather than an excuse for disappointed audience members to request refunds. The story is amusingly recounted in Tony Randall and Michael Mindlin's *Which Reminds Me* (New York: Delacorte Press, 1989), 33–34.

14. Season figures for 1948–49 from *Variety* (4 June 1975), p. 59; 1988–89 figures from *Variety* (31 May–7 June 1989), p. 72.

15. Brooks Atkinson, *Broadway*, rev. ed. (New York: Macmillan, 1974), 432.

16. "Anybody here remember collaboration? Once common practice, now defunct," *Variety* (28 December 1988–3 January 1989), pp. 39, 42.

17. Hummler, p. 39.

18. Marguerite Cullman's autobiography, *Occupation: Angel* (New York: W. W. Norton & Company, 1963) supplies a light-hearted account of the role of investors during the 1940s and 1950s.

19. Smith designed the musical *Candide* (opening 1 December 1956), *A Clearing in the Woods* (10 January 1957), *Visit to a Small Planet* (7 February 1957), and a revival of the hit musical *Brigadoon* at City Center (27 March 1957); details from Louis Kronenberger, ed., *The Best Plays of 1956–1957* (New York: Dodd, Mead & Company, 1957).

20. Thomas M. Disch, "The Death of Broadway," *The Atlantic*, 267 (March 1991): 98.

21. *Variety*, 14 March 1975, p. 161; 3 October 1956, p. 83.

22. William Goldman's *The Season: A Candid Look at Broadway* (New York: Harcourt, Brace and World, 1969) provides a detailed look at the 1967–68 commercial theatre season in New York, included extended analyses of the business of theatre.

23. Scrapbooks and financial records, Hartman Theatre Collection, Lawrence and Lee Theatre Research Institute.

24. See, for example, Julius Novick, *Beyond Broadway: The Quest for Permanent Theatres* (New York: Hill & Wang, 1969), and Joseph W. Zeigler, *Regional Theatre: The Revolutionary Stage* (Minneapolis: University of Minnesota Press, 1973).

25. The history of ANTA in its formative years under the executive directorship of Robert Breen remains to be written. During its greatest activity, ANTA produced experimental works in its own Broadway theatre, sponsored national conferences, sent professional actors and directors throughout the country, and provided literary and promotional support to its members nationwide.

26. David Ayers, letter, 10 February 1981; typescript in American Playwrights Theatre Collection, Lawrence and Lee Theatre Research Institute.

27. The production is fully documented in Laurence E. Fink, "From Thought to Theatre: Creation, Development, and Production of *The Night Thoreau Spent in Jail* by Jerome Lawrence and Robert E. Lee" (master's thesis, Ohio State University, 1988).

28. Galati's adaptation was first produced by the Steppenwolf Theatre on 17 September 1988 at the Royal-George Theatre in Chicago. With many of the Chicago actors, *The Grapes of Wrath* opened at the La Jolla Playhouse near San Diego on 9 May 1989; that production played in repertory for some dozen performances at the Royal National Theatre in London beginning June 22, 1989. *The Grapes of Wrath* opened at the Cort Theatre on Broadway on 22 March 1990, closing on 2 September 1990.

29. A full bibliography of published material by and about the playwrights is available in

Mark Winchester's "Jerome Lawrence and Robert E. Lee: A Classified Bibliography," *Studies in American Drama 1945 to the Present*, 7:1 (1992), 88–160.

30. John Chapman, reviewer for the *New York Daily News*, did eventually recognize Lawrence and Lee's contributions to *Auntie Mame* in print, as discussed below in the introduction to that play's text.

31. Both Rosalind Russell, the first Mame, and Eve Arden, who played the role in the West Coast company, recount amusing stories about the frantic action backstage during performances. Rosalind Russell and Chris Chase, *Life Is a Banquet* (New York: Random House, 1977), 193–94; Eve Arden, *Three Phases of Eve* (New York: St. Martin's Press, 1985), 127–28.

While this volume was in production, Robert E. Lee passed away after several years of ill health. Both Jerome Lawrence and Robert E. Lee were involved in each step of the preparation of this anthology, and I deeply regret that Bob will not see the finished volume. The anthology is dedicated to his memory, and to the achievements of the fifty-two year collaboration between Lawrence and Lee.

Alan Woods